# REALIZING UTOPIA

*The Future of International Law*

# Realizing Utopia

*The Future of*
*International Law*

Edited by
ANTONIO CASSESE

**OXFORD**
UNIVERSITY PRESS

# OXFORD
UNIVERSITY PRESS

Great Clarendon Street, Oxford OX2 6DP
United Kingdom

Oxford University Press is a department of the University of Oxford.
It furthers the University's objective of excellence in research, scholarship,
and education by publishing worldwide. Oxford is a registered trade mark of
Oxford University Press in the UK and in certain other countries

British Library Cataloguing in Publication Data
Data available

Library of Congress Cataloguing in Publication Data
Library of Congress Control Number: 2012932650

ISBN 978–0–19–969166–1 (HBK)
978–0–19–964708–8 (PBK)

Printed in Great Britain by
CPI Group (UK) Ltd, Croydon, CR0 4YY

# Contents

## II WHAT LAWMAKING TOOLS SHOULD BE USED TO BRING ABOUT THE NEEDED CHANGE?

## III CAN INTERNATIONAL LEGAL IMPERATIVES BE MORE EFFECTIVELY BROUGHT INTO EFFECT?

### (A) The Interplay of International and National Law

### (B) Major Obstacles to States' Compliance

### (C) The Role of International Judicial Bodies

(C)  Restraining Armed Violence in International and
Internal Armed Conflict

V  CAN INTERNATIONAL AND DOMESTIC JUSTICE PLAY
A MORE INCISIVE ROLE?

# Principal Abbreviations

| | |
|---|---|
| ACHPR | African Court on Human and Peoples' Rights |
| AJIL | American Journal of International Law |
| BIEN | Basic Income Earth Network |
| BIT | Bilateral Investment Treaty |
| BYIL | British Yearbook of International Law |
| BWC | Bacteriological Weapons Convention |
| CJTL | Columbia Journal of Transnational Law |
| COP | Conference of the Parties |
| CSA | Comprehensive Safeguards Agreement |
| CWC | Chemical Weapons Convention |
| ECtHR | European Court of Human Rights |
| ECJ | European Court of Justice |
| ECOMOG | Economic Community of West African States Monitoring Group |
| ECOSOC | Economic and Social Council (of the UN) |
| EJIL | European Journal of International Law |
| FAO | Food and Agriculture Organization (of the UN) |
| GA | General Assembly (of the UN) |
| GAOR | UN General Assembly Official Records |
| GATT | General Agreement on Tariffs and Trade |
| HR | Recueil des Cours de l'Académie de La Haye |
| HRLJ | Human Rights Law Journal |
| IAEA | International Atomic Energy Agency |
| I-ACHR | Inter-American Court of Human Rights |
| ICC | International Criminal Court |
| ICJ | International Court of Justice |
| ICJ Reports | Reports of the International Court of Justice |
| ICLQ | International & Comparative Law Quarterly |
| ICRC | International Committee of the Red Cross |
| ICSID | International Centre for Settlement of Investment Disputes |
| ICTR | International Criminal Tribunal for Rwanda |
| ICTY | International Criminal Tribunal for the Former Yugoslavia |
| IDL | international development law |
| IEL | international economic law |
| IFOR | Implementation Force (NATO) |
| ILC | UN International Law Commission |
| ILM | International Legal Materials |
| ILO | International Labour Organization |
| ILR | International Law Reports (since 1950; edited first by Sir H. Lauterpacht and at present by Sir E. Lauterpacht, C.J. Greenwood, and A.G. Oppenheimer) |
| IRRC | International Review of the Red Cross |
| JDI | Journal du droit international |
| JICJ | Journal of International Criminal Justice |
| LBO | law of belligerent occupation |

| | |
|---|---|
| LDC | least development countries |
| MEA | Multilateral environmental agreement |
| MLR | Modern Law Review |
| NCP | Non-Compliance Procedures |
| NGO | non-governmental organization |
| NIEO | New International Economic Order |
| NWS | Nuclear-Weapon State |
| NNWS | Non-Nuclear-Weapon State |
| NPMs | National Preventive Mechanisms |
| NPT | 1970 Treaty on the Non-Proliferation of Nuclear Weapons |
| OAS | Organization of American States |
| OAU | Organization of African Unity |
| OPCAT | Optional Protocol to the UN Convention against Torture |
| OSCE | Organization for Security and Cooperation in Europe |
| PCIJ | Permanent Court of International Justice |
| PSI | Proliferation Security Initiative |
| R2P | responsibility to protect |
| RBDI | Revue Belge de Droit International |
| RDI | Rivista di Diritto Internazionale |
| REDD | Reducing Emissions from Deforestation, Degradation and Forest Enhancement |
| RGDIP | Revue Générale de Droit International Public |
| RIAA | Reports of International Arbitral Awards |
| RUF | Revolutionary United Front of Sierra Leone |
| SC | Security Council (of the UN) |
| SPT | Subcommittee on Prevention of Torture (United Nations) |
| UN | United Nations |
| UNCITRAL | United Nations Commission on International Trade Law |
| UNCLOS | United Nations Convention on the Law of the Sea |
| UNCTAD | United Nations Conference on Trade and Development |
| UNEF | United Nations Emergency Force |
| UNEP | United Nations Environment Programme |
| UNFCCC | United Nations Framework Convention on Climate Change |
| UNESCO | United Nations Educational, Scientific and Cultural Organization |
| UNMIK | United Nations Mission in Kosovo |
| UNTAET | United Nations Transitional Administration in East Timor |
| WHO | World Health Organization |
| WIPO | World Intellectual Property Organization |
| WTO | World Trade Organization |
| YIHL | Yearbook of International Humanitarian Law |
| YILC | Yearbook of the International Law Commission |

# List of Contributors

**Philip Alston** John Norton Pomeroy Professor of Law, New York University School of Law; former Professor of Law, European University Institute; former member of the UN Committee on Economic, Social and Cultural Rights (Rapporteur, 1987–90) and Chairperson (1991–98); currently UN Special Rapporteur on Extrajudicial, Summary or Arbitrary Executions.

**José E. Alvarez** Herbert and Rose Rubin Professor of International Law at the New York University School of Law; former President of the American Society of International Law (2006–08); member of the US Council of Foreign Relations; since 2010 Special Adviser on Public International Law, Office of the Prosecutor, International Criminal Court.

**Orna Ben-Naftali** Professor of International Law and Dean of the Law School, the College of Management Academic Studies in Israel. A graduate of the Law Faculty of Tel-Aviv University, the Fletcher School of Law and Diplomacy, Tufts University and Harvard University, she taught at Brandeis University and at the Fletcher School of Law and Diplomacy, and worked in the Department of Peacekeeping Operations, the United Nations.

**Mohamed Bennouna** Judge at the International Court of Justice; former Ambassador of Morocco to the UN, former judge at the ICTY; Member of the UN International Law Commission (1986–98). First Special Rapporteur of the International Law Commission on the question of diplomatic protection (1997–98).

**Nehal Bhuta** Core Faculty member and Assistant Professor of International Affairs at the New School Graduate Programme in International Affairs, New York. He has previously worked with Human Rights Watch and the International Center for Transitional Justice, and at the Federal Court of Australia.

**Alan Boyle** Professor of Public International Law, University of Edinburgh, and barrister, Essex Court Chambers, London; General Editor of the *International and Comparative Law Quarterly* from 1998 until 2006; practises occasionally in the International Court of Justice and other international tribunals, most recently in the *Pulp Mills* case (ICJ, 2006–09) and the *Aerial Spraying* case (ICJ, 2008–).

**Antonio Cassese** Former Professor of International Law at Florence University; former President of the Council of Europe Committee for the Prevention of Torture and Inhuman and Degrading Treatment or Punishment; former Judge and President, ICTY; former President of the UN Commission of Inquiry on Darfur; Judge (and former President) of the Special Tribunal for Lebanon; formers member of the Institut de droit international.

**Andrew Clapham** PhD, European University Institute; Professor of International Law, Geneva Graduate Institute of International Studies and Development; Director of the Geneva Academy of International Humanitarian Law and Human Rights; former Representative of Amnesty International at the UN in New York; Special Adviser on Corporate Responsibility to High Commissioner for Human Rights Mary Robinson, and Adviser on International Humanitarian Law to Sergio Vieira de Mello, Special Representative of the UN Secretary-General in Iraq.

**Luigi Condorelli** Professor of International Law, University of Florence; Honorary Professor of Law at the University of Geneva; member of the OECD Admnistrative Tribunal; member of the Scientific Council of the Revue Générale de Droit International Public.

**Jérome de Hemptinne** Senior Legal Officer at the Special Tribunal for Lebanon; former legal officer, ICTY.

**Pierre-Marie Dupuy** Professor of International Law, Geneva Graduate Institute of International Studies and Development; former Professor at the University of Paris-II and at the European University Institute; an international arbitrator, he chaired the PCA International Tribunal in the *Abyei* case (Sudan/Southern Sudan) 2009; has participated in a number of ICC, ICSID, and PCA arbitrations dealing with international investment disputes.

**Souheil El-Zein** Senior Legal Officer, Chief of the Section of Administrative Legal Affairs, UNESCO.

**Malcolm D. Evans** was Head of the Bristol University Law School from 2003–05 and Dean of the Faculty of Social Sciences and Law at the University of Bristol from 2005–09. In 1999 he was appointed Professor of Public International Law. His areas of research interest now lie primarily in issues concerning the international protection of human rights, with particular focus on the freedom of religion and the prevention of torture, and also the law of the sea. He is currently Chair of the United Nations Sub Committee for the Prevention of Torture and is a member of the UK Foreign Secretary's Advisory Group on Human Rights. He is also a member of the Organization on Security and Cooperation in Europe's Advisory Council of Freedom of Religion and Belief and has worked extensively with numerous international organizations on a broad range of human rights issues.

**Bardo Fassbender** LLM (Yale), Professor of International Law at the Universität der Bundeswehr, Munich; co-editor of the series *Studien zur Geschichte des Völkerrechts* [Studies in the history of international law] founded by Michael Stolleis.

**Francesco Francioni** Professor of Law, European University Institute; Co-Director of the Academy of European Law; Member of the Board of Editors of the *European Journal of International Law*; President of the World Heritage Committee of the UNESCO (1997–98).

**Paola Gaeta** Professor of International Law and International Criminal Law, University of Geneva and Adjunct Professor, Graduate Institute of International and Development Studies; Director of the Geneva Academy of International Humanitarian Law and Human Rights.

**Bibi van Ginkel** LLM, PhD, Senior Research Fellow at the Netherlands Institute for International Relations 'Clingendael', and Research Fellow of the International Centre for Counter-Terrorism (ICCT), The Hague.

**Robert Howse** Lloyd C. Nelson Professor of International Law and Faculty Co-Director, Institute for International Law and Justice, NYU Law School.

**Massimo Iovane** Professor of International Law, University of Naples 'Federico II'.

**Emmanuelle Jouannet** Professor of International Law at the University of Paris I (Panthéon-Sorbonne), Deputy Director of the CERDIN, Paris; honorary member of the Board of Editors of the *European Journal of International Law*.

**Martti Koskenniemi** Professor of International Law, Helsinki University and Director of the Erik Castrén Institute of International Law and Human Rights; has been Global Professor of Law at New York University; member of the International Law Commission

(2002–06); served in the Finnish Diplomatic Service in 1978–96, lastly as director of the Division of International Law.

**Nils Melzer** Holds a PhD in law of the University of Zürich; currently Director of Research at the Centre for Business and Human Rights of the University of Zürich; former Legal Adviser for the International Committee of the Red Cross (ICRC).

**Jaykumar A. Menon** Adjunct Professor, McGill University Institute for the Study of International Development; Research Fellow, Center for International Sustainable Development Law, based at McGill University, Montréal, Québec; Senior Director, Education and Global Development, X PRIZE Foundation.

**Andrew Murray** Professor of Law, London School of Economics; as well as holding memberships of the Society of Computers and Law (SCL); the Institute for Learning and Teaching (ILT); the David Hume Institute and Associate Membership of the AHRB Research Centre for Research into Intellectual Property and Technology.

**Mauro Palma** A mathematician and Doctor in Law h.c., is founder and honorary president of *Antigone* (an Italian association which promotes respect for human rights in the criminal justice system); member and former chairman of the Council of Europe's European Committee for the Prevention of Torture and Inhuman and Degrading Treatment.

**Andreas Paulus** Professor of Public Law and International Law, Georg-August-University; Justice of the German Federal Constitutional Court.

**Anne Peters** Professor of International and Public Law, University of Basel; Legal expert for the Independent International Fact-Finding Mission on the Conflict in Georgia (2009); member of the executive board of the European Society of International Law, elected president in 2010; since 2011 member of the European Commission for Democracy through Law (Venice Commission).

**Giulia Pinzauti** PhD, European University Institute; associate legal officer, STL.

**W. Michael Reisman** Myres S. McDougal Professor of International Law, Yale Law School; Fellow of the World Academy of Art and Science; President of the Arbitration Tribunal of the Bank for International Settlements; former President of the Inter-American Commission on Human Rights; arbitrator in the Eritrea/Ethiopia Boundary Dispute and in the Abyei (Sudan) Boundary Dispute; member of the Advisory Committee on International Law of the US Department of State; member of the Institut de droit international.

**Laura Rockwood** Head of the Section for Non-Proliferation and Policy Making in the Office of Legal Affairs of the International Atomic Energy Agency (IAEA).

**Natalino Ronzitti** Professor of International Law, LUISS University, Rome; Member of the Italian delegation at the Second Session of the Diplomatic Conference on Humanitarian Law Applicable to Armed Conflicts (1973); Italian delegate at several sessions of the International Conference of the Red Cross; Legal adviser of the Italian Mission at the Conference on Disarmament, Geneva (1991–95).

**Philippe Sands** QC Barrister in the Matrix Chambers and Professor of International Law at University College London; Director of the Centre on International Courts and Tribunals at University College London.

**William Schabas** is Professor of International Law at Middlesex University in London.

He is also Professor of Human Rights Law at the Irish Centre for Human Rights of the National University of Ireland, Galway, and an honorary Professor at the Chinese Academy of Social Sciences in Beijing.

**Yuval Shany** LLB, Hebrew University, Jerusalem, LLM, New York University; PhD, University of London; he is the Hersch Lauterpacht Chair in International Law at the Law Faculty of the Hebrew University of Jerusalem.

**Sandesh Sivakumaran** Lecturer in law, Nottingham University; Associate Legal Officer to Judge M. Shahabuddeen at the Appeals Chamber of the ICTY; Law Clerk to Judges R. Higgins and P. Tomka at the ICJ. He is a co-editor of *International Human Rights Law* (Oxford University Press, 2010). His work has been cited by the Supreme Court of Israel and awarded the Giorgio La Pira Prize and the Antonio Cassese Prize by the *Journal of International Criminal Justice*.

**Christian J. Tams** Professor of International Law, University of Glasgow; Adjunct Professor at the Europa-Kolleg Hamburg; member of the German Court of Arbitration for Sports and of the ILA Committee on Non-State Actors; has held visiting positions at universities in China and Lithuania.

**Jorge E. Viñuales** Pictet Chair of International Environmental Law, Graduate Institute of International and Development Studies, Geneva; Counsel, Lévy Kaufmann-Kohler, Geneva; Executive Director of the Latin American Society of International Law.

**J.H.H. Weiler** Joseph Strauss Professor of Law, New York University; Director, Straus Institute for the Advanced Study of Law and Justice; Director, Jean Monnet Center for International and Regional Economic Law and Justice.

**Abdulqawi A. Yusuf** Judge at the International Court of Justice; former Legal Adviser to UNESCO; Assistant Director-General and Special Adviser on African Affairs (1998–2001), UNIDO; Founder and General Editor, *African Yearbook of International Law/Annuaire Africain de droit international*; member of the Institut de droit international.

**Salvatore Zappalà** Professor of International Law, University of Catania; currently Legal Adviser to the Permanent Mission of Italy to the United Nations, New York; editor-in-chief of the *Journal of International Criminal Justice*.

# Introduction

*Antonio Cassese*

## 1. Technicians v Utopians

In 1927, in one of his delightful short essays, Aldous Huxley, speaking of socio-logical writings, drew a distinction between two categories of sociologists. One category is that of the *Technicians*, who, 'like all critics of detail', are inclined 'to accept too complacently the main framework of the structure whose details they are trying to improve' and 'accept things as they are, but too uncritically; for along with the existing social institutions they accept that conception of human nature which the institutions imply'. The other category is made up of the *Utopians*, who

are much too preoccupied with what ought to be to pay any serious attention to what is. Outward reality disgusts them; the compensatory dream is the universe in which they live. The subject of their meditations is not man, but a monster of rationality and vir-tue...It is as though astronomers wrote books about what would happen if there were no such thing as gravitation and if the earth, in consequence, moved in a straight line and not in an ellipse.[1]

Huxley was aware that these two extreme mindsets were both ineffective and unhelpful to another category of scholars that he called the *Judicious Reformers*.

## 2. The need for judicious reformers

The approach we take in this book aims to avoid the extremes of both blind acquiescence to present conditions and the illusion of being able to revolutionize the fundamentals. Our approach reflects the attitude of the 'judicious reformer', whose contributions are not obfuscated by an overabundance of legal technicalities, though he moves on the solid ground of 'critical positivism' and knows how to use the traditional tools of jurisprudence (after all, two prominent positivists, Lassa Oppenheim and Heinrich Triepel, one prior to, and the other during the First World War, wrote essays on 'The Future of International Law'[2]). The 'judicious

---

[1] See A. Huxley, *Proper Studies* ([1927] London: Chatto and Windus, 1929), IX–XI.

[2] H. Triepel, *Die Zukunft des Völkerrechts* (Leipzig/Dresden: B.G. Teubner, 1916). The essay reproduces the text of a lecture he gave in Dresden on 11 March 1916. Given the circumstances in which he dealt with the future of international law, it is understandable that most of the lecture was devoted to the 'weaknesses' of the laws of warfare and their possible future amelioration (see in par-ticular at 32–56). L. Oppenheim, *The Future of International Law* (Oxford: Clarendon Press, 1921).

reformer' is also alert to the present—to its merits but also to its pitfalls—and suggests realistic and viable avenues in order to avoid, at least to some extent, those pitfalls encountered when trying to build a better path.

Within this general framework, and with specific regard to international law, this book is based on two theoretical, if self-evident, assumptions, both cogently spelled out by a distinguished international lawyer: Sir Robert Jennings.

The first assumption is that certainty and change are the two 'apparently irreconcilable essentials of law'.[3] By definition, law must be as unambiguous as possible, so as to constitute a stable and safe set of standards of behaviour for all legal subjects. Members of the community need to know what is permitted and what is prohibited. However, law should not be left to become obsolete either, by falling out of touch with reality. Evolving with changing historical, social, and political circumstances is a necessary precondition for any viable body of law, lest it should become an empty corpus of antiquated prescriptions.

The second assumption identified by Jennings is that in the international community 'there is almost no machinery for the reform of public international law; and there seems little prospect of such processes being achievable in the foreseeable future.'[4] Indeed, it is common knowledge that international law lacks an efficient institutional mechanism for the abolition of outdated legal rules and the formation of more modern and adequate prescriptions. Treaties need the concurrence of all contracting parties to be modified or amended, and customary law, as everyone knows, is not easy to identify, and, in any event, its updating requires the support or, at a minimum, the clear non-opposition, of most international legal subjects. The conspicuous difficulty in amending the UN Charter can be pointed out as quintessential evidence of all the obstacles in the way of peaceful legal change. Finally, the UN International Law Commission, however meritorious in the past in promoting the progressive development and codification of international rules, seems to have waned—at least in some respects. In any case, it does not constitute a mechanism for prompt and effective reform of some crucial areas of international law.

## 3. Sketching out the current most blatant inadequacies of the world society

Yet the international community is in dire need of change. Its inadequacies and inability to keep up with changing times have spurred a number of serious problems. I will mention only the main ones.

---

The book had been written in German (*Die Zukunft des Völkerrechts* in *Festschrift für Karl Binding* (Leipzig: Wilhelm Engelmann, 1911)) before the war, and was then translated into English after Oppenheim's death in 1919.

[3] R.Y. Jennings, 'Judicial Legislation in International Law', 26 Kentucky LJ (1938) 127.

[4] R.Y. Jennings, 'International Law Reform and Progressive Development', in *Liber Amicorum Professor Ignaz Seidl-Hohenveldern in Honour of his 80th Birthday* (The Hague: Kluwer, 1998), 325.

Many non-state entities (in addition to rebels) are participating, either peacefully or, more often, through violence, in international dealings or at any rate have imposed their presence on the international scene. Yet despite the steady increase of their impact on international relations, their legal status has remained uncertain, as have their rights and obligations. International civil society has similarly elbowed its way onto the scene and has come to exercise an important role in both exposing the individualistic, inward-looking attitude of the principal subjects of the international community, and prodding them to pay heed to community values such as peace, the rule of law, respect for human rights, and democracy. The bottom-up dynamic between civil society and governments or intergovernmental organizations continues to be unregulated, save for the role of NGOs within a handful of intergovernmental organizations. By the same token, individuals are dramatically carving a more visible role for themselves in international dealings and demanding respect for their interests and their human rights, both within their home country and on the international stage, where individuals have even advanced the claim that they should be entitled to trigger international procedures for the enforcement of their own rights.

These paradigmatic shifts have not succeeded in displacing states as the principal actors on the world stage, as the claims and demands of other, secondary actors continue to be routinely overlooked. Individuals may not institute proceedings at the universal level for states' breaches of the law which affect them. This, in a way, contrasts with the new trend of prosecuting and punishing individuals for gross violations of human rights amounting to international crimes. However, even international criminal justice is not fairing well. In spite of the recent mushrooming of international tribunals and courts, selective justice persists, and the ICC, which could dispense justice in a fair and absolutely even-handed manner, still seems to be a far cry from fulfilling its mission and using its enormous potential.

Another major problem is the current role of sovereignty. Although this old pillar of world society is far from waning, some traditional state prerogatives are being steadily eroded by the emerging universal values consecrated in peremptory international norms. Yet again, tensions between these two conflicting poles are not satisfactorily regulated by law. In addition, while globalization is gradually restricting state sovereignty, no legal regulatory mechanisms are replacing the void left behind as a result.

The question of change or stability in the legal framework of world society equally poses a panoply of problems. As noted above, traditional sources of law are unable to cope with the rapid shifts and developments in international dealings. Furthermore, the nationalistic and short-sighted outlook of most states means they still baulk at conferring direct binding value on international rules in their domestic legal orders. By leaving things as they are at present, they eventually manage to eschew compliance with those international rules. World society still lacks an institutional mechanism designed to ensure that international legal imperatives become immediately operational at the national level. In addition, domestic courts, which could be instrumental in implementing international rules by acting as 'guardians of international law' under Georges Scelle's famous theory of *dédou-blement fonctionnel* (role splitting), find it hard to discharge this role. Indeed, they are faced both with states' insistence on their being protected by the shield of functional, personal, and state immunities, and with broad and stubborn opposition to the exercise of universal criminal jurisdiction.

Moreover, much as judicial settlement of disputes between states is at present robust—a notable progress in the current world structure—many conflicts charged with strong political or ideological overtones are settled by non-judicial means. Monitoring, although it has become a potent substitute for judicial adjudication, does not manage to cope with all the problems posed by the lack of compliance with international standards.

What is even more striking is that major powers deliberately protect the vagueness and opacity of the legal regulation of some important areas related to the use of force, notably, self-defence; aggression either as an international wrongful act or as an international crime; the use of some modern weapons; protection of civilians in armed conflicts. Major sore spots involving entire populations and their fundamental human rights are left festering: chief among them are the over-protracted belligerent occupations of Palestine and Western Sahara. The world is rife with terrorism, but the primary and privileged response that states seem willing to display to this odious crime is a repressive one. In addition, global economic and financial upheavals occur free from any international legal restraint. The question of how to reconcile the right to self-determination of peoples oppressed by authoritarian governments, foreign domination, or prolonged and unwarranted belligerent occupation, with peace and stability in international relations, remains intractable. Also, the plague of underdevelopment has not yet been effectively tackled through reliance on an efficient international institutional mechanism.

Faced with these dramatic problems and all the attendant strictures, it may perhaps fall to international lawyers both to *identify*, for the benefit of politicians and diplomats, areas of international law more in need of radical change, and to *suggest* new ways and modalities to bring international legal institutions and rules up to date. This is precisely the (admittedly ambitious) task that we have set ourselves to accomplish in this book. Confronted with the current dramatic tensions between the old society of states hinging on self-interest, reciprocity, and 'a parochial spirit',[5] on the one side, and emerging community values, on the other, we intend to suggest how those values could be enhanced so as to gradually transform world society into a really international community endowed with paramount communal values and at least a modicum of community institutions so that public or collective concerns may prevail over private interests.

---

[5]  G. Fitzmaurice, 'The Future of Public International Law and of the International Legal System in the Circumstances of Today', in Institute de droit international, *Livre du Centenaire 1873–1973* (Basle: S. Karger, 1973), 259.

## 4. A plea for a realistic utopia: an oxymoron

This book—it is plain—is based on an oxymoron: the notion of building a realistic utopia. However, when we speak of utopia, we are consciously taking an approach that is miles away from the traditional conception of utopia. As Isahia Berlin explained so well, utopias are dreams where men imagine 'some ideal state in which there [is] no misery and no greed, no danger and no poverty or fear or brutalising labour or insecurity', in which all members of society

live in peace, love one another, are free from physical danger, from want of any kind, from insecurity, from degrading work, from envy, from frustration, experience no injustice or violence, live in perpetual, even light, in a temperate climate, in the midst of infinitely fruitful, generous nature.[6]

In contrast, we know that the international society will never be free from violence, poverty, and injustice. We do not dream of a peaceful international society based on comity, friendship, and cooperation. We simply intend to suggest in utopian terms new avenues for improving the major deficiencies of the current society of states.

## 5. The need for imaginative thinking

The book is a collection of essays by a group of innovative international jurists, chosen because they combine the two qualities that Herbert Hart so admired in Mr Justice Holmes: 'imaginative power' and 'clarity'.[7] The authors were not asked to engage in wild speculation about the future of the world society. Rather, they have been invited, more modestly, to (i) reflect on the condition of some of the major legal problems of that society and compendiously analyse inconsistencies or inadequacies of current law, (ii) highlight the elements—even if minor, hidden, incipient, or *in fieri*—that are likely to lead to future changes or improvements; in other words, contributors have been asked to discern the 'leaven', or potential, in the present legal construct of world society that might one day be brought to maturation in a better world; and (iii) suggest how these elements can be developed, enhanced, and brought to fruition *in the next two or three decades*, with a view to achieving an improved architecture of world society or, at a minimum, to reshaping some major aspects of international dealings.

In sum, we have deemed it necessary to abandon for a while the relatively comfortable analysis of existing legal institutions and the sophisticated construction of legal rules, engaging instead in imaginative thinking. However, as I have just pointed out, we have refrained from chasing unattainable dreams. We did not intend to go so far as to heed the exhortation of a distinguished international lawyer, B.V.A. Röling, who called upon international lawyers to propound 'the natural law of the atomic

---

[6] I. Berlin, 'The Decline of Utopias in the West', in *The Crooked Timber of Humanity* (H. Hardy ed., London: Fontana Press, 1990), 20.

[7] H.L.A. Hart, *Essays in Jurisprudence and Philosophy* (Oxford: Clarendon Press, 1983), 49.

age'.[8] We wanted to attain less forward-looking, yet more realistic goals. We have not looked at the stars, but closer to home, to the planets that turn around the earth. And we have charged our intellectual weapons with relatively short-range ammunition.

## 6. On the editor's tribulations

To collect all these chapters has proved an extremely arduous task, indeed a real nightmare: most invitees were too busy or overcommitted to deliver in time, and some dropped out at the last minute, in some cases compelling me to fill in (hence the multitude of essays by me, for which I seek the indulgence of the reader who, I hope, will not be led to think that that multitude is instead the result of an hypertrophic ego or even megalomania).

I have endeavoured to discuss each chapter with his or her author, to ensure that the general approach and format of the book is fairly uniform. However, although I had initially suggested guidelines for the drafting, the structure, and the thrust of the chapter, in the event each contributor has freely chosen his or her own path. As a result some chapters are longer than others, and there is much variation in the quantity and length of footnotes. In sum, the anarchy of the current world society has eventually reflected itself in the anarchy of our small community of contributors.

To ensure some sort of uniformity or consistency, I have written a summary for each chapter, to facilitate the reading and poring over of the various contributions by the patient reader (responsibility for such summaries is only mine). I have also taken the liberty of slightly changing the titles of many chapters proposed by their authors, with a view to more vividly bringing forward the purposes of the book. In my editorial work I have been greatly assisted, as far as editing and copy-editing is concerned, by Sandra Sahyouni, Margaret Gardner, and Valentina Spiga: to all of them I wish to express my appreciation and gratitude.

The reader will judge whether the efforts to publish this book have been worthwhile, and the ideas and suggestions advanced in it are of some value to scholars, diplomats, politicians, practitioners, and public opinion at large.

---

[8] Starting from the premise that 'A wide gap exists between our needs and our capacities', Röling held that

> Lawyers have a special responsibility in such circumstances. They are the experts who would recognize that present international law—measured according to its own values and goals—is bad law. They are also the ones who can formulate the 'natural law of the atomic age': the law capable of serving the goals and values of our present time. They can use this natural law as an inspiration and as a guiding principle to achieve a change in positive international law—a gradual change, a peaceful change—with the aim, not to create paradise on earth, but to make our world more livable, with a diminished fear of mankind's destruction and with the prospect of an end to mass starvation. Modest aims! But aims of vital importance. (B.V.A. Röling, 'Are Grotius' Ideas Obsolete in an Expanded World?', in H. Bull, B. Kingsbury, and A. Roberts (eds), *Hugo Grotius and International Relations* (Oxford: Clarendon Press, 1990), 298.)

# PART I

# CAN THE WORLD BECOME A GLOBAL COMMUNITY?

# 1

# The Subjective Dangers of Projects of World Community

*Martti Koskenniemi*

## SUMMARY

One should be careful with those who speak in the name of humanity and try to impose any particular blueprint on the world. Proposals for the legal-institutional architectures for the government of the whole world and other designs may seem appealing when stated in the abstract. However, their concrete realization always involves some distribution of power, and with it, some privileging of preferences and values. Claims to humanity are always infected by the particularity of the speaker, the world of his or her experience, culture and profession, knowledge and ignorance. A realistic utopia can only begin with the critique of present institutions. It is a mindset and an attitude that seeks to highlight the contingency and contestability of global institutions and their distributionary consequences.

## 1. Community through hierarchy

At the beginning of *Civilization and Its Discontents*, Freud tells the story of an 'exceptional individual' (from Freud's biography we know that this was Albert Einstein) who had commented on Freud's studies on religion by speculating that the source of religious faith is a 'peculiar feeling'—namely 'a feeling of something limitless, unbounded—as it were "oceanic"'. Freud admitted that he could find no such feeling in himself but that he could understand it as an intellectual perception, accompanied by a 'feeling of an indissoluble bond, of being one with the external world as a whole'.[1] Under Freud's cold eye, this feeling was part of what he considered the illusion of religion while its psychological source lay in an effort to perpetuate the life of the ego by lifting the wall between the self and

---

[1] S. Freud, *Civilization and Its Discontents* (J. Riviere trans.; J. Strachey rev. and ed., London: Hogarth Press, 1973), 1–2.

the external world. We need not, indeed cannot, examine the psychological origins or the reality of the 'oceanic feeling' here. Instead, there is reason to accept
that something like it has frequently received expression in ethical, religious,
and legal doctrines that emphasize altruism, love for one's fellow men or indeed
humanity as a whole as the basis of ambitious intellectual and political agendas
for world government. The desire for universal brotherhood or sisterhood is first
translated into descriptive theories about how all humans depend on each other
and share fundamentally similar hopes, fears, and objectives. Such descriptions
are then invoked to provide support to blueprints of political unity, the effort to
govern all humanity within a single structure of hierarchical rule. Surveying the
chaos in northern Italy in bitter exile from his native Florence, Dante Alighieri
had already made the familiar point that '[u]nity seems to be the root for what it
is to be good, and plurality the root of what it is to be evil'. But although unity
was good, it did not emerge automatically. In *De monarchia*, written sometime
between 1312 and 1314, Dante expressed his conviction that there was only one
way to attain it. For, he argued:

mankind is most a unity when it is drawn together to form a single entity, and that can only
came about when it is ruled as one whole by one ruler.[2]

The philosophical promise was supported by a historical observation. The presence
of two or more leaders on the world scene will automatically produce conflict. And
when there is conflict, judgment is needed. In other words, and as international
lawyers have written ever since, 'there must be a third party of wider jurisdiction who rules over both of these'.[3] Like most of the writers of this period, Dante
regarded monarchy as the best expression of this unity and the perfect image of
God's rule over the earth. In Dante's ideal, the represented—humanity—and the
representative—the emperor whose return to Italy he was advocating—could not
really be separated at all:

the whole of mankind in its ideal state depends on the unity which is men's wills. But this
cannot be unless there is one will which controls and directs all the others towards one
goal, since the wills of mortals require guidance on the account of the seductive pleaser of
youth, as Aristotle teaches at the end of the *Ethics*. Nor can such a single will exist, unless
there is one ruler who rules over everybody, whose will can control and guide all the other
wills.[4]

World government, for Dante, was necessary. But it required a unity imposed on
'men's wills' from above. It presupposed hegemony—which is why it has always
been opposed by critiques of universal empire. The history of Western international
political thought is a narrative about the clash of ambition and critique, hegemony
and counter-hegemony as these have appeared in debates about the institutional
form of world community.

---

[2] *De Monarchia*, Bk I, viii (13).    [3] Ibid, Bk I xii (21).    [4] Ibid, Bk I xv (27).

## 2. Origins: the role of providence

There is no other (Western) tradition of political and legal thought that would more consistently seek to translate the 'oceanic feeling' into proposals for world government than the law of nations, today's international law. Generations of religious, political, scientific, and legal thinkers, politicians, and diplomats from Western Antiquity to the founding fathers of the United Nations and the modern technicians of global governance have translated the oceanic feeling in themselves into theories of human unity, interdependence, world economy, the global environment, and so on in order to propose legal-institutional architectures for the government of the whole world. These theories often associate history with the tragic separation of humans, in the Christian narrative captured in the fall occasioned by original sin. Redemption, under this narrative, would mean the re-establishment of the once broken unity. Something like this inspired the first institutional proposals for a world governed by a universal natural law and *jus gentium* in the early sixteenth century, put forward from the University of Salamanca at the time of the worldwide expansion of the Habsburg Empire. How should Castilians think about the alien communities they encountered in the New World? Who had the rightful power to govern those communities? What about ownership over the resources that were found there?

Claims of universal lordship were made both by the emperor (who at this time was also the king of Castile-Aragon) as well as the pope. They were opposed by Dominican scholars such as Francisco de Vitoria and Domingo de Soto. God had created the world to be enjoyed by all humans in common, these scholars wrote, and even as the original commonality had been replaced by sovereign states and private property, this had taken place universally by human beings themselves as a realistic response to their circumstances. Sovereignty and private property arose under the *jus gentium* as necessary aspects of a functioning legal community among sinful humans. They did not contradict the idea of a single humanity, only gave institutional expression to its management by free individuals and discrete communities. Neither the *Respublica Christiana* nor myths of Roman power and glory could override the division of the world into separate communities and private properties that had arisen as an effect of God's will.[5]

Now the Dominicans did not leave it at that. They still accepted that the world was united by a right of everyone to travel and trade and that Christians (but not others) had the right to evangelize all over the world. To prevent this would be a cause for just war.[6] A humanity (tragically) separated by sovereignty and property would be united in a community of religion and economics. This image was immediately seized upon by Hugo Grotius who used it to argue against Iberian

---

[5] See F. de Vitoria, 'On the American Indians', in *Political Writings* (A. Pagden and J. Lawrence eds, Cambridge: Cambridge University Press, 1991) and D. de Soto, *Domingo de Soto, Relección 'De dominio'. Edición crítica y Traducción, con Introducción, Apéndices e Índices, por Jaime Prufau Prats* (Granada: Universidad de Granada, 1964).

[6] de Vitoria, n 3, 278–286.

trade monopoly in the East Indies in his youthful apology for the activities of the *Vereenigde Oostindische Compagnie* (VOC) written in 1604–06. Grotius agreed that the golden age had been one of freedom and common ownership and that this had been historically transformed into sovereignty and private property.[7] And yet, this separation was now being overcome by the universal right of navigation and trade.

For God has not willed that nature shall supply every region with all the necessities of life; and furthermore, he has granted pre-eminence of different arts to different nations. Why are things so if not because it was His Will that human friendship be fostered by mutual needs and resources, lest individuals, in deeming themselves self-sufficient, might thereby be rendered unsociable? In the existing state of affairs, it has come to pass, in accordance with the design of Divine Justice, that one nation supplies the needs of another, so that in this way … whatever has been produced in one region is regarded as a product native to all regions.[8]

Providence, in other words, pushed human beings to exchange goods in their own interest and so to create a community slowly, almost imperceptibly out of their separateness. And providence was now represented by the trading activities of the Dutch. Moreover, 'anyone who abolishes this system of exchange, abolishes also the highly prized fellowship in which humanity is united … In short, he does violence to nature herself.'[9] The Dutch war in the East Indies may have been in the immediate interests of the shareholders of the VOC. But as the Portuguese were 'imped[ing] the progress of international commerce', it was also waged on behalf of humankind.[10]

The universal laws put forward by Vitoria or Grotius emerged from the encounter by Europeans of peoples and cultures who, until then, had had little or no presence in the European imagination. After the regularization of those relations by colonization, the law of nations limited itself again to a 'public law of Europe'. Abbé de Saint-Pierre, for one, published his famous *Projet de rendre la paix perpétuelle en Europe* (1713) so as to decry the 'ineffectiveness' of present European diplomacy, advocating a '*Traité d'Union*' and a perpetual Congress of European states. In 20 articles his *Traité* was intended to freeze the territorial status quo and to set up a system of arbitration and free trade in Europe. Even if the proposal received no diplomatic support whatsoever, it was still a useful reminder for Europeans of the awkwardness of agreeing to a federal union under absolutist monarchies. As Rousseau later observed, a federal arrangement could only take place on this basis by revolution—but in that case, 'who among us would dare to say whether such a European league would be more to desire or to fear? It might perhaps do more evil in a moment than it could prevent in centuries.'[11]

---

[7] H. Grotius, *Commentary on the Right of Prize and Booty* (edited and with an introduction by M. van Ittersum, Indianapolis: Liberty Fund, 2006), on the origin of private property ch. XII, 315–18.                                      [8] Ibid, ch. XII, Thesis I, 302–3.
[9] Ibid, 303.
[10] Ibid, ch. XIV, 449.
[11] J.J. Rousseau, 'Jugement sur la paix perpétuelle', in *The Political Writings of Jean-Jacques Rousseau* (Cambridge: Cambridge University Press, 1915), 396.

## 3. 'Europe will probably lead the way'?

But cosmopolitan thought received one famous expression during the European enlightenment in the notion that all the nations of the world were naturally part of a *Civitas maxima*, put forward by the Professor of Philosophy from the University of Halle, Christian Wolff.[12] With characteristic optimism, Wolff assumed that 'law and politics were essentially concerned with the perfectibility of human nature as part of the general system of the world'.[13] Perfection, for him, meant participation in the pre-established harmony that arose from the creation of the world and could be grasped by reason itself—especially as expressed in the thick volumes of Prussian philosophy that would help us to see clearly how to calculate at each moment the maximal good that can be attained by a maximal number of human beings on earth.

Yet such harmony was hardly forthcoming. Wolff felt it himself as he was banished from the university after a public talk in which he had openly celebrated the enlightenment of Chinese society. His most important follower, Emer de Vattel, famously discarded the idea that the nations of the world were joined in a 'great state': this was pure fiction. On the contrary, all nations were equally directed by the law of nature to look out first for their own good. They were free and equal just like individuals were in their mutual relations.[14] No doubt in the ears of this Huguenot enlightener *civitas maxima* sounded too much like the 'universal monarchy' that everyone understood as a code word for the hegemonic pursuits of the most Christian (French) king. Vattel did accept that there existed a type of natural society of humankind. But he thought that the 'only means of securing the condition of the good, and repressing the wicked' lay in the organization of that society into separate, free, and equal nations.[15]

Something like this also underlay the opposition of German jurists at the beginning of the nineteenth century to French revolutionary universalism. While the National Assembly in Paris declared universal rights and freedoms, and even at one point debated a proposition on the universal rights of nations, the leading German internationalist, Georg Friedrich von Martens, writing in a Göttingen occupied by Napoleon's forces, repudiated such ideas as utopian nonsense. With the excuse of planting the trees of liberty they continued with their conquests, he wrote in a French preface to a work from 1801—'it is no invention of our day that the right of the most powerful has overridden all other considerations'.[16]

---

[12] C. Wolff, *Jus gentium methodo scientifica pertractatum, vol. II* (J.H. Drake trans., Oxford: Oxford University Press, 1934), Prolegomena §7-12, 11–14.

[13] K. Haakonssen, 'German Natural Law', in M. Goldie and R. Wokler, *The Cambridge History of Eighteenth-Century Political Thought* (Cambridge: Cambridge University Press, 2006), 260.

[14] E. de Vattel, *The Law of Nations, or Principles of the Law of Nature Applied to the Conduct and Affairs of Nations and Sovereigns* (Indianapolis: Liberty Fund, 2008), Preface, 13–16.

[15] Ibid, 15.

[16] G.F. von Martens, *Précis de droit des gens moderne de l'Europe fondé sur les traités et l'usage* (Gottingue, 1801), xvi.

The vocabulary of cosmopolitanism, including that of 'world community', was revived towards the end of the nineteenth century as the international law profession organized itself. Liberal lawyers from Europe, the United States, Latin America, and even from China, Japan, and Egypt, began to advocate the expansion of liberal legislation in Europe as well as the civilizing of what they called the 'Orient'. The ambivalence of their project was expressed in the way the members of the Institut de droit international celebrated what they felt to be a humanitarian impulse behind the establishment of the Congo Free State by King Léopold of the Belgians.[17] No doubt an 'oceanic feeling' was inspiring their imagination about what European law might accomplish in their 'Orient'. No doubt that feeling was part of their liberalism, their concern for domestic progress, equality of men and women, the advocacy of decent prison conditions, and the spread of liberal constitutionalism. And no doubt they saw all this as underwritten by a historical logic such as that sketched in Immanuel Kant's famous essay from 1784—'universal history with a cosmopolitan purpose'. The optimism of the international lawyers was built on the (Christian) myth of lost unity as the hidden object of a teleological history. Until the early years of the twentieth century no shadow hung over their assumption that their Europe and their civilization would represent history's avant-garde. As Kant had written, in progressive history, 'Europe will probably lead the way'.[18]

## 4. Into 'realism'?

After two world wars, genocide, and the final demise of formal colonialism, international lawyers became more careful in translating their oceanic feelings to institutional proposals of world government. Of course, some of the leading members of the profession, such as Hersch Lauterpacht, were quite open in their advocacy of world federalism, insisting nevertheless that this would have to come about through a long series of intermediate steps. Lauterpacht regarded the Covenant of the League of Nations as 'Higher Law', though he was very conscious of its imperfections.[19] In a famous piece on the 'Grotian tradition' published right after the Second World War, he restated his optimistic faith in the coming of world government through international law sometime in the future.[20] No doubt, after 1989 many lawyers felt this objective nearer than it had been in their lifetime, and their easy resort to the vocabulary of the 'international community' to justify fighter planes over Kosovo and Belgrade in the spring of 1999 testified to a change in the ideological atmosphere.

[17] See M. Koskenniemi, *The Gentle Civilizer of Nations. The Rise and Fall of International Law 1870–1960* (Cambridge: Cambridge University Press, 2001), 155–66.

[18] I. Kant, 'The Idea of Universal History with a Cosmopolitan Purpose', in *Political Writings* (Hans Reiss ed., Cambridge: Cambridge University Press, 1991).

[19] H. Lauterpacht, 'The Covenant as "Higher Law"', XVII BYIL (1936) 54–65. On Lauterpacht's federalism, see M. Koskenniemi, n 17, 389–91.

[20] H. Lauterpacht, 'The Grotian Tradition in International Law', 23 BYIL (1946) 1–53.

It is hard not to have sympathy with the representatives of the global South—as articulated by India as a member of the UN Security Council in 1999—when they expressed scepticism about the ease with which the West was ready to proclaim its preferences as those of an 'international community'. Equally, it is hard to blame the African countries for their recent insertion of the question of universal jurisdiction into the agenda of the UN General Assembly, suggesting that the practice of some (especially European) states to extend the application of their criminal laws to crimes against humanity or other serious violations of human rights irrespective of where they have been committed was a de facto attempt to discipline their former colonies.[21]

Such controversies especially between the developed North and the global South point to a continuing dialectic in the efforts to translate the oceanic feeling for humanity, felt by well-placed professionals travelling across cosmopolitan spaces, into institutional projects or policy programmes within such international institutions as the UN or the European Union. There is no genuinely or intrinsically universal position from which such proposals could be made. Every institutional proposal or policy initiative will always appear in the shape of some particular agenda, proposed by a particular actor in reaction to a particular situation. And the suspicion remains that it is the makers of those proposals that would be their designated beneficiaries as well. The 'war on terror', for example, may have been designed to counter a global threat—but despite the universal values it invokes, it is hard not to notice the way it has shifted institutional priorities in favour of the developed world. The same logic affects our understanding of human rights or environmental agendas, too. Even as they are formulated in universal terms, their implementation will require decisions on allocation of scarce resources that will necessarily favour some at the cost of others. Within the broad terms of universal languages, struggle continues about what they should mean, and whose preferences they should advance.[22] How then to traverse the gap that separates the inevitable particularity of any such institutional proposals, on the one hand, and the ideals of universal humanity and world community, on the other?

## 5. Community as hegemony

In the process of thinking about this, one might do worse than inject the question of *power* into the equation. The claim made by someone—the representative of a country, say, or a profession (such as international law)—to represent the universal

---

[21] General Assembly, Sixty-third Session, 2009 July 2009, A/63/237/Rev.1, Request for the inclusion of an additional item in the agenda of the sixty-third session, The scope and application of the principle of universal jurisdiction, Letter dated 29 June 2009 from the Permanent Representative of the United Republic of Tanzania to United Nations addressed to the Secretary-General. See also Assembly of the African Union, Twelfth Ordinary Session, 1–3 February 2009, Addis Ababa, Ethiopia, Progress Report of the Commission on the Implementation of the Assembly Decision on the Abuse of the Principle of Universal Jurisdiction, Assembly/AU/3(XII).

[22] This is the key point in M. Koskenniemi, *From Apology to Utopia: The Structure of International Legal Argument* (reissued with a new Epilogue, Cambridge: Cambridge University Press, 2005).

position (eg the world community) is also a claim to be taken as an *authority*, as someone with the capacity to speak in a voice that transcends the particularity of one's country or profession. It is a claim of objectivity and neutrality, a claim of occupying no particular viewpoint but the viewpoint of 'all'. This is what grounds the speaker's claim for institutional power: after all, he or she is not speaking only for themselves, but for everyone. Irrespective of the genuineness with which the speaker actually feels that he or she has reached such a viewpoint—that is to say, whether or not it arises from a genuinely 'oceanic feeling'—it is usually very hard for *others* to take it as such. This is so because for those others, the claim is always infected by the particularity of the speaker, the world of his or her experience, culture and profession, knowledge and ignorance.

For an analyst (such as Freud) this in itself is not a problem, merely a mark of the speaker's humanity. Grasping the particularity of the speaker is a necessary step towards understanding what the speaker is in truth proposing. But for those who are called upon to assent to that statement—diplomats in the UN, for example—this means giving the speaker the authority to occupy also *their voice*, to become the representative of *their experience*, to speak in their name. If the representative of a Western nation now makes that claim of universality, it is hard to see why the non-Western world would see it differently than when it was made in the languages of Christianity, civilization, 'modernity', or 'development' (among others). The claim to speak in the voice of the 'world community' is not only an innocent statement about how the world is (or what I happen to 'feel'), but also contains the implicit claim for special authority that belongs to the one who can speak on everyone's behalf.[23]

Political theory and international relations sometimes use the vocabulary of 'hegemony' to highlight the process whereby a powerful actor starts to speak in a universal voice without encountering serious opposition. It is common for political actors to try to do precisely that. In revolutionary history, Abbé Sieyès' 'third estate' once proclaimed itself as the representative of the 'nation' and, for a moment, was successful. In Marx, the 'working class' became the 'universal class' whose interests and history had an objectivity that transcended the interests and history of the bourgeoisie. With these proclamations, everyone was called upon to join the 'oceanic feeling' of being part of the third estate or the working class, and the representatives of the third estate and of the working class were no longer speaking just for themselves, but for everyone.

But history did not stop with liberal revolutionaries or with communism. Universal vocabularies proliferate. The language of Western 'modernity' once became a political Esperanto that lifted Western political and technical experts into positions of authority. Today, vocabularies of 'globalization', 'development', 'market', 'human rights', 'free trade', 'environment', 'fight against impunity', and so on each seek to become the new universal language of international law. They present themselves in universal terms so that their experts, their 'native language-speakers',

[23] M. Koskenniemi, 'International Law and Hegemony: A Reconfiguration', 17 Cambridge Review of International Affairs (2004) 197–218.

would become authoritative in the world community and would thus legitimately take over the government of the world. For surely only those who possess a universal language (who truly share an 'oceanic feeling') ought to guide the government of all. But as Freud knew, the fact that one has an 'oceanic feeling' is not proof of the truth of religion. The clash between the various universal languages is a political clash that plays with different, indeed contested, ideas of what the 'world community' should be like, how we should be governed. Today, that problem is addressed by the ubiquitous theme of international law's 'fragmentation'. That the International Law Commission proposed to address that problem through the complex construct of fragmentation—diversification—expansion is another expression of the ambivalence of ideas about world community.[24] We oscillate between joining Dante in desiring world unity and our historical experience that advocates of such unity have so far not only failed, but also usually wreak quite a bit of havoc on the rest of the world before failing or giving up. Diversification, separation, and distinctness are often at least as important as unity and community, and often more intensely felt. Not everyone may experience the 'oceanic feeling' as pure enjoyment.

## 6. Utopia as critique

Finally, it is important to note that to see the particular in the universal (to analyse the desires that give rise to 'oceanic feelings') is not entirely a criticism of the proposed universal. It does not even slightly suggest that what is being proposed is bad or unworkable or should be rejected. It is merely to make the point that the claim of the 'universality' of something goes nowhere as a justification of it. Although the 'oceanic feeling' may certainly be *real* to the extent that the speaker actually feels it, this is no proof of its *universal* reality, either in terms of it being available to others, or its having some objective presence in the world. It still needs a defence in moral, legal, or economic terms. The right response to those who speak in the name of humanity and on that basis advocate some institutional proposal is this: 'Yes, you feel it. That is wonderful for you. But is you proposal *right*, is it *useful, should we think of it as binding law?*'

This is why a realistic utopia for world government should not consist of ready-made technical institutions for the management of this or that global problem or for the realization of some substantive vision about the way the world should be. It should not be a system of rule by academic, technical, or legal experts. In the modernist, functional consciousness utopias tend to be petrified into bureaucratic institutions and architectures, rules and procedures. That is one of their great weaknesses and the reason why they tend to seem unattractive, or outright harmful from the perspective of alternative institutional designs and values. For however

---

[24] See Conclusions of the work of the Study Group on the Fragmentation of International Law: Difficulties arising from the Diversification and Expansion of International Law, United Nations, 2006.

much such designs may seem appealing when stated in the abstract, their concrete realization always involves some distribution of power, and with it, some privileging of preferences and values. To dress utopian imagination in the straightjacket of such functionalism is already to have given in to a particular, and therefore contestable, idea about human relationships in the world.

I have often wondered why Kant in his *Perpetual Peace* and elsewhere carefully refrained from outlining the concrete features of the cosmopolitan federation he so clearly preferred. The above history should provide the beginnings of an explanation. For Kant, law, constitutionalism, and the cosmopolitan federation were all secondary to what he called 'freedom', envisaged as the 'inner value of the world'.[25] This is a complicated idea but one of its illustrations lies in the transcendental character of Kant's own utopian imaginary—his effort to keep history's 'cosmopolitan purpose' open, to be constructed at each moment anew by real human beings themselves, as an offshoot of their freedom.[26] As such, it operated much more as a critical standpoint from which to attack any present (functional) architecture for falling short of the ideal of freedom than a constructive platform on which to impose any particular blueprint on the world. Instead of calling human beings to begin from scratch, with an ideal institutional project, it directs attention to the more humble (yet more realistic) avenue of working with institutions we have now—not because they are good, or because they already represent a utopian design, but because they are what real humans have to deal with when we try to make reality of our freedom now. Kant was critical of the lesson of the history of utopianism—namely, that it had always appeared necessary to break some eggs in order to make an omelette. For him, this undermined the effort to think of every human being as an end in himself or herself. To be faithful to the latter purpose, it was necessary to start from here and now, and to judge present institutions in view of the maximization of freedom tomorrow. This idea could not coexist with an arrogant functionalism, or any other view involving a conscious avant-garde pointing the way to what Vladimir Zinoviev once called the 'radiant future'—a future that would never arrive but for which the present would nevertheless be sacrificed.[27]

A realistic utopia can only begin with the critique of present institutions—the United Nations, the World Bank, the Kyoto Protocol, the operations of large multinational companies, the structures of public law and private ordering that decide on the distribution of material and spiritual values today. It is perhaps best seen not as an institution but a mindset and an attitude that seeks to highlight the contingency and contestability of global institutions and their distributionary consequences. To maximize freedom it would seek to invite the widest possible participation by everyone, but especially those in the global South, to reorient the

[25] I. Kant, *Lectures on Ethics*, as quoted in P. Guyer, 'Freedom as the Inner Value of the World', in P. Guyer, *Kant on Freedom, Law and Happiness* (Cambridge: Cambridge University Press, 2000), 96.

[26] I. Kant, 'Idea for a Universal History with a Cosmopolitan Purpose', in *Political Writings* (Hans Reiss ed., Cambridge: Cambridge University Press, 1991).

[27] A. Zinoviev, *The Radiant Future* (New York: Random House, 1980).

work of global institutions—including institutions of private law and ordering—so as to benefit those who have been deprived. It would seek to re-describe forms of global expertise as types of political power that are no less contestable than any other types of power. Participants in such re-politicization might well be inspired by an 'oceanic feeling' but that should not be necessary. After all, critique and contestation rarely fare well with that type of romantic sentimentalism.

# 2

# Is Leviathan Still Holding Sway over International Dealings?

*Luigi Condorelli and Antonio Cassese\**

## SUMMARY

Although the limits to the sovereignty of states are increasingly growing in quantity and depth, partly in consequence of delegations of authority to supranational institutions and agencies, it remains true in substance that those growing limits still ultimately arise from the choice of the states: the choice to bind themselves, the sovereign choice to accept limits to their sovereignty. The overall logic of the phenomenon does not, therefore, appear to be that of expropriation of state competences, but rather that of assignment, transfer, or delegation. The alleged 'crisis of the state' should be read as a crisis of a certain model of the state, given the easily detectable tendency in modern states to give the executive a free hand in the exercise of decision-making power in participating in international organizations, to exclude the mechanisms provided by national constitutions to ensure the balance of powers and to allow adequate controls and checks on government activities. Although the state has remained the master of international relations and the backbone of the world community, it has undergone drastic changes since 1945 that have dramatically restricted some of its traditional prerogatives. In this respect three major trends should be highlighted: (i) the spread of human rights doctrines; (ii) the increasing and more and more dramatic impact of globalization both on relations between states and on the intertwining of their domestic systems; and (iii) the growing tendency of internal strife (motivated by ethnic, religious, or social tensions) to disrupt many sovereign states and even to imperil their life. Two palliatives are suggested to increase the sway of restraints over state sovereignty. First, the domestic structure and organization of modern democratic states should be so reshaped as to avoid leaving the executive a free hand in all international dealings.

   \* This chapter is based on an article written in Italian by Professor Luigi Condorelli entitled 'Crisi dello Stato e Diritto Internazionale: *Simul stabunt simul cadent?*', forthcoming in a collective book on modern states. The original paper, translated by Iain L. Fraser, has been adapted for this volume, and supplemented by the addition of some paragraphs by Antonio Cassese.

Secondly, one should also democratize intergovernmental organizations, by among other things imposing upon them full respect for the rights of individuals.

## 1. The alleged crisis of the modern sovereign state

According to many commentators, the state is in crisis because it is undergoing a downright expropriation of the main prerogatives and functions associated with it, to the benefit of international agencies and organizations, on the one hand, and the business world, on the other. Regarding the latter, it is pointed out in particular that it increasingly escapes the grasp of 'state-centric' law—whether national or international—and ultimately operates under the exclusive dominion of the rules it gives itself: private law made by private persons, in the logic of '*leges mercatoriae*' (or the like).

Let us, then, consider first of all the evolution of international law, and then (more briefly) the autonomy of private economic power, as contributory causes of the alleged crisis of the state.

## 2. States are still the major international lawmakers

It is worthwhile—in discussing the first point—to start with some basic premises about what is usually regarded as the key structural feature of contemporary international law. We find it expressed in, for instance, Article 2 of the UN Charter, which in point 1 indicates as the first principle on which the UN (but really the whole international system) is founded the 'sovereign equality' of states. In fact, it is the states that 'make' international norms, at least those at the top of the system (treaties and customs), that commit themselves to respect them and run them, that create the so-called 'intergovernmental' international organizations and equip them with competences, powers (including legislative ones, if applicable), and appropriate means to work; it is the states that create the mechanisms for resolving disputes in various fields, be they courts, arbiters, or others. The constraints to which states are subject multiply incessantly, and international organizations, among which several have been given pervasive powers of action, are increasingly numerous. In short, the limits to the sovereignty of states are increasingly growing in quantity and depth, partly in consequence of delegations of authority to supranational institutions and agencies. However, it remains true in substance (as the Permanent Court of International Justice had already said in 1923, in the famous *Wimbledon* case,[1]

---

[1]  In its judgment of 17 August 1923 the Court states the following:

> The Court declines to see in the conclusion of any Treaty by which a state undertakes to perform or refrain from performing a particular act an abandonment of its sovereignty. No doubt any convention creating an obligation of this kind places a restriction upon the exercise of the sovereign rights of the state, in the sense that it requires them to be exercised in a certain way. But the right of entering into international engagements is an attribute of state sovereignty. (PCIJ, Series A, no. 1, 25)

and has since then been tirelessly repeated) that those growing limits still ultimately arise from the choice of the states themselves: the choice to bind themselves, the sovereign choice to accept limits to sovereignty. The overall logic of the phenomenon does not, therefore, appear to be that of expropriation, but rather that of *assignment*, *transfer*, or *delegation*.

### 3.  It is the states that set up and strictly control intergovernmental organizations

No one can doubt the exponential growth of international organizations and the progressive rise in their world of models that go well beyond the classic discussion and coordination fora, aimed at promoting and stimulating negotiations and agreements between states. There are in fact—as we know—a number of international bodies, both 'universal' and 'regional', that exercise administrative and regulatory powers in core areas that severely affect states, which find themselves addressees of all types of imperatives (rules, directives, requirements, regulations, decisions, and so on) from international, or otherwise 'external', sources they must comply with, even granting them—if required—primacy over domestic law. What sovereignty is there in these conditions?

Two sets of observations are called for in this connection.

The first set is: no international organization, even the best endowed, has bailiffs, police, or gendarmes, a fine-grained administrative and judicial apparatus, armed forces, etc. Even the UN 'blue helmets', for example, consist of 'national contingents' made available by the individual member states pursuing their own policy choices. In other words, cooperation—including that which is realized through the most powerful international organizations—needs, in order to function, sovereign states which, after having agreed to bind themselves at the international level, agree actually to implement what is decided at supranational level. The metaphor Antonio Cassese often uses, that international criminal justice has neither arms nor legs of its own, and therefore cannot operate if prostheses are not made available, namely the arms and legs of the states, actually applies to any entity, device, or structure of cooperation established by states. In this regard one should emphasize the need for states to be 'effective', that is to be based on the principle of effectiveness, if one wishes international law to function.

The second set of observations more directly concerns the source of the 'external' decisions to implement. While there is no doubt that international law absolutely needs states (indeed, 'effective' states) in order for what has been established at the 'supra-state' (or 'supranational') level to then be realized in practice, the aspect of the international institutions and the mechanisms by which decision-making power is exercised by them remains to be investigated. What is their relationship with the states and what is their *modus operandi*? It is curious (and superficial) that the international decisions to be implemented are presented by most commentators as data from which to start, without bothering to take into consideration—in developing the arguments on the crisis of the state—the actual operation of the decision-making apparatus and the role of the states in its midst. International (and/or supranational) law does not come down to states like the Ten Commandments to Moses on Mount Sinai. It is not the Lord that establishes it and imposes it from heaven on those who are called to respect it: it is the states themselves that make it and command it in their agreements.

The agreement between states—let us emphasize this point—is always, necessarily, there. In fact, first—upstream—there is the agreement by which the international body is created and its powers and functions regulated. It remains true today that all international organizations, even the most sophisticated and robust, are still creatures of the states, operating under the banner of what the International Court of Justice (ICJ) calls the 'principle of specialty': their powers and functions are those—and only those—limited ones that the states (entities with 'general' competence) have agreed to grant them.

But downstream too (so to speak) the role of states is very considerable, even decisive. In most cases, the organs called on, in accordance with basic international agreements, to take the decisions—at least the most important ones—that have to be implemented by the state apparatus are composed of the same member states of the international organization. The international decisions in question hide under another name their essence as international agreements between governments adopted through mechanisms other than the ordinary ones. This is undeniable, considering the current cases of international bodies that consist of states and decide unanimously or by consensus: a particularly good example is the 'North Atlantic Council', the NATO body that adopts all measures of note. *Mutatis mutandis*, the same can also be said about the international organizations to which we usually reserve the qualifier of 'supranational', in order to emphasize the capacity they have directly to affect the laws of the member states through their acts (legislative, executive, or judicial), whether they originate in organs composed of states or organs made up of individuals. The latter are undoubtedly endowed with very significant decision-making powers. Those powers are, however, to be defined as 'executive' in character, since the organs in question are still subjected to—and are called on to act within the limits of and in compliance with—agreements between countries: first, of course, those creating the organization, then those adopted under another name in the organs composed of states: in the case of the European Union, the Council of Ministers and, at the top, the European Council (or Council of Heads of State and Government). And it is hardly necessary to recall the cardinal role the unanimity rule still plays at this level for the exercise of decision-making power in key areas, not to mention the obvious need for real formal international agreements among all the member states in order to amend or improve or widen or deepen or enhance the organization's structure, its sphere of competence, etc. It is also not uncommon to use the system of 'contracting out', under which a majority decision is binding on all except those who opt out within a set time. However, it is a fact that, even if the international body has the power to take a binding decision by majority, the obligation for member states to comply with and implement it has its source and foundation in the sovereign decision of each of them to participate in the mechanism involved and to allow its operation.

This analysis can, with very similar results, be applied to the various international organizations to which we refer when discussing the expropriations of powers of the state effected by international law and because of the various decision-making mechanisms that operate at that level (in terms of political, financial, economic, etc. cooperation). The UN case deserves further brief consideration, however, since the Security Council—the only political body capable according to the founding treaty (the 'Charter') of imposing obligations, even heavy ones, on all countries in the world—certainly consists of states (but restricted, as we know, to 15) and decides by majority vote. It is clear that (only) decisions to establish measures to deal with threats to peace, breaches of the peace, or acts of aggression must compulsorily be implemented by all states to which they are addressed, including those which remain in the minority on the Council but do not enjoy the so-called 'veto', and those which do not sit on that body. There are, therefore, so to speak, five 'more sovereign' states, which have to endure much smaller limitations of sovereignty than the others. It should, however, be noted that this does not apply to measures involving the use of force. On the one hand, peacekeeping operations are carried out by military units which—although they must be regarded as 'organs' of the UN—are formed of contingents of the states' armed forces made available to the organization by them voluntarily (hence in sovereign fashion) from time to time. On the other hand, while actual military actions to combat aggression or massive violation of human rights are decided by the Security Council, it confines itself in such cases to granting the 'willing' states the mere permission to use all necessary means to the prescribed end: it is for these states to decide in sovereign fashion whether to participate or not in the operation and to what extent, and themselves to determine what means are to be deemed necessary in the case in point.

## 4. State sovereignty is not on the wane: rather, what is declining is the traditional model of the modern democratic state

It a truism to note that for the effective management of many important issues in the most varied areas, both 'foreign' and domestic (from security to the economy and finance, or the most varied social issues), the government dimension is increasingly inadequate and that states are increasingly affected—even in exercising functions belonging to the very core of sovereignty—by 'external' institutions (international and/or supranational). All the same, one should not forget to take into account what has just been highlighted about 'how' and 'by whom' decision-making power is actually exercised within these institutions. If it is true (or, if preferred, to the extent that is true) that those who really decide even at that level are still the states, then it is no wonder that if behind what is being labelled a 'crisis of the state' we are not instead essentially seeing phenomena related to changes taking place in the organization of states; in short, that we are dealing with a substantial alteration of the modes of exercising the sovereignty of states, rather than a real decline of it.

Put in these terms the issue has implications of no small importance: finding that the international decisions are at bottom agreements between states leads inevitably to questions about how these agreements are concluded, or about the legal regime which applies to the relevant decision-making powers. In short, the 'crisis of the state' should be read after all as a crisis of *a certain model of the state*, given the easily detectable tendency to favour governmental structures where state sovereignty is to be exercised through participation in international organizations and the conclusion in them of the agreements/decisions in question, and the related tendency in these cases to bypass the regulation of treaty-making power provided for by national constitutions, and in particular the mechanisms to ensure the balance of powers and to allow adequate controls and checks on government activities. Those who are sensitive to the type of considerations just underlined would do well to incorporate in their reflections on the crisis of the state the theme of 'international decision-making power'.

## 5. Intergovernmental organizations are not parties to human rights instruments

Subject to what will be pointed out later on the matter, it can be maintained that a further aspect not to be ignored concerns the protection of human rights. International instruments in this area are all designed in terms of states, are open to their participation only, and provide mechanisms that can be used to enforce their liability in case of violations: not that of the international organizations which—largely because of the developments we are discussing—now increasingly exercise powers and perform acts able directly or indirectly to affect fundamental rights and freedoms. Now, it would be absurd to pretend that human rights obligations on states vanish when, instead of each acting for themselves, they agree to cooperate by entrusting functions and powers to international organizations of their own creation.

## 6. Even international criminal justice does not hedge state sovereignty around with major limitations

There can be no doubt that international criminal justice is one of the most significant developments of contemporary international law. Many commentators suggest that such a development (even if it is rated by a majority as highly positive and encouraging) nonetheless implies a very considerable blow to one of the most characteristic attributes of state sovereignty: the monopoly of repressive power. But is that true? Can one truly say that the establishment of international criminal courts results—at least potentially—in a real diminution of sovereign state powers? That is to be doubted; indeed, those who argue in these terms are to be suspected of neglecting or overlooking highly relevant aspects of the current pattern of international law in this area.

We here refer mainly to the system of the International Criminal Court (ICC). The ICC is potentially competent to punish the most serious international crimes, or core crimes (genocide, crimes against humanity and war crimes, and one day, perhaps, the crime of aggression) wherever and by whomever committed. We should instead set aside for the purposes of our considerations the ad hoc international criminal tribunals established by the Security Council for specific situations of a transitory nature (those relating to events in the former Yugoslavia and Rwanda) and other international (or mixed) courts to deal with other special situations, also temporary, or even one-off (we are referring to the tribunals for Sierra Leone, Lebanon, Cambodia, and the like). It should be emphasized, in fact, that the ICC is not designed to 'hijack' the task of national courts to punish core crimes committed by individuals, but to judge and if necessary to sentence the perpetrators of such crimes when and only when states prove unable or unwilling to do so through their internal judicial systems. In other words, the Rome Statute confirms that the repressive function lies with the states and must be put in place by them also for the most serious crimes that endanger values essential to the entire international community: the Rome Statute makes the ICC essentially a strictly subsidiary mechanism to combat impunity, calling on it to operate only when necessary to remedy the states' omissions, detectable by the finding that they fail to comply through their own judges with the international obligations contracted by them regarding the prosecution of international crimes. Not an expropriation of the repressive function, in short, but, as it were, a type of sanction for failure to exercise it.

## 7. Private economic transactions only interstitially or tangentially escape state-centric legal regulation

It is now time for some considerations about private economic power and its auton-omy, understood as a tendency to escape the grip of state-centric law (both domes-tic and international) and to employ self-regulation.

Let us start with an elementary observation. We know that the world of international trade develops its own specific rules and practices to which economic actors (state and otherwise) conform when they negotiate, conclude, and execute both contracts between states and foreign public and private companies, and contracts between private companies of different countries. The name famously attached to this type of rules is *lex mercatoria* (often specified as 'new', to distinguish it from legal phenomena of other ages for which the term was originally coined). If disputes then arise, these contracts require the use of mechanisms such as 'transnational' (or international commercial) arbitration and call on the referee always to apply in resolving them the *lex mercatoria* itself, or, if this is insufficient, 'general principles of law', or other similar formulas. The world of the *lex mercatoria* has notoriously been growing dramatically over the years, and even multiplying: we now, in fact, speak of *lex informatica, lex sportiva, lex petrolea*, etc. That these 'third' laws (ie, neither internal nor international in nature) exist, have force, and apply is a real fact that no legal theory can deny; there are even those who, from this datum, develop imaginative ideas that preach the need to abandon the old and obsolescent argument that the law arises directly or indirectly from the state (or—with regard to international law—from the states) and claim we are instead seeing the gradual consolidation of an alternative *law without a state*, with no territorial connections, replacing (at least for international trade) the now outdated state-centric variety. But these (by nature, so to speak, hagiographic) visions are very approximate and naïve, given that they fail to notice that the relevance and application of the *lex mercatoria* are possible because (and as far as) international and national law leave room, opening up more or less extensive spheres of action for private autonomy: it is, in other words, an '*interstitial*' law, called upon to occupy the interstices left to it by domestic and international law. Its nature and its role are not changed by the fact that these gaps have—in today's context of 'globalization' in the name of the triumphant ideology of the 'free world market'—expanded dramatically.

It is true that the enlargement in question has ended up taking on abnormal proportions, since a number of economic and political factors have led to a sort of abdication of state-centric law, which too often refrains from appropriately adjusting the behaviour of markets, letting human rights, both individual and collective, largely be sacrificed on the altar of economic development and the logic of profit, especially, but not exclusively, with regard to the underdeveloped world. This does not mean, however, that 'governance' is impossible. One may certainly talk in this connection about a crisis of the state, in the sense that the sphere of national governance has proved inadequate to achieve it. But the same cannot be said of international law and cooperation mechanisms between countries: the operation of these mechanisms is, however, still (as noted above) dependent on the exercise of state power. If it does not succeed, that is because strong opposing interests among the states stand in the way of effective international action. However, there is growing awareness—in the face of events like the great financial crisis of 2008—that the era of so-called 'happy globalization' is over and that on the contrary the need is in fact to 'govern' the global economy. It is important to note, however, in this light, that this is not only a matter of plans for the future: work is in progress on several fronts, with instruments of all types, both hard and soft, and within the framework of various international organizations (UN, International Labour Organization, Organization for Economic Co-Operation and Development, European Union, UNIDROIT, etc.). This is, for example, the case in the fields of development cooperation, the fight against corruption, corporate social responsibility, environment protection, promotion of virtuous human rights practices by multinational companies, identification of mandatory rules the *lex mercatoria* must respect, and so on.

### 8. Nevertheless, the present sovereign state is not that of the Westphalian model: three extra-legal trends end up powerfully restraining the traditional sovereign prerogatives of states

What has been noted so far should not lead the reader to believe that the authors of this chapter feel that the state, although it has remained the master of international relations and the backbone of the world community, has not undergone drastic changes since 1945 that have dramatically restricted some of its traditional prerogatives.

In this respect three major trends should be highlighted: (i) the spread of human rights doctrines; (ii) the increasing and more and more dramatic impact of globalization both on relations between states and on the intertwining of their domestic systems; and (iii) the growing tendency of internal strife (motivated by ethnic, religious, or social tensions) to disrupt many sovereign states and even to imperil their existence.

Let us briefly consider each of these trends. The *spread of human rights* after the Second World War has meant that this new ideology has gradually if very slowly made it impossible for the sovereign state to behave as it pleases within the confines of its territory. Beforehand, state authorities could massacre their own nationals without other states meddling in the matter, or in a few extreme cases simply issuing protests, appeals, or exhortations. Now this is no longer possible: other states, normally congregated in international organizations or arrangements, either authorize the use of force against the wrongdoer (as in the case of Libya) or take economic sanctions against some leaders of the state at issue (think of the current attitude vis-à-vis Zimbabwe, Burma (Myanmar), and some Arab countries). What is even more important, hand in hand with the increasing rootedness of the ideology of human rights, *individuals* have emerged as new actors in international society. For centuries they were non-existent on the international scene. Then, after the Second World War, they gushed out on that scene thanks to two distinct but concurrent developments. *First*, the world community realized that it was individuals who had committed horrendous crimes during the war and who must therefore be brought to trial and punished, rather than (or in addition to) the states on whose behalf they had acted (hence the celebrated proposition of the Nuremberg International Military Tribunal that international law is also concerned with the acts of individuals, and that individuals, and not the states for which they act, bear responsibility for any gross violation of international law amounting to international crime).[2] The *second* development was the diffusion of the human rights

---

[2] The Tribunal stated the following:

> It was submitted that international law is concerned with the action of sovereign states, and provides no punishment for individuals; and further, that where the act in question is an act of state, those who carry it out are not personally responsible, but are protected by the doctrine of the sovereignty of the state. In the opinion of the Tribunal, both these submissions must be rejected.... individuals can be punished for violations of international law. Crimes against international law are committed by men, not by abstract entities, and

doctrine (prompted by the horrors of the war and President Roosevelt's famous speech on the Four Freedoms in 1941): the clear implication of the doctrine was that individuals were entitled to claim respect for their human rights; hence they could challenge their own governments as well as foreign governments for breaching their human rights. This doctrine entailed among other things that states could no longer legitimately claim immunity from prosecution for their officials accused of international crimes (a manifest inroad into state sovereignty) and that they had to accept being challenged before international bodies for the conduct they had taken within their domestic legal order towards nationals or foreigners (another major indentation of their sovereign authority). In short, states are no longer free to behave as they please vis-à-vis individuals.

The second extra-legal factor that has pushed towards a significant limitation of states' sovereign prerogatives resides in the increasing impact that *globalization* is having on international relations. Globalization, a more recent phenomenon than human rights (it began to loom large in its current forms and manifestations in the 1990s), means that thanks to modern technology there is an increasing interchange and interconnection at the economic, financial, commercial, cultural, and information level among states of the world. In addition, the unimpeded movement all over the world of goods, services, technology, information, and so on, means that no state can escape dramatic events that occur in other parts of the world. One of the many consequences of globalization is that *no individual state, not even the superpower, is able to decide everything by itself but must perforce rely upon other states, or at least agree with them upon what conduct to take in many specific areas.* In short, sovereign prerogatives of individual states are now eroded by this new extra-legal phenomenon.

The third trend that is restraining state authority is the mushrooming of rebellion in sovereign states. Admittedly this is not a new phenomenon. Hobbes epitomized well the tension between the sovereign state and insurgency by contrasting Leviathan to Behemoth:[3] two Molochs, one symbolizing the state, and the other what Kant later called 'an internal illness of the state',[4] namely civil war, or the attempt to break up the structure of sovereign states.[5] It is indeed no coincidence that no international rule evolved on civil wars while states dominated the structure of the international community, the matter being generally regarded as exclusively domestic and to be dealt with only by internal methods (rebels being seditious

---

only by punishing individuals who commit such crimes can the provisions of international law be enforced. (*Trial of the Major War Criminals before the International Military Tribunal*, vol. 1, Nuremberg, 1947, at 222–3)

[3] We are referring to *Leviathan* ([1651], ed. and with an introduction by C.B. Macpherson, Harmondsworth: Penguin, 1983), and *Behemoth or the Long Parliament*, 2nd edn ([1679], F. Tönnies ed., New York: Barnes and Noble, 1969). In *Leviathan*, Hobbes defined 'sedition' as a sickness and 'civil war' as 'death' (at 81).

[4] Kant speaks of a state in civil war as being 'a people independent of others, which only struggles with an internal illness' (*eines nur mit seiner innern Krankheit ringenden, von keinem andern abhängigen Volks*): see *Zum Ewigen Frieden* (Königsberg: Friedrich Nicolovius, 1795 (reprint 2004)), 12.

[5] However, for Hobbes, the Leviathan was an entity *indispensable* for modern society and to combat what for him was the really dangerous monster, namely civil strife.

criminals to be killed or hanged). Under this state-centric perspective of international law, third states must keep aloof from civil wars in other states: as noted by Wheaton, 'Until the revolution is consummated, whilst the civil war involving a contest for the government continues, other states may remain indifferent spectators of the controversy.'[6]

What is new, however, is the multiplication of instances where ethnic groups, minorities, or political organizations take up arms against the central authorities and promote insurgency and even secession. This trend is linked to the structure of many African and Asian countries whose borders had been arbitrarily shaped by colonial countries without attention to tribes, groups, nationalities, religion, and so on. It is also linked to the end of the Cold War and the demise of two blocs of states, which has released forces and scattered authority over the planet. What is also new is that in protracted civil wars, rebels often manage to acquire a state-like structure, with a functioning administration and courts of law that pass judgement on crimes by the government forces and even by rebels.[7] What is now new is that domestic tensions tend to become very strong and to blow up or break up many members of the world community. Strikingly, the aim of the rebels or insurgents is very often the establishment of a new state. Thus, if Behemoth trumps Leviathan, this is primarily to establish other new Leviathans.

In brief, the increase in internal strife perforce weakens the state even when state authorities react to rebellion by bolstering the authoritarian streak of the government and restricting civil liberties of all citizens.

## 9. What could be done to increase restraints on the sway of sovereignty?

It is indubitable that sovereign states will still for many decades to come be the overlords of the world community. Nevertheless, one should not rule out a slow dwindling of their immense power with the passage of time.

Globalization, by itself, will be the major driving force pushing states to get together and think up common strategies or work out joint defensive mechanisms—and all this will by necessity limit the authority of *each individual state*.

In the legal realm, only modest *palliatives* can be suggested.

First, the domestic structure and organization of modern democratic states should be so reshaped to avoid leaving the executive a free hand in all international dealings. Modern modalities of scrutiny or oversight should be put in place enabling democratic bodies not belonging to the executive branch to check that the executive

---

[6] H. Wheaton, *Elements of International Law, with a Sketch of the History of the Science*, vol. 1 (London: B. Fellowes, 1836), 92. Wheaton adds, however, that third states may then espouse the cause of one of the contestants, with the consequence that 'it becomes of course, the enemy of the party against whom it declares itself, and the ally of the other' (at 93).

[7] See S. Sivakumaran, 'Courts of Armed Opposition Groups—Fair Trials or Summary Justice?', 7 J Int'l Crim Justice (2009) 489–513.

does not decide everything by itself, and then face the whole national community with a fait accompli—on the pretext that indeed the decision challenged had been agreed upon or even imposed by an intergovernmental organization. In other words, if the state must remain the main actor in international dealings, let us at least democratize its domestic decision-making mechanisms, so that decisions formally taken at the international level (by organizations or groupings of states) are filtered at least at the domestic level. This would enable the domestic constituency to have a major say in foreign policy-making.

Secondly, one should also democratize intergovernmental organizations, by among other things imposing upon them full respect for the rights of individuals. As noted above, the international human rights instruments are all designed in terms of states, are open to the participation of these only, and provide mechanisms that can be used to enforce their liability in case of violations, but not that of international organizations. Now, it would be absurd to pretend that the human rights obligations that weigh on states vanish when, instead of acting each for themselves, they agree to cooperate by entrusting functions and powers to international organizations of their own creation. We must therefore firmly fight the tendency of states to 'shelter' behind international organizations, claiming that their responsibility does not come into play when it is agencies of the latter that fail to respect human rights. It is, in particular, important to ensure that the relevant international conventions in the area directly bind all international actors (states, international organizations, etc.) whose actions impact the lives and interests of individuals. The European Union's (future) full participation in the European Convention on Human Rights is an important first step in this direction, but only a first step: for example, the entire dossier relating to the UN and international measures to combat terrorism shows that other very important steps remain to be taken in order to obtain not only appropriate compliance with the principles in this connection by the world body, but also the opportunity for individuals affected by those measures to access appropriate mechanisms to oversee their legality.

# 3

# State Sovereignty is Not Withering Away: A Few Lessons for the Future

*José E. Alvarez*

## SUMMARY

The Westphalian system of nation-states remains the system that we have. State sovereignty, which even according to Bodin was not unfettered, is not withering away. States have pooled, shared, delimited, or delegated away some of their powers through treaties, but they but can always take back powers that they have previously negotiated away. The best illustration of this can be found in the investment regime. For long major states including the United States have favoured the most effective and sovereignty-intrusive of our international regimes at the global level: the international investment regime which protects the rights of foreign investors and consists of some 3,000 bilateral investment treaties (BITs) and free trade agreements (FTAs) with investment chapters, as supplemented by de facto regulators of capital markets such as the IMF. Now, however, nations are reasserting their 'sovereignty' vis-à-vis foreign investors through changes to their national laws or their treaties. Three lessons can be drawn for the future: (i) to the extent there are choices to be made between global regulation and sovereign control, the outcome may not reflect a progress narrative but a historical dialectic that periodically swings back and forth as international norms encounter resistance at the national level, thereby triggering re-evaluation and modification of the international regime or its rules; (ii) all international regimes, no matter how well constructed, ultimately rely on states to implement them at the domestic level; how that implementation occurs is subject to considerable state discretion; and much can occur to an international regime as its rules are translated for domestic consumption or application; and (iii) we need to remain vigilant when it comes to the North/South dimensions of international regimes and reactions to them.

# 1. Globalists v Sovereigntists

International lawyers are in a quandary when it comes to assessing the future of state sovereignty. Traditional international lawyers, particularly those based in Europe, have long been at war with Jean Bodin's and Thomas Hobbes' 'absolute' sovereignty. Many believe that the victories achieved by Europeans over 'outdated' forms of exclusive sovereign control—as institutionalized in relatively effective European Union institutions—ought to be emulated and even deepened further, if not globally at least at the regional level. For believers in a Grotian world order, international norms, particularly but not only its peremptory rules, need to penetrate deeper and supersede national jurisdiction and law. On this view, global progress is measured by the extent sovereignty yields to international rules designed to enhance community values.[1] For those bent on advancing world order through law, the state-centricity of international law is a burdensome constraint since generally the more international regulation, international institutions, and internationalized adjudication, the better.[2] Others, of a more 'critical' legal bent, have lauded the 'wonderful artificiality' of statehood, praising how governments have used their sovereignty to resist the dark sides of global governance.[3]

Such binary attitudes reflect opposing views of the benefits of global governance and not only distinct views of the value of the Westphalian system. Not everyone has been inspired, at the moral or intellectual level, by what Martti Koskenniemi has described in Chapter 1 as the 'oceanic feeling' endorsing universal brother/sisterhood. Some have found inspiration instead in old-fashioned statehood—on the premise that states, particularly but not only by those governed on democratic principles as defined by the West, provide a more reliable answer to those dissatisfied by the democratic and legitimacy deficits of international institutions.[4] What traditional international lawyers see as the culmination of international law's

---

[1] This point of view is suggested by Antonio Cassese's Introduction to this volume.

[2] For excellent examples in this volume of recipes for 'progress' along these lines, see Chapter 13, A. Cassese, 'For an Enhanced Role of *Jus Cogens*' (urging the use of *jus cogens* as a tool against state immunity); Chapter 24, id, 'Fostering Increased Conformity with International Standards: Monitoring and Institutional Fact-Finding' (urging greater adoption of these tools to ensure state compliance with international standards); Chapter 15, id, 'Towards a Moderate Monism: Could International Rules Eventually Acquire the Force to Invalidate Inconsistent National Law?' (recommending international and national measures, especially at the regional level, to secure the 'true superiority' of international over national norms).

[3] M. Koskenniemi, 'The Wonderful Artificiality of States', *ASIL Proceedings of the 88th Annual Meeting* (1994), 22. See also B. Kingsbury, 'Sovereignty and Inequality', 9 EJIL (1998) 599 (arguing that discarding sovereignty would intensify inequality, weaken restraints on coercive intervention, diminish critical roles of the state as the locus of identify and an autonomous zone of politics, and re-divide the world into zones, as between 'liberal' and 'non-liberal' states).

[4] For a useful survey of the democratic objections lodged against international institutions, see E. Stein, 'International Integration and Democracy: Love at First Sight', 95 AJIL (2001) 489.

progress narrative is criticized by the second group as ideologically captured and politically contestable governance by 'independent' experts from nowhere.[5]

Although the later 'crits' are associated with academic movements that originated in North American law schools, the debate on the future of state sovereignty (or indeed whether it ought to have a future at all) retains a North/South dimension. The mostly European defenders of global institutions on behalf of a 'world community', including the editor of this volume who sees such a world as a 'realistic utopia', find themselves pitted against those who purport to speak on behalf of the South and who see the hard-won sovereignty of the formerly colonized as a last bastion of protection against overweening global tools of the market and institutionalized hegemony laundered as 'international regulation'.[6]

As Martti Koskenniemi has suggested, both groups adhere to an instrumentalist or functionalist conception of sovereignty.[7] Both seek to maximize welfare for the greatest number but hold opposing views of how best to effectuate this goal. The globalist, citing innumerable historical examples, sees sovereignty as shielding tyrannical governments that violate human rights or incompetent rulers whose governance failings fail their populations in many other respects. The sovereigntist, armed with abundant, if more recent, failings of global institutions as varied as UN peacekeeping and the IMF, counters that governments are in a better position to improve the welfare of their own peoples.

Koskenniemi castigates globalists for failing to interrogate their own conception of the good. He argues that the laudable objectives of global institutions—security, the eradication of poverty, peace—are all highly contestable goals subject to inescapable political assessments and choices that cannot be reduced to mere technocratic, scientific, or juridical determinations by the 'international community'.[8] His argument for sovereignty is that the territorially defined peoples of the world are entitled to the 'thrill' of participating in their own respective forms of self-formation—whether or not defined in terms of republican self-rule:[9]

Sovereignty expresses frustration and anger about the diminishing spaces of collective re-imagining, creation and transformation of individual and group identities by what present themselves as the unavoidable necessities of a global modernity . . . [S]overeignty points to the possibility, however limited or idealistic, that whatever comes to happen, one is not just a pawn in other people's games but, for better or for worse, the master of one's life.[10]

Debates between sovereigntists and globalists have filled the pages of scholarly journals but more importantly they have helped to generate competing reactions

---

[5] See, eg, D. Kennedy, 'Challenging Expert Rule: The Politics of Global Governance', 27 Sydney JIL (2005) 5.

[6] For those associated with Third World Approaches of International Law (TWAIL), global governance institutions as diverse as the UN Security Council, UN human rights bodies, the IMF, or the WTO are neo-colonialist in orientation and/or effect. See, eg, M. Mutua, 'What is TWAIL?', *ASIL Proceedings of the 94th Annual Meeting* (2000), 31; R. Gordan, 'Saving Failed States: Sometimes a Neocolonialist Notion', 12 Am U J Int'l L &Pol'y (1997) 903. For an ideological critique, see S. Marks, 'Big Brother is Bleeping Us—With the Message that Ideology Doesn't Matter', 12 EJIL (2001) 109.  [7] Koskenniemi, n 3 (What use for sovereignty today?).

[8] Ibid, XXX.  [9] Ibid.  [10] Ibid.

to real-world dilemmas, as with respect to how best to handle the adjudication of mass atrocities. For some, such crimes should best be left to undisturbed domestic jurisdiction. For others, the history of immunity and amnesia at the national level compels international action but differences remain with respect to the continuing value of 'sovereign' control. The result is an ungainly assortment of international war crimes tribunals with primacy over national jurisdiction, an International Criminal Court subject to complementarity, and ad hoc 'hybrid' tribunals incorporating features of both international and national systems of justice—all of which are sometimes 'complemented' by other forms of accountability as diverse as Gacaca trials or truth commissions. For some globalists, this pragmatic outcome—reproduced in other regimes with proliferating international adjudicative fora operating in the absence of *stare decisis* or hierarchical means of control—encourages harmful fragmentation that de-legitimizes international law.[11]

## 2. The myth that the state is 'withering away'

A considerable number of scholars, including political scientists, have argued that sovereignty is 'waning', 'withering away', is in 'decline', 'retreat', is already 'dead', or even that it has always been a 'myth'.[12] They point to the steady accretion of international law and its impact on virtually every legal domain irrespective of categorization as 'public' or 'private' or potential effect on matters involving 'foreign affairs'. To the extent 'sovereignty' connotes, as classical writers suggested, supreme authority, or absolute, uncontested power over all matters within a territory, or freedom from outside interference, or the equivalent of a non-trespassing sign forbidding entry onto private property, or Greta Garbo's demand to be left alone, these sovereignty doubters are correct since no such thing exists today. Individual members of the European Union are not sovereign with respect to matters governed by EU law and, beyond Europe, modern sovereignty, as Abram and Antonia Chayes have noted, has been reduced to issues of status or membership in distinct international organizations—to which states have delegated away distinct (and growing) powers.[13] These international organizations have become 'autonomous' agents capable of exercising implied and un-enumerated powers as pedestrian as the capacity to exercise forms of diplomatic protection (see *Reparation for Injuries* case) and as grand as de facto control over a state's economic and

[11] See, eg, ILC Fragmentation Project.

[12] See, eg, E. Lauterpacht, 'Sovereignty—Myth or Reality?', 73 Int'l Affairs (January 1997); C. Schreuer, 'The Waning of the Sovereign State: Towards a New Paradigm for International Law?', 4 EJIL (1993) 447; T.G. Weiss et al, 'Sovereignty under Siege: From Intervention to Humanitarian Space', in G. Lyons and M. Mastaduno (eds), *Beyond Westphalia?: State Sovereignty and International Intervention* (Baltimore: John Hopkins University Press, 1995), 87; J.A. Camilleri and J. Falk, *The End of Sovereignty? The Politics of a Shrinking and Fragmenting World* (Cheltennam: Edwin Elgar, 1992); A. Rosas, 'The Decline of Sovereignty: Legal Perspectives', in J. Livonen, *The Future of the Nation State in Europe* (Cheltenham: Edwin Elgar, 1993). In addition, see the various papers published in the special issue of Daedalus: 'What Future for the Nation State?' 124(2) Daedalus (1995). See also N. MacCormick, 'Beyond the Sovereign State', 56 MLR (1993) 1.

[13] A. Chayes and A. Chayes, *The New Sovereignty: Compliance with International Regulatory Agreements* (Cambridge MA, London: Harvard University Press, 1995), 27.

social policies (eg IMF conditionality).[14] Thanks to the institutional practice of such organizations as well as decisions rendered by our proliferating body of international judges, there has been a steady diminution in conceptions of 'domestic jurisdiction'.[15]

Governments have found the premise in the *Wimbledon* case—the idea that entering into a treaty is an exercise of sovereignty not its diminishment—so alluring that treaties, inter-state organizations, and international tribunals have proliferated at a fast clip, overtaken only by other diverse forms of delegating sovereign power to others, such as hybrid intergovernmental organizations (eg the Internet Corporation for assigned Names and Numbers (ICANN)), private organizations governing and largely governed by market actors (eg the International Standardization Organization (ISO)), or transnational networks of sub-state actors or government regulators (eg the Basel Committee of central bankers). In other cases, states have authorized non-state third party beneficiaries of their treaties to bring claims against them in international tribunals, thereby generating the international 'case law' that has become the linchpin for ever-more developed international investment law and human rights law. The 'private attorney generals' charged with enforcing international investment law under Bilateral Investment Treaties (BITs) and Free Trade Agreements (FTAs) or international human rights law under human rights treaties have become, along with the adjudicators that accept their creative treaty interpretations, de facto lawmaking actors. Whether all of this is labelled 'global administrative law', species of 'global constitutionalism', 'humanity's law', or new forms of '*ius gentium*',[16] these diverse regulatory methods demonstrate the extent to which today's sovereigns, unlike Bodin's, are being governed by others. There is hardly an attribute of sovereignty—from the value of one's currency to the definition of one's nationals—that remains subject to absolute national control.[17]

But those who see in such developments the end of sovereignty have confused a normative agenda for reality. To use 'absolute sovereignty' as the starting point for measuring the 'decline' of the modern state is to deploy an old myth to propagate a new one. Even Bodin never really suggested that sovereigns were absolutely in control. He famously contended, on the contrary, that even sovereigns were bound by natural and divine law, including respect for customary and property rights— although he insisted that no human law could judge or appeal to it.[18] In the real

---

[14]  See generally, R. Collins and N.D. White (eds), *International Organizations and the Idea of Autonomy: Institutional Independence in the International Order* (London and New York: Routledge; 2011).

[15]  For evidence drawn from the practice of the UN General Assembly and Security Council concerning the shrinking domain of Art. 2(7) of the UN Charter, see, eg, J.E. Alvarez, *International Organizations as Law-Makers* (Oxford: Oxford University Press, 2005), 146–83.

[16]  See, eg, B. Kingsbury, N. Kirsch, and R.B. Stewart, 'The Emergence of Global Administrative Law', 68 L & Cont Prob (2005) 15 (describing forms of 'global administrative law' and '*ius gentium*'); R. Teitel, 'Humanity's Law: Rule of Law for the New Global Politics', 35 Cornell Int'l LJ (2002) 355; D. Schneiderman, *Constitutionalizing Economic Globalization* (Cambridge: Cambridge University Press, 2008); A. Stone Sweet and J. Matthews, 'Proportionality Balancing and Constitutionalism', 47 CJTL (2008) 73.

[17]  See, eg, D. Patterson and A. Afilalo, *The New Global Trading Order* (Cambridge: Cambridge University Press, 2008); Roundtable on Citizenship, *ASIL Proceedings of the 101st Annual Meeting* (2007), 89.

[18]  J. Bodin, *On Sovereignty* (J.H. Franklin ed. and trans., Cambridge: Cambridge University Press, 1992), 44–5.

world of states, sovereignty has never been an absolute but an accordion of powers subject to degrees of sovereign control. No single description of what 'state sovereignty' means is likely to satisfy because the set of attributes that defines a state changes over time and varies with the state in question. Sovereignty, never a legal term of art, is and remains a malleable concept. From Westphalia through to today, sovereigns have pooled, shared, delimited, or delegated away some of their powers.

The dictum in *Wimbledon* reflects reality. Sovereignty and global governance are not binary oppositions or the products of a zero sum game. Sovereigns may gain as much or more as they purportedly lose when they adhere to a treaty, join an international organization, or agree to binding international adjudication. Governments give their consent to such arrangements because these are in their interests, as where joining an international organization permits the centralization of the powers of members or permits them to find a neutral means to satisfy their mutual interests.[19] States delegated the most far-reaching international power of all—the power to use force—to the Security Council on the premise that this enhances the collective security of all states, for example.

At the same time, states may change their minds and attempt to take back powers that they have previously delegated away. International regimes may provoke sovereign backlash, particularly when Grotian aspirations fail to materialize. Consider what is arguably the most effective and sovereignty-intrusive of our international regimes at the global level: the international investment regime which protects the rights of foreign investors and consists of some 3,000 BITs and FTAs with investment chapters, as supplemented by de facto regulators of capital markets such as the IMF.[20] As is well known, the world of BITs and FTAs is touted as among the most legally effective treaty regimes in existence since, in most instances, its third party beneficiaries, foreign investors, have secure, direct access to binding international arbitration to enforce the rights that have been accorded to them, usually without the need to exhaust local remedies or secure the permission of their state of nationality (as was the case under diplomatic espousal).[21]

There is now overwhelming evidence that erstwhile defenders of this regime, such as the United States, prominent developing nations (such as Argentina, Bolivia, Ecuador, and Venezuela), and many nations in between, are now backtracking from the strong investment protections they once accorded foreign investors under treaties and conforming national laws. The United States Model Bilateral Investment Treaty, once a single-minded instrument designed to accord

[19] See K. Abbott and D. Snidal, 'Why States Act through Formal International Organizations', 42 J Conflict Resolution (1998) 3 (describing the functionalist attributes of international organizations in terms of centralization and independence).
[20] For an account of the rise and evolving nature of the international investment regime, see J.E. Alvarez, 'The Once and Future Foreign Investment Regime', in M.H. Arsanjani et al (eds), *Looking to the Future: Essays on International Law in Honor of W. Michael Reisman* (Leiden: Nijhoff, 2011), 607. For a description of IMF conditionality as a form of investment regulation, see D. Kalderimis, 'IMF Conditionality as Investment Regulation: A Theoretical Analysis', 13 Soc & Leg Stud (2004) 104, at 113–19.
[21] For an extended argument that the rise of investor-state arbitration through state contracts and BITs reflects the 'advancement' of international law, see C. Leben, *The Advancement of International Law* (Oxford: Hart Publ., 2010).

the strongest protection possible to the foreign investor, in the course of 20 years, has been 're-balanced' to narrow virtually every one of the rights given to foreign investors, to permit host states to assert broad exceptions to the guarantees that remain, to otherwise expand the scope for government regulation, and to narrow the discretion of or jurisdiction accorded to investor-state arbitrators.[22] Other countries' revised model BITs and FTAs are following the same path to sovereign re-empowerment.[23] The number of states engaged in 're-calibrating' their model investment protection agreements, attempting to renegotiate old agreements, or reviewing their investment policies—all with the intent of providing host states with greater latitude to take measures to protect health, safety, and the environment, respond (sometimes in a 'self-judging' fashion) to their 'essential security' interests, or otherwise pursue their notions of the public interest—has become a flood.[24] Nations are also reasserting their 'sovereignty' vis-à-vis foreign investors through corresponding changes in their national laws. (Thus, for the first time since 1992 when it began undertaking such surveys, UNCTAD's latest report on point found that more than 30 per cent of changes to national laws were in the direction of restricting not liberalizing the entry or treatment of foreign investment.[25]) States, including rich capital exporters such as the United States, Germany, and Canada, are reasserting or strengthening their rights to screen the entry of foreign investors, especially to the extent these are controlled by other states (such as China) or sovereign wealth funds.[26] Those states that have been on the receiving end of investor-state dispute settlement, or its threat most often, are having second thoughts about the sovereignty that they have ceded to arbitrators, or, in the case of the leading respondent state, Argentina, are even refusing to pay arbitral awards.[27]

The message being sent by the state creators of the investment regime is apparently being heard by the regime's other principal actors, namely investor-state arbitrators. A number of recent awards by the International Centre for Settlement of Investment Disputes (ICSID), including those issued by ICSID annulment committees, are responding to the threats posed to the regime—and the institution of

[22] For a detailed enumeration of the changes to the US Model BIT over time, see, eg, J.E. Alvarez, 'The Evolving BIT', in I.A. Laird and T.J. Weiler (eds), *Investment Treaty Arbitration and International Law* (New York: Juris Net, 2010), 1; K.J. Vandevelde, 'A Comparison of the 2004 and 1994 US Model BITs: Rebalancing Investor and Host Country Interests', Ybk Int'l Investment L & Pol'y (2008–09) 283.

[23] See, eg, UNCTAD, World Investment Report 2010, 81–90.

[24] See, eg, UNCTAD Reports.          [25] UNCTAD Report 2011.

[26] For a general overview of these developments, see J.E. Alvarez, 'Why are We "Re-calibrating" our BITs?', in *World Arbitration & Mediation Rev* (forthcoming 2011). For specific descriptions of national security screening, see M.E. Plotkin and D.N. Fagan, 'Foreign Direct Investment and US National Security: CFIUS under the Obama Administration', Columbia FDI Perspectives, No. 24, 7 June 2010; S. Bhattacharjeee, 'National Security with a Canadian Twist: The Investment Canada Act and the New National Security Review Test', available at <http://www.vcc.columbia.edu/content/national-security-canadian-twist-investment-canada-act-and-new-national-security-review-test>; M.E. Plotkin and D.N. Fagan, 'The Revised National Security Process for FDI in the US', available at <http://www.vcc.columbia.edu/content/national-security-canadian-twist-investment-canada-act-and-new-national-security-review-test>.

[27] See, eg, K. P. Sauvant, 'A Backlash against Foreign Direct Investment?', Economist Intelligence Unit, World Investment Prospects to 2010: Boom or Backlash? (2006).

investment arbitration—and are revisiting earlier awards seen as unfavourable to the interests of states. Some arbitrators are revisiting earlier expansive interpretations of investor guarantees or broadening their conceptions of permissible state defences.[28] Some arbitrators, along with a chorus of academics, are endorsing the return to sovereign discretion and state empowerment.[29] Indeed, one annulment decision goes so far in the direction of protecting the respondent state that it appears to endorse a considerable broadening of the general customary defence of necessity.[30]

The 'return of the state' that we are seeing within the investment regime reflects broader developments, including disillusionment with the formulas for 'good governance' pursued by international financial institutions and governments' desires to respond to the latest economic crisis through any means necessary. The latter has also driven states to re-enter the economic marketplace as both regulators and as entrepreneurs, that is, through new forms of 'state capitalism'.[31] In the investment regime and elsewhere, most prominently in the course of the post 9/11 'war on terror', states are also re-discovering Carl Schmitt's notoriously empowering 'law of the exception'.[32] In fora as distinct as UN human rights committees and investor-state arbitrations, states are now citing their need to protect 'security' (often redefined to extend to their economic, and not merely their military, needs) as an end-run against individuals' rights-based arguments. At least when it comes to security, and perhaps more generally, even the *Lotus* presumption—states can do what is not explicitly forbidden—may be staging a modest comeback.[33] In some cases we are now re-learning how periodic threats to the security of states can empower them and create new opportunities for state discretion with respect to even such well-established regimes as those governing the use of force or military occupation. Led by erstwhile defenders of the investment regime such as the United States, states are reasserting their rights to govern in a number of international regimes.

---

[28] See annulment rulings in *CMS v Argentina*, available at <http://icsid.worldbank.org/ICSID/FrontServlet?requestType=CasesRH&actionVal=showDoc&docId=DC687_En&caseId=C4>; *Sempra v Argentina*, available at <http://icsid.worldbank.org/ICSID/FrontServlet?requestType=CasesRH&actionVal=showDoc&docId=DC1550_En&caseId=C8>; *Enron v Argentina*, available at <http://icsid.worldbank.org/ICSID/FrontServlet?requestType=CasesRH&actionVal=showDoc&docId=DC830_En&caseId=C3>. For a critique of these decisions, see J.E. Alvarez, 'The Return of the State' (20 Minnesota J Int'l L (2011) 223).

[29] See, eg, O. Hall, Public Statement on the International Investment Regime, available at <http://www.osgoode.yorku.ca/public_statement/>.

[30] See, eg, Alvarez, n 28, discussing the annulment ruling in *Enron v Argentina*.

[31] See, eg, K. Pistor (with C. Milhaupt), *Law and Capitalism: What Corporate Crises Reveal about Legal Systems and Economic Development around the World* (Chicago: University of Chicago Press, 2008).

[32] C. Schmitt, *Political Theology: Four Chapters on the Concept of Sovereignty* ([1922] G. Schwab trans., Chicago: University of Chicago Press, 2005), 10–15. See also D. Dyzenhaus, *The Constitution of Law, Legality in a Time of Emergency* (New York and Cambridge: Cambridge University Press, 2006).

[33] See Separate Opinion by Judge Simma in ICJ Advisory Opinion in *Kosovo*.

## 3. Broader lessons for the future of sovereignty

For those trying to predict the future of sovereignty, contemporary developments suggest three lessons.

### (A) Lesson 1: global governance may be subject to a dialectic and is not (or is not merely) a progress narrative

The ongoing sovereign backlash against the international investment regime has divided international lawyers. Even some Grotian defenders of internationalism, including Europeans, support the move to restore 'sovereign policy space' in this instance.[34] The drive to establish global rules in defence of property rights, along with a scheme to enforce these internationally that was by most measures more effective than even regional systems for human rights protections has been seen by some as insufficiently deferential to sovereigns and to others whom sovereigns are committed to protect.[35] Even some Grotians are uncertain about whether in this case the turn to international governance and international adjudication truly enhances global welfare. Comparable doubts exist with respect to the net value added by other regimes, such as IMF conditionality or the turn to Security Council 'legislation'. In these cases, as with respect to the investment regime, the preferred solution seems to be to restore sovereign discretion and not to increase the number of international rules that we have. Even some erstwhile Grotians doubt the proposition that global progress is marked by progress in global law.

The backlash against the investment regime suggests that to the extent there are choices to be made as between global regulation and sovereign control, the outcome may not reflect a progress narrative but a historical dialectic that periodically swings back and forth as international norms encounter resistance at the national level, thereby triggering re-evaluation and modification of the international regime or its rules.[36] In the case of the international investment regime, there appears be a recursive cycle between champions of the market and regulation. If so, prognosticators of sovereignty should not be guided by those international lawyers who see only ever-rising levels of international regulation amidst steadily receding sovereignty such that one day, we would all banish, along with Louis Henkin, the 'S' word from our vocabulary. Perhaps those seeking to predict the future of sovereignty should be guided instead by historical prognosticators such as Karl Polanyi or describers of historical cycles' effects on developing states such as Amy Chua.[37]

---

[34] See, eg, O. Hall, Statement, n 29 (containing signatures of 37 prominent academics, including many international lawyers, from both sides of the Atlantic).

[35] For a comparison of the investment and human rights regimes, see G. Van Harten and M. Loughlin, 'Investment Treaty Arbitration as a Species of Global Administrative Law', 17 EJIL (2006) 121.

[36] For examples of the cycles of 'recursive change' in a number of international regimes, see G. Schaffer, 'Transnational Legal Process and State Change: Opportunities and Constraints', available at <http://ssrn.com/abstract=1612401>.

[37] K. Polanyi, *The Great Transformation* (Boston, MA: Beacon Press, 1944); A. Chua, *World on Fire: How Exporting Free Market Democracy Breeds Ethnic Hatred and Global Instability* (New York: Doubleday, 2002).

Notably, neither of these authors denies the possibility that both states and global regulators can learn lessons from the mistakes of the past. Those who see recursive change as the dominant trend do not suggest that historical cycles simply revert to prior reversions of the status quo without change. The key insight is that the interaction between global regimes and 'sovereign' actors (and sub-actors) is a key ingredient in the transnational legal process.

## (B) Lesson 2: sovereignty remains important even after a Grotian 'win'

As is implicit in lesson 1, the states which, after all, establish global legal regimes retain exit and voice options that can radically transform these regimes over time. While some of these options—such as withdrawing from ICSID, changing the texts of model treaties, or refusing to conclude more BITs—are obvious, others are far more subtle.[38] Those who built ICSID on the premise that this arbitration would 'de-politicize' the settlement of investor-state disputes probably did not anticipate that politics could re-emerge in the course of those arbitrations, albeit in a subtler form than the use of gunboat diplomacy to enforce diplomatic espousal of an investor's claim. They probably did not anticipate that party-appointed arbitrators and others would respond as much as they have to the needs of states—or to the prospect that states, if sufficiently threatened by arbitral awards, might pull the plug on the entire enterprise, including by failing to comply with such awards. They probably did not anticipate how the powerful legitimating forces urged on by international civil society in favour of transparency and acceptance of amicus briefs would help to transform perceptions of investor-state arbitration. They did not foresee how that institution—once seen as merely another form of commercial dispute settlement—would come to be seen as a high-profile venue for contestable forms of 'public adjudication'.[39] They did not foresee that as investor-state adjudications became regular sites for the proclamation of 'good governance', they would receive the same attention—and draw the same politicized contestation—as other forms of 'constitutionalization'.[40]

Global governance schemes are as malleable as sovereignty. Even when they do not elicit backlash on the magnitude as that evident in the international investment regime, they prompt reactions and are subject to periodic or continuous contestation. This is so if only because all international regimes, no matter how well constructed, ultimately rely on states to implement them at the domestic level. How that implementation occurs is subject to considerable state discretion. Much can occur to an international regime as its rules are translated for domestic consumption or application.[41]

---

[38] For an interesting analysis of the continuing power of states to influence the interpretation of their investment treaties over time, see A. Roberts, 'Power and Persuasion in Investment Treaty Interpretation: The Dual Role of States', 104 AJIL (2010) 179.

[39] See, eg, G. Van Harten, *Investment Treaty Arbitration and Public Law* (Oxford: Oxford University Press, 2007).

[40] See, eg, D. Schneiderman, *Constitutionalizing Economic Globalization* (Cambridge: Cambridge University Press, 2008).

[41] See, eg, Schaffer, n 36.

## (C) Lesson 3: there are flaws and continuing values in seeing the contest between sovereignty and global governance through a North/South lens

The United States' leadership role in re-storing 'sovereign' policy space in the investment regime runs somewhat counter to the usual North/South narrative. Critics of 'hegemonic' international law, and particularly of economic legal regimes such as the IMF or that governing investment, would not have predicted that the world's leading capital exporter, the state that has the most to gain from enhancing international protections for foreign investors, that has done the most to dismantle the Calvo doctrine that once barred investors from resorting to any forum other than local courts, and that produced the most investor-protective BIT in existence, would be leading the drive in the opposite direction. What these critics failed to anticipate was that the United States, along with other leading capital exporters *and importers* such as China, would eventually need to confront the reciprocal aspects of the investment regime. For the United States, repeated exposures as a respondent state within the North American Free Trade Agreement (NAFTA) has brought home the fact that it is not always easy to satisfy the legal conditions that it had blithely and for so long required of others.

As the example of the backlash now occurring against the investment regime suggests, it is too simple to portray supporters of global governance and its resisters in North/South terms—even when the underlying regimes were originally constructed by and for the interests of the North. Even a bilateral regime such as that of BITs constructed on model treaties drafted by Western states can acquire multilateral dimensions and come back to bite those very nations—particularly when the interpretation of investor protections is handed over to third party adjudicators.[42] Consider the once innocuous fair and equitable treatment (FET) provision in BITs and FTAs. As that guarantee has been transformed in the course of investor-state adjudication from a basic prohibition on egregious denials of justice by states with weak judicial institutions into a tool of 'global administrative law' requiring far more exacting standards of process and procedure, even wealthy 'rule of law' states have felt its sting.[43] At the same time, as some states of the 'global South' have developed their own multinational enterprises capable of investing abroad, those states—such as India, Egypt, China, and even Cuba—have become supporters of strong investment protections through BITs.[44] As this suggests, it is not always easy to predict which states will defend or resist an international regime. In any case, predictions may be refuted as conditions change and states change their minds over time, in either direction.

The example of the contemporary investment regime suggests that we need to remain vigilant when it comes to the North/South dimensions of international

---

[42] See generally, S. W. Schill, *The Multilaterization of International Investment Law* (Cambridge: Cambridge University Press, 2009).

[43] See, eg, B. Kingsbury and S. Schill, 'Investor-State Arbitration as Governance: Fair and Equitable Treatment, Proportionality and the Emerging Global Administrative Law', in B. Kingsbury et al (eds), *El Nuevo Derecho Administrativo Global en América Latina* (Buenos Aires: Rap, 2009), 221.

[44] See J.E. Alvarez, 'Contemporary Foreign Investment Law: An "Empire of Law" or the "Law of Empire"?', 60 Ala L Rev (2009) 943.

regimes and reactions to them. The extent of the backlash against the investment regime surely has something to do with the prominence and power of some of the states leading the charge. And how that backlash manifests itself—whether through defiant refusals to comply, withdrawals for ICSID, renunciations from BITs, or more subtle changes in the emerging case law— has a great deal to do with the respective powers of the states that are trying to exercise their 'exit and voice' options. Many states, particularly in Africa, are too disempowered to exercise these options or to do so without fear of severe consequence. Some states are more capable of 'exit and voice', in this regime as with respect to others.

For this reason, Koskenniemi's defence of sovereignty as enabling peoples to be 'masters' of their lives is subject to a significant caveat: the capacity to enjoy his 'thrill' of self-empowerment is not distributed evenly. Those who construct international regimes are very much aware, on the contrary, that states do not enjoy the sovereign equality that international law formally bestows upon them. Indeed, a common goal of globalists who construct such regimes is precisely to put more states on a more level playing field. Despite Koskenniemi's eloquent defence of sovereignty, Grotians may be on to something when they exalt the worth of their schemes for global governance.

## 4. Concluding remarks

These lessons do not provide clear guide-points for sovereignty's future. Like Koskenniemi's 'oceanic feeling' in favour of global brother/sisterhood, support for greater 'sovereignty' in particular instances—including within the investment regime—requires a defence in moral, legal, or economic terms. At the same time, the Westphalian system of nation-states—admittedly a blink of an eye in the scope of human history—remains the system that we have. How states react to global regimes over time remains the single greatest determinant of whether these regimes will succeed or fail, evolve or stagnate.

# 4

# The United Nations: No Hope for Reform?

*Philip Alston*

## SUMMARY

Utopia is a notion that is inevitably in the eye of the beholder, but the assumption of this analysis is that a strengthened and more efficient UN has the capacity to contribute in essential ways to more effective global governance arrangements. With some notable exceptions, most discussions of UN reform have taken up vast amounts of time and energy and generally yielded all too little. Nevertheless, there are significant reforms that could be undertaken if key states would back them and defeatism should not be permitted to prevail. This chapter identifies various steps that would promote the type of realistically utopian reforms that this volume seeks to identify. They include: (i) amending the Charter to eliminate the Trusteeship Council and ideally also the Economic and Social Council; (ii) ensuring sustainable financing for core UN activities; (iii) promoting a 'One UN' approach to on the ground service delivery, but complementing this with a more consultative approach to local actors; (iv) becoming more media savvy; (v) making vastly better use of new information and communications technologies; (vi) moving towards a 'smart' and knowledgeable Secretariat; and (vii) devoting more resources to three substantive areas (electoral assistance; development of a police rapid response capacity; tackling corruption at the national level).

## 1. Introduction

Utopia is a relative concept. One person's utopia is the next person's nightmare. This is clearly the case when one thinks of a utopian future for the United Nations. For some it would conjure up desirable images of a smoothly functioning system of global governance, possibly overseen by a global parliamentary assembly or peoples' chamber. For others, the less powerful the UN is the better, either for essentially nationalist or sovereigntist reasons[1] or because of a conviction that only decentral-

---

[1] See, eg, D. Gold, *Tower of Babble: How the United Nations Has Fueled Global Chaos* (New York: Three Rivers Press, 2005) (The UN is 'singularly unsuited to preserving global order' and 'has utterly failed to achieve its founders' goals: to halt aggression and assure world order...'.)

ized local solutions are really sustainable as responses to many of the major challenges confronting the world community.[2] Even if we assume that there is a strong and unavoidable need to strengthen global governance mechanisms in a very wide range of areas, the question still remains how central the UN should be to such a vision and how it should relate to more diffuse and less-encompassing specialist regimes and more or less structured networks.[3]

For experienced UN-watchers there is often an element of reform fatigue, epitomized by the endless and so far fruitless debates over Security Council reform, which has bred a deep scepticism about the feasibility of almost any far-reaching institutional reforms of the organization. For them, utopia begins to take the form of minor institutional adjustments, the creation of new bureaucratic units of one type or other, and the fashioning of new procedures that are assumed to have a chance of succeeding despite the fact that earlier efforts are widely considered to have failed. In short, the triumph of hope over experience.

The point is that utopia is in the eye of the beholder. The very idea of setting up a United Nations organization in the aftermath of the Second World War was utopian in many ways. The notion that all states would be treated equally in terms of their sovereign rights, that the use of force would be definitively outlawed, that a diverse array of functional international agencies in the economic and social fields would be established, and that their efforts would be coordinated in a systematic and meaningful way by an Economic and Social Council, and the plan to establish a Military Staff Committee consisting of the Chiefs of Staff of each of the Security Council's permanent members which would be able to coordinate, mobilize, and oversee the use of armed force: all this was utopian.

How much of this has really failed? How much more utopian do we need to be, or is it a matter of resiling from failed utopias to see the more mundane and banal needs of building an effective world organization? The answer, perhaps predictable when an author sets up such a choice, is probably a little of each. In other words, we need to acknowledge the failure and perhaps the unworkability of some of the utopian aspects of the existing Charter arrangements but we also need the infusion of a new dose of utopian thought inspired not just by the same 'never again' sentiment that moved the 'united nations' in 1945, but by a recognition of the new challenges and opportunities confronting the international community in the twenty-first century and the capacity of the UN to contribute significantly to their solution.

## 2. Defining the United Nations

The UN is many things to many people. To the poor in almost any least developed country the UN is the provider of last resort in emergencies requiring food, health

---

[2]  S. Zifcak, *United Nations Reform: Heading North or South?* (London, New York: Routledge 2008).
[3]  See generally G.C.A. Junne, 'International Organizations in a Period of Globalization: New (Problems of) Legitimacy', in J.-M. Coicaud and V. Heiskanen (eds), *The Legitimacy of International Organizations* (Tokyo, New York: United Nations University Press, 2001), 189.

care, shelter, and basic protection, and in the worst cases it may be seen as the provider of first resort. To American conservatives it seems to be a very powerful actor that has the capacity to ride roughshod over state sovereignty and to compel governments to do various things that they do not wish to do.[4] And to many in developed countries outside the United States it is a useful talking shop which also has the potential to tackle a range of problems that nations cannot deal with effectively on an individual basis. In 2004 a High-Level Panel on Threats, Challenges and Change identified the following areas as those in relation to which many in the international community expect the UN to take a lead role: 'poverty, infectious disease and environmental degradation; war and violence within states; the spread and possible use of nuclear, radiological, chemical and biological weapons; terrorism; and transnational organized crime.'[5]

In order to make sense of the topic of a realistically utopian role for the UN in the twenty-first century we need to recognize two different levels of analysis: (i) the various entities defined as coming under the umbrella of 'the UN' for these purposes and (ii) the different roles that the UN proper plays. In terms of the entities covered, the most basic distinction is between the UN family, which includes all the many specialized agencies and other bodies that coexist under a very broad umbrella (such as the International Labour Organization, the World Health Organization, the Food and Agriculture Organization, as well as the international financial institutions and many other agencies), and the UN itself defined as the UN Secretariat and the institutions and other functions that are funded, at least in part, from the regular UN budget. In terms of the second level of analysis we can distinguish at least three different principal functions: (i) a forum for debate, discussion, and decision; (ii) an actor to undertake a variety of specific functions such as peacekeeping and human rights promotion; and (iii) a catalyst to action by a diverse range of groups including civil society, national governments, local actors, corporations, and others. In addition to these levels of analysis there is an additional distinction to be drawn between the substantive outcomes and the processes and institutional arrangements through which the UN has sought to address them. This chapter cannot hope to address the substantive outcomes achieved, and is thus confined to examining the possible institutional arrangements that might contribute to promoting meaningful outcomes in the respective areas.

## 3. The never-ending reform process

To paraphrase Churchill, rarely have so many plans for reform been put forward by so many over such a long period of time and yielded so little. This is not the

---

[4] See generally B. Schaefer (ed.), *ConUNdrum: The Limits of the United Nations and the Search for Alternatives* (Lanham, MD: Rowman and Littlefield, 2009). In reviewing this Heritage Foundation-sponsored critique of the UN Doug Bandow of the equally conservative Cato Institute wrote in the *Washington Times* on 29 December, 2009: 'The last best hope of mankind. So the United Nations has been termed. If that's true, we should abandon hope.'

[5] Report of the High-Level Panel, UN Doc. A/59/565, 11.

place to review those well-intentioned endeavours.[6] Suffice it to note that the most recent comprehensive set of proposals was put forward by Kofi Annan in 2005. Referring to the UN's sixtieth anniversary as a historic opportunity, he called for what he termed the most sweeping overhaul in its history. Two years earlier, he had established a High-Level Panel on Threats, Challenges and Change which presented a lengthy and detailed set of recommendations in December 2004. Its report was premised on the need for a new consensus on a greatly expanded notion of collective security that included the need for far-reaching measures to address new and dramatic challenges.

By 2011, the talk about 'historic opportunities' and 'critical crossroads' in relation to UN reform had all but vanished. Thus in a statement that could hardly have been more low-key or less utopian, Annan's successor, Ban Ki-moon, told the General Assembly after his re-election to a second term of office that '[t]here is a great deal of work ahead. Millions of people around the world are looking to the United Nations with hope. We must answer their hopes with action.' At the same time Ban announced an austerity drive involving a 3 per cent cut in the organization's biennial budget. This ratcheting down of both the rhetoric and the aspirations reflects not only the personality of the respective UN leaders but also the lowered expectations of the times. Utopian optimism is in small supply.

But a realistic utopia cannot be built overnight and a reformed and revived UN remains critical to the future of global governance. Before turning to consider the main issues that have preoccupied would-be reformers in recent times it is appropriate to set some parameters. Perhaps the most important starting point relates to reasonable expectations. We thus need to acknowledge that the UN has never been, and will never be, the only game in town in relation to a great many of the most pressing challenges facing the international community. Nuclear non-proliferation provides as good an illustration as any in this respect. While the UN has a complex set of institutional arrangements for discussing nuclear issues, much of the recent work has been undertaken outside it. Bilateral discussions between Russia and the United States, and regional discussions between the European Union and the states that emerged from the former Soviet Union have been of vital importance. In addition, in April 2010 the United States convened 47 states to a first Nuclear Security Summit, in Washington DC. That process generated a range of specific commitments that have been monitored not by the UN but under the auspices of the United States.[7] It is generally assessed to have been relatively successful to date[8] and follow-up summits are envisaged. The UN itself remains relevant in terms of broader discussions over the future of the Nuclear Non-Proliferation Treaty but

---

[6] For a systematic and highly informative overview see Zifcak, n 2.

[7] The White House, Office of the Press Secretary, Highlights of the National Commitments made at the Nuclear Security Summit, 13 April 2010, available at <http://www.whitehouse.gov/the-press-office/highlights-national-commitments-made-nss>.

[8] It has been estimated that some 60 per cent of the national commitments undertaken were honoured within a year of the first summit. See 'Promises, Promises: A Progress Report One Year after the 2010 Nuclear Security Summit', Bulletin of the Atomic Scientists, 6 April 2011, available at <http://www.thebulletin.org/web-edition/columnists/fissile-materials-working-group/promises-promises-progress-report-one-year-af>.

significant breakthroughs are likely to come from outside that framework. By the same token, the Security Council and the International Atomic Energy Agency have been the principal fora for efforts to discourage Iran's nuclear weapons programme. The same sort of pattern of UN relevance and marginality can be found in relation to a great many other regimes or sectors. The lesson is that we need to remember that the UN's role is not necessarily the central or deciding one in relation to a great many of the matters that are on its agenda, but that it nonetheless does make a contribution.

The notion of limited expectations when reflecting on the UN's potential was well captured by Dag Hammarskjöld's comment in 1954 that the organization was 'not created in order to bring us to heaven, but in order to save us from hell'.[9]

We turn now to examine the principal issues of institutional reform that have been part of recent debates.

## 4. Options for institutional restructuring

Most of the UN reform literature has dwelt on proposals to create new institutions, to eliminate or fundamentally transform existing ones, or to make them more effective, more representative, and more efficient. It is difficult to escape the conclusion that too much time and energy have been devoted to such issues and too little to the consideration of more creative and more feasible alternative approaches. We shall return to those below, but no chapter on UN reform would be complete without an overview of the key institutional debates. Since the Security Council and the UN's human rights programme are both dealt with in separate chapters in this volume, those issues will not be considered here.

Before examining the principal problems it is important to acknowledge that the UN has, in fact, been reasonably adept at responding to a wide range of new and emerging issues through the creation or expansion of institutional capacity. For example, it has responded relatively rapidly to the various waves of enhanced environmental awareness beginning in the late 1960s and continuing into the twenty-first century by organizing highly effective international conferences, establishing a new agency (UNEP), generating important legal standards for dealing with a wide array of threats to environmental well-being (ozone, desertification, endangered species, deforestation, climate change, pollution of regional seas, etc.), and providing important scientific inputs into the climate change debates. It has been at the forefront of efforts to promote gender equality, to combat racism, to combat terrorism, to recognize and defend the rights of indigenous peoples, to combat torture, to reduce the spread and use of chemical weapons and other weapons of mass destruction, and has established or expanded institutional arrangements for overseeing these initiatives. A comprehensive list would be very long, and even more boring, but the point is simply that there has been no shortage of *institutional initiatives*. Whether they have been as effective as

---

[9]  B. Urquhart, *Hammarskjöld* (New York: Knopf, 1972), 48.

they might have been, and whether overlap and duplication have been part of the process, are issues considered below.

The focus of most discussions of institutional reform has been on some of the principal Charter organs, namely the Security Council, the General Assembly, the Economic and Social Council, and the Trusteeship Council. I explore each of these, except for the Security Council, in turn.

The *General Assembly* is the most democratic of the major bodies in the sense that all states are represented and can have their say on virtually any issue. It is easily dismissed as a 'talking shop', but such pejorative language misses the point that the promotion of ideas and the legitimation of emerging norms constitute potentially vital roles.[10] The long and arduous journeys of the 'responsibility to protect' concept, of the principles of the rule of law and democratic governance, of gender equality, and most recently of respect for the sexual-orientation preferences of individuals, all serve to illustrate the importance of these functions. Endless calls for agenda streamlining, for greater dialogue, and for more substantive debates have made little headway over a long period.[11] Calls for the Assembly to be replaced by a body of representatives elected in proportion to countries' populations are both utopian and entirely unrealistic. The more achievable utopia would see the General Assembly seeking to expand the range of inputs into its deliberations, making greater use of independent experts acting in its name, and opening up avenues of cooperation with civil society and with national power structures. A relatively simple starting point would be to authorize a Parliamentary General Assembly (PGA) to consist of one to three existing members of parliament from each state. The PGA would not require a Charter amendment, would (initially) exercise only advisory powers, and would provide an important complement to the work of the General Assembly itself. The equivalent parliamentary assemblies created by the Council of Europe and the Organization for Security and Cooperation in Europe (OSCE) provide an example of the strengths and weaknesses of such bodies.

President Obama told the General Assembly in 2010 that the Group of 20 (G20) had become 'the focal point for international coordination' in response to the global economic crisis[12] and it is now widely acknowledged that it has performed a crucial role in this regard. But even when accepting this reality, UN actors still tend to insist that the Assembly should nonetheless play a central role. Thus, for example, in 2011 the President of the General Assembly argued that economic matters should remain the sole preserve of the General Assembly, which, with its 193 states Members and its system of 'One state, one voice' is, par excellence, the democratic forum at the global level. It is therefore important to find ways of legitimizing the decisions that were taken by the G20.

---

[10] See R. Jolly, L. Emmerij, and T.G. Weiss, *UN Ideas that Changed the World* (Bloomington: Indiana University Press, 2009) arguing that ideas frame policy agendas, mobilize new coalitions, and eventually become embedded in institutions.

[11] For an accurately depressing review of such endeavours see Zifcak, n 2, 38–57.

[12] 'Obama's Remarks at the United Nations', *New York Times*, 23 September 2010, available at <http://www.nytimes.com/2010/09/24/us/politics/24obama-text.html>.

But as Weiss has noted, it is difficult to challenge the G20's legitimacy when it represents 70 per cent of the world's population, 80 per cent of its trade, and 90 per cent of its Gross Domestic Product.[13] The bottom line is that the General Assembly can remain an important forum, and can express its views on economic and financial matters, but there is little point in suggesting that it should be the central player that it could never be in such matters.

The most significant institutional reform to emerge from the 2005 process was the creation of a *Peacebuilding Commission*. The High-Level Panel harboured high-level hopes that such an initiative would serve an important early-warning function in relation to conflicts and that it would help to plan the contributions of the international community in the context of post-conflict transitions. But in designing the institution states watered down these goals to the point where the Commission became an advisory body, playing a coordinating role in bringing the key funding and troop-contributing states together with the representatives of the small number of states selected for attention. In 2010, Ireland, Mexico, and South Africa undertook a five-year review of the Commission's performance and warned that it had reached the proverbial crossroads, requiring either a serious recommitment to peace-building or settling for a very modest role. The report suggested that the Commission had failed to accord significant national ownership to the states being assisted, had achieved inadequate civil society involvement, had adopted unduly complicated procedures, had not been especially effective in mobilizing resources, had achieved little coordination with the international financial institutions, and had been largely ignored by the Security Council.[14]

The *Economic and Social Council* (ECOSOC) has always provided a major challenge to would-be reformers. Even in 2011 UN leaders were suggesting that the challenge is to strengthen it, to enable it to coordinate agency and programme mandates more effectively, and to make it 'an essential actor in global economic governance'.[15] But the reality is that the marginalization of ECOSOC began very early on in its existence. It then gathered speed as the Bretton Woods institutions became ever more powerful and as the World Trade Organization, the World Intellectual Property Organization, and a plethora of other specialist bodies dealing with trade, finance, intellectual property, and other economic issues flexed their muscles. The High-Level Panel graciously only went so far as to concede that ECOSOC would never become 'the centre of the world's decision-making on matters of trade and finance', and that it would never be able to direct the programmes of the various UN agencies. But this was a deep understatement. In a rational world ECOSOC would probably be put humanely to sleep, but the immense resistance to eliminating any UN body led the Panel to struggle valiantly to find a plausible role for it. It suggested that the Council should provide

[13] T.G. Weiss, 'Fundamental UN Reform: A Non-starter or Not?', 2 Global Policy (May 2011) 196, 199.
[14] Review of the United Nations Peacebuilding Architecture, UN Docs A/64/868 and S/2010/393 (2010).
[15] 'UN General Assembly President urges flexibility as UN debates stronger role in global governance', UN News Centre, 28 June 2011.

normative and analytical leadership, primarily through a new Committee on the Social and Economic Aspects of Security Threats. It could also take on the role of monitoring states' development-related commitments, and become a 'development cooperation forum' with an agenda built around the Millennium Declaration.[16] But the Panel's aspirations for the Council were hopelessly unrealistic and failed to take account of its principal shortcomings, which were a lack of any real source of power or authority, a lack of control over any resources, an absence of substantive expertise, and a deadly bureaucratic and statist culture. But even more unrealistic was the General Assembly's response. It not only ignored, and thus rejected, all of the Panel's suggestions, but reaffirmed the Council's role 'as a principal body for coordination, policy review, policy dialogue'[17] and so on. Given how little ECOSOC had achieved in any of these domains in recent memory, the Assembly did little more than provide evidence of its own inability to recognize existing shortcomings and promote even mild reforms in situations in which radically more is needed. An insightful diplomatic critique of ECOSOC's performance that echoed many of the criticisms expressed here concluded by suggesting that the Council could at least be transformed into civil society's 'portal of entry' into the UN.[18] But the question then becomes why civil society would want access through a portal that leads nowhere in terms of influence or significance, and what it could usefully do with any such access.

The problem remains that the UN and its supporters are unable to face the reality that it no longer has a significant role in relation to matters of major economic or financial importance. In addition to the revitalization of the International Monetary Fund in the wake of the global financial crisis that began in 2008, and the continuing strength of agencies such as the World Trade Organization and the World Intellectual Property Organization, groups entirely outside the UN structure have come to play the central roles in such matters. The most prominent example is the G20 consisting of the old G8 (United States, Britain, France, Germany, Italy, Japan, Canada, and Russia), along with four other OECD members (Australia, Mexico, South Korea, and Turkey), and the most influential of the developing countries (Argentina, Brazil, China, India, Indonesia, Saudi Arabia, and South Africa), along with the European Union.

The *Trusteeship Council* has been out of work since 1994 when Palau, the last of the UN trust territories, became independent. In fact it should be seen as a singularly successful UN organ because it accomplished in full the extensive responsibilities entrusted to it in an entire chapter of the UN Charter. While former Secretary-General Boutros-Ghali called for the Council's elimination, his successor picked up on states' apparent reluctance to do so and instead gently promoted a proposal by Malta that it be given new responsibilities relating to the environment

---

[16] Ibid, n 5, paras 274–8.

[17] GA Res. 60/1 (2005), para 155.

[18] G. Rosenthal, 'Economic and Social Council', in T.G. Weiss and S. Daws (eds), *The Oxford Handbook on the United Nations* (Oxford: Oxford University Press, 2007) (hereinafter '*Oxford UN Handbook*'), 136, 146. The 'portal of entry' metaphor comes from the Report of the Panel of Eminent Persons on United Nations–Civil Society Relations, UN Doc. A/59/354 (2004).

and areas of the global commons such as the oceans, atmosphere, and outer space. Other alternatives have also been proposed, including that it be used to address the plight of so-called 'failed states', but it seems unlikely that any such proposals will garner much support.[19] The precedent of actually terminating a major UN mandate because of the successful completion of its work would seem to be a highly desirable one, but the stumbling block remains the difficulty of securing a Charter amendment in order to do so.

The Charter has been amended only three times. All amendments occurred between 1963 and 1973 in the immediate aftermath of the massive influx of new members in the wake of decolonization, and each related to the size of the Security Council or ECOSOC. It has since been assumed that any further amendments would be impossible to accomplish, in part because of divergent political preferences, and in part because of the logistical difficulties involved in getting close to 200 states to pursue their own constitutional and other processes in order to agree to any amendment.

## 5. Broader challenges

The proliferation of agencies and other institutions has been a major problem for the UN, as has the seemingly inexorable expansion of each agency's mandate and range of activities. It has been suggested that this is partly due to an ideology according to which more international institutional expansion is good by definition, as well as to the flexibility of the law governing international organization which is said to do little to impede 'organizational wishes to expand and procreate'.[20] But because of the strength of the vested interests that tend rapidly to take over any international organization and to prevent either fundamental reforms or closure, the easiest way to deal with failure is to propose another organization which ends up being more or less superimposed on top of or beside the existing arrangements.

This then exacerbates another of the UN's major failings: its inability to coordinate disparate but closely related activities, and to rationalize overlapping and even directly competing programmes. Too little has changed since Robert Jackson's justly famous 1969 report in which he referred to the UN 'machine' as unmanageable, slow, and unwieldy and compared it to a 'prehistoric monster'. It was, he said, a machine without a brain.[21] The recent creation of UN Women as an agency to replace several significantly overlapping programmes is a positive example but one that was made feasible mainly because of the relatively low stakes involved (minor agencies with small budgets) compared to the major political pressures that could be generated in relation to an issue of fundamental importance (gender equity). It can be contrasted with the achingly slow progress

---

[19] See generally R. Wilde, 'Trusteeship Council', in *Oxford UN Handbook*, n 18, 149.

[20] J. Klabbers, 'The Changing Image of International Organizations', in Coicaud and Heiskanen, n 3, 221, at 245.

[21] R. Jackson, *A Study of the Capacity of the United Nations Development System* (UNDP, 1969), iii.

towards building a unified UN development profile. Competition among agencies with large budgets, significantly different constituencies and expertise bases, and almost entirely incompatible notions of their own self-interest in relation to reform, has led to the maintenance of a highly fragmented UN presence in the field in relation to development. There is no shortage of rational justifications for this fragmentation, such as the ability of a more diverse set of agencies to mobilize a larger range of actors, the building up of particular forms of expertise that might otherwise be marginalized or drowned out in a more unified system, the advantages of competition among ideas, personnel, and programmes, the provision of choice for governments, the ability to deal differently with different ministries at the national level, and so on. But, when all is said and done, it is almost inconceivable that anyone who has witnessed the day-to-day reality on the ground of an alphabet soup of UN agencies competing with and sometimes undermining one another could opt to maintain the existing system rather than moving towards a more 'utopian' system of centralized overall authority combined with a rational division of labour.[22] While seasoned observers seem resigned to riding on the never-ending merry-go-round of pseudo coordination driven by agency self-interest and turf battles,[23] it is governments that must be persuaded that they and more importantly their citizens are losing out badly under the current system.

## 6. Reforming the Secretariat

The UN Secretary-General and the staff under his or her direction constitute one of the principal organs of the organization set up by the Charter. In the early years, the principal challenge was thought to be to secure an independent and impartial Secretariat. As the organization expanded and developing countries came to make up the great majority of the membership, the representativeness of the Secretariat became the main concern. That principal is, however, a two-sided coin. On the one side is the need to ensure that the UN is truly representative of the diversity of the world's peoples, cultures, and values, while on the other side there is the desire on the part of the elites to ensure access to their 'share' of the plum jobs that the UN has to offer at all levels. Much neglected in this emphasis on independence and representativeness are the qualifications for the particular tasks that need to be performed.[24] Because of the need to struggle against nepotism and other forms of favouritism in recruitment, the UN has developed rigid, time-

[22] In 2010 the Funds Project published the results of an extensive survey of key actors, overwhelmingly from the global South, which showed some 70 per cent of respondents favouring a reduction in the number of UN agencies and the appointment of a 'single overall global head of the UN development system', and almost 80 per cent calling for a single development system representative at the country level. See *The Future of the United Nations Development System: A Global Perceptions Survey* (2010), available at <http://www.fundsproject.org/wp-content/uploads/funds-report-april2010.pdf>.

[23] J. Fomerand and D. Dijkzeul, 'Coordinating Economic and Social Affairs', in *Oxford UN Handbook*, n 18, 561, 579.

[24] See generally 'Reinvigorating the International Civil Service', in T.G. Weiss, *What's Wrong with the United Nations and How to Fix It* (Cambridge: Polity, 2008), ch. 8.

consuming, hierarchical, and highly inefficient personnel policies that rarely result in the appointment or promotion of very highly qualified individuals. Where the World Bank likes to style itself as 'the knowledge bank', the UN almost prides itself on having little room for original thinking, high-level knowledge production, or probing research. The result is a very high percentage of reports that are devoid of genuine research and substantive policy analysis, and are replete with banalities. There is a fear of confronting states with views that do not conform to those that have been expressed in advance, and a tendency for analytical reports to serve the primary purpose of justifying conclusions identified in advance. Where serious probing analysis is needed, the UN turns to extremely expensive and time-consuming 'high-level panels' and the like. We consider in the final section below the type of measures needed to break through this culture of producing stale, predictable, often undigested, and generally superficial reports.

### 7.  Some elements for a realistically utopian reform of the UN

The list that follows ranges from major efforts to amend the Charter and thus to change the basic structures, through various specific reforms of the way in which the organization functions, to several suggested substantive issues that need to be given greater attention in the years ahead.

1. A major effort to secure Charter amendment should be undertaken, although it would have to be entirely separate from efforts to restructure the Security Council since the latter have almost no chance of being accepted and have so far been used to hold hostage other initiatives. Some commentators acknowledge the need for a 'dramatic transformation [rather than] minor tinkering',[25] but others continue to counsel against any such efforts.[26] An endeavour to achieve a realistic utopia would surely confront such defeatism. The proposed amendment should eliminate the Trusteeship Council, either eliminate or fundamentally revise the functions of ECOSOC, elevate the Human Rights Council to the status of a principal organ, introduce a Parliamentary Assembly to operate side by side with the General Assembly, and state an obligation on the part of the Secretariat to promote transparency and accountability. While a much more extensive wish list could be drawn up, any more ambitious plan would surely fail.

2. Steps need to be taken to provide an assured and constant source of financing for core UN activities. Well under half the overall UN budget comes from the assessed contributions paid by states. The remainder must be raised from voluntary contributions. While these will always be important, they are never assured and they inevitably contribute to an uneven patchwork of programmes. To the extent that they fund what are in reality core programme expenses, they are a highly

---

[25] Ibid.
[26] E.C. Luck, 'Principal Organs', in *Oxford UN Handbook*, n 18, 653: 'The institution evolves and adapts to changing circumstances and needs more rapidly than it adopts structural reform. In the final analysis, that is the way the founders wanted it. In all probability, they would be pleased', ibid, 670.

inefficient way to run an organization, and raise major problems of donor influence. Many proposals have been made for global taxes to be levied on everything from international monetary transactions (the so-called 'Tobin tax'), air travel, internet usage, arms sales, and natural resource extraction activities. The United States has been the most adamant opponent of such initiatives,[27] but a serious commitment to a strong multilateral component of a diversified global governance regime will require a change of direction in this regard.

3. The effort begun immediately after the thaw brought by the fall of the Berlin Wall to create a single UN entity at the country level needs to be enhanced and developed. It was given a strong push by the High-Level Panel on System-Wide Coherence in 2006,[28] but the initiative seems to have stalled. Suggestions by some commentators to abandon such efforts in favour of even greater decentralization and individual agency competition, according to the principle of subsidiarity,[29] seem to be a recipe for exacerbation of the existing system of fiercely self-interested competition which does little to ensure optimal delivery of services on the ground to those most in need. It also weakens the UN's overall influence and encourages divide and conquer strategies on the part of government officials. Moving towards a 'One UN' approach in this regard is an indispensable element of a realistic utopia.

4. Directly linked to the development of the 'One UN' approach is the need for the UN to develop more effective mechanisms for consultation at the country level. The UN and its agencies in many developing countries too often tend to function as independent fiefdoms. The alternative is not to become the hand-maidens of the government of the day but to develop authentically consultative approaches in determining priorities and choosing among alternative approaches to programme delivery. While the rhetoric of participation is well developed, the reality of UN operations on the ground is often far divorced from it. There is also a need to build sustainable constituencies at the local level. While it is true, as the proponents of the power of civil society are keen to point out, that there has been a phenomenal growth in the number of NGOs that engage with the UN through consultative status mechanisms and attendance at meetings, there needs to be a much more deliberate outreach to grassroots level groups which act as 'agents' and 'pressure groups' in relation to the work of the UN in the field.

5. The UN needs to become more media savvy.[30] The vast majority of UN press releases are so dull they would not keep the average reader awake for more than a minute, let alone capture his or her attention. They are often bureaucratic documents of record, produced for the sake of it. The problem is partly the hypersensitivity of member states to anything remotely critical or insightful, but the problem also reflects the compulsive self-censorship of most officials and their addiction to blandness. They would not recognize a news story if they fell over one. The result is that the UN's message is poorly communicated, as is knowledge and understanding of the results achieved. A new strategy will require four elements. The first is

---

[27]  J. Laurenti, 'Financing', in *Oxford UN Handbook*, n 18, 675.
[28]  *Delivering as One* (New York, NY: United Nations 2006).     [29]  Zifcak, n 2, 192.
[30]  For an excellent critique see B. Crossette, 'Media' in *Oxford UN Handbook*, n 18, 275.

a change of mentality on the part of the Secretariat. Transparency is indispensable, bad news is not to be avoided at all costs, colourful language is essential, and meaningful information and commentary are needed. Perfunctory statements should be distinguished from real news. Secondly, the UN has to learn the lesson that personalities get coverage, not institutions. Kofi Annan and Jan Egeland, for example, always had something newsworthy to say and received a commensurate degree of coverage. Thirdly, the internal publicity machine can only do so much. The major source of publicity will inevitably be the external media and the UN needs to do more to cultivate and facilitate their interest in what is happening at the UN. Fourthly, the UN needs to start making effective use of the new media, in all its diverse forms. But a lumbering and inflexible public relations bureaucracy is not conducive to such initiatives.

6. The UN, along with diplomacy in general, still needs to be brought into the twenty-first century in terms of taking full advantage of the opportunities provided by new information and communications technologies. Many more 'meetings' should be held by satellite link, more consultations need to take place through new and emerging social networking approaches, more innovative approaches need to be adopted to the use of electronic language translation programs, and more meetings need to be broadcast in order to expose them to the real world, warts and all.

7. Secretariat reform is undoubtedly needed in a great many areas, including enhanced transparency, more effective oversight, and more systematic accountability. Significant steps have in fact been taken in these directions in recent years. But perhaps the biggest challenge is to transform the culture of the UN that assumes that high-level research and analysis, or knowledge promotion and dissemination, should be an indispensable function of the UN. It will only be achieved if more effective targeted recruitment takes place, more flexible contractual arrangements are introduced, specific demonstrated expertise rather than formal qualifications are valued, and a more sustained effort is made to draw upon external expertise in a systematic fashion. The *Human Development Report* stands as a tribute to what can be achieved, even under UN auspices, when there is a serious commitment to high-quality analysis and a preparedness to let the researchers go where their analysis takes them, rather than where their political masters would like them to go.

8. I turn now to three substantive issue areas in which the UN should become more involved. The first of these is *electoral assistance*. The organization already plays an important, although still rather fragmented and muted, role in this area. It needs to be given a higher political priority, perhaps through the appointment of a UN High Commissioner for Elections who can speak with authority and mobilize resources. Such an initiative would need to be accompanied by a stronger commitment on the part of all states to accept a degree of election monitoring as a matter of course.

9. A second substantive area is the development of *a police rapid response capacity*. Too often there is a focus on military intervention in situations in which more effective and better trained policing is what is really needed. Military intervention inevitably has very negative connotations in terms of concerns over sovereignty and an ability to work constructively with the political authorities in a situation.

10. The third and final substantive area is the need to do more to *tackle corruption at the national level.* A vast number of the principal challenges that the UN confronts—from civil wars to famine and general mortality—are due primarily to unhindered corruption on the part of key elites. An excellent place to begin is to act on the recommendation by Global Witness to appoint a high-level expert group to 'review international experience of responding to self-financing wars and draw up a comprehensive strategy for tackling them'.[31] The Security Council regularly confronts these issues and in some contexts, such as that of the Democratic Republic of the Congo, has established important mechanisms to explore and track the economic and other interests that fuel conflict. Given the ubiquity of resource-driven wars and the suffering and exploitation that accompanies them, this should become a major focus for the UN in the immediate future.

---

[31] Global Witness, *Lessons UNlearned: How the UN and Member States Must do More to End Natural Resource-fuelled Conflicts* (London: Global Witness, 2010), 42.

# 5

# The Security Council: Progress is Possible but Unlikely

*Bardo Fassbender*

## SUMMARY

In spite of all its shortcomings, there is broad agreement that it is better to have the Security Council with all its flaws than to have no such institution at all. It is difficult to envisage developments of the Security Council in the direction of an institution effectively promoting and sustaining a global community based on the values proclaimed by the UN Charter. Nevertheless, a set of fairly realistic measures can be suggested: (i) the Western members of the Council, especially the permanent members, should realize that their dominance is very fragile; (ii) the Security Council should attach more importance to collective goods and interests of all peoples inhabiting the earth than to the individual goods and interests of the states represented on the Council; (iii) the Council should have at its disposal more information from independent sources, gathered and evaluated in the Secretariat, instead of being dependent on information provided by member states, especially the permanent members, on the basis of the work of their secret services. The role of the Office of Legal Affairs in advising the Security Council in matters of international law should also be strengthened; (iv) action taken by the Council (in particular in the form of economic and military sanctions) needs to be more reliable and consistent, and less arbitrary. The Security Council should try to build a precedential case law which makes it possible to predict in general terms its course of action; and (v) sanctions imposed on individuals not belonging to a small circle of members of a government, military command, or the leadership of a non-state party to a conflict should remain an exception.

## 1. Introduction

Is there a place for the UN Security Council in a realistic utopia of international law? And, more specifically, can the Security Council substantially contribute to making the world a 'global community' based on peaceful relations, justice, and solidarity? These are, I believe, the two questions put by the editor of the present volume. In trying to answer them, I proceed on the assumption that both the present international legal order in general and the United Nations as an organization continue to function, something which is not to be taken for granted.

The Security Council is deeply intertwined with the reality of international power relations. It is a result of a war, a creation of the winners of that war, a part of the effort to maintain and defend the superiority of the victorious powers in the peacetime to come. It is perhaps the most realistic element of a project infused with a lot of idealism or, to others, utopianism. The preamble and Articles 1 and 2 of the UN Charter are an eloquent expression of that idealistic or utopian aspect of the United Nations. In the organizational structure of the UN, the realization of that aspect was assigned to the General Assembly and the Economic and Social Council, which are not by chance deliberative bodies without decision-making competences beyond the inner affairs (in particular the budget) of the organization. From the start, the idealistic supporters of the UN regarded the Security Council with suspicion. Accordingly, a realistic utopia with a place for the Security Council would have to be very realistic indeed, provided that the Council is expected to continue playing the role given to it by the Charter.

For most of the history of the United Nations, the expectations or hopes placed on the Security Council were rather low, even in the small circles of diplomats and international lawyers familiar with the work of the United Nations, not to mention the wider public opinion as it appears in the voices of politicians, journalists, and businessmen. That so little was expected from the Council had the effect that disappointment about its failures was also limited; criticism never rose to a demand that the Council be abolished, as happened in the case of other institutions. There were only two short periods of enthusiasm about the role the Security Council could play in international politics, advancing the goal of a world without war—the years following the founding of the organization up to the beginning of the Cold War, and the early and mid-1990s after the end of the East–West confrontation which had subjected the Council to a decades-long stalemate. The enthusiasm of the first period was mainly expressed in the United States, that of the 1990s mainly in Europe. In both instances, it was supported by a desire to reconstruct the world on the model of one's own political ideals—as a kind of world federation based on a US Constitution writ large, or a multilateral state system similar to the European Union, respectively.

If they were still alive, the American and British diplomats and lawyers who devised the Council as the realistic cornerstone of the new world organization at the end of the Second World War would be astonished to see it was still operating in 2011. Their astonishment would be even greater when they saw that the Council still functioned in the form and according to the rules as written in 1944–45 (with the only exception being a rise in the number of non-permanent members from six to ten in 1963). The international organization specialists in the State Department and the Foreign Office had surely hoped that the United Nations would fare better than its unhappy predecessor, the League of Nations, which effectively operated for barely 20 years. But a life of more than 60 years, or two generations, of an organization so deeply marked by the experience of the Second World War and the (mainly European) political developments leading up to it, was probably beyond their imagination. Even for a much shorter lifespan of the UN they had anticipated a need for major amendment of the Charter rules. The promise of a 'General Conference...for the purpose of reviewing the present Charter' (Art. 109(1)) was part of the compromise of the San Francisco Conference.

And, indeed, it is surprising that the compromises made more than 60 years ago (mainly between the United States and the Soviet Union, and between the 'Great Powers' and the 'smaller powers', respectively) with regard to the competences of the Council, its relationship with the General Assembly, and its voting procedure survived a number of fundamental changes in international relations and still last today. Of course, underneath the surface of the provisions of the UN Charter many changes occurred which modified the original rules and adapted them to changed circumstances. But there is enough old 'hard law' still in place, not suitable for such informal modification, to be astonished about, such as the rules about membership in the Council (Art. 23) and the Council's voting procedure (Art. 27), with the essential element of the right of veto of the permanent members.

## 2. Observations on the performance of the Security Council in the past

This is not the place to draw up a detailed balance sheet of the accomplishments and failures of the Council since it took up its work in 1946. To take stock is not at all easy. What is the standard against which to measure the performance of the Council? The Council was not conceived of as a 'world government' with a comprehensive responsibility for the well-being of the world population. Its very name, deliberately chosen in contrast to the 'Council' of the League of Nations, was meant to express its limited jurisdiction. However, the body was entrusted with the task of safeguarding what since the beginning of modern political thought has been regarded as the first and primary condition for any performance of governmental functions in a community, namely the absence of armed violence between the community members. In the case of the 'international community', this meant the prevention (and, if necessary, the suppression) of war between independent states. In the words of the UN Charter (Art. 24, para. 1), 'primary responsibility for the maintenance of international peace and security' was bestowed upon the Security Council.

Did the Council carry out this mandate? Did it live up to the expectation of its founders? It is true, since 1945 no war of the scale of the two world wars of the twentieth century took place—the kind of war which the Charter sought to prevent in the first place. Equally, there was no war between any of the states which in 1945 were regarded as 'Great Powers' and which were made permanent members of the Security Council. The defeated nations, Germany and Japan, did not go to war again and were integrated in the system of the United Nations. Except for the conflicts accompanying, and arising from, the break-up of Yugoslavia, no other war took place in Europe, the continent whose quarrels had been the source of the two world wars. Transatlantic peace between the United States and the European powers was preserved. Compared to the past (the nineteenth century and the first half of the twentieth century) the number of inter-state wars has decreased sharply. But it is hard to say whether, or to what extent, the existence and work of the Security Council contributed to those positive results. Have not other factors been much more decisive, such as the mutual fear of nuclear destruction during the time of the Cold War, or the common interest in economic stability and undisturbed world trade in the era since 1989–90, or the changes in military technology, or, as regards the absence of war in Europe, the demise of traditional nationalism and the growth of a European identity? Which outbreak of hostilities was actually prevented by measures taken by the Council? Which admonitions, warnings, and demands made by the Council were heeded by the parties to a conflict? What kind of positive effect on world peace had the secret discussions among members of the Council, and between Council members and states involved in a conflict? If we imagine a world without the Security Council, would it have been more violent in the last 60 years, or would the deals struck in the Council have just been made in other forms and fora? All these questions are difficult to answer. There is only a handful of careful case studies, not enough to form a basis for more general conclusions.

However, what can safely be said (in perhaps overly moderate language), looking back on the many wars of the past six decades, is that the Security Council accomplished its object of maintaining 'international peace and security' (understood as global peace) only very inadequately. War asserted its terrible presence. It did so not in the centre of 'Western civilization' but in the 'periphery'. The truth is that the founders of the UN had not intended to promise global peace in the sense that we think of it today. Colonialism limited the effective range of authority of the United Nations. The founders' Africa, in particular, was still a continent for which the colonial powers were responsible. 'War in Africa' could only become a business of the Council in the unlikely event of a transoceanic war between those powers. Further, violent conflict in Central and South America was tacitly left to the United States and the OAS. War between the East European states politically and militarily controlled by the Soviet Union seemed impossible, and in any case would be a matter for the USSR. Finally, and very importantly, the idea that international peace and security could be threatened by civil strife or serious violations of human rights had not yet arisen.

More often than not the failure attributed to the Council was not really a failure of 'the Council' but of the individual UN member states represented on it, in particular the five permanent members. This is certainly true for the 'proxy wars' instigated by the Soviet Union and the United States as part of their ideological struggle, as well as for the open or secret interventions of one of the P5 in its respective 'sphere of influence', including the former colonies. It is also true for the silence of the Council in many conflicts which were of no interest (neither political nor economic) to any of the P5, and, conversely, for its silence in conflicts in which one of the P5 was involved or took a strong interest.

A second observation which is hardly contestable is that the system of collective security envisaged by the drafters of the Charter never became effective. That system had a realistic and an idealistic component. The realistic pillar was a political and military hegemony of the 'Great Powers', in the first place the United States (supported by the United Kingdom, France, and China) and the Soviet Union. The idea was that those states would continue their close and successful cooperation of the wartime, which had brought about effective institutions both in the military and in the political field. The combined military power of the United States, Great Britain, and the USSR, made available to a Security Council controlled by the same states, would simply be irresistible, the post-war schemers thought. The idealistic component, on the other hand, was the idea of a universal solidarity of states resulting in collective action whenever a state became a victim of aggression: 'one for all, and all for one'. This component had been carried over from the League of Nations to the UN. The United States and the Soviet Union never believed in it; whether other states did is unclear. When the realistic pillar of the Charter system of collective security broke down at the beginning of the Cold War between the former allies, the idealistic pillar quickly followed suit. It became clear that its basis, a universal bond of solidarity between states, had been just a phantom. Consequently, whatever trust states had placed in the Security Council as a defender of their freedom and independence waned. Instead, states relied on the old means of their own standing armies as well equipped as they could afford, military alliances, and open or secret treaties about mutual assistance. Instead of Article 2(4) of the UN Charter, the general prohibition of war to be enforced by the Security Council, Article 51, the right to individual and collective self-defence, became the central effective norm 'regulating' the use of force in international relations. Both NATO and the Warsaw Pact were built on that right. In those circumstances, the veto power of the permanent members meant in practice that not only the P5 were effectively exempt from the Charter prohibition of the use of force but that any state relying on the argument of self-defence which was supported by any one of the P5 was given a free hand; such state could be sure that the Security Council would not interfere with its military operations.

The hope of the 1990s that the end of the Cold War would mean a 'rebirth' of collective security and a 'revival' of the Security Council was short-lived. The former antagonism between two inimical blocs was replaced by a more complicated concert of powers with shifting configurations and majorities—a concert, however, in which the United States is the central player. The United States cannot force the other players into performing, but when *it* does not appear on the stage the concert must be called off. What did not change after 1990 was the spirit of egoism dominating the political strategies of the states involved. The decisive aspect guiding a state's action and voting behaviour in the Security Council is still the 'national interest' of that state, that is, a consideration of what consequences a certain decision entails for the state's political, economic, and military situation and interests. Altruistic concern for the welfare of others, or for the 'common good' of all states and peoples, remains a rare exception. In addition, the political, economic, and military means necessary to enforce the Charter rules regarding international peace and security remain in the hands of individual states. The Security Council has no such means at its disposal. As a last resort, it can only 'authorize' the use of military force by particular states, thus completely relying on those states' willingness to make their armed forces available, and the course of military action chosen by those states.

In view of the ineffectiveness of the normative system at the centre of which the Security Council was placed it is rather astonishing that so far all states, including the powerful states, have clung to the Council. No state was ready to take the risk of testing the importance of the Council for the stability of the international order by calling for its abolition. This is even true for states which question the legitimacy of the Council, or states which see themselves as 'victims' of groundless sanctions imposed by the Council. States continue to invest much effort in obtaining a non-permanent seat on the Council. Some states have fought hard for a permanent seat. There is broad agreement that it is better to have the Security Council with all its shortcomings than to have no such institution at all. In other words, for lack of agreement on any alternative mechanism states prefer to keep the Council in existence as it is—a standing body observing certain rules of procedure, an institution every state can turn and appeal to, a body which under favourable circumstances can at least delay, confine, or keep within limits a use of force contrary to the rules of the UN Charter. States also realize that discarding the Council would mean destroying the United Nations as a whole because the balanced structure of the principal organs established in 1945 could not survive without the Council.

## 3. The place of the Security Council in a realistic utopia of international law

Let us return to the question of what kind of place the Security Council could find in a realistic utopia of international law. The conditions outlined above severely restrict a development of the Council in the direction of an institution effectively promoting and sustaining a global community based on the values proclaimed by the UN Charter. To put it differently, the contribution of the Security Council to such a utopia will probably be only a very modest one. Some would even say that we must consider ourselves lucky if the Council does not stand in the way of a development towards a better future for the international order.

One important limiting factor is the composition of the Council which is increasingly untenable but has proved unalterable. While there is almost universal agreement that the membership of the Security Council must be adapted to present conditions of international life, and that especially the circle of states which were made permanent members in 1945 cannot remain the same, all efforts of the past 20 years to arrive at an agreement on Charter reform have been fruitless. The reasons for this are manifold.

Basically, there is a deadlock between the states which would be the winners and those which would be the losers if the membership of the Council is changed. Among the potential losers are all present permanent members, either because they are likely to lose their permanent seat, or because their present position would be weakened by the addition of new permanent seats. This deadlock mirrors the present world situation in which the new and rising powers are not yet strong enough to dispossess the old, one of their weaknesses being the rivalries and antagonisms among themselves. The decisive question is how long the states and regions not adequately represented in the Council will tolerate the present composition. As said before, so far they prefer having a Council with a contestable membership to not having a Council at all. But that disposition could easily change. As with every rigid structure, the Council runs the risk of breaking into pieces as soon as it collides with a strong opposing force.

A second limiting aspect is the fact that the law the Security Council is meant to apply has become increasingly unclear. The prohibition of the use of force in international relations has become what Napoleon is reported to have said about a constitution: that it must be brief and obscure. Issues of cardinal significance (such as the use of force by non-state actors, the limits of the right of self-defence, the lawfulness of 'humanitarian interventions' in their different manifestations, the exact meaning of a 'responsibility to protect', or the work of private military companies engaged by states) are highly controversial, and agreement (preferably in the form of written law) is not on the horizon. The ground on which the Council is operating is shaky.

Thirdly, the Council is ill-prepared for new threats to international peace and security, in particular conflicts arising from environmental disasters, the scarcity of natural resources, including fresh water and grain, or large-scale migrations of people seeking a habitable climate. Rules about how to deal with such threats do not exist, and its weak legitimacy will hardly allow the Council to create them ad hoc.

In these conditions, what kind of conduct could one recommend to the Security Council, or its individual members, to strengthen the Council as a positive force in international relations?

First, the Western members of the Council, especially the permanent members, should realize that their dominance is very fragile. It must be handled with care as long as it is not openly rejected. The Council members representing the Northern industrialized world would act wisely if they increasingly, and credibly, had regard for the collective interests and the good of the world population.

Secondly, and more generally, one could hope for a Council which attaches more importance to collective goods and interests of all peoples inhabiting the earth than to the individual goods and interests of the states represented in the Council. Some states must begin to set aside their egoism for the benefit of the common good of the world even if that demands a price. Only then the 'international community' will stop being a rhetoric expression and turn into a real social phenomenon. In the work of the Council, all elements should be strengthened which promote such a turn towards community interest. For instance, the President of the Security Council should understand his or her office as a responsibility to bring to the Council's attention issues and perspectives reflecting the interests of the 'international community as a whole'. The President should not so much be a spokesperson for the 15 members of the Council but rather be a voice for the UN membership at large, and especially for interests and policy goals not expressed by the states represented in the Council. Further, the Council should rely much more often and consistently on the advice of independent experts and NGOs, and consult with representatives of other UN organs, in particular the General Assembly, the Human Rights Council, and the International Court of Justice. The open thematic debates of the Council held in the last few years set a good example. The Council should have at its disposal more information from independent sources, gathered and evaluated in the Secretariat, instead of being dependent on information provided by member states, especially the permanent members, on the basis of the work of their secret services. The role of the Office of Legal Affairs in advising the Council in matters of international law should also be strengthened.

Thirdly, while the Security Council was rightly given broad discretionary power to decide when and in what way it intervenes for the sake of international peace and security, action taken by the Council (in particular that in the form of economic and military sanctions) needs to be more reliable and consistent, and less arbitrary. The Council should try to build a precedential case law which makes it possible to predict in general terms its course of action. To that end, the Council could adopt resolutions providing a frame, or general structure, for its later action in specific cases. It could, for instance, spell out in which cases and under which conditions the Council feels obliged to intervene for the benefit of a population which is the victim of severe violations of human rights. With that proposal we reach, however, the limits of a realistic utopia because so far the Council has categorically refused to bind itself in the form of general commitments.

The fourth recommendation is that the Security Council should carefully consider whether it wants to take up a position on a particular situation or conflict. It should do so only if it is prepared to follow its words with action, that is, if it can muster the majority necessary for imposing economic or military sanctions, and if it is likely that those sanctions will be effectively implemented. Otherwise the Council will impair its authority and become the proverbial paper tiger. A realistic assessment of its means and resources should make the Council cautious about supporting the expectation that it will come to the assistance of every people suffering from internal conflict or human rights violations.

Fifthly, sanctions imposed on individuals not belonging to a small circle of members of a government, military command, or the leadership of a non-state party to a conflict should remain an exception, both in terms of numbers and time. Not only are such sanctions alien to the inter-state system of the UN Charter but the Council also lacks the means of identifying the persons it has defined in abstract terms as a threat to international peace and security, and it is unable to afford the targeted individuals the protection of the law to which they are entitled. Criminal law (national and international) and the mechanisms of international assistance in criminal matters (such as Interpol and the network of bilateral extradition treaties) offer better, and arguably more effective, methods of bringing to justice individuals charged with crimes of an international dimension, in particular terrorist activities.

I do not want to stop here without at least outlining a future for the Security Council beyond the narrow confines of what seems realistic today. In an 'unrealistic utopia', the Council would take a more proactive attitude and seek to identify and improve, in accordance with Article 34 of the UN Charter, situations 'which might lead to international friction or give rise to a dispute', including long-term developments like desertification, overpopulation, and climate change. The Council would no longer ignore the many arbitrarily defined borders between states which are a constant cause of disputes. In an 'unrealistic utopia', the Council would systematically determine which peoples, minorities, and other sections of a population are oppressed or deprived of their fundamental human rights by their respective governments, and demand and encourage improvements to their situation. In an 'unrealistic utopia', the Council would eventually take seriously the mission assigned to it in Article 26 of the UN Charter and formulate 'plans to be submitted to the Members of the United Nations for the establishment of a system for the regulation of armaments'. It would address the nuclear armaments piled up by states which menace the existence of humankind. In an 'unrealistic utopia', UN member states would agree on a fundamental reform of the UN Charter (including a reform of the membership, working methods, and voting procedure of the Security Council) so that the Charter could function as a viable constitution of a truly international community of the twenty-first century. Such Charter reform would preserve the provisions of the instrument which have been tested and proved good. It would maintain the Purposes and Principles of the United Nations which are by no means obsolete but add to them new objectives and fundamental rules made necessary by new challenges. At the same time, reform would overhaul the machinery of the organization established in 1945, examine the existing organs for repair or revision, improve their interaction and cooperation, and add new organs to the present structure if necessary. Such reform would bring about a Security Council that would wisely, justly, and impartially maintain international peace and security for the benefit of the entire world population. But, alas, the doors of such an unrealistic utopia will remain closed. Paradise, the dictionary tells us, is the name of a town in North California only.

# 6

# The Role International Actors Other Than States can Play in the New World Order

*Nehal Bhuta*

## SUMMARY

States remain the primary actors on the international scene. This remains true although at present numerous state functions appear to be disaggregated and delegated to, or calibrated by reference to, a variety of non-state entities, such as transnational networks of officials, public–private administrative bodies operating at the transnational plane, or treaty-based arbitral bodies with specific functional competences. In recent years three sets of actors have appeared on the world scene: (i) non-governmental organizations (NGOs); (ii) (violent) non-state armed groups; and (iii) multinational corporations. Can they be legitimately associated to sovereign states? Every argument about who is and ought to be recognized as a subject of international law is striated with a normative vision of what makes international law legitimate and what purposes should be served by it (peace, justice, order, etc.). Sweeping institutional prescriptions for expanding and consecrating the role of non-state actors such as NGOs in international lawmaking and international institutions (such as through a 'right to participate') are neither realistic nor normatively desirable. Yet the value of democratic legitimacy in international politics remains uncertain where no clear demos can be identified, and where the actors claiming to represent democratic values (NGOs) are themselves rarely created and maintained in a democratic manner. The function of NGOs is epistemic: their expertise, advocacy, and investigative capacity allows them to influence inter-state deliberations through 'behind the scenes' consultation and public opinion-oriented campaigning. As for non-state armed groups, the author shares Sivakumaran's suggestion that there is a need to work out an international agreement to which (violent) non-state actors can accede, and which codifies and progressively develops their human rights and humanitarian law obligations. As for multinational corporations, in the absence of treaty mechanisms which delineate and enforce corporate human rights responsibilities, an abstract finding that corporations are indeed subjects of international law is likely only to strengthen existing international law protections of corporate interests against state action.

## 1. International personality between realism and utopia: situating arguments over new actors

Whenever an epochal shift occurs in the international order, international law undergoes a period of crisis and renewal.[1] Fundamental questions about the nature and composition of the international legal order re-emerge, such as the nature of sovereignty, the foundations of legal obligation, and the proper boundaries of membership of international society. The last question in particular has consistently surfaced at moments of transformation. In her careful inquiry into the concept of international legal personality, Nijman[2] observes that Leibniz—the first jurist to coin the term *persona jure gentium*—developed the term as part of an argument for the *legitimacy of participation* of certain actors (the Duke of Brunswick-Luneberg) in international negotiations after the Peace of Westphalia.[3] At stake in the argument over legal personality was both an *empirical claim* about the nature of the international order (who or what is included in the set of entities acting internationally?) and simultaneously a *normative claim* about who can legitimately demand a seat at the table of lawmaking and benefit from the *dignitas*—and rights, privileges, and duties—of being a member of international society. The very notion of who or what is a legitimate actor, and the question of what theories and concepts of legitimacy are adequate to justify such a role, are inextricably part of the argument.

It is trite to observe that since the nineteenth century, at the latest,[4] the international legal order and its principles of legitimacy have been organized around the notion of the sovereign state as the fundamental legal person with rights, duties, and jurisgenerative capacity: their will was endowed with the authority to create legal obligations, and to enforce them through self-help or through standing before arbitral tribunals.[5] As a matter of historical reality, the practice of states was never so pure as the legal doctrine would appear to imply: a variety of persons, entities, and human collectivities which were not regarded as states continued to participate in legally governed relationships with sovereign states throughout the nineteenth century, and there was some basis to contend that these persons or entities held rights and duties immediately under international law—not mediately through

---

[1] See W. G. Grewe, *The Epochs of International Law* (Brussels: De Gruyter, 2000); A. Cassese, 'The Diffusion of Revolutionary Ideas and the Evolution of International Law', in A. Cassese, *The Human Dimension of International Law: Selected Papers* (Oxford: Oxford University Press, 2008), 70–98.

[2] J.E. Nijman, *The Concept of International Legal Personality: An Inquiry into the History and Theory of International Law* (The Hague: TMC Asser, 2004).                [3] Ibid, 36–7.

[4] As Osiander points out, the claim that the modern state system was inaugurated with the Peace of Westphalia is fictional. Westphalia 'confirmed and perfected...a system of mutual relations among autonomous political units that was precisely not based on the concept of sovereignty.' A. Osiander, 'Sovereignty, International Relations and the Westphalian Myth', 55(2) International Organization (Spring 2001) 251–87, 270.

[5] For a classic statement, see L. Oppenheim, *The Future of International Law* (Oxford: Clarendon Press, 1921).

a sovereign state.[6] But as a *theory* of international community, the implications of the modern doctrine were clear-cut: the society governed by and through international law was the society of states and, consequently, states were the most complete legal persons in that order. The legitimacy of the ensuing legal order derived from the consent of states; it was a thin, procedural legitimacy which did not presuppose much agreement on substantive values or purposes in international society and largely deferred to states' capacity for devastating organized violence as a background condition and limit upon the possibilities for law.[7]

Of course, it remained a matter of philosophical controversy as to exactly why states should be rendered sacrosanct in this way: nineteenth-century state theory was preoccupied with divining the substance of the state and providing rationales for the value accorded to its personality and its 'will'. Such state theories had a direct impact on international law, and also on arguments about whether other types of personhood were cognizable in the international legal order.[8] The idea of the state as the concrete apotheosis of national culture and civilization was distinctively European,[9] and the concept of the state at work in international law remained Eurocentric; other political organizations which did not conform to the European idea of the state were deemed uncivilized and thus ineligible for full legal personality.[10] Hence, while the principle of legitimacy underlying positive law was formal and procedural, the criteria for legitimacy of participating actors derived from thick standards concerning the form and substance of the state. As Hurrell points out, sovereignty had a double-sided character in the classical state system: 'on the one hand, it was central to the constitutional and constitutive bargain amongst European states; on the other, it established a system of authority and complex rules to determine who was and was not to be accorded the status of a legitimate political community.'[11]

The traumatic collapse of the nineteenth-century order after 1914 was an epochal shift of the kind mentioned above. With it came demands for revision and reform of the basic concepts of the international legal order, and an effervescence of criticism of the classical system of international law. A theme running through this criticism was

---

[6] See numerous examples cited in J.J. Paust, 'Non-State Actor Participation in International Law and the Pretense of Exclusion', University of Houston Public Law and Legal Theory Series 2010-A-34. See also G. Acquaviva, 'Subjects of International Law: A Power-Based Analysis', 38 Vanderbilt J Transnat'l L (2005) 215–67.

[7] See B. Kingsbury, 'Legal Positivism as Normative Politics: International Society, Balance of Power and Lassa Oppenheim's Positive International Law', 13(2) EJIL (2002) 401–36.

[8] See M. Koskenniemi, *The Gentle Civilizer of Nations: The Rise and Fall of International Law, 1870–1960* (Cambridge: Cambridge University Press, 2002), ch. 3. See also J.L. Brierly, *The Basis of Obligation in International Law* (Lauterpacht and Waldock eds, Oxford: Clarendon Press, 1958), ch. 1.        [9] See E. Kedourie, *Nationalism*, 4th edn (Oxford: Wiley-Blackwell, 1993).

[10] See the helpful overview in M. Mazower, 'An International Civilization? Empire, Internationalism and the Crisis of the Twentieth Century', 82(3) International Affairs (2006) 553–66.

[11] A. Hurrell, *On Global Order: Power, Values and the Constitution of International Society* (Oxford: Oxford University Press, 2007), 67.

a strong aversion to state omnipotence, as epitomized in the concept of sovereignty...In this setting, new doctrines emerged which attacked the notion of sovereignty at its roots. More particularly attempts were made to sever the law from the state ideologically, with the higher dignity in the law.[12]

What is interesting for our purposes here is that 'reconstructionist' visions of the international legal order developed in the 1920s frequently challenged the exclusive role of states as fully fledged international legal persons and demanded room for other actors. The logic of these earlier efforts to delineate a realistic utopia is worth briefly reflecting upon.

In his 1928 Hague Academy Lectures,[13] Brierly rejects a line of state theory that explained the international legal personhood of states as deriving from the natural or moral rights of states. Sovereignty does not imply some substantive, personalized state will, but is simply the term used to describe the fact that states successfully wield power and authority over territories and peoples.[14] The state cannot be reified as a corporeal person; it is a collection of institutions, which are in the end associations of individuals. States and their institutions have 'personality' only insofar as we attribute to them the acts and will of individuals, as a 'form of expression'.[15] This *disaggregation* of the state concept[16] leads at once to different theoretical possibilities as to who or what may be a legitimate international actor, and also a different theoretical foundation for the value of the state:

> On such a view the question whether states or individuals are the true subjects of international law loses most of its meaning... [I]t is true that the international juridical community has for its unit of membership the state, but it is not true that the unit is the state in abstraction from its individual members...And it is not true that the individual has no interests of an international character except those for which the state stands.[17]

Viewed through this lens, states' primacy in the international legal order is a matter of functional convenience, reflecting not ontological priority but expediency: to the extent that states do *in fact* wield great power and authority over territories and persons, it is practical to accord them a primary—but not exclusive—role.[18] In Brierly's argument, the correct understanding of the nature of the state (conceptually and empirically) leads to an expansion of the range of possible legal subjects and of the concept of international community as including both *civitates* and *genus humanum*. The expansion of subjects to include, at least, the individual, is predicted to enhance the prospects for peace,[19] because it expands the range of legitimate interests to be considered in the settlement of disputes and counteracts

---

[12] A. Nussbaum, *A Concise History of the Law of Nations* (New York: Macmillan, 1947), 282.

[13] Brierly, n 8, 1–67.                    [14] Ibid, 46.

[15] Ibid, 49.

[16] This was a common theoretical move by a variety of theorists in the early twentieth century. Parallels can be found in the work of Duguit, Scelle, and Laski.

[17] Brierly, n 8, 51.

[18] Ibid, 51: '[I]t becomes difficult to believe that there can be anything sacrosanct about a practice which treats states as the subjects of the international community. It is not a principle, but essentially a rule of expediency...'; see also ibid, n 8, 250–64, 254.                    [19] Ibid, 52.

the pernicious tendency of governments to identify 'the interests of a few powerful individuals with the interests of the whole community'.[20]

Politis similarly contends that the personality of states is 'pure fiction'.[21] The state is a 'purely abstract conception . . . it is not an end in itself, but a mere system of relationships among the men of which it is composed'.[22] This sociological perspective emphasizes the empirical nature of human relationships as the foundation upon which the international legal order stands: international law 'can be nothing but the sum total of the rules which govern the relations of men belonging to various national groups'.[23] Thus, as transnational interactions between individuals grow in depth and complexity, a new notion of legal personality is required, reflecting the direct role of the individual in the international community.[24] Interdependence among 'private international communities' will 'one day become the rule',[25] and so portends the need to render 'international law democratic by placing individuals in the first rank of its subjects'.[26]

The structure of both of these arguments is noteworthy. On the one hand, empirical claims are made about the nature of the state (a set of relationships, not a thing or person) and also about the nature of who acts in the international sphere (individuals and non-state communities). These facts about the nature of the state and international community are said to require new thinking in international law, if it is not to become unrealistic. On the other hand, both arguments are saturated with a normative vision about the promotion of certain values through an expansion of the range of legal subjects. For Politis, the expansion of membership of the international community to include individuals implies a new principle of legitimacy for international law, namely democracy. Brierly is more cautious, and more deferential to the enduring reality of the power of states, but also seeks to pierce the veil of state interest and permit the international legal order directly to incorporate individual interests in some form. For both writers, the disaggregation and functionalization of the state concept is a necessary step towards an international legal and political system more likely to realize peace and 'human perfection'.[27] The argument over the meaning of legal personality is inextricably linked with an argument about how international law can and should serve utopian ends. As Nijman points out, legal personality is at once a descriptive and evaluative term: when used in a 'descriptive way, [it] legitimizes the prevailing opinion and practice, but if used in a more evaluative way, the concept may serve to provoke change, to delegitimize the old and bring about new beliefs and practices'.[28]

---

[20] Ibid, 52.
[21] N. Politis, *The New Aspects of International Law* (Washington DC: Carnegie Endowment for International Peace, 1928), 13. [22] Ibid, 25.
[23] Ibid. [24] Ibid, 23–4. [25] Ibid, 20, 31.
[26] Ibid, 23. [27] Politis, n 21, 26. [28] Nijman, n 2, 26.

## 2. The twilight of the gods? Contemporary developments concerning new actors

In a 1986 essay, Cassese concluded—with some regret—that 'entities other than states contribute only marginally to the making of international law. States remain the main actors on the international scene. The twilight of the gods has not yet arrived.'[29] Within three years, the third major epochal shift of the twentieth century had unfolded: the end of the bi-polar stalemate and a decisive victory for liberal democracy and capitalist ideology. The post-Cold War period is rightly regarded as setting in motion dramatic changes in the accepted role of the state, and as inaugurating a new era of internationalization in trade, finance, and liberal economic policy prescriptions.[30] It also marks the beginning of renewed efforts to institutionalize realms of international politics, and of much greater expectations placed on existing institutions to resolve governance problems beyond the capacity of any one state.

The role of the Security Council in authorizing coercive and forceful measures against states and directly against individuals has expanded dramatically. International courts and tribunals have proliferated, and many more disputes seem amenable to judicial resolution than ever before—indeed, the range of international courts and tribunals granting standing to individuals to vindicate rights conferred by international law seems to be increasing. Numerous state functions themselves appear to be disaggregated and delegated to, or calibrated by reference to, a variety of non-state entities, such as transnational networks of officials, public–private administrative bodies operating at the transnational plane, or treaty-based arbitral bodies with specific functional competences. The regulatory and rule-making capacity of private actors and scientific and technical experts has a global reach through contracts and other forms of voluntary association, rather than sovereign mandates. Each transnational community of social, economic, and scientific expertise seems to produce its own set of norms and rules, only faintly legitimated through formal state consent.[31] Indeed, in certain cases, forms of voluntary standard setting in consultation with non-state actors and private associations seem the *only* politically feasible option for regulation of certain international concerns, such as private military contractors.[32] Developments such as these have led some

[29] A. Cassese, 'Civil War and International Law', in Cassese, n 1, 110–27.
[30] See L. Taylor and U. Pieper, 'The Revival of the Liberal Creed: The IMF, the World Bank and Inequality in a Globalized Economy', Center for Economic Policy Analysis, New School for Social Research, January 1998.
[31] For variations on this story, see R. Hofmann (ed.), *Non-State Actors as New Subjects of International Law* (Berlin: Duncker & Humboldt, 1999); A.-M. Slaughter and D. Zaring, 'Networking Goes International: An Update', *Annual Review of Law and Social Science*, vol. 2 (2006), 211–29; J. Klabbers, G. Ulfstein, and A. Peters, *The Constitutionalization of International Law* (Oxford: Oxford University Press, 2009), chs 1 and 3; G. Teubner, 'Global Bukowina: Legal Pluralism in World Society', in G. Teubner (ed.), *Global Law without a State* (Brookfield: Dartmouth, 1999), 3–28.
[32] See, eg, the Montreux Document on Private Military and Security Companies, in which states agreed on Principles of Law applicable to these non-state actors, through a roundtable format in which NGOs and companies participated. *The Montreux Document on pertinent international legal*

to conclude that 'the monopoly of the state as a political actor in the international system has entirely broken down'.[33]

A second post-Cold War trend which appears to challenge the empirical centrality of the state in the international legal order is the increase in numbers and forms of participation of NGOs. While the question of whether a true 'global civil society' exists remains controversial,[34] the proliferation of associations claiming to represent some constituency or issue at the international plane has been extraordinary. Since 1994, the number of NGOs accorded general consultative status with the Economic and Social Council has risen from 1,000 to almost 3,000, while the number of 'international NGOs' as defined by the Union of International Associations[35] has grown from 15,000 in 1996 to 23,300 in 2007–08.[36] Moreover, it has been widely observed that (well-resourced, northern-based) NGOs have played significant roles in shaping the agendas and negotiating dynamics of multilateral treaty texts and 'soft law' declarations[37]—although their capacity to participate directly or indirectly remains conditional upon states' acceptance of their role and international organizations' accreditation. There are also indications of an expanding role of NGOs as agents, implementers, and supervisors of treaty-based norms.[38]

Hurrell points out that such phenomenon raises deep challenges to how we understand the empirical reality of international society and international law-making today. This, in turn, raises questions about how we theorize the bases of legitimacy for international law's formation and its authority to bind:

All of these changes have diluted and clouded the idea of international law as a state-privileging system and have unsettled the concept of sovereignty...We increasingly find a variety of different kinds of rules, norms and principles, developed through the actions of a wide variety of actors, in a wide variety of national, international and transnational settings...As a result the interpretive community involved in law creation and

---

*obligations for States related to operations of private military companies and security companies during armed conflict*, Montreux, 17 September 2008.

[33] J. Delbrück, 'Prospects for a "World Internal Law?": Developments in a Changing International System', 9 Indiana J Global Leg. Stud. (2002) 401–31, 410.

[34] For a sceptical view from political theory, see J. Keane, *Global Civil Society* (Cambridge: Cambridge University Press, 2003).

[35] The UIA definition is similar to that employed by ECOSOC, see <http://www.uia.be/node/163545>.

[36] These numbers can be found in M. Albrow, H. Anheier, M. Glasius, M.E. Price, and M. Kaldor (eds), *Global Civil Society 2007–2008* (London/Thousand Oaks, CA: Sage, 2008), 318.

[37] See A. Boyle and C. Chinkin, *The Making of International Law* (Oxford: Oxford University Press, 2007), ch. 2; K. Anderson, 'The Ottawa Convention Banning Landmines, the Role of International Non-Government Organizations and the Idea of International Civil Society', 11 EJIL (2000) 91–120. See also examples cited by R. Wedgwood, 'Legal Personality and the Role of Non-Governmental Organizations and Non-State Political Entities in the United Nations System', in Hofmann (ed), n 31, 25 and in S. Charnovitz, 'Non-Governmental Organizations and International Law', 100 AJIL (2006) 348–72.

[38] See C. Pitea, 'The Legal Status of NGOs in Environmental Non-Compliance Procedures: An Assessment of Law and Practice', in P.-M. Dupuy and L. Vierucci (eds), *NGOs in International Law* (Northampton, MA: Edward Elgar, 2008), 181–203.

implementation is broadened very significantly—regulating states, but no longer wholly dependent on states for its existence, content and implementation.[39]

The distinction between law and non-law is blurred in practice, as is the distinction between binding 'hard' rules and influential 'standards' and 'principles'.

The result is a broad spectrum of norms exercising degrees of public authority in the international realm[40] and feeding into states' regulation of internal and external conduct through a great variety of channels. But as Bogdandy and others point out,[41] our theoretical apparatus for conceptualizing the authority and legitimacy of these diverse phenomena remain weak and highly contested. It may be that the twilight of the gods has arrived, but the owl of Minerva has not yet taken flight; the doctrine and theory of international law has not yet caught up with this new reality. The question for further consideration below is: what theoretical framework might become the basis for rationalizing and ordering this welter of actors, processes, and norms? What role should be retained for the state, and what concepts of legitimacy are pertinent and can become operative as rooted in practice and a basis for critique? Can we now answer in the affirmative an earlier generation's utopian claim that the international order need not and should not privilege states as its fundamental subject, author, and form of human political association?

A third important constellation of developments requires mention: the violence of non-state actors. In historical perspective, the problems posed for international law by organized violence from non-state actors are far from novel. Since the late eighteenth century, the de-legitimization and suppression of organized non-state violence (and the claims to incipient authority that it represents) has been a preoccupation of international law.[42] In certain respects, the right to wage war was constitutive of the idea of sovereign statehood, and the categorization of non-state violence as a merely domestic, criminal law issue underscored its irrelevance to the international legal order. But, as is well known, even in the classical period of the inter-state system, non-state groups could become the bearers of certain rights and duties if they were recognized by other states as belligerents in a civil war or insurrection.[43] Throughout the twentieth century, legal controversy con-

---

[39] Hurrell, n 11, 111.

[40] A. von Bogdandy, P. Dann, and M. Goldman, 'Developing the Publicness of Public International Law: Towards a Legal Framework for Global Governance Activities', in A. von Bogdandy et al (eds), *The Exercise of Public Authority by International Institutions* (Berlin: Springer, 2009), 3–32 and A. von Bogdandy, 'General Principles of International Public Authority: Sketching a Research Field', in von Bogdandy et al (eds), ibid, 727–60.

[41] Von Bogdandy, 'General Principles', ibid; B. Kingsbury, 'The International Legal Order', in P. Cane and M. Tushnet (eds), *The Oxford Handbook of Legal Studies* (Oxford: Oxford University Press, 2003), 271–98.

[42] See C. Schmitt, *The Theory of the Partisan* ([1963] New York: Telos Press, 2007); L. Benton, *A Search for Sovereignty: Law and Geography in European Empires, 1400–1900* (Cambridge: Cambridge University Press, 2010); K. Nabulsi, *Traditions of War: Occupation, Resistance and the Law* (Oxford: Oxford University Press, 2005), chs 1 and 2; H. Wilson, *International Law and the Use of Force by National Liberation Movements* (Oxford: Oxford University Press, 1988), 16–17.

[43] See A. Cassese, 'Civil War and International Law', n 29, 113. D. Kritsiotis, 'International Law and the Violence of Non-State Actors', in K.H. Kaikobad and M. Bohlander (eds), *International Law and Power—Perspectives on Legal Order and Justice: Essays in Honour of Colin Warbrick* (Leiden: Martinus Nijhoff, 2009), 343–86, 345.

tinued about how to classify non-state armed groups within the laws of war, and in international law generally. Progress was made through the increased acceptance of the application of fundamental principles of *jus in bello* to both sides in non-international armed conflicts, although a fundamental asymmetry remained: '[the] legal government permits its own forces to kill rebels but considers the latter to be common criminals who have violated the ... constitution.'[44] The legal status of armed groups as subjects remains ambiguous, but it is now clear that fighters from these groups are bound by the relevant norms of international humanitarian law and international criminal law and can be regarded as 'parties'. The much-noted prevalence of internal armed conflict over inter-state armed conflict since the late 1980s has made the violence of non-state actors a central preoccupation within international law's traditional concern to regulate and restrain organized violence. With increased international involvement in the settlement of internal armed conflicts through the brokering of peace accords, armed groups' capacity to be parties to agreements deemed effective and enforceable at the international level is now widely accepted.

Nevertheless, Cassese's observation in 1986 remains true today: international norms about such groups' status as subjects remains 'vague and uncertain'. The definition of what qualifies a group of fighters as an 'armed group' cognizable as a 'party' to a conflict remains controversial.[45] Equally uncertain is whether the practice of such groups can be considered to contribute to the formation of the *jus in bello* norms which are said to bind them.[46] To the extent that armed groups control territory and rule a population, they may be subject in principle to human rights obligations, but effective mechanisms for the enforcement of human rights laws in such situations rarely exist: no non-state actor can be considered a direct party to a human rights treaty body and, apart from forms of diplomatic engagement, the international system provides few incentives for human rights compliance by these actors.

The persistence of these ambiguities reflects the deep dilemmas posed by integrating armed groups into the legal order as subjects or participants: states and their governments have an interest in maintaining wide discretion in their dealings with such groups, and in having the last word as to whether and when to confer a certain political significance to their existence by negotiating with them. After all, such conflicts can represent a fundamental threat to the continuity of the state and undermine a government's claim to effective control. Clear rules expressing the subjecthood and status of such groups would accord them an immediate legitimacy as interlocutors and signal to the international community that a state with such groups faces severe challenges to its power—a signal that few states would want to send unless it was inescapable. Indeed, clear rules of this type may provide a strong incentive for states to escalate their repression of incipient armed groups,

---

[44] A. Cassese, 'Civil War and International Law', n 29, 111.

[45] See discussion in M. Sassòli, 'Transnational Armed Groups and International Humanitarian Law', Harvard Programme on Humanitarian Policy and Conflict Research, Occasional Paper No. 6, Winter 2006, 12–13.

[46] See S. Sivakumaran, 'Binding Armed Opposition Groups', 55 ICLQ (April 2006) 369–94.

with devastating human consequences. On the other hand, international law's consecration of states' will has always been tempered by (and is largely consistent with) the notion of *ex factis jus oritur*: effective power cannot be ignored, at the risk of rendering legal rules redundant in the face of a new reality. Legal adjustment may be preferable to a legal vacuum. Non-state armed groups which *succeed* in becoming a force which neither the state party to the conflict nor the international community can ignore must be engaged in order to find ways to restrain violence and limit the scope and intensity of conflict. They must also be engaged as indispensable actors in any conflict-resolution process, where the prospects for a military victory by either side are slim.

The extent of legitimacy and legal standing granted to non-state armed groups has varied enormously with the winds of international politics. National Liberation Movements achieved considerable rights of participation and much legitimation of their armed struggle, as a result of the geopolitical climate in which they emerged: the rise of the Third World majority in the General Assembly, and a Cold War dynamic in which each superpower sought to court, or avoid alienating, the newly emerging states, and so cooperated in different degrees with their normative agenda at the United Nations.[47] In the contemporary world, the pendulum appears to have swung far in the other direction. The utility of declaring armed groups as 'terrorist'—and thus confining them categorically to the status of criminals—appears widely understood among states facing internal armed conflicts, with few states willing to contest such labels even if the facts are more complex. Thus, while there is no doubt that the Islamic Resistance Movement in Palestine (Hamas) engages in terrorist tactics, it is equally beyond doubt that they now effectively control the Gaza Strip and its population, and conduct a full range of governance functions. Continuing to label the group terrorist as a means of inducing compliance with humanitarian and human rights law has had limited success, and greatly limits the avenues through which 'carrots' can be used to induce moderation, compromise, and conflict resolution. The pathologies of applying the terrorist label to any type of non-state armed group are exemplified by the continuing US view that they are in a worldwide non-international armed conflict with 'Al-Qaeda', wherever they may be found. The result is a 'war' in which one side (the state) is a party, but the other side consists entirely of 'unlawful combatants', criminals but not fighters. One side has recognized belligerency rights, including (controversially) a *jus ad bellum* right against the non-state group,[48] while the other has only duties. Such a profound asymmetry can only serve to diminish the prospects for compliance among non-state armed groups labelled terrorists—even though some of these groups can also be understood to have specific objectives of territorial and political control, in the same way as rebel groups conventionally understood.[49]

---

[47] See D.A. Kay, *The Politics of Decolonization: The New Nations and the United Nations Political Process* (New York: Columbia University Press, 1967).

[48] See C. Tams, 'The Use of Force against Terrorists', 20(2) EJIL (2009) 359–97. But see also *Armed Activities on the Territory of the Congo (Democratic Republic of the Congo v Uganda)*, Judgment of 19 December 2005, paras 146–7.

[49] Consider the Taliban in Afghanistan: evidently terrorist but also seeking a political role in Afghanistan. Hezbollah is another example of a group which has used terrorist tactics, but has achieved a quasi-state role in Lebanon.

## 3. Whither international community? Problems of legitimacy, values, and power

In *Fairness in International Law and Institutions*,[50] Franck observed presciently that

international law is only now beginning to think about the appropriate balance between the claims of the state, the individual, and the revived traditional and new groups? What sort of future do we want, what sort of governance should it have, and who or what will exercise power in it?[51]

Fifteen years later, these questions continue to lack clear answers in theory or in the practice of governments, international organizations, and other international actors. One of the anxieties underpinning the preoccupation with the fragmentation of international law is that, in fact, there may be no unitary conceptual and institutional framework—no metavalues or 'order of orders'—capable of rationalizing, ordering, and regulating the complex international environment and of satisfactorily integrating the multifarious new roles of non-state actors. As noted at the outset of this chapter, every argument about who is and ought to be recognized as a subject of international law is striated with a normative vision of what makes international law legitimate, who really constitutes the international community, and what purposes should be served by it (peace, justice, order, etc.). Yet, if one quality of international order remains relatively stable, it is continuing disagreement (outside Western Europe) about the significance of the state as a locus for identity, loyalty, and political agency, and continuing disagreement about fundamental values (notwithstanding widespread formal commitment to human rights, the historical and social meaning with which the words are endowed vary significantly in the 'lived politics' of different societies).[52]

For this reason, sweeping institutional prescriptions for expanding and consecrating the role of non-state actors such as NGOs in international lawmaking and international institutions (such as through a 'right to participate') are neither realistic nor self-evidently normatively desirable. Such prescriptions depend on the prior claim that reforms aimed at enhancing the democratic legitimacy of international law will conduce to the effectiveness and authority of the international legal order. Yet the value of democratic legitimacy in international politics—and, indeed, its very meaning—remain uncertain where no clear demos can be identified, and where the actors claiming to represent democratic values (NGOs) are themselves rarely created and maintained in a democratic manner. Similarly, the claim that, in the absence of a global demos, enhanced democratic legitimation

---

[50] T. Franck, *Fairness in International Law and Institutions* (Oxford: Oxford University Press, 1995).

[51] Ibid, 243.

[52] On this point see H. Englund, *Prisoners of Freedom: Human Rights and the African Poor* (Berkeley, CA: University of California Press, 2006); S.E. Merry, *Human Rights and Gender Violence* (Chicago, IL: University of Chicago Press, 2006).

requires an expanded role for democratically organized *states*[53] takes for granted the legitimating effects of a historically and institutionally specific set of political values and procedures, in a world where beliefs about legitimate world order 'vary enormously from [one place to another], reflecting differences in national and regional histories, in social and economic circumstances and in political contexts and trajectories'.[54] Likewise, it is doubtful that we have reached a point where the claim that 'the ultimate normative source of international law is—from a constitutionalist perspective—humanity, not sovereignty'[55] will be met with ready agreement outside very particular national and regional contexts. The risk of prioritizing democratic legitimacy as the organizing principle of any future international order is that it will serve mostly to underwrite the civilizational ethos and higher legitimacy of one, historically dominant, set of powers—the classic problem of claims of universal value in international politics.

The pathologies associated with a new generation of conflicts with non-state armed groups remind us that violence, heterogeneity, and problems of domination remain key features of international society. International order requires the organization of interests as much as it needs normative languages of morality and right. Perhaps one of the under-theorized dimensions of the classical system's prioritization of the state in international law, was the emphasis on the state's effective power as a means of reducing—or at least focusing—the complexity of human claims, interests, and political conflicts to those represented *through* the state. The state's representative function presupposed the capacity to speak for human political collectivities in ways that no other modern political form has succeeded in doing. To undertake legal obligations at the international level requires the capacity to bind an entire territory and population. This representativeness was not necessarily democratic, but did rely heavily upon the legitimacy derived from successful domination and the maintenance of order. The hope that new transnational mechanisms for deliberation and discussion could replace this decisive capacity seem far-fetched; for all its diffusion of norm-making authority, the contemporary international community continues to rely on the power of state apparatus to prescribe, persuade, and where needed, coerce, a population to act in accordance with these norms. The effective power of the state remains indispensable and, in some cases, we see efforts to strengthen states' coercive capacity to contain the threat posed by non-state armed groups.

There can be no return to the nineteenth century. But nor do we have successful alternatives to states as effective agents for concentrating political power, implementing decisions, and containing centrifugal violence. Indeed, to hold other international actors (NGOs, corporations, armed groups) accountable we continue to rely almost exclusively on the state's capacity to interpret, apply, and enforce the law. We also rely on states to use their resources and capacity to cajole, threaten, and promise, to mitigate violent conflict: the power of states to grant and

---

[53] See, eg, A. Buchanan and R. Keohane, 'The Legitimacy of Global Governance Institutions', 20(4) Ethics and Int'l Affairs (Winter 2006) 1–33.     [54] Hurrell, n 11, 46.
[55] A. Peters, 'Membership of the International Community', in Klabbers, Ulfstein, and Peters (eds), n 31, 155.

withhold legitimacy to non-state groups and to promote compromise by governments is essential to the peaceful settlement of civil wars.[56]

Brierly's observation that the 'vast power' of the modern state was a 'simple and obvious fact of which we have to take account'[57] remains valid. The state cannot yet be described as one actor on an equal footing with others; it remains *primus inter pares*, at the very least. Statism remains a fundamental organizing frame for international law, in as much as the latter remains tied to the realities of a power-political order. It is suggested that the new realities of complex governance, transnational norm creation, NGO participation, and non-state armed groups should be approached in the cautious, formalist method of a practice-oriented positivism. Careful attention should be paid to the *specific* challenges posed by each of set of developments, and how existing, functioning frameworks of norms and procedures can be adapted to address these concerns. For example, the concerns about transparency, accountability, and participation raised by new forms of governance should be addressed in the context of the institution and procedures in which they arise, and by drawing upon the values and forms of legitimacy already embedded in those institutions. Overarching principles drawn from human rights norms can also be used as a means of contesting specific outcomes and failures of transparency and accountability, as well as principles common to a variety of administrative law systems. To some degree, this is the approach favoured by the 'Global Administrative Law' literature, and seems promising.[58]

What might this mean for how we approach the status of NGOs? Lindblom rightly points out that the arguments concerning the personality of NGOs continue to obscure as much as they clarify.[59] But the absence of clarity concerning their legal status in international law has not prevented the emergence of a number of institutional mechanisms through which, in practice, they go far beyond mere 'observatory' status in inter-state bodies.[60] For example, the Permanent Forum on Indigenous Issues' advisory body has 50 per cent of its membership comprised of representatives of indigenous NGOs, nominated by civil society and chosen by the President of the Forum. These members sit as equals with government nominees. In a context where the Forum is concerned with the treatment of a distinctive kind of minority group within states, it is appropriate that those groups have some form of direct voice in an international body. But a 'representation' model would not necessarily be appropriate for, say, NGOs with a wider topical mandate, such as the protection of human rights in general or the promotion of environmental

---

[56] See, eg, J. Prantl, *The UN Security Council and Informal Groups of States: Complementing or Competing for Governance* (Oxford: Oxford University Press, 2006).

[57] Brierly, 'The Rule of Law in International Society', in *The Basis of Obligation in International Law*, n 8, 250–64, 254.

[58] See B. Kingsbury, N. Krisch, and R. Stewart, 'The Emergence of Global Administrative Law', 68 L & Contemp Prob (Summer/Autumn 2005) 15–61.

[59] A.-K. Lindblom, *Non-Governmental Organizations in International Law* (Cambridge: Cambridge University Press, 2005), 513.

[60] See the very insightful chapter by E. Rebasti, 'Beyond Consultative Status: Which Legal Framework for an Enhanced Interaction between NGOs and Intergovernmental Organizations?', in Dupuy and Vierucci (eds), n 38, 21–70.

standards. In such cases, the function of NGOs is *epistemic*: their expertise, advocacy, and investigative capacity allows them to influence inter-state deliberations through 'behind the scenes' consultation and public opinion-oriented campaigning. To a substantial degree, their capacity to pursue both types of strategy requires them to be 'outsiders' rather than members of intergovernmental bodies. Despite the limitations, the current, fragmentary approach to NGO presence and participation—varying in nature and extent depending on the specific treaty body, international organization, and mechanism—is to be preferred, with perhaps an enhanced emphasis on 'representativeness' in contexts where the rights and needs of particular communities are under consideration.

In the case of armed groups, there is a need to balance criminalization of terrorist tactics and other atrocities, with allowing the possibility for incentives for moderation and compromise through normalization of relations. Such incentives could include an effort at correcting aspects of the legal asymmetry between the state and the armed group by decriminalizing participation in hostilities per se.[61] Greater restraint is also needed in the use of the label 'terrorist' by states as a device to avoid the equal application of *jus in bello* and in order to delay attempts to address underlying grievances. Classical international law sought to restrain and limit violence in part by accommodating it. Aspects of this logic remain relevant today. There is much merit in the proposal to develop an international agreement to which non-state actors can accede, and which codifies and progressively develops their human rights and humanitarian law obligations.[62] However, the approach of 'standards before status' will do little to increase incentives for armed groups to comply with these obligations unless it also carries with it a strong implication that their claim to legitimacy as representatives of an aggrieved population also merits consideration, and thus provides a basis for negotiated dispute resolution. Otherwise, the existing asymmetry which provides states with rights, but armed groups only with responsibilities, is repeated. It seems to this author that the formulation of clear-cut definitions of the armed groups entitled to recognition as subjects of international law remains unpromising. At the same time, the deep internationalization of conflict-resolution processes and mediation efforts makes hard rules concerning the status of armed groups less significant: to the extent that international actors (governmental, intergovernmental, or non-governmental) regard them as necessary interlocutors, a soft form of legitimacy is conferred. The challenge is to combine these 'grey' forms of recognition with clearer *jus in bello* frameworks of application and accountability. An international agreement specifically addressing armed groups—combined with these political developments—may well be a way forward.

Attempts to extend human rights norms directly to corporations famously failed several years ago in the Human Rights Commission, leading to a reversion to a 'guiding principles' approach by the current Special Representative on Business

---

[61] See also Sivakumaran's suggestion that the practice of armed groups could be taken into consideration in the formation of humanitarian law, as a way of enhancing the legitimacy of the laws for these actors: n 46, 394.       [62] See S. Sivakumaran, Chapter 40 this volume.

and Human Rights. Yet, in the sphere of international investment arbitration, the standing of corporations directly to vindicate their treaty-guaranteed investment protections has led many to argue that corporations have now been recognized as subjects of international law. As José Alvarez has recently argued, the controversy concerning the personhood of corporations overlooks the fact that 'personhood may be a thin reed on which to rely for specific conclusions about what corporate responsibility actually entails under customary international law.'[63] In the absence of treaty mechanisms which delineate and enforce corporate human rights responsibilities as vigorously as they enforce corporations' investment guarantees, an abstract finding that corporations are indeed subjects of international law is likely only to strengthen existing international law *protections* of corporate interests against state action. But it is indeed the state to which we must turn if we are effectively to protect natural persons from human rights violations, whether by corporations or other non-state actors—something which the classical theorists of public law understood very well. The personhood of corporations under domestic law has long been uncontroversial, and as Ruggie argues, it is primarily through state legislation prescribing human rights norms—both domestic and extraterritorial—that we should strive to regulate corporate conduct affecting human rights and ensure remedies to victims.[64] That states rarely do so reflects a failure of international and domestic politics rather than law,[65] and it seems to me highly unlikely that a change in the international legal status of the corporation will do anything to change the political dynamics which currently provide strong disincentives to both capital-exporting and capital-importing states to regulate and hold accountable corporations for the negative human rights consequences of their activities.

These piecemeal approaches to dealing with the challenges posed by actors other than states may be unsatisfying: they lack conciseness and emotional appeal. But as Wight suggests, this method may 'correspond more accurately to the intractable anomalies and anfractuosities of international experience'.[66]

---

[63] J. Alvarez, 'Are Corporations "Subjects" of International Law?' (forthcoming in Santa Clara J Int'l L, available at <http://law.scu.edu/corplaw/file/Alvarez-Sept-2010.pdf> 38).

[64] Report of the Special Representative of the Secretary-General on the Issue of Human Rights and Transnational Corporations and other business enterprises, *Guiding Principles for the Implementation of the United Nations 'Protect, Respect and Remedy' Framework*, draft document, 31 January 2011, Principles 1–3.

[65] As Ruggie argues, existing international legal rules provide a sufficient foundation for regulating transnational corporate conduct.

[66] M. Wight, 'Western Values in International Relations', in M. Wight and H. Butterfield (eds), *Diplomatic Investigations: Essays in the Theory of International Politics* (London: Allen and Unwin, 1966), 96.

# 7

# The Possible Contribution of International Civil Society to the Protection of Human Rights

*Mauro Palma**

## SUMMARY

The author agrees agree with Manonelles in describing civil society as 'an actor defined by being non-governmental, non-profit, organized and genuine'. The non-governmental organizations (NGOs) that have specific relevance to action, for their impact in building more responsible public opinion, for their influence on governments and supranational institutions, are those involved in defending human rights. They tend to contribute to the functioning of international guarantee procedures, the identification of more advanced preventive, protective, and reparatory mechanisms, and the definition of standards to interpret in practice the rights formally recognized. In recent years authenticity, independence, and absence of profit interests have also been the basis for new patterns of combination. There are movements centred on the universality of fundamental rights, the abolition of torture, the death penalty and wars, and movements for universal access to common goods, to water and food, but also to information. Some positive developments stand out as new factors in the construction of public space: the movements on the non-negotiability of the commons, on participation in the delineation of patterns of development, and on building from the bottom up of ways to control and monitor the effectiveness of protection of human rights, on dialogue between different cultures, are all new forms of presence of an active civil society. At present social networks are a new form of group communication to be looked at with interest both as regards the means by which to affect the actions of governments and as regards the construction of more advanced stereotypes in society. Moreover, NGOs have benefited from the new opportunities offered by information and communication technologies to increase their visibility and consequently their presence in areas and countries that in the past were more objects of analysis than places of active presence, of direct membership of people living in

* Translated from Italian by Iain L. Fraser.

them. We are plunged into a global cultural flow that conveys not just information but also ideas, representations of the world, languages, and images. The role of civil society is to bring this immersion to life as a factor for overall growth in the cultural construction of a community. Two suggestions are made: (i) full and free access to the network and the construction through it of a diffused knowledge drawing on the experiences of individuals and associations and organizations; and (ii) emphasis on cooperation among NGOs, to overcome the risk of duplication or of competition, through the initiation of joint programmes aimed at raising social awareness and building common practices to monitor the actions of governments in the protection of rights.

## 1. The early years of the new century

Perhaps the silence with which international civil society watched many governments, in the early years of the new century, adopt emergency measures in the fight against international terrorism with only rather casual protection of guarantees is sufficient to highlight its weaknesses in two respects. First, in engaging in dialogue with institutional arrangements and power. Secondly, in building more advanced social views,[1] that is, in constructing a common sense more attentive to the preservation and dissemination of the hard-won gains over the years in terms of the inviolability of a set of rights to be granted to any individual, regardless of his being innocent or guilty, foreigner or citizen, regular or irregular, or any other possible description.

It is true discordant voices have not been lacking, but they have appeared unrelated, rather than as a web of views able to spread ideas; they were like voices of people who, to paraphrase Bertolt Brecht's aphorism, sit 'on the wrong side, since all the other seats are taken'.[2]

The tragedy of September 2001 in fact also brought, along with its dead and its opening of a new phase of military conflict, the start of an ambiguous debate on the relativity of absolute obligations and prohibitions, the usefulness of certain practices of torture, and the excessiveness of limits and constraints imposed by international conventions and guarantees in national law for the protection of persons suspected or detained.[3]

---

[1] M. Palma, 'La tortura nel panorama europeo e gli organi di prevenzione e controllo', in L. Bimbi and C. Rognoni (eds), *La tortura oggi nel mondo* (Rome: Edup, 2006); M. Palma, 'Inquietudini del nuovo millennio', in L. Zagato and S. Pinton (eds), *La tortura nel nuovo millennio. La reazione del diritto* (Milan: CEDAM, 2010).    [2] B. Brecht, *Arbeitsjournal* (Frankfurt: W. Hecht ed., 1942).
[3] Charles Clarke, UK Home Secretary, said in a speech to the European Parliament Plenary Session on 7 September 2005: 'Our strengthening of human rights needs to acknowledge a truth which we should all accept, that the right to be protected from torture and ill-treatment must be considered side by side with the right to be protected from the death and destruction caused by indiscriminate terrorism, sometimes caused, instigated or fomented by nationals from countries outside the EU. This is a difficult balance to get right and it requires us all as politicians to ask where our citizens—who elected all of us here—would expect us to draw the line.'

The debate on the *globalization of rights* seemed to give way to the practice of *globalization of violations*. Moreover, the fact that the first measures taken by the vast majority of governments after that September went in the direction of extending the time between an individual's detention and formal charges—in some cases, this extension was such as to blur the distinction—should give us pause. This implicitly linked efficacy and opacity: the signal sent to those working in the field of prevention and investigation was exactly the opposite of what should characterize the rule of law, where transparency, legality, and respect for rules are not only the elements that structure the full legitimacy of the coercive or punitive intervention of the state, but also the most productive in terms of ascertaining the truth.

This process, the cultural and theoretical implications of which are obvious, did not see a role by civil society organizations and structures that could rise to the challenge of the change that was triggered. Civil society instead fell back on denunciation, without the ability to set limits and bring the principles of rule of law to life as not mere statements, but tools to address the new issues in practice.

## 2. Where we are now

The elements of civil society always establish a complex dual relationship: with the institutions and with widespread ideas. As regards the institutions, they must constitute the organized forms of dialogue for the construction of more advanced normative scenarios and practices; as regards popular ideas, or more simply, common sense, they must be structures for building shared knowledge centred on respect and democratic participation. They are not bearers of sectoral interests, nor need their issue-orientation limit their action to the theme that characterizes them. This aspect distinguishes them from any lobby and gives them relevance beyond any thematic or territorial limit, making them supranational and inclusive.

In the light of these features, we may make an initial assessment of their current effect on the international scene, always bearing in mind their two aforementioned relationships, with the institutions and with common sense.

How is it that in a rich context full of NGOs and communication networks that place them in constant—and simultaneous—contact, a government representative of one of the founding states of the Council of Europe can assert that the use of weapons could be a way to stem the flow of irregular migrants from the coasts of Africa who venture across the Mediterranean to the edges of Europe, but is unfortunately not possible today,[4] without this statement arousing an immediate response from the mass of public opinion? Does this absence not perhaps show the weakness of the relationships both between the processes of the NGOs and the

---

[4] Statement by Roberto Castelli, Deputy Minister at the Italian Ministry of Infrastructures and Transport, on Radio 2, 12 April 2011: 'The violence of the immigrants, who could become millions over time, could require the authorities to use weapons', and later: 'We need to repel the immigrants, but we cannot shoot them, at least for now.'

institutional level, and between those processes and the construction of thought in society, as the basis of the capacity to become indignant?

It is this twofold weakness that characterizes the early years of the new century. Not only that, but the communication network and the extent of access to information do not always act to manufacture awareness, because they often instead induce desensitization. Thus, for example, the many images of torture and inhuman and degrading treatment from Abu Ghraib[5] that arrived on everyday domestic TV screens worldwide did not by themselves build an awareness of the fundamental necessity to ban the practice of torture. Instead, they built a familiarity with torture, downgrading it from a shameful practice to something that admittedly exists as an extreme way of conducting an interrogation, around which to build a slippery debate centred on its effectiveness, its inescapability in some contexts, and its potential regulation. Over and above some theoretical positions that have tried to justify this drift,[6] the fact remains that the deluge of information is not always a factor for increasing awareness in the direction of accepting the views of the very organizations that saw the spread of information as such a strength. Sometimes it can rebound as tolerance and acceptance of the phenomenon one would like to tackle.

Equally scarce and inadequate have been the questions raised about the extrajudicial solutions to such issues as the capture of militants or leaders of terrorist groups and their transfer to sites where interrogations can be conducted under torture away from international scrutiny ('extraordinary rendition'), or even their elimination, often presented as an effective and definitive way to eliminate the problem at the root. The few stunted words critical of such solutions, which are in fact symptoms of a profound defeat, are indicators of the weakness of international civil society in a turbulent context such as that which has characterized the last few years.

However, despite these limitations, the construction of an international civil society continues to be a central point for the affirmation of international humanitarian law, which if deprived of its contribution would remain a complex pattern of solemn commitments and regulatory formulations unable to produce an advance in the process of globalization of rights that it is not only solid, but also socially perceived as a value to defend and extend.

Accordingly, besides the negative elements in recent years, one should mention the positive factor of the re-appropriation of certain themes, through the construction of movements that make their generosity, social objectives, and affirmation of collective commitment into a point of strength to build new forms of presence in the societal debate, and that stand out as new factors in the construction of public space. The movements on the non-negotiability of the commons, on participation in the delineation of patterns of development, on scrupulous protection

---

[5] The first publication of photographs of torture and inhuman and degrading treatment in the prison of Abu Ghraib came on 28 April 2004; they had been made between spring 2003 and spring 2004. On subsequent occasions, first another 279 pictures and ten videos, then a number estimated by some sources at about 2,000, were circulated.

[6] A.M. Dershowitz, *Why Terrorism Works* (New Haven, CT: Yale University Press, 2002).

of individual rights, and on building from the bottom up of ways to control and monitor the effectiveness of such protection, on dialogue between different cultures, are all new forms of presence of a civil society that uses regulatory instruments and institutional spaces as ways to act concretely, so as to affirm its own leading role in building a common culture focused on these goals.

For alongside the silences about extrajudicial solutions, there is in fact progress of the commitment to a moratorium on and abolition of the death penalty. Beside the trivialization of interrogation practices that lead to torture there is the growing presence of organizations that act as watchdogs on the conditions of deprivation of liberty and call for acknowledgement. Alongside the acceptance of a fluidity of military conflict, there is the desire to establish supranational courts, as regulatory bodies that go beyond the narrow limits of a reductive concept of sovereignty; next to the gruesome statements about undocumented migrants to be excluded, there are chains of solidarity and movements for assertion of a right to mobility that can cross the defensive barriers of the states.

The landscape thus has many shadows, but also bright spots that should be investigated in order to encourage their gradual expansion.

## 3. The evolution of civil society as an actor

We would accordingly do well to reflect on what is meant by civil society today.

Civil society, as we know, is not simply the sum of the individuals composing a society. It is worth recalling how Tolstoy in *War and Peace* describes the flow of history not as the sum of the stories of individuals, separable from each other, but as overall trends that indicate general guidelines that can—he says—be described by using that branch of infinitesimal mathematics that was developing in his time, because

it is only by admitting to observation infinitely small units—the differentials of history, that is, the consistent aspirations of men—and achieving the art of integration, that is, of adding up infinitely small quantities, that we can hope to understand the laws of history.[7]

Similarly, it is only by understanding the forms that the infinitesimal individuals collectively assume in relation to the social goals they pursue that we can define that actor we call civil society. We can also thereby understand the limitations and potentials of the forms so far implemented and grasp the pointers to new ones; and especially, investigate the complex relationships between civil society, public space, political decisions, and disseminated social knowledge.

We may agree with Manonelles in describing civil society as 'an actor defined by being non-governmental, non-profit, organized and genuine'.[8] These features require some exclusions. They exclude, for example, lobbies acting in interests

---

[7] L.N. Tolstoy, *Voynai Mir* [War and Peace], published in 'Russkiy Vestnik', from 1865 to 1869.
[8] M. Manonelles, 'Civil Society Participation in Intercultural Dialogue', in *Pace diritti umani* (Padua: University of Padua, 2010).

peculiar to individual groups. Although sometimes organized forms of civil society can and should use sectoral pressure, their reference is always to general interests, much broader and more fundamental than those of a specific field, whether occupational or party political. They exclude paragovernmental organized forms or otherwise government-sponsored ones, depending on support for their work, or the construction, from above, of an otherwise absent civil society.

Being 'non-governmental' is a clear and unambiguous qualification: in fact there often occur on the social scene organizations claiming civil society as their reference, which are in fact articulations of political power and especially of government structures. Distinguished by the oxymoronic acronym GONGOs, for 'Governmental Non-Governmental Organizations', they are de facto financed and controlled by governments or sectoral lobbies to show their interest in social issues, but equally de facto support government policies. Their role is thus not to strengthen but weaken social potential, being not manifestations of civil society, but obstacles to its establishment as an independent and effective actor.

NGOs, in contrast, while indeed also characterized by having a defined, stable structure and a practice that often dialogues with government action, have a private constitution, a definition of their actions entirely independent of governments or other economic or political interest groups, and above all no profit objectives.

For this is the second distinguishing feature of civil society as an actor: to be 'non-profit'. It is not easy to preserve in a context where social investments are declining in many states, and government action aimed at providing tools to ensure the survival of associations and organizations through their involvement in projects that tend to bring them to an indirect and inappropriate dependence is accentuated.

Various NGOs have various aims, of course, from the cultural to technical or scientific research. Yet the ones that have specific relevance to action, for their impact in building more responsible public opinion, for their influence on governments and supranational institutions, notably the UN, are those involved in defending human rights. Marchesi notes[9] that 'it is particularly with respect to the latter that the question of possible international subjectivity or, more generally, of treating the role they play in terms of international law, arises.' In fact, they contribute—or at least tend to contribute—to the functioning of international guarantee procedures, the identification of more advanced preventive, protective, and reparatory mechanisms, and the definition of standards to interpret in practice the rights formally recognized.

Here we come to the other characteristic of civil society as an actor, its 'authenticity'. Its forms, in fact, although targeted at specific sectors, that is, oriented towards a particular direction of content and action, are founded on a value base that goes beyond the limit of their operations. This value base moves towards the emergence of possible societies based on the extension of recognition in practice, beyond geographical, political, and regulatory boundaries, to values theoretically

---

[9] A. Marchesi, 'Organizzazioni non governative (Diritto internazionale)', in S. Cassese (ed.), *Dizionario di Diritto pubblico* (Milan: Giuffrè, 2006).

established; towards a globalization of access to tangible and intangible assets recognized as fundamental to a more equitable society. In this sense, authenticity lies in the construction of a potentially limitless public space that can find ways to make accessible to all the public goods that constitute a democratic society.

The aspects of *authenticity, independence,* and *absence of profit interests* have in recent years characterized not only the traditional forms of NGOs. They are also the basis for new patterns of combination or for other reinterpretations of existing forms. First, there are *movements* centred on the universality of fundamental rights, effective access to their enjoyment, the abolition of torture, the death penalty, and wars, and *movements* for universal access to common goods, to water and food, but also to information. These are in part themes long present in the international humanitarian debate, but have taken on new forms and in part new issues, constituting a new generation of rights.

Historically, the movements are characterized by their radicalism, but also their fragility in time, due to difficulties in organizing and translating into stable forms the groupings they sparked off. Often in the past they have been typified by localism, regional, or thematic or in membership, which has reduced their impact on wider choices. However, Seattle in 1999 was a turning point,[10] and its effects marked the next decade, so that we can now identify some of the movements as structured forms of civil society. They in fact constitute a recognizable subject, less ephemeral and unstable than in the past, and tend to be a required partner for governments; for which they have often been subject to harsh repression.

At Seattle, diverse experiences of movements found themselves face to face, in a global dimension, from those fighting against the food multinationals to those monitoring detention systems calling for justice to those opposing the dependence of national economic policies on the directives of the IMF, to those fighting against war, or for the abolition of the death penalty, or for effective access to key natural assets. This multitude of demands did not require a synthesis, did not converge in a common assembly designed to outline a comprehensive policy line, yet showed a fluidly common direction, despite the differences in specificity. This convergence avoided the cacophony of possible different sectoral languages, and brought out a consistency that strengthened the perception in the individual instances of the correctness of the objectives.

That experience was a model for many movements of the last ten years, in methods, in forms of communication, in the construction of a thematic social presence differently from the more traditional NGOs.

The current context, moreover, increasingly tends to be describable through a dichotomy: between a society increasingly portrayed as a 'fluid' reality,[11] a 'multitude'[12] ungraspable through the usual tools of analysis and classification in predefined sectors and classes, and in contrast, a rigid, centralized government order, allergic to rules and to respect for the separation of powers as a criterion of balance

[10] Anti-globalization rally at the meeting of the World Trade Organization, 30 November 1999.
[11] Z. Bauman, *Liquid Life* (Cambridge: Polity Press, 2005).
[12] M. Hardt and A. Negri, *Multitude* (Harmondsworth: Penguin, 2004).

and restraint of the powers themselves, tending to simplify relationships in terms of dry response, use of harsh instruments of coercion, extension of the deprivation of liberty, overcoming of the absolute prohibition of such things as ill-treatment and torture, up to the extended use of war. In this dichotomous context, those wanting to give direction to the 'multitude', interpreting their needs, limitations, and aspirations, must be able to grasp their language, to create in it the public space for confrontation: here the movements play a role to which positive attention should be paid.

The form of communication and relationships with which movements were structured as from the late 1990s, just after the experience of Seattle, is not external to their content: the essential vehicle was the internet, which in recent years has become an indispensable tool and an equally indispensable way of bringing people together. The communication, in fact, came through it, and gradually expanded with the various *social networks* that allow the circulation of information in real time, making it more difficult for governments and their apparatuses to ensure opacity for their actions. But the social networks also let people come together around issues, even of great importance and scope, on which consensus can be built among the users of the network itself, as a pressure group transcending territorial limits. Its amplitude can be measured, and continuous updates given on individual results achieved and partial goals pursued. The networks also have their internal organization, and may constitute not just ways of recognizing a common objective, but of participating in and of sharing that authenticity and adherence to values that characterize the sectors of civil society committed to the globalization of rights.

So they are more than just a means available to organizations and movements, but are themselves part of the overall actor we refer to as civil society. It follows that *free access to the network* is a prerequisite for this form to be a constituent part of public space: it is no accident that one of the first demands pushed by the movements in the last decade was freedom of access to the network. The right to mobility is, therefore, something that refers not only to the right to travel, but also to virtual free movement of ideas, links, information, and goals.

Certainly, the network is a form of communication and combination to be 'handled with care', because its effects can cut both ways: it can be a vehicle for 'dumbing down', for generalizing and sharing opinions and points of view that would be silenced in more direct communication than occurs on-screen. Not only that, but—as already mentioned for the images of torture—it can be a vehicle for trivializing drama, for getting used to the violations, no longer thought out and responded to in the context of the unspoken and the unseen, but offered with a flood of information and images that ultimately neutralize their strength, and therefore the drama of the events and facts they document. However, networks do not cease to be a new form of group communication to be looked at with interest both as regards the means by which to affect the actions of governments, ever alert to the numbers and to ways of building consensus and dissent, and as regards the construction of more advanced stereotypes in society.

## 4. Some developments and potentials of the constitutive forms of civil society

As regards international humanitarian law, therefore, recent years have in my opinion seen convergence on statements of principle and a search for guidelines for democracy in globalization; corresponding practice to this has, however, been lacking. On the contrary, sometimes the gap between what is said and what is practised, between what is ratified in conventions and treaties and what is actually implemented, has been such as to suggest an inverse proportionality between affirmations and their embodiments: the more emphasis is given to affirming the centrality of principles and rights, the less seems to be their scrupulous observance.

Many states do not comply with commitments entered into nor act upon the recommendations made to them by the oversight bodies, and much of the public is inclined to turn a blind eye to these failures, convinced that the uniqueness of particular situations to face and fight requires or at least justifies less consistency.

The overall balance, however, has its light and dark sides, because in parallel new forms of participation have been built up which—as we have said—have led to outlining new modes of expression of civil society, with the potential of leading to positive developments.

First of all, NGOs, particularly those of international importance, have certainly benefited from the new opportunities offered by information and communication technologies to increase their visibility and consequently their presence in areas and countries that in the past were more objects of analysis than places of active presence, of direct membership of people living in them. Not only that, but along the lines of the major organizations, local ones have been created that are a source of essential information about what is happening in their country, sometimes the only source of information available. Consider, for example, the role played by Memorial,[13] a Russian NGO with its own offices and structures in the Caucasian republics, in making known first the many aspects of the two Chechen conflicts, then the current consequences in neighbouring countries, in particular the many cases of missing persons or allegations of mistreatment and torture by security forces in the area. These cases were not otherwise known, because to date the Government of the Russian Federation has never authorized the publication of reports on the fact-finding missions carried out by the European Committee for the Prevention of Torture,[14] so that very little is known beyond what the government officially reports. To the action of Memorial we owe journalistic investigations that have breached the opacity that has accompanied and still accompanies the situation in republics such as Ingushetia, Chechnya, and Dagestan.

---

[13] Human Rights Center 'Memorial', Moscow, available at <http://www.memo.ru/eng/memhrc/index.shtml>.

[14] European Committee for the Prevention of Torture and Inhuman or Degrading Treatment or Punishment, Strasbourg (<http://www.cpt.coe.int>). The Committee is composed of one member from each state that is a party to the Convention.

This process is destined to extend to other regions and territories still barely open to the presence of associations and organizations concerned with human rights and with making visible what has been learned and established.

Similarly, the new forms of organization we previously mentioned, such as international movements and communication networks, have produced new realities, which augur positive developments over the next decade. An example is the relationship between local situations of monitoring places of deprivation of liberty, often on a voluntary basis, tied to a particular territory and still with an organizational structure not comparable with that of an NGO, and the institutionalization of a networked system of preventive monitoring, provided for by some protocols to conventions. These can be the vehicle of their development and their connection to similar experiences in other countries.

Something to be carefully evaluated in this connection is the establishment of the National Preventive Mechanisms (NPMs), being set up in countries that have ratified the Optional Protocol to the UN Convention against Torture (OPCAT).[15] It is common knowledge that the Protocol provides for the establishment of a Subcommittee on Prevention of Torture and other Cruel, Inhuman or Degrading Treatment or Punishment (SPT) which has the power to visit places of deprivation of liberty in the countries that ratify it, unannounced and with unimpeded access to people and documentation. The model is similar to that of the Committee for the Prevention of Torture (CPT) of the Council of Europe, which has been operating for more than 22 years and has been accepted by 47 member states of the Council. The discussions around the development of the European Convention for the Prevention of Torture (ECPT) which established the Committee had highlighted the desirability of a global mechanism to exercise its function of prevention through continuous monitoring, with non-pre-agreed visits, of the various places where people could be deprived of their liberty by a public authority, even for very short periods such as for an informal interrogation. The process has come to an initial conclusion with the opening for signature in 2002 of OPCAT, which currently involves 57 countries. However, since the SPT's function cannot in practice be exercised with continuity throughout the world, the Protocol provides for the establishment of independent national mechanisms, with the same powers, to visit these places continually in their own countries, monitor the implementation of recommendations and act, even immediately, on violations reported; the Subcommittee is linked with them in its overall function.

The system thus established sets up, for European OPCAT member countries for example, three levels of monitoring and prevention of torture and ill-treatment— national, regional, and global—which should act synergistically, with consistent standards and cooperation, and avoiding duplication of effort.

In the most significant experiences of establishment of NPMs, the role of civil society is crucial: in many cases, the national machinery is nothing but an offshoot,

---

[15] OPCAT was approved by the UN General Assembly on 18 December 2002 at its 57th session, by Res. A/RES/57/199. It entered into force on 22 June 2006. Currently (September 2011) the Protocol has been ratified by 70 countries, while another 12 have signed it. SPT under OPCAT began work in February 2007 and is composed of 25 members.

with powers and resources, of previous experiences by local groups and NGOs and also movements that have arisen around the monitoring of custody. In these experiences—certainly not in all, but in those where independence from government is fully respected—we can see a renewed social protagonism that brings this new body to life as an enhancement to what the territory has already expressed, now finding new power of access as a more solid interlocutor both with institutions and with society. The years to come will show the effectiveness of the system introduced, but the institution itself can already be seen to have given visibility to issues previously confined within the limits of whatever field of action and interest an association could assemble around itself.

On a completely different thematic and organizational level, one relevant experience that demonstrates the role of networked linkage is that of the Basic Income Earth Network (BIEN),[16] an international network with strong European and Latin American roots calling for the institution in every country of a so-called 'basic income' or 'citizen's income' as a requirement to give everyone 'the right to live under worthy material conditions', as the 'Universal Declaration of Emerging Human Rights' adopted in 2007 at the Universal Forum of Cultures held in Monterrey (Mexico) says.[17] Outside the welfare logic and therefore the social-safety-net notion, the citizen's income is brought into the sphere of rights: as a prerequisite for the enjoyment of the other rights and as part of a network of fundamental rights around the specific notion of the personal dimension, 'overcoming the abstract subjectivity of law dear to legal positivism, and at the same time an ahistorical notion, too far from the social contradictions of equality, typical of traditional natural-law thinking'.[18] The path is still not linear, and not always fully supported doctrinally, but there is already wide membership, built up on the internet. This has led many local administrations and certain governments to confront the pressure of an organized network, with its own structures for studying and developing proposals for implementation, even in the absence of concrete, material visibility. Few specific events have in fact been organized, apart from a few international congresses, but comparison across the network is widespread and platforms of objectives are discussed institutionally.

What is important to see in this BIEN network is that it is goal-oriented and at the same time goes beyond the set objective to link up with the wider issue of how individual rights are to evolve in a globalized society. The value it expresses lies in the openness of a universalistic tension and shared options to tackle the changed scenario of the present with a positive outlook. To this value is added that of referring to national policies only as a possible realization of a goal that transcends them. How far it keeps this non-localistic, non-sectoral promise will have to be assessed in the coming years, according to how much the network

---

[16]  See <http://www.basicincome.org>.

[17]  The Declaration, of essentially symbolic value, was adopted in November 2007 in Monterrey.

[18]  G. Bronzini, 'Il diritto al reddito garantito come diritto fondamentale europeo', in *Reddito per tutti* (Basic Income Network Italia ed., Rome: Manifestolibri, 2009).

grows and affects policies adopted by countries. However, some signs are already encouraging.

A final example of possibly promising development in recent years of a new civil-society activism is the widespread cultural work, especially the 'intercultural dialogue'.[19] This is the construction of dialogue between different cultures, with full recognition of their diversity, taken as a value and not as a problem. It is the cornerstone of a redefinition of the relationship between indigenous people and migrants in societies, such as those in Europe, where immigration is often presented as a source of fear and debated in terms of security. This demand for security can, moreover, never be satisfied, taking on ever-new aspects and the contradictions they bring, with recourse to the most rigid instruments at its disposal: deprivation of liberty, expulsion, or work forms that go back to a past of lack of rights, often with a return to forms of slave labour.

The intercultural dialogue can be the way to build a positive social relationship centred on the dignity of each. A decisive part in this connection is played by the organizations that deal with the interfaith dimension, non-formal education and communication of experience: they gave substance to the year 2010 as 'International Year for the Rapprochement of Cultures'.

The *migrant* is in any case the emblematic figure of the present, not just because of the migration flows that characterize our society, but also because even those who always live in the same place are actors in an overall movement of 'migration' set going by information and communication technologies.[20] We are plunged into a *global cultural flow* that conveys not just information but also ideas, representations of the world, languages, and images. The role of civil society is to bring this immersion to life, with the comparisons it leads to, as a factor for overall growth in the cultural construction of a community, even when it is apparently succumbing to this phenomenon. Success in this effort means the construction of a deeply and necessarily contaminated, hybrid knowledge, built by linking various experiences. This hybridization is its strong point, without abandoning any roots. On these assumptions, the Council of Europe has launched the intergovernmental multilevel programme Intercultural Cities,[21] which is based on the activities undertaken for many years by the Council through youth centres that have become catalysts for building a culture so defined. The road has begun, and we shall increasingly have to measure up to it.

## 5. A provisional conclusion

How are we to leverage these positive elements to provide renewed impetus to effective globalization of rights in a context such as that outlined, in which both the commitment of governments in this direction and the public's attention to preserving what has been achieved in terms of civility and respect for the dignity of

[19] M. Manonelles, n 8.
[20] I. Chambers, *Migrancy, Culture, Identity* (London: Routledge, 1996).
[21] See <http://www.coe.int/t/dg4/cultureheritage/culture/cities/default_en.asp>.

everyone seem to be weakening? How are we to confront the new challenges with an approach that is not merely defensive, but positive? How are we to leverage the resources, including new forms, that civil society is developing?

A first point is certainly full use of what the contemporary world offers by way of support, first and foremost the information and communication potential we have today, which must increasingly be the tools to build a new society. *Full and free access to the network* and the construction through it of a diffused knowledge that draws on the experiences of individuals and associations and organizations is a key factor.

Another one—and this is a second point—is the *emphasis on cooperation among NGOs*, to overcome the risk of duplication or of competition between them, through the initiation of joint programmes aimed at raising social awareness and building common practices to monitor the actions of governments in the protection of rights.

These two aspects of organization and planning should help positively to develop the potential that we identify today and redirect a social awareness that has flagged during the first decade of this century. In particular, they should boost the discussion on how today to develop in an evolutionary direction the set of fundamental rights to do with the individual—always maintaining the principle that no alleged emergency and no reason of state can prevail over their scrupulous protection.

# 8

# Whether Universal Values can Prevail over Bilateralism and Reciprocity

*Andreas Paulus**

## SUMMARY

As long as the world order is based on a decentralized legal system, reciprocity remains one of the pillars of that order. However, community interests have emerged, which have some common features: (i) they do not (only) refer to individual interests or rights of certain states, but concern the community at large; and (ii) are of sufficient importance so that it is not enough to leave their implementation to the usual interplay between states. Some, but not all of those interests also fulfil a third criterion, that is (iii) they give rights to non-state actors that do not have the necessary international standing to see to enforcement themselves, such as interests related to the environment, the self-determination of peoples, or human rights. Community interests normally tend to implement universal values protected in international rules of *jus cogens*. At present, there is no reason why community interests should not be protected by the traditional means of reciprocity. However, in the last resort it is international institutions that have to take up collective concerns. This is the reason why the need for the bilateralization of community interests is the greatest in areas of international law that are not sufficiently institutionalized, such as environmental protection or human rights.

## 1. Introduction: universality v reciprocity

In current international law, the importance of reciprocity is due to international law's relative lack of effective central enforcement mechanisms.[1] Thus, reciprocity

---

* This chapter has been written by the author in his personal capacity only. Parts of this chapter have been published as A.L. Paulus, 'Reciprocity Revisited', in U. Fastenrath et al (eds), *From Bilateralism to Community Interest* (Oxford: Oxford University Press, 2011).

[1] B. Simma, 'Reciprocity', in R. Wolfrum (ed.), *Max Planck Encyclopedia of Public International Law* (online edn, Oxford: Oxford University Press, 2008), para. 1.

continues to be the basic proposition for the development of international law in a world of coexistent sovereigns or, in the words of the UN Charter, 'sovereign equality'. Whether the result is a 'primitive' legal system, though, is somewhat questionable in light of its rising complexity.[2] In any case, contemporary international law is a decentralized legal system, in which the central development and enforcement of the law is the exception rather than the rule.

Since the 1970s, however, international law has taken an almost revolutionary turn. Not only has globalization—for better or for worse—brought the world closer together than ever, but the advent of global warming and global terrorism has also increased the necessity of global regulation. As a result, national sovereignty itself seems to be at stake, and with it the separation of the domestic and international spheres, the first ideally being a realm of democracy and individual rights, the latter one of coexistence and cooperation between independent states.

The more centralized the international community becomes, the less important, it seems, is the reciprocity of rights and obligations between states. The title of Bruno Simma's 1993 Hague lectures 'From bilateralism to community interest'[3] implies that reciprocity is part of the 'old', traditional, or classic international law, whereas, in the new era, 'community interests' will confine reciprocity to a much more narrow space. For the central questions of our age, from arms control and environmental protection to human rights and financial regulation, reciprocity appears to do more harm than good. Insisting on reciprocity would result in legalizing rather than abolishing torture, in developing rather than banning weapons of mass destruction, or in destroying rather than protecting the environment, not to speak of the inevitable 'race to the bottom' in bilateral financial regulation, coupled with a perverse distribution of wealth between the super-rich and the hungry. This would all be due to the 'tit for tat' of classical international law, which, in a positive sense, can lead to a virtuous cycle of law abidance, but also, in a negative sense, to a downward spiral in which one violation follows the next and obligation and violation become indistinguishable from each other.

And yet, for the time being, we should not discard reciprocity altogether. Simma speaks of a 'bilateralist grounding' of community interests.[4] While there is much reason to be less than enthusiastic about the crude enforcement mechanism that is euphemistically termed 'countermeasures' by the International Law Commission (ILC),[5] the permissibility of such countermeasures for the enforcement of obligations towards the international community as a whole is a necessary corollary of

---

[2]  See, in particular, M. Barkun, *Law without Sanctions* (New Haven, CT/London: Yale University Press, 1968), 16ff, 34; R. Falk, 'International Jurisdiction: Horizontal and Vertical Conceptions of Legal Order', 32 Temple LQ (1959) 295; B. Simma, *Das Reziprozitätselement im Zustandekommen völkerrechtlicher Verträge* (Berlin: Duncker & Humblot, 1972), 19–20 with further references; see also H.J. Morgenthau, *Politics among Nations: The Struggle for Power and Peace*, 5th edn (New York: Knopf, 1972), 281.

[3]  B. Simma, 'From Bilateralism to Community Interest in International Law', 250 Recueil des Cours (1994) 217.    [4]  Ibid, 248–9, para. 16.

[5]  Responsibility of States for internationally wrongful acts, GA Res. 56/83, 12 December 2001, UN Doc. A/RES/56/83, Annex, Part III Ch. 2, Art. 49. See also J. Crawford (ed.), *The International Law Commission's Articles on State Responsibility: Introduction, Text and Commentaries* (Cambridge: Cambridge University Press, 2002).

their legal nature.[6] In spite of the weakness of an enforcement mechanism that is basically reserved for the strong states against the weak, the alternative that states could unilaterally react to violations of investment agreements, but not to genocide, is and remains unacceptable. As long as central institutions remain underdeveloped to implement community interests and values at the international level, we should be reluctant, even mistrustful, about attempts to leave the enforcement of community interests to international organizations alone. Thus, in a decentralized system, reciprocity is transformed, but should not be abandoned altogether.

The identification of community interests and universal values that would temper reciprocity is not simple. It begins with the delineation of community interests and universal values, on the one hand, and state interests, on the other. The term 'community interests' implies the possibility of an objective identification of interests that affect the whole of the international community.[7] However, this understanding hides the necessary choice involved in the identification of those interests shared by the community. In a democratic global legal system, identifying community interests would require a communal decision that would separate community interests from mere individual state interests. On the normative side, universal values also need to be identified by collective decision, not by philosophical speculation. Thus, both 'community interests' and 'universal values' require a collective, legitimate decision-making procedure.

In the following, I will first deal with reciprocity in contemporary international law and its (dis)contents, its failure to realize the most important interests shared by the international community. I will then look more closely into the identification of community interests and the more recent attempts to transform international law to better realize those interests. By way of conclusion, I will set out some reflections on a sort of dialectical 'resolution' of the juxtaposition of bilateralism and community interests through the further institutionalization of international law.

## 2. The role of reciprocity in international law

While there seems to be general agreement that reciprocity is a central feature of contemporary international law, there is great confusion regarding the exact meaning of the term. For some, reciprocity is a purely formal notion within the theory of the sources of international law, describing the synallagmatic, *do ut des* or tit-for-tat nature of the respective rights and duties between two or more parties, as well as

---

[6] The question is now left open, see ibid. For a previous draft that included them, see ILC Draft Articles provisionally adopted by the Drafting Committee on second reading, UN Doc. A/CN.4/L.600, 11 August 2000, 14, Art. 54.

[7] For a debate on the merits of the terms 'values' versus 'interests' see U. Fastenrath, 'Subsidiarität im Völkerrecht', 20 Rechtstheorie Beiheft (2002) 475, 488 n 88; contra A.L. Paulus, '*Jus Cogens* in a Time of Hegemony and Fragmentation', 74 Nordic J Int'l L (2005) 297, 308–9, n 40. For an interchangeable use see L. Henkin, *International Law: Politics and Values* (The Hague: Kluwer Law International, 1995), 97–108.

the legal consequences resulting from such a legal relationship. For others, reciprocity stands for the broader notion that states do not observe international law as an objective system of rules regardless of the other parties, but rather for more concrete gains commensurable with the burden undertaken by freely assuming an obligation. I will here employ the term in both the narrow and the broader sense, as described in the following section. I will then look to the legal ramifications of reciprocity in the classical, decentralized system of international law.

## (A) Narrow and broader notions of reciprocity

The analysis of the role of reciprocity in international law requires a broad terminology going beyond the mere exchange of benefits and burdens between two or more parties. Simma understands reciprocity in this sense 'as the status of a relationship between two or more states under which a certain conduct by one party is in one way or another juridically dependent upon that of the other party'.[8] One may further distinguish between *subjective* reciprocity, in other words when reciprocity is also the subjective reason or motivation for entering into an obligation, and *objective* reciprocity as an observation of the factual behaviour. When the motivation of the parties is known, it is relatively easy to identify the reciprocal obligations; otherwise, a judgement must be made as from the outside.

However, reciprocity can also remain purely formal rather than substantive. In this sense, any treaty is reciprocal, because every party that enters into a treaty is legally entitled to expect compliance from the other parties, and vice versa. In a substantive sense, however, parties may engage in a one-sided or unequal treaty because they expect to benefit from other aspects in the further legal or political relationship between the parties. For instance, one state may agree to the exploitation of the area of the sea under its jurisdiction or control by a stronger state in order to benefit from the stronger state's military protection, without spelling out this expectation in the treaty itself.

Equally important is the distinction between *positive* and *negative* reciprocity. The former leads states positively to engage in and implement international obligations, while the latter tries to induce a state back to compliance by suspending the observation of a rule the state has violated. Some would also include the notion of reprisals or countermeasures into reciprocity,[9] for example the non-observance of any rule of international law in response to a violation of any other rule by the other party with a view to inducing the violator to return to the observance of the law.

Finally, reciprocity may be legal or sociopolitical in character. The legal notion of reciprocity deals with the more or less formal relationship between an obligation or duty and the respective right, the obligation of one party corresponding to the right of the other. However, the sociopolitical term describes the rough equality of

---

[8]  See Simma, supra note 3, para. 2.

[9]  See, eg, M. Osiel, *The End of Reciprocity. Terror, Torture and the Law of War* (Cambridge: Cambridge University Press, 2009), 2. The book mainly deals with reprisals in a non-technical sense, including self-defence, targeting terrorists, and reprisals against civilians in armed conflict.

states in adopting a rule. Of course, this equality is formal rather than substantive. Thus, the United States can make a treaty with Haiti either on the formal basis of an inter-state relationship or by coercion, the former being the consequence of the principle of sovereign equality according to Article 2(1) of the UN Charter, the latter being a factual relationship.

The expectation of reciprocity is one of the prime reasons why states are engaging in international legal relations in the first place. However, such reciprocity can look very different depending on the power relationships between the parties involved. In this sense, one can distinguish between legal reciprocity, on the one hand, and social and political reciprocity, on the other.

## (B) Reciprocity in international law

The central role of legal reciprocity in the law of treaties is well established and does not require extensive elaboration here. The Vienna Convention on the Law of Treaties (VCLT) regulates this area of the law comprehensively and on the basis of the reciprocity of the undertakings by the parties. Only in the mutual relationship of the parties does a treaty provision come into practice; all parties need to observe the treaty equally, but only a party that directly benefits from the performance of an obligation can successfully invoke the duty of another party to perform. Such is the importance of reciprocity that one can ask whether a treaty that does not contain any concrete and mutual obligation is at all 'law' in the material sense of the term, with the intrinsic authority this designation implies.[10]

The 'mechanics' of treaty law almost all deal with the consequences of reciprocity, from the regime of reservations to the *inadimplenti non est adimplendum* clause in Article 60 VCLT. The latter contains, however, also the most characteristic exception to reciprocity, by excluding 'provisions relating to the protection of the human person contained in treaties of a humanitarian character' from its scope. Thus, the question of reciprocity cannot ignore the content of the obligation in question—if the obligation is strictly reciprocal between the state parties, reciprocity applies. If, however, the provision serves also the more general interest of the international community, or if it benefits other, third persons, it goes beyond the bilateral relationship between the parties and thereby also beyond reciprocity.

Reciprocity in the substantive sense is involved in the application of the *clausula rebus sic stantibus* (Art. 62 VCLT) and the question of the so-called 'unequal treaties'. In other words, when are the rights and duties so unequal regarding the burden imposed on the parties that the treaty becomes not only unjust, but non-existent? The International Court of Justice (ICJ) is remarkably reticent to allow for the application of the *clausula*, to the point of denying a practical solution to the parties for the implementation of a treaty that does not take present-day

---

[10] For a fuller elaboration of this argument using the example of the Treaty between the Russian Federation and the United States of America on Strategic Offensive Reductions (SORT) of 24 May 2002, 2350 UNTS 415 (2002), 41 International Legal Materials 799, concluded as a substitute for meaningful arms control, see A. Paulus and J. Müller, 'Survival through Law. Is There a Law against Nuclear Proliferation?', 18 Finnish YIL (2007) 83, 97–9.

environmental requirements into account.[11] In general, international law does not admit the argument that an unfair balance between the reciprocal rights and duties of the parties allows for the suspension or termination of a treaty. With regard to 'unequal treaties', legal certainty thus trumps justice.[12]

While treaties exemplify the formal aspects of reciprocity, customary law exemplifies the influence of reciprocity on the formation of international law by an informal process of tit for tat, in other words by the informal acceptance of claims by other states that are in the mutual interest. The best example is probably the Truman proclamation by which a unilateral US act codified the concept of the continental shelf and was generally accepted by other states.[13] It is this reciprocal process—namely, the formulation of a balanced and generally acceptable regime and its acceptance by other states—that characterizes successful customary lawmaking.

As to reciprocity of performance of international obligations, regardless from which source those obligations arise, the ILC's Articles on State Responsibility (ASR), which have become almost as authoritative as the VCLT, recently have enshrined reciprocity even further. One could read Part I of the ASR as suggesting that international law deals with violations of 'objective' law, as it were (see, in particular, Art. 12).[14] Parts II (see, in particular, Arts 34–7) and III (Arts 42–7, 49–53), however, make clear that the 'objective' wording of Part I was not intended to do away with requirements of reciprocity, by at least requiring an injury on the side of the other party to allow for the invocation of the breach and giving a right to demand reparation.[15] Only in the circumstance of obligations *erga omnes* does Article 48 provide an exception, and Article 54 leaves open the question of countermeasures in case of the violation of such community obligations.

It is highly questionable, however, whether the concept of reprisals or, more euphemistically, countermeasures (Arts 49–53 ASR) is itself an element of reciprocity, as some scholars believe.[16] Whereas Article 60 VCLT provides for the suspension of the very obligation that is not observed by the other party and is thus of a truly reciprocal character, bringing rights and obligations back into balance,

---

[11] See *Gabčíkovo-Nagymaros Project (Hungary v Slovakia)*, ICJ Reports 1997, 7, 65 para. 104, reserving the clause to 'exceptional cases'; see also ibid, 68 para. 114, rejecting reciprocal non-compliance. But see the Dissenting Opinion of Herczegh, ICJ Reports 1997, 176, invoking the 'fundamental changes in the attitude to the protection of the environment since the conclusion of the treaty'.

[12] On the rejection of the theory of unequal treaties in international law, see A. Peters, 'Unequal Treaties', in R. Wolfrum (ed.), *Max Planck Encyclopedia of Public International Law* (online edn, Oxford: Oxford University Press, 2007), paras 2, 34, 39, with further references.

[13] Presidential Proclamation No. 2667 und Executive Order No. 9633, in Laws and Regulations on the Regime of the High Seas, (1951) 1 United Nations Legislative Series, ST/LEG/SER.B/1, 39, 41.

[14] According to Art. 12, '[t]here is a breach of an international obligation by a State when an act of that State is not in conformity with what is required of it by that obligation.'

[15] See Art. 42 ASR, see also in Crawford (ed.), n 5, 69, 245, commentary, para. (1).

[16] See the references ibid. For a more sceptical view see Simma, 'Reflections on Article 60 VCLT', 19–22; similarly the ILC in Crawford (ed.), n 5, 282 paras 4 and 5.

reprisals are a means of enforcement—or, in the language of the ILC, inducement (Art. 49 ASR)—of the other party to return to lawfulness.[17]

In a broader sense, however, countermeasures are reciprocal in character by harming the other side as a consequence of its wrongdoing. But in the restrictive view of countermeasures advanced by the ILC, the ASR limit an existing practice rather than encouraging its further use for achieving compliance.[18] In addition, the Commission has explicitly rejected the distinction between reciprocal and other countermeasures.[19]

Thus, while not reciprocal in the legal meaning of the term, reprisals or 'countermeasures' continue to constitute an important feature of 'systemic reciprocity', in other words, the responsiveness of the international legal system with regard to its non-observance. 'Systemic reciprocity' of this type is still far away from a centralized international system that would be able considerably to curtail individual reactions to breaches of the law without regard for the harm done to others. In a certain sense, therefore, it seems justified to regard reprisals as part of the reciprocal nature of much of international law under which individual subjects, rather than a central enforcer, respond to breaches.

## (C) The deficits of bilateralism

The term 'bilateralism' distinguishes the reciprocal obligations between states from those between states and the international community at large.[20] Even in a multilateral treaty, concrete rights and duties only arise between pairs of states, and, in the words of the ICJ, 'only the party to whom an international obligation is due can bring a claim in respect of its breach'.[21] In other words, in a bilateralist system, legal norms do not define an objective standard against which to hold individual state behaviour to account, but rather a relative standard giving another party the right to demand compliance in case of breach. One may compare this to a domestic legal system without centralized enforcement. In addition, in such a system, obligations can only be derived from the consent of its legal subjects, or at least, as in customary law, from their acquiescence. General principles of law may apply to

---

[17] In addition, the ICJ explicitly excludes the termination or suspension of a treaty as such by countermeasures, see *Gabčíkovo-Nagymaros Project (Hungary v Slovakia)*, ICJ Reports 1997, 7, 65 para. 106.  [18] Crawford (ed.), n 5, 281 para. 2, 283 para. 6.

[19] Ibid, 282, para. 5, but see Air Services Agreement of 27 March 1946 between the United States and France, Decision of 9 December 1978 (1979) 18 RIAA 415, 443, para. 83 for the proposition that countermeasures 'must... have some degree of equivalence with the alleged breach'. However, the arbitral award does not clarify whether this simply alludes to the proportionality principle in general or whether it demands an additional connection between breach and countermeasure, ibid, para. 82.

[20] Simma, n 3, 230–1 para. 2, preferring 'bilateralism' to Verdross's use of 'relativity'. See already W. Riphagen, 'Third Report on State Responsibility', YILC (1982), Vol. II, Part One, 36, at 38; S. Rosenne, 'Bilateralism and Community Interest in the Codified Law of Treaties', in W. Friedmann (ed.), *Transnational Law in a Changing Society: Essays in Honor of Philip C. Jessup* (New York/London: Columbia University Press, 1972), 202ff.

[21] *Reparation for Injuries Suffered in the Service of the United Nations*, ICJ Reports 1949, 181–2.

the management of the system, as it were, but not to the creation of binding obligations of action or omission in the first place.[22]

Philipp Allott once denounced the immorality of the 'interstatal unsociety', in which 'governments...are able to will and act internationally in ways that they would be morally restrained from willing and acting internally'.[23] Alas, not much seems to have changed in this regard. And yet, the recent recognition of the 'responsibility to protect'[24] shows that there exists not only a general sentiment that states are prohibited from, again in Allott's words, 'murdering human beings by the million in wars, tolerating oppression and starvation and disease and poverty, human cruelty and suffering, human misery and attacks on human dignity',[25] but also that states are under an obligation to prevent the worst of international crimes from happening; and that if they are failing to do so, there is at least a 'soft law' obligation of the international community to intervene.[26] But because the Outcome Document does not oblige the international community actively to prevent violations of basic rights, it also signifies that institutional intervention cannot be relied upon even in the most egregious cases of the failure of states to fulfil their basic purpose, namely to safeguard the bare survival of their citizens.

Thus, the main problem with bilateralism and the concomitant legal order based on reciprocity between states lies in the lack of implementation of obligations that are undertaken for the benefit of subjects other than states, whether for the sake of humanity at large, such as protecting the atmosphere from global warming, or for the sake of non-state entities or individual human beings. It is not the benefits accruing to us—and even less so to contemporary states or their leaders—that motivate us to protect the environment, but the responsibility to protect (sic!) the necessary conditions for survival for all human beings, whether contemporaries or future generations. Neither do we fight poverty for investment purposes. The underlying rationale of a bilateralist system does not fit into the most important considerations of our time.

However, does this also imply the 'end of reciprocity'?[27] While sceptical regarding the current state of affairs, some writers have indeed argued for a continuous

---

[22] On the difficulties of dealing with general principles as codified in Art. 38 of the ICJ Statute, see the seminal article by B. Simma and P. Alston, 'The Sources of Human Rights Law: Custom, Jus Cogens, and General Principles', 12 Australian YIL (1992) 82.

[23] P. Allott, *Eunomia. New Order for a New World* (Oxford: Oxford University Press, 1990), 248.

[24] 2005 World Summit Outcome, UN Doc. A/RES/60/1 (24 October 2005), para. 139; see also SC Res. 1674 (2006), para. 4 ('reaffirms'), SC Res. 1706 (2006); Secretary-General's Report, Implementing the Responsibility to Protect, UN Doc. A/63/677 (2009), para. 3; C. Stahn, 'Responsibility to Protect', 101 AJIL (2007) 99.                [25] Allott, n 23, 248.

[26] According to para. 139 of the 2005 World Summit Outcome, UN member states,

> are prepared to take collective action, in a timely and decisive manner, through the Security Council, in accordance with the Charter, including Chapter VII, on a case-by-case basis and in cooperation with relevant regional organizations as appropriate, should peaceful means be inadequate and national authorities are manifestly failing to protect their populations from genocide, war crimes, ethnic cleansing and crimes against humanity.

This falls short of a legal obligation and only relates to the most heinous crimes, but is at least a beginning.

[27] Cf Osiel who refers, however, to the law of countermeasures rather than reciprocity in general.

development from bilateralism to the institutionalization or even constitutional-ization of the international community.[28] However, if 'community interests' are to be implemented effectively, international law needs to preserve the mechanisms in the bilateralist toolbox, so to speak, and among them chiefly the principle of reciprocity.[29]

## 3. From reciprocity to community interest?

As we have seen, reciprocity is the hallmark of a decentralized legal system whose subjects cannot rely on a centralized reaction to breaches of the law. While insti-tutionalization is the main feature of the development of international law in the twentieth century, however, it is far less clear that such institutionalization neces-sarily leads to the complete constitutionalization of the international system.[30]

While treaties establishing international organizations continue to be recipro-cal between the members of the organization, and the constituent treaty thus falls under the regime of the VCLT (Art. 5), this reciprocity is purely formal in nature. Rather, it is the relationship between the organization and the member which is more relevant. Thus, in principle, a treaty establishing an international organiza-tion transfers the reciprocal relationship between states members to a more general reciprocity between membership in the institution, on the one hand, and institu-tional protection by the institution, on the other.

However, in international relations, states hardly rely on an institutional reac-tion to violations of their rights. Thus, it would be naïve, to say the least, if a state faced with an aggression waited for the reaction of the Security Council to an invasion rather than defending itself in the exercise of its right under Article 51 of the Charter until the Security Council eventually steps in. In order to protect their interests, states are thus unlikely to renounce their capacity to react reciprocally to breaches of the law. For the same reason, the right to (peaceful) reprisals or coun-termeasures is still enshrined in contemporary international law.

Nevertheless, the new developments and challenges have had a profound impact on international law. In the following, I will look to various ways in which the new 'community interest' regime transforms international law and thereby also the role of reciprocity within the international legal system.

### (A) The identification of community interests

However, first we need to identify what constitutes community interests. As we have seen, while the term 'interests' seems to imply the objective qualification of

---

[28] See, eg, G. Abi-Saab, 'Whither the International Community?', 9 EJIL (1998) 248–65; and, recently, J. Klabbers, A. Peters, and G. Ulfstein, *The Constitutionalization of International Law* (Oxford: Oxford University Press, 2009). [29] Simma, n 3, 248–9, para. 16, 285 para. 45.
[30] For a more complete treatment, see A. Paulus, 'The International Legal System as a Constitution'. in J.L. Dunoff and J.P. Trachtman (eds), *Ruling the World? Constitutionalism, International Law, and Global Governance* (Cambridge: Cambridge University Press, 2009) 69, 75–81.

such interests, international law needs to define those subjects in which all states have a 'legal' interest beyond upholding international law as such.[31]

The usual place to look for the basic principles of international law is *jus cogens* or the peremptory norms of international law.[32] *Jus cogens* provides a loose, object- ive standard of a purely negative character, however. In its original version codi- fied in the VCLT, it is established by the 'international community of states as a whole' and voids any contrary international agreement. In spite of the uncertainty surrounding the 'international community of states as a whole',[33] there seems to have developed a general agreement as to the contents of *jus cogens*—the prohib- itions on the use of force and genocide, basic human rights such as the right not to be tortured, and the core rules of international humanitarian law are the main candidates commanding near-to-universal consent.[34] The ICJ also puts respect for the self-determination of peoples into the related category of *erga omnes* obli- gations.[35] The Inter-American Court and the Inter-American Commission on Human Rights have adopted a more expansive reading that integrates the larger part of human rights law into *jus cogens*, such as the prohibition on the death pen- alty against perpetrators younger than age 18, as well as the principles of equal- ity and non-discrimination.[36] As far as the present author can see, however, these precedents have not been followed elsewhere. Article 2 of the UN Charter defines basic states' rights and duties, and some of them, such as the prohibition on the use of force, probably also belong to *jus cogens*. Other norms of a *jus cogens* nature, such as the prohibition on genocide and the right not to be tortured, belong to human rights. Therefore, the core of the common value system cannot be derived from the 'structure' of the community interests, but requires a consensus of the 'inter- national community' as to the collective interest in their realization.

Such a constitutional consensus, however, seems to have eluded the international community at least since the San Francisco Conference of 1945; and as far as this consensus goes, it has not produced a complete ordering of 'community interests' but rather a piecemeal result in some areas that cannot be extended to others by logical implication alone. The 'Washington consensus' of the 1990s which some

---

[31]  This is the famous insight of *Barcelona Traction*, ICJ Reports 1970, 32, para. 33.

[32]  On *jus cogens* generally see recently, with further references to an abundant literature, A. Orakhelashvili, *Peremptory Norms in International Law* (Oxford: Oxford University Press, 2006); C. Tomuschat and J.-M. Thouvenin (eds), *The Fundamental Rules of the International Legal Order* (Leiden/Boston, MA: Martinus Nijhoff, 2006). For a theoretical perspective, see S. Kadelbach, *Zwingendes Völkerrecht* (Berlin: Duncker & Humboldt, 1992); R. Kolb, *Théorie du jus cogens inter- national* (Paris: PUF, 2001). See also my own view in Paulus, *'Jus Cogens'*, n 7.

[33]  See A. Paulus, *'Jus Cogens'*, n 7, 325–8.

[34]  Ibid, 306 with further references. For a more extended list (which is apparently due to its non- consensual character), see Orakhelashvili, n 32, 50 et seq.

[35]  *East Timor (Portugal v Australia)*, ICJ Reports 1995, 90, at 102, para. 29.

[36]  For the execution of minors, see Inter-American Commission of Human Rights, *Roach and Pinkerton v US*, Res. No. 3/1987, 8 HRLJ (1987) 353, para. 56; confirmed in *Domingues v US*, Rep. No. 62/2002, paras 84–5, available at <http://www.cidh.org>; for equality and equal pro- tection before the law and non-discrimination see IACtHR, *Juridical Condition and Rights of the Undocumented Migrants*, Advisory Opinion OC-18/03 of 17 September 2003, para. 101. But see the criticism by G.L. Neuman, 'Import, Export, and Regional Consent in the Inter-American Court of Human Rights', 19 EJIL (2008) 101 (arguing that the Court has gone far beyond state consent).

were regarding as the 'end of history'[37] has remained short-lived.[38] Nevertheless, one may note a certain convergence towards the view that a global interest in both human rights and democratic governance[39] exists, while attempts at a democratization by force from the outside—such as the wars in Iraq and Afghanistan—are rarely successful.

If we look at the substance of these community interests, such minimum rules are far away from any attempts to 'constitutionalize' international law[40] towards a system in which reciprocity only plays a limited role. It is still the comparative lack of central institutions in lawmaking and law implementation that leaves reciprocity, in Simma's words, as 'the principal leitmotiv'[41] of the international legal system.

## (B) The bilateral and multilateral realization of community interests, in particular human rights

The term 'community interests' connotes some 'objective' element in the designation of these interests.[42] Historically, of course, the 'objective' characteristics of human rights guarantees stood at the core of the term. Thus, in the *Pfunders* case, the European Commission of Human Rights insisted that the Convention was binding on Italy regardless of whether the other party to the case, Austria, had been bound, too, thus making an exception to the normal bilateral play of reciprocal rights and obligations between parties to a multilateral treaty.[43] Echoes of the 'objective' theory of fundamental rights may be visible in the jurisprudence of the German Federal Constitutional Court, too.[44]

However, is there something 'structural' to the notion of community interests, from which objective interests can be derived? Partly yes, one may say. Thus, the

---

[37] Cf F. Fukuyama, *The End of History and the Last Man* (New York: Free Press, 1992).

[38] For the original formulation that concentrated on economic policy, see J. Williamson, *What 'Washington Means by Policy Reform'* , in id (ed.), *Latin American Readjustment: How Much has Happened* (Washington DC: Institute for International Economics, 1989), available at <http://www.iie.com/publications/papers/paper.cfm?researchid=486>; cf M. Naim, 'Fads and Fashion in Economic Reforms: Washington Consensus or Washington Confusion?', 26 October 1999, available at <http://www.imf.org/external/pubs/ft/seminar/1999/reforms/Naim.htm>. Here the term is used in a more political connotation as embodiment of a consensus on the global applicability of a 'Western' combination of capitalism, democracy, and human rights. As such, it is not necessarily a negative term.

[39] See, in particular, the writings of the late T. Franck, 'The Emerging Right to Democratic Governance', 86 AJIL (1992) 46.

[40] For recent contributions to the constitutionalization debate see the contributions to J.L. Dunoff and J.P. Trachtman (eds), n 30; Klabbers, Peters, and Ulfstein, n 28; B. Fassbender, *The United Nations Charter as the Constitution of the International Community* (Leiden/Boston, MA: Martinus Nijhoff, 2009), each with further references.                [41] Simma, n 1, para. 1.

[42] A.L. Paulus, *Die internationale Gemeinschaft im Völkerrecht* (Münchener Universitätsschriften Reihe der Juristischen Fakultät; Bd 159, Munich: C.H. Beck, 2001), 251–2.

[43] *Pfunders, Austria v Italy*, decision of 11 January 1961, 4 Yearbook of the European Convention of Human Rights (1961) 116. On the significance of the case, see Simma, n 3, 366–75 paras 115–20.

[44] See the famous *Lüth* case that pioneered the 'objective dimension' of fundamental rights in the German Grundgesetz, *Lüth*, Judgment of the Federal Constitutional Court (15 January 1958), 7 Entscheidungen des Bundesverfassungsgerichts 198, 204ff.

preservation of the environment is indeed an interest that is communal, independent of any state involvement. The 'tragedy of the commons'—problem known from the economic sphere—comes to mind.[45] And it is certainly in the objective interest of all states to have the environment protected, at least by the others—free riding presupposes rather than contradicts the existence of a community interest.

However, with regard to human rights or self-determination, it is far less obvious that their protection is in the community interest—in particular if one limits the relevant community to states, as Article 53 VCLT does.[46] Why should a community of states be interested in allowing groups to secede—if only 'remedially' as exchange for the past and present violations of their rights?[47] Why should it be in its interest to oblige its members to protect the human rights of their own inhabitants? While it is certainly possible to give reasons for an affirmative answer to these questions, this is not necessarily so. As we all know, the answer that international law gives is decidedly positive: both the self-determination of peoples and fundamental human rights such as the prohibitions of torture and genocide are recognized as community interests.[48]

Nevertheless, such interests have certain structural characteristics in common: (i) they do not (only) refer to individual interests or rights of certain states, but concern the community at large and (ii) they are of sufficient importance so that it is not enough to leave their implementation to the usual interplay between states. Some, but not all of those interests also fulfil a third criterion, that is, they give rights to non-state actors that do not have the necessary international standing to see to enforcement themselves, such as interests related to the environment, the self-determination of peoples, or human rights. In fact, the only community interest generally recognized that does not meet this criterion is the prohibition on the use of force which protects individual states while at the same time being of interest to the whole community.

However, as the European Court of Human Rights itself has pointed out, just as in the domestic equivalent, the 'objective' dimension is not alternative but complementary in nature; in other words, while the community as a whole has an interest in the protection of those values and interests, they nevertheless are also in the interest of the states themselves.[49] Thus, the realization of human rights may occasionally be

---

[45]   G. Hardin, 'The Tragedy of the Commons', 163 Science (1968) 1243.

[46]   Interestingly enough, however, the ILC did not replicate this definition in its Articles on State Responsibility *verbatim*, speaking in its Art. 48(1)(b) of the 'international community as a whole' rather than the 'international community of states as a whole'. Rumour has it that this decision was made in committee by one single vote—hardly the broad-based legitimacy that such a move would require to be universally accepted.

[47]   To the chagrin of some, including Bruno Simma, the ICJ avoided the issue in *Accordance with International Law of the Unilateral Declaration of Independence in Respect of Kosovo*, Advisory Opinion, 22 July 2010, available at <http://www.icj-cij.org/docket/files/141/15987.pdf>, paras 82–3; cf Declaration of Judge Simma, <http://www.icj-cij.org/docket/files/141/15993.pdf>, para. 6.

[48]   See, eg, *Legal Consequences of the Construction of a Wall in the Occupied Palestinian Territory*, Advisory Opinion, ICJ Reports 2004, 199, paras 155, 157; I. Brownlie, *Principles of International Law*, 7th edn (Oxford: Oxford University Press, 2008), 511; American Law Institute (ed.), *Restatement of the Law. The Foreign Relations Law of the United States*, 3rd edn (St Paul, MN: American Law Institute Publishers, 1987), §102, Reporter's note 6.

[49]   *Ireland v UK*, Series A, no. 25 (1978), 90. On this point, see Simma, n 3, 358–75, paras 109–20.

against the immediate interest of the government of a state, but certainly continues to be in the interest of its inhabitants. Translated into international law, this subjective element implies that not only the community of states can demand respect for the prohibition on genocide, but a state can also bring a collective claim on behalf of its inhabitants to an international court, such as Bosnia-Herzegovina did against the former Yugoslavia.[50] In state-to-state proceedings before the European Court of Human Rights, only a few states have invoked the rights of citizens against another state; most state complaints have invoked rights of their own citizens against another state party.[51]

Are 'community interests' by themselves not amenable to reciprocity? If, for instance, human rights are enshrined in a treaty, that treaty remains a reciprocal promise of the state parties that testifies to the interest each of them takes in the observance of minimum rules of human rights by all the state parties, or maybe by all states. Thus, there is no reason why community interests should not be protected by the traditional means of reciprocity. Thus, states may adopt countermeasures not only against states violating the rights of the citizens of the claimant state, but also against those violating the rights of their own citizens.

As is well known, the international community had some difficulty with agreeing to so-called 'third party countermeasures' for the violation of community interests. While the ILC had suggested admitting them under narrow circumstances in 2000, they were dropped from the State Responsibility draft in 2001 due to heavy state opposition,[52] both relating to obligations in multilateral treaties towards all state parties (obligations *erga omnes partes*) and to those in customary law recognized as obligations towards the international community as a whole (obligations *erga omnes*). Instead, while introducing stringent requirements for any countermeasure, the Commission left the question explicitly open whether 'third parties' not directly injured by a violation of international law should be allowed to employ them.[53] It is highly understandable why weak states object to countermeasures since they will rarely be able to induce strong states to comply with international obligations by violating their own obligations in response. Nevertheless, if countermeasures are permitted in cases of simple breach of a bilateral obligation, it is inconceivable to provide a lower threshold of protection to those obligations considered *erga omnes* or even *jus cogens*. Protections against vigilantism should rather be found in the general limitations to countermeasures as contained in Articles 49 to 53 of the ASR.

---

[50] *Application of the Convention on the Prevention and Punishment of the Crime of Genocide, Preliminary Objections*, Judgment, ICJ Reports 1996, 623, para. 47 (affirming its jurisdiction).

[51] For a recent example, see *Georgia v Russia*, App. no. 13255/07, Admissibility decision, 3 July 2009.     [52] For the official explanation see Crawford (ed.), n 5, 305 para 6.

[53] Article 54 of the Articles on State Responsibility only contains a 'no-prejudice clause'. See generally C. Tams, *Enforcing Obligations Erga Omnes in International Law* (Cambridge: Cambridge University Press, 2005); D. Alland, 'Countermeasures of a General Interest?', 13 EJIL (2002) 1221; M. Koskenniemi, 'Solidarity Measures: State Responsibility as a New International Order?', 72 BYIL (2001) 337, 355–6 (against legal regulation of unilateral measures of this kind).

The necessity of such reciprocal protection of community interests is underlined by the failure of the ILC to come up with a convincing regime for serious violations of the most important rules of international law of the *jus cogens* variety. The ILC Articles provide for a rather minimal set of additional consequences for such heinous acts, relating to the duties of third states rather than additional consequences for the wrongdoing state. Thus, Article 41 asks other states to cooperate against such violations and not to recognize the consequences of such acts. At least the latter obligation can also be derived from the provisions of Article 16 of the ASR regarding aid or assistance in the violation of any rule of international law and from the ICJ *Namibia* Opinion with regard to violations of the prohibition on the use of force.[54] This is all that remains from the original proposition of 'international crimes of state' as contained in the first ILC draft on the matter, in 1996.[55]

As a consequence, the ILC did not satisfactorily solve the riddle of how to protect community interests in the framework of the bilateralist international law of state responsibility. It even seemed to take back some of the original strength of the *Barcelona Traction* judgment. Whereas the ICJ had insisted that any state has a legal interest in the protection of obligations *erga omnes* and can thus arguably also demand implementation,[56] the Commission now speaks of '[a]ny State other than an injured State' that is only exceptionally, under Article 48, entitled to invoke responsibility. Thus, the ILC does not recognize an injury, but exceptionally grants authority to invoke the observance of those rights. It thus fails to take up the original idea that obligations *erga omnes* can be invoked by all states in their collective interest in the implementation of the minimum rules for civilized state conduct.[57] While not explicitly referring itself to the Articles, the ICJ *Wall* Opinion suggests that the exception carved out in Article 48 for obligations *erga omnes* has achieved customary law status.[58]

The weak implementation of community interests also signifies something else: in the last resort, it is international institutions that have to take up collective concerns. 'Systemic reciprocity' of the kind envisaged in the ILC draft can only occasionally contribute to implementing obligations towards the community. Only the institutional pursuit of community interests will ultimately allow for a more regular response to violations of international law. Bilateralization of collective interests is inferior to institutionalization. This is the reason why the need for the bilateralization of community interests is the greatest in areas of international

---

[54] *Legal Consequences for States of the Continued Presence of South Africa in Namibia (South West Africa) notwithstanding Security Council Resolution 276 (1970)*, Advisory Opinion, ICJ Reports 1971, 16, 54, paras 117, 119 (based on a binding determination of the Security Council).

[55] Crawford (ed.), n 5, 348, 352, 361–2.

[56] 'In view of the importance of the rights involved, all States can be held to have a legal interest in their protection': *Barcelona Traction, Light and Power Company, Limited, Second Phase*, Judgment, ICJ Reports 1970, 32, para. 33.

[57] But see the proposal advanced by B. Simma, 'Staatenverantwortlichkeit und Menschenrechte im ILC-Entwurf 2001', in J.A. Frowein et al (eds), *Verhandeln für den Frieden Liber Amicorum Tono Eitel* (Berlin: Springer, 2003), 423.

[58] See *Legal Consequences of the Construction of a Wall in the Occupied Palestinian Territory*, Advisory Opinion, ICJ Reports 2004, 197–8, para. 159.

law that are not sufficiently institutionalized, such as environmental protection or human rights.

Where a comparably strong institution exists, such as the UN system for the maintenance of international peace and security or the World Trade Organization system in trade, the action will move to the institutional system. Certainly, such systems may have bilateral and reciprocal features,[59] but they go structurally beyond bilateralism towards institutionalization. Thus, the recent interest in the constitutionalization of international law may ultimately be the key towards a move from bilateralism to community interests. But the reverse is also true—as long as the institutionalization of the most important obligations that are so central to human survival remains shockingly incomplete, community interests will need the mechanism of reciprocity for their implementation.

## 4. Conclusion: reciprocity and beyond

Thus, in a world in which only states are legitimate lawmakers in the sense that they can make laws binding not only on themselves or on consenting third parties but also on others, in a world in which the central functions of lawmaking, adjudication, and enforcement are not sufficiently centralized, reciprocity remains firmly in place. It serves as extra-legal reason for states to make and observe international law, as intra-legal mechanism to induce compliance, to uphold the balance of rights and duties, and also to sanction non-compliance, even as leverage for implementing community interests when exercised by individual states acting for the international community. Thus, concepts such as *jus cogens* and obligations *erga omnes*, far from signalling an 'end to reciprocity', testify to its lasting relevance. For better or for worse, the news of the death of reciprocity is greatly exaggerated.

However, reciprocity is not everything. Certain considerations and values cannot be compromised by the non-compliance of some. States are not only the makers and breakers, but also the guardians of international law, in particular where courts or tribunals lack jurisdiction and competence. They must act as guardians not (only) for their own sake, but for the sake of all those whose interests are protected by international legal rules but who lack either the power or the legal standing to enforce those rights for themselves. As international lawyers—and as lawyers *tout court*—we must uphold the minimum core of civilization as a good in itself, as a condition for survival, and as an obligation towards future generations.

Only a world state could completely institutionalize the pursuit of community interests. For better or for worse, a world state is not forthcoming. It would have huge problems not only in implementing its decisions, but also in maintaining its unity in view of the diversity of actors and values. Nevertheless, when the intuition is correct that common interests require common, if not necessarily centralized

---

[59] See, eg, P.T. Stoll, 'The WTO as a Club: Rethinking Reciprocity and Common Interest', in U. Fastenrath et al (eds), *From Bilateralism to Community Interest* (Oxford: Oxford University Press, 2011), 172.

solutions, then institution-building is required. The bilateralization of community interests in the law of treaties—in particular by *jus cogens*—or state responsibility—obligations *erga omnes*—cannot substitute for institutionalized responses to the identification and implementation of community interests.

Nevertheless, as long as international law remains truly inter-national, reciprocal mechanisms remain necessary to remind states of their duties of implementation and compliance. Only by preserving reciprocity will our decentralized international law be able to survive. But changes such as the revolution in communications will necessarily also affect the role of reciprocity: non-state actors will increasingly contribute to enforcing international law, from mass demonstrations against wars to consumer boycotts against businesses violating core labour or environmental standards. To avoid vigilantism, however, such activities should be tempered by judicial or quasi-judicial means of control. Only when brought under a legal regime will those mechanisms help international law to enlist bilateralism to the service of community interests.

# 9

# Can Legality Trump Effectiveness in Today's International Law?

*Salvatore Zappalà*

## SUMMARY

Traditionally the principle of effectiveness represented a cornerstone of international law. Its role has been twofold: (i) it has been based on specific provisions of international law which require factual elements to be taken into account for legal consequences to arise and (ii) the factual dimension has been a broader distinctive trait of the international legal system as a whole. It follows that effectiveness has permeated the structure of international law and influenced it in its entirety by systematically connecting the world of law to its ability to display effects in the world of facts and vice versa. Today effectiveness has not been totally supplanted by the legality–legitimacy notions. Nonetheless, the aspiration of international law to impose itself as a legal system and the emergence of universal values which cannot be derogated from have inevitably entailed increasing limitations on effectiveness. Today there are three case scenarios: (i) there are cases in which facts can produce legal effects as provided for by specific rules of international law, in line with the traditional function of effectiveness; (ii) there are areas in which some of the new universal values that have emerged in the international community are of such importance as to bar any effect to factual situations in conflict with them (eg no foreign occupation can deprive peoples of their right to self-determination; no ethnic cleansing policy can be condoned; no government can be recognized if it is established on the basis of principles of apartheid and racial discrimination); and (iii) there are other cases in which the question is more doubtful since conflicting universal values may be at issue—a sort of grey area in which effects can materialize only where certain conditions are met. Recent examples relating to Iraq and to the birth of a new state in Kosovo seem to confirm the notion that, at least to a certain degree, effectiveness may still play an important role even when faced with universal values, provided it operates under the control of international institutions, so that it may lead to a better realization of such values (eg self-determination, peace and security, fundamental human rights protection). Furthermore, as shown by the case of Palestine and Western Sahara, effectiveness, coupled with the enactment of universal values and the commitment of international institutions, can help to determine how to strike the appropriate balance between the various competing universal values. The alternative would be the ongoing lack of any solution, with the added danger that the present, totally unsatisfactory conditions are likely to fester and thus to lead to new violence and bloodshed.

# 1. Effectiveness and legality

The principle of effectiveness has ancient roots and ultimately represents the foundation of any legal system since all legal orders presuppose the real ability of their rules to apply concretely (this is why, eg, the existence of a domestic legal order is essentially a de facto phenomenon and is measured by its effectiveness). However, in domestic legal systems this long-established traditional element has evolved. Effectiveness has been progressively eroded, being eventually supplanted by specific rules hinging on the notions of legitimacy, lawfulness, and legality, which place the legal dimension above any factual element. Against this background it is implied that institutions are there to ensure that the law is respected. Nonetheless, occasionally institutions can govern processes whereby originally illegal situations are somehow mended in order to bring about better solutions in terms of enactment of important values. In this perspective, facts may give rise to situations recognized by the legal system only insofar as there are legal provisions or procedures that authorize such legitimizing processes and regulate the limits within which certain facts may produce legal effects, requiring some sort of benefit for society.

The three notions of legitimacy, legality, and lawfulness[1] have become central in contemporary legal systems. Through appropriate procedures and specific institutions, they have fundamentally replaced effectiveness as a general tool for change in the legal order.

# 2. The traditional role of effectiveness in international law and the emergence of universal values

## (A) General remarks

Traditionally the principle of effectiveness (better known as *'principe d'effectivité'* or principle of *'ex factis jus oritur'*) represented a cornerstone of international law. The international legal order, given its lack of centralized structures, could have solid foundations as a legal system only insofar as its impact on reality was strong and concrete; it could not rely on legal constructs devoid of corresponding foundations in

---

[1] Here I do not want to engage in a semantic analysis given the necessarily multilingual character of international law. The notions of legitimacy (which has a strong political function in relationship to authority and power), legality (which refers to a more formal and rule-oriented discourse of justification), and lawfulness (which expresses a normative value judgement over specific facts or acts, for the determination of those which are lawful and those which are not) are grounded in a common postulate: they reject the attribution of normative force to mere facts. Facts (whether characterized by the system as legal or illegal) cannot per se bring about any change in the normative system, unless the system itself expressly provides that certain legal changes may attach to certain facts.

practice. When the universal authorities—the Pope and the Emperor—relinquished or lost their prerogatives to establish authoritatively the legality or illegality of all situations, there was no other alternative for the legal system of nations to be put in place (or to continue to exist): it was necessary to rely on the principle whereby the concrete existence of any given situation in the *real world* was to be considered as the strongest sign of its legitimate existence in the *legal world*.

The *role of effectiveness* in the international legal order is twofold. First, it is based on specific provisions of international law which require factual elements to be taken into account for legal consequences to arise (eg the existence of state practice as an element of custom; the requirement of actual opposition of state parties to bar the effects of reservations; proof of a genuine link to determine nationality, and so on). Secondly, the factual dimension is a broader distinctive trait of the international legal system as a whole, a trait which is inherent in the system. It follows that effectiveness permeated the fundamental structure of international law and influenced it in its entirety by systematically connecting the world of law to its ability to display effects in the world of facts and vice versa. Even today, in international law, effectiveness has not been totally supplanted by the legality–legitimacy notions mentioned above. Nonetheless, the aspiration of international law to impose itself as a legal system and the emergence of universal values which cannot be derogated from have inevitably entailed increasing limitations on the principle of effectiveness.

## (B) Effectiveness and universal values

The advent of universal values in the international community has changed the perception of the relationship between the various provisions of international law and introduced a clearer dichotomy between legality and effectiveness. In contemporary international law, there are provisions which possess a stronger resistance to change—they cannot be set aside by other provisions (apart from those which have the same character), and they represent a strong obstacle to change through effectiveness.

True, universal values have probably always been present in international law; however, after the Second World War it became clearer that certain rules, enshrining such values, enjoyed a unique status: the notions of obligations *erga omnes* and *jus cogens* were created. May facts affect these novel provisions? May the values behind these rules be set aside by inputs coming from the world of facts? May effectiveness alter the sphere of legality? In particular, may this occur when universal values are concerned? These are questions that arise as a result of the clash between the old and the new international law.

Against this background, it must be noted that often in the legal sphere mere facts are considered as the counterpart of values—normally *ex factis jus non oritur* because facts as such are devoid of a value dimension. However, in the old international community international legal provisions, and thus the values behind them, were not organized hierarchically but would rest at the same level and could reciprocally derogate from each other. Undoubtedly, the advent of universal values, which cannot be derogated from, has increased tension between effectiveness and legality, a bipolarity that is not always easy to solve in favour of one or the other. Hence, in today's international law there are, at least, *three case scenarios*.

First, there are cases in which facts can produce legal effects as provided for by specific rules of international law, in line with the traditional function of effectiveness (this is further examined in Section 3 below). Secondly, there are areas in which some of the new universal values that have emerged in the international community after the end of the Second World War are of such importance that they bar any effect to factual situations in conflict with them (eg no foreign occupation—no matter how long—can deprive peoples of their right to self-determination; no ethnic cleansing policy can be condoned; no government can be recognized if it is established on the basis of principles of apartheid and racial discrimination). Finally, there are other cases in which the question is more doubtful since conflicting universal values may be at issue—a sort of grey area in which effects can materialize only where certain conditions are met.

While the first and second scenarios bear strong similarities with the relevance and operation of the principle of effectiveness in domestic legal systems, the third hypothesis evidences the specificity of the role of effectiveness in contemporary international law. It also reflects the contradictions and tensions of the emergence of universal values in an individualistic society still based on a horizontal arrangement of the relationships between states.

## 3. The factual dimension of international law and the inherent function of effectiveness

Various *international law provisions* explicitly refer to factual elements for the purpose of recognizing a given situation or of granting rights or imposing obligations. For example, an entity exists as a state, and is considered to be able to engage actively in relationships with other existing states, insofar as its authority is exercised *with effectiveness* on a given community and a determined territory (with the consequence that this entity will also be able to ensure respect for international law over that territory and in that community). Similarly, insurgents may assume international personality insofar as they possess effective control over the territory (and hence can ensure respect for international law over that territory—and enter into agreements with the incumbent government or with other states concerning the protection of foreigners operating in that territory).

Continuing with the subjects of international law, international organizations can also possess international legal personality whenever they *effectively* have the powers and competences to act autonomously from member states (see the ICJ Advisory Opinion of 1949 on *Reparations*).

Moving on to the area of state responsibility, one may easily identify effectiveness as the main criterion to determine—beyond the formal classifications based on national law—the actual possibility to attribute the actions of a given individual to a state. In particular, Article 8 of the ILC Articles on State Responsibility clearly provides that 'the conduct of a person . . . shall be considered an act of a state under international law if the person . . . is *in fact* acting on the instructions of, or under the direction or control of, that state in carrying out the conduct' (emphasis added). This means that effectiveness is the criterion which allows the attribution of the actions of private individuals to a state.

Furthermore, to display its effects at the international level, nationality must be established by the existence of a genuine link, which clearly refers to a factual and substantial material element (an effective relationship between the individual and the state concerned).

Moreover, as for the law of treaties, the role of effectiveness is highlighted both in the area of reservations to treaties as well as in treaty interpretation. As far as the former is concerned, the opposition of a state party to a reservation is taken into account only insofar as it is effective. With regard to interpretation, effectiveness emerges in the doctrine of the *effet utile* which implies that where several different interpretative options are possible, the one permitting a broader range of effects should be preferred. Finally in the field of customary law, the element of practice (*usus*) is strongly linked to effectiveness.

All these examples confirm the persisting centrality of effectiveness in the international legal system, a centrality which has not been significantly affected by the emergence of universal values since it is the legal system itself, through specific legal rules, that takes into account the factual dimension for legal consequences to ensue. However, there are areas in which universal values may represent today a radical bar to effectiveness with a view to imposing greater respect for legality and ultimately for the fundamental values of the international community.

## 4. Universal values as a bar to effectiveness

The UN Charter and the gradual upholding of general principles, such as the prohibition of the use of force in inter-state relations, the proclamation of self-determination, the ban on apartheid, the increasing relevance of fundamental human rights, and the proscription and criminalization of genocide, have spawned a core of universal values that are indicative of the aspiration of the international community to bar any role for effectiveness in these areas, and certainly to exclude any role for effectiveness when it would conflict with such values.

There is a significant practice of pronouncements by the UN Security Council which shows the tendency not to recognize legal effects emanating from situations originating in illegal acts or otherwise unlawful roots. A few examples may be of assistance. With regard to the situation in Southern Rhodesia, the Security Council systematically affirmed the non-recognition of a government based on racial discrimination and apartheid policies through Security Council Resolution 216 (1965) of 12 November 1965. Similarly, in the context of East Timor, the Security Council never accepted the annexation of East Timor by Indonesia (although when it had to send a peacekeeping mission to the island in 1999, it turned to Indonesia to seek its consent prior to the adoption of Resolution 1264 (1999) establishing the International Force for East Timor (INTERFET), the military operation which preceded the creation of the UN transitional administration, the United Nations Transitional Administration in East Timor (UNTAET), by Resolution 1272 (1999) of 25 October 1999).

A similar approach had been taken in the Iraq/Kuwait conflict of 1990–91, though the factual situation was rapidly reversed by the armed intervention of coalition forces. The Council, however, already in its first resolutions had affirmed the refusal to recognize illegal situations; see for instance, Security Council Resolution 661 (1990) of 6 August 1990, whereby it explicitly 'calls upon all States:... (b) not to recognize any regime set up by the occupying Power' (operative para. 9), and Resolution 662 (1990) of 9 August 1990 whereby it clearly 'Decides that annexation of Kuwait by Iraq under any form and whatever pretext has no legal validity and is considered null and void' (operative para. 1) and further 'calls upon all states, international organizations and specialized agencies not to recognize that annexation and refrain from any action or dealing that might be interpreted as an indirect recognition of the annexation' (operative para. 2).

The Iraqi/Kuwait precedent shows that where there is no conflict between competing universal values and when the international community is determined to enforce such values, the illegality of effective situations is asserted and de facto situations may not prevail. A similar approach was taken by the International Court of Justice (ICJ) in its Advisory Opinion on the *Israeli Wall* built in Palestinian territory; in particular where it rejects the very idea that the international community can be placed before an unlawful situation, as well as where it rejects any justification for territorial changes brought about through the policy of 'fait accompli'.

On the other hand, where there are conflicting universal values at issue and the determination of the international community is not so clear, problematic situations arise and more nuanced solutions are needed. Arguably, in such cases it would be possible for effectiveness to play a role, particularly when coupled with the engagement of the international community through its institutions (typically the United Nations, but also regional organizations). In these instances, even starting from an originally unlawful de facto situation, effectiveness might allow a more rational enactment of universal values, as we shall see below.

## 5. Making effectiveness consonant with universal values to settle otherwise intractable situations

### (A) General

All the above examples should not be seen in isolation but as indicative of a general tendency to try to impose the paradigm of legality over effectiveness. However, this does not necessarily mean that today in international law *legality* as such simply prevails. It would be wrong to consider that the new universal values that have emerged after the Second World War and created a type of legitimacy paradigm for international law completely removed effectiveness as an overarching principle of international law, reducing its role to those areas in which the legal system, through specific provisions, pointedly attaches importance to factual dimensions.

On the contrary, when politicians or diplomats in the realm of difficult negotiations invoke a certain dose of 'realism' and call for pragmatic approaches, they very often unconsciously make an appeal for legal solutions inspired by 'effectiveness'. This is a necessary paradigm of international legality, even (and in particular) when universal values are at issue. However, it is indispensable that effectiveness be coupled with the action of international institutions, which are in a position to ensure that effectiveness eventually conforms with universal values.

Some recent examples relating to the Iraqi crisis and to the birth of a new state in Kosovo seem to confirm the notion that, at least to a certain degree, effectiveness may still play an important role even when faced with universal values, provided it operates under the control of international institutions, so that it may lead to a better realization of such values (eg self-determination, peace and security, fundamental human rights protection).

## (B) Iraq and Kosovo

A few events in the last decade have emphasized the clash between effectiveness and universal values: for example, the war in Iraq and its aftermath (2003–05) and the creation of a new state in Kosovo (1999–2010). These two cases have evidenced the power of factuality and the difficulties in assessing international reality merely on the basis of legality paradigms that do not recognize the role of effectiveness.

Much has been said on the invasion and the subsequent military occupation of Iraq by the Coalition forces (mainly the United States and the United Kingdom) and the empowerment of a new Iraqi government (after the military occupation). The purpose of this chapter is not to dwell on those events in great detail. However, a few elements which show the ambiguities of the relationship between effectiveness and legality in international law need to be highlighted.

On 20 March 2003 the Coalition forces invaded Iraq and occupied the country. Although the attack on Iraq has generally been regarded as contrary to the UN Charter, thereafter the evolution of the situation in Iraq has found no or very little opposition in the international community. The authority and legitimacy of the new Iraqi government has never been significantly challenged on the basis of the illegality of the use of armed force that triggered change in Iraq. Is this significant with regard to the relationship between effectiveness and legality? Some may argue that it is not, on account of the fact that the intervention was not illegal and thus no original sin affected the whole situation. However, considering the attack on Iraq as a violation of Article 2(4) of the UN Charter (or even as an act of aggression) and without engaging in a discussion on the level of illegality of that action, it is clear that in a system strongly reliant on legality none of the consequences of such an assertedly blatant violation of the provisions prohibiting the use of armed force would possibly be legalized.

In the Iraqi context there are at least three aspects which attract attention: first, the involvement of many states in the process of international assistance in rebuilding the Iraqi state; secondly, the general acceptance of the trials of the former leaders by a special court established by the new administration, but heavily relying on the authority and support of the (*pro tempore*) occupiers; and, thirdly, the very legitimacy of the new government (which received democratic support by the people of Iraq, but was also largely assisted by the occupiers).

A rigorous legality paradigm would tend to suggest that no assistance should have been lent to the reconstruction of the Iraqi state, no legitimacy should have been recognized in the activities of the Iraqi Special Tribunal, and no recognition should have been given to the new Iraqi government. Less rigour could still allow some consideration for the first two elements, but one could hardly deny that fully recognizing the new government necessarily implies condoning the illegality that may have surrounded its establishment.

On the other hand, the effectiveness paradigm suggests that a given situation exists in reality notwithstanding the origins of the situation, and all states as well as the international community at large are obliged to take that factual dimension into account. Why does this occur? Arguably the new Iraqi administration and the new Iraqi state as a whole have been supported and assisted and obtained broad recognition because ultimately—despite the violation of the ban on the use of force by Coalition forces—the whole process is fundamentally in keeping with *other universal values* protected by international law, such as for example improvement of human rights in Iraq; implementation of the principle of self-determination both in its external aspect (if one considers self-determination from the occupiers) and internal (if one considers the democratic process that ensued); and the establishment of a system based on respect for the rule of law.

Turning to the case of Kosovo, the following observations can be made. Looking at the case from a *legality* perspective, it is plain that Kosovo was an autonomous province within a sovereign state, and the territorial integrity of that state had been reaffirmed through Resolution 1244 (1999). Hence, the process of establishment of a new state in Kosovo seemed to be entirely against legality and destined to failure. Instead, from a *factuality* perspective one can stress (i) the situation on the ground, a consequence of the NATO war over Yugoslavia (March–June 1999) and the recognition of the factual marginalization of the authority of Belgrade over Pristina and (ii) the effective establishment (with some international assistance) of an autonomous entity—which no longer identified itself with the state of Serbia. This factual situation created the background for the declaration of independence by Kosovo. Moreover, Serbia itself contributed factually to altering the overall picture and the nature of the pre-existing state (the Federal Republic of Yugoslavia (FRY))—the territorial integrity of which was allegedly protected by Resolution 1244 (1999)—by agreeing with Montenegro on the dissolution of the last remnants of the FRY. In 2006 Montenegro became an independent state. It seems thus possible to suggest that when Kosovo proclaimed its independence, the territorial integrity of the State of Union of Serbia-Montenegro (previously the FRY) had already been modified.

Even the ICJ, in its Advisory Opinion of 22 July 2010, eventually downplayed the legality dimension and emphasized the factual dimension of international law. Of course, the Declaration of Independence was seen as a mere fact—there is nothing legal or illegal in Kosovo authorities proclaiming independence. However, the Court could have been more vocal about the role of Security Council Resolution 1244 (1999) and the principle of territorial integrity reaffirmed therein.

Instead, the choice was made to refrain from engaging in value judgements on the impact of UN legality over fundamental principles of international law. The solution chosen essentially rested on the factual dimension of the Declaration.

Arguably, the justification of such emphasis on effectiveness resides in the fact that the creation of Kosovo as a new state is the end result of a long process which started in the beginning of the 1990s and led to the dissolution of the Socialist Federal Republic of Yugoslavia (SFRY). This process showed that within a framework governed by legality principles in the form of direct involvement of the international community through the UN and on the basis of a UN Security Council resolution, effectiveness could still play a role (see eg Germany's oral submission before the ICJ).[2] The situation of Kosovo clearly shows that effectiveness can still be a powerful tool to effect change in international law. However, the whole situation is also evidence that effectiveness as such is not sufficient and can only produce some effects when it is assisted by a degree of 'blessing' by international institutions. Clearly, in the case of Kosovo the effective situation underlying the declaration of independence and the establishment of a new state resides in a number of factors: Resolution 1244 (1999), the effective administration of the territory of Kosovo by the United Nations Interim Administration Mission in Kosovo (UNMIK), and the continuing presence of international actors in Kosovo.

These examples prove, to my mind, that effectiveness does not operate alone, but must be coupled with an expression of commitment by the international community which ensures that the factual situation produces changes that are overall more consonant with universal values than the *status quo ante*. Effectiveness can produce the effect of legalizing an originally illegal situation, if some measure of legality is ensured both through the participation of international institutions and the improved implementation of universal values (first and foremost the values of peace and security, human rights, and self-determination).

## 6. May the combination of universal values and effectiveness contribute to the settlement of difficult crises? The cases of Palestine and Western Sahara

### (A) Competing universal values and the principle of effectiveness

As I have tried to emphasize above with regard to the two most recent cases where universal values and effectiveness seemed to be in conflict, universal values and effectiveness can be engaged in a positive partnership to try to contribute to the settlement of difficult and long-standing crises in the international community. As such, universal values must not be considered as a total bar to effectiveness. One must be aware that rhetorical insistence on universal values does not per se suffice to determine positive developments. Two situations stand out in this respect: the well-known Israeli/Palestinian situation and the often forgotten Western Sahara scenario. Both situations implicate universal values, such as

---

[2] See paras 28ff, at <http://www.icj-cij.org/docket/files/141/15714.pdf>.

the need to protect and preserve peace and security, the need to implement the principle of self-determination, as well as the need to ensure appropriate protection for the fundamental rights of the civilian population. The values involved are not always and entirely on one side, and in this respect the situations are far from clear, even from a pure legality perspective. It is true that there is a strong case for invoking self-determination in both situations, on the one hand; however, it is also true that consideration must be given in both cases to solutions that allow a better implementation of peace and security as well as fundamental human rights of all populations involved, on the other. Effectiveness, coupled with the enactment of universal values and the commitment of international institutions, can be a criterion which may help to determine how to strike the appropriate balance between the various competing universal values. The alternative to this simultaneous application of some universal values and a limited recognition of effectiveness would be the ongoing absence of any solution, with the added danger that the present, totally unsatisfactory conditions are likely to fester and thus to lead to new violence and bloodshed.

## (B) Palestine

In the context of the Palestinian situation, for example, one should take into account that the existence of an illegal de facto situation cannot be simply set aside, since there are also other universal values that ought to be taken into account. The reality in the field will have to influence the prospects for change. How to tackle it? For a realistic solution to be suggested it is necessary to strike the right balance between competing interests and to ensure that the main universal values are implemented, including the principles of self-determination of peoples and of respect for fundamental human rights. Should a solution be found that allows for the exercise of self-determination, while ensuring highest human rights standards, some concession could be imagined as to the existence of a de facto situation that may be originally tainted by illegality (eg concessions relating to originally unlawful territorial acquisitions).

In the Israeli/Palestinian scenario, the situation is still marked by a striking opposition of the two competing demands: legality and effectiveness. As mentioned above, in subsequent conflicts Israel has occupied several territories which fall within the territory over which the Palestinian state should be created. There have been numerous pronouncements of the Security Council emphasizing that modifications to the status of the territories cannot be based on violations of international law and cannot be condoned (see Security Council Resolutions 242 (1967) of 22 November 1967, 271 (1969) of 15 September 1969, and 681 (1990) of 20 December 1990, whereby the Council 'reaffirms the principle of the inadmissibility of the acquisition of territory by war'). However, the opposing claims that the territories should belong to Palestine brought the situation to a deadlock which is not productive for peace and security in the area, or for the exercise of self-determination, or for the fundamental rights of people living in those areas whether

Palestinian or Israeli. To overcome the current lack of perspectives, it would seem preferable to relinquish rigid legality and privilege instead a de facto situation that ensures implementation of several fundamental values. However, for this to occur, it is not sufficient merely to rely on a waiver of legitimate Palestinian claims—this could only be accepted on the condition that (i) there is an involvement of the international community through its institutions which ensures the full exercise of self-determination and the creation of the Palestinian state; (ii) Israel ensures appropriate compensation for all the territories involved, both for all individuals affected as well as for the state of Palestine; and (iii) there are appropriate guarantees of non-repetition (the details of which would have to be worked out with much specificity and could include appropriate economic guarantees). Any arrangement would have to entail that after this 'legalization' of an originally unlawful situation (the illegality of which should be recognized by the parties) no further violations of international law should be left unsettled between the two parties. This would require that the parties agree to one or more pre-established redress mechanisms to be activated in case of alleged violations (such as, eg, specific obligations binding on both parties to accept the jurisdiction of the ICJ to settle their disputes, or the establishment of a permanent joint claims tribunal).

## (C) Western Sahara

A similar pattern could be imagined for the situation of Western Sahara, where self-determination claims are still potent, but the situation on the ground tends to negate all fundamental values, including self-determination, and a prolonged military occupation filled with 'incidents'. This state of affairs does not seem satisfactory from any perspective. As is well known, since Spain relinquished colonial power over the area, Western Sahara has been the object of competing claims by Morocco, Mauritania, and the Polisario Front as a movement representing the people of Western Sahara in their quest for self-determination. Mauritania subsequently abandoned these claims after being defeated in military operations by Morocco. The situation as it stands now is one of military occupation of large portions of Western Sahara by Morocco. Various plans have been proposed and rejected; more recently a referendum should have been organized but the project failed since both parties opposed such a vote. The disagreement was essentially about who should have been allowed to vote. No decision has been taken, and while recent reports indicate that the parties are still willing to sit at the negotiating table and will meet again sooner or later, the situation is deadlocked and the option of the referendum seems at the moment unlikely. Meanwhile, the civilian population is forced to live in difficult conditions.

If one looks at this situation through the prism of the confrontation between facts and values in international law, one must recognize that there is, on the one hand, a strong legality claim based on universal values which points to the exercise of self-determination as the ultimate goal of the Sahrawi people; on the other hand, there is the effective control over the territory by Morocco, which insists on its claims to the territory, claims that hark back to a period prior to the relinquishment of colonial power by Spain. Would it not be better at this stage to abandon self-determination claims and try to realize better conditions for the population that lives in Western Sahara, thinking of possible forms of self-government within Morocco under international monitoring? In other words, one could imagine a settlement that would ensure a large measure of autonomy to Western Sahara, including control over natural resources (the income of which should be primarily spent for the benefit of this territory) in exchange for abandoning self-determination claims. One could add a strong form of international monitoring, the inclusion of arbitration clauses, and a clause establishing the option of a referendum and of exercising the right of secession should the autonomy pact be violated.

In both instances discussed so far, however, to overcome the long-standing situation of stalemate, it is indispensable that the international community becomes fully and directly involved and carries out a principled decision by which some sacrifice to legality principles can be accepted in the name of effectiveness, subject to the condition that improved implementation of universal values is ensured.

## 7. The continuing role of effectiveness in the world society: an outlook for the future

There is little doubt that the principle of effectiveness has been affected and restrained by the universal values that emerged in the twentieth century, referred to above. All these values are at the core of the international legitimacy–legality paradigm and represent distinctive traits of contemporary international law. However, effectiveness is an equally important principle and still plays a pivotal role in the international legal system. The most problematic aspects regard its relationship with the above-mentioned universal values.

At present, effectiveness does not operate against universal values but must rather be combined with them to protect them more concretely, to ensure the effective implementation of such values.[3] In this respect, it is hard to deny that in specific areas the importance of universal values may be evident. For example, the relevance of practice in the process of formation of customary rules may be less important in areas where the rules are the expression of universal values. As already emphasized by certain scholars, some customary rules which embody particularly important values may feature an objective element (the so-called practice or *usus*)

---

[3] Eg affirming the importance of effectiveness in the area of human rights can be done by assigning a factual dimension to the notion of jurisdiction provided for in many human rights treaties. In other words: what does the expression under the jurisdiction of a state means? The meaning of this notion should not be merely interpreted by relying on formal criteria but should take into account the factual dimension of the subjection of an individual to the jurisdiction of a state. There are a number of indications in the practice of the European and Inter-American Court of Human Rights which tend to show that the analysis of the requirement that an individual to be protected must be considered within the jurisdiction of a state party to the Convention must be undertaken by carrying out a careful examination of the effective situation.

that does not reach the degree of intensity normally required for a customary rule to be established. In other words, the suggestion is made that customary rules enshrining universal values may evolve even if the practice substantiating them is minimal. This could be read as a greater influence of the legality–legitimacy principles on the intimate structure of the international legal system. It can also be interpreted as a consequence of the prevalence of the legality–legitimacy paradigm over the normative force of facts, the effectiveness principle.

However, effectiveness is also an ideal tool for enabling the international community to strike the most appropriate balance between conflicting interests and values, and—if coupled with respect for some fundamental values of the international community—may contribute to defining the reaction of the international legal order to international crises. Since international law does not aim at transforming the world into a single legal order with coercive powers attributed to a 'world' government, the international legal system must preserve a central role for the principle of effectiveness. However, international institutions should be involved to ensure that effectiveness leads to an increased implementation of universal values. In some fashion, international institutions should monitor and guarantee the process of 'legalization' of originally unlawful situations. Ultimately universal values can only prevail on condition that they are assisted by some measure of effectiveness. Where original illegality is followed by the creation of an effective situation which, although in conflict with international law, may eventually result in the implementation of universal values, the fact that at the outset there might have been a violation of international law may be cured by the normative dimension of the de facto situation, coupled with the intervention of the international community as a guarantor of the process.

Universal values are toothless without effectiveness, and effectiveness remains brutal without appropriate connections with values, enshrined in legal norms but also in processes and institutions. The outlook in this area requires a progressive strengthening of institutional mechanisms for linking effectiveness to universal values, and vice versa. This perspective could be further improved by developing the role of regional organizations and by ensuring that all factual situations bearing some elements of illegality (or doubtful legality) in their origin are systematically addressed by international institutions, which should make an assessment as to whether the situation can be 'legalized', provided that such legalization would ensure a better implementation of universal values. Such process is not unrealistic. In certain regions of the world, for example in Europe, this is already happening under the auspices of the European Union. The efforts carried out in Kosovo by the EU indicates a move (probably unconscious) in this direction.

To sum up, at present effectiveness should be seen as a necessary partner of legality in international law, and should be made consonant with universal values through a collective effort (possibly by international organizations at global or regional level). Whenever a de facto situation, even though it might have its roots in an illegal act, is handled in such as way as to ensure better protection or implementation of universal values, and in addition international institutions are involved to monitor or steer the process, it may be acceptable for the general principle of effectiveness to contribute to legalizing that situation.

# 10

# Are we Moving towards Constitutionalization of the World Community?

*Anne Peters*

## SUMMARY

In the past 20 years international law has evolved quite dramatically. Many aspects of this evolution can be described and interpreted as constitutionalization in the sense of an evolution from an international order based on some organizing principles such as state sovereignty, consensualism, non-use of force to an international legal order which acknowledges and has creatively appropriated principles and values of domestic constitutionalism. Constitutionalization is a matter of degree. It is an ongoing but not linear process, and is often disrupted. It is not all-encompassing, but is accompanied by antagonist trends. The constitutionalization process of international law is mainly driven by academics and to some extent by international courts, not by governments and treatymakers. Nevertheless, the constitutionalist discourse has the merit of uncovering the structural deficiencies of current international law and assessing them in a new light. Thus the author points to a set of failings of the present 'constitutionalization' of international law and suggest ways of moving forward towards a more 'constitutionalized' international society.

## 1. Introduction: global constitutionalism

The core issue of constitutionalism is the relationship between governmental power and human liberty and flourishing. From a constitutionalist perspective, governmental arrangements are strictly instrumental, and must be so designed as to safeguard and promote as much as possible the well-being of natural persons not only as atomized individuals but also in their group relationships.

Constitutionalism claims that the principles of the rule of law, separation of powers, fundamental rights protection, democracy, and solidarity, together with institutions and mechanisms securing and implementing these principles are (comparatively) well suited to realize this overall objective. Global constitutionalism is an intellectual movement which both reads (or reconstructs) some features of the status quo of international relations as 'constitutional' and even 'constitutionalist' (positive analysis), and also seeks to provide arguments for their further development in a specific direction (normative analysis).

## 2. Current constitutionalization of international law

### (A) A legal process and a discourse

During the past 20 years, since the breakdown of the socialist bloc symbolized by the fall of the Berlin Wall, international law has evolved quite dramatically. Many aspects of this evolution can be described and interpreted as constitutionalization.[1] Constitutionalization in this sense is an evolution from an international order based on some organizing principles such as state sovereignty, consensualism, non-use of force to an international legal order which acknowledges and has creatively appropriated principles and values of constitutionalism.

When transposed to the international level, constitutionalist principles have been and must to some extent be modified, and the modes of their implementation as well. Also, they need not necessarily be united in one single document called 'World Constitution' but might be scattered in various legal texts and in the case law. These elements together might form a body of international constitutional law which is a specific subset of the international legal order, and which has a particular normative status.

The agents of this (putative) process of constitutionalization are the international lawmakers as political actors, most of all the international judiciary. But in a sense its agents are also academics who assert that constitutionalization exists. However, that positive claim is contested on empirical grounds, the objection being that there is no real trend of constitutionalization but only an academic artefact.

Moreover, the constitutionalist discourse normatively claims that the presumed constitutionalization process is laudable, most of all because it is needed to compensate for the de-constitutionalization on the domestic level which has been effected by globalization and global governance.[2] The argument here is that globalization has put the state and state constitutions under strain. Global problems have compelled states to transfer previously typically governmental functions, such as guaranteeing human security, freedom, and equality, to 'higher' levels. Non-state actors acting in a transboundary fashion are increasingly entrusted with the exercise of traditional state functions, even with core tasks such as military and police activity. All this has led to governance which is exercised beyond the states' constitutional confines. National constitutions are, so to speak, hollowed out; traditional constitutional

---

[1] J. Klabbers, A. Peters, and G. Ulfstein, *The Constitutionalization of International Law* (Oxford: Oxford University Press, 2009).

[2] A. Peters, 'Compensatory Constitutionalism: The Function and Potential of Fundamental International Norms and Structures', 19 Leiden JIL (2006) 579–610.

principles become dysfunctional or empty.[3] In consequence, if the achievements of constitutionalism are to be preserved, compensatory constitutionalization on the international plane is required, so the normative argument runs.

However, this normative claim is contested on various epistemic grounds (eg that globalization has not led to a de-constitutionalization of national governance, or that constitutionalization is unfeasible because of lacking preconditions in the international sphere), and on moral grounds (that the constitutionalization of international law is undesirable, eg because it is anti-pluralist or produces a sham legitimacy). Overall, constitutionalization is both a process and an accompanying academic discourse, and controversial in many dimensions.

## (B) From sovereignty to humanity

From a global constitutionalist perspective, the relevant society or community is humankind in its totality. The most important unit of government still is, as addressed by classic, domestic constitutionalism, the nation-state. But differently from domestic constitutionalism, global constitutionalism looks not only at the state institutions from the 'inside' but also at states from the 'outside', at the interplay between various levels of government, and at the coexistence and interaction of states among each other.

So on the international level, the two poles of power versus liberty and flourishment of natural persons, are encapsulated in two ideas: state sovereignty versus humanity. Much of the constitutionalist analysis turns around these two poles. It is analytically helpful to use these as a simplistic grid, even if sovereignty does not as such curtail human liberty but on the contrary also protects it, and is therefore profoundly ambivalent. It is a core claim of constitutionalism that the sovereignty of states no longer functions and should no longer be seen as a last principle (*Letztbegründung*) of the international legal order but that it already is and should be based on and derived from the principle of humanity.[4]

It is submitted that a principle of humanity underlies the entire international system of *human rights protection*, which is probably the most striking constitutionalist achievement of international law since 1945. The process of codification of human rights in internationally binding instruments possesses a constitutionalist significance in two regards. First, it has crucially modified the principle of state sovereignty by establishing that nation-states are not free to treat their own citizens on their own territory at whim, and that international minimum legal standards apply independently of state boundaries. Secondly, the international human rights covenants fulfil the constitutionalist core function of constraining states and preserving a space of liberty of natural persons.

---

[3] A. Peters, 'The Globalisation of State Constitutions', in J. Nijman and A. Nollkaemper (eds), *New Perspectives on the Divide between National and International Law* (Oxford: Oxford University Press, 2007), 251–308.

[4] A. Peters, 'Humanity as the A and Ω of Sovereignty', 20 EJIL (2008) 513–44.

The most important covenants have been ratified by more than four-fifths of all states.[5] The main problem of the current international human rights protection scheme is not a lack of formal acceptance but its deficient enforcement. Many states have ratified human rights covenants mainly for opportunistic reasons, in order to gain standing in the international community and obtain material benefits, without a real intention to implement them domestically. The international monitoring mechanisms, including the Universal Periodic Review through the UN Human Rights Council, are very weak.

More even than the international system of human rights protection which sees human rights as a mere limitation of sovereignty, the acknowledgement of the concept of *responsibility to protect* (R2P)[6] by the heads of government in the World Summit Outcome Document of 2005[7] manifests a full paradigm shift from sovereignty to humanity. The Outcome Document, some Security Council resolutions, and the 2009 Report of the Secretary-General on Implementing the Responsibility to Protect[8] have circumscribed R2P as relating (only) to the core crimes as defined in the Statute of the International Criminal Court (namely genocide, war crimes, and crimes against humanity including ethnic cleansing). While the (rather narrow) scope, the substance, and the pillar structure of the concept of a responsibility to protect are meanwhile settled, its precise legal status is not. It remains controversial whether R2P is a hard and fast legal obligation, only a political concept, soft law, or an emerging legal norm.[9]

Constitutionalists diagnose and praise the paradigm shift from sovereignty to humanity. However, they must keep in mind that state sovereignty in its traditional, Westphalian sense, is currently reasserted by important players such as the BRIC states (Brazil, Russia, India, and China).[10]

## (C) The constitutionalization of the international legal subjects

The creation of *states* and the international recognition processes have become constitutionalized. The traditional core element of statehood, the principle of effectiveness, which is in itself a legal, not merely a 'factual', requirement, has been supplemented

---

[5] Eg, the CERD has 174 state parties; the ICCPR has 167 state parties; the ICESCR has 160 state parties; CEDAW has 186 parties; the CAT has 146 parties; the CRC has 193 parties (figures as at January 2011).

[6] 'International Commission on Intervention and State Sovereignty' (ICISS), The Responsibility to Protect (2001), available at <http://www.iciss.ca/pdf/Commission-Report.pdf>.

[7] Resolution adopted by the General Assembly, World Summit Outcome Document, and UN Doc. A/RES/60/1 of 24 October 2005, paras 138–9.

[8] Report of the Secretary-General: Implementing the Responsibility to Protect, UN Doc. A/63/677 of 12 January 2009; GA Res. 63/208 (3 February 2009) takes note of the Secretary-General's Report.

[9] In a three-day-long General Assembly debate in July 2009 on R2P (GAOR (A/63/PV.97–100) of 23, 24, and 28 July 2009) in which 49 states took the floor, six governmental delegations (Brazil, Guatemala, Morocco, China, Venezuela, and Monaco) explicitly considered R2P not to be a legal principle, whereas three states (Liechtenstein, Canada, and Bangladesh) explicitly affirmed its legal quality.

[10] Xue Hanq in, 'Remarks on Andrew Hurrel's presentation', lecture of 2 September 2010, 4th biannual conference of the European Society of International Law, Cambridge (on file with the author).

and even substituted by international legal standards of self-determination, non-use of force, protection of human rights, minority rights, and even democracy. International actors, notably the United Nations and the Organization for Security and Co-operation in Europe (OSCE) have accompanied and shaped state-building processes and imposed the mentioned requirements. For example, both Security Council Resolution 1244 and the unilateral declaration of independence of Kosovo of 17 February 2008 relied on popular sovereignty.[11] Also all other states created since the 1990s, ranging from East Timor over the states emerging out of Yugoslavia and the Soviet Union to South Sudan, have been brought into existence through a democratic procedure, notably on the basis of a popular referendum. However, Kosovo, just like numerous African states, is currently hardly effective in the sense of having well-functioning governmental institutions and providing public goods such as human security and liberty to their inhabitants.

*Individuals* (both natural and moral persons under domestic law) have acquired more and more international rights and obligations, far beyond human rights. For example, victims of crimes are under various international instruments entitled to a remedy and reparation for gross human rights violations, foreign investors are creditors of secondary obligations arising out of the international responsibility of host states, and persons detained abroad have an international right to contact with their consular officer which is sanctionable through domestic criminal law remedies. In a variety of international fora, notably human rights bodies and investment tribunals, individuals act as enforcers of international law. However, their options to participate in international lawmaking (such as adopting treaties or decisions and resolutions within treaty regimes) mostly through non-governmental organizations (NGOs), remain limited.

Since the First World War, *international organizations and institutions* have proliferated. They have overall acquired more formal competences, and more autonomy from member states, although some are quite ineffective. This relative power gain raises the question of constraining and controlling the organizations, subjecting them to procedural and material standards, and of enforcing these standards—in short, the problem of the accountability of international organizations.[12]

A more recent problematic institutional development is the advent of informal and semi-institutionalized state cooperation in groups such as the G20. Here the issues of representativeness and inclusiveness, the delineation of competences and mission creep, the procedural propriety of decision-making, the inequality of the 'members', and the lacking accountability are amplified. The constitutionalist paradigm has contributed to the awareness of both problems, and provides tools for tackling them.

---

[11] SC Res. 1244, which created a legal and political framework for Kosovo pending a final political settlement, referred to the Rambouillet agreements which in turn referred to the 'will of the people'. The International Court of Justice (ICJ) found no violation of Resolution 1244 by the unilateral declaration of independence, and this resolution remained in force.

[12] International Law Association, First Report on the Accountability of International Organizations, Report of the 71st conference held in Berlin, 16–21 August 2004; J. Wouters et al (eds), *Accountability for Human Rights Violations by International Organisations* (Antwerp: Intersentia, 2010).

## (D) The constitutionalization of sources: *jus cogens* and *erga omnes* norms

Two special categories of norms, *jus cogens* and *erga omnes* norms, have acquired some practical significance in recent years. Many associate these two categories with international constitutional law.

*Jus cogens* norms can be said to operate as constitutional law because they establish a normative hierarchy based on material factors.[13] Their peremptory character flows from the importance of the particular moral values they embody. They constrain (at least) the states' treaty-making. The 'trumping' effect of peremptory norms over contrary 'ordinary' law would indeed resemble the supremacy of a written constitution in a (national) legal order where a constitutional court exists which has the power to declare unconstitutional norms invalid, such as in Germany or the United States. However, such a trumping effect of *jus cogens*, beyond the nullity of an incompatible treaty which is explicitly foreseen in Articles 53 and 64 of the Vienna Convention on the Law of Treaties is doubtful and controversial.

However, this lack of formal supremacy does not hinder ascribing a constitutional function to *jus cogens*, notably the function of expressing paramount values in a more symbolic and flexible way. This is how some domestic constitutions work. For example, the British constitution which is not codified in one document, is not superior to other English and Scots law, and can be amended or even undone through an ordinary parliamentary law. 'Higher law' in the United Kingdom is rather constituted by the European Convention on Human Rights (ECHR), the interpretation and enforcement of which is performed by the Strasbourg Court which is in turn to some extent beyond the control of the English parliament.

*Erga omnes* norms are associated with international constitutional law for a yet different reason. A norm's *erga omnes* quality in the sense of the International Court of Justice (ICJ)'s *Barcelona Traction* obiter dictum means that all states (and other international legal subjects) are entitled to invoke a violation of such a norm. The ILC Articles on State Responsibility have refined this idea.[14] It is, however, not clear whether not directly affected states have standing before an international court to enforce the violation of an *erga omnes* norm (probably not). Still, the basic acceptance of the idea of *erga omnes* might imply constitutionalism, because *erga omnes* norms protect community interests as opposed to specific national interests of one state.

## (E) The constitutionalization of legal processes: participation and transparency

A striking traditional feature of all types of international legal processes, ranging from treaty-making over decision-making within special regimes to international arbitration was their inter-state closedness and their relative intransparency.

---

[13] See A. Cassese, 'For an Enhanced Role of *Jus Cogens*', Chapter 13 in this volume; A. Orakhelashvili, *Peremptory Norms in International Law* (Oxford: Oxford University Press, 2006), 9–10 and 577; A. Bianchi, 'Human Rights and the Magic of Jus Cogens', 19 EJIL (2008) 491–508, at 495.
[14] ILC Articles on State Responsibility, Arts 42(b) and 48(1)(a) and (b).

Confidentiality and non-publicity was regarded as a necessary condition of successful negotiation and bargaining among states.

A constitutionalist perspective facilitated the formulation of the objection that limited participation and intransparency prevents public scrutiny and critique and runs counter to the constitutionalist ideals of democracy and rule of law. In response to this critique, various branches of the international (quasi-)judiciary, notably World Trade Organization (WTO) dispute settlement and arbitration by the International Centre for Settlement of Investment Disputes (ICSID), have recently been made more public, both in terms of participation of NGOs as observers and *amici curiae*, and in terms of publicizing sessions, files, and awards.

International lawmaking has been more resilient vis-à-vis claims for participation and transparency but is also opening up. For example, the climate conference in Cancùn in 2010 was explicitly guided by a strategy of transparency. Observers initially predicted a failure of the negotiations in particular because of this transparency. Ultimately, however, the strategy of openness worked out and yielded better results than the preceding climate conference of Copenhagen (2009), although these remain, on balance, meagre.

## (F) Constitutional goods and principles

An important factor of the constitutionalization of the international legal order is the emergence of new principles inspired by constitutionalist ideas and the ascription of constitutional functions to older principles, such as non-use of force (see below, Section 4(C)). In the 2005 World Summit Outcome Document the heads of state recommitted themselves 'to actively protecting and promoting human rights, rule of law and democracy', and recognized 'that they are interlinked and mutually reinforcing and that they belong to the universal and indivisible core values and principles of the United Nations'.[15]

With regard to the *rule of law*, the United Nations has set a broad agenda to 'strengthen engagement on the rule of law at the national *and international level*', as the most recent Secretary-General report formulated it.[16] With respect to strengthening the rule of law in the United Nations itself, the report mentioned the new system of administration of justice with the appointment of professional judges to the organization's administrative tribunal, and the improvements to the de-listing procedures concerning sanctions against individuals.

*Democracy* is viewed by the United Nations itself as an implicit principle of the UN, and the democratization of member states is one of the organization's objectives.[17] Notably the Secretary-General and the General Assembly have promoted

---

[15]   UN Doc. A/60/1 of 24 October 2005, para. 119.

[16]   Secretary-General's Annual Report on Strengthening and Coordinating United Nations Rule of Law Activities, UN Doc. A/64/298 of 17 August 2009, summary (emphasis added). But see critically U. Mattei and M. de Morpurgo, 'The Dark Side of the Rule of Law: Reassessing Global Law and Its Legitimacy', Juridikum (2010) 15–23.

[17]   See, eg, the preamble of GA Res. 50/133 (1996) and the Cardoso Report of 2004 (United Nations, We the Peoples: Civil Society, the United Nations and Global Governance, Report of

democracy as good governance.[18] In the World Summit Outcome Document, the heads of state and governments have asserted that 'democracy is a universal value.... [W]hile democracies share common features, there is no single model of democracy, ... it does not belong to any country or region ...'. The governments renewed their 'commitment to support democracy by strengthening countries' capacity to implement the principles and practices of democracy'.[19] Such implementation is sought through election monitoring and other assistance funded, inter alia, through the UN Democracy Funds established in 2005.

Other *global goods* (ie, goods that cannot be provided either by one state or by all states acting individually) are recognized and at least tentatively protected by international law. The most important ones are international peace and security (protected by the prohibition of the use of military force), the freedom of the high seas, natural resources in spaces outside the territorial jurisdiction of states (protected by the principle of common heritage of mankind), the global climate, free trade, and foreign (transborder) investment.

Within the constitutionalist paradigm, these goods can be qualified as constitutional goods. The principles providing the basis for institutions and procedures seeking to protect these goods are global constitutional principles. However, these principles are extremely vague, whereas the devil is in the detail. Governmental endorsement may be just cheap talk. Concrete steps to implement the principles are often lacking, as most glaringly demonstrated with regard to climate protection.

## (G) The constitutionalization of dispute settlement

Another element of constitutionalization is the legalization and even judicialization of dispute settlement. Especially after 1989, numerous new courts and tribunals have been established or activated (the International Tribunal of the Law of the Sea, ICSID arbitration, numerous ad hoc international or hybrid criminal tribunals, and the WTO dispute-settlement body). Legal and judicial, as opposed to political and diplomatic, dispute settlement means a strengthening of the rule of law, because it is more formalized, offers procedural guarantees, and applies legal (not political) standards. All this reduces the space for political pressure by the more powerful party to a dispute and favours an ultimate solution which respects the law.

---

the Panel of Eminent Persons on United Nations–Civil Society Relations) UN Doc. A/58/817 of 11 June 2004. UN Secretary-General Boutros-Ghali has interpreted the UN Charter's preamble 'We the Peoples' as invoking popular sovereignty, and thus as envisaging democratic member states (Secretary-General, Supplement to Reports on Democratization, Annex to UN Doc. A/51/761 of 20 December 1996, para. 28).

[18] UN Secretary-General, Agenda for Development, UN Doc. A/478/935, 1994, paras 118–38 on 'democracy as good governance'. See for the more recent position of the General Assembly, Promoting and Consolidating Democracy, UN Doc. A/55/96, 2001; Implementation of the United Nations Millennium Declaration, Part V: 'Human rights, democracy and good governance', UN Doc. A/57/270, 2002, paras 82ff.

[19] UN Doc. A/60/1 of 24 October 2005, paras 119 and 135–6, emphasis added.

The criminal tribunals and most of all the International Criminal Court which took up its work in 2003 are an important building block of the overall objective to combat impunity. The end of impunity is a core element of the rule of law.

The settlement of trade disputes through the WTO panels and appellate body in quasi-arbitral proceedings, as opposed to the previous diplomatic type of settlement under the old GATT before 1994, is generally considered as a success. In any case the mechanism is well used, and increasingly so by developing states.

Investor-state arbitration under ICSID is booming as well. But recent arbitral awards imposing high pecuniary damages on host states have triggered a backlash. The critique is that this dispute-settlement mechanism has been 'privatized' too far. Private investors have been empowered to request arbitration, public interests motivating investment regulation risk being marginalized, and the arbitrators might not be sufficiently independent from business. This type of critique demonstrates that a constitutionalist mindset helps to pinpoint deficiencies in existing legal arrangements and can be fruitfully employed to formulate a critique of the law as it stands.

The problem of conflicts of jurisdiction among the various courts and tribunals that was much feared at the beginning of the 1990s has turned out to be less serious than expected. Moreover, such conflicts can be resolved exactly by resort to procedural principles devised under the umbrella of the rule of law, such as subsidiarity and complementarity, *ne bis in idem* and *res iudicata*.

## 3. Problems of constitutionalization

### (A) Structural deficiencies of constitutionalization as a legal process

Besides the mentioned problems which persist inside the new tendencies which I counted as constitutionalization, bigger, structural problems persist. One of the most obvious ones is the *weak democratic legitimacy* of the international legal process,[20] to which I will return in Section 4(C).

The international legal order is overall *minimalist and soft*. In important issue areas, such as in environmental protection, including global warming and animal rights, the international legal standards are too low, too vague, formally non-binding, or are altogether lacking. Especially the increasing resort to international soft law in the form of summit declarations and the like instead of binding covenants is a symptom of lacking political consensus and a lack of commitment. Soft law can easily be used for camouflaging passivity, or as a fig leaf for the exercise of naked power.

*Enforcement* of international law is deficient. Moreover it is often handled unevenly in the sense that weaker states are forced to comply with international law, for example human rights or investment law, notably through economic sanctions. In contrast, stronger states can hardly be pressured by sanctions, and often

---

[20] A. Peters, 'Dual Democracy', in Klabbers, Peters, and Ulfstein, n 1, 263–341; S. Wheatley, *The Democratic Legitimacy of International Law* (Oxford: Hart Publishing, 2010).

even defy global public opinion, such as the United States when it used illegal military force against Iraq in 2003.

The international legal order is becoming much more differentiated. But what has been labelled the *fragmentation* of international law need not be overrated. The explosion of sub-branches of international law, such as international criminal law and international climate law, is as such not dangerous for the functioning of the international legal order, but simply a sign of its vitality and maturation. The constitutionalist paradigm is often depicted as an antidote to fragmentation, and as a search for an illusionary unity which must turn out to be futile. Indeed, traditional continental and US-American constitutionalism tended to be holistic in the sense that one single constitutional document was supposed to provide the complete legal and political basis for societal life. However, in the multilevel governance arrangements of the present, no state any longer possesses a total constitution which would govern all political actors. The existence of multiple constitutions is compatible with the idea of constitutionalism. Global constitutionalism admits the existence of specific international sub-constitutions, for example an international economic constitution.

Mention must be made of the increasing *refusal* of states, acting through their supreme courts, to accord *supremacy to all international law* (including judgments by international courts) over all domestic law, notably over core constitutional concepts. This attitude has been most prominently espoused by the European Court of Justice (ECJ) (which for this matter should be regarded as a 'domestic' court) in its *Kadi* decision which led to the non-implementation of Security Council resolutions by the EU (which for this matter should be regarded as a 'domestic' political entity).[21] However, this posture of 'constitutional resistance' should not be viewed as purely detrimental to the international legal order. It constitutes a challenge which might trigger constitutional progress at the international level. It is likely that the (slight) improvement of the listing and delisting procedures and the establishment of the sanctions ombudsman[22] have been motivated by the EU resistance. This interplay is at the same time an example of multilevel constitutionalism, with constitutionalist principles such as hearing and independent review being implemented on different levels of government.

A realistic assessment of these deficiencies and lacunae might lead to the conclusion that international law has not been constitutionalized. However, constitutionalization is a matter of degree. It is an ongoing, but not linear, and often disrupted and sometimes reversed process. It is not all-encompassing, but accompanied by antagonist trends.

---

[21] ECJ, Cases C-420/05P and C-415/05P *Kadi and Al Barakaat*, judgment of the Court (Grand Chamber) of 3 September 2008.

[22] SC Res. 1409 (2009); Kimberley Prost was appointed by the Secretary-General as Ombudsperson for a first period of office until 30 June 2011 (UN Doc. S/2010/282 of 4 June 2010).

## (B) Flaws of constitutionalization as a discourse

A different problem, besides the shortcomings of constitutionalization as legal processes, are the potential flaws of constitutionalization as a discourse, of the constitutionalist paradigm as such.

There is some danger that the hailed constitutionalist principles are too European, which would mean that the accompanying discourse might be a Eurocentric one. Eurocentrism or Western bias might end up bolstering a hegemony of the West over the rest. Furthermore, constitutionalism, an idea of the nineteenth century, might be too 'liberal' and too insensitive towards the enormous social inequality in the world, towards exploitation of large groups of persons and of natural resources. A related point is that the whole idea of constitutionalism might be anti-pluralist, and therefore particularly unsuited for application on a global scale to a world whose inhabitants have different moral and political views, and whose living conditions vary enormously.[23]

Another problem is that the supposedly constitutionalist principles are too general and imprecise to solve any concrete political problem or to guide legal reform. This seductive vagueness might even hinder the elaboration of concrete suggestions for concrete problems, when the constitutionalist vocabulary serves as a mere tranquilizer.[24]

Finally, the putative constitutionalization process is lopsided. It is mainly driven by academics and to some extent by international courts, but not by governments and treaty-makers. This means that constitutionalization is either an academic pipe dream, or—if it is real—raises the issue of democratic legitimacy vis-à-vis an undemocratic *gouvernement des juges* in which judicial self-empowerment is achieved with the help of a constitutional language.

On the other hand, the constitutionalist discourse has the merit of uncovering the structural deficiencies of international law and assessing them in a new light. The most conspicuous example is the democratic deficit of the international legal process. This issue was traditionally not perceived as a problem. The question of democracy was completely eclipsed by the focus on sovereignty and the belief that the basis of legitimacy of international law resided in state sovereignty. International lawyers did not care whether this sovereignty was internally bolstered by popular sovereignty or not. Global constitutionalism, in contrast, does care. On balance, I submit, the critical potential of the constitutionalization discourse outweighs its dangers. For this reason, its policy suggestions will be sketched out in the next section.

---

[23] N. Krisch, *Beyond Constitutionalism: The Pluralist Structure of Postnational Law* (Oxford: Oxford University Press, 2010).

[24] J. Dunoff and J. Trachtman, 'The Lotus Eaters', in Epilogue to J. Klabbers, A. Peters and G. Ulfstein, *The Constitutionalization of International Law* (expanded edn, Oxford: Oxford University Press, 2011).

# 4. Constitutionalist proposals *de lege ferenda*

## (A) Subjects

The constitutionalist approach offers a new foundation for the view that the ultimate international legal subjects are *individuals*. Constitutionalism postulates that natural persons are the ultimate unit of legal concern.

*States* are no ends in themselves, but merely instrumental for the rights and needs of individuals. This *finalité* makes states indispensable in a global constitutionalized order, as crystallization points for (collective) identity, as primary lawmakers and law-enforcers, and mediators between conflicting societal actors. But this *finalité* also calls for their constitutional containment. From a constitutionalist perspective, the equality of states in law is no abstract and absolute claim. Constitutionalism rather calls for proportional equality (*suum cuique tribuere*, not *idem cuique tribuere*). This means that a formally differentiated treatment of states, that is, legal distinctions among states, should be permissible if and as long as this is necessary and adequate to fulfil legitimate objectives of the global constitutional community. Put differently, the states' right to have equal rights within a concrete legal regime may be curtailed by countervailing considerations. Formal equality is thus subject to balancing against other concerns, such as concerns for security or of effective peacekeeping. Finally, state immunity should be curtailed so as not to shield crimes against humanity.[25]

*International organizations and other institutions* must be made more effective *and* more legitimate, with some help from the constitutionalist toolbox. To give an example, a new global institution should be set up in the field of environmental law. However, purely intergovernmental institutions are not always the most appropriate institutional response to global problems. In some fields, global public–private partnerships (PPPs) might work as well or better. For instance, the Global Fund, a global PPP created in 2002 to fight AIDS, malaria, and tuberculosis currently seems to be more efficient than the World Health Organization.[26]

The important recent phenomenon of outsourcing public functions—also on the international level—has no intrinsic or natural limits. Limits must be established normatively, and the value judgements should derive from constitutionalism. This means that the current privatization of international organizations such as the International Telecommunications Organization, and also the rise of informal institutions such as the G20 should be closely observed by international lawyers in order to uncover legitimacy deficits.

Private resources by *charitable individuals* should be tapped. Some moderate procedural and reporting requirements should be applied to their funding decisions without stifling their initiative.[27]

---

[25] Italian Corte Suprema di Cassazione, *Ferrini*, Appellate judgment of 11 March 2004, No. 5044/4; ILDC 19 (IT 2004).          [26] See <http://www.theglobalfund.org/en/>.
[27] T. Stein, 'Global Social and Civil Entrepreneurs: An Answer to the Poor Performance of Global Governance?', Social Science Research Center, Berlin, Discussion Paper No. SP IV 2008–304.

Micro-constitutionalization *within* international organizations will require first the realization of their legal and political accountability towards affected individuals (and not only towards member states), both through judicial review and through democratic (at least consultative) procedures (see on democratization below at Section 4(C)).

The irregular international status of *transnational corporations* (TNCs), and also of NGOs, is pernicious because it leaves space for the exploitation of their power for self-interested goals to the detriment of the public good and of affected individuals. With regard to TNCs it must be kept in mind that a complete constitutionaliza-tion of the private sector in the sense that private actors would be subject to the full panoply of (international) constitutional standards (eg human rights obligations), just like public actors, is not desirable. It might be useful to transfer some princi-ples and instruments of constitutionalism to the economic sphere, but only while respecting the own logics of that sphere. But overall, constitutionalism is in favour of formalizing the international legal status of those actors which are currently still devoid of international legal personality, because this would bring about legal clar-ity and containment, which is in a constitutionalist perspective laudable.

## (B) Sovereign responsibility

From a constitutional perspective, participants in the legal process and observers should insist on the responsibility pertaining to sovereignty. The focus should no longer be on third states' duty to refrain from action and intervention, but inversely on a possible duty to act internationally ('from non-intervention to non-indifference'). Such progressive reasoning can be based on four consecutive arguments. First, if we take human needs and human rights as a starting point, every state has the sovereign responsibility to protect its population from crimes that threaten their human exist-ence. Secondly, a state that grossly and manifestly fails to discharge these duties has its sovereignty suspended. This means that its sovereignty no longer functions as a shield against outside intervention. Thirdly, in a system of multilevel governance and under the principle of solidarity, the residual or subsidiary responsibility to protect falls on the international community. The explanation is that in the current global system of multilevel governance, competences and obligations must be allocated to that level of governance on which governance functions can be effectively performed. Fourthly, the international community may only step in through the Security Council, but not through individual states acting unilaterally. Anything else would open the door for abuse of the responsibility to protect by superpowers.

## (C) Other constitutionalist principles

Global constitutionalism crucially demands that constitutionalist principles must be applied not only within states *but also to the relations between states and to inter-national organizations.*

*Human rights*: it must be acknowledged that international organizations, and possibly 'private' international actors, such as armed groups, or even TNCs, may be bound (perhaps only in an indirect way) by human rights law, and the conditions and scope of this bindingness must be defined. Moreover, in the face of jurisdictional overlap and extraterritorial jurisdiction, the parameters for the extraterritorial applicability of human rights must also be worked out, and these parameters have a constitutional significance for the functioning of the entire system. However, the multidimensional (substantial, personal, and territorial) expansion of human rights risks debasing the human rights idea. From a constitutionalist perspective, caution is warranted. It seems important to acknowledge individual international rights other than human rights so as to avoid an inflation and devaluation, and also in order to underscore the increasingly complex structure of an international legal order consisting of a constitutional level and a level of ordinary international rules displaying criminal law, civil law, and administrative law features.

The principle of *separation of powers/checks and balances* can and should be brought to bear on the organs of international organizations. The international law notion of institutional balance should be fleshed out and applied in a constitutionalist manner so as to safeguard human liberty by checking power and establishing mutual control of different institutions, for example of the Security Council by the General Assembly.

Other global constitutionalist principles are genuinely international in origin, but they can be developed further in a constitutionalist direction. For example, the dubious qualification of the prohibition on the use of force as *jus cogens*,[28] which can hardly accommodate the exceptions to the prohibition, could be given up. The meaning of non-use of force is in my view better captured by calling it a constitutionalist principle. This qualification gives expression to the principle's functions as a fundamental precept which embodies the supreme value of international peace, contains state power, secures the peaceful coexistence and cooperation of states, and serves as a guideline for the interpretation of all international law. Conceived as a constitutionalist principle, the prohibition of force should not only be addressed at states but under certain conditions also at non-state actors such as stabilized de facto regimes.

The legal concept of *common heritage of mankind* should be refined and its application extended. It should not only be used to qualify goods situated outside the territorial jurisdiction such as the seabed and the outer space. It might usefully apply to goods spatially located within states such as tropical forests or endangered species. Thus it might justify prohibitions and limitations on their over-use and annihilation, which would have to be enforced by international bodies.

*Solidarity*: in the law as it stands, an international principle of solidarity is arguably inherent in some regimes.[29] For example, the common but differentiated responsibility in international environmental law[30] and the (controversial) right to

---

[28] Cf ICJ, *Military and Paramilitary Activities in and against Nicaragua (Nicaragua v United States)*, Merits, ICJ Reports 1986, 14, para. 190.

[29] R. Wolfrum and C. Kojima (eds), *Solidarity: A Structural Principle of International Law* (Heidelberg: Springer, 2009).        [30] See, eg, Art. 3(1) UN Framework Convention on Climate Change.

humanitarian assistance[31] can be interpreted as manifesting such a legal principle. For the time being, however, solidarity is no overarching general legal principle from which concrete legal obligations could be deduced. Further constitutionalization requires that solidarity should be spelled out as an international constitutional principle.[32]

*Democracy* as well must apply not only within states but also on the international level, that is, within international organizations and in the non-institutionalized relations between states. With regard to international law and decision-making (eg in the form of treaties and resolutions), the transitive democratic legitimacy derived from the participation of democratic states must be improved by strengthening the involvement of national parliaments in international governance.[33] Besides, the direct participation of natural persons in their role as global citizens, independently of their nation-state, must be improved. The democratization of international organizations could consist in the establishment of parliamentary or peoples' assemblies (as opposed to governmental assemblies).[34] Their composition should take due account of the size of the member states' populations, and their powers should be gradually extended from merely consultative to co-legislative.

The *global public opinion* which has expressed itself quite forcefully, for example against the Iraq war of 2003, will, in the age of the internet, have to be taken seriously as a factor of governance. The probably growing impact of public contestation of governmental decisions is, from a constitutionalist perspective, a positive development, because it functions as a (weak) control of abuses of power.

## (D) Procedures

Constitutionalism asks for inclusiveness and empowerment. Seen through the lens of constitutionalism, the transnational activities of NGOs and also of TNCs are manifestations of an emerging global civil society. The current discrepancy between the de facto influence of those actors and their formal incapacity is in a constitutionalist perspective problematic. The quest is therefore that the processes of developing and implementing international law must become more *inclusive*, that they should be made a shared endeavour among (inter-)governmental institutions, business, and NGOs whose participation should be intensified, streamlined, and more formalized.

---

[31] ILC, Protection of Persons in the Event of Disasters, Memorandum by the Secretariat, UN Doc. A/CN/590 of 11 December 2007 with Add. of 26 February 2008 (UN Doc. A/CN/590/ Add.1); ILC, Report of the International Law Commission on its 60th Session, UN Doc. A/63/10, ch. IX ('Protection of Persons in the Event of Disasters'), esp. paras 241–50 ('Right to humanitarian assistance').

[32] See in scholarship K. Wellens, 'Solidarity as a Constitutional Principle: Its Expanding Role and Inherent Limitations', in R. St MacDonald and D.M. Johnston (eds), *Towards World Constitutionalism: Issues in the Legal Ordering of the World Community* (Leiden: Martinus Nijhoff, 2005), 775–807.

[33] See notably the Cardoso Report of 2004, n 17.

[34] M. Krajewski, 'Legitimizing Global Economic Governance through Transnational Parlamentarization: The Parliamentary Dimensions of the WTO and the World Bank', Transtate Working Papers No. 136, 2010.

However, NGOs and TNCs should not participate on an equal footing with states, and more attention must be given to the disproportionate influence of 'northern' NGOs. Non-state actors should only obtain 'voice', not 'vote', because they are on average less representative and accountable than states. In this new form of 'civil regulation', the respective legitimacy deficits of the partly antagonist actors might cancel themselves out, but only when the parties remain independent from one another and sufficiently distant. Only then capture and collision are avoided, and only then the non-state actors can fulfil their watchdog and opposition function.

In order to improve the *effectiveness of rule- and decision-making* of some organizations, a practice of *majoritarian decision-making* should be introduced or revived, for example in the WTO. A different matter is the binding character of those rules and decisions. Measures taken by majority vote need not in any case be immediately binding on recalcitrant members. If they bind only those members that vote in their favour, the respective treaty regime or organization will become a multi-class regime. This leads to practical complications but might not inevitably undermine the functioning of the regime but might on the contrary incite gradual adherence—but only if free riding is effectively suppressed by smart mechanisms.

A persisting problem of majoritarian decision-making among a group of states is that any (international) measure taken by majority vote runs counter to the democratic preferences formulated on the domestic level within one democratic member state. This will only be acceptable to the members of the (democratic) sub-polity when international solidarity is strong enough and when the decision-making procedures are designed so as to offer each member state a fair chance to co-shape the outcomes. The latter feature is, for example, lacking with regard to the Security Council in its current set-up. This is why its activity as a rule-maker ('legislator') as opposed to a decision-taker should remain the narrow exception.

The *transparency* of the international legal process should be improved in order to assume the very constitutional and in particular democratic functions transparency performs in domestic law. Sessions of the international institutions, particularly the rule-making sessions, should become public as a rule (with due exceptions for security, business, and privacy reasons). Documents of global governance including drafts should be publicized via the internet, without confusing citizens and hiding important information through overflow. The facilitation of technical access to the internet in disadvantaged world regions should be a high priority of UN politics. However, governance designers must be aware of the costs created by more transparency. Most importantly, transparency in itself does not bring about democracy. It is only, but importantly, a precondition for democratic procedures. The Wikileak affair of 2010 has demonstrated that a critical mass of the global public yearns for more transparency especially with regard to foreign and military affairs.[35]

One aspect of transparency is the *obligation to give reasons* for legal acts. Under the rule of law, the authors of legal acts (lawmakers, decision-makers, and adjudicators) are obliged to state the reasons on which their acts are based (see, eg,

[35] See the so-called Wikileaks manifesto 'Conspiracy as Governance' of 3 December 2006.

Article 296 Treaty on the Functioning of the European Union (TFEU)). This should be demanded also from the Security Council members, for example when exercising their veto.[36] If we accept that the Security Council is operating under the rule of law, the Council's obligation to state the reasons for any legal act it adopts already exists as a matter of (unwritten) legal principle. The obligation to give reasons for a veto would leave its exercise within the realm of discretion of the permanent member, but would still force the member to rationalize its decision. This would allow other states and the public to criticize these reasons. In the long run, an obligation to justify the veto would rule out those most blatant abuses that simply cannot be rationalized.

### (E) Monitoring, adjudication, and enforcement

Enforcement of international law must be improved. In the field of human rights, the waste of human resources both in the national administrations and in the international institutions resulting from the coexistence of numerous human rights bodies with partly overlapping foci of scrutiny must be minimized by streamlining and bundling reporting obligations and possibly creating one human rights body or even human rights court with specialized chambers.

Generally speaking, the direct effect of those international treaty provisions which concern the legal status of individuals, and which are sufficiently clear and unconditional to be applied by (domestic) courts should be more readily acknowledged. Self-interested individuals are most motivated to go to court in order to terminate non-compliance with international law which negatively affects them personally. Transferring the business of complaints against violations of international law to private individuals also has the advantage of leaving intergovernmental political relations more or less intact.

The reluctance of domestic courts to apply international law seems to have less to do with concerns for a separation of powers and the courts' unwillingness to interfere with the executive branch than with the fact that these types of complaint are normally directed at the complaining individuals' home state without offering any guarantee that judges in other states will reach similar conclusions against their own governments. Domestic judges in that context are therefore, to the extent that they feel loyal to their state, probably more reluctant to tie the hand of their own government than in the purely domestic context of an administrative or constitutional lawsuit.

Would it be a remedy to allow for complaints of individuals of whatever nationality before domestic courts against breaches of international law by foreign states or state actors and to narrow the scope of state immunity for that purpose (such as under the US American Alien Tort Claims Act)? This is doubtful because the neutrality and expertise of domestic courts passing sentences on foreign states

---

[36] Proposal by Costa Rica, Jordan, Liechtenstein, Singapore, Switzerland (UN Doc. A/60/L.49 of 17 March 2006). See the Security Council's reaction in declaration of 19 July 2006 (annex to the Note by the President of the Security Council, S/2006/507).

will always be called into question by critics and therefore the authority of such judgments is too easily undermined, leaving aside the fact that they can hardly be enforced.

The better option seems to be to create more access for individuals to international courts, tribunals, and monitoring bodies. But then the question of the *legitimacy of the international judiciary* must be asked upfront. It may be that any dynamic and teleological interpretation of international instruments, such as the ECHR, by a powerful and activist court such as the European Court of Human Rights, will be acceptable only upon modifications of the judges' appointment procedures in the direction of more representation of global society's concerns and less of nationality. Also, courts' and tribunals' procedures need to be speedy and open to the participation of affected groups (usually represented by NGOs, eg through *amicus curiae* briefs) in order to secure acceptance of awards and judgments.

## 5. Conclusion: constitutionalization and community

The emergence and extension of a constitutional world community (of individuals, states, NGOs, and business actors) is both a manifestation and a driver of global constitutionalism, while the constitutionalization of international law is at the same time an explanation and a promoter of this communitarization. A more constitutionalized world community would normatively rely on the principle of sovereign responsibility as described above, which means that its basis of legitimacy would be human security, freedom, and flourishment. Institution-wise, the constitutionalized world community would display multiple levels of governance consisting in local, regional, national, supranational, and global public actors. It would leave space for private co-governance activity through NGOs and public–private partnerships. The international legal obligations of states and other governance actors vis-à-vis other states and even individuals would not be only negative ones, but increasingly positive ones, such as the obligations actively to promote human rights or to intervene against the commission of core crimes.

The basic constitutional principle of pluralism calls for accepting as much diversity as possible in this community. This means that different standards, for example of fair trial, in different regimes (eg the UN as opposed to the EU) should be mutually recognized as long as a minimal threshold is not undercut. Of course the question remains where this standard lies and most of all who defines it.

The vocabulary of global constitutionalism allows raising the pressing question of the legitimacy of international law and facilitates constructive criticism. Formulating both criticism and alternatives to the law as it stands is an intellectual obligation of legal scholars, not 'only' a political and hence potentially unscholarly activity. But the normative and practical power of international law ultimately does not depend on the use of the term 'international community' as such or on the use of the concepts of constitution and constitutionalism, but rather on concrete institutions, principles, rules, and enforcement.

# 11

# A Plea for a Global Community Grounded in a Core of Human Rights

*Antonio Cassese*

## SUMMARY

Although the doctrine of human rights is inherently universalistic, the stark reality of the world society shows that there is huge variety in the implementation of human rights by the various states. To promote the gradual formation of a world community based on a core of universal values, it is suggested that a double-track approach should be taken, dealing both with the values at stake and with the means for translating them into living reality. As for values, one should emphasize the existence of peremptory rules of international law (*jus cogens*) on human rights, which are at the summit of the international legal order and may not be derogated from by any state. Such rules are gradually constituting the constitutional principles of the world society. As for means for implementing those rules of *jus cogens*, three distinct avenues are suggested. First, one should set up a system of inquiry capable of verifying how and when violations occur. Secondly, one should enhance the criminal responsibility of the authors of gross violations of those fundamental values. Thirdly, one should rely upon international civil society to tenaciously and steadfastly prod all international subjects to abide by the law.

## 1. The doctrine of human rights is inherently universalistic

The doctrine of human rights has aspired from the outset to be universal, to be a doctrine that applies everywhere to everyone, irrespective of nationality, culture, tradition, ideology, or social conditions. The Frenchman René Cassin, one of the fathers of the Universal Declaration of Human Rights who so much contributed to the drafting of that text, looked at human rights from a universal perspective in a groundbreaking and seminal article he wrote in

1940.[1] He wrote that the existence of Leviathan-states embracing ideologies based on violence, oppressing individuals, and only aiming at expansionist hegemonies was a pernicious phenomenon of our age. He hoped that at the end of the Second World War the world community would be ready to adopt a universal declaration that would put people before states. In his view it was necessary, among other things, to create 'rules common to all human groupings, whether regional or universal'.

In the same vein, when President Roosevelt, on 6 January 1941, made his celebrated State of the Union Address to the US Congress propounding the four freedoms (freedom of speech and expression, freedom of worship, freedom from want, and freedom from fear), he described the new doctrine as valid for the whole world, declaring: 'In the future days, which we seek to make secure, we look forward to a world founded upon these freedoms.' And he deliberately repeated four times the phrase 'everywhere in the world'.

Also, during the drafting process of the Universal Declaration, René Cassin was aware that one could not simply transpose onto the international level the bill of rights of one or another country. In a report of 27 February 1947 to the French Foreign Ministry he wisely noted that 'a Universal Declaration cannot be the simple photographic enlargement of a national declaration. It cannot ignore the calling of any human being to have a native country or, if he expatriates voluntarily or by force, to have a homeland or to be granted asylum.'[2] The rights in the Declaration would transcend the cultural or political framework of any one country.

The Universal Declaration of 1948 confirms this outlook not only by its very name, but also in its contents. It envisages the same human rights for all individuals of the earth, whatever their historical conditions and traditions. It addresses itself to 'all members of the human family' and posits itself as 'a common standard of achievement for all peoples and all nations'.

This universalistic aspiration, I believe, was right. You cannot proclaim a new religion, albeit secular, which should be valid for any human being, and then start drawing distinctions between the various categories of persons, peoples, or states, lest the new set of principles should lose its moral force as a corpus of imperative guiding standards. However, the drafters of the Universal Declaration were aware that they were not speaking to an amorphous mass of individuals. Their awareness that individuals of the earth were distributed among states, and that states were not equal in condition and history is reflected in Article 2, which proclaims among other things that 'no distinction shall be made on the basis of the political, jurisdictional or international status of the country or territory to which a person belongs, whether it be independent, trust, non self-governing or under any other limitation of sovereignty.' Nevertheless those drafters, while aware of the *hic et nunc* (here and

---

[1] R. Cassin, 'L'État-Léviathan contre l'homme et la communauté humaine', *Les Nouveaux Cahiers*, April 1940, 13–16.

[2] The original typewritten text is reproduced photographically in É. Pateyron (ed.), 'René Cassin et la Commission consultative des droits de l'homme', *La Documentation Française* (Paris: 1998), 181–90.

now), that is, of the prevailing historical conditions, deliberately chose, and rightly so, to speak *sub specie aeternitatis* (for eternity).

## 2. The stark realities of the world

We all know that the 'common standard of achievement' is far from realized: not only do human rights continue to be violated if not unabated, with stunning frequency, but the values preached by Roosevelt and Cassin and enshrined in the Universal Declaration have also not trickled down to all states of our planet. Too many governments still turn a blind eye to the universal values that should guide all countries of the world. Consider Sudan as an example. When I was in Sudan in 2004 for the UN Security Council Commission of Inquiry on Darfur, I was told by the Minister of Justice and some senior judges that crucifixion is still one of the legal penalties for the most serious crimes (it is provided for in Art. 27(3) of the Criminal Act 1991[3]), although such penalty—he added— is rarely inflicted and only in the countryside, not in towns. Sudan's Criminal Code also does not uphold the principle that criminal responsibility is personal: it provides in Article 30(1) that 'an individual shall be executed for a group and a group for an individual'. Let me add that also in the New Sudan (that is, South Sudan), where a more modern Criminal Code was adopted in 2003, this Code nonetheless includes a provision (Art. 76) which authorizes courts to pass 'a sentence of whipping not exceeding ten strokes' on male offenders in lieu of imprisonment.

Sudan is not the only country whose penal code still regards stoning and mutilation of parts of the body as lawful ways of punishing culprits. Furthermore, sexual mutilation of women is a legal practice in many countries. The same applies to some forms of modern slavery. A few years ago Iran asserted that, if it were to choose between the Universal Declaration and shari'a law, it would opt for the latter. In many states freedom of expression and of assembly are not considered as important as the right to work. In addition, in spite of all the international customary and treaty rules prohibiting torture, even major Western countries sometimes condone this practice, either by putting forward odd and manipulative interpretations of the international ban, or by simply refraining from punishing those who engage in torture (a clear signal to torturers that what they do will not fall under the sword of the law).

In short, human rights are not truly universal in practice. Even the most fundamental rights are subjected to cultural, religious, and ideological constraints—as well as political expediency. What are the principal reasons for this intolerable state of affairs? There are many, of course, but I will emphasize only two: the *persistent impact of sovereignty*, and the *ineradicable role of self-interest* resulting in the lack of a real community sentiment in the world society.

---

[3] 'Death sentence with crucifixion shall not be passed except for armed robbery (*hiraba*).'

### 3. What should be done to move gradually towards a global community of human rights?

If we do not want to resemble persons painting still lifes on the walls of a sinking ship (to take up a famous metaphor by Bertold Brecht) we must strive to move, even if slowly, towards a global community where human rights tend to be universally upheld. Thus, even if human rights are (and they undoubtedly will be) violated, at least there will be an awareness that they are breached, and public opinion can raise its voice and call the perpetrators to account.

What type of action should we endeavour to engage in? I would suggest that we should take *a double-track approach*, dealing both with the *values* at stake and with the *means* for translating them into living reality.

### (A) Enhancing fundamental and intransgressible values

We should first of all *draw a distinction* between (i) a core of fundamental values which must be common to all nations, states, and individuals and may not, therefore, be derogated from and (ii) other values, the application of which may need to take into account national conditions. The fundamental values of the world society are those enshrined in that core of rules that constitute the international *jus cogens*, a set of peremptory norms that may not be derogated from.

As I have pointed out in another chapter in this volume, in the 1960s for the first time in world history the notion was accepted that there should be a hierarchy in the body of rules of the international community and that some principles or norms should be at the summit of the legal system. States could not transgress or derogate from these principles inter se. This marked a conspicuous progress. For the first time a set of legal principles having a higher rank than any other international rule was contemplated. They could be equated to the constitutional principles of a domestic legal order; that is, principles that are higher than laws normally adopted by parliaments and may not be deviated from or infringed upon except by subsequent norms having the same rank. Thus, for the first time in the world society peremptory norms restrained the hitherto unlimited lawmaking power of states.

With this new development came a clear understanding that *jus cogens* rules included norms concerning human rights: those banning genocide, slavery, racial discrimination, and forcible denial of self-determination. Over the years national or international bodies have suggested that other international rules also enjoy the status of peremptory norms: the ban on torture, the prohibition of the slave trade, the right to life, the right of access to justice, the right of any person arrested or detained to be brought promptly before a judge (the so-called habeas corpus right), the ban on *refoulement* (refusal of entry of refugees at the frontier), the prohibition of collective penalties, and the principle of personal responsibility in criminal matters. I would also add the right to a fair trial. Other norms are likely gradually to rise to the level of *jus cogens* through a process of accretion. This normative process unfolds through judicial decisions (be they national or international), pronouncements by collective bodies such as the UN General Assembly, and declarations of states and other international legal subjects. The formation of a norm possessed with *jus cogens* force results from the convergence of a wide number of factors, all expressing in different forms and to varying degrees the legal view (the *opinio juris*) that the international rule at issue enshrines values so fundamental that no deviation from it is admissible.

The existence of a host of norms on human rights having the nature of *jus cogens* shows that there exists in the international society a two-tier set of values: some rights are regarded as more crucial than others, and are therefore enshrined in peremptory norms. These norms can be considered as those which have universal scope and bearing. They must be obeyed by all nations, states, and individuals of the planet. Other values, consecrated instead in international rules deprived of the nature of *jus cogens*, although still important, can be restrained in their incidence and scope by individual states, or adjusted to some extent to national conditions—as long as, however, such interpretation or adjustment does not appear to be absolutely arbitrary or unwarranted to other states or the relevant international bodies.

The existence of two different sets of values and corresponding international norms can make allowance for the coexistence of a core of indispensable and absolute values and a set of other, less imperative values. The gradual *expansion* over time of the first group of norms might eventually lead in the future to the formation of a global community where all the basic norms on human rights must be equally respected by everyone in any part of the planet.

This trend will be furthered by the meritorious work of the UN Human Rights Committee and the UN Committee on Economic, Social and Cultural Rights regarding the two 1966 Covenants on Human Rights. These Committees, as is well known, point in their General Comments and in the UN Human Rights Committee's decisions on individual communications to the right interpretation to be placed on the various provisions of the Covenants. They thereby propound a notion of the various international rights that should be uniformly applied by all states.

Let me add that the existence of this *two-tier system of human rights values* in the international society is not per se a pernicious phenomenon. It simply reflects the reality of that society, where states with a different history, outlook, and philosophy coexist. In the interim, it is crucial to entrench in the international ethos and in the international legal mindset the notion that there exists a core of fundamental values which must be complied with by any state or other entity, whatever its history, culture, religion, or civilization.

## (B) Inducing compliance with *jus cogens* norms on human rights

We must not, however, confine ourselves to discussing normative developments. The international society is teeming with impressive normative constructs that are not matched by reality and remain magnificent dreams. It is as if states, after much discussion and interminable polemics on its placement and configuration, had built a stupendous skyscraper, provided with an entrance, floors, stairs, lifts, fully furnished rooms, and even vases overflowing with freshly cut flowers, and then left the building empty, for no one dares or wishes to enter and live there.

Hence, it is also necessary to propose that some sort of supervisory or enforcement mechanisms be set up, capable at least of ensuring respect for the *jus cogens* rules on human rights. I would like to point out that to my mind one should not pursue, or at least should entertain doubts about pursuing, two particular avenues for achieving this end: establishing a universal international court of human rights and providing for humanitarian intervention whenever human rights are grossly violated. The former option should be discarded because it is simply naïve to think that states will submit their own domestic relations with individuals living on their territory to binding international judicial scrutiny. The second option (humanitarian intervention) should be taken with a pinch of salt for it is likely to lend itself to dangerous abuses and manipulations. Nevertheless, the use of force has recently been authorized by the UN Security Council with regard to the Ivory Coast (where the Council authorized both the UN peacekeeping forces and the French forces supporting them to use force for the protection of civilians)[4] and to Libya (where again all states were authorized to use force for the sake of protecting civilians).[5] These are important precedents. Were the Security Council to insist on this approach in future instances, a new vista would open up and possible ways of conceptualizing and institutionalizing the Security Council's authorization to use force to pursue humanitarian goals would be worth exploring.

Setting aside these two oft-suggested options, I would suggest *three distinct avenues*. First, one should set up a system of inquiry capable of verifying how and when violations occur. Secondly, one should enhance the criminal responsibility of the authors of gross violations of those fundamental values. Thirdly, one should rely upon international civil society tenaciously and steadfastly to prod all international subjects to abide by the law.

## *(i) Monitoring respect for* jus cogens *norms on human rights*

I would first suggest the possible establishment of a Commission of Inquiry available to states and individuals alike. This suggestion is grounded on three assumptions. First, currently states are no less reluctant than in the past to submit the possible misconduct of their agents to international adjudication. Secondly, states are instead more amenable to fact-finding, which is felt to be less intrusive and hence less prejudicial to their sovereign prerogatives. Thirdly, fact-finding would have the great merit of establishing in an impartial and authoritative manner the

---

[4]  See SC Res. 1967 of 19 January 2011 and SC Res. 1975 of 30 March 2001. The Security Council authorized the peacekeeping forces 'to use all the necessary means to carry out its mandate to protect civilians'. France was included in the authorization.

[5]  See SC Res. 1973 of 17 March 2001, where states were authorized 'to take all necessary measures to protect civilians'.

facts at issue, thereby laying the indispensable ground for a peaceful settlement of the matter and return to normality.

It would thus seem that an *international non-judicial oversight mechanism* could usefully fulfil the task of rapidly establishing whether gross violations of human rights norms of *jus cogens*, in particular acts of torture, genocide, crimes against humanity, or terrorism, have been perpetrated. A Commission of Inquiry made up of independent experts having impeccable professional credentials and great moral authority could be established by the UN Secretary-General. It could consist of a roster of experts, from which in each case the Secretary-General could draw a certain number of commissioners. The Commission could be activated either by the victims or by the territorial state (or even by the national state of the victim if they belong to a state other than the territorial one). The Commission would have the advantage of acting promptly and discharging its task expeditiously. In addition, it might be more acceptable to states if its findings were devoid of any legally binding force. Such findings could even be handed over confidentially to the relevant state, while the individual complainants might be given only a summary account of the findings. Under such a scheme, it would however, be wise to allow for the Commission's right to disclose its findings whenever the state in question contumaciously failed to comply with the conclusions articulated in the Commission's report. If this Commission were absolutely impartial and independent as well as very authoritative, its findings would carry much weight.

### (ii) Bolstering international accountability mechanisms

There is no doubt that bringing the authors of serious and large-scale violations of human rights to justice constitutes one of the most efficacious means of reacting to such violations. Plainly, to hold perpetrators personally accountable strikes at the root source of grave misdeeds and prevents culpable individuals from hiding behind the state. *Individual criminal liability* is more effective than *state responsibility* for the purpose of both preventing future violations and alleviating the suffering of the victims or their next of kin. However, criminal justice is far from a panacea. Indeed, the deterrent effect it aims to produce is less apparent than the other two effects attaching to international conviction and sentence: stigmatization of the criminal conduct and retribution.

In spite of these limitations, criminal accountability processes remain a valid tool for addressing the whole range of gross violations of human rights norms of *jus cogens*, in particular those violations which, being uniquely odious in character and collective in nature, amount to such international crimes as torture, crimes against humanity, genocide, war crimes, or terrorism.

What should be done to enhance the existing accountability procedures and bolster their effectiveness? I would suggest a number of different avenues: (i) to make the *International Criminal Court* more effective so as better to use its universal potential; (ii) strongly to urge the exercise by national courts of *universal criminal jurisdiction* over such international crimes and (iii) to insist on the notion that no *amnesty* for gross violations of human rights amounting to international crimes is permissible under current international law.

## (iii) Activating international civil society

To push states and other international subjects to respect human rights and, generally speaking, behave in consonance with the universal values enshrined in the norms of *jus cogens*, one cannot rely too much on states. They are too concerned with pursuing economic, commercial, political, or military interests to prioritize safeguarding fundamental values or to take principled positions. We must therefore turn to international civil society.

In earlier times this society substantially coincided with public opinion. Indeed, in 1931 a distinguished British international lawyer, J.L. Brierly, stressed the importance of public opinion as a sanction, noting that in the international society public opinion

is intrinsically a weaker force than opinion in the domestic sphere, yet it is in a sense more effective as a sanction of law. For whereas an individual law-breaker may often hope to escape detection, a state knows that a breach of international law rarely fails to be notorious; and whereas again there are individuals so constituted that they are indifferent to the mere disapproval, unattended by pains and penalties, every state is extraordinarily sensitive to the mere suspicion of illegal action.[6]

Today international civil society must guide public opinion more actively. At present public opinion is too frequently distracted by the media, and the media bombardment is also intensive but shallow, for it jumps each day to a new subject. We have thus been made accustomed to tragedies occurring every day in some part of the world, with the risk of becoming indifferent or even cynical.

We must therefore turn to that international civil society, which is chiefly incarnated in the most independent, impartial, and proactive non-governmental organizations. By gathering and disseminating information, by drawing publicity to issues, and by acting as the moral voice of the international community, international civil society might play a significant role in prodding states and other international subjects as well as national courts increasingly to proclaim and comply with fundamental values upheld in *jus cogens* rules.

---

[6] J.L. Brierly, 'Sanctions', in *The Basis of Obligation in International Law* ([1931] Oxford: Clarendon Press, 1958), 203.

# PART II

# WHAT LAWMAKING TOOLS SHOULD BE USED TO BRING ABOUT THE NEEDED CHANGE?

# 12

# Customary International Law:
# The Yesterday, Today, and Tomorrow of
# General International Law

*Luigi Condorelli**

## SUMMARY

It would simplistic to speak of a merely supplementary or 'interstitial' role of customary international law. Treaties are subject to a legal regime of customary law that regulates and also limits their power of derogation. In short, the life of international relations requires and presupposes the existence of a single legal framework, a sort of 'backdrop' represented by the general customary law, from which the agreement may if necessary deviate. Three developments may be observed in current international relations. First of all, in fact courts, and in particular the International Court of Justice (ICJ), tend to attach overriding importance to *opinio juris* over *usus*. Secondly, at present a broad correspondence can be found between general customary rules and those provisions written down in large international conventions of (basically) universal character. Thirdly, among customary rules of international law some have emerged that have a special legal force: they may not be derogated from by treaty law. This set of 'constitutional rules' is made up of rules that are all connected to principles of the UN Charter and constitute their logical, ideological, and value extension. There are three possible ways of improving upon the current role of customary law. First, the widely lamented fragmentation of international law in separate and self-contained legal regimes, in fact depends, in large measure, on the as it were 'fragmented eye' of the observer, rather than on the fragmentation of the observed object. Hence, the best way to counter this fragmentation would reside in training practitioners in general international law, rather than in (or in addition to) specialist areas. Secondly, it is necessary to promote compliance with *jus cogens*, by ensuring that all members of the international community have effective tools at their disposal for the removal of treaties affecting

* Translated from Italian by Iain L. Fraser.

the fundamental rights of each and all. Thirdly, mechanisms should be put in place for monitoring compliance of Security Council decisions with the principles of the UN Charter including *jus cogens*.

## 1. Introduction

No one has ever doubted that among the components of the law governing international relations there is—and always has been—international custom. For everyone recognizes that international law does not end in the written rules formulated in the treaties and other international instruments of a normative nature, but that alongside these there are others, which can be identified by 'induction'. These are rules that are not created by preordained procedures, whose operation is subject to a specific legal regulation, but inferred from the actual practices of international actors: rules, in other words, whose existence is considered proven once their actual social effect is established, that is, once it is found that the actors in question generally behave in a manner consistent with those provisions, in the belief that the conduct in question is socially obligatory.

It is a real cliché to say that international custom is the result of two elements (the *opinio juris ac necessitatis* and *repetitio facti*), and there is no reason to oppose this very traditional and popular way of speaking—as long as it is made clear, however, that these wise, though approximate and indicative, formulas, are seeking in essence to explain what 'induction' means: it is the operation that consists in gathering evidence to prove the social effect of the rules in question. This evidence may be multiple, and the weight of each piece may also be different in different situations: an extended period may sometimes be necessary, or at other times the evidence may work synchronously. In all cases it should be deemed sufficient if it enables the assessment that the rule sought indeed has social effect in the international community. In short, the object sought is single, and there is also a single method to use, but paths to go through to find it may be different: longer and more difficult here, faster there, and sometimes, perhaps, very fast.

It is widely accepted that 'international custom' may have a general reach, when it is addressed to all international actors, or 'local' (about two states only) or 'regional' (with regard to a particular group of states) scope. In the pages that follow I shall focus on customary law of the first type. Let us immediately note the widespread usage, also adopted by the ICJ, of considering the two terms '(general) international custom' and 'general international law' as substantially equivalent.

## 2. The role of international custom: some basic concepts

In an international society which—as proclaimed (with reference to the UN) by Article 2(1) of the Charter—continues to be 'based on the principle of the sovereign equality' of states, and where the lawmaking function is still exercised (at least primarily) by those states, it is natural that we tend to keep the traditional idea that the role of custom is, in essence, secondary, or if you will, integrative (not to say 'interstitial'). Article 38 of the Statute of the ICJ is emblematic in this regard when, in describing the sources of law which the Court must draw on 'to decide in accordance with international law such disputes as are submitted to it', it requires the Court first to apply the 'international conventions, whether general or particular, establishing rules expressly recognized by the contesting states', and secondly, calls on it to use 'international custom, as evidence of a general practice accepted as law'. The priority thus apparently given to agreement over custom does not, however, reflect superior rank compared to the latter. If the Court is asked to begin by applying the existing treaties between the parties and only then custom, if and insofar as what is necessary is not to be found in the former, the practice is not because the former are higher ranking than the latter: if there is a treaty, that means it relates to a specific legal regime explicitly chosen ('expressly recognized') by the parties to the dispute, and there will then be no need to resort to custom. In the absence of applicable conventional rules, however, one turns to custom, given that its rules too are essentially to be classified as 'accepted as law'. So, to give an account of the relationship between treaty and custom and the ability of the first to derogate from the second, it seems only logical to call into question the notions of, respectively, *jus speciale* and *jus generale*.

However, only slightly deeper reflection can immediately highlight just how shallow and simplistic it is to speak of a merely supplementary or 'interstitial' role of customary international law as compared to conventional law, and how full of meaning treating as synonymous the terms 'international custom' and 'general international law' is. In truth, the various international agreements create rights and obligations for the parties only and are not capable of producing effects for third countries. The set of rules put in place with the myriad of bilateral and multilateral agreements that bind pairs or groups of different countries is therefore insufficient to sustain the totality of international relations. Moreover, the capacity of the individual treaty to depart from custom cannot be manifested except on condition that the treaty has been duly formed and remains in force: to verify this, we must resort to legal rules on the 'law of treaties' that obviously cannot all be found in the treaty itself. No one, in fact, doubts that it is for general international law to regulate the making, effects, and termination of treaties, as well as their possible invalidity: treaties are therefore subject to a legal regime of customary law that regulates and also limits their power of derogation. In short, the life of international relations requires and presupposes the existence of a single legal framework, a sort of 'backdrop' represented by the general customary law, from which the agreement may if necessary deviate. This is only apparently a vicious circle, but really makes it obvious that between the universes of treaty law and customary law there is an equal relationship of interdependence and mutual support, resulting from the fact that both are 'autonomous' law emanating—through different processes—from the actual addressees of legal rules. In short, it follows from the absence in the international community of an institutional apparatus with authority over the states that all the law they employ—through acts of will or otherwise—to regulate their relations has *the same rank*. It is precisely for this reason that the role of the relationship between treaty law and customary law seems effectively expressed by reference to the binomial *jus speciale/jus generale*.

Customary international law thus has a central role to play in the life of inter-national relations, since it has the task of providing the unitary legal framework of principles and rules by which to ensure coherence in the system as a whole. The exponential growth of the contemporary international set of rules, its increasingly marked expansion and diversification, the formation of a whole number of sec-toral subsystems provided with specific legal rules and autonomous institutional devices, bring out ever more clearly how essential that role is, but at the same time make its proper performance increasingly difficult.


## 3. Tendencies and developments in international custom: the preponderance of *opinio juris, consuetudo scripta,* and peremptory general international law

### (A) The preponderance of *opinio juris*

If one tries to reply to the question 'How do you detect the existence and con-tent of customary rules?' using the methodology currently used by international judges, and in particular the ICJ, one finding compels itself. The Court usually begins by declaring allegiance to the 'dualist' concept of custom (*opinio juris* plus *repetitio facti*), but then carefully refrains from actually doing what it says it should: in most cases, it will not carefully review the practice of states, under-stood as the sum of the actual conduct of those through which the state acts, but opt instead to highlight factors that at first glance are among the *opiniones juris*. In short, it tends to accept the actual social power of the rule sought as proved if it finds a widespread belief in its existence, deducing this from, for example, pos-itions solemnly taken, widespread recognition consecrated in documents adopted by large majorities, or even unanimously, multilateral agreements with very broad participation, and the like.

Typically, this is what is found, for example, in human rights and international humanitarian law: no one today denies that at least their basic principles are bind-ing on all states, including those that have not signed international treaties devoted to them, despite the fact that violations are unfortunately known to be frequent. In fact, the undoubted existence of such violations is not sufficient to exclude the existence of the customary rules in question, when such conducts are contrasted, on the one hand, by a huge number of documents, instruments, solemn declar-ations, and domestic laws attesting to a widespread conviction about the validity of the rules and, on the other, by the absence of dispute as to their binding nature. It should also be noted that the assessment of practice should not be done in short-sighted and incomplete fashion: it is not enough, in fact, simply to compute the contrary behaviours, disregarding the fact that violations of international stand-ards are always very visible, but compliant behaviour is undoubtedly less so: in addition to counting and weighing the former, the latter should also be weighed and counted, and then the results compared. In other words, even repeated and serious violations of a customary rule in no way justify the conclusion that the rule itself has lapsed, where there is reason to believe that it continues to be respected in most cases, demonstrating its broad, persistent, and effective social influence.

Nor is it necessarily the case that the accumulation of data necessary for a finding that the customary rule is proved requires a prolonged period. One should not at all exclude, in fact, the possibility that it may happen in a very short time if necessary, when the evidence of its validity accumulates synchronically (rather than diachronically). One should in fact note visible—though not very frequent—phenomena of acceleration of the evolution of custom, due to factors that deserve highlighting. First, the fulgurant speed of circulation of information makes any event instantly become known throughout the world and allows immediate reactions. But above all there is now a range of international fora (the plenary bodies of large international organizations, continual diplomatic conferences and meetings, the annual meetings of the UN International Law Commission (ILC), and the debates between states commenting on the results at the Sixth Committee of the UN General Assembly, etc.) representing places and occasions of choice for a collective and ongoing debate about the state of international law, and the scope and need for reform. It happens in particular that documents adopted in these fora proclaim normative statements entirely suitable to be the content of actual legal rules (conventional or customary), as well as candidates for them. However, the stages, procedures, and conditions necessary to achieve the status of treaty provisions are provided for and governed by international legal rules, while things are otherwise for any transformation into customary law. Everything here depends on the acceptance the international community gives the normative statement in question, that is, on whether it acquires (or consolidates) wide effect as a regulator of social relations. Now, such acquisition (or consolidation) may be greatly facilitated by the size and solidity of the consensus that has formed at the time, the favourable attitudes of third parties (states, international organizations both governmental and non-governmental, public opinion, etc.), possible consecration in case law, and so on. It is not impossible, then, that the accumulation of such practice (as a set of 'evidentiary facts' of the social basis or impact of the norm) is brought to completion in synchronous fashion; hence the possibility of seeing much faster consolidation of the customary rule, compared to a treaty provision of similar content.

## (B) The emergence of written customary law

Closely connected with what we have just noted, we may find a further, growing phenomenon. More and more nowadays, international custom is perceived as '*consuetudo scripta*': we find, that is, a broad correspondence between general customary norms and those written down in large international conventions of (basically) universal character. There are, in fact, growing numbers of cases where we may (with massive case law) talk of a 'double value' in the sense that the wording of many provisions in relevant international agreements ends up being seen as suitable faithfully to represent the content of customary law too. Entire chapters of contemporary international law appear to consist (at least in large part) of normative statements in which the conventional and the customary dimensions live together harmoniously, thanks to procedures that the ICJ has taught us to identify by means of a now codified terminology: I am referring to the processes that give rise to the so-called 'consecration' of custom (where the agreements merely acknowledge and confirm an existing practice), or its 'crystallization' (where the treaty completes the process of formation of a custom that was still not fully defined, but can now be considered fixed), or 'new formation' (where the conventional provisions, innovative at the time of their adoption, are then appreciated as the starting point or a stage of the process leading to the formation of a corresponding new customary rule). What is certain is that today, in order to recognize the principles of general international law on the subject—for example—of the law of treaties, international humanitarian law, diplomatic law, law of the sea, law of outer space, or law on the use of force and self-defence, we turn to the major international conventions on the subject, assuming that what is proclaimed in them corresponds (at least in large part) to general international law.

## (C) *Jus cogens* (peremptory rules of international law)

One of the areas of contemporary international law in respect of which is particularly easy to talk about *consuetudo scripta* is undoubtedly the law of treaties: as we know, the Vienna Convention of 1969 is now currently used (except for certain rare provisions) as a reliable transcription of general international law on the subject. This can now be said, despite undoubted persisting resistance (to a declining extent, however), with reference to Article 53, which declares the radical invalidity of treaties where they conflict with a peremptory norm of general international law. This implies a belief that one can consider as established the existence of rules of general international law which, instead of being derogable (as usually happens), may not be derogated from: namely, customary law that not only cannot be superseded or set aside by contrasting treaty rules, but instead invalidates them. Thus, the existence is recognized, at the top of the international order, of a kind of 'material constitution', protecting supreme and universal values which are not at the disposal of states: if they attempt to modify them even by an agreement with strictly limited *inter partes* effects, that would still injure legitimate interests of the entire international community to be conceived as indivisible. The absolute and irremediable nullity of such an agreement, provided for by the Vienna Convention, is a 'penalty' in terms of the law of treaties of this injury inflicted simultaneously on all. The view that international custom can in some cases be peremptory and therefore prevail over treaties may seem at odds with the concept highlighted earlier that all law that states use to regulate their relations has the same rank: a concept from which it logically follows, as mentioned, that rules posed by agreement—and hence expressly recognized by the states concerned—prevail over customary *jus generale*. From the very wording of Article 53 of the Vienna Convention it can, however, be inferred why there is actually no real contradiction: the peremptory nature of the binding customary rule depends on whether it is 'accepted and recognized by the international community of states as a whole as a norm from which no derogation is permitted.' In other words, in order for a rule of general international law to be assessed as peremptory in nature it has to be found that the entire international community (and not just a segment) agrees that it is. This is not to require unanimity, but it is necessary that all the significant components of the international community concur in accepting and recognizing the binding nature of the principle in question, that is, show that they perceive that principle as aiming to protect an essential common interest and therefore see its breach as *indivisibly violating the rights of each and all*. One can certainly speak of a 'hierarchy', but not in the formal sense: this was why we used the term 'material constitution' just now.

It is well known that the identification of the principles of general international law belonging to *jus cogens* is currently proceeding, in practice and case law, very slowly. But it is interesting to note that the principles thus far identified (eg the prohibition of aggression, genocide, torture, slavery and forced labour, crimes against humanity, and the like) are all connected to principles of the United Nations Charter and are logical, ideological, and value extensions of them.

## 4. How can general international law be made to perform its functions better?

International custom therefore has a dual role of a fundamental nature to play: that of offering international relations principles and rules appropriate to ensuring unity and coherence to the system, and that of providing them with a 'material constitution' which identifies the principles which, by the very fact of protecting interests perceived as supreme and universal, shall be designated as mandatory. What suggestions can be made in order to achieve improvements in the performance of this dual role?

### (A) Fragmentation of the object v fragmentation of the observing eye

As to the first, it is hardly necessary to recall the great debate that has taken place in recent years about the 'fragmentation' of international law, its 'explosion' into sectors and subsystems the sum of which—since, as already mentioned, each often has a special legal regime and an appropriate institutional apparatus—tend to appear chaotic, a sort of assemblage of heteroclite and random fragments. It is a debate that will surely continue, but it is undeniable that it has gradually allowed us to become increasingly aware of the impossibility of asserting the existence of truly 'self-contained' regimes, that is, areas of international law whose separateness from others is so pronounced as to have to exclude their subjection to the common principles of general international law by which an essential unity and fundamental cohesion can be maintained.

However, it is one thing to understand that the principles of general international law are and remain essential in order to avoid contradictions and resolve conflicts between the rights and obligations arising for the same subjects from the rules belonging to different areas, ensuring a basic consistency between these, and quite another to know and recognize adequately the content and *modus operandi* of the principles in question. In fact, as we know, the phenomena already mentioned of relentless expansion and diversification of international law are increasingly leading to specialization: international law practitioners tend to shut themselves up in the various sectors in which they work and to ignore all or nearly all of the others, including those adjacent, thus becoming owners of a markedly specialist culture. A culture that makes us unable to recognize the bridges between the various area of specialized knowledge, and then cross them: which is the only way forward to identify the links and contact points of convergence between them, and the only way to let us detect the common principles to which they are subjected. It is strange that so few voices have been raised so far to suggest that the fragmentation of international law may depend, in large measure, on the as it were 'fragmented eye' of the observer, rather than on the fragmentation of the observed object.

If this diagnosis is agreed with, then we would suggest not just thinking about how to combat the 'fragmentation of the observed object', but also looking for cures for the 'fragmentation of the observing eye'. In the writer's opinion, one of the primary causes of this fault (certainly not the only one, but not the most marginal one either) lies in the inadequate legal training of many practitioners in international law (of all types and levels): we allude to the harmful consequences of the widespread lack of generalist courses in international law in the curricula of legal studies in many university systems, where specialized, and even highly specialized, courses are offered instead, sometimes in large numbers. This promotes the mentality that nothing prevents you from becoming a major expert in, say, human rights, international humanitarian law, the law of the sea, international environmental law, international law on investments, or international criminal law without ever having taken cognizance of the principles of the UN Charter, the law of treaties, law of international responsibility, or law on the settlement of international disputes.

## (B) For the establishment of more forceful means for ensuring compliance with *jus cogens* rules

We come now to the second aspect mentioned: that of peremptory rules of general international law. We have already noted the slow progress in identifying the principles of *jus cogens*, and how limited at present are the number of those one can definitely say seem to be accepted and recognized as binding by the international community of states as a whole. It is, however, clear that this number should grow, especially with regard to the protection of human rights both collective and individual: we must surely go beyond the prohibitions of gross violations or proscription of the most heinous and serious crimes, such as genocide or crimes against humanity. But the growth of peremptory general international law must be accompanied by a clear improvement of the mechanisms effectively to realize its primacy over all other international norms, and in particular over conventional ones, which currently reveal a glaring inadequacy. There is indeed a striking gap between the international norms that protect collective interests of a fundamental nature and the 'operational' means that should be used to compel compliance and to remedy violations, a gap it is essential to seek to bridge.

As regards the instruments available to interested parties under the law of treaties in order to assert that a given treaty is contrary to a peremptory rule of international law, it is well known that the Vienna Conventions of 1969 and 1986 did not respond at all adequately to the need for the protection of collective interests. In fact, the mechanisms for resolving disputes concerning the invalidity of treaties which are provided by these Conventions not only may be sidelined through reservations, but are also organized to be accessible only to the parties (states, and if appropriate, international organizations) to the treaty the invalidity of which, for contrast with *jus cogens*, is to be established. All other bearers of the collective interest to compliance with the peremptory rules of general international law are instead totally ignored. Here, then, is a front on which to engage, in the perspective of ensuring that all members of the international community have effective tools at their disposal for the removal of treaties affecting the fundamental rights of each and all.

But the law of international responsibility too is clearly lacking when it comes to striking at wrongful acts in serious breach of legal obligations under the peremptory rules of general international law. It is true that the principles contained in the Articles on State Responsibility adopted by the ILC in 2001 outline—in very incomplete fashion, however—the general characteristics of the regime applicable in the case of illegal acts of this kind, indicating in particular what types of claims against the author of the offence states other than the one directly affected can make. The fact remains, however, that the Commission had to give up the ambition to propose mechanisms to take into account the general interest at stake, to be used to target illegal conduct detrimental to the entire international community.

The gaps and inadequacies mentioned are serious, and have to be removed to ensure that peremptory general international law can truly carry out its essential function effectively. In the face of breach of obligations *erga omnes*, all these *omnes* (including individuals or groups of individual victims) should be allowed access to effective mechanisms to obtain appropriate remedies.

## (C) Using Article 103 of the UN Charter to ensure the primacy of the general principles of the Charter including *jus cogens*

But that is not all: the UN system too should be mentioned in this regard, given that the Charter proclaims the primacy of the principles enshrined in it over any obligations under any other international agreement (Art. 103). Of course, Article 103 says nothing about a possible primacy of the principles of the Charter over the rest of international law, and in particular general international law. It goes without saying, however, that primacy cannot be seriously questioned with regard to customary norms that can be classified as '*dispositives*' (ie, norms that they themselves allow their addressees to regulate the matter differently), from which any treaty may derogate: *a fortiori* the Charter. It is instead clear that the obligations under the Charter cannot prevail over those arising from the peremptory rules of general international law. Rather, it should be stressed that no contradiction is conceivable between the principles of the Charter and those of *jus cogens*, which should instead be seen as in a relation of continuity and mutual integration.

We must, then, reflect on the means UN law offers to ensure the primacy of the principles of the Charter (incorporating those of peremptory general international law). Of course, here things should go differently from that mentioned above, since the entire system of agencies and all the mechanisms of the organization can become active to enforce that primacy. But looking at the practice, one can easily see that Article 103 is not used—as would, however, be perfectly conceivable—in order to put in place regular monitoring of international agreements concluded by states and other international actors in order to verify compliance with the principles of the Charter (including *jus cogens*); it is not used to 'moralize' the universe of treaty law by overseeing consistency with the 'material constitution' of the international community. In fact, Article 103 has thus far served a single purpose: to reinforce the obligation of states, enshrined in Article 25, to 'accept and carry out the decisions of the Security Council'. In short, the primacy over agreements that Article 103 provides is in reality operated only in favour of the obligations imposed on states by decisions of the Security Council.

Of course, to produce the effects provided for in Article 25 the decisions of the Council must be in accordance with the purposes and principles of the United Nations (Art. 24(2)): thus also in accordance with the peremptory norms of general international law. Everyone knows, however, that the Charter does not establish any mechanism to check the legality of Council decisions, even if it were to be accused of violating the 'material constitution' of international law. Certainly, the great debate on this subject since the early 1990s, catalysed in particular by the few cryptic phrases of the ICJ in the Orders of 14 April 1992 relating to the *Lockerbie* case and then by the clear and courageous position of the ICTY in its decision of 2 October 1995 on the *Tadić* case, has highlighted some byways that could be used for the purpose, at least in specific situations: they are, however, of doubtful effectiveness and highly uncertain access. In short, the gap remains very serious, and it is vital for the future development of the system that it be filled. But this hope must seem essentially utopian and very unrealistic, if one only recalls that no proposal in this direction was made during the—essentially abortive—debate on reform of the UN (and the Security Council in particular) that took place in the early years of the new millennium.

A final observation. Until the hoped-for mechanism for monitoring compliance of Security Council decisions with the principles of the Charter (including *jus cogens*) has been organized, that is, until such review falls within the exclusive jurisdiction of an appropriate mechanism set up within the UN system, it is perfectly legitimate to infer that any court (domestic or international) called on to apply any such decision is to be considered entitled to satisfy itself, incidentally (*incidenter tantum*) whether or not that decision is valid: that is, to make sure that the decision does not contradict the principles that the Security Council is bound to respect under the Charter. Obviously, if the court in question should be persuaded that the Security Council has acted *ultra vires*, it certainly could not cancel the decision, but should confine itself to refusing its application *in casu* by reason of its illegality. This is an idea that is beginning timidly to make inroads with some judges, despite the undoubted problems that may arise: for example, different courts could take different lines, and the international responsibility of the state (or international organization) of which the court is a body might also come into play, in the event of a dispute with the UN. These are serious drawbacks, which should not, however, be avoided by abandoning the principles of the Charter and of *jus cogens* to the uncontrolled and unlimited discretion of the Security Council; instead, a centralized control system that is reliable and accessible should be set up.

# 13

# For an Enhanced Role of
# *Jus Cogens*

*Antonio Cassese*

## SUMMARY

There is general consensus on the existence of a string of overarching inter-national legal principles. In addition, there also is a large measure of agreement of the fact that some principles have acquired the special status of *jus cogens*. Furthermore, there has so far been no objection to the notion that *jus cogens* has or may have an impact on certain areas of international law other than treaty-making (such as recognition of states, reservations to treaties, immunity from jurisdiction, and so on). There is, however, disagreement on: (i) how to deter-mine the birth and force of a peremptory norm; (ii) the extent to which such a norm may have a direct or indirect impact on domestic legal orders; and (iii) the international judicial remedies available in case of dispute on the existence and scope of a peremptory norm. These are three areas where some progress could be achieved. For point (i), the determination of the existence of a peremptory norm should primarily be allocated to courts. As for the method by which to ascer-tain the birth of a peremptory norm, it may suffice for the majority of members of the world community to evince their 'acceptance' of a customary rule as having the rank of a peremptory norm. Such 'acceptance' does not necessarily involve actual conduct, or a positive assertion; it may involve an express or tacit manifestation of will, which can take various forms. No consistent practice of states and other international legal subjects (*usus*) is necessary. For point (ii), the most efficacious way of rendering *jus cogens* operational at the national level would reside in states passing legislation to the effect that peremptory norms are automatically binding within their municipal legal order and indeed over-ride any contrary legislation; (iii) any time one party asserts that its legal claims are based on a peremptory norm and the other party disputes its existence, the community interest in the peaceful settlement of disputes should prompt states to accept adjudication of such dispute, if possible by the International Court of Justice (ICJ).

## 1. An overview of the current condition

### (A) The impact of *jus cogens* on treaty-making: an outright failure?

Indubitably the introduction of a hierarchy in the body of rules of the international community marked a conspicuous progress. For the first time legal principles having a higher rank than any other international rule were contemplated. They could be equated to the constitutional principles obtaining in any domestic legal order, that is, principles that are higher than laws normally adopted by parliaments and may not be derogated from.

This breakthrough did not, however, come without shortcomings. Three major points were left in the shadow: (i) the content of *all* the norms that had already evolved; (ii) the way new imperative norms emerge; and (iii) the judicial determination of a new imperative norm in case of dispute between international legal subjects.

This is why, faced with the enthusiasm of many developing and socialist countries, some lawyers wisely counselled prudence. In particular E. Jiménez de Aréchaga, a leading international lawyer and one of the draftsmen in Vienna, stressed that one should not make of *jus cogens* either a mystique 'that would breathe fresh life into international law' or 'an element of the destruction of treaties and of anarchy'.[1]

It is therefore not surprising that, although the notion of *jus cogens* has been in existence for almost 50 years in the world community, so far it has never had the effect proper to the notion, namely: (i) to bring about the nullity of a treaty contrary to a peremptory norm, or at a minimum (ii) to be relied upon in legal disagreements between states as one of the major issues in dispute, or (iii) to be used by an international judicial body as the *ratio decidendi* of one of its judgments. *Jus cogens* has only been invoked in states' pronouncements, or upheld in obiter dicta of international judicial bodies, or relied upon in declarations or statements of international bodies, or used in legal arguments of some litigants before the ICJ. In contrast, in domestic cases it has been frequently invoked, and occasionally has constituted part of the *ratio decidendi* of the court.

Two reasons may account for this state of affairs. First, states, while engaging in conduct contrary to peremptory norms, as a rule avoid entering into agreements providing, if only implicitly, for such conduct. It is more convenient for them to breach those norms in actual fact, without any need for a prior legal cover or authorization laid down in a treaty. Secondly, the mere existence of the notion of *jus cogens* has perhaps fulfilled a deterring role, forestalling the conclusion of agreements contrary to peremptory norms.

Should we conclude that consequently what is normally asserted to be a major advance accomplished by the 1969 Vienna Convention (with its follow-up: the 1986 Vienna Convention on the Law of Treaties between States and International Organizations and between International Organizations) has in fact proved over

---

[1] See UN Conference on the Law of Treaties, First session (1968), *Official Records*, at 303, para. 48.

the years to be an outright flop? In other words, and to take up a metaphor by Ian Brownlie,[2] should we consider that 'the vehicle does not often leave the garage'?

I would contest this conclusion. Let us not underestimate a primary feature of *jus cogens*: for the first time in the world community peremptory norms restrain the hitherto unlimited lawmaking power of states. Now at long last the old formula of the Digest (II, 14, 38) *jus publicum privatorum pactis mutari non potest* (a public law cannot be altered by the agreements of private persons) holds sway: public law, that is, the expression of the will of the society (or of the society's majority) prevails over and curtails the will of two or more legal subjects. In addition, and more importantly, the concept of *jus cogens* carries a significance for the international community that goes beyond its impact on treaty-making. It would be short-sighted to appreciate only the more visible aspect of *jus cogens*: its restraining incidence on the major source of law of the international community. In fact, *jus cogens* is one of the hallmarks of the *new* international community, together with *erga omnes* obligations, the possession by individuals of internationally recognized human rights, the notion of aggravated state responsibility and that of individual criminal liability for international crimes. *Jus cogens* is indicative of a novel approach to international relations, where 'community concerns' to some extent prevail over states' self-interests. None better than Jiménez de Aréchaga has highlighted the general and indeed groundbreaking dimension of *jus cogens*, by stressing its 'dynamic' dimension.[3]

That the concept of *jus cogens* is now firmly entrenched in the world legal order is tellingly testified by the circumstance that indisputably the relevant provisions of the 1969 Vienna Convention (Arts 53 and 64) and of the 1986 Vienna Convention (Arts 53, 64, and 71) have been accepted by the whole 'international community' and have thus turned into customary international rules, although—*qua* customary rules—they are of course disconnected from the provision subjecting the invocation of *jus cogens* to resort to the ICJ.

## (B) Practice has breathed new life into *jus cogens*

Fortunately states, national courts, and international judicial bodies have invoked peremptory norms with regard to *areas other than treaty-making*. By so doing, these entities have expanded the scope and normative impact of peremptory norms.

---

[2] I. Brownlie, 'Comments', in A. Cassese and J.H.H. Weiler (eds), *Change and Stability in International Law-Making* (Berlin/New York: Walter de Gruyter, 1988), at 110. Brownlie's metaphor has been taken up by B. Simma, 'Universality of International Law from the Perspective of a Practitioner', 20 EJIL (2009), at 273.

[3] He rightly noted:

> What…is the essence of the rules of jus cogens? The international community recognizes certain principles which safeguard values of vital importance for humanity and correspond to fundamental moral principles: these principles are of concern to all states and 'protect interests which are not limited to a particular State or group of States, but belong to the community as a whole'….[T]he concept of jus cogens represents a signal achievement both from a scientific and a practical point of view. It introduces into international law a dynamic concept, capable of future development and a new perspective. (E. Jiménez de Aréchaga, 'International Law in the Past Third of a Century', 159 HR (I-1978) at 64 and 66)

First, *jus cogens* has been relied upon with regard to *recognition of states*. It has been stated that when an entity with all the hallmarks of statehood emerges as a result of the breach of a peremptory norm (eg on the use of force or on respect for minority rights), other states are legally bound to withhold recognition.[4]

Secondly, peremptory norms may play a role in the making of *reservations to treaties*. Inconsistency of a reservation with a peremptory norm (eg the norm on access to justice or on the ban on racial, ethnic, or religious discrimination) would make the reservation inadmissible.[5]

Thirdly, *jus cogens* can authorize states to *refrain from complying with a treaty*. For instance, although an extradition treaty may impose the obligation to hand over an accused to another state, the detaining state may be obliged by the peremptory norm banning torture not to surrender a person who is likely to be tortured in the requesting state.[6]

Fourthly, *jus cogens* has been relied upon to argue that even the highest political body of the world community, the UN *Security Council*, may not derogate from it.[7]

Fifthly, *jus cogens* may have a bearing on *state immunity from jurisdiction of foreign states*. It has been maintained that a state is never entitled to immunity from

---

[4] See Opinion no. 3, of 4 July 1992, of the Arbitration Commission on Yugoslavia (in 4 EJIL (1993) at 90).

[5] See *North Sea Continental Shelf*, ICJ judgment of 20 February 1969, Separate Opinion of Judge Padilla Nervo ('Customary rules belonging to the category of *jus cogens* cannot be subjected to unilateral reservations', at 97), and the Dissenting Opinions of Judges Tanaka (at 182) and Sørensen:

> The acceptance, whether tacit or express, of a reservation made by a contracting party does not have the effect of depriving the Convention as a whole, or the relevant article in particular, of its declaratory character. It only has the effect of establishing a special contractual relationship between the parties concerned within the general framework of the customary law embodied in the Convention. Provided the customary rule does not belong to the category of jus cogens, a special contractual relationship of this nature is not invalid as such. (at 248)

See also General Comment no. 24 of 1994, rendered by the UN Human Rights Committee, at para. 8.

See also the Joint Separate Opinion of Judges Higgins, Koojimans, Elaraby, Owada, and Simma in ICJ, *Armed Activities on the Territory of the Congo (New Application 2002) (Congo v Rwanda)*, judgment of 3 February 2006, at para. 29. The Court took instead a negative position (see judgment, para. 67).

[6] See the decisions of the Swiss Federal Tribunal in *Bufano et al*, judgment of 21 May 1986 at 8a; *Sener*, judgment of 22 March 1983 at 6aa, *P v Office fédéral de la police*, judgment of 21 May 1986 at 2; *X v Office fédéral de la police (recours de droit administratif)*, judgment of 3 November 1995 at 3-5; *X v Office fédéral de la police (recours de droit public et de droit administratif)*, judgment of 28 November 1995 at 2d.

See also the decision of the same Federal Tribunal in *Y. Nada v Staatssekretariat für Wissenschaft*, of 14 November 2007, where the Federal Tribunal, after stating that Switzerland is bound by the decisions of the Security Council to the extent that they are not contrary to *jus cogens* (at 7.1), held that *in casu* it could not comply with a decision of the Council concerning economic sanctions against an alleged terrorist, for it seriously restricted fundamental rights of the addressee without affording him any judicial safeguard against such sanctions (at 7–8). The Tribunal said:

> Es ist dem Beschwerdeführer einzuräumen, dass in dieser Situation keine effektive Beschwerdemöglichkeit besteht: Das Bundesgericht kann zwar prüfen, ob und inwiefern die Schweiz an die Resolutionen des Sicherheitsrats gebunden ist; dagegen ist es nicht befugt, die Sanktionen gegen den Beschwerdeführer wegen Grundrechtsverletzungen aufzuheben. (at 8.3)

[7] See Judge E. Lauterpacht, Separate Opinion in *Application of the Convention on Genocide (Provisional measures)*, judgment of 11 July 1996, paras 100 and 102; ICTY, Appeals Chamber, *Tadić*, judgment of 15 July 1999, para. 296.

foreign jurisdiction for acts of its agents that contravene an international peremptory norm.[8] Assertedly *jus cogens* also has an impact of the *functional immunity of state agents* when such agents are accused of international crimes.[9]

Finally, peremptory norms have been held to have *an impact on the domestic legal orders of states*. One can infer from them the obligation of states to refrain from applying, or even to take positive measures to nullify, national laws manifestly contrary to them. This has been held to occur with regard to laws providing for amnesty for international crimes such as genocide or crimes against humanity, or with regard to national laws that somehow implicitly authorize torture or inhuman or degrading treatment.[10]

## (C) New peremptory norms have been identified

International practice has made some headway in another area: the identification of norms eligible for the category of *jus cogens*. When the new notion emerged, a clear understanding took place that a core of international rules belonged to *jus cogens* (those banning genocide,[11] slavery, racial discrimination, aggression, forcible denial of self-determination, the acquisition of territory by force). Over the years national or international bodies have suggested that other international rules also enjoy the status of peremptory norms: the ban on torture,[12] the ban on the

---

[8]  See P. Wald, Dissenting Opinion in US Court of Appeals of the District of Columbia Circuit, *Princz v Federal Republic of Germany*, judgment of 1 July 1994, 26 F3d 1166 (1994) at 1176–85. In the *Ferrini v Germany* case the Italian Court of Cassation, meeting in plenary (judgment of 11 March 2004), held that a foreign state may not invoke immunity from jurisdiction whenever it has committed an international crime on the territory of the forum state (paras 5, 9–10). The immunity is set aside by a peremptory norm of international law.

See also the Joint Dissenting Opinion of Judges Rozakis and Caflisch, joined by Judges Wildhaber, Costa, Cabral Barreto and Vajić, in the *Al-Adsani v United Kingdom* case, at para. 3. The Court took a contrary position (judgment, at para. 61).

[9]  See again the *Ferrini v Germany* case, at para. 11. In *R v Bow Street Stipendiary Magistrate and Others, ex p Pinochet Ugarte (No. 3)*, judgment of 24 March 1999 [2000] AC 147, the House of Lords (majority) considered that torture was an international crime prohibited by *jus cogens*. The coming into force of the UN 1984 Convention had created a universal criminal jurisdiction in all the contracting states in respect of acts of torture by public officials, and the state parties could not have intended that an immunity for ex-heads of state for official acts of torture would survive their ratification of the UN Convention. The House of Lords (and, in particular, Lord Millett, at 278) made clear that their findings as to immunity *ratione materiae* from criminal jurisdiction did not affect the immunity *ratione personae* of foreign sovereign states from civil jurisdiction in respect of acts of torture.

[10]  See ICTY, Trial Chamber, *Furundžija*, judgment of 10 December 1998, at 153–7. See also Spanish *Audiencia nacional*, order of 5 November 1998 in *Pinochet*, legal ground no. 8; Argentina, Federal Judge Gabriel R. Cavallo, decision of 6 March 2001 in *Simon Julio, Del Cerro Juan Antonio*, at 64–104.

[11]  See ICJ, *Armed Activities on the Territory of the Congo (new Application 2002) (Congo v Rwanda)*, judgment of 3 February 2006, para. 64; *Application of the Convention on genocide (Bosnia and Herzegovina v Serbia and Montenegro)*, judgment of 26 February 2007, para. 161.

[12]  See ICTY, Trial Chamber, *Furundžija*, n 10, at 153–7; House of Lords, *R v Bow Street Metropolitan Stipendiary Magistrate and Others, ex p Pinochet Ugarte (No. 3)*, judgment of 24 March 1999 [2000] AC 147; European Court of Human Rights, *Al-Adsani v United Kingdom*, judgment of 21 November 2001, para. 61.

slave trade, the right to life, the right of access to justice,[13] the right of any person arrested or detained to be brought promptly before a judge,[14] the ban on *refoulement* (refusal of entry at the frontier), the prohibition of collective penalties,[15] the principle or personal responsibility in criminal matters.[16]

## (D) Summing up

In summary, the existence of a string of overarching legal principles is no longer contested by any international legal subject. In addition, there is also a large measure of agreement on the fact that some principles have acquired this special status. Furthermore, there has so far been no objection to the notion that *jus cogens* has or may have an impact on certain areas of international law other than treaty-making.

There is, however, disagreement on: (i) how to determine the birth and force of a peremptory norm; (ii) the extent to which such a norm may have a direct or indirect impact on the domestic legal order, thereby piercing the shield of state sovereignty; and (iii) the international judicial remedies available in case of dispute on the existence and scope of a peremptory norm.

These are three areas where some progress could be achieved.

## 2. Could some headway be made?

### (A) How to determine the existence of a peremptory norm

Here two distinct problems arise: (i) which entity or body is competent to satisfy itself that a peremptory norm of international law has taken shape? and (ii) by what legal means or methods should it determine that a norm possessed with *jus cogens* force has evolved?

---

[13] See Inter-American Court of Human Rights, judgment of 22 September 2006 in the *Goiburú et al v Paraguay* case, para. 131. Similar statements had been made, prior to that judgment, by Judge Antônio Cançado Trindade in various Dissenting and Separate Opinions attached to judgments of the same Court (see *Masacre de Pueblo Bello v Colombia*, judgment of 31 January 2006, Separate Opinion, paras 8, 13, 64–5; *Baldeon Garcia v Peru*, judgment of 6 April 2006, Dissenting Opinion, paras 5, 7, 9–10; *Trabajadores Cesados del Congreso v Peru*, judgment of 24 November 2006, Separate Opinion, paras 4–7; *Trabajadores Cesados del Congreso v Peru* (interpretation), 30 November 2007, Dissenting Opinion, paras 35–43). See also Special Tribunal for Lebanon (STL), President's Order of 15 April 2010, paras 31–5.      [14] See STL, Pre-Trial Judge, Order of 15 April 2009, para. 4.
[15] See UN Human Rights Committee, General Comment no. 29, adopted on 24 July 2001, at para. 11.

L. Hannikainen, *Peremptory Norms (Jus Cogens) in International Law* (Helsinki: Ninnish Lawyers Publishing Co, 1988), at 495–8 argues that the ban on taking of hostages and on imposing collective punishments have become peremptory norms of international law. This view is, however, based only on the opinion of the writer.

[16] Some of these new norms have been proclaimed by the Swiss Federal Tribunal in its judgment of 14 November 2007 in *Nada v Staatssekretariat für Wirtschaft* (IA 45/2007; DTF 133 II 450):

> Allgemein werden zum *ius cogens* elementare Menschenrechte wie das Recht auf Leben, der Schutz vor Folter und erniedrigender Behandlung, die Freiheit von Sklaverei und Menschenhandel, das Verbot von Kollektivstrafen, der Grundsatz der persönlichen Verantwortung in der Strafverfolgung sowie das *non-refoulement*—Gebot. (para. 7.3)

As for the first question, I submit that the task of authoritatively determining whether a peremptory norm exists cannot be entrusted to either the UN General Assembly or to any other political body. Nor can pronouncements of individual states or by other members of the international society be tantamount to more than expressions of legal views by such international subjects, expressions which of course may have powerful weight for any international organ pronouncing on the issue. To make such an authoritative determination requires being endowed with judicial powers. It is therefore chiefly for international judicial courts and tribunals to make such a finding. Both inter-state and international criminal courts are empowered to undertake this task. Of course, the persuasive force of their findings and indeed their authority as judicial precedent very much depends on how persuasively they make their findings. Here, as in any other matter, the cogency of the court's reasoning has a decisive bearing on its likelihood to be taken up by other courts and tribunals.

The second question amounts to asking by which means an international court or tribunal should ascertain whether a general rule or principle of international law has acquired the status of a peremptory norm. Logically, this presupposes the existence of such a *customary* rule or principle[17]. The task of the body charged with inquiring into *jus cogens* would only consist of establishing whether, in addition to being a customary rule or principle, the norm at issue has also been endowed with the higher rank of a peremptory norm. However, in fact often the inquiry deals both with the question of whether a *general* rule or principle has evolved and, if so, of whether such rule or principle also has the *status of jus cogens*. In other words, in practice the two logically distinct phases of investigation may tend to merge.

Nevertheless, I shall discuss here only the second stage, since the question of whether a customary rule or principle has taken shape is part of the more general problem of the formation of custom—an issue that I can leave open. The question then boils down to asking: for the purpose of establishing whether a *jus cogens* rule or principle has evolved, should we resort to the habitual method for establishing whether a customary rule of international law has emerged, namely determine whether *usus* and *opinio juris* show that such a rule has taken root in the world community? Or should we rather resort to a different method?[18] Of course, should

[17] A.Orakhelashvili, *Peremptory Norms in International Law* (Oxford: Oxford University Press, 2006), at 119 considers instead that although the method for finding a customary rule is different from that for finding whether a rule is endowed with *jus cogens* value, the customary nature of a rule can be proved *after* finding that the rule is of peremptory nature. This proposition seems to me illogical.

[18] As rightly pointed out by K. Zemanek ('The Metamorphosis of Jus Cogens: From an Institution of Treaty Law to the Bedrock of the International Legal Order?', in E. Cannizzaro (ed.), *The Law of Treaties beyond the Vienna Convention* (Oxford: Oxford University Press, 2011), at 384–91) at least three different theories have been advanced for the identification of peremptory norms: (i) those norms that find their source in natural law; (ii) the concept of *ordre public* should be used, similarly to that which occurs in the domestic legal orders of states; (iii) the method to be resorted to is the same as that normally used to identify a customary rule, namely reliance on *usus* and *opinio juris*. I would add that other commentators have instead emphasized the need to differentiate between the method for establishing the existence of a customary rule and that for ascertaining whether a general rule of international law also possesses *jus cogens* nature: R.St.J. Macdonald, 'Fundamental Norms in Contemporary International Law', 25 Canadian YIL (1987), at 130–1; Orakhelashvili, n 17, at 119. These authors, however, do not explain why two different methods should be utilized. In other words, they do not point to the legal reasons justifying the choice of two different methods.

the court or tribunal opt for the method applicable to the formation of customary rule, it would have to apply such a method *mutatis mutandis*, and thus ascertain whether the practice of international legal subjects and their legal views show that a certain general rule has the legal force of *jus cogens*.

Some indications as to the method can be inferred from Article 53 of the Vienna Convention on the Law of Treaties setting out the definition of *jus cogens*. That provision requires that a norm be '*accepted* and *recognized* [as peremptory that is non-derogable] by the international *community of States as a whole*'. What is meant by 'the international community of States as a whole'? Of course, the 'community of States as a whole' is not a distinct subject from the members of that community, a sort of 'legal personification' of those members. The reference to the 'community' must therefore be taken to encompass its members. However, does it mean '*all states*' of the international community'? Or does it rather prescribe the approval of the 'majority' of states? It can be inferred from authoritative statements of some of the protagonists of the Vienna Conference that what is required is the *acceptance* by the *majority* of states provided that such majority includes states which are representative of the various political and geographic areas of the world.[19] We can conclude that, unlike the customary process, the two elements of *usus* and *opinio juris* are not required. It may suffice for the majority of members of the world community in some way to evince their 'acceptance' of a customary rule as having the rank of a peremptory norm. Such 'acceptance' does not necessarily involve actual conduct, or a positive assertion; it may involve an express or tacit manifestation of will, which can take the form of a statement or declaration, or acquiescence in statements by other international legal subjects or in recommendations or declarations by intergovernmental organizations or in decisions by judicial

---

[19] An authoritative interpretation of that expression favourable to the former option was suggested in Vienna by the President of the Drafting Committee, K. Yasseen. He noted that

> There was no question of requiring a rule to be accepted and recognized as peremptory by all States. It would be enough if a very large majority did so: that would mean that, if one State in isolation refused to accept the peremptory character of the rule, or if that State was supported by a very small number of States, the acceptance and recognition of the peremptory character of the rule by the international community as a whole would not be affected. (UN Vienna Conference on the Law of Treaties, First session (1968), *Official Records*, at 472, at para. 12)

This statement was not challenged in Vienna or subsequently. In addition, it has been cited approvingly by authoritative scholars (see Jiménez de Aréchaga, n 3, 65). We can therefore be justified in holding that it reflects the right interpretation of Art. 53. If this is so, we can consider that a large majority of states (as well as other international legal subjects) may suffice, and the possible opposition or silence of one or more states (or other legal subjects) does not bar the norm from acquiring *jus cogens* status.

It should be added that, as stressed by the President of the Vienna Diplomatic Conference, Roberto Ago, in a lecture he gave in 1971, the states that are taken into account for their consent to or acquiescence in a peremptory norm ought to include the most important and representative states from the various areas of the world (see R. Ago, 'Droit des traités à la lumière de la Convention de Vienne', 134 HR (1971-III), at 323 (with regard to the clause whereby a peremptory norm must be accepted by the whole international community), Ago pointed out that

> Cela revient à dire, notamment, qu'il faut que la conviction du caractère impératif de la règle soit partagée par toutes composantes essentielles de la communauté internationale et non seulement, par exemple, par les États de l'Ouest ou de l'Est, par les pays développés ou en voie de développement, par ceux d'un continent ou d'un autre.

bodies. No consistent practice of states and other international legal subjects (*usus*) is necessary.

However, despite this advance in our research, if we look at the current state of affairs, we are taken back to square one: for, very few *states* and *other legal subjects* take a stand on the peremptory nature of international rules, and authoritative pronouncements on the matter are few and far between.

Should we conclude that no new peremptory norms exist or are in the process of formation? I think not. To my mind, while by no means discounting the importance of declarations by states, by such international organs as the UN General Assembly or by other international legal subjects, one should primarily rely upon *three parameters*.

First, one should see whether there exist judicial decisions rendered by either international or national *courts*: normally judges are in a better position than states, international organizations, and other international legal subjects to assess whether a general rule or principle has acquired the rank and force of *jus cogens*.

Secondly, one should determine whether the international society (acting through such collective bodies as the UN General Assembly) regards the value protected by a general rule or principle as fully *congruous* with the universal goals or values upheld by that community (peace, respect for human rights, respect for the right of peoples to self-determination, democracy, pre-eminence of the rule of law).

Thirdly, one should establish whether the value safeguarded in a rule or principle has the same *prominence*, and is as crucial to the world community, as those enshrined in other, undisputed peremptory norms, such as the norms banning genocide, slavery, racial discrimination, and so on. A comparison with existing and unquestioned peremptory norms can permit a better assessment of the importance of the norm at issue and more persuasively lead to the conclusion that it does (or instead does not) uphold a value essential to the world community.

I should add that one should dissent from the methodological approach advocated by some domestic courts (eg the Swiss High Court, the *Tribunal Fédéral*[20]) with regard to peremptory norms relating to human rights. Under this approach, one should see whether treaties on human rights consider a specific human right laid down in such treaties as subject to derogations. In the affirmative, the customary rule on the right (corresponding to the treaty provision enshrining the same right) is not eligible for the status of peremptory norm. In contrast, if the right may not be subjected to derogations, the corresponding customary rule may be held

---

[20]  See the Swiss Federal Tribunal, judgment of 14 November 2007 in *Nada v Stattssekretariat für Wirtschaft* (IA 45/2007; DTF 133 II 450) :

> Indizien für den absoluten Charakter einer Norm sind Vertragsklauseln, die bestimmte Rechte oder Pflichten als unaufhebbar bezeichnen, z.B. indem sie es den Vertragsstaaten untersagen, anderslautende Vereinbarungen zu treffen, gewisse Vertragsbestimmungen wegen eines Notstands zu suspendieren oder indem sie Vorbehalte ausschliessen. (para. 7.1)

See also *A v Départment Fédéral de l'Économie*, judgment of 23 January 2008 (2.784/2006), paras 8.2–8.4; *A v Segreteria di Stato dell'Economia*, judgment of 22 April 2008 (IA.48/2007/bis), paras 7.1 and 7.3 (in Italian). It would seem that the same approach is taken by Hannikainen, *Peremptory Norms (Jus Cogens) in International Law*, n 15, at 429–34.

to belong to *jus cogens*. This approach should be faulted, for it is conceivable, and indeed has been held,[21] that a peremptory norm concerning a human right provides itself for possible restrictions on the exercise of such right.

## (B) Can *jus cogens* have a decisive impact on national legal orders?

In Vienna the draftsmen of the Convention on the Law of Treaties had in mind only the effect of *jus cogens* on treaties. However, while not underestimating the impact of *jus cogens* on the whole ethos of the world community (see Section 1), it is a fact that, like all international rules, international peremptory norms may play a real role only if they have an effective bearing on the domestic legal orders of sovereign states. Even if this aspect of *jus cogens* was totally neglected in Vienna, can we maintain that nevertheless peremptory norms can directly influence or have some impact on the national legal order of states?

In *Furundžija* the ICTY Trial Chamber, discussing torture, derived from the force of *jus cogens* the following legal consequences at the domestic level: (i) states are under the obligation to pass legislation prohibiting the illegal conduct and imposing the prosecution of the culprits; (ii) they may not pass amnesty laws concerning the crime prohibited by *jus cogens*; (iii) they have to refuse extradition or expulsion of individuals to states that act or are likely to act contrary to *jus cogens*; (iv) any other state has universal jurisdiction over the crime prohibited by *jus cogens*; and (v) any other state is duty-bound to refrain from attaching legal values to acts contrary to *jus cogens*.[22] Thus, the Chamber contemplated, and offered a compelling justification for,[23] a significant impact of peremptory norms on national legal systems. However, faced with the 'dualist' approach still prevailing among states, the Chamber did not go so far as to hold that *jus cogens* had a *direct and immediate bearing* on national law so as to nullify any law, administrative act, or judicial decision taken at the domestic level and contravening *jus cogens*.

---

[21] See UN Human Rights Committee, General Comment no. 29, adopted on 24 July 2001:

the category of peremptory norms extends beyond the list of non-derogable provisions as given in article 4, paragraph 2. States parties may in no circumstances invoke article 4 of the Covenant as justification for acting in violation of humanitarian law or peremptory norms of international law, for instance by taking hostages, by imposing collective punishments, through arbitrary deprivations of liberty or by deviating from fundamental principles of fair trial, including the presumption of innocence. (at para. 11)

See also EU, Tribunal of First Instance, *Yassin Abdullah Kadi v Council of the European Union and Commission of the European Communities*, judgment of 21 September 2005, paras 286–8 (however, this judgment has been set aside by the European Court of Justice, judgment of 3 September 2008); STL, Pre-Trial Judge, Order of 15 April 2009, para. 14; STL, President, Order of 15 April 2010, paras 31–4.

[22] See ICTY, Trial Chamber, *Furundžija*, n 10, paras 155–7.

[23] The Trial Chamber held that

It would be senseless to argue, on the one hand, that on account of the *jus cogens* value of the prohibition against torture, treaties or customary rules providing for torture would be null and void *ab initio*, and then be unmindful of a State say, taking national measures authorising or condoning torture or absolving its perpetrators through an amnesty law. (para. 155)

It would seem that the view propounded by the ICTY in that case is logical and consistent. However, it has been taken up by only a few other courts. One should fervently hope that other courts will follow suit and thus the view becomes generally acceptable so that domestic legal effects also follow from those peremptory norms.

However, the most efficacious way of rendering *jus cogens* operational at the national level would reside in states passing legislation to the effect that peremptory norms are automatically binding within the municipal legal order and indeed override any contrary legislation including any piece of legislation aimed at implementing treaties contrary to *jus cogens*. Plainly, such a national rule would perforce have constitutional rank. It would produce the following legal effects: (i) it would invalidate any legislative or administrative act contrary to *jus cogens* and (ii) it would prevent the lawmakers from passing in future any law contrary to *jus cogens*.

So far only Switzerland has proclaimed respect for *jus cogens* at the constitutional level.[24] Admittedly, it would be difficult for states to uphold at the constitutional level international peremptory norms, given that they are not contemplated *nominatim* in any treaty or other international instrument. States are likely to baulk at self-imposing domestic limitations without reference to specific international norms. To induce states to take such a step without any fear of assuming undetermined national obligations, a constitutional rule could be passed referring to those categories of peremptory norms that are already widely accepted (ban on genocide, slavery, torture, forcible denial of the right to self-determination), while adding also that any other international norm classified in future by the ICJ as belonging to *jus cogens* would become automatically binding at the national level. Thus the national constitutional norm would consist of two parts: one making reference to a set of well-specified international norms, the other subjecting any reference to other peremptory norms to the ICJ determination that such norms do have the rank and status of *jus cogens*.[25]

## (C) What judicial remedies should be available in case of dispute on *jus cogens*?

Article 66(a) of the Vienna Convention (and Art. 66(2) of the 1986 Convention) provides for resort to the ICJ in the event of disputes on the contents of *jus cogens*

---

[24] On 18 April 1999 new provisions were incorporated into the Swiss Constitution. Article 139(2) provides that if a popular initiative for partial revision of the Constitution does not respect, among other things, 'the peremptory norms of international law', the Federal Assembly shall declare the initiative null and void, in whole or in part. Article 193(4) provides that, in the case of the total revision of the Constitution, 'the peremptory norms of international law shall not be violated'. Article 194(2) stipulates that any partial revision of the Constitution 'shall not violate the peremptory norms of international law'.

[25] See Ago, n 19, at 297.

in specific instances.[26] However, this provision may only be invoked by a state that is party both to the Vienna Convention and to a bilateral or multilateral treaty it intends to have declared, in whole or in part, contrary to (or instead consistent with) *jus cogens* (in this respect it should be remembered that a number of prominent states have so far refrained from ratifying or acceding to the Vienna Convention).[27] Since, as I pointed out above, at present the rule on *jus cogens* born out of the 1969 Vienna Convention has turned into customary international law, even a state *not* party to the Vienna Convention can bring a dispute concerning *jus cogens* before the ICJ provided: (i) it is a party to the bilateral or multilateral treaty under dispute and (ii) both such state and the other state party against which the claim concerning the consistency or inconsistency with a peremptory norm has been advanced have accepted the compulsory jurisdiction of the Court.

Plainly, this state of affairs is utterly unsatisfactory. A significant segment of the international community, composed of Western countries, accepted the notion of *jus cogens* on condition that its functioning be anchored to international judicial scrutiny so as to prevent abuses. This demand, I submit, was well founded, for both the novelty of the concept and the lack of any legally binding enumeration of the existing peremptory norms made the concept an empty container susceptible of being filled at whim. An authoritative third party determination of *jus cogens* would constitute a welcome safeguard against any abuse.

How could one prompt states and other international legal subjects to submit to international judicial scrutiny?

It stands to reason that no one can impose on states the obligation to submit their disputes to the jurisdiction of the ICJ. However, the very spirit of the doctrine of *jus cogens* is grounded in the requirement that whoever invokes *jus cogens* qua *ratio decidendi* must be prepared to submit to arbitral or judicial determination: the linkage of *jus cogens* with third party determination of whether a claim based on peremptory norms is well founded is integral to the very concept of *jus cogens*.[28] If one party asserts that its legal claims are based on a peremptory norm and the other party disputes its existence, the 'community interest' in the peaceful settlement of disputes

---

[26]

> If no agreement has been reached through conciliation, within a period of 12 months following the date on which the objection to the applicability of *jus cogens* was raised, any one of the parties to a dispute concerning the application or the interpretation of Article 53 or 64 [of the 1969 Convention] may, by written application, submit it to the International Court of Justice for a decision unless the parties by common consent agree to submit the dispute to arbitration.

[27] The 1969 Vienna Convention can count on 111 contracting states. Important states such as the United States, Israel, Iran, Pakistan, as well as Afghanistan and Bolivia are still outside the Convention.

[28] Jiménez de Aréchaga rightly noted that the provision for compulsory jurisdiction of the ICJ was 'the compromise achieved at the [Vienna] Conference as an indispensable condition for the consensus finally reached in respect of the acceptance of jus cogens as a ground for the invalidity of treaties' (n 3, at 67). And he goes on judiciously to observe that 'It may be asserted that even before the entry into force of the Vienna Convention a valid application of this ground of nullity, when the alleged infringement of a rule of jus cogens is disputed, requires the claimant State to be willing to submit the controversy to judicial determination' (ibid).

(a corollary of the emphasis on peace so strongly laid in the UN Charter) should prompt states to accept adjudication of such disputes. Indeed, a dispute on this issue is not tantamount to a difference in the interpretation or the application of a treaty provision or of a customary rule of international law where *bilateral or reciprocal interests* are at stake. For such a dispute it is right for states to accept the compulsory jurisdiction of the ICJ or an arbitral tribunal only if their national interests prompt them to do so. Instead, in the case we are discussing, the dispute would involve alleged universal values binding on the whole international community; it would be a dispute that affects *collective concerns.* If this is so, there is a collective interest in the judicial settlement of such disputes. In other words, in this case we are not faced with a dispute over an 'ordinary' legal provision or rule of international law; rather, we are faced with a controversy over fundamental values of the whole world society. It follows that states should not be allowed to rely on their sovereign prerogatives and refuse to submit to the ICJ. They must be prepared to go to court.

The states' general commitment to the ICJ judicial determination could be laid down in a resolution adopted by the UN General Assembly declaring that all member states of the world community as well as other international legal subjects having standing before the ICJ accept to submit any dispute over *jus cogens* to the Court. In light of what I have pointed out on the 'community concern' for the judicial settlement of any dispute on peremptory norms, this resolution—I submit—might constitute a sufficient basis for the Court to exercise its jurisdiction.

## 3. A blueprint for action

In sum, how could the role of *jus cogens,* a concept so crucial to the new international society, be enhanced in the next decades?

I think that *three paths* could be taken. First, international and national courts should increasingly rely on this notion, so as to contribute to the consolidation of existing peremptory norms and to the identification and recognition of emerging or incipient norms. As states and other international legal subjects are unlikely to insist on the notion or invoke it in international disputes, one should perforce turn to courts for this important action. Areas where promising developments are likely include human rights, humanitarian law (where the banning of cruel weapons causing unnecessary suffering, and the urgent need to step up the protection of civilians are likely to lead sooner or later to the formation of *jus cogens*) as well as international criminal law (where the norms banning and penalizing war crimes and crimes against humanity, and attributing universal jurisdiction over such crimes, can be considered as nascent peremptory norms in need of consolidation and specification) as well as environmental law.

Another crucial area is that of state immunity and immunity for state agents. State immunity and functional immunity of state agents are concepts belonging to the old international society. International dealings broke down into bilateral relationships, consequently there was a need to protect states from interference in domestic or international affairs by other states, and no collective body existed representing the whole membership of the society and proclaiming universal and non-derogable values. The world order is now different. Universal values have emerged, and the concept of accountability has firmly established itself. There is therefore no longer a need for the safeguards deriving from state immunity and functional immunity of state agents, at least when fundamental and universal values are at stake. This holds true in particular for serious international crimes (genocide, war crimes, crimes against humanity, torture, aggression, terrorism): where one such crime is at stake, a *state* or a *state agent* may not invoke immunity. It (or he) must stand trial and answer for their alleged misdeeds.

Also the area of treaty-making can be affected or influenced by *jus cogens*. For instance, reservations should increasingly be subjected to the scrutiny imposed by peremptory norms, with the consequence that any reservation inconsistent with such a norm should be held to be inadmissible (see Section 1(B)). Furthermore, *jus cogens* should be taken into account when interpreting treaties or other international instruments such as resolutions adopted by international organizations. If one of the various possible constructions runs counter to a peremptory norm, it should be rejected and another interpretation should be preferred that would be consistent with that norm.

The second avenue that should be taken relates to the domestic implementation of peremptory norms. As pointed out above (Section 2(B)) the best way of ensuring national respect for those norms lies in passing national legislation imposing compliance with those norms. As noted, for such legislation to have a realistic chance of being passed, it would be necessary both to refer specifically in it to a set of peremptory norms that have widely been accepted in the world community and to provide that, with regard to any other norm of *jus cogens* asserted by a party, the ICJ must have the final say.

Finally, international civil society might play a significant role in prodding states and other international subjects as well as national courts increasingly to proclaim and comply with fundamental values upheld in *jus cogens* rules. This role should not be underestimated. Non-governmental organizations, as well as distinguished scholars and practitioners could underline the crucial importance of *jus cogens* for the new reality of the world community. Given the importance of the 'acceptance' of those principles and the way in which such 'acceptance' may take shape (see Section 2(A)) those organizations could stimulate international intergovernmental organizations and other international entities to pronounce on such principles. They could stress that a core of constitutional principles has revolutionized the mere 'contractual dimension' of the international law of the past and now yields sway in the world society, setting standards that no one, not even the UN Security Council, may shun. These principles, besides restraining the previous unfettered normative autonomy of sovereign states, also have a crucial impact of the daily conduct of states in international dealings and in their own domestic legal systems. To consolidate and expand them means to strengthen the collective will of the international community and make universal values override short-term national interests.

# 14

# International Lawmaking:
# Towards a New Role for the Security Council?

*Alan Boyle**

## SUMMARY

Climate change represents one of the greatest challenges to international lawmaking the UN has ever faced. It is politically unrealistic to set up a new environmental organization and, on the other hand, the process frequently resorted to in the field of environmental law, namely inclusive consensus, is frequently unattainable. A possible alternative may lie in asking the UN Security Council to legislate on the matter, under its general power to deal with questions relating to the maintenance of peace and security. Admittedly, to give the Security Council an enhanced role as an international legislator in areas such as climate change would be a tenable option only if the process can be legitimized and made generally acceptable to all states. At present it is questionable whether the unreformed Security Council can be said to have the right process to make itself legitimate as a lawmaking body. Whether viewed in terms of accountability, participation, procedural fairness, or transparency of decision-making, it remains a seriously deficient vehicle for the exercise of legislative competence. Nevertheless, this authority could be given to the Council subject to the condition that the involvement and the approval of the General Assembly would be required. Security Council resolutions should be debated and adopted in the General Assembly first, before giving them binding force in the Council. It would also be necessary to maintain and enhance deliberative and transparent processes in both the General Assembly and the Security Council when such resolutions are under discussion but there is no reason why observers and accredited non-governmental organizations (NGOs) should not be involved at this stage as they are in the General Assembly.

---

\* This chapter draws heavily on A. Boyle and C. Chinkin, *The Making of International Law* (Oxford: Oxford University Press, 2007).

## 1. The challenge to international lawmaking, with particular reference to climate change

Climate change represents one of the greatest challenges to international lawmaking the UN has ever faced. Few topics provide a better illustration of the importance of a globally inclusive regulatory regime focused on preventive and precautionary approaches to environmental harm—or of the problems of negotiating one on such a complex subject. It is par excellence a global problem, potentially affecting all states, and for which global solutions are essential. That was the reason for negotiating the two principal multilateral environmental agreements (MEAs) on the subject—the UN Framework Convention on Climate Change (UNFCCC) and the Kyoto Protocol. It was the reason for trying to negotiate a replacement global treaty at Copenhagen in 2009.

The fragmented structure of international lawmaking is obvious when viewed from a climate change perspective. It might be thought that regulation of climate change and the coordination of international lawmaking should therefore be the responsibility of a dedicated international environmental organization. Proposals to create such a body or to turn the United Nations Environment Programme (UNEP) into a UN specialized agency have not so far found the necessary support, but the idea has not gone away and it remains strongly supported by some states, most notably France and Germany. The main arguments in favour are first that its standing, funding, and political influence would be enhanced. Secondly, coordination and policy coherence would be improved if it hosted the secretariats of the major environmental treaties. This, it is said, would reduce overlaps and duplication, while improving effectiveness. Protagonists rightly point to fragmentation of existing structures, the relative weakness of UNEP as the principal UN body with general environmental competence, and the powerful focus the International Monetary Fund (IMF), the World Bank, and the World Trade Organization (WTO) bring to economic development. Several models are canvassed by those in favour. The most radical would merge existing bodies into a powerful new intergovernmental environmental organization with decision-making and enforcement powers. A less radical vision would merge existing environmental institutions and treaties into a new organization similar to the WTO. The least radical choice would simply upgrade UNEP into a UN specialized agency rather like the International Maritime Organization (IMO).

Sceptics remain unconvinced by some of these arguments. To them a new environmental organization is politically unrealistic and would not be any better at securing the necessary decisions. Insofar as reform is necessary to enhance the efficiency of the present eclectic system, they favour a simple clustering of MEAs within UNEP and greater efforts to coordinate international action.[1] A

---

[1] The arguments are comprehensively addressed in F. Biermann and S. Bauer, *A World Environment Organization* (Aldershot: Ashgate, 2005). On clustering see K. von Moltke, in G. Winter (ed.), *Multilevel Governance of Global Environmental Change* (Cambridge: Cambridge University Press, 2006), 409–29.

UN environment agency could not monopolize the field. It could not take over the environmental responsibilities of other specialized agencies, such as the Food and Agriculture Organization (FAO) or IMO: the work of these bodies has an important climate change dimension which cannot be separated from their general responsibilities. Nor is it evident how coordination of environmental treaty regimes would be any easier under a specialized agency than it is at present. States are no more likely to negotiate or revise such agreements under a new agency than they are at present, and the agency could not impose change unless given unusual powers. There may well be efficiencies to be gained from a 'clustering' of secretariat services and non-compliance procedures within UNEP. Certainly, there is a need for a system that can ensure the integration of environmental and development objectives in a more balanced and efficient manner,[2] but a more centralized, bureaucratic, and entrenched institution may be less likely to influence the system as a whole, or to facilitate the cross-sectoral integration that Agenda 21 seeks to promote. It is thus far from obvious that this idea represents a viable alternative to the present system, whether for regulation of climate change or in respect of any other environmental topic. Moreover, it does not overcome the more fundamental systemic problems faced by any attempt to legislate on a globally inclusive basis.

Although international lawmaking often proceeds within the constitutional structures of international organizations, international law itself lacks an identifiable constitutional structure.[3] The lawmaking system is eclectic, unsystematic, overlapping, and often poorly coordinated. The UN is a central element, but by no means the only one, or even the principal one in certain contexts, such as international economic law. Moreover, the UN is not a coherent whole but comprises multiple organs, specialized agencies, working groups, programmes, etc., which operate through various procedures and mechanisms. Constitutionalism, however defined, is not the most obvious perspective from which to address legitimacy in this fragmentary setting, and we have not focused on it as a major element of our analysis.[4] This is not to suggest that we should overlook academic debate about the constitutionalization of particular institutions, most notably the WTO. Nevertheless, none of these bodies, including the WTO, has become part of some separate constitutional order. On the other hand, the existence of multiple institutions promoting international lawmaking within their own specialized areas poses an obvious challenge for the coherence and integrity of international law.

[2] J. Ayling, 'Serving Many Voices: Progressing Calls for an International Environmental Organisation', 9 Journal of Environmental Law (1997) 243–70, at 268; W. Bradnee Chambers (ed), *Reforming International Environmental Governance* (Tokyo: UNU Press, 2005), 13–39.
[3] But there have been many sophisticated attempts to envisage one: see, eg, E. de Wet, 'The International Constitutional Order', 55 ICLQ (2006) 51; D.M. Johnston, in R.St.J. Macdonald and D.M. Johnston (eds), *Towards World Constitutionalism* (Leiden: Martinus Nijhoff, 2005), 3; B. Fassbender, 'The United Nations Charter as Constitution of the International Community', 36 Col JTL (1998) 529–619.
[4] For a powerful but sceptical assessment of the concept see D. Cass, *The Constitutionalisation of the WTO* (Oxford: Oxford University Press, 2005), and more positively N. Walker, 'The EU and the WTO: Constitutionalism in a New Key', in G. de Búrca and J. Scott (eds), *The EU and the WTO: Legal and Constitutional Issues* (Oxford: Oxford University Press, 2001), 31.

It is tempting to suggest that the present international lawmaking 'system'—in reality more bric-a-brac than system—should evolve into something closer to the European Union, the only functioning model of a multilateral legislative system currently available. On that model the UN General Assembly might become the Parliament, the Security Council would be the equivalent of the Council of Ministers, and the Secretariat would perform the functions of the European Commission. Analogies of this kind are potentially misleading, and the context is clearly very different. Nevertheless, the institutions of European lawmaking have themselves evolved, most notably in the present sharing of legislative functions by the Parliament and the Council of Ministers, a power originally exercised by the Council alone. The institutions of international lawmaking also evolve; currently the most important development is the emergence of the Security Council as a significant legislator. How to legitimize and democratize the involvement of such a body is perhaps the most interesting challenge posed in this chapter. One obvious answer might be to accept that the Security Council should be empowered to legislate, but only with the involvement and approval of the General Assembly. Another answer looks to a more democratic composition of the Security Council, a reform mooted by the Secretary-General but not accepted by the General Assembly's 2005 Summit. Both would require a significant reform of the UN Charter, or at least a change in the practice of the two principal organs and the acquiescence of member states to that change, but if carried out would constitute a genuine legislative body. Whether the world needs such an institution is another question, but the point should remind us that the UN's centrality in the present system for international lawmaking has come about despite, not because of, the institutional architecture created in 1945. As Oscar Schachter pointedly observed, 'Neither the United Nations nor any of its specialised agencies was conceived as a legislative body'.[5] This is true insofar as the authority of international organizations to adopt binding rules remains limited. Nevertheless, in the modern world, the United Nations has in practice assumed the role of principal promoter of international lawmaking.

It is potentially well suited for this purpose, for several reasons. First, in the eyes of many member states it has legitimacy. As an intergovernmental organization with universal membership, all states have in theory an equal voice and an equal vote in the General Assembly. Their right to participate in its lawmaking activity is assured. However, as we shall see below, the same cannot be said of the Security Council, nor of other elected bodies with limited membership such as the Human Rights Council established in 2006.[6] Secondly, the UN is a political organization. Deliberation, negotiation, and compromise are its working currency and the principal rationale of its existence. If greater inclusivity and consensus are thereby

---

[5] In C. Joyner (ed.), *The United Nations and International Law* (Cambridge: Cambridge University Press, 1997), 3. See generally P. Szasz, ibid, 27–64; R. Higgins, *The Development of International Law through the Political Organs of the United Nations* (Oxford: Oxford University Press, 1963); J. Alvarez, *International Organizations as Law-Makers* (Oxford: Oxford University Press, 2005).

[6] Membership consists of 47 states elected by the General Assembly taking into account candidates' contribution to 'the promotion and protection of human rights': GA Res. 60/251, 3 April 2006.

facilitated, then global lawmaking is more likely to be successful. Thirdly, it has universal competence. The powers it possesses under the UN Charter embrace, potentially, all areas of political, economic, and social affairs.[7] Some important areas of UN lawmaking, such as human rights, are explicitly envisaged in the Charter. Others, such as suppression of international crime, or the promotion of sustainable development and environmental protection, have emerged through subsequent interpretation to meet the evolving needs of international society. The Charter has proved a very flexible instrument for accommodating such needs.

While the UN General Assembly has no lawmaking power as such, its ability to adopt resolutions, convene lawmaking conferences, and initiate codification projects has given it a central role in the development of international policy and law relating to many aspects of the environment.[8] General Assembly resolutions on such diverse matters as high seas fisheries, the legal status of the deep seabed and outer space, friendly relations between states, and global climate change have influenced the evolution of treaties, general principles, and customary law on these and many other topics. In the environmental field, lawmaking conferences on, inter alia, the Human Environment (Stockholm, 1972), the Law of the Sea (1973–82), Environment and Development (Rio, 1992), and Fish Stocks (New York, 1993–95) have been convened and their results endorsed by the General Assembly. An important component of the Rio Conference was the adoption of the UNFCCC, which has provided the principal institutional architecture for subsequent negotiations, including adoption of the Kyoto Protocol, the Copenhagen Conference in 2009, and the Cancún Conference in late 2010.

Both the UNFCCC and the Kyoto Protocol were negotiated by consensus as an interlocking whole or 'package deal' the integrity of which is protected by a prohibition on reservations—in effect an all or nothing bargain. In essence this meant that there was no voting and a text was adopted only when states no longer had any objections to the deal as a whole. Bringing the negotiations to that stage required delicate diplomacy to produce a deal which balanced the vital interests of all the main groups in the negotiations. Every group of states had to be accommodated in this process—none could be ignored. Powerful states or groups of states could not simply dictate what should be in the treaty without risking ultimate breakdown. The concerns of small or otherwise insignificant states had to be accommodated. This explains the influence of the Association of Small Island States (AOSIS) during the UNFCCC negotiations, but also the need to keep the United States on board. The subsequent ratification of the treaty by nearly all the negotiating parties demonstrates the value of the process and reflects the 'politics of interdependence' that characterize regulation of world trade, the oceans, and the global environment—illustrated in particular by the 1993 Marrakesh Conference which established

---

[7]   UN Charter, Art. 1.
[8]   On the UN's general contribution to international law see Joyner (ed.), n 5, and on the environment see P. Birnie, in A. Roberts and B. Kingsbury (eds), *United Nations, Divided World*, 2nd edn (Oxford: Oxford University Press, 1993), ch. 10.

the WTO, the 1992 Rio Conference on Environment and Development, and the 1973–82 UNCLOS III Conference.

Most modern international lawmaking processes are deliberative and transparent to some degree, and the UNFCCC/Kyoto process is no exception. Deliberation is an essential lubricant of any lawmaking process because it facilitates discussion, negotiation, compromise, persuasion, influence, and participation. It is what allows participants a voice, whether or not they also have a vote. Just as importantly, contemporary international lawmaking has also become generally more transparent than in earlier times. This is partly a consequence of wider participation, but it also reflects a significant change in the way governments and international organizations view their role as international lawmakers. Transparency is an essential ingredient if these institutions are to be made responsive to a wider public. That entails a willingness to facilitate NGO participation, and to publish reports and findings.

Processes of the type just described tend to enhance the legitimacy of what has been agreed and make it more likely that states will comply, but they also make it harder to reach agreement. There is little doubt that it is quicker and easier to negotiate a new text by majority vote, but there is also little point in doing so. If global problems require global solutions then the process must be capable of delivering. Even two-thirds majorities are not enough for that purpose, and that is why the climate regime is not in principle a process of majority decision-making. But if the compromises necessary to engineer consensus cannot be reached then nothing will be agreed, and some way must be found to overcome that outcome. For that reason the option of adopting a text by majority vote is normally retained as a fallback if all else fails.

A consensus procedure therefore has benefits and drawbacks.[9] The success of the procedure, still uncertain in 1982, can be gauged inter alia from its use in negotiating the 1992 Climate Change and Biological Diversity Conventions, the 1994 Uruguay Round agreements establishing the WTO, and many other subsequent agreements. It allows complex, comprehensive, and inclusive agreements to be negotiated, relying on the 'politics of interdependence' that characterizes regulation of world trade, the oceans, or the global environment.[10] At the same time, as the stalemate in WTO negotiations in 2005–09, and the failure of the Copenhagen Climate Change negotiations in 2009 illustrate, consensus requires compromises that may be unobtainable, or may result in a text that is weaker or more ambiguous than might be thought desirable by some states or NGOs. Whether to join in a consensus is thus a potentially delicate decision. A state that refuses to do so may find itself ignored, or it will simply be a tiny minority if it forces matters to a vote. But if its participation is essential to the deal under discussion then other states may have no option but to keep negotiating if stalemate is to be avoided. Thus to stand any chance of success any deal on climate change will have to enjoy

---

[9] See generally, K. Zemanek, 'Majority Rule and Consensus Technique in Law-Making Diplomacy', in R.St.J. Macdonald and D.M. Johnston (eds), *The Structure and Process of International Law* (Dordrecht: Martinus Nijhoff, 1986), 857–87; B. Buzan, 'Negotiating by Consensus: Developments in Technique at the United Nations Conference on the Law of the Sea' 75 AJIL (1981) 324; R. Sabel, *Procedure at International Conferences* (Cambridge: Cambridge University Press, 1997).

[10] Buzan, n 9, 329.

the support of the EU, the United States, China, India, Brazil, Canada, Australia, Japan, the major oil-producing states, the Association of Small Island states, and the grouping of developing states. A simple majority of votes will not be sufficient to produce a globally inclusive outcome.

## 2. UN Security Council lawmaking?

If an inclusive consensus is unattainable, could the UN Security Council become an alternative international legislature in order to fill the vacuum left by any failure in the global lawmaking process? Some authors have used the concept of 'environmental security' to envisage a greater role for the Security Council in dealing with environmental threats and emergencies.[11] The Council has more power, but a narrower role, than the General Assembly. Composed of 15 states, and dominated by the five permanent members, its decisions on measures to restore international peace and security under Chapter VII of the Charter are binding on all UN member states unless vetoed by one of the permanent members.[12] The scope of Security Council powers is plainly confined to the maintenance of international peace and security and the Council must also act within the 'purposes and principles of the UN' (Art. 24 Charter).

Nevertheless, measures to promote environmental protection may in some circumstances be necessary for the maintenance of international peace and security, thus potentially giving the Security Council power to take mandatory action under Chapter VII, but 'the language of the Charter, not to speak of the clear record of the original meaning, does not easily lend itself to such an interpretation'.[13] The Council has acted cautiously in this respect, using its Chapter VII powers only once, to hold Iraq responsible in international law for environmental damage inflicted on Kuwait during the 1991 Gulf War.[14] In 2007 it also held its first ever debate on climate change.

Its post-Cold War practice shows how broad an interpretation can be given to the phrase 'international peace and security',[15] and a purposive construction of the powers of UN principal organs has so far survived all challenges before international courts.[16] Moreover, although the Security Council is not formally a lawmaking body, since 9/11 it has started to use its mandatory powers to adopt a small number of binding resolutions

---

[11] A. Timoshenko, in E. Brown Weiss (ed.), *Environmental Change and International Law* (Tokyo: UNU Press, 1992), ch 13; L. Elliott, 'Expanding the Mandate of the United Nations Security Council' in Chambers (ed.), n 2, 204, but for contrary views see P.C. Szasz, in Brown Weiss (ed.), 359–61; C. Tinker, ' "Environmental Security" in the United Nations: Not a Matter for the Security Council'. 59 Tennessee LR (1992) 787.          [12] UN Charter, Arts 23–5, 27, 41–2.
[13] Szasz, in Brown Weiss (ed.), n 11, 359.          [14] SC Res. 687.
[15] For differing views of the limits to Security Council powers see V. Gowlland-Debbas, 'The Functions of the United Nations Security Council in the International Legal System', and G. Nolte , 'The Limits of the Security Council's Powers and its Functions in the International Legal System', in M. Byers (ed.), *The Role of Law in International Politics* (Oxford: Oxford University Press, 2000).
[16] *Expenses Case, Namibia Case, Lockerbie Cases, Tadić Case*—but ECJ decision in *Kadi* does show that there are limits to the powers of the Security Council.

on anti-terrorism measures laying down general rules for all states.[17] Although such resolutions necessarily have a treaty basis—otherwise they would not be binding—it is usually assumed that they are nevertheless not treaties and states have not sought to register them as such under Article 102 of the UN Charter. Michael Wood rightly notes that many Security Council resolutions are not intended to have legal effects and for that reason cannot be treaties, but he does not explain why those that *are* binding cannot or should not be regarded as treaties. He simply asserts that they are not treaties.[18] He nevertheless relies by analogy on the Vienna Convention as the best source of rules and guidance on interpretation of Security Council resolutions. Does it matter whether we view binding resolutions of international organizations as treaties? Apart from the question of registration, the answer would seem to be no. What does seem clear, however, is that a small number of binding resolutions share the same characteristics as lawmaking treaties and have been adopted for the same purpose.

It is also worth recalling that resolutions were regarded as extensions of the UN Charter in the *Lockerbie Case*—one characteristic feature being that they override other treaties pursuant to Article 103 of the UN Charter. As Kelsen explains: 'The Charter does not provide that decisions...in order to be enforceable must be in conformity with the law which exists at the time they are adopted.'[19] Reviewing Security Council resolutions which expressly or by implication assert priority over other treaties, Bernhardt concludes that 'the principle that binding SC decisions taken under Chapter VII supersede other treaty commitments seems to be generally recognised...'[20] The significance of this conclusion cannot be overestimated. Unlike any other international organization, it gives the Security Council the power to rewrite or dispense with existing international law in particular situations, and possibly in more general terms. Potentially, Security Council resolutions may thus have as great or greater significance than the concept of *ius cogens*.

The Security Council has no express power to legislate and it is doubtful if the drafters intended it to have such a role. Thus the conventional view is that the Security Council 'is not, properly speaking, an organ that creates law', but merely one that interprets and applies existing law.[21] Nevertheless, the capacity to override other treaties and general international law potentially amounts to a claim to formal legislative capacity. Two unprecedented post-9/11 resolutions have shown how the Council can legislate in general terms on matters within its mandate to maintain international peace and security. Security Council Resolutions 1373 (2001) and 1540 (2004) on terrorist financing and proliferation of weapons of mass destruction are clearly lawmaking resolutions and it is not plausible to argue otherwise—they may be unusual and limited precedents, based on a fleeting moment of global

---

[17] SC Ress 1373 (2001) and 1540 (2005) both Chapter VII resolutions passed in the aftermath of the 9/11 attacks in New York and Washington and later atrocities. See below.

[18] M. Wood, 'The Interpretation of Security Council Resolutions', 2 Max Planck YB of UN Law (1998) 73, 79.

[19] H. Kelsen, *The Law of the United Nations* (New York: Praeger, 1950), 294–5.

[20] In B. Simma (ed.), *The Charter of the United Nations*, 2nd edn (Oxford: Oxford University Press, 2002), 455. See also T. Sato, 'The Legitimacy of Security Council Activities', in J.-M. Coicaud and V. Heiskanen, *The Legitimacy of International Organisations* (Tokyo: UNU Press, 2001), 309, 321–3.          [21] M.P. de Brichambaut, in Byers (ed.), n 15, 275. See also Wood, n 18, 73, 79.

consensus and never to be repeated, but they do lay down general rules applicable to all states and they are binding by virtue of Article 25 of the Charter.

In Resolution 1373 (2001) the Security Council decided that states must take a range of anti-terrorist activities, including prevention and suppression of the financing of terrorism; refraining from any form of support for persons involved in terrorism; providing early warning to states by exchange of information; denying safe havens to those who finance, plan, support, or commit terrorist acts; and affording the greatest measure of assistance in criminal investigations. Such obligations would previously have been adopted by treaty, leaving states free to participate or not. The resolution calls upon (although it does not require) states to become parties to the 1999 Convention for the Suppression of the Financing of Terrorism,[22] the provisions of which are in significant respects similar to those found in Resolution 1373. States are required to report to a Counter-Terrorism Committee explaining how they have implemented the resolution. The Committee may take further measures where it deems the response to be inadequate. Yet the resolution provides no definition of international terrorism, which had long been debated within the United Nations and other international arenas. In effect this Security Council committee makes authoritative determinations on what constitutes international terrorism and adequate steps to counter it. All UN member states must comply with these decisions.

In Resolution 1540 (2004) the Council again legislated in general terms to ensure that non-state actors are prevented from obtaining nuclear, chemical, or biological weapons. Implementation is also monitored by the Security Council. Resolution 1540 adds to rather than changes existing treaty law. Its terms expressly disavow any conflict with the rights or obligations of state parties to the Nuclear Non-proliferation Treaty, the Chemical Weapons Convention, and the Biological and Toxic Weapons Convention, and it leaves unchanged the responsibilities of the International Atomic Energy Agency (IAEA) and the Organization for the Prohibition of Chemical Weapons (OPCW).

The exercise of what might be termed legislative or quasi-legislative power by the Security Council is not unproblematic, and the objections should not be underestimated.[23] Pushed too far, its legislative actions may quickly lose acceptability among the wider community of states and challenges to their validity may be an inevitable response.[24] Thus to give the Council an enhanced role as an international legislator in areas such as climate change would be a tenable option only if the process can be legitimized and made generally acceptable to all states. At present it is questionable whether the unreformed Security Council can be said to have the right process to make itself legitimate as a lawmaking body. Whether viewed in terms of accountability, participation, procedural fairness, or transparency of decision-making, it remains a seriously deficient vehicle for the exercise of legislative competence. It presents a stark contrast to consensus treaty negotiations like UNCLOS or the International

---

[22] The Convention did not enter into force until 10 April 2002. See P. Szasz, 'The Security Council Starts Legislating', 96 AJIL (2002) 901, 903.

[23] M. Happold, 'SC Resolution 1373 and the Constitution of the UN', 13 Leiden JIL (2003) 593.

[24] See D. Caron, 'The Legitimacy of the Security Council', 87 AJIL (1993) 552 and Szasz, n 22.

Criminal Court, or to the adoption of resolutions by the General Assembly. The vast majority of General Assembly member states would in effect be excluded from the lawmaking process. This may be justifiable in cases where urgent action is required to maintain or restore peace and security, but should the General Assembly be excluded even when less urgent lawmaking is undertaken? Further resort to Chapter VII lawmaking would also evade national control over the process of treaty ratification and may on that basis be regarded as undemocratic. It has already encountered problems of acceptability before other courts.[25] For all these reasons expansive use of Chapter VII powers by an unreformed Security Council is more likely to be resisted by some states regardless of the binding character of these resolutions.

The problems are obvious if we consider current Security Council membership from the perspective of major GHG emissions: the United States, China, and Russia are already on the Council, but India and Brazil are not permanent members. The EU is fully represented only if the United Kingdom, France, and the one other EU member state on the Council can present a coordinated European position. Most of the other GHG emitters and oil-producing states are only represented in the General Assembly: a Security Council lawmaking process would have to involve General Assembly participation to be inclusive.

But if we get the process right then the Council could and should be seen as an appropriate and legitimate forum for international lawmaking when the need arises. It could thus be one way of breaking any deadlock in UNFCCC negotiations. In this context legitimacy, constitutionality, and process are intimately connected. The most effective way to engage in Security Council lawmaking would be to ensure that such resolutions are debated and adopted in the General Assembly first—before giving them binding force in the Security Council.[26] It would also be necessary to maintain and enhance deliberative and transparent processes in both the General Assembly and the Council when such resolutions are under discussion but there is no reason why observers and accredited NGOs should not be involved at this stage as they are in the General Assembly.

A process of this type may slow down the adoption of binding law by the Security Council, but that would be a small price to pay for greater acceptability and legitimacy. It would reflect the needs of global governance by promoting greater accountability, openness, and inclusivity in the way the Council carries out a lawmaking function—and would ensure that Security Council lawmaking rests on a broader consensus than at present by involving the General Assembly. It would give both bodies acting together the chance to impose greater coherence in a decentralized lawmaking system which currently lacks any institution capable of doing so and to make law in areas of pressing concern—such as terrorism or climate change—if necessary against the wishes of a minority of dissenting states, leaving no room for opt-outs, persistent objectors, or reservations. Such a joint lawmaking

---

[25] Joined Cases C-402/05 P and C-415/05 P, *Yassin Abdullah Kadi and Al Barakaat International Foundation v Council of the European Union and Commission of the European Communities*, ECJ (2008).

[26] On possible ways of involving the General Assembly in Security Council decisions see Caron, n 24, at 575–6, and Happold, n 23.

procedure could be implemented without revising the Charter—although changing membership and voting rights in the Security Council would require Charter amendment.

There are some obvious advantages to the Security Council making law by resolution, rather than the more formal processes of negotiation through the General Assembly or a treaty conference. First, where there is political support within the Council it can quickly produce universal and immediately binding obligations in a manner that no treaty negotiation or General Assembly resolution could replicate.[27] The Council can if necessary act in days. In the period after 9/11 this evidently appeared to be a more appropriate and effective lawmaking process in a situation of immediate threat to peace and security. Secondly, all UN member states are bound to comply with Chapter VII resolutions—there is no room for the opt-outs, reservations, or non-participation that bedevil many multilateral treaties. Thirdly, as we saw above, such resolutions prevail over other international agreements—they do not have to conform to existing general international law. Security Council lawmaking could thus enhance the coherence of international law if used appropriately. To that extent the Council could become an instrument of law reform, overcoming the problem of the 'persistent objector' in customary law and the 'free rider' in multilateral treaties.

Are there any limits on the power of the Security Council to take binding decisions? Herein lies a profound debate on the constitutional limits of an admittedly powerful institution. It is not necessary to explore this debate in depth here,[28] but some understanding of the issues is necessary because they impact directly on the lawmaking potential of the Council. The Council does not have absolute power; two obvious limitations are suggested by the wording of the Charter itself. First, Article 24 provides expressly that in carrying out its duties the Security Council 'shall act in accordance with the Purposes and Principles of the United Nations',[29] while Article 25 refers to the obligation of member states to 'accept and carry out the decisions of the Security Council in accordance with the present Charter'. Delbruck gives this phrase a narrow reading limited to procedural compliance with the Charter,[30] but as Martenczuk argues, the treatment by the International Court of Justice (ICJ) of the *Lockerbie* cases suggests that it has 'resisted all attempts to remove Chapter VII of the Charter from the ambit of legal interpretation'.[31] It might thus be argued that the Council's assumption of a more general lawmaking authority under Chapter VII falls outside the substantive scope of its powers as intended by the negotiators of the Charter.[32] More probably, however, the

---

[27] The General Assembly adopted resolutions on terrorism in 1994 and 1996: see GA Res. 49/60, 9 December 1994 and GA Res. 51/210, 17 December 1996, respectively.

[28] The literature is extensive. See T. Franck, 'Who is the Ultimate Guardian of UN Legality?', 86 AJIL (1992) 519; V. Gowlland-Debbas, 'The Relationship between the ICJ and the Security Council', 88 AJIL (1994) 643; J. Alvarez, 'Judging the Security Council', 90 AJIL (1996) 1; D. Akande, 'The ICJ and the Security Council', 46 ICLQ (1997) 309.

[29] See ICTY, Appeals Chamber *Prosecutor v Tadić* decision of 2 October 1995, paras 28–9.

[30] In Simma, n 20, 455.

[31] B. Martenczuk, 'The Security Council, the International Court and Judicial Review', 10 EJIL (1999) 517.                    [32] See M. Happold, n 23.

purposive reading of the Charter adopted by the ICJ in the *Certain Expenses* case[33] would lend support to the Council's lawmaking activities so long as they can reasonably be related to the maintenance or restoration of international peace and security under Article 39.[34] We saw earlier how the Council has made generous use of Chapter VII, asserting the right to act even in respect of internal humanitarian crises, civil war, governmental breakdown, or racist oppression. In some of these cases the threat to 'international peace and security' is tenuous. Given the breadth of the discretion afforded to the Council, however, it is not surprising that judicial decisions have shown considerable deference to its political judgments and treated its decisions as presumptively valid.[35] Nevertheless, it is possible that the legality of a resolution could be challenged on the ground that it is far removed from peace and security.

A second limitation may flow from the concept of *jus cogens*. Some of the Council's resolutions relating to the war in Bosnia have been challenged on this basis because, it was argued, they facilitated genocide by denying Bosnia the right to defend itself.[36] This argument would at least support the conclusion that Council resolutions cannot legitimize torture, genocide, war crimes, or any other activity falling within the narrow category of *jus cogens* presently supported by judicial decisions. In the context of possible Security Council action against international terrorism these may prove to be significant limitations.

More questionably, it might be argued that in using its powers the Council must respect general international law. A possible example is the *Tadić* case, which addresses human rights limitations on the Council's power to establish criminal tribunals. However, interpreting and applying Council resolutions in accordance with human rights law, or with other relevant rules of international law, does not tell us that the Council cannot lawfully pass resolutions inconsistent with general international law; it merely compels it to do so in appropriate terms. More pertinently, it has been suggested that the Council cannot force states to agree to third party settlement of disputes, or impose territorial boundaries, or compel states to extradite suspected terrorists, because to do so would be inconsistent with existing law, procedural due process, or treaty commitments.[37] If that were correct, then the Council's power to legislate generally about such matters would be similarly constrained. It is doubtful that this is a good argument, however. In Resolution 687 the Council carefully refrained from imposing a boundary on Iraq, but it is not clear that its reasons for doing so were constitutional rather than political.[38] In *Lockerbie* incompatibility with an existing treaty did not persuade the ICJ to

---

[33] ICJ Reports 1962, 151.

[34] UN Charter, Art. 39. See F. Kirgis, 'The Security Council's First 50 Years', 89 AJIL (1995) 506, 520–8.

[35] *Namibia Advisory Opinion*, ICJ Reports 1971, 16, para. 20; *Prosecutor v Tadić* n 29, para. 29.

[36] See *Prevention and Punishment of the Crime of Genocide*, ICJ Reports 1993, 3, especially the Separate Opinion of Judge Lauterpacht.

[37] I. Brownlie, 'The Decisions of Political Organs of the United Nations and the Rule of Law', in R. Macdonald (ed.), *Essays in Honour of Wang Tieya* (Dordrecht: Martinus Nijhoff, 1993), 91.

[38] M. Mendelson and S. Hulton, 'The Iraq–Kuwait Boundary', 64 BYBIL (1993) 135, 144–50.

restrain implementation of a Council resolution regarded by the court as prima facie valid.[39]

Moreover, if the Council is bound to act within existing international law then its power to act at all will be severely compromised and open to challenge in most, if not all, cases. Why, for example, should a state which claims to be acting lawfully in self-defence pay any attention to a resolution imposing a ceasefire? Why should it evacuate territory it believes to be lawfully its own, however implausibly? Why should it do anything that general international law does not already require or empower it to do? On that basis the Council would find itself constantly embroiled in endless arguments about the legality of its decisions, with serious consequences for its effectiveness. This outcome is a recipe for emasculation, and appears inconsistent with Article 103 of the UN Charter as interpreted by the ICJ. It is unlikely to appeal to any international tribunal. In his classic work on the United Nations, Kelsen concluded that 'The Charter does not provide that decisions…in order to be enforceable must be in conformity with the law which exists at the time they are adopted.'[40]

A UN more committed to the more effective exercise of collective responsibility could scarcely avoid enhancing its own lawmaking role. In this context there is a clear need openly to consider the way the Security Council makes new law and whether and how it should continue to do so. It seems unlikely that the Council will be called upon to legislate for climate change in the near future. Nevertheless, like climate change itself, it is far better to ponder the problems now and adopt a precautionary approach to solving them before they become insoluble. What the example does show, however, is the dynamic character and diversity of contemporary international lawmaking.

---

[39] (Provisional Measures) ICJ Reports 1992, 114.
[40] Kelsen, n 19, 294–5.

# PART III

# CAN INTERNATIONAL LEGAL IMPERATIVES BE MORE EFFECTIVELY BROUGHT INTO EFFECT?

# 15

# Towards a Moderate Monism: Could International Rules Eventually Acquire the Force to Invalidate Inconsistent National Laws?

*Antonio Cassese*

## SUMMARY

International law still proves unable effectively to bring about the necessary changes of domestic legislation at odds with international rules. Four measures would be necessary to change this state of affairs. Two of them would operate at the international level only: (i) there should be an international judicial body (endowed with compulsory jurisdiction) charged with authoritatively establishing (a) whether in a specific instance a state has breached a rule imposing to amend national legislation so as to make it consistent with international rules and (b) in the affirmative, enjoining the state to modify its legislation forthwith. The power to set in motion proceedings before such a court should be granted not only to all parties to a multilateral treaty and any international body monitoring the implementation of the treaty, but also to any natural or legal person showing a direct legal interest in the implementation of the international rule; (ii) a monitoring body should be entrusted with ascertaining whether the state has followed up that ruling. Two other sets of devices would instead function at the domestic level; they would be more incisive: (i) states should pass a constitutional provision stating that any time a national piece of legislation is in conflict with an international norm, such legislation is automatically repealed or, at a minimum, courts, administrative bodies, and individuals are bound to disregard it, and (ii) whenever there is a doubt or a dispute on whether national legislation conforms to international rules, national courts as well as natural and legal persons should be empowered to bring the case before an international court, tasked to pass on the matter with legally binding effect. However, the current condition of the world community renders the implementation of the suggested reforms very difficult. Based on the experience of some regional courts, it is suggested that any progress may only occur within regional groupings, not at the universal level.

## 1. Introductory remarks: international rules prevail over contrary national laws

One of the various thorny problems that international law has to face is the relative impermeability of national systems to international legal imperatives: many states fail to translate *international rules* into *national* legislative commands so as to make those rules operational. Too often states do not pass legislation in order to comply with international rules or, when under their constitution such legislation is not needed (because international rules are automatically incorporated into domestic law), they simply ignore them. How does the international legal system cope with this problem?

It is a truism that when an international rule expressly or implicitly imposes upon a state the obligation to change a law in order to comply with that rule, the state is duty-bound to put in place all the international procedures necessary to repeal or amend the law. The Permanent Court of International Justice (PCIJ) put it pithily in its Advisory Opinion of 21 February 1925 on *Exchange of Greek and Turkish Populations*: it spoke of

a principle which is self-evident, according to which a state which has contracted valid international obligations is bound to make in its legislation such modifications as may be necessary to ensure the fulfilment of the obligations undertaken. (Series B, no. 10, at 20)

A closely connected principle is that a state may not invoke the status of its legislation to justify its failure to fulfil an international obligation: Article 27 of the 1969 Vienna Convention on the Law of Treaties codifies this principle ('A party may not invoke the provisions of its internal law as justification for its failure to perform a treaty. This rule is without prejudice to article 46' [on the possible invalidity of a treaty for the breach of the internal law of a contracting state regarding competence to conclude treaties]).

However, too often the aforementioned 'self-evident principle' is not abided by and international rules remain a dead letter. I propose to discuss the principle first from a *historical* perspective and then from a *theoretical* viewpoint. I will then try to suggest a possible way forward.

## 2. The primacy of international rules in historical and theoretical perspective

If the above 'principle' is looked at in its historical context, it appears that in the old international community, where the so-called Westphalian model prevailed, generally speaking states were not interested in the national legislation of other states per se, unless such legislation led to a violation of a foreign state's right. A state had no authority to call upon another state to bring its legislation into line with international rules, unless a *private interest* of the former state was at stake. And when national laws in some way breached the right of another state, this state was only interested in the cessation of the breach, which did not necessarily lead to the repeal or modification of the whole piece of relevant legislation. If the breach was not terminated the aggrieved state could set in motion the law of state responsibility and thus either request reparation or, if need be, take sanctions—an occurrence that realistically could not materialize if the victim country was a small or middle state and the delinquent party was a major political and military power.

Luckily, things have changed in the new international community, under the so-called UN Charter model. Now, international multilateral conventions often impose on contracting states not only the obligation to change their legislation so as to make it consistent with the provisions of the convention; they also set up a mechanism to supervise compliance by contracting states with their international obligations, including that of modifying domestic legislation. If a state party does not implement its obligations, the supervisory mechanism is empowered to issue exhortations, recommendations, moral and political censure, and so on. Sometimes the collective body also has the right to demand of state parties the repeal or change of their national legislation in order for it to be consonant with the convention's provisions.

As noted in another chapter in this volume (Chapter 24), the need for such supervisory mechanisms has been motivated by the fact that modern treaties normally do not necessarily protect reciprocal interests; they often safeguard community concerns (frequently in addition to reciprocal interests): this applies in particular to conventions on human rights, on the environment, and similar matters. Since normally any contracting party has no direct and immediate interest of its own in the implementation of the convention (eg it has no direct interest in a contracting state refraining from ill-treating its nationals), a collective body is established to take care of the matter, in the interest of the whole collectivity of contracting states.

One should not, however, be unmindful of the major limit of such 'collective' action: it is unable effectively to lead a recalcitrant state to change its laws.

The legal principle embodied in the dictum of the PCIJ cited above has also been the occasion for an interesting debate on the relationship between international law and domestic legal systems: we can thus move to a brief theoretical discussion of this thorny matter. For the supporters of the 'dualist' or 'pluralist'[1] theory, that dictum proves beyond any doubt that international law makes up a legal system that is totally separate and distinct from domestic legal orders, which

---

[1] The term 'dualist' was first suggested by A. Verdross in 1914 ('Zur Konstruktion des Völkerrechts', 8 Zeitschrift für Völkerrecht (1914), 334–5, 337, 359). See also A. Verdross, *Die Einheit des rechtlichen Weltbildes auf Grundlage der Völkerrechtsverfassung* (Tübingen: J.C.B. Mohr (Paul Siebeck), 1923), at VI. In 1927 Verdross, however, regretted having proposed that expression, and pointed out that it would have been more appropriate to speak of a 'pluralist construction of law' ('Le fondement du droit international', 16 HR (1927) at 289). As for the supporters of the pluralist view, it may suffice to refer to H. Triepel, 'Les rapports entre le droit interne et le droit international', 1 HR (1923) at 79–195; D. Anzilotti, *Cours de droit international*, vol. 1 (Paris: Sirey, 1929), 49–65.

are autonomous from international law, have their own subjects and sources of law, and can abide by international imperatives only if domestic authorities decide so. It follows, among other things, that international law cannot as such quash or invalidate a national piece of legislation contrary to international rules. If such inconsistency arises, international law can only enjoin a state to change its legislation, and it will be for such state to decide whether or not to comply, and, in the affirmative, through which domestic mechanisms.

The legal principle under discussion has been viewed in a different way by a leading international lawyer, Alfred Verdross. Criticizing the approach of his mentor, Hans Kelsen, the author of the 'monistic' conception, Verdross rightly emphasized as crucial an issue already dealt with by Kelsen, noting that admittedly the international legal system is unable to render null and void national legislative or administrative acts contrary to international rules. Contrasting his 'moderate monism' to the 'extreme legal monism' advocated by Kelsen, Verdross emphasized that international law acknowledges the relative autonomy of national legal systems. For Verdross the fact remains, however, that international treaties (and customary rules) are 'superior' to national legal systems, and domestic procedures are subjected to international law: compliance by a contracting state with a treaty (or a customary rule) is subject to scrutiny by the aggrieved state and indeed if a dispute is brought before an international court, the relevant international rule will always be found to override the contrary domestic legislation. It follows, according to that prominent international lawyer, that national law cannot but produce its effects within the framework established by international law.[2]

I will not engage in a theoretical discussion of the conflict between the two theories (the 'dualist' or 'pluralist', on the one hand, and the 'moderate monist', on the other). It may suffice here to point out that the former approach in the end propounds a picture of legal systems *juxtaposed* to one another. Instead, the latter theory better expresses the notion that international rules are *superimposed* upon and should prevail over national domestic orders. In short, it is more internationally oriented. However, its drawback is that it remains at the level of aspiration. In fact, it turns a blind eye to the reality of sovereign states' recalcitrance to obey international commands in their daily dealings and accordingly change their laws to meet international requirements. The international legal system is still powerless in its endeavour to penetrate national legal systems and make its commands operative there. If it is a bilateral treaty protecting interests of mutual concern to two states that imposes on the parties the requirement to change their national legislation, each party will do so under the impetus of *reciprocity*. If the treaty is multilateral but protects reciprocal interests, or such interests are solely taken into account at the level of customary law, only the state that is injured by the lack of

---

[2] A. Verdross, *Die Einheit des rechtlichen Weltbildes auf Grundlage der Völkerrechtsverfassung*, n 1, 126–35, 159–71; 'Le fondement du droit international', n 1, 287–96; 'Coïncidences: deux théories du droit des gens apparues à l'époque de la création de l'Académie de droit international', in *Livre jubilaire de l'Académie de droit international—1923–1973* (Leiden: Sijthoff, 1973), at 86–9.

change in the legislation of another state will set in motion mechanisms, if any, for inducing compliance with the obligation. If the multilateral treaty or the customary rule protects *community* concerns, in practice no state will demand that another contracting state change its legislation. True, as noted above, whenever there exists a collective body charged with monitoring respect for the treaty, it will be for such mechanism to prompt the failing state to live up to its obligations. This, however, only applies to *some* multilateral treaties and in addition, as mentioned above, monitoring mechanisms have no enforcement power. Even when a *private interest* of a state is infringed by foreign internationally unlawful legislation, few aggrieved states—particularly if they are minor countries facing major powers—will set in motion an enforcement mechanism.

In short, in actual practice international law still proves unable effectively to bring about the necessary changes of domestic legislation at odds with international rules.

## 3. What would be needed to improve upon the current state of affairs

Four things would be necessary to change this state of affairs. Two sets of measures would operate at the international level only and would prove—at least in some respects—to be less audacious. Two other sets of devices would instead be more incisive and function at the domestic level.

Let us first consider the international mechanisms. For one thing, there should be an international judicial body (endowed with compulsory jurisdiction) charged with authoritatively establishing (i) whether in a specific instance a state has breached a rule expressly or implicitly requiring to amend national legislation so as to make it consistent with international rules and (ii) in the affirmative, enjoining the state to modify its legislation forthwith. The power to set in motion proceedings before such a court should be granted not only to all parties to a multilateral treaty and any international body monitoring the implementation of the treaty, but also to any natural or legal person showing a direct legal interest in the implementation of the international rule. This broadening of the range of subjects entitled to institute proceedings would *a fortiori* be required when the implementation of a customary rule were at stake, and it might therefore happen that no other state has a private interest in the implementation of that rule.

Secondly, a monitoring body should be entrusted with ascertaining whether the state has followed up that ruling and, if it has not, exposing this failure and restating the obligation to revise national legislation.

The limit of these two measures lies in the fact that any change in national laws still remains contingent upon the will of the failing state. If such a state persists in its failure to adjust its national legal system to international rules, no action can be taken to prompt it to do so against its will. A more effective action can be taken at the national level, provided of course that it is undertaken, if not by all states of the world, at least by the overwhelming majority of them. Two main measures could be envisaged.

First, it would be necessary for states to pass a constitutional provision stating that whenever a national piece of legislation is in conflict with an international norm (be it customary or conventional), such legislation is automatically repealed or, at a minimum, courts, administrative bodies and individuals are bound to disregard it.

This action could be accompanied by another measure, to take account of the difficulty of establishing the scope and purport of international customary rules as well as the fact that some treaty provisions lend themselves to conflicting interpretations, and, in addition, national laws themselves may be susceptible to more than one construction. Whenever there is a doubt or a dispute on whether national legislation conforms to international rules, national courts as well as natural and legal persons should be empowered to bring the case before an international court, tasked to pass on the matter with legally binding effect. In these cases, if the matter has been referred to the international institution by a national court, proceedings before such court would be suspended until the international ruling is made.

In sum, a change in international legal mechanisms would not suffice. What would ideally be needed is a combination of international and national measures designed to bring about the implementation of the tenets of moderate monism, that is, true superiority of international law over national legal systems.

Clearly, putting into effect the measures just mentioned could only be predicated on a dramatic change in the domestic and international ethos—a process which is likely to occur only over many decades.

## 4. Are there institutions that have already taken the right path towards alignment of domestic law with international rules?

While, as I have just noted, the realization of the necessary international and national institutions to ensure full international superiority is a long shot, it is worth establishing whether some steps have already been taken in the right direction and, if so, what could be done to make them more effective.

Novel measures have indeed already been carried out, but only *within a regional context*. It may suffice to mention, for Europe, the Court of Justice of the European Union and the European Court of Human Rights, as well as for Latin America, the Inter-American Court of Human Rights. In addition, these are all *international* mechanisms that have been instituted. At the national level very few states have adopted constitutional provisions automatically incorporating international rules into their legal systems and in addition granting such incorporated rules higher standing than their domestic legislation.[3]

---

[3] Some states (eg Germany, Italy) automatically incorporate international customary rules solely but confer a higher status than legislative acts on them. Other states (eg Spain, the Netherlands) provide for the automatic incorporation of treaties duly ratified and approved by Parliament (whenever

I propose briefly to take a critical look at some aspects of these institutions.

## (A) The Court of Justice of the European Union

It is common knowledge that this Court, which operates within the 27-member European Union and only with regard to the relatively *limited matters* subjected to its jurisdiction, has, among other things, the power to find that a national law or some of its provisions are contrary to EC rules. In this case the state is required to revise or amend the law.[4] By virtue of the ratification of the relevant EU treaties,

---

this is needed), and also grant them supra-legislative value. Very few states have constitutions referring both to customary and treaty law: see, eg, Greece and Russia.

Article 28(1) of the 1975 Greek Constitution provides that

> The generally recognised rules of international law, as well as international conventions
> as of the time they are sanctioned by statute and become operative according to their
> respective conditions, shall be an integral part of domestic Greek law and shall prevail
> over any contrary provision of the law. The rules of international law and of international
> conventions shall be applicable to aliens only under the condition of reciprocity.

Article 15(1) of the 1993 Russian Constitution stipulates that

> The commonly recognized principles and norms of the international law and the inter-
> national treaties of the Russian Federation shall be a component part of its legal system. If
> an international treaty of the Russian Federation stipulates other rules than those stipu-
> lated by the law, the rules of the international treaty shall apply.

[4] In many rulings the ECJ has asserted the primacy of EU law over national law in relation to
matters covered by the Treaties. Eg see *Costa v ENEL*, judgment of 15 July 1964, Legal Grounds. The
Court said:

> By contrast with ordinary international treaties, the EEC Treaty has created its own legal
> system which, on the entry into force of the Treaty, became an integral part of the legal
> systems of the Member States and which their courts are bound to apply. By creating a
> Community of unlimited duration, having its own institutions, its own personality, its
> own legal capacity and capacity of representation on the international plane and, more
> particularly, real powers stemming from a limitation of sovereignty or a transfer of powers
> from the States to the Community, the Member States have limited their sovereign rights,
> albeit within limited fields, and have thus created a body of law which binds both their
> nationals and themselves. The integration into the laws of each Member State of provi-
> sions which derive from the Community, and more generally the terms and the spirit of
> the Treaty, make it impossible for the States, as a corollary, to accord precedence to a uni-
> lateral and subsequent measure over a legal system accepted by them on a basis of reciproc-
> ity. Such a measure cannot therefore be inconsistent with that legal system. The executive
> force of Community law cannot vary from one State to another in deference to subsequent
> domestic laws, without jeopardizing the attainment of the objectives of the Treaty set out
> in Article 5 (2) and giving rise to the discrimination prohibited by Article 7.

See also *Amministrazione delle Finanze dello Stato v Simmenthal SPA*, judgment of 9 March 1978,
paras 13–24 (at para. 21 the Court said:

> It follows from the foregoing that every national court must, in a case within its jurisdic-
> tion, apply Community law in its entirety and protect rights which the latter confers on
> individuals and must accordingly set aside any provision of national law which may con-
> flict with it, whether prior or subsequent to the Community rule'); *R v Secretary of State
> for Transport, ex p Factortame Ltd and others*, judgment of 19 June 1990, paras 18–22 (at
> para. 21 the Court stated that 'the full effectiveness of Community law would be just as
> much impaired if a rule of national law could prevent a court seised of a dispute governed
> by Community law from granting interim relief in order to ensure the full effectiveness of
> the judgment to be given on the existence of the rights claimed under Community law. It
> follows that a court which in those circumstances would grant interim relief, if it were not

each member state has attached automatic binding effects to the Court's judgments within the legal system of each of such states, thereby ensuring that such rulings are duly complied with. Nevertheless, if a state fails to abide by the Court's judgments, the Court may act again, pursuant to Article 228 and, if it finds that the member state concerned has not complied with its judgment 'may impose a lump sum or penalty payment on it'. The practice of the Court has proved that the system works well and is effective in bringing about the necessary changes in national legislation.

## (B) The European Court of Human Rights

At first sight the 1950 European Convention on Human Rights meets most of the conditions I mentioned above for a full adjustment of national law to international rules in a *broad field*: human rights. The Convention is a typical treaty imposing community-oriented *erga omnes* obligations: each of the 47 contracting states undertakes to respect human rights in territories subject to its jurisdiction, to the benefit not only of its nationals but also of all individuals, whatever their nationality, falling under its jurisdiction. This obligation entails that contracting states must not only treat individuals consistently with the Convention but also change the national legal system in such a way as to live up to all the Convention's provisions. The European Court of Human Rights, which can be triggered by states or by the victim of an alleged breach of the Convention, ensures that the state complained of remedies the breach. Under Article 46(1) 'The High Contracting Parties undertake to abide by the final judgment of the Court in any case to which they are parties'. Under Article 46(2) 'The final judgment of the Court shall be transmitted to the Committee of Ministers, which shall supervise its execution'. Thus, another body, the Committee of Ministers, through a specialized sub-body, monitors respect for the Court's rulings, can call upon the failing state to heed those rulings, and also has some forms of 'sanctions' at its disposal. One would think that, pursuant to these provisions, each contracting state must not only change its legislation whenever it is inconsistent with the provisions, but also, if it fails to do so, the Court can enjoin it to make the necessary changes subject to the supervision of the Committee of Ministers.

Alas, in actual fact even the Convention and its supervisory bodies have not succeeded in breaking new ground and setting a seminal precedent. Indeed, Article 41 of the Convention stipulates that

If the Court finds that there has been a violation of the Convention or the protocols thereto, and if the internal law of the High Contracting Party concerned allows only partial reparation to be made, the Court shall, if necessary, afford just satisfaction to the injured party.[5]

---

for a rule of national law, is obliged to set aside that rule'); *Peterbroeck, Van Campenhout & Cie SCS v Belgian State*, judgment of 14 December 1995, paras 12–22.

[5] How the provision was born is worth a brief reminder. When the powers of the Court were discussed in the Council of Europe Consultative Assembly, it was held that the Court should be endowed with extensive powers, including that of requesting the amendment of laws (eg the French

This provision leaves a huge loophole in the whole implementation system of the Convention. The provision lends itself to two different interpretations. One could first construe it to the effect that the Court, once it has made a finding of a breach of the Convention (eg on account of inhuman or degrading treatment of detainees, or of unlawful deprivation of the life of individuals by enforcement agents, or of a denial of fair trial, or for implementing national legal provisions that run counter to the Convention), may enjoin the state concerned to take all measures necessary to repair the damage (repeal of the inconsistent law, arrest and prosecution of the responsible state officials, adoption of judicial measures aimed at making good the denial of justice, and so on). Whenever the domestic measures necessary to remedy the breach of the Convention require a change in legislation, the Court may request such change, pending which it can order the state to pay to the victim 'just satisfaction'.

Under a different, less liberal and more sovereignty-oriented construction, once it has satisfied itself that the Convention has been contravened, the Court can make such a finding and, without going into the specific national (legislative, administrative, or judicial) measures to be taken to make reparation, can grant 'just satisfaction' to the victim.

Regretfully, from the outset the Court has chosen the second interpretation and is continuing to do so.[6] This unfortunate state of affairs is somewhat attenuated in

---

MP Teitgen said: '[The Court] could set aside governmental decisions, and legislative, administrative or legal measures which were clearly contrary to the principle of the guaranteed rights', in *Collected Edition of the Travaux Préparatoires*, vol. 1 (The Hague: Martinus Nijhoff, 1975), at 48. The British MP Foster held that 'The Court can prescribe measures of reparation, or it may require that the State concerned shall take penal or administrative action in regard to the persons responsible for the infringement, or it may demand the repeal, cancellation or amendment of the Act', ibid, at 94. These suggestions were substantially upheld in Art. 23 of the Report submitted by Mr Teitgen on 5 September 1949 (ibid, at 212). There was no objection in the first session of the Consultative Assembly (see *Collected Edition of the Travaux Préparatoires*, vol. II, at 126 and 218). However, in the Committee of Experts that was called upon to review the initial draft, in the sitting of 7 February 1950 the Italian expert, Mr Perassi, proposed what in substance became (after some changes) the present Art. 41 (see *Travaux Préparatoires of the European Convention on Human Rights*, vol. 3, at 228–30). The proposed Art. G stipulated as follows:

> If the Court finds that a decision or a measure taken by a legal authority, or any other authority of one of the Contracting parties, is completely or partially opposed to the obligations arising from the present Convention, and if *the constitutional law of the said party* only allows the consequences of this decision or measure to be imperfectly repaired, the decision of the Court shall, if necessary, accord just satisfaction to the injured party. (emphasis added)

However, in the event the Drafting Sub-Committee adopted the text as Art. 28, but the expression 'the constitutional law' was replaced by 'the internal law' (see ibid at 232 and 246). In the second session of the Consultative Assembly the text was endorsed by the Italian MP Azara (*Travaux Préparatoires of the European Convention on Human Rights*, vol. 5, at 248), but was harshly attacked by the French MP Teitgen (ibid, at 300–92).

[6] As for cases where the Court found that a national law was in breach of the European Convention, see among others *Marckx v Belgium* (1979), para. 31; *Airey v Ireland* (1979), para. 26; *X and Y v Netherlands* (1985), para. 23; *Castello Roberts v United Kingdom* (1993), para. 53; *A v United Kingdom* (1998), para. 22; *Goodwin v United Kingdom* (2002), para. 18; *MC v Bulgaria* (2003), para. 153; *Babylonova v Slovakia* (2008), para. 51; *I v Finland* (2009), paras 47–8; *Ku v Finland* (2009), para. 46.

two respects. First, in a few instances the Court has indeed indicated the specific measures to be taken by the respondent state to remedy the breach.[7] Secondly, the Committee of Ministers, through a subsidiary body,[8] has somehow tried to substitute for the lack of specificity of the Court's determinations, and called upon states to comply with judgments.[9]

Faced with this condition, some member states that uphold the rule of law at the international level as well, after being found in breach of the Convention have amended or repealed the law impugned.[10] Other states, in spite of the Committee of Ministers' supervision, have instead ignored the findings of the Court, confining themselves to paying to the victim the just satisfaction imposed by the Court. Yet other states have found seemingly more astute ways out: for instance Italy, faced with hundreds of the Court's rulings that its civil and criminal trials were too lengthy contrary to Article 6 of the Convention, instead of changing the relevant legislation, has passed a law which entrusts Italian courts of appeal with the task of paying compensation for the excessive length of proceedings. Thus, instead of complying with the Court's rulings, it simply avoids being shamed at the international level.

---

[7]  Eg see *Assanidze v Georgia*, judgment of 8 April 2004, and *Ilascu v Russia*, judgment of 13 May 2005, where the Court ordered the release of applicants who were being arbitrarily detained. See also the so-called pilot judgments where the Court requested the adoption of wide-ranging measures: *Broniowski v Poland*, judgment of 19 June 2006 (Grand Chamber), and *Huten-Czapask v Poland* (judgment of 19 June 2006 (Grand Chamber)).

In *Saghinadze v Georgia* (judgment of 27 May 2010), the Court, after finding various violations of the Convention, with regard to the breach of the right to property stated:

> As it transpires from the formulation of that claim, the first applicant seeks, in principle, *restitutio in integrum*, which the Court finds reasonable. It must be reiterated in this connection that a judgment in which the Court finds a violation of the Convention or its Protocols imposes on the respondent State a legal obligation not just to pay those concerned the sums awarded by way of just satisfaction, but also to choose, subject to supervision by the Committee of Ministers, the general and/or, if appropriate, individual measures to be adopted in its domestic legal order to put an end to the violation found by the Court. The respondent State is expected to make all feasible reparation for the consequences of the violation in such a manner as to restore as far as possible the situation existing before the breach (see, amongst others, *Apostol v. Georgia*, no. 40765/02, § 71; *FC Mretebi v. Georgia*, no. 38736/04, § 61, 31 July 2007; and *Assanidze v. Georgia*, cited above, § 198).

[8]  This is the Department for the Execution of Judgments of the Court, belonging to the Council General of Human Rights and Legal Affairs.

[9]  Eg see the excellent 3rd Annual Report of the Committee of Ministers *Supervision of the execution of judgments of the European Court of Human Rights*, April 2010. However, it must be stressed that in many instances states do not heed the appeals of the Committee of Ministers. Eg see the Committee's Interim Resolution CM/ResDH (2010) 83, of 3 June 2010, relating to the case *Ben Khemais v Italy*, where the Committee deplored that Italy had failed in many instances to abide by interim measures indicated by the Court and urged once again Italy to fulfil its obligations.

[10]  Eg as a result of the *Marckx v Belgium* judgment of 1979, Belgium amended its family law in 1987 (see Committee of Ministers Resolution DH (88) no. 3 of 4 March 1988). Interestingly, the Netherlands had already changed its own law in 1982 to take account of that judgment against Belgium. Furthermore, in 1980 Ireland changed an Irish law on legal aid as a result of the *Airey v Ireland* judgment of 1979 (the law was further revised and meliorated in 1990). In 2003 and 2004 the United Kingdom amended its laws on corporal punishment of children as a result of the *A v United Kingdom* judgment of 1998.

Admittedly the entry into force of Protocol 14 and the strengthening of the supervisory powers of the Committee of Ministers are a step in the right direction.[11] However, it would be necessary for the Court to place a strict interpretation on Article 41 and always indicate the measures to be taken (albeit when necessary in non-specific terms), while in addition affording 'just satisfaction', if need be. In other words, the Court should, after finding that a breach of the Convention has occurred on account of an inconsistent national law, *enjoin* the responsible state to change that law. This bolder stand, not barred by the text of the European Convention, is in my opinion imposed by a teleological interpretation.[12]

---

[11] Article 46 of the Convention, as amended by Protocol 14, after providing in para. 1 that 'The High Contracting parties undertake to abide by the final judgment of the Court in any case in which they are parties', adds in paras 4 and 5 the following:

> If the Committee of Ministers considers that a High Contracting Party refuses to abide by a final judgment in a case to which it is a party, it may, after serving formal notice on that Party and by decision adopted by a majority vote of two thirds of the representatives entitled to sit on the Committee, refer to the Court the question whether that Party has failed to fulfil its obligation under paragraph 1. (para. 4)
>
> If the Court finds a violation of paragraph 1, it shall refer the case to the Committee of Ministers for consideration of the measures to be taken. If the Court finds no violation of paragraph 1, it shall refer the case to the Committee of Ministers, which shall close its examination of the case. (para. 5)

In this way the Court may be requested by the Committee of Ministers to pronounce on non-compliance with one of its judgments. Although this is a welcome step, it remains to be seen whether the required majority of two-thirds is reached in the Committee, and in addition what 'enforcement' measures the Committee can take in case of non-compliance.

[12] Taking into account the very *object and purpose* of the Convention, one can note that the Convention aims at safeguarding the fundamental rights of individuals in the territory of the contracting states and wherever such states exercise their jurisdiction over them; to this end, an important supervisory body, the Court, has been tasked to guarantee that human rights are *really and fully* respected by those States. It therefore follows that whenever a state infringes upon one of the rights, it must subsequently make good the damage and also *ensure* again, to the maximum possible extent, respect for the rights violated. This cannot be done solely by obliging the state concerned to pay money to the victim of the violation. If this were the case, in future the material and moral authors of the violation might simply escape any responsibility, with the consequence that they would be likely to commit the same breach anew, knowing that in any case they would not incur any responsibility and therefore would escape punishment. To realize human rights it is instead necessary to prevent perpetrators of serious human rights violations from repeating the same or other breaches by making their conduct illegal and punishing them at the domestic level.

The interpretation in question is also consonant with the *very notion of justice*. Where an individual is deprived of a fundamental right on account of a national law, how can one think that monetary satisfaction is sufficient to remedy an intolerable attack on his rights? Perhaps in some cases a monetary response can contribute to placating the suffering of the victim. However, it will not restore the national and international 'public order' (*ordre public*) injured by the misconduct. The possible meeting of *subjective* exigencies will not be matched by the *objective* need to provide a congruous and proportionate response to a blatant deviation from universal values. The only way to restore 'public order' is to impose upon the state concerned the requirement to take action at the national level to ensure that similar acts will not be repeated.

## (C) The Inter-American Court of Human Rights

This Court is much better off than its European 'sister', although it lacks a supervisory body such as the Council of Europe Committee of Ministers.[13]

First of all, the American Convention on Human Rights includes a provision that unequivocally demands that member states adjust their laws to the Convention.[14] Furthermore, in many cases the Court has explicitly enjoined a defendant state to change its legislation to bring it into line with the Convention;[15] in addition, where the necessary legislative changes have not been made, the Court has again pronounced on the matter, requesting the state to comply with the previous judgment.[16]

---

[13] However, the Court has constantly declared, in orders by which the Court's President ruled on compliance by states with the Court's judgments, that 'That monitoring compliance with its decisions is a power inherent in the judicial functions of the Court.' In addition, Art. 69 of the Court's Rules of Procedures provides for a complex mechanism designed to ensure that states abide by the Court's judgments.

[14] This is Art. 2, pursuant to which

> Where the exercise of any of the rights or freedoms referred to in Article 1 is not already ensured by legislative or other provisions, the States Parties undertake to adopt, in accordance with their constitutional processes and the provisions of this Convention, such legislative or other measures as may be necessary to give effect to those rights or freedoms.

[15] In *Barrios Altos v Peru* (*Merits*), Series C, no. 75 (14 March 2001), the Court, after examing the amnesty laws at issue (paras 41–3), held that

> Owing to the manifest incompatibility of self-amnesty laws and the American Convention on Human Rights, *the said laws lack legal effect* and may not continue to obstruct the investigation of the grounds on which this case is based or the identification and punishment of those responsible . . . (para. 44)

In *Olmedo Bustos et al v Chile* ('*The last temptation of Christ* case'), *Merits*, Series C, no. 73 ((5 February 2001), only in Spanish), after mentioning Art. 2 of the Convention, the Court stated that both an international customary rule and the Convention imposed on states the requirement to change their domestic laws to give effect to international rules (para. 87). It went on to say that Chile was bound to change its laws on the preventive censorship of films to comply with Art. 13 of the Convention (paras 97–8).

In *Paniagua Morales et al v Guatemala (Reparations)*, Series C, no. 76 ((25 May 2001), only in Spanish), after mentioning Art. 2, the Court said that Guatemala had to change its laws on personal freedoms to forestall further violations similar to those found by the Court (para. 203).

In *Del Caracazo v Venezuela (Reparations)*, Series C, no. 95 (29 August 2002, only in Spanish), the Court held that Venezuela was duty-bound to avoid applying amnnesties or statutes of limitation or rely upon circumstances excluding criminal responsibility in instances of serious and gross violations of human rights (para. 119). It concluded that the Venezuelan authorities were therefore to introduce into national legislation all the changes necessary to live up to its obligations, as set out in the previous paragraphs (para. 120).

[16] See, eg, the Order of the Court of 28 November 2003 (relating to the Court's judgment on *Olmedo Bustos et al v Chile*, n 15) at paras 19 and 25, finding that on 10 July 2001, the National Congress had adopted the draft constitutional reform designed to establish the right to freedom of artistic creation and the elimination of cinematographic censorship. See also the Court's Order of 22 September 2005 (relating to the Court's judgment in *Barrios Alto v Peru*, n 15), at paras 8(f) and 15(a), finding that the respondent state had passed amendments of the Criminal Code to comply with the judgment. See also the Order of 21 November 2007 (relating to the judgment in *Trujillo Oroza v Bolivia (Reparations)*, Series C, no. 92 (27 February 2002)), at para. 5, finding that in 2006 Bolivia had approved the law that classifies the crime of forced disappearance of people. See further the Order of 27 November 2007 (relating to the Court's judgment in *Paniagua Morales et al v*

## 5. What could be done to move forward?

As I pointed out above, given the present structure of the world community, international law by itself does not possess the force to amend or repeal internationally unlawful domestic legislative acts. At present, states would baulk at any such authority being conferred on the corpus of international rules, lest they should be deprived of some of their sovereign prerogatives, chiefly that of disregarding international legal prescriptions whenever they are in stark conflict with national short-term interests. To achieve the suggested result, it would also be necessary for domestic legal orders to change dramatically and accord international rules immediate and binding effect within each national legal system.

This, however, as noted above at Section 3, may only occur in future times. What, then, can be suggested in the shorter term?

Based on our current experience, as indicated in the above section, I would suggest that any progress may only occur within *regional groupings*, not at the universal level. Within such groupings one should endeavour to rely primarily on *international* mechanisms. It would fall to international judicial institutions to impose on member states the requirement to amend specific domestic laws or legal provisions conflicting with international rules and also subsequently to verify whether such a judicial determination has been brought into effect. Also, those states should try to introduce—albeit gradually—into their own legal systems a mechanism whereby any international ruling determining the inconsistency of a law with international rules would render that law null and void or, at a minimum, would oblige the competent national bodies to forthwith take all measures necessary to bring about a change in domestic legislation.

Admittedly, it would not be an epoch-making change. It would nevertheless improve the chances of international rules effectively guiding the conduct of states, at least within regional systems.

*Guatemala (Case of the White Van)*, Reparations, of 25 May 2001), at paras 27–8. The Court pointed out that

> The State submitted during the private hearing a copy of the Decree No 33–2006 whereby the State approved the 'Prisons Act'.... The information system should allow knowing the identity of the detainee by means of the photograph and the period of time that the detention of each of the persons entered to the center lasts.... The Commission, despite the fact that it valued the adoption of said law, stated that the same refers only to the prisons system and interpreted that the Court's decision regarding this issue 'does not make any specific reference to the persons detained in the prison system but to a register of detainees technically speaking, that is to say, to every person deprived of freedom in Guatemala.

> At para. 31 the Court concluded that

> as a result of the foregoing, the Court considers that the State has partially complied with the operative paragraph four of the Judgment on the reparations and that, as a consequence, the State must set up a register to include all people who are deprived of freedom.

# 16

# Should the Implementation of International Rules by Domestic Courts be Bolstered?

*Yuval Shany\**

## SUMMARY

In recent years there has been a considerable overlap in the substantive fields of operation of domestic and international courts. In addition, the relaxation of the rules of standing applicable before several international courts and the removal of a number of obstacles that used to prevent domestic courts from addressing questions touching upon foreign policy has approximated the procedural opportunities for pursuing litigation before both sets of fora. As a result, both domestic and international courts may now serve as guardians of international legality. In spite of the many hurdles existing in this matter, there would exist many advantages in bolstering the role of domestic courts. First, it could dramatically increase the prospects of enforcing international obligations. Secondly, the growing judicial treatment of international law texts by national courts may lead to increased international norm-elucidation. Thirdly, the democratic credentials of many domestic legal systems may confer upon their courts' international law-applying decisions a greater degree of democratic legitimacy than that associated with the decisions of international courts. With a view to enhancing the role of domestic courts, the author makes a few suggestions: (i) incentivizing domestic courts to apply international law should be made part of new and existing treaty regimes; (ii) states and international institutions should allocate more resources to develop the capacity of domestic courts to adjudicate cases involving international law norms; (iii) a more rational set of principles governing the division of labour between domestic and international courts ought to be developed, especially in fields where international courts are inundated with cases; (iv) new international standards should be developed that would try to regulate the application of international law in domestic courts; and (v) serious conceptual work should be undertaken with the aim of

\* This chapter is based on research conducted with the support of a European Research Council Starting Grant for Frontier Research.

redefining international law sources in a way that captures the various domestic legal ways in which international law standards are actually being implemented.

# 1. Introduction

Our traditional outlook on the world of adjudication regards domestic and international courts as two very different sets of institutions. Whereas domestic courts apply national law to disputes brought before them and are part of the local institutions of government, international courts apply international law and resolve disputes between two or more states. It appears, however, that the traditional view of the dividing line between national and international adjudicatory bodies is increasingly hard to reconcile with ongoing legal and political developments—in particular, the increased occurrence of jurisdictional overlaps, the assumption of a stronger international law-applying role by national courts, and the emergence of hybrid courts. The erosion of the boundaries between the said two categories of judicial institutions generates new opportunities for the future evolution of international law, but also entails a number of serious challenges.

The present chapter seeks to describe in its first section the principal contours of the process leading to the meshing of the domestic and international adjudicatory powers to apply international law. In Section 2 I discuss the principal implications of bolstering the international law-implementing role of domestic courts. In Section 3 I conclude by asking whether and how the international law-implementing role of domestic courts should be further encouraged.

# 2. The erosion of traditional legal boundaries

Under classic dualism, domestic and international courts operate in dichotomously distinct legal spheres.[1] The former are national institutions grounded in national law, whereas the latter are international institutions operating within the realm of international law. Though some functional similarity between domestic and international courts no doubt exists, this similarity is not greater than the one existing between domestic courts of different nations; hence, domestic and international courts operate in separate legal universes. The dicta employed by the Permanent Court of International Justice (PCIJ) in the *Certain German Interests* case is illustrative of this dualistic approach:

From the standpoint of International Law and of the Court which is its organ, municipal laws are merely facts which express the will and constitute the activities of states, *in the same manner as do legal decisions* or administrative measures.[2] (Emphasis added)

---

[1] See, eg, G. Gaja, 'Dualism—A Review', in A. Nollkaemper and J.E. Nijman (eds), *New Perspectives on the Divide between National and International Law* (Oxford: Oxford University Press, 2007), 52.

[2] *Certain German Interests in Polish Upper Silesia (Germany v Poland)*, (*Merits*), PCIJ, Series A, no. 7 (1926), at 19.

In other words, the separate sphere of operation of domestic courts renders their work normatively meaningless from the international court's viewpoint and vice versa.

As has been acknowledged by several authors, the traditional view on the legal gulf separating domestic and international courts has become over time less and less tenable.[3] For one, the jurisdictional powers of domestic and international courts have both expanded considerably—due to the development of domestic laws and legal doctrines permitting their extraterritorial application (eg universal jurisdiction[4] or Alien Tort Statute (ATS) litigation[5]), and the parallel development of international law norms regulating issues previously regarded as internal state matters (eg human rights[6] and numerous norms governing economic relations[7]). This has resulted in a considerable overlap in the substantive fields of operation of domestic and international courts.

In addition, the relaxation of the rules of standing applicable before several international courts[8] and the removal of a number of obstacles (or 'avoidance techniques') that used to prevent domestic courts from addressing questions touching upon foreign policy,[9] has approximated the procedural opportunities for pursuing litigation before both sets of fora. This does not merely render domestic and international courts functionally similar institutions; it also transforms them, at times, into actual jurisdictional alternatives to one another.

Another important development contributing to the erosion of legal boundaries between domestic and international courts involves a change in their respective ethos. Some domestic courts have displayed in recent years a growing willingness to apply international law, including in cases involving governments and government officials (be they their own governments or foreign governments).[10] The

---

[3] See, eg, J.E. Nijman and A. Nollkaemper, 'Introduction', n 1, at 1; Y. Shany, *Regulating Jurisdictional Relations between National and International Courts* (Oxford: Oxford University Press, 2007), 78ff.

[4] See, eg, *Attorney-General v Eichmann*, 36 ILR (1961) 5 (Israeli District Court), aff'd 36 ILR 277 (1962) (Supreme Court); *R v Bow Street Magistrates, ex p Pinochet (Nos 1 & 3)* [2000] 1 AC 147.

[5] See, eg, *Filártiga v Peña-Irala*, 630 F2d 876 (2d Cir., 1980); *Sosa v Álvarez Macháin*, 542 US 692 (2004).

[6] See, eg, Convention for the Protection of Human Rights and Fundamental Freedoms, 4 November 1950; International Covenant on Civil and Political Rights, 16 December 1966.

[7] See, eg, Treaty Establishing the European Economic Community, 25 March 1957; Convention on the Settlement of Investment Disputes between States and Nationals of Other States, 18 March 1965.

[8] See, eg, Protocol 11 to the Convention for the Protection of Human Rights and Fundamental Freedoms, restructuring the control machinery established thereby, 11 May 1994, ETS 155; Rome Statute Establishing the International Criminal Court, 17 July 1998, art 68, 2187 UNTS 90.

[9] For a discussion of resort to avoidance techniques limiting the application of international law by national courts, see E. Benvenisti, 'Judicial Misgivings Regarding the Application of International Law: An Analysis of the Attitudes of National Courts', 4 EJIL (1993) 159; E. Benvenisti and G.W. Downe, 'National Courts, Domestic Democracy and the Evolution of International Law', 20 EJIL (2009) 59.

[10] See, eg, *A (FC) v Secretary of State for the Home Department* [2004] UKHL 56 (holding foreign terrorists in indefinite detention violates international law); *Hamden v Rumsfeld*, 548 US 557 (2006) (military commission procedures violate international law); *Ferrini v Germany*, Appeal decision, no. 5044/4; ILDC 19 (IT 2004) (damages can be claimed from a foreign government for violations of international law in the forum state's territory); *Simón v Office of the Public Prosecutor*, Appeal

increased robustness of the manner in which international law is being applied by these domestic courts appears to rest, at least in part, on the notion that compliance with international law is supported by the same 'rule of law' justifications that were originally developed to support the judicial application of national laws.[11] This change in attitude towards international law, which has features of both a quantitative (more domestic courts applying more international law more frequently), and qualitative nature (domestic courts applying international law as a meaningful restraint on government power), may provide a late-in-coming validation for Georges Scelle's classic *dédoublement fonctionnel* theory, which envisioned national institutions as fulfilling governance roles under both national and international law.[12]

At the same time, the role of international courts has also undergone a significant evolution, which affects, in turn, their operational ethos. Classic inter-state courts such as the PCIJ, the International Court of Justice (ICJ) and, to a large extent, also the International Tribunal for the Law of Sea, have focused on resolving inter-state conflicts—offering thereby an institutionalized alternative to inter-state arbitration. Still, a subsequent generation of courts active in the fields of economic integration law (eg the European Court of Justice), human rights law (eg the European and Inter-American Courts of Human Rights), and international criminal law (eg the International Criminal Court (ICC)) are operating pursuant to a different guiding ethos, concentrating less on dispute resolution, and more on

judgment, S. 1767. XXXVIII; ILDC 579 (AR 2005) (a national amnesty law violates international law); *Denton v Director General National Intelligence Agency*, Decision on Application for Declaratory Relief, Civil HC 241/06/MF/087/F1; ILDC 881 (GM 2006) (prolonged detention without trial violates international law); *German Consular Notification Case*, Joint constitutional complaint, BVerfG, 2 BvR 2115/01; ILDC 668 (DE 2006) (existing consular notification practices in Germany fall short of international law standards); *Adalah v General Officer Commanding Central Command, Israeli Defense Force*, Original Petition, HCJ 3799/02; ILDC 155 (IL 2005) (IDF order permitting the utilization of Palestinian civilians in military operations violates international law).

[11] See, eg, *R v Horseferry Road Magistrates' Court, ex p Bennett* [1994] 1 AC 42 at 67F–H (per Lord Bridge): ('There is, I think, no principle more basic to any proper system of law than the maintenance of the rule of law itself. When it is shown that the law enforcement agency responsible for bringing a prosecution has only been enabled to do so by participating in violations of international law and the laws of another state in order to secure the presence of the accused within the territorial jurisdiction of the court, I think that respect for the rule of law demands that the court take cognisance of that circumstance'); *Tavita v Minister of Immigration* [1994] 2 NZLR 257, 266 (per President Cooke) (the court should require the government to meet its international obligations, or else adherence to international instruments may be regarded as 'window dressing'); *Minister of Education and Another v Syfrets Trust Ltd NO*, 2006 SACLR LEXIS 29, 49 (Cape of Good Hope Provincial Division) ('South Africa—including this Court—is bound by international law to give effect to the provisions of [various] conventions'); *Re Colonel Aird, ex p Alpert*, 209 ALR 311 (2004), at para. 116 (per Justice Kirby) ('Ignoring international law will sometimes result not only in chaos and futility. It will reduce the enlargement of the international rule of law, to which municipal, regional and international law together contribute'); HCJ 3451/02 *Almandi v Minister of Defense*, 56(3) PD 30, at para. 9 (per President Barak), available in English at <http://elyon1.court.gov.il/files_eng/02/510/034/a06/02034510.a06.htm> ('This combat is not taking place in a normative void. It is being carried out according to the rules of international law, which provide principles and rules for combat activity…The state fights in the name of the law and in the name of upholding the law').

[12] See, eg, G. Scelle, II *Précis de droit des gens: principes et systématique* vol. II (Paris: Receuil Sirey; 1934), 10–12; G. Scelle, 'La phénomène juridique de dédoulement fonctionnel', *Rechtsfragen der Internationalen Organisation* (Frankfurt: Vittorio Klostermann, 1956), 324.

law-interpretation and law-application. Their activities in these areas have, in fact, been associated with the notion of global governance—the application of law and other forms of power, by supranational institutions, and with it the development of safeguards against abuse of law and power in the form of judicial review and an 'international rule of law' principle. The upshot of these transformations may be a growing functional parallelism between domestic and international courts—both serving as guardians of international legality; both involved in addressing related legal aspects of multilevel governance.

The traditional division between domestic and international courts has become even harder to sustain with the emergence of coordinated systems of judicial review involving both sets of institutions (eg the preliminary ruling procedure under EU law[13] and the positive complementarity policies embraced by the ICC Office of the Prosecutor and Assembly of State Parties in order to foster domestic criminal prosecutions[14]), and with the creation of hybrid judicial institutions comprising both domestic and international judicial features (eg the internationalized criminal courts[15] and the Caribbean Court of Justice[16]). Such combined and interlocked legal structures underscore the overlapping purposes of domestic and international judicial institutions, and give expression to a move from doctrinal separation to functional convergence—necessitating, in turn, a new articulation of legal doctrine.

## 3. Potential and limits

The emergence of a domestic judiciary willing and able to apply international law vis-à-vis national and international actors may have significant implications for the future of international law and the international rule of law. First, the availability of domestic fora could dramatically increase the prospects of enforcing international obligations: unlike their international counterparts, whose work is often governed by restrictive and/or cumbersome *jus standi* rules (sometimes investing the right to initiate proceedings with states only—notwithstanding their reluctance to sue one another),[17] domestic courts are easily accessible to a vast number of potential liti-

---

[13] Consolidated Version of the Treaty on the Functioning of the European Union, Art. 267, OJ (C 083) 47, 30 March 2010.

[14] See, eg, 'Paper on Some Policy Issues before the Office of the Prosecutor' (September 2003), available at <http://www.icc-cpi.int>; Kampala Declaration of 4 June 2010, Review Conference of the Rome Statute, at para. 5, ICC Doc. RC/4 (2010).

[15] See, eg, Agreement between the United Nations and the Government of Sierra Leone on the Establishment of the Special Court for Sierra Leone, 16 January 2002, available at <http://www.sc-sl.org>; SC Res. 1757 (2007), UN Doc. S/RES/1757 (2007) (endorsing the Agreement between the United Nations and the Lebanese Republic on the establishment of a Special Tribunal for Lebanon).

[16] Agreement establishing the Caribbean Court of Justice, 14 February 2001, available at <http://www.caribbeancourtofjustice.org/courtadministration/ccj_agreement.pdf>.

[17] The contentious jurisdiction of the ICJ being only available under Art. 35 of the ICJ Statute to states is the classic example of a restrictive *ratione personae* approach to adjudication. The difficult path through which victim complaints are channelled to the Inter-American Court of Human Rights (requiring the espousal of such claims by the Inter-American Commission) illustrates the

gants, who may seek to uphold through them their international law-related interests and grievances. The opening up of the doors of domestic courts to this 'army of private attorney-generals' may lead to a surge in the volume of international law cases. The recent experience of US courts dealing with a booming number of ATS claims[18] and the experience of European countries in receiving a growing number of requests to exercise universal jurisdiction[19] illustrate the potential growth in the international law caseload, which changes in the laws governing the international law jurisdiction of domestic courts and in their actual practices may foster.

In addition, since the enforcement facilities available at the domestic level are generally superior to the inadequate remedial and enforcement facilities existing at the international level, increasing the role of domestic courts in litigating international law cases is likely to lead to higher enforcement rates. This too has significant implications for the 'bite' attendant to international obligations and for the international rule of law.

Increasing the involvement of domestic courts in the project of international law-application is likely to result in additional beneficial outcomes—the growing judicial treatment of international law texts may lead, inter alia, to increased international norm-elucidation and to a greater degree of legal accountability of the reviewed international actors. In the same vein, domestic courts may employ their fact-finding capabilities, which often exceed the parallel facilities available to international courts, and produce thereby an improved fit between applied norms and ascertained facts on the ground. Moreover, domestic courts may share some of the burden of work currently assumed by international courts (which in some cases—most notably, the European Court of Human Rights—far exceed their capabilities). Such burden-sharing could allow international courts to concentrate their limited resources on a relatively small number of cases involving the most difficult questions of principle, where international judicial intervention could be most useful.[20]

---

cumbersome nature of some international adjudicative procedures concerning individual right-holders. See, eg, *Viviana Gallardo*, I/A CHR Series A No. 101 (1981) (per Piza Escalante, at para. 11) ('the American States in drafting [the American Human Rights Convention] did not wish to accept the establishment of a swift and effective jurisdictional system but rather they hobbled it by interposing the impediment of the Commission, by establishing a veritable obstacle course that is almost insurmountable, on the long and arduous road that the basic rights of the individual are forced to travel'). See also M. Pena, 'Victim Participation at the International Criminal Court: Achievements Made and Challenges Lying Ahead', 16 ILSA J Int'l & Comp L (2010) 497, 511

[18] J. Davis, *Justice Across Borders: The Struggle for Human Rights in US Courts* (Cambridge: Cambridge University Press, 2008), 127–8 (more ATS cases were filed during George W. Bush's presidency than during all previous presidencies combined).

[19] FIDH/Redress, Universal Jurisdiction Developments: January 2006–May 2009, available at <http://www.unhcr.org/refworld/pdfid/4a26393f2.pdf>.

[20] Eg, under Protocol 14 of the European Convention on Human Rights, the Court is authorized to reject cases dealt by domestic courts in which the victim was not significantly disadvantaged. Protocol No. 14 to the Convention for the Protection of Human Rights and Fundamental Freedoms, amending the control system of the Convention, 13 May 2004, Art. 12, ETS 194 (amending Art. 35 of the Convention). In the same vein, the ICC is expected to address only cases of particular gravity, leaving less serious cases to prosecution before domestic courts. ICC Statute, Art. 17; F. Jessberger, 'International v National Prosecution of International Crimes', in A. Cassese (ed.), *The Oxford Companion to International Criminal Justice* (Oxford: Oxford University Press, 2009), 208, 212.

Finally, the democratic credentials of many domestic legal systems may confer upon their courts' international law-applying decisions a greater degree of democratic legitimacy than that associated with the decisions of international courts, afflicted by real or perceived democratic deficits. This too has considerable significance for the success of international law in general, and global administrative law in particular.

Still, a number of problems associated with increasing domestic courts' international law-application role should be readily acknowledged.

First, many domestic courts lack the professional capacity correctly to apply international law norms, as most domestic judges have little, if any, international law experience or training.

Secondly, the independence and quality of some domestic courts and judges is questionable; such problems of limited capabilities and politicization may be exacerbated if domestic courts were to deal more and more frequently with international law norms, often characterized by a high degree of politically sensitive and legal complexity.

Thirdly, past international law-application exercises by domestic courts have sometime been coloured by the forum state's national interests, if not by an outright chauvinistic bias.[21] In the same vein, international norms have been applied, at times, by domestic courts through the prism of national law provisions and subject to the conflicting norms of the latter—thus rendering such an international law-application exercise subsidiary and interstitial in nature (if not somewhat haphazard).[22] So, the rise in the volume of international law decisions by domestic courts may come at the cost of reduced quality, increased politicization, and norm-fragmentation.

At a more fundamental level, the assumption of an international law-application role by domestic courts may raise a *quis custodiet ipsos custodes* problem: since domestic courts continue to function as state organs even when they apply international law, their role as custodians of international legality may be in tension with their other responsibilities under domestic law (which may push them, for instance when applying national law, in a direction incompatible with international legality). Bolstering the role of domestic courts in implementing international law may thus lead to more legal accountability in some areas, but to the perpetuation of accountability gaps in other areas, where the ability (or willingness) of domestic courts to invoke international standards in a satisfactory manner may be restricted by national laws or interests.

Finally, one should note that the movement towards increasing the international law-applying capabilities of domestic courts and the greater utilization of that

---

[21] See, eg, H. Lauterpacht, 'Decisions of Municipal Courts as a Source of International Law', 10 BYIL (1929) 65, 65; E. Benvenisti, 'Reclaiming Democracy: The Strategic Uses of Foreign and International Law by National Courts', 102 AJIL (2008) 241.

[22] See, eg, A.F. Bayefsky, 'International Human Rights Law in Canadian Courts', in B. Conforti and F. Francioni (eds), *Enforcing International Human Rights in Domestic Courts* (The Hagve: Martinus Nijhoff, 1997), 295, 323; S.H. Fisherow, 'Follow the Leader?: Japan Should Formally Abolish the Execution of the Mentally Retarded in the Wake of *Atkins v Virginia*', 14 Pac Rim L & Pol'y J (2005) 455, 481.

capacity in actual practice is by no means universal. Perhaps paradoxically, two groups of states have been largely left out of the process of increased international law-application: states that strongly resist the penetration of international law into their domestic legal system, and states whose domestic laws already reflect to a large extent international norms—thus rendering redundant the invocation of the latter.[23] Any long-term strategy for integrating domestic courts within the international judiciary by bolstering their role in implementing international law must therefore account for the uneven geographical and political prevalence of the international law-applying project.

## 4. Conclusion: the way forward

Ultimately, bolstering the international law-applying role of national courts may complement the judicial structures of the international legal system and narrow, to some extent, the gaps existing between its normative and institutional components.[24] Given the increased work burdens assumed by international institutions in general, and international courts in particular,[25] and in view of the low prospect of a significant investment of resources on the part of states or international organizations in the creation of new international courts, or the expansion of existing ones,[26] increased resort to domestic courts for international law-application appears to me to be an inescapable consequence of international law's increased normative density. In fact, the continued viability of the project of expanding international law, empowering its norms, and sustaining their long-term legitimacy may depend on the bolstering of such domestic avenues of application.

A number of measures—conceptual and factual— may need to be taken in order to support and streamline the application of international law in domestic courts, while addressing, at least to a certain degree, some of the associated problems mentioned above.

First, incentivizing domestic courts to apply international law should be made part and parcel of new and existing treaty regimes. Such incentives may include both 'sticks' and 'carrots'—such as the threat of international censure and intervention by international institutions in the absence of domestic international law-application, on the one hand, and assistance to states willing to harness their domestic courts for international law-application purposes and international

---

[23] See, eg, G. Hudson, 'Neither Here nor There: The (Non-)Impact of International Law on Judicial Reasoning in Canada and South Africa', 21 Can J L & Juris (2008) 321, 350–2.

[24] See G. Abi-Saab, 'Fragmentation or Unification: Some Concluding Remarks', 31 NYU J Int'l L & Pol (1999) 919, 925.

[25] See, eg, Interlaken Declaration and Action Plan to Reform the European Court of Human Rights, 19 February 2010, paras 7–10, available at <http://www.eda.admin.ch/etc/medialib/downloads/edazen/topics/europa/euroc.Par.0133.File.tmp/final_en.pdf>.

[26] See, eg, S.D. Murphy, 'Biotechnology and International Law', 42 Harv Int'l LJ (2001) 47 (alluding to 'institution fatigue' at the international level); R. Cryer, *Prosecuting International Crimes: Selectivity and the International Criminal Law Regime* (Cambridge: Cambridge University Press, 2005), 210 (alluding to 'tribunal fatigue' at the Security Council).

deference to the international law-based domestic decision-making processes, on the other hand. Arguably, states interested in preserving a margin of independent decision-making authority as to the manner in which their international law obligations ought to be applied may be inclined to facilitate the involvement of their domestic courts in such matters (or, at least, tolerate such an involvement by their judiciaries).

The upshot of this may be that the introduction of a positive complementarity rule, *à la* ICC, should be considered in new treaty regimes introduced in diverse fields, such as human rights, international criminal law (ie, beyond the core crimes currently covered by the ICC Statute), international investment law, and international environmental law. Under such a proposed structure, international courts (and other suitable international institutions) would be expected to exercise a predominantly monitoring role. Hopefully, a stronger set of incentives would increase the number of domestic courts able and willing properly to apply international law.

Secondly, states and international institutions could allocate more resources to develop the capacity of domestic courts to adjudicate cases involving international law norms. This may involve the wide dissemination of international norms and focused judicial training, but also supporting domestic legal reforms, aimed at strengthening the local judiciary and at internalizing international norms within the domestic legal system. In some cases, the creation of new internationalized judicial structures (eg special criminal courts) or the establishment of other forms of judicial cooperative networks (such as the EC preliminary rulings procedure or other forms of inter-judicial dialogue, such as judicial exchange programmes) can be considered. Arguably, an investment of resources into domestic legal systems could also improve the quantity and quality of international law-applications by domestic courts.

Thirdly, a more rational set of principles governing the division of labour between domestic and international courts ought to be developed, especially in fields where international courts are inundated with cases. Such principles should, as a rule, allocate to international courts the more important, difficult or sensitive international cases, as well as conferring upon them monitoring functions over domestic courts. International law cases exhibiting more mundane features—raising less politically sensitive and legal complex issues—would be handled, whenever possible, by domestic courts. Arguably, the gravity criteria of the ICC Statute,[27] and the 'significant disadvantage' test under the revised Article 35 of the European Convention on Human Rights,[28] offer a modality for labour division that could be extended to other international law regimes as well.

Fourthly, new international standards could be developed that would try to regulate the application of international law in domestic courts. Hence, for example, the development of international standards on the exercise of universal jurisdiction, designed to minimize and monitor alleged abuses of the doctrine by domestic authorities, could be a useful step towards encouraging greater application of the

---

[27] ICC Statute, Arts 17(1)(d), 53.    [28] Protocol 14, Art. 12.

doctrine in a less objectionable manner than has been the case up until now.[29] Clearer rules on the proper standards for conducting investigations of allegations of violation of international humanitarian law in the course of military operations, would also improve the prospects of serious law-application exercises by domestic courts, especially if complemented by some international review mechanism.

Finally, serious conceptual work needs to be undertaken with the aim of redefining international law sources in a way that captures the various domestic legal forms in which international law standards are actually being implemented. A more pluralistic approach towards international law could consider domestic laws not couched in the form and language of international law, but reflective nonetheless of international standards in their substantive contents, as possible tools for international law-application and as potential sources for international law-interpretation. Such a reconceptualization of international law's sphere of substantive application would go a considerable way towards integrating domestic courts applying such norms in a multilevel international judiciary. As a result, the decisions of such courts—even if based on domestic law—may attract deference by other judicial bodies (in other states, and at the international level), and could affect the future development of international law.

Although this list of measures proposed hereby is by no means exhaustive in nature or problem free, it could foster, I believe, the evolution of a more robust and, yet, prudent international law-applying role for domestic courts. Moreover, such developments are, to some extent, already occurring. Thus, the further bolstering of the international law-applying role of domestic courts may be fairly characterized as a realistic utopia.

---

[29] See, eg, Report of the Secretary-General on the scope and application of the principle of universal jurisdiction, UN Doc. A/65/181 (2010), at paras 108–14 (describing concerns of certain states against abusive exercise of universal jurisdiction and surveying proposals for future norm-elaboration).

## (B) MAJOR OBSTACLES TO STATES' COMPLIANCE

# 17

# The Deficiencies of the Law of State Responsibility Relating to Breaches of 'Obligations Owed to the International Community as a Whole': Suggestions for Avoiding the Obsolescence of Aggravated Responsibility*

*Pierre-Marie Dupuy*

## SUMMARY

The 2001 International Law Commission (ILC) Articles on State Responsibility are a valuable but incomplete project which, to some extent, relied on the dream of an 'international community'. One of the main weaknesses of the ILC Articles is that, after eliminating the concept of 'crime of state', substituted by the notion of 'breach of an obligation owed to the international community as a whole', they do not provide a comprehensive and substantial legal regime for the responsibility of one state vis-à-vis other states, whether they belong to a specific group or simply to the international community as a whole. The Articles say very little about the so-called 'non-injured states' referred to under Article 48 vis-à-vis the responsible state. In particular, this Article does not indicate which type of measures they are legally authorized to invoke and carry out against the responsible state. Three general aims should be pursued. First, it is necessary to avoid the obsolescence of the very principle of a specific and aggravated responsibility. Secondly, one should ensure that any legal regime of this type is not used in an anarchic way by individual states (or by a group of states acting collectively) to take measures outside any international control by turning the alleged defence of a community interest into a convenient alibi for the realization of specific political strategies. Thirdly,

---

* This chapter was finalized in January 2011, before armed actions in Libya and Côte d'Ivoire were taken. Whatever the case may be, the present text focuses on situations in which no UN organ, including the Security Council, was able to decide any measure in the name of the international community.

it is necessary to strive to define with as much precision as possible cumulative legal criteria for enabling recourse by states to countermeasures as a reaction to the violation of peremptory and *erga omnes* obligations. The author also suggests three specific steps to be taken: (i) any reaction from the states 'objectively' or 'indirectly' injured by a breach of an obligation towards the international community should be reserved only to those situations where the Security Council is unable to take any efficient measures; (ii) if the breach of any such obligation does not constitute the object of a procedure for the peaceful settlement of disputes the member states of the international community must be able to invoke the responsibility of the responsible state and take countermeasures against it aimed at obtaining (a) the cessation of the internationally wrongful act, and assurances and guarantees of non-repetition; and (b) the performance of the obligation of reparation in the interest of the injured state and of all the beneficiaries of the obligation breached; and (iii) any such countermeasure must be commensurate with the injury suffered, taking into account the gravity of the internationally wrongful act and the rights in question.

## 1. Introduction: Roberto Ago's four forward-looking suggestions

In 1945, the Charter purported to herald in a new era founded upon the affirmation of a common fate for the Peoples of the United Nations, who declared their determination to share the same political interests and ethical values, converging in the promotion and maintenance of international peace. On this basis, the multilateral dimension of an ever growing number of international obligations gave rise to a need to take stock of classical international law on state responsibility, which had originally been designed in the context of bilateral inter-state relationships.[1] Even as late as 1961, Professor Paul Reuter, an expert in the field of the law of state responsibility and a member of the ILC, maintained that this fundamental branch of public international law was grounded on the simple and direct relationship between two equal sovereigns, one being the author of the wrongful act or omission, the other being the injured holder of subjective rights and material interests.[2]

In line with the codification of the law of treaties, which culminated in 1969 in the adoption of the Vienna Convention on the Law of Treaties,[3] a treaty which openly launched the notion of 'peremptory norms of international law', defined as norms 'accepted and recognized by the international community of states as a whole', the ILC was obliged to follow in the footsteps of this inspiring development in its work on state responsibility. Indeed, the distinguished Special Rapporteur on state responsibility after 1969 was none other than Roberto Ago, the former

---

[1] See P.-M. Dupuy, 'General Stocktaking of the Connections between the Multilateral Dimension of Obligations and Codification of the Law of Responsibility', 13 EJIL (2002) 5, 1053–83.

[2] P. Reuter, 'Principes de droit international public', 103 RCADI (1961-II) 425.

[3] See J. Verhoeven, 'The Law of Responsibility and the Law of Treaties', in J. Crawford, A. Pellet, and S. Olleson (eds), *The Law of International Responsibility* (Oxford: Oxford University Press, 2010), 105–15.

President of the Vienna Conference on the Law of Treaties. He stated that 'it would be hard to believe that the evolution of the legal consciousness of states with regard to the idea of the inadmissibility of any derogation from certain rules had not been accompanied by a parallel evolution in the domain of state responsibility.'[4]

In order to put this assumption to work, and as part of his new design project for the modern international law of state responsibility, Ago took *four novel steps*.

First, taking issue with the parameters originally imposed on the work of the ILC by Mr Garcia Amador, his predecessor,[5] Ago clearly distinguished—as Hart did at the same time within the general theory of law—between 'primary' and 'secondary' rules of law. The norms governing the law of state responsibility belong to the second category as they are obligations deriving from the prior violation of other obligations, or in other words, they dictate the consequences of a breach of a primary obligation to act or refrain from acting.

Secondly, Ago reduced the very definition of the responsibility of a state for its international wrongful acts to a purely normative dimension, by removing the requirement of *damage*—either material or legal—as an element of responsibility or as a condition for responsibility to be triggered. According to Article 1 of the ILC Articles, 'every internationally wrongful act of a state entails the international responsibility of that state'. Period. What is also noteworthy here, and of fundamental importance—in addition to the elimination of damage as a condition of responsibility—is that Ago remained in agreement with Anzilotti's positivist and objective definition of a wrongful act, given in 1906, that was opposed to the old vision of *culpa* or fault (in the subjective sense of the term), and which was still a fashionable idea at that time for the legal analysis of the underlying theory of the international responsibility of the state. For Ago, as well as for Anzilotti, who had become the highly influential President of the Permanent Court of International Justice at the time of the celebrated *Lotus* and *Chorzów* cases, a state cannot commit a fault in the same way as an individual; the legally pertinent question for state responsibility is to assess the measure of the discrepancy, in a given case, between the state's actual conduct and that conduct which is or which would have been dictated in the same circumstances by the applicable primary rule of international law.

The third step taken by Roberto Ago, and perhaps his most famous, must be understood in the light of the two preceding ones. It is a move that takes directly into account the major innovation of the 1969 Vienna Convention on the Law of Treaties, which is not to be understood as strictly limited to the legal validity of treaties since it defines a new category of legal norms within the overarching international legal order: that of *jus cogens* or peremptory norms of international law.[6] In a paradoxical twist, Ago, despite remaining faithful to the elimination of any reference to subjectivity or 'fault' as a basis for the responsibility of the state,

---

[4]  R. Ago, 'Fifth Report', YILC (1976), Vol. II, Part One, at 33–4, para. 57.

[5]  See D. Müller, 'The Work of Garcia Amador on State Responsibility for Injury Caused to Aliens', in Crawford, Pellet, and Olleson (eds), n 3, 69–74.

[6]  For the contrary view, see D. Alland, 'Countermeasures of General Interest', 13 EJIL (2002) 5, 1221–40.

nevertheless introduced, and the ILC with him, the notion of a state 'crime', that is, the gravest form of fault, in an attempt to establish a modern statement on the international law of state responsibility. As the breach of an international obligation had to be defined by the codifier, the ILC logically had to distinguish, within the generic category of internationally wrongful acts and their respective consequences in terms of responsibility, whether the breach affected an 'ordinary' obligation (ie, a bilateral one in a classical inter-state understanding of the term) or an 'essential' obligation (ie, one which threatened fundamental interests of the international community). Ago called breaches of obligations belonging to the first category 'delicts', and breaches of the obligations falling under the second category, 'crimes'. Of particular interest is the relationship between this second category of wrongful acts, and the nature and identity of the subject(s) entitled to invoke the responsibility of the 'guilty' state. No longer was *only* the state directly injured by the commission of the wrongful act entitled to invoke the responsibility of a state, but in addition to this state, *all states* affected by the breach of an obligation safeguarding the interests of the international community *as a whole*, could implement the legal consequences to which the wrongful conduct gave rise. They would be acting either qua organs legitimately representing the international community, or as individual states acting in defence of community interests. It is from this third initiative that the fourth and last proposal by Ago derives all its meaning and reach.

Fourthly, after having reduced state responsibility to its essence, that is, a wrongful act attributable to a specific state, Ago enlarged the *scope* of the legal relations triggered by this wrongful act. For the ILC (following the conclusions of its Special Rapporteur), the legal relations ensuing from the breach of a primary norm are not only limited to the bilateral dimension established between the wrongdoer and the victim. They are broadened so as to encompass

every kind of new relations which may arise, in international law, from the internationally wrongful act of a state, whether such relations . . . are centred on the duty of the guilty state to restore the injured state in its rights and repair the damage caused, or whether they also give the injured state itself *or other subjects of international law* the right to impose on the offending state a sanction admitted by international law.[7]

This broadening entails several consequences. It includes the law of reprisals, enlarged under the concept of 'countermeasures' in the framework of international responsibility, broadening the focus from the obligations of the wrongdoer to include the rights of the 'injured state'. At the same time, it admits as part of the same law of responsibility the reactions of all those acting in defence of the interests of 'the international community as a whole'.

As will be recalled, the ILC draft finally adopted in 2001 and approved by the UN General Assembly only gives partial answers to the questions raised by the four Ago initiatives. As it is, this draft is a valuable but uncompleted project (Section 2)

---

[7] YILC (1973), Vol. II, at 175. See M. Spinedi, 'From One Codification to Another: Bilateralism and Multilateralism in the Genesis of the Codification of the Law of State Responsibility', 13 EJIL (2002) 5, at 1112ff.

which—to some extent—relied on the dream of an unrealized and even unrealistic institutional integration of the concept of an 'international community', which very much seems to be an institutional mirage (Section 3). In light of this assessment, and confirmed by the trends manifested in the current practice of states and international case law, different scenarios are considered in order to answer the question posed in the title of this chapter (Section 4): is the multilateral dimension of the modern law of state responsibility just a dream based on an optimistic vision born during the second half of the last century? Or is there still a chance to make this dream a reality in the future?

## 2. A project left incomplete

On the basis of the four initiatives of its first Special Rapporteur, the ILC was able to develop and clarify a number of important rules while at the same time leaving unanswered some questions and even raising new ones. One such question relates to the fourth initiative addressed above, namely the issue of the right of an injured state to take countermeasures in a situation in which a state has breached an obligation it owes to the international community as a whole and refuses to fulfil this obligation.

### (A) Conditioning the taking of countermeasures, but for whom?[8]

Article 52 of the ILC Articles lays down a number of procedural conditions relating to resort to countermeasures by the injured state. This state must call on the responsible state to comply with its obligations and—in the absence of a positive answer—notify it of its intention to take measures aimed at obtaining the fulfilment of the obligations in question, the obligation to repair the damage caused being at the core of them. Furthermore, countermeasures should not be taken or, if already decided, should be suspended if the responsible state has put an end to its wrongful conduct or the dispute is already before a competent court.

That being said, countermeasures primarily deal with the reaction of an *individual* injured state, even in cases where the obligation breached by the responsible state has a multilateral or even a universal scope.[9] It is true that Article 42, the formulation of which is far from being a masterpiece of clarity, also deals with violations of collective obligations, that is, obligations that apply between more than two states 'and whose performance in the given case is not owed to one state individually, but to a group of states or the international community as a whole'.[10] Indeed, outside the hypothesis under which, in a given situation, a state is specially

[8] See H. Lesaffre, 'Countermeasures', in Crawford, Pellet, and Olleson (eds), n 3, 469–75.

[9] See J. Crawford, *The International Law Commission's Articles on State Responsibility: Introduction, Text and Commentaries* (Cambridge: Cambridge University Press, 2002), 297–300.

[10] Ibid, 259, (11); G. Gaja, 'The Concept of an Injured state', in Crawford, Pellet, and Olleson (eds), n 3, 941–9.

affected by the breach of an obligation owed towards a group of states (covered by Art. 42(b)(i)), Article 42(b)(ii) deals with a special category of obligations 'of such a character that a material breach of its provisions by one party radically changes the position of every party with respect to the further performance of its obligations.'[11] This is a situation concerning what may be termed a violation of an 'interdependent obligation'. Nevertheless, as evidenced by the comments provided by the last Special Rapporteur on state responsibility, James Crawford, Article 42 is focused on the 'injured state' perceived on a individual basis whatever the nature of the obligation breached, even though the Article's cumbersome formulation, by its reference to 'the international community as a whole', gives the troublesome impression of an overlap with the situations covered under Article 48.

## (B) The lack of a comprehensive regime of responsibility in case of breach of an obligation belonging to *jus cogens*

The true multilateral dimension of the international responsibility of a state appears to be fundamentally covered not by Article 42, but by Article 48.[12] The title of this provision is awkward for the purpose of legal analysis. It is entitled: 'Invocation of responsibility by a state *other than an injured state*', another demonstration of the fact that the ILC, until the very completion of its work, could not rid itself of the idea that an 'injured state' was basically an individual state, directly affected by the wrongdoing of another; a persistent idea inherited from the time when the responsibility of states was solely viewed from a bilateral perspective between the delinquent and the victim states, and prior to the affirmation of the existence of *community interests*. It makes little sense to say that '*non*-injured states' have a right of action against another state. If they are not injured, what is the legal ground for them legitimately (and legally) to take remedial action? Rather, more accurately, they are not affected in their individual and subjective interest, contrary to the 'injured state' in the sense of Article 42(1), but in their *objective* interest in the adherence to those obligations that are of essential importance for the international community. The legal basis for their action against the responsible state lies merely in their belonging to the international community. They may act on an *actio popularis* basis. Speaking of initiatives taken by so-called 'non-injured states' runs counter to the fundamental principle that no right of action exists when no legal interest has been infringed ('*pas d'intérêt, pas d'action*'), simply because no one possesses the legal quality (or, more narrowly, in procedural terms, the *locus standi*) for taking any initiative in defence of an absent interest. A more suitable turn of phrase could have been found, the best one most probably being a distinction between 'objectively' and 'subjectively' injured states, or, at least, it would have been better to speak of states being either 'directly' or 'indirectly' injured.[13] Be that as it may, the serious terminological and theoretical deficiencies of the ILC Articles are most

---

[11] Ibid, 259 (13).

[12] Ibid, 276–80.

[13] For further developments on this critics, see P.-M. Dupuy, 'Le fait générateur de la responsabilité internationale des Etats', 188 RCADI (1984-V) and of the same author, n 1, at 1060ff.

likely due to the input of states that discussed earlier versions of the ILC project within the context of the Sixth Commission of the UN General Assembly.[14]

We are thus faced with one of the main weaknesses of the ILC Articles. After having eliminated (for quite understandable reasons of legal policy) the concept of 'crime of state' from its last version, substituted by the notion of 'breach of an obligation owed to the international community as a whole', *the Articles do not provide a comprehensive and substantial legal regime for the responsibility of one state vis-à-vis other states, whether they belong to a specific group or simply to the international community as a whole*. Systematically, it says very little about the so-called 'non-injured states' referred to under Article 48 vis-à-vis the responsible state. In particular, it does not indicate which kind of measures they are legally authorized to invoke and carry out against the responsible state.

As a matter of fact, the formulation of Article 49, which deals with the 'object and limits of countermeasures', specifically reserves the right of taking such measures to 'the injured state' in the limited, individual, and narrow sense earlier provided by Article 42. This leads to the conclusion that the states allegedly said to be 'non-injured' under the title of Article 48, cannot take the type of 'countermeasures' dealt with by Article 52 in reaction to a breach of an obligation towards a group of states or towards the international community as a whole. Article 48 provides that these 'third' states may only claim the cessation of the internationally wrongful act, and request assurances and guarantees of non-repetition, or performance of the obligation of reparation in the interest of the injured state or 'of the beneficiaries of the obligation breached'.[15] In addition, Article 41(2) provides that the 'serious' breach by a state of an obligation arising under a peremptory norm of general international law entails for all other states within the international community an obligation *not* to recognize a situation created by this breach[16] as well as an obligation of non-assistance to the responsible state.[17] The distinction established by the ILC Articles between the rights of the 'injured' state and those of the others in the face of a breach of a community obligation can be criticized as it does not reflect the actual practice of states, in a number of concrete cases. In particular, during the 1980s, when confronted with the illegal use of force to invade the territory of a third state, states not directly injured nevertheless took true countermeasures in the sense of classical reprisals and did not limit themselves to asking for the cessation of the wrongful act or the non-recognition of the situation created. The same can be said for reactions to other serious breaches of community obligations.[18]

---

[14] See G. Gaja, 'States Having an Interest in Compliance with the Obligation Breached', in Crawford, Pellet, and Olleson (eds), n 3, at 957–65.

[15] This last formulation remains quite ambiguous. Strictly speaking, any so-called 'state other than an injured state' falls under this designation. Why was it not made more precise?

[16] See M. Dawidowicz, 'The Obligation of Non-Recognition of an Unlawful Situation', in Crawford, Pellet, and Olleson (eds), n 3, at 677–87.

[17] See N. Joergenzen, 'The Obligation of Non-Assistance to the Responsible State', in ibid, n 3, at 687–95.

[18] See A. Cassese, 'The Character of the Violated Obligation', in ibid, n 3, at 417–18. For illustrations, see P.-M. Dupuy, 'Observations sur la pratique récente des sanctions de l'illicite', RGDIP (1983), 505ff.

Even if this caution in establishing new progressive developments in the law may be understood as designed to avoid any anarchic and uncontrolled unilateral reaction, the fact is that the restrictive provisions of Articles 41 and 48 are by themselves insufficient to establish a full and complete regime of responsibility for the breach of *erga omnes* obligations of a peremptory nature. This leads to the conclusion that, on the basis of the Articles analysed above, the international legal order is left in the twenty-first century with a situation in which the multilateral dimension of the law of state responsibility is affirmed without at the same time providing states with a clear indication of what would be the content of this responsibility and, in particular, what would be the measures to be taken and how they should be implemented.

The reason for this lies in the fact that the codifiers, starting with Ago and continuing with the majority of states that discussed the progressive series of drafts within the Sixth Committee, remained more or less as if they were attracted to an unattainable dream: that of an institutional integration of the notion of 'international community'; an integration which, instead of leaving the invocation of community interests and values to the individual initiative of its members, would empower an organ provided with universal legitimacy necessary to act in its name.

## 3. The illusions of an institutional response

Special Rapporteur Roberto Ago, when drafting the provisions on countermeasures, was perfectly aware of the danger of anarchy represented by the possibility left to each state to intervene against a state that had infringed a peremptory norm of international law, which at the same time is, by definition, an *erga omnes* obligation. He understood

that a community such as the international community, in seeking a more structured organization, even if only an incipient 'institutionalization', should have turned ... towards a system vesting in international institutions other than states the exclusive responsibility for determining the existence of a breach of an obligation of basic importance to the international community as a whole, and thereafter, for deciding what measures should be taken in response and how they should be implemented. Under the United Nations Charter, those responsibilities are vested in the competent organs of the Organization.[19]

Even more than his predecessor Ago, the second Special Rapporteur, Willem Riphagen, referred quite systematically to the organs of the United Nations and in particular to the Security Council, when dealing with what would have become, still at the time of his reports, the content and legal regime of the international

---

[19] R. Ago, 'Eighth Report on State Responsibility', YILC (1979), Vol. II, Part One, at 43, paras 91 and 92; on this matter see in particular Spinedi, n 7, esp. at 1115–19, and P. Klein, 'Responsibility for Serious Breaches of Obligations Deriving from Peremptory Norms of International Law and United Nations Law', 13 EJIL (2002) 5, 1241–55, esp. 1242–3.

responsibility for the crime of state, as defined in the 1976 Report of Ago.[20] For his part, Ago had been able to remain extremely vague on the issue, as his specific mandate was limited to the first part of the codification process, and was restricted to considering the wrongful act, without approaching even the basic features of the content and implementation of the responsibility for state crimes. As for the third Special Rapporteur, Mr Gaetano Arangio-Ruiz, he presented to the ILC quite a complete set of proposals for the establishment of a true procedure for the implementation of the responsibility for breach of community obligations, which will be further examined below in Section 4.

When going through the list of crimes identified by former Article 19(3), Riphagen had no difficulty, when tackling the 'crime of aggression', in concluding that the competent organs of the UN, and in particular the Security Council under Chapter VII, were the appropriate bodies to organize and enforce the responsibility of the delinquent state.[21] In practice, one may notice that such was indeed the case in a few concrete situations, in particular for Iraq after its invasion of Kuwait. After the end of the Gulf War, led by the Allied powers on the mandate delivered by Security Council Resolution 678 based on Chapter VII of the Charter, the international community recognized this very organ as its faithful representative. As a consequence, the Council was able to extend beyond the collective use of force the determination of, and strict international control over, the effectiveness of reparations, by creating in particular the UN Compensation Commission.[22]

The increasingly broad vision developed by the Security Council of the concept of 'maintenance of peace' made it possible for it to act, at least during the first half of the last decade of the twentieth century (1990–95) in defence of the interests—and even more of the values—held to be those belonging to the 'international community as a whole'.[23] As stated by Marina Spinedi, who served during the entire period of Ago's membership in the ILC as his research assistant,[24] this broad vision of the early 1990s seemed to meet the views of Ago and the majority of the ILC members at the time of the elaboration of the first part of the Draft in the 1970s.

Be that as it may, the progressive crumbling of UN authority in the Balkans affair, and its ultimate rejection by the military allies during the 1999 Kosovo crisis, clearly showed the marked tendency of the strongest states to have recourse to force *outside* the UN framework, and hence no longer to recognize the Security Council

---

[20] W. Riphagen, 'Third Report on the Content, Forms and Degrees of International Responsibility', YILC (1982), Vol. II, Part One, at 48, para. (4).          [21] Ibid.
[22] See Klein, n 19, at 1245; P.-M. Dupuy, 'Après la guerre du Golfe...', 95 RGDIP (1991) 635; by the same author, 'Sécurité collective et organisation de la paix', 97, RGDIP (1993) 619–33; J.M. Sorel, 'L'élargissement de la notion de menace contre la paix', in Société Française pour le Droit International (ed.), *Le Chapitre VII de la Charte des Nations Unies* (Paris: Pedone, 1995), 3–57.
[23] See G. Gaja, 'Réflexions sur le rôle du Conseil de sécurité dans le nouvel ordre mondial', 97 RGDIP (1993) 297–320; P. Picone, *Interventi delle Nazione Unite e diritto Internazionale* (Padua: CEDAM, 1995), 517–78.
[24] Spinedi, n 7 at 1099–125.

as the political body with the necessary legal and moral authority to promote and enforce *erga omnes* obligations.

This development of state practice is still likely to change. It is possible that, in the future, if the political preconditions are met, the Security Council will recover for a time the position of being the true protector of the interests and values of the international community. The core of the issue is the following: how to reconcile legal security with the political nature of the Security Council and its discretionary power to act or to refrain from acting if it considers that, given the political context, it is not appropriate to intervene in the face of a serious breach of an *erga omnes* obligation of essential importance for the international community as a whole.

As rightly noted by Pierre Klein,

the risk then would be of replacing one subjectivity (of states) by another (of the SC), a risk that would be only slightly attenuated by the more collective nature of the decision-making processes of the SC, without it being possible for the state concerned to employ any outside review mechanism.[25]

The Security Council possesses extensive discretionary power in classifying as well as implementing the coercive measures it may adopt under Chapter VII with a view to maintaining peace and security. As demonstrated by its practice, it also has discretion to reinterpret on a case-by-case basis what falls within its mandate in terms of 'threats to the peace' under Article 39 of the Charter, as well as 'peacekeeping', a notion which is subject to its sole interpretation and to successively broader or more restrictive versions.[26]

This structural and organic dimension leads to the conclusion that the ILC Articles' confidence in the existing institutions for promoting an efficient regime of responsibility for breaches of community interests and values remains without any clearly stable and sustainable solution. In order to appreciate whether this goal will ever be attainable in the future, a number of different scenarios may be invoked.

## 4. Possible future scenarios

It is of course quite risky to venture a description of what could possibly happen in the decades to come, from the viewpoint of the affirmation and development of the legal regime of state responsibility for breaches of peremptory norms of international law, that is, norms the violation of which infringe the interests of each and every member state of the international community. The following should only be taken for what it is: simply an exercise aimed at trying to reduce uncertainty by imagining, on as realistic a basis as possible, a tentative typology of situations that offer different legal perspectives with a view to reconciling as much as possible what should be with what will be. To simplify, the following scenarios focus on

[25] N 19, at 1249.
[26] See V. Gowlland-Debbas, 'Responsibility and the United Nations Charter', in Crawford, Pellet, and Olleson (eds), n 3, at 115–39.

situations in which the obligations breached are not only *erga omnes* but also peremptory in character.[27]

*The first scenario*, and by no means the least plausible, is that things remain as they are, however unsatisfactory this may be! No further developments, either institutional or purely normative, will take place. On the occasion of a review of the ILC Articles, states will consider that there is no need further to develop the content of the responsibility of states for this kind of breach, and that any development in this respect, either within or outside the UN framework, may appear not only premature but also inappropriate. To be sure, the notion of 'state crimes' has already been formally removed from the Articles;[28] but there still remains an echo of its presence in the text of Article 48 in the form of a 'breach of an obligation towards the international community as a whole', a notion which may appear to be—in particular, for at least one or two of the permanent members of the Council, if not more—a dangerous remainder of the second part of the twentieth century. Would it be too adventurous to say that a good number of other countries, including major developing countries, share the same scepticism at the present time? The question at least warrants being raised.

Under such a scenario, the situation would be far from stable. On the contrary, the weaknesses and loopholes of the regime of international responsibility for this kind of breach of the law would leave room for the sporadic development of unilateral or collective initiatives more or less inspired by the provisions set out in Article 48(2) of the ILC Articles. However, state responsibility would remain outside any institutional control, at least at the universal level. One may nevertheless add that, despite the fact that countermeasures are in principle only designed to be used by the 'injured state' in the strict sense of Article 42, states could nevertheless apply by analogy the conditions set out under Articles 50 to 52, and in particular the condition of proportionality under Article 51, when acting in defence of community interests and values against the perpetrator of a violation of an *erga omnes* obligation. The regulation of such practice would nevertheless remain under states' sole initiative. As a consequence, there is absolutely no guarantee that states would act with a sense of self-restraint and respect for the international rule of law. The danger of anarchical conduct ensuing and of a 'hijacking' of the argument of acting in defence of the world community then could hardly be avoided.

*The second scenario*, contrary to the previous one characterized by the absence of institutionalization, would be that of a systematic development of new procedures within the UN system. Such exercise had already been proposed by the third Special Rapporteur, Gaetano Arangio-Ruiz, in his seventh report (1995). He

---

[27] As it is known, the two notions only overlap with each other partially. All peremptory norms of international law are *erga omnes* ones but the reverse is not true. Some authors take nevertheless another view and consider that *erga omnes* obligations and obligations deriving from *jus cogens* norms not only overlap but indeed coincide. See Cassese, n 18, at 416–18.

[28] See E. Wyler, 'From "State Crime" to "Responsibility for Serious Breaches of Obligations under Peremptory Norms of General International Law"', 13 EJIL (2002) 1147; J. Crawford, 'International Crimes of States', in Crawford, Pellet, and Olleson (eds), n 3, at 405–15.

submitted to the ILC a highly elaborate proposal for a new institutional structure based on the existing principal organs of the UN, with a view to implementing the international responsibility of states for acts that at the time were still classified as 'state crimes', on the basis of the original version of Article 19 as adopted in Ago's reports.[29] The mechanism proposed was highly sophisticated and recommended that:

First, any state member of the UN (and party to an eventual codification treaty on state responsibility) 'claiming that an international crime has been or is being committed by one or more states shall bring the matter to the attention of the General Assembly or the SC . . . in accordance with Chapter VI of the Charter'.

Secondly, the International Court of Justice (ICJ) could be seized by any UN member state party to the codification treaty, after a vote adopted by a qualified majority of either the General Assembly or the Security Council justifying the grave concern of the international community. It would be for the Court to decide 'whether the alleged international crime has been or is being committed by the accused state'.[30]

A judgment of the ICJ would then authorize any UN member state party to the codification treaty to implement the 'special or supplementary legal consequences of international crimes of states as contemplated in the present part'.

The advantage of this proposal lay in using three of the permanent organs of the UN according to their respective capacity without any need for revising the Charter. It is nevertheless significant to note that the proposal was not adopted by the ILC itself mainly because it was considered too unrealistic. Indeed, this appraisal already seemed justified in 1995 and it is still the case, not only today but most probably for decades to come. Nevertheless, this does not mean that all the content of the proposals made by Professor Arangio-Ruiz should be cast aside. His proposal seems to remain a useful contribution as it provides politicians, diplomats, and scholars with a model regime that could serve at least as a source of reflection if not even of inspiration.

*In search of a third and more realistic scenario*: at this stage, it seems necessary to review what truly is at stake when we discuss the question of how to develop and consolidate a viable legal regime for state responsibility for breaches of 'obligations owed to the international community as a whole'. There appear to be three major concerns. First, to avoid the obsolescence of the very principle of a specific and aggravated responsibility for this type of serious breach, a development which, if realized, would jeopardize the very survival of states' respect for peremptory norms of international law, if not also the legal significance of any reference to 'the international community as a whole'. Secondly, to ensure that any legal regime of this kind would not be used in an anarchic way by individual states (or by a group of states acting collectively) to take measures outside any international control by turning the argument of defence of a community interest into a convenient alibi for the realization of very specific political strategies. Thirdly, and additionally,

---

[29] G. Arangio-Ruiz, 'Seventh Report on State Responsibility', YILC (1995), Vol. II, Part One.
[30] See YILC (1995), Vol. II, Part Two, at 46, no. 117.

to strive to define with as much precision as possible cumulative legal criteria for enabling recourse by states to countermeasures as a reaction to the violation of peremptory and *erga omnes* obligations.

## 5. The importance of the Kosovo case (1999)

Keeping in mind these three concerns, one may reflect upon a past experience which could reoccur in the future, if circumstances allow, and which may be viewed as a kind of precedent, with all the legal consequences attached to it. This experience was provided by the way in which the Western Allies, grouped under the umbrella of NATO, had recourse to air strikes in order to stop the blatant violation by what was at that time the Federal Republic of Yugoslavia (FRY) of its humanitarian obligations towards the ethnic Albanians in Kosovo. In March 1998, acting under Chapter VII, the Security Council adopted Resolution 1160 (1998) in which the FRY and the Kosovar Albanians were called upon to reach a political solution through negotiation. At the same time, an arms embargo was imposed on both sides. On the ground, the situation continued to deteriorate, causing significant civilian casualties as well as the massive displacement of innocent populations and a massive flow of refugees into neighbouring countries.

As a consequence, on 23 September 1998 the Security Council adopted Resolution 1199, again on the basis of Chapter VII of the UN Charter, in which it declared that what was happening in Kosovo constituted a 'threat to peace and security in the region'. The Council urged the parties to apply a ceasefire as well as to take urgent steps to improve the humanitarian situation and enter into negotiations with international involvement. The resolution also contemplated the possibility of taking additional measures in the event that the two sides, starting with the FRY, refused to comply with the binding requests of Resolutions 1160 and 1199. The following weeks demonstrated, in particular due to the attitude adopted by Russia, that the Security Council would not be in a position to adopt these new measures which would have logically comprised authorization to have recourse to force in order to address the growing threats to international peace, in particular the massive flow of refugees across the border.

Although nothing in the terms of the aforementioned resolutions made it legally possible, this was the context in which, absent any authorization given to the UN member states to have recourse to such steps, the NATO countries nevertheless decided to take military action if the FRY did not comply with the Security Council resolutions. In an attempt to legitimize this initiative, the NATO Secretary-General based this decision on violations by the FRY of the two Council resolutions, the continuation of the humanitarian crisis, and the assessment that the Council was unable in the near future to adopt any new resolution. He concluded 'that the Allies believe that in the particular circumstances with respect to the present crisis in Kosovo as described in UNSC Resolution 1199, there are legitimate grounds for the Alliance to threaten, and if necessary, to use force.'[31] A few months later, after the adoption of another resolution by the Council, the terms of which nevertheless did not contain an authorization for UN member states to have recourse to force, the NATO Allies, in the face of the further deterioration of the humanitarian situation on the ground and the refusal of the FRY to abide by the injunctions contained in the resolutions, decided to have recourse to a comprehensive series of air strikes.

The actual fact of this recourse to force outside the strict conditions defined by the UN Charter as further interpreted in particular during the early 1990s raised the issue of the *legitimacy* of the NATO members' action as contrasted to its formal *illegality*. Interestingly enough, this gave rise in particular to a debate among several eminent scholars and in particular Professors Bruno Simma and Antonio Cassese.[32]

According to the former of these two scholars, taking into consideration the fact that the Alliance 'had made every effort to get as close to legality as possible' by linking its efforts to the existing Council resolutions, 'only a thin red line separates NATO's action on Kosovo from international legality'.[33] Nevertheless Simma warned against the 'boomerang effect' which could result from such breaches of the Charter even if 'this danger can at least be reduced by indicating the concrete circumstances that led to a decision ad hoc being destined to remain singular'.[34]

For his part, Cassese, while sharing the view that the use of force by NATO countries against the FRY was contrary to the UN Charter since NATO had acted without any authorization of the Security Council, nevertheless disagreed with Simma when the latter considered that this resort to illegality should not set any precedent and remain as an isolated exception if one wanted to avoid the risk of damaging the Charter. Taking advantage of the fact that 'in the current framework of the international community, three sets of values underpin the overarching system of inter-state relations: peace, human rights and self-determination',[35] Cassese reflected upon the strategic, geopolitical, and ideological context in which the NATO countries had taken their decision while mainly insisting on the analysis of the justifications given by them for such military action.

Their main justification has been that the authorities of FRY had carried out massacres and other gross breaches of human rights as well as mass expulsions of thousands of their citizens belonging to a particular ethnic group, and that this humanitarian catastrophe would most likely destabilize neighbouring countries such as Albania, Bosnia and Herzegovina and the Former Yugoslav Republic of Macedonia, thus constituting a threat to the peace and stability of the region. (at 25)

---

[31] Letter from Secretary-General Solana, addressed to the permanent representatives in the North Atlantic Council, dated 9 October 1998.

[32] Both published an article in 10 EJIL (1998) 1: B. Simma, 'NATO, the UN and the Use of Force: Legal Aspects', 1–22; A. Cassese, *Ex injuria ius oritur*: Are We Moving towards International Legitimacy of Forcible Humanitarian Countermeasures in the World Community?', 23–31; see also Cassese, n 18, at 415–20.

[33] See B. Simma, n 32, at 22.    [34] Ibid.    [35] See A. Cassese, n 32, at 24.

The same author continued by asking

faced with such an enormous human-made tragedy and given the inaction of the UN SC due to the refusal of Russia and China to countenance any expulsions, should one sit idly by and watch thousands of human beings being slaughtered or brutally persecuted? Should one remain silent and inactive only because the existing body of international law proves incapable of remedying such a situation?

His answer is that 'from an ethic viewpoint resort to armed force was justified' even if manifestly contrary to current international law.[36]

That being said, with a view to overtaking the present state of the law and adopting a kind of a *de lege ferenda* approach, Cassese was careful to foresee an evolution 'based on ... nascent trends in the world community' making it legally possible in the future for states to take collective action to prevent new humanitarian catastrophes as a substitute for a paralysed Security Council. He set out in a cumulative and rather restrictive way the conditions under which such a substitution of action would become not only legitimate but even legal: gross and egregious breaches of human rights 'involving loss of life of hundreds or thousands of innocent people; amounting to crime against humanity'; resulting from anarchy in a sovereign state where the central authorities would evidently be utterly unable to put an end to those crimes; while 'the SC is unable to take any coercive action to stop the massacres because of disagreement among the Permanent Members'; and all peaceful avenues to achieve a solution based on negotiation having been explored and exhausted without success.

Two remarks can be made by way of commentary to the stimulating proposals of the former President of the ICTY in this respect, which in no way contradict his approach, but rather try simply to see how to make use of them for the purposes of presenting the states with a possible legal regime of responsibility for breach of peremptory norms of international law.

First, it should not be forgotten that in 1999 the aim of this kind of unilateral collective substitution of action was not, and would not necessarily be in the future, to implement an international regime of responsibility for crimes, however they would or could be characterized. Rather, this action was a way of addressing the paralysis of the Council so that it did not lead to the continuation or aggravation of a humanitarian catastrophe. One is here on the same ground as the general position taken with respect to all actions taken by the Security Council. These actions are not primarily aimed at judging or condemning a state declared responsible for not implementing its obligation of reparation. Rather, Security Council initiatives are legally taken according to the Charter with a view to re-establishing a situation so that it no longer constitutes a threat to the peace by the very fact of its incompatibility with the international rule of law. Within the framework of the law of the UN Charter, the Council discharges the function to maintain international peace and take the measures necessary when the peace is threatened or breached. The Council is neither a prosecutor nor a judge, even if the measures which it is able to take are a response to the commission of a wrongful act constituting a danger for the international community as a whole.[37]

---

[36] Ibid, 25.        [37] See V. Gowlland-Debbas, n 26, fn 22.

That being said, Cassese is right in stressing that the legal grounds for actions in substitution for those which the Security Council would have been able to take in Kosovo in 1998 and 1999, had it not been paralysed by the veto, should be seen within the framework of the nascent trends in the world community with regard to the protection of human rights, the respect of cardinal principles of humanitarian law and respect for the rights of people—all rights the violation of which constitutes precisely a breach of obligations 'owed to the international community as a whole'. In other words, one should take into account the aims and the underlying basis in any analysis of the relationship between actions of the type undertaken by the NATO countries in Kosovo, and any future regime of responsibility in this field. Furthermore, as for the respective aims (of actions of the Kosovo type, and actions designed to react to a breach of a peremptory norm), there may be a partial overlap between the two inasmuch as both are (also) taken in order to attain the cessation of the wrongdoing.

The second observation is that the Kosovo experience dealt with the ultimate level of reaction conceivable for members of the international community acting without authorization from the Security Council, that is, *recourse to force*. Other measures are of course possible which would not constitute an exception to the customary international law rule established on the basis of Article 2(4) of the UN Charter, namely the prohibition of force which falls under the classical concept of 'reprisals', today repackaged under the less precise notion of 'countermeasures', the intrinsic illegality of which is negated by the very fact that they respond to the previous commission of a wrongful act by another state.

## 6. A few constructive suggestions

The two above observations should be borne in mind when envisaging the main features of a potential regime of state responsibility for breaches of peremptory obligations owed to the international community. Based on all the considerations set out above, including the three concerns expressed in relation to the search for a viable scenario, three remarks are warranted:

First, any reaction from the states 'objectively' or 'indirectly' injured by a breach of an obligation towards the international community should be reserved only to those situations in which the Security Council is unable to take any efficient measures due to the persistent use of the veto by one or more permanent members. This, of course, is premised on a general assumption: that any breach of this type of obligation may be interpreted as constituting at least a 'threat to the peace', enabling the Security Council to take action. This assumption may be understood on the basis that this organ is, by virtue of the Charter, the one that best represents 'the international community as a whole'. In other words, the Council is, as a question of priority, the one organ that would have as its task: (i) to characterize the wrongful act and (ii) either to decide the measures to be taken by UN member states, or to authorize them to take such measures.

Secondly, it may happen that the breach of any such obligation does not constitute the object of a procedure for the peaceful settlement of disputes, either upon the unilateral initiative of the responsible state itself or on the initiative of this same state and another state (or states) acting individually or collectively, by way of negotiation, mediation, conciliation, or judicial means. If this is so, the member states of the international community will be able to invoke the responsibility of the state they deem responsible. They will also be able, under the conditions recalled above, to take countermeasures against this state aimed at obtaining (i) the cessation of the internationally wrongful act, and assurances and guarantees of non-repetition and (ii) the performance of the obligation of reparation in the interest of the injured state and of all the beneficiaries of the obligation breached.

Thirdly, any such countermeasure must be commensurate with the injury suffered, taking into account the gravity of the internationally wrongful act and the rights in question. It does not exclude recourse to force, but such recourse is limited exclusively to the case in which the persistent wrongful conduct of the responsible state would lead to a situation seriously affecting human rights, the rights of a people and/or of civilian populations, involving loss of life of hundreds or thousands of innocent people and amounting to crimes against humanity.

In contrast to the provisions of the current Article 48, the main but, it is submitted, fundamental difference of the regime proposed above is that it attempts to fill the gap between the mere *invocation of responsibility* by any member of the international community—as is already envisaged by the ILC under Article 48—and the actual *taking of measures or 'countermeasures'* listed currently under Article 52, the use of which is, however, reserved for the time being to the individually injured state(s) as defined under Article 42, with the negative consequence that the responsibility for breach of obligations towards the international community as a whole is for now restricted to a 'right of invocation' without any indication of the measures that the states invoking the responsibility may take with a view to having this responsibility effectively implemented if not always enforced.

As seen above, it is in particular on the basis of state practice developed by at least a part of the international community of states in the Kosovo crisis that one may consider such a scenario as plausibly feasible in the future, taking due account, on the one hand, of the substantial developments that the law is confronted with, and on the other hand, the organic limits still affecting the United Nations, starting with the Security Council, with no real hope that any specific development in this respect may be realistically expected.

This chapter could well be interpreted as an imperfect and still incomplete way of tracing a rough outline of a legal regime of state responsibility still not deeply rooted in positive international law. However, it is at least an attempt to provide some food for thought, so that the defence of community values and interests, which are more and more dramatically evident at a time of globalization, will not remain a dead letter.

# 18

# Immunity of States and State Officials: A Major Stumbling Block to Judicial Scrutiny?

*Paola Gaeta*

## SUMMARY

The international legal order lacks a universal and compulsory system for enforcing international responsibility, and therefore the role that domestic courts play in this regard is crucial. The various facets of the doctrine of international immunities, however, can make the domestic judicial system unavailable in cases of claims against foreign states and (former or sitting) foreign state officials. The application of this doctrine to domestic claims concerning egregious violations of human rights has given rise to controversy. As for foreign state immunity, it has been argued that the *jus cogens* nature of international rules protecting human rights should prevail over those granting immunities. However, it is suggested that a better theoretical foundation can be found in the content and normative structure of the international rules on human rights. Since these rules protect fundamental rights of private individuals against abusive exercise of state sovereignty, it appears highly contradictory to call for the application of the rules of foreign state immunity for the sake of protecting state sovereignty when what is at stake is the application of international rules protecting individuals from the abuse of state sovereignty. In addition, if international rules on human rights are considered to confer rights upon individuals, it is only logical to contend that individuals are also the holders of the ensuing right to reparation in cases of violation. Domestic courts cannot therefore deny access to justice to the individual victims by opposing the doctrine of international immunities since this would amount, in most cases, to leaving the victims without a remedy. Finally, the doctrine of foreign state immunity must be brought into conformity with the development of international law and of the notion of sovereignty, which now has a functional and normative content and requires states to exercise their powers respecting the fundamental rights of human beings. As for personal immunities, international customary law does not seem to provide for an exception to their applicability in cases of serious violations of human rights amounting to international crimes.

It is, however, argued that, *de lege lata*, there can be cases where domestic courts can refuse to apply the rules on personal immunities in order to avoid a denial of justice. Finally, with regard to functional immunities, the general contention is made that they do not apply for domestic claims concerning international crimes. Nonetheless it would be wrong to consider that this constitutes a derogation from, or an exception to, the customary rules of international law on functional immunities. Arguably, there exists a rule of customary international law of *jus cogens* nature that obliges states not to recognize the fact that international crimes have been committed in an official capacity, and as a consequence not to recognize functional immunities with respect to claims related to the commission of these crimes.

## 1. The role of domestic courts in enforcing international responsibility

It is perhaps trivial to observe that the international legal order lacks a centralized enforcement mechanism. The progressive development of an international institutional framework, with the establishment of an impressive number of international institutions, bodies, and organizations endowed with a variety of competences in a variety of fields, not to mention the UN collective security mechanism and the International Court of Justice (ICJ), have not redressed the situation: the international community still lacks a centralized judicial and enforcement system for international responsibility, which is universal and compulsory in character.

When it comes to international state 'responsibility as answerability',[1] namely the possibility for states to be called to account for their allegedly internationally illegal conduct, the role that domestic courts are allowed to play is therefore crucial. Were national judicial apparatus empowered to deal with domestic claims based on alleged violations by states of their international obligations, the international legal order could count upon a high number of 'generals'[2] to ensure that wrongdoers are accountable for their internationally illegal behaviour. As has been correctly emphasized, this model, that finds its theoretical foundations in Georges Scelle's theory of role-splitting, is not so utopian as it might appear at first sight.[3] On the contrary, there are many tangible signs of the progressive organic integration of the domestic judicial apparatus within the international legal system: by

---

[1] See J. Crawford and J. Watkins, 'International Responsibility', in S. Besson and J. Tasioulas (eds), *The Philosophy of International Law* (Oxford: Oxford University Press, 2010), 283.

[2] The metaphor of international law as a field marshal who can only give orders to generals (states), with the consequence that it is only through 'generals' that international law orders can reach the 'troops' (individuals and state organs operating within a national legal system) goes back to H. Triepel, 'Les rapports entre le droit interne et le droit international', HR (1923), at 196. It was taken up by A. Cassese, *International Law in a Divided World* (Oxford: Clarendon Press, 1986), 15.

[3] P.-M. Dupuy, 'Unity in the Application of International Law at the Global Level and the Responsibility of Judges at the National Level: Reviewing Georges Scelle's "Role Splitting" Theory', in L. Boisson de Chazournes and M. Kohen (eds), *International Law and the Quest for Its Implementation: Liber Amicorum Vera Gowlland-Debbas* (The Hague: Martinus Nijhoff, 2010), 417.

way of examples, one may think of the systems of complementarity and of subsidiarity with regard to the International Criminal Court (ICC) and human rights bodies respectively,[4] and the more active role taken by some domestic courts in this respect.[5]

Nonetheless, impediments and obstacles to domestic judicial scrutiny over internationally wrongful acts do exist. These can be based entirely on national rules and doctrines, or can have an international origin. When it comes to international wrongs committed by foreign state and foreign state officials, the various facets of the doctrine of international immunities can make the national judicial system unavailable, unless the foreign state waives its own immunities or those of its officials, to allow national proceedings.[6]

Admittedly, the doctrine of international immunities has gone through a progressive erosion. With respect to foreign state immunity from civil jurisdiction, it is generally accepted that it is not available with respect to claims unrelated to the exercise of sovereign powers (*acta iure imperii*), or at least with respect to some specific claims (the so-called commercial exception). Similarly, with respect to diplomatic immunities, it is well known—and codified in the 1961 Vienna Convention—that they do not apply in cases of civil or administrative claims concerning specific activities of the foreign diplomat. However, controversy exists with respect to the availability of foreign state immunity and diplomatic immunities when it comes to domestic claims concerning egregious violations of human rights amounting to international crimes. As for functional immunities of foreign state officials, it seems to be less controversial that they do not apply in relation to such claims, although the scope and purport of their unavailability seems not to have been fully grasped.

## 2. Why foreign state immunity shall not apply in cases of serious violations of human rights and the subsidiary role of domestic civil jurisdiction

The question that must be assessed is whether domestic jurisdictions are in fact obliged to respect the traditional rule on immunity of foreign states in respect to domestic civil claims related to serious violations of human rights. The general wisdom is that they are, and consequently that domestic courts have to deny access to justice to the individuals who have suffered injuries because of serious violations

---

[4] Dupuy, n 3,
[5] See in this volume J.A. Menon, Chapter 47, 'The Low Road: Promoting Civil Redress for International Wrongs'.
[6] The view, however, has been put forward according to which foreign international customary law does not oblige domestic jurisdictions to recognize foreign state immunity and that this is a privilege that can be denied by domestic law (L.M. Clapan, 'State Immunity, Human Rights and *Jus Cogens*: A Critique of the Normative Hierarchy Theory', 97 AJIL (2003) 741).

of human rights attributable to a foreign state.[7] However, a perusal of national case law shows that a different position can be taken. Suffice here to mention the dissenting opinion of Judge Patricia Wald to the ruling of the US Court of Appeals in *Princz v Federal Republic of Germany*,[8] the decision of the Greek Areos Pagos in the *Distomo* case,[9] and the case law of the Italian Court of Cassation, starting with the *Ferrini* case,[10] in relation to claims concerning alleged wrongful behaviour by Germany during the Second World War (a case law which has given rise to a controversy between Italy and Germany that at the time of writing is pending before the ICJ).[11]

Various arguments have been put forward to justify that in cases of serious violations of human rights (in particular those that can be described as international crimes) states are not internationally obliged to recognize foreign state immunity. The main argument focuses on the *jus cogens* nature of the rules of international law prohibiting international crimes and asserts that, given the hierarchical normative supremacy of these rules with respect to all other rules of international law (including those concerning state immunity), the former must prevail.[12]

Arguably, however, the theoretical foundation of the unavailability of the doctrine of foreign state immunity is related more to the content and the normative structure of the rules protecting fundamental human rights from serious abuse, and to the legal notion of sovereignty, rather than to normative hierarchy.

As for the content of the international rules protecting human rights, it is well known that they aim at protecting fundamental rights of private individuals against abusive exercise of state sovereignty. As a consequence it logically makes no sense to oppose the doctrine of foreign state immunity as a bulwark protecting sovereignty exactly when it comes to its abuse in respect to private individuals. It would, indeed, be highly contradictory to call for the application of the rules of state immunity for the sake of protecting state sovereignty, when what is at stake is the application of international rules which protect individuals from abuses of

---

[7] See, among others, C. Tomuschat, *Human Rights: Between Idealism and Realism*, 2nd edn (Oxford: Oxford University Press, 2008), 379–86, who after an articulated reasoning contends that '[t]o lift the ban of immunity would certainly open up a bonanza for lawyers, but would not really benefit the victims' and advocates 'some coordination with reparation measures at the inter-state level' to pay financial compensation to the victims.

[8] *Princz v Federal Republic of Germany*, United States, Court of Appeals of the District of Columbia Circuit, 1 July 1994, 26 F3d 1166 (1994), Dissenting Opinion of Judge Wald, in 103 ILR 612–21.        [9] *Prefecture of Voiotoia v Germany*, Judgment of 4 May 2000, in 129 ILR 513.

[10] Corte di Cassazione (Sezioni Unite), Decision of 6 November 2003, no. 5044, in 87 Rivista di diritto internazionale (2004) 539. For subsequent case law see Order of 29 May 2008, no. 14201 *Germany v Giovanni Mantelli et al*, available at <http://www.cortedicassazione.it>; *Milde v Italy*, Decision of 21 October 2008, no. 1072, in 92 Rivista di diritto internazionale (2009) 618; *Germany v Prefecture Vojotia*, Decision of 12 January 2011, still unreported (on file with the author).

[11] *Jurisdictional Immunities of the State* (*Germany v Italy*), proceedings instituted by Germany on 23 December 2008.

[12] See, eg, the authors quoted by Tomuschat, n 7, at 382 fn 111. The distinguished author, however, criticizes this view, which would fail to distinguish between 'substantive rules of *jus cogens* and the substantive and procedural consequences of their breach' (ibid at 383).

state sovereignty![13] Furthermore, this position is strengthened if we start from the assumption that these international rules protecting fundamental human rights impose upon states obligations vis-à-vis individuals. Violations of these rules would therefore by necessity give rise to the international obligation of the responsible state to repair the damage caused to the individuals, who will therefore be the bearers of the corresponding international right. Just to be clear, this does not mean that individuals automatically have *locus standi* before international bodies or that they can directly bring a claim against the responsible state at the international level. However, this is precisely where the role-splitting theory must come into play. Private individuals may indeed enforce their international right to reparation before a competent national tribunal.[14] The extent to which domestic legal systems allow victims of serious violations of human rights to sue the responsible state may of course vary, and in some cases reparation claims can and have been dismissed on national procedural grounds.[15] This, however, does not mean that the doctrine of foreign state immunity must constitute a stumbling block to the hearings of those domestic claims.

On the other hand, one has to consider that the doctrine of foreign state immunity has developed at a time when international law merely regulated inter-state conduct and the positivistic view, according to which states are born free to behave as they wish subject to respect for the equal freedom of their peers, was predominant. It was therefore only natural to conceive that states had to be protected by the exercise of national (civil) jurisdiction, since it was considered that only at the intergovernmental level issues of state responsibility could and should have been solved, in accordance to the *adagio par in parem non habet judicium*. Today, this view is no longer tenable. As the Italian Court of Cassation has rightly put it in a recent judgment, to contend that foreign state immunities are meant to protect this notion of sovereignty is still to conceive the international legal order as 'an empty space',[16]

---

[13] See in this vein the Italian Court of Cassation in *Milde v Italy*, n 10, where the Court states:

> non avrebbe senso proclamare il primate dei diritti fondamentali della persona e poi, contraddittoriamente escludere la possibilità di accesso al giudice negando, in tal modo, agli individui la possibilità di usare i mezzi indispensabili ad assicurare l'effettività e la preminenza di quei diritti fondamentali conculcati nell'azione criminosa di uno Stato.

[14] One clear example of the individual right to compensation vis-à-vis the state can be found in EU law, and relates to the right that individuals possess with regard to member states which have violated European Union law and have caused them damage. As the European Court of Justice has noted, this substantive individual right to compensation can only be enforced within the competent domestic legal system, due to the absence of European legislation in this regard. See P. Gaeta, 'Are Victims of War Crimes Entitled to Compensation?', in O. Ben Naftali (ed.), *International Human Rights and Humanitarian Law* (Oxford: Oxford University Press, 2011), 305–27, and the authors quoted in fn 63.                                         [15] Ibid, and for further reference fn 65.

[16] *Germany v Prefecture Vojotia*, above n 10, where the Court rightly observes:

> Le teorie che fondano l'immunità sul principio di eguaglianza degli Stati sono portate a configurare un diritto assoluto all'immunità che, come dimostra l'esperienza statunitense, non è, in realtà, mai esistito. Si tratta di una visione astratta dello spazio internazionale, inteso come spazio vuoto piuttosto che come spazio di cooperazione. Mentre la storia degli ultimi decenni ha visto affermarsi, sempre di più, una sfera di normazione sovranazionale intesa al rispetto e alla tutela dei diritti umani.

which is entirely at odds with contemporary reality. The international legal order has evolved to become a normative legal order which also contains rules directed at regulating the exercise of sovereign powers vis-à-vis the individuals, who are becoming more and more (paraphrasing Kant) the ends of states' conduct, and not the means to states' ends. In other words, although the doctrine of foreign state immunity might still find its place in contemporary international law to protect state sovereignty, what has dramatically changed is indeed this notion: state sovereignty has a functional and normative content, which among other things require states to exercise their powers respecting the fundamental rights of human beings.

Admittedly, in cases of serious violations of human rights there could be a very large number of victims, and therefore of potential plaintiffs, with all the ensuing practical problems that might arise in the absence of an appropriate system for class action in the relevant domestic legal order. In addition, since the amount of financial compensation in relation to each claim will be determined by the judges, the responsible state can be condemned to pay an unknown and very large total amount of money to repair the wrongs caused to each individual victim. In all probability, these uncertainties would put the responsible state in the impossible position of establishing *ex ante* the necessary fiscal measures to face its reparative obligations. Finally, from the point of view of the individual victims, one cannot underestimate the difficulty of going through a lengthy and complicated civil procedure, which would surely need the assistance of qualified lawyers. In the absence of pro bono legal assistance and other measures that can facilitate recourse to civil proceedings, for many of the victims to sue the responsible state before the civil courts is simply not a feasible option. It is for these reasons that, even if the doctrine of foreign sovereign immunity would not be applied as a rule, recourse to national civil courts would prove not to be the panacea for ensuring reparation of serious violations of human rights. Resort should be made to other traditional mechanisms which should take precedence, such as diplomatic protection and lump-sum agreements. In addition, since serious violations of human rights also allow non-injured states to request reparation on behalf of the injured state or injured victims, a collective body could be established (eg a commission within the UN) with the task formally to request the responsible state to comply with its reparative obligations and, if necessary, to negotiate the various aspects to put compliance into practice (eg calculation of the lump-sum to be paid, damage to be covered, etc.). Domestic civil claims should therefore play a subsidiary role, when the victims are left without any remedy, due to the failure of their state of nationality and of the international community to exercise their right to demand reparation and to induce the responsible state to repair the wrongs caused to them.[17]

---

[17] On the residual role of domestic compensation claims in cases of serious violations of human rights by foreign states, see also M. Frulli, 'When States Are Liable towards Individuals for Serious Violations of International Humanitarian Law? The *Markovic* Case', 1 JICJ (2003) 406, at 426.

## 3. Personal immunities and international crimes: are they really untouchable?

Following the judgment of the ICJ in the *Arrest Warrant* case,[18] it is usually maintained that the rules of customary international law on *personal immunities* (of which diplomatic immunities could be considered a category) would continue to apply even in relation to serious violations of human rights amounting to international crimes. Clearly these rules can be derogated from by treaties, as is the case with the Rome Statute, which renders them inapplicable among state parties in relation to a request of arrest and surrender issued by the ICC.[19] With respect to customary international law, however, state practice clearly indicates that these rules are not subject to exceptions in the matter of international crimes.[20] This view has also been confirmed by the ICJ in the *Arrest Warrant* case. Although the issue is usually discussed with respect to criminal charges and proceedings, one could speculate that the same conclusion is also intended to apply to civil claims.[21]

Elsewhere, I have already expressed the view that *de lege lata* this situation appears to be sound.[22] Personal immunities are designed to safeguard state sovereignty by shielding those state officials representing the state abroad from undue interference in the local state, so that no obstacle or impediment is set to the performance of their official functions abroad. The need to protect states from undue interference by other states in the official activity of their organs acting abroad is crucial for the smooth conduct of international dealings. It therefore appears that the safeguard of personal immunities should be given pride of place, even in the case of the alleged commission of international crimes. This is even more so if one considers that personal immunities are of a temporal nature, and therefore in principle they do not protect forever their beneficiaries from the criminal or civil jurisdiction of the forum state.

One could, however, wonder whether these remarks necessarily apply across the board, so to speak, and whether situations might be envisaged *de lege ferenda* where personal immunities can exceptionally be set aside to hear domestic civil or criminal claims related to the commission of international crimes. Clearly, the rules on procedural immunities (as personal immunities under international law are) constitute the outcome of a delicate balance between two sets of conflicting values: the principle of equality before the law and the need to safeguard the exercise of some specific state functions from abusive prosecution. With the evolution of international criminal law, another element has come into the picture, namely the

---

[18] ICJ, *Arrest Warrant of 11 April 2000 (Democratic Republic of Congo v Belgium)*, judgment of 14 February 2002, ICJ Reports 2002, 3.

[19] P. Gaeta, 'Official Capacity and Immunities', in A. Cassese, P. Gaeta, and J.R.W.D. Jones (eds), *The Rome Statute of the International Criminal Court: A Commentary* (Oxford: Oxford University Press, 2002), 975, at 990–6.

[20] For an analysis of the state practice in this regard, see M. Frulli, *Immunità e crimini internazionali* (Turin: Giappichelli, 2004), 210–44. See also A. Cassese, *International Law*, 2nd edn (Oxford: Oxford University Press, 2005), 119–20. [21] Frulli, n 20, at 237–40.

[22] Gaeta, n 19. The views expressed in this section are based on the view contained therein.

need to ensure that serious crimes do not go unpunished. The question therefore is to what extent this recent development can modify the balance between the two aforementioned conflicting values which was reached in the past through the formation of customary rules on personal immunities.

To answer this question, an interesting starting point is the little-known exception to the otherwise absolute nature of the international rules on diplomatic immunities, in the field of both civil and criminal jurisdiction. Article 38(1) of the 1961 Vienna Convention provides that these immunities are not absolute if the foreign diplomat has the nationality of the receiving state, because they only apply to official acts accomplished by the diplomat in the exercise of his functions.[23] As an authoritative commentator correctly noted, the rationale behind the denial of diplomatic immunity in such cases is the need to avoid *risking a denial of justice.*[24] For the state of which the individual is a diplomat will not usually have criminal and civil jurisdiction over the illegal acts committed by him in the territory of the receiving state. For the receiving state, therefore, to confine itself to declaring him *persona non grata* and to sending him back to the state he represents could mean that he would never face criminal or civil proceedings in the sending state, or that—whenever they can be prosecuted *in absentia* in the territorial state—the punishment will never be executed.

One could rely upon the rationale behind this traditional exception to the diplomatic immunities rules in order to establish whether another possible exception can be added in cases of domestic claims in relation to international crimes. Arguably, the general contention is warranted that personal immunities cease to operate whenever the courts to which the individual organ belongs lack jurisdiction over the crimes or torts allegedly committed by that organ. This proposition applies *a fortiori* when the alleged crimes have been committed on the territory of the receiving or host state, since this state has a particular interest in the prosecution and punishment of the crimes in question and/or to ensure that the victims are not left without a remedy. In addition, personal immunities should not be granted when, although the state to which the organ belongs does have jurisdiction over the crimes allegedly committed, nevertheless the receiving state has compelling

---

[23] 'Except insofar as additional privileges and immunities may be granted by the receiving State, a diplomatic agent who is a national of or permanently resident in that State shall enjoy only immunity from jurisdiction, and inviolability, in respect of official acts performed in the exercise of his functions.'

[24] G. Sperduti, *Lezioni di diritto internazionale* (Milan: Giuffrè, 1958), 131–2. He notes:

L'immunità, a chiunque riconosciuta, incontra come limite costante che non siano sacrificati superiori esigenze di giustizia.... Questa sicura tendenza del diritto internazionale ad armonizzare le esenzioni dalla giurisdizione con le esigenze della giustizia, e soprattutto [sic] ad evitare che l'immunità si risolva in un diniego di giustizia (o, come si è anche detto, in un *juridical vacuum*) trova espressione in vari atti internazionali...Appare, così, del tutto giustificato che il diritto internazionale non imponga ad uno stato di accordare l'esenzione dalla giurisdizione agli agenti diplomatici di Stati esteri, aventi la nazionalità di tale Stato:...gli agenti diplomatici aventi la cittadinanza dello Stato, in cui esplicano le loro funzioni, se fossero esenti dalla giurisdizione di questo Stato, sarebbero esenti dalla giurisdizione praticamente in senso assoluto, almeno fino a quando durino in carica. Ciò darebbe luogo ad una situazione giuridica contraria ad ogni criterio di giustizia.

reasons to believe either that the sending state will not exercise it (eg because the relevant state authorities have been implicated, either actively or passively, in the commission of the crimes), or that the exercise of criminal or civil jurisdiction will be barred by specific national rules pertaining to the particular status of the individual in question (eg personal immunity or statute of limitation under national law).

However, the aforementioned exception should not apply in cases of criminal charges against a sitting head of state or sitting head of government. This conclusion is not based on the notion that for heads of state the *ne impediatur legatio* principle should prevail over the demands of justice. The rationale behind the above proposition is that to arrest and to bring to trial before a foreign court a sitting head of state or head of government might seriously jeopardize the structure and functioning of the foreign state, since those individuals discharge important and sensitive constitutional functions. Therefore, with regard to these two categories of state officials, the two counter-weighing values at stake are no longer the need to enable foreign dignitaries freely to fulfil official functions abroad, on the one hand, and the necessity to ensure justice by prosecuting and trying alleged international criminals, on the other hand. Rather, we are faced here with the need to strike a balance between the demands of justice, on the one side, and the need to avoid any conduct which might lead to the disruption of the highest institutions of a foreign state, on the other side. In addition, the possibility for heads of state and heads of government to be arrested and prosecuted abroad might lend itself to serious abuse, and this of course could put international peaceful relations in considerable jeopardy. These considerations warrant the conclusion that in the case under discussion personal immunities should prevail. Faced with allegations that a foreign head of state or head of government has perpetrated international crimes, the authorities of other states should either deny entry into the territory or, if the charges have been made after entry, request the foreign dignitary immediately to leave the country.[25]

## 4. Some misunderstandings on functional immunities and international crimes

On the face of it, the question of the applicability of the international rules on functional immunities for international crimes-related claims seems to be less unclear, from a strict legal point of view, than the one concerning state and personal immunity. It is usually contended that the rules of customary international law on *functional immunities*—protecting state officials from foreign jurisdiction for acts committed in their official capacity—would not apply, with the consequence that they could be held responsible for international crimes before the domestic courts

---

[25] The question could be raised whether the proposition set forth above also applies to ministers for foreign affairs, on the assumption that under customary international law they are entitled to personal immunity.

of a foreign state.[26] Here again, as in the case of personal immunity, the matter is often debated only with respect to criminal charges, but the contention can be made that the invoked inapplicability of functional immunities also concerns domestic civil suits based on international crimes.[27]

What is worth noting is the approach taken to the issue at hand. The question which is debated—and that generally receives an affirmative answer by the majority of scholars—is whether customary international law provides for an exception to the applicability of the rules on functional immunities in cases of charges of international crimes. Discussing functional immunities as an exception to otherwise applicable rules, however, could be misleading. Functional immunities in international law serve to determine the 'irresponsibility' of the agent of the state for acts accomplished in the exercise of his function before foreign domestic jurisdiction, to make only the state responsible under international law. The very birth of international criminal law is based on the rejection of such a paradigm, since—as the Nuremberg Tribunal forcefully put it—'crimes against international law are committed by men, not by abstract entities, and only by punishing individuals who commit such crimes can the provisions of international law be enforced.' In other words, in Nuremberg the principle of irrelevance of having acted in an official capacity has been asserted as the necessary postulate for the assertion of personal criminal liability for serious violations of international law amounting to international crimes. The impact of the new paradigm set forth in Nuremberg is that, at least for some specific conduct, states are not the exclusive duty-bearers under international law, and that also individuals must be internationally liable. In a way, the Nuremberg paradigm partially responds to what is one of the main criticisms raised against the theory of international responsibility as a form of 'collective' responsibility, namely that of its ineffectiveness in promoting compliance with international obligations: why should a state agent be induced to comply with international parameters and values if he knows that he will never personally incur any sanction, at the international level, for his illegal behaviour?[28]

In light of the above, it is apparent that to describe the principle of the irrelevance of having acted in an official capacity as an exception of, or a derogation from, the customary rules of international law on functional immunities, is patently wrong. In international law states are free to dispose of the scope of their criminal and civil jurisdiction, and of many other aspects related to their sovereignty, with the only exception of respect for *jus cogens* rules. This means that states are at liberty, if they wish, not to exercise their criminal and civil jurisdiction beyond what is imposed on them by customary international law. To maintain that, in cases of international crimes, there is an exception to or derogation from the rules of international law

---

[26] See, among others, Cassese, n 20, at 113. A contrary view has, however, been put forward by the Special Rapporteur of the International Law Commission, Roman Anatolevich Kolodkin, in his Second Report on immunity of state officials from foreign criminal jurisdiction, 10 June 2010, A/CN.4/631.         [27] For a lucid analysis of state practice in this regard see Frulli, n 20, at 143–72.

[28] See P. Allot, 'State Responsibility and the Unmaking of International Law', 29 Harv Int'l L Rev (1988) 14, and the remarks by Crawford and Watkins, n 1, who correctly observe that this criticism has radical implications, since it would require that 'states should surrender their standing as principal duty-bearer under international law in favour of individuals' (at 291).

on functional immunities could lead to the contention or belief that states retain their freedom not to exercise it in relation to claims concerning the commission of crimes committed by foreign state officials in the exercise of their official capacity, as a matter of self-restraint, act of courtesy, or in application of treaties concluded to that effect. This construction would be incorrect. It would run counter to the fabric of international criminal law, which is based on the assumption that—for given acts amounting to international crimes—every individual can be held liable, regardless of whether he has acted qua state official. If states were at liberty to dispose of this basic postulate, the whole logic of the system of international criminal justice would simply collapse.

This is the reason why, far from constituting a derogation from or an exception to the rules of international law on functional immunities, the proper interpretation of the principle of the irrelevance of official capacity for international crimes is that it gives rise to an international obligation of a *jus cogens* nature. Consequently, states cannot claim or obtain respect for the rules of international law of functional immunities when their state officials are accused of having committed an international crime in the exercise of their function. On the other hand, states having jurisdiction over the crime cannot refuse to exercise it on account of the official nature of the act.[29]

## 5. By way of conclusion

International law as a normative system has impressively evolved with the formation of customary rules prohibiting the commission of serious violations of human rights. When these violations are attributable to a foreign state, international responsibility as a system of 'liability'[30] provides that the wrongdoer state must repair the injuries caused, and that all the non-injured states can also claim reparation in favour of the victims and induce compliance through 'lawful measures'.

---

[29] In addition, if construed with the meaning propounded above, the principle of the irrelevance of official capacity would also imply the obligation for states not to apply the national rules on immunity sheltering some categories of state officials from criminal responsibility for acts committed in an official capacity. This is an obligation that already stems from the Rome Statute and other treaties, such as the Genocide Convention. However, it is submitted that it also constitutes an obligation stemming from international criminal law as such, and from its basic principle of the irrelevance of official capacity. Indeed, it would be illogical to contend that this principle only applies with respect to the exercise of criminal jurisdiction over foreign state officials, leaving the states of nationality and/or of territoriality (which are usually the states to which the state official responsible for international crimes belongs) free to shelter from criminal responsibility the alleged authors of international crimes before their own courts. The consequence is that it would be contrary to the rule of *jus cogens* if national jurisdiction were to be barred from prosecuting a particular category of individuals, on account of the immunity attached to the official nature of the activity.

[30] See again Crawford and Watkins, n 1, at 284, who note that the term 'responsibility as liability' conveys the idea that a person has violated his obligations and becomes liable to some negative consequence such as punishment, censure, or enforced compensation. In this sense, it must be distinguished from 'responsibility as answerability', which does not necessarily imply that a wrong has been done since the person called to account for his conduct can offer a valid justification for it, and deflect any imputation of wrongdoing (ibid at 283).

However, the institutional gaps in the international legal order to bring states to account for their alleged internationally wrongful behaviours in respect of individuals make it necessary to rely upon domestic civil proceedings. International responsibility as 'accountability' needs therefore to rely on domestic judicial scrutiny, although in a subsidiary manner. The doctrine of foreign state immunity, which is considered still to apply in relation to domestic civil claims related to violations of international rules protecting fundamental human rights, cannot however be invoked to hamper this scrutiny, not without incurring an inherent normative inconsistency. If individuals are protected by international law against abuse of sovereignty, it is clear that to oppose the doctrine according to which foreign states are not accountable before domestic courts for sovereign acts that are abusive in nature really makes little sense.

When it comes to individuals accused of having committed international crimes, again the doctrine of personal immunities might hamper the system of responsibility as 'accountability' through national judicial scrutiny in the host state. Here, it is perhaps sound to assert that the protection of the exercise of official functions abroad ensured by the rules on personal immunities shall prevail over the demands for accountability, but not in all circumstances. Arguably, *de lege ferenda*, personal immunities can be deemed inapplicable where, in relation to serious violations of human rights, there is a reasonable ground to believe that the protection afforded by these immunities will eventually lead to a denial of justice or impunity.

Finally, with regard to functional immunities, one cannot fail to observe that their asserted inapplicability in cases of international crimes constitutes an enormous progress in the system of international responsibility as 'liability'. It is therefore necessary forcefully to reject the arguments that these immunities must instead be maintained, because there are risks of abuse to pursue, through judicial scrutiny, political agendas. These risks are exaggerated and are put forward precisely to shield from liability those who, while in power, have abused their official capacity and committed acts that the international community considers criminal in nature, and therefore deserve no protection under international law. The temptation to listen to these concerns must be resisted, because they are akin to the *Odyssey's* sirens in that they attempt to entice and misdirect us from our ultimate destination—in this case to assert the principle of personal liability for conduct by state officials constituting serious crimes against international law.

# (C) THE ROLE OF INTERNATIONAL JUDICIAL BODIES

# 19

## The International Court of Justice: It is High Time to Restyle the Respected Old Lady

*Antonio Cassese*

## SUMMARY

The essential recipe for reviving the Court and bringing it into the twenty-first century is to turn it from a substantially arbitral court, a late nineteenth-century institution oriented to unrestricted respect for outmoded conceptions of state sovereignty, into a proper court of law, with all the attributes and trappings of a modern judicial body. A number of legal and practical measures are suggested for improving the Court. Some changes would need an amendment of the Court's Statute: (i) the suppression of the ad hoc judges system or the duty for a national judge to recuse himself or herself where a state is not 'represented' on the Court; (ii) the expansion of contentious jurisdiction to intergovernmental organizations; (iii) the granting of the right to request advisory opinions to subjects other than states; and (iv) the endowing of the Court with the power to decide on referrals from national or international courts. Other changes would instead require only amendments of the Court's Rules or even only changes in the Court's practice directions: for instance, improving on the current restrictive practice concerning third party intervention with a view to departing from the current 'arbitral' approach; setting up small panels of judges within the Court, each dealing with, and possibly specializing in, specific issues; inviting or allowing albeit prudently, *amici curiae* to submit written statements on legal issues arising before the Court.

## 1. A success, in spite of many wrinkles

The current success of the International Court of Justice (ICJ) among many states, particularly developing and middle-sized states, is no doubt one of the few positive hallmarks of the current international society. No one could deny that the Court authoritatively contributes to the settlement of some international disputes between states, thereby defusing quite a few situations that might fester and lead to stronger friction and even to threats to the peace. Similarly, there is no gainsaying that the Court is playing an important role in the area of lawmaking. Since at present, and on a number of political grounds, states are loath to create new rules by treaties, the scope and impact of customary law on international relations is expanding at a rapid pace. However, the difficulty with custom is that, apart from traditional rules, which are undisputed, emerging rules or rules that are indicative of new trends in the world community need, in order to be recognized, the formal imprimatur of a court of law. No other court is in a better position than the ICJ to play this role. Once the ICJ has stated that a legal standard is part of customary international law, few would seriously challenge such a legal finding.

Nevertheless, there is considerable unease about how the Court is conducting its business. The Court's proceedings are relatively slow and excessively cumbersome, and often the Court's output fails to meet the expectations of the world community. Also, however important and compelling the legal reasoning of the Court may be, one is often left with the impression that its reasoning may be more fully persuasive if it gave more extensive consideration to state practice, legal arguments, and the views of other courts. Instead, all too often the Court relishes re-citing its own jurisprudence without exploring new avenues, and leaves readers of its judgments with the impression that the legal reasoning has been constructed to allow a particular outcome to be reached—an outcome that, most of the time, is inspired by great deference to state sovereignty. Furthermore, it is increasingly doubtful that the current practice of always electing a national of the five permanent members of the Security Council (plus, it would seem, a national of Japan and Germany, two de facto quasi-permanent members) adds to the legitimacy of the Court, the more so because those states tend to nominate former legal advisers of their Foreign Ministry or persons who have been actively engaged in advising that state in a professional capacity, that is, persons used to defending the legal views of their own government. It is submitted that while it is important for the five permanent members to make full use of their leverage in political matters, it is not necessary that they also take the lead or have a say in legal matters at the judicial level. As long as all the major legal systems of the world are duly represented on the Court, there is no longer a need for these particular states to be always represented on that judicial body.

Despite defects and shortcomings, many, including the present writer, entertain a tincture of hope that things may gradually improve and the Court will achieve all the potential that it has available—by among other things broadening the number of states that accept its compulsory jurisdiction (currently limited to only 66 out of 193 member states of the United Nations).

The Court is indeed like a prepossessing lady, who has been little courted for many years in spite of her indisputable youthful charm and now, at old age, all of a sudden has found herself much sought after and indeed insistently wooed, although at present her beauty is somewhat dimmed by many wrinkles and a few liver spots.

At present, she does not need any make-up nor a fanciful, fashionable dress full of frills. She has already proved to have much vitality. She only needs some peptone in her arteries and greater grit. It is high time to rejuvenate the old lady and to bring out her best, to make her attractiveness more arresting than before. This becomes all the more relevant as other suitors increasingly grace the world stage.

## 2. How to rejuvenate the Court: from an accomplished arbitral court to a true court of law

To my mind, the essential recipe for reviving the Court and bringing it into the twenty-first century is to turn it from a substantially *arbitral* court, a late nineteenth-century behemoth oriented to unrestricted respect for outmoded conceptions of state sovereignty, into a proper *court of law*, with all the attributes and trappings of a modern judicial institution. The Court should be re-invented and re-shaped to be no more the archaic arbitral instrument of sovereign states, as it was in the 1920s and thereafter,[1] but the judicial institution of the *new international society*, which at present is made up not only of states but also of intergovernmental organizations, non-state entities such as the International Committee of the Red Cross (ICRC) and even (some categories of) rebels. The Court should be cautiously open—within the limits I will endeavour to outline below—to *all these new international subjects*, so as to extend its peace-making role to them as well. Why, indeed, should only the *old subjects* of the world community, sovereign states, benefit from the enormous advantages for peace and justice offered by the Court, while the *new* international subjects, the recently arrived actors that now play an increasing role in the world community, are not allowed to reap any benefit from the availability of an important judicial institution?

Also, given the Court's success in the modern age, it would be advisable to endow it with all the powers that a modern international institution can have.

Below, I will briefly enumerate some changes that appear to me to be necessary.

---

[1] It is probably the arbitral nature of the Court and the prevailing notion that the Court had been set up as a tool in the hands of sovereign states that probably led in 1923 one of the most distinguished judges, the Italian Dionisio Anzilotti, to do something that normally would not be permitted to a member of a judicial body, namely to allow an Italian diplomat to consult him on whether it was advisable for Italy to bring the Corfu island case before the PCIJ. It is now apparent from recently published documents that, following instructions from B. Mussolini (who, besides being Prime Minister, was also Minister of Foreign Affairs), the Italian Ambassador to the Netherlands asked Judge Anzilotti whether Italy should bring the Corfu case (Italian bombardment of the island following the assassination of General Tellini) before the Court (see cable of 3 September 1923 from the Italian diplomat to Mussolini, in O. Ferrajolo (ed.), *Il caso Tellini—dall'eccidio di Janina all'occupazione di Corfù* (Milan: Giuffrè, 2005), at 152–3). On 5 September 1923 the Italian diplomat again cabled Mussolini to report Anzilotti's opinion advising against any resort to the Court, since Italy among other things 'had done justice by itself' by occupying Corfu contrary to the provisions of the Covenant ('*appariamo esserci fatta giustizia da noi mediante occupazione isola contro spirito e lettera del Patto (Articoli 12 e 15)*'), ibid at 154.

### 3. Suggestions for stripping the Court of the old restraints dictated by the twentieth-century sovereignty-oriented vision

#### (A) Doing away with ad hoc judges

The mainstay of the ICJ's arbitral dimension is the provision (Art. 31 of the Statute) whereby, if in a dispute between two or more states, one of the contenders does not have a judge of its nationality sitting on the bench, that state may appoint an ad hoc judge. Thus, the Court is still looked upon as an arbitral panel, where all contestants must be represented. Plainly, a court consisting of 15 judges is and cannot but be impartial. To object to the need to discard ad hoc judges by recalling the practice of the European Court of Human Rights would be misleading. There, the reason for the national judge sitting on a case is different: the national judge may contribute to casting light on the national legislation and case law, thereby helping the other members of the bench to adjudicate the case. Whatever the rationale behind the norm, it is a fact that at Strasbourg the national judge most of the time sides with the majority. This outcome is indicative both of the weight of the majority of judges and of the independence of national judges.

In short, it is suggested that the system of ad hoc judges be scrapped. Were this measure not regarded as sufficient, one could suggest that any time there is a dispute between two states, only one of which has a judge of its nationality on the Court, that judge should be automatically disqualified from sitting on the case or should recuse himself or herself.

#### (B) Making greater allowance for third states that have a legal interest in a dispute to intervene before the Court

As is well known, at present Article 62 of the Court's Statute provides that a state considering 'that it has an interest of a legal nature which may be affected by the decision' of the Court on a dispute between two or more other states may ask the Court to intervene, and the Court decides. However, the Court's practice in matters of third party intervention has been very restrictive. As early as 1984 Judge Roberto Ago, in his Dissenting Opinion in the *Case Concerning the Continental Shelf (Libyan Arab Jamahiriya v Malta, Application by Italy for permission to intervene)*, assailing the Court's decision not to allow the requesting state to intervene, noted that that decision might 'well sound the knell of the institution of intervention in international legal proceedings' (*sonner le glas de l'institution de l'intervention dans les procès internationaux*).[2] Recently, in *Territorial and Maritime Dispute (Nicaragua v Colombia), Application by Costa Rica for permission to intervene*, the Court has gone so far as to state, in rejecting Costa Rica's request to intervene, that 'a third party's interest will, as a matter of principle, be protected by the Court, without it defining with specificity the geographical limits of an

---

[2] *Continental Shelf (Libyan Arab Jamahiriya v Malta, Application to intervene)*, judgment of 21 March 1984, at para. 22.

area where that interest may come into play.'[3] It would seem that in the end by so reasoning the Court has largely deprived the institution of third party intervention of its principal *raison d'être*. Hence, the views forcefully set out by Judges Cançado Trindade and Yusuf in their joint Dissenting Opinion seem compelling: they rightly conclude that

> The Court's practice to date seems to amount to a slow-motion asphyxiation of the institution of intervention . . . as such practice appears reminiscent of traditional bilateral arbitral proceedings where a barrier against third party intervention may be considered desirable. It is our view that such practice is not in line with contemporary demands of the judicial settlement of disputes, nor with challenges faced by present-day international law within the framework of a universalist outlook. (para. 29)

One cannot but earnestly hope that the Court will gradually change its practice on third party intervention and depart from its current 'arbitral' approach (however, in the Order of 4 July 2011 in *Jurisdictional Immunities of the State (Germany v Italy), Application of the Hellenic Republic for Permission to Intervene*, the Court took a more liberal approach, so much so that in his Separate Opinion Judge Cançado Trindade spoke of a 'resurrection of intervention', at paras 56–61).

## (C) Cautiously allowing *amici curiae* to submit memorials and participate in proceedings

At present, pursuant to Article 66 of the Court's Statute, whenever the Court is requested to give an advisory opinion, states and intergovernmental organizations, duly notified by the Court, may submit written statements on the question of which the Court has been seized, as well as make oral statements in the Court's proceedings. These statements may of course prove of great assistance to the Court.

I do not see why the Court, when dealing with *contentious* cases, should not invite or allow albeit prudently, *amici curiae* to submit written statement on legal issues arising before it. Memorials by national or international academic institutions (suffice it to think of the celebrated Max Planck Institute in Heidelberg or the Cambridge Centre on International Law), states, or intergovernmental and even non-governmental institutions might help the Court clarify some questions of law (eg the existence of a customary rule on a particular matter, the question whether a general norm belongs to the *jus cogens* category, the interpretation of a particularly obscure treaty provision, the legal value of a promise or of an act of recognition, the question whether in a particular instance one may be faced with acquiescence or estoppel, and so on). Three points need to be made in this connection. First, the Court would in no way abdicate its function to rule on existing law, for ultimately it could ignore or disregard the *amici curiae* briefs. Secondly, allowing *amici curiae* briefs would mean opening up to the international society at large, heeding the exigencies in the field of law emanating from that society,

---

[3] *Territorial and Maritime Dispute (Nicaragua v Colombia), Application by Costa Rica for permission to intervene*, judgment of 4 May 2011, para. 86.

and stimulating the interest of both international civil society and intergovernmental actors in making the rule of law prevail in international relations. Thirdly, the experience of other tribunals shows that resort to *amici curiae* may prove of momentous assistance to courts: suffice it to mention the importance of reliance by the ICTY on *amici curiae* briefs in *Tadić (interlocutory decision)*, in 1995, and in *Blaškić (subpoena)*, in 1997.

### (D) Opening up the contentious jurisdiction of the Court to international subjects other than states

Since the current world order is different from that existing a century ago, there is no reason why the Court should be accessed only by states and not also by at least intergovernmental organizations, which should be allowed to submit to the Court disputes between two or more organizations or a dispute between one of them and a state (be it a member state or otherwise).

### (E) Opening up the advisory jurisdiction of the Court to international subjects other than intergovernmental organizations

Also, there is no longer any reason why the advisory jurisdiction of the Court should not be open to subjects other than organizations. As a first step, it would be necessary to do away with the clause of Article 96(2) of the UN Charter, whereby 'other organs [than the General Assembly and the Security Council] and specialized agencies' may request an advisory opinion only if the General Assembly gives its prior authorization. Any intergovernmental organization should be authorized *a priori* to request an advisory opinion on an issue of law, provided the Court does not declare the request inadmissible or inappropriate. In addition, I do not see why the Court should not be empowered to issue advisory opinions at the request of other international subjects, such as states and also the ICRC (which, eg, might seek advice on the scope and purport of one or more customary rules of international humanitarian law, or on the entitlements of its officials in third countries, and so on), or even an insurgent group endowed with stability (which might be interested in knowing which rules of international humanitarian law bind it, or to what extent it may enter into international agreements, or what status its officials may have when captured by the incumbent government or when exercising official functions abroad, and so on).

## 4. Enhancing the judicial role of the Court

I submit that the Court has a lot of potential that should be actuated in order to grant it the crucial role in present international dealings that it rightly deserves. A few ameliorations, certainly not easy to implement, would nonetheless be appropriate.

## (A) Clarifying the legal impact of advisory opinions

By definition advisory opinions rendered by the Court are not legally binding. However, it is striking that in most instances the Court is called upon to state the law on a particular issue. While it may be conceded that the application of the relevant law to the facts at issue, if any, should not be binding, it is difficult to understand why the Court's dictum on the relevant international law should not amount to an authoritative judicial finding of the relevant law, and thus be binding, at least de facto, on all subjects of the international community. Let me give an example. In its Advisory Opinion on *Legal Consequences of the Construction of a Wall in the Occupied Palestinian Territory* (2004), the unanimous view of all judges, including that of the (otherwise) dissenting Judge Buergenthal,[4] was that the building of settlements on the West Bank was contrary to international law. If this is so, why should one deny that according to the highest judicial authority international law prohibits the building of settlements in occupied territory? This substantive rule of international law is already binding on all states by the mere fact of its existence—in a sense, it 'precedes' the ruling of the court. Due to the procedural rule on the value of advisory opinions, however, the Court's findings that Israel's construction of the 'Wall' was in breach of a number of rules of international humanitarian law is, at the present stage of development, not binding on states.

In sum, its seems to me incontrovertible that, although the specific factual finding of the Court in a particular case on which it pronounces in its advisory capacity may not be binding, any 'abstract' finding on issues of law cannot but be binding on the international community as a whole.

## (B) Issuing preliminary decisions on legal issues of international law at the request of national or international courts

There exists much bemoaning about the possible fragmentation of international law, and in particular about the dangers of each international court propounding its own interpretation of international rules. Suffice to mention the speech of the then-President of the ICJ, Gilbert Guillaume, to the UN General Assembly.[5] I, for one, believe that this danger is greatly exaggerated. Nevertheless, if we really want to ensure a uniform interpretation and, to some extent, consistent application of international law, the best means to do so resides in granting the ICJ the power to pronounce on any issue of international law at the request of national or international courts. This 'referral jurisdiction' could be exercised any time a national or international court seeks the views of the ICJ on a point of international law relevant to the issues brought before the requesting court (which of course would have to stay proceedings until the Court determines the relevant legal issue).

---

[4] See his Declaration appended to the Advisory Opinion, paras 2 and 9. As for the Advisory Opinion, see para. 120.

[5] See the statement President Guillaume made in 2000 before the General Assembly, to be found on the ICJ website (<http://www.icj-cji.org>) under Presidents' statements.

The advantages of this referral system cannot escape the careful observer of international relations. Admittedly the system would start working slowly and in a haphazard manner for, of course, once changes are made at the international level, states and international courts would need to adjust their own legal systems to account for the new opportunity. This would take much time, especially as far as states are concerned. Nevertheless the groundwork would be set for the achievement of a gradual, increasing uniformity in the interpretation and application of international law. De facto the Court would come to exercise the 'judicial function' that, like the other two functions of governance (lawmaking and enforcement), is now lacking in the world community. The advantages for a better understanding of and greater compliance with international law would be incommensurable.

## 5. Restructuring the Court and streamlining its procedures

Of course, the granting of new tasks to the Court would require a restructuring of its methods and procedures, to avoid the Court drowning in a flood of applications for judgments and requests for advisory opinions. Some reforms would therefore be needed. A precondition to any reform would consist in considerably bolstering the Court's staff. For instance, it would become imperative to assign at least two legal officers to each judge, and the Registry would have to be staffed up.

### (A) Dividing the Court into small panels of judges

At present the Court has an environmental disputes Chamber, and a summary procedure Chamber. However, neither of them has ever been used. Even suggestions to states to use chambers instead of plenary are often rejected by such states.

It would instead be crucial to set up small panels of judges within the Court, each dealing with, and possibly specializing in, specific issues. Thus, for instance, one panel could adjudicate disputes between international organizations, another could deal with referrals from national courts, yet another could adjudicate referrals from other international courts. It would fall to the President, with the assistance of one or more Vice Presidents, to set up one or more panels of five judges, to assign cases to the panels, or to decide that instead a case should go to the plenary bench.

Obviously, the streamlining of the Court's procedures and the whole process of multiplying and speeding up the Court's handling of cases would presuppose, as noted above, a dramatic strengthening of the Court's staff.

### (B) Setting up a fact-finding body

In at least three recent cases[6], it has become apparent that the Court lacks the right tools for ascertaining facts. Indeed, in the *Wall* case at least one judge felt that

---

[6] *Legal Consequences of the Construction of a Wall in the Occupied Palestinian Territory* (2004), the case on *Application of the Convention on the Prevention and Punishment of the Crime of Genocide (Bosnia-Herzegovina v Serbia-Montenegro)* (2007), and the case on *Application of the International*

the Court had not had available all the requisite facts,[7] whereas in the *Genocide* case the Court had to rely heavily on the findings of the International Criminal Tribunal for the former Yugoslavia. More recently, Judge Simma, in his Separate Opinion in *Application of the Convention on the Elimination of All Forms of Racial Discrimination*, cogently criticized the way the Court had reviewed and assessed the documentary evidence submitted to it by the applicant.

It would therefore be appropriate for the Court to develop its procedures for dealing with issues of fact. The Court would need to establish clear rules on the admissibility of evidence, provide proper arrangements for the examination of witnesses and experts, and renew its procedures for appointing its own experts in a manner that is transparent and meets minimum due process requirements. It could also set up a fact-finding body, consisting of one or more judges heading a team of investigators and fact-finders (possibly to be recruited on an ad hoc basis), to establish facts in dispute and report to the Court thereon.

## (C) Streamlining the internal functioning of the Court

At present written proceedings are rather archaically organized. They involve the filing by each party of lengthy memorials, counter-memorials, and, if necessary, replies, pursuant to Article 43(2)–(4) of the Court's Statute. In fact, states tend to file voluminous documents. Then the oral proceedings follow, where the agents and counsel for each party need to file their oral pleadings, which they then read out before the bench. This whole system wastes time and resources. At no point before the oral hearings are the parties given any indication by the Court as to issues it would like to be addressed at the hearings. Judges, having read the written documents and knowing that in a matter of a few hours they will be handed the written texts of the oral pleadings, may doze off during the hearings. This is in fact allowed, the more so because Court practice requires that any question asked by a judge (after obtaining permission from the President) shall not be answered by the relevant party forthwith, but only some time later, out of respect for the sovereign prerogatives of the parties. Although parties do sometimes answer immediately or the day after (it is only when the questions are asked at the end of the oral proceedings that they are given a week or so to reply in writing), it is a fact that they are not legally *bound* to answer right away. Thus, under the present procedure, all the benefits of having a state appear 'in person'—questioning, testing of arguments, refinement of positions, etc.—are effectively lost.

The suggestion can respectfully be made that the Court could easily impose upon, or request, or call upon, the parties to a dispute to submit short memorials (with a set ceiling of pages), which go to the essentials, and in addition, in the oral

---

*Convention on the Elimination of All Forms of Racial Discrimination (Georgia v Russian Federation)* (2011).

[7] Strikingly, in his declaration the *Legal Consequences of the Construction of a Wall in the Occupied Palestinian Territory* (2004), the dissenting Judge Buergenthal lamented the failure of the Court to have before it 'the requisite factual bases for its sweeping findings' (para. 1).

hearings, to refrain from reading out their prepared texts. The practice of some domestic Supreme Courts comes to mind in this respect. The Court has indeed available quite a few excellent interpreters who could easily translate the orally delivered text into the other official language. In addition, hearings could be drastically shortened. The judges should be free to ask questions in the course of the hearings, and the parties required to answer them on the spot, as happens before other international courts and also in inter-state arbitral proceedings. In order to facilitate this project, the Court could also provide the parties—in advance of the hearings—with an indicative list of issues that it would be useful to address during the course of the hearings.

## (D) Rendering the Court's pronouncements more impactful

At present all too often the Court takes a sort of oracular attitude on the applicable law. It frequently states that a rule belongs to customary law without providing any evidence or argument to support the proposition. Similarly, it often states that 'it is not convinced' by the argument of a party, but then fails to adduce any demonstration or proof of its not being convinced.[8] In addition, it is striking that as a rule the Court does not refer to decisions of other international tribunals or courts, either to controvert them, or instead to adhere to them.

I submit that more extensive consideration of the relevant points of law and the articulation of arguments in support of or against a legal finding would render the Court's decisions more persuasive, hence more compelling. In all instances, the Court should provide full reasoning for all findings of fact and legal conclusions.

## 6.  How to carry out all these possible ameliorations?

Whoever has patiently read so far the above considerations will object that, whether or not they are apposite, they amount to a dream book. Indeed, many of the changes suggested require an amendment of the ICJ Statute, a text which is an integral part of the UN Charter and therefore, under Article 69 of the Court's Statute, may only be changed pursuant to the procedure envisaged in Article 108 of the UN Charter: adoption of amendments by the General Assembly by a vote of two-thirds of the member states, plus ratification by two-thirds of the member states including all permanent members of the Security Council. However, a distinction can be made between the various categories of changes.

Some changes will, of course, need an amendment of the Court's Statute: (i) the suppression of the ad hoc judges system or the duty for a national judge to recuse himself or herself where a state is not 'represented' on the Court; (ii) the expansion of contentious jurisdiction to intergovernmental organizations; (iii) granting of the

---

[8] This point was made among others by Judge Buergenthal in his declaration in the *Legal Consequences of the Construction of a Wall in the Occupied Palestinian Territory* (2004), see para. 7 *in fine*.

right to request an advisory opinion to subjects other than states; and (iv) endowing the Court with the power to decide on referrals from national or international courts. Here, however, the Court could play a considerable role in prompting the passing of those amendments: under Article 70 of the Court's Statute, the Court may propose amendments to its Statute by written communication to the UN Secretary-General. The Court could also try to find methods or develop techniques (in the same way it developed the notion of *forum prorogatum* to deal with consent issues), which might allow it, through practice, to pave the way for dealing with such issues in the future.

The other changes would instead require only amendments of the Court's Rules or even only changes in the Court's practice directions. Were most members of the Court persuaded of the need to embark upon its modernization, time and patience, but also perseverance would make it possible gradually to attain a more vital and vibrant judicial institution. In this way, the Court could maintain its leading position as the principal judicial organ of the United Nations. In order more efficiently to achieve this goal the Court should, however, modernize its procedures. It should update, streamline, and render more expeditious its working practices, in line with other international courts and tribunals. Otherwise there is a risk that more cases will go elsewhere (eg to arbitral courts or to specialized tribunals such as the International Tribunal for the Law of the Sea) and the Court will become a less attractive institution. That would not be a good thing.

# 20

# The International Criminal Court: Struggling to Find its Way

*William Schabas*

## SUMMARY

In spite of the initial success in the establishment of the International Criminal Court (ICC), the Court is facing difficulties in becoming operational and effective. Many procedural defects stand out. In addition, the idea that the choices of 'situations' falling under the Court's jurisdiction is left to one unaccountable individual, who employs vague concepts of 'gravity' and 'interests of justice' to explain these, is the Court's greatest flaw. The Court remains confronted by the need to address shortcomings that have manifested themselves in its first years of operation. Nevertheless, there are many encouraging signs that it continues to enjoy the confidence of a large number of states.

## 1. Three distinct phases in the initial years of the Court

Three distinct phases signpost the history of the ICC. The negotiation and adoption of the Rome Statute, completed on 17 July 1998, is the first. It was a phenomenally dynamic period driven by a process pumped up with oxygen from post-Cold War political developments and a constantly strengthening international human rights regime. The cautious, conservative draft statute proposed in 1994 by the International Law Commission (ILC), characterized by fealty to the Security Council, was radically transformed into a tribunal with the power to select its targets for prosecution and to refuse them when they had been selected by the Council. This was largely the work of so-called 'like-minded' middle powers who were buttressed by energetic non-governmental organizations (NGOs). The result at the Rome Conference could hardly have been imagined when the project began less than a decade earlier.

The second is the process of ratification and entry into force, a phase completed on 1 July 2002. At the Rome Conference, there was great scepticism, even from the keenest supporters of the project, that the threshold of 60 ratifications could ever be attained within a reasonable time. Some argued that the 60-state requirement proposal was a scheme by opponents of the Court to ensure that the Statute would never enter into force. Many states argued persuasively, but unsuccessfully, that the Court's jurisdiction be premised on universality, given the perceived unlikelihood that any significant number of states—other than developed democracies from the global North—would join the Court. These pessimistic misperceptions became evident in the years following adoption of the Statute. Not only was the 60-state target relatively easy to attain, the club of founding members included many conflict-torn states in Africa such as Sierra Leone, Fiji, Colombia, and the Democratic Republic of the Congo.

The third phase began with the entry into force of the Statute. It followed a euphoric decade of extraordinary progress in the creation of the Court. By 1 July 2002, the Court had already surpassed the most optimistic forecasts of the keenest supporters. Something almost magical was at work. Commentators recalled Victor Hugo's famous words: 'On résiste à l'invasion des armées; on ne résiste pas à l'invasion des idées.'

## 2. Frustration and underperformance in the second decade

However, the dynamism that marked the initial ten years of this idea stands in stark contrast to its second decade, marked by frustration and underperformance. Nearly ten years after the Rome Statute's entry into force, the Court has still been unable to complete its first trial. Afflicted with a cumbersome and inflexible procedural regime, there is nevertheless resistance to contemplation of any reforms. The Court lacks vision and leadership. It employees exude frustration and even demoralization. The ardour of the African states that ratified the Statute in large numbers, proving its appeal to countries of the South confronted with internal conflict, has cooled.

Compare this with the accomplishments of the UN tribunals at a similar stage in their development. Nine years after the adoption of the Security Council resolution establishing the International Criminal Tribunal for the former Yugoslavia, it had issued 76 indictments, about three times the number of the ICC. Forty-six people were in detention in The Hague, compared with five for the ICC. The Tribunal was conducting six simultaneous trials, compared with three for the ICC. Perhaps most telling, the Yugoslavia Tribunal had completed the trials of 25 accused persons.[1] In 18 of these cases, even the appeals were finished.[2] The International Criminal Tribunal for Rwanda cannot claim to have been quite as productive, but its performance is still rather stellar when set beside that of the ICC. Nine years after its

---

[1] Erdemović, Tadić, Mucić, Delić, Landžo, Delalić, Furundzija, Jelisic, Krstic, Blaskić, Aleksovski, Kordić, Cerkez, Kunarac, Kovac, Vukovic, Josipović, Šantić, Zoran Kupreškić, Mirjan Kupreškić, Vlatko Kupreškić, Papić, Sikirica, Došen, and Kolundžija.
[2] Tadić, Aleksovski, Mucić, Delić, Landžo, Delalić, Erdemović, Furundzija, Jelisic, Kunarac, Kovac, Vukovic, Josipović, Šantić, Zoran Kupreškić, Mirjan Kupreškić, Vlatko Kupreškić, and Papić.

establishment, it had completed the trials of 13 accused. Several appeals had also been adjudicated. And at the same age, the Special Court for Sierra Leone had completed three trials of nine defendants through to the appeals stage.

Is it unfair to compare the pace of the ICC with that of the ad hoc tribunals? When I suggested this at a conference in Mexico City a few years ago, the Prosecutor of the ICC took umbrage. He said that the procedural regime at the Court was much more complex, especially in the preliminary phase, with its triggering requirements and tests of admissibility. That is, of course, true, but it does not explain all of the problems. The first trial at the ICC began in January 2009. By then all of the preliminaries that the Prosecutor invoked to distinguish the two regimes had been completed. The *Lubanga* trial at the Court is a relatively minor matter, concerning one accusation of child soldier recruitment and a single defendant. The evidentiary phase of the proceedings took almost 30 months to complete. By that time, the accused had been in detention in The Hague for more than five years. Even if he is convicted, 'time served' will probably be an appropriate sentence.

The first trial at the Yugoslavia Tribunal, of DuškoTadić, began on 7 May 1996. The verdict was issued exactly one year later. Several charges and several different crimes were involved, and many novel issues of international criminal law confronted the Tribunal in this first effort since Nuremberg and Tokyo. At the Rwanda Tribunal, the first trial began on 9 January 1997 and final judgment was delivered on 2 September the following year, some 21 months later. For the first time, a tribunal contemplated by Article VI of the 1948 Genocide Convention had to explore the interpretation of 'the crime of crimes'. Difficult issues involving evidence of sexual crimes confronted the tribunal. Thus, even when the playing field is level, and the only variable being measured is the length of the first trial itself, the ICC finishes last. Its first trial will take a minimum of three years.

The Prosecutor's dismissal of criticism about the Court's poor performance does not correspond to some of his own exceedingly optimistic forecasts. A year after taking office, the Prosecutor proposed a budget based upon the proposition that '[i]n 2005, the Office plans to conduct one full trial, begin a second and carry out two new investigations.'[3] A flow chart derived from the Prosecutor's forecasts indicated that the first trial before the Court would be completed by August 2005.[4] He became somewhat less ambitious in 2006, when a three-year strategic plan proclaimed the expectation that the Court would *complete* two 'expeditious trials by 2009, and…conduct four to six new investigations'.[5] In fact, as has been explained above, only one trial started in 2009. No reasonable observer would use the adjective 'expeditious' to describe its glacial pace.

In February 2010, a new three-year strategic plan from the Office of the Prosecutor said the Court would finish the three trials then underway or about to begin, and start 'at least one new trial'. In addition, the Prosecutor said he intended to continue ongoing investigations in seven cases, and conduct 'up to four new

---

[3]  Draft Programme Budget for 2005, ICC-ASP/3/2, para. 159.     [4]  Ibid, at 49.
[5]  Report on Prosecutorial Strategy, 14 September 2006, at 3.

investigations of cases'.[6] In fact, by early 2011 not even one trial was even close to completion. Given that holding trials is the core activity of the Court, these mistaken projections reflect an unrealistic assessment of the difficulties facing the institution.

But the Prosecutor is not the only Doctor Pangloss associated with the ICC. There had been expectations that the Review Conference promised by Article 123 of the Rome Statute would provide a forum for reflection on the Court's perform-ance. As the June 2010 Kampala Conference approached, it became clear that there was no stomach for any soul-searching, in public or in private. The Court's institu-tions and the Assembly of States Parties agreed not to talk about any shortcomings. Some said it was out of concern that this would only nourish Africa's simmering malaise with the Court. But if anything feeds disappointment and cynicism, it is a refusal to acknowledge that the emperor has no clothes. The Review Conference indulged in some 'stocktaking', but there was no introspection. The four stocktak-ing sessions mainly consisted of hectoring states about pulling their weight, as if that is what holds back the Court's performance.

## 3. Procedure in need of repair

It is often overlooked that when the Rome Statute was adopted, the Yugoslavia and Rwanda tribunals had been operational and engaged in trial work for only a few years. Most of the rich lessons from their activity in the procedure (and substance) of international criminal law had yet to be learned. Thus, when the first trial began at the ICC in 2009 it was operating on the basis of a ten-year-old procedural model that had not benefited from the invaluable experience of the ad hoc tribunals.

Although some of the procedural law is in the Rome Statute itself, making amendment difficult, the Rules of Procedure and Evidence and the Regulations of the Court provide the ICC with flexible instruments enabling adjustments as pitfalls are identified. At the UN tribunals, the Rules of Procedure and Evidence have been subjected to a constant process of fine-tuning and amendment, as judges adjust in light of experience and changes in the nature of the caseload. Although the same should be possible at the ICC, in practice there is nothing of the sort. The Rules of Procedure and Evidence have never been amended. When provided the opportunity for changes, in the context of the Review Conference, the Court refused even to allow the discussion. Actually, it takes little imagination to see how the procedure can be improved, the pre-trial and trial activity simplified, and the Court made more efficient.

One of the innovations in the Rome Statute is the confirmation hearing, which is a preliminary proceeding at which the Pre-Trial Chamber is to determine whether there are 'substantial grounds' to go to trial. There is nothing similar at the ad hoc tribunals. The confirmation hearing probably adds close to a year to the length of the proceedings as a whole. Its enthusiasts explain that it adds a layer of protection

---

[6] Prosecutorial Strategy, 2009–2012, 1 February 2010, at 2.

against abusive trials, which may well be true. But in all such arguments, a cost–benefit analysis is central. Is the added length to the proceedings, especially if the accused is in custody, worth the investment in time and resources that is involved? Fortunately, the Regulations of the Court require that the decision on the confirmation hearing be issued within 60 days of its conclusion. Working within this requirement, the Pre-Trial Chambers have issued lengthy rulings in which the facts and law are reviewed. The time limit is useful, because where one is not imposed, the judges generally take much, much longer to issue written rulings. On the arguably simpler issue of whether or not to issue an arrest warrant, they have sometimes taken several months. By comparison, issuance of an arrest warrant at the ad hoc tribunals is a matter of a few days.

Questions about the utility of the confirmation hearing inexorably lead to thoughts about the value of the Pre-Trial Chamber itself. Again, this is a feature introduced in the Rome Statute that has no equivalent at the ad hoc tribunals, where the same issues are very adequately dealt with by a single pre-trial judge. A minimum of one-third of the entire cohort of judges at the ICC is tied up with this pre-trial work. If the Chamber were abolished, there would be more judges for trials which are, after all, the bread and butter of the institution.

At the other end of the system sits the Appeals Chamber. There was no appeal at Nuremberg or Tokyo. When the Yugoslavia Tribunal was established in the early 1990s, the text of the International Covenant on Civil and Political Rights made an effective right of appeal a *sine qua non*. Article 14(5) of the Covenant promises this right to 'everyone convicted of a crime'. Although it was not entirely apparent from the text of the Statute of the ICTY, the judges themselves soon determined that in addition to an appeal of conviction—the only requirement imposed by human rights law—that interlocutory matters could also be dealt with. The idea stuck, and was incorporated in the Rome Statute.

By the time the ICC completes its first full cycle of judicial elections, in early 2012, a full-time five-judge Appeals Chamber (together with professional assistants and secretarial help) will have occupied a floor of the Court's premises for nearly the entire period without ever engaging in the fundamental reason for its existence: appeal by an accused of a conviction. The Appeals Chamber has barely managed to keep itself occupied with interlocutory appeals. The occasional decisions are generally sparsely reasoned and there are few separate or dissenting opinions. The job could very well have been accomplished with a panel of part-time or standby judges, called to The Hague as required and remunerated according to the work that they actually accomplish.

Would the sky fall in if there was no interlocutory appeal at all? There might be variations in procedure from one chamber to another, but that is something that many justice systems accept as a fact of life. Some argue the virtue of 'clarifying' the law so as to ensure 'legal certainty'. But it might be more constructive for a court in its early years to 'let a hundred flowers bloom', and to encourage experimentation and innovation. The Rome Statute contemplates a division of labour whereby the Pre-Trial and Trial Chambers are enriched by a large proportion of judges with criminal trial experience. That makes sense. But the consequence may be that there is less criminal trial experience at the Appeals Chamber, and a tendency for it to be top-heavy with judges from the international law stream. This means that tricky determinations about trial procedure made by experienced judges working at the coalface are being second-guessed by those who are probably less familiar with daily life in the courtroom.

A much-heralded innovation in the Rome Statute is the recognition of a role for victims of crime. The Statute's provisions concerning victim participation might well have been interpreted relatively narrowly. Instead, an elaborate and costly regime of victim representation and participation has developed. Much of the institutional energy of the Court in its first decade has been devoted to addressing this. But it is not apparent that the right scheme for victim participation has been found. One suspects that if the victims understood that many millions had been invested—mainly in professional salaries and international travel—in order to ensure the respect of their rights, they might ask if they could simply be given the money instead. The continental procedural model of the *partie civile* on which victim participation was premised seems very remote from what we actually see in the Chambers of the ICC.

One example of this indulgence is the Trust Fund for Victims, the establishment of which is called for by Article 79 of the Rome Statute. As it was understood, this was to provide a mechanism for seizing the assets of the wealthy warlords and tyrants upon successful prosecuted by the Court. Of course, to date it has collected nothing of the sort, because no trials have been completed. It was probably unrealistic to view the defendants as a reliable source of resources for the Fund. At the ad hoc tribunals, most of the defendants have been declared indigent for the purposes of legal aid. Even the notorious Charles Taylor, said to have billions tucked away in foreign bank accounts, was not declared to be capable of paying his own lawyers' fees because the money could not be found. And proof of assets for the purposes of legal aid should not be nearly as demanding as for the seizure of bank accounts and other assets.

The Fund itself gets a limited income in the form of voluntary contributions from the wealthier state parties. The money is being spent on a range of projects in regions where the Court is active. For the year 2010, the Fund expected an income of something under €2 million in such gifts. It had budgeted an operating cost of €1.2 million. It is an expensive way to do what amounts to overseas development assistance. Maybe states should give their money to the UNDP or Oxfam, and let the Trust Fund become inoperative until such time as the Prosecutor is astute enough to catch a wealthy defendant.

## 4. Policy and politics: the fabled de-politicized Prosecutor has in fact not been immune to political factors

Although the procedural issues pose interesting challenges, it may be that the crux of the difficulty facing the ICC is essentially substantive. After all, this is where the real differences lie between the Court and the ad hoc institutions. James Crawford, who chaired the ILC drafting committee in the early 1990s, has said that the statute it prepared was what the Commission thought would meet general acceptance. He has suggested that the world may not have been ready for the more radical concepts that emerged from the Rome Conference. If he is right, this may help to understand the difficulties that the Court faces in becoming operational and effective.

The Rome Statute makes an important distinction between 'situations' and 'cases'. The process of prosecution begins with identification of a 'situation' rather than a 'case'. Thus, we have the 'Situation in the Democratic Republic of the Congo' and the 'case' of Thomas Lubanga, leader of a combatant faction in a civil war accused of recruiting child soldiers. There is the 'Situation in northern Uganda' and the 'case' of Joseph Kony, head of the Lord's Resistance Army.

The great originality of the ICC compared with all of its predecessors is that the Prosecutor selects both the 'situation' and the 'case'. At the other institutions, starting with Nuremberg, the 'situation' has been selected by the political body that created the tribunal. The Prosecutor at these institutions only selects the 'case'. In 1945, the four-power London Conference charged the International Military Tribunal with delivering justice to 'the major war criminals of the European axis'. The four prosecutors concurred about the individuals they would prosecute. Even there, it seems they were instructed by their various governments in making this choice. In the course of the trial, the judges heard evidence of war crimes perpetrated by the Allied forces— the Katyn massacre, unrestricted naval warfare—but were without jurisdiction to address these issues. Had one or more of the prosecutors suggested that these matters be dealt with in the interests of 'balance' and fairness, he would have been quickly replaced by someone prepared to live within the Tribunal's mandate.

When the ICTY was established in 1993, it was said that the shortcomings at Nuremberg had been corrected. A specific provision in the Statute enshrines the independence of the Prosecutor. The Prosecutor is appointed by the Security Council, and 'shall not seek or receive instructions from any Government or from any other source'. But he or she must still live within the confines of the narrow jurisdictional scheme established by the Council. At the ad hoc tribunals, the Prosecutor's discretion is limited to the choice of 'cases'. The 'situation', on the other hand, is part of his job description and he cannot change it. This was also the vision of the prosecutor of an international criminal court that the ILC envisaged, but on which the Rome Conference turned its back.

The Prosecutor of the ICC selects both the 'cases' and the 'situations'. Although there is some degree of political involvement in the choice of situations, to the extent that the Security Council or a state party may 'trigger' the jurisdiction of the Court, the Prosecutor has the last word. He or she may even decline to pursue the agenda set by the Council or a state party, subject to a vague and untested degree of judicial supervision. The Prosecutor may also decide to act *proprio motu*, proceeding in a 'situation' of his or her choice, provided of course that the Court is already empowered to exercise jurisdiction.

The *proprio motu* Prosecutor was vaunted as one of the great achievements of the Rome Conference. This was the result of two different and perhaps somewhat disparate objectives: to free the Court from the hegemony of the Security Council, and to create an institution where the decisions about targets for prosecution are based upon judicial rather than political criteria. One nourished the other. Adversaries of the Council invoked the goal of an apolitical prosecutor without giving much thought to how this would work in practice. Fans of the independent and impartial prosecutor transposed models from domestic justice systems, where all serious crimes against the person receive attention, without adequate reflection about the different imperatives of an international system.

When Luis Moreno-Ocampo took office in June 2003, he could build on much experience from his predecessors at Nuremberg, Tokyo, The Hague, and Arusha. But in the selection of 'situations', no path had been cleared. A team of lawyers hired to set up the Office had prepared draft Regulations that attempted to parse the matter of selecting situations. The initial draft Regulations contemplated a highly transparent process of the selection of situations based upon objective judicial standards. The Prosecutor himself quickly understood that the Rome Statute did not provide much guidance on what those standards really were. Moreover, he was astute enough to recognize that mechanistic application of regulations such as those drafted by the advance team might have unexpected consequences that would be politically unwise.

Some students of the Rome Statute have read Article 15 as suggesting that the Prosecutor is required to proceed relying upon information received, from whatever source, as long as there is a 'reasonable basis'. This is an absurdly unrealistic interpretation in light of the resources of a court that is barely able to deal with a handful of cases in a decade. Although the drafters at Rome gave little thought as to the basis on which the Prosecutor would exercise his phenomenal discretion, there can be no doubt that he or she must make such hard choices.

The Rome Statute itself advances three concepts that may assist in the application of prosecutorial discretion: *complementarity*, *gravity*, and the '*interests of justice*'. The first of these creates a presumption in favour of national jurisdictions, directing the Court not to proceed when national jurisdictions are willing or able to prosecute. Article 17 of the Statute offers some instruction about the scope of 'unwillingness' and 'inability'. The issues lend themselves to a reasonably objective assessment. The same cannot be said of such stunningly nebulous concepts as 'gravity' and the 'interests of justice'. These notions are so malleable as to provide any imaginative prosecutor with a rationale for what may be, in reality, rather arbitrary choices.

In order to avoid the challenge of selecting situations, early in his term the Prosecutor essentially abdicated the responsibility. He rather quietly encouraged some states to refer situations to the Court and then proceeded on this basis without challenging the validity of such choices. He used a novel interpretation of Article 14, by which states could 'self-refer' situations within their own territory. The Prosecutor explained that state parties had decided to refer the situations in Uganda, the Democratic Republic of the Congo, and the Central African

Republic, and acted as if he was virtually bound to proceed in the absence of evidence that the situations were inadmissible. The Prosecutor did the same when the Security Council referred the 'situation in Darfur', in March 2005.

This was an expedient by which the Prosecutor avoided selecting a situation on his own. But even then, it soon became apparent that situations were a Matryoshka doll, and that there were situations within situations. When he obtained the first arrest warrants, in 2005, in the 'situation in Uganda', the targets were the Lord's Resistance Army rebels. The big human rights NGOs took the Prosecutor to task for failing to proceed against the pro-government forces as well. It was at this point that he discovered 'gravity', a term buried in the Statute and essentially forgotten or overlooked, until that point, by academic writers in the major commentaries. He said the rebels were killing many more people than the government forces, and this meant they should be prioritized by the Court. He suggested he would get to the pro-government forces later, but never did. There was the lingering suspicion of an agreement, or perhaps only a tacit understanding, by which Museveni's helpful 'self-referral' of the situation in Northern Uganda meant the focus would be on Museveni's enemies rather than on himself.

In practice, it seemed that the fabled de-politicized Prosecutor was in fact not immune to political factors. Soon, gravity was invoked once again to explain why the Prosecutor had decided to reject the numerous complaints about violations of the Rome Statute perpetrated by British troops in Iraq. He explained that many more people were being killed in Uganda and in the Congo, so these areas deserved the attention of the Court as a priority. The explanation was unconvincing, because the evidence of massive death in Iraq was notorious. The Prosecutor seemed to be confusing 'situations' and 'cases', comparing the 'cases' of alleged deaths in British custody in Iraq with the 'situations' of mass killings in Uganda and the Congo. Days later, he announced that he was proceeding against Thomas Lubanga, a Congolese warlord, on charges of recruitment of child soldiers. But if the Democratic Republic of the Congo was inherently more serious than Iraq, because of the number of deaths, why was the Prosecutor not dealing with murder rather than the arguably less important crime of recruitment?

James Crawford may well have been right to suggest that the world is not ready for a court with an independent and impartial prosecutor, analogous to what we expect in the national justice system of a functional, democratic society that is based upon the rule of law. International human rights courts, like the European Court of Human Rights, have held that there is a procedural obligation upon states to investigate and prosecute all serious crimes against the person. But the theory does not lend itself to a simplistic application in the international criminal law environment. The ICC cannot prosecute all atrocities that go unpunished at the national level. Choices are inevitable. The Prosecutor claims he makes them on the basis of judicial standards. But the whiff of politics is inescapable.

Possibly this is what really ails the Court. Seductive as the vision of an independent Prosecutor may be, the idea that the choices of situations are left to one unaccountable individual, who employs vague concepts of 'gravity' and 'interests of justice' to explain these, is perhaps not the Court's greatest strength but rather its greatest flaw. At the Rome Conference, the drive to eliminate a role for the Security Council in the determination of 'situations' was understandable. But it may have caused another problem in the neglect of the ineluctable role of politics. The challenge, as the Court enters its second decade, may be to find ways to remedy the situation by governing and regulating the role of political factors in the choice of 'situations' rather than pretending that they are simply absent.

The other big challenge to the Court comes from Africa, where it initially found so much support. Understandably frustrated with the ability of existing international organizations and mechanisms, such as the Security Council and the African Union, to address the desperate situation of international and non-international armed conflict on the continent, African states quickly turned to the ICC in the hope that it might better serve their interests. Initially, they welcomed the attention of the Prosecutor and the judges, as one by one the African situations consumed the resources of the Court. Things soured when the Prosecutor announced he was seeking an arrest warrant against President Al-Bashir of Sudan. It is worth noting that there had been no objection in Africa at the time the situation in Darfur was referred to the Court, nor any when arrest warrants were issued against a senior government official and a militia leader. Prosecution of a head of state, however, seemed to transform the debate, and several African governments urged the Prosecutor to reconsider. He paid no real attention to their concerns. His answer was that while the selection of situations fell within his remit, the 'de-selection' was a matter for the Council in accordance with Article 16. This was not a good answer, and only made relations worse. After all, most states at the Rome Conference would have preferred to have no Article 16 in the Statute at all. It was a watered-down version of the provision in the ILC draft that had given the Security Council full control over the proposed court's docket. In the course of negotiations, Article 16 emerged as a compromise that tolerated some role for the Council, despite the desire of most states that there be none at all. Thus, presenting Article 16 as if it is part of a holistic and comprehensive legal regime does not sell very well in Africa. It was not the answer that African states wanted to hear. Later, they reacted by proposing that if the powers of the Council were essential to the Court's operation, Article 16 might be amended so as to share such authority with the General Assembly.

The proposal was ridiculed for being incompatible with the Charter of the UN. Be that as it may, it was a technique by which African states underscored their disappointment with a court that seemed bent on a seamless and complementary relationship with the Security Council, rather than one that would try as best it could to work outside the frame altogether. Of course, to the extent that those within the Court insist upon the significance of the relationship with the Council, some previously lukewarm or even antagonistic governments, notably that of the United States, warm to the institution. But the Court seems to obey a law of thermodynamics: an increase in heat comes at the price of cooling elsewhere in the system. As Washington's temperature rises, Africa gets chillier.

## 5. Nevertheless, an optimistic conclusion

Although the ICC confronts something of a crisis as it prepares for its second decade, there are many encouraging signs that it continues to enjoy the confidence of a large number of states, including many who have yet to join the Court. In early 2011, the Court presented itself as one of the useful options to deal with evolving crises in Libya and the Ivory Coast. When the Security Council referred Libya to the Court, both the Prosecutor and the Pre-Trial Chamber reacted with a sense of urgency that neither had shown years earlier when it had been asked to do the same thing in Darfur. Another sign of health is the successful adoption of amendments at the Kampala Conference that will eventually permit the Court to exercise jurisdiction over the crime of aggression. While the pace of ratification has slowed, political changes such as the jasmine revolution in the Arab countries open up new opportunities. Tunisia's accession to the Rome Statute in June 2011 is a positive indication in this respect.

But the Court remains confronted by the need to address shortcomings that have manifested themselves in its first years of operation. Other international courts and tribunals—the International Court of Justice and the European Court of Human Rights, for example—also face challenges to adjust as the world changes around them. But there is confidence in their continued existence as a more or less permanent fixture of the global order. This cannot yet be said as safely about the ICC. The Court must address its problems with a greater sense of urgency. One of the concerns is that if there is a failure to do so adequately, states may begin to lose the enthusiasm for the institution with which it has been blessed since the 1990s. Although international criminal justice has a secure place in the realistic utopia, the precise role that is to be played by the ICC may still require some fine-tuning.

# 21

# The Future(s) of Regional Courts on Human Rights

*Malcolm D. Evans*

## SUMMARY

UN human rights bodies tend to avoid drawing in the work of the regional courts of human rights, largely in order to underline the extent to which theirs is a global remit and not to be overly influenced by the concerns or approaches of a particular region. Given that the approaches to some key questions vary from region to region, this is perhaps hardly surprising. Where regional courts of human rights have developed they have done so in a way which reflects both the nature of the regional organization to which they owe their being, and at a pace and in a manner which is consonant with the legal and political realities that they serve. Where that pace has, perhaps, been 'forced' by outside pressure to proceed more swiftly than the constituency it serves is prepared to accept, the resulting institutions are, as in the case of the African Court relatively weak for the want of support. The experience of the Inter-American system suggests that slow, organic growth over time produces a system which is both relatively robust and enjoys a relatively high degree of political legitimacy. There is no single 'future' for regional courts of human rights as such. There are as many futures as there are Courts, and each must take its own path, informed by the institutional parameters, jurisdictional competencies, and substantive criteria which are of relevance to it. These futures will be different and vary for each from time to time as the configurations and ambitions of the various regional bodies evolve over time. The future of the regional courts themselves is of considerably less significance than the realization of the tasks they were established to fulfil. While, then, it remains important that they are as well equipped as possible to fulfil their functions within their discrete regional and institutional settings, it is equally important to recognize that they must remain responsive to the changing political and intellectual configurations which continue to shape and reshape not only those regional and institutional settings themselves but which also form and reform the nature of the international community as a whole, in the interest of the human person which that community is there to serve.

# 1. Introduction

This chapter offers a reflection on the future—or rather, the futures—of regional courts of human rights. It would be possible to undertake this task in a number of different ways. Most obviously, and perhaps most usefully, one could look at each of the existing regional courts, explore the challenges which they face and consider how best they might be responded to. There is, however, a significant drawback in adopting such an approach, this being that it has the effect of isolating the consideration of each from the other and reinforcing the tendency to treat the regional courts as if they were 'hermetically sealed units' operating in some form of vacuum. It must be admitted that this is not merely the 'vice of commentators': the regional courts themselves appear to be reluctant to draw on each others' work when developing their own approaches and jurisprudence. While it remains true that the work of the various regional courts does have mutual influence and impact, this is not really because they themselves are seen as, or see themselves as, part of a more general system of regional courts of human rights. Such cross-fertilization of thinking that has occurred seems to owe more to the indirect transplanting of ideas and arguments by others—civil society, counsel, academics, etc.—than to the direct work of the courts themselves as a collective of judicial bodies. Thus a chapter which focuses on how each of the Courts might best tackle the particular challenges which they face sidesteps the *a priori* question of whether those are indeed the challenges which ought to be addressed and this the manner in which they ought to be addressed.

In short, adopting this familiar approach to the work of and prospects for regional human rights courts has the practical effect of assuming that they neither do, nor ought, to cohere as a part of a broader system and so does not contribute much to a debate about regional courts of human rights per se. Such an exercise would be largely comparative in nature and fall short of what might be expected of a chapter intended to reflect upon the future of regional courts of human rights in general, rather than upon the possible futures for each individual regional court in particular. That being said, the conclusion reached in this chapter is that regional courts must be considered to be exactly that—regional courts—and this conclusion has the practical effect of re-confirming the worth of the many such exercises which have already been undertaken. However, the aim of this chapter is to reflect on the wider question of why it is that the futures of the regional courts are best approached in this fashion even when viewed from a more general perspective. It would, then, be premature to constrain this particular consideration of regional human rights courts by limiting it to the particular concerns and challenges which the existing Courts face individually when it is the appropriateness of such an approach which needs to be considered.

It is implicit in all of this that there is another way of considering the future of regional courts, stepping back from the particularities of each of the existing bodies and evaluating their work and their possible futures from a more holistic viewpoint. It is also implicit in what has been said that pursuing a more holistic approach should be the precursor of any more focused 'court by court' analysis and prognosis—and this is indeed the premise upon which this chapter is based and informs how it proceeds. That being said, it must be acknowledged that such an approach is 'artificial' to the extent that it ignores the reality that regional courts do exist, do function, and do have their own 'futures' which need to be considered, no matter what the outcome of any more 'holistic' appraisal of the idea of regional courts might be. Regional courts of human rights are not about to go away, and neither are the particular practical and institutional constraints which bear upon them and which need to be faced as a matter of day-to-day reality.

There are, then, a number of complementary exercises which might be undertaken. At the most abstract, this might concern the general question of what the very existence of regional courts of human rights might mean and imply for the future of international law and the international community (bearing in mind that the very idea of 'international community' may itself be bound up in, or influenced by, that discussion). At the most specific lie questions concerning the future of each court as a body in its own right, operating within the system of which it forms a part. What is the connection—if any—between these extremes within the exercise? Is a holistic appraisal of regional courts to be driven by an analysis of their work and practice? Or is it to be driven by other factors, such as a consideration of the place of regional courts in the developing architecture of international human rights protection?

It seems to me that the appropriate way of proceeding is to acknowledge that any overarching consideration of the future of regional human rights courts must take account of their experience, their successes, and their limitations in order to inform our understanding of what reasonably might be expected of them—but not to drive our understanding of what they should be or should become. It is not so much a question of determining what might make the existing regional courts 'better' from their current standpoint (whatever that might mean) but a question of considering what factors ought to inform thinking about such developments from a more general standpoint. Most literature on the Courts tends to focus on the former rather than the latter. This contribution seeks to consider the future of regional courts of human rights from this more general perspective. Rather than focus on 'improving' the functioning of the regional courts, it asks what 'improvement' might mean in the light of more general developments relating to human rights protection. A short chapter such as this cannot possibly engage with these questions in depth. Rather, it seeks to make some general observations and offer some general thoughts on a number of issues which have a relevance to the question posed, in the hope that these will inspire further and more detailed reflection on the future of regional human rights courts in a similar vein.

## 2. Regional human rights courts and regional systems

For the purposes of this chapter, the principal regional human rights courts are taken to be the European Court of Human Rights (ECtHR), the Inter-American Court of Human Rights (I-ACHR) and African Court on Human and Peoples' Rights (ACHPR), as it currently is. Each of them is the product of a distinct political and legal process and is intimately connected with the various regional organizations which gave them birth—the Council of Europe in the case of the ECtHR, the Organization of American States in the case of the I-ACHR, and the African Union in the case of the ACHPR. These organizations provide both the practical as well as political context in which each 'regional' court works, shaping the parameters of their jurisdictional reach and providing systems of enforcement and oversight of their work. They also provide the funding and, in varying degrees, the professional staff which service them. Since the significance of their being rooted in regional organizations is often overlooked, this is the first factor which this chapter seeks to highlight.

The regional courts of human rights 'belong' to particular regional systems, and each system may well place different emphases on the enterprise of human rights protection in general and upon the role of 'their' Court in particular. This is, perhaps, least apparent in the case of the ECtHR for the very simple reason that the Council of Europe is now so often portrayed (if it is portrayed at all) as being primarily the 'life-support system' of the Court, and as a result the Court is widely perceived as providing the *raison d'être* of the organization. To the extent that the European Convention on Human Rights is the centrepiece of the Council of Europe, this is not altogether untrue. Moreover, while it is most certainly true that there is a great deal more to the Council of Europe than the Convention and the Court, it is also true that the work of the Council of Europe as a regional organization coalesces around the core objectives of preserving and promoting the protection of human rights, democracy, and the rule of law within the legal space of the Council of Europe. Without in any way seeking to ignore or downplay the significance of the many other strands of the work of the Council, and bearing in mind the manner in which our understanding of what the promotion and protection of human rights entails, it does not seem unfair to describe the Council of Europe as being (or as having become) primarily a regional human rights organization with the ECtHR its most visible and single most significant organ. Or, if this is going too far, it is a regional organization which approaches those issues which it addresses from within a markedly human rights-oriented perspective.

As a result, the European Convention and Court of Human Rights tend to overshadow the Council of Europe as a whole. In one sense, this does not really matter if the Council is, essentially, a 'human rights' organization. It does matter, however, insofar as it gives a misleading picture of the situation of other regional human rights courts which may not be rooted in quite so human rights-oriented a regional organization. For example, one has only to consider the disquiet which the forays of the European Union (which manifestly is not primarily a regional human rights organization) into the arena of human rights protection have occasioned to understand the difficulties: there has been particular concern that vesting the European Court of Justice with oversight of the human rights commitments of EU member states might result in their being put in positions incompatible with their Convention obligations. There is no shortage of cases before the ECtHR in which the issue at stake concerns the compatibility of a member state's conduct undertaken in order to fulfil its EU obligations with its obligations under the Convention. The post-Treaty of Lisbon process by which the EU will become a party to the European Convention, and thus itself subject to the jurisdiction of the ECtHR, appears to offer some prospect of addressing this difficulty, but the more general issue of competing and potentially conflicting obligations remain.

It might be argued that the entire point of 'human rights courts' (regional or otherwise) is to ensure that decisions which are taken at a national level and which bear upon the enjoyment of human rights are subject to appraisal from a human rights-centred body in order to ensure that the human rights perspective has been properly respected in the decision-making process. If so, it is important that the regional human rights courts are firmly rooted in a human rights-focused framework, as is the European Court within the Council of Europe. However, this is not the case with all of the regional organizations which provide the frameworks within which some regional human rights courts are located. It should be stressed that this is not to suggest that the Courts themselves may not be 'human rights focused'. Rather, it is to suggest that what might be expected of or be achieved by the various regional human rights courts may differ as a result of the particular focus of the organizations of which such institutions form a part.

## (A) The African Court

This is most obvious in the case of the regional Court within the African system. The ACHPR was established by virtue of the 1998 Protocol to the African Charter on Human and Peoples' Rights and came into being with the election of its judges in January 2006, although it had entered into force two years earlier in January 2004. The establishment of this Court was widely perceived as necessary to address a 'gap' in the African Charter, which had provided for the establishment of a Commission but not of a Court of Human Rights. The Court, as established by the 1998 Protocol, was very much a 'treaty body' located within the overall framework of the Charter: indeed, in both Article 2 and the Preamble of the Protocol the Court is described as being established in order to 'complement' the mandate of the African Commission on Human and Peoples' Rights, its jurisdiction is limited to matters concerning the Charter, the Protocol itself, 'or any other human rights instruments' and, importantly, the sources of law which it might apply are likewise limited to the provisions of the Charter and other relevant human rights institutions ratified by the states concerned.

Both the Charter and the Protocol were, of course, products of the Organization of African Unity (OAU). In 2000 the OAU reformed itself as the African Union

(AU) and as a part of its new institutional architecture the AU established a Court of Justice by means of a Protocol in 2003 and which finally entered into force in 2009. In July 2004, before the 2003 Protocol had entered into force, but after the 1998 Protocol had done so (but before its actual 'constituting' had occurred), the AU Assembly decided to merge the two Courts into a single body, and after a series of complex discussions both the 1998 and 2003 Protocols were replaced by the 2008 Protocol on the Statute of the African Court of Justice and Human Rights, which has yet to enter into force. When it does so, the 'African Court' of Human Rights will be a section of a more general court, which according to the Constitutive Act will be the main judicial organ of the AU, the Statute of which grants it an extraordinarily broad jurisdictional competence in relation to the interpretation and application of the Constitutive Act and a broad range of other questions. Given that Article 2 of the Constitutive Act itself lists some 14 different objectives of the Union (one of which, (h), concerns the promotion and protection of human rights in accordance with the African Charter and other relevant human rights instruments) and Article 3 contains a list of some 16 principles which are to guide it in the pursuit of them (one of which, (m), is 'respect for democratic principles, human, rights, the rule of law and good governance') it may be wondered if it will be really possible for the Court as an institution to approach its work primarily through the lens of human rights, even though it is to have a discrete human rights 'section'. The probability is that it will not, and this concern is further reinforced by Article 31 of its Statute, which provides that when applying the law the Court (and thus its sections) will have regard to the Constitutive Act itself, treaties, custom, general principles or law, and judicial decision and writings 'as well as the regulations, directives and decisions of the Union'.

## (B) The European Court

The African Court is very different from the ECtHR, the purpose of which, according to Article 19 of the European Convention on Human Rights is to 'ensure the observance of the engagements undertaken by the High Contracting Parties in the Convention'. This is not to suggest that the European Court is insulated from broader influences in a way which the African Court will not be. The Council of Europe remains vital to the functioning of the European Convention system and as an intergovernmental organization it is prone to precisely the same tensions and pressure which affect all others. For example, any significant alternation to the structure or functioning of the Court requires the adoption of an amending Protocol and thus the political assent of all members of the Council of Europe. This has significantly hampered the ability of the Court to respond to the practical problems which it faces, not only in terms of the changes which might be effected but the speed with which they can be brought into effect. Put simply, not all member states seem equally committed to enhancing the effectiveness or efficiency of the European Court and there is a long history of ECtHR procedural reforms being more or less outdated before they have entered into force. Thus Protocol 14, containing the latest set of amendments to the procedural functioning of the Convention system, was concluded in May 2004 but did not enter into force until July 2010. All except Russia had ratified by the end of 2006, but Russia did not ratify until February 2010, when the adoption of the 'Interlaken' Declaration which heralded the need for yet another reappraisal of the Court's functioning. Moreover, the delay in the entry into force of Protocol 14 prompted the adoption of the 'Madrid' Agreement in May 2009 which permitted the provisional application of parts of the Protocol as between consenting states—a move which threatened the universal application of a common court system across the Council of Europe. Moreover, the Court is not immune from the more political dimensions of the Council when considering substantive issues—so, for example, its conception of such key questions as what comprises a 'common European consensus' for the purposes of its jurisprudential determinations is inevitably influenced by the outputs of the political organs of the Council itself, the Parliamentary Assembly and the Committee of Ministers. While this is not illegitimate, it does underline the nexus between the organization and the Court. Indeed, it is sometimes forgotten that, no matter what might be said of their origins and underpinnings from a philosophical perspective, the 'human rights' which are protected by the regional courts are those which are either set out or referred to in the treaties or protocols which create them and which are themselves the product of state activity.

## (C) The Inter-American Court

In some ways, it is the Inter-American Court which has the most 'distance' between itself and the organization to which it relates. The Organization of American States (OAS) claims, with good cause, to be the oldest regional organization in the world and the purpose of which according to Article 1 of its Charter is 'to achieve an order of peace and justice, to promote their solidarity, to strengthen their collaboration, and to defend their sovereignty, their territorial integrity and their independence'. The promotion and protection of human rights figures neither in its objects nor in the list of 'essential purposes' set out in Article 2—though there is no doubt that some of those purposes reflect human rights concerns. Nevertheless, the OAS today describes its four main pillars as being democracy, human rights, security, and development and Article 106 of the Charter itself provides for the creation of the Inter-American Commission on Human Rights 'whose principal function shall be to promote the observance and protection of human rights and act as a consultative organ of the Organisation in these matters'. The Commission was established in 1960 and was subsequently re-crafted within the framework of the 1969 American Convention on Human Rights, which also established the Inter-American Court. The Convention entered into force in 1978 and the Court came into being in 1979. Article 1 of its Statute stresses that the Court is 'an autonomous judicial institution whose purpose is the application and interpretation of the American Convention on Human Rights'. Nevertheless, it is notable that, unlike the European Court, the Inter-American Court has no jurisdictional capacity to receive cases at the behest of individuals itself: it may only consider contentious cases referred to it either by state parties or by the Commission. The reason for this is often said to lie in the political situation within the region at the time of the drafting of the Charter, and reflected a more 'state-centric' paradigm of human rights, coupled with a sense of regional solidarity which made members more comfortable with the idea of fellow states raising concerns directly before a court than of their citizens being able to do so.

## 3. Some implications of the relationship of the Courts to their regional organizations

There is no need to engage in a further or fuller comparative analysis of the three regional Courts in order to illustrate the point that they are all very much the product of, and reflective of, the regional organizations which created them. Indeed, why would they not be? The problem is that many commentators have acquired a rather idealized notion of what a regional court can or should be. This has largely been modelled on the ECtHR and tends to reduce the role of the regional body which stands behind it, if not to vanishing point, at least to a point where its sole *raison d'être* is the support of the work of a court which 'looks like' the ECtHR. For example, it is possible that one of the reasons for the relative dearth of interest in the work of the Inter-American Court may at least in part be due to its not being able to receive individual petitions. It is certainly the case that the African Court (in all its manifestations) is routinely examined against the model of the European Court and found wanting to the extent that it departs from it. The deficiencies in the European model are rarely held against the validity of the ideal which it is said to represent: rather, they are seen as flaws in its practical operation, rather than in its design. So a regional human rights court which is manifestly unable to handle its workload in an effective and timely fashion, has been the playground of litigation strategists and which does not function in the languages spoken by the bulk of those whose cases it determines is nevertheless projected as setting the standard in terms of international judicial protection of human rights and provides the model to which others must aspire.

Why? In the context of the Council of Europe, the answer seems clear: as has been said, the European Court through many years of development has achieved a position of primacy within the panoply of protection which the European Convention offers. While there are many other important conventions, treaty bodies, organs, and agencies operating within the framework of the Council to fulfil its objectives of promoting and protecting human rights, democracy, and the rule of law—such as the office of the Commissioner for Human Rights, the European Committee for the Prevention of Torture, the European Commission against Racism and Intolerance, the Monitoring Committee established under the Framework Convention on Minority Rights, the European Social and Economic Council, and many others—the Council has itself elevated the Court to a position of de facto primacy, making it the 'centrepiece' organ of its 'centrepiece' instrument. It is worth reminding ourselves that it was not always so. In retrospect it is hugely significant—and fortuitous, that when Turkey accepted the then optional jurisdiction of the European Court back in 1983, it meant that for the first time in the Convention's history all of the Council of Europe member states accepted all of the 'optional' elements that the test of the Convention then provided for. This paved the way for the subsequent amendment of the text in Protocol 11 (which did not enter into force until 1998) which abolished the European Commission on Human Rights and the 'judicialized' system of oversight. It also allowed the Council to put pressure on all newly joining member states not only to accede to the Convention but also to accept the jurisdiction of the Court when it expanded to embrace the former communist countries of Central and Eastern Europe in the 1990s. Had that unanimity among the existing members not been achieved, this would hardly have been possible and a more variegated pattern of jurisdictional competence, including the retention of the Commission, would have been almost inevitable. In short, the current primacy of the Court within the regional system is as much a product of chance as of design. It is, then, a matter of concern that the frustration caused by the delay in the entry into force of Protocol 14 induced states to risk fragmenting this unified approach in the Madrid Agreement, mentioned above.

The other regional courts are not in a similar position. The Inter-American Court continues to serve only a subset of state parties to the American Convention, which is itself only in force for a subset of the membership of the OAS: of the 35 member states of the OAS, 25 are parties to the Convention, of which only 21 recognize the jurisdiction of the Court. The position in Africa is a little different, in that while all 53 members of the AU are a party to the African Charter by no means all are a party to the protocols establishing the Courts. The 1998 Protocol establishing the ACHPR has been signed by 51 of the 53 member states but ratified by only 25, whereas the 2008 Protocol establishing the merged Court is yet to enter into force: indeed, the 2003 Protocol establishing the Court of Justice of the African Union which entered into force in 2009 has so far only attracted 16 ratifications. Does this mean that the American and African systems are, in some sense, either 'imperfect' or 'incomplete'?

The same question might be asked as regards the situation in other regions, where there are no regional human rights courts and little immediate prospect of their being any. For example, ASEAN was established in 1967 and now has ten member states. While its original aims and purposes, as set out in the ASEAN Declaration of 1967 refer to justice and the rule of law, they made no mention of 'human rights' as such, and neither did the 1997 Kuala Lumpur Declaration setting out the '2020 Vision' for ASEAN. However, Article 1(7) of the ASEAN Charter, which entered into force in 2008, now includes the promotion and protection of human rights as one of the purposes of the organization, alongside supporting democracy, enhancing good governance and the rule of law, and 'respect for fundamental freedoms, the promotion and protection of human rights and the promotion of social justice' as one of its basic principles (Art. 2(i)). This was operationalized by Article 14 of the Charter, which provides for the establishment, by the committee of ASEAN Foreign Ministers, of an 'ASEAN Human Rights Body', the nature of which is left unspecified. The following year, the terms of reference of the ASEAN Intergovernmental Commission on Human Rights (AICHR) were established. As its name implies, the Commission is 'intergovernmental' in nature and is focused on facilitating cooperation between member states on matters concerning human rights. The Commission has the capacity to undertaken thematic studies on matters concerning human rights but it does not have any powers to consider communications or allegations of human rights abuses by member states. This is not to minimize the significance of the AICHR, which may well be an important milestone in the development of a human rights structure within the ASEAN region. What is clear, however, is that at the moment vision for that structure does not extend to the creation of a regional court (though this is not to say that it might not).

The picture in the Arab world is not dissimilar. The Arab League had adopted the Arab Charter on Human Rights in 1994 but this never entered into force. A revised charter was adopted in 2004 and entered into force in 2008. The revised charter provides for the establishment of the 'Arab Human Rights Committee', a seven-member Committee of experts who serve in their personal capacities, and this came into being in March 2009. Its role, as set out in Article 49 of the Charter, is to consider reports which are submitted to it by contracting states setting out the measures they have taken to give effect to the rights and freedoms set out in the Charter. It has no jurisdiction to consider complaints of any form and, as with the AICHR neither purports to be, nor has the capacity to develop into, a 'regional court of human rights' in its current guise. The Commonwealth of Independent States (CIS), which was formed in 1991 and comprises 12 of the 15 states which were formed from the former USSR (the three Baltic states not being a part of the CIS) and is headquartered in Minsk, presents a slightly different picture. Article 33 of its Charter established a Commission on Human Rights comprised of state representatives which is to 'supervise the observation of obligations on human rights assumed by the member states within the framework of the Commonwealth', this being the 1995 CIS Convention on Human Rights and Fundamental Freedoms. The Regulations of the Commission permit it to consider complaints submitted by other state parties as well as both collective and individual complaints, but its governmental nature means that it is not an independent regional court.

## 4. 'Sub-regional' and 'cross-regional' courts of human rights

It is, then, clear that practice from the various regions varies greatly. But what *is* a region for these purposes? They can and do change, and over time may have a greater or lesser degree of coherence. For example, the 'regional' divisions which still operate within the UN context, and which are also used to gauge the achievement of 'equitable geographic representation', no longer bare a particularly close resemblance to the geography of contemporary geopolitics or, indeed, to the geography of regional approaches to human rights: for example, in what sense is 'Eastern Europe' a distinct regional configuration? Until the mid-1990s the states of Central and Eastern Europe were outside the reach of the Council of Europe but—with the exception of Belarus—are now firmly within its fold. Indeed, the UN 'Eastern Europe' grouping now includes states which are members of the European Union.

More importantly, if some states no longer form a part of the 'regions' to which they are nominally assigned, there are other states still which lie outside the natural orbit of the principal 'regional' organizations which are the focus of international attention. The most prominent of these states would be India and China, which between them contain approaching one-third of the world's population. Yet these states do not obviously 'belong' to a regional organization which operates within the human rights sphere, and so somehow manage to 'disappear' from view when regional approaches to human rights are being considered—a quite remarkable (but rarely remarked upon) situation.

It is equally obvious, but worth recalling, that numerous states 'belong' to more than one regional systems: some East European states are within both the Council of European and the Commonwealth of Independent States and are bound by both of their respective Conventions on Human Rights, while some Arab states fall within the reach of both the African and Arab system, and so on. Perhaps less obviously, but equally importantly from the perspective of the 'geography' of human rights, some of the major political blocs which influence the international human rights landscape either cut across the boundaries of the regional organizations and their human rights treaties and courts or have major players which are outside them. The 'Western European and other group' (WEOG) at the UN embraces states from the European, American, and Asia Pacific regions and regional organizations. The Organization of Islamic Cooperation (OIC) likewise cuts across regional boundaries. In terms of the diplomacy of international human rights protection these groupings (and others) are of major significance and comprise elements of what might best be termed a 'regionalism of ideas' rather than a regionalism based on geography, and which is all the more potent for that. One might pause to ponder how elements of the international human rights community might react to the creation of an 'Islamic Court of Human Rights'. Such an entity would be a regional human rights court, after a fashion.

Indeed, there are already 'other' regional courts of human rights, though not of this nature, which operate in parallel to other regional courts. An obvious example is the ECOWAS Community Court of Justice, which commenced work in 2001 as the chief legal organ of the Economic Community of West African States. In 2005, by means of a supplementary Protocol, the Court was given competence to determine cases of violation of human rights that occur in any ECOWAS member state, and it has already decided cases and has shown itself willing to consider whether states are in breach of their obligations under not only the African Charter but other international instruments as well. Also within Africa, the regional courts which form organs of the East Africa Community—the East African Court of Justice—and of the South African Development Community—the SADC Tribunal—though not expressly endowed with a jurisdictional competence over human rights issues, have both crafted a form of 'human rights' competence through an expansive reading of their jurisdictional provisions. Other regional organizations have developed court structures and it is to be expected that each will, over time, either be vested with a human rights jurisdiction or will follow the example of others and find a means of developing such a role.

Finally, and by no means exhaustively, it is worth recalling that other regional bodies have a very clear human rights focus but do seek to exercise it through courts, or court-like structures. Perhaps the best example is the Organization for Security and Co-operation in Europe (OSCE), which owes its very being to the recognition of human rights issues as a matter of international political concern at the time of the Helsinki Accords between the countries of NATO and the Warsaw Pact back in 1975 at the height of the Cold War. The OSCE continues to exercise a major role in human rights protection through the work of its field missions and of its Warsaw-based Office for Democratic Institutions and Human Rights (ODIHR), the latter providing a particularly useful forum for the coming together of civil society and participating states within a political rather than legal framework. As a political rather than legal process it naturally eschews the formal trappings of legalism, such as courts and judges. Nevertheless, its practical work is firmly grounded in international human rights law and serves as an important reminder that the realization of human rights protections can be achieved through non-legal as well as legal methodologies. Its *modus operandi* also illustrates the point that the means of human rights protection pursued by regional organizations will inevitably reflect the nature and rationale of those organizations themselves.

Once one opens up the discussion in such ways, other regional initiatives also become germane, since the question becomes not so much one of thinking about the future of regional courts of human rights but of regional protection of human rights. This ushers in the potential role of regional configurations of civil society which can play a part in the protection as well as in the promotion of human rights, and particularly so where there may be a regional nexus but as yet no regional body: a prime example would be the Asia Pacific Forum which has emerged as a strong voice for human rights protection based on the work of national human rights institutions operating on a cohesive regional basis.

Finally, there remains the question of the United Nations. It is notable that the UN human rights bodies tend to avoid drawing in the work of the regional courts of human rights, largely in order to underline the extent to which theirs is a global remit and not to be overly influenced by the concerns or approaches of a particular region. Given that the approaches to some key questions vary from region to region, this is perhaps hardly surprising and it is beyond the scope of this contribution to dwell on the relationship between the regional and 'universal' human rights bodies. Nevertheless, it is worth recalling that there is an inevitable overlap and that, for some, the future lies in the creation of an international court of human rights. This writer doubts both the practicality and the wisdom of such aspirations. Yet even were such a body to come into being, it would not displace the regional bodies which currently exist. Just as there is no suggestion that the emergence of the International Criminal Court displaces the need for criminal justice to be dispensed—even in relation to international crimes—at the national level and through regional and international judicial cooperation, so there is neither prospect nor need for the emergence of an international human rights jurisdiction to displace the regional. This certainly has not happened in the sphere of international economic law—where the WTO and regional economic organizations continue to operate and interact with each other, sometimes solving and sometimes generating legal disputes. It is congruence and coherence, rather than jurisdictional convergence, which is the goal to be sought. Moreover, the effective implementation of any legal regime requires a multi-tiered approach in order to be effective: within any single domestic jurisdiction there will be a multiplicity of judicial and non-judicial institutions which serve different constituencies, have different jurisdictional competencies, and operate within different institutional parameters. This is quite normal. What appears to be happening as regards the international protection of human rights is that a similarly variegated and complex pattern of jurisdictional networks is emerging as the normative system which it serves matures. For the older and more established Courts this doubtless can appear threatening as it may seem to undermine their place in the established order, challenging their primacy and authority. Perhaps they are right. But perhaps this is no bad thing.

## 5. Conclusion

The lesson to be learned from this review of practice is as simple as it is unsurprising. It is that where regional courts of human rights have developed they have done so in a way which reflects both the nature of the regional organization to which they owe their being, and have done so at a pace and in a manner which is consonant with the legal and political realities that they serve. Where that pace has, perhaps, been 'forced' by outside pressure to proceed more swiftly than the constituency it serves is prepared to accept, the resulting institutions are, as in the case of the African Court relatively weak for want of support. The experience of the Inter-American system suggests that slow, organic growth over time produces a system which is both relatively robust and enjoys a relatively high degree of political legitimacy.

It is instructive to compare this with the European Court which, despite the prestige which it carries, struggles with the burden of expectation which is placed upon it and whose legitimacy as the ultimate arbiter of European mores is increasingly called into question both in its former European heartlands to the west and in Russia to the east. One might speculate that the European system has developed past the point at which it offers a tier of regional appraisal of the realization of human rights standards within the member states of the organization and has become a vehicle for the articulation and implementation of regional human rights standards, as opposed to human rights approaches. Perhaps there is less danger of this occurring in other regional contexts for the reasons previously canvassed, but it remains an important watershed: once a regional human rights court begins to see itself as generating the standards, rather than adjudicating the extent to which those subject to the jurisdiction of states contracting to its relevant constituting instruments have had their rights entrenched upon by those contracting parties, it is engaging in a very different exercise and, perhaps, runs the risk of undermining the enterprise they were constructed to support. At that point, it becomes worthwhile recalling that there is nothing inevitable about regional courts of human rights and they have no special status in the system of human rights protection that justifies their existence other than that which flows from the legitimacy which they enjoy in the service of the organizations which have given them life in pursuit of their realization of human rights and fundamental freedoms, in whatever guise and whatever configuration that might take.

As was suggested at the outset, and implied by the title of this chapter, there is no single 'future' for regional courts of human rights as such. There are as many futures as there are Courts, and each must take its own path, informed by the institutional parameters, jurisdictional competencies, and substantive criteria which are of relevance to it. These futures will be different and will vary for each from time to time as the configurations and ambitions of the various regional bodies evolve. Human rights thinking has not remained static and neither have the institutional structures through which such rights are promulgated, promoted, and adjudicated. The future of the regional courts themselves is of considerably less significance than the realization of the tasks they were established to fulfil. While, then, it remains important that they are as well equipped as possible to fulfil their functions within their discrete regional and institutional settings, it is equally important to recognize that they must remain responsive to the changing political and intellectual configurations which continue to shape and reshape not only those regional and institutional settings themselves but which also form and reform the nature of the international community as a whole, in the interest of the human person which that community is there to serve.

# 22

# The Future of International Investment Law and Arbitration

*W. Michael Reisman*[*]

## SUMMARY

In the contemporary world, a satisfactory rate of development cannot be secured without the participation of foreign capital, technology, and enterprise. However, the introduction of capital, alone, would not necessarily produce multipliers with economic benefits for the local economy. An appropriate normative infrastructure is also required. Thus international agreements and their dispute-resolution mechanisms have assumed a role in, first, establishing the minimum standards for the governance of foreign investment by host states and, secondly, supervising and implementing them. There are now some 2,800 bilateral investment treaties (BITs). Most of which allow the qualifying investor itself, acting without the intervention or permission of its state of nationality, to invoke an international tribunal to review host state action, in terms of, inter alia, whether it has constituted 'fair and equitable' treatment. This is a procedural change with far-reaching substantive implications which make international investment law unique in international law. In addition to appraising the adequacy of the total administrative structure of a respondent state, international investment tribunals are increasingly appraising the propriety of specific national administrative action with respect to a foreign investor in terms of the law of that respondent state. In theory, international arbitration tribunals are well positioned to make ad hoc adjustments in disputes precipitated by changed circumstances but factors such as the limits on arbitral authority and the ever-present peril of annulment for *excès de pouvoir* constrain their ability to redesign long-term economic arrangements so that an appropriate balance of the benefits and burdens of the transactions can be re-established. To respond to current stresses within the legal arrangements now collectively referred to as international investment law, five alternative futures are delineated: (i) global integration (more and more direct foreign investment would be made worldwide,

[*] I acknowledge with gratitude the assistance and critical comments of Mahnoush H. Arsanjani.

on the basis of economic rather than political considerations; in addition, there would be more decisions by international investment tribunals with respect to the quality of governance within states which hosted foreign investment); (ii) regional and sub-regional integration; (iii) recrudescence of protectionism and mercantilism; (iv) revival of the New International Economic Order system; and (v) continuation of the present heterogeneous system. According to the author future (i) is the most desirable, for its promise of enhanced production and the efficient use of the resources of our planet and the resulting interdependence which, one hopes, will act as a restraint on the use of violence.

## 1. The need for direct foreign investment

Direct foreign investment is one of the girders of the *Unterbau* (foundation) of the international political and economic system. Its practice dates back to ancient Egypt and Lebanon; there are references to direct foreign investments in the Old Testament.[1] In the current global era, direct foreign investment outstrips international trade.[2] It is probable that it will continue to be important in the international system—and to be controversial.

At its best, an economic transaction is reciprocally enriching, with each participant net better off thanks to the exchange. But that was not how foreign investment was always viewed. From the rise of European imperialism, in particular, direct foreign investment acquired an image, in some circles, as an exploitative instrument of mercantilism and foreign domination. Later, the Industrial Revolution enabled European transportation and communications companies to carry their technology to comparatively less developed countries: key parts of direct foreign investment were henceforth dedicated to and often controlled infrastructural development and its management in national economies that had yet to experience industrialization. To many citizens of those states, it seemed that the great corporations and mighty banks of the Metropolitan 'owned' their countries.

The Russian Revolution, installing the command economy as a model for equitable development, reinforced the perception of direct foreign investment as an instrument of exploitation. After the Second World War, as the great European empires were dismantled, many of the new states that emerged from them adopted the command economy model, and, along with it, the conception of foreign investment as one more instrument for neocolonialist exploitation and domination. The most explicit normativization of this view of foreign investment was to be found in the General Assembly's Declaration on the Establishment of a New International

---

[1] R.D. Bishop, J. Crawford, and W.M. Reisman, *Foreign Investment Disputes: Cases, Materials and Commentary* (The Hague: Kluwer Law International, 2005), 2.

[2] Economist Intelligence Unit, *World Investment Prospects to 2011: Foreign Direct Investment and the Challenge of Political Risk* (Economist Intelligence Unit, 2007), 18–29.

Economic Order (NIEO)[3] and its Charter of Economic Rights and Duties of States.[4]

Ironically, this burst of economic nationalism in many of the newer states coincided with a demand for national economic development. The nearly universal political imperative for elites there was to grow their national economies, increase the national wealth, and, through some form of distribution, whether by provision of opportunity, entitlement, or some mix of both, to expand the economic and other life opportunities of their citizens. For non-democratic elites, the promise of economic development became a substitute for political legitimacy. No surprise then that in 1986, the UN General Assembly resolved not only that 'the right of development is an inalienable human right' but that 'states have the duty to take steps individually and collectively to formulate international development policies with a view to facilitating the full realization of the right to development'.[5]

Efforts to achieve development autochthonously, on the model of Chairman Mao's oxymoronic 'Great Leap Forward' demonstrated conclusively that, in the contemporary world, a satisfactory rate of development cannot be secured without the participation of foreign capital, technology, and enterprise. The community of new states, which had advanced, at least terminologically, if not factually from the rubric of 'underdeveloped states' to 'developing countries', looked to international organizations for assistance.

The International Bank for Reconstruction and Development (IBRD), the original name of the World Bank, had been established as a specialized agency of the United Nations, with the task of assembling and then lending the public international funds necessary for the reconstruction of a Europe that had been devastated by the Second World War. The IBRD project succeeded brilliantly. By the late 1950s, Europe's economies had bounded back. In the meanwhile, however, more and more of Europe's former colonial territories which were emerging to independence desperately needed to develop. Because the demand for development capital for the new states exceeded the supply of public international funds available to meet that demand, the only available source that could realistically address the shortfall was private direct foreign investment. But, this was the heyday of a pseudo-socialist rhetoric among the governments in developing countries: foreign investment was more often vilified as a neo-imperial tool of exploitation than as a potential adjunct tool for national development. In this impasse, the latent significance of the Washington Convention of 1965, which established the World Bank's International Centre for the Settlement of Investment Disputes (ICSID),[6] was seen as a consensus decision according public international law's seal of approval to private direct foreign investment. And it did so because of the indispensability

---

[3] GA Res. A/RES/S-6/3201, adopted 1 May 1974.

[4] GA Res. A/RES/40/182, adopted 17 December 1985.

[5] Declaration on the Right to Development, GA Res. A/RES/41/128, adopted 4 December 1986.

[6] Convention on the Settlement of Investment Disputes between States and Nationals of Other States—International Centre for Settlement of Investment Disputes, Washington 1965 (ICSID), entered into force 14 October 1966.

of private investment to the now international legally sanctioned goal of national economic development.

It quickly became clear, however, that foreign capital was not a magic bullet. The introduction of capital, alone, would not necessarily produce multipliers with economic benefits for the local economy. An appropriate normative infrastructure, the 'rule of law', was also required. In short order, international agreements and their dispute-resolution mechanisms assumed a role in, first, establishing the minimum standards for the governance of foreign investment by host states and, secondly and equally as important, supervising and implementing them.

## 2. The need for the rule of law: the spread of bilateral investments treaties

There are now some 2,800 BITs, including Free Trade Agreements with investment chapters. Although there are variations between them, each seeks to establish an orderly framework for investment by creating, in the language of a typical United Kingdom BIT, 'favourable conditions for greater investment by nationals and companies of one state in the territory of the other state'.[7]

This focus on the local environment for investment contrasts with Friendship, Commerce and Navigation (FCN) treaties, the genre of investment instrument that preceded the BIT generation. FCN treaties had operated on a rather simple theory of economic development: only bring foreign investment into an underdeveloped economy and as long as the host state does not expropriate it, the investment will generate profits while the host state will enjoy the benefits of a multiplier effect.

After much experience, it became clear that 'favourable conditions' are comprised of more than natural phenomena, such as climate, ecology, geography, and natural and human resources. Critically, 'favourable conditions' must also encompass appropriate internal legal, administrative, and regulatory arrangements, conducted through procedures designed to ensure that the arrangements are applied as they are supposed to be applied. This, in turn, requires an effective system of implementation, comprised of impartial courts, an efficient and legally restrained bureaucracy, and the measure of transparency in decision-making which is now recognized as a necessary control mechanism over governments and a component of the international minimum standard of governance.

Indeed, by the beginning of the twenty-first century, it was accepted that one of the functions of international direct investment was the attainment of Rule of Law transformations within developing countries. Without these 'favourable conditions', there may be investor profits, but the potential for robust multiplier effects for the host state is limited. Thus, contemporary international investment law and its instruments and institutions began to play a more particularized and increasingly

---

[7] W.M. Reisman and R.D. Sloane, 'Indirect Expropriation and Its Valuation in the BIT Generation', 74 BYIL (2004) 115.

assertive role in supervising internal arrangements within state parties. BITs, in the aggregate, were raising international law's bar for the way states conducted their internal affairs. Matters have gone from the *Neer v Mexico*[8] standard (a case actually unrelated to foreign investment) of 'an outrage...bad faith...to wilful neglect of duty...an insufficiency of governmental action' to a lower and more nuanced standard which involves a more searching inquiry into the administrative actions of the respondent government in a specific case. *Waste Management II*, which undertook to summarize and synthesize the case law until that time, spoke generally of conduct that was 'arbitrary, grossly unfair, unjust or idiosyncratic...'.[9]

## 3. The granting of an independent international standing to the investor

As all international lawyers can attest, international law is replete with injunctions for such high-minded standards. Most of them remain unfulfilled; indeed, some may have been enacted with such an expectation.[10] What has distinguished these new developments in international investment law is that most BITs allow the qualifying investor itself, acting without the intervention, permission, or blessing of its state of nationality, to invoke an international tribunal to review host state action, in terms of, inter alia, whether it constituted 'fair and equitable' treatment. This is a procedural change with far-reaching substantive implications which make international investment law unique in international law.

In his 'Early Law and Custom', Sir Henry Maine observed that 'so great is the ascendancy of the Law of Actions in the infancy of Courts of Justice, that substantive law has at first the look of being gradually secreted in the interstices of procedure.'[11] The insight is particularly relevant to this stage of the evolution of international investment law, for the procedural addition—the ascription of a meaningful independent international standing to the investor—has transformed what was heretofore soft, aspirational, and only intermittently applied law into effective law which, moreover, cuts ever more deeply into domestic legal arrangements. The initiation of the process of enforcement of investor rights is transferred entirely to the investor, a party that is driven only by an economic interest in the outcome. Thus the possibility of the investor's state's 'national interest' (or disinterest) or its short-term political objectives which might have led that state to refrain from pressing its national's claim and, thus, the realization of the rights on which it purported to be based is excluded. With more effective invocations of third party decision, there is more effective application of international investment law.

---

[8]  *L.F.H. Neer and Pauline Neer (USA) v United Mexican States*, 15 October 1926, RIAA Vol. IV, 60–6, para. 4, at 61–2.

[9]  *Waste Management, Inc. v United Mexican States (No. 2)*, ICSID Case No. ARB(AF)/00/3 (NAFTA), Final Award, 30 April 2004, at para. 98 (emphasis added).

[10]  W.M. Reisman, *Folded Lies: Bribery, Crusades, and Reforms* (Chicago: Collier-Macmillan, 1979).

[11]  Sir Henry Sumner Maine, *Dissertations on Early Law and Custom* (London: John Murray, [1883] reprint 2009), 389.

I would emphasize that the revolution here is not only in the right of the private initiation of claims but in the scope of their content as well. Scope has expanded dramatically. Compare the high thresholds set in the *Neer*[12] and *Chattin*[13] cases, which were very indulgent to the state, with some widely cited current formulations: in *Metalclad v Mexico*, the tribunal found that '[t]he totality of these circumstances demonstrates a lack of orderly process and timely disposition in relation to an investor of a Party acting in the expectation that it would be treated fairly and justly.'[14] In *Tecmed v Mexico*, in a paragraph that has been cited and recited by many other tribunals, the tribunal said:

The foreign investor expects the host state to act in a consistent manner, free from ambiguity and totally transparently in its relations with the foreign investor, so that it may know beforehand any and all rules and regulations that will govern its investments, as well as the goals of the relevant policies and administrative practices or directives, to be able to plan its investment and comply with such regulations. Any and all state actions conforming to such criteria should relate not only to the guidelines, directives or requirements issued, or the resolutions approved thereunder, but also the goals underlying such regulations.[15]

Even more far-reaching is the statement in *Occidental Exploration v Ecuador*, where the tribunal said

The relevant question for international law in this discussion is not whether there is an obligation to refund VAT, which is the point on which the parties have argued most intensely, but rather whether the legal and business framework meets the requirements of stability and predictability under international law.[16]

In addition to appraising the adequacy of the total administrative structure of a respondent state, international investment tribunals are increasingly appraising the propriety of specific national administrative action with respect to a foreign investor in terms of the law of that respondent state. Consider one other paragraph from the *Occidental Exploration v Ecuador* award:

The Tribunal agrees with the SRI [Internal Revenue Service of Ecuador] that Article 69A grants the right to a tax refund to exporters of goods involved in activities such as mining, fishing, lumber, bananas and African palm oil. The Tribunal does not, however, agree that the oil industry is excluded from the application of Article 69A.... As has been explained above, the Tribunal has concluded that VAT reimbursement was not included in OEPC's [Occidental's] Contract. It follows that under Ecuadorian tax legislation the Claimant is entitled to such a refund.[17]

---

[12] Above n 8.

[13] *B.E. Chattin (United States) v United Mexican States*, Award of 23 July 1927, RIAA, Vol. IV, 282–312.

[14] *Metalclad Corporation v The United Mexican States*, ICSID Case No. ARB(AF)/97/1, Award of 30 August 2000, para. 99, 27 (emphasis added).

[15] *Tecnicas Medioambientales Tecmed S.A. v The United Mexican States*, ICSID Case No. ARB(AF)/00/2, Award of 29 May 2003, para. 154, 61 (emphasis added).

[16] *Occidental Exploration and Production Company v The Republic of Ecuador*, UNCITRAL Arbitration (London Court of International Arbitration Administered Case No. UN 3467), Final Award of 1 July 2004, para. 191, 64–5 (emphasis added).

[17] Ibid, at paras 136 and 143.

Thus, some international investment tribunals seem to be moulting into what are essentially *international courts of appeal over the administrative actions of the respondent state*, appraising not only (i) the adequacy of the entire administrative framework in terms of international law standards but even (ii) the specific applications of national law by the national administration in terms of its legal accuracy under that law.

This expanded scope of review of matters which, until now, had been deemed quintessentially domestic, is all of a piece with other developments in international law: for example, the international human rights programme and the World Bank's vision of inculcating Rule of Law in domestic settings. In a broader sense, it is part of the remarkable constriction of the sphere of 'domestic jurisdiction' in general international law, which, as the Permanent Court of International Justice famously observed, is a function of the state of international relations.[18] But in investment law, as in many other spheres, it is now being resisted by many governments because of three coinciding factors.

## 4. Growing resistance to the expansion of the scope of review over national administrative action

The first of these factors is the administrative revolution that has taken place within states seeking development. The early ideal of the laissez-faire state has yielded to the current model of the regulatory state. It is now universally appreciated that accommodating an efficient economy to the complex political demands of democratic states, the protection of the most vulnerable strata of the population, and the preservation of the environment is a task beyond the powers of the 'Invisible Hand'. Rather, it requires continuing managerial oversight and episodic adjustments by governmental agencies of the national regime that regulates economic activity. So just as the developing state is learning, as did the states which went through this process in the early twentieth century, to manage its political economy through a panoply of regulatory agencies, the international investment law system is subjecting those efforts to greater and greater scrutiny by external decision-makers who apply a set of international standards that was shaped by laissez-faire values.

The second factor is the empowerment in many of the host states of a multipartite civil society and the remarkable extent to which that new 'E-state' is now capable, thanks to the political potentialities afforded by the revolution in electronic communications, of pressing their own versions of the national interest; many of those versions are not congruent with the programmes pursued by the national government. In some instances, this private political activity works in favour of international law; some groups within civil society press their governments to adjust policies and practices so as to more closely approximate the requirements

---

[18] *Nationality Decrees Issued in Tunis and Morocco on 8 November 1921*, Advisory Opinion, PCIJ, Series B, no. 4 (7 February 1923), 21.

of international investment law. In other instances, however, non-governmental entities agitate against compliance with particular decisions and even against the regime of international investment law itself.

The third factor is the blurring of the line between capital-importing and capital-exporting states. Many developed states, which had essentially been capital-exporters, are now hosts to significant amounts of foreign investments; many of those investments are, moreover, of increasing importance to their economic infrastructure. Earlier these states had been champions of an international investment regime which provided protections to investors. In that role, they had insisted on international supervision of domestic regulatory competences insofar as they impacted foreign investors. Now, however, many of these states are beginning to behave like traditional capital-importing states, who have been jealous of trespasses on their own regulatory competences. The result, reflected in new generations of Model BITs and in negotiating positions, is a move toward a constriction of investor protections and a greater tolerance for governmental actions against foreign investors. As a consequence of the operation of these three factors, the interventionist role and transformative ambitions of international investment law are now being resisted in different ways by a surprisingly heterogeneous coalition of states.

One major response, until now only on the part of developing countries, has been an attempt to revive the Calvo Doctrine in a new raiment. Its vehicle is not a formal 'Calvo Clause' but, rather, an insistence that choice-of-law and choice-of-forum clauses in contracts with foreign investors should prevail over international treaty commitments. If the investor has accepted such clauses after arm's length negotiation, it is argued, then it has freely agreed that the matter is to be decided only in local courts according to local law and has waived any treaty-based rights it might otherwise have had to an international tribunal in accordance with a bilateral investment treaty and general international law. That argument has won some support. Thus the extent of the future effectiveness of international supervision over domestic administration has been put into question.

The causes of tensions within international investment law are part of the very fabric of this sector of law. Governments are different from other actors. Even when they enter the marketplace, their responsibilities to internal communities and constituencies continue; in all but the most brutally totalitarian of them, governmental power is temporary and often shaky. Even strong governments are beholden to internal constituencies which may have little appreciation of or respect for the international arrangements that their governments have concluded but which later come to be popularly perceived as affecting their own lives and aspirations. Compensation metrics in international investment law have always been somewhat mysterious and they come under intense pressure in circumstances in which awards, which are easily justified in terms of ordinary commercial standards, are not politically feasible. Yet, here, as everywhere else, there is, in Milton Friedman's words, 'no free lunch'. Redressing compensation quanta in favour of respondent governments which claim *'non possumus'* simply passes the losses through to the ultimate investors, the pension funds of vast numbers of individuals in the developed world or, even, ironically, to sovereign wealth funds in developing countries. The mere prospect of such a reassignment of losses could well chill the appetite for foreign investment by the very international market which ICSID had sought to mobilize.

In theory, international arbitration tribunals are well positioned to make ad hoc adjustments in disputes precipitated by changed circumstances but factors such as the limits on arbitral authority and the ever-present peril of annulment for *excès de pouvoir* constrain their ability to redesign long-term economic arrangements so that an appropriate balance of the benefits and burdens of the transactions can be re-established.

## 5. Five alternative futures

The fact that there are stresses within the legal arrangements now collectively referred to as international investment law should occasion no surprise. All law is dialectical in nature and every arrangement, which provides comparative benefits to some and less to others, immediately generates pressure to adjust or to terminate it and to replace it with a different value configuration. Some of the adjustments that result from this dialectical process operate within the established constitutive structure of international investment law. Others are truly revolutionary, rejecting the constitutive structure, as a whole, or particular arrangements within it. One cannot, as a result, assume a straight-line projection from the past or an organic extension of the current situation into the future. Without according excessive importance to the economic vicissitudes which the world economy is now experiencing, one can identify five alternative Futures, each based on latent tendencies of current trends, any one of these constructive futures could emerge from the current system of international investment law. Let us consider them briefly.

### (A) Future One: global integration

One possible future would involve the reinforcement of the trends toward globalization, with English functioning as the lingua franca, within a context of a planetary-wide civilization of science and technology. In such a future, more and more direct foreign investment would be made worldwide, on the basis of economic rather than political considerations. The lawmaking and law-applying functions of international investment law and the national decision processes influencing them, would continue to fall within the jurisdiction of international arbitral tribunals, whether under the aegis of ICSID, the Permanent Court of Arbitration, or as ad hoc tribunals operating under UNCITRAL Rules administered by private transnational arbitral associations. This future would witness new generations of bilateral investment treaties, with common provisions affording identical enhanced protections to investors. It would also include the pluralization or multilateralization of investment treaties, in place of much of the current network of bilateral instruments and an explicit investment role for the World Trade Organization

(WTO). It would likely include the installation of an appeal mechanism, perhaps on the model of the WTO's Appellate Body, which would make arbitral applications more uniform.

A future of global integration would include more decisions by international investment tribunals with respect to the quality of governance within states which hosted foreign investment with a view to moving steadily toward a homogenization of national practice in accordance with increasingly robust international standards.

### (B) Future Two: regional and sub-regional integration

A second possible future would be marked by regional and sub-regional integration rather than the high level of global integration as the central feature of the preceding future. Regional blocs in Europe, North and Central America, in the southern cone of South America, Africa, and Asia would trade and principally invest among themselves. In place of a single lingua franca, dominant regional languages would operate. Extra-regional investment might continue but it would be relatively reduced, as compared to the more intense regional and sub-regional investment. New generations of bilateral investment treaties and Free Trade Agreements, instead of running North and South or East and West, as in the recent past, would tend to be between members of the same regional bloc. Instead of international standards, regional standards would emerge, on the model of 'regional customary international law'. As for the tribunals charged with deciding disputes, they would be increasingly composed of members of a single region, on the model of the Chamber-system of the International Court of Justice.

### (C) Future Three: recrudescence of protectionism and mercantilism

A third possible future would be characterized by increased protectionism and mercantilism, driven by economic uncertainty and perceived resource scarcities. Protectionism would manifest itself in limitations on outward foreign investment as well as increased restrictions on inward foreign investment. Both limitations would be justified as measures necessary for the protection of national security and other vital national interests.

A recrudescence of mercantilism could be exacerbated by a perception of a critical shortage of key natural resources in a world whose population has grown and the demands of whose members for a better material lifestyle have universalized. Such a future is likely to see a new generation of bilateral investment treaties, marked by enhanced competences assigned to host states, including rights of counterclaim by the host state against foreign investors. In such a future, the amount of general foreign investment would be expected to decline significantly, to be replaced by 'diaspora networks'.[19]

---

[19]  D. Leblang, 'Familiarity Breeds Investment: Diaspora Networks and International Investment', 104 APSR (2010) 584.

## (D) Future Four: revival of the NIEO system

A fourth possible future would see the return of an effective coalition of developing countries and developed mineral-exporting countries, trying to use their numerical superiority within international organizations to enact international instruments comparable to the Charter of Economic Rights and Duties of States of the New International Economic Order. In this future, states would insist on the right of expropriation for a broad range of self-judging reasons with 'appropriate' compensation to be determined exclusively by institutions of the host state. This future would see significant withdrawals from ICSID and its consequent decline as the central institution in international investment dispute resolution (without regard to decline due to endogamous factors such as loss of confidence in its control mechanism). Many bilateral investment treaties would also be denounced. Insofar as mineral-extraction industries would still be obliged to pursue natural resources wherever they might be found, the system of international investment law based on the provision of protections for investors and their implementation by international arbitration tribunals would decline, to be replaced by alternative risk-management or risk-abatement methods. Thus political risk insurance might be more widely used with the consequent additional costs of investment passed through to consumers. At the international organizational level, in this future construct, the Multilateral Investment Guarantee Agency (MIGA) and its private counterparts would supersede ICSID in importance.

## (E) Future Five: continuation of the present heterogeneous system

A final possible future would involve a continuation of the present mixed and contradictory system in which international law continues to commit itself to the encouragement and protection of international investment through the maintenance of international standards and some soft supervision of the practices of host states in terms of those standards. In this future, many of the antinomies that are characteristic of contemporary international investment law would continue.

## 6. By way of conclusion

One engages in the intellectual task of the creation of alternative images of futures in order to refine strategies that will increase the likelihood of achieving desirable or utopic futures and decreasing the likelihood of the eventuation of dystopic ones. I consider Future One the most desirable, for its promise of enhanced production and the efficient use of the resources of our planet and the resulting interdependence which, one hopes, will act as a restraint on the use of violence. By contrast, the third and fourth futures are, in my view, undesirable.

In navigating through the present towards any of the imagined futures, the emergent future of the international investment system and its role in the growth and maintenance of the global economy will depend on the statesmanship and wisdom of national leaders as well as those who are charged with managing arbitration tribunals and applying and elaborating international law in this regard. National leaders will, in the main, be the critical actors in determining, through their behaviour, which of the futures is most likely to eventuate. But, with respect to the maintenance of the international investment regime, arbitration tribunals have the potential of being important agents, whether of regression, stabilization, or change.

# 23

# How to Cope with the Proliferation of International Courts and Coordinate Their Action

*Mohamed Bennouna*

## SUMMARY

The problem of coordination between international courts and tribunals arises as a result of the existence of numerous tribunals interpreting and applying international law. This problem is due to the horizontal, autonomous, and non-hierarchical relationships between these courts. This does not mean, however, that in international law every court is a 'self-contained system'. It is difficult to imagine that an international tribunal could carry out its duties on its own, without contact with other international tribunals. The need for coordination arises in two respects: (i) the jurisdiction of certain courts may overlap and (ii) the substantive law that each court 'produces' can cause disparities in the interpretation and application of international law. For the purposes of coordination, one should consider the creation by the UN General Assembly of a new expert body, modelled on the International Law Commission, which would ensure 'the progressive development of international law and its codification' (Art. 13, UN Charter). The task of this expert body would be to identify and analyse the potential divergences in the interpretation and application of general international law, as well as the consequences thereof. They would submit their study to the UN General Assembly, to international courts, as well as to the bodies entrusted with the codification of international law. These periodical studies, carried out by an expert body, would have the advantage of demonstrating to the judges issues relating to the diversified implementation of general international law by different international jurisdictions.

## 1. Introduction: the increasing judicialization of international relations

We live in a world where a growing number of international tribunals are increasingly being used; this is what has been called the judicialization of international relations. This phenomenon can be said to have originated in the 1990s, after the end of the Cold War. Since then, the judicialization of international relations has developed in parallel with their globalization.

The end of the clash of ideologies has probably favoured more frequent recourse to international courts, especially when dealing with disputes which do not concern questions of vital importance to concerned parties.

This chapter is limited to the institutionalized courts and tribunals which are required to achieve a certain level of coherence in the adoption of their decisions, to the extent that their statutes provide for some continuity in their functioning. These institutionalized entities certainly differ from the arbitration tribunals established by the parties for a specific matter and dissolved once the award is rendered. Nonetheless, international arbitration also developed with globalization, particularly in the fields of trade and investment. Moreover, this study will not discuss what has been termed 'quasi-judicial' organs composed of international experts, and created especially in the context of major international conventions on human rights.

We must not lose sight of the fact that international courts are very diverse in reach (universal, regional), jurisdiction (general, special), composition (international or hybrid judges: ie, a mix of international and national judges), and subjects (states or other entities, legal entities or natural persons). For example, only states can refer a matter to the International Court of Justice (ICJ) (general jurisdiction) and to the Appellate Body of the World Trade Organization (special jurisdiction). On the other hand, the international criminal courts are either universal in reach (International Criminal Court (ICC)), or created to deal with a particular conflict (ad hoc courts), and can either be composed of international judges (International Criminal Tribunal for the former Yugoslavia (ICTY) and Rwanda (ICTR)), or a mix of international and national judges (Court for Sierra Leone, Cambodia, Lebanon). As for human rights courts, they are regional in reach (European, Inter-American, African) and are open to individuals as well as states.[1]

In spite of this variety, this chapter essentially deals with the problem of coordination that arises as a result of the existence of numerous tribunals interpreting and applying international law. This problem is due to the horizontal, autonomous, and non-hierarchical relationships between these courts. This does not mean, however, that in international law every court is a 'self-contained system' as has been asserted, particularly in the jurisprudence of the ICTY.[2] It is difficult to imagine that an international tribunal could carry out its duties on its own, without contact with other international tribunals. At the very least, by professional duty, the judges keep themselves abreast of the evolution in the practice of other institutions in charge of interpreting and applying international law.

---

[1] C.P.R. Romano, 'A Taxonomy of International Rule of Law Institutions', 2 J Int'l Dispute Settlement (2011) 241–77.

[2] ICTY, *Prosecutor v Duško Tadić*, Decision on the defence motion for interlocutory appeal on jurisdiction (2 October 1995), Case No. IT-94–1-T, para. 11.

Indeed, judges cannot ignore the case law of other tribunals, either to repudiate it and deviate from it or, on the contrary, to find support for their own reasoning[3] or even rely on their findings. For example, the ICJ relied on the case law of the ICTY in order to characterize the massacre of Srebrenica as genocide. On the other hand, the ICJ preferred to diverge from the ICTY rulings and stand by its own case law when attributing certain acts to the state, providing each time a specific justification for its choice.[4] Nonetheless, it is true that each of the international courts, in the end, operates independently, subject only to the intellectual scrutiny of scholars.

Along with the increasing number of international tribunals, it is possible to identify a trend of specialization in their field of competence. As a consequence, some have feared that such trends would bring about the *fragmentation* of international law, as a result of different application of principal sources of law depending on the field of international relations. This fear is based on the postulate of unity of international law; such postulate, in my opinion, cannot be raised *a priori*.[5] Indeed, international law's unity and diversity should emerge as the by-product of the practice of tribunals.

## 2. Risks of overlaps of jurisdiction

However, the jurisdiction of certain courts may overlap: this is the case with the ICJ and the International Tribunal for the Law of the Sea (ITLOS, based in Hamburg), with regard to the resolution of disputes on the delimitation of maritime boundaries or on marine environmental protection. Concerns have arisen due to the fact that states were left with the choice between different judicial proceedings ('forum shopping'), and such choice might be motivated in light of these courts' practice. I deem it certainly appropriate that litigants have the opportunity to choose which particular tribunal to seize, when this option is available to them, as it is convenient for them. The United Nations Convention on the Law of the Sea of 10 December 1982 leaves to parties the possibility to choose between various procedures for the settlement of their disputes relating to its interpretation and its application: that is, ITLOS, ICJ, an arbitral tribunal established under Annex VII, and a special arbitral tribunal constituted in accordance with Annex VIII (Art. 287, Convention).

---

[3] The Court noted, in its Judgment of 10 November 2010 on the *Ahmadou Sadiou Diallo* case, that the interpretation by the European Court of Human Rights and the Inter-American Court of Human Rights of provisions close in substance to those of the International Covenant on Civil and Political Rights and the African Charter on Human and Peoples' Rights which the Court was applying, was consistent with what it found in respect of the latter provisions (*Ahmadou Sadio Diallo (Republic of Guinea v Democratic Republic of the Congo)*, judgment of 10 November 2010, para. 68).

[4] *Application of the Convention on the Prevention and Punishment of the Crime of Genocide (Bosnia and Herzegovina v Serbia and Montenegro)*, Judgment, ICJ Reports 2007, 206–11, paras 396–407.

[5] P.-M. Dupuy, 'L'unité de l'ordre juridique international', 297 RCADI (2002-V) 9.

Nevertheless, it is possible that one of the parties to a dispute decides to resort to one of the procedures under the Convention of Montego Bay, while the other party considers that this dispute comes within the exclusive jurisdiction of another international tribunal. This issue has been raised before the arbitral tribunal constituted in accordance with Annex VII of the UN Convention on the Law of the Sea, in a dispute between Ireland and the United Kingdom in the case of *MOX Plant* case. In its Order no. 3, the arbitral tribunal observed that the European Commission had drawn its attention to the fact that the European Court of Justice could have been seized of the same dispute and could declare its exclusive jurisdiction thereon. For these reasons, the arbitral tribunal considered that its decision on its own jurisdiction would ultimately depend on the jurisdictional findings of the European Court. Also, in order to avoid the adoption of conflicting decisions on the same case, the arbitral tribunal decided to suspend its proceedings until the issues of European Union law were resolved.[6]

## 3. Coordination of courts based on comity and other principles

The *MOX Plant* case provides a telling example of the potential conflicts of jurisdiction between international courts whose decisions are compulsory and final, but this is only one of the elements of the necessary coordination of their activities.

In the *MOX Plant* case, the arbitral tribunal referred to 'considerations of mutual respect and comity which should prevail between judicial institutions' (para. 28). This method of coordination is especially well known in common law: the court, as a courtesy, takes into account the risks of conflict with another judicial institution. Nevertheless, comity potentially amounts to a discretionary power of the first seized court, and cannot prevent every possible jurisdictional clash. It must be noted, however, that at present there is no other method of coordination to rely on. This does not mean we cannot improve it, in particular by including specific mechanisms in the statutes of international jurisdictions, allowing them to stop the proceedings so as to prevent jurisdictional conflicts, and by regulating continuation of the proceedings with particular attention to the relationship between jurisdictions involved. One could also envisage a multilateral international convention laying down the procedures necessary to manage potential conflicts of jurisdiction between judicial international institutions. Granted, this would not be an easy task, in light of the variety of situations and interests at stake, but insofar as this attempt regards only the technique of coordination itself and its essential elements, it should be possible to draw a general framework that international tribunals could implement.

---

[6] Permanent Court of Arbitration, Arbitral Tribunal Constituted Pursuant to Art. 287, and Art. 1 of Annex VII, of the United Nations Convention on the Law of the Sea for the Dispute Concerning the MOX Plant case, *Ireland v United Kingdom*, Order no. 3, 24 June 2003, Suspension of Proceedings on Jurisdiction and Merits, and Request for Further Provisional Measures, para. 29.

In this regard, the case of former Chadian president, Hissène Habré, is also indicative of necessities of coordination between different tribunals and courts. While the African Union was seeking an African solution by mandating Senegal to prosecute and judge the former president,[7] the Court of Justice of ECOWAS opposed this solution by invoking the risk of violation of the human rights of Mr Habré (the guarantees of a fair trial, the authority of *res judicata*, and the principle of non-retroactivity of criminal law).[8] While acknowledging that the ICJ has not had its last word on the issue of prosecution of Mr Habré, which set Belgium and Senegal against each other,[9] the Court of Justice of ECOWAS considered, in its Judgment of 18 November 2010, that the African Union mandate to Senegal is to judge the former President within the scope of an ad hoc special procedure with an international character.[10] Although, in general, all states concerned and all institutions involved adhere to the objective of fighting against impunity, what is lacking in this case is the coordination not only between states but also between international institutions and tribunals.

## 4. The need for coordination with regard to the applicable substantive law

The second aspect of coordination between international tribunals concerns their legal production, the substantive law that each 'produces' and the disparities in the interpretation and application of international law that could result. How, indeed, is it possible to harmonize this production, including the establishment of certain practices as customary norms, in a decentralized judicial system?

However, one can ask first whether such harmonization is necessary. Indeed, there is a doctrinal debate between those advocating a status of competition between international courts—which would have beneficial effects for the production of fairer and more pertinent norms—and those who believe that the adoption of norms and interpretations by different courts may ultimately weaken the legitimacy of the international legal order as a whole.[11] Granted, the former rely on the assumption that this legal order does not have a proper legal coherence, whereas

---

[7] In July 2006, the heads of state of the African Union mandated Senegal 'to prosecute and ensure that Hissène Habré is tried, on behalf of Africa, by a competent Senegalese court with guarantees for a fair trial' (African Union Conference, *Decision on the Hissène Habré Case and African Union*, Doc. no. Assembly/AU/3 (VII), 2 July 2006, para. 5-ii). This decision has been confirmed by another decision (*Decision on the Hissène Habré Case*, 1–3 February 2009, Doc. no. Assembly/AU/Dec. 240 (XII)).

[8] Court of Justice of ECOWAS, *Hissène Habré v Republic of Senegal*, Judgment no. ECW/CCJ/JUD/06/10, 18 November 2010.

[9] *Questions relating to the Obligation to Prosecute or Extradite (Belgium v Senegal)*, provisional measures, Order of 28 May 2009.

[10] It should also be noted that the decisions taken so far are not in harmony with the decision of the Committee against Torture of 17 May 2006. UN Committee against Torture, *Suleymane Guengueng v Senegal*, Communication no. 181/2001, Doc. CAT/C/36/D/182/2001, 17 May 2006.

[11] W.T. Worster, 'Competition and Comity in the Fragmentation of International Law', 34(1) Brooklyn JIL (2008) 119–49.

the latter deem that such consistency can only be read between the lines, and needs an effort to reinforce it. Among the latter, some even argue for a 'constitutional-ization' of the international dispute-settlement system.[12] This categorical position clearly takes its inspiration from national legal systems by suggesting a hierarch-ical system of international dispute settlement in which the ICJ should play the role of a supreme court. As former President Gilbert Guillaume recalled, the ICJ could either reconsider, by way of appeal or review, the judgments of other inter-national tribunals, or these tribunals could seize the ICJ for an advisory opinion on general issues of international law raised during their proceedings. Thus, as in the European law model, international tribunals could stay proceedings until the ICJ gives its opinion on the question of international law under discussion, ensuring their consistent application.[13]

Apart from the difficulties inherent in any in-depth reform of the Charter of the United Nations and the statute of the ICJ, the scheme of a system of international dispute settlement organized into a hierarchy supposes the evolution, beforehand, of decision-making processes, on a global scale, towards greater integration. The globalization of certain economic and financial activities did not come along with a globalization of the decision processes, which remains dependent on the still-existing sovereignty of states.

Any prospective study of the phenomenon of proliferation of international tri-bunals should necessarily take into account states and their sovereignty.

In this context, I think a minimum of harmonization of the legal production process is essential to preserve the credibility of international law and its legi-timacy. Because, regardless of the type of international court, and its degree of specialization, the court does not operate in a vacuum, and does not settle disputes in a given field of international relations that would be completely impenetrable and separated from all others.

Thus, according to Martti Koskenniemi in his Report on fragmentation of inter-national law: '[i]f international law is needed as a structure for coordination and cooperation between (sovereign) States, it is no less needed in order to coordinate and organize the cooperation of (autonomous) rule-complexes and institution.'[14] This is why I think it desirable that, at least, the international courts harmonize their references on the basis of general international law. It does not necessarily mean that dissonant voices will not be expressed from time to time as part of the functioning of international tribunals, but this should only be a temporary dis-cordance. I have in mind, as an example, the positions taken by the ICJ and the ICTY on the issue of attribution of international responsibility in relation to acts of private persons. The ICJ has attempted to limit the subject of controversy by

---

[12] E.-U. Petersmann, 'Constitutionalism and International Adjudication: How to Constitutionalize the UN Dispute Settlement System?', 31(4) NYU J Int' L & Pol (1999) 763.

[13] Gilbert Guillaume, Speech by President of the ICJ to the sixth Committee of the General Assembly of the United Nations, 27 October 2000.

[14] Report of the Study Group of the ILC, 'Fragmentation of International Law: Difficulties Aris-ing from the Diversification and Expansion of International Law', finalized by Martti Koskenniemi, 13 April 2006, Doc. A/CN.4/L.682, para. 487.

underlining that the criterion of 'overall control' made by the ICTY in the case of *Duško Tadić*, if applicable when characterizing an internal or international armed conflict, cannot be extended to the issue of attribution of state responsibility. However, this issue has not been raised before the ICTY.[15] There has therefore been an attempt to circumscribe the discordance between two courts, but has the problem been solved?

## 5. A plea for a new expert body

That is why I believe that coordination between international courts is necessary to move beyond simply exchanging information between judges and taking into account as much as possible their respective positions.

It would be possible to consider the creation by the UN General Assembly of a new expert body, modelled on the International Law Commission (ILC), which would ensure 'the progressive development of international law and its codification' (Art. 13, UN Charter).

Granted, all this concerns the implementation of international law by international courts. This would not exclude the possibility that a group of experts, representing the international community and the different branches of international law, could carry out a study on the legal production of different international tribunals. Their task would be to identify and analyse potential divergences in the interpretation and application of general international law, as well as the consequences thereof. They would then submit their study to the UN General Assembly, to the international courts, as well as to the bodies entrusted with the codification of international law. These periodical studies, carried out by a body composed of independent experts, would have the additional advantage of demonstrating to the judges the issues relating to the diversified implementation of general international law by different international jurisdictions. Nonetheless, it would be for each to decide what weight to give to these studies and, where necessary, to adjust their own action accordingly, in full autonomy.

Judges could at least rely on a set of shared documents, from which they would be able to draw the consequences they deem appropriate.

There are, of course, plenty of scholarly works on the activity of international tribunals, but they are very unstructured, of unequal value, and not exhaustive! In any event, there can be a beneficial complementarity between the works of the scholars and those produced by a representative group of independent experts. I believe that it would be helpful if a similar body could, from time to time, take stock of the current status of the implementation of general international law in a decentralized legal order.

---

[15] *Application of the Convention on the Prevention and Punishment of the Crime of Genocide (Bosnia and Herzegovina v Serbia and Montenegro)*, Judgment, ICJ Reports 2007, 206–11, paras 396–407.

We should not forget that we can currently rely on certain groups of experts established within the framework of the major international conventions, particularly those on human rights. Their task is periodically to evaluate the application of these conventions by state authorities, including national courts.

The group of experts monitoring the coordination between international tribunals could address not only the issues of conflicting case law, but also the instances of conflicts of jurisdiction, and the procedures through which these could (or could not) be resolved.

In any event, the General Assembly could even assign this task to the ILC, subject to the effect of making it a subsidiary body. In all cases, the experts should have at their disposal a powerful database comprised of the case law of international tribunals.

## 6. Concluding remarks

In conclusion, I take a rather favourable view of the phenomenon of the proliferation of international tribunals, which reflects a state of vitality of international law and its peaceful dispute-settlement mechanisms. However, it must be noted that such proliferation has taken place in a very pragmatic way, depending on international contingencies and without a clear plan regarding the development of new jurisdictional actors and the legal framework within which they operate. Who would have foreseen that the ad hoc tribunals on the former Yugoslavia and Rwanda would still be operating some 20 years after their creation? This is why it is time to put some order into the unprecedented expansion of the activity of international tribunals which has occurred in the last two or three decades. In order to do so, the issue of coordination must be treated with flexibility, bearing in mind that the jurisdictional nature of the institutions concerned evolves within a system that is based on the dynamics of sovereignty.

# 24

## Fostering Increased Conformity with International Standards: Monitoring and Institutional Fact-Finding

*Antonio Cassese*

## SUMMARY

Given that international adjudication, even in its modern forms and manifestations, is unable to ensure compliance by states with international rules, it is proposed to step up resort to two existing methods, which seem indicative of the new international society and more attuned to its needs: (i) monitoring (a modern process of verifying compliance with and inducing respect for international legal standards) and (ii) institutional fact-finding (a method of establishing facts resort to which is not contingent on the will of the states concerned). Monitoring should be expanded and strengthened. It should be expanded to all multilateral treaties, by establishing within the UN a Committee of experts entrusted with overseeing the implementation of multilateral treaties to be made in future. In addition, follow-up to monitoring should be envisaged, so as to ensure that states take into account the reports of monitoring bodies. Monitoring should be strengthened in at least four areas: armed conflicts, use of nuclear energy, human rights, and environment. As for fact-finding, the relevant bodies should not be established by states, but by international organizations, and not necessarily with the consent of the state or states concerned.

## 1. The traditional setting: the limits of international adjudication

It is a trite observation that from the outset the rules of the world society have been based on self-limitation, for no outside authority existed capable of imposing heteronomous rules. In addition, the lack of an international judiciary proper, comparable to that existing within the legal system of each state, has resulted in a dire condition: the judicial settlement of disputes is based on the previous (or contemporaneous) acceptance of the jurisdiction of a judicial body by all the states involved in a dispute. The requirement both for the existence of a legal dispute (a clash between opposing legal claims) and consent of the states concerned has been the hallmark of judicial adjudication in the world society. As a result, arbitration and jurisdiction have always been triggered by a *private* claim; there was no *collective* interest in the judicial determination of law, although of course one of the side effects of arbitration has always been to contribute to defuse a situation that otherwise might have led to war. This state of affairs still persists today.

## 2.  Past attempts to break the deadlock: commissions of inquiry

An attempt to depart from the traditional approach to judicial determination of disputes was made back in 1899 and then in 1907, at the behest of an imaginative international lawyer and diplomat, F. F. Martens. The Hague Peace Conferences gave birth to the notion of 'commissions of inquiry' (Arts 9–14, 1899 Convention no. 1 and Arts 9–36, 1907 Convention no. 1).[1] The proposal was astute: since states baulk at being bound by a judicial body, why not entrust an international mechanism simply with the task of establishing facts? The inquiry was to 'facilitate a solution ... by elucidating the facts by means of an impartial and conscientious investigation' (Art. 9, 1907 Convention). It was added that the report of the Commission of Inquiry was to be 'limited to a statements of facts and has in no way the character of an award. It leaves to the parties entire freedom as to the effect to be given to the statement' (Art. 35).[2]

Plainly, this mechanism was still based on respect for sovereignty and the notion of reciprocity. It was simply intended to oil the relations between sovereigns so as to render them smoother, if the disputants were prepared to go for peace rather than for war. The third party (the commission of inquiry) was only a broker; it was dependent on the goodwill of the disputants, and had no force of its own, except for the authority deriving from its impartiality. Despite its merits, this mechanism as well, even in its more modern versions[3] (ie, trimmed

---

[1]  Article 9 of the 1899 Convention no 1 stipulated that

 ... the Signatory Powers recommend that the parties, who have not been able to come to an agreement by means of diplomacy, should as far as circumstances allow, institute an International Commission of Inquiry, to facilitate a solution of these differences by elucidating the facts by means of an impartial and conscientious investigation.

[2]  Article 14 of the 1899 Convention provided that

 The report of the International Commission of Inquiry is limited to a statement of facts, and has in no way the character of an Arbitral Award. It leaves the conflicting Powers entire freedom as to the effect to be given to this statement.

[3]  See, eg, Art. 33 of the UN Charter, which enumerates inquiry among the various forms of dispute settlement available to states, and does not include the old clauses protecting states interests and so on.

of the old clauses hinging on outright prostration before sovereign preroga-tives of states[4]), has come up against the hurdle of sovereignty. True, in many instances commissions of inquiry have been set up and have yielded good results. Nevertheless, in some crucial areas where states' concerns are more prominent, they have failed. Two circumstances bear out this conclusion. First, when in 1967 the Netherlands proposed in the UN General Assembly to establish a per-manent commission of inquiry, the proposal was rejected, and General Assembly Resolution 2329 (XXII) simply requested the UN Secretary-General to prepare a 'register of experts...whose services the States parties to a dispute may use by agreement for fact-finding in relation to the dispute'. Secondly, the International Fact-Finding Commission established under Article 90 of the First Additional Protocol of 1977, although it exists on paper, has never been activated by states (this, however, is also due to its cumbersome structure and its being modelled on the arbitration scheme).

## 3. Current attempts to innovate in the field of adjudication

One could think that the traditional paradigm of international adjudication has currently been superseded in at least some instances: at the *regional level*, the European Court of Justice (ECJ) of the European Communities and the European Court of Human Rights (ECtHR); at the *universal level*, the International Criminal Court (ICC), at least when the Prosecutor institutes criminal proceed-ings *proprio motu*. However, on close scrutiny, only the ECJ functions as a truly judicial body capable of both being seized by individuals or legal persons (Art. 230(4), Treaty Instituting the EC) and of issuing decisions which are directly binding in the legal orders of each of the 27 member states (Art. 228(1)). Instead, in the case of the other two judicial bodies, sovereignty, thrown away through the door, climbs back in through the window. A few words on these two institutions may suffice.

Many features of the ECtHR could induce one to believe that it is a truly judicial body which has disbanded sovereignty. For instance, ratification of the European Convention on Human Rights (ECHR), which established the Court, is in fact considered a *sine qua non* for adherence to the Council of Europe. The Court has compulsory jurisdiction over the 47 member states of the Council, and each of them may be the object of a complaint by other states or individuals (including its own citizens) for a breach of the Convention. The Court's judgments are binding (Art. 46 ECHR). However, as I have already pointed out in Chapter 15 (4 B), the sovereignty paradigm, expunged by all these groundbreaking innovations, resur-faces at the end of the process: the Court has consistently construed its powers to the effect that, if it finds that a state has violated the Convention, it says so and may

---

[4] Article 9 of the 1899 and 1907 Conventions limited the role of the commissions of inquiry to disputes 'of an international nature involving neither honour nor vital interests' of the contending states.

grant the victim 'equitable satisfaction', that is, a sum of money. In contrast, the Court has never stated that the state found in breach of human rights must take all the national measures (legislative, administrative, and judicial) to efface the breach. It would have been natural for the Court to take more incisive action. In particular, where it makes a finding of a grave breach of a substantive or a procedural obligation flowing from some crucial provisions of the ECHR (in particular, of Arts 2, on the right to life, 3 on the right to be free from torture, and 4 on the right to be free from slavery or forced labour), the Court should enjoin the state to institute criminal proceedings to punish the individuals responsible for the unlawful taking of human life, or for torture or slavery.

As for the ICC, admittedly the Prosecutor is vested with the enormous power of setting in motion court proceedings on his or her own initiative, that is, not at the behest of a member state. The Prosecutor is thus endowed with the authority to act on behalf on the whole community of state parties and of international justice more generally. In a way, he or she is the holder of a sort of *actio popularis contra auctores criminum* in that he or she acts to safeguard a twofold collective concern: to prosecute and punish the culprits thereby protecting the rights of the victims, and to incarnate the interest of the world community (*populus* or *societas populorum*) sternly to react against gross breaches. However, the Prosecutor's action, besides being subject to the Pre-Trial Chamber's scrutiny (see Art. 15(3)–(4) of the Court's Statute), can be blocked by the Security Council, pursuant to Article 16 of the Statute.

## 4. Alternative paradigms to ensure greater compliance with international standards

### (A) Monitoring

Traditional adjudication and traditional inquiry processes set up by states are emblematic of the state-centric, Westphalian paradigm. Instead, monitoring and institutional fact-finding are indicative of the new international society and more attuned to its needs.

Why and how were these new mechanisms established? Let us start with monitoring. After the First World War new treaties were concluded that regulated matters which until then had remained within the domestic jurisdiction of each state. These treaties were not based on reciprocity but rather safeguarded general interests: the protection of minorities; the regulation of labour conditions and the rights of workers; the establishment of international mandates over territories which up to that time had been under the exclusive control of sovereign powers; the regulation of narcotic drugs; and such unique matters as the relations between the Free City of Danzig (now Gdansk) and Poland and more generally the protection of the rights of the City laid down in the Treaty of Versailles. The unique features of the subject matter meant that adjudication was scarcely appropriate. Indeed, the non-reciprocal character of the obligations laid down in those rules meant that infringement of one of them might be passed over in silence, if it was only the other contracting states that had the right to demand compliance. It would have been only logical to bestow the right to exact respect for the rules upon the very entities for whose benefit they had been agreed. However, it was impossible for states to accept the granting of *locus standi* before international judicial or quasi-judicial bodies to individuals or groups. To satisfy the conflicting requirements, it was thus thought necessary to devise new ways of scrutinizing the behaviour of state parties to such treaties. The new scheme was monitoring.

This system differs from international adjudication and inquiry in four crucial respects. First, the scrutiny (which is carried out through the examination of periodic reports, or on-site inspections, or contentious proceedings) is not triggered by a dispute between two or more parties, that is, as a result of a *private* action; it is instead inspired by a *collective* interest in supervising states' abidance by international standards. Secondly, it is not undertaken by an organ accepted ad hoc by, or set up ad hoc at the behest of, the states concerned, but is carried out by *pre-existing international institutions*. Thirdly, monitoring is not occasional, but *permanent and automatic*; it functions on a steady basis, that is, even before any violation occurs and regardless of whether or not a party complains about an alleged violation. Fourthly, the party or parties concerned *are not free* to give any follow-up to the result of supervision: unlike that provided for in the aforementioned Article 35 of the 1907 Hague Convention, they have no choice but to comply with the finding or assessment of the supervisory body.

To make international scrutiny acceptable to states, it was, however, deemed necessary to take up some of the features of the old commissions of inquiry. Thus, in order to water down their possible impact on state sovereignty, no binding force was attached to the final assessment of supervisory bodies. In addition, side by side with organs consisting of impartial individuals, bodies composed of state representatives were set up (obviously they are more sensitive to states' exigencies and, therefore, more inclined to attenuate possibly harsh evaluations). It was also decided that the meetings or sessions of the monitoring bodies should normally be held *in camera*, for the manifest purpose of shielding states from public exposure.[5]

Plainly, the expansion of supervision to many important areas is testimony to its responsiveness to states' needs. In addition, it also proves that all groups of states are ready to submit to supervision, for even those countries which are loath to accept other international means of investigation do not oppose international

---

[5] For the main features of monitoring I take the liberty of referring to A. Cassese, *International Law*, 2nd edn (Oxford: Oxford University Press, 2005), at 291–5. Supervisory systems proved a balanced and relatively effective means of impelling states to live up to their international undertakings. It is, therefore, not surprising that certain of them survived the Second World War (eg the ILO mechanisms for monitoring the application of international labour conventions, and the systems for scrutinizing conventions on narcotic drugs). In other areas new control machinery was instituted. The fields in which supervision is at present most widespread are (i) international labour conventions; (ii) treaties and other international standards on human rights; (iii) the peaceful use of atomic energy; (iv) the manufacturing and use of chemical weapons; (v) the environment; (vi) the Antarctic and outer space; (vii) international economic law; and (viii) international and internal armed conflict.

monitoring. This, of course, is mainly due to its flexibility and to the fact that supervisory bodies do not put states in the dock, but tend to persuade them, even before any possible breach occurs, by dint of cautious diplomatic and moral pressure, to abide by those rules which they may be inclined to disregard.

It is, however, important to emphasize that, although monitoring shares with traditional commissions of inquiry the lack of any binding force of its assessments, it is different in one decisive respect. The traditional commissions of inquiry played an ancillary role to states; after all they were still part and parcel of a state-centric system. Instead, monitoring is 'external' to states; it is an emanation of the world society and is indicative of the pressure that international organizations, as an expression of the collective body of that society, put on individual states to lead them to comply with international standards.

## 5. Areas of monitoring in need of expansion and strengthening

For many years the international society will lack a judiciary proper, endowed with compulsory jurisdiction over any dispute and over any international legal subject: the current structure and configuration of the community make it unlikely to have such a judiciary in the next decades. As long as this is the prevailing state of affairs, monitoring will remain crucial. It is indeed the only way, acceptable to states, of overseeing their observance of international standards.

Monitoring should be expanded and strengthened. It should be expanded to all multilateral treaties. To this end it would be necessary to establish within the UN structure a committee of experts entrusted with overseeing the implementation of all multilateral treaties to be made in future (on the assumption that states, when working out such treaties, include a clause granting the power to monitor their respect to that committee). This addition to the UN bureaucracy, if relatively expensive, would certainly be salutary, for states would start taking multilateral treaties more seriously and would begin to implement them fully at home.

Furthermore, it should be agreed that all treaties providing for a supervisory mechanism (such as the UN Covenants on Human Rights, the Convention Against Torture, and other conventions) should rule out the power of contracting states to accept the jurisdiction of the supervisory body only partially. States would thus be prevented from excluding from their acceptance the power of the monitoring body to receive 'communications' from individuals.

Monitoring should be strengthened in at least four areas: armed conflicts, use of nuclear energy, human rights, and environment. Monitoring mechanisms should be rendered more incisive. In this respect a distinction must be made. When the result of supervision is automatically made public, some sort of *follow-up* should be envisaged for instances of failure of the targeted state to live up to its commitments. It is not enough to make a (non-binding) finding of a breach and to exhort the failing state to comply with the relevant standards. It is also necessary to pursue the matter further so as not to leave the state with the feeling that, once a possible breach has been spotted and the necessary recommendations have been issued, the matter is laid to rest. It is imperative to 'breathe down' the states' necks, as it were, so as to keep them under steady pressure. When instead the appraisal of the monitoring body is confidential, it would be judicious, in cases of repeated contraventions, to make a public statement denouncing the failing state. Possibly, the methods of the Council of Europe Committee for the Prevention of Torture should be taken as a model. There, the rule of confidentiality of the Committee's reports has been bypassed in fact by persuading states to decide on their own to make the reports public. In addition, the provision for the possibility to make a public statement in cases of repeated non-compliance with the Committee's reports has strengthened the supervisory role of the Committee.

Since the three areas where in my view monitoring should be strengthened (human rights, environment, and use of nuclear energy) are being dealt with in this book by other commentators, I will limit myself to setting out a few considerations with regard to armed conflicts.

## 6. In particular: armed conflicts

It is time to abandon the mechanism adopted in Geneva in 1977, when Article 90 of the First Additional Protocol was approved. As I have hinted above, this provision follows an outdated, quasi-judicial logic and lays down a quite cumbersome procedure. In contrast, what is needed are flexible bodies, not quasi-judicial ones but rather organisms adapted for the minute and daily monitoring of the conduct of combatants. These supervisory mechanisms should obviously be impartial beyond any doubt and should be composed of military and medical experts as well as specialists in humanitarian law who do not come from countries involved in the armed conflict at issue. They should moreover be able to operate *right from the start* of the conflict: their intervention in the conflict should indeed be *automatic*. For example, as soon as armed conflict breaks out, the International Committee of the Red Cross, or another authoritative humanitarian organism, could ask the belligerents to ensure that small monitoring organs can operate in their respective territories. Presumably, refusal of access to such an organ would be a huge embarrassment for a state or an insurgent party. If accepted by the parties, these organs would be responsible for monitoring the conduct of the belligerents and for preparing factual reports. Initially these reports should be confidential and disclosed only to the parties to the conflict. However, they could be made public in cases of repeated violations of international humanitarian law. At the conclusion of the conflict all reports should automatically be published.

It could also be useful to provide for the creation of ex post verification mechanisms at the national level for the purpose of ascertaining whether the killing of civilians has been, under the circumstances, disproportionate.

On whom could one count to carry such an enterprise forward? In my view we cannot rely on states or intergovernmental organizations. Even the states most sensitive to humanitarian needs, such as Switzerland, the Netherlands, or the Nordic European countries, cannot by themselves make changes to international law, let alone establish international monitoring mechanisms. In this domain, more than in others, it is the Great Powers that have the final word. And it is hardly in the Great Powers' own interests to tie their hands. It is therefore necessary to turn, above all, to non-governmental organizations (NGOs) such as the International Committee of the Red Cross or other entities whose moral authority places them on higher ground than that of states, including, for example, the Holy See. There are also other NGOs of high prestige that could be involved in the effort, such as the US-based Human Rights Watch or Amnesty International. These organizations have already achieved a great deal in their quest to 'humanize' war. One of these bodies or organizations might invite a group of military and legal experts and request that they study these themes carefully and formulate proposals along the lines I have just indicated.

I realize that it will not be easy to travel down these roads. It will take courage and imagination. But I am hopeful that some authoritative humanitarian body of great moral prestige will take affirmative steps to drive forward or otherwise support this humanitarian enterprise.

## 7. The other modern mechanism for ensuring better compliance with international standards

### (B) Institutional fact-finding

Another area that looks promising is that of fact-finding established not by states, but by international organizations, and not necessarily with the consent of the state or states concerned (these indeed are the main features that differentiate these bodies from the traditional commissions of inquiry mentioned above).

These mechanisms were born out of the attempt to perfect traditional commissions of enquiry, chiefly by disentangling such commissions from the will of the states concerned. In recent years the UN, through the Security Council, the Human Rights Council, or the Secretary-General, has set up various commissions composed of a few independent experts charged with looking into specific matters or situations and reporting thereon. Suffice it to mention the Commissions established by the Security Council to investigate human rights abuses or gross violations of international humanitarian law.[6]

These Commissions have many merits: (i) they are not dependent on individual states involved in the matter at issue, but result from majority decisions of international bodies; (ii) they are made up of independent experts; (iii) they report to international organs, which may decide to take follow-up action; (iv) often, in

---

[6] Reference can chiefly be made to those on the conflict in the former Yugoslavia (SC Res. 780 (1992)), in Rwanda (SC Res. 935 (1994)), in Burundi (SC Res.1012 (1995)), in Darfur (SC Res. 1564 (2004)), as well as that charged with investigating the assassination in Lebanon of former Prime Minister Hariri (SC Res.1595 (2005)). Other Commissions have been established by the Human Rights Council: eg, that on East Timor (HRC Res. 1999/S-4/1) and A (54/728-S/2000/59) or on the Gaza conflict of 2009 (A/HRC/S-9- 2009).

addition to establishing facts, they also characterize such facts in light of the relevant international standards, thereby determining whether or not they amount to violations of those standards; and (v) frequently they also propose to the 'parent body' how to deal with the matter, that is, what possible steps could be taken in light of the Commission's conclusions.

I would think that this is an area where there is a lot of potential. To enhance the role of institutional fact-finding three avenues could be taken. First, the UN Secretary-General should establish a roster of experts specializing in various fields and prepared to be called upon to undertake a mission. This would avoid the UN wasting much time in the selection and appointment of competent persons. Secondly, a fund should be set up to finance such fact-finding, so as to prevent states or organs from hampering or delaying missions on account of financial problems. Thirdly, regulations should be passed to outline the structure, powers, and functioning of fact-finding commissions, so that, once the need arises to investigate a situation, all the relevant rules are already in place. I submit that such a commission should be granted extensive powers, and in this respect the Inquiry Commission on Darfur (established in 2004 by the UN Security Council) could be taken as a model: the Commission was given three tasks: to establish whether serious violations of human rights had been committed; to identify the perpetrators; and to propose accountability mechanisms. Whether or not one considers that the Commission did a good job, indisputably its extensive powers allowed it to undertake an in-depth examination and also point to possible perpetrators and propose suitable means for achieving accountability. Thus the Commission, although charged with heavy tasks, was nevertheless in a position to examine the whole spectrum of problems and act indeed as a pre-judicial body capable of clearing the ground for a court of law.

## 8. Concluding remarks

As I noted above, both monitoring and institutional fact-finding are expressions of a new relationship existing in the world society between each individual state and the whole society. Each state is no longer master of his own, but strongly depends on multilateral relations and is subject to the pressure and weight of the collectivity. True, the world legal order does not have yet the various means available in each domestic legal system to centralize authority. To induce compliance with international standards it cannot therefore resort to compulsory judicial determination let alone to collective enforcement. Monitoring and institutional fact-finding are thus the best way of bringing the weight of the community to bear on each member state (and other international legal subjects).

We cannot hope for a dramatic amelioration of the world community in the next decades—unless of course new macroscopic violence erupts at the world level, bringing in its aftermath similarly dramatic changes. Hence, for the time being we can only strive to invigorate and expand the two ways of putting pressure on states and other subjects, discussed above.

# 25

# Ensuring Compliance with Standards on the Peaceful Use of Nuclear Energy

*Laura Rockwood*[*]

## SUMMARY

The International Atomic Energy Agency (IAEA) has provided unbiased independent verification for over 50 years, within the legal authority granted to it by its member states and the resources which it has been given to carry out that authority and has been able to respond to shifting perceptions of proliferation threats. It has also been engaged in verifying the disarmament of nuclear weapon programmes in Iraq, South Africa, and Libya, and developed 'black box' techniques for verifying material dismantled from nuclear weapons in non-nuclear states. To ensure the continued adherence by states to the 1970 Treaty on the Non-Proliferation of Nuclear Weapons and to their respective safeguards agreements and to reduce the risk that additional states attempt to circumvent their non-proliferation undertakings, it is suggested that it is necessary: (i) to strengthen the IAEA's verification capabilities; (ii) to minimize the risk of break-out; and (iii) to address the underlying motivations of states. A set of concrete steps that could be taken under each of these headings are then suggested by the author.

## 1. Introduction

The dawning of the nuclear age—and the introduction of a new and powerful source of energy—was heralded with the devastating brilliance of the flash of nuclear weapons and the destruction of the cities of Hiroshima and Nagasaki in August 1945. The peaceful exploitation of this energy will forever be marked by

[*] The views expressed in this chapter are the author's own personal views and not those of the IAEA.

its birth. However, while acknowledging conflicting views about the benefits and risks of nuclear energy, it must be assumed, in the context of a realistic utopia, that nuclear is here to stay for the foreseeable future. And, in the nuclear world, there is no effective alternative to international verification for ensuring that nuclear energy is used exclusively for peaceful purposes.

The IAEA has provided that service since its creation in 1957. Just over a half century old, the IAEA's safeguards system has demonstrated the efficacy of monitoring in the verification of compliance by states with legally binding undertakings. While enforcement of compliance is ultimately for the organ with primary responsibility for the maintenance of international peace and security, the UN Security Council, the value of credible, independent international verification in limiting—if not preventing altogether—the further spread of nuclear weapons has been demonstrated. Instead of the 15 to 25 states estimated by US President John Kennedy as possibly obtaining military nuclear capabilities by the 1970s, the world has but nine states which currently have, or are believed to have, nuclear weapons capability, and another three which have acknowledged and given up programmes to acquire such weapons.

If one accepts on this basis that safeguards have contributed to limiting the number of states possessing nuclear weapons, it is equally reasonable to assume that, the more effective the safeguards system is in the early detection of indicators of non-compliance with legally binding non-proliferation commitments, the greater is its value in terms of deterrence and, accordingly, the assurance of compliance.

Notwithstanding, there exists today resistance to measures designed to ensure a fully effective safeguards system. From the point of view of an avowed safeguards 'utopian', such resistance is counter-intuitive. However, the 'Technician' must confront—and address—the reality of that resistance.

## 2. The origins of the nuclear non-proliferation regime and the IAEA

It is the view of this author that the nuclear non-proliferation regime came about as a function of the collective perception of the world community that, while nuclear energy could be exploited for the benefit of mankind—not just for power generation, but for medical, agricultural, and industrial applications as well—its unconstrained development and unverified use could give rise to the further proliferation of nuclear weapons: a threat not only to the security of states, but to the security of mankind. The regime has continued to evolve as a function of shifting perceptions of the nature and source of that threat.

Between 1945 and 1953, there was plenty of demand for this new technology. Associated with that demand was the risk that nuclear trade could give rise to proliferation threats. To address that risk, the technology holders required, as a condition of supply, bilateral verification agreements with their trading partners. While mutual verification might have satisfied the parties to the relevant transactions that the recipient states were not misusing supplied material or items for weapons purposes, these bilateral agreements did not necessarily provide states not party to those agreements with the level of assurance required for their individual and collective security: what was needed was international multilateral verification.

This common cause found its voice in the 1953 proposal by US President Dwight Eisenhower, in his 'Atoms for Peace' speech before the UN General Assembly, for the creation of an agency responsible for promoting atomic energy and verifying the safe and peaceful uses of nuclear material and facilities. This initiative eventually gave rise to the IAEA, which came into being in 1957 following the entry into force of its Statute.[1]

## 3. The IAEA

The IAEA was created as an independent international organization whose objective is to seek to accelerate and enlarge the contribution of atomic energy to peace, health, and prosperity throughout the world. Article III.A.5 of the IAEA Statute authorizes the Agency to establish and administer safeguards: (i) in connection with special fissionable material, and other materials, services, equipment, facilities, and information, made available by the Agency or at its request or under its supervision or control to ensure that they are not used in such a way as to further any military purpose; (ii) at the request of the parties, to any bilateral or multilateral arrangement; and (iii) at the request of a state, to any of that state's activities in the field of atomic energy.

The drafters of the Statute anticipated a verification system involving measures that were novel and surprisingly far-reaching, given the chilling climate of the Cold War during which they were negotiated, demonstrating the willingness of states to cede national sovereignty in the interest of a common threat. Those measures, as set out in Article XII of the Statute, include extremely broad rights of access at all times to all necessary places and data, and to any person who dealt with items required to be safeguarded.

The drafters also foresaw, in Article XII.C, reporting to the UN Security Council and General Assembly by the IAEA Board of Governors on non-compliance by a state with its safeguards obligations. That Article provides further that, in the event of failure of the recipient state to take fully corrective action within a reasonable time, the IAEA may also direct the curtailment or suspension of assistance being provided by the Agency or by a member state and/or call for the return of materials and equipment made available to the recipient member state. The Agency may also, in accordance with Article XIX of the Statute, suspend any non-complying member from the exercise of the privileges and rights of membership.[2]

---

[1] For a detailed account of the early events leading to the creation of the IAEA, see P. Szasz, *The Law and Practices of the International Atomic Energy Agency*, Legal Series No. 7 (Vienna: IAEA Publications, 1970), ch. 1.

[2] Article XIX of the Statute provides that a member of the Agency which has persistently violated the provision of the Statute or of any agreement entered into by it pursuant to the Statute may be suspended from the exercise of the privileges and rights of membership by the General Conference,

The safeguards provisions of the Statute, however, are not self-executing. Thus, IAEA safeguards may only be applied with the consent of the state concerned. In most instances, that consent is made manifest in the form of an agreement with the Agency—a safeguards agreement (or in the case of Agency assistance, a project and supply agreement containing safeguards obligations).[3] These safeguards agreements thus regulate the relationship between the Agency and the other party or parties to the agreement.

## (A) The evolution of IAEA safeguards

As indicated above, the initial verification efforts were focused on addressing the risk that exports of nuclear material, or the technology to produce it, might be misused. Thus, the early safeguards system was focused on verifying only that the supplied items (which were specified in the relevant safeguards agreement), and any nuclear material produced, processed, or used in or by the use of supplied items, were not used for any military purpose: so-called 'item specific safeguards'.[4] Agreements based on this early system were thus not comprehensive, nor did they require that a state forswear nuclear weapons.

However, with expanding interest in all aspects of nuclear energy—non-peaceful as well as peaceful—it rapidly became clear that states were able to develop their own nuclear programmes indigenously, and that what was needed were legally binding commitments by states not to acquire or develop nuclear weapons using *any* nuclear material in the country—whether produced indigenously or with the help of imported items and technology—and a mechanism for verifying compliance with such commitments.

The product of that perception was the 1970 Treaty on the Non-Proliferation of Nuclear Weapons (NPT), and the consequential development by the IAEA of a new safeguards system.

In short, the NPT provided that, in exchange for disarmament undertakings by nuclear-weapon states (NWSs),[5] Non-Nuclear-Weapon States (NNWSs) would agree not to manufacture or otherwise acquire nuclear weapons and would accept safeguards, as set forth in an agreement with the IAEA, 'for the exclusive purpose of verification of the fulfilment of [the NNWS's] obligations assumed under [the

---

acting by a two-thirds majority of the members present and voting, upon recommendation by the Board of Governors.

[3] A state may also voluntarily accept the implementation of safeguards measures not routinely foreseen in its safeguards agreement, as did South Africa, which cooperated fully with Agency verification of South Africa's dismantlement of its nuclear weapons. In addition, a state which is a member of the United Nations may be bound, by virtue of its adherence to the UN Charter, to accept safeguards measures as a function of a decision by the Security Council (as in the case of Iraq and SC Res. 687 (1991)).

[4] The safeguards procedures incorporated in these early agreements are reflected in a document currently known as INFCIRC/66/Rev.2, or 'the Safeguards Document', which evolved in the 1960s to address increasingly diverse nuclear trade.

[5] Art. IX.3 of the NPT defines a nuclear weapon state as a state which had manufactured and exploded a nuclear device prior to 1 January 1967. They are China, France, the Russian Federation (the successor state to the USSR), the United Kingdom, and the United States.

NPT] with a view to preventing diversion of nuclear energy from peaceful uses to nuclear weapons or other nuclear explosive devices' (Art. III.1). The NPT provided further that the procedures for such safeguards were to be applied on all source or special fissionable material in all peaceful nuclear activities within the territory of such state, under its jurisdiction, or carried out under its control anywhere, regardless of whether it was being produced, processed, or used in any principal nuclear facility or is outside any such facility.

To ensure that nuclear trade did not contribute to the unsafeguarded production of nuclear material for nuclear weapons, the NPT also included export controls, which obliged all state parties not to provide source or special fissionable material, or 'equipment or material especially designed or prepared for the processing, use or production of special fissionable material' (so-called 'EDP' or 'single use'), to a NNWS for peaceful purposes, unless the source or special fissionable material is subject to Agency safeguards (Art. III.2). The NPT did not, however, provide for IAEA verification of states' compliance with the export controls, as such controls were seen to be a matter for regulation by the states, rather than by an international organization.

Following the entry into force of the NPT, the IAEA, through an open-ended committee of its Board of Governors,[6] negotiated a document entitled 'The Structure and Content of Agreements between the Agency and States required in Connection with the NPT' (INFCIRC/153 (Corr.)), which was approved by the Board in 1971. Agreements based on INFCIRC/153 cover all nuclear material in a state, and are thus commonly referred to as Comprehensive Safeguards Agreements (CSAs).[7]

The negotiation history of INFCIRC/153 makes clear that the Agency's role in the implementation of CSAs was not intended to be limited to verifying only nuclear material that is declared by the state. Nowhere is that made more explicit than in paragraph 2 of INFCIRC/513, which establishes the 'right and obligation' of the IAEA to ensure that safeguards will be applied, in accordance with the terms of the Agreement, on '*all* source or special fissionable material' (emphasis added), and in the provisions related to special inspections, which grant the IAEA access to information and locations in addition to that provided for in connection with other inspections under the agreement if the Agency considers that information made available by the state is not adequate for the Agency to fulfil its responsibilities under the agreement.[8]

Notwithstanding, between 1971 and 1990, there developed a self-perpetuating myth that the IAEA's authority was limited to the nuclear material and facilities actually declared by the safeguarded state. How could that have happened? As one of the negotiators of INFCIRC/153 once in exasperation queried, 'What was it about the word "all" that people didn't get?' Could it have been the influence of

---

[6] Committee 22, the 'Safeguards Committee'.

[7] As of December 2010, safeguards were being implemented in 168 of NPT NNWSs under CSAs (also referred to as 'full scope' safeguards agreements).

[8] INFCIRC/153 (Corr.), para. 73(b).

'strict constructionist' lawyers interpreting treaties on behalf of their governments? Or the result of fears about an inspectorate out of control—fears perhaps compounded by industry's perception of possible negative impacts on trade? Legitimate concerns by states about national sovereignty or security—behaviour frequently indistinguishable from that of states interested in minimizing safeguards to evade detection? Maybe a little of each, all of which perhaps exacerbated by an inspectorate which, aware of member states' resistance, focused more on getting a good job done than on establishing legal precedent and running the risk of a collective push-back from member states. While the Agency's right to implement safeguards procedures under CSAs is clearly not unlimited, the constraints imposed on the Secretariat, some of which were self-imposed, resulted in the practical development of a facility-based approach to safeguards, rather than a holistic state-based approach.

The discovery by the IAEA in 1991 of Iraq's clandestine nuclear weapons programme, using the extensive tools available to it under relevant Security Council resolutions, called into question some of the fundamental assumptions upon which verification approaches under CSAs had been premised, clearly demonstrating that: (i) focusing only on *declared* nuclear material was not sufficient to ensure that a state is complying with its non-proliferation obligations; (ii) even small quantities of nuclear material could be useful in developing sensitive parts of the nuclear fuel cycle; (iii) focusing on nuclear material *alone* was not sufficient for detecting undeclared nuclear material and activities: the whole infrastructure of a state's nuclear programme needed to be addressed; (iv) export controls on *single-use items* alone were not effective: a state could import dual-use items and create its own single-use items for the undeclared production of fissionable material; and (v) non-state actors could play a significant role in nuclear proliferation.

Motivated by these revelations, member states reassessed their national and collective security needs in relation to the assurances which they required in connection with Agency safeguards: specifically, assurances not only of the non-diversion of declared nuclear material, but of the absence of undeclared nuclear material and activities in a CSA state. One of the first steps taken by the Board of Governors following those revelations was to confirm that, pursuant to paragraph 2 of INFCIRC/153, the IAEA not only had the right, but the obligation, to provide such assurances.

As a consequence of this reassessment, the Secretariat of the Agency, working closely with the member states, worked on a programme to strengthen IAEA safeguards under CSAs. In 1995, the Board of Governors took note of those measures which could already be implemented under existing legal authority, which included: the Agency's right of access to undeclared information and locations under special inspections; the state's obligation with respect to the early provision of design information on nuclear facilities; the Agency's right to use state-of-the-art technical measures, such as environmental monitoring and satellite imagery analysis; and the Agency's right to make use of intelligence information.[9] Together with the Secretariat, they subsequently developed a new legal instrument intended to supplement that authority: the Model Additional Protocol (INFCIRC/540 (Corr.)), which was approved by the Board of Governors in 1997.

While the basic right and obligation of the Agency to verify the non-diversion of all nuclear material in a state, whether declared or undeclared, derived from the safeguards agreement itself, the additional tools ultimately incorporated in the Model Additional Protocol—expanded declarations by states about their nuclear activities, along with more routine and broader access to locations within the state—were designed to permit the Secretariat to fulfil its responsibilities under CSAs more effectively by enabling the Agency to detect indicators of possible non-compliance at an earlier stage.

## 4. Detection and response

### (A) The law

Key to understanding how CSAs work is an appreciation of the twofold technical objectives of such agreements: the timely detection of the diversion of significant quantities of nuclear material to nuclear weapons or nuclear explosive devices, or for purposes unknown; and the deterrence of such diversion through the risk of early detection. The process of detecting and responding to indicators of diversion involves four general stages (which do not necessarily involve a straight linear chronology): inspection and information-gathering, evaluation, decision-making, and consequences.

As with most verification/monitoring regimes, the implementation of Agency safeguards starts with declarations by the state concerned. Under a CSA, the state is obliged to submit to the Agency an initial report on all nuclear material subject to safeguards thereunder. The state is also required to provide the Agency with design information in respect of all nuclear facilities in the country. The information provided by the state regarding the nuclear material and facilities is then verified through ad hoc and routine inspections, as well as design information verification (DIV).

Based on an evaluation of all of the information available to it, including state declarations, inspection, and DIV results, publicly available information and information from other states through national technical means (ie, intelligence information), the Agency attempts to identify any indications of the diversion of

---

[9] Less than two decades later, it is dismaying to hear challenges, by those who are either uninformed or those who perhaps wilfully choose to disregard the record, to the fact that these basic measures are possible within the scope of CSAs, and assertions that such measures (including the authority to seek access to undeclared information and locations) are only available under the Model Additional Protocol. What has somehow been lost on such proponents is that each one of these measures was approved long before the Model Additional Protocol was even conceptualized, let alone approved by the Board of Governors in 1997.

declared nuclear material and any indications of undeclared nuclear material or activities. If, in implementing the tools available to it in a CSA and an Additional Protocol, the Agency finds no such indications, it is able to draw the conclusion that all nuclear material in the state is in peaceful activities.

Should the Agency find indications which give rise to doubts about the correctness and the completeness of the state's declarations, the matter is, in the first instance, discussed with the state with a view to resolving the issue. Should those discussions not resolve the matter, the Agency is entitled, in accordance with the provisions for special inspections in CSAs, to request access to information, or to locations, in addition to the access provided for in connection with ad hoc and routine inspections.

Historically, the Agency has been able to negotiate the necessary additional access to information and/or locations, and to resolve most safeguards-related issues, in consultation with the state concerned without invoking special inspections. While that is certainly a positive result, an unfortunate unintended consequence is that special inspections have come to be seen as highly political and only to be formally invoked when a serious safeguards violation is suspected or has been detected.

While the Agency is required to consult with the state concerned before requesting a special inspection, it is not required to seek Board approval before doing so. Should the state decline to provide access to the additional information or locations, the Director General could report the matter to the Board of Governors, seeking a Board decision, in accordance with paragraph 18 of INFCIRC/153, that such access is 'essential and urgent in order to ensure verification that nuclear material is subject to safeguards under the Agreement is not diverted'. If the Board determines that an action is 'essential and urgent', it may call on the state to take the required action without delay, irrespective of whether procedures for the settlement of dispute are invoked. A difficulty may arise if the Board is divided, insofar as most decisions by the 35-member Board of Governors are, as a matter of practice, taken by consensus. In the absence of consensus, the Board could take a vote, by simple majority, with respect to such a decision.

If the Board were to decide that the requested access is 'essential and urgent', and the state were to decline to provide such access, the Director General would then inform the Board of Governors. Paragraph 19 of INFCIRC/153 provides that, if, upon examination of relevant information reported to it by the Director General, the Board finds that the Agency is not able to verify that there has been no diversion of nuclear material required to be safeguarded under the Agreement, it may make the reports provided for in Article XII.C of the Statute and may also take, where applicable, the other measures provided for in that paragraph. Again, depending on the degree of unity in the Board, decisions about such findings and actions may be taken either by consensus or by a vote.

CSAs contain disputes-settlement procedures which contemplate the possibility of the state requesting that any question arising out of the interpretation or application thereof be considered by the Board, and participating in the Board's discussion of that question. They also provide for the possibility of disputes resolution through binding arbitration (except a dispute with regard to a finding by the

Board under para. 19, or an action taken by the Board pursuant to such a finding). Not surprisingly, neither of these procedures has ever been invoked: with respect to requesting consideration by the Board, this would hardly be necessary if, as would probably be the case, the Board is already engaged with the issue; with respect to the latter, requesting arbitration in a matter of what would probably be of significant political and security sensitivity is not likely a risk states would consider worth taking (not to mention that arbitration does not stay the requirement for the state to take an action the Board considers to be essential and urgent, and cannot be invoked with respect to findings that the Agency is unable to verify that there has been no diversion of nuclear material).

In terms of sanctions, the reach of the Agency's arm is not long: the Board may decide, as indicated in Article XII, to curtail or suspend Agency assistance and call for the return of materials and equipment made available to a member state. It may also recommend to the General Conference the suspension of a non-complying member state from the exercise of the privileges and rights of membership. The sanctions available to the Security Council under Chapter VII of the UN Charter, however, can be much more substantial, and all states which are members of the United Nations are bound to implement the decisions taken by the Council in that regard.

## (B) The practice

The Board of Governors has requested the Director General to report non-compliance to the Security Council in connection with the implementation of safeguards in connection with only five states: Iraq (1991), Romania (1992), the Democratic People's Republic of Korea (1993, 1994, 2003), Libya (2004), and Iran (first reported in 2006). In the case of Romania and Libya, the Board requested that the reports be provided 'for information purposes'.[10] The Board has also considered reports of the Director General in connection with findings of failures by North Korea and Egypt to report in a timely fashion certain nuclear material and activities, but chose not to report those findings to the Council largely in light of the small quantities of material involved, the cooperation and corrective actions of the states, and the fact that there did not appear to be any attempts to conceal the material and activities. The Director General has also submitted reports to the Board of Governors on the implementation of safeguards in Syria as a consequence of inspectors having found, at the site of a building alleged to have been a nuclear reactor which was destroyed in 2007, particles of nuclear material not consistent with Syria's declared inventory of nuclear material. The matter remains ongoing at this time.

Although the Security Council has adopted resolutions under Chapter VII of the UN Charter in response to reports of safeguards non-compliance, compliance with those resolutions by the states concerned has been mixed. Iraq ultimately

---

[10] In the case of Romania and Libya, the Board chose to report its findings on non-compliance 'for information purposes' only, in light of the fact that, in both instances, the state itself had revealed its past non-compliance and renewed its respective commitment to nuclear non-proliferation.

cooperated with the IAEA in the mapping out and dismantlement of its nuclear weapons programme, after some years of resistance. In the case of North Korea, the state not only withdrew from membership of the Agency, but has declared itself to have also withdrawn from the NPT, and has carried out a number of nuclear weapon tests. Iran has challenged the legality of the Agency's reporting to the Council, as well as the legality of the Security Council's resolutions, has not suspended the ongoing enrichment activities or its heavy water-related activities as requested by the Security Council, and has reduced its cooperation with the IAEA in the implementation of its Safeguards Agreement.

All things considered, however, it can be seen as positive that, since the beginning of the nuclear non-proliferation regime, there have been only three instances where the Council has felt that the circumstances warranted the adoption of Chapter VII resolutions in connection with the maintenance of international peace and security in relation to nuclear non-proliferation. The predictions of the early 1960s of 15 to 25 new nuclear weapon states have, fortuitously, not been fulfilled. However, it should be a matter of global concern that there is even one state which has withdrawn from the nuclear non-proliferation regime and publicly announced that it has nuclear weapons. It is likewise troubling to see states rejecting the authority of the Security Council to enforce compliance with legally binding international treaty obligations.

What can be done to ensure the continued adherence by states to the NPT and to their respective safeguards agreements and to reduce the risk that additional states attempt to circumvent their non-proliferation undertakings?

## 5. Pre-empting non-compliance

There are three areas which bear consideration in promoting compliance with non-proliferation undertakings: strengthening the IAEA's verification capabilities, minimizing the risk of break-out, and addressing the underlying motivations of states.

### (A) Strengthening the IAEA's verification capabilities

The IAEA has provided unbiased independent verification for over 50 years, within the legal authority granted to it by its member states and the resources which it has been given to carry out that authority and has been able to respond to shifting perceptions of proliferation threats. It has also been engaged in verifying the disarmament of nuclear weapon programmes, in Iraq, South Africa, and Libya, and developed 'black box' techniques for verifying material dismantled from nuclear weapons in NWSs, without proliferating sensitive weapons information.[11] Thus,

---

[11] In 1996, the Russian Federation, the United States, and the IAEA embarked on the Trilateral Initiative to address, inter alia, the technical and legal issues associated with implementing IAEA verification of weapon origin and other fissile material released from defence programmes. By 2002,

there is no need to establish a new or different institution for monitoring compliance with non-proliferation (or, for that matter, disarmament) commitments.

One of the most challenging aspects of the Agency's safeguards system is in verifying the absence of undeclared nuclear material and activities: proving that something does *not* exist is always more difficult than proving that it *does* exist. Its ability to detect indications of such material and activities is obviously dependent on the scope and nature of the information available to it which, in turn, is dependent on the scope of the Agency's authority to demand relevant information, and to seek access to locations to verify such information.

In recent years, there have been renewed efforts to constrain the Agency's rights under CSAs. As indicated at the outset of this chapter, such constraints are counter-intuitive to the 'Utopian', and should be even to the 'Technician', for the effective implementation of IAEA safeguards is in the collective interest of all states, and its deterrent value is only as good as its detection capabilities.

To ensure effective safeguards, the system needs to be dynamic—it needs to evolve. In the face of new challenges to the nuclear non-proliferation regime, the *following steps would facilitate that evolution*:

(i)     the Agency's authority under CSAs to detect the non-diversion of declared nuclear material and the absence of undeclared nuclear material should be reconfirmed;

(ii)    states should assist the Agency in developing state-of-the-art technologies for detecting undeclared nuclear material and activities;

(iii)   the Agency's authority under CSAs to pursue the verification of possible nuclear weapons-related activities (eg weaponization activities) should be confirmed;

(iv)    states should ensure the implementation of effective export controls, translate the nuclear supplier guidelines into legally binding treaty obligations, and provide the Agency with more information about nuclear trade;

(v)     the nuclear industry should share more information with the Agency, on a voluntary basis, on nuclear trade, in particular in connection with suspected efforts illegally to acquire controlled items;

(vi)    a CSA with an Additional Protocol should be established as the verification standard for NNWSs party to the NPT;

(vii)   in accordance with Security Council Resolution 1540 (2004), states need to improve security controls and implement effective measures (including putting into place an appropriate legislative framework) for deterring, detecting, and responding to the threat posed by non-state actors, not sim-

---

the Joint Working Group of the Trilateral Initiative had succeeded in developing technical measures that would allow the IAEA to draw meaningful verification conclusions while ensuring the protection of classified weapons-related information, and the legal framework for such a verification agreement.

ply because of their involvement in illicit nuclear transactions, but by the challenge which they pose to the very notion of deterrence.

As the idea of 'getting to zero' gains traction, and even the most sceptical of the non-utopian 'Technicians' seem to be coming to terms with the possibility of a world free of nuclear weapons, an essential element in that process will be the assurances that can only be provided through an effective verification system.

## (B) Minimizing the risk of break-out

The case of North Korea has heightened concerns about the risk of a NNWS party to the NPT acquiring a complete nuclear fuel cycle while simultaneously developing a parallel, but separate, programme for weaponization, and then withdrawing from the NPT and marrying the two programmes. This risk becomes more acute with the expansion of nuclear programmes, and a growing interest of a greater number of states in developing their own advanced fuel-cycle facilities and nuclear know-how.

One possibility for reducing that risk is the development of multilateral approaches with a view to minimizing the need for a state to develop its own capability to carry out the most proliferation-sensitive aspects of the nuclear fuel cycle, in particular enrichment and reprocessing. Among the many proposals for such approaches are international supply guarantees, with the IAEA acting as a guarantor of services or supplies.[12] In 2009, the Board of Governors approved an initiative proposed by the Russian Federation to establish a reserve of low enriched uranium (LEU) for the supply of LEU by the IAEA to its member states. In 2010, the Board approved another proposal for the establishment of an LEU bank to be owned by the Agency. Both of these initiatives are intended to provide assurances of the supply of enriched uranium, thereby reducing the incentive for states to develop sensitive fuel-cycle capabilities at the national level. While it is unlikely that a state bent on developing a nuclear weapons programme would be deterred by such initiatives, the LEU reserve and the IAEA LEU bank could serve to minimize the number of new enrichment and reprocessing facilities in the world.

The Security Council could also take steps to demonstrate strengthened resolve in the face of non-compliance by a state with its safeguards obligations or threats to withdraw from the NPT. One author has proposed that the Council consider the merits of adopting a generic resolution stating that, if a state is found to be in non-compliance with its CSA, the Council would, at the request of the IAEA, automatically adopt a resolution under Chapter VII of the UN Charter requiring that the state grant the Agency temporary extended access rights to resolve outstanding

---

[12] This proposal and other options are discussed in detail in the 2005 report, *Multilateral Approaches to the Nuclear Fuel Cycle*, of an international expert group, convened by the then-Director General of the IAEA, Mohamed El Baradei, to identify and provide an analysis of issues and options.

issues.[13] The Security Council could likewise adopt a resolution asserting that any withdrawal from the NPT by a non-compliant state would be treated as a threat to international peace and security, and establish, outside the context of an ongoing conflict, specific steps which it might take in the event of such a withdrawal.

## (C) Addressing underlying motivations

States' motivations to acquire a nuclear weapons capability are complex. For some it is regional hegemony, for others it is the perception of a threat to their national security; for others, it may be a matter of prestige. It is important for the world to address the underlying insecurities which give rise to the perceived need for such weapons. A recently published collection of theoretical perspectives regarding the sources of and propensity for nuclear proliferation, provides a valuable analysis in much greater academic detail of various sociopolitical theories about proliferation motivations.[14]

But perhaps one of the most significant impediments to the universal implementation of safeguards and non-proliferation is the perceived lack of commitment to disarmament by the states possessing nuclear weapons. Disgruntlement about the lack of progress in disarmament has fuelled concerns by developing countries that proposals to strengthen the Agency's verification authority, or to establish mechanisms for the assurance of supplies, are simply disguised efforts by the 'nuclear haves' to limit the legitimate development of peaceful nuclear fuel cycles by the nuclear 'have-nots'. As a consequence, a deep political divide has developed, which threatens the very existence of the nuclear non-proliferation regime.

A number of immediate measures could be taken by the NWSs which would demonstrate a renewed commitment to disarmament and a world free of nuclear weapons: verified reductions in stockpiles of nuclear weapons, through such measures as the Trilateral Initiative; bringing into force the Comprehensive Test Ban Treaty; negotiation and entry into force of a Fissile Material Cut-Off Treaty; and de-emphasis of nuclear weapons as part of their respective security strategies.

## 6. Concluding thoughts

In his commencement address at American University in June 1963, in which he announced the initiation of high-level discussions with the Soviet Union and the United Kingdom on a comprehensive test ban treaty, John F. Kennedy said:

While we proceed to safeguard our national interests, let us also safeguard human interests. And the elimination of war and arms is clearly in the interest of both. No treaty, however much it may be to the advantage of all, however tightly it may be worded, can provide abso-

---

[13] P. Goldschmidt, 'IAEA Safeguards: Dealing Preventively with Noncompliance', Carnegie Endowment for International Peace, 12 July 2008.

[14] W.C. Potter and G. Mukhatzhanova (eds), *Forecasting Nuclear Proliferation in the 21st Century* (Stanford, CA: Stanford University Press, 2010), 2 vols.

lute security against the risks of deception and evasion. But it can—if it is sufficiently effective in its enforcement and if it is sufficiently in the interests of its signers—offer far more security and far fewer risks than an unabated, uncontrolled, unpredictable arms race.

The international political, diplomatic, and legal community has shown that it can rise to the occasion in response to a crisis—it happened in connection with nuclear safety, in response to Chernobyl, with the rapid conclusion of not one, but two, international treaties on early notification and assistance in the event of nuclear incidents and accidents; the watershed for nuclear security was 9/11, in response to which the nuclear community developed improved security standards and dedicated major financial and technical resources to improving the security of nuclear material and facilities; and, in the case of nuclear safeguards, Iraq triggered unparalleled unity among member states to achieve the most significant improvements in the Agency's safeguards system since its inception.

However, we cannot simply wait for the next crisis. If we are unable to detect the diversion of nuclear material in another NNWS before it builds a nuclear weapon, it will be too late.

# 26

# Overseeing Human Rights Compliance

*Andrew Clapham*

## SUMMARY

In imagining a realistic utopia for human rights compliance it is not enough to stress independent non-governmental organizations (NGOs), judicial training, treaty monitoring, periodic reviews, and national protection systems to hold governments accountable. We need also to address violence which emanates from beyond the state and which often has transnational dimensions. This is violence brought about by: (i) private security companies; (ii) companies entrusted with public functions such as water supply or guarding detainees and prisoners; (iii) clothing manufacturers relying on sweatshop conditions and union free zones; (iv) rebel groups and armed gangs operating; and (v) some activities of international organizations. Although monitoring is crucial, monitoring does not really lead to compliance, which depends on incentives. While some governments are sensitive to exposure and findings of violations, others are seemingly impervious to the recommendations of UN mechanisms. To carry out effective monitoring, a combination of transnational and national NGOs are crucial. Furthermore, there is a need for a World Court for Human Rights. To consider an international court as the final guarantor may seem naïve, but this destination is simply the logical development of the project to protect human rights through international law. The establishment of a World Court would have many merits: (i) the Court would encompass all human rights, including subsistence rights, collective rights, and the welfare rights that are central to addressing inequality; (ii) transnational actors would be both plaintiffs and defendants; NGOs would be entitled to complain that they were victims of human rights violations; and complaints could be brought against non-state actors such as transnational corporations, intergovernmental organizations, or rebel groups; and (iii) as the key to future protection lies in access to justice at the national level, the proposal for the World Court recognizes that, in thinking about human rights compliance, we need to take into account a multiplicity of priorities, actors, and national systems.

## 1. On the way to utopia

Emphasis on national protection systems is now the priority for the international human rights system. This emphasis is found in the UN programmes addressed to capacity building, technical assistance and judicial training, through the work of regional and UN treaty-monitoring bodies and Courts and Commissions, up to the most recent device: the UN Periodic Review of countries' national records. The emphasis on strengthening national capacity is even found in the arena of the International Criminal Court and the fashion for focusing on transnational cooperation to ensure 'positive complementarity' with regard to national prosecutions of international crimes.[1] Is compliance, then, a simple matter of guaranteeing existing international rights by ensuring a simplified rule of law at the national level? I would suggest not.

If we step back and consider what our current human rights preoccupations actually are, we will find a series of different lists depending on our circumstances and our country. I would suggest that of course there are continuing traditional concerns with regard to: prison conditions, unfair trials, racial and sex discrimination, access to health care, education, and adequate housing; but contemporary concerns also relate to newly discovered transnational threats from beyond the state, and that the country-by-country approach is now seen as inadequate. A realistic utopia would have to address these challenges. This wider agenda was already heralded in 1979 by Antonio Cassese in the following way:

> The grave violations of human rights so widespread today do not arise only from the whim of despots or the desire for power of select oligarchies. They may *also* arise from these phenomena, but the essential reasons for these grave violations lie in the 'structural violence' so widely diffused in the world, in the essence of socio-political structures that are incapable of guaranteeing respect for human dignity.[2]

Although Cassese's solution stresses the transnational promotion of human rights through NGOs, we can also say that compliance requires not only transnational NGOs 'naming and shaming' human rights violators, but also a focus on certain transnational actors as potential violators themselves.

Asked in 1974 to consider the future of international law Sir Gerald Fitzmaurice suggested that there are:

> fields in which it is becoming clear that the nation-state alone cannot assure the protection of the individual—even its own particular subjects or citizens—from the prospect of serious harm,—and where in the long run only international action, internationally

---

[1] See, eg, the approach of the US government as explained by Ambassador Rapp, he concludes:

> We now know that it is not enough to *hope* that international courts will catalyze domestic justice; we must actively *work* to assist States ravaged by violence to strengthen their own systems of protection and accountability. (7 December 2010, 6th Assembly of States Parties ICC)

[2] A. Cassese, 'Progressive Transnational Promotion of Human Rights', in B.G. Ramcharan (ed.), *Human Rights: Thirty Years after the Universal Declaration* (The Hague: Martinus Nijhoff, 1979), 249–62, at 249.

organized and carried out, will suffice, since the mischief knows no natural boundaries, and cannot be kept out by any purely national barriers;—such things as overpopulation and its consequences in overcrowding, malnutrition and disease; the pollution of waters, rivers, seas and airspace; the overexploitation and potential exhaustion of the earth's mineral resources and stores of fuel and power; the extinction of species and devastation of fish stocks; problems of drought, famine and hurricane damage; problems of poverty and underdevelopment; the possible misuse of outer space; terrorist activities that cross all frontiers, and 'hi-jacking' of aircraft and other threats to the safety of communication; the traffic in arms, narcotic drugs and slavery; forced labour; migration, emigration, conditions of work and other labour problems, etc.[3]

It is suggested therefore that in imagining a realistic utopia for human rights compliance it is not enough to stress independent NGOs, judicial training, treaty monitoring, periodic reviews, and national protection systems to hold governments accountable. We need also to address violence which emanates from beyond the state and which often has transnational dimensions. As we shall see the existing regime addresses these issues in an inadequate way.

## 2. Transnational actors

The types of transnational actors that threaten the enjoyment of human rights are quite well known. In the business world we can simply mention recent preoccupations with the activities of private security companies operating in Iraq and Afghanistan, the companies entrusted with public functions such as water supply or guarding detainees and prisoners, and clothing manufacturers relying on sweatshop conditions and union-free zones. In another register there is concern over the rape, killing, and mayhem caused by rebel groups and armed gangs operating with levels of violence which negate the notion that we live in a world of human rights. And, shifting again, we need now to address the threats to human rights that can emanate from the activities of international organizations. The literature has tended to shy away from treating international organizations as human rights violators, perhaps this is because so many human rights experts themselves are intimately bound up with the human rights work of the UN and the regional organizations, or perhaps it is because there is an assumption that there will always be a way to ensure compliance by addressing the member states. But the time has come to consider human rights compliance by the UN, NATO, the EU, the WTO, the World Bank, the IMF, and so on.

Compliance in this context could be seen as having three dimensions. First, a clear admission by all concerned that the entity itself has obligations under international human rights law; secondly, that the entity has to ensure that it has the internal mechanisms to adjust policies to bring its activities into compliance with these obligations (in a way not so different from the techniques adopted to ensure that each country has a national human rights protection system); and, thirdly,

---

[3] G. Fitzmaurice, 'The Future of Public International Law and of the International Legal System in the Circumstances of Today', in Institut de droit international, *Livre du Centenaire 1873–1973: Evolution et perspectives du droit international* (Basle: Karger, 1973), 196–329, at 260.

that the entity submits to external human rights accountability mechanisms. In a realistic utopia the scope of these obligations will not depend on the result of doctrinal debates over international legal personality, or the subjects of international law. Obligations will be simply determined taking into account the capacity of the entity to infringe on the enjoyment of rights.

## 3. Transnational monitors

Some might argue that instead of worrying about improving the monitoring of human rights violations we should be creating societies where they do not occur in the first place. In More's *Utopia* there would be no recourse to human rights violations because everyone has been trained as a farmer and food is plentiful; everyone wears the same clothes (with some variation for sex and marital status); and most people spend their free time on further education attending early morning lectures.[4] Those who transgress the law are fairly and humanely punished for having violated a rule which was just in its aims, and clear in its ambit. But, if we are realistic, we know that we are stuck with structural violence, including poverty, discrimination, and unequal access to education and health care. Monitoring is therefore crucial, but we need to pause and ask does monitoring really lead to compliance? Monitoring works where the transgressor is dissuaded from action for fear of exposure, or where violations are exposed and the violator feels the need to redress the situation. Both situations depend on the relevant entity wanting or needing to change their behaviour. While the regional human rights mechanisms provide a compliance mechanism where states do effectively adjust their behaviour due to a sense that they should respect their international obligations, they do not represent universal coverage. Suffice it to mention that China and India are not subject to any such mechanism, and the United States and Canada do not allow for complaints before the Inter-American Court of Human Rights. Moreover, none of the regional human rights mechanisms allow for complaints against the non-state entities referred to in the previous section.

The United Nations has an impressive array of human rights monitoring mechanisms: treaty bodies, the Human Rights Council's Universal Periodic Review, the Special Rapporteurs of the Human Rights Council, ad hoc Commissions of Inquiry, and field monitors in around 50 countries.[5] But if we focus on compliance, and not just monitoring, we could be disappointed. Compliance depends, as suggested above, on incentives. While some governments are sensitive to exposure and findings of violations, others are seemingly impervious to the recommendations of these UN mechanisms. The authority of the High Commissioner for Human Rights and the Secretary-General can be used to considerable effect, but again there are limits where governments carry on regardless.

---

[4] T. More, *Utopia* ([1516] P. Turner trans., London: Penguin Classics, 2003), at 55–6.
[5] For a detailed introduction see C. Krause and M. Sheinin (eds), *International Protection of Human Rights: A Textbook* (Turku: Institute for Human Rights, Abo Akademi University, 2009).

National protection systems can work to ensure compliance, but we have to admit that the worst situations today often have national systems that are unwilling or unable to confront human rights violations, hence the emphasis on the transnational and the supranational. But intergovernmental organizations are hard-wired to respect their members, so we come to the unsurprising conclusion that a combination of transnational and national NGOs are crucial to effective monitoring. Monitoring, however, is not compliance, and again we are faced with partial results. To better the compliance record in a realistic utopia there would need to be greater incentives for governments to change. One could imagine developing targeted sanctions, denial of trade preferences, boycotts, abolishing state and personal immunity for human rights violations, and deploying significant numbers of UN civilian police and human rights monitors to the worst cases. But we are enjoined to remain realistic, and even if there were the political will for such initiatives, there may be reasons to be cautious about the efficacy of such measures. For example, sanctions have had only limited success when used to attempt to bring recalcitrant states into compliance. The initial sanctions on Iraq seemed to reinforce Saddam Hussein's grip on power, and had such an effect on the civilian population that they simply led to further denials of basic rights to adequate health care. The best hope is for national and international human rights organizations to be able patiently to work (using the monitors' reports) to build the national structures that will prevent and punish human rights violations.

## 4. Transnational rights, responsibilities, and remedies

One of the challenges facing human rights compliance is the denial by some governments and courts that human rights obligations apply transnationally. The issue arises for example when government agents act abroad.[6] The United States argues that it is not bound by its human rights treaty obligations under the International Covenant on Civil and Political Rights when it acts abroad; and it has been held that the UK Human Rights Act only protects those held in detention facilities, while actions on the streets of Baghdad, or in the homes of Iraqis, remain beyond the scope of the Human Rights Act. In other words, human rights are being seen as rights against one's own government at home, and not rights that belong to all human beings enforceable against a foreign presence. This in turn suggests that

---

[6] See, eg, Third Report of the United States to the UN Human Rights Committee, UN Doc. CCPR/C/USA/3, 28 November 2005, esp. Annex I; M.J. Dennis and A.M. Surena, 'Application of the International Covenant on Civil and Political Rights in Times of Armed Conflict and Military Occupation: The Gap between Legal Theory and State Practice', 6 EHRLR (2008) 714–31, compare N. Rodley, 'The Extraterritorial Reach and Applicability in Armed Conflict of the International Covenant on Civil and Political Rights: A Rejoinder to Dennis and Surena', 5 EHRLR (2009) 5, 628–36; European Court of Human Rights: *Bankovic et al v Belgium et al* (19 December 2001); House of Lords: *Al-Skeini and others v Secretary of State for Defence* [2007] UKHL 26 and *Al-Jedda et al v Secretary of State for Defence* [2007] UKHL 58; Supreme Court of Canada: *R v Hape* [2007] SCC 26.

states will not generally be held responsible for human rights violations committed abroad.

The extraterritorial question also arises in the context of the failure of states to tackle the activities of 'their' transnational corporations acting abroad. While there may be provisions to ensure compliance in fields such as corruption and pollution, the notion of states taking more responsibility for ensuring redress for violations committed by companies incorporated in their jurisdictions remains controversial.[7] Although there have been some out of court settlements (totalling several million dollars) in the context of allegations of complicity in human rights violations with regard to Shell in Nigeria, Unocal in Myanmar/Burma, and Blackwater in Iraq, the US Federal Courts have most recently rejected the idea that they should have jurisdiction over such corporate violations of international human rights law or international criminal law.[8]

## 5. Arriving in utopia: a World Court for Human Rights

In this last section we turn to a new proposal for an accountability mechanism that would go some way to answering some of the problems raised above. The proposal for a World Court of Human Rights is a revived idea which will be seen by many as utopian, but which nevertheless repays careful reading.[9] Such a Court is said to represent the missing piece in the institutional jigsaw designed at the end of the Second World War. The other pieces were an International Criminal Court and a High Commissioner for Human Rights. As recounted by Nowak and Kozma:[10]

the Working Group on Implementation of the Commission on Human Rights, on the basis of an Australian proposal,[11] recommended that an International Court of Human Rights be established and 'empowered to constitute the final guarantor of human rights.[12]

To consider an international court as the final guarantor may today seem hopelessly naïve, not to say unrealistic, but this destination is simply the logical development

---

[7] See report by Special Rapporteur of the Secretary-General John Ruggie to the 2010 Human Rights Council, UN Doc. A/HRC/14/27, 9 April 2010, at paras 46–50; see also 'Exploring Extraterritoriality in Business and Human Rights: Summary Note of Expert Meeting', 14 September 2010, the Mossavar-Rahmani Center for Business & Government, Harvard Kennedy School. These and other related documents on this aspect of extraterritoriality are all available at <http://www.business-humanrights.org/SpecialRepPortal/Home>.

[8] See *Kiobel et al v Shell et al*, Docket nos 06–4800-cv, 06–4876-cv, 17 September 2010 (US Court of Appeals Second Circuit).

[9] J. Kozma, M. Nowak, and M. Scheinin, *A World Court of Human Rights—Consolidated Statute and Commentary* (Vienna: Neuer Wissenschaftlicher, 2010).

[10] M. Nowak and J. Kozma, *A World Court of Human Rights* (Report for the Swiss Initiative to Commemorate the 60th Anniversary of the UDHR, available at <http://www.udhr60.ch/report/hrCourt-Nowak0609.pdf>).

[11] See, eg, A. Devereux, 'Australia and the International Scrutiny of Civil and Political Rights: An Analysis of Australia's Negotiating Policies, 1946–1966', 22 Australian YIL (2003) 47 (fn in original).

[12] [Report of the Commission on Human Rights on its second session held in Geneva from 2 to 17 December 1947] UN Doc. E/600, 58ff. See also H. W. Briggs, 'Implementation of the Proposed International Covenant on Human Rights', 42 AJIL (1948) 389, at 395 (fn in original).

of the project to protect human rights through international law. Fears of compliance at the time (1947) were absent: the Group chose to emphasize that 'cases have hitherto been rare of states deliberately going against international judicial decisions or arbitral awards'.[13] The Group also preferred that the guarantor of the guarantor be the General Assembly rather than the Security Council due to its broader mandate covering economic and social cooperation.[14]

At this point we might pause again and wonder whether, as international lawyers, we are on the right path. The UN architecture and the inter-state treaty regime are the bread and butter of teaching human rights in the context of international law. Such a focus comes naturally; but are we in danger of missing the opportunity for a more meaningful engagement with the idea of human rights?

Two new books (one from a historical perspective and one from an anthropologist) have highlighted how our seduction by the idea of a human rights utopia risks undermining alternative projects for emancipation and human flourishing. In *The Last Utopia: Human Rights in History* Samuel Moyn argues that the human rights movement in the 1970s shifted the focus from self-determination to cases of individual religious persecution, and so 'the attractions of Amnesty International in the decisive decades depended on leaving behind political utopias and turning to smaller and more manageable moral acts'.[15] Moyn considers that the modern attractiveness of human rights owes much to the disenchantment with promised utopias:

what the substitution of moral for political utopianism meant is that human rights came to the world as its partisans abjured the maximalism that had once lent utopias glamour—especially utopias that required profound transformation, or even revolution and violence.[16]

Moyn's history of human rights leads him to conclude that the disconnect from democratic revolution, and the turn from the political to the moral, mean the project is incapable of delivering utopia.

Because they were born at a moment when they survived as a moral utopia when political utopias died, human rights were compelled to define the good life and offer a plan for bringing it about precisely when they were ill-equipped by the fact of their suprapolitical birth to do so.[17]

In *Surrendering to Utopia: An Anthology of Human Rights* Mark Goodale appeals for less postwar triumphalism and more sensitivity to the multiplicity of social practices we find in the world.[18] He also highlights the transnational over the international:

But the extent to which a transnational human rights regime interconnects people beyond the boundaries of nation states, promotes norms that are derived from the apolitical idea of human rights (and not the logics of international relations), and lays the foundation for legitimacy by establishing networks that are organized around human, rather than

[13]  UN Doc. E/600, at para. 55.
[14]  Ibid, para. 54.
[15]  (Cambridge, MA: Belknap Harvard, 2010) at 147.
[16]  Ibid, 171.
[17]  Ibid, 214.
[18]  (Stanford, CA: Stanford University Press, 2009).

national or political, principles—like the principle of human dignity, or the imperative to protect human rights—it at least has the virtue of cohering with (rather than contradicting) the idea of human rights.[19]

Bearing in mind these appeals from history and anthropology, does the idea of a World Court undercut the prospect of political transformation and ignore the significance of the emerging transnational human rights regime? Are we being enticed off the road to utopia by a modernist architectural mock-up?

The answers to these questions deserve careful reflection, but for present purposes let us simply highlight the extent to which the proposed World Court does surprisingly attempt to meet some of the challenges highlighted throughout this chapter. First, the Court would encompass all human rights, including subsistence rights, collective rights, and the welfare rights that are central to addressing inequality.[20] Secondly, transnational actors would be both plaintiffs and defendants. NGOs would be entitled to complain that they were victims of human rights violations; and complaints could be brought against non-state actors such as transnational corporations, intergovernmental organizations, or rebel groups.[21] Thirdly, it is recognized that the key to future protection lies in access to justice at the national level, and the Commentary to the draft reminds readers to continue to bear in mind the proposal (from one of the constituent drafts) that states be required to establish their own national courts of human rights.[22] The proposal for the World Court therefore recognizes that, in thinking about human rights compliance. we need to take into account a multiplicity of priorities, actors, and national systems. The concept of such a Court may therefore stimulate us in envisioning ways of building an effective human rights compliance regime fit for utopia.

Fears will continue to be expressed that building a new shrine to international human rights will distract from political mobilization to tackle structural violence. This may even be the case, but the history of human rights protection through the courts is replete with instances where laws and practices have had to be abandoned (and one can certainly find instances of governments changing course for fear of being challenged on human rights compliance in court). Ensuring human rights compliance through transnational monitoring and human rights courts may not be sufficient to construct a realistic utopia—but it is a start.

---

[19] Ibid, 98.

[20] The consolidated statute (above) foresees a total of at least 21 human rights treaties being annexed to the Statute (Art. 5(1) Applicable Law).

[21] See Arts 51 and 4(1) '"Entity" refers to any inter-governmental organization or non-State actor, including any business corporation'. The Commentary explains that the list is non-exhaustive and could include non-governmental organizations should they too choose to make the relevant declaration:

> But there is no doubt that this provision primarily aims at transnational corporations, international non-profit organizations, organized opposition movements and autonomous communities within States or within a group of States. An 'Entity' does not necessarily have to be a juridical person recognized under domestic or international law. (Commentary to Art. 4, at 30)

[22] Nowak and Kozma, n 10, at Art. 10.

# 27

# Managing Abidance by Standards for the Protection of the Environment

*Jorge E. Viñuales*

## SUMMARY

There are two core ideas underpinning international environmental law, namely 'prevention' and 'balance'. The idea of prevention is enshrined in an array of principles such as those of no-harm, prevention, precaution, cooperation, prior informed consent, and environmental impact assessment which, in turn, can be found at the basis of many multilateral environmental agreements. The basic message carried by these principles is that environmental damage may be irreversible. Therefore, it is of vital importance to foster compliance with environmental standards, through monitoring and other means, rather than to determine responsibility through an adjudication mechanism once damage has occurred. One can identify various stages of compliance: (i) gathering information regarding state conduct; (ii) focusing on facilitating compliance; (iii) managing non-compliance; and (iv) thoroughly characterizing a situation of breach and deriving the legal consequences attached to it. In the view of the author, the main focus of a judicious reformer should be on strengthening the means to monitor, facilitate, and manage compliance, as well as to carve out sufficient space for environmental considerations to be taken into account in specialized adjudication mechanisms. Four principal avenues are suggested for action to enhance compliance with environmental standards: (i) the monitoring powers of the bodies set up by multilateral environmental agreements should be expanded to include the ability of these bodies to verify the information submitted by states, to request additional information, to gather their own information, to assess compliance, and, when necessary, to adopt binding measures to manage compliance; (ii) the scope and modalities of technical and financial assistance should be significantly revisited; (iii) it would be necessary to clarify the basic legal principles that currently characterize the respective contribution of developed and developing states to the protection of the environment; and (iv) although international environmental law is geared towards the prevention of environmental damage, adjudication mechanisms have a role to play, and resort to them should be increasingly made.

# 1. Compliance as a process

Those interested in the means that can be used to ensure compliance with international law will no doubt find abundant food for thought in the arrangements most often contemplated in international environmental instruments. Compliance is envisioned in this context as a process that starts with the adoption, by a subject of international law,[1] of a legally binding commitment (or one which is not legally binding[2]) and continues throughout the life of the international 'regime'. As a process, compliance needs to be 'managed' and it admits different 'degrees' which, in turn, influence the overall 'effectiveness' of an international regime.

Thus characterized, the term compliance has a broader meaning than the one which is ascribed to it in more traditional approaches to international environmental law.[3] Not surprisingly, the means contemplated to manage compliance are also considerably different. To make this point clear, one may refer to the framework described by Antonio Cassese in his introductory chapter to Part III. Such framework refers to the existence (i) of one traditional approach to ensuring the respect of international law, namely the different forms of adjudication, the main role of which is deciding whether a state is in breach of an international obligation and determining the consequences of such a breach (in accordance with the general rules on state responsibility or with a specific regime operating as *lex specialis*) and (ii) of two alternative approaches, namely monitoring and institutional fact-finding, which seek to fill the gaps left by the inadequacy of adjudication to a new range of subject matters regulated by international law. The means used in international environmental law are also an attempt to fill some of the gaps; gaps

---

[1] Other entities the international legal personality of which is controversial, such as non-governmental organizations (NGOs) or transnational corporations, may also be involved in a process of compliance with international environmental standards. This is the case, eg, in connection with the mechanisms to monitor compliance with the OECD Guidelines on Multinational Enterprises (the conformity of the activities of transnational corporations with such guidelines can be examined by 'National Contact Points' set up in their home countries, if these latter have adhered to the OECD Guidelines; *Decision of the OECD Council on the OECD Guidelines for Multinational Enterprises (June 2000)*, 40 ILM 237 (2000)) or under the monitoring system created by the North-American Agreement on Environmental Cooperation (NAAEC) (pursuant to Art. 14(1) of the NAAEC 'The Secretariat may consider a submission from any non-governmental organization or person asserting that a Party is failing to effectively enforce its environmental law [if certain conditions are met]', 32 ILM 1480 (1993)).

[2] Such as the commitments arising from the OECD Guidelines, above, which include recommendations relating, inter alia, to transparency, respect of human rights and decent labour conditions, the taking into account of environment, public health and safety standards.

[3] Traditionally, a more restrictive definition of 'compliance' has been used in international legal scholarship. Eg, UNEP's Manual on Compliance with and Enforcement of Multilateral Environmental Agreements defines compliance as the '[f]ulfillment by a Party of its obligations under an international agreement'. See United Nations Environment Programme, *Manual on Compliance with and Enforcement of Multilateral Environmental Agreements*, available at <http://www.unep.org/DEC/OnLineManual/Resources/Glossary/tabid/69/Default.aspx?high=compliance#high>. On newer approaches to compliance, see A. Chayes et al, 'Managing Compliance: A Comparative Perspective', in E. Brown Weiss and H.K. Jacobsen (eds), *Engaging Countries: Strengthening Compliance with International Environmental Accords* (Cambridge, MA: MIT Press, 1998), 39–62; A. Chayes and A. Handler Chayes, *The New Sovereignty: Compliance with International Regulatory Agreements* (Cambridge, MA: Harvard University Press, 1995), 1–28.

that have been left open not only by adjudication but also by monitoring and institutional fact-finding. More precisely, although international environmental law contemplates monitoring, fact-finding, and even adjudication mechanisms as part of the palette of means to manage compliance, a number of other means focusing on the 'soft-belly' of the compliance process are also available, means that are based on a different understanding of the reasons why a state complies (or not) with a commitment.

## 2. Stages and means of compliance

The compliance process can be understood as an axis along which one could tentatively identify four different 'stages' of compliance, each with its own basic methods of managing compliance. Of course, in reality, the compliance process is a continuum and some means may operate at more than one point of such continuum. The identification of four stages is, however, convenient for analytical purposes.

The initial stage is concerned with gathering information regarding state conduct. This is the natural place of monitoring systems broadly defined to include not only regular reporting systems but also other systems such as the establishment by states of domestic inventories or mechanisms capable of gathering the information that must be reported.[4] Depending on each regime, the monitoring system may be limited to a reporting obligation imposed on states, with limited or no follow-up processes for prompting, verifying, or completing the information reported by states, or extend to more sophisticated mechanisms with significant information-gathering powers.

The second stage focuses on facilitating compliance. Facilitation mechanisms can seek to channel diplomatic or moral pressure to persuade a state inclined to disregard a commitment to abide by it. In international environmental law, however, their main objective is often to assist states which are willing to abide by

---

[4] Eg Art. 9 of the Convention on Long-Range Transboundary Air Pollution of 13 November 1979 (LRTAP Convention) states in relevant part:

> The Contracting Parties stress the need for the implementation of the existing 'Cooperative programme for the monitoring and evaluation of the long-range transmission of air pollutants in Europe' (hereinafter referred to as EMEP) and, with regard to the further development of this programme, agree to emphasize: ... (c) The desirability of basing the monitoring programme on the framework of both national and international programmes. The establishment of monitoring stations and the collection of data shall be carried out under the national jurisdiction of the country in which the monitoring stations are located. (18 ILM 1442 (1979))

See also, Arts 6 (Assessment and Review of Control Measures), 7 (Reporting of data), and 8 (Non-compliance) of the Montreal Protocol on Substances that Deplete the Ozone Layer of 16 September 1987 (Montreal Protocol), 26 ILM 154 (1987); Art. 10 of the Basel Convention on the Control of Transboundary Movements of Hazardous Wastes and Their Disposal of 22 March 1989 (Basel Convention), 28 ILM 657 (1989); and Art. 12 of the United Nations Framework Convention on Climate Change of 9 May 1992 (UNFCCC), 31 ILM 849 (1992).

their commitments but lack the necessary resources/capabilities to do so.[5] Unlike the commitments undertaken in some other fields of international law, environmental commitments (eg in the areas of chemical or hazardous waste regulation, ozone depletion, or climate change) may indeed require specialized knowledge and significant resources to be implemented. A state that would be willing to comply but lacks such resources would be unable fully or reasonably to comply with some or even most of the commitments which it has undertaken under the treaty. Moreover, even states that do have the resources to comply may benefit from the establishment of 'facilitation' mechanisms seeking to render compliance more cost-effective. For these reasons, many multilateral environmental treaties contemplate mechanisms to provide financial, technical, and/or managerial assistance to member states that are willing but unable to comply or to make compliance more cost-effective. As I will discuss later, these mechanisms may take a variety of forms ranging from financial or technical assistance, to sophisticated 'flexibility mechanisms',[6] to self-triggered supervisory systems (the so-called 'non-compliance procedures' or NCPs).

The third stage is concerned with managing non-compliance. This stage is premised on the inability or the unwillingness, as the case may be, of a state to comply with its commitments under a given environmental treaty. The means operating at this third stage pursue four main objectives, namely detecting a case of non-compliance, identifying the likely reasons underlying such non-compliance, solving the situation through non-adversarial means (assistance), and, if necessary, applying pressure on the state concerned to cease its non-compliance. Multilateral environmental treaties often provide for advanced 'non-compliance procedures', of different scope and sophistication, to meet these objectives. I will discuss the operation of these mechanisms later. However, let me note at this point that, despite their potentially adversarial features, NCPs are primarily aimed at detecting non-compliance, investigating its causes, and facilitating the return to a situation of compliance, even by granting renewed assistance.

---

[5] The Commission on Sustainable Development (CSD) sought to address this problem as early as 1996:

> Concern exists...about the need to reduce the reporting burden placed on countries, particularly developing countries, by international legal instruments and various intergovernmental decisions. This marks a growing trend towards coordination and streamlining of the reporting process and cooperation at international and national levels for the purpose of data collection, analysis and dissemination. (UN Doc. E/CN.17/1996/17, para. 13)

[6] The term 'flexibility mechanisms' is commonly used to refer to the mechanisms set up in the Kyoto Protocol to the United Nations Framework Convention on Climate Change of 11 December 1997 (Kyoto Protocol), 37 ILM 22 (1998), to make compliance with the commitments adopted by state parties thereunder more cost-effective. Some commentators would consider that these mechanisms are not, as such, mechanisms of compliance. Underlying such a view is a more restrictive definition of compliance than the one adopted in this chapter. The *travaux préparatoires* of the Kyoto Protocol suggest, however, that such mechanisms were adopted to facilitate compliance with emission reduction commitments. See J. Depledge, 'Tracing the Origins of the Kyoto Protocol: An Article-by-Article Textual History', Technical Paper FCCC/TP/2000/2, 25 November 2000, para. 349.

The fourth stage focuses on thoroughly characterizing a situation of breach and deriving the legal consequences attached to it. The basic means used for this purpose are adjudicatory or quasi-adjudicatory mechanisms, deciding disputes on the basis of law and reaching legally binding decisions. Many multilateral environmental treaties provide for such mechanisms, although, in practice, they have rarely been implemented, if at all. The legal consequences to be derived from a finding of breach may be those generally described in the ILC Articles on the Responsibility of States for Internationally Wrongful Acts[7] and/or those set out in other more specific regimes, such as those established in connection with liability for oil pollution or nuclear accidents.[8]

The reasons explaining the inadequacies of the traditional adjudicatory approach to ensure compliance with international environmental standards are important to understand why multilateral environmental treaties have focused on the means identified in connection with the first three stages of compliance.

### 3. Some observations on environmental adjudication

In the last decades, the development of international adjudication has marked an evolution in many fields of international law, ranging from human rights, to international criminal law, to trade and investment disputes. As discussed in other chapters in this volume, this emerging trend has been based on the establishment of specialized adjudicatory bodies with jurisdiction over particular subject matters.

A conspicuous absence in this trend is international environmental adjudication. Despite initiatives to establish an adjudicatory body with a special focus on environment-related disputes (eg adjudicatory systems contemplated in multilateral environmental agreements, the special environmental chamber in the International Court of Justice, an international environmental court, or, at least, a set of arbitration rules specifically designed for environment-related disputes), such attempts have yielded limited results.[9] Instead, and aside from a small number

---

[7]  Responsibility of States for Internationally Wrongful Acts, YILC (2001), Vol. II, Part Two.

[8]  See, eg, Convention on Third Party Liability in the Field of Nuclear Energy, 29 July 1960, 956 UNTS 251; Convention on Civil Liability for Nuclear Damage, 21 May 1963, 1063 UNTS 265; Joint Protocol Relating to the Application of the Vienna Convention and the Paris Convention, 21 September 1988, 42 Nuclear Law Bulletin 56 (1988); Convention Relating to Civil Liability in the Field of Maritime Carriage of Nuclear Material, 17 December 1971, 944 UNTS 255; International Convention on Civil Liability for Oil Pollution Damage, 27 November 1992, 973 UNTS 3; Convention on Civil Liability for Damage Resulting from Activities Dangerous to the Environment, 21 June 1993, 32 ILM 1228 (1993); International Convention on Liability and Compensation for Damage in Connection with the Carriage of Hazardous and Noxious Substances by Sea, 3 May 1996, 25 ILM 1406 (1996); Protocol to the International Convention on the Establishment of an International Fund for Compensation for Oil Pollution Damage, 16 May 2003, IMO Doc. LEG/CONF.14/20 (2003).

[9]  For an overview see T. Stephens, *International Courts and Environmental Protection* (Cambridge: Cambridge University Press, 2009), 7–17; E. Hey, *Reflections on an International Environmental Court* (The Hague: Kluwer Law International, 2000), 1–25.

of cases brought before the International Court of Justice,[10] environment-related disputes have 'borrowed fora' normally devoted to other fields, such as human rights courts and commissions, the World Trade Organization Dispute Settlement Body or investment tribunals.[11] Even the International Tribunal on the Law of the Sea (ITLOS), whose mandate covers substantial environmental aspects, has so far played a limited role (mostly in connection with provisional measures) in adjudicating environment-related disputes. One may therefore wonder why international environmental adjudication has followed a different path.

The answer must be sought, in my view, in the two core ideas underpinning international environmental law as a field, namely 'prevention' and 'balance'. The idea of prevention is enshrined in an array of principles such as those of no-harm, prevention, precaution, cooperation, prior informed consent, and environmental impact assessment, which, in turn, can be found at the basis of many multilateral environmental agreements. The basic message carried by these principles is that environmental damage may be irreversible. Therefore, it is of vital importance to foster compliance with environmental standards, through monitoring and other means, rather than to determine responsibility through an adjudication mechanism once damage has occurred.

However, adjudicatory means do have a role when it comes to finding a balance between the scope of environmental standards and that of other rules of international law. Indeed, the principles and concepts provided by international environmental law in this respect, such as the principle of common but differentiated responsibilities or the concept of sustainable development, are broad enough to admit very different interpretations and, therefore, call for the intervention of a body which can solve potential conflicts between environmental and other standards authoritatively, with an eye to the future. More specifically, I believe that it is very useful and even necessary that international courts and tribunals established to decide disputes arising in other fields of international law pay attention to the environmental dimensions of such disputes and, as necessary, allow some room for environmental considerations to be taken into account in their own jurisprudence.

---

[10] The first cases touching upon environmental issues are the two *Nuclear Tests* cases (*Nuclear Tests (Australia v France)*, Judgment, ICJ Reports 1974, 253 and *Nuclear Tests (New Zealand v France)*, Judgment, ICJ Reports 1974, 457) and the *Case Concerning Certain Phosphate Lands in Nauru (Nauru v Australia)*, discontinued by Order of 13 September 1993 (ICJ Reports 1993, 322). The first cases expressly dealing with environmental questions are the *Legality of the Threat or Use of Nuclear Weapons*, Advisory Opinion, ICJ Reports 1996, 226 and *Case Concerning the Gabčíkovo-Nagymaros Project (Hungary/Slovakia)*, Judgment, ICJ Reports 1997, 7. The last environment-related case to have been decided by the International Court of Justice is *Case Concerning Pulp Mills on the River Uruguay (Argentina v Uruguay)*, Judgment, 20 April 2010. Two environment-related cases are pending before the Court: *Aerial Herbicide Spraying (Ecuador v Colombia)* and *Whaling in the Antarctic (Australia v Japan)*. See J.E. Viñuales, 'The Contribution of the International Court of Justice to the Development of International Environmental Law: A Contemporary Assessment', 32 Fordham ILJ (2010) 232.

[11] The most complete overview so far is provided by the five-volume collection published by Cambridge University Press: *International Environmental Law Reports* (vols I–V). This collection does not make reference to investment disputes. For a study of the impact of environmental considerations on investment disputes see: J.E. Viñuales, 'Foreign Investment and the Environment in International Law: An Ambiguous Relationship', 80 BYIL (2010) 244–332. On disputes concerning other areas see Stephens, n 9.

Such a need may explain, at least in part, the phenomenon of 'borrowed fora' referred to above. But even in these cases, the function of adjudication mechanisms remains geared to the idea of prevention, because their efforts to clarify the relations between environmental and other standards are mainly important to balance different demands with an eye to the future.

The preceding considerations suggest that the main focus of a judicious reformer should be on strengthening the means to monitor, facilitate, and manage compliance, as well as to carve out sufficient space for environmental considerations to be taken into account in specialized adjudication mechanisms. In order to see what could be adjusted or added, the following section provides an overview of the palette of means available in international environmental law.

## 4. Compliance's 'soft-belly': reporting, facilitation, and management mechanisms

### (A) Reporting

The use of monitoring and reporting systems is widespread in multilateral environmental agreements.[12] The basic characteristics of such mechanisms are comparable to those presented by monitoring systems in human rights and arms control regimes. For analytical purposes, a distinction can be made between three different reporting systems according to their scope.

The most basic systems, such as the one applicable to the reduction and control of sulphur and nitrogen oxide emissions under the 1979 Convention on Long-Range Transboundary Air Pollution,[13] as completed by its 1985 Sulphur Emissions Protocol[14] and its 1988 Nitrogen Oxides Protocol,[15] only provide for the regular submission by states of reports communicating, inter alia, their level of emissions. A similarly limited approach was initially followed by the 1989 Basel Convention on the Control of Transboundary Movement of Hazardous Wastes and their Disposal, until a more robust system was adopted in 2002 by the Conference of the Parties (COP).[16]

---

[12] See R. Wolfrum, 'Means of Ensuring Compliance with and Enforcement of International Environmental Law', 272 RCADI (1998) 36–55.

[13] Art. 9(e), LRTAP Convention, n 4.

[14] Art. 4 of the Protocol on the Reduction of Sulphur Emissions or their Transboundary Fluxes by at least 30 per cent, 8 July 1985, 27 ILM 707 (1988); and Art. 5 of the Protocol to the 1979 Convention on Long-Range Transboundary Air Pollution on Further Reduction of Sulphur Emissions, 14 June 1994, 33 ILM 1542 (1994).

[15] Art. 8 of the Protocol to the 1979 Convention on Long-Range Transboundary Air Pollution Concerning the Control of Emissions of Nitrogen Oxides or Their Transboundary Fluxes, 31 October 1988, 27 ILM 698 (1988).

[16] An Implementation and Compliance Committee was established at the sixth Conference of the Parties in Geneva in 2002. COP Decision VI/12 on Establishment of a Mechanism for Promoting Implementation and Compliance, 'Final Report of the Sixth Conference of the Parties to the Basel Convention', UNEP/CHW.6/40 (2003), 45. See A. Shibata, 'Ensuring Compliance with the Basel Convention—its Unique Features', in U. Beyerlin, P.T. Stoll, and R. Wolfrum (eds), *Ensuring Compliance with Multilateral Environmental Agreements: A Dialogue between Practitioners and Academia* (The Hague: Martinus Nijhoff, 2006), 69.

Other more sophisticated systems entitle an administrative body of the environmental treaty in question to verify the information submitted, to request additional information, and/or to gather its own information (in some cases through inspection systems). For instance, the COP of the 1971 Convention on Wetlands of International Importance,[17] in its fourth meeting in 1990, established an inspection procedure, conditional upon the consent of the state party concerned.[18] Similarly, the 1973 Convention on the International Trade of Endangered Species provides for an inspection system to assess whether trade in a given species has put such species in danger.[19]

Still other mechanisms entitle the relevant administrative body, on its own motion or at the request of a state party or another entity, to assess the compliance of the reporting state with the obligations arising from the treaty and, in some cases, also to take a number of steps (eg conciliate the parties, provide assistance, or apply sanctions) to manage non-compliance. The mechanisms falling under this third category arguably go beyond the common understanding of reporting or monitoring systems. Their operation spans indeed 'stage 1' to 'stage 3' of the compliance process identified in Section 2 above, taking different forms in each stage, as I shall discuss next.

## (B) Facilitating compliance

The mechanisms designed by multilateral environmental agreements in this connection can, for the main part, be organized under two main categories: financial and technological assistance, and efficiency increasing mechanisms.

Concerning the first category, those who have followed the climate negotiations over the last three years can appreciate the importance of providing financial and technological assistance to developing countries in order for them to undertake more ambitious mitigation commitments and/or to adapt to the consequences of climate change. The provision of financial and technological assistance can be seen as a reflection of the understanding that, in some cases, even those states inclined to abide by their commitments, may not have the necessary capabilities to do so. Such an understanding has two major implications for the effectiveness of multilateral environmental treaties. On the one hand, it is important in order to incorporate financial and technological assistance as an

---

[17] Convention on Wetlands of International Importance Especially as Waterfowl Habitat, 2 February 1971 (Ramsar Convention), 11 ILM 963 (1972).

[18] Recommendation 4.7: Mechanisms for Improved Application of the Ramsar Convention, 1990, REC. C.4.7 (Rev.) Annex 1. The Ramsar Advisory Mission was formerly known as the Monitoring Procedure (prior to Res. IV.14 (1996)) and the Management Guidance Procedure (prior to Res. VII.12 (1999)).

[19] Arts XII(2)(d) and XIII(2) of the Convention on International Trade in Endangered Species of Wild Fauna and Flora (CITES), 12 ILM 1085 (1973). In accordance with Art. XII(2)(d), the CITES Secretariat's functions include 'to study the reports of the Parties and to request from Parties such further information with respect thereto as it deems necessary to ensure implementation of the present Convention'. See E. Milano, 'The Outcomes of the Procedure and their Legal Effect', in T. Treves et al (eds), *Non-Compliance Procedures and Mechanisms and the Effectiveness of International Environmental Agreements* (The Hague: TMC Asser Press, 2009), 407, 412.

integral part of the treaty regime. This may take different forms, including the provision of funds to poor states to enable them to participate in the meetings of the treaty bodies,[20] or to cover the so-called 'incremental costs' of compliance,[21] or to help them modernize their infrastructures and development model.[22] As a rule, the resources enabling such funding are contributed by developed states on a voluntary basis,[23] although in some cases contributions have been made more automatic.[24] On the other hand, the often unspecified relation between the provision of such assistance and the exigibility of the commitments undertaken by developing countries may undermine the overall effectiveness of a multilateral environmental regime.[25]

Regarding facilitation by means of reducing the cost of compliance, a number of mechanisms have been introduced or are currently being discussed in order to make compliance with commitments relating to climate change mitigation or forest conservation more efficient. The basic idea had already been introduced in 1987, with the adoption of the Montreal Protocol. Article 2(5) of the Montreal Protocol allowed indeed for inter-party transfers of the excess in production of regulated substances 'for the purpose of industrial rationalization'. Also, Article 2(8) provided for the joint fulfilment of the obligations of state parties which are members of a regional economic integration organization, a mechanism often referred to as the 'bubble'. The most sophisticated mechanisms for facilitating compliance by reducing the costs of compliance so far have

[20] Such provisions are mostly found in so-called 'first-generation' financial mechanisms, such as the CITES Trust Fund (Decision 13.1, *Strategic Vision and Action Plan*, CoP13 Decisions (2003), Annex 1, Goal 7) or the Basel Convention's Technical Cooperation Trust Fund (Decision V/32, *Enlargement of the Scope of the Technical Cooperation Trust Fund*, Doc. UNEP/CHW.5/29 (1999)). See L. Boisson de Chazournes, 'Technical and Financial Assistance', in D. Bodansky, J. Brunnée, and E. Hey (eds), *The Oxford Handbook of International Environmental Law* (Oxford: Oxford University Press, 2007), 947, 962.

[21] Art. 10(1) of the Montreal Protocol, n 4, provides that the Protocol's financial mechanism 'shall meet all agreed incremental costs of [Art. 5] Parties in order to enable their compliance with the control measures', without defining the term 'incremental costs'. It only states that the Meeting of the Parties should adopt an indicative list of the categories of incremental costs, which it did in 1992; see Doc. UNEP/OzL.4/15. Incremental costs are the costs incurred by Art. 5 States when converting from ozone-depleting technology to ozone-benign technology in order to comply with the provisions of the Protocol. The Multilateral Fund for the Implementation of the Montreal Protocol is entrusted with the task of managing the financial mechanism and providing funds for the progressive phase out of the use of ozone-depleting substances.

[22] See, eg, the Multilateral Fund for the Implementation of the Montreal Protocol; or the Global Environment Facility (Agreement Establishing the Global Environmental Facility, 33 ILM 1273 (1994)). See also Art. 10A Montreal Protocol, n 4; Art. 18 of the Convention on Biological Diversity (CBD), 31 ILM 818 (1992); Arts 6(e) and 16–18 of the Convention to Combat Desertification, 33 ILM 1016 (1994).

[23] See, eg, Art. 11 UNFCCC, n 4; Art. 11 Kyoto Protocol, n 6.

[24] See, eg, Art. 10(9) Montreal Protocol, n 4; or the Adaptation Fund of the Kyoto Protocol where a portion of the certified emission reduction units granted under the clean development mechanism is set aside as a contribution to the Adaptation Fund (Decision 10/CP.7, *Funding under the Kyoto Protocol*, FCCC/CP/2001/13/Add.1, 10 November 2001, para. 2).

[25] See R.E. Benedick, *Ozone Diplomacy. New Directions in Safeguarding the Planet* (Cambridge, MA: Harvard University Press, 1998), 241. See also Art. 5(5), Montreal Protocol, n 4; Art. 20(4) CBD, n 22; Arts 3(1) and 4(7) UNFCCC, n 4; and Art. 13(4) of the Convention on Persistent Organic Pollutants, 22 May 2001 (POP Convention), 40 ILM 532 (2001).

been introduced with the adoption of the Kyoto Protocol to the UN Framework Convention on Climate Change (UNFCCC). Articles 4 (bubble), 6 (joint implementation), 12 (clean development mechanism), and 17 (emissions trading) all provide for mechanisms to make compliance with the emission reduction commitments undertaken by Annex I countries more cost-effective. Still another mechanism currently under negotiation is the so-called 'REDD-plus' mechanism (REDD-plus stands for Reducing Emissions from Deforestation, Degradation and Forest Enhancement). The basic idea of this mechanism is to channel funds to developing countries in order for them to conserve their forests, which are extremely valuable resources not only for biodiversity purposes but also for the capture and storage of carbon dioxide. The underlying rationale is that conserving forests in developing countries would be an effective and much cheaper way to reduce global emissions of carbon dioxide as compared with other approaches, such as technological changes in the way energy is produced or in the transportation sector. There are, however, a number of problems with the use of flexibility mechanisms to the extent that they may create perverse incentives to increase emissions precisely in order to receive the resources devoted to emission reduction mechanisms. This issue has arisen, for instance, in the context of certain projects under the clean development mechanism of Article 12 of the Kyoto Protocol in connection with the elimination of a very powerful greenhouse gas known as HFC23, which is created as a by-product of the production of an ozone-depleting gas, HFC22, still in the process of being phased out.[26] Similarly, it has been noted that the implementation of a REDD-plus mechanisms would create a much higher supply of emission rights, which would produce a decrease in the price of such rights. This, in turn, would send the wrong signal to markets, as companies and states would be incited simply to purchase emission rights to meet their obligations instead of adopting long-term technological strategies.

## (C) Managing non-compliance

In case the preceding mechanisms prove insufficient to ensure compliance, multilateral environmental agreements often contain additional procedures to manage instances of non-compliance. NCPs span almost the entire compliance process, from the initial efforts to gather information, to providing assistance to facilitate compliance, to the management of situations of non-compliance, either through facilitative or adversarial methods.[27] NCPs can be characterized by reference to four main aspects of their establishment and operation, namely their legal basis, the ways in which the procedure can be triggered, their structure, and the measures that they can adopt.

---

[26] M. Wara, 'Measuring the Clean Development Mechanisms's Performance and Potential', 55 UCLA L Rev (2008)1759.
[27] On NCPs in general, see Treves, n 19.

Regarding the legal basis of NCPs, most often they are created by the COP to a given multilateral environmental agreement acting pursuant to a delegation clause contained in the treaty.[28] NCPs have also been adopted in the context of older environmental agreements, which did not contain a delegation clause, on the basis of the implicit competences of the COP under the agreement.[29] The legal basis of the NCP may be important to determine the binding nature of the outcomes of the procedure. This point has been controversial, for instance in connection with the decisions adopted by the body in charge of the NCP set up pursuant to Article 18 of the Kyoto Protocol. According to this Article: 'Any procedures and mechanisms under this Article entailing binding consequences shall be adopted by means of an amendment to this Protocol.' Effectively, this provision makes ratification (acceptance) a requirement for an NCP to be authorized to adopt binding decisions. However, this procedure has not been followed in the setting up of the NCP of the Kyoto Protocol, which would suggest that any decisions reached by the body in charge of the NCP would not be binding. The limited practice of this NCP so far does not allow reaching any practical conclusion on how things will evolve, although at least in one case (Greece) the decision of the enforcement branch of the NCP was complied with.[30]

The second feature characterizing NCPs is the way in which the procedure can be triggered. In most cases, NCPs can be triggered both by the state which is in a situation of non-compliance (a feature that stresses the non-adversarial nature of NCPs)[31] and by other state parties (either all other state parties[32] or only those state parties which can show a specific interest[33]). In some cases, NCPs can also be triggered by a body set up by the treaty, especially the Secretariat (either in connection with non-compliance of specific obligations (reporting[34]) or of most (unspecified)

---

[28]  Examples include Art. 8 Montreal Protocol, n 4; Art. 18 Kyoto Protocol, n 6; Art. 34 of the Cartagena Protocol on Biosafety to the Convention on Biological Diversity (Biosafety Protocol), 39 ILM 1027 (2000); Art. 17 POP Convention, n 25.

[29]  Examples include the NCPs adopted on the basis of the implied competence of the COP arising from Art. 15(5) of the Basel Convention, n 26, or from Art. 10(2) LRTAP Convention, n 4.

[30]  CC-2007–1-6/Greece/EB, 6 March 2008 (preliminary finding); CC-2007–1-8/Greece/EB, 17 April 2008 (final decision); CC-2007–1-10/Greece/EB, 7 October 2008 (decision on the review and assessment of the plan submitted under para. 2 of section XV); and CC-2007–1-13/Greece/EB, 13 November 2008 (decision under para. 2 of section X).

[31]  See, eg, Montreal Protocol NCP (*Decision IV/5 on Non-Compliance Procedure*, doc. UNEP/OzL.Pro4/15 (25 November 1992) at 13, and Annex IV, at 44; subsequently amended by *Decision X/10 on Review of the Non-Compliance Procedure*, doc. UNEP/OzL.Pro.10/9 (3 December 1998) at 23, and Annex II, at 47), para. 4; Basel Convention NCP (*Decision VI/12 on Establishment of a Mechanism for Promoting Implementation and Compliance*, Appendix, doc. UNEP/CHW.6/40 (10 February 2003) at 45), para. 9(a); Kyoto Protocol NCP (*Decision 27/CMP.1 on Procedures and Mechanisms Relating to Compliance under the Kyoto Protocol*, doc. FCCC/KP/CMP/2005/8/Add.3 (30 March 2006) at 92), section VI.1(a); Biosafety Protocol NCP (*Decision BS-I/7 on Establishment of Procedures and Mechanisms on Compliance under the Cartagena Protocol on Biosafety*, doc. UNEP/CBD/BS/COP-MOP/1/15 (27 February 2004), Annex I, at 98), section IV.1(a).

[32]  See, eg, Montreal Protocol NCP, n 31, para. 1; Kyoto Protocol NCP, n 31, section VI.1(b).

[33]  See, eg, Basel Convention NCP, n 31, para. 9(b); Biosafety Protocol NCP, n 31, section IV.1(b).

[34]  See, eg, Basel Convention NCP, n 31, para. 9(c).

obligations).[35] More rarely, the NCP can be triggered by a private party, such as an NGO.[36] This latter possibility could provide an interesting avenue to increase public pressure for states to comply with their obligations under an environmental agreement. However, as has happened in the human rights field, direct access by individuals may also have the undesirable consequence of politicizing or overburdening the bodies in charge of the NCP if adequate safeguards are not introduced.

The third feature of NCPs is their structure. In most cases, the management of the NCP is delegated to a subsidiary body created by the COP, the function of which may be either to make recommendations to be subsequently adopted (or not) by the COP[37] or, in some cases, to itself adopt decisions.[38] The composition of such a body varies from one case to another. Some bodies consist of representatives of state parties,[39] whereas others consist of independent experts appointed by the COP.[40] Moreover, according to the reach and sophistication of the NCP in question, procedures may involve a facilitative phase (focusing on providing assistance to the non-complying state) and an enforcement phase (focusing on imposing 'measures'—in fact, sanctions—to the non-complying state), sometimes managed by different 'branches' of the administrative body in charge of the NCP.[41] The more an NCP is structurally complex the better it seems to be adapted to manage the two main hypotheses of non-compliance, that is, involuntary and wilful non-compliance.

This latter point takes me to the fourth feature of NCPs, namely the types of measures that they can adopt in order to manage non-compliance. As already noted, NCPs may lead to the provision of financial/technical assistance,[42] but also to a number of more adversarial consequences, including the issuance of warnings, requests for the submission of information or plans, declarations of non-compliance, suspension of the advantages granted by the treaty in question, and even sanctions, such as penalties or trade bans.[43] The differing adversarial character of

---

[35] See, eg, Montreal Protocol NCP, n 31, para. 3.

[36] See, eg, Alpine Convention NCP (*Decision VII/4 Mécanisme de vérification du respect de la Convention alpine et de ses protocoles d'application* (Seventh Alpine Conference, 2002), reprinted in 33 Environmental L & Pol'y (2003) 179), para. 2; Aarhus Convention NCP (*Decision I/7 on Review of Compliance*, doc. ECE/MP.PP/2/Add.8 (2002)), para. 18.

[37] Montreal Protocol NCP (1998), n 31, paras 7(f), 9, 13, and 14.

[38] Kyoto Protocol NCP, n 31, sections II.8–9, VIII.7, IX.9. In the context of CITES, both the body in charge of the NCP—the Standing Committee—and the COP can adopt decisions. See Art. XIII(3) CITES, n 19; CITES NCP (*Resolution Conf. 14.3*, Fourteenth Meeting of the COP (June 2007) Annex), 46 ILM 1178 (2007), paras 11, 12(d), and 30.

[39] Montreal Protocol NCP (1998), n 31, para. 5.

[40] Kyoto Protocol NCP, n 31, section V.1–3.

[41] Ibid, section IV (Facilitative Branch) and section V (Enforcement Branch).

[42] Basel Convention NCP, n 31, para. 20(a); CITES NCP, n 38, para. 30(a) and (d); Kyoto Protocol NCP, n 31, section XIV.

[43] For the issuance of warnings, see Montreal Protocol NCP (1998), n 31, para. 2; Basel Convention NCP, n 31, para. 20(b); CITES NCP, n 38, para. 29(c) and (g); Biosafety Protocol NCP, n 31, section VI.2(b); Aarhus Convention NCP, n 36, section XII.37(f). For the request of further submissions of information, see Montreal Protocol NCP (1998), paras 3 and 5(c); Basel Convention NCP, para. 22(a); CITES NCP, para. 29(b); Biosafety NCP, section VI.1(d); Kyoto Protocol NCP, n 31, section IX.3; Aarhus Convention NCP, section VII.25(a). For declarations of non-compliance, see Montreal Protocol NCP, para. 9; Kyoto Protocol NCP, section IX.4(a) and (7), and section

these measures provides considerable room for the bodies in charge of NCPs to graduate their response according to the type of non-compliance situation that they have to manage.

## 5. Enhancing compliance: four recommendations

The foregoing observations suggest that, whereas a number of innovative mechanisms have been developed to ensure compliance with international environmental standards, there are still several avenues that could be explored in order to enhance the performance of some of these mechanisms as well as of the more traditional methods of enforcement of international law. In what follows, I would like to summarize what I see as the four main and most realistic avenues that should be considered in this regard.

First, the monitoring powers of the bodies set up by multilateral environmental agreements should be expanded to include, to all the extent possible, the ability of these bodies to verify the information submitted by states, to request additional information, to gather their own information, to assess compliance and, when necessary, to adopt binding measures to manage compliance. One interesting approach to provide these bodies with an additional flow of information would be to increase their openness to civil society groups, particularly by amending the provisions relating to the triggering of procedures. Also, bodies in charge of NCPs should consist of independent experts appointed by the state parties rather than of state representatives. Their structure and potential outcomes should match the types of non-compliance situation that are most likely to arise in practice. This is particularly important taking into account that some types of non-compliance situation are best addressed in a non-adversarial manner, by the provision of technical and financial assistance.

Secondly, the scope and modalities of technical and financial assistance should be significantly revisited. The provision of public funds by industrialized states remains very important both as 'initial' resources and as a display of genuine commitment, and should be made less dependent on voluntary contributions, which are too subject to changes of governments and/or priorities. However, it should also be understood that in order for environmental finance to reach the scale required by the daunting environmental challenges now facing the international community, a major role will have to be played by the private sector. The private sector should in turn be incentivized to take part in the global protection of the environment, not merely as a sign of 'good citizenship' (which was the essence of corporate social responsibility efforts) but also, and mainly, for economic reasons. Schemes for the channelling of private funds towards environmental projects (eg the clean development mechanism, the joint implementation mechanism, REDD-

XV.1(a); CITES NCP, para. 29(g); Aarhus Convention NCP, section XII.37(e). For suspension of advantages and sanctions, see Aarhus Convention NCP, section XII.37(g); CITES NCP, paras 30 and 34; Kyoto Protocol NCP, section XV.5.

plus, benefit-sharing agreements for the exploitation of genetic resources, etc.), despite the difficulties relating to their implementation, should be maintained and adjusted to enhance their operation. More generally, domestic and foreign investment in environmental opportunities should be encouraged through a variety of means, ranging from environmental taxes, cap-and-trade systems, insurance schemes, and reasonable foreign investment protection.

Thirdly, at a less operational level, it appears important to clarify the basic legal principles that currently characterize the respective contribution of developed and developing states to the protection of the environment. Whereas the concept of sustainable development or the principle of common but differentiated responsibilities were important tools in the quest for integrating as many countries as possible in the efforts to protect the environment, the very vagueness of these tools that facilitated consensus may undermine the operation of the environmental agreements thus adopted. In particular, it seems important to determine with some precision the relations between, on the one hand, the provision of financial and technical assistance and, on the other hand, the reporting as well as substantive obligations of the receivers of such assistance.

Fourthly, and relatedly, the fact that international environmental law is geared towards the prevention of environmental damage must not lead to the conclusion that adjudication mechanisms have no role to play in this context. As noted above, despite the absence of an international environmental court, the environmental dimensions of human activities are increasingly being taken into account by other specialized fora in the context of human rights, trade, investment, and other types of dispute. In this regard, it seems important that sufficient space is left by these 'borrowed fora' to integrate environmental considerations, by means such as the systemic integration rule codified in Article 31(3)(c) of the Vienna Convention on the Law of Treaties[44] or the introduction of environmental clauses in treaties focusing on other areas of international law.

Incorporating (some of) the preceding recommendations into international law may not always be politically feasible. It is, however, not unrealistic, as suggested by the fact that each one of them has already crystallized in one or more specific contexts. Compliance with international environmental standards is an incremental, slow, and patient process, and the mechanisms that seek to enhance this process should not misapprehend its nature.

---

[44] Vienna Convention on the Law of Treaties, 1155 UNTS 331, 8 ILM 679.

# PART IV

# WHAT LAW SHOULD BE CHANGED?

# (A) ENHANCING THE LAWFUL USE OF FORCE TO MEET MODERN CHALLENGES

# 28

# Operationalizing the UN Charter Rules on the Use of Force

*Philippe Sands*

## SUMMARY

More than six decades after the UN Charter was adopted it is difficult to see how the formulation of the Charter provisions on the use of force might usefully be altered. They are—on their merits—no more inadequate than those governing the prohibition of violence at the national level. There is little to be served in fine-tuning the language of Articles 2(4) and 51, and it is unlikely that states would easily reach agreement on a generalized meaning of 'imminent attack' legitimizing self-defence, a concept that will necessarily fall to be interpreted and applied by reference to the particular facts of a given situation. Utopian efforts must recognize that where vital interests are seen to be at stake no drafting exercise will be able to finesse away major differences, or impose real solutions. Instead, utopian efforts would do better to focus on the operationalization of the Charter rules, chiefly through: (i) domestic legal debate (in many countries around the world the interface between an unlawful use of force and the crime of aggression has begun to generate increased debate; greater public and political attention to legal considerations may be said to reflect the operationalization of Security Council resolutions and the relevant international rules in a domestic political context); (ii) international judicial consideration (the rules governing the use of force as well as the consequences of their violation have been the subject of recent judicial consideration before various international instances, chiefly the International Court of Justice (ICJ) but also an Arbitral Court established under the 1982 Law of the Sea Convention); and (iii) international legislative efforts, such as the definition of the crime of aggression agreed upon in 2010 by the Assembly of the States Parties to the Rome Statute.

## 1. The UN Charter restraints on the use of force

In September 2010, the respected American commentator Jeffrey Goldberg imagined different scenarios responding to the prospect of a nuclearized Iran.[1] The most likely option, he suggested, was that Israel would use military force to prevent the threat from actually materializing. A far-fetched scenario? Perhaps not. Leaked diplomatic cables have indicated that King Abdullah of Saudi Arabia had repeatedly urged the United States to attack Iran to destroy its nuclear programme.[2] When Tony Blair gave evidence to Britain's Chilcot Inquiry on the Iraq war, he made much of Iran's actions, stating that Iran presented 'very similar issues to [Iraq], which is why learning the lessons of this is so important'.[3]

Some six decades after the adoption of the UN Charter's new rules governing the use of force, this scenario raises familiar issues: are the existing international rules governing the use of force adequate to address the challenges posed by new technologies and new actors? Does international law permit force to prevent a state from manufacturing a nuclear weapon, assuming such actions to be in violation of obligations under the 1968 Treaty on the Non-Proliferation of Nuclear Weapons?

These and other questions relate to the *jus ad bellum*, the circumstances in which military force may be used, and this chapter addresses some recent lessons of Iraq and the challenges of Iran for the existing system of rules.[4]

Until the last century, there were no generally applicable rules of international law that prohibited the use of force by one state against another. The 1919 Covenant of the League of Nations made a start but fell short of outlawing war. In 1928, renunciation of war as 'an instrument of national policy' was taken a step further by the Kellogg–Briand Pact, committing signatories to renounce war as between themselves. The Second World War re-ignited idealist—if not utopian—spirits. In August 1941, Franklin Roosevelt and Winston Churchill agreed an Atlantic Charter, expressing a belief 'that all of the nations of the world, for realistic as well as spiritual reasons must come to the abandonment of the use of force'.[5] The aspiration featured as a central part of the Charter of the United Nations, adopted in San Francisco in April 1945, when some 50 states acted to outlaw the use of force, except under the most limited of conditions. Article 2(4) of the Charter articulates a rule of general application:

---

[1] J. Goldberg, 'The Point of No Return', available at <http://www.theatlantic.com/magazine/archive/1969/12/the-point-of-no-return/8186/>.

[2] I. Black and S. Tisdall, 'Saudi Arabia urges US attack on Iran to stop nuclear programme', *The Guardian*, 28 November 2010, available at <http://www.guardian.co.uk/world/2010/nov/28/us-embassy-cables-saudis-iran>.

[3] Tony Blair, evidence before the Chilcot Inquiry, 29 January 2010, transcript, p 55 (also p 29), available at <http://www.iraqinquiry.org.uk/transcripts/oralevidence-bydate/100129.aspx>. See also T. Blair, *A Journey* (London: Random House, 2010), 674.

[4] On the use of force in relation to Iraq see P. Sands, *Lawless World* (London: Penguin, 2006), chs 8 and 12. This chapter focuses largely on the particular experience of the United Kingdom, recognizing that while each national jurisdiction's appreciation of the issues will turn on its own legal, political, and cultural situation, there are nevertheless broader conclusions that may be drawn.

[5] The Atlantic Charter, Common Principle No. 8 (14 August 1941).

All Members shall refrain in their international relations from the threat or use of force against the territorial integrity or political independence of any state, or in any other manner inconsistent with the Purposes of the United Nations.

Putting to one side the possibility of using force to protect human rights (addressed in the following chapter by Christian Tams),[6] this general rule is subject to two established exceptions. A first exception is where force is authorized by the UN Security Council, acting under Chapter VII of the UN Charter: Article 42 allows the Security Council to authorize force 'to maintain or restore international peace and security'. For nearly 50 years, until 1990, the Cold War prevented the Security Council from exercising its Article 42 powers. With the collapse of the Soviet bloc, a newly invigorated Security Council emerged. In November 1990 the Council acted for the first time to authorize force under Chapter VII, in response to Iraq's unlawful invasion of Kuwait.[7] Resolution 678 authorized member states 'to use all necessary means' to uphold and implement previous Security Council resolutions and to restore peace and security in the area.[8] Since then, Chapter VII powers have been relied upon quite regularly to authorize different measures, for example in relation to Somalia, the Balkans, Liberia, Sierra Leone, Haiti, and East Timor. In March 2003 the United States and United Kingdom led a small coalition arguing that Resolution 678 had 'revived' so as to justify renewed force against Iraq.

The second exception is self-defence: Article 51 of the UN Charter affirms that nothing in the Charter 'shall impair the inherent right of individual or collective self-defence if an armed attack occurs against a member of the United Nations'. The right is not open-ended, existing only until such time as the UN Security Council 'has taken measures necessary to maintain international peace and security'. And the carefully crafted compromise language of Article 51 is not free from ambiguity: more than six decades of practice and case law and countless volumes and essays of academic commentary confirm that Article 51 raises a great number of questions. Can self-defence be invoked *before* an armed attack has taken place? If there is a right of 'anticipatory self-defence', as it has been called, can it be invoked where another state acquires—or is in the process of acquiring—weapons of mass destruction?[9] Since the events of 11 September 2001, the issue of anticipatory defence has become even more pressing, as President Bush's 2002 National Security Strategy committed the United States to act *pre-emptively* to forestall or prevent hostile acts.[10] In March 2004, British Prime Minister Tony Blair seemed to give some support to this, affirming the existence of a 'duty and a

---

[6] See C. Tams, Chapter 29, 'Prospects for Humanitarian Uses of Force'.

[7] In 1966, Art. 42 had provided the basis for the Security Council's authorization for Britain to use force against tankers discharging oil from Rhodesia.

[8] Resolution 678 does not mention Art. 42, which has led to different views as to whether that provision was indeed the legal basis on which force was authorized. Although that seems to be the more compelling view, there is some academic support for the view that the Council was acting on the basis of Arts 42 and 51 of the Charter: see B. Simma, *The Charter of the United Nations: A Commentary*, 1st edn (London: Routledge & Kegan Paul, 1995), 635.

[9] See Sands, n 4.

[10] United States, 'The National Security Strategy' (September 2002), at 15, available at <http://georgewbush-whitehouse.archives.gov/nsc/nss/2002/>.

right to prevent the threat materialising' of the proliferation or illegal acquisition of WMD.[11] The Bush doctrine—and Mr Blair's support for it—remain live issues in the face of the 'nuclearization' of Iran, even if the self-defence justification was not invoked in relation to Iraq and President Obama's May 2010 National Security Strategy adopts a different language and tone.[12]

## 2. Avoiding the constraints of Article 2(4) of the UN Charter: the 2003 Iraq war and the British experience

The 2003 Iraq war confirmed the currency of the UN Charter's rules on the use of force. While the events demonstrated that international law cannot prevent military force when powerful states are committed to its use, it is a striking feature of the early twenty-first century that when states do use force they feel bound to seek to find a justification in law. The legality of the Iraq war was—and remains—a live political issue, in Britain and many other countries. Public concerns at the time caused the British government to make an unprecedented parliamentary statement on 17 March 2003, by then Attorney General Lord Goldsmith, devoted to the issue of legality and asserting that force against Iraq was unambiguously lawful. This was said to be on the ground that force had been authorized by the Security Council.

What was not known at the time—in Parliament, in Cabinet, or by the public—was that just ten days earlier, on 7 March 2003, Lord Goldsmith had written a secret memorandum to the Prime Minister, and that it contained a rather different message. I learnt about the memorandum while researching my book *Lawless World*, which also revealed the details of the resignation letter of Foreign and Commonwealth Office deputy legal adviser Elizabeth Wilmshurst, noting that Lord Goldsmith had changed his mind 'again'. Ms Wilmshurst wrote that she could not

in conscience go along with advice…which asserts the legitimacy of military action without such a resolution, particularly since an unlawful use of force on such a scale amounts to the crime of aggression…in circumstances which are so detrimental to the international order and the rule of law.[13]

Lord Goldsmith's secret memorandum was published by Mr Blair in April 2005, making clear the gulf between the private advice of 7 March 2003 and the public statement of 17 March 2003. It underscored the fact that the Prime Minister was not accurate when he said that the Attorney General had given 'clear' advice, and had been 'consistent' in his approach. The lack of candour, which was emphasized by Ms Wilmshurst's resignation letter, fuelled speculation as to what happened between

---

[11] Tony Blair, Speech in Sedgefield, *The Guardian*, 5 March 2004, available at <http://www.guardian.co.uk/politics/2004/mar/05/iraq.iraq>.
[12] See <http://www.whitehouse.gov/sites/default/files/rss…/national_security_strategy.pdf>.
[13] See <http://news.bbc.co.uk/1/hi/4377605.stm>.

7 and 17 March 2003, and also what occurred in the period before 7 March 2003. The issue of the legality of the use of force had given rise to considerable internal debate.

After years of prevarication, in June 2009 Prime Minister Gordon Brown announced an inquiry, to coincide with the departure of British troops from Iraq. It would be chaired by a retired senior civil servant, Sir John Chilcot and would work behind closed doors. Sir John summarized the inquiry's mandate as considering 'the UK's involvement in Iraq, including the way decisions were made and actions taken, to establish, as accurately as possible, what happened and to identify the lessons that can be learned'. Issues of law and legality have been at the heart of the Inquiry, although the five-member panel includes no lawyers. A combination of a sceptical public, media interest, and political pressures have combined to force greater openness. Curiouser and curiouser, the issue of legality—in particular, the interpretation of Resolution 1441 and the question of Security Council 'authorization'—continue to attract considerable interest.

It is now clear that the 337 words of the parliamentary statement were nothing more than an advocacy document for which Lord Goldsmith required the assistance of no fewer than nine lawyers and senior civil servants. The statement had the great merit of reductionist simplicity: it claimed that Security Council Resolution 678 authorized the 1990 Iraq intervention and was 'revived' as a result of Saddam's 'material breach' of the terms of the subsequent ceasefire. At the heart of the argument is Resolution 1441, adopted unanimously by the Security Council in November 2002. According to Lord Goldsmith, Resolution 1441 gave Iraq 'a final opportunity to comply with its disarmament obligations' and determined that a failure to so comply and cooperate would constitute a further material breach of those obligations. 'It is plain,' wrote Lord Goldsmith, 'that Iraq has failed so to comply', thus giving rise to a material breach and the revival of the original authority to use force. But plain to whom? For Lord Goldsmith's short parliamentary statement skated over the crucial question: who decides whether Iraq is in material breach, is it the Security Council or can one or more individual members such as the United States or the United Kingdom so decide? It has been virtually impossible to find any seasoned international lawyer in Britain who agrees with Lord Goldsmith's parliamentary statement to the effect that the Security Council did not have to make this decision in the form of a new resolution or by other means. It is now clear that, until shortly before he put his name to the 337-word statement, he did not agree with it either.

Well before the Chilcot Inquiry, it was known that the Attorney General had changed his mind just days before the war.[14] His 7 March 2003 secret advice concluded that although a 'revival' argument could be made, it would probably not be successful if it were to reach a court of law. He seems to have recognized that the better view was that the war was unlawful. The 7 March 2003 memo was never put before the Cabinet, which, like Parliament, had no inkling about the Attorney General's serious doubts. The Inquiry has teased out that it was Foreign Secretary

---

[14] See *Lawless World*, n 4, at ch. 8.

Jack Straw who talked Goldsmith out of sharing his doubts with the Cabinet.[15] Nor was the Cabinet aware of the decisive role played by senior Bush Administration lawyers in contributing to Lord Goldsmith's change of mind. 'We had trouble with your attorney,' the legal adviser to Condoleezza Rice—John Bellinger—later told a visiting British official, 'we got him there eventually'.[16] Nor did the Cabinet learn of the terms of the resignation letter of the deputy legal adviser at the Foreign Office, Elizabeth Wilmshurst, that referred to Lord Goldsmith's late change of mind without revealing details.

Lawyers—even international lawyers—are entitled to change their minds, and frequently do. New facts emerge, or new legal arguments come to the fore. Between 7 and 17 March 2003, there were, however, no new facts and no new legal arguments on which Lord Goldsmith could rely. In the intervening seven years, no convincing explanation has been provided to rebut the inference that the Attorney General succumbed to political pressures. Lord Goldsmith's appearance before the Chilcot Inquiry on 27 January 2010 did not dispel the doubts. He reiterated the claim that the change was largely due to the persuasive arguments of senior Bush Administration lawyers, with whom he had met in early February 2003. These are many of the same lawyers who failed to prevent the Bush Administration's descent into serial illegalities during 2001 and 2002, ditching the Geneva Conventions, imprisoning suspects at Guantánamo without granting them minimum rights, and embracing waterboarding and other acts of obvious torture. Tantalizingly, during Lord Goldsmith's appearance, new information did emerge about the views he had expressed in writing *before* 7 March 2003, suggesting that the Inquiry had before it other documents that were not publicly available.

Then, in May 2010 Labour lost the general election and a new government came into office. A few weeks later came a decision to declassify documents for which the Inquiry, as the Cabinet secretary put it, had waited for 'some time'.[17] On 25 June 2010 the Inquiry quietly published a set of documents that laid bare the clear and consistent legal advice that Lord Goldsmith had provided from July 2002 up to 12 February 2003. The documents show law in action and the active engagement of the Attorney General on issues more usually associated with a law school seminar, but they also paint a picture that emphasizes the Attorney General's sudden, late, and total change of direction. Following a year of consistent advice, he made a 180-degree turn in the space of a month.

The paper trail is an unhappy one. On *30 July 2002*, Lord Goldsmith wrote to the Prime Minister that self-defence and humanitarian intervention were not admissible, and that military action without explicit Security Council authorization

---

[15] S. McDonald, 'Iraq: Meeting with the Attorney General' (17 March 2003), available at <http://www.iraqinquiry.org.uk/media/43523/doc_2010_01_26_11_06_14_637.pdf>.

[16] *Lawless World*, n 4, at p x.

[17] Gus O'Donnell, Letter to Sir John Chilcot regarding declassification of draft legal advice (25 June 2010), available at <http://www.iraqinquiry.org.uk/media/46469/ODonnell-to-Chilcot-re-declassification-250610.pdf>.

would be 'highly debatable'.[18] On *18 October 2002*, he told Foreign Secretary Jack Straw that the draft of Security Council Resolution 1441 'did not provide legal authorization for the use of force', and that the British government must not 'promise the US government that it can do things which the Attorney considers to be unlawful'.[19] On *11 November 2002*, immediately after Resolution 1441 was adopted, he told Jonathan Powell (Blair's chief of staff) that 'he was not at all optimistic' that there would be 'a sound legal basis for the use of force against Iraq'.[20] At a Downing Street meeting on *19 December 2002*, Goldsmith declined to tell those present that they would have a green light for war without a further resolution.[21] On *14 January 2003*, he wrote a draft memo that concluded without ambiguity that 'resolution 1441 does not revive the authorisation to use of force contained in resolution 678 in the absence of a further decision of the Security Council'.[22] These words contradict what he would later tell the Cabinet and Parliament.

Which brings us to Lord Goldsmith's 30 January 2003, one-page memo to Mr Blair, written the day before a vital meeting with President Bush at the White House. Lord Goldsmith told the Prime Minister that he wished to explain where he stood on the question of whether a further decision of the Security Council was legally required in order to authorize the use of force against Iraq. His conclusion? 'I remain of the view,' he wrote, 'that the correct legal interpretation of resolution 1441 is that it does not authorise the use of military force without a further determination by the Security Council.' The advice is clear, unambiguous, and without caveat. The published version of the document includes the handwritten reactions of three key players.

In the top left-hand corner, Sir David Manning, Blair's principal foreign policy adviser, notes: 'Clear advice from Attorney on need for further Resolution.' Alongside, Matthew Rycroft, who served as Blair's private secretary, sounds an irritated note: 'Specifically said we did not need further advice this week' (appearing to confirm that Blair did not want a paper trail of early, unhelpful advice). And on the left-hand side of the document, alongside Lord Goldsmith's unhelpful conclusion is to be found this comment: 'I just don't understand this.' The handwriting is Blair's, and it is difficult to see quite what he might have had trouble understanding. Lord Goldsmith's words—consistent with the views expressed since March

---

[18] Lord Goldsmith, Letter to Prime Minister Tony Blair regarding Iraq (30 July 2002), p 3 at 13, available at <http://www.iraqinquiry.org.uk/media/46499/Goldsmith-note-to-PM-30July2002.pdf>.

[19] David Brummel, Record of Attorney General's conversation with the Foreign Secretary on 18 October (11 November 2002), 1, at 4, available at <http://www.iraqinquiry.org.uk/media/46478/AGO-note-of-Goldsmith-Straw-telecon-18October2002.pdf>.

[20] David Brummel, Note of telephone conversation between the Attorney General and Jonathan Powell on 11 November 2002 (11 November 2002), 1, at 2, available at <http://www.iraqinquiry.org.uk/media/46475/AGO-note-of-Goldsmith-Powell-telecon-11November2002.pdf>.

[21] See David Brummel, Note of meeting at No. 10 Downing Street on 19 December 2002 (19 December 2002), available at <http://www.iraqinquiry.org.uk/media/46472/AGO-note-of-Goldsmith-No10-meeting-19December2002.pdf>.

[22] Lord Goldsmith, Draft legal advice to Prime Minister Tony Blair regarding the interpretation of resolution 1441 (14 January 2003), 5, at 13, available at <http://www.iraqinquiry.org.uk/media/46493/Goldsmith-draft-advice-14January2003.pdf>.

2002—admit of no doubt, adopting the views taken by the United Kingdom since 1990 by the Foreign Office legal advisers, and by virtually every international lawyer in Britain (if not the world, outside the United States).

Blair seems to be saying that he does not understand why this wretchedly unhelpful view was put in writing at that critical moment. The timing could not have been worse. The next day, on 31 January 2003, Blair met Bush, accompanied by Manning and Rycroft. Manning prepared a widely reported five-page note of the meeting that is before the Chilcot Inquiry but has not yet been made public in full.[23] Sir David records the President telling Blair that the United States would put its full weight behind efforts to get another Security Council resolution but if that failed, 'military action would follow anyway'; that the 'start date for the military campaign was now pencilled in for 10 March', which was 'when the bombing would begin'; and that the 'diplomatic strategy had to be arranged around the military planning'. Sir David then sets out Blair's response, noting that he was 'solidly' with the President and ready to do whatever it took to disarm Saddam. He wants a second resolution 'if we could possibly get one', because it would make it much easier politically to deal with Saddam, and to provide an insurance policy 'against the unexpected'. It seems that the Prime Minister has completely ignored the previous day's memo from the Attorney General, advising him that a further resolution is necessary to act lawfully, not merely desirable.

The Chilcot Inquiry has already popped the utopian bubble that is sometimes associated with Britain's famed system of governmental decision-making. The issue is not the adequacy or appropriateness of the rules being applied, but rather their interpretation and application. Given its composition, the Chilcot Inquiry has no particular authority to express any view on the lawfulness of the war (in January 2010, a parallel Dutch inquiry chaired by a retired Supreme Court judge and largely composed of lawyers concluded that the war was illegal, contributing to the downfall of the Dutch government).[24] Yet in the court of public opinion it seems that minds have already been made up. The general view seems to be that the rules are clear, and that they were clearly violated. This view has been set out with particular clarity and force by Lord Alexander of Weedon (the former Chairman of the Bar Council), in the Justice/Tom Sargant Annual Memorial Lecture (2003), and by Lord Bingham (the former Senior Law Lord) in his book *The Rule of Law*.[25]

This was reflected in July 2010 when Deputy Prime Minister Nick Clegg, standing in for Prime Minister David Cameron in Parliament, described the Iraq war as 'illegal'[26] (he subsequently repeated that view in September 2010 in a speech

---

[23] D. van Natta, 'Bush Was Set on Path to War, British Memo Says', *New York Times*, 27 March 2006, available at <http://www.nytimes.com/2006/03/27/international/europe/27memo.html>.

[24] *Rapport Commissie Van Onderzoek Besluitvorming Irak*, January 2010 (summary and Conclusions in English at pp 519ff). See also A. Hirsch, 'Iraq Invasion Violated International Law, Dutch Inquiry Finds', *The Guardian*, 12 January 2010, available at <http://www.guardian.co.uk/world/2010/jan/12/iraq-invasion-violated-interational-law-dutch-inquiry-finds>.

[25] T. Bingham, *The Rule of Law* (London: Penguin, 2010), 120–9.

[26] Nick Clegg, Address before the House of Commons on 21 July 2010 (21 July 2010), col. 346, available at <http://www.publications.parliament.uk/pa/cm201011/cmhansrd/cm100721/debtext/100721-0001.htm#10072126001991>.

to the UN General Assembly).[27] When asked for clarification about whether this was now British government policy, the British Government's official spokesman conspicuously failed to back Blair and Goldsmith and to defend the war as lawful, indicating instead that the new government would prefer to await the outcome of the Chilcot Inquiry.[28] A spokesman for the Inquiry was then reported as saying that Sir John would not make a conclusion on whether the war was legal.[29] That provides a telling confirmation that the adequacy of the rules is not in issue. There is no challenge to the general rule reflected in Article 2(4) of the UN Charter, or the exception provided by Security Council authorization. While there may be an issue as to the interpretation of Resolution 1441, there is no claim that the rules have, in this regard at least, been shown to be inadequate.

## 3. Anticipatory self-defence and the notion of 'imminent attack'

Iraq has emphasized the significance of processes of governmental decision-making, including in relation to the preparation, use, and presentation of intelligence material and of legal advice. Those issues will be even more acute on the self-defence exception under Article 51 of the UN Charter, and in particular with regard to claims of 'anticipatory self-defence' or pre-emption of the kind envisaged by the Bush Administration's US National Security Strategy of 2002.[30] The possibility that terrorist organizations or rogue states might obtain WMD has concentrated minds on the circumstances under which a state may be entitled to use force in anticipation of an actual armed attack, where it is determined that an imminent threat exists. There is no real dispute as to the existence of a right of anticipatory self-defence in international law, or that it may be invoked against non-state actors.[31] Professor Thomas Franck has, however, emphasized the challenge:

---

[27] See Nick Clegg, Speech to the UN General Assembly (24 September 2010), available at <http://www.number10.gov.uk/news/speeches-and-transcripts/2010/09/deputy-pms-speech-to-the-un-general-assembly-55287>.

[28] See UK Government, Press briefing of 21 July 2010 (21 July 2010), available at <http://www.number10.gov.uk/news/press-briefings/2010/07/afternoon-press-briefing-from-21-july-2010–53769>.

[29] See Iraq Inquiry Committee discussion of the inquiry's outcome, indicating it 'is not a court of law'. Iraq Inquiry Committee, 'Frequently Asked Questions', available at <http://www.iraqinquiry.org.uk/faq.aspx>.

[30] 2002 US National Security Strategy, p 15. This stated that:

> The greater the threat, the greater is the risk of inaction—and the more compelling the case for taking anticipatory action to defend ourselves, even if uncertainty remains as to the time and place of the enemy's attack. To forestall or prevent such hostile acts by our adversaries, the United States will, if necessary, act pre-emptively.... in an age where the enemies of civilisation openly and actively seek the world's most destructive technologies, the United States cannot remain idle while dangers gather.

[31] See SC Res. 1368 of 12 September 2001, recognizing the inherent right of individual or collective self-defence in relation to acts of terrorism that threaten international peace and security.

The problem with recourse to anticipatory self-defence is its ambiguity. In the right circumstances, it can be a prescient measure that, at low cost, extinguishes the fuse of a powder keg. In the wrong circumstances, it can cause the very calamity it anticipates.[32]

In what circumstances might a threat be said to be imminent? Does it encompass threats which have not yet materialized but which might materialize at some time in the future? These are live issues. It is noteworthy that in the United Kingdom there is a broad agreement as to the basic principles, even among those who may not have agreed on Iraq. In October 2002, Professor (now Judge) Christopher Greenwood told the House of Commons Select Committee on Foreign Affairs that 'so far as talk of a doctrine of "pre-emption" is intended to refer to a broader right to respond to threats which might materialise some time in the future, I believe that such a doctrine has no basis in law'.[33] In April 2004, in the House of Lords, then Attorney General Lord Goldsmith was asked whether the Government accepted the legitimacy of pre-emptive armed attack under Article 51. He responded that it was 'the Government's view that international law permits the use of force in self-defence against an imminent attack but does not authorise the use of force to mount a pre-emptive strike against a threat that is more remote'.[34] He recognized—rightly in my view—that these rules had to be applied in the context of the particular facts of each case, so that the 'concept of what constitutes an "imminent" armed attack will develop to meet new circumstances and new threats', and 'that states are able to act in self-defence in circumstances where there is evidence of further imminent attacks by terrorist groups, even if there is no specific evidence of where such an attack will take place or of the precise nature of the attack'. Even here, military action had to be a last resort, and the force used proportionate to the threat faced and limited to what is necessary to deal with the threat. The key issue is whether an attack is 'imminent'. In the *Caroline* incident in 1837 the US Secretary of State famously set out the circumstances of a 'necessity of self-defence, instant, overwhelming, leaving no choice of means and no moment for deliberation'.

The concept of imminence is a flexible one, as it must be in an age in which technology allows massive devastation and great loss of life to be wrought in a very short period of time. 'Imminence' is determined by two key factors: capability and intent. There may be circumstances in which *capability* could, for example, include the acquisition (by a state or a terrorist organization or even an individual on behalf of a terrorist organization) of material or component parts to be used in the manufacture of WMD, and not possession of the finished product, all the more so where it is violation of an international obligation (such as that imposed by the Treaty on Non-Proliferation of Nuclear Weapons). Might possession of nuclear weapons or components thereof, as such, amount to threat of use in violation of Article 2(4) of the UN Charter? In 1995, in its Advisory Opinion on *Legality of the Use of Nuclear*

---

[32] T. Franck, *Recourse to Force: State Action against Threats and Armed Attacks* (Cambridge: Cambridge University Press, 2002), 107.

[33] Professor Christopher Greenwood, Memorandum on Legality of Using Force Against Iraq, 24 October 2002, at para. 24, available at <http://www.publications.parliament.uk/pa/cm200203/cmselect/cmfaff/196/2102406.htm>.

[34] Hansard, 21 April 2004, col. 370.

*Weapons*, in response to the argument put forward by some states that possession of nuclear weapons is itself an unlawful threat to use force, the majority did not exclude the possibility; the Court recognized that possession 'may indeed justify an inference of preparedness to use them'. However, the question of whether this amounted to a 'threat' that was contrary to Article 2(4) depended

upon whether the particular use of force envisaged would be directed against the territorial integrity or political independence of a state, or against the Purposes of the United Nations or whether, in the event that it were intended as a means of defence, it would necessarily violate the principles of necessity and proportionality. In any of these circumstances the use of force, and the threat to use it, would be unlawful under the law of the Charter.[35]

In the case of Iran, the determination of whether its possession of nuclear weapons 'would be directed against the territorial integrity or political independence' of Israel or of any other state, is essentially a question of fact. It turns, among other factors, on the nature of the weapon, the delivery mechanism, and an assessment of whether there is truly an intent to use it. In this context, it has to be said that Iran has not helped itself: repeated statements by its current President—to the effect that he would like to see Israel destroyed—provide support for those who seek to use military force to prevent a future threat from arising. Whether these words amount to a statement of intent, and if so whether they reflect an actual capacity on the part of that particular leader to actualize an order to use nuclear weapons, requires the most careful consideration, given the potentially catastrophic consequences of an erroneous assessment, either way.

## 4. Operationalizing the prohibition on the use of force: the consequences of non-compliance and the crime of aggression

More than six decades after the rules established in the UN Charter were established it is difficult to see how their formulation might usefully be altered. Without being starry-eyed about international law, the rules prohibiting the use of force are—on their merits—no more inadequate than those governing the prohibition of violence at the national level. There is little to be served in fine-tuning the language of Articles 2(4) and 51, and it is unlikely that states would easily reach agreement on a generalized meaning of 'imminence', a concept that will necessarily fall to be interpreted and applied by reference to the particular facts of a given situation. Utopian efforts must recognize that where vital interests are seen to be at stake no drafting exercise will be able to finesse away major differences, or impose real solutions. Over time the drafters of these well-established rules have shown themselves to be remarkably prescient. Instead, utopian efforts would do better to focus on the operationalization of the rules—including decision-making at national and international levels, including the Security Council—and on the consequences of non-compliance. Our hope must be that increasingly, over time the formulation of policy and the taking of decisions on such matters might be fixed around the

---

[35] ICJ, *Legality of the Threat or Use of Nuclear Weapons*, ICJ Reports 1996, 226, at para. 48.

law, and not—as appears to have been the case in London in the early months of 2003—the other way round.

There is ample evidence that—in some places at last—efforts to operationalize the rules are gaining ground. This may be seen in a number of developments, including domestic political debate as to the legality of the use of force in particular cases, judicial consideration of these issues, and legislative efforts at the international level.

## (A) Domestic political debate

In many countries around the world—but by no means all—the interface between an unlawful use of force and the crime of aggression has begun to generate increased attention and debate. This was highlighted by Elizabeth Wilmshurst's letter of resignation in relation to Iraq, and by a little noted paragraph at the end of Lord Goldsmith's opinion of 7 March 2003, drawing Tony Blair's attention to the fact that aggression is 'a crime under customary international law which automatically forms part of domestic law'. Since then, Lord Bingham and the Judicial Committee of the House of Lords have confirmed that 'the core elements of the crime of aggression have been understood, at least since 1945, with sufficient clarity to permit the lawful trial (and, on conviction, punishment) of those accused of this most serious crime'.[36]

The difficulties engendered by the 2003 war in Iraq have caused greater attention to be paid to the legal issues in Britain. This was illustrated in early 2011, when Britain supported and led efforts to use military force to protect civilians from attacks by Colonel Gaddafi's government. The debate as to what steps Britain should take, as a political matter, was accompanied by extensive consideration of the legality of possible responses: what did international law allow? Many calls supporting the use of force made it clear that such actions would require explicit Security Council authorization, in the absence of any right to exercise self-defence. The Security Council's initial reaction to the situation was to adopt Resolution 1970, on 26 February 2011: the resolution included travel bans and asset freezes, and referred the situation in Libya to the Prosecutor of the International Criminal Court (ICC). It also included an arms embargo to prevent the supply of arms 'to the Libyan Arab Jamahiriya', apparently embracing both sides of the conflict, as the Bosnian arms embargo had done with such catastrophic consequences in the early 1990s. Significantly, Resolution 1970 included a line in its preamble—'*Acting* under Chapter VII of the Charter of the United Nations, and taking measures under its Article 41'—that was inserted by Russia to avoid any possibility that Britain and the United States could claim that the Security Council had justified the use of military force. That line made clear that no use of force—even the

---

[36] *R v Jones*, Judgment of 29 March 2006 [2006] UKHL 16, per Lord Bingham, at para. 19 (the Law Lords concluded that in the absence of legislation establishing the crime of aggression into English law the customary obligation as such would not be actionable).

enforcement of a no-fly zone—had been authorized by the Security Council to prevent the commission of more crimes against humanity.

A few weeks later, on 17 March 2011, the Security Council followed up with Resolution 1973, that authorized UN members 'to take all necessary measures . . . to protect civilians and civilian populated areas under threat of attack' in Libya. The formulation gave rise to competing interpretations that were actively debated, by parliamentarians and in the media: did the resolution allow Colonel Gaddafi to be targeted? Could the UK provide arms to opposition forces? Against this background, the British government released a summary of the legal opinion prepared by the Attorney General, Dominic Grieve, to inform parliamentary debate and public opinion.[37] At the time of writing, there appears to be stronger support in the United Kingdom for the proposition that Britain's role should be tightly constrained by a narrow reading of what the relevant Security Council resolutions may or may not permit. There can be little doubt that such caution as exists is largely informed by the Iraq experience. Such greater public and political attention to legal considerations may be said to reflect the operationalization of Security Council resolutions and the relevant international rules in a domestic political context.

## (B) International judicial consideration

The rules governing the use of force—and the consequences of their violation—have also been the subject of recent judicial consideration before various international instances. In 2005, the ICJ gave a notable judgment that found Uganda responsible for having used force against the Democratic Republic of the Congo in such a manner as to occasion a 'grave violation of the prohibition of the use of force expressed in Article 2, paragraph 4, of the Charter'. There is nothing in the judgment to indicate that the Court considered the rules set forth in the UN Charter to pose any particular difficulties of application, or that they are somehow inadequate for current situations. Of particular interest, however, is the fact that the Court declined to characterize Uganda's actions as amounting to aggression.[38] In a Separate Opinion Judge Simma noted that

One deliberate omission characterizing the Judgment will strike any politically alert reader: it is the way in which the Court has avoided dealing with the explicit request of the DRC to find that Uganda, by its massive use of force against the Applicant has committed an act of aggression. . . . After all, Uganda invaded a part of the territory of the DRC of the size of Germany and kept it under its own control, or that of the various Congolese warlords it befriended, for several years, helping itself to the immense natural riches of these tormented regions. . . . If there ever was a military activity before the Court that deserves to be qualified as an act of aggression, it is the Ugandan invasion of the DRC . . . It is true that the United Nations Security Council, despite adopting a whole series of resolutions on the situation in the Great Lakes region (cf. paragraph 150 of the Judgment) has never gone

---

[37] P. Winter and O. Bowcott, 'Libya: The Legal Case for Deployment', *The Guardian*, 21 March 2011, available at <http://www.guardian.co.uk/world/2011/mar/21/libya-arab-and-middle-east-protests>.
[38] *Armed Activities on the Territory of the Congo (Democratic Republic of the Congo v Uganda)*, ICJ Reports 2005, 168, at para. 147.

as far as expressly qualifying the Ugandan invasion as an act of aggression, even though it must appear as a textbook example of the first one of the definitions of 'this most serious and dangerous form of the illegal use of force' laid down in General Assembly resolution 3314 (XXIX). The Council will have had its own—political—reasons for refraining from such a determination. But the Court, as the principal *judicial* organ of the United Nations, does not have to follow that course. Its very *raison d'être* is to arrive at decisions based on law and nothing but the law, keeping the political context of the cases before it in mind, of course, but not desisting from stating what is manifest out of regard for such non-legal considerations. This is the division of labour between the Court and the political organs of the United Nations envisaged by the Charter![39]

It is a matter of speculation as to why the Court desisted, as Judge Simma put it, 'from stating what is manifest out of regard for ... non-legal considerations'. Judge El Araby also put in a powerful Separate Opinion on the subject of aggression, noting its centrality to the Democratic Republic of the Congo's Application and 'the seriousness of the violation of the use of force in the present case and the broader importance of repressing aggression in international relations'. He concluded that he was

unable ... to appreciate any compelling reason for the Court to refrain from finding that Uganda's actions did indeed amount to aggression. The International Court of Justice has not been conceived as a penal court, yet its dicta have wide-ranging effects in the international community's quest to deter potential aggressors and to overcome the culture of impunity.[40]

The majority's silence was a reflection, perhaps, of the long shadow of Iraq: the hearings before the ICJ, and the Court's deliberations, took place against the backdrop of an Iraq war in which considerable attention was being given to issues of legality and criminality, and it seems unlikely that the consequences of characterizing Uganda's actions as amounting to aggression (with all that implied for the potential individual criminal responsibility of Uganda's political leaders) could have been far from the minds of the judges.

A couple of years later, the Charter's restraints on the use of force were addressed by a more unlikely tribunal, namely that established under Annex VII of the 1982 UN Convention on the Law of the Sea, in the dispute between Guyana and Suriname. Having concluded that it had jurisdiction to adjudicate alleged violations of the UN Charter and general international law, having regard to Article 293 of the Convention,[41] the tribunal recognized that 'in international law force may be used in law enforcement activities provided that such force is unavoidable, reasonable and necessary'. It concluded, however, that 'in the circumstances of the present case, ... action mounted by Suriname on 3 June 2000 seemed more akin to

---

[39] Separate Opinion Judge Simma, ibid, 335, at paras 2–3.

[40] Ibid, 332, at para. 20

[41] Arbitral Award, 17 September 2007, para. 406 (Art. 293 provides: 'A court or tribunal having jurisdiction under this section shall apply this Convention and other rules of international law not incompatible with this Convention'). The award is available at <http://pca-cpa.org/showpage. asp?pag_id=1147>.

a threat of military action rather than a mere law enforcement activity', and ruled that

The expulsion from the disputed area of the CGX oil rig and drill ship *C.E. Thornton* by Suriname on 3 June 2000 constituted a threat of the use of force in breach of the Convention, the UN Charter, and general international law.[42]

The fact that the tribunal decided to address—and rule in favour of—a claim concerning the unlawful threat or use of force in the context of a maritime delimitation case will be seen as surprising by many. Nevertheless, the approach may be said to reflect a recognition of the broad currency of the rules prohibiting the use of force, to the point that they are able to be accommodated and applied through the instrumentality of a convention that includes no explicit rule on that subject. This may be seen as the rather creative operationalization of the rules by more indirect means.

## (C) International legislative efforts

The factors that caused the ICJ to refrain from touching on the crime of aggression in its 2005 judgment might also be thought to limit the possibility of legislating on that subject. Domestic legislation on the crime of aggression has been adopted by a number of states, which means that the possibility cannot be excluded that those most responsible for the Iraq war may yet feel a 'tap on the shoulder', depending upon the range of their foreign travels. The nefarious effects of the Iraq war have also limited the ability of the Security Council to adopt necessary resolutions on other matters (for fear that certain states might again seek to accord to themselves the right unilaterally to re-interpret such resolutions), and limiting the necessary development of the responsibility to protect (given the reasonable fear of smaller states that this might open the door to more unwarranted actions). The two recent resolutions in relation to Libya could be seen as a modest opening towards future actions.

Against this background it was, therefore, somewhat surprising that in the summer of 2010 the Assembly of States Parties to the ICC managed to reach agreement on the adoption of a resolution to amend the Rome Statute, by inserting an agreed definition of the crime of aggression.[43] It is equally surprising that it did so in a manner that could, in definitional terms, encompass the circumstances of the Iraq war in 2003. The crime is defined by Article 8*bis*(1) of the ICC Statute as

the planning, preparation, initiation or execution, by a person in a position effectively to exercise control over or to direct the political or military action of a State, of an act of aggression which, by its character, gravity and scale, constitutes a manifest violation of the Charter of the United Nations.[44]

---

[42] Ibid, paras 445 and 488(2).
[43] RC/Res.6, The Crime of Aggression, 11 June 2010; Depositary Notification C.N.651.2010 Treaties-8, dated 29 November 2010.
[44] ICC Statute, Art. 8*bis*(1).

Article 8*bis*(2) defines an act of aggression as 'the use of armed force by a state against the sovereignty, territorial integrity or political independence of another state, or in any other manner inconsistent with the Charter of the United Nations', and identifies certain acts that will, in accordance with UN General Assembly Resolution 3314, qualify as acts of aggression.

This rare example of legislative agreement on the use of force will not, however, have immediate effect under the ICC Statute, and various 'safeguards' have been inserted that will limit the role of the Prosecutor. Thus, a new Article 15*bis* provides that the Court will only be able to exercise jurisdiction after 1 January 2017, once a decision has been taken by the same majority of state parties as is required to amend the Statute. Moreover, in the absence of a referral to the ICC Prosecutor by the Security Council, the Prosecutor will only be able to proceed with an investigation if the Security Council has made a determination of an act of aggression by a state concerned.[45] The restrained approach taken by the Security Council in the case of the Democratic Republic of Congo and Uganda, as noted by Judges El Araby and Simma, underscore the reasons for caution. However welcome Kampala's moment of legislative impulse might be, these and other limitations will severely constrain the circumstances in which the statutory crime of aggression can be operationalized within the framework of the ICC.

## 5. Conclusions

The developments here described are not without consequence. They confirm the currency of the existing rules of international law on the use of force, and flesh them out. The hope must be that they make it more (and not less) likely that the formulation and application of policy will be fixed around the UN Charter rules establishing restraints on the use of force. In this measure utopians might find some degree of comfort, at least over the longer term. They should not, however, expect a magical transformation.

---

[45] ICC Statute, Art. 15*bis*(7).

# 29

# Prospects for Humanitarian Uses of Force

*Christian J. Tams*

## SUMMARY

How to strike a balance between the desire to restrict the availability of force and the need to protect human rights depends on the relative importance that a normative system accords to each of these values. The international legal system has adopted a rather differentiated approach that distinguishes between institutional and private uses of force, privileges certain values over others, and lives with grey areas of legal uncertainty. The Security Council is competent to authorize humanitarian interventions in order to maintain international peace and security. In the Rhodesian and South African cases, and more regularly from the 1990s onwards including recent resolutions on Libya, the Council has characterized situations of massive human rights abuse as a 'threat to peace', thus authorizing UN member states to use force in order to remove the threat. The major problem relates to the cases where states resort to force on humanitarian grounds outside and without any Security Council authorization. Different humanitarian uses of force have been treated rather differently. The international community has accepted that force can be used in two cases: (i) to rescue nationals abroad and (ii) to provide military assistance to end colonial domination. Instead, international law does not recognize a right of states to forcible humanitarian intervention. Prospects for the future: (i) within the UN system, the organization might be able to make more frequent and more effective use of its existing competences; in addition, Council practice may help to develop agreed standards governing the auto-interpretation of equivocal mandates. Furthermore, a reinvigorated General Assembly might assume a more active role in the field of peace and security again. (ii) Outside the UN system, the most likely scenario is that the international community will continue to reject humanitarian interventions while at the same time tolerating breaches in exceptional circumstances. Nevertheless, one type of humanitarian intervention outside the UN system is likely to be accepted: regional interventions based on Article 4(h) of the African Union's Charter.

# 1. Introduction

Whether force can be used to protect human rights of others is a major question occupying lawyers, but also philosophers, theologians, and political scientists. In essence, any normative system seeking to answer it has to strike a balance between two considerations: (i) the desire to restrict the availability of force and (ii) the interest in seeing human rights effectively protected.

Both considerations are important, but not absolutely valid. As far as international law is concerned, many have dreamed of a world without military force, but unless minimum standards of human rights protection are met, a state of 'negative peace'[1] is today seen as insufficient. Conversely, effective human rights protection is essential, but in most instances 'the use of force [will] not be the appropriate method to monitor and ensure such respect':[2] force may worsen a human rights situation and humanitarian motives have often been a pretext for interventionism.

How the balance between the two considerations is struck depends on the relative importance that a normative system accords to each of them, as well as on the modalities of the use of force. The subsequent discussion shows that the international legal system has adopted a rather differentiated approach that distinguishes between institutional and private uses of force, privileges certain values over others, and lives with grey areas of legal uncertainty.

The starting point, however, seems clear. Even though humanitarian uses of force have long been discussed, contemporary debates take place within the normative framework of the United Nations Charter. The Charter has set the parameters by prohibiting the use of military force in the international relations between states (Art. 2(4)) and by explicitly recognizing two relevant[3] exceptions—the inherent right to self-defence (Art. 51) and military enforcement mandated by the Security Council (Chapter VII). What is uncertain is whether these express rules, or possible unwritten rules that have evolved alongside them, accommodate humanitarian concerns, or ought to do so. This question has prompted much debate, notably under the rubric of 'humanitarian intervention'. The subsequent considerations reflect on these debates, but adopt a broader approach that includes other humanitarian uses of force—resort to military violence with a view to protecting human rights of others—as well, notably UN-mandated interventions, armed struggles against colonialism, and military operations to rescue nationals from abroad. It is hoped that this broader focus will enable us to avoid the 'tunnel vision' besetting entrenched contemporary debates about humanitarian intervention, and to appreciate the dynamic evolution of the Charter regime.

---

[1] Cf J. Galtung's distinction, explored eg in 'Violence, Peace, and Peace Research', 6 J Peace Research (1969) 167.

[2] Cf ICJ, *Nicaragua case*, ICJ Reports 1986, 14, at 134–5.

[3] The subsequent discussion ignores the Charter's now obsolete enemy clauses.

## 2. Where do we stand?

As noted above, the contemporary debates are shaped by the UN Charter. The Charter regime was designed to ban 'the scourge of war'[4] and reflects that design. Since 1945, it has been consolidated, but also applied in a dynamic normative context characterized by the rise to prominence of human rights.

### (A) The Charter regime

The Charter rules governing resort to force mark one of the rare quantum leaps of international law: 'fifty States, [then] representing the vast majority of the members of the international community'[5] renounced their right to use military force in their international relations and thus transformed the traditional *liberum jus ad bellum* into a *jus contra bellum*. Article 2(4) of the Charter, agreed in 1945, imposes a comprehensive ban on military force, subject only to the two exceptions: it covers not only force directed against the territorial integrity or political independence of another state, but any use of force, irrespective of its motivation and direction.[6] This implies that humanitarian uses of force are prima facie unlawful and require to be justified.

As for justifications, as is well known, the Charter regime does not codify an express 'humanitarian exception'. It endorses the idea of human rights in principle,[7] but lacking specific human rights guarantees, the Charter was to be a catalyst for future developments rather than a bill of rights in its own right. Still less did it translate human rights concerns into a licence to use force unilaterally against other states. The matter was considered,[8] but barely five years after the Hitler regime had justified its intervention in Sudetenland on humanitarian grounds, drafters needed little reminding that such an exception might be open to abuse. Instead, they placed great trust in the system of collective security set up under Chapter VII of the Charter, which envisaged the Security Council as a world policeman able to combat threats to international peace and security. In the drafters' vision, collective action (including by forcible means) was to be the main exception to Article 2(4). Chapter VII did not expressly mention Security Council enforcement measures in defence of human rights; however, in line with the spirit prevailing at the time, it was envisaged mainly to apply to inter-state conflicts.[9]

---

[4] UN Charter, first preambular para.
[5] Cf ICJ, *Reparations Opinion*, ICJ Reports 1951, 171, at 185.
[6] ICJ, *Corfu Channel* case, ICJ Reports 1949, 4, at 34–5.
[7] See notably Art. 1(3), which refers to human rights among the purposes of the organization.
[8] For references see T. Franck, *Recourse to Force* (Cambridge: Cambridge University Press, 2002), 14–19.
[9] E.J.A. Frowein and N. Krisch, 'Commentary to Article 39', in B. Simma (ed.), *The United Nations Charter*, 2nd edn (Oxford: Oxford University Press, 2002), 720.

## (B) An evolving legal context

Sixty-five years after the adoption of the Charter, Articles 2(4), 51 and Chapter VII stand textually unchanged. What is more, over time, the Charter regime, revolutionary in 1945, has been consolidated. The ban on force is considered 'the very cornerstone of the human effort to promote peace in a world torn by strife'.[10] It is included, almost as a matter of course, in the various categories of 'higher law' invented since 1945—*jus cogens*, obligations *erga omnes*, crimes of states, etc.—and has spilled over into a range of ancillary rules, for example prohibiting the recognition of territorial gains procured by force,[11] or of forcible reprisals,[12] and perhaps imposing individual criminal liability on those responsible for grave breaches of the prohibition.[13]

And yet, notwithstanding this ostensible consolidation, the regime set up in 1945 has come under pressure. To some extent it had to, as it simply did not work as planned. For more than 40 years, the Security Council was unable to live up to the drafters' expectations, and the Charter's preferred option of enforcing peace and security through collective mechanisms was not realized meaningfully. Not surprisingly, then, second-best options were explored—a process that, for example, led to the 'invention' of peacekeeping or the General Assembly's arrogation of subsidiary enforcement powers pursuant to General Assembly Resolution 377 (V) (Uniting for Peace).

What is more, just as the UN Charter transformed the *jus ad bellum,* so has subsequent practice transformed the normative status of human rights. Drawing on the Charter's general references, multilateral treaties, international practice and judicial decisions have forged a widely accepted international bill of rights. In fact, so decisive has been the shift that fundamental human rights today are recognized as peremptory and form the core of an international *constitutional* order based on a 'human-being-oriented approach',[14] with the individual as 'the ultimate unit of all law'.[15]

The question remains whether the phenomenal rise to prominence of human rights has been translated into enforcement rights—rights of protection that can be exercised against another state that violates human rights. At some level, this seems difficult to dispute: international law since 1945 has clearly provided the human rights regime with some 'teeth'. Depending on the circumstances, states violating human rights are today liable to face institutional sanctions; they may lose benefits accruing to them under treaties (with or without conditionality clauses); they can find themselves dragged before foreign courts (in which their plea of immunity may be challenged on human rights grounds); and they may be

---

[10] ICJ, *Nicaragua* case, ICJ Reports 1986, 14, Separate Opinion of President Singh, at 153. Cf also *Armed Activities (DRC v Uganda)* case, ICJ Reports 2005, 201, at para. 148.

[11] ILC, Articles on State Responsibility, Commentary to Art. 41, paras 6–7.

[12] Ibid, Art. 50(1)(a); GA Res. 2625 (XXV), principle I.6.

[13] See notably Arts 8*bis* and 15*bis* of the Rome Statute, as amended during the Kampala Review Conference.

[14] ICTY, Appeals Chamber, *Tadić* case (Interlocutory Appeal), at para. 97.

[15] H. Lauterpacht, 'The Grotian Tradition in International Law', 23 BYIL (1946) 1 at 27.

subjected to third party reprisals short of force.[16] The recognition of human rights in many respects has modified the enforcement structure of international law. But of course it is one thing for a legal system to allow for, for example, treaty suspension and quite another to authorize the use of force against another state. So it is an entirely open question whether contemporary international law has struck a new balance between the two considerations outlined above—whether the 'cornerstone' has been moved.

## (C) Humanitarian interventions with UN mandate

In one respect, it clearly has. It is widely accepted that the Security Council is competent to authorize humanitarian interventions in order to maintain international peace and security. In the Rhodesian and South African cases, and more regularly from the 1990s onwards, the Council has qualified situations of massive human rights abuse as a 'threat to peace';[17] this in turn has allowed it to authorize UN member states to use force in order to remove the threat.[18] Over time, such determinations have lost much of their exceptional character: unlike 15 years ago, the Security Council today no longer feels obliged to draw attention to cross-border flows of refugees, or attendant risks to regional stability, to justify the application of Chapter VII; instead, the systematic violation of human rights in itself can amount to a threat to peace if the Security Council so determines. In fact, in its recent resolutions on Libya, the Council has expressly emphasized the responsibility of a government to protect its population and thereby linked its sanctions practice to the debate about 'R2P' (Responsibility to Protect).[19]

At the legal level, this practice is based on an expansive interpretation of Article 39 that accommodates the rise to prominence of international human rights and that, while considerably expanding the Security Council's powers, has met with surprisingly little protest. As a consequence, UN-authorized humanitarian interventions are fully in line with contemporary international law—in fact, they have become the preferred option, and there is even talk about a duty to intervene in the face of grave humanitarian crises.[20]

All this may seem trite, as the evolution of Chapter VII has been widely discussed. And yet it is important, because it illustrates the primary approach by which contemporary international law resolves the tension between restricting

---

[16] See C. Tams, 'Individual States as Guardians of Community Interests', in *Festschrift Simma* (Oxford: Oxford University Press, 2011), 379.

[17] Cf Frowein and Krisch, n 9, at 722–6; and further G. Nolte, 'Practice of the UN Security Council with Respect to Humanitarian Law', in *Weltinnenrecht: liber amicorum Jost Delbrück* (Berlin: Duncker & Humblot, 2005), 487.

[18] On a more technical level, this has been facilitated by the 'uncoupling' of Arts 42 and 43: see Franck, n 8, at 24; and further T. Gazzini, *The Changing Rules on the Use of Force in International Law* (Manchester: Manchester University Press, 2006), 35–7.

[19] See SC Res. 1970 and 1973 (2011). For brief comments on 'R2P' see below, Section D.

[20] O. Corten and P. Klein, *Droit d'ingérence ou obligation de réaction?* (Brussels: Etablissements Emile Bruylant, SA, 1992); M. Bettati, *Le droit d'ingérence. Mutation de l'ordre international* (Paris: Editions Odile Jacob, 1996).

force and ensuring human rights. Rather than balancing substantive criteria or weighing values that are at stake in a given case, it has opted for a 'procedural way'. What distinguishes the desired (viz. Security Council enforcement) from the controversial (viz. other humanitarian uses of force) is a procedural *imprimatur*, a decision taken by a competent organ. Of course, that organ is not entirely free, but must seek to phrase its determination in the terminology of 'peace and security' used in Article 39. However, as the terms are vague and the Council's political discretion hardly disputed, the language of Article 39 has ceased to be a serious substantive constraint: a threat to peace is what the Council says it is.

This does not mean that the Council was quick to authorize humanitarian uses of force. In the regular course of events, the procedural requirements continue to act as a major hurdle: in order for the Council to 'say' something, the veto powers need to agree (or at least refrain from disagreeing). But even this procedural requirement has on occasion been applied rather pragmatically. Outside the regular course of events,[21] interventions have been authorized *ex post facto* (Economic Community of West African States Monitoring Group, ECOMOG);[22] and on occasion, the international community has accepted the auto-interpretation of ambiguous Security Council mandates by intervening states.[23] Finally, at least in theory, nothing precludes a majority of states, acting through the General Assembly, from reviving the Uniting for Peace doctrine to authorize enforcement action outside the Security Council.[24]

In short, behind the façade of continuity, the Charter regime has undergone a remarkable re-interpretation: the international community today accepts, even encourages, humanitarian uses of force agreed within the UN, and it has been prepared to apply the procedural conditions pragmatically. And yet, in practice, these continue to pose a major challenge. The General Assembly has all but forgotten about the military dimension of Uniting for Peace, and the Security Council is regularly chided for its failure to act efficiently. Put differently, contemporary international law has opened up to embrace humanitarian uses of force authorized by the UN, but the political will required to make use of the legal options is often lacking.

---

[21] This 'regular approach' is of course itself very pragmatic, as it construes abstentions as 'concurring votes' for the purposes of Art. 27(3).

[22] See SC Res 788 and SC Res. 1132. For comment see C. Walter, *Vereinte Nationen und Regionalorganisationen* (Berlin/Heidelberg: Springer-Verlag, 1996), 289–309; for a more critical assessment contrast T. Gazzini, n 18, 89–92.

[23] The United Kingdom, the United States, and France, eg, attacked Iraqi weapons factories in 1993, relying on a 'revived' SC Res. 687 (1991). In the specific instance, their interpretation was endorsed by the Secretary-General. Many other auto-interpretations have met with greater resistance, notably the subsequent attempts, by the United States and its allies, to portray the 2003 Iraq war as the implementation of a Security Council mandate. For a cautious, but extremely detailed account see C.D. Gray, *International Law and Use of Force*, 3rd edn (Oxford: Oxford University Press, 2008), 348–66.

[24] Cf GA Res. 377 (V). For comment on its current relevance see D. Zaum, 'The Security Council, the General Assembly, and War: The Uniting for Peace Resolution', in V. Lowe et al (eds), *The United Nations Security Council and War* (Oxford: Oxford University Press, 2008), 154.

## (D) Outside the UN framework

The question of humanitarian uses of force without UN authorization therefore remains with us. As is well known, it continues to prompt heated debates, which especially in the case of humanitarian intervention (the most controversial instance) have become rather entrenched.

Two features of these debates stand out. One is the continuing popularity of simple truths: notably, there is much support for an approach that sees the Charter rules (textually unchanged as they are, consolidated over time, peremptory in nature) as a rather rigid regime. As this regime—so the argument runs—does not enshrine an express humanitarian exception, and as it has been officially affirmed rather than changed, contemporary international law excludes humanitarian uses of force outside the UN framework.[25] This is a powerful argument of appealing clarity and rigour. Yet it may simply be too clear; offering black and white solutions where the reality of international relations displays shades of grey. On the other end of the spectrum, many works on humanitarian uses of force present a strange blend of the *lex lata* and a *lex ferenda* shaped by perceived moral or political imperatives. Frequent resort to extra-legal categories (notably legitimacy) is one indicator of this trend, assertions that an international legal system worthy of its name *must* tolerate a certain conduct another.[26]

Both features illustrate the complex nature of the legal issues, but are problematic. The Charter rules are more flexible than proponents of simple truths are ready to admit. By the same token, legitimacy is an important category but no substitute for a legal assessment. On the basis of these considerations, the following comments on the debate of humanitarian uses of force outside the UN framework seem in order.

### (i) 'Privileged' humanitarian uses of force: (1) rescuing nationals abroad, (2) ending colonialism

The first point to make is that different humanitarian uses of force have been treated rather differently. While the concept of humanitarian intervention has remained very controversial, the international community seems to have accepted that force could be used to defend a number of specific humanitarian objectives. Two specific (if disparate) humanitarian uses of force have met with considerable approval—in between the black and the white, they occupy the 'light grey' area. Forcible measures taken to rescue nationals abroad are the first example in point, military assistance to end colonial domination the second. Both remain controversial, but in each case, powerful arguments suggest that the Charter regime does not preclude resort to force.

---

[25] Powerful versions of this argument appear in O. Corten, *Le droit contre la guerre* (Paris: Pedone, 2008), 741ff; and A. Randelzhofer, in B. Simma (ed.), n 9, 130–2.

[26] See, eg, F.R. Téson, *Humanitarian Intervention. An Inquiry into Law and Morality,* 2nd edn (New York: Transnational Publishers, 1997); F. Kofi Abiew, *The Evolution of the Doctrine and Practice of Humanitarian Intervention* (The Hague: Kluwer Law International, 1999).

With respect to rescuing nationals abroad, states have traditionally considered themselves entitled to intervene on foreign territory to avert danger to their citizens. Unless consented to by the host state, such 'rescue missions' are very difficult to bring in line with the Charter regime. Still, the international community—especially since the late 1980s—has been prepared to accept low-intensity operations that seemed necessary to avert a serious risk to citizens' lives and that were limited in time and scope.[27] Recent examples include France's operations in Chad (1990), (then) Zaire (1991), the Central African Republic (1996); US missions in Sierra Leone (1997) or Liberia (1998), and the evacuation of foreign nationals from Tirana by German, American, and Italian troops (1997). It is by no means clear how this practice—which unlike earlier incidents has met with little opposition—could be squared with the Charter regime. Intervening states have usually not asserted a new humanitarian exception to Article 2(4) of the Charter, and from the International Law Commission debates on diplomatic protection,[28] it is clear that proposals expressly recognizing a right of forcible diplomatic protection will not be endorsed. Instead, the approach has been one of 'muddling through': intervening states have sought to portray their rescue missions as self-defence operations, and even though that requires a very dubious construction of the 'armed attack' requirement, the international community has been willing to look the other way if, on the facts, a given operation did not lead to clashes with the territorial state's forces and if it seemed genuinely necessary and proportionate.

The use of military force to end colonialism raises matters of a more complex nature.[29] It is largely of historical relevance today, as the 'anti-colonial reasoning' has not been applied to other self-determination claims; however, re-visiting the old debates provides interesting insights into the malleability of the *jus contra bellum* where it seemed to stand in the way of a major political objective. As is well known, anti-colonialism from the 1960s became one of the key priorities for a majority of states of the world. Where colonial powers resisted decolonization, they frequently faced armed liberation movements. Whether these movements should be entitled to use force themselves became a divisive issue, as was the question whether third states were entitled to assist liberation movements by forcible means. These questions defy an easy answer: Western states in particular long resisted any softening of the *jus contra bellum*. However, from 1973 onwards,[30] UN General Assembly resolutions (as well as documents emanating from the G77 and the Non-Aligned Movement (NAM)) for two decades affirmed the legality of 'armed struggle' to overthrow colonial regimes, and also (albeit in more guarded language) urged

---

[27] The following argument largely follows Gazzini, n 18, 170–4. The traditional view has been shaped by D. Bowett, *Self-Defence in International Law* (Manchester: Manchester University Press, 1958); and id, 'The Use of Force for the Protection of Nationals Abroad', in A. Cassese (ed.), *The Current Regulation of the Use of Force* (Dordrecht: Martinus Nijhoff, 1986), 39. For more cautious readings cf. Corten, n 25, at 788ff and 803ff; and Gray, n 23, at 156–60.

[28] Cf ILC, Report of the International Law Commission on the Work of its Fifty-Second Session, UN Doc. A/55/10, at paras 430–9.

[29] See the helpful discussion in Gray, n 23, 59–64 (who, however, adopts a more sceptical approach than the one advocated in the text).

[30] Cf GA Res. 3070 (1973).

third states to provide support for liberation movements. Just as in the case of rescue operations, international debates about the legality of anti-colonial struggles are characterized by a considerable degree of conceptual uncertainty.[31] As far as the use of force by liberation movements themselves is concerned, one might have of course argued that these movements were not bound by the ban on force in the first place, but curiously, the most common approach was to portray their struggle as an exercise of self-defence against the colonial regime's permanent armed attack.[32] With respect to foreign support, third states regularly provided military support for liberation movements (often without meeting major opposition), but typically refrained from expressly asserting a right to do so. Yet their practice was hard to ignore, and in the *Nicaragua* case, even the International Court of Justice seemed sympathetic with the view that intervention in support of decolonization was governed by a special rules regime:[33] as Judge Schwebel noted in his dissent, the majority judgment seemed to 'inferentially endors[e] an exception to the prohibition against intervention, in favour of the legality of intervention in the promotion of so-called "wars of liberation"'.[34]

From today's perspective, the heated debates of the past are of limited practical relevance, as the decolonization rationale has not been applied outside the colonial context and states have abandoned the dramatic rhetoric of the 1970s and 1980s. And yet, one cannot help but notice that three decades ago, a majority of states seemed prepared to accept that the particular humanitarian objective of decolonization could be promoted through forcible means, and expressly said so in a host of legally relevant documents.

### (ii) Humanitarian intervention

Humanitarian intervention proper has met with much greater resistance—on the spectre of black and white, it is at best a case of 'dark grey'. It does of course present a greater challenge to the Charter regime than the two privileged instances discussed in the preceding section: the self-defence analogy (which could possibly be stretched to cover rescue operations) is of no real help;[35] and the use of force cannot be linked to a transformative struggle to end colonialism. In these circumstances, and notwithstanding the rise to prominence of human rights, the available evidence makes it extremely difficult to argue that contemporary international law recognizes a right of humanitarian intervention. The more convincing view is that it does not—but that the international community in exceptional circumstances has decided not to insist on the application of the law.

---

[31] For a clear account see A. Cassese, *Self-Determination of Peoples* (Cambridge: Cambridge University Press, 1995), 150–8.

[32] H. Bokor-Szegö, 'The Attitude of Socialist States towards the International Regulation of the Use of Force', in Cassese (ed.), n 27, 435 at 467–9.

[33] *Nicaragua* case, ICJ Reports 1986, 14, at para. 206.

[34] Ibid, Dissenting Opinion of Judge Schwebel, at para. 179.

[35] Although it is occasionally invoked: see *North Atlantic Assembly, Res. 283*: 'Recasting Euro-Atlantic Security: Towards the Washington Summit' (November 1998), at para. 15(e).

The legal case against a right of humanitarian intervention is rather straightforward. In essence, it rests on three propositions:

(i) To assess the legality of humanitarian intervention, one cannot draw support from pre-Charter practice, as the Charter has ushered in a new era.[36]

(ii) Since 1945, intervening states have been very reluctant to invoke the concept, even where they ostensibly used force to protect human rights.[37] The classical cases of Tanzania/Uganda, Vietnam/Cambodia, and India/Bangladesh were presented as instances of self-defence, at best reinforced by references to the humanitarian catastrophe. More recently, some states have begun to use the concept as an official justification, but this practice is by no means consistent, and when push comes to shove (as eg in court proceedings such as those brought by Yugoslavia against NATO members), states prefer to avoid a clear stance.[38]

(iii) Most importantly, a majority of states has consistently rejected the concept. This, in fact, seems the key difference between debates about humanitarian intervention proper and the privileged instances discussed above. Whereas the majority of states has at times been unconcerned by concrete assertions of, for example, a right to rescue nationals abroad, it has resolutely dismissed real or potential precedents of humanitarian interventions. Nowhere could this be seen more clearly than in the international reaction to the bombing of Yugoslavia in 1999: as is well known (and still often disregarded conveniently), a clear majority of UN member states officially rejected the view (cautiously advanced by some, but by no means all, intervening states) that humanitarian grounds should justify resort to force.[39] It almost seemed as if the majority of states felt that the potential 'Kosovo precedent' required a principled response. Lastly, a very similar pattern of behaviour can be seen in debates about the concept of 'responsibility to protect': over the course of debates, the initial, 'interventionist' thrust of the concept has been channelled into the safe haven of Chapter VII—so that R2P has become a doctrine justifying (or even requiring) institutional UN action rather than unilateral humanitarian interventions.[40]

As is the case with grey areas, there is some room for argument. With respect to the more recent developments, Article 4(h) of the Constitutive Act of the African Union provides the most interesting piece of evidence. In this provision, AU

---

[36] Y. Dinstein, *War, Aggression and Self-Defence*, 4th edn (Cambridge: Cambridge University Press, 2005), 71.

[37] Gray, n 23, 33–9.

[38] Ibid, 44–7.

[39] See notably Ministerial Declaration of the Meeting of Foreign Ministers of the Group of 77, New York, 24 September 1999 (rejecting 'the so-called right of humanitarian intervention, which had no basis in the UN Charter or in international law').

[40] See notably para. 203 of the High-Level Panel Report and para. 126 of Kofi Annan's 'In Larger Freedom'. For much more on R2P see C. Stahn, 'Responsibility to Protect', 101 AJIL (2007) 99. In SC Res. 1970 and SC Res. 1973, the Security Council expressly refers to the concept and thus seems to accept the link between violations of 'R2P' and institutional sanctions.

member states expressly recognize the Union's right to 'intervene in a Member State pursuant to a decision of the Assembly in respect of grave circumstances, namely war crimes, genocide and crimes against humanity'.[41] This provision indeed marks an interesting departure from the Charter regime: it seeks to minimize abuse by requiring a collective decision, but substitutes regional security for the UN's universal system. And it *expressly* grants an enforcement power where for decades debates had been about unwritten exceptions to the ban on force. In both respects, it could indeed point towards future developments. Whether it will be influential, or merely flowery rhetoric, however, is too early to tell. And so, for the time being, proponents of a right of humanitarian intervention continue to face an uphill battle.

If, nevertheless, humanitarian interventions come within the (dark) grey area of legal uncertainty, then it is because the international community has occasionally displayed a remarkable ease in accepting their effects.[42] To be clear, not every form of toleration can be construed as acceptance; very often, the international community simply has no choice but to come to terms with illegal outcomes, and in the absence of duties of non-recognition, it typically is free to do so. However, in exceptional instances, the international community's response to a humanitarian use of force seems to have gone beyond (reluctant, gradual) toleration and amounted to tacit acceptance. Acceptance can take various forms and, as the international community typically responds in an uncoordinated way, it may be a matter of degree. It can be seen, for example, in the absence of protests against France's military intervention in the coup toppling Emperor Bokassa. It is one explanation for the willingness with which the international community accepted Tanzania's dubious reliance on self-defence as a justification for its removal of Idi Amin, in a situation in which its operation was—to say the least—obviously disproportionate, or the Western powers' intervention aimed to protect Northern Iraqi Kurds. It is implicit in the denial, by the Security Council, to address claims by the state on whose territories interventions have taken place. And many read it into the reasonably quick validation of NATO's bombing campaign through Security Council Resolution 1244 (1999).[43]

All this, of course, is 'muddling through' of a new level, especially since state responses are often more difficult to read than tea leaves. But what is difficult to ignore is that notwithstanding its rejection of a right to humanitarian intervention, the international community has occasionally decided not to apply the law and instead condoned conduct violating its 'cornerstone rule'. This in turn suggests that despite the constant affirmations of the importance of the Charter regime, states will exceptionally be considered to have crossed no more than a 'thin red line'.[44]

---

[41] Constitutive Act of the African Union, Art. 4(h). For comment see B. Kioko, 'The Right of Intervention under the African Union's Constitutive Act: From Non-interference to Non-intervention', 85 IRRC 852 (2003), at 807.

[42] The following draws on Franck, n 8, at 139–70.

[43] See notably A. Pellet, 'Brief Remarks on the Unilateral Use of Force', 11 EJIL (2000) 385.

[44] B. Simma, 'NATO, the UN and the Use of Force: Legal Aspects', 10 EJIL (1999) 1, at 6.

This pragmatic handling is problematic in at least two respects. For one, it makes for an uneasy tension between the law as proclaimed (and peremptory law at that) and the law as applied (or rather, *not* applied). But more importantly, as acceptances take the form of discretionary responses, it is extremely difficult to predict which humanitarian interventions are likely to be condoned. One would of course hope that in its response to a given use of force, the international community were to be guided by humanitarian considerations, taking into account the magnitude of the suffering, the extent and duration of the use of force, and the bona or mala fides of the intervening state. This indeed is what it should do if recent studies on legitimate or justified uses of force are to be believed: these accept that humanitarian interventions could be undertaken to prevent or stop systematic and large-scale abuses of essential human rights, if they involve targeted and limited force and are in some way procedurally 'hedged in', for example, because the Security Council has already determined that a certain situation amounts to a threat of peace, or because the action is undertaken by a regional organization.[45] But these guidelines—plausible as they sound—have so far not been borne out by practice. As for the substantive rights at stake, Vietnam's intervention in Cambodia in retrospect seems a strong candidate, as it effectively ended a brutal regime's reign of terror—and yet, Vietnam was harshly condemned by a curious *mésalliance* of Third World and Western states. What is more, it is much easier to recognize in the abstract that a certain human right must be protected (with freedom from genocide as a key example) than to agree, in a concrete case, whether there is indeed an imminent threat of massive abuse justifying forcible action. Debates in Western states in the run-up to NATO's 1999 bombing campaign suggest that even where it is genuinely felt, a humanitarian imperative may derive from dubious factual premises. This of course explains the popularity of procedural safeguards—such as collective action; but again, practice does *not* bear them out: the best examples of 'accepted humanitarian interventions' involved strictly unilateral action (Idi Amin, Bokassa), while notwithstanding their 'collective' character, the campaigns against Yugoslavia, or later Iraq, have proven highly divisive. All this suggests that the international response to a particular humanitarian use of force has often been determined by political ideology more than by the legitimacy criteria put forward in international documents.

## 3. Looking ahead

The preceding considerations suggest that the Charter regime governing resort to force has been applied with more flexibility than is sometimes recognized: UN competence to authorize resort to force has been construed liberally; in the 'light

---

[45] For variations on this theme see, eg, A. Cassese, *Ex iniuria ius oritur*, 10 EJIL (1999) 23, at 27; International Commission on Intervention and State Sovereignty, *Responsibility to Protect: Report of the International Commission on Intervention and State Sovereignty* (2001), esp. ch. 6; Independent International Commission on Kosovo, *Kosovo Report: Conflict, International Response, Lessons Learned* (2000), at ch. 6.

grey' area, privileged humanitarian uses of force have been accepted without a clear conceptual basis; and even where the international community has resisted normative drift, as in the 'dark grey' case of humanitarian intervention, it has accepted occasional breaches of the law. This flexibility has modified or at least mollified the system devised in 1945. It has enabled the international community to maintain its support for the Charter regime while at the same time accommodating the increased concern for human rights. At the same time, the unprincipled manner in which the international community has dealt with humanitarian uses of force has obfuscated the law in an area in which one would hope for clear normative guidance.

Seen against this background, how will the international law of the future deal with humanitarian uses of force? It seems safe to say that the tension underlying the present regime will not simply disappear. The future legal system will continue to uphold the ban on force as a 'cornerstone principle'; at the same time, we may realistically expect human rights to remain a key element of the international legal order. What may be hoped is that a realistically utopian international law of the future will be able to balance these competing concerns in a more principled and consistent way. If past practice is any guide, this is unlikely to be achieved by a textual change of the Charter regime. Decades of affirmation have immunized the Charter regime against textual amendment—for example the recognition of an Article 51*bis* enshrining a new 'humanitarian exception'. Conversely, it seems also unlikely that the Charter should be modified so as to exclude humanitarian uses of force expressly. However, as the preceding discussion shows, the international community is quite capable of adapting the textually unchanged Charter regime to new challenges. The following considerations suggest how it might do so in the future.

## (A) The United Nations

Much will depend on how the UN will deal with the Darfurs and Rwandas of the future. The UN's role is crucial because even proponents of unilateral enforcement accept the primacy of institutional action, and because international law embraces humanitarian uses of force with a UN mandate. At the UN level, the challenge is not a normative one, not even one of interpretation. As far as its authority is concerned, the UN is well equipped to handle humanitarian crises of the future: Chapter VII has been 'humanized' surprisingly quickly, and the procedural requirements for UN authorizations applied pragmatically. The key question therefore is whether the UN will be able to make more frequent and more effective use of its existing competences. This to a large extent depends on whether the member states allow it to do so—by providing the UN with the resources it needs to protect human rights in times of crises and by taking decisions authorizing humanitarian uses of force. As regards the latter aspect, one should not rule out change. It is by no means excluded that Security Council members that at present remain sovereignty-minded will open up and accept that human rights protection may occasionally require intrusive action, including, exceptionally, by force. More fundamentally, the UN of the future may be different from the one we know today. Its present decision-making procedures in particular are not set in stone. Institutional reforms could render the use or threat of the veto (which at present is the biggest obstacle to effective Security Council action) more difficult. Below the threshold of 'constitutional reform', Security Council practice may help *develop agreed standards* governing the auto-interpretation of equivocal mandates or regularize the relationship between the Council and regional agencies willing to take enforcement action subsequently approved by the Council. Finally, future decades could see *a reinvigorated General Assembly assume a more active role* in the field of peace and security again. Of course, none of this can be taken for granted. However, the current regime is already quite flexible and allows for many different types of UN decisions authorizing humanitarian uses of force. This requires political will, but would clearly be the most acceptable way of alleviating the tensions besetting contemporary international law. Past experience suggests that solutions that can somehow be portrayed as having 'UN imprimatur' are much more readily accepted, and thus should be explored.

## (B) Outside the UN

As regards humanitarian uses of force outside the UN, the international law of the future cannot content itself with focusing on questions of political will, but will have to address the normative uncertainties—the grey areas—of the current regulation.

With respect to the two privileged uses of force, this may be done by simply acknowledging that the Charter regime is at times flexibly applied. While anti-colonial struggles seem of limited relevance today, recent practice indeed suggests that the international community is willing to recognize a right of states to use limited, low-intensity force to rescue nationals abroad. The international law of the future may simply stop ignoring this body of practice or desperately trying to explain it away. Rescue missions might then be accepted as either a new, self-standing exception to the ban on force, or (presumably) a curious sub-category of self-defence. The Charter regime would presumably survive this adaptation—just as it has survived the challenge of colonialism and the opening up of Chapter VII.

Whether the same could be said for humanitarian intervention is a different matter. In this respect, it is by no means clear which direction the international law of the future should take, which 'realistic utopia' one should hope for. Yet, at a basic level, just as with rescue missions, one might hope for *a more honest and transparent debate.* In the past, reliance on semi-legal categories of legitimacy or culpability served a useful purpose, just as the portrayal of humanitarian uses of force as self-defence operations—it was the most convenient way to avoid outright condemnation.[46] But the convenient practice of the past has weakened the normative pull of the law. As states traditionally rarely invoked the concept of humanitarian intervention, practice provides remarkably little guidance. As noted above,

---

[46] Franck, n 8, 145.

though, matters seem to be evolving. Since the 1990s, states have gradually begun to use the forbidden word of humanitarian intervention and even codified the concept in a major regional treaty. One would hope that in a realistically utopian international law of the future, debates about humanitarian uses of force would be moved out of the grey areas of normative obscurity.

This should not be read as a plea for a debate in the abstract, which would only deepen divisions. Most likely, international law will continue to be shaped by the international community's response to specific incidents, specific assertions of the right to intervene in defence of human rights of others. As noted above, the strength of such claims will to a large extent depend on the evolution of UN practice: the more the UN shows itself capable of responding effectively, and the more it opens up its decision-making procedures, the more difficult it will become for states to argue that they had to move out of the system. Conversely, if the UN continues to be seen as not realizing its potential, future crises will continue to prompt calls for humanitarian interventions outside the Charter framework. In this case, in view of the major concerns raised by the concept, the most likely scenario presumably would be for the international community to *continue to reject humanitarian interventions while at the same time tolerating breaches in exceptional circumstances.* However, one may hope that it rises above the present 'muddling through' towards a more principled approach that draws distinctions between acceptable and unacceptable humanitarian interventions.

One type of humanitarian intervention outside the UN system in fact seems likely to become accepted: *regional interventions* based on Article 4(h) of the African Union's constitutive document. This provision is hard to reconcile with the UN Charter regime (unless AU interventions are endorsed by the Security Council). And yet, it seems to strike an acceptable balance: it deals with enforcement within a recognized (regional) collective security system (as opposed to envisaging 'out of area' interventions); it defines the circumstances justifying intervention rather narrowly; and it requires the collective decision of the AU Assembly of States. In so doing, it goes a considerable way in alleviating fears of abuse. Of course, even this regionalization requires a flexible adaptation of the Charter regime. Yet as shown above, the regime is already being applied rather pragmatically, and the line between regional humanitarian interventions on the one hand, and liberally construed UN authorizations (*ex post facto* approval, General Assembly mandates, etc.) may be rather fine. On that basis, Article 4(h) may indeed pave the way for the gradual recognition of humanitarian interventions within the framework of regional organizations. In the realistically utopian international law of the future, these would presumably be 'elevated' to the status of (light grey) privileged humanitarian uses of force: not beyond doubt, but highly likely to be accepted.

Outside this specific case, it is much less likely that humanitarian interventions without UN mandate should become accepted in the foreseeable future. The more honest debates of the last decade have helped to clarify some the conditions under which one could discuss their legality, but the general climate has not been conducive to building consensus around a cautious modification of the Charter regime.

As for the former aspect, even proponents claim that they should only be acceptable in extreme circumstances, namely 'the most serious humanitarian emergency involving large scale loss of life'.[47] By the same token, recent debates have stressed the need for some form of collective decision-making as a procedural safeguard against abuse.[48] However, while some of the preconditions now seem clear(er), little progress has been made with respect to their operationalization. Even if it were possible to agree in the abstract on the requirement of 'the most serious humanitarian emergency',[49] a future regime seeking to prevent abuse would need to include *more effective mechanisms of fact-finding and inspection* that can actually verify or falsify assertions about the alleged imminence of a humanitarian emergency. But unfortunately, outside specific treaty regimes, international verification and inspection mechanisms are so far underdeveloped and typically not capable of producing quick results. The Security Council's practice of establishing the Darfur Commission[50] is no doubt a step in the right direction, but a much more regular practice will be required. By the same token, reform proposals acknowledge that force must exclusively be used to stop the atrocities.[51] However, it is by no means clear how a regime accepting humanitarian interventions could ensure compliance with this condition. Perhaps one could think of reporting obligations along the lines of Article 51 or envisage mandatory Security Council debates during which the intervening state(s) would be expected to disclose information about the operation. But at present, no serious attempt has been made to implement such models.

From a broader perspective, this lack of progress should perhaps not come as a surprise. The last decade has not been conducive to a reform of the *jus ad bellum*. The general impression has been that of a beleaguered Charter regime— threatened by US unilateralism, new assertions of anti-terrorist self-defence, or forcible regime change. This general climate has quite naturally deepened fears that human rights concerns might be abused as a pretext for interventionism. And so the cautiously optimistic tone dominating much of the Western literature in the wake of the Kosovo crisis—that over time, genuine humanitarian interventions would become acceptable—has subsided. From the perspective of today, it therefore seems unlikely that a realistically utopian international law of the future should come to recognize humanitarian interventions outside the specific context of regional organizations.

---

[47] C. Greenwood, 'Humanitarian Intervention: the Case of Kosovo', 10 Finnish YIL (1999) 141 at 177.

[48] See references in n 44.

[49] Cf n 46.

[50] SC Res. 1564 (2004).

[51] See references in n 44.

# (B) OTHER GLOBAL PROBLEMS BADLY IN NEED OF SUBSTANTIVE LEGAL REGULATION

# 30

## The Role That Equal Rights and Self-Determination of Peoples can Play in the Current World Community

*Abdulqawi A. Yusuf*

## SUMMARY

There are two strands of self-determination, one based on Lenin's anti-coloni-alist principles, the other on Wilson' insistence on the right of a people freely to select its own government. These two strands have been referred to as external and internal self-determination. However, there is also a third normative strand of the principle that was not foreseen in the earlier conceptions of self-determination. This is the right of peoples freely to pursue their economic, social, and cultural development, and to participate, contribute to, and enjoy such development. Together with internal self-determination, this third strand, which may be called socio-economic self-determination, is likely to contribute in the future to a better realization of human rights and fundamental freedoms. Indeed, when implemented together, these two strands may, on the one hand, protect peoples from anti-democratic or oppressive actions by their own state, while, on the other hand, they may provide the preconditions necessary to the fulfilment of indi-vidual human rights, particularly in the economic, social, and cultural sphere. Two aspects of this third strand are likely to assume growing legal importance in the twenty-first century: one based on the evolution of the principle of per-manent sovereignty over natural resources, and the other related to the realiza-tion of the equal rights of peoples through the mitigation or elimination of the inequalities inherent in the international economic system. One can assume that, in the future, actions involving the exploitation of natural resources taken by non-representative or autocratic governments and manifestly contrary to the interests of the peoples concerned could be open to challenge as violations of international law. The gradual coming together of the two strands of internal political self-determination and socio-economic self-determination will render obsolete the need for secession and separation of certain peoples from existing states.

## 1. Introduction

The principle of equal rights and self-determination of peoples has, over the past 60 years, acted as a force for the humanization and democratization of international law. It is one of those pioneering principles of the UN Charter which have contributed to the break with the classical conception of international law as a law which concerned itself solely with the relations between states. By piercing the veil of state sovereignty, it has enabled international law to pay closer attention to the rights of the individuals and groups living within the state and subject to its authority, and to view them as bearers of international legal rights. As observed by a commentator, it also marked a break with

the pre-war framework of international law which drew a sharp distinction between Europeans or people of European descent and non-Europeans: only the former were unquestionably entitled to sovereign statehood. The latter were assumed not to be qualified at least prima facie, and the burden of proof was on them to justify it in terms of standards defined by western civilization.[1]

In the same way that it substantially contributed to the liberation of peoples subject to colonial oppression or alien domination, could one expect it to break new ground and play a prominent role in the future in the emancipation of peoples from authoritarian and non-democratic rule within their own states? Could it legally enable such peoples in the future to throw off the shackles of poverty and underdevelopment, freely to participate in and enjoy economic, social, and cultural development of their countries; and to achieve equal rights in the economic field? Could these expectations constitute a realistic utopia for the twenty-first century in light of the meteoric evolution that the concept of equal rights and self-determination of peoples has gone through in the twentieth century?

It may indeed be recalled that although self-determination was strongly advocated both by V.I. Lenin and President Wilson of the United States in the aftermath of the First World War, it was not incorporated either as a principle or as a right into the Covenant of the League of Nations. The Committee of Jurists on the Aaland Islands Question went so far as to state specifically that self-determination had not yet attained the status of a positive rule of international law.[2] Nevertheless, both the Leninist notion of self-determination in the sense of the political separation of

---

[1] R.H. Jackson, *Quasi-States: Sovereignty, International Relations, and The Third World* (Cambridge: Cambridge University Press, 1990), 16.

[2] League of Nations, Report of the Committee of Jurists on the Aaland Islands Question, LN Doc. B.7 21/68/106, 1921.

a people from an existing national state or imperial power, and the formation of its own independent state, and the Wilsonian concept of the right of a people freely to select its own government, were later to find concrete expression in two strands of self-determination which evolved under the UN Charter. These were the right of peoples to independence from colonial and alien domination and the right of peoples within a state to choose a representative government. These two strands have been referred to in the literature as external and internal self-determination.

There is also a third normative strand of the principle of equal rights and self-determination of peoples that was not foreseen in the earlier conceptions of self-determination, but was exclusively developed under the UN Charter. This is the right of peoples freely to pursue their economic, social, and cultural development, and to participate, contribute to, and enjoy such development. Together with internal self-determination, this third strand, which may be called socio-economic self-determination, is likely to contribute in the future to a better realization of human rights and fundamental freedoms. Indeed, when implemented together, these two strands may, on the one hand, protect peoples from anti-democratic or oppressive actions by their own state, while, on the other hand, they may provide the pre-conditions necessary to the fulfilment of individual human rights, particularly in the economic, social, and cultural sphere. The various ways in which the above-mentioned different strands of the principle of equal rights and self-determination of peoples might evolve in the future will determine its further contribution to the development of international law as well as to the progress of humanity.

## 2. The birth of a right

There is no doubt that the principle of equal rights and self-determination of peoples, as laid down in the UN Charter, had its most important impact in international law with regard to decolonization and the right to independent sovereign statehood of peoples subjected to colonial oppression and alien domination. This might not have been the original intention of the drafters of the Charter. Nor did the Charter provide for a legal right to self-determination, as such. This right has emerged as a result of subsequent practice by the United Nations. It is, in my view, the pairing of 'self-determination' with 'equal rights' of peoples in the Charter that provided the legal basis for such subsequent practice giving rise to the consecration of self-determination as a positive right against colonization, oppression, and alien domination. It may indeed be argued that it is from the strength of the interaction between the two concepts that the subsequent right has arisen. Once the 'equal rights of peoples' was recognized in the Charter, there was no way in which some peoples and their powerful states could be allowed to continue to oppress and dominate other peoples who were much weaker either in terms of arms and weaponry or in economic and financial terms. By virtue of their equal rights under the Charter, the colonized or oppressed peoples became entitled to self-determination and independent statehood.

Neither the Charter nor the subsequent resolutions of the UN General Assembly provide us with a definition of 'peoples', but, contrary to the views of certain authors, one thing which the concept of 'equal rights and self-determination of peoples' in the Charter does not provide for is the rights of states. It clearly provides for the rights of 'peoples', distinct from the state, and mentioned, as such, in various parts of the Charter. The peoples in question may live in a sovereign independent state of their own, and may therefore coincide with the population of such a state or be only a part of such population. They may be subjected to colonial rule by a foreign power; or they may find themselves under foreign occupation or alien domination. But, in all the above-mentioned cases, they constitute a collective entity, distinct from the state itself, and entitled to equal rights and self-determination under international law. The specific nature of such rights and their normative content will depend on the actual circumstances and conditions of the peoples concerned.

Even before the UN General Assembly adopted its 1960 Declaration on the Granting of Independence to Colonial Countries and Peoples, the equal rights and self-determination of peoples proclaimed in the Charter fired up the hopes and aspirations of all those whose equal rights as a people had been forcibly taken away through colonial subjugation and who were treated, sometimes through the invocation of international law itself, as inferior peoples, lacking history, civilization, or statehood, and consequently neither having rights nor obligations at the international level. The added value of the resolutions adopted by the General Assembly, particularly Resolutions 1514(XV),[3] 1541(XV),[4] and 2625(XXV),[5] was to render operational the Charter principles by specifying their legal implications both in normative and practical terms, as reflected in the practice of the organs of the United Nations. The rights and duties established under these resolutions are now deemed to have become part of customary international law.[6]

From a normative perspective, the proclamation of the principle of equal rights and self-determination of peoples in the Charter made the continued colonization or domination of one people by another legally and politically impermissible. Thus, in Resolution 1514(XV), the General Assembly first declared that 'the subjection of peoples to alien subjugation, domination and exploitation' constitutes a denial

---

[3] GA Res. 1514(XV), Declaration on the granting of independence to colonial countries and peoples, 14 December 1960, available at <http://daccess-dds-ny.un.org/doc/RESOLUTION/GEN/NR0/152/88/IMG/NR015288.pdf?OpenElement>.

[4] GA Res. 1541(XV), Principles which should guide Members in determining whether or not an obligation exists to transmit the information called for under Article 73e of the Charter, 15 December 1960, available at <http://daccess-dds-ny.un.org/doc/RESOLUTION/GEN/NR0/153/15/IMG/NR015315.pdf?OpenElement>.

[5] GA Res. 2625(XXV), Declaration on Principles of International law concerning Friendly Relations and Co-operation among States in accordance with the Charter of the United Nations, 24 October 1970, available at <http://daccess-dds-ny.un.org/doc/RESOLUTION/GEN/NR0/348/90/IMG/NR034890.pdf?OpenElement>.

[6] See ICJ, *Legal Consequences for States of the Continued Presence of South Africa in Namibia (South West Africa) notwithstanding Security Council Resolution 276 (1970)*, Advisory Opinion, ICJ Reports 1971, 31–2, para. 53, *Western Sahara*, Advisory Opinion, ICJ Report 1975, pp 30–7; and the more recent *Accordance with International Law of the Unilateral Declaration of Independence in Respect of Kosovo*, Advisory Opinion, ICJ Reports 2010, 30, para. 80.

of human rights contrary to the UN Charter and an impediment to the promotion of world peace and security. The Assembly then proclaimed that 'all peoples have the right to self-determination; by virtue of that right they freely determine their political status and freely pursue their economic, social and cultural development'; thereby underlining the symbiotic relationship between equal rights and self-determination of peoples in the Charter. Colonization, foreign occupation, and alien domination were declared, first, to constitute a violation of the equal rights of peoples, and thus contrary to the Charter; and, secondly, to give rise to a right of the peoples concerned to determine their political status and decide on their destiny free from foreign pressure. This is indeed the manner in which the interaction between the two concepts operates in the context of the principle, with the violation of equal rights of peoples giving rise to a right to self-determination, while the exercise of the latter leads to the realization or restoration of the equal rights of the peoples concerned.

The 'equal rights of peoples' has emerged in recent years from the shadows of its applicability to colonial and alien domination only, and appears to be increasingly acquiring legal significance in all situations of domination and oppression of a people by other peoples, as well as situations of institutionalized inequalities among peoples, irrespective of whether such situations exist inside the state or in the relations between states. An early indication of this trend is to be found in Article 19 of the African Charter on Human and Peoples' Rights,[7] which provides that '[a]ll peoples shall be equal; they shall enjoy the same respect and shall have the same rights. Nothing shall justify the domination of a people by another.'

In practical terms, Resolution 1514(XV) prohibited certain practices of colonial powers, such as the pretext often used by such powers to delay or deny independence due to an alleged inadequacy of political, economic, social, or educational preparedness; or their attempts to dismember a non-self-governing territory so as to hold on to a part of such territory, or to use armed action and repressive measures against peaceful liberation movements or political parties. More importantly, it called for immediate steps to be taken by such colonial powers to 'transfer all powers' to the peoples of non-self-governing territories, 'without any conditions or reservations, in accordance with their freely expressed will and desire . . . in order to enable them to enjoy complete independence and freedom.'[8] It also banned the use of force against dependent peoples striving for the realization of their right to self-determination, declaring that 'all armed action or repressive measures of all kinds directed against dependent peoples shall cease in order to enable them to exercise peacefully and freely their right to complete independence, and the integrity of their national territory shall be respected.'[9]

The normative principles and practical measures thus established for the realization of the right of peoples to self-determination from colonization, foreign

---

[7] See the African Charter on Human and Peoples' Rights, available at <http://www.africa-union.org/official_documents/treaties_%20conventions_%20protocols/banjul%20charter.pdf>.
[8] Principle V, n 3.
[9] Principle IV, n 3.

occupation, and alien domination cannot be held to be devoid of significance for other situations where the equal rights of peoples are violated. Indeed, it may be argued that whenever such violation occurs, it gives rise to the right of peoples to exercise their self-determination, and the corresponding duty of every state to respect that right, in accordance with Resolution 2625(XXV) of the General Assembly, which has consolidated and codified the legal implications of the principle of equal rights and self-determination of peoples, as developed in the practice of states as well as of UN organs.

### 3. Is the external strand exhausted with decolonization?

Notwithstanding the near-completion of the process of decolonization in the world, the right of self-determination continued to acquire, in the last four decades, renewed significance following its consecration in the two covenants on human rights of 1966, the 1970 Declaration on Principles of International Law Concerning Friendly Relations and Co-operation among states in accordance with the Charter of the United Nations, the Final Act of the Conference on Security and Co-operation in Europe of 1975, (Helsinki Declaration),[10] the 1981 African Charter on Human and Peoples' Rights and the Vienna Declaration and Programme of Action adopted by the World Conference on Human Rights, June 1993.[11] But, does this renewed significance apply also to external self-determination, in the sense of entitlement to independence and separate statehood? Or, does it mainly concern the two other strands mentioned earlier?

The continued applicability of the right to self-determination, and its underlying principle of equal rights and self-determination of peoples, to situations of colonial domination or foreign occupation is generally admitted and has been confirmed on several occasions by the International Court of Justice.[12] However, doubts have often been expressed in the literature on its relevance and application within the framework of relations between peoples and their own state, particularly in the form of external self-determination or separation from such state. This is principally due to the fact that international law primarily protects, and gives priority to the territorial preservation of states and seeks to avoid their fragmentation or disintegration due to separatist forces. Secession may occur as a matter of fact, and may even be recognized by the international community, but it is neither encouraged by international law nor is it viewed, in all instances, as an entitlement based on the right to self-determination. So, although the right of

---

[10]  Available at the website of the Organization for Security and Co-operation in Europe, <http:// www.osce.org/mc/39501>.

[11]  See <http://www.unhchr.ch/huridocda/huridoca.nsf/(symbol)/a.conf.157.23.en>.

[12]  See, eg, *Legal Consequences for States of the Continued Presence of South Africa in Namibia (South West Africa) notwithstanding Security Council Resolution 276 (1970)*, Advisory Opinion, ICJ Reports 1971, 31–2, paras 52–3; *East Timor (Portugal v Australia)*, Judgment, ICJ Reports 1995, 102, para. 29; *Legal Consequences of the Construction of a Wall in the Occupied Palestinian Territory*, Advisory Opinion, ICJ Reports 2004 (I), 171–2, para. 88, *Western Sahara*, Advisory Opinion, ICJ Reports 1975, 31–3, paras 54–9.

external self-determination has not become obsolete and continues to apply to situations of foreign occupation and domination, a few cases of which still appear to persist in the world, particularly in the form of military occupation or forceful annexation of territory; its standing as the predominant strand within the right of self-determination is bound to diminish. This is likely to occur partly because of its gradual eclipse by the growing importance of internal self-determination, both in the political and socio-economic fields, and partly because of the fact that a claim to self-determination leading to separation from an existing state and creation of a new state has come to be viewed as a very exceptional, and most often an undesirable, occurrence in international relations. Indeed, the tendency in the world today is much more towards regional integration rather than fragmentation of existing states.

Yet, a racially or ethnically distinct group within a state may still claim external self-determination in those cases where the state to which it belongs not only denies it the exercise of the right of internal self-determination, but also subjects it to discrimination, persecution, and egregious violations of human rights or humanitarian law, amounting to a denial of equal rights of peoples. Under such exceptional circumstances, the right of peoples to self-determination, in its external strand of separate statehood, may be available to such a group provided the conditions prescribed by international law are specifically met in the situation regarding such a group. Such conditions may be gleaned from various instruments, including the 1970 Declaration on Principles of International Law Concerning Friendly Relations and Co-operation among states in Accordance with the Charter of the United Nations,[13] which is considered to have become part of customary international law, as well as the African Charter on Human and Peoples' Rights. The Declaration contains, under the principle of equal rights and self-determination of peoples, the following saving clause:

Nothing in the foregoing paragraphs shall be construed as authorizing or encouraging any action which would dismember or impair, totally or in part, the territorial integrity or political unity of sovereign and independent states conducting themselves in compliance with the principle of equal rights and self-determination of peoples as described above and thus possessed of a government representing the whole people belonging to the territory without distinction as to race, creed or colour.

This provision makes it clear that so long as a sovereign and independent state complies with the principle of equal rights and self-determination of peoples, its territorial integrity and national unity should neither be impaired nor infringed upon. However, the clause in its latter part implies that if a state fails to comport itself in accordance with the principle of equal rights and self-determination of peoples, an exceptional situation may arise whereby the ethnically or racially distinct group denied internal self-determination may claim a right of external

---

[13] General Assembly, *Declaration of Principles of International Law Concerning Friendly Relations and Co-operation among States in Accordance with the Charter of the United Nations*, 24 October 1970, available at <http://www.un-documents.net/a25r2625.htm>.

self-determination or separation from the state which could effectively put into question the state's territorial unity and sovereignty. Indeed, as pointed out above, the equal rights of peoples makes it legally impermissible that one people should dominate or oppress another people, even in those cases where both peoples are part of the same state. The domination or oppression of one people by another within the boundaries of the state does not legally differ from oppression across the oceans (or saltwater domination) insofar as it constitutes an infringement of the equal rights of peoples.

Similarly, Article 20 of the African Charter on Human and Peoples' Rights distinguishes between the right to self-determination of colonized peoples and the right of '[a]ll peoples to existence' and to 'the unquestionable and inalienable right to self-determination' under which they 'shall freely determine their political status and shall pursue their economic and social development according to the policy they have freely chosen.' Nevertheless, the latter type of self-determination, though generally available to all peoples, cannot be claimed by peoples resident in a state where they are treated in conditions of equality and non-discrimination with other component peoples of the state, and are allowed to participate in the choice of a representative government, however ethnically or racially distinct they may be. The African Commission on Human and Peoples' Rights in the case concerning the *Katangese Peoples' Congress v Zaire* described as follows the exceptional circumstances in which a claim to external self-determination and separation from an existing state may be advanced:

In the absence of concrete evidence of violations of human rights to the point that the territorial integrity of Zaire should be called to question and in the absence of evidence that the people of Katanga are denied the right to participate in government as guaranteed by Article 13 (1) of the African Charter, the Commission holds the view that Katanga is obliged to exercise a variant of self-determination that is compatible with the sovereignty and territorial integrity of Zaire.[14]

In other words, the Commission held that the Katangese people should exercise their right to self-determination internally unless it could be clearly demonstrated that their human rights were egregiously violated by the Government of Zaire (now DRC) and that they were denied the right to participate in government.[15]

---

[14] African Commission on Human and Peoples' Rights, Case 75/92 *Katangese Peoples' Congress v Zaire*, 1, available at <http://www.achpr.org/english/Decision_Communication/ DRC/Comm.%20 75-92.pdf>.

[15] The Canadian Supreme Court came to a similar conclusion in the case on the Secession of Quebec, see *Reference by the Governor-General concerning Certain Questions relating to the Secession of Quebec from Canada* ([1998] 2 SCR 217; 161 DLR (4th) 385; 115 ILR 536).

The African Commission has relied on several instances, including the above case, on Article 13(1) of the African Charter on Human and Peoples' Rights[16] as a fundamental criterion in deciding whether a people is so oppressed or discriminated against, or otherwise excluded from participation in government within its own state, that it becomes entitled to the right of external self-determination and separation from that state. It appears that the denial of the right of a people to participate in its own government, and the consequent non-existence of a government which represents its entire population would constitute, in the view of the Commission, a crucial element of the exceptional circumstances that may justify resort to external self-determination within an existing state. In this sense, the saving clause of Resolution 2625(XXV) mentioned above and the interpretation of the African Charter by the Commission appear to coincide on the conditions for the exercise of external self-determination.

It may therefore be concluded that, even in a post-colonial context, a claim to an external right to self-determination may be considered justifiable in exceptional circumstances attesting to a violation of the equal rights of peoples within the state. All possible remedies for the realization of internal self-determination must, however, be exhausted before the issue is removed from the domestic jurisdiction of the state which had hitherto exercised sovereignty over the territory inhabited by the people making the claim. In this context, the role of the international community, and in particular of the Security Council and the General Assembly of the UN as well as regional organizations such as the African Union, is of paramount importance. Such external self-determination may also occur through mutual agreement between the peoples concerned and the government of the state, particularly as a means of bringing to a peaceful end a long-lasting internal conflict. Recent cases of this type of consensual separation include those of Eritrea and Southern Sudan, respectively from Ethiopia and the Republic of Sudan.

Nevertheless, through the increasing application and realization within states of the internal right to self-determination enabling the entire population of the state to determine its own political, economic, and social destiny and to choose a representative government, it might be realistic to assume that resort to external self-determination, in the sense of separation from an existing state, will gradually disappear in the future, except in its consensual form, giving way to the increasing prevalence of internal self-determination of peoples, both in the political and socio-economic fields, as a cornerstone of international law and relations.

.

---

[16] Art. 13 reads:

1. Every citizen shall have the right to participate freely in the government of his country, either directly or through freely chosen representatives in accordance with the provisions of the law.
2. Every citizen shall have the right of equal access to the public service of his country.
3. Every individual shall have the right of access to public property and services in strict equality of all persons before the law.

## 4. Internal self-determination: respecting the will of the people

The right of self-determination, in its post-colonial conception, chiefly operates today inside the boundaries of existing states in various forms and guises, particularly as a right of the entire population of the state to determine its own political, economic, and social destiny and to choose a representative government; and, equally, as a right of a defined part of the population, which has distinctive characteristics on the basis of race or ethnicity, to participate in the political life of the state, to be represented in its government, and not to be discriminated against. These rights are to be exercised within the state in which the population or the ethnic group live, and thus constitute internal rights of self-determination. They offer a variety of entitlements to the concerned peoples within the borders of the state without threatening its sovereignty. The most important of these is respect for the will of the people freely to choose a genuinely representative government. This right is manifestly opposable to unconstitutional forms of government such as military governments, as well as to authoritarian or despotic governments, although until recently such governments have always tried to hide behind the principle of non-interference in the domestic affairs of states to ward off any claim of the applicability of international legal rules such as the right of self-determination to the choice of government by their own people. For such governments, this choice was a matter of domestic law and policy, and not of international law.

It might however be realistic to assume that this situation is in the process of changing and that the twenty-first century will most likely witness the emergence of a legal guarantee at the international level, in the form of a duty not only of the state concerned, but also of other states and international organizations, to ensure the respect of the rights of peoples freely to choose a government which truly represents them and reflects the expression of the will of the majority in free and fair elections. Such legal obligation of other states could consist of the withholding of recognition, individually or collectively, from governments which are not respectful of the will of their peoples or the suspension of their membership in universal or regional organizations. In other words, regional institutions or the international community as a whole would have the legal authority and obligation to effect the isolation of illegitimate and unrepresentative governments without necessarily resorting to intervention or the use of force to overthrow them.

The will of the people as the basis of the legitimacy of governments and as an internal right of self-determination was already recognized in the Universal Declaration of Human Rights, in which it is stated, under Article 21, paragraph 3, that: '[t]he will of the people shall be the basis of the authority of government; this will shall be expressed in periodic and genuine elections which shall be by universal and equal suffrage and shall be held by secret vote or by equivalent free voting procedures.' It is perhaps with reference to this provision that Cassese was able to state in 1995 that: 'a contention could...be warranted that at the present time a customary rule on the subject is in *statu nascendi*, that is, in the process of formation.' He warned, however, of the 'stumbling blocks which lie in the way of the birth of this emergent customary rule'.[17] He attributed these stumbling blocks mainly to the attitude taken by third world countries which, in his view, did not show 'a convinced and consistent acceptance that national government should be based on the consent of the governed, expressed at periodic, free and genuine elections'.[18] It could perhaps be affirmed, a decade and a half after Cassese's observations, that those stumbling blocks are on their way to disappearing, if they have not already disappeared.

We may not yet be at a point where the existence of despotic and tyrannical governments, not based on the freely expressed will of the people, would be considered to constitute an infringement of the right of peoples to self-determination; but we seem to be gradually, but clearly, moving in that direction with the establishment of certain standards and criteria the violation of which is now bound to give rise to economic and political sanctions or other measures against the concerned illegitimate or unrepresentative government either at the regional or at the global level. First, the African Union in its Constitutive Act of 2000 outlawed the unconstitutional change of government in the continent,[19] and has since then suspended from participation in the work of the organization any government brought to power by a coup d'état. Thus, although a military government or a civilian government installed by the army might be effectively in control of the territory of a state, the African Union does not recognize it, nor does it allow it to exercise its membership rights in the organization until such time as it re-establishes, most often with the assistance of the organization, a democratically elected and representative government which assumes power with the consent of its own people through free and fair elections. Similarly, the heads of state and government of the Americas, adopted on April 2001 in Quebec city, a 'democracy clause' which establishes that any unconstitutional alteration or interruption of the democratic order in a state of the hemisphere constitutes an insurmountable obstacle to the participation of that state's government in the Summits of the Americas process.[20]

Secondly, the member states of both organizations adopted charters on democratic governance. The Inter-American Democratic Charter, adopted on 11 September 2001,[21] is in the form of a declaration adopted by the General Assembly of the Organization of American States; nevertheless, it clearly states that '[t]he peoples of the Americas have a right to democracy and their governments have an obligation to promote and defend it' (Art. 1), and also establishes that '[t]he effective exercise of representative democracy is the basis for the rule of law and of the constitutional regimes of the member states of the Organization of American States' (Art. 2). The African Charter on Democracy, Elections and Governance,

---

[17] A. Cassese, *Self-determination of Peoples: A Legal Reappraisal* (Cambridge: Cambridge University Press, 1999), 306–7.

[18] Ibid.

[19] See Arts 4(p) and 30 of the African Union Constitutive Act 2000 available at <http://www.africa-union.org/about_au/AbConstitutive_Act.htm>.

[20] The Declaration of Quebec City, available at <http://www.summit-americas.org/iii_summit/iii_summit_dec_en.pdf>.

[21] Available at <http://www.oas.org/charter/docs/resolution1_en_p4.htm>.

adopted in 2007,[22] is in the form of a convention which will enter into force once it is ratified by 15 member states of the organization. It stipulates, inter alia, that 'States Parties shall commit themselves to promote democracy, the principle of the rule of law and human rights'[23] and that 'states Parties shall recognize popular participation through universal suffrage as the inalienable right of the people'.[24]

In a similar vein, the Protocol on Democracy and Good Governance of the Economic Community for West African States (ECOWAS)[25] proclaims among the shared constitutional principles of the member states of this sub-regional African organization that: (i) every accession to power must be made through free, fair, and transparent elections; (ii) zero tolerance for power obtained or maintained by unconstitutional means; and (iii) popular participation in decision-making, strict adherence to democratic principles, and decentralization of power at all levels of governance.

The African Charter on Democracy, Elections and Governance makes it very clear that accession to power through non-democratic means is no longer a matter of domestic jurisdiction but a situation which triggers the adoption of certain measures or sanctions by the organs of the African Union. Thus, according to Article 24 of the Charter:

When a situation arises in a State Party that may affect its democratic political institutional arrangements or the legitimate exercise of power, the Peace and Security Council shall exercise its responsibilities in order to maintain the constitutional order in accordance with relevant provisions of the Protocol Relating to the Establishment of the Peace and Security Council of the African Union, hereinafter referred to as the Protocol.

The types of situation which may draw sanctions from the African Union are described in Article 23 of the Charter as follows:

States Parties agree that the use of, *inter alia*, the following illegal means of accessing or maintaining power constitute an unconstitutional change of government and shall draw appropriate sanctions by the Union:

1. Any putsch or *coup d'État* against a democratically elected government.
2. Any intervention by mercenaries to replace a democratically elected government.
3. Any replacement of a democratically elected government by armed dissidents or rebels.
4. Any refusal by an incumbent government to relinquish power to the winning party or candidate after free, fair and regular elections; or
5. Any amendment or revision of the constitution or legal instruments, which is an infringement on the principles of democratic change of government.

---

[22] Available at <http://www.au.int/en/sites/default/files/AFRICAN_CHARTER_ON_DEMOCRACY_ELECTIONS_AND_GOVERNANCE.pdf>.

[23] Ibid, Art. 4(1).

[24] Ibid, Art. 4(2).

[25] Available at <http://www.comm.ecowas.int/sec/en/protocoles/Protocol%20on%20good-governance-and-democracy-rev-5EN.pdf>.

All these situations are likely to be considered in the future, not only under the instruments of the African Union, but in international law in general, as an infringement upon the right of peoples freely to determine their political status and to choose the form of government most appropriate for the management of their affairs. With the upcoming entry into force of this Charter, such an infringement will not only be outlawed in Africa, but will also draw sanctions by the African Union, and most probably by the UN, against those governments responsible for the violation of the right of internal self-determination in the form of suspension from membership of the organization. Such sanctions are already being applied by the African Union. They were recently imposed on the Governments of Madagascar,[26] Guinea,[27] and Niger[28] following their accession to power through a coup d'état, and on that of the Côte d'Ivoire for the refusal of its incumbent President to relinquish power to the winning candidate after elections the results of which were certified by the UN Special Representative in accordance with Security Council resolutions.[29]

It might equally be realistic to assume that in the future the normative principles and practical measures specified in Resolution 1514(XV) of the General Assembly with regard to the realization of the right to self-determination in situations of colonization, foreign occupation, and alien domination may find appropriate application in internal situations involving a violation of equal rights and self-determination of peoples, particularly their right to a representative government. This would imply the outlawing of the use of force by an unrepresentative and authoritarian government against its own people, and its obligation to respect the free and peaceful expression of the will of the people, as well as the right of other states, acting collectively in the UN or through regional organizations, to protect such people in order to ensure its existence and its inalienable right to self-determination. Moreover, besides the sanctions mentioned above, we are likely to witness in the future increasing resort to international criminal justice to hold the political leadership accountable for repressive measures against its own people, particularly when such measures involve massive violations of human rights or humanitarian law, or crimes against humanity. Recourse by representatives of the peoples concerned, or by non-governmental organizations on their behalf, to human rights jurisdictions, such as the African Court on Human and Peoples' Rights and the Inter-American Court of Human

---

[26] See Communiqué of the African Union Peace and Security Council, 17 March 2010, available at <http://www.africa-union.org/root/ua/conferences/2010/mars/psc/17mars/221st%20communiqu%E9%20cps%20madagascar%20eng.pdf>.

[27] See Communiqué of the African Union Peace and Security Council, 29 October 2009, available at <http://www.africa-union.org/root/au/organs/207%20Communique%20Guinee%20_Eng._.pdf>.

[28] See Communiqué of the African Union Peace and Security Council, 19 February 2010, available at <http://www.africa-union.org/root/au/organs/216%20Communique%20Niger%20_eng.pdf>.

[29] See Communiqué of the African Union Peace and Security Council, 10 December 2010, available at <http://www.africa-union.org/root/au/Conferences/2010/december/Communiqu%C3%A9%20of%20the%20252nd.pdf>.

Rights, is also likely to increase to find judicial remedies to situations involving a breach of the internal self-determination of peoples within states.[30]

## 5. Socio-economic self-determination: the right of peoples to shape their destiny in the social, economic, and cultural field

In the same way that internal self-determination contributes to the realization of individual rights in the civil and political domain, socio-economic self-determination can provide the preconditions necessary to the fulfilment of individual human rights in the economic, social, and cultural sphere. It must, however, be recognized that socio-economic self-determination, despite its consecration in various international instruments, has not moved as significantly, both at the international and domestic levels, as internal self-determination in promoting peoples' rights and protecting them from foreign domination and exploitation or from domestic oppression and dispossession. Socio-economic self-determination involves the right of peoples to 'freely pursue their economic, social and cultural development',[31] and to 'freely dispose of their natural wealth and resources'.[32]

Two aspects are likely to assume growing legal importance in the twenty-first century: one based on the evolution of the principle of permanent sovereignty over natural resources and its implications for internal self-determination in the socio-economic field, and the other related to the realization of the equal rights of peoples through the mitigation or elimination of the inequalities inherent in the international economic system. The latter reference is not so much to the inequalities that arise from unequal resource endowments, but the inequalities which result from foreign exploitation or economic domination by other peoples, or by foreign institutions and enterprises, or due to patterns of global trade and investment underpinned by inequitable rules. In both instances, it should be recalled that in view of the interplay between internal and external factors in matters of socio-economic self-determination, the state acts as an intermediary in dealings with external interests on behalf of the people as well as a trustee of the people in the management of the national wealth and resources. As stated by Umozurike:

For the 'peoples to benefit from the advantages derived from their national resources' an atmosphere must be created that rectifies the shortcomings of economic relations with international monopolies as well as those of internal leadership.[33]

---

[30] See most recently the decision of the African Court on Human and Peoples' Rights in the matter of *African Commission on Human and Peoples' Rights v Great Socialist People's Libyan Arab Jamahiriya*, App. no. 004/2011 Order for Provisional Measures, 4, para. 3. The African Commission following the receipt of complaints against the Libyan Government concluded that the Government had violated rights enshrined in Arts 1, 2, 4, 5, 9, 11, 12, 13, and 23 of the African Charter.

[31] Art. 1(1) of the International Covenant on Economic, Social and Cultural Rights 1966, available at <http://www2.ohchr.org/english/law/cescr.htm>.

[32] Ibid, Art. 1(2).

[33] U. Oji Umozurike, *The African Charter on Human and Peoples' Rights* (The Hague: Martinus Nijhoff, 1997), 55.

The question, however, arises whether an unrepresentative and non-democratic government can fulfil such requirements. This is where the essential link between internal self-determination, in the sense examined above, and socio-economic self-determination needs to be recognized, since the full realization of the latter often presupposes the existence of the former.

When the principle of permanent sovereignty over natural resources was proclaimed by the General Assembly in 1962, it was thought that control over the natural resources would enable the newly independent countries to achieve 'economic independence' from the former colonial powers and their enterprises.[34] It was also envisioned that such states would use their resources for the economic empowerment of their peoples and for the pursuit of their social, economic, and cultural development. In many cases, however, the benefits derived from these resources were either diverted by the political leadership for their own personal ends, or otherwise misused by autocratic ruling elites, resulting in what has been referred to as the 'resource curse', particularly in African countries, where it has been observed that an inverse relationship often exists between resource endowment and economic development. It should, however, be recalled that General Assembly Resolution 1803 (XVII) made it clear that the permanent sovereignty over natural resources belonged to the people and not to the state, nor to its governmental authorities. This was later confirmed by Common Article 1 of the two Covenants on Human Rights[35] which provides in paragraph 2 that 'All peoples may, for their own ends, freely dispose of their natural wealth and resources without prejudice to any obligations arising out of international cooperation, based upon the principle of mutual benefit, and international law.' Similarly, it is stipulated in Article 21(1) of the African Charter on Human and Peoples' Rights that 'All Peoples shall freely dispose of their wealth and natural resources. This right shall be exercised in the exclusive interest of the people. In no case shall a people be deprived of it.' This is a reaffirmation of the fiduciary relationship which exists between the state and its citizens in the management and utilization of natural resources. This fiduciary relationship implies certain rights and duties, in the sense that the peoples' rights specified in the above-mentioned provisions impose corresponding duties on the state and its institutions. First, the government has to manage such resources for the benefit of the people, as a whole, and ensure that they are not diverted for the use of a section of the population or of individuals exercising political power. Secondly, state institutions have an obligation not to use such resources in a way that may cause substantial harm to the health and environment of the people.[36] Thirdly, it is the duty of the state to protect intergenerational rights, particularly with respect to non-renewable resources. Since the source of wealth created by non-renewable resources vanishes with the exploitation of such resources, it is the

---

[34] See generally, N. Schrijver, *Sovereignty over Natural Resources* (Cambridge: Cambridge University Press, 1997).

[35] Available at <http://www.ohchr.org/EN/ProfessionalInterest/Pages/InternationalLaw.aspx>.

[36] The Social and Economic Rights Action Center and the Center for Economic and Social Rights/ Nigeria Communication 155/96, available at <http://www.achpr.org/english/activity_reports/ activity15_en.pdf>.

obligation of the state to safeguard the rights of future generations through the establishment of mechanisms that can store part of the wealth derived from the resources in assets that will continue to yield earnings even after the exhaustion of the resources.[37] The rights and duties implied in this fiduciary relationship have yet to find widespread application and enforcement at the international level.

It may, however, be realistic to assume that in future actions involving the exploitation of natural resources taken by non-representative or autocratic governments and manifestly contrary to the interests of the peoples concerned could be open to challenge as violations of international law. Indeed, according to Article 21(2) of the African Charter, 'In case of spoliation the dispossessed people shall have the right to the lawful recovery of the property as well as to an adequate compensation.' A policy of exploiting the resources of another country against the interests of its own inhabitants, and for the benefit of foreign enterprises or states, may equally qualify as an infringement of the right of such peoples freely to dispose of their resources for their own ends. Affording international legal protection through the right of peoples to socio-economic self-determination to the utilization of such resources by the people holding the ownership rights for their own ends may put an end to the irresponsible use of resources by unrepresentative governments or corrupt ruling elites and, at the same time, expand the pool of financial resources available for the realization of individual human rights in the economic, social, and cultural field as well as for the fight against poverty and underdevelopment.

As regards the realization of equal rights of peoples, a better recognition and application of the right to socio-economic self-determination and its relevance to international economic relations, as a peoples' right freely to pursue their economic, social, and cultural development, may equally contribute in the future to the identification of appropriate remedies to the lingering inequalities in the international economic system, and, in particular, to have the basic concerns of underdeveloped countries reflected in the asymmetrical rules which continue to govern international trade. The imbalances of the multilateral trade rules, enshrined in the General Agreement on Tariffs and Trade (GATT)/World Trade Organization (WTO) legal framework, with regard to the trade and development interests of underdeveloped economies have long been recognized by almost all participants in the system. The latest attempts to rectify such imbalances through the launching of the Doha Development Round of the WTO have not yet achieved a successful conclusion. As developing states, acting as intermediaries for the realization of the equal rights of their peoples in the socio-economic field, try to integrate more closely into the world economy, and fully partake in international economic cooperation, it may not be unrealistic to assume that the architecture, contents, and coverage of the multilateral trade rules will be subjected to fundamental changes so as to turn international trade into an engine of growth for all countries and extend its benefits to all peoples to enable them to realize their socio-economic self-determination, and to combat poverty and economic marginalization.

---

[37] See, eg, the creation of sovereign wealth funds in Norway and Kuwait. Additional information on global sovereign wealth funds can be found at <http://www.swfinstitute.org/about/>.

It may therefore be concluded that the gradual coming together of the two strands of internal political self-determination and socio-economic self-determination for the peoples of the world will not only render obsolete the need for secession and separation of certain peoples from existing states, but will contribute to the realization of equal rights of peoples at the international and domestic levels and create an environment in which individual human rights and fundamental freedoms can be fully exercised; or is this too much to assume realistically in the future development of international law?

# 31

# How to Depart from the Existing Dire Condition of Development

*Emmanuelle Jouannet**

## SUMMARY

Classical International Development Law (IDL) has not kept its promises despite continuing attempts to implement it. Major legal principles such as the right of peoples to self-determination, sovereignty over natural resources, and the right to nationalize against just compensation have helped to found and consolidate the sovereignty of newly independent states and let them properly consider their development. However, the set of legal norms that were subsequently adopted, which are legally binding and have been provided with some effectiveness, have proved extremely disappointing in their application. Not only do they maintain a real dependency on the helper and donor states or international organizations but they also seem to have had virtually no impact on the development of poor states. The same applies to the principle of double standards, public support, cooperation, technology transfer, the principle of common but differentiated obligations, or the famous Structural Adjustment Programmes (SAPs) run in authoritarian fashion under the leadership of large financial institutions. None of these legal and economic practices has been convincing. The new IDL of the post-Cold War years, which currently applies concurrently with conventional law on the matter seems no more effective. To change the existing dire condition, three options are open: (i) sticking to the neo-liberal pro-market paradigm—an economically efficient but socially unfair solution; (ii) jettisoning any model of development—a blind alley; and (iii) changing the rules of the global economic system, and creating a new and fair New International Economic Order. This third option aims at changing the rules of the global economic system, recasting the Bretton Woods financial institutions, changing the rules of the General Agreement on Tariffs and Trade (GATT), and revising the World Trade Organization (WTO) in a more equitable direction so that it finally refocuses relations between the various North(s) and

* Translated from French by Iain L. Fraser.

South(s). The point is to rethink the core of the economic system in its dual normative and institutional aspects. This reform seeks not the mirage of equality between states, but to make the principle of fairness the legal basis for all future discussions between the North(s) and South(s), so as to change a profoundly unjust system—the interests of the North(s) must be taken into account as well as those of the South(s), because poverty and inequality have also increased in the North. A new New International Economic Order (NIEO) is the necessary condition for sustainable human development that is effective, and it is only at this price that the enchanted discourse of IDL can finally become a reality, and utopia can perhaps finally become incarnate.

## 1. The international situation: a new world, but inequities persist

With the end of the Cold War and the advent of the new globalization, a series of utopian projects emerged with regard to the developing countries and overall world development. They interwove national and international doctrines and policies, legal practices involving free trade, open markets, the expansion of democratic institutions, human rights, and the opportunities offered by new communications media. They were intended to liberalize and to rid the world of the old barriers, especially collectivist and socialist ones, to promote freedom and good governance in all states and to mitigate the social and economic inequalities between states through a new general era of abundance that would benefit everyone. They promised developing countries freedom along with prosperity, two goals the realization of which communism and the Cold War had prevented. These projects supported and encouraged the new globalization, which was considered the main factor for success and development. They were also designed drastically to reduce world poverty. This was the time of faith in the blessings of liberal globalization, which some believed, and still believe firmly, would make the world more prosperous and more peaceful.

Experience gained during the past two decades, however, contradicts some of these expectations. The balance sheet is in fact highly contrasting. On one side there is the spectacular success of large emerging countries like India, Brazil, the countries of Southeast Asia and especially China, which in 2010 became the world's second economic power. Concomitantly, not only is the world perhaps becoming post-Western, but also, the so-called Third World broke apart, was divided and reconstructed, with some countries leaving it forever. It is now necessary to speak of North(s) and South(s), to denote sets of states that are increasingly divided and composite, and comparative analysis, once confined to North–South relations, now includes South–South and South–North relations.[1] This success of former developing countries is a new element that partly changes the data of the problem as they were assumed for decades, because now the economic model of

---

[1] S. Brunel, *Le Sud dans la nouvelle économie mondiale* (Paris: PUF, 1995), 245ff.

development from the North seems to really be bearing fruit in the South, raising living standards in the big emerging countries. It has helped lift hundreds of millions of people out of poverty. The failure on the part of some people to acknowledge this is, to say the least, surprising and perhaps displays an excessive contempt for the facts.[2]

On the other hand, there are poverty, hunger, and social and economic inequalities between states which retain frightening and unacceptable proportions, stopping us thinking that, as Robert Zoellick recently suggested, the Third World has completely disappeared.[3] Developing countries are still there, marked by hunger, misery, and poverty, and entirely dependent on international aid. The numbers show it. The latest UN Conference on Trade and Development (UNCTAD) report on least developed countries (LDCs) in 2010 is particularly dark, and says that everything in development should be reviewed.[4] World hunger was at its highest level in 2009, to decline only slightly in 2010, as 925 million people still suffer from chronic hunger.[5] While progress had been made in recent years, 64 million additional people fell into poverty in 2010 because of the crisis in the global financial and economic system.[6] The fact is that the recent financial crisis has further undermined hopes for a happy globalization, because it demonstrated how fragile the whole system was, capable at repeated intervals of leading to widespread social tragedies generating unemployment, insecurity, social exclusion, poverty, and hunger.

The question, then, is why we are still facing these problems and what we can or cannot do to address them. This question can be split in two. First, what might be the role of international law and particularly what is called IDL, which has been termed the 'social law of nations',[7] in eventually resolving the socio-economic inequalities between countries, ensuring the development of the developing countries, and thus bringing so many people out of poverty (Section 2)? Then, assuming that this law is a failure and has not kept its promises regarding the current situation, can we envisage a legal alternative that is realistic (Section 3)?

---

[2] For the facts see, eg, *Pays émergents: vers un nouvel équilibre mondial? Problèmes économiques*, April 2010, No. 29993. And for a denial of this bridging of the North–South gap through the economic development of countries of the South see, eg, G. Rist, *Le développement. Histoire d'une croyance occidentale*, 3rd edn (Paris: Sciences Po les Presses, 2007), 441ff.

[3] Robert Zoellick is the current President of the World Bank. See his speech in Washington, 14 April 2010. Full text available at <http://www.voltairenet.org/article164965.html>.

[4] UNCTAD, The Least Developed Countries Report 2010, *Towards a New International Development Architecture for LDCs*. See text at <http://www.unctad.org/en/docs/ldc2010_en.pdf>.

[5] According to the UN Food and Agriculture Organization (FAO) figures for 2010, 925 million people suffer from hunger. They represent 16 per cent of the population in developing countries and 30 per cent in the states of sub-Saharan Africa, but they are also increasing in developed countries. See the FAO website at <http://www.fao.org/hunger/hunger-home/en/>.

[6] Ie living on less than $1.25 per day. See World Bank figures quoted in *Le Monde*, 16 September 2010, available at <http://www.lemonde.fr/idees/article/2010/09/16/c-est-la-croissance-qui-eradiquera-la-pauvrete_1411907_3232.html>.

[7] To use a term from A. Pellet, in *Le droit international du développement*, 2nd edn (Paris: PUF, 1987), 4.

## 2.  Stocktaking of practice: development law in the fight against poverty

Law and development have for decades been in almost dialectical relations, which varied according to the times and development patterns within states. Whether in the English- or French-speaking worlds, essentially three major periods can be distinguished, characterized broadly as, first, the 'all-state' period of the years 1950–70, with an instrumental public law serving state interventionist policies, then the 'all-market' one of the 1980s dominated by the private rights of private actors, and finally the 'rule-of-law' one as from the 1990s, combining public law and private law and making the primacy of law (rule of law) into the actual goal of development. But interesting as these may be to go further into, our object is not to ponder these classifications. We wish to refocus attention on international law in relation to development, and more precisely on what is called IDL.

### (A) Classical international development law and new international development law

Two comments by way of a stocktaking:

First, it is clear that *classical IDL* has not kept its promises despite continuing attempts to implement it. Nothing makes it possible to believe that the various legal principles and practices that were grouped together in the 1970s as *the* international law of development were or currently are of any use in developing any countries. Remember that what is called IDL was built around the years 1960–70 thanks to the very new decolonized countries.[8] It consisted of a set of specific rules that sought to re-articulate the relations between North and South and especially to confer a special set of legal rules on the newly independent states regarded as 'underdeveloped', so as to give them the chance, legally, to play on equal terms with developed countries and thus to 'take off', then 'catch up' economically. Apart from the NIEO, which never gained legal force, these rules were designed to both strengthen the newly decolonized sovereignty and establish affirmative-action mechanisms in order ultimately to establish greater equality of economic and social situation between developed and underdeveloped countries.

Indeed, major legal principles such as those of the right of peoples to self-determination, sovereignty over natural resources, and the right to nationalize against just compensation have undoubtedly helped to found and consolidate the sovereignty of newly independent states and let them properly consider their development. But the set of legal norms that were subsequently adopted, those which are legally binding and have been provided with some effectiveness, have proved

---

[8]  Here, therefore, we study not the general relationship between law *and* development, which go beyond mere international law *of* development and concern how domestic just as much as international law can be used for the development of countries following different development strategies in vogue at a given time. For a discussion, cf eg D.M. Trubek and A. Santos (eds), *The New Law and Economic Development: A Critical Appraisal* (Cambridge: Cambridge University Press, 2008).

extremely disappointing in their application if one takes stock today. Not only do they maintain a real dependency on the helper and donor states or international organizations (IOs), but also they seem to have had virtually no impact on the development of poor states. The same applies to the principle of double standards, public support, cooperation, technology transfer, the principle of common but differentiated obligations, or the famous SAPs run in authoritarian fashion under the leadership of large financial institutions. None of these legal and economic practices has been convincing. On the contrary, although the situation of certain states means that they cannot do without them, they are part of a system that maintains dependency and does not give access to development.

First, it is not these legal practices of classic IDL that let the big states like China, India, and Brazil, or the countries of Southeast Asia, emerge. Many endogenous and exogenous factors explain this development, and will be discussed, but certainly not the few practices and legal principles of IDL.[9] Even more striking: the countries that have most dramatically developed, like those in Asia, were precisely those that did not submit to the dictates of the international financial institutions. Secondly, these practices, whether the Generalized System of Preferences (GSP), Official Development Assistance (ODA) or SAPs are always set unilaterally, either by the helping country (for GSP or ODA), or by financial institutions (for SAPs), and the mentions of partnership or the semblance of negotiation cannot hide the imposition of a hegemonic power relationship. So these are actually legal practices that perpetuate dependency of the recipient country, not only in the short to medium term due to the unilateral imposition, but also in the long term, as the states which benefit can no longer do without them, though not on that account gaining access to the status of emerging country. Among this set of practices, the SAPs imposed by the World Bank and the International Monetary Fund (IMF) are sadly famous for their devastating effects. They have been the object of very harsh criticism because of their incredible brutality in social terms but also their inefficiency. One witness against them was economist Joseph Stiglitz, describing what he calls his 'great disillusionment' after his experience at the World Bank, from which he resigned in November 1999.[10] His extremely precise indictment against the World Bank's neo-liberal policies and especially IMF policy is overwhelming.

However, it is even more disturbing and worrying to see that the legal principle of the GSP on trade, based on the principle of double standards and therefore positive discrimination in favour of developing countries, seems not to have borne fruit. It can probably prevent some countries from foundering in the face of increasingly liberalized trade, and it remains essential in this, but it seems in no way to be the lever for development. Recently, several studies have been carried out showing the ineffectiveness of such measures.[11] For example, the GSP of the

---

[9] Cf on this point C. Jaffrelot (ed.), *L'enjeu mondial. Les pays émergents* (Paris: Sciences Po les Presses, 2008), and esp. the references below at nn 48 and 49.

[10] J.E. Stiglitz, *Globalization and Its Discontents* (New York: W.W. Norton, 2002).

[11] Eg H. Gherari, 'Tendances récentes des préférences commerciales', in *Mélanges Madjid Benchik* (Paris: Pedone, 2010), 465ff and C. Vidcar, 'Le traitement spécial et différentiel. Plaidoyer contre le système des préférences généralisées', JDI (2005) 319–39.

European Union, which is the oldest and most comprehensive, has been criticized on both theoretical and practical grounds because of excluding some countries that are non-beneficiaries (threshold effects) and actually benefiting, moreover, only those developing countries with the highest income levels. Due to the continuing trend towards lower tariffs, we also see a new opposition forming between developing countries which want to maintain their GSP and those which are not beneficiaries and seek the widest possible liberalization without GSP, with the largest drop in tariffs possible. This is one aspect of the new South–South struggles that continue to multiply. But the record of recent years shows especially that we are perhaps seeing the end of the GSPs so emblematic of classic IDL, because of both their economic inefficiency and the legal uncertainty that they create because of the numerous disputes that have crystallized around them, as with bananas.[12] Moreover, with the combined effect of more and more extended free trade and the rise of emerging countries that constitute harder and harder competition, we see that the trend is very much to reserve GSPs only to LDCs, while GSPs granted to other developing countries will be replaced by the establishment of regional free-trade areas with the opposite philosophy. We go from the double standards and discriminatory preferential principle to a strengthening of free trade on the basis of reciprocity, now considered the only effective instrument for growth in developing countries. The example of the Economic Partnership Agreements (EPAs) that the EU countries are currently forcing African countries to adopt is its direct translation. They are in effect aiming to reinstate the most-favoured-nation clause status as an equal, enabling free trade between the two regions of Europe and Africa. However, under pressure from the EU, the African countries concerned, which began by rejecting them, eventually accepted them even though they regard them as deeply unfair.

Given this, we could show the same problems with regard to some other principles, weakly legalized but legalized all the same, of classical IDL, such as public assistance, commodities, cooperation, or technology transfer; to say the least, they did not make poor countries take off. Their shortcomings, their narrow reach, and several major factors local to developing countries reinforce the impression of the almost complete failure of classical IDL. Emblematic of this sense of failure, the latest UNCTAD report on LDCs in 2010 has sounded the death knell for hopes of the latest strategies for development through trade in the poorest countries in the world.[13] UNCTAD concludes that the economic development model used for these 49 countries has failed and must be totally reviewed, particularly regarding the dependence of these countries on food imports, which according to UNCTAD's Secretary-General has 'devastating' consequences.[14]

---

[12] Gherari, n 11, at 478ff.

[13] Available at <http://www.unctad.org/Templates/WebFlyer.asp?intItemID=5737&lang=1>.

[14] He indicates that spending on food imports from these countries increased from $9 billion in 2002 to $23 billion in 2008. Text available at <http://www.lemonde.fr/international/article/2010/11/26/le-nombre-de-pays-tres-pauvres-a-double-en-quarante-ans_1445160_3210.html>.

Such a finding must be taken particularly seriously if we want to redirect thinking and explore new hypotheses to find the appropriate legal instruments to remedy the situation of profound inequality between rich and poor countries, but also the classical IDL which, by a tragic paradox of its effects, has never done anything other than perpetuate dependency and the underdevelopment of the latter vis-à-vis the former. What is IDL really worth if the alleged purpose is constantly postponed and its only effects are to avoid the country's financial and commercial collapse? What relevance can be given to these legal principles and practices if they do not lead to development? Classical IDL was supposed to lead so-called 'underdeveloped' countries to genuine independence and to economic and social development. But if, contrary to what was proclaimed, IDL maintains underdevelopment, then it is a law not of development but of underdevelopment. If it does not make the countries more independent, then it is a law of dependency.[15]

Secondly, the *new IDL* of the post-Cold War years, which currently applies concurrently with conventional IDL, seems no more convincing or effective. Since the 1990s, IDL has expanded and become more complex in the light of the new consensus of the international community in favour of human rights, good governance, and the need to fight together against the adverse effects of economic development on our environment. IDL has thus been redeveloped following guidelines aimed at highlighting the hitherto ignored multidimensional nature of development. We shall here summarize by way of example two of these new guidelines that appeared to open up new perspectives.

The first direction is that of the 'human development' law that redirects development towards the service not of states but of individuals, meaning that the human being is regarded as being the ultimate beneficiary. Thus, in 1990 the United Nations Development Programme (UNDP) launched a 'human development index' designed to assess the state of development and performance of a state in terms not only of income (GDP per capita), but also of the capacity which each individual has to make 'choices'. To do this, it inserts two other non-economic indicators: the first is health (life expectancy and infant mortality) and the second is educational (school enrolment of children and adult literacy). Human IDL also includes all the rules on what is known in UN parlance as 'good governance' that are recommended or imposed for application within developing countries wishing to develop. Good governance is defined by several legal rules on the operations of government, reminiscent of the rule of law in the English sense of the term: transparency, responsibility, the obligation of accountability, participation, and taking into account the needs of the population. Usually, we find the idea that 'good governance' is inseparable from democratic governance and respect for the civil, economic, and social rights of the individual.[16] The reversal of perspective from classical IDL is then obvious: where classic IDL is entirely focused around the traditional framework of international law and respect for the sovereignty of

---

[15] As already noted by M. Benchik, *Droit international du sous-développement. Nouvel ordre dans la dépendance* (Paris: Berger-Levrault, 1983), 12.

[16] See eg <http://www.institut-gouvernance.org/index.html>.

the state, advocating the customary principle of tolerance and neutrality vis-à-vis the political regime of developing states, the current law of development is built around the central figure of the individual, his rights, and his basic needs.[17]

A second shift which partially incorporates the concept of 'human development' has also been brought to the classical concept of IDL. The concept of 'sustainable development' law is the new face of IDL. It addresses the deep concerns of the time in relation to the devastation caused to the environment through our economic development pattern and the cascading effects that are expected in the more or less long term. We have finally realized that it is growth itself that ultimately implies the occurrence of the serious environmental damage affecting the climate, the planet, its biosphere, and its ecosystem. So there has gradually emerged, particularly given the essential role of non-governmental organizations (NGOs), the need to subordinate implementation of economic development to respect for the environment; hence the introduction into the legal texts of the principle of 'sustainable development'. The law of 'sustainable development' results more specifically from a series of initiatives, ranging from the Stockholm Conference on the Human Environment in 1972 to the last Earth Summit in Johannesburg in 2002, via the June 1992 Rio Declaration on Environment and Development, Agenda 21, and the Framework Conventions on Biological Diversity, to the Kyoto Protocol, which came into force in 2005. This development is called 'sustainable' because it corresponds to a mode of development with an intergenerational dimension: it must meet the current needs of development without compromising the ability of future generations to meet their own needs. Several legal principles, more or less well characterized, and with a more or less binding scope, frame this sustainable development law: the principle of participation, the precautionary principle, the principle of common but differentiated responsibilities, and the polluter-pays principle. But if it means a form of development that respects the environment, it also incorporates the principle of sustainable development that respects basic human rights.[18] When teamed with 'human development', it therefore further aims at making sustainable development policies that are environmentally acceptable also socially equitable and respectful of basic human rights. Finally, it continues to attempt a response, in part legal, to the question of economic development of states, primarily with regard to developing countries. In other words, it is particularly encompassing as it generates rules and legal practices in the three areas it seeks to reconcile: the economic (growth and production), the social (fight against poverty, good governance), and the ecological (preserving nature, or rather the planet).

---

[17] Recognizing that the human rights approach is different from and sometimes opposed to the basic needs approach. See P. Meyer-Bisch, 'Les violations des droits culturels, facteur d'appauvrissement durable: pour une observation des pauvretés culturelles', in E. Decaux and A. Yotopoulos-Marangopoulos (eds), *La pauvreté, un défi pour les droits de l'homme* (Paris: Pedone, 2009), 185ff.

[18] As indicated in eg the UN Agenda 21, Principle 1, in 1992: 'Human beings are at the centre of concerns for sustainable development. They are entitled to a healthy and productive life in harmony with nature.' Available at <http://www.un.org/esa/sustdev/documents/agenda21/french/action0. htm> and English text available at <http://www.unac.org/en/link_learn/monitoring/susdev_background_sustain.asp>.

The new model of development and the new law (more soft than hard) that can be linked with it therefore reflect an attempt to renew the old. They are interesting for the human and environmental progress that they bring together so as to consider not just the states but individuals and the environment. They are also interesting in their extremely broad scope, because while in most cases they apply to developing countries, they are nevertheless intended to apply to all states in the world, both North and South, emphasizing that we all share a common fate.

However, this new IDL too has many limitations. Suffice it here to mention two.

The first limitation is that the new IDL remains—at least temporarily—a law of dependence. The dependence of developing countries is growing very significantly. Poor countries are increasingly forced to accept the new principles of respect for the environment, good governance, democracy, and respect for human rights if they wish to continue to benefit from development assistance and cooperation. The obligations on the beneficiary state are considerably heavier, as are the possible restrictions and limitations on the preferences granted if the conditions are not met. Let us take the case of the special incentive arrangement for sustainable development and good governance (GSP+) established at European level. To benefit from this system of preferences that is more favourable than the classic version, it is in particular necessary for the beneficiary state to ratify no less than 27 conventions: 16 International Labour Organization (ILO)/UN conventions on human rights and workers' rights and 11 conventions relating to the environment and principles of good governance. Secondly, the state must make a commitment to legislation and measures for the internal application of these 27 conventions, and finally, it must accept that this implementation be subject to periodic review. Added to this are the principles of good governance and the penalties if either party violates its obligations, ranging up to suspension of the system of preferences. This new type of legal arsenal leads many commentators to believe that we have entered a new development paradigm where the primacy of law and the rule of law are not only new ways of development but also the very object of development.[19] We would then be witnessing a rise in power of the law which, far from reflecting the decline of politics, on the contrary strengthens the politicization of development.[20]

How can one fail to see the strong politicization of these new legal practices associated with this new face of IDL, or the intensified interventionism in the poor countries? As we know, it is the poorest African states that have principally been targeted by these measures and that have been subjected to sanctions, giving new reasons to maintain resentment at a policy of 'one law for the rich and another for the poor' compared to other countries and regions worldwide. It also follows that the complexity of the historical, political, and cultural processes of development, respect for indigenous forms of development, the social choices of each state, are

---

[19] See, eg, A. Perry-Kessaris, 'Introduction', in A. Perry-Kessaris (ed.), *Law in the Pursuit of development* (London/New York, Routledge, 2010), 2ff.

[20] *Contra* D. Kennedy, 'The "Rule of Law", Political Choices and Development Common Sense', in Trubek and Santos (eds), n 8, at 95ff.

all erased in favour of one and the same vision of a politically liberal free-market society considered as a place of exchange between free and equal individuals, and as embodying in itself progress and modernity. By the same token, the generalization of this liberal, humanist, mercantile view of development is based on a positive portrayal of the West, which values its own standards for education, knowledge, economy, autonomy, and politics. In saying this, we are not pushing a radical critique of this vision, as a culturally situated model can be not only valid but can also be generalized if there is widespread acculturation of populations and international agreement among states. But the fact is that for the moment this face of development is much more intrusive.

The second limitation of the new IDL is that beyond this intensified political interventionism IDL still seems both ineffective and inefficient. Disregarding the environmental aspects that are marginal to the most crucial problems for developing countries, given the current situation mentioned in the introduction, we must fear that this new IDL changes inequality between states very little and hence does not have any impact on the actual economic and social development of poor countries. As Sylvie Brunel tersely summarized it, the problem is that 'the rich focus on sustainability but the poor still think development'.[21]

## (B) The turn in favour of the fight against poverty

Moreover, it seems that policymakers have realized the rhetorical nature of the new IDL, which finds it very hard to get beyond mere discourse and furthermore does not address the economic and social development of developing countries and LDCs. At the same time as they proliferated the new texts on sustainable social and human IDL, the major international players have for more than a decade adopted much more precise goals, much more focused on social issues such as health, hunger, and poverty; as if all the time they were multiplying their non-binding texts on sustainable human and social global development, with their particularly ambitious and wide scope, they were becoming aware of their ineffectiveness and backing down from the objectives. Among these objectives, translated under the name of the Millennium Development Goals (MDGs),[22] the main one is certainly the fight against poverty.

It may seem strange to make the fight against poverty a new trend in the years 1990–2000, when it has since 1950 been one of the major goals of development law. However, it is indeed a crucial contemporary development, since the fight against poverty has everywhere been taking precedence over IDL. An emblematic instance is how the UN General Assembly did not proclaim a new Development Decade, but in 1995 launched the First United Nations Decade for the Eradication

---

[21] S. Brunel, *A qui profite le développement durable?* (Paris: Larousse, 2008), 9.
[22] *Déclaration du Millénaire* [United Nations Millennium Declaration, GA Res. of 8 September 2000 (A/55/L.2)]. Text available at <http://www.un.org/french/millenaire/ares552f.htm> and English text available at <http://www.un.org/millennium/declaration/ares552e.htm>.

of Poverty.[23] Hence, also, the introduction of the new classification into 'emerging countries' and 'poor countries'. The former (MICs) benefit from IMF loans; the others, supported by the International Bank for Reconstruction and Development, have the priority aim of reducing the extreme poverty and destitution of their populations. An International Day for the Eradication of Poverty was also decreed by the UN in 1993. And the MDGs have set the international community the very precise objective of halving poverty by 2015. The main international and regional organizations concerned have followed suit, making it the top priority and reorienting their activities and aid in this direction. In 2000, the World Bank report was entitled 'Attacking Poverty' and the UNDP's 'Overcoming Human Poverty'. In 2010, the European Year was called European Year for Combating Poverty and Social Exclusion. At the state level it is the same, and there are countless statements of heads of state calling for overcoming poverty. The external legal policies have been adapted to the new goal. Thus, in France, as in many other countries, the fight against poverty was defined in 1999 by the Ministry of Foreign Affairs as 'the priority reference of all cooperation policy'. This results in legal practices that are no longer conditional but selective according to poverty of the population and much more targeted and precise as to figures than the grand pronouncements of IDL.

But by narrowing the aims it reflects, the current fight against poverty and extreme poverty contributes in any event to endorsing the idea that it is impossible to find political and legal solutions for the all-round development of developing countries.[24] However, if the MDGs are more focused and precise and thus seem more realistic, it is doubtful they will be more satisfactory. First, the question of the effectiveness of the commitments made at international, regional, and national level arises. The 2010 report to the UN taking stock of the MDGs is very mixed: it announces that extreme poverty has declined, but hunger in the world nonetheless increased.[25] Moreover, the MDGs seem unattainable for 2015, and if nothing changes nearly one and a half billion people will continue to live in poverty. Then, the priority and urgency of these goals can have a perverse effect, hiding the underlying causes of poverty and preventing reflection on the overall development of states. As Zaki Laïdi rightly notes,[26] at this stage we no longer reason in terms of urgency because the problems are urgent, but just

---

[23] Res. A/RES/50/107, 26 January 1996. It also covered the observance of the International Year for the Eradication of Poverty. Text available at <http://www.un.org/documents/ga/res/50/a50r107.htm>. See also Section III of the Millennium Declaration and the World Summit for Social Development.

[24] Certainly, the MDG 8 provides for a 'global partnership for development' which is much broader, but as shown by a recent report submitted to the UN in September 2010, a weakening of that goal is feared, due to both the rich countries' economic difficulties because of the crisis and the constant delays in payment of aid or carrying out transfers and cooperation. See on this the UN website at <http://www.un.org/millenniumgoals/pdf/10–43282_MDG_2010%20(E)%20WEBv2.pdf>.

[25] The Millennium Development Goals Report 2010, September 2010. Text available at <http://mdgs.un.org/unsd/mdg/Resources/Static/Products/Progress2010/MDG_Report_2010_En_low%20res.pdf>.

[26] Z. Laïdi, 'Le basculement du "nous" vers le "je". Réflexions sur le système social mondial', in Y. Daudet (ed.), *Les Nations Unies et le développement social international* (Paris: Pedone, 1996), 35ff.

because we no longer have a long-term perspective, because there is no longer any global project to transform international society and, unable to project ourselves into such a goal, we focus only on immediate problems. Accordingly, this logic is an obstacle to finding substantive solutions. We thus no longer speak of socio-economic inequalities in the texts relating to poverty, as the problem has gone. LDCs and developing countries are regarded as now having only one central problem, that of poverty, so that the fight against poverty will be the key to everything, along with the market. But the fight against poverty is not economic and social development, and ways to address social and economic inequalities are far more difficult and challenging for states than the means needed to eradicate poverty.[27]

The contemporary turn towards poverty cannot, however, be reduced to this one dimension. The fight against poverty remains a goal of social justice and the standards adopted for this purpose try to compensate for the extreme imbalances in the world.[28] This refocusing on the fight against poverty can also, as we said, be understood as being due to a crisis of legal policies on global development. It is the failure of these prior legal policies, a sense of helplessness. and of the inefficiency of certain legal and economic principles or rules, that also led to this focus on poverty alone, and on humanitarian action alone.

## (C) General assessment

Faced with the dual finding of the ineffectiveness of both conventional IDL and new IDL and the limited character of the fight against poverty, an inevitably bleak general assessment can be drawn up.

For all this shows that the tragic fate of IDL and of all the principles, traditional and new, by which it sought to change the socio-economic inequalities between states and peoples since the 1970s continues today: they simply do not work. They are mostly legally non-binding, and if they are binding they are largely ineffective. Legal policies are ineffective, and the most progressive standards are never adhered to. Some allow the poor states not to founder, others worsen the situation. None can be cited as having actually helped to develop a state harmoniously or restrain socio-economic inequalities between states. And yet year after year, decade after decade, numerous standards, rules, and practices relating to an IDL able to save the developing countries are produced. We continue to develop material that, for decades, has explained that 'the way to go' 'is long' because 'the gap keeps widening' between rich and poor countries; that, however, there 'is progress' or even that 'great progress has been made', that we are going to 'eradicate poverty', because if we recognize the 'failures' we are finally going to 'learn from the past' and 'take up new challenges' with the whole 'international community'. The recommended

---

[27] As an example of this type of comparison, see F. Mestrun, 'OMD: lutte contre la pauvreté ou développement?'. Text on the CADTM website at <http://www.cadtm.org/Objectifs-du-Millenaire-lutte>.

[28] See T.W. Pogge, 'Priorities of Global Justice', in T.W. Pogge (ed.), *Global Justice* (London: Blackwell, 2007), 16ff.

solution is then certain principles, mostly abstract and vague, sometimes specific and quantified, which, if faithfully followed, will finally open the 'road to development'. And we go on to cite the 'technological advances', the 'information age', the 'new media', the 'processes', the 'flows', the 'dynamics', as so many characteristics of a new complex historical reality that no one controls but seems to make future success inevitable.[29] But who can still believe in the enchanted world of UN resolutions, summit declarations, and solemn commitments by states to 'economic', 'human', 'sustainable', or 'social' development? While we continue to proclaim Days and Decades against poverty, disease, and hunger, just as we once multiplied development days and decades, the hollowness of this repetitive rhetoric is in the image of the IDL on the developing countries: it is devoid of meaning.

In fact, since 1970, regardless of how IDL was dressed up, it remained ineffective and totally dependent on the implementation of a neo-liberal-type capitalist economic system which has always greatly limited its *possibilités*. This is why Maurice Kamto is absolutely right, in our view, in saying that IDL was a 'stillborn' law and a 'great illusion'[30] that it is time to become aware of. Insufficiently legalized and never fully accepted, IDL has never succeeded in establishing itself completely, and in so doing, it has unfortunately created a lot more misunderstanding than it has led to advances. Behind the good intentions of those who defended it and who believed in it, it was most often used as a diversion to serve the interests of dominant states and of a global system that has certainly made possible the economic growth of some states, but also continues to reproduce huge inequities, create poverty, and maintain the dependency and underdevelopment of other states.

The current economic–legal system is economically efficient: this is what the success of the emerging states teaches us, and this new fact is fundamental. When it is made possible, the economic and financial integration of developing countries in a globalized market economy seems to be a source of economic growth and social development of states, as well as of significant reduction of poverty, hunger, and mortality. However, contrary to the neo-liberals' belief, this system remains deeply socially unfair, and will always be deeply unfair if one does not intervene to correct its excesses. And this observation is not by radical ideologues or fanatics, but shared by some of the most prominent figures in international society. So it is with the Director General of the WTO himself, Pascal Lamy:

International relations today remain marked by unbearable injustices... This situation is no accident. It is the legacy of a bygone world on a political level, but not yet economically: colonialism. Political colonialism ended in the 60s of the last century; economic colonialism has not ended fifty years later. This is a reality we must describe as such, analysing both its elements and its origins.[31]

---

[29] We directly summarize here the analyses developed in G. Rist (ed.), *Les mots du pouvoir. Sens et non-sens de la rhétorique internationale, Nouveaux cahiers de l'IUED* (Geneva: IUED, 2002), Coll. Enjeux, no. 13, esp. 11ff.

[30] M. Kamto, 'Requiem pour le droit international du développement', in *Mélanges Benchik*, n 11, at 495.

[31] P. Lamy, 'Comment sortir de l'injustice des rapports Nord/Sud?', in Semaines sociales de France, *Qu'est-ce qu'une société juste?* (Paris: Bayard, 2007), 173.

According to the 2004 Report of the ILO World Commission, based on a study of 63 countries:

we have reached a crisis stage in the legitimacy of our political institutions, whether national or international. There is an urgent need to rethink current institutions of global economic governance, whose rules and policies are largely shaped by powerful countries and powerful players. The unfairness of key rules in the field of trade and finance reflects a serious democratic deficit at the heart of the system.[32]

As an example of this unfairness of the existing legal–economic framework, we shall confine ourselves here to mentioning some aspects of international trade. The trade agreements reached are neither free nor fair. Large numbers of trade barriers have remained in place in rich countries, and large numbers of subsidies remain, at the same time as we have forced developing countries to open their markets. The scandal of the agricultural market is well known, and yet so far no real progress has been achieved towards changing it. The subsidies in industrialized countries in this area are estimated at over $1 billion per day, while 70 per cent of people in poor countries depend on agriculture and live on less than $1 per day. Subsidies thus create a situation of gross injustice. Only a few really interesting commitments were introduced in the new WTO Round launched in Doha, but as we know the Round is blocked. However, the issue is still further complicated because even if trade barriers were removed, even if trade agreements were free and fair, not all states are in a position to benefit because of their starting point, their inadequate resources, their lack of transport infrastructures, lack of efficient technology, etc. When in 2001 Europe took the welcome initiative to unilaterally open its markets to the poorest countries, there was virtually no new trade, because these countries are not able to take advantage of such an opportunity. Finally, while South–South trade may have indisputable advantages, market logic means that new inequalities deepen among southern states because of the private operators and the expansionist logic of the new rich. The states called 'emerging' are now the first to claim the enforcement of all rules favouring maximum free trade. Far from wanting to really change the rules in a fairer way for everyone including the poorest, the emerging states seek primarily to defend their own interests. Certainly, they can at least balance the opposing forces and get better representation for developing countries in international fora, but so far they confine themselves mainly to using the unfair rules for their own benefit. Thus they perpetuate the same unfair legal and economic system. And this explains why classic and new IDL have been constantly neutralized in their scope and effect.

## 3. What is the solution for the twenty-first century?

From that starting point, three options seem open to us. They concern the existing economic legal system, and are underpinned by opposing economic theories.

---

[32] *A fair globalization—Creating opportunities for all*, 2004, available at <http://www.ilo.org/fair-globalization/report/lang—en/index.htm>.

They revive at global level the controversy between social justice and economic efficiency.

## (A) First solution: sticking to the neo-liberal pro-market paradigm—an economically efficient but socially unfair solution

This is to bet everything on International Economic Law (IEL) and on maintaining the existing global system, considering it as the long-term solution to the problems of the developing countries, and its unfairness as part of a natural process carrying forward to more equality between states. It became totally dominant once the fall of the Berlin Wall meant the failure of alternative paths to capitalist development and the superiority of a global market system able to offer all countries the possibility of sustainable growth on condition of adapting to the legal norms and economics of this globalized economy. This means that we must continue to practise openness of markets, maintain the existing WTO rules, changing them only at the margin based on existing power relations, and maintain the course adopted by the international financial institutions. In this perspective, the law of choice is private law, or public law of simple regulation. This is not a law claiming to determine or introduce fairness in the material conditions of peoples and states. What matters most is that private property rights are assured, that contracts are protected, trade secured, and loans repaid so as to encourage people to work and invest.[33] It also means that the responsibility for the 'lag' in development is attributed to the developing countries themselves, to their poor governance, their instability, their corruption, lack of rule of law, etc., but never to the system itself.

One cannot underestimate the strength of this current or automatically disqualify it as some do, thus underestimating some of its assets. The existing system is based on a neo-liberal ideology that, contrary to what has been suggested, does not abandon justice to society (internal and international) but simply considers that justice will result from the spontaneous play of the market. The inequality of material conditions among states is part of the market order that we should not interfere with because market forces will promote opportunity for all and lead by themselves to an overall improvement in the condition of each. The demand for a NIEO, a just and equitable international order based on interventionist development law and discriminatory practices, is considered a total misunderstanding and a mistake, because it not only disturbs the order of the world market, which spontaneously creates wealth, but also, by favouring one particular group of states, goes against equal opportunities for everyone to benefit from the market. The case of India, Brazil, China, and Southeast Asia is given as the perfect example of the success of this system. And it must be stated with clarity and admitted that their spectacular development is due not to IDL nor to the more specific and targeted

---

[33] J. Brasseul, *Introduction à l'économie du développement*, 3rd edn (Paris: A. Colin, 2010), 80ff.

measures of the MDGs, but to economic, social, cultural, and historical factors specific to these states.[34]

Moreover, it is striking to see how the contemporary turn towards poverty is part of the same pattern. It does not signal the failure of the dominant neo-liberal economistic paradigm; on the contrary, it may be regarded as being closely linked to it. The fight against poverty (against hunger, for health and education) is indeed a much more consensual project than all former IDL; it is also a much less revolutionary project for states than a NIEO, and far from ending the famous 'Washington consensus', it seems to be an inevitable aspect of it. There is a real neo-liberal tradition in this direction. A thinker like Friedrich von Hayek, who has so influenced the practices and thoughts of the Washington consensus, is useful for understanding how international legal practices solely in favour of poverty combine with the neo-liberal discourse of the international institutions. According to Hayek, it is important above all not to interfere in market forces to establish some sort of social justice, but the fact remains that action in cases of 'extreme poverty' to ensure minimum resources to the poorest is still perfectly acceptable.[35] However, it is more an ethical than a truly legal obligation. He states that this minimum of resources must be provided 'off-market', suggesting that the point should be primarily to coordinate private initiatives that directly recall the moral duty of charity that has always been part of classical liberal thought. But is it not this ethical side of globalization that is found both in international policies and in the private actions of some company executives like Bill Gates, NGOs, and movements of public opinion?

In addition, the high-profile displaying by financial institutions of international action for the elimination of poverty pursues less avowed goals. It helps to defuse potential crises of legitimacy of the dominant neo-liberal economic model that could arise due to the dismantling of the old social protections that this development model implies. If the adjustment plans are to the detriment of the poorest people, too big a social deficit can create challenging conditions. To gain acceptance, they must therefore give priority to helping governments that will establish 'safety nets' for those most affected. We can take as an example the new loans from the IMF under the Poverty Reduction and Growth Facility which was established in 1999. As noted in the 2007 report of the Independent Evaluation Office (IEO), they are indeed more favourable to public expenditure (reduced drastically with SAPs) and to poverty alleviation programmes.[36] In other words, they let the laws of economics operate, according to the neo-liberal doctrine that continues to prevail, but work on the most visible and extreme social consequences. And, finally, the focus on the fight against poverty can thus strengthen the existing neo-liberal model. There is therefore a direct and consistent relationship between the ethical fight against poverty and the neo-liberal pro-market paradigm.

[34] See below nn 49 and 50.
[35] F. Hayek, *Law, Legislation and Liberty, Vol. 2: The Mirage of Social Justice* (Chicago, IL: University of Chicago Press, 1976), 62–100.
[36] See the indications given by the IMF's website at <http://www.imf.org/external/np/exr/facts/fre/prgff.htm>.

For lack of space, we cannot discuss in detail the validity of this initial solution and the ideological trend that supports it, but at the very least we can argue the facts and the existing international situation. They tell us that this first solution is economically efficient but socially unfair. And both aspects must be taken into account without, because of ideology, deliberately pushing one aspect at the expense of the other. If the current economic–legal system has shown it can promote the development of some emerging countries, it therefore contains in itself some elements of a solution. But it is also a large part of the problem, because it continues to maintain and generate new forms of poverty and inequality in unacceptable proportions. In fact, IEL produces neither solely development nor solely underdevelopment, but both at once, and the whole difficulty today is to take into account the contradictory nature of this observation, which somehow puts the former pro-third-world and anti-third-world positions back to back. But who can really be satisfied with that?

### (B) Second solution: jettisoning any model of development—a blind alley

It is the opposite of the first, though at bottom the two come together to condemn any IDL. It is offered by the post-developmentalists and involves advocating the abandonment of any model of development, even any idea of development, but also of the global economic system and thus of both any IDL and all existing IEL. The strongest criticisms concern the development paradigm itself. Because of this development paradigm, linked to a liberal economic vision of the world, the whole world is still engaged in an ongoing chase after development of the countries, in a collective task called 'catch-up' which mobilizes considerable financial resources while very often being thwarted because it helps to maintain the exclusion and increased poverty that it claims to eliminate. Thus, it continues to widen the gap it is supposed to fill.[37] IDL is considered as a machine for manufacturing the excluded and poverty at the same time as the developed and wealth, precisely because of the economic assumptions of liberal capitalism and free trade on which it is based. By a kind of cynical ruse of history, it has always been the means of perpetuating a state of balance of power in favour of those who really benefit, namely the strong and the rich.

As we can see, the charges are strong, and the critique is convincing in denouncing this chase for ever-increasing growth, which can have no end and will ultimately mean the depletion of the planet and therefore its own extinction. But the question is what alternative to offer if we want out of both IDL and IEL. Now, it is clear that the solutions advanced are much less convincing. They most often advocate a type of romantic anti-modernist and culturalist economics, law and society, and a policy of downsizing as well, the effects of which would appear to be particularly expensive for the peoples in a world as interdependent, acculturated, and mixed as ours. The problem is that currently, when all societies are interdependent,

---

[37] See, eg, S. Latouche, *Le pari de la décroissance* (Paris: Fayard, 2006) and G. Rist, *Le développement. Histoire d'une croyance occidentale*, 3rd edn (Paris: Sciences Po Les Presses, 2007), 17ff.

it is hardly conceivable to envisage a return to a strictly traditional and quasi-autarkic communitarization of societies, with a minimum of international law that is not only viable but in addition reflects the real aspirations and the actual lives of the populations. Leaving the South in a poverty/frugality supposed to be blessed as being far from Western industrial troubles is a myth that can be in every respect as degrading as the converse evolutionary myth based on economic growth at any cost. It also means considering that the development progress evident in Europe, North America, and now in Asia should be reserved for those who have already benefited, and keeping the rest of the planet as a sort of conservatory of fauna, flora, and traditional human communities, to be sure not to harm them. In short, the positions of those who want to escape development bring us back, we believe, in symmetrically opposite fashion, to the radical position of those who advocate all-out economic development. And they seem to lead to so radical a solution given our current context that this solution seems to be neither economically efficient nor socially equitable.

Thus while the criticisms of the development paradigm have the merit of raising serious questions, they are too excessive, calling on us to consider a third alternative. Critical as it may be of past mistakes and of the illusions generated by the institutional normative law of IDL and IEL, it nevertheless remains on the same ground of the development principle and a market economy.

## (C) Third solution: changing the rules of the global economic system, and creating a new and fair NIEO

This option means embarking on a reform of the existing IEL to establish a new NIEO, a legal–economic system compatible with the establishment of an international social justice; to ensure that the global economy is subordinated to the purpose of social justice, and that we can bring out a set of legal practices that is both economically efficient and socially equitable. If different standards of IDL and more targeted struggles against poverty and hunger are mere stopgaps that do not change the socio-economic inequalities and the system in place, this means that any new resolution or agreement, any new legal commitment that does not address the unfairness of the system, will always be biased and inevitably limited in its effects, and we shall continue to see Decades and World Days devoted to poverty or hunger or development, and legal policy incantations that tell a reassuring consensus story, but in reality only repeat the errors and illusions of the past. Put another way: where IDL remains a corrective solution which aims to correct unequal situations but never gets there because it is still stuck at the margin of an unfair economic system of which it is inherently part, then questioning the world legal and economic system through a new and fair NIEO would be a transformative solution, tackling the economic system itself by changing its legal, formal, and substantive rules.

This third option therefore aims not at some new IDL but at a new NIEO, that is, changing the rules of the global economic system, recasting the Bretton Woods financial institutions, changing the GATT rules, and revising the WTO in a more equitable direction so that it finally refocuses relations between the various North(s) and South(s). The point is not to redo the façade of the building yet again, to wave new lures by introducing a new slogan on development or adding exception schemes and ineffective provisional discriminatory measures to the existing system, but to rethink the core of the economic system in its dual normative and institutional aspects. And this reform seeks not the mirage of equality between states, but to make the principle of fairness the legal basis for all future discussions between the North(s) and South(s), so as to change a profoundly unjust system— the interests of the North(s) must be taken into account as well as those of the South(s), because poverty and inequality have also increased in the North.

Indeed, we see that the idea of a fair globalization has precisely become the watchword of the last ten years, directly recalling the general demand for fairness which accompanied the call for the NIEO in the 1970s. A new discourse centred on economics thus seems to prevail as from the 2000s. Already in 1992, Agenda 21 talked about the need to 'make the world economy more efficient and equitable' and in 1995, in San Francisco during the celebration of the fiftieth anniversary of the UN, the Secretary-General of the organization, Boutros Boutros-Ghali, called for a 'new social contract' between North and South in order to obtain a better distribution of global wealth.[38] In 2001, the WTO launched in Doha, Qatar, a new round of negotiations, still on trade liberalization, but this time in the service of 'development'.[39] This programme recognizes the linkages between trade and development and puts the needs and interests of developing countries at the heart of future negotiations. In 2002, at the World Summit on Sustainable Development in Johannesburg, delegates adopted a resolution in which they committed themselves to 'building a humane, equitable and caring global society, cognizant of the need for human dignity for all'.[40] In 2006, the new Nobel Peace Prize winner, an economist and founder of the first micro-credit institution, Muhammad Yunus of Bangladesh, was rewarded for his efforts to 'create economic and social development from below', and he called for the creation of a High Committee for a Fair Globalization. The same year, the World Bank published a report entitled 'Equity and Development'.[41] In 2007, at the ILO Forum, the EU undertook to promote measures in favour of 'fair globalization'.[42] On 12 April 2008, UNCTAD called for a 'globalization of solidarity'. On 10 June the same year, the ILO unanimously voted for the Declaration on Social Justice for a Fair Globalization, inspired by

---

[38] See text at <http://www.liberation.fr/monde/0101145567-boutros-ghali-veut-ranimer-la-flamme-onusienne-pour-le-cinquantenaire>.

[39] Ministerial declaration adopted on 14 November 2001, including a 'Work Programme' (WT/MIN (01)/DEC/1).

[40] See text at <http://www.unctad.org/en/docs//aconf199d20&c_en.pdf>.

[41] World Development Report 2006, *Equity and Development* (Washington DC: World Bank, 2006). See text at <http://siteresources.worldbank.org/ INTANNREP2K6/Resources/2838485–1158333614345/AR06_final_LO_RES.pdf>.

[42] At the 2007 ILO Forum. See <http://www.politiquessociales.net/Mondialisation,3658>.

the Philadelphia Declaration of 1944, which defends the 'need for a strong social dimension to globalization to achieve better results shared equitably by all'.[43]

It remains to be seen whether these statements regarding the fairness of globalization and the economic system will remain an 'enchanted' order of discourse with the actors of international society, making a diversion while leaving the system to continue to impose itself further. We would see an oscillation without consequences, where after a very liberal period we return to a more social one, but at bottom nothing really changes in terms of practical legal and economic dominance. Worse, the notion of fairness may be used by key decision-makers and international institutions for the sole purpose *of* getting the same neo-liberal policies better accepted.[44] And there *are* ground*s for* caution when we note the multiple statements without effects made by major international players. The fact that the Doha Round is a failure for now—despite the 2005 Hong Kong conference—is not reassuring. The commitments of the last G20 in Seoul, not binding, are not very encouraging either, and even less when you realize the enormous tensions that underlie this group of states. Only the IMF reform can be seen as actual progress.

To really move forward and not remain at the level of discourse, we must precisely define *the nature and legal scope of fairness* in this context. What exactly do fair globalization, an equitable economic order, or a fair society mean in international law? How are we to translate this into legal terms? The formulations included in resolutions or non-binding commitments suggest a new, very general, direction, for which it is difficult to see the practical applications, not only in economics but also in the form of legal rules. However, we can imagine enhancing the nature and scope of the principle of fairness by making it the basic legal principle acting as mandatory target for any discussion of the substantive and formal norms of the international economic system. Fairness as an objective and as a foundation will result *in ensuring that all states are not only formally considered equal, but beyond this formal equality also actually have equal opportunities to address the market and thus fully participate in the economic system*. It is seen as the means of correcting formal equality in order that we can move towards a certain real equality. But, contrary to the rules of classical IDL which already in a limited way provided this, in this new context anything that seeks to restore equality of opportunity for developing countries and LDCs can no longer maintain the status of mere exceptions to a system that renders them ineffective. Consideration of equity, and therefore the consideration of the special, disadvantaged situation of some states—which may vary according to contexts and situations in both South and North—should be the heart of any revision of existing agreements, the heart of the existing legal and economic system. It must become a fundamental legal rule of the international order, at both institutional and normative level, and hence in the dual form of a *guiding principle* of the WTO, IMF, and World Bank, and a *general principle of international*

---

[43] See text of the Declaration at <http://www.ilo.org/wcmsp5/groups/public/@dgreports/@cabinet/documents/publication/wcms_099766.pdf>.
[44] See below at n 61.

*economic law* to guide the negotiation of any bilateral or multilateral agreement.[45] It would relate to both the substantive rules and the formal procedures.

With regard to substantive rules, we can only cite a few avenues without being exhaustive, whereas the issues of investment and the financial system should also be covered, as should the issue of international taxation, which has never been so topical.[46] Above all, it is necessary to look back at the very principle of free trade, which has become the alpha and omega of the WTO, just as at the IMF or the World Bank. For the history, past and present, shows that the economic and social development of states was not built on general free trade, the very thing we want to impose on everyone. The development of Euro-American States yesterday, like that of the major emerging countries today, came about in two stages, reinforced and supported by the international law of their time.[47] Initially, these states raised protective barriers to consolidate local agriculture and industry that would be strong enough to face full opening to the world market. In a second stage, this opening was made, with market liberalization, the lowering of tariffs, a framework of good governance and direct investment, all generating strong growth. The backward movement we see today thus illuminates the spectacular development of four Asian Dragons, and it has too quickly been overlooked that the states which have been so successful have enjoyed outstanding benefits and historical circumstances, something the World Bank report, for example, totally underestimates.[48] By virtue of their geographical location and their colonial past, which has been beneficial for them this time, these states did not really suffer from the ravages of history, and enjoyed massive Western aid during the Cold War, a strong state inherited from their past,[49] which is the origin of structural reforms—especially in agriculture— and a growing integration into world trade due to low labour costs and the welcome that they have offered to multinational corporations. Similarly, the situation in China, India, or Brazil is not comparable, historically or sociologically, with that of other states in Asia, Latin America, and especially Africa. Africa is the con-

---

[45]   Some propose to make it a global public good, but it is not certain that a specific concrete and operational system in economic matters can be inferred from it. See L.L. Martin, 'L'économie politique de la coopération internationale', in I. Kaul, I. Grunberg, and M. Stern (eds), *Les biens publics mondiaux. La coopération internationale du XXIème siècle* (Paris: Economica, 2002), 55ff.

[46]   For investments and the notion of 'fair and equitable treatment' that is becoming ever more crucial in the case law, see P.-M. Dupuy and Y. Kerbrat, *Droit international public*, 10th edn (Paris: Dalloz, 2010), 795ff. On international taxation and the fairness debate see, eg, T. Pogge, 'Human Flourishing and Universal Justice', 1 Social Philosophy (1999) 16ff; C.R. Beitz, *Political Theory and International Relations*, 2nd edn (Princeton, NJ: Princeton University Press, 1999), 65ff; and J.-M. Ferry, *L'Europe, l'Amérique et le monde* (Paris: Pleinsfeux, 2004), 46ff. And for the opposite position see J. Rawls, *The Law of Peoples: with 'The Idea of Public Reason Revisited'* (Cambridge, MA: Harvard University Press, 1999), 113–20.

[47]   See E. Jouannet, *Le droit international libéral-providence* (Brussels: Bruylant, 2011).

[48]   On this crucial issue for understanding development, see A. Amsden, *Asia's Next Giant: South Korea and Late Industrialization* (Oxford: Oxford University Press, 1989); R. Wade, *Governing the Market: Economic Theory and the Role of Government in East Industrialization* (Princeton, NJ: Princeton University Press, 1990); and G. Rodan, *The Political Economy of Singapore's Industrialization: National State and International Capital* (Petaling Java: Forum, 1991).

[49]   For Taiwan and South Korea see, eg, A. Leftwitch, 'Bringing Politics Back in: Towards a Model of the Development State', V.31(3) J Development Stud (1995) 410ff.

tinent that has experienced the heaviest historical past, with not only slavery and trafficking, but also a very brutal colonization over the centuries. It is the continent where, in contrast to what happened elsewhere, the fight against poverty seems to have replaced development and where the trend has more and more been, as we have said, to liberalize markets without actually aiming at the role of the state—although recently international policies seem to be changing on this point.[50]

In addition, experience teaches that it is not the major emerging states nor Western states that must protect themselves, but rather the developing countries and LDCs, which must have the legal right to protect their economies before being in a position to face international competition, and in which the role of the state must be restored.[51] It is an option, or in other words a right, that they should have, not an obligation, because the lesson of all these decades is that there is no single model and that each developing country, each LDC, is a special case needing a particular solution. This implies a revolution in the philosophy of the WTO, but it is a reform that could be negotiated concretely on the basis of fairness as the guiding principle, according to category of state, once the Northern states and the new rich ones in the South agree to take seriously the interests of individual developing countries or LDCs. If such measures were taken, one might think of restoring real equality of opportunity between states in respect of market access, which is fundamental.

To reinforce this more equitable access, it is also essential finally to make effective the measures to remove the advantages of rich countries. The WTO Doha Declaration with an eye to future trade negotiations thus provides as an objective a 'fair market' in agriculture (paras 13 and 14), that is, a substantial improvement in the agricultural market access of some disadvantaged states, reducing all forms of export subsidies, with substantial reduction of domestic support measures that have obvious distortion effects on agricultural trade. Equal access to markets should also be promoted by enhanced measures in favour of developing countries, that is to say, affirmative action, compensatory and discriminatory. Far from having to be abandoned, GSPs should be extended and made effective through an economic environment that no longer distorts their implementation.[52] This was recommended in the 2002 Report of the High Level Panel at the Financing for Development conference in Monterrey.[53] And the Doha Declaration provides for special and differential treatment for developing countries to be part of all negotiations, to make it more operational and effective or even give it the form of a binding legal obligation. But even in a world where we offer a level playing field for market access in these different ways, we have seen that many developing countries would still not manage to succeed in the global economy, to benefit from opportunities at

---

[50] See Brasseul, n 33, at 246 ff.

[51] For the very lively debates on this topic see J.E. Stiglitz and A. Charlton, *Fair Trade For All: How Trade Can Promote Development* (Oxford: Oxford University Press, 2005), 171 ff.

[52] On the evolution and the economic controversies concerning the effectiveness of SDT, see ibid at 154 ff.

[53] Report of the International Conference on Financing for Development, March 2002, A/CONF.198/11, p 8. Available at <http://www.unctad.org/en/docs/aconf198d11_en.pdf>.

world level, and thus to develop satisfactorily. As Denis Cogneau and Jean-David Naudet have again shown, some countries suffer from structural handicaps to growth and institutional weaknesses that anyway exclude them from equal access to markets and the global development process.[54] And as Robert Zoellick pointed out, it is perhaps this latter aspect that is most critical of all and the one that should bring all the efforts of the international community to bear.[55]

That being said, the overhaul of rules for a new NIEO also comes about through the formal rules. The mere existence of a procedural unfairness in representation and negotiation produces substantive rules that are unfair—precisely the characteristic of the current system. It is always the rich countries that write the texts that form the basis for negotiation and settle the key economic issues, including those relating to development, while the LDCs and developing countries are continually being asked to improve in order to develop. The legal rules that govern economic activities are the outcome of very complex negotiation processes, when they take place at the multilateral level, at which developing countries have little influence. It is indeed an understatement to say this, when we know the multiple pressures and measures of constant intimidation to which they are subjected to induce them to sign agreements they do not want. The first conference of the Doha Round provided the most pitiful example, with the smug decision to name it the 'development round'. The way to achieve a real situation of equity between rich and poor countries is therefore to revive an ancient and essential claim of the developing countries: the call for better representation in international bodies and a fair weight in negotiations on standards and in their implementation. But the extreme complexity of technical issues today means that, even were they properly represented through a level playing field (eg at the WTO), the LDCs would be greatly disadvantaged in international negotiations on international rules. A fair system must be capable of helping them in this sense: that is, not only strengthen their representation but also their ability to negotiate on equal terms. This *a priori* implies equitable access to information in order to have the means to make choices by being well informed. Developing countries can hardly make the situation of inequality in commercial and financial respects change as long as the power to be well informed and to be heard and the power of influence remain in favour of the dominant group. For example, global warming threatens to disrupt the lives of people in low-lying coastal areas, small islands, and semi-arid zones, and yet the states of these potential victims actually cannot make their voices heard in major negotiations on climate. Their ability to act with international organizations may itself be problematic, and their retaliatory capability in the framework of existing mechanisms at the commercial level is derisory given existing power relations.

Moreover, as we know, poor countries are still further disadvantaged when they engage in bilateral agreements, which is just why some rich countries prefer this second option. As unfair as the TRIPS Agreement, written mainly by lawyers in

---

[54] D. Cogneau and J.-D. Naudet, 'Who Deserves Aid? Equality or Opportunity, International Aid and Poverty Reduction', 35(1) World Development (2007) 104–20.
[55] N 3.

the industry, may seem, it represents an international multilateral standard subject to studies and in-depth checks, whereas a number of recent bilateral agreements between the United States and developing countries (Chile, Jordan, Vietnam, Morocco, etc.) contain rules for the protection of intellectual property rights that are more restrictive for poor countries. The Declaration on the TRIPS Agreement and Public Health, adopted at Doha by the WTO Ministerial Conference on 14 November 2001, shows that the process of multilateral WTO discussions and negotiations can better mobilize public opinion and obtain advances that are impossible at the bilateral level. For the first time ever an official text of the WTO clearly states that the protection of public health takes precedence over intellectual property and should be used to interpret the TRIPS Agreement in this specific area.

Procedural fairness should be able to drive the adoption of more balanced institutional principles such as voting rights, the adoption of principles other than representation, access to information, transparency, strengthening the capacity of developing countries to participate effectively in decision-making, improving international institutions' own responsibility, and development of judicial procedures. And progress has nonetheless been made in recent years in terms of representation, as shown in the novel compositions of the new Council for Financial Stability and the Basel Committee on Banking Supervision, or the recent IMF reform.

All these substantive and formal reforms are now well known and should be finally realized in the framework of a new NIEO where *equity would replace equality as a founding principle of the system*.[56] But how far does this new utopia recast the rules of the existing economic–legal system? Can this new NIEO be considered more realistic than in 1974, at the proclamation of the first NIEO? Two elements are to be considered here.

First, the challenge of this new NIEO is to reconnect with the presuppositions of a critique of the prevailing economic system but without lapsing into the bad habits of collectivist analysis and planning. The international context has completely changed anyway. What is needed is a consolidation of existing economic rules, based not on the repetition of soft law, on resolutions that ultimately create bitterness and disillusionment, on an ideological basis that has become very questionable, but on an overhaul of rules based legally on the principle of equity, and based pragmatically on focused legal battles and negotiation of the revision of existing agreements and statutes of the international economic institutions in all major sectors: trade, investment, finance, and, something new, international taxation.

Secondly, one may think that using equity coincides with the interest of states and even private operators to such an extent that it is actually preferred. We know that any change in this area is possible only if it corresponds to the interest of states or a fundamental motivation of public opinion in them.[57] But for the moment

---

[56] We cannot develop this question here. For contemporary domestic debates also found internationally, refer to eg T. Lambert et al, *Egalité et équité. Antagonisme ou complémentarité?* (Paris: Economica, 1999).

[57] See J. Habermas, *The Postnational Constellation* (Oxford: Polity Press, 2000).

only the realistic interest motive predominates.[58] Yet perhaps it is precisely here that things can change from previous years. It is indeed the case that the latest economic theories now seem to reinforce the introduction of fairness into economics. They show that ultimately a more equitable situation is conducive to the economic efficiency of markets and thus benefits all.[59] If global society became more equal, it would provide more opportunities for all, rich states and poor states: 'fundamentally, good economic institutions are fair institutions: to prosper, a society must create conditions to encourage a wide... majority to invest and innovate.'[60] Too large inequalities result in conflicts, frustrations, distorted competition among states themselves, the inability of some to access markets, lack of innovation and creativity, and total economic unproductivity. We also know that the economic and social policies advocated can really work only if the developing countries and their peoples take them up and are actually participating. Yet this process of appropriation can come about only if the states and peoples have the feeling that it contains principles of social justice both within states and between states. Mobilization of the different development actors in these countries depends largely on the degree of fairness with which these players expect to be treated. This is especially important to consider given that so far many of the measures imposed by the system—compliance, the balance of power, etc.—feed a tremendous sense of powerlessness, frustration, and resentment.

These new analyses thus show that only a socially equitable model can be truly effective economically, since equity is a factor for greater efficiency. So that even the dominant states and large private operators of the moment may have a well-understood interest in its application, making the idea of this new NIEO as the indispensable solution to the problems of the developing countries and poverty in the world less utopian. However, the utmost vigilance is still required in the face of this new discourse that uses the rhetoric of equity. Equity can stay at the level of rhetoric and argument to justify measures that sometimes have absolutely nothing fair about them, in the endeavour to make them look more acceptable. In this case, the new economic and legal discourse of 'fair globalization' may be directed not at reversing the neo-liberal model of development, but rather at making it easier to accept the painful consequences.[61]

---

[58]  That poverty currently persists in such disproportionate terms is because states and their publics do not find the situation morally intolerable. The majority of the people in rich or newly rich countries do not see any relation between the present situation and their own attitudes or the dominant economic system. See T. Pogge, *World Poverty and Human Rights* (Cambridge: Polity Press, 2008), 3ff.

[59]  For details of these new theories see World Development Report 2006, n 41, at 260ff.

[60]  Ibid, 11.

[61]  See in this connection B. Gosovic, 'L'hégémonie intellectuelle mondiale et le développement', 166 Revue internationale des sciences sociales (UNESCO) (December 2000) 507ff ; F. Lapeyre, 'Le rêve d'un développement sans conflit', in Rist (ed.), n 29, at 101ff; O. Favereau, 'Conventions et régulations', in R. Boyer and Y. Saillard (eds), *Théories de la régulation: l'état des savoirs* (Paris: La découverte, 1995), 65ff ; and R. Boyer, 'Justice sociale et performances économiques: de la synergie au conflit?', in J. Affichard and J.-B. Foucauld (eds), *Justice sociale et inégalités* (Paris: Esprit, 1992), 33ff.

## 4. Brief concluding remarks

Would a new NIEO based on a legal principle of fairness be adequate alone to meet the challenges of development? Certainly not. The warning of the post-developmentalists should not be forgotten. If a new NIEO can come about, it must be accompanied by the implementation of all principles of the new IDL in its social, human, and environmental dimensions in order to ensure that the overall development of all does not come at the expense of the planet and future generations and that it actually makes human beings its ultimate beneficiary. A new NIEO is the necessary condition for sustainable human development that is effective, and it is only at this price that the enchanted discourse of IDL can finally become a reality, and utopia can perhaps finally become incarnate.

# 32

# The WTO:
# Already the Promised Land?

*J.H.H. Weiler**

## SUMMARY

There are deep inequities in the current system—the most notable and justly notorious being the one rooted in an inequitable distribution of tariff reductions and other barriers (including subsidies) which continue to exclude agriculture to the detriment of many poorer economies (and consumers in the richer countries). There was a distinct political deception in the Uruguay process whereby important systemic reform was pushed and accepted as the multilateral 'Single Undertaking', whereas the actual negotiations of terms of trade was left to the usual multi-lateralized (MFNed) bilateralism where each state is on its own and which favours the rich consuming economies with plenty of trade leverage, at the expense of the poorer ones with less leverage or none at all. Two major issues must be tackled: (i) whether the World Trade Organization (WTO) has a 'constitutional' future and (ii) whether a global approach will prevail over a regional one. (i) Within the General Agreement on Tariffs and Trade (GATT) and, more recently, WTO the official mantra is still that it is an organization which belongs

 * This is, by the nature of the project, a work of synthetic reflection drawing on two decades of research and writing on the world trading system. I have drawn particularly on *European Constitutionalism and Its Discontents* (with J. Trachtman), 17 Northwestern J Int'l L & Bus (1997) 354; 'Law, Culture, and Values in the WTO—Gazing into the Crystal Ball', in D. Bethlehem, D. McRae, R. Neufeld, and I. Van Damme (eds), *The Oxford Handbook of International Trade Law* (Oxford: Oxford University Press, 2009), ch. 27 at 750–72; *EC—Asbestos. European Communities—Measures Affecting Asbestos and Asbestos-Containing Products* (with H. Horn) in H. Horn and P. Mavroidis (eds), *The WTO Case Law of 2001* (Cambridge: Cambridge University Press, 2003); 'The Rule of Lawyers and the Ethos of Diplomats: Reflections on the Internal and External Legitimacy of WTO Dispute Settlement', Harvard Jean Monnet Working Paper 9/00, Cambridge, MA (2000); also in 35 J World Trade (2001) 191; 'Towards a Common Law of International Trade', in J.H.H. Weiler (ed.), *The EU, the WTO, and the NAFTA: Towards a Common Law of International Trade?* (Oxford/New York: Oxford University Press, 2000), Epilogue; 'Europe: The Case against the Case for Statehood', 4 European LJ (1998) 43; also 'Europe: The Case for Statehood…And the Case against: An Exchange' (with G.F. Mancini), Harvard Jean Monnet Working Paper 6/98, Cambridge, MA (1998).

to its members which is taken to mean the governments of its members. Discourse of change of the WTO in the direction of constitutionalization cannot, to be normatively credible, decouple the legal from the political, the exercise of rights from the responsibilities of power. Only if the WTO develops its institutional framework could a constitutional future become normatively compelling. (ii) Regional Free Trade Area Agreements continue to offer significant political benefits which spill over beyond the partners themselves. They often comprise regional states with a history of conflict, even violence. When successfully concluded and implemented, they enhance a welcome stabilizing interdependence. In conclusion, although in the WTO there is much room for improvement (dispute settlement can be improved by introducing the power to remand cases back to panels; the Appellate Body can rid itself of its fetishistic textual hermeneutics and love of dictionaries; there can be a better system of sanctions which do not depend on trade leverage and which do not reduce trade rather than increase it; transparency, efficiency, and legitimacy can be improved) the WTO of today is Utopia Now. One should, however, eschew widening and deepening the constitutional which replaces the international.

## 1. Between reform and utopia

The WTO[1] seems a bit like the Jewish Messiah for whom one prays fervently, and is obligated to believe that he *will* come. But that of course means that the Messiah who actually *does* come is always false. From its very conception back in the 1940s as the would-be ITO (International Trade Organization), through its 'doctor assisted' birth as the GATT 1947 employing the Protocol of Provisional Application (a 'provisional' application which lasted a full 47 years), through the further agonies of successive 'Rounds' culminating in the Uruguay Round and the compromises of the Marrakech Agreements and bringing us to the present on-again-off-again trials and tribulations of Doha, the WTO/GATT has always been an incomplete project—with a reform agenda—a never-ending search for an illusive Promised Land being part of its very ontology.

In addition to the endless official 'Rounds'—there has been a stream of secondary literature. The titles of the studies comprising this literature tell the story. The excellent Warwick Commission Report of 2007—*The Multilateral Trade Regime: Which Way Forward?*[2] Or the authoritative so-called Sutherland Report of 2004—*The Future of the WTO: Addressing Institutional Challenges in the New Millennium*.[3] Or the earlier influential Leutwiler Report of 1987—*Trade Policies*

---

[1] All references to the WTO, unless specified should be read as a short cut to the GATT in its guise as its institutional precursor.

[2] The Warwick Commission, 'The Multilateral Trade Regime: Which Way Forward?', Report of the First Warwick Commission, University of Warwick, 2007.

[3] The Sutherland Report, A Report by the Consultative Board to the Director-General Supachai Panitchpakdi, 'The Future of the WTO: Addressing Institutional Challenges in the New Millennium', Geneva, WTO, 2004.

*for a Better Future.*[4] And the list goes on.[5] Looking for realistic utopias has been to the WTO a way of life.

There is a common thread to this future-looking literature. With differing nuances it tends to share the premises concerning the virtues of a multilateral trading system driving towards greater liberalization of the terms of trade and consolidating the associated disciplines which are designed to stamp out protectionisms and similar market-distorting state measures. The premise notwithstanding, this literature is not oblivious to several of the trade-related 'discontents' of globalization—as the WTO itself is not oblivious. Addressing these is always part of the Agenda. It is a very 'Reform', somewhat idealist, admonishing and optimistic at the same time (of the 'If you do . . . But if you don't' type) and fully within the utopian tradition: a better world should be imagined and can be had.

There is, too, a normatively critical literature which is not reformist, but challenges the premises. The critical literature is curious. There is, of course, the 'Rivers of Babylon' variant, that avalanche of lamentations on the woes of 'Globalization' in a never-ending stream of articles and books—some more serious than others[6]—in which somehow the WTO is to a greater or lesser degree presumptively assumed to be a principal source of all that is evil in Globalization. If you turn to the blogosphere the decibels just grow.[7] But if you look for seriously analytical literature which actually seeks to explore and document the nexus between WTO/GATT legal disciplines and systemic social and economic injustice resulting from international trade, with the exception of fine work on TRIPS-related issues, one comes up with very little indeed. To my knowledge the case for that nexus has simply not been made. In my view it cannot be made: globalization has, indeed, many discontents but they are not primarily or even secondarily caused by the legal disciplines of the WTO—thousands of protesters in Seattle, Genoa, or elsewhere notwithstanding. Admittedly it is difficult to prove a negative, but I await any serious study which will prove me wrong.

Make no mistake: this is not to claim that there are no deep inequities in the current system—the most notable and justly notorious being the one rooted in an inequitable distribution of tariff reductions and other barriers (including subsidies) which continue to exclude, say, agriculture to the detriment of many poorer economies (and consumers in the richer countries). There was in my eyes a distinct political deception in the Uruguay process whereby important systemic reform was pushed and accepted as the multilateral 'Single Undertaking', whereas the actual negotiations of terms of trade was left to the usual multi-lateralized (MFNed) bilateralism where each state is on its own and which favours the rich consuming

---

[4] The Leutwiler Report, *Trade Policies for a Better Future* (Amsterdam: Martinus Nijhoff, 1987).

[5] See, eg, E. Zedillo, P Messerlin, and J. Nielson, *Trade for Development, UN Millennium Project Task Force on Trade* (London: Earthscan, 2005).

[6] J. Stiglitz, *Globalization and Its Discontents* (New York: W.W. Norton, 2002); L.L. Raynolds, D. Murray, and J. Wilkinson (eds), *Fair Trade: The Challenges of Transforming Globalization* (London: Routledge, 2007); W. Bello, *De-Globalization: Ideas for a New World Economy* (New York: Zed Books, 2002).

[7] See, eg, <http://www.focusweb.org>.

economies with plenty of trade leverage, at the expense of the poorer ones with less leverage or none at all.

However, from a legal perspective, the fact that someone struck a very bad bargain when buying a car, does not necessarily mean that there is a flaw in the law of contracts which legally embodies that bargain. It is not a change of the rules that is called for to address this very real issue, but a change of the content of the bargain, and of the negotiating strategy and tactics under the rules, a lesson that seems to have been learnt. One might complain today of the hard line taken by, say, India or Brazil in relation to Doha. But that hard line taken by the developing world under Doha is bred by the bitter experience of Uruguay.

In most of the Reform literature, law is treated as instrumental, derivative, and heteronomous—the medium through which the economic and political bargains are articulated and implemented and not as an independent and autonomous variable which in and of itself bestows certain qualities on the system.

There is, typically, a 'legal' chapter, focusing almost invariably on dispute settlement (and enforcement). How to make it more efficient and predictable, how to give it more teeth, how to make it more equitable in addressing differences in legal resources. How to address the problems of sanctions classically based on withdrawal of concessions and thus on consumption leverage and which penalizes individual importers and exporters arbitrarily. There are also institutional issues: in the current round of negotiations the suspects on the agenda are, well, the usual ones. Institutionalize the Panels in some more fixed and permanent structure? Give the Appellate Body the power of remand? Et cetera.

It would be futile to replicate or summarize the above-mentioned excellent Reform literature. The Sutherland and Warwick Reports, to mention but two, still maintain their freshness and relevance with the militancy and occasional stridence of Sutherland being matched by the nuanced and sobriety of Warwick.

Equally futile would be to summarize the critical literature. I cannot make the case that the WTO legal framework as such (outside TRIPS) is in any direct way linked to the meaningful inequities of globalization, for the simple reason that I do not believe that to be the case. I do not think the gnomes of Geneva stand in the dock. (In any event if anyone is to be stood in the dock, it would be the gnomes of Brussels, and Washington, and Peking, and Sydney masquerading as the gnomes of Geneva.)

Instead, I want to focus on two issues which go to the very 'operating system' of the WTO and seem to be posited at a more profound level of future casting— than the important but efficiency-driven reform agenda—the realization of either or both is truly a case in utopian terms. These are issues that go to identity and systemic self-understanding—the Id/Ego of the WTO, its essential identikit. Even though they do not directly dictate policies, they undergird, sometimes *sub silentio*, both the scope for, and discussion of, much future-oriented policy discourse. I should warn that the themes selected are not the only or even most important systemic identity or self-understanding markers of the WTO. They are, however, in my view the ones where *legal* discourse as such conditions reality; the ones where the lawyer or legal theorist rather than the economist or political economist are the necessary interpreters and interlocutors.

## 2. The WTO: a constitutional future?

The GATT was born into an international legal system which understood itself as thoroughly intergovernmental. The state was not disaggregated both externally and internally. Externally, there was an uncritical conflation of state (the primary unit of authority) and its government. Individuals could be the direct or indirect objects of agreements among states/governments—but were not, in and of themselves, subjects. Internally, too, fresh in the wake of the Second World War and following a rather short democratic tradition for most countries in the system, democracy stopped short or ground to an inefficient crawl when it came to issues of foreign policy. The government, the executive branch, was given very high degree of leeway in conducting the foreign affairs of the state—it was acting, after all, in the 'national interest' which demanded political loyalty.

Within the GATT and, more recently, WTO the official mantra is still that it is an organization which belongs to its members which is taken to mean the governments of its members. Disaggregation is, on the whole anathematized.

By contrast, in the literature the sirens of disaggregation have been particularly seductive with a substantial chorus calling for one form of disaggregation—constitutionalization. Almost invariably it is the advent of the European Community (EC) which represents expressly or implicitly a model. One has learnt to be cautious—to repeat religiously that the WTO is not the EC and could/should not become one. But having said that, some of the principal 'constitutional' features of the WTO are pined after.

At the core of the EC 'constitutionalization' was the affording a growing number of its Treaty Articles (as well as secondary legislation) direct effect, namely endowing them with a legal quality which would allow individuals to plead them before national courts in disputes with conflicting state norms, and oblige these national courts to vindicate them in such situations against such conflicting state norms. This, in and of itself, is not such a unique move and is known in many a monist system. The drama of EC 'constitutionalization' was the coupling of such an effect with the principle of supremacy (grafted from general public international law) so that provisions of the Treaties instituting the EC were not, through direct effect, merely the law of the land, but, through supremacy, the 'higher law' of the land. Through the jurisprudence of its principal judicial organ, the European Court of Justice, in collaboration with the highest courts of its member states, the EC acquired one of the principal features of constitutional federal systems. It should be noted that here we are dealing with a self-referential autonomous legal development. The Treaties were not negotiated as such; there was even some resistance—not by the state (suddenly a meaningless concept as such) but by their governments in representation to the Courts who claimed that they were the Masters of the Treaty. It was driven by a certain legal logic much discussed in the famous early cases in which these developments took place.[8] It is

---

[8] See generally J. Weiler, *The Constitution of Europe* (Cambridge: Cambridge University Press, 1998).

easy to understand the seductiveness of these developments to some or many in the WTO interpretative community.[9] Practically, there is no more efficient system of monitoring and compliance than that achieved through domestic courts giving effect, 'higher law' effect, to treaty provisions. It is the ultimate in the 'private attorney-general' model of judicial review. Each and every trader becomes a policeman of his or her country's compliance with their obligations. And the habit of obedience of national governments to their domestic court is far higher than such habit vis-à-vis international fora. Compliance pull is enhanced by orders of magnitude in such a regime. Conceptually, it appears at least, to elevate individuals to the status of subjects, which are the direct bearers of rights under the international legal regime. The rhetorical combination of 'Individuals as Subjects' and the conflation of direct effect with 'rights' gives constitutionalization not only a practical efficiency attractiveness, but a normative moral patina, derived from the elevation of individuals from objects to subjects and the transformation of the system from *a set of intergovernmental mutual promises* to a *disaggregated legal system* based on rights, with 'higher law' status and where governments are but one actor of the states and can be the authors of violations not only vis-à-vis their WTO partners but also their very own citizens. The fact that these developments in the EC emanated from legal actors based on a specific way of interpreting the legal instruments make them all the more attractive—a way of not only circumventing the difficulties of the WTO political process, but of compensating for its weaknesses.

An influential literature, even most contemporary, continues not only to posit some form of constitutionalization as a future desideratum for a future WTO but detects signs of steps in that direction.[10]

It is not an attractive future, if it is to come. This is not because of the self-serving arguments of governments and their WTO delegates that the WTO belongs to its members—its members meaning them (as if a treaty is really the property of the executive branch and not a projection into the (international) public space of legislatures, citizens, and all other societal actors as well). It is also not because, a very common notion, there is some fundamental intrinsic difference between the EC Treaty and the WTO Treaty which justifies a 'constitutional hermeneutics' for the EC but not to the WTO.[11] The unattractiveness is rooted

---

[9] There is a very rich literature on the issue of constitutionalization of the WTO. See, eg, D. Cass, *The Constitutionalization of the World Trade Organization* (Oxford: Oxford University Press, 2005).

[10] See the illuminating exchange between U. Petersmann and R. Howse—a classic in the literature, 'Trade and Human Rights—An Exchange', in Jean Monnet Working Papers 12/02, available at <http://www.Jeanmonnetprogram.org>. See, more recently for an attempt to identify constituitionalizing moves in the jurisprudence of the Appellate Body, S. Cho, 'Constitutional Adjudication in the World Trade Organization', Jean Monnet Working Paper 04/08, available at <http://www.Jeanmonnetprogram.org>.

[11] I have tried to demonstrate that the 'constitutional' outcome of the famous ECJ decisions in the 1960s could have been achieved by using the very hermeneutic sensibilities and methods of the Appellate Body: J. Weiler, 'Rewriting Van Gend & Loos: Towards a Normative Theory of ECJ Hermeneutics', in O. Wiklund (ed.), *Judicial Discretion in European Perspective* (Stockholm: Norstedts Juridik/The Hague: Kluwer, 2003).

in many reasons but principally in the decoupling of the political and lawmaking process from its legal normative output.[12]

The problem is apparent even in the EC which has far more developed political institutions than the WTO but continues nonetheless to suffer from a persistent democracy deficit. How does one justify according higher law status and direct effect to norms, the democratic provenance of which is suspect? Giving individuals 'rights', even rights defensible in courts, does not make them subjects, if they have no appreciable participation in, or control over, the authorship of such rights. The bearers of such rights are no more subjects that the various 'subjects' of the Roman Empire who enjoyed rights granted them by others. There is really no principle reason to grant slaves certain rights. Does that make them subjects? Moreover, all such 'rights' are not, of course, value neutral or outside the political process of distributing advantages and disadvantages to competing interests of our societies. They are the outcome of two sets of flawed political processes of bargaining among unequals. The flawed process of the WTO itself, but also the internal flawed process by which, say, the EU or the United States or the Canadian authorities come to craft what will be their position within the WTO negotiating game. The capture by Special Interests of governmental positions which are then enshrined in WTO obligations is notorious. Is there really moral advantage in constituionalizing such? And is there pure political advantage in the judicial empowerment which results from such constitutionalization? I think only the blind fail to see that in the international legal system, sometimes the only meaningful checks and balances (to which we are accustomed and take not simply as normal but as indispensable within our domestic legal systems) take place at the *implementation* stage. On this reading, the international system of State Responsibility is a subtle mediating mechanism which assures states/governments respect for their mutual promises but allows wriggle room at the domestic implementing level. Often, the violation is the result of a Special Interest compromising a broader societal advantage in compliance. But again, only the wilfully blind, will not accept that the right too, can be the result of Special Interest influence in the first place.

This is not a *plaidoyer* for the status quo. The status quo must change and will change. But discourse of change in the direction of constitutionalization cannot, to be normatively credible, decouple the legal from the political, the exercise of rights from the responsibilities of power. Only should the WTO develop its institutional framework (and whether and how this is to take place is itself a delicate issue) could a constitutional future become normatively compelling. Even then one may wonder if one wants to empower yet another level of governance and give it Higher Law status and direct effect within one's legal system. If some believe that the protectionism is an evil akin to violation of human rights, a case could be made. Otherwise why not leave the operating system of the WTO, rooted in

---

[12] The most trenchant and convincing critique, the *locus classicus* of the genre is R.L. Howse and K. Nicolaides, 'Enhancing WTO Legitimacy: Constitutionalization or Global Subsidiarity?', 16 Governance (2003) 73.

*international* rather than *constitutional* vocabulary, in its present configuration. If it works, why fix it?

## 3. The Global v The Regional

This is an even better known story. Article XXIV was considered a marginal exception and for years commanded little attention. It is only in the mid-1970s, that the number of Regional Trade Agreements (RTAs) began to rise; it has now exceeded 200, a number which is growing at a furious pace. The language of Article XXIV—which seems to regard Free Trade Agreements (FTAs) and Custom Unions as positive— notwithstanding, the orthodox view is that at best RTAs are a transient evil to be tolerated pending a more universal and global liberalization of terms of trade. A more aggressive view[13] regards them not simply as a menace to the efficient producers in countries outside this or that FTA, but as having a chilling effect on more global negotiations premised on Most Favoured Nations (MFN) because the trade advantages within the FTA erode as the gap between RTA tariffs and general tariffs narrows.

Here the dissonance between the literature and the political practice is reversed. Whereas the academic desideratum of constitutionalization is oft met with indifference or hostility from the principal state actors, the academic critique of *regionalism* is met by an ever growing popularity of such. As India scuttles chunks of Doha, she gives the nod to an ASEAN FTA. Does the future look bleak?

There is no doubt that RTAs strike at the primordial norm of MFN and that RTA-induced trade diversion militates against some of the core benefits liberalized trade is designed to produce. Additionally, the proliferation of RTAs with disparate regimes of Rules of Origin add an additional distorting effect on trade patterns and the allocation of resources. But RTAs, *stricto sensu*, that is, excluding bilateral Free Trade Area Agreements, offer some distinct global systemic advantages beyond any ill-gained benefits to intra RTA-inefficient producers vis-à-vis outsiders.

Regional Free Trade Area Agreements continue to offer significant political benefits which spill over beyond the partners themselves. They often comprise regional states with a history of conflict, even violence. When successfully concluded and implemented, they enhance a welcome stabilizing interdependence. The experience of negotiations of the RTA and of subsequent management create habits of cooperation, compromise-seeking, and even constructivist transnational communities—COREPER (Committee of Permanent Representatives) style—of civil servants that has a beneficial effect which may transcend any economic benefits measured by trade volume or enhanced efficiencies. Internally, it instructs governments in the art of resisting special interests.

---

[13] See recently, J. Bhagwati, *Termites in the Trading System: How Preferential Agreements Undermine Free Trade* (New York: Oxford University Press, 2008).

Likewise, powerful RTAs, especially among the less powerful, may help somewhat in redressing the classical negotiating disparities characteristic of the GATT and WTO history.

A future of growth in RTAs is not necessarily to be regarded as a problem getting out of control and a menace to the international trading system, especially if, willy-nilly, the gaps between generalized tariffs and intra RTA tariffs continues to fall. 'Man shall *not* live by *bread alone*' (Deuteronomy 8:3). Indeed.

## 4. For a realistic utopia

Maybe it is not the WTO which can be compared to the Jewish Messiah, but it is I who has a sceptical view of utopia, realistic or otherwise. With the WTO we have reached the Promised Land. Sure, it can and will be reformed. Its *dispute settlement*, to give but one example, can be improved by, say, introducing the power to remand cases back to panels; the Appellate Body can rid itself of its fetishistic textual hermeneutics and love of dictionaries. There can be *a better system of sanctions* which do not depend on trade leverage and which do not reduce trade rather than increase it. But all that, and similar reforms, are within the existing paradigm and do not require utopian stretches. The inequalities and inequities of globalization are not rooted in the legal architecture of the WTO. Bad and iniquitous contracts, are not to be equated with bad and iniquitous contract law. Enhanced international governance comes with a price—not least the reduction in the specific gravity of individuals and societies and the further empowerment of judges and lawyers.

Let us decide that the WTO of today is, modestly, the Promised Land, Utopia Now. And let us humbly simply work to *improve its transparency, efficiency, and legitimacy.* Let us eschew widening (a globalizing that obliterates the regional) and deepening the *constitutional* which replaces the *international*.

# 33

# Fragmentation and Utopia: Towards an Equitable Integration of Finance, Trade, and Sustainable Development

*Robert Howse**

## SUMMARY

The concept of equity is inescapable in the interpretation and application of the law of the international trade and financial systems. The author assumes that we can help to achieve more equitable outcomes through better appreciating the elements of equity implicit or sometimes explicit in the existing rules of international law, interpreting and applying them together with or in light of other norms of international law, such as those entrenched in the UN human rights covenants. In the field of exchange controls and convertibility the original International Monetary Fund (IMF) Articles were premised on a world of largely fixed exchange rates adjusted through IMF supervision and as against an objective standard (gold reserves). The world that the IMF represents today is a very different one: because of speculation-driven currency markets and the widespread liberalization of capital controls, there is no agreed international standard against which a currency can be viewed as over- or undervalued, thus triggering a reasonable obligation to adjust economic fundamentals through means that do not impose unreasonable costs on other countries. The thrust of the Declaration on Coherence and the subsequent Agreement between the IMF and the World Trade Organization (WTO) is that issues that arise from possible inconsistencies between measures taken in relation to Fund programmes, on the one hand, and WTO obligations, on the other, ought to be addressed through consultations and cooperation between the WTO Secretariat and the IMF. In the field of trade restrictions for balance-of-

* This chapter draws on work I did for UNCTAD, where I was grateful for the support and encouragement of Rico Zampetti. My broader view on fragmentation and the nature of international law (along with much else) owes more than I can say to my endless conversation with Ruti Teitel. I am also grateful for the opportunity to present the earlier work at Stanford Law School on which this chapter is based, and particularly for reactions to that work from Al Sykes and Bob Staiger.

payment purposes, it is suggested that even though a developing country could address its balance-of-payments difficulties through exchange rate adjustments or tighter macroeconomic policies, it should not be expected to do so given the harm to development that may come from the resultant decline in needed imports. According to the author, the concept of coherence reflected in the relevant WTO instruments and activities concerning balance of payments and exchange matters is too narrowly focused on relations between the IMF and the WTO and does not include cooperation with those international institutions concerned with equity in development. The concept of coherence should be revised to reflect the relationship between equity and coherence as implied in the Millennium Declaration and related instruments.

In the history of political and legal philosophy the notion of utopia, at least since Plato's *Republic*, has been associated with the quest for justice or equity—for a human community where each is given his or her due. As international law visibly shifts from a state sovereignty to a humanity orientation,[1] the aspiration to equity in this sense is increasingly evident within its norms, structures, and institutions; even if the meaning of equity is much contested, and its application to different fields of international law complex and varied. In the case of the field of international finance, an appropriate beginning point for understanding the aspiration to equity is the Millennium Declaration.

In Section III of the Millennium Declaration entitled 'Development and Poverty Reduction', UN member states committed themselves 'to create an environment—at the national and global levels alike—which is conducive to development and to the elimination of poverty'. This depends on 'good governance within each country' and on 'good governance at the international level, and on transparency in the financial, monetary and trading systems'. Hence, they 'are committed to an open, equitable, rule-based, predictable and non-discriminatory multilateral trading and financial system'.

## 1. Equity in international finance and trade

The concept of equity in international trade and financial rules and institutions has not been explicitly defined and is the subject of debate and speculation among philosophers and political theorists.[2] Economists are often sceptical of whether the trade and financial systems should be understood at all in terms of justice rather than as instruments of economic policy coordination. Nevertheless, it will be observed that the actual rules often do depend, explicitly or implicitly, on a concept of fairness. For instance, one of the rules that will be discussed in this chapter, contained in Article IV of the IMF Articles of Agreement required that IMF members

---

[1] R. Teitel, *Humanity's Law* (Oxford: Oxford University Press, 2012).

[2] For a critical discussion, focusing on the approach of T. Pogge to these matters, see R. Howse and R. Teitel, 'Global Justice, Poverty, and the International Economic Order', in S. Besson and J. Tasioulas (eds), *The Philosophy of International Law* (Oxford: Oxford University Press, 2010).

not 'manipulate exchange rates or the international monetary system in order to prevent effective balance of payments adjustment or to gain an *unfair* competitive advantage over other members' (emphasis added). In the trading system, the WTO rules on subsidies, including fiscal measures such as tax incentives, suppose a conception of fair competition; as the WTO Appellate Body noted in one case, there are situations where market-based benchmarks for fairness will be inapplicable given the pervasive interconnection of public policies and market structures.

The concept of equity is then inescapable in the interpretation and application of the law of the international trade and financial systems. The question is whether there are legal and policy sources that allow us to give a definite meaning to this concept as we apply it to particular rules and disputes in the trade and financial systems. Once one looks for these sources, they appear more various and more instructive than one might have originally imagined.

The approach pursued in this chapter can usefully be contrasted to that of Thomas Pogge, who seeks to judge (and condemn) the existing system of rules in international economic law against an abstract conception of global justice, emphasizing the priority of eliminating poverty.[3] Rather, I begin without assuming the manifest injustice of the existing norms of international economic law, and assume that we can help to achieve more equitable outcomes through better appreciating the elements of equity implicit or sometimes explicit in those rules, and interpreting and applying them together with or in light of other norms of international law, such as those entrenched in the UN human rights covenants, for example. Thus the beginning point is not radical critique with a view to radical and comprehensive reconstruction, but a careful consideration of how relevant conceptions of equity have been sidelined or distorted in the way the existing rules have been applied and interpreted within and across international economic and other regimes under conditions of fragmentation. The end point might well be characterized as realistic utopia—a more perfect expression or elaboration of the ideals of equity already reflected in a range of positive international legal norms, through the interpretative transcendence of 'self-contained regimes'.

This last point requires some elaboration. The international financial system does not have its own 'court'. As will be discussed, its rules and practices may take effect as legal norms through their interpretation within the trade regime, which does have a highly developed dispute-settlement arrangement, including an appellate tribunal.[4] Attached to the trade regime, which is not integrated into the UN system, this dispute-settlement arrangement risks viewing the rules of global finance from a rather narrow perspective on growth, development, and equity, without consideration of the norms that have emerged from the UN institutions concerned with human rights and development.

---

[3] For an elaboration of this approach and a critique of its abstract utopianism, see Howse and Teitel, n 2.

[4] On the way in which the legal norms in one regime may have effects through their interpretation and application by another, see R. Howse and R. Teitel, 'Beyond Compliance', 1(2) Global Policy (2010) 127.

One ingredient of equity that is widely reflected in international instruments concerning trade, finance, and development (eg the Doha Declaration and its references to Special and Differential Treatment) is the notion that rules should be adjusted to the different situations of different states, in terms of their development needs. Thus, there is widespread agreement that formal legal equality, treating everyone the same regardless of their particular situation, is *not* equitable. At the same time, there is disagreement among states on how much *differential treatment* is justified in a given situation. The WTO rules on the balance of payments, designed to work in close relation to IMF principles, allow, for example, additional policy space to developing countries to use trade restrictions for purposes of monetary stability, in recognition that the alternative of tight monetary and fiscal policies to achieve stability might be at odds with development goals (as we shall see below, these flexibilities have been unfortunately not interpreted broadly enough in dispute settlement).

There is an interesting parallelism between the conception of equity as treating 'unlikes' *differently* and the recognition, in recent economic literature, that—contrary to what was implied in the Washington Consensus orthodoxy of the international financial institutions—there is not a single formula or pathway to development that will work for all countries.

Another dimension of equity that is reflected in international human rights instruments is that of voice and participation. These instruments suggest that people should not have a vision of development forced on them or decided by others. The Declaration on the Right to Development stipulates that the Right to Development includes 'free and meaningful participation in development'.

Further, there is a concept of equity implicit in the Millennium poverty reduction goals. Acceptance of these goals implies that existing inequalities of wealth, to the extent that they leave billions in dire poverty, are unacceptable. The focus on reducing *poverty* not just increasing *growth*, implies that increased wealth does not necessarily lead to an acceptably just or equitable distribution of wealth without positive redistributive measures.

Closely related to this notion of equity is the concept of social and economic justice or equity expressed in the United Nations Covenant on Social and Economic and Cultural Rights. Article 11 of the Covenant provides:

1. The States Parties to the present Covenant recognize the right of everyone to an adequate standard of living for himself and his family, including adequate food, clothing and housing, and to the continuous improvement of living conditions. The States Parties will take appropriate steps to ensure the realization of this right, recognizing to this effect the essential importance of international co-operation based on free consent.[5]

While not all states—most notably the United States—have embraced the rights in the Covenant as treaty or customary international law, even the United States has participated in the Declaration on the Right to Development, which incorporates

---

[5] See R. Howse and R. Teitel, 'Beyond the Divide: The Covenant on Economic, Social and Cultural Rights and The World Trade Organization', Occasional Paper No. 30, Friedrich Ebert Stiftung, Geneva, April 2007.

to a large extent and affirms these rights. It is important to note that the Covenant does require a specific notion of redistribution between countries as a means of realization of the rights in question. The primary obligation is of states to their own peoples. However, a concrete implication of this notion of equity is that the rules of the international trade and financial system at a minimum should not *undermine* and ideally should *facilitate* the ability of states to discharge their obligations under the Covenant to implement social and economic rights. In this respect, the UN human rights organs have correctly grasped that they have a mandate to evaluate the rules of the trade and financial system against their impact on the ability of states, individually and collectively, to fulfil their obligations under the Covenant.[6]

Finally, equity has been considered by UN members to imply a fair global distribution of burdens and benefits from the operations of the international economic system. This goes beyond a notion that the system(s) should enable states to achieve social and economic justice within their borders to a conception of *global solidarity*. Thus, according to the Millennium Declaration, solidarity requires that 'global challenges must be managed in a way that distributes the costs and burdens fairly in accordance with basic principles of equity and social justice. Those who suffer most, or who benefit least, deserve help from those who benefit most.'[7]

## 2. Coherence as the logical implication of the recognition of equity

Coherence—the normatively justified bridging of self-contained regimes—seems a logical implication of the recognition of equity as a fundamental ingredient of the international trade and financial system. While, as noted, there are rules and policies in the system that are *expressions* of equity, mostly those rules and policies leave unarticulated—and in some sense presuppose—relevant conceptions or articulations of equity. These are found, as we have seen, in the instruments and institutions primarily of the United Nations that address human rights and development. Coherence, then, means in the first instance coherence between, on the one hand, the rules and policies of the institutions where equity is articulated and defined normatively, and the rules and policies of the international trading system, on the other.

But there is a further aspect to the relationship between equity and coherence: inequity may result from *uncoordinated rules as between* the trading system and

---

[6] See, eg, 'Liberalization of Trade in Services and Human Rights', Report of the High Commissioner for Human Rights (E/CN.4/Sub.2/2002/9); 'Globalization and its Impact on the Full Enjoyment of Human Rights', Report of the High Commissioner for Human Rights (E/CN.4/2002/54)—the report considers the WTO's Agreement on Agriculture; 'Human Rights, Trade and Investment', Report of the High Commissioner for Human Rights (E/CN.4/Sub.2/2003/9); 'Impact of the TRIPS Agreement on the Enjoyment of all Human Rights', Report of the High Commissioner for Human Rights (E/CN.4/Sub.2/2001/13).

[7] See for an elaboration of these notions, Teitel, n 1, at ch. 6.

the financial system.[8] For example, the IMF may ask a country to improve its balance of payments and the trading system may prevent the use of certain instruments for doing so, such as import surcharges or concessional export financing. Furthermore, there may be strong reasons why these policy options have been constrained by the international trading system. However, without greater sensitivity by the IMF for the constraints imposed by that system *and their underlying policy reasons* and a broader and more palatable range of policy options, developed to accommodate the trading system while achieving the IMF's goals for a given client state, such states may well feel those policy options are their only viable choices. If these options remain foreclosed without the provision of other viable trading-system-friendly options, states may then be forced to have recourse to policy instruments that threaten social equity, and result in poverty and unemployment if they are to obey the prescriptions of the financial system as well as respect the rules of the trading system.

An early explicit attempt to address coherence at the WTO is the Uruguay Round Declaration on the Contribution of the World Trade Organization to Greater Coherence in Global Economic Policymaking.

Paragraph 2 of the Declaration reads, in relevant part,

Trade liberalization forms an increasingly important component in the success of the adjustment programmes that many countries are undertaking, often involving significant transitional social costs. In this connection, Ministers note the role of the World Bank and the IMF in supporting adjustment to trade liberalization, including support to net food-importing developing countries facing short-term costs arising from agricultural trade reforms.

The most important text in the Declaration is arguably to be found in paragraph 5:

The interlinkages between the different aspects of economic policy require that the international institutions with responsibilities in each of these areas follow consistent and mutually supportive policies. The World Trade Organization should therefore pursue and develop cooperation with the international organizations responsible for monetary and financial matters, while respecting the mandate, the confidentiality requirements and the necessary autonomy in decision-making procedures of each institution, and avoiding the imposition on governments of cross-conditionality or additional conditions. Ministers further invite the Director-General of the WTO to review with the Managing Director of the International Monetary Fund and the President of the World Bank, the implications of the WTO's responsibilities for its cooperation with the Bretton Woods institutions, as well as the forms such cooperation might take, with a view to achieving greater coherence in global economic policymaking.

It is to be noted that, while paragraph 2, for example, mentions the important social costs of trade liberalization and economic reform and singles out the situations of developing countries, the Declaration does not extend the idea of coherence to cooperation with those international institutions whose mandate

---

[8] 'Economic Policy Challenges in an Open Economy: Coherence between Trade and Finance', Communication of UNCTAD to the WTO Working Group on Trade, Debt and Finance (WT/WGTDF/W/27), 24 November 2004.

is development policy such as the United Nations Conference on Trade and Development (UNCTAD) and the United Nations Development Programme (UNDP) nor those concerned with social equity and justice in particular, such as the UN human rights institutions. Instead, the need for coherence is limited to those international institutions 'responsible for monetary and financial matters, . . .' Nevertheless, paragraph 5 does state the imperative of avoiding 'cross-conditionality', a situation where a government is forced to pursue a harmful policy or set of policies or even inconsistent policies because otherwise it will fall foul of uncoordinated conditions or strictures imposed by different international economic institutions.

In 1996, the WTO entered into a cooperation agreement with the IMF: this agreement provides for consultations between the WTO and the IMF and the exchange of information. Paragraph 10 of that agreement provides:

The Fund's staff shall consult with the WTO Secretariat on issues of possible inconsistency between measures under discussion with a common member and that member's obligations under the WTO Agreement. The WTO Secretariat shall consult with the Fund's staff on issues of possible inconsistency between measures under discussion with a common member and that member's obligations under the Fund's Articles of Agreement.

This provision would appear to be of very great importance for coherence; it appears to both strengthen and implement paragraph 5 of the Uruguay Round Declaration on Coherence by requiring (the obligatory 'shall' is used here) discussions about possible inconsistency while measures are 'under discussion', that is, to avoid a conflict in the first place. As we shall see, however, in at least one prominent WTO dispute it became clear that this consultation requirement had not been followed and unfortunately the Appellate Body of the WTO did not attach much importance to it.

The WTO Doha Declaration provided for the establishment of a new Working Group on Trade, Debt and Finance:

We agree to an examination, in a Working Group under the auspices of the General Council, of the relationship between trade, debt and finance, and of any possible recommendations on steps that might be taken within the mandate and competence of the WTO to enhance the capacity of the multilateral trading system to contribute to a durable solution to the problem of external indebtedness of developing and least-developed countries, and to strengthen the coherence of international trade and financial policies, with a view to safeguarding the multilateral trading system from the effects of financial and monetary instability. The General Council shall report to the Fifth Session of the Ministerial Conference on progress in the examination.

## 3. Exchange controls and convertibility

The General Agreement on Tariffs and Trade (GATT) rules on exchange controls and convertibility reflect the international financial and monetary system designed at Bretton Woods at the end the Second World War. The post-war Bretton Woods arrangements contemplated a system of fixed exchange rates tied to the gold standard. Under this system, a country would in theory be required to hold sufficient reserves of gold to back the quantity of its currency in circulation. Where a temporary imbalance of payments occurred (ie, where a country could not meet payments for imports with its receipts of foreign currency from export sales without selling gold for foreign currency), this would be financed by a country borrowing from the IMF. In the case of a structural or persistent imbalance, a country would devalue its currency under the supervision of the IMF, which might recommend domestic policy adjustments to ensure that further devaluations were not required in order to maintain the balance of payments. While it had already been under tension for some time, the Breton Woods system broke down in the 1970s when the United States unilaterally opted out of the system by refusing to back the dollar with gold reserves.

In the case of developing countries, rapid progress towards convertibility and the removal of exchange controls became the economic orthodoxy in the 1980s and 1990s. Such reforms were thought to have the effect of encouraging foreign investment and creating domestic financial systems as well as access to global financial networks that would underwrite growth and development. The Asian and Latin American financial crises of the 1990s led to considerable rethinking of this story. Some economists, such as Jagdish Bhagwati of Columbia University believe that too rapid financial liberalization contributed to the crises, which led to widespread human misery in a number of countries. According to Bhagwati,

Per capita incomes tumbled to almost one-third their 1996 level in Indonesia, with the other crisis-stricken Asian countries showing declines ranging from a quarter to nearly half of the 1996 levels. . . . This crisis, precipitated by panic-fueled outflows of capital, was a product of hasty and imprudent financial liberalization, almost always under foreign pressure, allowing free international flows of short-term capital without adequate attention to the potentially potent downside of such globalization.[9]

Nobel Prize-winning economist Joseph Stiglitz takes a similar view, and when he was at the World Bank he resisted the IMF-led orthodoxy of rapid financial liberalization, largely predicting the kind of consequences discussed by Bhagwati.[10] Both Stiglitz and Bhagwati, economists of the first rank who disagree on many issues, nevertheless see capital controls as a valuable instrument in stemming a panic flight of short-term capital and thereby preventing the kind of financial collapse that sent millions back into poverty in the late 1990s. The Report of the UN Commission chaired by Stiglitz in the wake of the recent global financial crisis has re-emphasized these considerations.[11]

At the same time, more recently, the United States has placed considerable pressure on China to either revalue or 'float' its currency, the renminbi, on the theory that the exchange rate was 'unfair', rigged somehow to keep Chinese

---

[9] J. Bhagwhati, *In Defense of Globalization* (Oxford: Oxford University Press, 2004), 199–200.
[10] J. Stiglitz *Globalization and Its Discontents* (New York: W.W. Norton, 2002).
[11] United Nations, 'Report of the Commission of Experts of the President of the United Nations General Assembly on Reforms of the International Financial system', New York, 21 September 2009.

exports artificially cheap. The implication is that a 'fair' exchange rate would be one based upon the currency markets. Certainly, in a world of floating exchange rates, where there is no objective standard such as gold reserves, the concept of a 'correct' exchange rate is an elusive one. Economists have attempted various estimates of the 'correct' exchange rate between the renminbi and the US dollar, but these estimates vary considerably depending on the methodology used. Unless China moves further than it has already to a market-base, floating exchange rate, it will thus always be vulnerable to criticisms that, according to some methodology, its exchange rate is not 'correct', or unfair to US trading interests. Bhagwati has, however, suggested that China's fixed exchange rate with the dollar and cautious approach to financial liberalization contributed positively to its development strategy, providing needed stability in a dynamic economy, and sustaining policies that led to millions being brought out of poverty: 'It is noteworthy that both India and China escaped the Asian financial crisis; they did not have capital account convertibility.'[12]

The GATT rules concerning exchange measures and convertibility are contained in Article XV of the General Agreement. Article XV:4 states that 'Contracting parties shall not, by exchange action, frustrate the intent of the provisions of this Agreement, nor by trade action, the intent of the provisions of the Articles of Agreement of the International Monetary Fund.'

Article XV:9 of the GATT further provides:

Nothing in this Agreement shall preclude: (a) the use by a contracting party of exchange controls or exchange restrictions in accordance with the Articles of Agreement of the International Monetary Fund or with that contracting party's special exchange agreement with the CONTRACTING PARTIES, or (b) the use by a contracting party of restrictions or controls on imports or exports the sole effect of which, additional to the effects permitted under Articles XI, XII, XIII and XIV, is to make effective such exchange controls or exchange restrictions.

According to Article XVI:2 of the GATT, there shall be deference to 'the determination of the Fund as to whether action by a contracting party in exchange matters in accordance with the Articles of Agreement of the International Monetary Fund . . .'.

These provisions suggest that, where measures have been taken with respect to exchange controls or restrictions, even if such measures would otherwise be considered trade restrictions because of their effect on import and export transactions, *the intent of the GATT is not to impose disciplines beyond those required by the IMF.* Nevertheless, it is inaccurate to view these provisions, as some commentators have, essentially *ceding jurisdiction* to the IMF. The reason is that, where an exchange measure is not consistent with the IMF Articles then the 'safe haven' of Article XV disappears and the measure may well then fall foul of a provision of the GATT, such as Article XI. Thus, where a country disagrees with the Fund on the best course for solving a financial crisis, including in a manner that does not worsen the plight of

---

[12] Bhagwati, n 9.

the least advantaged, there is a risk that the GATT will allow for that country to be 'punished' through being found in violation of GATT rules; in other words, added to the punishment that the IMF can dish out, is the punishment that can be dished out through possible retaliatory sanctions for a violation of the GATT. In other words, the GATT/WTO sets itself up as a residual enforcer for the IMF.[13] Thus, while IMF consistency may well be a 'safe haven' in the GATT, the fact that a WTO member is pursuing a strategy in disagreement with the IMF should not serve to *de*-legitimate its trade measures, or create a presumption of GATT *illegality*.

The original IMF Articles were premised on a world of largely fixed exchange rates adjusted through IMF supervision and as against an objective standard (gold reserves). The world that the IMF represents today is a very different one, where because of speculation-driven currency markets and the widespread liberalization of capital controls, which IMF economists have generally wholeheartedly endorsed, there is no agreed international standard against which a currency can be viewed as over- or undervalued, thus triggering a reasonable obligation to adjust economic fundamentals through means that do not impose unreasonable costs on other countries.

The IMF Articles of Agreement provide that an IMF member shall not 'manipulate exchange rates or the international monetary system in order to prevent effective balance of payments adjustment or to gain an unfair competitive advantage over other members' (IMF Agreement, Art. IV, Section 1(iii)). Currency manipulation as such is defined in the surveillance provisions of the IMF Articles as 'protracted large-scale intervention in one direction in the exchange market'.

However, the concept of an *'unfair'* competitive advantage is not defined. Thus, the international community is here required to supply a relevant conception of 'equity'. Is China's purchase of dollars with renminbi aimed at maintaining an exchange rate that constitutes an 'unfair' competitive advantage? Arguably, under an approach to fairness influenced by conceptions of sustainable development and the right to development, one essential aspect of the question would be whether China's exchange rate policy represents a legitimate exercise of its right to development, and thus the way in which the policy figures in its development needs and strategies. For example, as Erik Denters argues, pegging the renminbi to the dollar may well have encouraged foreign investment, a crucial part of China's development strategy.[14] At the same time, one would have to ask if China's exchange rate actions undermine the development policies of other WTO members.

In GATT/WTO practice and jurisprudence, the justifiability of measures under Article XV has been considered on a number of occasions. In the *Argentina—Textiles and Apparel* case, Argentina argued that a 3 per cent ad valorem tax that it collected was for purposes of funding the collection of accurate statistical data on import and export transactions as part of its overall understanding with the IMF on stabilization and adjustment. The Panel held that there was no exception

[13] This kind of double jeopardy or cross-regime magnifying effect is what Teitel and I have labelled 'ultra-compliance'. See Howse and Teitel, n 5.

[14] E. Denters, 'Manipulation of Exchange Rates in International Law: The Chinese Yuan', ASIL Insights, November 2003.

under the GATT that would, for these reasons, limit Argentina's obligations under Article VIII with regard to customs fees. The Panel did not consider whether, given that Argentina was maintaining the tax in the context of its arrangements with the IMF, the tax could be deemed to be an exchange measure within the meaning of Article XV:9 of the GATT. The fact that the tax applied to all imports indicates that it was not intended as a protectionist measure to shelter Argentine industries from competition while lending plausibility to its connection to Argentina's exchange arrangements. The Appellate Body upheld the Panel's approach.[15]

Argentina had argued that the Declaration on Coherence and the subsequent 1996 Agreement between the IMF and the WTO, discussed above, were 'legislative developments' in the WTO which had the effect of creating a meta-norm of avoidance of 'cross-conditionalities', such that its relations with the IMF would require a state to engage in conduct that would violate WTO law. The Appellate Body first of all observed that Argentina had not shown to the Panel's satisfaction that the tax had been requested of it by the IMF or there was a conflict of *legal obligation*, that is, that Argentina had a legally binding agreement with the IMF that would be violated if it did not impose the tax.

These findings of the Appellate Body suggest a far too narrow and formalistic view of the problem of coherence and conflicting conditionalities. In many cases the IMF's requirements are of a general nature, and linked to the achievement of certain results. The IMF leaves the specific instrumentalities up to the state in question. The fact that the IMF has not requested 'x' policy does *not mean* that 'x' policy does not result from requirements imposed by the IMF—the policy in question may be one of the only feasible ways of satisfying the IMF demands at reasonable social cost, for example. The notion of legal conflict suggested by the Appellate Body is equally problematic. It reduces the challenge of coherence to a notion of avoiding conflicting treaty requirements. However, international law is not the only or even the primary lever that the IMF uses to 'enforce' conditionality; rather, the IMF will simply not disburse further funds to a state that does not meet its conditions, regardless of whether those conditions are formalized as legal requirements or expressed as is typically the case in 'memoranda' or 'letters of intent' from the state in question.[16]

The Appellate Body placed considerable emphasis on the notion that neither the Declaration on Coherence nor the subsequent Cooperation Agreement between the WTO and the IMF added to or diminished the rights and obligations contained

---

[15] *Argentina—Measures Affecting Imports of Footwear, Textiles, Apparel and Other Items*, Report of the Appellate Body, WT/DS56/AB/R (adopted 22 April 1998), paras 69–74.

[16] See O. Eldar, 'Reform of IMF Conditionality; a Proposal for Self-Imposed Conditionality', IILJ Working Paper 2005/10, New York University Law School, Centre for Global Administrative Law Series; D. Siegel, 'Legal Aspects of the IMF/WTO Relationship: The Fund's Articles of Agreement and the WTO Agreements', 96 AJIL (2002) 561 at 581:

> even those measures that constitute Fund conditionality do not entail legal obligations to implement the policies in the program. As a legal matter, failure to complete those measures results solely in the non-fulfillment of a condition for the use of Fund resources. Political ramifications may stem from this failure, but the legal consequences are limited to the suspension of financing absent further action by the Executive Board; they do not give rise to a breach of obligation or the possibility of sanctions.

in the WTO Agreements. The Appellate Body noted that the effect of cross-conditionalities or possible conflicts between measures that might result from IMF programmes and WTO obligations was specified as 'consultation' between the Fund and the WTO. Yet when it considered whether the Panel's failure to consult with the Fund constituted a violation of its obligation to make an objective assessment of the matter, the Appellate Body *ignored* the consultation requirement as set out in the paragraph 10 of the Agreement between the IMF and the WTO. In the *Dominican Republic—Cigarettes* case, the Dominican Republic argued that a foreign exchange fee charged on certain import transactions was an exchange measure within Article XV:9(a) of the GATT and thus justified even if otherwise inconsistent with GATT Article II, because

it is prescribed by monetary authorities, not by trade or customs authorities; it applies to exchange actions, not to import transactions as such; and it is a charge on foreign exchange transactions imposed through the banking system, not a charge on import transactions levied by customs authorities. (para. 7.124)

The Panel rejected the Dominican Republic's defence under Article XV:9 on the grounds that

since Article XV:9 of the GATT exempts exchange restrictions measures that are applied in accordance with the Fund Articles, from obligations under other Articles of the GATT, the guiding principle that the IMF prescribed as the criterion for the determination of what constitutes an 'exchange restriction' should be respected by this Panel. (para. 7.132)

This is the same non sequitur evident in a Panel ruling on a Greek import charge in the 1950s—the leap from the textual requirement of the GATT that a measure justified under Article XV:9 be consistent with the IMF Articles, the constitutional treaty of the IMF, to the conclusion that the IMF and its policies should be determinative *in other respects* of whether the measure falls into Article XV.

In jumping to various IMF documents to assess whether the Dominican Republic's measure was an 'exchange restriction' within the meaning of those documents, the Panel failed to consider the meaning of the text of Article XV, especially the language, 'exchange restrictions', in light of the purpose and object of the WTO agreements. It looked at Article XV:9 as if it simply ceded jurisdiction or deferred to the IMF, rather than being intended to fulfil goals of the WTO itself, such as the achievement of full employment and improving standards of living, through allowing a country to safeguard the stability of its currency and payments as a sovereign matter, and not on account of the authority of the IMF.

## 4. Trade restrictions for balance-of-payments purposes[17]

Articles XII to XIV of the GATT elaborate a complex code designed to govern and discipline the use of trade restrictions for balance-of-payments purposes. Article XII:1

---

[17] The following draws from M.J. Trebilcock and R. Howse, *The Regulation of International Trade*, 3rd edn (London/New York: Routledge, 2005), ch. 5, 'Trade, Exchange Rates and the Balance of Payments'.

states the basic right of any contracting party to impose quantitative restrictions in derogation from Article XI 'in order to safeguard its external financial position and its balance of payments'. Article XII:2 establishes that such restrictions shall be limited to what is 'necessary: (i) to forestall the imminent threat of, or to stop, a serious decline in monetary reserves, or (ii) in the case of a Contracting Party with very low monetary reserves to achieve a reasonable rate of increase in its reserves.' As well, such restrictions must be progressively relaxed as the balance of payments improves.

Furthermore, contracting parties 'undertake, in carrying out their domestic policies, to pay due regard to the need for maintaining or restoring equilibrium in their balance of payments on a sound and lasting basis' (Art. XII:3). At the same time, no contracting party is obligated to take domestic balance-of-payments measures that would threaten the objective of full employment (ie, contracting the domestic money supply to dampen demand for imports, Art. XII:3(d)).

In the case of *developing countries*, there is a much broader exemption for balance-of-payments-based trade restrictions. Hence, Article XVII:2(b) states the principle that developing countries should have additional flexibility 'to apply quantitative restrictions for balance of payments purposes in a manner which takes full account of the continued high level of demand for imports likely to be generated by their programmes of economic development'.

What this suggests is that even though a developing country could address its balance-of-payments difficulties through exchange rate adjustments or tighter macroeconomic policies, it should not be expected to do so given the harm to development that may come from the resultant decline in needed imports. In the *India—Balance of Payments* case, the exception relied on by India required that balance-of-payments restrictions be removed as soon as the crisis conditions to which they were addressed had passed, unless the removal were likely to provoke the return of those conditions. However, a further proviso was that, in any case, a developing country should not be required to remove balance-of-payments import restrictions, if doing so could require a change in that country's development policies. India's reliance on this provision required the Appellate Body to determine what is a development policy and whether if India were to remove its balance-of-payments restrictions it would be required to change its policies. What the Appellate Body did was to rely entirely on a judgment of the IMF that India did not need to change its development policies because it could address the consequences of removing its balance-of-payments-based import restrictions through 'macroeconomic' policies.

Had the Appellate Body considered development policy informed by a conception of equity that includes the notion that development policy is a matter in the first instance for participation of those who are affected, it would have analysed the legal issue quite differently.

First of all, the Appellate Body would not have accepted that one institution, and particularly, the technocrats in that institution have 'ownership' of the meaning of a 'development' policy.

Secondly, the Appellate Body would not have embraced the stark contrast between 'development policy' and macroeconomic policy. This implies that development policy is restricted to a series of techniques that 'experts' view as formulae for 'development', rather than including all those policies that people—in this case, at a minimum, India and Indians—see as affecting the fulfilment of their approach to development. From the perspective of equity, as informed by the social and economic rights recognized in the UN Covenant on Social, Economic and Cultural Rights, it would be obvious that macroeconomic policies, which affect revenues available for government programmes to fulfil social and economic rights, as well as the cost of imported goods and services needed to fulfil such rights and the reserves of currency with which to pay for them, are 'development policies'.

Thirdly, on the question of whether India would be required to change its development policy in order to be able to remove the balance-of-payments restrictions without a return to the crisis conditions that led to their imposition, the Appellate Body and the Panel ought to have, for purposes of equity and coherence, considered and indeed solicited the views of a broader range of institutions and social actors—at a minimum the international organizations with express mandates on development, such as UNCTAD and the UNDP.

Finally, the Appellate Body might have considered that the provision in question is largely a matter of self-declaration—that it empowers India and above all Indians to chart their own course in development policy, and therefore that the provision is not intended to invite the dispute settlement organs to examine *de novo* India's judgment that if it removed the restrictions, it would have to change its development policy.

In sum, even *if* the overall orthodox economic preference for macroeconomic measures over trade restrictions is correct, in the realm of the second best, trade restrictions at least of a temporary nature may be a desirable alternative to a macroeconomic policy move that leaves very severe social and economic consequences.

## 5. Conclusions and recommendations

The aspiration to equity, providing to each his or her due, is inseparable from the utopian idea. We can help to achieve more equitable outcomes through better appreciating the elements of equity implicit or sometimes explicit in the existing rules of international law, interpreting and applying them together with or in light of other norms of international law, such as those entrenched in the UN Human Rights Covenants. The WTO rules on exchange actions and balance-of-payments justifications for trade restrictions clearly reflect a conception of equity that takes into account the particular needs and situations of developing countries. A *realistic* utopia implies fully recognizing that equitable considerations are not narrow exceptions to technocratic governance of finance, or merely a form of aspirational rhetoric or soft law but are central to the task of an international financial system embedded in the general project of international law. In the way that WTO dispute-settlement organs have interpreted the provisions in question, especially as they relate to developing countries, equity understood as differential treatment has too often been marginalized or even dismissed. In part this is because the relationship of the norms in question to international legal regimes that appear 'external' to trade and finance has been inadequately appreciated. Thus the task is to main-stream these regimes into the interpretation and application of the law of inter-national finance and trade.

In certain, very precisely defined, matters, the WTO rules entail deference to judgments of the IMF. In dispute settlement, however, those elements in the rules that reflect equity in particular as concerns developing countries have been minimized or ignored. Moreover, the dispute-settlement organs have gone well beyond the explicit limits of deference to the IMF such that they have deferred to the IMF even in such a matter as the meaning of a country's 'development policy' (the *India—Balance of Payments* case). From the perspective of equity as participa-tion in decision-making concerning development, these tendencies of the dispute-settlement organs are of considerable concern, since developing countries have limited and unequal representation and voice in the IMF.

More generally, the concept of coherence reflected in the relevant WTO instru-ments and activities as concerns balance of payments and exchange matters is too narrowly focused on relations between the IMF and the WTO and does not include cooperation with those international institutions concerned with equity in development. The concept of coherence should be revised to reflect the relation-ship between equity and coherence as implied in the Millennium Declaration and related instruments.

At the same time, it appears that even within the narrow conception of coherence embraced in the WTO, the agreed mechanism for avoiding cross-conditionalities, namely obligatory consultations between the WTO Secretariat and the IMF prior to either taking decisions that could result in cross-conditionalities, has not been closely followed. A comprehensive review should be carried out of the situations where and where not these consultations have occurred and whether they have been effective in the avoidance of cross-conditionalities.

# 34

# Realism, Utopia, and the Future of International Environmental Law

*Francesco Francioni*

## SUMMARY

If one looks at the contemporary scene of international environmental law, three basic features stand out as elements capable of influencing future developments of this law, both as a distinct branch of international law and as a legal discipline: (i) the meaning and role of 'sustainable development', a concept that for more than 20 years has been at the heart of diplomatic and judicial efforts at reconciling environmental protection with the demands of economic growth; (ii) the increasing polarization of the academic debate and judicial practice around the dilemma of environmental protection versus scientific and technological advancement; and (iii) the continuous search for an institutional framework to ensure environmental governance in a world of increasing economic and social interdependence. The most serious weakness of international environmental law is the lack or deficiency in enforcement mechanisms. Other branches of international law have proved helpful. In some instances. The World Trade Organization (WTO) dispute-settlement Panels and especially the Appellate Body have wisely reconciled their responsibility to guarantee the observance of the specific obligations arising for the member states under the WTO agreements with the need to give proper consideration to the legitimate goals pursued by member states in protecting their local environment or even the general environment beyond the limits of their national jurisdiction. Other times, however, the WTO Dispute Settlement Body has been impervious to environmental sustainability and has mechanically applied WTO rules even in the face of legitimate environmental concerns raised by the rigid implementation of free trade rules. In the field of investment law progressive incorporation of environmental issues within the sphere of investment arbitration has taken place in the past ten years. The International Court of Justice (ICJ) has had the opportunity to adjudicate an increasing number of cases with a distinct environmental law dimension. However, international environmental law, in spite of its impressive development at the level of treaty law and notwithstanding the abundance of soft law instruments, declarations, and 'understandings', remains an immature and underdeveloped body of law. What are the prospects for further developments? At the normative level, a 'realistic utopia' entails the recouping of the original promise of the environmental movement, that is the conceptualization and the legal treatment of the natural environment as a 'public good' to be administered in the interest of all and of the generations to come. At the institutional level two approaches are possible: (i) consciously to shun the need for institutional reform as too costly and ineffective and rely on market mechanisms of self-regulation and transnational private enforcement and (ii) a reform of the institutional system of environmental governance by creating effective multilateral institutions that can mirror what has been done in the international economic law and human rights. The two approaches are not mutually exclusive. They should be complementary because the first one can hardly work without the other.

# 1. The method

In his introduction, Antonio Cassese invites the contributors to this book to engage in imaginative thinking about the future of international law. But he warns that we should strive to avoid wishful thinking and apply our imagination to the hard reality on the ground. This advice seems especially pertinent to the topic of this chapter: international environmental law. In spite of its spectacular development in terms of quantity of treaties and other normative instruments dealing with environmental protection that have been adopted in the past 40 years or so, the identity of environmental law as a legal discipline and its maturity as a branch of international law are still contested.[1] Its efficacy is put to a difficult test in light of the glaring failures to prevent the continuous degradation of the natural environment. Consensus still eludes the international community on what system of environmental governance should be set up to tackle global environmental problems such as climate change. At the same time, the language of environmental law is increasingly penetrating into every aspect of our economic, social, and cultural life and, paradoxically, the growing awareness of the importance of environmental preservation for our life and welfare seems to go hand in hand with the perception of a decline and failure of environmental law.

To grasp this complex reality and at the same time to pay heed Cassese's advice, the best approach is to undertake a retrospective analysis of the achievements and shortcomings of international environmental law and then try prospectively to set out, hopefully as a 'realistic utopia', a path for progress and innovation. This approach fits also this writer's conviction that any imaginative leap forward can

---

[1] E. Fisher, B. Lange, E. Scotford, and C. Carlarne, 'Maturity and Methodology: Starting a Debate about Environmental Law Scholarship', 21 J Env L (2009) 213–50, with a response by R. Macrory.

only come from a full comprehension of the past, from the awareness and state of mind that combines 'wisdom and youth'.[2]

## 2. The *acquis*

There is general agreement that the origin of international environmental law—that is, the branch of international law dealing with the protection of the natural environment—can be traced to the early 1970s with the organization by the United Nation of the first conference on international law and the environment and the adoption of the Stockholm Declaration on the Human Environment.[3] The Stockholm Declaration contained innovative elements and had the potential for progressive development of international law. It contributed to the consolidation of the idea that the conservation of the environment is a concern of the international community, thereby removing environmental law from the narrow confines of private law regulating reciprocal relations between neighbouring states.[4] It gave substance to the novel concept of *erga omnes* obligations, enunciated just two years earlier in the famous dictum of the International Court of Justice (ICJ) in the *Barcelona Traction* case.[5] It proclaimed the responsibility of every state to prevent damage to the environment, not only of other sovereign states but also of the common environment beyond the bounds of national jurisdiction.[6] It linked the safeguarding of environmental quality to fundamental rights and human dignity and to the duty 'to protect and improve the environment for present and future generations'.[7]

The wave produced by the Stockholm Declaration in the 1970s and 1980s led to the adoption of the first generation of treaties and conventions dealing with the protection of the environment. Among them one can recall innovative treaties, such as the World Heritage Convention,[8] which combines the protection of cultural and natural heritage of outstanding importance; the Washington Convention on trade in endangered species;[9] the MARPOL system on the prevention of marine pollution from ships and Part XII of the Law of the

---

[2] I borrow these felicitous words (in English in the original Italian text) from Cesare Pavese, who in his diary (12 June 1939) observed that 'La vitalità creatrice è una riserva di passato. Si diventa creatori—anche noi—quando si ha un passato. La giovinezza...è una ricca vecchiaia (genius is wisdom and youth)', *Il mestiere di vivere* (Turin: 1962), 148.

[3] Adopted 16 June 1972, 11 ILM 1416 (1972).

[4] *Trail Smelter Arbitration* (Canada-US), 16 April 1938–11 March 1941, RIAA Vol. III, 1905–82.

[5] *Barcelona Traction, Light and Power Ltd*, judgment, ICJ Reports, pp 3ff, paras 33–4.

[6] Principle 21.

[7] Principle 1.

[8] Convention Concerning the Protection of the World Cultural and Natural Heritage, adopted by the UNESCO General Conference on 16 November 1972. For the text and analytical commentary see F. Francioni with F. Lenzerini (eds), *The 1972 World Heritage Convention—A Commentary* (Oxford: Oxford University Press, 2008).

[9] Adopted 3 March 1973, 12 ILM 1085 (1973).

Sea Convention;[10] the Geneva Convention on Long-Range Transboundary Air Pollution;[11] and the evolving system of protection of Antarctic fauna and flora.[12] These and many other treaties adopted in this period have contributed to the emergence of some general principles of environmental protection, as well as to the consolidation of international environmental law as a discrete area of legal study and research. At the same time, there is no denying that this first wave of legal instruments presents some significant defects and shortcomings. With few exceptions,[13] these legal instruments address environmental problems following a sector-by-sector approach, resulting in a multiplication and fragmentation of legal regimes, which does not take into account the interdependence of various elements of the biosphere and the need for an ecosystem approach to the preservation of environmental quality. Another weakness is the inadequate integration of environmental standards into economic development policies. To this, one has to add the systemic avoidance in this first generation of environmental treaties of 'secondary rules' on liability for breach of the substantive obligations to respect and protect the environment.[14]

A second wave of international environmental law coincides with the emergence of global ecological issues at the end of 1980s and with the Earth Summit that led to the Rio Declaration of 1992. This was the era of the discovery of the relentless erosion of the ozone layer and of the adoption of the related Vienna Convention and the Montreal Protocol on the control of substances that deplete the ozone layer;[15] of the emergence of global warming as a scientific, political, and economic issue, with the attendant adoption of the 1992 UN Framework Convention on Global Warming;[16] and of the perception of biodiversity degradation as a 'common concern' of humankind.[17] Increased awareness about the dangers posed by the irreversible degradation of the environment spurred in this period the emergence of the 'precautionary approach' in its twofold expression as a radical ban on activities deemed to be harmful to the environment—as in the case of the 1991 Madrid Protocol on the protection of the Antarctic environment[18]—and, in its moderate

---

[10] International Convention for the Prevention of Pollution from Ships, 1973 (with following Protocol and Annexes), 21 ILM 1319 (1973); UNCLOS, 21 ILM 1261 (1982).

[11] Adopted 13 November 1979, 18 ILM 1442 (1979).

[12] See *Handbook of the Antarctic Treaty System*, US Department of State, especially chs X and XI.

[13] One such exception is the Canberra Convention on the Conservation of Antarctic Marine Living Resources, which inaugurated the so-called 'ecosystem approach' to the conservation of fisheries in the Antarctic seas, see *Handbook*, ibid, at fn 13.

[14] The well-known example of deliberate avoidance of liability and responsibility implications in the footnote attached to the Geneva Convention on Long-Range Transboundary Air Pollution of 13 November 1979 (reprinted in 18 ILM 1442 (1979)) which explicitly declares that it does not cover issues of responsibility.

[15] Montreal Protocol of 16 September 1987, reprinted in 26 ILM 1550 (1987), additional to the Vienna Convention on the Protection of the Ozone Layer, 22 March 1985, ibid, at 1529.

[16] Rio de Janeiro, 9 May 1992, reprinted in 31 ILM 849 (1992).

[17] See the Convention on Biological Diversity, adopted in Rio de Janeiro on 5 June 1992, reprinted in 31 ILM 818 (1992).

[18] Protocol on Environmental Protection to the Antarctic Treaty, *Handbook*, n 12, Art. 7 of which establishes a ban on mineral resource activities in Antarctica for a period of 50 years from the entry into force of the Protocol, with the possibility of further extension, thus reversing the earlier decision of the Antarctic Treaty Consultative Parties to proceed with opening Antarctica to mineral activities

form, as an obligation to provide a prior assessment of the foreseeable environmental impact of planned industrial, technological, and scientific activities.

Another important feature of environmental law in this period is the 'constitutionalization' of some fundamental principles in regional economic integration in systems, notably the European Community and later in the North American Free Trade Agreement (NAFTA). In the former, the Single European Act of 1987 first and the Maastricht Treaty later gave the status of fundamental norms to several principles, including not only the already mentioned precautionary approach, but also the principle of prevention, the 'polluter pays principle', and the principle of correction of adverse environmental impacts at the source, which provide the 'constitutional' framework for the development of one of the most advanced systems of environmental legislation in the world.

If we look at the contemporary scene of international environmental law, three basic features stand out as elements capable of influencing future developments of this law, both as a distinct branch of international law and as a legal discipline.

The first concerns the meaning and role of 'sustainable development', a concept that for more than 20 years has been at the heart of diplomatic and judicial efforts at reconciling environmental protection with the demands of economic growth. As we shall see later in this chapter, this concept, in spite of its initial indeterminacy, is increasingly acquiring a normative content. This is especially reflected in the arbitral and adjudicatory practice of the past ten years.

The second feature is the increasing polarization of the academic debate and judicial practice around the dilemma of environmental protection versus scientific and technological advancement. In no other area has this dilemma caused as much friction and disagreement as in the field of commercial application of biotech products, which has provided a fertile field of disputes before the World Trade Organization (WTO),[19] the EU courts,[20] and national courts. Beyond the technical aspects of the legal dispute over the extent of free trade and the applicability of the precautionary approach, looms a more radical clash between the different world views of those who, on the one hand, see traditional methods of agriculture and local control over food production as an essential condition for the preservation of environmental quality and socio-cultural cohesion, and of those who, on the other hand, support the progressive industrialization of agriculture and downplay the risk of putting food production in the hands of a few biotech companies.

The third feature one has to consider is the continuous search for an institutional framework to ensure environmental governance in a world of increasing economic and social interdependence. Some limited progress has been achieved by the establishment of quasi-institutional arrangements in global environmental

and adopting a specific convention aimed at regulating such activities. See the Convention on the Regulation of Antarctic Mineral Resource Activities, adopted in Wellington, June 1988, *Handbook*, above n 12.

[19] See the the *Biotech* dispute between the EU and the United States, Argentina, and Canada, Dispute Settlement Body, Panel report of 29 September 2006.

[20] See, eg, *Commission v Poland*, ECJ (Second Chamber), judgment of 16 July 2009.

treaties—such as the Convention on Biological Diversity, the UN Framework Convention on Climate Change and the Montreal Protocol on the ozone layer. These arrangements, although they fall short of amounting to a traditional international organization with distinct legal personality, have produced Conferences of the Parties (COPs) and Meeting of the Parties which ensure continuity in the implementation of the environmental standards and monitoring of the parties' compliance with the treaty obligations. At the same time, innovative solutions have been introduced in this embryonic institutional setting to deal with cases of failure by state parties to abide by treaty obligations, short of specific procedures to enforce international responsibility and liability. I am referring to the alternative methods (alternative to liability) introduced with the so-called 'non-compliance procedures', which entail the examination by ad hoc treaty bodies (the non-compliance committees) of cases of suspected or ascertained breach by state parties of treaty standards or commitments with a view to assisting in redressing the wrongful conduct rather than to enforcing liability or securing some form of reparation.

## 3. The context

Given this origin and this less than robust evolution, what is the place of environmental law within the larger context of international law today? The answer to this question is that, surely, environmental law has become an established branch of international law—in the sense that it is constituted of a coherent set of norms having the common goal of establishing obligations for states and other actors in the international community to respect and protect the environment. At the same time, unlike other areas of international law that have undergone a dynamic evolution, such as human rights and international economic law, international environmental law remains a weak body of law. This is due to various factors.

First, the object of protection remains elusive. It is not easy to find general consensus over what constitutes a 'safe', 'healthy', or 'good' environment. This uncertainty hinders the consolidation of general principles and norms laying down precise obligations for states and other international law actors to respect, protect, and redress the environment. In addition, even after 40 years of development, international environmental law is still comprised mainly of treaties and soft law instruments, with the consequence that even in relation to global issues such as climate change and biodiversity degradation, regulatory gaps persist due to the inability to co-opt important actors within the relevant treaty system.

But the most serious source of the weakness of international environmental law is the lack or deficiency in enforcement mechanisms. In other areas of international law, such as the already mentioned human rights and international economic law, the progressive development at the normative level has been accompanied in the past half-century by a parallel development of dispute-settlement institutions and enforcement procedures.

In the field of human rights law this has led to the constitution of regional courts—notably, the European,[21] Inter-American,[22] and African[23] Courts of Human Rights—and of quasi-judicial treaty bodies competent for the supervision of state compliance with treaty obligations.[24] The existence of enforcement procedures, sometimes open to individual applications, has proved to be not only a guarantee of the effectiveness of the law; it has provided the platform for the elucidation of the law, its jurisprudential development into a living body of norms and principles beyond the bare skeleton of the constitutive treaty. It is thanks to this jurisprudential development that today we can speak of a true 'international legal order' of human rights protection. This legal order is constantly renewed and refined thanks to inter-judicial dialogue and comparative analysis of different adjudicatory experiences. This feature contributes in no small measure to the universality of international human rights law.

The ethical and legal strength of the human rights jurisprudence has positively reflected upon the protection of the environment. This has happened by way of the development of an 'environmental dimension' of human rights through an expansive interpretation of the human rights obligations incumbent upon state parties to the relevant conventions. The European Court, in particular, has made extensive use of Article 2[25] and Article 8,[26] concerning respectively the right to life and the right to private and family life, to extend the protection of the European Convention on Human Rights to persons exposed to hazardous industrial and technological activities incompatible with the respect of such rights. It has developed the concept of 'positive obligations' of state parties effectively to enforce legal, administrative, and judicial measures designed to prevent or remedy harmful environmental interferences by private parties with the sphere of protected rights. Further, in the absence of specific treaty provisions, the Strasbourg Court has fashioned a procedural requirement of information and consultation with affected parties as a condition for the fulfilment of the obligations arising under specific human rights provisions, such as Articles 2 and 8.[27] Similar development can be

---

[21] European Convention for the Protection of Human Rights and Fundamental Freedoms (as amended) 213 UNTS 221.

[22] American Convention on Human Rights, adopted 22 November 1969 and entered into force, 18 July 1978, 1144 UNTS 123.

[23] African Charter on Human and Peoples' Rights, 26 June 1981, with its 1998 Protocol establishing an African Court on Human and Peoples' Rights, OAU Doc. OAU/LEG//MIN/AFCHPR/PROT.1Rev 2 (1997).

[24] The United Nations Human Rights Committee, established pursuant to Art. 28 of the International Covenant on Civil and Political Rights is competent, under its additional optional Protocol, to receive and consider communications from individuals—subject to the jurisdiction of a State Party—who claim to be victims of a violation of the rights set forth in the Covenant. For the text of the Covenant and of the additional Protocol, 999 UNTS 171

[25] *Oneryildiz v Turkey*, App. no. 48939/99, Judgment of 18 June 2002.

[26] *Lopez Ostra v Spain*, App. no. 16798/90, ECtHR, Series A, no. 303C; *Guerra v Italy*, App. no. 14967/89, ECtHR Reports 1998-1, 210; *Fadeyeva v Russia*, App. no. 55723/00, Judgment of 9 June 2005, ECtHR Reports 2005-iv, 255.

[27] For a detailed analysis of this case law, see F. Francioni, 'Human Right in an Environmental Horizon', 21 EJIL (2010) 41, at 48ff.

found in the system of the American Convention on Human Rights[28] and of the African Charter on Human and Peoples' Rights.[29]

In the field of international economic law the 'weakness' of traditional norms on trade and investments has been overcome by the setting up of a worldwide system of dispute settlement and arbitration. In the domain of trade, such system is guaranteed by the compulsory and binding dispute settlement procedure of the WTO, which is binding upon the overwhelming majority of the states controlling the world economy. In the field of investments, compulsory and binding arbitration is now a permanent feature of bilateral investment agreements, national laws, regional agreements such as NAFTA,[30] and of the International Centre for Settlement of Investment Disputes (ICSID) under the 1965 World Bank Convention.[31] It is hardly necessary to recall that, with respect to investment, the 'strength' of the law is further guaranteed by the possibility for private individuals and entities to bring claims directly against the host state of the investment. This possibility has spurred a vast jurisprudence and arbitral practice that has contributed to the consolidation and strengthening of international investment law especially in the period following the end of the Cold War and the almost universal acceptance of free movement of capital as a vehicle for economic growth and development.

## 4. Asymmetries and imbalances

The asymmetry between international environmental law and these other areas of international law, besides disclosing the weakness and deficiencies of the former, produces further distortion and imbalances, especially with regard to the area of international economic law.

In this field, the lessons drawn from the WTO dispute-settlement practice and from international investment arbitration are particularly instructive.

As for the WTO, since the establishment of the new organization in 1995, many commercial disputes involving the legitimacy of national measures to protect the environment have been drawn within the sphere of the adjudicatory competence of the Dispute Settlement Body. This is quite understandable, since the WTO provides a compulsory system of dispute resolution and gives binding force to the rulings adopted on the basis of the Panels' and Appellate Body's findings. However, the absence of a comparable universal forum competent to adjudicate on the environmental law aspects of international disputes inevitably influences the normative perspective in which such disputes are adjudicated. That normative perspective is trade law, and more precisely the relevant WTO agreements, which

---

[28] See the groundbreaking judgment in *Mayagma Sumo Awas Tngni Community v Nicaragua*, IACHR Series C, no. 79, 31 August 2001.
[29] *Social and Economic Rights Action Center v Nigeria*, Case N0 ACHPR/COO/AO44/1, OUA Doc. CAB/LEG/67/3 rev. 5.
[30] North American Free Trade Agreement, ch. 11, ILM.
[31] Convention on the Settlement of Investment Disputes between States and Nationals of Other States, Washington, 18 March 1965.

is the applicable law of the WTO Dispute Settlement Body. Thus the very existence of a strong system of international enforcement of trade rules exerts a powerful attraction and influence with regard to the settlement of disputes which arise or are related to questions of environmental law, for which no international forum is normally available.

In some instances, the WTO dispute settlement Panels and especially the Appellate Body have wisely taken upon themselves the complex task of reconciling their responsibility to guarantee the observance of the specific obligations arising for the member states under the WTO agreements with the need to give proper consideration to the legitimate goals pursued by member states in protecting their local environment or even the general environment beyond the limits of their national jurisdiction. This task has been accomplished by resorting to the interpretive tool offered by Article 31(3)(c)[32] of the Vienna Convention on the Law of Treaties,[33] by an expansive interpretation of the general exceptions under Article XX of the General Agreement on Tariffs and Trade (GATT),[34] and by giving relevance to the Preamble of the WTO constitutive treaty. The first clause of the Preamble recognizes, as one of the purposes of the organization, the need to conduct trade and economic relations 'in accordance with the objective of sustainable development, seeking both to preserve and protect the environment'.

Other times, however, the WTO Dispute Settlement Body has been impervious to the consideration of environmental sustainability and has mechanically applied WTO rules even in the face of legitimate environmental concerns raised by the rigid implementation of free trade rules. The apex in this attitude can be found in the notorious *Biotech* case[35] involving the claim by the United States and other countries that the precautionary procedure adopted by the European Community (now European Union) for the authorization of the import and marketing of genetically modified products amounted to a violation of the WTO obligations because of the undue delay in the administrative procedure followed in the authorization process. In spite of the fact that the EU procedure was motivated by legitimate environmental and health concerns and that it was prima facie consistent with the Cartagena Protocol on Biosafety, binding on the EU and other parties to the dispute, the ruling of the Panel concluded that the precautionary approach followed in the EU procedure would not justify departure from the timely observance of the obligations arising from the WTO Sanitary and Phytosanitary Agreement because the United States was not a party to the Cartagena Protocol. That Protocol's relevance

---

[32] This Art. lays down the general rule of treaty interpretation and provides that

3. There shall be taken into account, together with the context .... (c) any relevant rule of international law applicable in the relations between the parties.

[33] Signed in Vienna, 23 May 1969, entered into force 27 January 1980, 1153 UNTS 331.

[34] See *Shrimps and Turtle* case, WTO Doc. WT/DS58/AB/R, 12 October 1998, extending the application of the 'exhaustible natural resources' exception (Art. XX(g)) to living resources of the sea, and *Brazilian Retreaded Tyres,* finding that environmental and health considerations may justify the adoption of an import ban on retreaded tyres. See Panel report WT/DS 332/R (12 June 2007) and Appellate Body Report WT/DS 332/AB/R (17 December 2007).

[35] *European Communities—Measures Affecting the Approval and Marketing of Biotech Products,* WT/DS291/R, WT/DS292/R, WT/DS 293/R (29 September 2006).

as a legal tool to interpret the applicable WTO rules could be justified, in the opinion of the Panel, only in the event that all members of the WTO were also parties to the Protocol.

It is regrettable that this ruling has never been challenged before the Appellate Body because it is wrong in terms of law and unacceptable in terms of sound environmental policy. From a strictly legal point of view, since WTO obligations are typical reciprocal obligations binding on member states in their mutual relations, the Panel should have recognized that the Cartagena Protocol was applicable in the relations between the EU and any other disputing parties which were also parties to the Protocol. This is consistent with the Vienna Convention on the Law of Treaties, Article 30(3) and (4). A different solution could have been reached for those disputing parties which (like the United States) were not parties to the Cartagena Protocol. From a policy point of view, a more appropriate solution would have been to try to accommodate the legitimate environmental and health concerns of the EU with the rules of the game applicable to the free movement of goods. This is the approach followed in more advanced regional economic integration systems, such as NAFTA, with its side agreement on environmental cooperation, and the EU, where the Court of Justice has always assessed the legality of measures entailing restrictions to the free circulation of goods to the twofold test of (i) the measure's necessity to accomplish a legitimate environmental goal and of (ii) the proportionality of the measure's impact on trade with the environmental goal pursued.[36] At the same time, this approach would have been more consistent with the emerging principle of 'mutual supportiveness' between trade liberalization and environmental protection which is already codified in a number of important normative instruments of recent adoption and the function of which is clearly to avoid or minimize the risk of fragmentation of international law.[37]

In the field of investment law a similar phenomenon of progressive incorporation of environmental issues within the sphere of investment arbitration has taken place in the past ten years. Even more frequently than in the field of trade, regulatory measures adopted for the purpose of environmental protection have given rise to investment disputes because of the direct or indirect impact that such measures were deemed to produce on the rights of the investor. One may recall that the first claim brought before an investment panel under Chapter 11 of the NAFTA Agreement, *Metalclad*,[38] concerned a bitter dispute between a US investor who had planned the construction of a landfill for the disposal of hazardous waste in Mexico and the local government of the Mexican State of San Louis de Potosí, which strenuously opposed the use of its land for such purpose. In the end, the adoption by the local authorities of an administrative decision declaring

---

[36] See the seminal case, Case 302/86 *Commission v Denmark*, European Court of Justice, decision of 20 September 1988.

[37] For a timely analysis of the principle of mutual supportiveness and of its role in resolving conflict between WTO norms and environmental norms, see R. Pavoni, 'Mutual Supportiveness as a Principle of Interpretation and Law Making: A Watershed for the "WTO-and-Competing Regimes" Debate', 21 EJIL (2010) 649–79.

[38] *Metalclad v Mexico*, arbitral award 30 August 2000, Case ICSID No. ARB(AF)/97/1.

the area that included the planned site for the landfill to be a nature reserve, and thus not susceptible to industrial development, triggered the investor's request for arbitration and led to an award adverse to Mexico. The environmental decision to designate the area as a nature reserve was deemed to be an interference with the property rights of the US investor, thus giving rise to an obligation to pay compensation.[39] Similarly, in the *Santa Elena* arbitration,[40] the measures adopted by Costa Rica in order to enlarge a nature reserve in compliance with international obligations arising under the UNESCO World Heritage Convention were not deemed sufficient to exclude the liability of the government to pay compensation to the US investors for loss of investment opportunity in a tourist development project. The arbitral award in this case went so far as to reject that even the amount of compensation could be equitably affected by the legitimate environmental goal pursued by Costa Rica.

More recent arbitral practice, and the growing concern that investment arbitration may go too far in reviewing legitimate national regulation under the international parameter of investor's rights, has led to a more cautious attitude and to the opening of investment arbitration to environmental considerations. Two recent cases are especially relevant in this context. In *Glamis Gold*,[41] a Canadian mining company had brought a complaint against the United States under NAFTA Chapter 11 on investment protection because of the alleged damage to its property rights and economic interests as a consequence of the adoption of regulatory measures both at the level of state law and federal regulation (Department of the Interior). Such measures were aimed at regulating the environmental impact of gold mining, particularly at ensuring proper rehabilitation of the land after extraction activities, taking into account also the rights of native tribes for whom the territory targeted for mining represented protected ancestral land. In its 2009 arbitral award, the NAFTA Panel concluded that the environmental legislation adopted by the United States, even if it had some adverse impacts on the investor's economic interests, could not be considered in breach of NAFTA investment obligations because it pursued a legitimate public interest and did not disclose any discriminatory treatment. Similarly, in an earlier case, *Methanex*,[42] the United States was confronted with a complaint by a foreign company engaged in the production of a fuel additive banned under legislation passed by the State of California—a state whose record of cutting-edge legislation in the field of environmental protection is well known—because of its polluting effects on groundwater. The complaining company claimed loss of property rights, loss of market share, and discriminatory treatment because of the alleged unfair advantage that the new environmental

[39] The claimant company was awarded $16.7 million in damages, which were later reduced to $15.6 million at the execution stage by the courts of British Columbia, the jurisdiction of the arbitration..

[40] *Compania del Desarrollo de Santa Elena v Costa Rica*, Case No. ARB/96/1, Final Award, 17 February 2000.

[41] *Glamis Gold Ltd v Government of the United States*, available at <http://www.state.gov/s/l/c10986.htm>.

[42] *Methanex Corp v United States*, Final Award, 3 August 2005, 44 ILM (2005) 1345.

legislation would give to US producers of alternative fuel additives. Again, the legitimate goal pursued with the environmental legislation, its abstract and general character, and the open and democratic process of its adoption, which also involved proper evaluation of independent scientific advice, led to an arbitral award favourable to the United States.

These are modest steps towards the desirable goal of a full integration of environmental considerations in the settlement of economic disputes. But they remain precarious steps because environmental protection in WTO dispute settlement and in investment arbitration comes only as an exception to the rule, which is the enforcement of the economic rights of states and of investors.

This raises the question of the role of the ICJ, as a court of general jurisdiction, in the development and consolidation of international environmental law.

## 5. The International Court of Justice

In spite of the unhappy ending of the 'environmental chamber', which was never utilized and was finally abolished in 2006, the ICJ has had the opportunity to adjudicate an increasing number of cases with a distinct environmental law dimension. In the well-known 1997 *Gabčíkovo-Nagymaros* case,[43] the Court had to adjudicate a complex dispute between Slovakia and Hungary arising from Hungary's refusal to follow up on a Communist-era project involving the construction of a series of dams on the Danube. In its judgment, the Court recognized the binding nature of the obligation to prevent damage to the environment,[44] thus reaffirming a principle already enunciated in the Advisory Opinion on the *Legality of the Threat or Use of Nuclear Weapons*.[45] At the same time, the Court elaborated at length on the importance of the principle of sustainable development as a legal tool to couple economic development and the protection of environmental quality. Yet, when the Court came to address the question of whether the adoption of measures which are necessary to preserve the environment may justify non-compliance with prior treaty obligations (as maintained by Hungary), the answer was negative. The Court preferred to shun the uncertain path of progressive development of international law, as outlined in the bold Dissenting Opinion of Judge Weeramantry, and disappointingly reiterated traditional principles of the law of treaties and of state responsibility. No wonder that this has provided little help to settle the dispute, which remains pending 13 years after the judgment.

In the recent case *Pulp Mills on the River Uruguay*,[46] concerning a typical transborder environmental dispute between Argentina and Uruguay, the Court has correctly focused on the importance of procedural obligations, which include disclosure, consultation, negotiation, and environmental impact assessment prior to

[43] Judgment of 25 September 1997, ICJ Reports 1997, 7–84.
[44] Ibid, para. 53.
[45] Opinion of 8 July 1996, para. 29 available at <http://www.icj-cij.org>.
[46] Judgment of 20 April 2010.

the initiation of a planned industrial project, but in the end the judgment does not mark any significant progress in the elucidation and consolidation of general international law on environmental protection. This is so essentially for two reasons. First, the judgment is based exclusively on specific treaty commitments undertaken by the disputing parties with respect to the management and conservation of the shared resources of the River Uruguay.[47] Secondly, despite the positive approach taken by the Court in clarifying the procedural obligations incumbent upon a state planning or authorizing[48] industrial activities in a transboundary context, in the end the judgment falls short of providing a meaningful connection between the breach of such procedural obligations and the substantive obligation to prevent environmental damage. On the contrary, the Court somewhat artificially separates the procedural and substantive obligations, and the ascertained breach of the former has no influence—in the reasoning of the Court—on the latter. Furthermore, the Court did not deem reparation necessary for the breach of procedural obligations: the finding of the wrongfulness of Uruguay's conduct in this respect was considered sufficient satisfaction for Argentina. This may be formally correct. However, in environmental disputes such as this, where complex questions of scientific evidence are posed to the Court, it may not be a good judicial policy rigidly to separate the procedural and the substantive dimensions of environmental obligations. Procedural obligations of prior impact assessment, notification, and consultation are meant to avoid the fait accompli and to address environmental concerns before damage occurs. Therefore they are in a close functional relationship with substantive obligations to respect and protect the environment. Thus their breach should entail a careful scrutiny of the way in which the breach affects the overall conduct of the parties and their degree of compliance with substantive obligations. The approach followed by the Court risks giving an incentive to be negligent or even wilfully to ignore procedural environmental guarantees in the expectation that once the planned works are realized, the procedural breach will not affect the legality of the project and no meaningful sanction or obligation to provide reparation will ensue.

## 6. Reclaiming legal imagination

The above analysis indicates that international environmental law, in spite of its impressive development at the level of treaty law and notwithstanding the abundance of soft law instruments, declarations, and 'understandings',[49] remains an immature and underdeveloped body of law. Its immaturity, and consequent weakness, is reflected in the implementation 'deficit': the lack of a strong generalized enforcement mechanism and the consequent reliance on voluntary procedures of

[47] Treaty of Salto of 26 February 1975 establishing the Statute of the River Uruguay, UNTS Vol. 1295, N. I-21425, 340.

[48] In this case the potential environmental impact originated from a foreign private investment.

[49] The last in time being the inconclusive 'Understanding' covering up the Copenhagen fiasco on post-Kyoto agenda to combat climate change.

non-compliance verification, and its 'incidental' enforcement by other compulsory mechanisms of dispute settlement and, on rare occasion, by the ICJ. This comes at a price. The main price is the lack of coherent jurisprudential development and its insufficient integration into the adjudication of international economic disputes, as well as the lack of a systemic character of international environmental law adjudication.

Can international law develop into a more mature and effective system of environmental governance, similar to the one which has evolved in the field of international economic law and, to a lesser extent, of human rights? The answer to this question depends on how much in the epistemological assessment of the observer the balance will tilt on the side of utopia or on the side of hard realism. In any event, for the purpose of the present analysis, I think it is necessary to distinguish between two different but interconnected perspectives: the normative perspective and the institutional perspective on the future of international environmental law.

## (A) The normative perspective

At the normative level, a 'realistic utopia' on the future of international law entails the recouping of the original promise of the environmental movement, that is the conceptualization and the legal treatment of the natural environment as a 'public good' to be administered in the interest of all and of the generations to come. The innovative project of the 1972 Stockholm Declaration was that of the progressive consolidation of a body of norms and principles governing the collective action of states and other international actors with the goal of safeguarding the essential elements of the environment as a 'public good', including water, air, climate, and the biosphere. From a legal point of view this agenda brought to the fore the very idea of *erga omnes* obligations, that is, obligations of solidarity of each towards all, of individual states towards the international community as a whole. The crisis and the decline of international environmental law go hand in hand with the failure of this original idea. Very little solidarity has materialized in this respect in the almost 40 years that have passed since the Stockholm Declaration. The adjudication of environmental disputes, as illustrated above, has provided little contribution to the elaboration of international environmental law as a system of *erga omnes* obligation. On the contrary, despite some abstract declarations of principle, the technique of adjudication has systematically followed the traditional path of reciprocal obligations—mainly arising from treaty law—binding the disputing parties in their mutual relations, with hardly any consideration of the collective dimension of the international community interest.

However, it would be wrong to attribute to the shortcomings of international adjudication the sole responsibility of the failure to give legal form to the need for collective action in the environmental field. The main responsibility lies with the major economic powers, which have pursued their national economic interests and their agenda of unsustainable growth by effectively withholding global environmental matters from the realm of international relations for which legally binding regulation is acceptable. This attitude may change under the pressure of the global environmental crises. However, the persistent refusal by the major economic actors, such as the United States and China, to adhere to the Kyoto Protocol, and their continuing reluctance to undertake legal commitments in the post-Kyoto agenda, do not facilitate the emergence of a new solidarity—which has contributed to the Copenhagen demise and to the inconclusive results of the 2010 Cancún meeting.

Legal scholarship in the field has not been of much help either in overcoming these normative limits of international environmental law. Study and research in environmental law and policy have proliferated, giving rise to countless specialized journals, books, and even specialized law faculties.[50] But this has produced an increasingly fragmented scholarship, overspecialized in distinct areas of the law, self-concluded and self-referential, with a strong 'militant' attitude and yet unable to bring the environmental value to the top of the globalization agenda, where economic growth and development still dominate.[51] This does not mean that study and research in the field of environmental law have not influenced policy-making at the level of international negotiations and within competent intergovernmental organizations. In this respect the influence has been significant and, together with scientific expertise and non-governmental organization (NGO) activism, has provided the necessary support to specific lawmaking initiatives and environmental regimes.[52] However, judging from the results obtained by the environmental law community in terms of overall progress of international law, the conclusion is inevitable that doctrinal elaboration in this field has remained confined within the horizon of state sovereignty as the seat of the power to make environmental decisions. Sovereignty and democratic decision-making within the nation-state provide the political–legal framework for the legitimation of environmental measures that restrict human freedom. The will of the majority may override individual interests. But this framework presupposes the persistence of people's loyalty to national institutions and interests, primarily economic interest, rather than a loyalty to a remote 'international' public interest in the preservation and protection of the general environment. It is this state-centred perspective that has hindered the passage of the idea of *erga omnes* obligation from a purely theoretical concept to a practical legal tool codifying the commitment of every state actively to engage in the promotion and protection of environmental quality as an essential public good. The shortcomings of international legal scholarship in facilitating this passage are revealed in the International Law Commission Articles on the Responsibility of

---

[50] This has occurred especially in the United States.

[51] This is made evident by UN documents indicating that more than 60 per cent of the countries of the world consider environmental protection as an obstacle to economic development rather than one of its necessary components. See UNDP, 'Human Development Report 2005', New York, 2005.

[52] This is suggested especially by the experience of this writer in the Antarctic Treaty system, where environmental protection has always been elaborated with the support of highly skilled legal experts capable of devising innovative models of environmental protection in order to accommodate conflicting views over the legal status of Antarctica and of the legal regime of its natural resources. See in this respect, the Convention on the Conservation of Antarctic Marine Living Resources, the 1991 Madrid Protocol on environmental protection of Antarctica, and the Annex on liability for damage to the Antarctic environment.

States for Internationally Wrongful Acts,[53] where even the expressions 'environment' and *'erga omnes'* obligations are avoided and the hypothesis of state responsibility for breach of an obligation owed to the international community as a whole remains marginal and confined to Article 48(1)(b).

Placing the idea of the environment as an international 'common good' at the centre of a hypothetical agenda of 'realistic utopia' entails certain legal implications.

First, it is necessary to reconsider critically certain categories of past international law, such as permanent sovereignty over natural resources. It is clear that if such a concept was justifiable in the wake of de-colonization to allow newly independent states to recoup control over their natural resources, today it may not be used to justify an irresponsible use of such resources, especially when this happens under the pressure of the insatiable demand of industrial production that leads to the unsustainable use of air, water, and minerals, within the legal framework of international investment law and trade liberalization.

Secondly, the idea of the environment as an international common good illuminates the limits of the economic theories that tend to reduce the natural world to a pure economic resource to be submitted to the logic of the market. This logic has gone very far in recent years. Hand in hand with the development of knowledge in the field of molecular biology, it has supported the claim to the propertization of genetic resources, both as a channel of information and as material valuable for the production of goods and services. This race to the enclosure of the most intimate essence of the natural world, our genetic patrimony, reduces life itself to merchandise to produce profit. It makes us lose the sense of what is the common good.[54] This enclosure cannot be morally justified, as in the past, with the need to increase productivity for the benefit of humankind, since the world today experiences an excess of production of goods but an uneven and inequitable distribution of them among the peoples of the earth.

This last point introduces the third and perhaps most important implication of our idea of the environment as an international common good. That is the necessity of looking at the environment also as a dimension and an essential condition for the enjoyment of human rights. As indicated in Section 2 above, the connection between environmental protection and human rights has already been captured in the case law of human rights courts. But this practice eludes the essential nature of the environment as a public good: it remains confined within the traditional conception of human rights as individual rights. In this perspective, forms of environmental degradation become relevant only to the extent that they amount to unlawful interferences with the sphere of human rights of a single individual claimant.[55] Today, such an individualistic approach is no longer adequate

---

[53] Adopted by the International Law Commission at its 53rd session, 2001, GAOR, 56th session, Supp. No.10(A/56/10), ch. IV, E.1.

[54] For in-depth analysis of the legal implications of the propertization of the genetic patrimony, see A. Rouvroy, EUI thesis; F. Francioni (ed.), *Biotechnologies and International Human Rights* (Oxford: Hart Publishing, 2007).

[55] Cf Francioni, n 27.

to counter the tendency to subtract essential components of the natural environment, such as water and air, from the public domain and treat them as tradeable commodities. Nor can it effectively contend against the many unsustainable forms of pollution that affect the general environment in an indeterminate and diffused form, with risks for the health, integrity, and life of people at large and not just single individuals. This is made evident by the current debate about access to water as a fundamental right of every person, a right that would be foolish to consider in a purely individualist dimension, since it is the fundamental component of our life and of the functioning of society as a whole.[56] It is made evident also by the emerging human rights implications of the worsening of global warming with its devastating effects in terms of desertification, flooding, and environmental disasters that affect the enjoyment of fundamental human rights of entire peoples and not only of single persons.

## (B) The institutional scenario

As I have pointed out at the beginning of this chapter, the insufficiency of global institutions for the monitoring of environmental compliance and the lack of compulsory mechanisms of dispute resolution are the true Achilles' heel of the present system of international environmental law.

To overcome this deficit two approaches are possible within the perspective of a progressive development of the law. The first approach would consciously shun the need for institutional reform as too costly and ineffective, and would rely on market mechanisms of self-regulation and transnational private enforcement. The second approach would entail a reform of the institutional system of environmental governance by creating effective multilateral institutions that can mirror what has been done in the other areas of international law examined in this chapter, namely international economic law and human rights.

It is the opinion of this writer that the two approaches are not mutually exclusive. They should be complementary because the first one can hardly work without the other. The reason is simple. International–transnational private regulation (eg trade in emission allowances, the clean development mechanism, and forest conservation), however effective it may be, intrinsically operates outside the sphere of state control, and in the long term it may pose an undesirable challenge to the very idea of sovereignty over the national territory and its resources. Besides, a 'realistic utopia' approach cannot ignore the bitter lesson of the contemporary financial crisis, the decline of confidence, or sheer market failure of the 'private' self-control mechanisms, and the contemporary shift of focus back to the role of the state in regulating and controlling essential aspects of economic and social life in its relation to the vital components of the earth's environment.

---

[56] On 28 July 2010, the UN General Assembly adopted a resolution introduced by Bolivia on the human right of access to clean water and sanitation. The resolution was adopted by 122 in favour, no votes against, and 41 abstentions.

For this reason, it is necessary to re-examine *de lege ferenda* what kind of improvements are needed and are politically feasible in order to modernize and strengthen the institutional framework of environmental governance. In this respect, an opportunity for institutional reform and for improved global environmental governance was offered by the 2005 UN reform. Several critical issues were on the table at that time, and had been clearly articulated also with the support of academic studies and research.[57] In the end, however, the 2005 UN mini-reform did not produce any meaningful improvement to the UN architecture of global environmental governance, and the institutional deficit remains unresolved at a time when we are facing the most dangerous of environmental threats, climate change.

How can imagination contribute to the improvement of the institutions of global environmental governance?

The simplest way would be to proceed with the strengthening of the existing institutions, in particular the United Nations Environmental Programme (UNEP). This was the route which was indicated by the UN Secretary-General in his 2005 Report on the reform of the UN system[58] and which UNEP itself is exploring at the time of writing.[59] This route is certainly still feasible. However, to yield a reasonable expectation of effective improvement, certain functional conditions should be kept in mind.

First, if UNEP were to remain a 'programme' as it is today, it would need to rely on adequate, predictable, and stable funding. This is not the situation today. From the mid-1990s funding has declined, both because of creeping dissatisfaction of some major contributing countries and because of increasing competition by other UN programmes, such as the United Nations Development Programme, which has an important role in promoting environmental sustainability.

Secondly, an enhanced role of UNEP would be possible only to the extent that it is given real authority and operational capacity with regard to the mounting complexities of the threats to the global environment. Since the time of its creation, following the 1972 Stockholm Conference, the UNEP mandate has been quite limited. It was meant to provide monitoring of environmental developments, serve as a 'clearing house' for environmental information, and provide impetus and coordination for the development and implementation of international environmental agreements. UNEP has performed these functions quite well; in some

[57] See, among them, F. Biermann, 'The Emerging Debate on the Need for a World Environmental Organisation: A Commentary', 1 Global Environmental Politics (2001) 45; S. Charnowitz, 'A World Environmental Organization', 27 Columbia J Env L (2002) 321; F. Francioni and P.-M. Dupuy, 'Preliminary Feasibility Study for the Establishment of a UN Environmental Organisation or Agency', Study commissioned by the French Ministry of Foreign Affairs, European University Institute, Florence, 2005; F. Francioni, 'The Role of the EU in Promoting Reform of the UN in the Field of Human Rights and Environmental Protection', Chaillot Paper no. 78, ISS, EU, Paris, 2005, pp 32ff; R.G. Tarasofsky and A.L. Hoare, *Implications of a UNEO for the Global Architecture of the International Environmental Governance System* (London: Chatham House, 2004).
[58] K. Annan, 'In Larger Freedom—towards development, security and human rights for all', 20 March 2005.
[59] See UNEP Governing Council Decision 25/4 on International Environmental Governance of February 2009, and Governing Council Decision SS XI/1 of February 2010.

respects it has outperformed its original mandate, notably in its normative role as a sponsor of a great variety of multilateral environmental agreements ranging from hazardous waste to trade in dangerous chemicals, air pollution, land degradation, regional seas and water resources management. Today, however, it seems that it has stretched to its limits, and it is doubtful that more authority and enhanced operational capacity can be achieved without institutional reform and substantial upgrading.

This brings us to the examination of the second option, that is, the creation of a new environmental organization. This project could be pursued in two alternative directions. One would be the creation of a UN environmental agency, which would be an organization endowed with its own legal personality but placed within the UN system. The other alternative would be the creation of an independent world environmental organization on the model of the WTO with a distinct member- ship, secretariat, and implementing mechanisms. In spite of the intrinsic differ- ences between these two models, they have in common several advantages. First, they would place the current system of international environmental governance on a more stable institutional basis. Secondly, they would bring under the same institutional umbrella the vast and diversified array of multilateral environmental agreements which today are served by sector-specific and often competing secre- tariats. Thirdly, they could work as a catalyst for stronger environmental solidarity and for the development of a fiduciary spirit among participants in view of greater coherence in the efforts for environmental protection. Finally, they could provide a single forum for global environmental monitoring, an issue that is acutely felt in the current post-Kyoto negotiations on climate change, and for dispute settlement.

There is no hiding that the creation of any of these environmental organizations would entail the investment of enormous political capital, in terms of limitations of national sovereignty necessary to establish a system of effective multilateral cooperation. It would entail also technical obstacles linked to the intractable issue of the reform of the UN Charter, or to the adoption of a new multilateral treaty, for which complex negotiations would be required. But that would also be an oppor- tunity for a fresh approach involving in the negotiation process not only states, but also relevant UN agencies and programmes, the main secretariats of multilateral environmental agreements, the World Bank, the private sector, and the leading environmental NGOs. This is not an easy task. But I see no easy solution to the daunting challenge posed to the international community by the global environ- mental crisis. This is time to rebuild consensus, not to drift in the hope that some- thing good will come from the creative destruction of the planet.

# 35

# Combating Terrorism: Proposals for Improving the International Legal Framework

*Bibi van Ginkel**

## SUMMARY

This chapter assesses the bottlenecks and pitfalls identifiable in the counter-terrorism system of the UN as we know it today, as well as in the international legal system. Two key uncertainties influence the way the international community will deal with combating international terrorism in the future. They are the strength of states and the willingness and intensity of international cooperation. For the purpose of engaging in a realistic utopia concerning counterterrorism in 20 to 30 years, it is submitted that the rule of law and the body of universal values such as human rights should be respected, as they form the fundamental requirements for developing an effective and comprehensive counterterrorism policy. Although so far the UN has accomplished much in the fight against terrorism, it is faced with three legal challenges, the right response to which might contribute to a greater degree of legitimacy and effectiveness in the battle against terrorism. These challenges are: (i) the lack of definition of terrorism; (ii) the monitoring systems of the implementation of Security Council resolutions; and (iii) the potential for adjudication of terrorism by an international tribunal. The lack of a universal definition of terrorism plays a role in many international initiatives and undermines the legitimacy of these policies. The Security Council oversight of the blacklisting

* For the ideas developed in this chapter the author took inspiration from previously published work, namely B. van Ginkel, 'How to Repair the Legitimacy Deficit in the War on Terror: A Special Court for Dealing with International Terrorism?', in J. de Zwaan, E. Bakker, and S. van der Meer (eds), *Challenges in a Changing World; Clingendael Views on Global and Regional Issues* (The Hague: TMC Asser Press, 2009), 145–62; B. van Ginkel, *The Practice of the United Nations in Combating Terrorism from 1946–2008; Questions of Legality and Legitimacy* (Antwerp/Oxford/Portland, OR: Intersentia, 2010); B. van Ginkel, 'Towards a Comprehensive and Effective Counter-terrorism Policy within the United Nations', in G. Molier, A. Elllian, and D. Suurland (eds), *Terrorism: Ideology, Law and Policy* (Dordrecht: Republic of Letters Publishing, 2011).

The author wishes to thank Professor Antonio Cassese for the fruitful discussion they had which formed a source of inspiration when writing this chapter, and also Dr Jair van der Lijn for his valuable comments on an earlier version of this chapter.

system is not adequate, nor is the working of the Sanctions Committee. The recent appointment of an Ombudsperson does not change much, even though its establishment might potentially improve some of the flaws in the system. Although the creation of an international criminal tribunal might not be a major deterrent for terrorists, states that intend to fight terrorism would stand stronger if their trials were fair and their fight legitimate. The author suggests the following avenues with regard to the three questions at issue: (i) the Security Council could decide on a definition of terrorism that would apply to all other resolutions in which the term is used, and which would thus limit their scope. Such definition could, of course, develop into customary international law over the years; (ii) it should be possible to appeal the listing of an individual or an organization as 'terrorist' to an independent and impartial organ with the authority to order appropriate compensation, and in accordance with procedural principles; and (iii) three options for an international tribunal for terrorism stand out: (a) an ad hoc tribunal established pursuant to a Security Council resolution; (b) the broadening of the subject matter jurisdiction for the International Criminal Court (ICC); or (c) the setting up of a special court for terrorism.

## 1. Introduction

Imagine... in 20 years, Al-Qaeda—again at full strength—has scattered over the world, and established major headquarters in countries such as Somalia, Yemen, Pakistan, Algeria, Chechnya, India, and Indonesia. Since the governments of these countries will not have enough control over their territory, these areas will become safe havens for terrorist training camps. Meanwhile the United States has lost its economic hegemony to China. As a consequence, the United States is no longer in the position to use its military power to control terrorism, and China is not willing to do so. Europe is still a strong economic power, but too divided to play a decisive role in power politics. Europe's purpose is nevertheless to seek multilateral cooperation, but for lack of a strong military power, they do not succeed in controlling the Al-Qaeda threat.

This scenario, quite clearly, is just a wild guess as to how the world might develop in the future. What is interesting from the viewpoint of this intellectual exercise, is that it is less important how terrorism has developed, but it is far more important to understand how the strength of state power to control its own territory, as well as the position of states in relation to each other, has shifted. It is these developments that will determine the general character of future counterterrorism policies. Terrorism has been a threat in all centuries, albeit in different forms, which makes it almost a 'given' for this intellectual exercise. Surely, the counterterrorism policies will be shaped to face the specific threats, be it, for example, a religiously or nationally motivated terrorist group, but the general character of these policies will depend on other factors. It is thus important to try to understand how the position of states might develop, and how that might influence the development of international legal counterterrorism instruments, in particular those of the United Nations.

This chapter assesses the bottlenecks and pitfalls identifiable in the counter-terrorism system of the UN as we know it today, as well as in the international legal system. The success rate of any possible suggestions for improving these measures will depend on the evolution geopolitics and the power structures as we know them today. Thus, before anything else, the scenarios of different developments in geopolitics will be elaborated upon. Finally, some proposals for improving the current system will be made, thereby taking into account the circumstances necessary to make that happen.

## 2. Possible future scenarios

Instead of just gazing into a crystal ball, and trying to see the future, one could use a model for sketching different scenarios which depend on several factors that are most likely to change or at least influence major changes in geopolitics and power structures, generally identified as the 'key uncertainties'. These exercises have proved to be very helpful in providing insight into the security risks that follow from different power structures and are, for example, being used to plan defence budgets.

In the field of combating terrorism, one could use this model to determine how terrorism as a threat might develop, depending on a selection of key uncertainties. These key uncertainties could be found, for instance, in the world of technical developments when studying the means used by terrorists, or in the choice of targets, depending on—for instance—the openness of borders (providing opportunity) or the political position and actions of certain states against whom the terrorists are reacting. One could also use this model to study the way the international community will deal with international terrorism in the future. In this chapter, the latter will be the case.

There are probably two key uncertainties that influence the way the international community will deal with combating international terrorism in the future. These factors are the *strength of states* and the *willingness and intensity of international cooperation*. These uncertainties could be placed on different axes in a model, which will then create through various combinations four quadrants. The strength of states is placed on the vertical axis, and the willingness and intensity of international cooperation is placed on the horizontal axis. Clockwise, the upper left quadrant would then show a situation of strong states, with little ambition for intensive international cooperation. This quadrant represents a *multipolar* situation. The upper right quadrant will show yet another situation of strong states but which—this time—invest a lot in intensive international cooperation. This represents a situation of *multilateralism*. The lower right quadrant shows a situation of weak state power, but with still extensive international cooperation. In this situation, key players would include all kinds of non-state actors, such as civil society organizations, international organizations, or multinational cooperations. This form of international cooperation is mainly *network*-driven. The lower left quadrant shows a situation of weak states and no form of international cooperation, and is thus qualified as a situation of *fragmentation*.

The four quadrants will probably represent the dominant situation in different regions. The developments in the United States and China, as we can assess them now, will fit the description of the multipolar quadrant, whereas the situation in Europe will probably best fit the description of the multilateral quadrant. Certain regions of Africa, in particular, fit the description of the fragmentation quadrant. Clearly, in a situation of fragmentation we are mostly dealing with failed states, which will be considered by other states and systems of cooperation to pose a serious security threat, since they provide opportunities for extremists and terrorists to set up training camps in these so-called black holes. In the lower right quadrant, which is characterized by a lack of dominant state power and in which civil society organizations, private security companies, as well as international organizations also form major factors of influence, the key word is not so much control, but rather networking. This networking can take a rather informal character, or could also be shaped through quasi-legislation, such as codes of conducts or memoranda of understanding.

For the purpose of engaging in a realistic utopia concerning counterterrorism in 20 to 30 years, it is submitted that the rule of law and the body of universal values such as human rights should be respected, as they form the fundamental requirements for developing an effective and comprehensive counterterrorism policy. If that understanding forms the starting point of this intellectual exercise, then the most favourable scenario for reaching a realistic utopia would be the situation of multilateralism. After all, in this situation it is most likely that the rule of law is well respected and monitored; there is a balance between providing security and respecting human rights; there is intensive international cooperation in counterterrorism, including in international criminal justice; and there will be an engagement with civil society and other non-state actors to find shared agendas to end conditions conducive to the spread of terrorism.

## 3. Identifying the challenges for the future

Before suggesting any directions for changes and improvements of the counterterrorism regulations of the UN and other international legal measures, it is first necessary to identify the challenges that need to be addressed. Clearly, the UN has been very active in dealing with issues related to combating terrorism over the last years. The topic has been on the agenda of the General Assembly since 1972. The UN is very well equipped to play a key role in the international combat against terrorism because of its universal membership and the vast variety of topics that are related to combating terrorism and that fall under the scope of its powers. These ingredients seem to offer a perfect recipe for a comprehensive and effective counterterrorism policy. Furthermore, the UN has motivated member states to adopt and implement international conventions, as well as to intensify international judicial cooperation. The question remains, however, whether the UN has indeed contributed to a comprehensive and effective counterterrorism policy, and whether the international legal system dealing with terrorism can be considered efficacious.

The answer to this question is related to the degree of legality and legitimacy of the measures and policies adopted by the UN and its member states.[1] The UN has accomplished much in the field of combating terrorism. Among other things, the adoption of the UN Global Counter-Terrorism Strategy, as well as the establishment of the Counter-Terrorism Implementation Task Force, have contributed substantially to the comprehensiveness and the effectiveness of UN measures in the field of combating terrorism. Nevertheless there still remain some major challenges that need to be faced both within the UN and by the member states. For the purpose of this chapter, I have selected three legal challenges in the field of combating terrorism, the improvements of which might contribute to a greater degree of legitimacy and effectiveness in the battle against terrorism. These challenges are: (i) the (lack of) definition of terrorism; (ii) the monitoring systems for the implementation of resolutions; and (iii) the potential for adjudication of terrorism by an international tribunal.

## (A) The (lack of) definition of terrorism

Threat perceptions of terrorism are different in every corner of the world. Moreover, domestic political agendas often influence the degree of adherence to the agreed international policy goals. Human rights reports of different non-governmental organizations (NGOs) also point out that in some situations governments might even try to get international support for dealing with their internal problems under the heading of fighting international terrorism.[2] In order to find a common ground for laying down these policy goals on an international level, the difficult issues, such as defining terrorism, are commonly avoided.

This lack of a (legal) definition of terrorism is at the heart of many problems resulting from the need to improve the measures countering terrorism. Notwithstanding many attempts, so far the international community has not been able to agree on a comprehensive, universal definition.[3] Negotiations on a universal definition have been ongoing within the United Nations for almost 15 years now.[4] The reason for this lies in the fact that most Third World states retain their conviction that a definition of terrorism should explicitly exclude from its scope

---

[1] See, on this question in more depth, B. van Ginkel, *The Practice of the United Nations in Combating Terrorism from 1946–2008; Questions of Legality and Legitimacy* (Antwerp/Oxford/Portland, OR: Intersentia, 2010).

[2] Clear examples are the Russian Federation with regard to Chechnya, and China with regard to the Uighurs in the province of Xinjiang. See, eg, Human Rights Watch, *World Report 2007, World Report 2008*; D. Cortright et al, 'Friend not Foe: Civil Society and the Struggle against Violent Extremism', report to Cordaid from the Fourth Freedom Forum and Kroc Institute for International Peace Studies and the University of Notre Dame, October 2008; F. van Lierde, *Countering the Politics of Fear* (The Hague: Cordaid, 2010).

[3] See, in further depth, B. van Ginkel, 'The United Nations: Towards a Comprehensive Convention on Combating Terrorism', in M. van Leeuwen (ed.), *Confronting Terrorism; European Experiences, Threat Perceptions and Policies* (The Hague/London/New York: Kluwer Law International, 2003).

[4] In 1996 India submitted a proposal for a Comprehensive Convention on Combating Terrorism to the Legal Committee of the UN General Assembly, including a definition of terrorism. See UN Doc. A/C.6/51/.

the use of force in the struggle for self-determination. Western states, on the other hand, are reluctant to agree on a definition that suggests a legitimization of the use of force in the struggle for self-determination, arguing that this would legitimize the use of terrorist violence for that cause.

Thus, there is no agreement yet on a comprehensive convention on combating terrorism. Instead, there are several comprehensive regional conventions and a series of universal issue-specific conventions.[5] Although, within the UN, both the

---

[5] The 1963 Tokyo Convention on Offences and Certain Other Acts committed on Board Aircraft, UKTS 126 (1969), Cmnd 4230, entered into force 4 December 1969; the 1970 Hague Convention for the Suppression of Unlawful Seizure of Aircraft, UKTS 39 (1972), Cmnd 4965; (1971) ILM 133, entered into force 14 October 1971; the 1971 Montreal Convention for the Suppression of Unlawful Acts Against the Safety of Civil Aviation, UKTS 10 (1971), Cmnd 5524, entered into force 26 January 1973; and its 1988 Protocol for the Suppression of Unlawful Acts of Violence at Airports Serving International Civil Aviation, 27 ILM 627 (1988); the 1973 UN Convention on the Prevention and Punishment of Crimes Against Internationally Protected Persons, Including Diplomatic Agents, Misc. 19 (1975), Cmnd 6176, entered into force 20 February 1977; the 1979 UN Convention Against the Taking of Hostages (1979) 18 ILM 1456, entered into force 4 June 1983; the 1980 IAEA Convention on the Physical Protection of Nuclear Material, Misc. 27 (1980), (1979) 18 ILM 1419, entered into force 8 February 1987; the 1988 IMO International Convention for the Suppression of Unlawful Acts Against the Safety of Maritime Navigation and its Protocol on the Suppression of Unlawful Acts Against the Safety of Fixed Platforms Located on the Continental Shelf (1988) 3 IJECL 317; the Convention on the Marking of Plastic Explosives for the Purpose of Detection of 1 March 1991, entered into force 21 June 1998, UN Doc. S/22393, Annex; the International Convention for the Suppression of Terrorist Bombings, adopted by the General Assembly of the United Nations on 15 December 1997, UN Doc. A/Res/52/164, entered into force 23 May 2001; the International Convention for the Suppression of the Financing of Terrorism, adopted by the General Assembly of the United Nations on 9 December 1999, UN Doc. A/Res/54/109, entered into force 10 April 2002; the International Convention for the Suppression of Acts of Nuclear Terrorism, adopted by the General Assembly of the United Nations on 15 April 2005, UN Doc. A/RES/59/290, entered into force 7 July 2007; the Amendment to the Convention on the Physical Protection of Nuclear Material, 2005, adopted at the Diplomatic Conference of the IAEA on 8 July 2005 (Vienna), not yet in force; the 2005 Protocol to the Convention of the Suppression of Unlawful Acts against the Safety of Maritime Navigation, adopted on 14 October 2005, not yet in force; the 2005 Protocol to the Protocol for the Suppression of Unlawful Acts against the Safety of Fixed Platforms Located on the Continental Shelf, adopted on 14 October 2005, not yet in force. At the regional level: the 1971 OAS Convention to Prevent and Punish Acts of Terrorism Taking the Form of Crimes Against Persons and Related Extortion that are of International Significance, (1971) 10 ILM 225, entered into force 16 October 1973; the 1977 European Convention on the Suppression of Terrorism, ETS No. 90, UKTS 93 (1977), entered into force 4 August 1978; the SAARC (South Asian Association for Regional Cooperation) Regional Convention on the Suppression of Terrorism, signed at Kathmandu on 4 November 1987, entered into force on 22 August 1988; Treaty on Cooperation among States Members of the Commonwealth of Independent States in Combating Terrorism of 4 June 1999 (Minsk), entered into force on 3 October 2000; Arab Convention on the Suppression of Terrorism of 22 April 1998 (Cairo), entered into force on 7 May 1999; Convention of the Organisation of the Islamic Conference on Combating International Terrorism of 1 July 1999 (Ouagadougou), entered into force on 7 November 2002; OAU Convention on the Prevention and Combating of Terrorism of 14 July 1999 (Algiers), entered into force on 6 December 2002; the Shanghai Convention on Combating Terrorism, Separatism and Extremism, adopted on 15 June 2001 (Shanghai), entered into force on 29 March 2003; the Inter-American Convention against Terrorism, Doc. A-66, adopted at the 32nd regular session of the OAS General Assembly on 3 June 2002, entered into force on 10 July 2003; the Amending Protocol to the European Convention on the Suppression of Terrorism, adopted on 15 May 2003 (Strasbourg), ETS No. 190, not yet in force; the Additional Protocol to the SAARC Regional Convention on Suppression of Terrorism, adopted on 6 January 2004 (Islamabad), entered into force on 12 January 2006; the Protocol to the OAU Convention on Prevention and Combating of Terrorism, adopted on 8 July 2004 (Addis Ababa), not yet in force; the European Convention on the Prevention against Terrorism, adopted on 16 May 2005 (Warsaw), CETS No. 196, entered

General Assembly and the Security Council have adopted resolutions with formulations explaining the term 'terrorism' that come close to qualifying as a universal definition,[6] they were never intended to have that effect.

So far, the most powerful states, which in most cases dictate the international agenda, have found greater benefit in *not* defining terrorism, since this provides them with more freedom in drafting their policies. However, lessons learned from the most recent years of combating terrorism have demonstrated that the international community should enhance the legitimacy of the anti-terrorism policies in order to be more effective. One of the needed improvements is the formulation of a definition of terrorism, which would contribute to the transparency of the governance in this field and would henceforth facilitate the establishment of a special international tribunal (see below).

The argument that a lack of a definition of terrorism offers more flexibility in the response to terrorism, has especially been used by states which believe that effectively dealing with security issues is only possible if there are no restrictions on their powers. This was certainly the case with the adoption of Security Council Resolution 1373 (2001),[7] which ordered states to take measures against the financing of terrorism without defining terrorism, and also mandated the Counter-Terrorism Committee to monitor the implementation of the resolution. The absence of a clear definition of terrorism delimiting the scope of applicability of the measures, however, can render the policy vulnerable to abuse. This has even resulted in violations of human rights and the discrimination of certain groups.[8] As mentioned, several states have reportedly used the 'global war against terrorism' as a justification to neutralize or target political opponents, and to limit the political space in which civil society organizations can function.[9]

The lack of a universal definition thus plays a role in many international initiatives and undermines the legitimacy of these policies. It furthermore complicates the drafting of any legal instrument regarding terrorism. The general principle of

---

into force on 1 June 2007; the Council of Europe Convention on Laundering, Search, Seizure and Confiscation of the Proceeds from Crime and on the Financing of Terrorism, adopted on 16 May 2005 (Warsaw), CETS No. 198, entered into force 1 May 2008.

[6] See, eg, GA Res. 40/61 (1985) and 49/60 (1995), both adopted without a vote, and SC Res. 1566 (2004) and 1624 (2005).

[7] See on this issue E. Rosand, 'Resolution 1373, the Counter-Terrorism Committee, and the Fight against Terrorism', 97 AJIL (2003) 333–41.

[8] See, eg, 'In the Name of Counter-Terrorism: Human Rights Abuses Worldwide', Human Rights Watch Briefing Paper for the 59th Session of the United Nations Commission on Human Rights, 25 March 2003.

[9] B. van Ginkel, F. van Deventer, and L. van Broekhoven, 'The Role of Civil Society in Implementing the Global UN Counter-Terrorism Strategy', Discussion paper on the occasion of the CTITF Office Side-Event during the Second Review of the Implementation of the UN Global Counter-Terrorism Strategy, Panel on the Role of the Civil Society in Implementing the Global UN Counter-Terrorism Strategy, 7–9 September 2010, available at <http://www.clingendael.nl/publications/2010/20100909_cscp_paper_ginkel.pdf>; M. Tiwana and N. Belay, 'Civil Society: The Clampdown is Real; Global Trends 2009–2010', Civicus paper, December 2010; D. Cortright et al, 'Friend not Foe; Opening Spaces to Civil Society Engagement to Prevent Violent Extremism', report to Cordaid from the Fourth Freedom Forum and the Kroc Institute for International Peace Studies at the University of Notre Dame, 2nd edn, May 2011.

legality, after all, prescribes that any punitive measure should find its basis in law and can only be inflicted upon proof of the described criminal act. Thus a definition of the criminal act of terrorism is a prerequisite for drafting any criminal code and for effective international judicial cooperation, including extradition.

## (B) The monitoring system

One of the important instruments in the fight against terrorism adopted by the UN, and copied by regional organizations such as the EU as well as by individual states, is *blacklisting*, namely targeted sanctions that freeze financial assets of individuals and entities.[10] In an attempt to become more effective in pressuring states to change policies in order to remove threats to international peace and security, the Security Council has developed the model of targeted sanctions against individuals, instead of the more comprehensive sanction system it used to adopt, which harmed the civilian population while not effectively influencing the targeted governments.[11] While the system of targeted sanctions originally only targeted government officials, this changed with the adoption of Security Council Resolution 1267(1999) instituting a sanctions regime against individuals and entities associated with Al-Qaeda and Osama bin Laden. Since then the Council no longer uses its enforcement powers only against states, but also acts as a quasi-judicial body, albeit without the procedural guarantees that would normally be in place in such bodies.

The problem with this mechanism is twofold. In the first place, the mechanism is defective with regard to guaranteeing procedural protections for listing and delisting individuals and entities. In the second place, the mechanism is based on confidential information that cannot be verified.

In short, the instrument works as follows. The UN Sanctions Committee, charged with implementing the Resolution 1267(1999) regime established by the UN, places an individual or entity on the sanction list, which obliges states to freeze the individual's or entity's financial assets. In general, individuals and entities can be listed if they may be 'associated' with Al-Qaeda or Osama bin Laden. It is, however, not specified what qualifies as 'associated with'. Member states submit requests for listings based on intelligence. This information is rarely shared with other states. The other states are merely presented with the information that they need to know to support the nomination for the sanction list. Sources are not shared, nor is the information very detailed. Meanwhile, as resolutions adopted by the Security Council under Chapter VII of the UN Charter are binding for the member states, and even override other international obligations, member states are thus obliged to implement this regime into their national system. The

---

[10] SC Res. 1267 (1999) and 1333 (2000) and follow-up resolutions have in effect been copy-pasted into EU Regulations: Common Position 2001/931/CFSP of 27 December 2001 and Regulation (EC) No 2580/2001 of 27 December 2001 and follow-up Regulations.

[11] See D. Cortright and G.A. Lopez, 'Assessing Smart Sanctions, Targeting Sanctions: Lessons from the 1990s', in M. Brzoska (ed.), *Smart Sanctions: The Next Steps* (Baden-Baden: Nomos, 2001).

European Union, following the decision of the Sanctions Committee, adopted several Regulations to give effect to the Security Council resolutions, and in essence copy-pasted the list of the Sanction Committee.[12]

Within the system of the Regulation 1267 (1999) regime, since 2005 the Sanctions Committee has been required to issue a statement of reasons to explain the listing of individuals,[13] and since 2006 individuals are also able to file a request for delisting directly at a focal point.[14] A request for delisting, however, does not allow the listed individual to get full access to the evidence that provided the reason for the original listing, and this makes it impossible to question the reliability and veracity of the information. This information is furthermore not reviewed by an independent and impartial body that could decide whether the listing is justified. The individual seeking delisting must also submit evidence to support his request. Moreover, the decision on the request for delisting is made by the Sanctions Committee, which is a political and not an independent and impartial body. The recent appointment of an Ombudsperson[15] does not change anything in this respect, even though the establishment of the Ombudsperson might potentially improve some of the flaws in the system. As of May 2011, the Ombudsperson has ten cases under consideration. Two comprehensive reports have been submitted to the Sanction Committee. In order to provide some form of transparency in the work of the Ombudsperson, the Office of the Ombudsperson has drafted a 'standard for analysis, observations and principled arguments' to be considered when assessing the facts that should lead to listing or delisting.

The freezing instrument has been termed a preventive and temporary rather than a punitive and confiscatory measure by the Security Council.[16] However, this characterization has been disputed on many occasions, among others by the Special Rapporteur on the Promotion and Protection of Human Rights and Fundamental Freedoms while Countering Terrorism, Martin Scheinin, in his report of 2006.[17] Also Switzerland and the Like-Minded States submitted a document to the Council in April 2011 to argue in favour of a fair and effective UN sanctions system.[18] The instrument as adopted by the Council in 1999, and amended to also target individuals associated with Osama bin Laden and Al-Qaeda in January 2002,[19] has already been in place for ten years. For those individuals who have been on the list since the beginning, the consequences of the measure are very severe. Without

---

[12] Ibid.
[13] SC Res. 1617 (2005).
[14] SC Res. 1730 (2006).
[15] SC Res. 1904 (2009).
[16] SC Res. 1735 (2006).
[17] Report of the Special Rapporteur on the Promotion and Protection of Human Rights and Fundamental Freedoms while Countering Terrorism, Martin Scheinin, 'Protection of Human Rights and Fundamental Freedoms while Countering Terrorism', UN Doc. A/61/267, 16 August 2006.
[18] 'Improving fair and clear procedures for a more effective UN Sanctions system', Document submitted to the Security Council by Switzerland and the Like-Minded States in April 2011.
[19] SC Res. 1390 (2002).

going into an in-depth discussion on the qualification of the measure,[20] it is nevertheless important to point to the absence of procedural guarantees for individuals in the listing and delisting procedures.

## (C) Adjudication of terrorist crimes by international tribunals

A proposal for an international criminal court with jurisdiction to deal with crimes of terrorism was made as early as 1937.[21] This initiative coincided with a draft international convention on the combating of terrorism which was submitted under the auspices of the League of Nations.[22] However, the problem which prevented the convention from becoming operational in those days is still the same problem besetting the international community now: there is no internationally accepted definition of terrorism.[23]

Apart from this major impediment to the realization of an international criminal court dealing with the crime of terrorism, an international tribunal might offer a solution to the fact that national prosecution and extradition can easily be thwarted by threatening the government of unstable or weak states with adverse political consequences or even more violent repercussions.[24] Such a situation might, for example, occur in Pakistan. Another problem could be that a state is suspected of being involved to some extent in the attacks, as was the case with Libya after the Lockerbie bombing. It could, moreover, be an advantage for less developed states, which lack financial resources to prosecute terrorism, to be provided with an international forum with jurisdiction to prosecute these crimes.[25] After all, terrorist cases are likely to be complex, and the evidence trail may run through different states, involving significant travel, translation, and other investigation expenses. Furthermore, since in many cases impartiality of states is now doubted, establishing a criminal court with jurisdiction over international terrorism could create a neutral forum for prosecution. In any event, it would offer a solution to the problem that, as a general rule, a country's domestic court only has jurisdiction to prosecute perpetrators who have committed acts of terrorism against its nationals or on its territory, and sometimes if the perpetrators are themselves nationals. In this last case prosecution is, to a great extent, dependent on extradition.

In addition, judicial systems usually vary across nations in regard to the impartiality of courts and the severity of punishments. Hence, this might create legal uncertainty as well as friction between states.[26] Even though the creation of an

[20] See on this topic Van Ginkel, n 1, at 120–1 and 320–35.

[21] E. Chadwick, *Self-determination, Terrorism and the International Humanitarian Law of Armed Conflict* (The Hague: Martinus Nijhoff, 1996), 97.

[22] M.O. Hudson (ed.), 'International Legislation', Vol. 7, No. 499 at 862; League of Nations Official Journal, Vol. 62, January 1938, at 23.

[23] See in more depth on this issue Van Ginkel, n 3, at 207–25.

[24] M. Banchik, 'The International Criminal Court & Terrorism', 3 Peace Conflict & Development (2003) 9.

[25] Ibid.

[26] R.J. Goldstone and J. Simpson, 'Evaluating the Role of the International Criminal Court as a Legal Response to Terrorism', 16 Harv Hum Rts J (2003) 16.

international criminal tribunal might not be a major deterrent for terrorists, causing them to change their mind about a planned attack out of fear of prosecution by such a tribunal,[27] states that intend to fight terrorism would stand stronger if their trials were fair and their fight legitimate.

## 4. Facing the challenge: some proposals for improving the international legal framework

It has been submitted that a realistic utopia in counterterrorism can only be realized if there is full respect for the rule of law and universal values such as human rights. The challenges for the future that have been identified in the previous sections have therefore been scrutinized in that light, and the proposals for improving international counterterrorism policies are thus also tailored to best fit the international legal framework.

### (A) The definition of terrorism in international law

To overcome the lack of an international legal definition of terrorism, there are several possibilities, besides the obviously needed agreement on the text of the draft Comprehensive Convention on Terrorism.

One relatively easy solution could be for the Security Council to decide on a definition of terrorism that would apply to all other resolutions in which the term is used, and which would thus limit the scope of these resolutions. This possibility had already presented itself, when Security Council Resolution 1566 (2004) formulated a definition of terrorism,[28] but neglected to declare that it was applicable to all other actions of the Council in the area of combating terrorism.[29] The text of the definition could, of course, also develop into customary international law over the years. In fact, according to the Interlocutory Decision of the Appeals Chamber of the Special Tribunal for Lebanon, a definition of terrorism in times of peace has already emerged in customary international law.[30] The conclusion of the Appeals

---

[27] S. C. Roach, 'Courting the Rule of Law? The International Criminal Court and Global Terrorism', 14 Global Governance (2008) 17.

[28] SC Res. 1566 (2004), para. 3 reads:

> Criminal acts, including against civilians, committed with the intent to cause death or serious bodily injury, or taking of hostages, with the purpose to provoke a state of terror in the general public or in a group of persons or particular persons, intimidate a population or compel a government or an international organization to do or to abstain from doing any act, which constitute offences within the scope of and as defined in the international conventions and protocols relating to terrorism, are under no circumstances justifiable by considerations of a political, philosophical, ideological, racial, ethnic, religious or other similar nature...

[29] Van Ginkel, n 1, 258–9.

[30] Special Tribunal for Lebanon, Appeals Chamber, *Interlocutory Decision on the Applicable Law: Terrorism conspiracy, homicide, perpetration, cumulative charging*, Case no. STL-11–01/I, 16 February 2011, paras 83–123.

Chamber is partly based on the assessment that the passing of robust resolutions by the General Assembly and has contributed to the requisite practice and *opinio juris*.[31] Irrespective of the question whether the argument of the Appeals Chamber will be followed by others, it probably goes too far to turn the argument around and apply it to the status of the definition of Resolution 1566 (2004), in view of the fact that states still openly advocate the preference not to limit the scope of the other resolutions on terrorism by defining the issue.

In any event, from an analysis of numerous legal definitions, it becomes clear that an international definition of terrorism should in one way or another deal with six elements: (i) the *mens rea aspect*, addressing the intentional character of the act; (ii) *the purpose of the act*, in the sense of intimidating a civilian population, or compelling a government or other formal institution to do or abstain from doing something; (iii) *the characterization of the act* itself as criminal, or more specifically involving some form of violence irrespective of the result, or requiring a particular result of the act such as bodily injury or material damage and economic loss; (iv) *the target of the act*, and whether it has to be civilian or whether it could also be military; (v) *the perpetrators* as individuals, non-state actors, or state actors; and (vi) *the scope of the definition* in time or place, and whether any exception or justification could be applicable.[32]

As mentioned earlier, the difficulty with the definition relates to the elements (v) and (vi), namely the disagreement on whether the struggle for self-determination should be explicitly excluded from the scope of a definition and whether state actors could also fall within the scope of the definition. This problem could possibly be avoided, if one were to decide to draw a distinction between terrorism committed in times of peace and in times of conflict.[33] For the former category, it should be possible to get consensus on a definition. After all, the politically sensitive issue of the struggle for self-determination is not applicable to this situation. As stated, the Appeals Chamber of the Special Tribunal for Lebanon indeed argued that a rule of customary law has already developed in this respect.[34] It concluded that three key elements appear to be common in state practice and *opinio juris*: (i) the perpetration of a criminal act (eg murder, kidnapping, hostage-taking, arson, and so on), or threatening such an act; (ii) the intent to spread fear among the population (which would generally entail the creation of public danger) or directly or indirectly coerce a national or international authority to take some action, or to refrain from taking it; and (iii) when the act involves a transnational element.[35] All the same, it should also be considered that the international community in the negotiations on a comprehensive convention on combating terrorism decided that the international definition of terrorism should also include elements regarding perpetrators and the scope of the definition. The fact that there seems to be state practice and *opinio iuris* on three elements surely

---

[31]  Ibid, para. 104.

[32]  Van Ginkel, n 1, at 26–9.

[33]  See in more depth on this topic, A. Cassese, 'The Multifaceted Criminal Notion of Terrorism in International Law', 4 JICJ (2006) 933–58.

[34]  Special Tribunal for Lebanon, *Interlocutory Decision*, n 30; Cassese, n 33, at 935.

[35]  Special Tribunal for Lebanon, *Interlocutory Decision*, n 30, at para. 85.

means that a customary rule is emerging on the definition of national terrorism, or on the issue-specific forms of terrorism that have been dealt with in numerous conventions. This conclusion in itself was probably enough for the Appeals Chamber to argue that the interpretation of international customary law should influence the meaning of the definition of terrorism as laid down in the Lebanese criminal code, the specific question the Chamber was considering. However, whether the authorities cited by the Appeals Chamber satisfy the criteria for the formulation of a definition of international terrorism is debatable, especially since the consequence of this position could be a more restrictive interpretation of the scope of several operative Security Council resolutions.

For terrorist acts committed in times of conflict, it would be much more difficult. However, the definition of terrorism used in the International Convention for the Suppression of the Financing of Terrorism could provide guidance.[36] In this Convention, the definition of terrorism reads:

Any other act intended to cause death or serious bodily injury to a civilian, or to any other person *not taking an active part in the hostilities in a situation of armed conflict*, when the purpose of such act, by its nature or context, is to intimidate a population, or to compel a Government or an international organization to do or to abstain from doing any act. (Emphasis added)[37]

Clearly, for acts committed against persons who do take part in hostilities, the legal regime of the Hague and Geneva Conventions applies. For those who do not take part in the hostilities and against whom attacks are committed, it will depend on the character of the attack and the motivation of the perpetrators whether it will qualify as a war crime or as a terrorist attack, or as both.

## (B) Monitoring in accordance with the principles of fair trial

Notwithstanding the different proposals for improving the listing and delisting procedures that have been submitted to the UN in various reports and in numerous opinions,[38] the changes made over the years to these procedures by the Security

---

[36] The International Convention for the Suppression of the Financing of Terrorism, adopted by the General Assembly by Resolution 54/109 of 25 February 2000, and entered into force on 10 April 2002.

[37] Ibid, Art. 2(1)(b).

[38] See, eg, the Watson Institute for International Studies of Brown University, Providence, Rhode Island, White Paper, *Strengthening targeted sanctions through fair and clear procedures*, March 2006, UN Doc. A/60/887—S/2006/331, 14 June 2006; B. Fassbender, *Targeted Sanctions and Due Process*, 20 March 2006; Report of the Independent Expert, Robert Goldman, on the Protection of Human Rights and Fundamental Freedoms while Countering Terrorism, UN Doc. E/CN.4/2005/103, 7 February 2005; Report of the Special Rapporteur on the Promotion and Protection of Human Rights and Fundamental Freedoms while Countering Terrorism, Martin Scheinin, 'Protection of Human Rights and Fundamental Freedoms while Countering Terrorism', UN Doc. A/61/267, 16 August 2006; Report of the Special Rapporteur on the Promotion and Protection of Human Rights and Fundamental Freedoms while Countering Terrorism, M. Scheinin, 'Protection of Human Rights and Fundamental Freedoms while Countering Terrorism', UN Doc. A/63/223, 6 August 2008; Report of the Special Rapporteur on the Promotion and Protection of Human Rights and Fundamental Freedoms while Countering Terrorism, Martin Scheinin, 'Promotion and Protection

Council[39] still do not rectify the currently insufficient procedural guarantees. This conclusion was also drawn by the General Court of the EU in the *Kadi II* case.[40] In its judgment of 30 September 2010, the General Court concluded that the mere sending of the statement of reasons, drafted by the UN Sanctions Committee but only listing the allegations against an individual without substantiating them with evidence or granting the individual the possibility to comment on them, did not qualify as 'the full review' intended by the Court of Justice in its earlier judgment in the *Kadi I* case.[41] As a result, the applicant's rights of defence had not been observed. The Court clarified that

the few pieces of information and the imprecise allegations in the summary of reasons appear clearly insufficient to enable the applicant to launch an effective challenge to the allegations against him so far as his alleged participation in terrorist activities is concerned.

The Court even considered the impact on the procedure of the establishment of the Ombudsperson by Resolution 1904 (2009), and concluded that this still does not repair the lack of effective judicial procedures for review of decisions.[42]

The absence of an effective judicial procedure for review of decisions clearly seems to be the most important problem with the targeted sanctions regime. In the White Paper by the Watson Institute,[43] an analysis was made of the applicability of fair trial principles to the regime of targeted sanctions. The White Paper makes several recommendations for improving the different stages of the

of Human Rights and Fundamental Freedoms while Countering Terrorism', UN Doc. A/65/258, 6 August 2010; A.P. Schmid, 'Terrorism and Human Rights: A Perspective from the United Nations', in M. Ranstorp and P. Wilkinson (eds), *Terrorism and Human Rights* (London: Routledge, 2008), 16–26; E. Rosand, 'The UN's Counter-Terrorism Efforts', in R.S. Lee (ed.), *Swords into Plowshares: Building Peace through the United Nations* (The Hague: Martinus Nijhoff, 2006), 73–83; G. Nesi, 'Reflections on the Security Council's Counter-Terrorism Resolutions', in R. S. Lee (ed.), ibid, at 85–91; A. Hudson, 'Not a Great Asset: The UN's Counter-Terrorism Regime: Violating Human Rights', 17(5) Berkeley JIL 881–919; R. Wessel, 'Debating the "Smartness" of Anti-Terrorism Sanctions: The UN and the Individual Citizen', in C. Fijnaut, J. Wouters, and F. Naert (eds), *Legal Instruments in the Fight against International Terrorism: A Transatlantic Dialogue* (Leiden/Boston, MA: Martinus Nijhoff, 2004), 633–60; I. Cameron, 'UN Targeted Sanctions, Legal Safeguards and the European Convention on Human Rights', 72(2) Nordic JIL (2003) 159–214; Van Ginkel, n 1; I. Johnstone, 'Legislation and Adjudication in the UN: Bringing Down the Deliberative Deficit', 102 AJIL (2008) 275–308; K. Harper, 'Does the United Nations have the Competence to Act as a Court and Legislature?', 27(1) J Int'l L & Politics (1994) 103–57; M. Heupel, 'Multilateral Sanctions against Terror Suspects and the Violation of Due Process Standards', 85(2) International Affairs (2009) 311; E. Rosand, 'The Security Council's Efforts to Monitor the Implementation of Al Qaeda/Taliban Sanctions', 98(4) AJIL (2004) 760–1; A. Bianchi, 'Assessing the Effectiveness of the UN's Anti-Terrorism Measures: The Quest for Legitimacy and Cohesion', 17(5) EJIL (2006) 904–5; I. Johnstone, 'The UN, Counterterrorism and Human Rights', in A. Bianchi and A. Keller (eds), *Counterterrorism: Democracy's Challenges* (Oxford: Hart Publishing, 2008), 335–53, at 343.

[39] SC Res. 1452 (2002), 1455 (2003), 1526 (2004), 1617 (2005), 1730 (2006), 1735 (2006), 1822 (2008), and 1904 (2009).

[40] Judgment of the General Court, Case T-85/09 *Kadi v European Commission (Kadi II)*, 30 September 2010.

[41] Judgment of the European Court of Justice, Joined Cases C- 402/05 P and C-415/05 P *Kadi and Al Barakaat v Council and Commission (Kadi I)*, 3 September 2008.

[42] *Kadi II*, para. 128.bbb.

[43] Watson Institute White Paper, n 38.

implementation of the sanctions regime. With regard to the delisting procedure, it concluded that three criteria should be met in order for the procedure to qualify as an effective remedy: it should be possible to appeal a listing to (i) an independent and impartial organ, (ii) with the authority to order appropriate compensation, and (iii) in accordance with procedural principles.[44] The White Paper subsequently refers to five options that may contribute to an effective appeal procedure. These options are: (i) extending the scope of the powers of the 1267 Monitoring Team to deal with delisting requests; (ii) establishment of an ombudsman; (iii) establishment of a panel of experts; (iv) establishment of an independent arbitration panel; and (v) establishment of an independent and impartial tribunal. The first three options would be mechanisms that would fall under the authority of the Security Council, and the other two options would work autonomously.

Also Professor B. Fassbender, in his report to the Legal Service,[45] pointed to the right of a person or entity to have access to an effective legal remedy before an independent organ.[46] With regard to the latter, Fassbender made several suggestions for models that would fulfil these requirements, such as an independent international tribunal, an ombudsman, an inspection panel, a research committee, or a committee of experts.[47]

Although both reports mention the option of appointing an ombudsperson, the establishment of an ombudsperson by the Council in Resolution 1904, apparently still does not meet the criteria for an effective judicial procedure for review, as noted in both reports.

In order to improve the legitimacy and the effectiveness of the procedures, it is required that more fundamental changes are made to the listing and delisting system. Much depends on whether the future will bring a willingness for more or less international cooperation, and whether there is any chance that the Security Council would move towards a fully fledged independent review of listings, which clearly would qualify as an effective judicial review mechanism. Meanwhile, much can be done to improve the transparency of the procedures. The most simple improvement would be to allow the Ombudsperson to submit public advice to the Sanctions Committee with regard to delisting requests. But it would clearly be a more thorough improvement to set up a mechanism for independent oversight of the veracity and credibility of the confidential information that lies at the basis of the listings. The General Court of the EU also noted that a procedure might be needed to allow for review of confidential information,[48]

---

[44] Ibid, 47.

[45] The Secretary-General had requested the Legal Service to carry out inter-departmental research on this topic and to submit recommendations and guidelines that would take the statements made during the World Summit into account. See 'Implementation of Decisions from the 2005 World Summit Outcome for Action by the Secretary-General', UN Doc. A/60/430, para. 20, 25 October 2005. The Legal Service subsequently requested Professor B. Fassbender to carry out the research called 'Targeted Sanctions and Due Process', 20 March 2006.

[46] Fassbender, ibid, para. 12.

[47] Ibid, para. 12.9.

[48] *Kadi II*, para. 147.

to do justice to the rights of the defence. Examples of clearing house systems or national oversight commissions on the work of the intelligence services could be used as models for such adjustments to the procedures. Furthermore, several states have adopted legislation allowing the use of intelligence information in criminal court cases through special procedures, authorizing for instance the use of anonymous witnesses, or installing special advocates to attend closed hearings and to assess classified material. These constructs allow the use of intelligence information, which by its nature is designed to shield its sources and thus conflicts with the fair trial principle of equality of arms, by building in certain checks and balances.

## (C) An international special tribunal for terrorism

The question of what would have happened if Osama bin Laden had been arrested instead of killed by US Special Forces on Pakistani territory on 2 May 2011 reveals multiple dilemmas concerning the execution of a legitimate and fair trial, such as the competition for jurisdiction and whether a request for extradition would be granted, the impartiality and independence of the trial, the question of a civil versus military court, and the political and public pressure on the trial. If, on the other hand, there were an international tribunal to prosecute the alleged culprits, these problems would not arise.

If geopolitics move in the direction of multilateralism, in which strong states with the ambition of intense international cooperation decide to confront the dilemmas just mentioned, three options for an international tribunal for terrorism stand out: (i) an ad hoc tribunal established pursuant to a resolution; (ii) the broadening of the subject matter jurisdiction for the ICC; or (iii) the setting up of a special court for terrorism.

An ad hoc tribunal for dealing with cases of terrorism could be established pursuant to a binding resolution of the Security Council. According to Articles 39 and 41 of the UN Charter, the Council is empowered to take decisions that entail non-military measures to maintain or restore international peace and security, after a determination of a threat or a breach of the peace. The establishment of the ad hoc International Criminal Tribunal for the Former Yugoslavia occurred after such a resolution.[49] The only requirement that needs to be met is the Council's determination of a threat or breach of the peace. Since several resolutions have already been adopted stating that international terrorism, in general, amounts to such a threat,[50] this requirement does not pose an impediment. Furthermore, the Council has even determined that several terrorist attacks with a more national character qualify as threats to international peace and security.[51] With this option, one would avoid the dragging process of negotiations by the interested states.

---

[49] SC Res. 827 (1993).

[50] See, eg, Res. 1377 (2001) in which the Council declares terrorism as one of the most serious threats to international peace and security in the twenty-first century.

[51] Examples are the resolutions issued in relation to the hostage taking in the Moscow theatre, SC Res. 1440 (2002); the bomb attack in Bogota, SC Res. 1465 (2003); and the bomb attack in Istanbul, SC Res. 1516 (2003).

Surely, the Council should agree upon a definition of terrorism to set the scope of the jurisdiction of the tribunal, but since various previous resolutions already contain formulations that come very close to a definition, this might not be as big a problem as formulating a definition of terrorism in other situations. The problem of distinguishing between terrorism and the legitimate struggle for self-determination can be avoided.

Another option would be to extend the ICC subject matter jurisdiction to encompass crimes of terrorism. The ICC's jurisdiction now covers genocide, crimes against humanity, and war crimes.[52] Directly after the attacks of 9/11, several argued that the attacks would qualify as crimes against humanity[53] and, as such, could subsequently fall under the subject matter jurisdiction of the ICC.[54] These claims did not take stock of the fact that the Rome Statute did not enter into force until after the attacks[55] and the United States withdrew its signature from the Statute prior to its entry into force.[56] In order for acts of terrorism to fall within the scope of crimes against humanity, several requirements have to be fulfilled. According to Article 7 of the Rome Statute, any such attack must be inhumane in nature and character, causing great suffering or serious injury to body or mental or physical health. Moreover, the act must be committed as part of a widespread or systematic attack against members of a civilian population. Furthermore, the perpetrator must have knowledge of the widespread or systematic character of the attack. The widespread or systematic practice of the act entails that it can never be a single act, but it should always be part of the 'multiple commission of acts... pursuant to or in furtherance

---

[52] Arts 6, 7, and 8 of the Rome Statute of the ICC. The Statute was adopted on 17 July 1998 by the UN Diplomatic Conference of Plenipotentiaries on the Establishment of an International Criminal Court, UNTS, vol. 2187, p. 3. The Stature entered into force on 1 July 2002.

[53] See, inter alia, Alia Mary Robinson, UN High Commissioner for Human Rights, on 17 October 2001, while speaking at the US Institute of Peace in Washington, expressed the opinion that the attacks of 9/11 would constitute a crime against humanity. Also former ICTY Judge Antonio Cassese is of the opinion that the international community should revisit the Rome Statute with regard to crimes against humanity. See A. Cassese, 'Terrorism is Also Disrupting Some Crucial Legal Categories of International Law', 12 EJIL 2001 993, 994. See also P. Kirsch, the author and Chairman of the Preparatory Commission for the ICC, who argues that although international terrorism does not fall under the jurisdiction of the ICC, it could qualify as a crime against humanity, and thus be subject to international punishment: P. Kirsch, *Terrorisme, crimes contre l'humanité et Court Pénale Internationale* (Paris: SOS-Attentat, 2001). See for another overview of arguments V.-J. Proulx, 'Rethinking the Jurisdiction of the International Criminal Court in the Post-September 11th era: Should Acts of Terrorism Qualify as Crimes against Humanity?', 19 Am U Int'l L Rev (2004) 1009–89.

[54] Art. 7 of the Rome Statute encompasses the Court's jurisdiction for crimes against humanity.

[55] The Rome Statute entered into force on 1 July 2002.

[56] On 6 May 2002 the Bush Administration declared it would no longer cooperate with the ICC. See also S.C. Roach, 'Courting the Rule of Law? The International Criminal Court and Global Terrorism', 14 Global Governance (2008) 13–19. Moreover, not only did the United States withdraw its signature, but it also adopted the American Service-Member's Protection Act (signed by the President on 2 August 2002, H.R. 4775, 107th Cong. (2d Sess. 2002)), which includes the prohibition of cooperation with the ICC. And the United States remains a persistent objector to any international tribunal, see also R.F. Perl, CRS Report for Congress, 'International Terrorism: Threat, Policy, and Response', 3 January 2007, p 20.

of a state or organisational polity to commit such an attack'.[57] The central theme is thus the connection between the single act and the widespread act.[58] And even though developments within customary international law show that it has evolved to include non-state actors as a category of 'policymakers', it will remain difficult to prove a systematic policy of destruction.[59] Questions that should thus be raised, include: Can there be intervals between the attacks? What if the attacks are carried out by different groups? How many attacks are needed before one can speak of a regular pattern? And how many victims are needed before the attack qualifies as a widespread attack?

To include terrorist crimes as a separate crime under the subject matter jurisdiction of the Rome Statute of the ICC, an amendment to the Rome Statute would be needed. Herewith, the high threshold that has to be met when prosecuting terrorism crimes under the subject matter jurisdiction of crimes against humanity could be lowered. There is, however, still the issue of the definition. An interim solution could be to provide for subject matter jurisdiction with regard to those acts of terrorism that have been described in the existing sectoral conventions, with a back-up option of using crimes against humanity for those widespread systematic attacks that do not fit any of the already existing definitions.

As for the option of a new special court for prosecuting acts of international terrorism, this would probably be the most time-consuming option. In terms of international lawmaking, however, this option is probably most in accordance with the classical principle of state sovereignty.

The key question that needs to be answered before any agreement on a special court for international terrorism can be reached, relates to the scope of the subject matter jurisdiction of this court. It is thus necessary to decide whether the court will only deal with large-scale terrorist attacks, the ones that shock the international community at large, or whether all terrorist attacks that match the definition in the treaty can be dealt with. Should the agreement under discussion list various forms of terrorist activities or acts comparable to the acts that are already covered by the existing international conventions? Or should it strive for a general definition? Another question regarding the scope of jurisdiction is whether or not the tribunal can only deal with acts of terrorism that involve an international or cross-border element, or whether local acts of terrorism can also be the subject of investigations by the tribunal's prosecutor. And finally, it must be decided whether this tribunal's jurisdiction will be autonomous or complementary to domestic jurisdictions. In the latter case, similar to the arrangements of the ICC, the international tribunal will only have jurisdiction if a state is unwilling or unable to prosecute.

If all these hurdles are overcome, the creation of an impartial tribunal with a geographical representation of the different legal systems would be possible. There

---

[57]  Rome Statute, Art. 7(2)(a).
[58]  Banchik, n 24, at 12.
[59]  Ibid at 13.

would be no political involvement in the procedures and, moreover, absolute transparency and the highest respect for the fair trial principles would be ensured.

## 5. Conclusions

Much has been accomplished in the international struggle against terrorism. But much more needs to be changed, if the international community wishes to be effective in combating this scourge. Some of the areas in which improvements can be made are of a legal character. In this chapter, three topics have been selected that suffer from a legitimacy deficit. Repairing this legitimacy deficit might not only contribute to the effectiveness of counterterrorism policies, but also improve the overall image of the international coalition and the way in which it deals with terrorism issues. The importance of this image is not to be neglected. After all, a bad image might in some instances even contribute to the motivation of potential terrorists. The question is thus how to repair the legitimacy deficit in our struggle against terrorism.

An absolute requirement for the answer to this question is the conviction that the response to terrorism should have a long-term character, taking into account all human rights principles and preventing measures from having a negative effect on, for example, radicalization processes. Even though the panic after the attacks of 9/11 explains the short-term solutions adopted with less respect for liberty rights, repairs to these flaws have to be made in order to remain credible as defenders of freedom and the rule of law. Part of the answer to the question on how to repair the legitimacy deficit can thus be found in limiting the possibility of political abuse of the situation by defining terrorism, and in better guarantees of respect for fair trial principles during the different legal procedures that relate to terrorism. Both national procedures as well as international procedures, such as the Security Council's sanction regime on blacklisted individuals,[60] would benefit from procedural improvements. However, notwithstanding these possibilities, there will always be concerns with regard to the procedures in terrorist trials in certain states. Whether that stems from the political bias associated with a certain conflict, or just because the state's human rights level is not particularly high, the impact on the international community's image in the struggle against terrorism will continue, since after 9/11 all joined in the campaign of the global war on terror. These concerns have triggered the call for a special international court for international

---

[60] This sanction regime was first adopted with Res. 1267 (1999) to pressure the Taliban, inter alia, to surrender Osama bin Laden, and members of the Al-Qaeda organization. Financial freezes had to be installed on the assets of the individuals on the blacklists. Later the regime was revised on many occasions to also include Osama bin Laden and members of Al-Qaeda as well as others associated with them on the sanction list. A delisting procedure had first been adopted on 7 November 2002 in the Guidelines of the Security Council's Sanction Committee established pursuant to Res. 1267 (1999) concerning Al-Qaeda and the Taliban and associated individuals and entities, and amended on 10 April 2003 and revised on 21 December 2005. See <http://www.un.org/Docs/sc/committees/1267/1267_guidelines.pdf>.

terrorism as a possible answer to the legitimacy deficit.[61] Such a tribunal could contribute to the reparation of the bad image, because it would be impartial and independent and respect procedural guarantees.

What changes will be made to the selected topics, depends on the developments in geopolitics. The best climate for these improvements can be found if multilateralism prevails. It is in this situation that strong states are willing to cooperate and to strive for a comprehensive and balanced approach to combating terrorism, while limiting their otherwise untrammelled power both by defining terrorism and by respecting human rights. And it is in this situation, moreover, that a definition is a prerequisite for international criminal cooperation. The multilateral system, furthermore, offers a guarantee for respect for the rule of law and human rights, since state actors will check and correct one another if breaches or deviations are committed, either on their own account, but even more likely within the framework of an international organization or monitoring system.

[61] Recently the Dutch Parliament adopted a resolution in which the government was encouraged to look into the options for creating a special tribunal. Resolution adopted in Dutch Parliament in November 2007 (*Kamerstukken* 31200 V 51, 8 November 2007), in which it is stated that human rights should be respected while countering terrorism, and that terrorist suspects also deserve a fair and transparent trial, and the parliament therefore requests government to promote the implementation of universal jurisdiction, and explore as an interim measure the possibility of establishing an international tribunal to prosecute international terrorism.

# 36

# Genetic Manipulation: How to Strike the Right Balance between Technology and Respect for Human Rights

*Souheil El-Zein*

## SUMMARY

The rapid increase in scientific and technological advances in the areas of genetic manipulation and genetic engineering or biotechnology, mainly applied to medicines and foodstuffs, poses considerable risks (to biodiversity, human health, the environment, etc.) and has raised regulatory challenges under both regional and international law. While free trade imposed its universal values and its permissive regulations through many instruments developed under the auspices of the World Trade Organization (WTO), the question arises of the compatibility of this tendency with human rights instruments, built on the concept of human dignity. The only hard law in this field is regional: the Council of Europe Convention on Human Rights and Biomedicine and all its additional protocols, and European Community Directive 98/44/EC of 6 July 1998 on the legal protection of biotechnological inventions. A string of UNESCO Declarations are not legally binding and may thus be described as 'soft law'. To ensure that humans are not dominated by their tools, UNESCO's legal instruments refer systematically to human rights instruments. The aim is to ensure better compatibility between the 'universal' freedom of research or trade, applicable under the WTO framework to human genetic resources, and the universal human rights law. As a result, the rights of each patient must be respected. In particular, research and application must respect: (i) the right not to be subjected without free consent to medical or scientific experimentation; (ii) the right to the highest attainable standard of physical and mental health and associated rights to health care; (iii) the right to protection against arbitrary interference with privacy or with the family; and (iv) the right to enjoy the benefits of scientific progress and its application. The proclamation in the UNESCO Declarations of the concept of the human genome as part of the heritage of humanity was designed to establish a dynamic balance between the protection of the inalienable rights of the individual and the common interests of humanity as covered by the concept of human dignity. As a result the rights of the individual with regard to his or her genome are subject solely to those constraints arising from the need to respect the rights of others. Notwithstanding the uncertainties about the feasibility of a single hard law instrument embracing all the questions that arise and are linked to the extraordinary and rapid development of science and technology, the instruments of the Council of Europe and UNESCO reflect potential norms that could build customary international law and address the best balance between fast technology and secure law, ethical and legal norms, and norms in the trade field and in the field of medical or technological research. The conceptual contribution of the instruments of the Council of Europe and UNESCO can enable future decision-makers to revise the law, which is sometimes judged permissive or vague and sometimes restrictive or poorly adapted.

## 1. Introduction

There has been a rapid increase in scientific and technological advances in the areas of genetic manipulation and genetic engineering or biotechnology[1] in the past 30 years, and there is still a great deal that remains to be discovered.

Although this fast-growing technology, mainly applied to medicines and foodstuffs, has been promoted for its potential benefit for welfare and growth in the field of life sciences and the economy, it poses considerable risks (to biodiversity, human health, the environment, etc.) on which research is still scarce and thus has raised regulatory challenges under both regional and international law. The first question we might have in mind is: what was the reaction of international law to those challenges?

The evaluation of the impact of the treatment of biotechnology under international law requires a plurality of approaches and different levels of inquiry, depending on the fundamental legal, social, and cultural distinction between human genetic resources and other genetic resources (plants and animals), even if the gene of animals and human beings are scientifically similar.

## 2. A fragmented and pluralistic regulation of biotechnology looking for its universality

Torn between conflicting tendencies during the negotiation of many instruments through the appropriate mechanisms of competent international organizations (the UN, the WTO, the UN Food and Agriculture Organization (FAO), the

---

[1] Genetic manipulation and genetic engineering refer to the direct manipulation of an organism's genes as a subject of biology and life sciences that involves the use of living things in technology, medicine, and other useful applications. Those terms applied to plants and animals or human beings are used in accordance with the definition provided in the UN Convention on Biological Diversity. which also defines biotechnology as 'any technological application that uses biological systems, living organisms, or derivates from them, in order to make or modify products or processes for specific use.' (See Art. 2, 'Use of terms'.)

World Health Organization (WHO), the Council of Europe, and UNESCO), international law appears fragmented in its treatment of genetic resources and biotechnology in general.

While free trade imposed its universal values and its permissive regulations through many instruments[2] developed under the auspices of what became the WTO, the UN Convention on Biological Diversity (CBD) tried to resist the powerful attraction of the WTO on this issue[3] and was followed in this regard by the FAO International Treaty on Plant Genetic Resources.[4]

The presumption that these treaties should be implemented in a mutually supportive and consistent manner with the WTO agreements was not problematic for the majority of states, except when the principle of 'equitable sharing of benefits' proclaimed by the CBD was confronted with the practices allowed by the free negotiation of agreements between private companies and developing countries.[5]

The elusive language of 'sustainable development' as a common goal of all these treaties was used as an argument for their presumed compatibility, as was the fact that access to genetic resources is subject to the sovereign rights of states over their natural resources, whether by reference to general international law or by reference to the treaties of the UN system and the WTO.

This above tendency was also used by analogy to regulate the exploitation of human genetic resources in order to open this new 'market' for competition and production of biomedicines.[6] The dilemma brought by this extension of technological advances to human genetic resources was the unsolved question of compatibility of that tendency with human rights instruments, built on the concept of human dignity.[7]

Consider stem cell research, genetic testing, and cloning, as examples of progress in the life sciences. These may be presented as giving human beings new power to improve health and to control the development processes of all living species, but the concerns about the social, legal, and ethical implications of such controversial

---

[2] The General Agreement on Trade in Services was established in 1994 and was one of the trade agreements adopted for inclusion when the WTO was formed in 1995. See also the relevant provisions of the Trade-Related Aspects of Intellectual Property Rights (TRIPS) and Art. XX(a) of the GATT Agreements relating to moral exceptions and public health.

[3] See A. Yusuf, 'The UN Convention on Biological Diversity', in *International Legal Issues Arising under the United Nations Decade of International Law* (The Hague: Kluwer Law International, 1995), 1163–95. See also the Cartagena Protocol on Biosafety, available at <http://www.biodiv.org>.

[4] See the International Treaty on Plant Genetic Resources for Food and Agriculture adopted by the FAO Conference on 3 November 2001 and entered into force on 29 June 2004. This treaty was based on the recognition of the 'sovereign rights of states over their phyto-genetic resources' (Arts 10–13). See also Directive 2001/18//EC and Council Directive 90/220/EEC, 2001 OJ L/106/1.

[5] See L. Boisson de Chazournes and M.M. Mbengue 'Trade, Environment and Biotechnology: On Coexistence and Coherence', in D. Wüger and T. Cottier (eds), *Genetic Engineering and the World Trade System* (Cambridge: Cambridge University Press, 2008), 205–45.

[6] S. El-Zein, 'The Regulation of Human Genetics by International Soft Law and International Trade', in Wüger and Cottier (eds), ibid, at 315.

[7] See F. Francioni 'Genetic Resources, Biotechnology and Human Rights: The International Legal Framework', in Francioni (ed.), *Biotechnologies and International Human Rights* (Oxford: Hart Publishing, 2007), 3.

progress have led to one of the most significant debates of the past century, in particular in the field of human genetic resources (the bioethics debate).

However, the response to challenges of misuse of human genetic resources was neither unified nor uniform in terms of normative action, and international law did not succeed in providing a universal mandatory framework coherent enough to face the current issues identified by bioethics studies.[8]

The only legally binding instrument (hard law) dealing with such issues is regional rather than universal. It consists of the Council of Europe Convention on Human Rights and Biomedicine and all its additional protocols dealing with research, cloning, transplantation of organs, genetic data, and the related technology,[9] without prejudice to European Community Directive 98/44/EC of 6 July 1998 on the legal protection of biotechnological inventions.

It would seem difficult to advance much further towards binding international instruments in the field of bioethics at the beginning of the twenty-first century in the absence of consensus on the relevant issues.

For example, there has been no consensus on criminalizing cloning on a global level, and the attempt of the United Nations to produce hard law in the field of international criminal law was unsuccessful. After the failure to adopt any draft convention on cloning owing to lack of consensus on the scope of such an instrument (regarding the permissibility of therapeutic cloning versus reproductive cloning), the UN General Assembly adopted a resolution in March 2005 to call for a ban on all forms of human cloning and on genetic engineering techniques 'that may be contrary to human dignity'.[10] That resolution also refers to UNESCO's instruments on this item. In addition to the UN resolution, the corpus of this 'emerging universal law' dealing with human genetics mainly consists of:

(*i*) The Universal Declaration on the Human Genome and Human Rights[11] drafted by the International Bioethics Committee of UNESCO (hereinafter referred to as IBC), which was adopted by the UNESCO General Conference in 1997 and endorsed by the United Nations General Assembly in 1998;

---

[8] Since the creation of International Bioethics Committee (IBC) following Res. 27 C/5.15 (15 November 1993) of the UNESCO's General Conference to follow progress in the life sciences, many important reports have been produced: genetic screening and testing (1994), human gene therapy (1994), ethics and neurosciences (1995), human population and genetics research (1995), experimental treatment and experimentation on human subjects (1996), the use of embryonic stem cells in therapeutic research (2001), the cooperation between developed and developing countries concerning the human genome (2001), intellectual property and genomics (2002), and pre-implantation genetic diagnosis and germ-line intervention (2003). All these reports are available at <http://www.unesco.org>.

[9] See Council of Europe website at <http://conventions.coe.int/> in particular Oviedo Convention CETS No. 164 (1997) and its additional protocols CETS No. 168 (1998), CETS No. 186 (2002), and CETS No. 195 (2005).

[10] The text of the resolution (A/RES/59/280) is available at <http://www.un.org/Depts/dhl/resguide>.

[11] The text of this Declaration, adopted by the UNESCO General Conference at its 29th session in 1997 (Res. 29 C/16), is available at <http://www.unesco.org/legal_instruments>.

(*ii*) The International Declaration on Human Genetic Data[12] adopted by the General Conference of UNESCO on 16 October 2003; and

(*iii*) The Universal Declaration on Bioethics and Human Rights, which was adopted at the General Conference of UNESCO during its 33rd session (17 October 2005) (hereinafter referred to as UDBHR).

The UNESCO Declarations constitute a first, but very important, step in the pursuit of the universal regulatory goals in the field of biotechnology, even if they are considered legally as non-binding instruments and thus described as 'soft law'.[13]

In this regard, the purpose of this chapter will not be to review in detail[14] the provisions of that soft law or to identify all the conditions necessary for creating new customary rules of international law in each field of biotechnology and life science.

Ensuring the Declaration's effectiveness will depend on the practices of the states and all the decision-makers of international law, including the UN specialized agencies, in particular UNESCO and its monitoring system based on reports to be presented by the member states on the implementation of the declared legal and ethical principles to which the Declaration are addressed.

My focus will be on the priority which should be given *de lege lata* and *de lege ferenda* to the criteria proclaimed by both the Council of Europe's conventions and the UNESCO 'Declarations' to establish certain basic principles and standards on which there is broad consensus among the members of the international community and that can serve as the basis for internationally acceptable rules and regulations capable of being incorporated into national legislation.

---

[12] The text of this Declaration, adopted at the 32nd Session of the General Conference in 2003 (Res. 32 C/22) is available at <http://www.unesco.org/legal -instruments>.

[13] To avoid more detailed comments on the legal value of the 'soft law' of these declarations, it is important to mention that the Universal Declaration of Human Rights raised the same question in general international law. In its Advisory Opnion of 8 July 1996 on the *Legality of the Threat or Use of Nuclear Weapons*, the International Court of Justice (ICJ) stated that

> The Court notes that General Assembly resolutions, even if they are not binding, may sometimes have normative value. They can, in certain circumstances, provide evidence important for establishing the existence of a rule or the emergence of an *opinio juris*. To establish whether this is true of a given General Assembly resolution, it is necessary to look at its content and the conditions of its adoption; it is also necessary to see whether an *opinio juris* exists as to its normative character. Or a series of resolutions may show the gradual evolution of the *opinio juris* required for the establishment of a new rule. (para. 70)

[14] See S. El-Zein, 'La Déclaration universelle sur le génome humain et les droits de l'homme', in *Treizièmes Rencontres Internationales d'Aix-en-Provence*, a Symposium organized by the Institut d'Études Politiques d'Aix-en-Provence, *La communauté internationale et les enjeux bioéthiques* (Paris: Pedone, 2006), 18.

## 3. Incorporation of biotechnology regulation into the international law of human rights

Both the title and the content of the Council of Europe's instruments or the UNESCO Declarations, as described above, are indicative of the link between all the normative standards regulating the research or the exploitation of human genetic resources and the human rights instruments.[15]

The general approach of the decision-makers of these instruments was to globalize the benefits of technical progress and its use in a way that is compatible with respect for human rights—which confirms what Albert Einstein put more simply when he said: 'Science is a powerful instrument. How it is used...depends on mankind and not on the instrument.'

To ensure that humans are not dominated by their tools, the legal instruments of UNESCO refer systematically to human rights instruments. As a result of this approach, the framework of the new ethical–legal normative system regulating the use of human genetic resources is rooted in international human rights law.

This approach is illustrated by two proclamations relating to cultural diversity and to what we could call 'bio-rights'. These proclamations sought to ensure better compatibility between the 'universal' freedom of research or trade, applicable under the WTO framework to human genetic resources, and the universal human rights law as redefined and extended specifically to biotechnology by the Council of Europe conventions and the UNESCO Declarations.

Concerning cultural diversity, Article 12 of the UDBHR states that

such considerations [relating to pluralism of ethical views[16] or to the principles of UNESCO's Declaration on Cultural Diversity of 2001] are not to be invoked to infringe upon human dignity, human rights and fundamental freedoms, nor upon the principles set out in this Declaration or to limit their scope.

This proclamation, based on the need for a universal shared position, is completed by another proclamation stating that 'The interests and welfare of the individual should have priority over the sole interest of science or society' (Art. 3, UNDBHR), which matches Article 2 of the Oviedo Convention of the Council of Europe.[17]

However, the added value of the instruments of the Council of Europe and UNESCO resides in the emergence of a set of 'bio-rights'. These rights

---

[15] Eg the first Council of Europe instrument is entitled the 'Convention on Human Rights and Biomedicine', while the title of the last instrument of UNESCO was changed during the General Conference of 2005 from 'Declaration on Universal Norms on Bioethics' to 'Universal Declaration on Bioethics and Human Rights'.

[16] See R. Brownsword, 'Genetic Engineering, Free Trade and Human Rights: Global Standards and Local Ethics', in Wüger and Cottier (eds), n 5, at 287. In his view, different opinions in this field exist not only between Europe and the rest of the world, but also inside Europe and inside every country where the decision-makers can be categorized into three groups: the dignitarian, the utilitarian, and the human rights fighters.

[17] Art. 2 of this convention proclaims that 'the interests and welfare of the human being shall prevail over the sole interests of society and science'.

are derived from the subjective rights recognized by the two UN international Covenants (Covenant on Civil and Political Rights and Covenant on Economic, Social and Cultural Rights) as well as the Universal Declaration of Human Rights. Indeed, the UNESCO Declarations referred expressly to the Universal Declaration in concretely applying those universal rights in the specific field of biotechnology.

Admittedly, the Council of Europe's Convention on Human Rights and Biomedicine, as well as its additional protocol relating to biomedicine research, have paved the way for reconciling the freedom of scientific research and the dignity of the human being by highlighting the roots of the freedom of research in international human rights law. It should be noted also that the UNESCO Declarations on the human genome and on human genetic data as well as the one on bioethics in general reaffirm the principle of freedom of scientific research while stressing that 'such research and developments occur within the framework of ethical principles set out in this Declaration' (Art. 2(iv), UDBHR).[18]

Therefore, freedom of research on the human genome or any other elements of the human body and the resulting applications may open up vast prospects for progress, but only if the individual rights of each patient are respected. In particular, research and application must respect: (i) the right not to be subjected without free consent to medical or scientific experimentation; (ii) the right to the highest attainable standard of physical and mental health and associated rights to health care; (iii) the right to protection against arbitrary interference with privacy or with the family; and (iv) the right to enjoy the benefits of scientific progress and its application, etc.

In other terms, for the decision-makers concerned by biotechnology projects to benefit from the protection of international law, all research, treatment, genetic testing, or diagnosis affecting an individual's genome must be undertaken and applied with respect for the principles of free consent, privacy, and confidentiality, and without prejudice to the principle of non-discrimination. In addition, a risk assessment pertaining to the intended biotechnological project must be undertaken in advance.

Furthermore, the collection, processing, treatment, use, and storage of human genetic data, in accordance with Articles 5 and 12 of the Human Genetic Data Declaration, are permissible only for purposes of diagnosis and health care, including screening and predictive testing, and medical and other scientific research.[19]

Consequently, any biotechnology project on human genetics should be compatible with the principles dealt with in the UNESCO Declarations in such a way as to render indivisible the three generations of human rights instruments, if one

---

[18]  See also Art. 12 of the Human Genome Declaration and Art. 1 of the Human Genetic Data Declaration.

[19]  This should be without prejudice to the purposes of forensic medicine, civil, criminal, and other legal proceedings, taking into account the conditions spelled out in Art. 1(c) of the Declaration.

considers its reference to vulnerable persons (individuals, families, and population groups who are particularly vulnerable to or affected by disease or disabilities of a genetic nature) and the sharing of the benefits of scientific research and its provisions relating to social responsibility with respect to the right to health and to development.[20]

However, the fact that all the above instruments are substantively rooted in international human rights law brought to this new biotechnical regulation the tensions of conflicts between the freedom of research and the subjective rights of the individuals concerned, since the reference to human rights instruments could not itself resolve all the problems of interpretation.

Therefore, the task of balancing the various rights in order to ensure the compatibility between these two branches of law cannot be addressed on the basis of generalities, but will require in-depth analysis of different fields in which biotechnology plays an important role.

In this regard, the instruments of the Council of Europe and UNESCO not only refer explicitly to the principles applied by the international law of human rights but also go further to establish procedural principles in order to give states guidance for solving such conflicts between different human rights-holders.[21] For example, Article 27 of the UDBHR provides that

If the application of the principles of this Declaration is to be limited, it should be by law, including laws in the interests of public safety, for the investigation, detection and prosecution of criminal offences, for the protection of public health or for the protection of the rights and freedoms of others. Any such law needs to be consistent with international human rights law.

We are very far from the proclamation of 'un-derogable bio-rights'. However, hard law (customary law) still bears on the legality of limiting any subjective right such as the right to life, to privacy, and to withhold consent. Further, the importance of human dignity and the heritage of humanity has been reaffirmed by the instruments of the Council of Europe and UNESCO.

---

[20] All the preambles to the UNESCO Declarations refer to the UN Convention on the Elimination of All Forms of Discrimination against Women of 18 December 1979, the UN Convention on the Rights of the Child of 20 November 1989, and the Standard Rules on the Equalization of Opportunities for Persons with Disabilities adopted by the General Assembly of the United Nations in 1993. The purpose is to ensure that, when selecting a group for experimentation or research, special care is taken in obtaining the consent of particularly vulnerable individuals. This requirement is clearly provided for by Art. 8 of the UDBHR of 2005, which proclaims that

In applying and advancing scientific knowledge, medical practice and associated technologies, human vulnerability should be taken into account. Individuals and groups of special vulnerability should be protected and the personal integrity of such individuals respected.

[21] The reference to procedural mechanisms such as the ethical committees, the process of decision-making following open consultation, and the reference to the general principles of law such as proportionality or good faith are important to confer a legal effect that transcends the role normally ascribed to customary law or to declarations as normative instruments in the international arena.

## 4. The reconfirmation of human dignity as a fundamental legal concept and as a standard constraining the tendency for permissive actions in the manipulation of human genetic resources

Recalling Article 1 of the Universal Declaration of Human Rights (UDHR),[22] the preamble and Article 1 of the Oviedo Convention (Council of Europe) refer to the protection of 'dignity and identity of all human beings'. So does the preamble and Article 1 of the Universal Declaration on the Human Genome and Article 2 of the UDBHR, which aims to 'to promote respect for human dignity and protect human Rights'. It is important to note the juxtaposition of the term 'dignity' to the term 'human rights' in those instruments.

Considering the value of respect for human dignity through the lens of bio-rights as referred to in the instruments of the Council of Europe and UNESCO has produced a very important debate on the concept of dignity.

In the well-known case of *Netherlands v European Parliament and Council*, Advocate General Jacobs stated that human dignity is 'perhaps the most fundamental right of all, and is now expressed in Article 1 of the Charter'.[23] However, for David Feldman, dignity is not a right per se but a value underpinning all fundamental rights and constitutional principles.[24] In a rather similar vein, Bertrand Mathieu suggested that safeguarding dignity can be best viewed as a sort of meta-value or 'matrix' providing a guiding pathway for the configuration of other specific rights and duties or their reconciliation.[25] Finally, Roger Brownsword completed this interesting debate by identifying two different roles for the concept of dignity: under a rights-driven ethic, the idea of dignity acts in support of individual autonomy (human dignity as 'empowerment')[26] while under a duty-driven ethic, it acts as a constraint on autonomy (human dignity as 'constraints').[27]

This debate was intense when permissive actions to legitimate euthanasia where linked to the 'right to die in dignity', or when actions where proposed for the use of embryonic stem cells in therapeutic research (so-called therapeutic cloning).[28]

---

[22] Art. 1 of the UDHR provides that 'all human beings are born free and equal in dignity and rights', giving solid ground for the concept of dignity whether linked or separated from human rights.

[23] Opinion of AG Jacobs of 14 June 2001 in Case C-377/98 *Netherlands v European Parliament and Council* [2001] ECR I-7079, para. 197.

[24] D. Feldman 'Human Dignity as Legal Value', Part 1, in Public L Rev (1999) 682–702 and Part II, in Public L Rev (2000) 61–76.

[25] B. Mathieu, 'Pour une reconnaissance de "principes matriciels" en matière de protection constitutionnelle des droits de l'homme', 27 Dalloz chronique (1995) 211–12 and *Génome humain et droits fondamenteaux* (Paris: Economica, 2000).

[26] See D. Beyleveld and R. Brownsword, *Human Dignity in Bioethics and Biolaw* (Oxford: Oxford University Press, 2001).

[27] See R. Brownsword, n 16, at 287, and 'Ethical Pluralism and the Regulation of Modern Biotechnology', in *Biotechnologies and International Human Rights* (Oxford: Oxford University Press, 2007), 45–70.

[28] Or when Art. 5, para. 2, of Directive 98/44/EC on the Legal Protection of Biotechnological Inventions admitted that 'an element isolated from the human body or otherwise produced by means

Regardless of whether human dignity is properly viewed as a fundamental right (as opposed to a constitutional principle or objective) or as empowerment or as constraint for the right-holders, it is a fact that the hard law of the Council of Europe has been gradually supplemented by other references to dignity in the additional protocols which use human dignity to justify the prohibition of human cloning.[29] Even the EC Directive on the Legal Protection of Biotechnological Inventions emphasizes the need for patent law to respect dignity (Art. 5(1)).[30]

Such use of the concept of dignity as a constraint on reproductive cloning also has many objective justifications derived from the UNESCO Declarations which demonstrate a real dualism in the concept of dignity. In that sense, the Declarations of UNESCO were in the vanguard of attempts to forge a worldwide bioethical consensus in order to 'moralize' international trade and to ban human reproductive cloning. Thus Article 11 of the Universal Declaration on the Human Genome and Human Rights[31] proclaims and states in its Article 2(b) 'that dignity makes it imperative not to reduce individuals to their genetic characteristics'.

Those of the UNESCO Declarations that state that 'a person's identity should not be reduced to genetic characteristics, since it involves complex educational, environmental and personal factors and emotional, social, spiritual and cultural bonds with others and implies a dimension of freedom'[32] seek to affirm the reality of the dualism in the legal concept of the human being. From this perspective, the human being is considered both as an individual and as part of the human family, to which the concept of dignity is attached and introduced in law in order to reconcile the international public order with human rights. What is protected here is 'humanity', construed as both the species and the family. But the concept also covers the indivisibility of the individual human being, who should not be reduced to separate aspects of his or her identity. This means that 'dignity' as a legal standard for the concept of public order has an interpersonal dimension that modifies the scope of the principle of consent (eg the free will of any individual seeking to be cloned, even with his or her own consent).

It is not the first time that international law has imposed such a restriction on the principle of individual autonomy. For example, Article 11 of the Geneva Protocol prohibits experimentation on the civil population even if a member of the

---

of a technical process . . . may constitute a patentable invention.' Furthermore, the failure at the UN to achieve a treaty consensus against cloning has been attributed in part to the tension between human dignity as empowerment and human dignity as constraint. See R. Brownsword, n 16, at 296.

[29]  In the preamble to this additional Protocol signed 12 January 1998 it is stated that 'the instrumentalisation of human beings through the deliberate creation of genetically identical human beings is contrary to human dignity and thus constitutes a misuse of biology and medicine.' The same could be said about the Council of Europe Protocol of 24 January 2002 concerning Transplantation of Organs and Tissues of Human Origin.

[30]  Directive 98/44/EC, 1998 OJ.

[31]  Art. 11 of this Declaration provides that 'Practices which are contrary to human dignity, such as reproductive cloning of human beings, shall not be permitted.'

[32]  See Art. 3 of the International Declaration on Human Genetic Data. In the same spirit, Art. 3 of the Universal Declaration on the Human Genome and Human Rights of 1997 states that the human genome 'contains potentialities that are expressed differently according to each individual's natural and social environment [including health and education].'

population has given his or her consent to such experimentation. The same could be said about the prohibition of slavery.

In fact, the public order nature of dignity occasionally makes it possible to conceal in legal guise an ethic similar to that of the notion of accepted standards of behaviour or of decency, the meaning of which is both variable and imprecise in any legal system.

However, this analogy is limited in that dignity cannot be reduced to a simple situation of fact, and implies a duality that is central to its value. The dual nature of the principle of dignity is illustrated by the fact that the rights arising from it must be made compatible with other rights and freedoms. On the one hand, the subjective right is what gives value to the dignity and personality of the individual. On the other hand, human dignity, the matrix principle underlying all human rights, seems in the legal instruments of Council of Europe and UNESCO to go beyond the subjective rights arising from it, to merge with the notion of an international public order governing humanity as a whole or to establish a normative standard in which freedom and subjective rights can be reconciled. The legal discourse of the Council of Europe and UNESCO has thus transformed human dignity into a legal standard modifying the concept of international public order, which is at the origin of the limitation on both scientific power and the principle of the autonomy of the patient's will.

## 5. The tentative emergence of the concept of the human genome as part of the common heritage of humanity

In comparison with the instruments of the Council of Europe in this field, the added value of the UNESCO Declarations is the linkage between the concept of the common heritage of humanity and that of human dignity. This connection is made right at the beginning of the Universal Declaration on the Human Genome and Human Rights, where the concept of 'heritage of humanity' reflects a deep change in the approach to human dignity proclaimed for humanity as a whole.

This idea is also reflected by Article 1 of the Human Genome Declaration, which proclaims that

The human genome underlies the fundamental unity of all members of the human family, as well as the recognition of their inherent dignity and diversity. In a symbolic sense, it is the heritage of humanity.

Under international law, the expression 'common heritage of humanity' is applicable to resources the use of which it is deemed desirable to regulate in the interests of humanity as a whole. The concept of common heritage was introduced for the purpose of characterizing property considered to be of universal interest and which the international community is duty-bound to safeguard, for example as in the UN Convention on the Law of the Sea or the UNESCO Convention for the Protection of the World Cultural and Natural Heritage of 16 November 1972.

Thus, by symbolically characterizing the human genome as the heritage of humanity, the Declaration was following the tradition of these prior legal texts to ensure the preservation of universal values in the future exploitation of human genetics, without trying entirely to assimilate the human genome or human resources as an object of law like any other good.

Generally speaking, the import of the proclamation that the human genome is common heritage of humanity was not immediately clear because of the dispute among the UNESCO governmental experts as to who was entitled to dispose of or to take advantage of the said heritage, as well as on the legal status of the genome itself, that is, on whether or not it should be considered as a good over which one could have property, or intellectual property, rights.

In 1997 during the discussions of the International Bioethics Committee (IBC) group of experts, it was suggested that the Declaration should emphasize that the human genome was first and foremost the 'property' of the individual. Other experts felt that, legally speaking, the notion of common heritage could create tension between the individual heritage of a person and the heritage of the species, for each gene is thus deemed to be both the property of an individual, and at the same time an inalienable property of humanity. Several experts felt it necessary to consider the specific legal consequences of the adoption of such a notion. Mrs Noelle Lenoir, Chairperson of the IBC, pointed out that it would be difficult to state in a declaration that the individual was the 'owner' of his or her genome, since this would go against the legislation of certain countries, which did not recognize ownership of the human body.

The same tension was raised about the status of human embryos which has not previously been determined by human rights instruments. In fact, those secular instruments do not recognize a direct human right to life for an embryo, since the legal personality enabling the human being to be subject of law is only recognized for a person who has been born. It is thus legally inconsistent to speak about the individual human dignity of the embryo.[33] For this reason, the experts considered the necessity of a legal principle other than dignity to protect the human embryo.

The concept of the human genome as part of the heritage of humanity was therefore designed to establish a dynamic balance between the protection of the inalienable rights of the individual and the common interests of humanity as covered by the concept of human dignity. The indivisibility of these values must be emphasized: the rights of the individual with regard to his or her genome are subject solely to those constraints arising from the need to respect the rights of others.

On this basis, it was agreed that the symbolic reference to the genome as being part of the heritage of humanity must be maintained in order to emphasize the

---

[33] Eg the preamble to the Convention on the Rights of the Child adopted on 20 November 1989 and which entered into force 2 September 1990, declares that 'Bearing in mind that, as indicated in the Declaration of the Rights of the Child . . . the child, by reason of his physical and mental immaturity, needs special safeguards and care, including appropriate legal protection, before as well as after birth.' But this legal protection is considered as an obligation of the parents and the scientists dealing with the health of the unborn child and does not create a subjective right of an unborn child to decide whether or not he or she has the right to born.

moral obligation to preserve the universal dignity of mankind. It is highly significant that the concept of the heritage of humanity was used for the first time not to limit the excess of states' sovereignty over spaces of communal interest, but explicitly as a limitation on the potential of individuals to dispose of their human genome at will, as well as an attempt to secure the broadest possible protection of the human genome against damage that might endanger the very survival of humankind. In addition, the notion of heritage covers the knowledge accumulated by men and women about themselves as a source of potential for the progress of humankind.

This idea appears later on, in other provisions of the Universal Declaration on the Human Genome and Human Rights, as a restriction on the practice of the free exploitation of human genetics by any individual, like the provisions of Article 4 stating that 'the human genome in its natural state shall not give rise to financial gains'.

In addition to this ban, the new UDBHR[34] refers in its preamble to 'the principles already stated in the Universal Declaration on the Human Genome and Human Rights and the International Declaration on Human Genetic Data' and provides by its Article 21(e) that

States should take appropriate measures, both at the national and the international level, to combat bioterrorism, illicit traffic in organs, tissues and samples, genetic resources and genetic-related materials.

Those Articles emphasize the principle of the 'inalienability' of the human body, including the human genome, and especially prohibit the commercialization of human genes.

Despite the above-mentioned constraints, the prohibitions are not absolute. There is a continuum from ban, to restrictions, to permissive actions, with the position along that continuum depending on the purposes of the medical or biotechnological research or practices, including those relating to genetic resources.

In fact, the principle of non-appropriation of the human body and its elements, as acknowledged by the UNESCO Declarations as well as other hard law regional instruments and many national laws, is designed to retain the indivisibility of the legal personality of the human person, considered as a subject of law and not as an object. The slave trade, as prohibited by the human rights instruments, is another example of that principle and of the danger of considering the human being as an object of law like any other 'good' or property, including animals and plants.

Surely, the use of the qualifying phrase 'heritage of humanity... in a symbolic sense' has been understood as weakening the legal strength of this Article. However, a more convincing explanation given by Francesco Francioni is that

the adjective 'symbolic' is rather intended to stress that the human genome is not to be treated in a patrimonial sense, like the mineral resources of the sea bed, and that it is not subject to forms of individual or collective appropriation. Its value for humanity is thus not so much in its potential to yield economic benefits, as is the case for the tangible natural resources to which the same concept had previously been applied, but rather in its reflexive

---

[34] It is important to note that Art. 2(viii) of this Declaration proclaims that its aim is 'to underline the importance of biodiversity and its conservation as a common concern of humankind'.

capacity to establish an ethical obligation, owed to humanity as a whole, to preserve and safeguard the continuity of the human species when faced with the unfathomable applications of biotechnologies to human genetic engineering.[35]

## 6. Prospects for the future

Can such body of law, rich in potential legal concepts—where the human genome could form a symbolic part of the heritage of humanity, where dignity could serve both as a democratic ideal and as the foundation for the prohibition of the use of the human body for financial gain. and, finally, where bio-rights could be attributed both to the individual and to communities—serve as the basis for a coherent international order regulating the use of human genetics?

Notwithstanding the uncertainties about the feasibility of a *single hard law instrument* embracing all the questions raised above and linked to the extraordinary and rapid development of science and technology, the instruments of the Council of Europe and UNESCO reflect potential norms that might build customary international law and address the best balance between fast technology and secure law, between ethical and legal norms, and finally, between compatible norms in the trade field and in the field of medical or technological research.

This trend in international law is not specific to regulation of biotechnology and human genetics, since the soft law approach exists also in the field of misuse of other new technology (such as the internet) or in the field of climate change,[36] despite many appropriate recommendations going beyond the self-regulation promoted by the providers of those new technologies.[37]

Time is a very important factor in this field, not only to determine the effectiveness of those new rules in the field of biotechnology but also—and perhaps more importantly—to check whether the therapeutic promises of science and technology materialize as expected before questioning the rationale of the restrictions introduced in this fragmented corpus of mixed hard law and soft law.

The instruments of the Council of Europe and UNESCO are in fact serving as an experimental normative mechanism. The results of this can be observed only after a certain period of time, within the framework of an evaluation process aimed at establishing compatibility between the biotechnological regulations and trade regulations.

---

[35] Francioni, n 7, at 11.

[36] UNESCO created the World Commission on the Ethics of Scientific Knowledge and Technology (COMEST) as a specific subsidiary body, tasked with drafting a study on the advisability of preparing a declaration of a code of conduct for states and other actors in relation to the consequences of climate change, even if the Kyoto Protocol were adopted in 1997, since the UN Framework was built on cycles of negotiation leaving wide discretion for the parties (like the soft law) in dealing with substantive items.

[37] See S. El-Zein, 'L'indispensable amélioration des procédures internationales pour lutter contre la criminalité liée à la nouvelle technologie', in *The Law of Cyberspace*, Lyons University (Lyon III), 2000.

Confronted with the current dramatic tensions between the old society of states hingeing on self-interest and reciprocity,[38] on the one side, and emerging community values, on the other, the issues surrounding bioethics raised openly the need gradually to transform the world society into a real international *community* so that *public* or collective concerns may prevail over *private* interests. Otherwise, a supermarket where human beings could change parts of their body and replace them by other parts could exist at the price of more legal simplicity.

In fact, legal simplicity has been generated as a result of strong industrial and scientific pressure to provide a broad interpretation of the scope of free trade in services and goods. However, in this case this is not sufficient to encompass the complexity of the scientific stakes and their relationship with the economy while solving the problem of the status of genetic resources, the scope of patients' rights, and the principle of sharing benefits by means of a new reconciliation of all the principles confirmed by the international treaty law relating to human rights and trade. Excluding the ethical dimension in the emergence of the new law, or reducing the concept of heritage of humanity or human dignity to simple questions of free choice of each individual may in certain situations produce disadvantages of which we must become aware now, in order to avoid finding later that it generates more problems than it solves.

In this sense, the conceptual contribution of the instruments of the Council of Europe and UNESCO is indubitably rich, in particular in the following fields: establishing that human genes may be used for scientific purposes only in a way that endangers neither the value of humanity as a common heritage nor the concept of human dignity, construed both individually and collectively; reconciling the principle of non-appropriation of the human body and its elements with benefits of scientific progress for humanity as a whole, in a spirit of solidarity, equal treatment, and the sharing of benefits; enhancing the idea of an international public order that monitors bioethics practices with the involvement of the states and that may request those states to acknowledge new duties that will also be the future rights of the individual or of humanity in this area.

This conceptual contribution will enable the future decision-makers to revise the law, which is sometimes judged permissive or vague and sometimes restrictive or poorly adapted. Such revision will depend on the technological and human issues at stake, even if in this field it is reasonable to adopt a *gradual approach* in the codification of universal legal frameworks, due to the rapid scientific and technological development.

---

[38] G. Fitzmaurice, 'The Future of Public International Law and of the International Legal System in the Circumstances of Today', in Institut de droit international, *Livre du Centenaire 1873–1973* (Basle: S. Karger, 1973), 259.

# 37

# Uses and Abuses of Cyberspace: Coming to Grips with the Present Dangers

*Andrew Murray*

## SUMMARY

Of key importance to the challenge of cyberspace to all areas of law is the distinction between space and cyberspace. Space is the lawyer's natural environment. It represents our place in the physical environment and is the cornerstone of our legal systems domestic and international. Concepts such as jurisdiction, domicile, and enforcement of rights (and duties) are bordered by one's physical location in space. Cyberspace is the global network of interdependent information technology infrastructures, telecommunications networks, and computer processing systems. How does the rule of law apply in cyberspace? There are several examples of international cooperation. In the criminal law field there is the Council of Europe Convention on Cybercrime (with protocol). This is a framework convention which attempts to harmonize the criminal legal regimes of the 47 signatory states, on a number of key issues including computer misuse (or hacking), system and data interference, computer fraud, and child pornography. Another example of such traditional international cooperation can be found in taxation where the Organization for Economic Co-Operation and Development (OECD) Ottawa Taxation Framework attempts to harmonize rules on the imposition, collection, and transfer of taxation revenue from online activities through a series of framework general principles. Also, there are a number of domestic cases in which successful cross-jurisdictional enforcement has been effective. If we are to have any hope of producing effective de facto jurisdiction for cyberspace content, international lawyers must first accept there is a distinction between space and cyberspace. Cyberspace may (when viewed from the space of the physical environment) look like a communications media. The author suggests there are areas where international cooperation and perhaps even formalization of law through treaty obligations are likely to be successful. They include (i) e-commerce where the UNCITRAL Model Law on Electronic Commerce has been extremely successful in bringing harmony and international recognition; (ii) intellectual property rights where a number of the World Intellectual Property Organization (WIPO) treaties and others such as the recently finalized Anti-Counterfeiting Trade Agreement have been or are likely to be effective; and (iii) a number of criminal law measures where the Council of Europe Convention on Cybercrime has been effective in providing cooperation on matters of illegal interception and computer-related fraud. However, if lawyers want to create de facto control over content it cannot be through legal documents; it must be through a web of terms and conditions of service and through Lessigian code-based solutions. Content may just be beyond the direct control of the international legal community, as predicted by the cyberlibertarians.

## 1. The Wikileaks scandal, legal change, and legal certainty

As I write this in early December 2010 the world is gripped by the Wikileaks scandal.[1] Julian Assange the Wikileaks founder is in Wandsworth Prison in southwest London while he awaits a bail hearing pending a full hearing on a European Arrest Warrant issued in Sweden on charges of serious sexual assault. The media debate and opine as to whether this is a politically motivated act undertaken by the Swedish state on behalf of the Government of the United States. Assange believes that upon his removal to Sweden (if permitted) he will be handed over to the US government, and meanwhile a group of online activists identified by the moniker 'Anonymous' have carried out Distributed Denial of Service Attacks (DDOS) on a number of sites seen to be involved in attempts to stifle Wikileaks including Amazon, PayPal, and MasterCard. Throughout the fog of the media war the Wikileaks site has remained online through the support of web users globally who have provided hosting, mirroring, and internet protocol (IP) and domain name services. This serves to illustrate perhaps more clearly than any academic argument Jennings's assumption that one of the 'irreconcilable essentials of law' is change.[2] Here we have a serious international event. One that if contained wholly within the United Kingdom would involve a number of potential criminal offences including the original offence committed by the individual who obtained the data, believed to be defence analyst Bradley Manning, which in the United Kingdom would be a breach of section 2 of the Computer Misuse Act 1990 (as well as no doubt an offence under the Official Secrets Acts 1911 to 1989), while the leaking of data by the Wikileaks site would likely be an offence under section 55 of the Data Protection Act

---

[1] In the unlikely event any reader is unfamiliar with the Wikileaks scandal, in November 2010 intermediary site Wikileaks began to reveal a number of private, confidential, and even secret US government diplomatic cables both via its website and via partner media organizations. This led to a considerable public affairs debate across politics, the media, and academia.

[2] R.Y. Jennings 'Judicial Legislation in International Law', 26 Kentucky LJ (1938), at 127.

1998. Yet adding the international element changes this. The data were gathered in the United States and is being leaked via servers in Sweden and several other countries globally. Thus it is no longer clear if European data protection rules apply given that the data were released in the United States and given that it may be publicized via Wikileaks servers in almost any global location. Even setting aside complex policy arguments on whether the details Wikileaks are releasing may be covered by either whistle blowing or public interest protections it is almost impossible for a lawyer to say with certainty whether the actions and activities of Wikileaks are legal or illegal.[3] This suggests the change noted above is as Jennings predicted adversely challenging the other 'irreconcilable essential of law', certainty.[4]

## 2. Space and cyberspace

Of key importance to the challenge of cyberspace to all areas of law, not just international law is the distinction between space and cyberspace. Space is the lawyer's natural environment. It represents our place in the physical environment and is the cornerstone of our legal systems domestic and international. Concepts such as jurisdiction, domicile, and enforcement of rights (and duties) are bordered by one's physical location in space. Thus to turn to the Wikileaks example again we see that if personal data on European-domiciled individuals were to be published via a Wikileaks server in the United Kingdom this may lead to a prosecution under section 55 of the Data Protection Act 1998, but as the data were released in the United States, then published at any number of global server sites the certainty of domicile jurisdiction, and most importantly enforcement of duties is undermined. The same accusation may be laid at the legal failure to curb the activities of the 'Anonymous' cyber activist community. Their actions are a clear breach of section 3 of the UK Computer Misuse Act 1990. Why are they not prosecuted? Well some of these activists are certainly UK resident and may at some future time be prosecuted. But the distinction between space and cyberspace again causes problems for enforcement of the legal settlement. There is a large number of activists involved in the campaign with some estimates suggesting up to 300,000 people have downloaded the necessary software to take part in DDOS protest attacks and at least 9,000 were involved in attacks on the MasterCard site. To ingather evidence on 9,000 protesters and to then identify and prosecute them would be a massive task if the investigation were limited to a single jurisdiction but given the cross-border nature of the campaign it becomes an impossible task.

---

[3] Anecdotally discussions with several colleagues in a number of fields including media law, human rights, torts, public law, and public international law provided no common answer.

[4] Jennings, n 2, at 127.

## 3. The rule of law and cyberspace

How then does the rule of law apply in cyberspace? Some commentators point to traditional efforts to extend principles of international cooperation such as treaty formation and cooperation on policing and recognition of enforcement orders.[5] There are several examples of such international cooperation. In the criminal law field there is the Council of Europe Convention on Cybercrime (with protocol).[6] This is a framework convention which attempts to harmonize the criminal legal regimes of the 47 signatory states, which although mostly Council of Europe states includes external parties such as the United States, South Africa, Japan, and Canada, on a number of key issues including computer misuse (or hacking), system and data interference, computer fraud, and child pornography. Another example of such traditional international cooperation is to be found in taxation where the OECD Ottawa Taxation Framework attempts to harmonize rules on the imposition, collection, and transfer of taxation revenue from online activities through a series of framework general principles.[7] Although these measures broadly provide for some level of international cooperation on key principles there remains a weakness in that they still assume principles of jurisdiction, domicile, and enforcement of rights (and duties) bordered by one's physical location in space, that is, space principles not cyberspace principles. This is the heart of a debate surrounding effective jurisdiction in cyberspace. The key distinction here is between de jure jurisdiction and de facto jurisdiction. While there may be de jure jurisdiction granted to a particular court or tribunal by either international settlement, or even under traditional rules for the finding of jurisdiction the de facto situation may be rather different. This debate has been characterized as a debate between cyberlibertarians and cyber-legal positivists.

## 4. Cyberlibertarianism and cyber-legal positivism

The belief that the activities of individuals online may de facto escape the control of traditional legal settlements is founded in the cyberlibertarian movement of the 1990s. The totem of cyberlibertarian thought is usually taken to be two works. David Post and David Johnson's 1996 paper 'Law and Borders—The Rise of Law in Cyberspace',[8] and John Perry Barlow's 'A Declaration of the Independence of

---

[5] H.K. Spang-Hanssen, 'A Just World under Public International Law in Cyberspace: Jurisdiction', 13 Annual Survey of Int'l & Comp L (2007) 1; R. Azam, 'E-Commerce Taxation and Cyberspace Law: The Integrative Adaptation Model', 12 Virginia J L & Tech (2007) 5.

[6] CETS No. 185, Budapest, 23 November 2001; CETS No. 189, Strasbourg, 28 January 2003.

[7] The Ottawa Framework may be accessed at <http://www.oecd.org/dataoecd/46/3/1923256. pdf>.

[8] 48 Stanford L Rev (1996) 1367. See also D.G. Post and D.R. Johnson, 'Chaos Prevailing on Every Continent: Towards a New Theory of Decentralized Decision-Making in Complex Systems', 73 Chicago-Kent L Rev (1998) 1055.

Cyberspace'.[9] Johnson and Post in giving the foundational definition of cyber-libertarianism claimed that 'the Net radically subverts a system of rule-making based on borders between physical spaces'.[10] They argued that cyberspace undermined the ability for a state to assert de facto jurisdiction over online activities, and that cyberspace should therefore be recognized as a separate legal jurisdiction from the 'real world'. Classical cyberlibertarianism contends that regulation founded upon traditional state sovereignty, based as it is upon notions of physical borders, cannot function effectively in cyberspace as individuals may move seamlessly between zones governed by differing regulatory regimes in accordance with their personal preferences. Simply put, they claimed the internet was unregulable as de jure legal controls were confined to the jurisdiction in which they were promulgated and/or recognized while content hosted and carried on the internet flowed seamlessly over these borders. Their legal formulation of cyberlibertarianism found political voice in John Perry Barlow's classic 'A Declaration of the Independence of Cyberspace'. Here using powerful and politically evocative language he asserted that governments of the world had no sovereignty on the internet, as cyberspace does not fall within the borders of any jurisdiction.

> We have no elected government, nor are we likely to have one, so I address you with no greater authority than that with which liberty itself always speaks. I declare the global social space we are building to be naturally independent of the tyrannies you seek to impose on us. You have no moral right to rule us nor do you possess any methods of enforcement we have true reason to fear.
>
> Governments derive their just powers from the consent of the governed. You have neither solicited nor received ours. We did not invite you. You do not know us, nor do you know our world. Cyberspace does not lie within your borders. Do not think that you can build it, as though it were a public construction project. You cannot. It is an act of nature and it grows itself through our collective actions.

Thus Barlow uses the same systemic argument employed by Johnson and Post to develop a political argument to counterpoint their legal one. Not only are attempts to impose external legal controls in cyberspace doomed to fail because de facto legal controls cannot be imposed on a space with no physicality and no borders (and which is therefore open to regulatory arbitrage), but according to Barlow any attempt also lacks legitimacy as there is no recognized lawmaking authority for this space. This argument may be seen as a historical one. Made in the mid-1990s when the internet was a less regulated space and when movements to regulate online activities were in their infancy we may wish to dismiss cyberlibertarians as libertarian romantics but to do so would be a mistake as we shall see.

The question thus becomes: are the cyberlibertarians right? This is not an inquiry into the accuracy or otherwise of Barlow's political argument but rather are Johnson and Post correct in claiming that there are no de facto legal controls emanating from sources external to the cyberspace sphere? The immediate response to this

---

[9]  Made at Davos, Switzerland, 8 February, 1996, available at <http://www.ibiblio.org/netchange/hotstuff/barlow.html>.

[10]  'Law and Borders: The Rise of Law in Cyberspace', 48 Stanford Law Review (1996), at 1370.

may be found in the works of a number of lawyers who follow a legally positivistic approach and who argue that effective de jure controls may be easily converted into de facto controls via the application of traditional rules of international private law. These cyber-legal positivistic arguments are common and may be seen in a number of sources but most commonly may be centred around the so-called 'fallacy' arguments common to Professor Chris Reed in the United Kingdom[11] and Professor Jack Goldsmith in the United States.[12] Goldsmith is probably the first academic lawyer to present the fallacy arguments. He identified three, in his words persistent, fallacies which infected cyberlibertarianism. These were: (i) the fallacy that cyberspace is a separate space; (ii) the fallacy that territorial governments cannot regulate the non-territorial net; and (iii) over-optimism that there will be cheap, plentiful information.

For our purposes it is the first two fallacies and in particular fallacy (i) which is important. Goldsmith points out that:

> Net users are not removed from our world. They are no more removed than telephone users, postal users, or carrier-pigeon users. They are in front of a screen in real space using a keyboard and scanner to communicate with someone else, often in a different territorial jurisdiction.[13]

This is the key to enforcement of rights (and duties) and may be instrumental in solving problems of both jurisdiction and domicile. Effectively Goldsmith is saying that cyberspace is a *communications media* not a *physical space*—he denies the distinction between space and cyberspace and instead treats cyberspace as an extension of pre-existing (and legally regulable) communications media. This view has many supporters including Professor Chris Reed who defines Goldsmith's fallacy (i) as 'the cyberspace fallacy', saying 'the human and corporate actors and the computing and communications equipment through which the transaction is effected, all have a real-world existence and are located in one of more physical world legal jurisdictions.'[14] In this Reed and Goldsmith are essentially correct; there is no doubting that individuals and corporations undertake actions from within sovereign jurisdictions. However, the transborder nature of internet activity has presented a significant challenge to traditional legal institutions in enforcing jurisdiction over online activities. At times, the law has struggled to establish effective jurisdiction,[15] for as Gillies notes the 'dematerialised nature of online commercial activities renders the location of the parties and the place where those activities take place difficult to determine.'[16] This issue is none more prevalent than in the related

---

[11] C. Reed, *Internet Law: Text and Materials* (Cambridge: Cambridge University Press, 2000). Note: page refs are to the 2nd edn, 2004. See also L.E. Gillies, 'Addressing the "Cyberspace Fallacy": Targeting the Jurisdiction of an Electronic Consumer Contract', 16 Int'l J L & Inf Tech (2008) 242.

[12] J.L. Goldsmith, 'Regulation of the Internet: Three Persistent Fallacies', 73 Chicago-Kent L Rev (1998) 1119. See also C.M. Kelly, 'The Cyberspace Separatism Fallacy', 34 Texas Int'l LJ (1999) 413.

[13] Goldsmith, n 12, at 1121.

[14] C. Reed, *Internet Law: Text and Materials*, 2nd edn (Cambridge: Cambridge University Press, 2004), 188.

[15] J. Reidenberg, 'Technology and Internet Jurisdiction', 153 U Penn L Rev (2005) 1951.

[16] Gillies, n 11, at 242.

cases of *Licra et UEJF v Yahoo! Inc and Yahoo! France*,[17] and *Yahoo Inc v LICRA*[18] an action described by one US commentator as 'a backlash response to the cultural and technological hegemony of the United States in the on-line world'.[19]

## 5. Space and cyberspace:
### *Licra et UEJF v Yahoo! Inc and Yahoo! France*

This inter-jurisdictional dispute arose because Nazi memorabilia was being offered for sale on a Yahoo! auction site, which was accessible in France. The Ligue Internationale Contre le Racisme et l'Antisémitisme (LICRA) and the Union des Étudiants Juifs de France (UEJF) brought an action against Yahoo! on the ground that offering the sale of Nazi memorabilia was illegal under Article R645-1 of the French Criminal Code. This case presented a challenge for establishing jurisdiction over online activities. As Yahoo! was a US company operating within the United States, the Tribunal de Grand Instance de Paris had to assess whether the actions undertaken on foreign soil fell under its jurisdiction. Yahoo! argued that the French court was 'not territorially competent over the matter because the alleged fault is committed on the territory of the United States', but the court ruled otherwise: 'the harm is suffered in France; our jurisdiction is therefore competent'.[20] In addition to the local harm, the court found that Yahoo! were able to identify French customers. Yahoo! were using IP numbers to identify—with significant accuracy—French visitors in order to display relevant advertising to them. A panel of technical experts gave evidence that it was technically possible for Yahoo! to use IP numbers to filter out French users, and the court ordered Yahoo! to install such filters or face a daily fine.

However, without the ability to enforce its will, the law has no real power. As Shultz notes: the territorial nature of enforcement jurisdiction is such that 'the state can enforce its laws only against in-state actors, against entities with a presence on the territory of the state or with assets there.'[21] This was exemplified in actions of Yahoo! immediately after the order was made. Instead of appealing the decision within the French legal system, Yahoo! took action against LICRA and

---

[17] Tribunal de Grande Instance de Paris (Superior Court of Paris). There are three separate orders in this case. To make sense of the case you should read all three. Order of 22 May 2000 at <http://www.lapres.net/yahen.html>; Order of 11 August 2000 at <http://www.lapres.net/yahen8.html>; Order of 20 November 2000 at <http://www.lapres.net/yahen11.html>.

[18] There were three hearings in California. A hearing before the District Court in which a decision was filed on 7 November 2001, *Yahoo Inc v LICRA*, 145 F Supp 2d 1168 (ND Cal. 2001), an appeal to the 9th Circuit in which a ruling was filed on 23 August 2004, *Yahoo Inc v LICRA*, 379 F3d 1120 (9th Cir. 2004), and an *en banc* rehearing before the 9th Circuit in which a ruling was filed on 12 January 2006, *Yahoo Inc v LICRA*, 433 F3d 1199 (9th Cir. 2006).

[19] M. Fagin, 'Regulating Speech across Borders: Technology vs Values', 9 Mich Telecoms & Tech L Rev (2003), at 421.

[20] A. Murray, *Information Technology Law: The Law and Society* (Oxford: Oxford University Press, 2010), 113.

[21] T. Schultz, 'Carving up the Internet: Jurisdiction, Legal Orders, and the Private/Public International Law Interface', 19 EJIL (2008), at 813.

UEJF in the US District Court of California, seeking a 'declaratory judgment that two interim orders by a French court are unrecognizable and unenforceable'. They successfully argued that enforcement of the French ruling would violate the First Amendment in the United States. The District Court ruled in Yahoo!'s favour, undermining the jurisdiction of the French court. Yahoo! eventually ended the dispute by removing all Nazi material from their auction sites, citing public opinion as the reason. While the District Court's decision was eventually reversed (in LICRA and UJEF's favour),[22] the issue of establishing effective jurisdiction seized the courts for almost six years and across two continents.[23]

It may be argued that the Yahoo! decision offers support for the long-disregarded cyberlibertarian argument by illustrating how the issue of enforceable jurisdiction has been affected by the borderless nature of the internet. Johnson and Post said: 'The rise of the global computer network is destroying the link between geographical location and . . . the legitimacy of the efforts of a local sovereign to enforce rules applicable to global phenomena.'[24] The information one contributes on the internet can be retrieved in virtually any jurisdiction throughout the globe, and the de jure rules where one is domiciled are bound to be in conflict with the de jure rules elsewhere, for as highlighted by Shultz:

seen from the perspective of Internet content providers, the problem is that they may be subject to regulations of states to which they had no intention of sending information and to local laws the application of which they could thus not legitimately be expected to foresee.[25]

Reed and Schultz both point out that if one were to expect de jure jurisdiction to be converted into de facto jurisdiction, then in order to prevent breaking the law of at least one state, one must comply with the most stringent laws found around the globe, or at least the most stringent laws among the nations where you have assets.[26] This seems to place too much emphasis on a positivistic analysis which places an unrealistic burden on internet users.

## 6. Space and cyberspace: *R v Sheppard & Anor*— The issue of de facto jurisdiction over cyber-presence

Cyber-legal positivists often suggest that the Yahoo! case is an extraordinary case and point to a number of cases in which successful cross-jurisdictional enforcement has been effective: cases such as defamation actions *Dow Jones & Co Inc v*

---

[22] *Yahoo Inc v LICRA*, n 18, at 1199.

[23] Although an intelligent international law audience will recognize this is not unusual in the sphere of conflicts of law what is interesting is that the case was not finally settled by the courts but by the voluntary actions of Yahoo!. Had Yahoo! continued to host Nazi memorabilia the conflict would have remained extant with them in breach of the order of the Tribunal but shielded by the First Amendment.

[24] Post and Johnson, n 10, at 1370.        [25] Schultz, n 21, at 815.

[26] Reed, n 14, at 257; Schultz, n 21, at 814.

*Gutnick,*[27] *Loutchansky v Times Newspapers Ltd,*[28] and *King v Lewis,*[29] or copyright cases such as *MGM Studios Inc v Grokster Ltd,*[30] and *Universal Music Australia Pty Ltd v Sharman License Holding Ltd.*[31] Recently attention has been turned to an English case as the classical example of how one cannot escape de facto jurisdiction by simple 'offshoring' content. It is argued by cyber-legal positivists that the case of *R v Sheppard & Anor*[32] has shown that unlawful activities undertaken in cyberspace can be subject to successful prosecution within a real world jurisdiction. While domiciled in the United Kingdom, Mr Sheppard posted racially inflammatory material on a website hosted in California, and was subsequently convicted under section 19 of the Public Order Act 1986, whereby 'a person who publishes or distributes written material which is threatening, abusive or insulting is guilty of an offence if he intends thereby to stir up racial hatred.' Mr Sheppard appealed his conviction on the grounds that as the website was hosted outside the United Kingdom, the publication of the material fell outwith the jurisdiction of the courts of England and Wales. Cyberlibertarian thought would deem this to be a classic example of the inability to regulate cyberspace activity. The technology within cyberspace has essentially removed the physicality of the traditional 'hard copy' publication and distribution model. People accessing the racially inflammatory material were essentially being delivered material from California, via a number of physical servers in various locations. The court ruled against the appellant, noting that a 'substantial measure' of the activities constituting the crime took place in England. By operating and editing the website from within England, Mr Sheppard was found to be acting within the jurisdiction of England and Wales, rendering the physical location of the server irrelevant. Furthermore, the judge also noted that Mr Sheppard targeted the jurisdiction in question, having a dedicated page for British customers on the website (the only nationality with its own dedicated area), and having also offered publications for sale with the price in pounds sterling.

It may be argued that the ruling dismisses Johnson and Post's argument that 'the power to control activity in Cyberspace has only the most tenuous connections to physical location.'[33] The case appears to show that there is in fact a real and direct connection between activities undertaken in cyberspace and the physical location in which one is located. Had the judge upheld the appeal, individuals within the jurisdiction of England and Wales would essentially be able to circumvent section 19 of the Public Order Act by publishing racially inflammatory content via servers located in the United States using the shield of the First Amendment. This hypothetical world would entail a true realization of cyberlibertarian theory. However, this judgment proved that jurisdiction can be established even if the content in question is hosted in cyberspace.

That is, it may have established that if it were effective. However, while Mr Sheppard sits in a jail cell, his website still stands and may be accessed from any point on the globe with an internet connection including the United Kingdom.

---

[27]  [2002] HCA 56.          [28]  [2002] 2 WLR 640.          [29]  [2004] EWCA Civ 1329.
[30]  545 US 913 (2005).          [31]  [2005] FCA 1242.          [32]  [2010] EWCA Crim 65.
[33]  Post and Johnson, n 10, at 1370.

What we see here is an essential distinction in space and cyberspace. The courts of England and Wales have taken de facto jurisdiction over Mr Sheppard's corporeal person but not his *incorporeal identity*. Thus the distinction between the cyberlibertarian ethos and the cyber-legal positivists is drawn into sharp relief. The cyberlibertarians were defining the inability of traditional states-based regulators to leverage de facto jurisdiction around the incorporeal identity of the individual which is made up of their online postings, accounts, and alter egos. The cyber-legal positivists were meanwhile focusing upon the corporeal identity of the individual which, of course, will be subject to de facto jurisdiction wherever they are domiciled and wherever they hold assets which may be seized. The issue of enforcement then simply becomes one of international private law. We are returned to Goldsmith's rather arbitrary distinction that the internet is a communications media not a physical space. What *R v Sheppard & Anor* demonstrates is that this is not strictly true, as has been the common theme of this chapter there is space and cyberspace. While the courts of England and Wales take jurisdiction over Mr Sheppard's corporeal presence in space, they have been denied de facto jurisdiction over his virtual identity (or presence) in cyberspace and as a result the harm which section 19 of the Public Order Act seeks to prevent continues to occur in the United Kingdom every time an individual accesses Mr Sheppard's website from the United Kingdom. How then is de facto jurisdiction established over his cyberpresence?

By placing his content on a Californian server Mr Sheppard effectively exported the de facto jurisdiction over his content to the United States, and in particular to the State of California. There, following the US Supreme Court decision in *Reno v ACLU*,[34] it is protected by the First Amendment. This allows US servers to be used as a safe haven for online hate speech.[35] If an individual anywhere in the world is willing to take the risk and publish hate material to a US web server, the material is likely to stay there unmolested. Furthermore, the constitutional status of the Supreme Court decision in *Reno v ACLU* renders the US government unable to enter into any international treaty or agreement, or recognize an order of another court or jurisdiction which would restrict the right of individuals awarded under *Reno* for, as explained by Douglas Vick,

The *Reno* decision will constrain the international community's efforts to establish a comprehensive body of common rules for regulating Internet content. Under American law, treaties and other international accords are hierarchically inferior to the provisions of the US Constitution. A treaty provision, just like a congressional statute, is unenforceable if it fails to conform with First Amendment law.[36]

This handicap could clearly be seen in negotiations to draft the Council of Europe Convention on Cybercrime.[37] The Convention deals with only one 'content-related offence', that being the production or distribution of child pornography using a computer system. We know several of the states that took part in

---

[34] 521 US 844 (1997).    [35] Reidenberg, n 15, at 1958.
[36] D. Vick, 'The Internet and the First Amendment', 61 MLR (1998), at 419.
[37] CETS No. 185, Budapest, 23 November 2001.

the drafting process were keen to include further content-related offences, but that these never made the final text. The reason for this is to be found in the Explanatory Report:

> The committee drafting the Convention discussed the possibility of including other content related offences, such as the distribution of racist propaganda through computer systems. However, the committee was not in a position to reach consensus on the criminalisation of such conduct. While there was significant support in favour of including this as a criminal offence, some delegations expressed strong concern about including such a provision on freedom of expression grounds.[38]

Although the identity of the delegations in question is not revealed, it is clear that at least one of these would be the US delegation, for the US delegation could not, as Douglas Vick had predicted, sign the US government up to any treaty provisions which would conflict with First Amendment protection.


## 7. Space, cyberspace, and international law

The present author is not an international lawyer by training or practice and therefore begs indulgence over his simplistic view of international law. If we are to have any hope of producing effective de facto jurisdiction for cyberspace content, international lawyers must first accept there is a distinction between space and cyberspace. For too long cyber-lawyers have debated whether or not effective legal controls may be leveraged into cyberspace without facing up to this distinction. Yes cyberspace may (when viewed from the space of the physical environment) look like a communications media. It is this perspective which leads cyber-legal positivists to announce that of course the activities of an individual may be regulated in cyberspace as the individual remains domiciled in real space. Equally when one looks at cyberspace as a separate space by looking at the content of the place, one may erroneously imagine that it is unregulable as the cyberlibertarians did. The example of both Mr Sheppard and Mr Assange show that while the body may be regulated the outpourings of the mind may not, unless one takes a holistic view that space and cyberspace are two separate but connected places. Where does this leave the international lawyer? It suggests there are areas where *international cooperation* and perhaps even formalization of law through *treaty obligations* are likely to be successful. These areas include: (i) e-commerce where the UNCITRAL Model Law on Electronic Commerce has been extremely successful in bringing harmony and international recognition;[39] (ii) intellectual property rights where a number of WIPO treaties[40] and others such as the recently finalized Anti-Counterfeiting

---

[38] Council of Europe, ETS No. 185, *Explanatory Report on the Convention on Cybercrime.*

[39] The UNCITRAL Model Law on Electronic Commerce (1996) with additional Art. 5*bis* as adopted in 1998.

[40] Including the WIPO Performances and Phonograms Treaty of 1996, the WIPO Copyright Treaty of 1996.

Trade Agreement[41] have been or are likely to be effective; and (iii) in a number of criminal law measures where the Council of Europe Convention on Cybercrime has been effective in providing cooperation on matters of illegal interception and computer-related fraud[42] Unfortunately content-related issues are more complex due to the effect of *Reno v ACLU*. Here US-based servers will act as safe havens, as we saw in *Sheppard* (and perversely in reverse in the Wikileaks case). Content can be instantly mirrored and moved, as the Wikileaks case has shown to contain data when it is on the web is almost impossible. If lawyers want to create de facto control over content it cannot be through legal documents; it must be through a web of terms and conditions of service and through Lessigian code-based solutions.[43] Content may just be beyond the direct control of the international legal community, as predicted by the cyberlibertarians, after all.

[41] Final text available at <http://trade.ec.europa.eu/doclib/docs/2010/december/tradoc_147079.pdf>.

[42] A. Murray, *Information Technology Law: The Law and Society* (Oxford: Oxford University Press, 2010), 391.

[43] L. Lessig, *Code 2.0* (New York: Basic Books, 2006).

## (C) RESTRAINING ARMED VIOLENCE IN INTERNATIONAL AND INTERNAL ARMED CONFLICT

# 38

# Bolstering the Protection of Civilians in Armed Conflict

*Nils Melzer\**

## SUMMARY

In virtually all contemporary armed conflicts—whether conducted by professional, well-resourced, and disciplined armed forces, or by poorly trained, equipped, and organized armed groups—a staggering 90 per cent of all victims are civilians. A comprehensive and constructive clarification of international law relating to the protection of civilians in armed conflict requires that both academics and practitioners take a step back from an overly technical, political, or positivist analysis of the law and look at the questions presenting themselves through the prism of general, well-established principles of law, most notably the principles of: (i) necessity; (ii) proportionality; (iii) precaution; and (iv) humanity, which underlie the entire normative framework governing the use of force. Indeed, wherever states resort to force, whether in self-defence against armed attacks, in the conduct of hostilities against belligerent adversaries, or in exercise of their law-enforcement authority, it is always these four principles which circumscribe the permissible scope and intensity of their action. In short, these four principles reflect general principles of law which govern the use of force by states in all circumstances. They could be regarded as a normative superstructure from which a unified use of force regime can be derived for all situations ranging from peacetime policing to all-out international armed conflict. A major problem arises with regard to the lack of any incentive for rebels to comply with international humanitarian law. A viable alternative to the introduction of a full combatant privilege for non-state belligerents

\* Dr Nils Melzer is former legal adviser for the International Committee of the Red Cross (ICRC). This contribution reflects the views of the author alone and not necessarily those of the ICRC.

would require a two-pronged approach. In accordance with the respective logic of the *jus in bello* and the *jus ad bellum*, the conduct of hostilities and the exercise of power and authority over persons in compliance with international humanitarian law should be encouraged and legitimized (first objective), whereas the initiation of, or participation in, an armed conflict in contravention of domestic law should be discouraged (second objective). The first objective could be obtained by providing immunity from prosecution under ordinary criminal law for all activities carried out for reasons related to an armed conflict provided that they are in compliance with international humanitarian law. The second objective could be achieved by introducing a *jus contra bellum* for non-state actors. To that end states could create, in their domestic criminal law, an offence penalizing the mere fact of having engaged in acts of rebellion which, although in compliance with international humanitarian law, would be unlawful under domestic law. This offence could be named 'breach of the public peace'.

# 1. Introduction

Today it is universally recognized that, in times of armed conflict, belligerents must distinguish between civilians and combatants and may direct their operations only against legitimate military targets. Civilians must not be directly attacked, and all feasible precautions have to be taken to protect them from the incidental infliction of harm. Civilians can lose this protection only if, and for as long as, they themselves take a direct part in hostilities. Once detained or otherwise exposed to the authority and control of a belligerent party, civilians must be treated humanely in all circumstances. In sum, as far as the protection of civilians in armed conflict is concerned, contemporary international law seems to be fairly straightforward and clear.

The reality, however, looks different. In virtually all contemporary armed conflicts—whether conducted by professional, well-resourced, and disciplined armed forces, or by poorly trained, equipped, and organized armed groups—a staggering 90 per cent of all victims are civilians. They become 'collateral damage' of aerial bombardments, artillery, and mortar fire; they lose life, limb, and property to landmines and unexploded ordnance; they are deliberately made 'soft targets' by snipers and suicide-bombers; or they are erroneously or arbitrarily attacked by forces pursuing an elusive adversary. Moreover, once the fighting is over, civilians often suffer untold abuse at the hands of their captors. The reasons for the tragic failure of international law to deliver upon its promise of civilian protection in armed conflicts are manifold, but most of them can be traced back to a few seminal problems, two of which shall be addressed here. First, there is a growing sense of uncertainty and confusion as to the standards governing the use of force in contemporary contexts of armed violence and, secondly, there is a marked lack of incentive for the compliance of non-state belligerents with international humanitarian law. Both problems shall be briefly described, each followed by a proposal as to how the conceptual resources of existing international law could contribute to resolving them with a view to improving the protection of civilians in armed conflict.

## 2. Confusion and controversy on use of force standards

Contemporary conflict environments have very little in common with the traditional inter-state wars for which the categories, standards, and distinctions of international humanitarian law were originally conceived. Today, many situations where states resort to military force may not, or not necessarily, qualify as armed conflicts. Cases in point are the current 'drug wars' raging in Mexico, northern Colombia, and the Brazilian Favelas, the multinational counter-piracy deployments in the Gulf of Aden, and the extraterritorial drone attacks conducted by the United States as part of its transnational counterterrorism campaign. While all of these contexts are marked by levels of violence and organization clearly exceeding the scope of classic law enforcement, none of them comfortably fits the traditional mould of 'armed conflict'. Even where the existence of an armed conflict is undisputed, the rise of loosely organized and clandestinely operating armed groups, the widespread outsourcing of traditional military functions to private contractors and civilian intelligence personnel, and a more general trend towards increased civilian involvement in military operations have blurred the distinction between legitimate military targets and persons protected against direct attack. In operational practice, all of these developments have given rise to a growing sense of uncertainty as to the standards governing the use of force in a given situation. As a result, armed forces bear an increased risk of being attacked by persons they cannot distinguish from the civilian population, whereas civilians are more likely to fall victim to erroneous targeting and arbitrary violence.

This situation has led to widespread controversy over the accurate interpretation, and even the continued adequacy, of existing treaty rules and concepts in contemporary armed conflicts. Although there is universal agreement that, in situations of armed conflict, civilians are protected by the principles of distinction, precaution, proportionality, and humanity, and that they may not be attacked unless and for such time as they directly participate in hostilities, there is significant disagreement on what each of these terms means in practice. Not only is there fierce debate as to what activities should amount to 'direct participation in hostilities' and, thus, lead to loss of civilian protection, but also on who qualifies as a civilian or as a combatant in the first place, and on whether there is a separate status of 'unlawful combatant' falling outside existing humanitarian protections. Once a person has been determined to be a legitimate military target, there are divergent views as to whether humanitarian law provides an unfettered 'right' to kill such persons, or whether there is an obligation to capture rather than kill. Once persons are deprived of their liberty, on the other hand, disputes focus on the permissibility of certain interrogation methods, of indefinite internment without review or trial, and of transfers to third states with doubtful human rights records. In fact, there is not even consensus as to the threshold at which armed violence linked to organized crime would have to be regarded as an armed conflict, and as to whether the ensuing applicability of international humanitarian law is confined to the territories of the involved states, or whether it extends to belligerent relations wherever they may occur. Similarly, in human rights law, there are deadlocked technical debates not only as to whether the treaty term 'jurisdiction' should be interpreted to imply, or to exclude, the extraterritorial scope of human rights obligations, but also as to the formal applicability and practical relevance of human rights treaties in situations of armed conflict. Finally, there is continued debate on the meaning of the term 'armed attack' used in the UN Charter as a trigger of the inherent right of self-defence, resulting in fierce disagreement as to whether states are entitled to resort to force in self-defence in cases of sporadic cross-border incidents, pre-emptively against less than imminent threats, or against non-state actors within the territory of a third state.

## 3. Towards a unified use of force regime

Most of these debates have not been conducive to resolving the underlying legal controversies, mainly because they are driven by conflicting policy interests and preconceptions, but also because they are generally confined to a positivist analysis of existing treaty provisions and treaty-specific case law without much consideration for the integrity, coherence, and equilibrium of the international normative framework as a whole. For instance, if the rights and duties of belligerents continue to be interpreted exclusively in light of treaty provisions that were formulated with the large-scale conflicts of the twentieth century in mind, and if human rights obligations continue to be interpreted exclusively through the lens of standards developed in jurisprudence for the purposes of peacetime policing, the result will be two legal frameworks imposing virtually irreconcilable standards on the use of force. As a consequence, questions of whether a situation amounts to an armed conflict, whether someone qualifies as a civilian, combatant, or civilian directly participating in hostilities, and how exactly international humanitarian law and human rights law interrelate will gain almost artificial importance and give ample opportunity for unfruitful polarization.

It is here submitted that a comprehensive and constructive clarification of international law relating to the protection of civilians in armed conflict requires that both academics and practitioners take a large step back from an overly technical, political, or positivist analysis of the law and look at the questions presenting themselves through the prism of general, well-established principles of law, most notably the principles of necessity, proportionality, precaution, and humanity, which underlie and inform the entire normative framework governing the use of force. Indeed, wherever states resort to force, whether in self-defence against armed attacks, in the conduct of hostilities against belligerent adversaries, or in exercise of their law-enforcement authority, it is always these four principles which circumscribe the permissible scope and intensity of their action. It may therefore be justified to draw the conclusion, through inductive reasoning, that these considerations amount to general principles of law which govern the use of force by states in all circumstances and, thus, provide a normative superstructure from which a unified use of force regime can be derived for the entire spectrum ranging from peacetime policing to all-out international armed conflict.

*Necessity*: according to the principle of necessity, the type and degree of force used in a specific situation must not exceed what is reasonably necessary to achieve the desired goal in the circumstances ruling at the relevant time and place. This is a general principle which governs any interference by state authorities with individual or collective rights and interests in virtually all national jurisdictions. It would therefore be preposterous to argue that, in the absence of a positive treaty norm to the contrary, international humanitarian law should be interpreted to permit the needless slaughtering of enemy combatants or civilians directly participating in hostilities where the circumstances are such that they could easily have been captured without resort to lethal force. On the other hand, it would be just as absurd to interpret the human right to life as subjecting law-enforcement operations against heavily armed drug-traffickers in the jungle of northern Colombia to an overly strict and inflexible standard of necessity derived from case law dealing with police operations conducted in relatively controlled and peaceful environments. The point is that, as a matter of operational necessity, both law-enforcement and military personnel must be authorized to use the type and degree of force which is reasonably required to complete their task. However, the legal authority in which both police and military power is vested cannot possibly provide a justification for the use of force which would be excessive in relation to the exigencies of the situation. Even though the urgency and difficulty of the operational circumstances may require a considerable margin of judgement, considerations of necessity as such are an indispensable part of any use of force assessment.

*Proportionality*: according to the principle of proportionality, in addition to considerations of necessity, the harm likely to result from the use of force must always be justified by the expected benefit. In this generic sense, although at times phrased in different terms, considerations of proportionality restrict the exercise of public power in virtually all national jurisdictions and, thus, can be regarded as a general principle of law. It is erroneous to argue that international humanitarian law, contrary to human rights law, knows the concept of proportionality only in relation to the infliction of 'collateral' harm on civilians but does not take the harm caused to combatants into account. Accurately understood, the principle of distinction simply predetermines in advance that, to the extent reasonably necessary to achieve a legitimate military purpose and not otherwise prohibited by international humanitarian law, the use of force against combatants and civilians directly participating in hostilities is never considered disproportionate, even if they have to be killed in the process. Direct attacks against peaceful civilians, on the other hand, have been predetermined not to be justifiable (ie, proportionate) in any circumstances, even if such attacks were to yield considerable military advantage. The only question which international humanitarian law leaves open to operational determination is the proportionality of collateral harm in view of the military advantage expected to result from an attack against a legitimate military target. In short, there is no basis for the claim that international humanitarian law does not take into account the harm inflicted on combatants or civilians directly participating in hostilities and that, therefore, there must be a positive 'right' to kill them in combat without any further considerations. As the debate surrounding the permissibility of shooting down hijacked renegade aircraft may illustrate, however, it is just as unrealistic to claim that human rights law categorically prohibits the infliction of any 'collateral' harm on innocent bystanders simply because human rights treaties remain silent in this regard. The point is simply that, as a matter of fundamental juridical equity, any harm likely to be caused by the public use of force must always be justified by the benefit expected to result from the achievement of a legitimate purpose, irrespective of whether this assessment is made on the spot or, where circumstances permit, predetermined in advance.

*Precaution*: the principle of precaution requires that those responsible for the planning and conduct of operations take all reasonable precautions to avoid erroneous, unnecessary, or disproportionate use of force. Without this requirement, the principles of necessity and proportionality cannot be implemented effectively, so that it is part and parcel of any use of force regime subjected to the rule of law. It would not only be morally unacceptable, but also legally inaccurate to claim that belligerents have no duty to take precautionary measures to avoid inflicting unnecessary suffering on combatants and civilians directly participating in hostilities or incidental harm on those *hors de combat* simply because, in treaty international humanitarian law, the principle of precaution is expressed exclusively with a view to avoiding or, in any event, minimizing incidental harm to civilians. On the other hand, it would be just as absurd to interpret human rights law to require all law enforcement personnel to identify themselves, give advance warnings, and, where the use of force or firearms is unavoidable, to ensure the immediate availability of medical care for the wounded without taking into account the urgency and difficulty of the circumstances and terrain in which they may be operating.

*Humanity*: in a very general sense, the principle of humanity pervades the entire normative framework of international law—including the preceding principles of necessity, proportionality, and precaution—in the form of elementary considerations aiming to preserve human life, dignity, and well-being. In international humanitarian law, the principle finds one of its more specific expressions in the unconditional duty of belligerents to ensure humane treatment to all persons finding themselves under their authority or control for reasons related to an armed conflict. While the principle of humanity is generally acknowledged as one of the seminal principles underlying all international humanitarian law, the International Court of Justice in the *Corfu Channel* case has even recognized that elementary considerations of humanity constituted a general principle of law, 'even more exacting in peace than in war'. It is therefore repulsive, for example, to engage in artificial debates as to whether or not interrogation methods clearly designed to induce physical suffering and anxiety—such as sleep deprivation, prolonged uncomfortable positions, and waterboarding—technically qualify as torture or inhumane or degrading treatment within the meaning of certain treaty provisions, failing which such methods would be acceptable under international law. The same concern arises, of course, with regard to the acceptability of indefinite internment without review or trial, and of the transfer of detainees to third states with doubtful human rights records. After all, elementary considerations of humanity attach to every person *qua human being* irrespective of the formal categorization of a particular context, person, or treatment in treaty law.

In sum, it is submitted that the principles of necessity, proportionality, precaution, and humanity outlined above reflect general principles of law which govern the use of force by states in all circumstances. These principles thus could be regarded as a normative superstructure from which a unified use of force regime can be derived for all situations ranging from peacetime policing to all-out international armed conflict. It is clear that specific circumstances, such as the intensity of ongoing military hostilities or the complete breakdown of public order after a natural disaster, will strongly influence the concrete interpretation and application of these principles. Nevertheless, the recognition of a unified use of force regime governed by these four principles may have the potential of avoiding sharp paradigm shifts and artificially created 'gaps' between parallel, overly strict, and inflexible criteria for the legality and legitimacy of force. Arguably, therefore, the recognition of a unified use of force regime would represent a large step forward in clarifying international law in a manner conducive to improving the protection of the civilians in situations of armed conflict.

## 4. Lack of incentives for non-state belligerents

While violations of international humanitarian law are generally committed by all parties to a conflict, state armed forces are, at least in theory, subject to a comparatively sophisticated disciplinary and judicial system provided by their domestic law. Moreover, where captured state armed forces are likely to be exposed to the jurisdiction of an opposing state—in international armed conflict—international humanitarian law provides them with the so-called 'combatant privilege'. The combatant privilege guarantees members of state armed forces immunity from domestic prosecution for lawful acts of war, but not for war crimes and other violations of international humanitarian law. This privilege is an important incentive for state armed forces to comply with international humanitarian law. It is also an incentive for them to distinguish themselves from the civilian population at least to the extent that failing to do so may entail loss of combatant privilege or may amount to a perfidious violation of international humanitarian law. In non-international armed conflict, national law generally provides them with a comparable incentive in the form of immunity from prosecution for lawful acts of state. Dysfunctions in that system may be due to the inability or unwillingness of states to provide or enforce adequate national legislation, or to submit to the jurisdiction of the International Criminal Court, but are not usually due to shortcomings on the level of international law. This observation also applies, for example, to the recent insertion of tens of thousands of private contractors or civilian intelligence personnel and other civilian government employees into the reality of modern-day conflicts. Existing international law is fairly unambiguous as to the fact that states remain responsible for the conduct of all those acting under their instruction and control, including private military or security contractors. It is therefore up to the contracting states to ensure that their national legislation provides for extra-territorial jurisdiction and disciplinary authority over all personnel operating on their behalf.

The issue of incentives and accountability becomes more complicated with non-state actors, be they individual civilians, groups of criminals, or organized insurgents. While it is generally recognized that non-state belligerents are subject to international humanitarian law and international criminal law and, thus, are legally obliged to protect and respect the civilian population in situations of armed conflict, international law provides them with few incentives for complying with this obligation. Contrary to state armed forces, non-state actors are not entitled to the combatant privilege, but remain exposed to the full force of national criminal law even for lawful acts of war. Thus, insurgents having caused death and destruction among governmental armed forces and infrastructure may not have violated international humanitarian law but, nevertheless, remain subject to domestic prosecution for crimes such as rebellion, murder, or arson. While treaty international humanitarian law does encourage the belligerent parties to provide a 'broadest possible amnesty to persons who have participated in the armed conflict' at the end of hostilities, the non-binding nature of this recommendation hardly provides for a sufficient incentive for non-state belligerents to respect international humanitarian law and to distinguish themselves from the civilian population. The lack of any form of combatant privilege for non-state actors engaging in lawful acts of war also further facilitates the current trend in unilateral and multilateral state practice to extend stigmatizing blanket labels such as 'terrorism' to all armed violence attributable to non-state actors, regardless of their compliance with international humanitarian law. In other words, armed non-state belligerents essentially have the rather unsatisfactory choice of being 'bad criminals' or 'good criminals'. In the following it shall therefore be explored as to what extent the lack of incentives could be remedied through developments of existing international humanitarian law.

## 5. Towards a modified combatant privilege for non-state belligerents

*Extending the full combatant privilege to non-state belligerents*: the first option to remedy the absence of any form of 'privilege' for non-state belligerents in return for compliance with international humanitarian law would be to replace the discretion left to states with regard to post-conflict amnesties by a formal entitlement of all fighting forces to immunity from domestic prosecution for lawful acts of war. In the course of the twentieth century, governments have successively extended combatant privilege in international armed conflict beyond members of their regular armed forces also to participants in a levée en masse (1907), irregular militia and volunteer corps (1907) including organized resistance movements (1949), and even to armed forces of certain national liberation movements representing territorial entities not yet having attained statehood (1977). The extension of the combatant privilege to non-state belligerents, however, although discussed and re-examined on countless occasions, was never adopted by states. The main reason for this reluctance has always been the fear of governments that providing insurgents with immunity from prosecution for lawful acts of war may encourage and legitimize armed rebellion against the state.

Indeed, in the absence of an international *jus ad bellum* for non-state belligerents, the introduction of a full combatant privilege would be highly problematic. With the prospect of escaping the reach of domestic criminal law for all anti-governmental activities not prohibited by international humanitarian law, even otherwise peaceful opposition movements may be tempted to resort to organized armed force in order to trigger the applicability of international humanitarian law rather than engaging in peaceful political opposition which may be severely penalized under domestic law. Overall, therefore, the introduction of a full privilege equivalent to that afforded to state combatants also for non-state belligerents would hardly be acceptable to states and, by encouraging armed violence, would hardly be beneficial to the protection of the civilian population.

*Modifying the combatant privilege*: during the 1974–77 Diplomatic Conference compromise proposals had been made which would have required courts to take into account compliance with international humanitarian law in sentencing non-state belligerents, would have excluded the death penalty for lawful acts of war, or deferred the execution of such death penalty until after the end of hostilities. According to these proposals, states would still have applied their domestic criminal law to non-state belligerents, but would have been obliged to do so more leniently compared to ordinary criminals. For example, a robber having murdered a single person could be sentenced to death, whereas a rebel having killed several soldiers could not. Ultimately, these proposals did not sufficiently address the concerns of states as to the equitable application of their domestic criminal law and the potential encouragement or legitimization of rebellion and did not find their way into the final treaty text. This historical background illustrates that, in considering potential alternatives to full immunity from prosecution *de lege ferenda*, the necessary incentive for insurgents to respect international humanitarian law must be carefully balanced against the equally important interests of not encouraging the initial escalation of force by non-state actors and of maintaining the domestic rule of law.

It is submitted that a viable alternative to the introduction of a full combatant privilege for non-state belligerents would require a two-pronged approach loosely analogous to, and fulfilling essentially the same functions as, the mechanism of the *jus ad bellum* and the *jus in bello* in conflicts between states. More specifically, in accordance with the respective logic of the *jus in bello* and the *jus ad bellum*, the conduct of hostilities and the exercise of power and authority over persons in compliance with international humanitarian law should be encouraged and legitimized (first objective), whereas the initiation of, or participation in, an armed conflict in contravention of domestic law should be discouraged (second objective). The first objective could be obtained by providing immunity from prosecution under ordinary criminal law for all activities carried out for reasons related to an armed conflict provided that they are in compliance with international humanitarian law. In order to encourage full compliance with international humanitarian law, this privilege could not be limited to the conduct of hostilities, but would also have to include the exercise of power and authority over persons for reasons related to an armed conflict. The second objective could be achieved by introducing a *jus ad bellum* or, more accurately, a *jus contra bellum* for non-state actors. To that end states could create, in their domestic criminal law, an offence penalizing the mere fact of having engaged in acts of rebellion which, although in compliance with international humanitarian law, would be unlawful under domestic law. This offence could be named 'breach of the public peace', inspired by the offence of '*Landfriedensbruch*' recognized in the penal codes of Switzerland, Germany, and Austria, which originally aimed to outlaw feuds and similar organized violence between non-state actors. It would enable states to prosecute and punish non-state actors having initiated or participated in an armed conflict even if they fully respected international humanitarian law. At the same time, it would allow avoidance of both the stigmatization related to ordinary crimes such as 'murder', 'arson', and 'terrorism', and the contradictions related to an inequitable application of the same domestic penal provisions to non-state belligerents and ordinary criminals.

In order not to defeat the purpose of the immunity granted for compliance with international humanitarian law, punishment for this offence should exclude not only the death penalty, but also life sentences and should always be kept in proportion to the gravity of the case and personal culpability. Contrary to the proposals made in the 1970s, proceedings and sentencing should not be postponed until after the end of the hostilities, as this may lead to undesirable long-term detention without either trial or periodic review. Instead, the detaining authority should be obliged to provide for a fair trial and, once a person is serving a sentence, should be required (instead of only encouraged) periodically (instead of only initially) to consider the possibility of an amnesty, rehabilitation, release, and re-integration into society. Negative decisions in such review proceedings should be made subject to an appropriate form of judicial review. In terms of a preliminary text proposal for a possible future codification, this two-pronged approach could be formulated as follows:

No one, whose activities in support for a party to the conflict were carried out in compliance with applicable customary and treaty IHL, shall be prosecuted, sentenced, or punished under the penal or administrative law of the authorities in power, except for the offence of having breached the public peace.

Punishment for breaches of the public peace must be proportionate to the gravity of the specific offence and of personal culpability. In no case shall breaches of the public peace be punished by the death penalty, nor by imprisonment for life.

Any penal, administrative, or preventative deprivation of liberty for breaches of the public peace shall be periodically, and in any event annually, reviewed by the detaining authority with a view to favourably considering the granting of amnesty, release, or rehabilitation. Negative decisions shall be subject to judicial review by a regularly constituted court.

The proposal outlined above would have the advantage of discouraging and de-legitimizing resort to organized armed force by leaving the (domestic) criminalization of breaches of the public peace intact. At the same time, it would provide an effective incentive for non-state belligerents to respect international humanitarian law by liberating lawful acts of war from the stigma and full weight of domestic criminal law. It may therefore significantly contribute to improving the protection of civilians in situations of armed conflict.

## 6. Conclusion

As has been shown, the concepts, rules, and principles of existing international law (*lex lata*) can contribute decisively to improving the protection of civilians in situations of armed conflict. First, interpreting the *lex lata* regulating the use of force by states in situations of law enforcement, self-defence, and hostilities in light of general, well-established principles of law allows the emergence of a single use of force regime which—through juridical coherence and intuitive simplicity—would have the potential of avoiding erroneous targeting and arbitrary violence against civilians. Secondly, existing rules and concepts of the *jus contra bellum, jus in bello*, and national criminal law could be joined *de lege ferenda* to afford non-state actors immunity from domestic prosecution for lawful acts of war (*jus in bello*), while at the same time permitting their prosecution for a less stigmatized, and more leniently sanctioned, offence of 'breach of the public peace' (*jus contra bellum* and national criminal law). Such a modified combatant privilege could provide non-state belligerents with a potent incentive to comply with international humanitarian law and, as a consequence, help better to protect civilians in armed conflict.

# 39

# Should Rebels be Treated as Criminals? Some Modest Proposals for Rendering Internal Armed Conflicts Less Inhumane

*Antonio Cassese*

## SUMMARY

Governments against whom rebels fight regard them as persons engaging in seditious action hence as criminals deserving to be punished. As a result rebels, knowing that in any case upon capture they will be punished not only for any war crime they may have committed but also for the simple fact of taking up arms against the government, have no incentive to comply with humanitarian law rules, in spite of recent trends to the contrary and the imperatives stemming for the whole body of international humanitarian law. No international customary rule exists suppressing or curtailing the freedom of every state to treat as it pleases (subject of course to the requirements of human rights law) its own nationals and other individuals participating in a civil strife. However, a customary rule is gradually crystallizing. Two conditions should be met for rebels to acquire a special status under customary international humanitarian law: (i) such status should only be granted when the insurgent group is (a) organized; (b) shows some degree of stability; (c) conducts sustained and concerted military operations; with the consequence that (d) the hostilities are not sporadic or short-lived. It is also necessary (ii) for the rebels to distinguish themselves from the civilian population when engaging in an attack or in a military operation reparatory to an attack. For the purpose of this requirement of distinction, it would be necessary for the combatants to carry their arms openly, or at least to have a distinctive sign recognizable at a distance. In addition, rebels as a group must comply with the rules of humanitarian law. The emergence of the new customary rule can be powerfully promoted by statements or declarations of the International Committee of the Red Cross (ICRC) and the UN General Assembly as well as by the case law of international and national courts.

## 1. The problem

It is common knowledge that, while in international armed conflicts combatants who fulfil the necessary requirements must be accorded prisoner of war status upon capture, in internal armed conflicts normally combatants opposing government forces do not enjoy any privileged status.

What should be done to introduce a modicum of humanity into non-international armed conflicts? In the following paragraphs an effort will be made to show: (i) how inconsistent the current situation is with the whole spirit and purpose of humanitarian law and (ii) how some new trends in the international community could lead to better legal regulation of the matter.

## 2. The current condition is utterly at odds with international humanitarian law

The situation sketched above is in conspicuous contrast with the whole spirit of international humanitarian law, in many respects.

First of all, since the seminal Interlocutory Decision of the ICTY Appeals Chamber in *Tadić* (1995) the previously widely upheld dichotomy between two markedly different classes of armed conflicts, that of international and that of internal conflict, has gradually been eroded and is fading away. In that decision the Court held that serious violations of international humanitarian law amount to war crimes, whether perpetrated within the context of an international or an internal armed conflict, with the consequence that the author of such crimes may be prosecuted and punished. More generally, the Court held that in recent times

A state-sovereignty-oriented approach has been gradually supplanted by a human-being-oriented approach. Gradually the maxim of Roman law *hominum causa omne jus constitutum est* (all law is created for the benefit of human beings) has gained a firm foothold in the international community as well. It follows that in the area of armed conflict the distinction between interstate wars and civil wars is losing its value as far as human beings are concerned. Why protect civilians from belligerent violence, or ban rape, torture or the wanton destruction of hospitals, churches, museums or private property, as well as proscribe weapons causing unnecessary suffering when two sovereign states are engaged in war, and yet refrain from enacting the same bans or providing the same protection when armed violence has erupted 'only' within the territory of a sovereign State? If international law, while of course duly safeguarding the legitimate interests of States, must gradually turn to the protection of human beings, it is only natural that the aforementioned dichotomy [between international and internal armed conflicts] should gradually lose its weight. (para. 97)

Clearly, it is the very logic of humanitarian law that to a large degree blurs the distinction between the two classes of conflict with a view to demanding of all parties to a conflict, whether internal or international, the requirement strictly to abide by that body of law if they intend to avoid prosecution and punishment for gross violations. To attain this goal it is, however, necessary for the rebels to benefit from some privileged status so that they may not be punished for the simple act of taking up arms against the central authorities.

Another reason for the granting of some type of special status to rebels resides in the fact that when insurgents make up an organized group enjoying control over part of the state territory and the armed hostilities are protracted, under customary international law they acquire international legal personality, as evinced by their frequent conclusion of international agreements with either the central authorities or third parties. Qua international subjects they are beneficiaries of rights but also holders of international obligations relating to or deriving from humanitarian law. All this shows that rebels are not a conglomerate of loose dissidents or criminals bent on murdering state officials and attacking government institutions, but make up an international interlocutor who claims to operate as an actor in international dealings. If this is so, it is illogical and contradictory not to promote persons fighting on behalf of rebels to the status of combatants entitled not to be treated as common criminals.

These humanitarian tendencies are borne out by practical reasons. It would seem that states, although on principle they refuse to acknowledge any particular status to rebels, in fact are induced to refrain from treating them as persons responsible for sedition or high treason and consequently from trying and executing them as criminals. Most often during internal armed conflicts government forces that capture rebels detain them in prisons or detention camps without bringing them to trial; they tend to treat them as rebels, rather than common criminals. In addition, states also refrain from trying rebels for any war crime they may have committed. They prefer instead to hold them in legal limbo for the duration of hostilities, as detainees who are looked upon and treated *neither* as common criminals (eg thieves, rapists, murderers) *nor* as war criminals. There is a practical reason for that. If governments were to try to execute rebels in the course of the armed conflict, their adversaries would take revenge by killing any member of the armed forces in their hands or would retaliate against the civilian population loyal to the government. To avoid this plunge into barbarity, governments prefer to keep captured rebels in a shadowy legal condition for the duration of the hostilities. Very often at the end of the conflict, if rebels have not succeeded in overthrowing the government or seceding from the state, they are granted amnesties. It is notable that the granting of amnesties for the mere fact of participating in rebellion is provided for in Protocol II of 1977 (Art. 6(5)).[1] It also appears consonant with the spirit of international humanitarian law and—it would seem—is borne out by state practice.

---

[1] 'At the end of the hostilities, the authorities in power shall endeavour to grant the broadest possible amnesty to persons who have participated in the armed conflict, or those deprived of their liberty for reasons related to the armed conflict, whether they are interned or detained.'

It bears adding that recently some international criminal tribunals have appeared to be sensitive to an extension of the status of prisoner of war to armed combatants in internal armed conflicts. This, for instance, can be deduced from an admittedly somewhat uncertain holding of the Appeals Chamber of the International Criminal Tribunal for the Former Yugoslavia (ICTY) in *Mrkšić and Šljivančanin* (judgment of 5 May 2009):

> it is well established that Common Article 3 of the Geneva Conventions, which is applicable to both international and non-international armed conflicts, is part of customary international law and therefore binds all parties to a conflict. Common Article 3 enshrines the prohibition against any violence against the life and person of those taking no active part in the hostilities, including members of armed forces who have laid down their arms and those placed *hors de combat* by sickness, wounds, detention, or any other cause. The Appeals Chamber considers that Common Article 3 of the Geneva Conventions reflects the same spirit of the duty to protect members of armed forces who have laid down their arms and are detained as the specific protections afforded to prisoners of war in Geneva Convention III as a whole, particularly in its Article 13,247 which provides that:

> > Any unlawful act or omission by the Detaining Power causing death or seriously endangering the health of a prisoner of war in its custody is prohibited, and will be regarded as a serious breach of the present Convention. (para. 70)

Although this ruling has rightly been faulted on account of its relative ambiguity,[2] it is a fact that it is grounded in the notion that even in non-international armed conflict rebellious combatants must upon capture enjoy a treatment equivalent to that of prisoners of war.

The above confirms that states are aware that the situation of rebels may not always be automatically equated to that of common criminals.

## 3. Do states have an international obligation to grant a special status to rebels?

We should now ask ourselves whether the aforementioned humanitarian and practical reasons that warrant the conferment of a special status on rebels have solidified to such an extent as to bring about a change in customary international law. In other words, can one argue that at present states are under an *international obligation* to treat rebels as combatants deserving special treatment in that they may not be punished for the mere fact of participating in the hostilities? I would answer this question by noting that, in spite of recent trends to the contrary and the imperatives stemming from the whole body of international humanitarian law, no customary rule has yet emerged suppressing or curtailing the freedom of every state to treat as it pleases (subject of course to the requirements of human rights law) its own nationals or any other individual on its territory participating in a civil strife.

---

[2] See G. Pinzauti, 'Protecting Prisoners of War', 8 JICJ (2010), at 210.

I believe, however, that a customary rule is emerging. It is justified by the humanitarian and practical reasons illustrated above, and its incipience is borne out by the aforementioned attitude of states during and after internal armed conflicts. It is worth emphasizing briefly the conditions that, in light of international humanitarian law, should be met for this rule to become applicable.

## 4. The two conditions necessary for rebels to be entitled to a special status

For the purpose of assisting in the crystallization of the nascent customary rule, it is perhaps advisable to set out the conditions that should be met for rebels to acquire a special status under international humanitarian law.

It would seem reasonable to argue that a privileged position cannot be afforded to combatants any time a group of persons decide to gang up and engage in armed hostilities against the central authorities of a state. To do otherwise would mean undermining the authority of any state and cancelling, in practice, the criminal offences of high treason and insurrection. A special status for rebels can only be granted when the insurgent group is: (i) organized; (ii) shows some degree of stability; (iii) conducts sustained and concerted military operations; with the consequence that (iv) the hostilities are not sporadic or short-lived.

This, however, would not be sufficient. It is also necessary for the rebels to distinguish themselves from the civilian population when engaging in an attack or in a military operation preparatory to an attack. For the purpose of this requirement of distinction, it would be necessary for the combatants to carry their arms openly, or at least to have a distinctive sign recognizable at a distance. In addition, rebels as a group must comply with the rules of humanitarian law.

Plainly, the rationale behind these requirements is the need to protect civilians. As long as rebels do not distinguish themselves from the civilian population, they must be treated as civilians and therefore are immune from attacks by governmental forces. However, were they to enjoy such immunity and then suddenly take up arms and shoot at the adversary army, this would create an unwarranted advantage for them as well as a dangerous condition for civilians: governmental forces, not being able to see which civilians are real civilians and which are instead rebels pretending to be civilians, in case of doubt would be led to fire on civilians for fear that they might actually be combatants. This would expose the civilian population to unnecessary peril.

If the two aforementioned requirements are met, rebels, while forfeiting of course immunity from attack, may, however, be entitled in case of capture to the status of 'captured combatants'. This entails that: (i) they may not be prosecuted and punished for the mere fact of taking up arms against the central authorities and (ii) they are entitled to all the safeguards laid down in Articles 4 and 5 of II Protocol of 1977, which by now can be considered as having turned into customary international law.

## 5. How could one promote the crystallization of this nascent customary rule?

The question arises of who could push for a rapid transformation of the aforementioned requirements into a fully fledged rule of customary international law and how this could be effected.

This is, of course, an area where one cannot expect a customary rule to grow out of treaty law: states would never enter into an agreement granting rebels combatant status, for fear of encouraging sedition and undermining state prerogatives. Sovereignty rhetoric would always stand in the way of such a treaty. One should therefore turn to other entities for the purpose of acting as 'midwives'. The ICRC should be the first and foremost of such entities. Faced with specific internal armed conflicts it could encourage both states and insurgents alike to enter into agreements designed both to safeguard the civilian population and to request rebels to meet the aforementioned requirements if they wish to be treated as combatants. The ICRC could also promote the signing by states, following international conferences, of statements or declarations upholding the principles and requirements mentioned above. The ICRC could in addition draft a declaration on internal armed conflicts with a view to laying down a set of general principles to be respected by states and rebels for the purpose of rendering internal strifes less inhumane. The agreements, statements, and declarations, if supported by a broad number of states and insurgents, would prove to be conspicuous testament to the formation of a customary rule on the matter.

Similar declarations could and should also be promoted by the UN General Assembly. Since this body might encounter political difficulties in enhancing the legal status of rebels, it could confine itself to adopting one or more resolutions on the matter.

Another powerful factor contributing to the consolidation of a customary rule of international humanitarian law could be constituted by the case law of international and national courts, along the lines of, but hopefully with less ambiguity than, the ICTY Appeals Chamber judgment in *Mrkšić and Šljivančanin* above.

It bears noting that all the statements and declarations referred to above should also urge states to prosecute and punish rebels (as well as members of the governmental armed forces) who commit war crimes. This would highlight the need to protect the civilian population by both according rebels a particular status when they act in consonance with international humanitarian law and by instead trying and punishing them whenever they grossly deviate from the rules of that body of law.

# 40

# How to Improve upon the Faulty Legal Regime of Internal Armed Conflicts

*Sandesh Sivakumaran*

## SUMMARY

There are two major gaps in the law governing non-international armed conflicts: (i) not infrequently, armed groups do exercise territorial control, yet international humanitarian law has little to say on the point and (ii) rebels lack combatant immunity and the associated prisoner of war status; whether or not such individuals respect the law of internal armed conflict, they may be prosecuted and even sentenced to death. Another problem is that there is a growing view that human rights law offers greater protection to the individual and should therefore replace international humanitarian law in the regulation of internal armed conflict, at least when the violence is below the threshold of Protocol II. However, the consequences of a shift from regulation through international humanitarian law to regulation through human rights law have not been fully explored. For example, one would need to turn attention to whether, and in what circumstances, armed groups have human rights obligations. There would also need to be a forum before which these obligations could be enforced. Another problem is the methodological approach by which the international law of internal armed conflict has developed. The development has taken place primarily by analogy to the law of international armed conflict. Rarely have norms been created to govern internal armed conflicts; rather, it has been a question of how far the law governing international armed conflicts can be extended. Yet there are important differences between internal armed conflicts and their international counterparts, principal among which are the actors that take part in each of them. A study needs to be undertaken to determine whether all rules now applicable in internal armed conflicts are within the capacity of armed groups, whether certain rules need tailoring to meet the involvement of this category of actor, and whether other norms are needed. To improve upon the current condition greater regard should be had to the ad hoc regulation of internal armed conflict through unilateral declarations, bilateral agreements, and the like, which is more prevalent than may be thought. In the area of enforcement three recent initiatives suggest that although traditional enforcement approaches may be of limited value, more creative approaches may prove workable. A way forward might reside in working out a new instrument designed to bind armed groups in each situation. The instrument would draw from international humanitarian law, international human rights law, and other relevant bodies of international law. Armed groups should be able to sign up to the instrument as signature coupled with participation in the process may imbue armed groups with a greater sense of investment in the process as well as the norms that result from that process. Potentially, this could have a beneficial impact on compliance. The International Committee of the Red Cross (ICRC) could prompt armed groups to declare that they will abide by this instrument. Monitoring and enforcement of the instrument should take place through a number of complementary means, not being reliant solely on any particular one.

## 1. Characterization of the violence

It is well known that states frequently deny the existence of an internal armed conflict on their territory. This is not a new trend. When the ICRC attempted to involve itself in the violence in Ireland in 1922, it was met with a frosty response from the Minister of Foreign Affairs:

Refuse [to] discuss measures considered necessary by my Government to repress rebellion in Ireland. They are internal in character...Your attempt to intervene [is a] hostile act excusable only by ignorance of facts or false information from anti-Irish source.[1]

Sometimes, the denial may be disingenuous; however, on other occasions, the violence may be such that reasonable individuals can disagree on its characterization. Accordingly, denial of the existence of an internal armed conflict cannot automatically be put down to bad faith on the part of the state concerned. This makes an impartial assessment of the characterization of the violence all the more crucial.

Historically, the lack of an impartial assessment was compounded by the lack of a definition of an internal armed conflict. The ICRC commentaries on Common Article 3 provided some 'convenient criteria',[2] but these had the potential to mislead given that they were no more than a compilation of the suggestions made at the 1949 Diplomatic Conference, all of which had been rejected. Today, we do have a definition of an internal armed conflict and one that has been used extensively, namely the definition contained in the *Tadić* Interlocutory

---

[1] Telegram from Minister of Foreign Affairs, Desmond Fitzgerald, to President of the ICRC, Gustave Ador, 26 January 1923, reproduced and translated in A. Durand, *From Sarajevo to Hiroshima: History of the International Committee of the Red Cross* (Geneva: Henry Dunant Institute, 1984), 227.
[2] See, eg, J. Pictet (ed.), *The Geneva Conventions of 12 August 1949, Commentary: IV Geneva Convention Relative to the Protection of Civilian Persons in Time of War* (Geneva: ICRC, 1958), 35–6.

Appeal on Jurisdiction.[3] However, while this greater clarity over the definition is to be welcomed, it does not obviate the need for an impartial assessment of the situation.

More difficult is identification of the entity that could take on the role of assessing the character of the violence. Certain states have taken the view that the characterization of the violence is a purely subjective matter for the state on whose territory the violence is taking place.[4] Others have suggested that there can be no room for a subjective assessment of the situation and that the decision should be an objective one.[5] As already indicated, an objective assessment by a neutral body is to be preferred, but who could take on this role? It will not suffice for domestic courts or tribunals to make the determination as procedural constraints may prevent the issue from arising before them and allegations of partiality may also arise. International courts and tribunals may be ruled out as the matter may reach them many years after a determination is most needed. UN entities have made such determinations implicitly in the past, but some of these have subsequently been withdrawn after opposition from the states concerned.[6] For understandable reasons, in 1971, the ICRC declined to take on the role.[7] It may be, then, that a body consisting of independent and impartial legal and military experts has to be established under the auspices of an existing institution. That body would be tasked with determining whether the threshold for the application of international humanitarian law has been met in a particular instance at the request of the ICRC or by one of the parties to the violence.

Ideally, any such determination would be binding on the parties involved in the violence. Should this prove impossible, other approaches could still prove useful. For example, determinations could be of persuasive value to the parties to the violence, or to third states and international organizations for their dealings with the parties concerned.

An alternative approach would be for the relevant assessor to act as an accurate provider of the facts, documenting incidents of violence and clarifying the level of organization of the armed group. It would then be up to others to draw their own conclusions from these facts as to the characterization of the violence. This has the advantage of appeasing certain states' concerns while still providing the necessary information for others to make their own informed decisions.

---

[3] *Prosecutor v Tadić*, Decision on the Defence Motion for Interlocutory Appeal on Jurisdiction, IT-94-1-AR72, 2 October 1995, para. 70.

[4] See, eg, *Official Records of the Diplomatic Conference on the Reaffirmation and Development of International Humanitarian Law Applicable in Armed Conflicts, Geneva 1974–1977* (Bern: Federal Political Department, 1978), Vol. 7, p 72, para. 75 (Delegate of Chile).

[5] Ibid, p 75 (Delegate of Argentina).

[6] Compare Children and Armed Conflict: Report of the Secretary-General, UN Doc. A/58/546-S/2003/1053 of 30 October 2003, with its two corrigenda, UN Doc. A/58/546/Corr.1-S/2003/1053/Corr.1 of 20 February 2004 and UN Doc. A/58/546/Corr.2-S/2003/1053/Corr.2 of 19 April 2004.

[7] *Conference of Government Experts on the Reaffirmation and Development of International Humanitarian Law Applicable in Armed Conflicts: Vol. V* (Geneva: January 1971), 42.

## 2. The substantive rules

Were this chapter written at any point prior to the late 1990s, no doubt its focus would have been on the substantive law of internal armed conflict, berating its dearth. Today, the point can still be made, but to a far lesser degree, for there has been nothing short of a wholesale transformation of the applicable law. International humanitarian law instruments tend to extend to internal armed conflicts almost as a matter of course; and through the medium of customary international law in particular, very real developments have taken place. In terms of custom, two contributions stand out, namely the jurisprudence of the ad hoc international criminal tribunals and the customary international humanitarian law study concluded under the auspices of the ICRC.[8] Between the extension of conventional law and the growth of customary law, there exists a substantial body of international law applicable to internal armed conflicts.

The fact that the bulk of the transformation has taken place through the medium of custom has led to certain difficulties. We cannot point to a piece of paper containing the relevant rule and so evidencing its existence becomes rather more difficult. This leaves the existence of the rule open to challenge and predictably, on occasion, states have so challenged.[9] However, the general thrust of the transformation—that there is a body of international law of internal armed conflict—has been accepted by states and the broader international community. This in itself is a significant accomplishment. At some future point, the international community may wish to codify the customary law. However, it will be important to choose a propitious moment at which to do so, for the danger is that any codification exercise will end up proving regressive.

Given that we now have an international law of internal armed conflict, it is perhaps time to ask whether that body is fit for purpose, a question that involves various assessments. In particular, are there any gaps in the law? Two immediately stand out. The first relates to territory under the control of armed groups. Not infrequently, armed groups do exercise territorial control, yet international humanitarian law has little to say on point. This is surprising given the existence of the law of belligerent occupation. To be sure, there are important differences between that body of law and the situation at hand. However, the law of belligerent occupation could provide useful guidance in certain areas even if it cannot be drawn upon in others. For example, drawing on the law of belligerent occupation, armed groups could be considered under an obligation to keep law and order in the territory under their control and maintain orderly governance. This may require them to maintain existing administrative and local government structures. However, the law of belligerent occupation cannot be applied wholesale to internal

---

[8]  J.-M. Henckaerts and L. Doswald-Beck, *Customary International Humanitarian Law* (Cambridge: Cambridge University Press, 2005).

[9]  See, eg, J.B. Bellinger III and W.J. Haynes II, 'A US Government Response to the International Committee of the Red Cross Study *Customary International Humanitarian Law*', 89 IRRC (2007)443.

armed conflicts, to the taking of property, for example, given the tripartite relationship between the occupying power, occupied people, and displaced sovereign relationship in the law of belligerent occupation and the state and armed group relationship in the law of internal armed conflict. Armed groups that exercise territorial control may also be under an obligation to respect customary international human rights law, at least insofar as they have the capacity to do so. This would require them to refrain from torturing, restricting freedom of movement, and the like, even if they cannot actively provide food, education, and housing.

The second gap is that of combatant immunity and the associated prisoner of war status.[10] The traditional view is that persons taking up arms against the state cannot benefit from combatant immunity. Whether or not such individuals respect the law of internal armed conflict, they may be prosecuted and even sentenced to death. Accordingly, we are only able to appeal to the conscience of such persons when invoking international humanitarian law. Yet, self-interest is a hugely important motivating factor. Whether we like it or not, incentives make compliance with the law a more attractive option. Incentives could take the form of combatant immunity, ruling out of the death penalty, mitigation of sentence, anything that may motivate compliance.

A second assessment concerns the nature of the body of law that governs internal armed conflict. Today, a body of international law governs internal armed conflicts rather than a more limited body of international humanitarian law. Yet this broadening of scope has certain consequences that remain under-appreciated. For example, there is a growing view that human rights law offers greater protection to the individual and should therefore replace international humanitarian law in the regulation of internal armed conflict, at least when the violence is below the threshold of Protocol II, Additional to the 1949 Geneva Conventions. However, the consequences of a shift from regulation through international humanitarian law to regulation through human rights law have not been fully explored. For example, we would need to turn our attention to whether, and in what circumstances, armed groups have human rights obligations. There would also need to be a forum before which these obligations could be enforced.

At least the human rights–humanitarian law nexus is well recognized. The same is not true of other areas of international law from which there remains a reluctance to draw. For example, we apply the provisions on environmental protection contained in the law of armed conflict while only rarely turning to international environmental law to interpret them. International humanitarian law provisions on environmental protection tend to focus on modification of the environment or aspects of the environment that impact on humans.[11] Yet, if we were to consider international environmental law definitions of the environment, the air, water, soil, flora, and fauna would all be included. In international humanitarian law,

---

[10] See A. Cassese, Chapter 39, 'Should Rebels be Treated as Criminals?', in this volume.
[11] Convention on the Prohibition of Military or Any Other Hostile Use of Environmental Modification Techniques (1977); Protocol Additional to the Geneva Conventions of 12 August 1949 and Relating to the Protection of Victims of International Armed Conflicts (1977), Arts 54 and 55(1), as applicable to internal armed conflicts through customary international law.

the protection of fauna, for example, tends to be overlooked despite the very real impact of armed conflicts on fauna. If there is truly to be an international law of internal armed conflict, other areas of international law, to the extent relevant, need to be embraced.

A third assessment relates to the methodological approach by which the international law of internal armed conflict has developed. The development has taken place primarily by analogy to the law of international armed conflict. Rarely have norms been created to govern internal armed conflicts; rather, it has been a question of how far the law governing international armed conflicts can be extended. Yet there are important differences between internal armed conflicts and their international counterparts, principal among which are the actors that take part in each of them. International armed conflicts are traditionally fought between states; internal armed conflicts involve at least one armed group. A study needs to be undertaken to determine whether all rules now applicable in internal armed conflicts are within the capacity of armed groups, whether certain rules need tailoring to meet the involvement of this category of actor, and whether other norms are needed. This study could then be used by actors that enforce the law of armed conflict, such as national and international courts and tribunals. This leads neatly to a set of issues concerning armed groups themselves.

## 3. Armed groups

Armed groups are sometimes treated as if they are not *parties* to internal armed conflicts but as having some secondary status. Interaction with them on the part of the international community is limited. We frequently lack knowledge of their practice and have little sense of their views on the law. More often than not, at least insofar as the creation of the law is concerned, they are simply ignored. Some armed groups have purported to sign, ratify, or accede to treaties; however, these attempts have been turned down. Others have sought to enter into correspondence with international actors on issues of the law of armed conflict but that correspondence has been ignored.

At another level, armed groups are frequently called upon to comply with humanitarian law norms. If they genuinely seek to do so but fail to meet international standards, they are (understandably) criticized. But if armed groups then seek assistance in order to meet the relevant standard, the assistance tends not to be forthcoming. This is symptomatic of a broader issue. Armed groups, and to an extent states, too, are often criticized but rarely encouraged. If they violate a particular rule, this fact will be seized upon, but if they comply with a particular norm, this barely registers.

At still another level, armed groups are increasingly characterized as terrorists. In some respects, this is not new; in an earlier era, armed groups were characterized as criminals and bandits. However, in light of the present climate, characterization as terrorists has very real consequences, for example in certain states engagement with the group, even on humanitarian ideals, may fall foul of domestic legislation.[12]

There may be good reason for each of these approaches or reactions. From the perspective of traditional international law, it may well be correct to limit ratification of humanitarian law treaties to states alone. However, an explanation ought to be given to the armed group as to why their purported ratification was rejected and an alternative approach suggested. For example, 'only states may ratify the Geneva Conventions but you could indicate your acceptance of the norms contained therein through the issuance of a unilateral declaration of adherence.'

Greater regard should also be had to the ad hoc regulation of internal armed conflict through unilateral declarations, bilateral agreements, and the like, which is more prevalent than may be thought. One approach would be to give these materials a certain legal weight. Alternatively, they could be used as an indication of which humanitarian law rules are generally accepted and which are rather more troublesome while leaving the normative status of the rules intact. At the very least, they should provide a sense of what is possible, for example that amnesties are frequently granted. They may also help to dispel certain received wisdom, such as armed groups rarely accept the applicability of international humanitarian law.

Engagement with armed groups is an admittedly sensitive issue. States, the depositary of the Geneva Conventions included, need to maintain political relations with other states, as do UN entities. Non-governmental organizations (NGOs) may depend on the government in question for visas and the like. These third parties may be rightly fearful of being accused of intruding in the domestic affairs of states, or of legitimizing or increasing the status of armed groups by interacting with them. Third parties also may be reluctant to provide assistance to armed groups for fear of entrenching their control over territory or populations. However, the counterpart to lack of engagement and demonization is that, if armed groups are systematically ignored, consistently met with negative responses, or criticized even when good faith efforts are made, this will fail to induce compliance. Not only that, but it may lead to a decline even in attempts to meet humanitarian standards. An excessive focus on violations may also present a picture of total non-compliance, suggesting that only if the law is violated will the desired outcome—winning the conflict—be achieved.

## 4. Enforcement of the law

Enforcement of the law of armed conflict is rightly considered one of its principal failings. As just noted, the point should not be overstated; however, it remains a pertinent one. With the law of internal armed conflict in particular, an enforcement gap is evident. The Protecting Power system is inapplicable in situations of internal armed conflict. The International Humanitarian Fact-Finding Commission is

---

[12] See, eg, *Holder, Attorney General, et al v Humanitarian Law Project, et al,* Supreme Court of the United States, Judgment of 21 June 2010.

now accepted as applicable but to date has not been used. Belligerent reprisals, to the extent lawful, are not to be encouraged. Prosecution is important but cannot be relied upon by itself whether for jurisdictional constraints in the case of international courts or potential bias in the case of national courts. Monitoring and reporting by international organizations and NGOs is useful but gaining access is sometimes difficult. Dissemination and training are critical but provide no substitute for a strong enforcement system. This is not to say there is a total absence of possibilities.

Three relatively recent, novel, initiatives deserve greater attention, not least since they have had a certain measure of success. The first is a Swiss-based organization, 'Geneva Call'. Geneva Call has drawn up a 'Deed of Commitment' designed for armed groups (or 'armed non-state actors' in the language of Geneva Call), which contains obligations equivalent to those contained in the Ottawa Convention on Anti-Personnel Mines. At the time of writing, the Deed has been signed by 41 armed non-state actors. Signatories to the Deed have certain reporting obligations and a verification mechanism monitors allegations of non-compliance. Geneva Call reports that the vast majority of signatories have complied with the Deed,[13] and it is in the process of expanding its work to encompass children and gender.

The second novel approach has been undertaken by the UN Security Council. The Security Council has required certain listed state and non-state actors to conclude 'action plans' on the halting of the recruitment and use of child soldiers.[14] A working group of the Council monitors the development of, and compliance with, these action plans. Should action plans not be concluded or should they be violated, the Security Council has indicated that certain sanctions may be imposed.[15] In practice, a number of states and armed groups have concluded action plans and this has led to the demobilization and reintegration of child soldiers.[16] However, others have failed to conclude action plans and sanctions have not proven forthcoming. The process has recently been expanded to include killing, maiming, and sexual violence against children.[17]

The third initiative of interest is the arbitration between the Government of Sudan and the Sudan People's Liberation Movement/Army on the delimitation of the Abeyi area.[18] The particularities of the arbitration—between two recognized entities engaged in a territorial delimitation prior to two important referenda—may make it a unique situation rather than a potential precedent. Nevertheless, the possibility of arbitration in respect of allegations of violations of international humanitarian law may be worth further inquiry. A roster of independent legal and military experts could be drawn up, the services of whom would be triggered

---

[13]  See Geneva Call, *Engaging Armed Non-State Actors in a Landmine Ban: The Geneva Call Progress Report (2000–2007)*.

[14]  SC Res. 1539 (2004). For the listed entities, see Children and Armed Conflict: Report of the Secretary-General, UN Doc. A/63/785-S/2009/158 of 26 March 2009.

[15]  SC Res. 1539 (2004).

[16]  See, eg, Action Plan between the Moro Islamic Liberation Front (MILF) and the United Nations in the Philippines regarding the issue of Recruitment and Use of Child Soldiers in the Armed Conflict in Mindanao (1 August 2009).                    [17]  SC Res. 1882 (2009).

[18]  Final Award of 22 July 2009.

upon the request of the parties to the conflict. Each of the parties could select two members from the list, such members then selecting a fifth, presiding, arbitrator. The parties—or other affected and interested persons—would then present their case and the arbitrators would provide a binding opinion on point. This would not take the place of international criminal prosecution, but would form a complement to it.

These three initiatives suggest that although traditional enforcement approaches may be of limited value, more creative approaches may prove workable.

## 5. A possible way forward

The international law of internal armed conflict has gone through a wholesale transformation in recent years. However, this chapter has shown that gaps in, and difficulties with, the law remain. This section seeks to provide a concrete proposal that addresses the various concerns and which may allow us to move forward.

Armed groups are bound by international humanitarian law but international humanitarian law presupposes the existence of an armed conflict. Given the disinclination of states to recognize the existence of an armed conflict, and in the absence of a binding neutral assessor, international humanitarian law may prove inapplicable. Insofar as states are concerned, this is not overly problematic as international human rights law would fill any normative gap. With respect to armed groups, however, there may be a gap in protection. That armed groups have human rights obligations is a contested issue and one progressive view limits human rights obligations to armed groups that exercise territorial control.[19] However, it is unlikely that armed groups would exercise territorial control in situations of low intensity violence. Accordingly, in such situations, a normative gap exists. A new instrument designed to bind armed groups in all situations ought to be concluded. Of course, it would remain the case that armed groups are bound by their pre-existing obligations. The ICRC could also prompt them to declare that they will abide by this instrument.

The instrument would draw from international humanitarian law, international human rights law, and other relevant bodies of international law. It would also bring together the patchwork of treaty norms that pertain to internal armed conflicts, customary international law, as well as certain soft law standards such as the Guiding Principles on Internal Displacement. In order to conclude such an instrument, the various assessments considered in Section 2 necessarily would have to be undertaken. Accordingly, the creation of a new instrument would also afford an opportunity to assess the existing state of affairs.

The 'Fundamental Standards of Humanity' initiative could form a useful starting point in this regard. However, it would be but a starting point. It is crucial that

---

[19] See, eg, 'Human Rights in Palestine and Other Occupied Arab Territories', Report of the United Nations Fact-Finding Mission on the Gaza Conflict, UN Doc. A/HRC/12/48 of 25 September 2009, paras 305 and 1370.

armed groups be involved in the formulation of any new instrument that concerns them, for, as has been aptly remarked, '[n]o one would suggest revising the law of naval warfare without speaking with the navies'.[20] Inclusion of representatives of armed groups in the drafting process would provide certain actors within the armed group with increased exposure to international humanitarian law. It would also afford the international community points of contact within the group for engagement on humanitarian issues at a later stage. More importantly, the international community would get a better sense of the norms that armed groups find controversial, those norms that they have difficulty meeting, and those that are uncontested. This is not to say that the normative content should be sacrificed or watered down in light of the comments of armed groups. Indeed, the text should be drawn up by a group of experts. However, ultimately, the involvement of armed groups would provide the rules with a greater sense of realism.

Armed groups should also be able to sign up to the instrument as signature coupled with participation in the process may imbue armed groups with a greater sense of investment in the process as well as the norms that result from that process. Potentially, this could have a beneficial impact on compliance. This is not to suggest that states should not be involved in the creation of the instrument. On the contrary, they too should play an important role, whether in the form of meetings of state representatives, government experts, or as participating observers in meetings of armed groups. Particular use could be made of the views of those governments or states that were, until recently, armed groups, for example Kosovo (KLA), East Timor (FRETILIN), and Rwanda (RPF). It is unfortunate that more use is not made of the knowledge of such states in the period immediately after they gain statehood. Regardless of how the instrument is characterized—as a treaty, an agreement subject to international law, or a declaration—it would be binding on its signatories.

Given the relative dearth of enforcement measures, the instrument would need to contain strong provisions on implementation, dissemination, and enforcement. The instrument should require its signatories to 'translate' the instrument into orders, regulations, or directives internal to the armed group and in language that is understood by its members. It is of little use to the ordinary fighter to have detailed provisions drafted in an international instrument that are formulated in complicated legal terms. Without legal training—and even with—these provisions can be difficult to comprehend. The requirement of translation would ensure that the relevant norms are captured in simple language understandable to everyone. The translation imperative also serves a second purpose. Representatives of armed groups who participate in the creation of the instrument will probably be the elite of the group and members of the group's political wing or human rights division. For the law of internal armed conflict fully to realize its purpose, humanitarian dialogue should not be limited to elites but should include the ordinary fighter. The norms thus need to be translated across from the political wing, which in any

---

[20] M Sassòli, 'The Implementation of International Humanitarian Law: Current and Inherent Challenges', 10 Yearbook of IHL (2007) 45, 64.

event is often based outside the state in which the actual fighting takes place, to the military wing, and translated down the chain of command to the rank and file. Only in this way will the norms have a chance of being respected.

The instrument should also contain provisions on dissemination. Creative thinking is needed in this regard. For example, dissemination need not be limited to the written form. Rather, means of communication with which fighters are familiar should be utilized as far as possible, even at the expense of books and manuals to which lawyers would instinctively turn. Norms could be presented pictorially if there is a high level or illiteracy among fighters, for example in the form of comic books aimed at child soldiers. They could be broadcast by radio if, as in many places, radio is the predominant means of communication. Alternatively, they could be distributed by text message, if mobile phones are commonplace but writing materials are in short supply.

Monitoring and enforcement of the instrument is, of course, crucial. This should take place through a number of complementary means, not being reliant on any single one alone. Signatories to the instrument should have obligations of self-reporting. This would include the submission of progress reports on the obligations of translation and dissemination. More importantly, there would be an obligation to submit periodic reports responding to allegations of violation of the instrument and it would be incumbent on the armed group to explain the measures it has taken in response to the allegations. These allegations could come from the state, a third state, NGOs, or individual victims. This self-monitoring has the potential to continue fostering a sense of investment in the humanitarian law process and may lead to greater exposure of humanitarian norms amongst a broader community. It would also counter the idea that enforcement always comes from the outside, whether the state, NGOs, or international organizations.

Of course, self-monitoring cannot be relied upon alone for enforcement of the instrument. Rather, there needs to be an external monitoring mechanism in place to complement self-monitoring. Armed groups have to be aware that signing the instrument brings with it certain responsibilities and commitments that have to be honoured. Accordingly, there would be no possibility of opting out of the monitoring mechanism—with signature comes monitoring. There are various possible modalities for this external monitoring. Monitoring could be carried out by a standing body created by the instrument for that specific purpose. It could be a neutral body but with input from a representative of the armed group provided confidentiality allows. The armed group could even select the composition of the neutral monitoring body from a list of designated experts or organizations.

It should be stressed that this proposal is entirely realistic, for some of its aspects are already taking place, albeit on an ad hoc basis and to differing degrees. Armed groups often do commit themselves to various rules of international humanitarian law. Numerous armed groups have issued unilateral declarations committing themselves to the Geneva Conventions. Others have concluded bilateral agreements on international humanitarian law issues with the opposing state, the UN, or an NGO. Still others have codes of conduct, penal codes, or internal regulations which contain international humanitarian law ideals. Thus, there is certainly scope for the creation of an instrument to which armed groups would sign on.

Given the experience of the International Humanitarian Fact-Finding Commission, it may be thought that monitoring or enforcement of the instrument would be its failing. However, this does not have to be the case. In terms of monitoring, many signatories to the Geneva Call Deed of Commitment have reported on measures taken by them to implement the Deed. Other armed groups have responded to reports of UN entities and NGOs, countering allegations or disagreeing on what the law requires of them. These groups may be willing to undertake self-reporting. The same is true of enforcement. Some armed groups do discipline their members for committing violations of international humanitarian law. Furthermore, not infrequently, armed groups call on the international community to verify particular allegations made against them or issue what would seem to be standing invitations to investigate.[21] Armed groups should be taken up on these invitations and to the extent that they are bluffing, the bluff should be called. However, it may turn out that at least some armed groups are not bluffing, for Geneva Call has undertaken verification missions in response to allegations that certain signatories have not complied with their obligations under the Deed.[22]

Certainly, not all armed groups will sign on to an instrument. Others may sign on but with no intention of complying with their obligations. In this respect, armed groups are not unlike state parties to treaties. A mechanism that separates out those armed groups that take their obligations seriously from those that do not, and one which differentiates between those groups that claim to respect the law of internal armed conflict and those that actually do so would be an accomplishment in and of itself.

The principal disadvantage of this proposal is that some of the reciprocity between the parties to the conflict gets lost. The normative obligation for states continues to be derived from the mix of treaties and custom. For armed groups, the obligations stem from these same sources as well as the new instrument. However, as the armed groups would remain bound by treaties and custom, reciprocity of obligation is not in fact lost. Rather more difficult is the loss of reciprocity in respect of enforcement. For states, enforcement would be limited to the existing mechanisms; for armed groups, it would extend to the enforcement mechanisms of the newly created instrument. Viewed in this manner, states may not object to the creation of a new instrument. The instrument would be binding on armed groups at all times, thus characterization of the violence would be less important. Similarly, questions of status of the armed groups should not arise.

---

[21] See, eg, Karen National Union, 'Press Statement on Report of United Nations Secretary-General' (27 April 2009); Justice and Equality Movement, 'Accusations of UNICEF regarding use of child soldiers in the Sudan' (1 January 2009); Letter from Abd al-Malik Badr al-Din Al-houthi to Human Rights Watch (29/Jumada II/1430).

[22] Geneva Call, *Report of the 2009 Verification Mission to the Philippines to Investigate Allegations of Anti-Personnel Landmine Use by the Moro Islamic Liberation Front* (2010).

The better alternative would be to create a treaty open to states and armed groups alike, adopting the same framework as that set out above. Only this would ensure true reciprocity. However, serious thought needs to be given to whether the present climate is conducive to the creation of a new treaty involving states, particularly one in need of strong enforcement mechanisms. That may prove a little too utopian at the present time.

# 41

# Belligerent Occupation: A Plea for the Establishment of an International Supervisory Mechanism

*Orna Ben-Naftali*

## SUMMARY

Three main lessons can be drawn from some recent cases (the occupation of Gaza and that of Iraq): (i) an occupation is not an either/or situation—the decisive fact of 'effective control' (potential and actual) rather than the tag 'occupation' should determine the applicability of the law of occupation; (ii) the scope of the obligations of the foreign power which exercises effective control should derive from and relate to the scope of the control actually exercised; and (iii) an authoritative characterization of the situation by the Security Council—which took place in the case of Iraq but not in the case of Gaza—may often be required to delineate respective legal obligations and ensure no void in governance, including during transitional periods. It is undisputed that effective control by foreign military forces suspends, but does not transfer, sovereignty. The prohibition on annexation of an occupied territory is the normative consequence of this principle. Under current international law, and in view of the principle of self-determination, sovereignty remains vested in the occupied people. Belligerent occupation is a *sui generis* form of trust insofar as it carries with it a potential conflict of interests between the security needs of the occupant and the welfare of the inhabitants. The occupant is barred from instituting major changes in the occupied territory; this notion has its historical origins in the preservation of sovereignty, inclusive of the domestic governmental system, of the ousted rulers in Europe. The notion that an occupation is a temporary form of control that may not generate permanent results is undisputed. Indeed, it is implicit in both the principle that occupation does not confer title and in the conservation principle. The notion of limited duration further coheres with the exceptionality of the regime and highlights the need to resume as quickly as possible the normal international order of sovereign equality. Major shortcomings of the present legal regime are: (i) the lack of a rule setting time limits on the duration of an occupation and the attendant failure to determine the illegality of an indefinite occupation and (ii) the lack of congruence between self-determination and transformative objectives pursued by the occupant. While it is neither feasible nor desirable to renegotiate the law of belligerent occupation in order to rectify its shortcomings, the *sine qua non* for enabling some advancement of this law is the establishment of an international supervisory mechanism equipped with the means to fulfil a number of tasks including (a) monitoring that the occupying power applies the law on belligerent occupation by governing the territory and facilitating the re-establishment of local governance while protecting the humanitarian interests of the inhabitants and (b) holding the occupant accountable for violations of the relevant law through resort to reporting, judicial review, and, when necessary, enforcement. The oversight mechanism should be a standing, neutral body of professional experts (military and legal) established by and reporting to the Security Council.

## 1. Introduction

Belligerent occupation interrupts the international order. The international legal order seeks to regulate this interruption. This regulation is classified as part of international humanitarian law. Accordingly, it reflects the sensibility of 'the lesser evil':[1] the very phenomenon of occupation is assumed to be a necessary evil, and on the basis of this assumption, the law seeks to regulate it in a manner designed to minimize its painful consequences for the occupied civilian population and its disruptive effect on the international order.

The very reference to 'the lesser evil' raises a problem. This is partly because 'evil'—rather than 'good'—is accepted as the proper realm of thought and action and partly due to the strong affinity thereby suggested to cost–benefit analysis. The first reason tends to curb our political imagination (and to push the law even further towards its apologetic edge); the second, to pollute our moral and legal reasoning, at least in the context of humanitarian and human rights concerns. In a 'realistic utopia', the law of belligerent occupation (LBO) would work to prevent both effects: in order to guard against the first, it is imperative to make a clear distinction between the phenomenon of occupation as an interruption, an exception to the normal order of the international society, and to ensure that the legal order provides as quick as possible a return to normalcy. In order to prevent the second effect, it is necessary to ensure that the LBO is applied in a manner that distinguishes between utilitarianism (ie, the cost–benefit analysis that applies equally to both the giving and the receiving entities) and care for the well-being (and the minimization of suffering) of the weaker party, and gives preference to the latter. This contribution assesses whether the legal regime of occupation responds

---

[1]  See, eg, H. Arendt, *Responsibility and Judgment* (Jerome Kohn (ed.), New York: Shocken Books, 2005); M. Ignatieff, *The Lesser Evil: Political Ethics in an Age of Terror* (Princeton, NJ: Princeton University Press, 2004).

adequately to these challenges, identifies areas where change is required, and proposes ways to introduce it.

## 2. The international legal order's response to the challenge of occupation

The underlying principle of the international legal order rests on a presumption of sovereign equality between states, each exercising effective control over its territory and people.[2] Under current international law, sovereignty is understood as vested in the people, giving expression to their right to self-determination, a right conceived as the *sine qua non* for realizing freedom in its negative (freedom from coercion) and positive (freedom of choice) senses. This fundamental principle reflects the inherently pluralistic nature of the international order. This pluralism accounts for its fragility while simultaneously serving as a leitmotif for its enduring validity and further development. By the same token, utopian crusaders, each attempting to impose its particular vision on reality (often camouflaged as representing universal values), present the greatest threat to this order.[3]

An occupation consists of foreign military force exercising effective control over a territory over which it has no sovereign title and without the volition of the sovereign.[4] Analytically, an occupation presents the international order with the challenge of the exceptional: the severance of the link between sovereignty and effective control entailed in an occupation, suspends the normal order as it relates to the occupied territory.[5] International law seeks to regulate this interruption. Such regulation signifies both the need to distinguish between order and chaos and the need to distinguish between the rule and the exception: in distinguishing between order and chaos, its function is to govern the situation; to prevent anarchy by entrusting the occupying power with governing the occupied territory; in distinguishing between the rule and the exception, its function is to establish the conditions that would enable as swift as possible a return to the normal order of the international society. This is the role of the LBO which, unsurprisingly, transplants the basic tenets of a domestic emergency regime to the international sphere.[6] Any assessment of this law should thus begin with an understanding of its normative

---

[2] Art. 2(1) of the UN Charter.

[3] It is unnecessary in this context to dive into the deep waters of the dialectics between the universal and the particular. It is sufficient to point out that in a pluralistic world order a properly constituted collective actor is a better agency for safeguarding universal values than a single power. This 'second order' solution is discussed in the concluding section.

[4] E. Benvenisti, *The International Law of Occupation*, 2nd edn (Princeton, NJ: Princeton University Press, 2004), 4.

[5] This notion of suspension was already recognized in the first attempt to codify the LBO, in the Brussels Declaration. See Final Protocol and Project of an International Declaration Concerning the Laws and Customs of War, 27 August 1874, reprinted in D. Schindler and J. Toman (eds), *The Laws of Armed Conflicts: A Collection of Conventions, Resolutions and other Documents*, 3rd edn (Dordrecht: Martinus Nijhoff, 1988), 25.

[6] An emergency regime, the roots of which date back to the Roman-Commissarial model, rests on three precepts: exceptionality; limited scope of powers; and temporary duration. See O. Ben-Naftali,

framework and proceed to evaluate the degree to which the rules and procedures comprising it adequately provide for the desired outcome in the light of the lessons learned from the practice of occupations.

## 3. The normative regime of belligerent occupation

### (A) The normative framework

The normative regime which governs this exceptional situation is the LBO. This law is part of the laws of war (*jus in bello*), currently referred to as international humanitarian law, to convey a shift in emphasis from regulating relations between states to protecting the human person. This branch of law is distinct from the law regulating the initial use of force (*jus ad bellum*). While the latter inquires whether the initial use of force was legal, international humanitarian law does not concern itself with this question and prescribes rules applicable to all parties to a conflict regardless of their responsibility for the initial use of force. The relevant normative framework of the LBO consists of the 1907 Hague Regulations Respecting the Laws and Customs of War on Land; the Fourth Geneva Convention Relative to the Protection of Civilians Persons in Times of War (GCIV) and its Additional Protocols I and II of 1977. Over the past decades it has been accepted that international humanitarian law provides the specific, but not the exclusive law governing occupation (*lex specialis*), and that it is complemented by international human rights law.[7]

### (i) Triggering the LBO

The application of the LBO is triggered, in the language of Article 42 of the Hague Regulations, once a 'territory is actually placed under the authority of a hostile army. The occupation extends only to the territory where such authority has been established and can be exercised.'

This text fails to clarify the relationship between actual ('actually placed under the authority') and potential ('can be exercised') authority. Later developments have clarified that three cumulative conditions have to be met to initiate the application of the LBO: (i) physical presence of hostile troops in a foreign territory; (ii) the troops have the potential of exercising effective governmental authority; and (iii) the previous government is incapable of exercising its authority effectively.[8]

---

A.M. Gross, and K. Michaeli, 'Illegal Occupation: The Framing of the Occupied Palestinian Territory', 23(3) Berkeley Int'l. LJ (2005) 551–614.

[7] See, eg, *Legality of the Threat or Use of Nuclear Weapons,* Advisory Opinion, ICJ Reports 1996, 226, para. 25; *Consequences of the Construction of a Wall in the Occupied Palestinian Territory,* Advisory Opinion, ICJ Reports 2004, p 136, para. 106; *Armed Activities on the Territory of the Congo (Democratic Republic of the Congo v Uganda)*, Judgment, ICJ Reports 2005, 168, paras 216–17. See, generally, O. Ben-Naftali (ed.), *International Humanitarian Law and International Human Rights Law* (Oxford: Oxford University Press, 2011).

[8] Eg *US v List (Hostages Case)*, VIII Law Reports of Trials of Major War Criminals 38 (1949), at 55–6; *Prosecutor v Naletilić,* Judgment of 31 March 2003 (ICTY Trial Chamber), para. 217; HCJ 102/82 *Tsemel v Minister of Defense* 37(3) PD 365 (1983) (Israel); the *US Army Field Manual,*

The explicit inclusion of the potential for control was designed to ensure that there is no void in governing the area by obligating an occupant to shoulder governmental responsibilities vis-à-vis the inhabitants.[9] Article 47 of the GCIV, forbidding the transfer of governmental authority from the occupant to a pliant government, which lacks effective control, underscores this rationale.

The relationship between these three conditions is dynamic. Thus, for instance, it could be posited that given the potential effectively to control an area without physical presence of troops on the ground, the condition related to the potential for control should have greater weight in determining the application of the LBO. The 2005 Israeli disengagement from the Gaza Strip provides an excellent example: Israel withdrew its forces from the Gaza Strip, but continues to exercise effective control over the Strip's air and maritime space, land borders, population registration records, and economy. Israel's at-will incursions and operations in the area further attest to its potential effectively to control it. A dynamic approach would not relieve it of responsibility as an occupant, at least as regards the issues over which it exercises its control effectively and precludes the local government from exercising effective control.[10]

The proclaimed end of the occupation of Iraq and the concurrent assumption of authority by the Iraqi Interim Government on 28 June 2004, lend further support to the merits of a dynamic approach. In this case, foreign forces remained very much present in the territory, and the authority of the Interim Government of Iraq was limited in key areas where the occupying powers had retained effective control. Even assuming that the Interim Government was neither a sham nor otherwise a client government and that it genuinely invited the continued presence of foreign troops, the fact remains that effective control was shared by the hitherto occupying powers and the local government.[11]

Both these examples further identify a lacuna in the LBO: as the law assumes that the occupying power shoulders the responsibility for maintaining governmental structures and services throughout the occupation, it does not provide a framework for transferring power from the occupying to the local authorities.[12] Given

---

Department of the Army, Field Manual 27–10: The Law of Land Warfare, 18 July 1956 (rev. 15 July 1976); the UK Ministry of Defence, *Manual of the Law of Armed Conflict*, ch. 11 (2004).

[9] It is for this reason that the dictum of the International Court of Justice which considered that physical presence of foreign troops and lack of authority on the part of the previous government are sufficient conditions lacks persuasive power. See *Armed Activities on the Territory of the Congo*, n 7, at para. 173.

[10] Report of the Special Rapporteur on the situation of human rights in the Palestinian territories occupied since 1967, John Dugard, UN Doc A/62/275, paras 10–11; N. Stephanopoulos, 'Israel's Legal Obligations to Gaza After the Pullout', 31 Yale JIL (2006) 524–8 at 525–6. For a view that Israel no longer occupies the Gaza Strip see Y. Shany, 'Faraway, So Close: The Legal Status of Gaza after Israel's Disengagement', 8 YIHL (2006) 369–83.

[11] See A. Roberts, 'The End of Occupation: Iraq 2004', 54(1) ICLQ (2005) 27–48.

[12] Art. 6 of GCIV assumes that authority would be transferred back to the local government within one year after the general close of military operations, but fails to provide either a framework for this transfer or guidance for occasions where the assumption is defied by reality. See text below and n 33.

the dynamic relations between the three conditions upon which the applicability of the law depends, such a framework is required.

Three main lessons can be drawn from these examples: first, an occupation, unlike pregnancy, is not an either/or situation. The decisive fact of 'effective control' (potential and actual) rather than the tag 'occupation' should determine the applicability of the law of occupation.[13] Secondly, the scope of the obligations of the foreign power which exercises effective control should derive from and relate to the scope of the control actually exercised.[14] Finally, an authoritative characterization of the situation by the Security Council—which existed in the case of Iraq[15] but not in the case of Gaza—may often be required to delineate respective legal obligations and ensure no void in governance, including during transitional periods. The role the Security Council could play is discussed in Section 5.

## (B) The basic tenets of the LBO

### (ii) Sovereignty is distinct from occupation and occupation does not confer title

Effective control by foreign military forces suspends, but does not transfer sovereignty. The prohibition on annexation of an occupied territory is the normative consequence of this principle.[16] Under current international law, and in view of the principle of self-determination, sovereignty remains vested in the occupied people.

This principle is currently undisputed. Its development merits attention for two reasons: first, because change over time is hardly ever a linear process of progression and present unease with the phenomenon of occupation resonates past conflicts. Secondly, because changes that did occur over time demonstrate the adaptability of the LBO to political realities, a quality it still retains. It is thus worthwhile to take count, albeit briefly, of this development.

The roots of the principle of the inalienability of sovereignty date back to the post-Napoleonic wars and the restoration of a European order designed to protect the sovereignty of the ruler from intervention by another state. Given that the political legitimacy of European rulers at the time was based on either dynastic monarchy or popular democracy, the principle was designed to accommodate both systems and minimize disruption by preventing one from overthrowing the other.[17] In the relationship between the European and the non-European world, conquest remained a legally valid way to acquire sovereignty until the twentieth century.[18] The gradual renunciation by the international community of the use of force as an acceptable policy coupled with decolonization processes and the

---

[13] See F.S. Cohen, 'Transcendental Nonsense and the Functional Approach', 35(6) Columbia L Rev (1935) 809–49.        [14] Art. 6 of GCIV supports this construction.

[15] SC Res. 1546 (2004).

[16] S.P. Sharma, *Territorial Acquisition, Disputes and International Law* (The Hague: Kluwer Law International, 1997), 148.

[17] E. Benvenisti, 'The Origins of the Concept of Belligerent Occupation', 26(3) L & Hist Rev (2008) 621–48; N. Bhuta, 'The Antinomies of Transformative Occupation', 16(4) EJIL (2005) 721–40.

[18] S. Korman, *The Right of Conquest: The Acquisition of Territory by Force in International Law and Practice* (New York: Oxford University Press, 1996), 9.

ensuing right to self-determination, have internationalized the hitherto exclusively European order. Accordingly, the LBO prohibition on annexation of territory, differentiating between occupation and sovereignty, coheres with the corpus of general international law core principles of sovereign equality, self-determination, and non-intervention.[19] Given, however, that such principles have not been inscribed on a *tabula rasa*, it is little wonder that the very occurrence of an occupation echoes the sorry story of the 'civilizing mission' and that 'alien occupation' of whatever type has been grouped together with colonial domination, racist regimes,[20] and related practices of subjugation, domination, and exploitation.[21] This sensibility is the Ariadne's thread that runs through the divide between sovereignty and foreign occupation. It implies that the very phenomenon of occupation is viewed with suspicion and is likely to generate resentment and resistance. This is *a fortiori* the case with prolonged occupations and with occupations that purport to replace the sociopolitical system of the occupied territory with a system akin to that of the occupying power, that is, 'transformative occupations'. The association between such attempts and imperialism may well explain why the various international interventions of the 1990s shied away from either describing themselves as occupations or indeed from referring to the LBO. From this perspective, the admission by George W. Bush that the US and British troops occupying Iraq were 'welcomed, but it was not a peaceful welcome',[22] and the subsequent resurgence should not have come as a surprise. Foreign occupation connotes subjugation, not liberation. The distinction between sovereignty and occupation, and the consequential limits placed on the governmental authority of the occupant, discussed below, reflect this understanding.

### (iii) Occupation is a form of trust that precludes the introduction of major systemic change

The basic rule regulating the governmental authority of the occupant is articulated in Article 43 of the Hague Regulations. Under this rule, the occupant is vested with the authority 'to take all the measures in his power to restore, and ensure, as far as possible, public order and safety/civil life, while respecting, unless absolutely prevented, the laws in force in the country.'[23] This rule, thus, imposes two categories of obligations on the occupant: (i) to protect the inhabitants' life, property, and livelihood and (ii) to respect the existing legal, economic, and sociopolitical institutions in the territory.

---

[19] See UN Charter, Arts (2), 2(1), 2(4), 2(7), and 55.     [20] Art. 4, Additional Protocol I.

[21] See the Declaration on Principles of International Law Concerning Friendly Relations and Co-operation among States in Accordance with the Charter of the United Nations, GA Res. 2625, 25th Session (1970).

[22] In an interview with Brian Williams, NBC News, 12 December 2005, cited in A. Roberts, 'Transformative Military Occupation: Applying the Laws of War and Human Rights', 100 AJIL (2006) 580–622, at 616.

[23] For the discussion between the French and the English versions of Art. 43 of the Hague Regulations see Y. Dinstein, 'Legislation under Article 43 of the Hague Regulations: Belligerent Occupation and Peace-Building', Harvard Program on Humanitarian Policy and Conflict Research, Occasional Paper No. 1, 2004, at 2–4.

The first category reflects humanitarian concerns.[24] It has evolved over time to incorporate the concept of trusteeship, the beneficiaries of which are the inhabitants of the territory.[25] Admittedly, this is a *sui generis* form of trust insofar as it carries with it a potential conflict of interests between the security needs of the occupant and the welfare of the inhabitants. In the nineteenth-century context, this framework produced two primary rules: the occupant was mainly incumbent with the negative duty of refraining from infringing on the most basic rights of the inhabitants, while the latter were incumbent with a duty of obedience to the occupant.[26] Over time, the scale began to tip to the side of the inhabitants: the GCIV seems to reject the idea that the occupied population was under any obligation to obey the occupant.[27] In parallel, it has considerably expanded the protection due to the inhabitants, in respect of both negative and positive duties. This process has culminated with the co-application of international humanitarian law and international human rights law, inclusive of the right to self-determination, to occupied territories. Nevertheless, the GCIV explicitly subjects some of the guarantees afforded to the population to military necessity and conditions[28] and empowers the occupant to take various measures against protected persons.[29] It is thus clear that situations where the occupation is met with strong resistance in general (eg the occupation of Iraq), or produces such resistance due to its prolonged duration (the occupation of the Palestinian territory being the quintessential example) threaten the viability of this precarious balance.

The second category of obligations, which prohibits the occupant from instituting major changes in the occupied territory, has its origins in the above discussed preservation of the sovereignty, inclusive of the domestic governmental system, of the ousted rulers in Europe. This limitation on the authority of the occupant was incorporated and further detailed in the GCIV.[30] Currently known as the 'conservation principle', it highlights the distinction between temporary occupation and sovereignty.[31] Given that the latter is attached to the occupied people, the principle protects local self-determination. In this context,

---

[24] Originating in the principle of distinction between civilians and combatants, see Benvenisti, n 17, at 624–7.

[25] *Construction of a Wall*, n 7, at para. 88; Separate Opinion of Judge Koroma, para. 2, explicitly stated that occupied territories 'constitute...a sacred trust, which must be administered as a whole in the interests both of the inhabitants and the legitimate sovereign or the duly constituted successor in title'; Cf Separate Opinion of Judge Higgins, para. 2; Separate Opinion of Judge Kooijmans, para. 33.

[26] R.R. Baxter, 'The Duty of Obedience to the Belligerent Occupant', 27 BYIL (1950) 235–66.

[27] Eg the terms 'war rebellion' and 'war treason' were not incorporated in the Convention. Furthermore, while providing the occupant with the right to take measures against protected persons who carry out acts detrimental to the security of the occupant, (Arts 27, 64), it nevertheless preserves most of their rights under the Convention (Arts 5 and 68).

[28] Eg Arts 27, 49, 51, and 53 of the GCIV.

[29] Promulgating penal laws (Art. 64), assigning residence (Art. 78), and internment (Art. 42).

[30] Article 64.

[31] J.L. Cohen, 'The Role of International Law in Post-Conflict Constitution-Making: Toward a Jus Post Bellum for "Interim Occupations"', 51 NY Law School L Rev (2006–07) 496–532 at 498–9.

too, both transformative and prolonged occupations threaten the viability of this principle: the former because the objective of redesigning the existing system stands in direct conflict with its conservation; the latter because maintaining the status quo may well become a mandate for stagnation and defy the obligation to promote the welfare of the inhabitants. This point invites a discussion of the third tenet of the LBO.

### (iv) Occupation is a temporary form of control

The idea that an occupation is a temporary form of control that may not generate permanent results is undisputed. Indeed, it is implicit in both the principle that occupation does not confer title and in the conservation principle. The notion of limited duration further coheres with the exceptionality of the regime and high-lights the need to resume as quickly as possible the normal international order of sovereign equality.

The greatest challenge to this principle comes not only from reality,[32] but from law itself: the law of occupation, while providing for the provisional status of the occupation regime, does not set time limits on its duration. This absence of time limits has been construed to mean that an occupation can continue indefinitely. This construction obfuscates the crucial distinction between the 'temporary' and the 'indefinite': a temporary situation definitely has an end; an indefinite situation may, or may not, have an end. Indeed, if an occupation could continue indefinitely, the interests it is designed to protect would all become meaningless: (i) the interest of the inhabitants in regaining control over their life and exercise their right to self-determination; (ii) the interest of the international system in resuming the normal order of sovereign equality between states; and (iii) the interest of the very international rule of law in maintaining the distinction between and the norm (the principle of sovereign equality) over the exception (occupation) and the superiority of the former over the latter.[33]

---

[32] Eg the Israeli occupation of the Palestinian Territory, the occupation of northern Cyprus by Turkish forces. See, generally, A. Roberts, 'Prolonged Military Occupation: The Israeli Occupied Territories Since 1967', 84 AJIL (1990) 44–103 at 50–1.

[33] Art. 6 of the GCIV is the only provision that tackles directly the issue of the duration of an occu-pation. It does so, alas, in an implausible manner, providing for the continued applicability of only some of the Convention's provisions. This may well be construed by occupying powers as limiting their obligations towards the inhabitants precisely in situations where greater protection is needed. Indeed, the text indicates the drafters' assumption that occupations would normally be of short duration. Once it became clear that this assumption was defied by reality and that it may generate counter-productive results, the provision was abrogated: Art. 3(b) of Additional Protocol I provides for the application of the LBO until the termination of the occupation. It does not, however, provide for time limits for its duration. See *Construction of a Wall*, n 7, Separate Opinion of Judge El Araby, para. 3.1; Separate Opinion of Judge Koroma, para. 2; O. Ben-Naftali, '"À La Recherche du Temps Perdu": Rethinking Article 6 of the Fourth Geneva Convention in the Light of the Construction of the Wall Advisory Opinion', 38(1–2) Israel L Rev (2005) 211–29.

# 4. Evaluating the normative regime

## (A) The question

The normative regime of occupation is over a century old. It was subject to two legislative revisions, each responding to lessons learned from then prevailing political realities, while nevertheless enacted within the existing legal framework. Is it feasible and is it desirable to maintain this framework for the twenty-first century? The answer depends on an evaluation of both the achievements and the drawbacks of the current regime and on appreciation of alternatives.

## (B) The major accomplishments of the present normative regime

### (i) The position of the LBO within the framework of the jus in bello

The positioning of the LBO within the framework of the *jus in bello*/international humanitarian law is an important asset to be maintained. This is so because (i) the distinction between the *jus ad bellum* and the *jus in bello* underscores the importance of humanitarian protection regardless of the justification for the initial use of force; (ii) the distinction between occupation and *jus post bellum* remains important: transformative/nation-building occupations aspire to effect fundamental change after forceful interventions in an area. This very attempt, however, often triggers violent insurgency, thus defying any post-*bellum* reality and requiring the application of humanitarian law; (iii) the application of international humanitarian law to both international and internal armed conflicts allows for a modified extension of the law of occupation to armed groups that occupy a territory; and (iv) international humanitarian law is one of the oldest branches of international law. While pedigree itself does not guarantee obedience, it nevertheless commands respect and legitimacy.[34] These are meaningful assets.

### (ii) The merits of the core principles of the LBO

The core principles of the LBO, making a clear distinction between the norm of sovereign equality and the exception of occupation, have acquired more, not less, persuasive force over the years. This is so especially in view of the right to self-determination. The fact that the international community generally withholds recognition from annexation (eg the reaction to the annexation of East Jerusalem and the Golan Heights by Israel; the attempt by Iraq to annex Kuwait) and the concurrent demand that the inhabitants remain protected under the LBO, attest to the validity of this point.

### (iii) The adaptability of the law to change over time

The existing framework has proved to be extremely adaptable to changing realities. This is mainly due to: (i) the elasticity of the concept of occupation which,

---

[34] T. Franck, *The Power of Legitimacy among Nations* (New York: Oxford University Press, 1990).

once defined in terms of (actual and potential) effective foreign control can accommodate and apply to varying types of occupations; (ii) the amenability of Article 42 of the Hague Regulations, qualifying the substantive limitations on the occupant's regulative authority by the 'unless absolutely prevented' proviso, to expansive interpretation; (iii) the realistic recognition, explicit in numerous rules, of the need to balance the occupant's responsibility for the welfare of the inhabitants' with its own security considerations; and (iv) the introduction of international human rights law into the law of occupation as both an interpretative tool and as a complementary system of rights, obligations, and compliance mechanisms. Security Council Resolution 1483 on the composite legal framework applicable to the occupation of Iraq underscores the enduring quality of an adjustable LBO. At the same time, this very resolution has arguably stretched the contours of the regime of occupation beyond its proper boundaries. This brings us to consideration of the limitations and lacunae of the existing framework.

## (C) The major shortcomings of the present normative regime

### (i) Lack of time limits on the duration of occupation

The elasticity of the legal regime of occupation comes at some cost, the highest of which may be the blurring of its boundaries and, ergo, the obfuscation and even the reversal of the relationship between the norm and the exception. The regime is least susceptible to such transgression when the antinomy between sovereignty and foreign control is most determinate. The clear rule that occupation does not confer title and that annexation is illegal meets this standard. By the same token, the lack of a rule setting time limits on the duration of an occupation and the attendant failure to determine the illegality of an indefinite occupation fails to meet this standard and renders the regime most susceptible to substituting the exception for the rule. This is a clear defect in the law.

### (ii) Lack of congruence between self-determination and transformative objectives

In the shadowland between the exception and the rule lies the difference in the substantive scope and substance of the governing authority between an occupant and a sovereign. The presumption against institutional change underlying the 'conservation' principle (and, currently, safeguarding self-determination) was designed to maintain this difference; 'transformative' occupations obscure it. It is at this point of interpretative indeterminacy that both the malleable classification of an 'occupation' and the introduction of the human rights discourse into the law of occupation become a double-edged sword. This predicament requires some clarification.

A belligerent occupation, much like that famous rose, is still an occupation even if by any other name.[35] The common denominator of all types of occupations is

---

[35] 'What's in a name? that which we call a rose by any other name would smell as sweet', Shakespeare, *Romeo and Juliet* (Act II, Scene II).

the exercise of various degrees of effective control by foreign power(s) against the volition of the sovereign. More often than not, the more changes introduced by the foreign power(s), the greater the resistance they trigger. The LBO should apply to all such situations. If, however, the foreign presence is welcomed and meets neither meaningful resistance from the population nor strong opposition from the state the territory of which is occupied, the situation is not, or ceases to be that of, belligerency and the presence of the troops should properly be classified as *occupatio pacifica*, to which the LBO does not apply. This distinction means that it is neither the initial intervention, nor the objective of the foreign presence, nor indeed an authorization by the Security Council, that determines the applicability of the LBO. Thus, the UN presence facilitating nation-building in Cambodia was not an occupation subject to the LBO, but such presence in Somalia, Liberia, Haiti, East Timor, and Kosovo was up to a point subject to that law, as was the coalition's occupation of Iraq and as remains, among others, the Israeli occupation over Palestinian territories. The distinction underscored by the GCIV's provision against the construction of fake consent, further means that the application of the LBO is case-sensitive and highlights the need to fill a lacuna in the LBO by providing for a gradual transfer of governmental authority from the occupant to the local population.

This classification of situations that fall within the framework of the LBO means that transformative and nation-building occupations may well be subject to that law. This, in turn, begs the question of the relationship between transformative objectives and the conservation principle.

Viewed from the perspective of the conservation principle, a 'transformative occupation' mocks the law. Indeed, when measured against the idea that an occupation is distinct from sovereignty and that, therefore, it is necessary to preserve the decision-making capacity of the sovereign in matters pertaining to its socio-political and economic profile, that is, its right to self-determination, the very concept of 'transformative occupation' is an oxymoron which challenges the basic assumptions of the LBO.[36]

Viewed from the perspective of human rights, however, 'transformative occupations', designed to substitute a democratic for a despotic form of government, arguably create the conditions of possibility for self-determination. From this perspective, the argument has been made that a law that fails to advance this objective is anachronistic and should be updated.[37] A somewhat less radical variation of this view holds that resort to dynamic interpretations allows for the reconciliation of transformative objectives with the conservation principle without a legislative reform.[38]

---

[36] Bhuta, n 17; N. Bhuta, 'New Modes and Orders: The Difficulties of a Jus Post-Bellum of Constitutional Transformations', 60(3) U Toronto LJ (2010) 799–854.

[37] See, eg, G.H. Fox, 'The Occupation of Iraq', 36(2) Georgetown JIL 196 (2004–05) 195–298.

[38] Eg a liberal interpretation of the 'unless absolutely prevented' proviso of Art. 43 of the Hague Regulations; reading the law of occupation in the broader context to align it to developments in international human rights law and ensure the harmonization of international legal obligations, as sanctioned by Art. 31(3)(c) of the Vienna Convention on the Law of Treaties and indeed in the light

Legal texts are often susceptible to creative interpretations. It does not follow that such interpretations are always either convincing or advisable. Indeed, occupying to bring about self-determination seems as sensible and genuine as divorcing to save a marriage. There is a huge difference between repealing existing laws and institutions that are unacceptable from a human rights perspective and transforming the sociopolitical system in an occupied territory: the former is reconcilable with the conservation principle; the latter is not. It is in fact a project that defies the LBO, may well generate abuse of human rights and jeopardize the legitimacy of both the human rights discourse and the very rule of international law: it defies the LBO because it substitutes the occupant for the sovereign; it often generates abuse of human rights committed by occupying powers fighting to squash violent resistance which the attempted transformation generates; insofar as the human right to self-determination is violated, rather than advanced, by a foreign occupation, it renders hollow the human rights discourse. In sacrificing the pluralism inherent in the international system at the altar of a utopian (and self-interested) vision of a hegemonic power, it replaces an imperialistic for an international rule of law. It does not follow that the LBO does not continue to govern 'transformative occupations', but it does mean that the law is violated by the occupying power. An authorization by the Security Council, its political wisdom notwithstanding, may well render transformative actions legal, but such legality neither resides in nor, well, transforms the LBO.[39]

## 5. The way forward

The LBO has been designed to manage an emergency situation in a manner that would facilitate the resumption of the normal order of the international society. Its tacit assumptions are that: (i) managing a bad reality is better, from a humanitarian perspective, than anarchy; (ii) external self-determination is better, from the perspective of both freedom and equality, than foreign rule; and (iii) the pluralistic Westphalian order is better, from a realistic perspective, than any post-Westpahlian self-ordained, allegedly universal consciousness which purports to mould foreign experience in its own image. Change over time has vindicated the sensibility and enduring validity of these assumptions while simultaneously clarifying areas where the legal regime of occupation falls short of realizing its objectives.

It is neither feasible nor desirable nor indeed necessary to renegotiate the LBO in order to rectify its shortcomings. It is not feasible primarily because there is no consensus over the core issues ranging from humanitarian/transformative intervention and occupation, to the scope of the right to self-determination, the

---

of the co-application of human rights law and international humanitarian law. See, eg, Roberts, n 22, at 620–2.

[39] Art. 103 of the UN Charter.

definition of sovereignty, and the notion of asymmetrical conflicts, to name a few. It is undesirable because underlying these disagreements are not merely conflicts over territory and other resources but the deep resentment associated with ethnicity, identity, culture, and the North–South divide. Such passions may well generate the cutting of the nose of the LBO to spite the face of international humanitarian law in its entirety. The debacle of the 2001 Durban Conference—poignantly followed by the 9/11 spectacle—and the consequential shifting of priorities from international justice to national security (and to 'transformative' occupations), all advise against such a move. Finally, such renegotiation is unnecessary because there are better alternatives to advance the objectives of the regime of occupation.

The *sine qua non* for enabling such advancement is the establishment of an *international supervisory mechanism* entrusted with the responsibility and equipped with the means to:

(i) determine that the situation qualifies as an occupation;

(ii) receive from the occupant a clear plan for the governing of the territory, for the envisioned duration of the occupation, and for the orderly transfer of authority to the local population

(iii) review and, when necessary, revise the plan;

(iv) supervise the implementation of the plan;

(v) monitor that the occupying power(s) apply the LBO by governing the territory and facilitating the re-establishment of local governance while protecting the humanitarian interests of the inhabitants; and

(vi) hold the occupant(s) accountable for violations of the LBO through resort to reporting, judicial review, and, when necessary, enforcement.[40]

In the case of state(s) occupation, as distinct from an occupation by an international agent, it should be possible to determine that the occupation has become illegal; demand withdrawal and, when necessary, replace the occupant with an international force.

The oversight mechanism should be a standing, neutral body of professional experts (military and legal) established by and reporting to the Security Council. Its membership should rectify some of the glaring inadequacies of the composition of the Councl (ie, the coexistence of permanent and non-permanent members), reflect the plurality of experience with occupation (ie, some members should be drawn from nations that have been occupied and occupants), but exclude, in the case of a specific state occupation, experts from that state. Such a body, while not replacing the Security Council and indeed subject to it, would nevertheless operate

---

[40] The need for an international oversight mechanism and the role the Security Council should assume has been identified by various scholars, eg B.C. Parsons, 'Moving the Law of Occupation into the Twenty-First Century', 57 Naval L Rev (2009) 1–49; S.R. Ratner, 'Foreign Occupation and International Territorial Administration: The Challenges of Convergence', 16(4) EJIL (2005) 695–719; Cohen, n 13; R. Falk, 'Some Legal Reflections on Prolonged Israeli Occupation of Gaza and the West Bank', 2(1) J Refugee Stud (1989) 40–51 at 46.

as a constraining force (especially necessary when the Council is dominated by one power) on both the Council and on occupying power(s). The resulting substantive and procedural *multilateralization* of occupation may well enjoy greater legitimacy and ensure a better attainment of the objectives of the occupation regime, that is, that the 'lesser evil' of foreign rule is effectively superseded by a better reality of self-government.

# 42

# Modern Means of Warfare: The Need to Rely upon International Humanitarian Law, Disarmament, and Non-Proliferation Law to Achieve a Decent Regulation of Weapons

*Natalino Ronzitti*

## SUMMARY

The problem with traditional criteria for restricting the use of certain weapons is that they are unclear and thus unable to set a prohibition, or that they are obsolete, since they regulate weapons no more in use or of no specific military value. At present disarmament and international humanitarian law employ two different techniques for regulating weapons. While disarmament prohibits the build-up and stockpiling of weapons, humanitarian law regulates their use. The modern law on weapons is a combination of disarmament and humanitarian law. There are three techniques for prohibiting weapons and making their use a criminal offence: (i) simply listing prohibited weapons; (ii) listing such weapons and asking states to enact penal legislation for their prohibition; or (iii) making the use of such weapons an international crime. A topical issue is that of the use of drones. They should be operated in conformity with rules of international humanitarian law and kept under control. For instance, if they drop weapons against a military target in a populated area, the collateral damage caused by the attack should be in keeping with the principle of proportionality. With regard to possible future changes, it must be said that international humanitarian law is not the only way to achieve decent regulation of weapons. Arms control, non-proliferation, and disarmament instruments should be used to achieve a more suitable result. The choice of instruments available is also important. The indeterminacy and lacunae of customary international law makes it ill-suited for disarmament. Treaties are necessary for international humanitarian law, that is, for prohibiting the use of specific weapons. However, one should also rely on soft law for managing non-proliferation regimes and even arms control. As far as disarmament is concerned, one may rely on treaties for stating the obligation of non-production and stockpiling and on soft law for verification, whenever treaty obligations on monitoring are difficult to negotiate. Moreover, soft law instruments may be transformed into hard law as soon as the political conditions make the transformation feasible. In the framework of non-proliferation, Security Council resolutions are of paramount importance.

## 1. The traditional principles

The law of armed conflict does not grant belligerents the right to employ whatever weapons they like. Certain weapons are prohibited. There are two main ways to achieve prohibition. One involves a general criterion forbidding weapons which may cause consequences contrary to international humanitarian law, and the other is a treaty specifically identifying the weapons which are prohibited. While the former has the advantage of keeping the prohibition up to date with technological developments, it is often too vague and difficult to apply. The latter does not suffer from this shortcoming, since the weapons that are prohibited are listed. However, states often try to circumvent the prohibition by developing new weapons that cannot be deemed as falling under the prohibition.

Both methods are reflected in earlier codification. Article 22 of the Regulations annexed to the IV Hague Convention of 1907 states that the right of belligerents to adopt means of injuring the enemy is not unlimited. This principle is generally understood as implying that belligerents should employ only those weapons which conform to the criterion of military necessity, that is, those weapons that are necessary to overcome the enemy.

The criterion of superfluous injury dates back to the 1868 St Petersburg Declaration and is stated again in the Regulations annexed to both the II Hague Convention of 1899 and the IV Hague Convention of 1907. This criterion is generally regarded as declaratory of customary international law.

Weapons specifically identified as prohibited by treaty provisions include: (i) explosives or incendiary projectiles of a weight below 400 grams if used against military personnel. The prohibition, contained in the St Petersburg Declaration of 1868, is regarded as declaratory of customary international law; (ii) bullets which easily expand or flatten in the human body, such as bullets with a hard case that does not cover the entire core or that has an incision (dum-dum bullets). The prohibition stems from the Hague Declaration No. 3 of 1899; (iii) poison or poisoned weapons. The prohibition is contained in Article 23(a) of the Regulations appended to the IV Hague Convention of 1907.

As stated above, the problem with traditional criteria for restricting or limiting the use of certain weapons is that they are unclear and thus unable to set a prohibition, or that they are obsolete, since they regulate weapons no more in use or of no specific military value. Take, for instance, the criterion of superfluous injury, now referred to as superfluous injury/unnecessary suffering[1] because of the difference in translation into English from the French authentic text of the Regulation,

---

[1] See Art. 35(2) of the 1977 Protocol I additional to the 1949 Geneva Conventions.

which is annexed both to the II Hague 1899 Convention and the IV Hague 1907 Convention. There is much uncertainty about its sphere of application, namely whether it covers only combatants or both combatants and civilians. In her Dissenting Opinion in the International Court of Justice (ICJ) *Nuclear Weapons* Advisory Opinion, Judge Higgins stated that the criterion is aimed at protecting only combatants since the civilian population is protected by other norms of international humanitarian law.[2] The criterion has been endorsed by the International Criminal Court (ICC) Statute, Article 8(2)(b)(xx) of which qualifies as a war crime the use of projectiles 'which are of nature to cause superfluous injury or unnecessary suffering'. The provision wisely adds that the punishment of this conduct as a war crime is conditional upon an amendment, adopted according to the procedure established by the ICC Statute, which should indicate the precise weapons the use of which falls under the prohibition. At the 2010 Kampala Conference, revisions to the ICC Statute included the introduction of a definition of the crime of aggression and the inclusion as a war crime of the use of chemical and bacteriological weapons during a non-international armed conflict, but no amendment regarding Article 8(2)(b)(xx) was adopted. In contrast, Article 3(a) of the Statute of the International Criminal Tribunal for the Former Yugoslavia (ICTY) makes the employment of 'weapons calculated to cause unnecessary suffering' a war crime. The inclusion was due to the circumstances under which the ICTY was adopted and the instrument embodying it, a Security Council resolution, which is not grounded in the balanced views that only an international conference may ensure.

## 2. The new principles

Additional Protocol I to the 1949 Geneva Conventions (API) adds a new set of principles for forbidding the use of certain weapons. In Article 35 it enunciates three basic rules. It states that the right of belligerents to choose means of warfare is not unlimited (para. 1); then states the traditional principle of prohibiting weapons, projectiles, and material of a nature to cause superfluous injury or unnecessary suffering; and lastly adds a new prohibition banning weapons intended, or which may be expected, to cause widespread, long-term, and severe damage to the natural environment.

The protection of the environment has become paramount and the ICJ, in its Advisory Opinion on *Nuclear Weapons*, has stated that the obligation to protect the environment against widespread, long-term, and severe damage belongs to customary international law.[3] The insertion of the prohibition of weapons aimed at causing damage to the environment is a laudable endeavour. However, the provision suffers from three weakness: (i) the meaning of harm that is so widespread, long-term, and severe as to fall under the prohibition is still controversial; (ii) there

---

[2] *Legality of the Threat or Use of Nuclear Weapons*, Advisory Opinion, ICJ Reports 1996, 225, Dissenting Opinion of Judge Higgins, 583, 585.
[3] *Legality of the Threat or Use of Nuclear Weapons*, n 2, at 242–3.

are important countries which have not ratified API; and (iii) the lack of ratification by important countries is not without consequences for further codification, even at the level of soft law. The Air Warfare rules drafted by the Program on Humanitarian Policy and Conflict Research (HPCR) at Harvard University do not contain any stringent prohibition on harming the environment, mainly because of the opposition of US experts.[4]

API addresses another category of prohibited weapons: indiscriminate weapons. The rule, which is regarded as belonging to customary international law even if it was not precisely codified until the conclusion of API,[5] is now embodied in Article 51 of the API, which clarifies that a weapon may be indiscriminate by its nature when it cannot be directed at a specific military objective (Art. 51(4)(b)) or may be indiscriminate in its use since its effects cannot be limited as required by the Protocol (Art. 51(4)(c)). The prohibition of indiscriminate weapons does not mean that belligerents are obliged to only use precision-guided weapons. This type of weaponry is available only to the most developed countries. In a situation of asymmetrical warfare, imposing the sole use of precision-guided weapons would run counter to the principle of equality of belligerents.

The law on weapons is today enriched by a new provision inserted in API Article 36 establishing that in the study, development, and acquisition of a new weapon, states should determine whether its use would in some or all circumstances be prohibited by API or by other applicable rules of international law. Article 36 states a 'due diligence' obligation, but it is not easy to verify since the development of new weapons is a jealously kept secret by states, unless they want to disclose it for deterrence purposes. The International Committee of the Red Cross has, however, suggested criteria for a review process.[6]

*Disarmament* and *international humanitarian law* employ two different techniques for regulating weapons. While disarmament prohibits the build-up and stockpiling of weapons, humanitarian law regulates their use. The modern law on weapons is a combination of disarmament and humanitarian law. This is a new and promising trend. Unlike the Bacteriological Weapons Convention (BWC), which prohibits only the production and the stockpiling of biological weapons, the Chemical Weapons Convention (CWC) both prohibits the production and stockpiling of chemical weapons and their use. Also reprisals in kind are prohibited, since the CWC forbids the use of chemical weapons in all circumstances. The CWC model has been followed by other disarmament/humanitarian conventions, such as the Ottawa Convention on anti-personnel landmines (1997) and the Oslo Convention on cluster weapons (2008), even though the latter regime contains serious loopholes with regard to coalition warfare when one or more

---

[4] See Arts 88 and 89 of the HPCR *Manual on International Law Applicable to Air and Missile Warfare* (2010).

[5] W. Boothby, *Weapons and the Law of Armed Conflict* (Oxford: Oxford University Press, 2009), 77.

[6] ICRC, 'A Guide to the Legal Review of New Weapons, Means and Methods of Warfare. Measures to Implement Article 36 of Additional Protocol I of 1977', 88 IRRC (2006) 931.

coalition partners are not parties to the Convention. This point will be considered below.

## 3. The Oslo Convention on cluster weapons: a step forwards or backwards?

Cluster weapons have been widely employed in recent conflicts, both international and non-international. The United States has used them in Afghanistan, and Israel made recourse to such weapons in 2006 at the time of its intervention in Lebanon. The Russian Federation used them in Chechnya, as did the NATO coalition in its intervention against the Federal Republic of Yugoslavia (1999). The problem with such weapons is that when they explode, they release a number of submunitions (bomblets) which represent a danger for the civilian population and remain on the ground for a long period, unless equipped with a self-destructive mechanism.

As previously noted, the Oslo Convention follows the new trend of disarmament/international humanitarian law regulation in that its Article 1 prohibits production and stockpiling of cluster weapons as well as their use. The prohibition of reprisals in kind constitutes another sound prohibition in line with the modern notion of international humanitarian law. As with the Ottawa Convention on landmines, the Oslo Convention represents an example of popular diplomacy in that it was negotiated under the pressure of public opinion and NGOs. The Norwegian government took the lead by convening a conference and starting negotiations and the Convention entered into force on 1 August 2010.[7]

The main problem with conventions like these is that their effectiveness is modest if they are not universally accepted. The best example of a universally accepted disarmament/international humanitarian law convention is the CWC, which has been ratified by the major powers; only countries in the Middle East are not party to it, since the possession of chemical weapons is linked to the issue of Israeli atomic deterrence. The negotiators of the Oslo Convention were obliged to make concessions in order to pursue the goal of universality. The compromise formula, which was reached at the very last moment of negotiations, is embodied in Article 21 (Relations with states not party to this Convention), paragraph 3 of which reads:

Notwithstanding the provisions of Article 1 of this Convention and in accordance with international law, States Parties, their military personnel or nationals, may engage in military cooperation and operations with States not party to this Convention that might engage in activities prohibited to a State Party.

As the drafting history of the Oslo Convention shows, this clause saved the negotiating process at the very last moment during the final stage of negotiations in Dublin. The United Kingdom and a number of other European Union countries

---

[7] The process for a Convention on cluster weapons was initiated in Oslo in 2007 and the Final Draft was concluded in Dublin on 30 May 2008. The Convention was opened for signature at Oslo on 3 December 2008. For this reason the CWC is also referred to as the Dublin Convention.

tabled the proposal in order to allow for war-fighting coalitions made up of states party and states not party to the Oslo Convention. The compromise proposal came from a number of EU countries, but they had in mind NATO operations rather than Common Security and Defence Policy missions by the EU.

The compromise formula is praised by the HPCR Manual on International Law Applicable to Air and Missile Warfare, which for coalition warfare enunciates the following rule (Art. 164):

A State may participate in combined operations with States that do not share its obligations under the law of international armed conflict although those other States might engage in activities prohibited for the first State.

The clause follows the interpretative declaration made by Australia, Canada, and the United Kingdom when they ratified the Ottawa Convention on anti-personnel landmines. This does not help to clarify the doubts originating from reading Article 21(3) of the Oslo Convention. In principle, paragraph 3 seems an innocent provision aimed at ensuring the legal interoperability of a coalition force. In a coalition, states are only obliged to abide by instruments they have entered into. It happens, for instance, within NATO regarding API, which has not been ratified either by the United States or by Turkey. However, the Oslo clause poses a more complicated set of problems. It may happen that the weapons prohibited by the Oslo Convention are stored in a place under the jurisdiction of a state party, for instance on its territory. May an aircraft equipped with cluster weapons be stored on the territory of a state party? May nationals of a state party be employed to store cluster weapons in a military facility located in a state party? What about bombing with cluster weapons when the aircraft is operated by a mixed crew belonging both to a state party and to a non-state party? The clause is qualified by reference to international law, in that any activity of a state party should be carried out in accordance with international law. The use of cluster weapons by a non-state party is not a violation of international law; but what about a state party that contributes substantially to conduct that if carried out by that state would be a violation of international law?

## 4. The criminalization of use of prohibited weapons

There are three techniques for prohibiting weapons and making their use a criminal offence: (i) simply listing prohibited weapons, as does the CCW;[8] (ii) listing such weapons and asking states to enact penal legislation for their prohibition; or

---

[8] The 1980 UN Convention on Prohibitions or Restrictions on the Use of Certain Conventional Weapons Which May be Deemed to be Excessively Injurious or to have Indiscriminate Effect contains a number of annexed Protocols. Three of them were negotiated together with the 1980 Convention: Protocol I on Non-detectable Fragments, Protocol II on Prohibition or Restrictions on the Use of Mines, Booby-traps and Other Devices (amended in 1996), and Protocol III on Prohibition or Restrictions on the Use of Incendiary Weapons. Two other Protocols were added respectively in 1995 (Protocol on Blinding Laser Weapons, Protocol IV) and in 2003 (Protocol on Explosive Remnants of War, Protocol V).

(iii) making the use of such weapons an international crime. For instance, both the Ottawa Convention on anti-personnel landmines and the Oslo Convention on cluster weapons contain only an obligation to adopt penal legislation when state parties enact implementing legislation (Art. 9 of both Conventions). On the contrary the ICC Statute considers as international crimes the use of: (i) poison or poisoned weapons; (ii) bullets that expand or flatten easily in the human body, such as bullets with a hard envelope which does not entirely cover the core or is pierced with incisions; and (iii) weapons, projectiles, and material which are of a nature to cause superfluous injury or unnecessary suffering or which are inherently indiscriminate in violation of the international law of armed conflict. However, because of the indeterminacy of this latter criterion, an amendment to the ICC Statute is needed in order to individuate precisely such weapons and make their use an international crime.

As for weapons of mass destruction (WMD), the Non-Proliferation Treaty (NPT) does not criminalize the use of atomic weapons. During the negotiation of the ICC Statute India tried to insert a provision making the use of such weapons a war crime. However, its proposal was rejected.

The BWC does not contain any provision rendering the use of biological weapons an international crime. This is in line with the thrust of the Convention which is a genuine disarmament instrument and does not contain any provision of humanitarian law.

The criminality of chemical warfare is now an established principle of international law. Article 8(2)(b)(xviii) of the ICC Statute qualifies as a war crime 'employing asphyxiating, poisonous or other gases, and all analogous liquids, material or devices'. The language employed is similar to that of the 1925 Geneva Protocol (even though biological weapons are not mentioned). As far as the criminality of employing prohibited weapons, Article 8 of the ICC Statute covers only international armed conflict and does not address non-international armed conflict. One could therefore argue that the use of chemical weapons during an international armed conflict is not only prohibited, but also amounts to a crime of war, while the use of the same weapons during a non-international armed conflict is only prohibited but cannot qualify as a crime of war. This conclusion, however, would run counter to the case law of the ICTY, which established that the prohibition of non-permitted means of warfare should be regarded as a war crime whether the forbidden weapons are used during an international or internal armed conflict.[9] It is felicitous that the amendment adopted at Kampala revised ICC Statute Article 8 and characterizes the use of chemical weapons during a non-international armed conflict as a war crime. The amendment, however, has not yet entered into force.

Article VII(1)(a) of the CWC obliges state parties to enact penal legislation in order to impede individuals from undertaking an activity prohibited by the Convention. However, the CWC does not itself qualify the prohibited activity as a crime of war.

---

[9] *Prosecutor v Tadić*, ICTY-94-1, decision of 2 October 1995, para. 124.

The Iraq of Saddam Hussein, which employed chemical weapons during the Iran–Iraq War in order to stop the counteroffensive of the Iranian army, was a major importer of substances destined for the production of chemical weapons. Western exporters shipped these substances to Iraq in contravention of the prohibition. On 23 December 2005, The Hague District Court (Criminal Section) condemned Mr van Anraat to 15 years' imprisonment for having supplied Iraq with chemicals used to produce chemical weapons. The criminal activity was committed before the entry into force of the CWC and the judgment applied Dutch criminal law of the time.[10] The sentence was confirmed by The Hague Court of Appeal (9 May 2007) and the penalty increased to 17 years' imprisonment.

## 5.  Weapons in international and non-international armed conflict

As a rule, the law on weapons has been developed in connection with international armed conflicts. This is in line with the codification of the international law of armed conflict, which initially did not recognize the category of non-international armed conflicts. Therefore the St Petersburg Declaration on the prohibition of projectiles below 400 grams applied only in an international war, as did the 1899 Hague Declaration on projectiles which flatten in the human body and the Regulations annexed to the Hague IV Convention. Even the 1925 Geneva Protocol on the prohibition of toxic gases and bacteriological means applied in war, clearly indicates an international conflict. The first codifications of law regarding non-international armed conflict are those of Common Article 3 to the Geneva Conventions and Additional Protocol II. However, they do not contain any provision on weapons. The first occasion to expand the regulation of arms to non-international armed conflicts was the Protocol amending Article I to the CCW, adopted on 21 December 2001. Both the Ottawa Convention on anti-personnel landmines and the Oslo Convention on cluster weapons prohibit the use of these types of weapons in all circumstances, thus even during a non-international armed conflict.

The CWC does forbid the use of riot control agents as a method of warfare,[11] but still allows their use for 'law enforcement including domestic riot control purposes'.[12] The 1925 Geneva Protocol does not state any particular prohibition of riot control agents (eg tear gas), and several states, including the United States, affirmed that such agents are not prohibited by the Protocol, even though these states declared that they would not resort to first use of riot control agents in war, since this would provoke an escalation of the conflict. The CWC thus helps to clarify an issue on which, however, some doubts remain. It is certain that riot control agents may be employed for law enforcement, and it is now equally certain that they may not be employed as a method of warfare. The definition

---

[10] S. Onate, B. Exterkate, L. Tabassi, and E. van der Borght, 'Lessons Learned: Chemicals Trader Convicted of War Crimes', *Chemical Disarmament Quarterly* (December 2006) 19.

[11] CWC, Art. I(5).          [12] CWC, Art. II(2)(d).

of riot control agents by the CWC is also of some help in clarifying the subject. Article II(7) gives the following definition of riot control agents: 'any chemical not listed in a schedule, which can produce rapidly in human sensory irritation or disabling physical effects which disappear within a short time following termination of exposure.'

Also the quantity detained in stock is important, since a large quantity of riot control agents might be suspicious as it could be employed for a purpose prohibited by the CWC.

It is certain that riot control agents cannot be employed as a method of warfare in times of an international armed conflict, but it is not clear that the same prohibition applies in the event of a civil war, since the established government can always state that it is using such chemical agents for law enforcement. The regulation of international armed conflict, too, is not exempt from uncertainty. A state is obliged not to use tear gas in the battlefield, but what about its use to quell a rebellion in a prisoner of war camp or in an occupied territory? A further doubt is related to peacekeeping operations. Are peacekeepers authorized to use tear gas in a non-combat situation? The UN Secretary-General *Bulletin*, issued on 8 August 1999 on the principles of international humanitarian law to be applied by peacekeeping forces, outlaws 'the use of asphyxiating, poisonous or other gases', but does not clarify the point under consideration.[13] According to some authorities, riot control agents may be lawfully used in normal peacekeeping operations, counterterrorism, and hostage-rescue operations. The same is true for controlling riots in areas under the control of the occupier, quelling the rioting of prisoners of war, rescue missions for downed pilots, and other non-combat situations.[14]

## 6. Non-lethal weapons

In recent years armies have shown an increasing interest in non-lethal weapons and not only in the traditional category of riot control agents.[15] Non-lethal weapons allow the selection of the target, without causing the death of civilians: a useful effect particularly when a military target is intermingled with a civilian population. Another advantage is that they are in principle not deadly and are thus tolerated by public opinion. The UK *Manual of the Law of Armed Conflict* gives this definition of non-lethal weapons:

---

[13] K. Annan, 'Observance by United Nations Forces of International Humanitarian Law' Secretary-General's Bulletin, UN Doc. ST/SGB/1999/13, 6 August 1999, para. 6.2, section 6.

[14] K. Watkins, 'Chemical Agents and "Expanding" Bullets: Limited Law Enforcement Exceptions or Unwarranted Handcuffs?', in A.H. Helm (ed.), *The Law of War in the 21st Century: Weaponry and the Use of Force*, International Law Studies, vol. 82 (Newport, RI: Naval War College, 2006), 193, 205–6.

[15] See, generally, D.A. Koplow, *Non-Lethal Weapons, The Law and Policy of Revolutionary Technologies for the Military and Law Enforcement* (Cambridge: Cambridge University Press, 2006).

Non-lethal weapons are weapons that are explicitly designed and developed to incapacitate or repel personnel, with a low probability of fatality or permanent injury, or to disable equipment, with minimal undesired damage or impact on the environment.[16]

The Manual gives as an example, 'water cannon, plastic bullets, CS gas, stun grenades, electronic jammers and laser weapons'. CS gas belongs to the category of riot control agents and its use is lawful, provided that it is not employed as a method of warfare—CS gases produce their effect on the skin and not inside the body. There are other gases which cause effects inside the body at the brain level, such as disorientation, sedation, or even unconsciousness. Malodorous or calmative substances are also referred to as examples of non-lethal weapons. The problem with these weapons is whether they are compatible with the prohibitions laid down by the CWC or by the BWC.[17] Non-lethal weapons cause only temporary incapacitation. However, chemical weapons are those chemicals which cause death or other harm through their toxic properties. It follows that a non-lethal weapon may fall within the category of prohibited chemical weapons if it causes temporary incapacitation or permanent harm to humans through its chemical action.

May non-lethal weapons, which are not riot control agents, be categorized as chemicals employed for purposes not prohibited under the CWC, as enumerated by Article II(9) of that Convention? In this connection, the main problem is the definition of 'law enforcement'. For instance, the execution of a death penalty with a lethal injection falls within the notion of law enforcement. On the contrary, the use of non-lethal weapons in warfare is not law enforcement. Between the two, there are grey areas, which are properly neither law enforcement nor warfare, for instance a peacekeeping operation. What about the use of non-scheduled chemicals? On 26 October 2002, the Russian Federation employed fentanyl, a non-scheduled chemical under the CWC, in order to free the hostages held by Chechen rebels in a theatre in Moscow. The anti-terrorist squad successfully accomplished its mission. A number of people were killed, including both hostages and terrorists: two were shot dead by the Chechen rebels and 129 died as a consequence of chemicals employed; others were subjected to medical treatment. The Russian storming of the theatre was not raised before the Organization for the Prohibition of Chemical Weapons (OPCW) as an illegal use of chemical and a CWC violation. The OPCW only asked for information from the Russian authorities about the type of chemical used.[18]

---

[16] UK Ministry of Defence, *The Manual of the Law of Armed Conflict* (Oxford: Oxford University Press, 2004), 118.

[17] See M. Sossai, 'Drugs as Weapons: Disarmament Treaties Facing the Advances in Biochemistry and Non-Lethal Weapons Technology', 15 J Conflict & Security L (2010) 5.

[18] See J. Hart et al, 'Chemical and Biological Weapon Developments and Arms Control', 34 SIPRI Ybk (2003) 645, 660–1.

## 7. Robots in warfare and international humanitarian law

Robotics is gaining currency in contemporary military operations and its employment is preferred since it does not expose soldiers in the battlefield.[19] Robots do not operate autonomously, and behind them there is always a person responsible for programming or conducting their operation in conformity with international humanitarian law. Robots do not pose new problems for international humanitarian law, and the recent outcries are greatly exaggerated. A robot out of control of the army is a blind weapon and its use may involve the international responsibility of the belligerent and even criminal responsibility for the operator if a war crime ensues. Robots used for rescuing wounded soldiers obviously do not pose any particular problem.

UAV (unmanned air vehicles)/UCAV (unmanned combat aerial vehicles) are the best-known examples of robots used in armed conflict. There are also UGV (unmanned ground vehicles) and UUV (underwater unmanned vehicles). Usually robots are remotely controlled from a long-distance platform and are employed by the most technologically advanced states. Drones, for instance, are useful not only for reconnaissance, but also when there is a need to singularize a military objective and may be preferred to a commando operation.

The US army has employed drones in a number of operations in Afghanistan, but also in other areas such as in Pakistan or Yemen to conduct anti-terrorist operations and targeted killing. UAV are more common than UCAV, which are operated only by very advanced technological powers, mostly the United States.

From the point of view of *jus in bello*, drones should be operated in conformity with rules of international humanitarian law and kept under control. For instance, if they drop weapons against a military target in a populated area, the collateral damage caused by the attack should be in keeping with the principle of proportionality. The same is true, *mutatis mutandis*, for the law of neutrality. Drones may overfly a neutral strait, but cannot overfly a neutral territory.

From the perspective of *jus ad bellum*, overflying a state for hitting a target (ie in an anti-terrorist operation) is a violation of the rule on prohibition of the use of force, unless the consent of the interested state is given.

Cyber war is a method of warfare rather than a weapon. For this reason it is not dealt with here. Using cyber methods to blind the defence of an adversary is not a prohibited means of warfare. The problem with cyber war is one of *jus ad bellum* rather than one of *jus in bello* and raises the question of whether a cyber attack is equivalent to an armed attack violating Article 2(4) of the UN Charter and consequently allowing the aggrieved state to react in self-defence.[20]

---

[19] See, generally, A. Krishnan, *Killer Robots: Legality and Ethicality of Autonomous Weapons* (Farnham: Ashgate, 2009).

[20] M.N. Schmitt, 'Cyber Operations in International Law: The Use of Force, Collective Security, Self-Defense, and Armed Conflict', in *Proceedings of a Workshop on Deterring Cyber Attacks Informing Strategies and Developing Options for US Policy* (Washington DC: National Academic Press, 2010), 163–5.

## 8. A world free from weapons of mass destruction?

Is a world free from WMD a realistic utopia or an impossible dream? There are three treaties regulating the three classes of WMD: *biological, chemical,* and *nuclear.* The first two classes of weapons are the object of an absolute prohibition, since it is forbidden to produce, acquire, and stockpile biological or chemical weapons. The CWC explicitly forbids use, but this prohibition should also be considered as implicitly included in the treaty banning biological weapons, even though it is not spelled out. For nuclear weapons it is different. They are forbidden to non-nuclear states and allowed for the five nuclear states party to the NPT. However Article VI of the NPT obliges nuclear states to engage in negotiations in order to arrive at a world free from nuclear weapons.

Disarmament treaties should be universal, that is, ratified or acceded to by all states of the international community, and verifiable, that is, under strict international control. The BWC and the CWC are quasi-universal: a few countries are not party to them. As far as verification is concerned, only the CWC has a true and reliable system of verification, which is not the case with biological weapons. The NPT is quasi-universal and its verification system has been entrusted to the International Atomic Energy Agency. The North Korea case proves that the NPT verification system has a number of holes. This perception is backed by the Iranian case and the suspicion that Iran is trying to build up a nuclear arsenal in violation of the NPT.

The WMD treaties suffer from two main setbacks. The first is that they contain a withdrawal clause which allows states to end their obligations under the treaty very easily. The treaties are stipulated for unlimited duration; however, each contain a clause allowing a party to withdraw if its 'supreme interests' are in jeopardy. In the case of the NPT, the withdrawal is conditional upon notification of the intention to withdraw to the UN Security Council and the other parties three months in advance. The same is true for the BWC. In the case of the CWC, notice should be given not only to the other parties and to the Security Council but also to the Executive Council (an organ of the CWC Organization), and the withdrawal takes effect only 90 days after the notification. The notified entities, and in particular the Security Council, may intervene to cool off the crisis. However, as North Korea shows in connection with its intention to withdraw from the NPT, a state cannot be prevented from abandoning a disarmament treaty. In case of withdrawal from the BWC and the CWC, the 1925 Geneva Protocol becomes very important, since the withdrawing state still has the obligation not to use biological or chemical weapons if it is party to the 1925 Protocol.

The second setback is related to war. In the case of war between two or more parties, the fate of disarmament treaties is doubtful. They are terminated or at least suspended. This conclusion may be applied to all three WMD treaties, including the CWC, even though the effect of war on this particular treaty was not raised during its negotiation (one may refer to the control system of the CWC regime: it would be nonsense to claim to execute a 'challenge inspection' during a war, which might jeopardize the security of the inspected state!). Even if the treaty is not automatically terminated in times of war, a party might always withdraw invoking extraordinary events (ie, war) jeopardizing its security. Unlike disarmament treaties, international humanitarian law treaties, such as the 1925 Protocol, continue to apply in wartime. Indeed, they were adopted taking into account that they should be applied in war, as is made explicit in the text of the Protocol.

It is obvious that the above perspective may change if one opts instead for the customary law nature of the provisions inserted in WMD treaties. However, it is difficult to contend that the obligation *not to produce* WMD is now embodied in a customary rule. Rather it is easier to be in favour of the customary nature of the rule prohibiting the *use* of WMD. But this assertion demands clarification. Take, for instance, chemical weapons. Even if one assumes that the prohibition of the use of chemical weapons is nowadays embodied in a norm of customary international law, it is not certain that their use in reprisal is forbidden, if reprisals in kind are considered. Egypt, for instance, has not ratified the CWC since it considers the potential use of chemical weapons against Israel as a valid deterrent against nuclear weapons in the hands of Israel. As for nuclear weapons, the ICJ, after having held that nuclear weapons are subject to international humanitarian law, concluded with a *non liquet* stating that it did not say whether the use of nuclear weapons in extreme circumstances of self-defence was lawful.[21]

## 9. Has Obama's vision of a world without nuclear weapons already waned?

During the celebration of NATO's 60th Anniversary, President Obama traced the way for the complete elimination of nuclear weapons. States should reduce the role of nuclear weapons in their national strategies with the aim of achieving a world without such weapons. The road to the zero option would require a number of important steps: the entry into force of the Comprehensive Test Ban Treaty, the creation of a bank for the distribution of fissile material for the peaceful use of atomic energy, the end of the production of fissile material for military purposes, and the negotiation of a cut-off treaty. At the same time non-proliferation regimes, such as the Proliferation Security Initiative and the Global Initiative to Combat Nuclear Terrorism should be reinforced.

On 24 September 2009 the landmark Security Council Resolution 1887 (2009) was adopted, and the Council was chaired for the first time in its history by a US President. Paragraph 5 of the resolution calls upon the NPT parties to pursue negotiations in good faith on a treaty on general and complete nuclear disarmament under strict and effective international control, an obligation stemming from Article VI of the NPT, and at the same time called upon NPT non-parties to join the treaty. But the road laid out was uphill, and on 13 April 2010 the Washington Nuclear Security Summit emphasized the importance of the nuclear security

---

[21] *Legality of the Threat or Use of Nuclear Weapons*, n 2, at 266.

instruments as essential elements of the nuclear security architecture. After two unsuccessful NPT review conferences the most recent one—held in New York on 3–28 May 2010—adopted a number of commitments. The nuclear weapons states reaffirmed their unequivocal understanding to accomplish, in accordance with the principle of irreversibility, the elimination of their nuclear arsenal leading to nuclear disarmament, to which all state parties are committed under Article VI of the NPT. At the same time the New York meeting delineated the steps for convening in 2012 a conference for eliminating all WMD from the Middle East.

Is a world free from nuclear weapons a viable option? One main theoretical point is how deterrence should be ensured in a world without nuclear weapons, in which a wrongdoer may threaten the equilibrium. President Obama stated that a nuclear-weapons-free world should be under the strict control of a structure he did not delineate. At the same time deterrence should be ensured by new and powerful conventional weapons, whose destructive effect is by no means less than that of nuclear weapons.

Subsequent developments put into question the zero option. One may wonder if it is really being pursued or whether President Obama paid only lip service to the cause of NPT Article VI. While the politics of non-proliferation and arms control is progressing with the conclusion of the Treaty between the United States and the Russian Federation on the reduction of strategic offensive weapons and their launchers (2010), entered into force in 2011, the importance of nuclear deterrence has not been reduced. The Nuclear Posture Review, released by the United States in April 2010, states that the United States will retain the capability to forward-deploy nuclear weapons, even though their importance as a deterrence against biological and chemical weapons is diminished since the threat of the use of those weapons has decreased.[22] It is also significant that NATO, in its strategic doctrine released at the Lisbon Summit on 19–20 November 2010, affirmed that it relies on the strategic nuclear forces of the Alliance as the supreme guarantee for the security of NATO's member states, with the consequence that deterrence is based on an appropriate mix of nuclear and conventional weapons, even though the goal of the NPT Article VI is still pursued.[23]

## 10. Is non-proliferation a useful tool for limiting the use of dangerous weapons?

Unlike international humanitarian law, which only forbids the use of certain weapons, and disarmament, that imposes the non-production and destruction of a class of weapons, non-proliferation regimes are aimed at impeding the spread

---

[22] US Department of Defense, *Nuclear Posture Review Report* (April 2010), 33–5.
[23] *Active Engagement, Modern Defence: Strategic Concept for the Defence and Security of the Members of the North Atlantic Treaty Organization*, adopted by Heads of States and Governments in Lisbon (19 November 2010), para. 1, available at <http://www.nato.int/lisbon2010/strategic-concept-2010-eng.pdf>.

of weapons, since their possession by a large number of states increases the risk of their deployment. Often non-proliferation is the object of 'unequal treaties' such as the NPT, which allows only declared states (China, France, Russian Federation, the United Kingdom, and the United States) to possess nuclear weapons, although the inequality is balanced by the duty of the possessor states to achieve complete and general disarmament. Non-proliferation regimes are not an exclusive feature of WMD, but may encompass other classes of weapons. Moreover, they are often the object of soft law or of Security Council resolutions. The increased threat of terrorism is at the origin of non-proliferation regimes tailored against non-state actors. For instance, Security Council Resolution 1540 (2004), which falls under the controversial category of 'legislative' resolutions, obliges states to enact domestic legislation in order to curb proliferation and prevent WMD from falling into the hands of terrorists.

The Security Council has passed resolutions targeting specific countries responsible for proliferation or suspected of carrying out activities inconsistent with the duty not to produce WMD. The main targeted countries are North Korea and Iran. North Korea decided to withdraw from the NTP on 10 January 2003.[24] Since then action by the Council has been aimed at impeding North Korea from acquiring nuclear capability by requesting it to retract its decision to withdraw from the Treaty. After the North Korean nuclear test, on 9 October 2006, the Council requested North Korea to abandon all nuclear weapons and to return under the NPT umbrella.[25] Sanctions were adopted against the country by banning the export of weapons and freezing financial assets of individuals to be designated by a competent committee. Iran did not withdraw from the NPT and is still a state party. The Security Council has nevertheless adopted a series of resolutions imposing sanctions,[26] as Iran has not halted its uranium enrichment programme and is accused of diverting it to military purposes in defiance of Security Council Resolution 1696 (2006). Again, sanctions hit the country and the listed individuals and entities involved in the nuclear programme or in the construction of ballistic missiles.

States have undertaken a number of initiatives outside the UN framework. *Multilateral* initiatives should be preferred to *unilateralism*. Unilateralism may lead to the use of force or to measures short of force, while state parties to a multilateral process consult each other and take joint action, which is a result of a political understanding. Powerful members of the coalition may be moderated by less powerful states. Whenever force is used, it is in some manner authorized by the coalition.

The Proliferation Security Initiative (PSI) is the most well-known example of a multilateral non-proliferation action. It was launched in Kraków on 31 May 2003 by the United States. Although the 11 founding states were all Western states, other countries have joined and nowadays the PSI counts a substantial number of

---

[24] As a matter of fact the intention to withdraw from the NPT had already been notified in March 1993, but suspended immediately before its effectuation.     [25] SC Res. 1718 (2006).
[26] SC Res. 1737 (2006); 1747 (2007); 1803 (2008).

partners, including all the permanent members of the Security Council with the exception of China, which has declared that it is not interested in joining. States are free to abandon the coalition but until now no state has withdrawn. It seems, on the contrary, that a number of states are unofficially collaborating on an ad hoc basis with the more powerful members of the coalition, namely the United States. In total about 97 countries, including the Holy See, are now supporting the PSI.[27]

The PSI is not aimed at creating new law or a new organization and does not have a permanent structure. It is based on a set of principles which should be regarded as political commitments or soft law. They are not at odds with international law, although a number of countries, namely those belonging to the Non-Aligned Movement (NAM), assert the contrary. The PSI is aimed at impeding the transfer of WMD, their means of delivery (such as missiles), and related material to states and non-state actors. The PSI is implemented through measures of land, air, and sea interdiction. From a legal point of view, air and sea interdictions raise the most delicate issues. Air interdiction of an overflying aircraft may involve the opening of fire and destruction of the aircraft, if it does not obey an order to land.[28] Sea interdiction is not allowed under the current provisions of the law of the sea, since those provisions do not contemplate in times of peace the power to stop and search a foreign vessel, except for the grounds established under Article 110 of the 1982 Law of the Sea Convention. Proliferation does not fall within such exceptions. Thus a foreign ship, suspected of having WMD on board, may be stopped only with the consent of the flag state. The United States has concluded a number of boarding agreements with states having an open registry. They allow the US Navy to stop and visit a suspect ship flying the flag of a country party to the boarding agreement.

Soft law regimes often include export control mechanisms to impede the trans-shipment of dual-use items for producing WMD or other strategic offensive weapons and their launchers. The most well-known examples are the Australia Group, tailored for impeding the spread of biological and chemical weapons, and the Wassenaar Arrangement, now including nearly 40 states. Other arrangements, aimed at curbing the spread of nuclear weapons and WMD launchers, are the Nuclear Suppliers Group and the Missile Technology Control Regime. Third World countries consider these control regimes to be highly discriminatory. However, the main problem consists in measuring the regimes' success in curbing the proliferation of WMD. They might help but cannot be a substitute for a true disarmament policy, which implies the conclusion of treaties that are universal, non-discriminatory, and under strict and effective control.

---

[27] M.B. Nikitin, 'Proliferation Security Initiative (PSI)', US Congressional Research Service RL 34327 (18 January 2011).

[28] In 2006, a judgment by the German Constitutional Court stated that the *Luftsicherheitgesetz* was contrary to the German Constitution and should be repealed.

## 11. By way of conclusion: the prospects for realistic restraints on weapons

A world without weapons is not feasible even for the most optimistic utopia. A world without weapons would have to be founded on a world without wars! This is unthinkable, and no responsible state may seriously consider the perspective of unilateral disarmament without adequate and realistic guarantees. Since the international community is still made up of states and an international organization having a monopoly of force does not exist, a 'realistic' utopia should be based on instruments which discourage aggression and at the same time make available to states the means to deter potential aggressors. One has to take into account also the threat coming from non-state entities such as terrorist organizations.

International humanitarian law, as has been seen, has a limited impact on the law of weapons. The main principles, such as the superfluous/unnecessary suffering criterion and the one on the prohibition of weapons having indiscriminate effects, were considered by the ICJ in its Advisory Opinion on *Nuclear Weapons* as 'intransgressible' principles of international law. However, they have only a limited role unless rendered effective in an international convention. The same is true for the Martens Clause, the role of which is too often emphasized but which cannot in itself be a source of law in relation to weapons, unless translated and developed into sound provisions of conventional law. It is difficult or almost impossible to regulate new weapons relying only on traditional criteria. They may too easily be circumvented.

One of the major results of the ICJ Opinion on *Nuclear Weapons* is that the use of nuclear weapons is subjected to the rules of international humanitarian law. More than a decade has passed since the Opinion was delivered and no state party to the API that had made a reservation stating that the API does not apply to nuclear weapons has withdrawn its reservation.

International humanitarian law is not the only way to achieve decent regulation of weapons. *Arms control, non-proliferation*, and *disarmament* instruments should be used to achieve a more suitable result. For a whole class of weapons—that is, chemical weapons—both international humanitarian law and disarmament have been employed with success and the BWC may be interpreted as prohibiting not only the production of biological weapons, but also their use. Disarmament treaties, to be effective, should be universal and verifiable under strict international control. Is a world free from WMD really achievable? The CWC is a success story and this is also partially true for the BWC. As far as nuclear weapons are concerned, the ICJ Advisory Opinion proves that international humanitarian law is not enough for achieving a positive result. *Disarmament* is the main road. As an intermediate step, arms control and non-proliferation might help.

The choice of instruments available is also important. Leaving apart customary international law, the indeterminacy and lacunae of which makes it ill-suited for disarmament, treaties are not the sole instrument to be employed. Treaties are necessary for international humanitarian law, that is, for prohibiting the use of specific weapons. However, one may rely not only on treaties, but also on *soft law* for managing non-proliferation regimes and even arms control. As far as disarmament is concerned, one may rely on treaties for stating the obligation of non-production and stockpiling and on soft law for verification, whenever treaty obligations on monitoring are difficult to negotiate. Moreover, soft law instruments may be transformed into hard law as soon as the political conditions make the transformation feasible.

In the framework of non-proliferation, Security Council resolutions are of paramount importance. The same is true for a moratorium on nuclear testing pending the Comprehensive Test Ban Treaty's entry into force.

In conclusion, the 'Law on Weaponry' cannot be exclusively within the international humanitarian law domain, but should be coupled with the law of disarmament, arms control, and non-proliferation. Soft law is helping and should be a part of a realistic utopia. It is also to be pointed out that *public opinion* and *NGOs* might help. Popular diplomacy was successful in driving states to negotiate the Ottawa Convention on landmines and the Oslo Convention on cluster weapons. This is particularly true for new weapons.

# 43

# Good Time for a Change: Recognizing Individuals' Rights under the Rules of International Humanitarian Law on the Conduct of Hostilities

*Giulia Pinzauti*

## SUMMARY

Given the current state of international law and international relations, in the near future it would be impossible, though highly desirable, to improve the situation of all civilians adversely affected by the outbreak of an armed conflict. It is, however, both necessary and realistic to address the condition of at least those individuals who suffer damage as a result of violations of the rules of *jus in bello* on the conduct of hostilities (the so-called 'Hague law'). A belligerent violating international humanitarian law bears responsibility for the breach of such rules and is liable to make reparation for the consequences thereof. Arguably, the time is ripe for recognizing that the rules of the Hague law also protect individuals' rights, and that injured individuals are therefore entitled to remedy and reparation for the wrong suffered. The shift from the traditional paradigm of inter-state responsibility to responsibility of the state vis-à-vis individuals could be achieved through the creation of ad hoc international mechanisms (such as claims commissions) for the processing of individual complaints. In addition, the task of making a major breakthrough would fall to domestic courts and human rights supervisory bodies, which have ample potential for affirming the existence of individuals' rights under the rules of international humanitarian law regulating means and methods of warfare.

## 1. Justice for war victims: a realistic utopia

In a utopian world, war would most certainly exist only as a chapter in books dealing with the history of the earth, or inspire science fiction novelists and filmmakers. The inhabitants of utopia would know no grievance, no suffering, no injury, nor destruction caused by military operations. However, for us earthlings, war is a cruel reality, which inevitably causes death, injury, and destruction. In the face of such suffering, one naturally questions what can be done to improve the condition of the victims of armed conflict. Importantly, assisting individuals who have been injured by the unlawful conduct of military operations is both a growing need and a realistic possibility.

Part of the destruction or damage caused by military operations to civilian objects is incidental damage resulting from legitimate attacks on military objectives, provided that it is proportional to the military advantage gained by the attacker. This is also known, in common language, as 'collateral damage'. Likewise, loss of civilian life and injury to civilians can be the lawful by-product of military operations, although this should be avoided as far as possible. That is the case if the belligerents fully abide by the applicable rules of the *jus in bello*,[1] which prescribe that hostilities shall only be conducted between opposing armed forces and against military objectives. These rules also provide that civilians, the civilian population, and civilian objects must be protected from direct attack and against dangers arising from military operations. However, when belligerents disregard the prohibitions of international humanitarian law laying down restrictions on the use of means and methods of warfare, the loss and destruction caused are in violation of international law. The belligerent who carried out the unlawful acts of war bears responsibility for them under international law and is obliged to make reparation as far as possible for the consequences of the breach.

The problem is that the rules of the Hague law lay down rights and obligations only for the belligerent parties, and do not clearly spell out that individuals—who undoubtedly have certain obligations under international law with regard to the conduct of hostilities—also enjoy rights under this body of law. As a result, civilians whose homes are unlawfully destroyed during an armed conflict, or who lose their loved ones in the course of an attack, have no remedy under international or national law. Not only do they suffer a loss that cannot be repaired, but also, most probably, they will not obtain any compensation for the wrong suffered, nor hear any words of apology from those responsible. The alternative scenarios for the injured individuals are as follows.

If the violation was carried out by members of an armed group, the practical difficulties in enforcing the responsibility of the group would be enormous.[2] I will therefore focus this discussion primarily on the responsibility of states, which has greater prospects of actual enforcement, even though it is still defective in many respects. In addition, it should be stressed that, under certain conditions, the

---

[1] The belligerent parties are not free to use whatever weapons or military tactics they want to defeat the enemy. The conduct of hostilities is regulated by a body of legal rules of international humanitarian law spelling out the restrictions applicable to the use of means and methods of combat. The majority of those rules apply in both international and non-international armed conflicts as a matter of customary international law, and are thus binding on both states and armed groups. See, eg, J.-M. Henckaerts et al, *Customary International Humanitarian Law. Vol. I: Rules* (New York: Cambridge University Press, 2005), according to which 66 out of 72 (pertaining to the regulation of means and methods of warfare) apply equally to all types of armed conflicts.

[2] On the accountability of armed opposition groups see S. Sivakumaran, Chapter 40, 'How to Improve Upon the Faulty Legal Regime of Internal Armed Conflicts', in this volume.

responsibility of states extends to their failure to prevent or punish international humanitarian law violations committed by armed groups or other non-state actors, even when the wrongful conduct cannot be attributed to the state.[3] Therefore, there is merit in focusing on the responsibility of states in such circumstances.

If the violation was perpetrated by state organs or agents, and is thus attributable to the state itself, the injured individuals will still face enormous hurdles in attempting to secure reparation. Indeed, individuals acting on their own account cannot file a complaint against the delinquent state at the international level, because there are no individual complaints procedures for violations of international humanitarian law. Existing fora, such as the International Court of Justice (ICJ) and mixed arbitral tribunals and claims commissions, are only accessible to states. Thus, individuals would have to rely on the goodwill of their national state, or of another state willing to take up their cause, to bring a claim against a wrongdoing state. The fact is that states that could pursue injured individuals' claims have no legal obligation to do so, and in any event they will be reluctant to do anything that does not directly benefit and promote their own interests. Thus, the call for justice is often overridden by political, strategic, or financial considerations. Moreover, even if a state successfully pursued injured individuals' claim, it would then be up to that state to distribute the compensation eventually obtained to the victims.

Turning to those human rights supervisory bodies that are competent to adjudicate individual applications (such as the European Court of Human Rights, the Inter-American Commission and Court of Human Rights, the African Commission of Human and Peoples' Rights, and the UN Human Rights Committee), the common wisdom is that they have no jurisdiction over international humanitarian law issues. In any event, these bodies can only provide a remedy within the limits of the substantive claim (*petitum*) set forth in the applications brought before them. In addition, they are subject to jurisdictional constraints, and applications can only be held admissible after the exhaustion of local remedies. Thus, only a limited number of complaints are examined in the merits. In addition, the procedures are quite lengthy; thus, the wait is long, before individuals manage to have their applications examined by the competent human rights body.

Finally, individuals have only slim prospects of succeeding in their claims before their national courts, or those of a wrongdoing state. Harm resulting from armed conflict, and particularly from the conduct of military operations, is a particular kind of damage originating from state conduct that in certain legal systems is excluded from the ordinary regime of state responsibility, particularly when it occurs in a foreign country.[4] In some countries (most notably, in Japan and the United States) courts have had recourse to the doctrine of the 'irresponsibility of

---

[3] That is the case when the primary obligation breached imposes on the state the obligation to *protect* certain rights or entities. Those obligations of diligent conduct are often referred to as 'positive obligations'.

[4] That is so, eg, in the United States, the United Kingdom, and Germany. See C. Tomuschat, 'State Responsibility and the Individual Right to Compensation before National Courts', in A. Clapham and P. Gaeta (eds), *Oxford Handbook of International Law in Armed Conflict* (Oxford: Oxford University Press, forthcoming), at 8–9.

the state', which excludes liability for particular kinds of state conduct. In other instances, individuals' claims have been dismissed because the court found that they revolved around non-justiciable 'political questions'. Where victims have attempted to sue a wrongdoing state before their own courts, the most remarkable obstacle has been the rule whereby states enjoy immunity from the jurisdiction of foreign courts.[5] In those few cases where the responsibility of a state has been asserted, the judgment has not been enforced (either owing to a decision of the executive,[6] or pending the ICJ's judgment on the matter).[7]

In sum, it is apparent that state practice denies the existence of individuals' rights under the rules of international humanitarian law regulating the conduct of hostilities. For those international lawyers who, although they are living down-to-earth, still dream of making the earth a bit more like utopia, that is unacceptable. In that regard, it is argued that recognizing that the rules of the Hague law, in addition to protecting belligerents' rights, also safeguard individuals' rights (to life and physical integrity, property, and private and family life) is a realistic utopia. If that conception were accepted, individuals injured by the unlawful conduct of military operations would be entitled to reparation for the wrong suffered, including access to justice and compensation.

In the following paragraphs, I will first briefly recall the nature of the rules of international humanitarian law on the conduct of hostilities, which is reflected in the way in which these rules have been interpreted and applied in traditional international law. That is still, to a great extent, the prevailing understanding of these rules by the courts of numerous states. I will then pinpoint the elements signalling the possibility of changes in the interpretation and application of the rules of the Hague law in the near future, to the benefit of individuals. Finally, I will set out some tentative proposals for making these emerging trends a reality.

## 2. Traditional international law

The rules governing warfare represent the original nucleus of international humanitarian law, dating back to the end of the nineteenth century. They are formulated as prohibitions addressed to the parties to the conflict, and for a long time have been interpreted as only conferring rights or imposing obligations on those parties, to the exclusion of individuals affected by the conflict. Clearly, at the time of their

---

[5] Victims of massacres perpetrated by Nazi occupation forces in Greece (at Distomo, Lidoriki, and Kalavryta) and Italy (in the villages of Civitella, Cornia, and San Pancrazio) during the Second World War, together with the victims' descendants, have brought lawsuits against Germany before Greek and Italian courts, respectively, for the recovery of damages. See, eg, Greece, Supreme Civil and Criminal Court (*Areios Pagos*), *Germany v Prefecture of Voiotia, Representing 118 Persons from Distomo Village*, 4 May 2000 (henceforth '*Distomo* case'); Greece, Special Supreme Court, *Germany v Margellos*, 17 September 2002 (both judgments are available in English at Oxford Reports on International Law in Domestic Courts, online at <http://www.oxfordlawreports.com>); Italy, Court of Cassation (*Corte di Cassazione*), *Germany v Milde*, 21 October 2008, 92 RDI 618 (henceforth '*Civitella* case').

[6] See the *Distomo* case, in Greece, n 5.          [7] *Civitella* case, in Italy, n 5.

codification those rules were conceived as rules applicable in the relations between belligerents only, consistent with the then prevailing conception of international law as a law between states.

The rules spelling out certain restrictions on the use of weapons and military tactics were motivated by considerations of chivalry and fair play between the warring parties, as well as by the need to alleviate the suffering of those who were disabled in the fighting. Individuals, who have always been the ultimate beneficiaries of the rules of international humanitarian law governing warfare, did not enjoy rights proper under that body of legal rules but were merely entitled to a certain standard of treatment. In traditional international law, when 'bilateral relations' prevailed and no notion of 'community concern' had yet evolved, a state having recourse to prohibited means and methods of warfare was only responsible towards the other international subjects to which the obligation breached was owed, namely other states. Individuals who suffered harm as a result of the violation were not granted the right to claim on their own account that the rules protecting them be respected, or to demand reparation for the wrong suffered.

## 3. Signals of change

This conception of the Hague law acutely jars with the ongoing trend towards the progressive humanization of international humanitarian law. The advent of human rights in the post-Second World War era introduced a new paradigm in the international community, which has progressively eroded state sovereignty in many respects. In addition, individuals have emerged as the holders of rights under international law, and also—with the development of international criminal law—as holders of international obligations. It would thus seem that the rules governing the conduct of hostilities—rules that protect highly sensitive state interests—are the last stronghold of state sovereignty against the overwhelming and unstoppable advance of human rights.

Arguably, at present there are several elements that warrant an interpretation of those rules in light of human rights norms, as indicated below.

First, there is an impressive corpus of jurisprudence where human rights supervisory bodies have upheld respect for human rights in time of armed conflict, including during the conduct of military operations by state organs or agents (eg in the event of indiscriminate air strikes against civilians and civilian objects, mopping-up operations, direct attacks against civilian villages, and patrol operations in occupied territory).[8] By so doing, these bodies have de facto adjudicated serious violations of the rules on the conduct of hostilities even when they did not make reference at all to international humanitarian law or to the existence of an armed conflict. The very fact that victims of the unlawful conduct of military operations were able to bring claims alleging the violation of their internationally protected

---

[8] The case law of human rights monitoring bodies is so vast that it cannot be recalled or summarized here.

human rights shows that the rules of the Hague law ultimately protect human rights (eg the right to life and physical integrity, the right to property, and the right to private and family life). Moreover, if we take into consideration the overlap of the substantive provisions of international humanitarian law and human rights law, it is contradictory to maintain that individuals enjoy *rights*, and can claim redress for the violation of those rights, under human rights law, whereas they are only the mere *beneficiaries* of rights (accruing only to states) under international humanitarian law, when the same act runs contrary to both bodies of law.[9]

Secondly, the practice of UN organs supports an emerging consensus that individuals enjoy both primary (substantive) and secondary (procedural) rights under the rules of international humanitarian law, including those regulating means and methods of warfare. A significant example is the adoption, by the UN General Assembly, of the Basic Principles and Guidelines on the Right to a Remedy and Reparation for the Victims of Gross Violations of International Human Rights Law and Serious Violations of International Humanitarian Law (2000).[10] Moreover, in the *Wall* Opinion the ICJ held that Israel was obliged 'to make reparation for the damage caused by the construction of the wall in the Occupied Palestinian Territory, including in and around East Jerusalem'.[11] The Court furthermore identified individuals as the beneficiaries of Israel's obligation to make reparation.[12] In addition, in 2005 the International Commission of Inquiry on Darfur in its Report to the UN Secretary-General firmly held that victims of serious violations of international humanitarian law have a right to reparation.[13]

Thirdly, a number of soft law instruments have also recognized the right of victims of international humanitarian law to remedy and reparation, such as the Chicago Principles on Transitional Justice[14] and the International Law Association's Declaration on International Law Principles on Reparation for Victims of Armed Conflict (2010).[15] Although these texts are not as authoritative as the practice and *opinio juris* emanating from UN organs, they nevertheless signal the growing attention of international civil society to the issues under consideration.

Fourthly, the emergence of the principle of individual criminal responsibility for breaches of the Hague law proves that the rules that were originally only applicable in inter-state relations have gradually been interpreted as imposing obligations directly on individuals. However, there has not yet been any parallel development

---

[9] C. Droege, 'The Interplay between International Humanitarian Law and International Human Rights Law in Situations of Armed Conflict', 40 Israel L Rev (2007) 310, at 353.

[10] UN Commission on Human Rights, 'Basic Principles and Guidelines on the Right to a Remedy and Reparation for the Victims of Gross Violations of International Human Rights Law and Serious Violations of International Humanitarian Law', UN Doc. E/CN.4/2000/62, 19 April 2005.

[11] ICJ, *Legal Consequences of the Construction of a Wall in the Occupied Palestinian Territory*, Advisory Opinion, 9 July 2004, ICJ Reports 2004, para. 163(3)(C).    [12] Ibid, paras 152–3.

[13] International Commission of Inquiry on Darfur, 'Report of the International Commission of Inquiry on Darfur to the United Nations Secretary-General', 25 January 2005, para. 597. The Commission also recommended the creation of a compensation commission to the victims' benefit.

[14] International Human Rights Law Institute, 'Chicago Principles on Post-conflict Justice' (2008).

[15] ILA, 'Declaration on International Law Principles on Reparation for Victims of Armed Conflict', Resolution No. 2/2010, August 2010.

with respect to the other side of the issue, namely the recognition of individual *rights* under those rules. There is thus an imbalance in the legal position of individuals under the rules of the Hague law, which at some point must come to an end.

Fifthly, national judicial practice, once very firm in defending state sovereignty against attempts by individuals to bring reparation claims, is now beginning to waver. The best example is the judgment handed down by The Hague Court of Appeal on 5 July 2011 against the state of the Netherlands, where the Court held the respondent state liable to pay compensation for the deaths of three Muslims in the Srebrenica massacre, in 1995.[16] In addition, the domestic courts of some states have also taken the bold stance that the need to safeguard fundamental values of concern to the international community as a whole (values which are embodied in rules of *jus cogens*) should prevail over the recognition of immunity of foreign states. In other cases (particularly in Germany), courts have left the door open to the recognition that the rules of international humanitarian law on the conduct of military operations protect individual rights, or may give rise to individuals' complaints, although in those instances the claims were struck down on their facts.[17] It should also be emphasized that the practice of domestic courts denying individuals' right to reparation mostly related to atrocities committed during the Second World War, and to the law in force at that time. No court has ever denied that, under contemporary international law, individuals have standing to invoke the responsibility of a state that uses prohibited means or methods of warfare.

Finally, the new interpretation of the rules on the conduct of hostilities suggested in this contribution is warranted under the rules on treaty interpretation as set forth in the Vienna Convention on the Law of Treaties. For one thing, such evolutionary interpretation would be more in conformity with the object and purpose of international humanitarian law. This body of law is designed to protect human beings who find themselves in situations of armed conflict against abusive conduct by their national state (in non-international armed conflict) or by a foreign state(s)

---

[16] The Hague Court of Appeal, *Mustafic v The State of The Netherlands*, Case No. 200.020.173/01, 5 July 2011; and *Nuhanović v The State of The Netherlands,* Case No. 200.020.174/01, 5 July 2011.

[17] See, eg, two cases decided by Dutch courts: Court of Appeal of Amsterdam, *Dedović and 28 Others v Kok and Others*, 6 July 2000, available in English in 35 YIHL (2004) at 508 (concerning a request for compensatory damages lodged by 29 citizens of the former Federal Republic of Yugoslavia against members of the Dutch government for alleged violations of international humanitarian law committed by the Netherlands during NATO's air campaign in the FRY); Supreme Court of The Netherlands, *Danikovic and 6 Others v The State of the Netherlands*, 29 November 2002, available in English in ibid at 522 (on the claim of seven Yugoslav military personnel against the Netherlands for the allegedly unlawful use of force by the state against the FRY). Another important statement that certain international humanitarian law provisions protect individual rights comes from the judgments of both the German Federal High Court of Justice and the Federal Constitutional Court in the cases concerning, respectively, the *Bridge of Varvarin* and the *Distomo* massacre. See Federal High Court of Justice (*Bundesgerichtshof*), *35 Citizens of the former Federal Republic of Yugoslavia v Germany*, 2 November 2006; Federal Constitutional Court (*Bundesverfassungsgericht*), *Distomo*, 15 February 2006 (both judgments are available online, in English, at Oxford Reports on International Law in Domestic Courts, at <http://www.oxfordlawreports.com>). See also Israel's Supreme Court, sitting as High Court of Justice, *Physician for Human Rights and the Palestinian Centre for Human Rights v Almog (Commander of the Southern Command) and Israel*, HCJ 8990/02, 27 April 2003, available online in English at Oxford Reports on International Law in Domestic Courts (concerning the legality of the use of flechette shells by the Israeli Defence Force in the Gaza Strip).

(during inter-state wars). In order to grant individuals a more effective protection, it would be preferable to allow them to assert their interests independently of the assistance of their state of nationality. For another thing, departing from the traditional interpretation that the rules of the Hague law are only addressed to belligerent states is also warranted in the light of the ICJ's holding in *Namibia* that a treaty should be interpreted and applied 'within the framework of the entire legal system prevailing at the time of the interpretation'.[18]

## 4. Suggestions for the realization of individuals' rights

The above elements foreshadow the emergence of new trends whereby human rights norms are progressively reshaping the interpretation of the Hague law, although that body of legal rules is clearly the 'hard core' of international humanitarian law, the kernel that is less amenable to be redesigned by human rights values. If practice develops coherently with the interpretation suggested above, individuals' rights could emerge also under the rules at stake. Individuals injured by the unlawful conduct of military operations would thereby acquire legal entitlements vis-à-vis the wrongdoing state, matched by corresponding obligations of remedy and reparation on the part of the state.

I will now elaborate on the practical consequences of the emergence of individuals' rights, and set out some tentative proposals for fostering this development.

### (A) Preliminary remarks

Three preliminary considerations are in order. First, any proposal supporting the emergence of individuals' rights under the rules of the Hague law needs to be *realistic*, or it will remain on paper. For instance, the various proposals for the creation of new enforcement mechanisms of international humanitarian law at the international level, endowed with the authority to hear individual complaints and order reparatory measures, have not yet yielded any tangible results. Those proposals are probably too forward-looking for the current state of international law and international relations. It seems, therefore, more realistic to focus on the possibility of enforcing individuals' rights through mechanisms that are already in place (eg human rights supervisory bodies and domestic courts), or whose setting up would be less ambitious than the creation of an 'International Humanitarian Law Committee' with general competence.[19]

Secondly, to the extent that individuals will only be able to exercise their substantive 'humanitarian rights' within the domestic sphere, as opposed to the

---

[18] ICJ, *Legal Consequences for States of the Continued Presence of South Africa in Namibia (South West Africa) notwithstanding Security Council Resolution 276 (1970)*, Advisory Opinion, 21 June 1971, ICJ Reports 1971, para. 53.

[19] The proposal of creating the Humanitarian Law Committee was launched at the Hague Appeal for Peace and Justice in the 21st Century, in May 1999.

international legal order, those rights would only have a *national dimension*. In other words, they will not be international rights proper.

Thirdly, the content of state responsibility towards individuals for violations of international humanitarian law is still, to a great extent, uncharted territory, in the sense that it has not yet been explored by legal scholars. Arguably, the content of the relationship of responsibility existing under international law between the wrongdoing state, on the one side, and the injured individuals, on the other, is not the same as that of state-to-state responsibility. By the same token, such responsibility is also different from that arising between the state and individuals under national law. The example of reparations may help to clarify the matter.

In a typical inter-state reparation scheme, international law mandates the wrongdoing state to provide *full* reparation to the injured state. A similar attempt may prove unfeasible with respect to state responsibility arising towards individuals for violations of the rules on the conduct of hostilities. Breaches of those rules are likely to cause a large number of victims, and hence to give rise to mass claims. A standard of 'adequate reparation', to be determined on the facts of the case, may thus prove more realistic, as well as more useful, than an illusory criterion of 'full reparation'. The idea of adopting a standard of proportionality to the gravity of the offence should equally be discarded as it may bankrupt the respondent state (an occurrence contrary to international law, since reparation should not deprive the population of the delinquent state of its own means of subsistence). It has therefore been suggested that compensation to injured individuals be afforded on the basis of additional criteria, such as the economic capacity of the respondent.[20] It could also be argued that courts could reach their decisions on the basis of principles of equity.

Courts may also insist on forms of reparation other than monetary compensation, including restitution, rehabilitation, and satisfaction.[21] For instance, it could be more appropriate to order *collective* reparation measures rather than the payment of monetary compensation to individual claimants. It is further submitted that the measures to be adopted in reparation should be tailored to the specificities of each context, taking into consideration factors such as: (i) the culture of the country or countries involved, and particularly the values that are most cherished by the community; (ii) the impact of the conflict on the local population (ie, whether a significant number of people were injured or killed, whether the conflict caused the displacement of those who survived, the destruction of villages and livestock, the contamination of residential or agricultural areas due to the use of prohibited weapons, and so on); and (iii) the available resources. For instance, in certain contexts the creation of refugee camps, the rebuilding of villages that were destroyed during the conflict, and the maintenance of security in those camps or villages could be a pressing need, whereas in different environments those measures might

---

[20] J. Kleffner and L. Zegveld, 'Establishing an Individual Complaints Procedure for Violations of International Humanitarian Law', 3 YIHL (2000) 384, at 399.

[21] 'All states are capable of public apologies for having violated international humanitarian law, or of allowing organizations such as the ICRC to disseminate international humanitarian law.' Ibid at 400.

not be necessary, or at least not as a primary concern. In contrast, in certain cultures people need to know what happened to their loved ones who have gone missing in order to move on and start rebuilding their lives. Thus, establishing the facts of such armed conflicts in an independent and impartial manner would be of crucial importance to those communities. In almost every situation, building schools, promoting education, and ensuring access to hospitals would be appropriate reparatory measures. Finally, in certain areas (eg where belligerents made extensive use of landmines or cluster munitions) it might be appropriate to order that mines be cleared, and to set up medical clinics for the physical rehabilitation of victims.

I will now address some potential ways of making individuals' rights practical and effective in an attempt to strike the right balance between realism and utopia.

## (B) The practice of human rights supervisory bodies

Human rights bodies addressing human rights violations resulting from the unlawful conduct of military operations could apply their power of judicial oversight to also uphold international humanitarian law rules. Assuredly, such bodies cannot apply international humanitarian law directly, nor declare that a respondent state violated its obligations under that law. However, human rights supervisory bodies have the inherent power to, and should, apply international humanitarian law incidentally (*incidenter tantum*) when dealing with human rights violations committed in the course of military operations. Indeed, the relevant provisions of human rights treaties contain an explicit or implicit *renvoi* to the laws of war. These references authorize the interpreter to look to, and apply, the provisions of international humanitarian law to the extent necessary to pronounce on the violation of the relevant human rights treaty.

If human rights bodies were to apply international humanitarian law in the exercise of their incidental jurisdiction, they would contribute to the enforcement of at least some rules of international humanitarian law for the benefit of victims. In addition, human rights bodies can demand that respondent states pay monetary compensation to victims, or indicate other forms of reparation.

One can therefore argue that human rights bodies may—within the limits of the specific claim (*petitum*) submitted to them—provide an avenue for victims of violations of international humanitarian law to defend their rights. This could lead, in the long run, to the gradual affirmation of individuals' rights under the rules on the conduct of hostilities.

## (C) The role of domestic courts

Domestic courts are in a position to make a breakthrough in the interpretation and application of the rules governing the conduct of hostilities. These courts are, in my view, the driving force behind the chances for a change in the future: whereas it is highly improbable that states will adopt new primary rules foreseeing the responsibility of states towards individuals, interpreting the old rules in a new way is instead a practicable step. This would have several important consequences in practice.

First, in the short term, by interpreting international humanitarian law rules through the lens of human rights doctrines, national courts could affirm the responsibility of states towards individuals, at least within their national legal orders. By so doing, injured individuals could obtain reparation. Secondly, in the long run, the consequences of a change in attitude with respect to the rejection of individuals' reparation claims could be even more far-reaching. National judicial practice represents state practice, which is key to the formation of customary rules. Thus, if domestic courts begin to recognize individuals' rights under international humanitarian law in the future, their judgments could help to buttress the formation of new rules of customary international law.

The emergence of individuals' rights under the rules of international humanitarian law on the conduct of hostilities would radically change the paradigm whereby states, in traditional international law, used to reach postwar settlements where they waived the claims of their nationals for violations of the *jus in bello* by the adversary. If individuals emerge as bearers of subjective rights under international law, autonomous from those of their national state, states would no longer be entitled to renounce the claims of their nationals.[22] Indeed, that would unveil a different legal relationship, opposing the wrongdoing state, on the one hand, to the injured individuals, on the other.

It could also be argued that in line with the emergence of individuals' rights under international humanitarian law, delinquent states would no longer be entitled to invoke immunity from jurisdiction of the courts of foreign states. Indeed, states allegedly responsible for infringing individuals' rights under international law, if sued before the courts of another state, would no longer be subject to the *imperium* (ie, the law) of one of its peers (*pares*), but to the law of the international community.

Recognizing that the rules defining permissible and impermissible means and methods of warfare are also addressed to individuals could potentially change the role of national courts, from being guardians of the domestic legal order to judicial organs of the international community. This would be the realization of Scelle's theory of role splitting (*dédoublement fonctionnel*). If individuals' rights are directly laid down and protected by the international legal order, domestic courts would assume a critical role in implementing the responsibility of states under international law. Moreover, they would also be entitled to pronounce on pending cases according to principles of international law, as opposed to (domestic) tort law only.

---

[22] In this sense see also F. Kalshoven, 'Article 3 of the Convention (IV) Respecting the Laws and Customs of War on Land, Signed at The Hague, 18 October 1907. Expert Opinion by Frits Kalshoven', in H. Fujita, I. Suzuki, K. Nagano (eds.), *War and the Right of Individuals: Renaissance of Individual Compensation* (Tokyo: Nippon Hyoron-sha, 1999), 31, at 47.

## (D) Establishing claims commissions for the processing of individuals' claims

Another way of supporting the emergence of individuals' rights under the rules governing the conduct of military operations would lie in the creation of mechanisms at the international level where victims of violations of international humanitarian law could file complaints without the intermediary role of a state. These mechanisms could be set up on an ad hoc basis in the aftermath of a conflict, either at the initiative of the belligerents (on the model of the Eritrea–Ethiopia Claims Commission), or under the auspices of the international community, represented by a regional organization (eg the Council of Europe or the Organization of American States) or a universal one (the UN). Such mechanisms would unquestionably be the most effective way of promoting the emergence of individuals' rights under the body of law under consideration. Obviously, these commissions should not be restricted to adjudicating violations of the rules on the conduct of hostilities, but should also be competent on other matters (eg violations of human rights law).

It is further submitted that, as far as the functions of those organs are concerned, emphasis should be given to granting reparation to victims. In order to enhance the role of these claims commissions, their mission should not be limited to ascertaining the responsibility of states, but also, arguably, that of armed groups in non-international armed conflict.

These claims commissions could have at their disposal funds coming from different sources, depending on the specificities of each case: voluntary contributions by states or other donors; the administration of the natural resources of the country (eg oil or gas) according to the rules of usufruct; or they could be financed by contributions from their relevant parent organizations. In this way, affirming the responsibility of one or more parties to a conflict would be more symbolic than real (in the sense that, if the case demands, payment of compensation to victims would be made out of the trust fund). Such an approach would also eliminate the risk of draining the financial resources of poor countries.

Handling war-related settlements in this manner would also contribute more effectively to restoring peace and reconciling warring parties. In certain countries, bringing individual claims before domestic courts is not even an option, as the necessary judicial organs are not in place, or are dysfunctional due to corruption or to the effects of armed conflict. In addition, even when domestic courts function properly, bringing individual complaints tends to perpetuate ill feeling and risks upsetting relations between the countries concerned. That being so, a claims commission simultaneously adjudicating violations committed by all parties to a conflict and ordering collective reparation measures would perhaps ensure a smoother and faster transition to peace.

# PART V

# CAN INTERNATIONAL AND DOMESTIC JUSTICE PLAY A MORE INCISIVE ROLE?

# 44

# The Future of International Criminal Justice: A Blueprint for Action

*Jérome de Hemptinne*

## SUMMARY

New ways must be found significantly to increase the cohesion, efficiency, and transparency of the international criminal justice system without disrupting the decentralized structure of the international order in which it operates. Two avenues of action should be pursued. On the one hand, a large number of international criminal cases should be decentralized on the basis of precise rules of jurisdictional allocation, that is, brought before local, ad hoc internationalized or possibly regional courts that are located as close as possible to the populations concerned. In addition, this process should be strengthened by the involvement of truth and reconciliation commissions. On the other hand, a number of investigative and judicial activities of the International Criminal Court (ICC) should be devolved, that is, conducted by the Court, not in The Hague, but in the countries concerned. These two processes of decentralization and devolution should be implemented in parallel according to well-defined criteria.

## 1. Utopian v realistic approach

It would be *utopian* to advocate the establishment of a fully organized international criminal judicial order grounded on a clearly defined hierarchy of courts. At the top, an international supreme court composed of judges from all over the world would adjudicate, on a global scale, a few emblematic cases of mass crime. It would also act as a constitutional court answering preliminary questions of general, criminal, or humanitarian international law raised by regional tribunals. At the intermediate level, regional criminal tribunals made up of judges from the states in each continent or sub-continent would try political and military 'leaders' who cannot be prosecuted at the national level. It would also operate as a supreme court, guaranteeing that national courts abide by the highest standards of a fair and impartial trial. At the lower level, domestic courts composed of national judges—when necessary assisted by international judges—would adjudicate, in the first instance and appeal stages, international crimes falling within their jurisdiction. Such a system would not only give rise to many practical difficulties, but it would also presuppose a strong political will among the states of the international community. However, this intent is currently lacking and unlikely to emerge in the near future in such a sensitive area as criminal justice that pertains to the very core of their sovereignty.

Conversely, an overly *realistic* approach would satisfy itself with the current system of international criminal justice and promote the status quo, perhaps with some minor changes. After all, this system has only existed since the end of the last century and has already undergone considerable change. Moreover, several levels of justice similar to those described above already exist. The ICC sits alongside international ad hoc tribunals established by United Nations Security Council resolutions (the Tribunals for the former Yugoslavia and for Rwanda), hybrid ad hoc tribunals created by treaties (the courts for Cambodia and for Sierra Leone), and international judges appointed by the United Nations within national courts (the Special Panel for East Timor and the international judges sitting in Bosnia's war crimes chamber and Kosovo's courts). The ICC is also helped by several national tribunals (acting within the specific framework of complementarity) and supplemented by truth and reconciliation commissions. Furthermore, many reforms have been undertaken at these courts and tribunals to improve their operational efficiency and fairness.

Nonetheless, the delineation of the relationship between the ICC and other judicial or quasi-judicial bodies is so complex and the reforms undertaken within these bodies so limited in scope considering the huge backlog of as yet unpunished war crimes and crimes against humanity that potentially lie within their jurisdictions, that the present 'model' of justice has almost reached its limits. Additionally, international criminal justice—with its current focus on Africa—is increasingly perceived by the states of that continent as a form of imperialism or neocolonialism in judicial disguise. These states feel dispossessed of their sovereign power by a system of justice controlled by Western countries.

Against this backdrop, new ways must be found significantly to increase the cohesion, efficiency, and transparency of the international criminal justice system without disrupting the decentralized structure of the international order in which it operates. Towards that goal, two avenues of action should be pursued. On the one hand, a large number of international criminal cases should be *decentralized* on the basis of precise rules of jurisdictional allocation, that is, brought before local, ad hoc internationalized or possibly regional courts that are located as close as possible to the populations concerned. In addition, this process should be strengthened by the involvement of truth and reconciliation commissions. On the other hand, a number of investigative and judicial activities of the ICC should be *devolved*, that is, conducted by the ICC, not in The Hague, but in the countries concerned. These two processes of decentralization and devolution should be implemented in parallel according to well-defined criteria.

## 2. Decentralizing international justice

Decentralizing cases that may fall within the ICC's competence in favour of local, ad hoc, or regional courts and truth and reconciliation commissions satisfies three necessities. First, the Court clearly does not, on its own, have the means and resources to try all war crimes, crimes against humanity, and crimes of genocide over which it may have jurisdiction. At most, it is able to prosecute a limited number of crimes committed at the highest level of the political and military hierarchy of states or organized groups. Secondly, the more national authorities take part in the administration of justice, the more their citizens will learn to defend democratic values and expect abidance with international norms. In other words, by working closely with national courts, the ICC, sitting in The Hague—far from the preoccupations of local populations and authorities—will achieve greater transparency and better contribute to restoring the rule of law. Finally, in the context of the progressive globalization of criminal law and procedure, decentralization offers interesting means for the international community to encourage states to respect universal principles of justice while preserving the diversity of their national legal traditions. Indeed, decentralization must be deployed according to the most fundamental standards of international criminal justice. Accordingly, as states conform to these standards, a certain harmonization of national criminal law will be achieved. But equally, and perhaps more importantly, the decentralization process must respect national legal traditions and their diversity.[1]

However, implementing the decentralization process creates legal, political, and structural difficulties. They must be examined before outlining concrete proposals for reform.

First, from a legal perspective, decentralization must rely on a set of clear rules governing the allocation of cases between the ICC and other courts. That is by no means an easy task. Everyone shares the view that the ICC should try only the most serious crimes.[2] However, there is no agreement on the definition of what these 'most serious crimes' are. Several features, including the scale, the nature, the manner of commission, the impact of these crimes, or the number of victims have been proposed by the Prosecutor[3] and the judges at the ICC[4] in an attempt to delineate the notion. However, these elements are very relative and thus cannot

---

[1] M. Delmas-Marty, 'L'influence du droit comparé sur l'activité des Tribunaux pénaux internationaux', in A. Cassese and M. Delmas-Marty, *Crimes internationaux et juridictions internationales* (Paris: PUF, 2002), 95ff.          [2] See Preamble and Art. 17(1)(d) of the ICC Statute.
[3] See ICC Prosecutor, *Report on the activities performed during the first three years (June 2003—June 2006)*, 12 September 2006, 6.
[4] Pre-Trial Chamber I of the ICC has considered that some crimes are not sufficiently serious to fall within the Court's jurisdiction, in particular because the accused in question was not one of the more senior leaders in the Congo situation (ICC, Pre-Trial Chamber I, *Situation in the Republic Democratic of Congo, Decision on the Prosecutor's Application for Warrant of Arrest, Article 58, 10 February 2006*, Doc. ICC-01/04-02/06-20-Anx2, paras 64 and 89). The Appeals Chamber overturned this decision and rejected this criterion, considering it to be flawed, without, however, offering an alternative (ICC, Appeals Chamber, *Judgment on the Prosecutor's appeal against the decision of Pre-Trial Chamber I entitled 'Decision on the Prosecutor's Application for Warrants of Arrest, Article 58'*, Doc. ICC-01/04-169, 13 July 2006, para. 82).

serve as the precise benchmarks which are essential to implementing a coherent and transparent international policy of criminal justice. Rather, the primary criterion should be the rank held by the accused. In other words, only officials at the highest political and military level of states or organized groups should be prosecuted by the ICC. Indeed, only a court such as the ICC has the authority and the impartiality required to try these individuals. With a few exceptions, all other crimes should fall under the jurisdiction of local, or where applicable, regional courts. As J. Graven rightly pointed out as early as 1950,

Le jugement par une juridiction de l'État national, tacitement solidaire de ces crimes ou intéressés à les couvrir, serait totalement illusoire et ne conduirait qu'à la répétition, d'une dérision tragique, de ce qu'on a pu appeler la 'farce' et le 'fiasco' des jugements par la Cour allemande de Leipzig, après la Première Guerre mondiale. On ne voit pas un chef d'État comme Guillaume II ou Hitler, ni de 'grands criminels' comme Göring, Himmler, Sauckel ou Bormann, ainsi que les grands chefs militaires et fonctionnaires des affaires étrangères et intérieures, comparaître devant un tribunal national allemand pour y répondre des actes décidés par eux ou accomplis en exécution de leurs ordres ou plans de caractère national. Les 'grands criminels' contre la paix, les lois de la guerre et celles de l'humanité doivent répondre de leurs actes devant la Cour suprême internationale, gardienne du 'droit des nations' et garantes de la 'paix et sécurité de l'humanité'... [5]

Of course, in cases of civil wars where leaders of states and of autonomous entities together with military and paramilitary groups are likely to spread terror on a large scale, determining abstractly and precisely the level of responsibility required for an accused to be tried by the ICC may be difficult. All the same, three levels of responsibility should be distinguished:[6] the highest, that is, the level of political or military decision-makers who are accused of devising war plans and/or systems of terror and of setting out general guidelines to achieve them; the intermediate level, that is, individuals (eg officers or camp commanders) who are accused of giving orders to implement these plans or systems; and the lowest level, that is, those who are accused of physically committing the crimes. No one would question that the political and military decision-makers should be tried exclusively by the ICC. Nor would anyone question that those who carry out the misdeeds, and who would not have done so if others had not deliberately planned and organized such crimes, should be tried by domestic courts (possibly with the assistance of the international community). But what about the persons comprising the middle category? Should they fall under the ICC's jurisdiction in spite of the risk that the court may be materially unable to judge them all and may become rapidly overwhelmed? Should they instead be referred to domestic courts which, although not themselves members of the first group, may nonetheless have played a major role in large-scale wrongdoing? Would that not entail a true risk of unjustified acquittals and questionable convictions?

---

[5] J. Graven, 'Les crimes contre l'humanité', RCADI (1950-I), 589 and 590.

[6] See *Report attached to the draft Statute of the International Criminal Tribunal from the permanent representative of France to the United Nations addressed to the President of the Security Council*, 10 February 1993, S/25266, paras 22 and 23.

One could imagine that these questions would be answered by a panel of three independent ICC judges who would 'filter' the seriousness of cases falling under the Court's jurisdiction and would therefore exercise control over the Prosecutor's criminal policy. For any case brought before the ICC, the panel would assess whether suspects do indeed fall into the category of senior political or military leaders on the basis of the effective role they played during a conflict, regardless of the ability and willingness of domestic courts to try them. This suggestion will be revisited later.

Secondly, from a political perspective, a requisite for decentralizing the ICC's work is the ability to count on reliable courts, ones that are able and willing to administer independent, impartial, and effective justice. Countries recently affected by war cannot reasonably be expected to benefit from such courts. They often need to undertake major political and judicial reforms in order to restore a democratic foundation and bring their institutions into compliance with international standards. Clearly, such a process of reconstruction is time-consuming, often taking several years, thereby failing to satisfy the requirement of expeditious justice. It would be a mistake to believe that switching back and forth between the ICC and national authorities—the so-called complementarity mechanism—could decisively improve the credibility of these courts in any way. On the contrary, by placing them under the constant threat of withdrawal of cases due to failure to abide by international standards, this complementarity mechanism fosters a relationship of mistrust and potential conflict not conducive to improving national judicial systems. Complementarity could even work against the very interests of the ICC by placing it in the sensitive situation, for a judicial institution, of having to make a political judgement about the democratic character or legitimacy of the national institutions concerned. This position is made even more uncomfortable by the fact that the ICC, not having a police force of its own, relies entirely on cooperation with states to apprehend accused and gather evidence.

To overcome these political difficulties, several options can be recommended. As already pointed out, the ICC's jurisdiction should be confined to individuals who, due to their high level of responsibility, cannot and never will be tried fairly and impartially by national, or even regional, courts. This approach would heighten the transparency of the ICC's prosecutorial policy while shielding the Court from external contingencies arising from the functioning of national courts, as required under the complementarity procedure. Indeed, by definition, these individuals would be excluded from this process.

However, the fact that cases relating to intermediate or lower-level accused would not fall within the ICC's scope does not mean that they can simply be swept under the carpet. As soon as any concrete ICC investigation is initiated, the United Nations, any competent regional organizations, and any relevant state authorities should, in partnership with the ICC Registry, set out a clear policy for processing related cases. One possibility is to continue with the past policy of establishing ad hoc internationalized tribunals to try the intermediate and lower-level accused. If so, then, whenever the political circumstances would allow, the seats of these tribunals should be located in the states where the conflict occurred so as to be as close as possible to the populations affected. As domestic courts, they should employ primarily local judges and apply national procedural law. However, if the political situation in the countries concerned precludes the establishment of such courts locally (eg because the countries are still at war), they could be located in neighbouring states that are willing to be involved and, where necessary, could be composed of international judges in whole or in part so as to guarantee the courts' independence and impartiality.

As experience with the Tribunals for the former Yugoslavia, Rwanda, Sierra Leone, and Cambodia has shown, to set up an ad hoc tribunal, with its own mandate and rules, every time the circumstances so require is an awkward, lengthy, and costly process. It might therefore be more appropriate for the UN Secretary-General to set up, within the United Nations, a committee composed of experts in international criminal justice charged with the following duties: establishing and regularly updating a list of international prosecutors, judges, and defence counsel specializing in international criminal justice, who can be called upon at short notice; deploying them within domestic courts alongside national judicial actors, to prosecute and try sensitive and complex cases; and coordinating the proper functioning of these courts with other regional and international bodies, in particular the ICC.

Furthermore, in line with a marked tendency towards regionalization of international law, in the longer term, permanent regional or sub-regional courts could be established in the more troubled regions of the world. International criminal law—with the exception perhaps of procedural law—is in principle universal in scope and, unlike human rights law, should not need to be adjusted to cater to political, social, cultural, and economic needs of the region concerned. However, the creation of regional courts primarily designed to alleviate the ICC's workload might contribute to reassuring states and strengthening their confidence in international criminal justice if, following the example of the European Court of Human Rights, every state could appoint a judge of its own nationality entitled to sit on cases concerning that state. These courts could be established by international agreements or, if necessary, by a resolution of the Security Council taken under Chapter VII of the UN Charter. The states and, where appropriate, the Security Council or the regional organizations concerned could refer cases to the regional courts, particularly those falling within the second category of perpetrators and which are too sensitive to be handled domestically.

Cases of lesser importance could be entrusted to courts in third countries that are competent to try them under the principle of universal jurisdiction. This solution could be implemented without having to wait for the judicial systems in states devastated by conflict to be reformed or for the establishment of ad hoc international or regional tribunals. However, such an approach creates two difficulties: it is based on a controversial principle (universal jurisdiction), and it does not help to bring the citizens of the affected country closer together or to encourage the country to reform its judicial institutions. At least, the principle of universal jurisdiction should not raise controversies when applied to a suspect who is already present on the territory of the state where the trial is to be held.

Finally, extrajudicial national reconciliation commissions made up of representatives from civil society should play a prominent role in societies that are sufficiently stable to host commissions of this type and manage their functioning. This could be an effective means to supplement and indeed boost the action of international criminal justice at the local level. By inviting perpetrators to testify or confess to their crimes, these commissions could relieve international or national courts of some cases of lesser priority. Perpetrators would be encouraged to participate in this work if commissions recommend to local prosecutors and, in some cases, the ICC Prosecutor, about how to treat persons who have made a full confession of their crimes, particularly in terms of prosecution.[7] In addition, by exercising broad powers in the area of reparation (in particular symbolic reparation) of damage caused to victims, these commissions could make up for the shortcomings of the ICC in this domain. Furthermore, these commissions could supplement the ICC's strictly judicial and criminal approach by examining the origins and the historical, political, sociological, and economic causes of the conflicts from an educational perspective. Finally, these commissions are 'a forum open to all. The forum should be covered by the media and be a place for collective discussion about the past. Its ultimate objective would be to fashion a collective memory of the war, that is, one shared by all the citizens...'.[8] They venture beyond the strictly judicial rationale of justice, which can sometimes be perceived as too black and white.

Thirdly, from a structural perspective, decentralizing international criminal justice could lead to some inconsistencies in the application and interpretation of international humanitarian and criminal law between the ICC and the other courts. For instance, if two or more courts are called upon to try war crimes, crimes against humanity, and crimes of genocide, they are likely to define and interpret the elements of these crimes and the principles that govern criminal responsibility of the perpetrators differently. This problem is aggravated by the fact that the ICC and other courts would often be adjudicating the same criminal facts but committed by individuals who held different levels of responsibility. Such a situation could bring about unequal treatment among the accused and divisions in public opinion that could be damaging to the credibility of international, regional, and domestic justice. It could also challenge the uniformity of international criminal law at a time when it is still developing and is, in many respects, in need of consolidation.

To overcome this difficulty, a system could be devised that guarantees compliance with the guidelines provided by the ICC by local, ad hoc international, or regional tribunals while respecting their independence. It would indeed be inappropriate for these local and regional bodies to be paralysed by excessive interference from the ICC at a moment when the affected state's sovereignty is in the

---

[7] ICTY, Press Release of 17 May 2001: President Jorda's speech made on 12 May 2001 in Sarajevo, 'The ICTY and the Truth and Reconciliation Commission'. Available at the 'Press—Archive' of the ICTY website at <http://www.un.org/icty>.    [8] Ibid.

process of being rebuilt. On the basis of these imperatives, when called upon to administer a territory in the wake of a conflict, the United Nations (eg through the previously mentioned committee of experts) or any other competent body could take the necessary measures to: guarantee that all serious infringements of humanitarian law and the principles of individual criminal responsibility enshrined in the ICC Statute are transcribed into national criminal law; adapt some aspects of domestic criminal procedure to the needs of international criminal procedure, in particular as concerns the protection of victims and witnesses; and acquaint national judges better with the rules of international criminal law by means of regular training, information programmes, and awareness initiatives, together with the appropriate documentary facilities. Above all, however, it is important that the ICC itself strives not only to punish the most serious crimes, but also, by issuing clear, instructive rulings based as much as possible on customary international law, to shape the constitutive, evolving elements of an international criminal order able to command credibility with states. Such rulings can then serve as examples and anchoring points for the jurisprudence of states' own courts and tribunals.

If these courts and tribunals are to enjoy some freedom in applying the principles of international criminal and humanitarian law, they cannot be required to conform fully to the jurisprudence of the ICC. However, if, as has been recommended, regional tribunals were to be established, they could be expected to refer to the ICC for preliminary rulings on the interpretation of provisions, both on the merits and procedure, which are the subject matter of controversy or, at the very least, to be allowed to seek an opinion from the Court on such issues. Of course, while greater uniformity in international criminal and humanitarian law would be achieved with a binding system of preliminary referral, such a system would place national courts under the ICC's control and would thus be detrimental to their autonomy.

These structural difficulties might be compounded if truth and reconciliation commissions are utilized. It is quite likely, since these commissions will examine the causes and origins of conflicts from the political, historical, sociological, and economic standpoint, that their perceptions of the war-related events would be quite different from those of the ICC or of other courts tasked with determining the criminal responsibility of individuals and, where appropriate, providing for reparation to the victims. It will be no easy matter to devise institutional links between these bodies (and possibly reconcile their respective approaches), considering their very different natures and mandates. It is therefore essential that both types of institutions also undertake major outreach programmes in order to foster greater awareness among the subjects of those jurisdictions, the victims, and, more generally, the populations concerned about the different goals of these institutions and the different rationales on which their respective missions are based.

## 3. Devolving international justice

As a natural extension of the decentralization mechanism just described, a parallel process of devolution of certain activities of the ICC should be implemented.

These activities would remain in the hands of the ICC but would be carried out in the countries concerned, or at least in the neighbouring areas, rather than in The Hague.

Clearly, this process meets the same requirements as those that justify setting up a policy of decentralization, that is, to enhance the effectiveness of international criminal justice and its transparency, and to bring it closer to the populations concerned. These purposes could be achieved through devolution at the stages of investigation and trial, each of which will be examined separately.

Two options can be considered with respect to investigations: one that is more in line with the ICC Statute and Rules of Procedure and Evidence but less efficient, and the other which is more ambitious because it requires these texts to be revised, but could have a far greater impact on the effectiveness of proceedings.

Under the first option, one trial attorney per state concerned would be appointed right at the start of an investigation and would conduct his work in that state. He would be assisted by a local deputy and as many investigators as necessary. He would be responsible for independently conducting the investigations in that state and reporting regularly to the Chief Prosecutor on developments in the investigation. The Chief Prosecutor, as the guarantor of the unity of all investigations undertaken by the ICC, would remain in The Hague, and his role would be confined to: devising the principal guidelines for his office's criminal policy and, namely, determining where and when investigations should be undertaken in accordance with the jurisdictional criteria set out by the Statute and by ICC case law; appointing the trial attorneys responsible for implementing those policies in the field and supervising the conduct of their activities; and establishing stringent timetables for bringing investigations to a close. This solution does not require any fundamental alterations to the checks and balances established by the Court's texts. Roles would be revised such that the trial attorneys can exercise their duties independently and under their own responsibility in the countries concerned according to well-defined rules.

The second option is more ambitious as it would require a complete revision of the adversarial system applied at the ICC. This solution is based on the idea of establishing investigation chambers that would conduct investigations in the countries involved. Indeed, in spite of the extensive reforms that have already been undertaken, international criminal trials are complex, too cumbersome, lengthy, and costly. The judges at the ICC do not, as such, conduct investigations. These are left entirely in the hands of the Prosecutor and of defence counsel. Therefore, the judges do not prepare, as is the case in some Roman law systems, an investigation file which, when completed, serves as the basis for the trial judges to select the witnesses that will be heard or set the duration of the trial. Under the ICC's procedure, this choice is mainly in the hands of the parties. These parties have legitimate concerns other than ensuring the effectiveness and expeditiousness of the proceedings. It is unquestionable that in-depth investigation of cases performed by independent judges would simplify and speed up trials. With investigation files that have been drawn up on a neutral basis prior to the trial stage, the trial judges would no longer need to hear all of the Prosecutor's or defence counsel's witnesses. A small selection of representative witnesses would be chosen according to the needs of each case and called to appear before the court.

That being said, before setting up investigation chambers of this type locally, it is important to draw lessons from the difficulties encountered with this institution in domestic systems. To avoid situations that would be fatal to international criminal justice at this embryonic and vulnerable stage, a number of safeguards should be implemented. For instance, investigations should be conducted by chambers comprising at least three judges who are experts in the area of international investigations, in contrast to the single judge system used in places such as Belgium and France. Furthermore, to ensure that the adversarial principle is upheld, defence counsel should, in principle, be present in the field when evidence is collected and should take part in interviews with their clients, witnesses, and victims. They should also have full access to the investigation file and the option of requesting additional inquiries. In addition, to ensure full compliance with the rights of suspects and accused, these chambers must defer to an independent judge in The Hague to rule on whether such suspects should be placed in detention. Finally, any important decision taken by the investigation chambers, such as refusal to proceed with investigations, must be appealable.

Along the same lines, the Trial Chambers could conduct the trials, not in The Hague, but in the states concerned or, in the event of political instability, in neighbouring states. Devolution at the trial stage would enhance the ICC's visibility in the field. It would also facilitate cooperation with the local authorities and reduce the operating expenses of this Court (there would no longer be any need to bring witnesses to The Hague for hearings). As for the Appeals Chamber, being the chamber that rules on all cases that fall within the ICC's jurisdiction and the guarantor of the consistency of case law, it should continue to sit in the Netherlands regardless of the circumstances.

# 4. Conclusion

Ideally, if the processes of decentralization and devolution were to be conducted concurrently, very few cases would continue to be referred to the ICC: those relating to the top political and military leaders, that is, those who are accused of devising war plans and/or systems of terror and of setting out general guidelines to achieve them. Among those few cases, most should be investigated and then tried by judges of the ICC sitting where the crimes were committed. Only under very exceptional circumstances—open warfare; strong political, military, or social tensions; or in appellate proceedings—would cases be heard in The Hague. Establishing this system presupposes that the United Nations and the competent regional organizations would take every step to ensure that the other cases are tried at the local level, including those in the intermediate category involving people who are accused of playing a major role in carrying out wholesale criminal plans. This would require new solutions. Indeed, experience with international courts has taught us that to set up ad hoc or hybrid tribunals *de novo* to remedy special situations is extremely cumbersome, lengthy, and costly. The simplest option would doubtless be to establish permanent regional courts placed under the control of the states in that region or of the UN Security Council. However, in the absence of political consensus and of resources, it is unlikely that these courts will emerge in the near future. In the meantime, setting up a committee within the United Nations in charge of seconding competent international judges, prosecutors, and defence counsel to domestic courts to investigate and try sensitive cases might in the short term make a major contribution to instituting a more credible, efficient, and transparent system of international justice.

# 45

# The Need Reasonably to Expand National Criminal Jurisdiction over International Crimes

*Paola Gaeta*

## SUMMARY

Since recourse to the territorial and active nationality principles is unlikely with respect to 'core' international crimes, the emerging culture of accountability for these crimes necessitates the expansion of domestic criminal jurisdiction on the basis of other principles. Whether and to what extent this is possible under international law ultimately depends on the approach one takes in relation to the notion of sovereignty and the competences of sovereign states under international law. Paradoxically, the positivistic approach followed by the majority of the judges of the Permanent Court of International Justice (PCIJ) in *Lotus* will be more favourable to the expansion of criminal jurisdiction over international crimes. By contrast, the more modern approach, according to which criminal jurisdiction is principally territorial, would imply that one should point to a rule of international law expressly allowing extraterritorial criminal jurisdiction. In any event, it seems undisputable that for the repression of international crimes customary international law allows extraterritorial jurisdiction also on the basis of the passive personality and the protective principles. As for universal jurisdiction, controversy exists, inter alia, as to the need for a jurisdictional link to the forum state, in particular the presence of the suspect in the territory of the state. It is suggested that to put the exercise of universal jurisdiction in conformity to the principle of legality the presence of the suspect should be at least a requirement for the exercise of adjudicatory/enforcement jurisdiction (while this requirement is not strictly necessary for legislative jurisdiction). In addition, the judge exercising universal jurisdiction should be allowed to apply substantive criminal law which is most favourable to the accused among those of the forum state, the state of nationality, and the territorial state to fill the lacunae of international criminal law particularly in relation to penalties. It is hoped that the UN will start a process of codification that will take into account these solutions, which can help to challenge the suspicions levelled by some states that universal jurisdiction is a tool of legal imperialism, and to build a true international community for the repression of international crimes.

# 1. The problem outlined

The concept of international crimes seems to be ineluctably predicated on the necessity to expand the reach of national jurisdiction beyond the traditional bases of territoriality and active nationality. These two jurisdictional principles, the legality of which under international law is indisputable, are scantly used for the repression of international crimes usually described as core crimes, or international crimes proper: namely genocide, war crimes, and crimes against humanity. These are crimes that express a sort of 'system criminality',[1] in that they are normally perpetrated by state officials with the acquiescence, tolerance, or support of the authorities of the state, which makes domestic prosecution in the state of the *locus commissi delicti* or of the nationality of the alleged perpetrators unlikely.[2] It comes therefore as no surprise that the emerging culture of accountability with respect to international crimes increasingly necessitates the exercise of criminal jurisdiction on the basis of extraterritorial principles other than active nationality.

The notion of international crimes also unavoidably calls for the necessity to expand the jurisdictional reach of domestic courts *ratione personae*, by virtue of the inapplicability of the national and international rules on immunities. As noted above, these crimes are usually committed by state officials. Hence, to uphold the doctrine of immunities in respect of these crimes not only 'may lead to ensuring impunity for the perpetrators', but also

would mean to bow to and indeed strengthen traditional concerns of the international community (chiefly, respect for state sovereignty), which in the current international community should instead be reconciled with new values, such as respect for human dignity and human rights.[3]

Clearly, were domestic courts to be empowered to prosecute international crimes on the basis of wide titles of extraterritorial jurisdiction, in particular universality,

---

[1] B.V.A. Röling, 'The Significance of the Laws of War', in A. Cassese (ed.), *Current Problems of International Law* (Milan: Giuffrè, 1975), 137–9.

[2] When committed in the state's own territory (as could be the case for crimes against humanity, genocide, or war crimes in non-international armed conflicts), domestic prosecution grounded on the territoriality principle probably depends on a change of government, as well as on the lack of amnesty laws or other legal impediments expressly set out to avoid criminal repression. Similarly, when committed by a state's national abroad, eg in the context of an international armed conflict, it is unlikely that domestic courts will act on the basis of the active nationality principle, as state authorities would tend to shield their nationals (usually state officials) from criminal responsibility. In the last scenario, even the territorial state might tend to avoid prosecution of crimes committed by enemy belligerents, in particular at the end of hostilities, because of the necessity to restore peaceful relations with the former enemy.

[3] A. Cassese, 'When May Senior State Officials Be Tried for International Crimes? Some Comments on the *Congo v Belgium* Case', 13 EJIL (2002) 853, 873–4.

and at the same time permitted to disregard the international rules on immunities, they could be at the forefront of the struggle against impunity for international crimes.[4]

In Chapter 18 of this volume, I discuss the question of the applicability of the doctrine of international immunities in cases of international crime. I therefore focus here only on the question of the extraterritorial expansion of criminal jurisdiction over international crimes.

## 2. The *Lotus* approach to extraterritorial criminal jurisdiction and beyond

Back in 1927, in the *Lotus* case, the PCIJ delivered a judgment which still constitutes the inescapable starting point for any discussion about the relationship between public international law and states' jurisdiction in criminal matters, in particular the legality under international law of the exercise of extraterritorial criminal jurisdiction by domestic courts.[5]

---

[4] It is, however, precisely because of this combined effect that the application of the principle of universality, which has never been disputed for the repression of forms of criminality such as piracy, money laundering, trafficking of human beings, or attacks against marine cables, has been challenged instead with respect to international crimes. Once the inapplicability of the rules of international law on immunities is admitted, domestic courts acting on broad extraterritorial titles could accuse former or sitting foreign state officials, regardless of their seniority, of international crimes, with all the ensuing serious political consequences. There is also the fear that national courts may abuse this possibility. International immunities are therefore perceived as a necessary bulwark to protect sitting or former state officials (especially those holding senior positions) from abusive prosecution in foreign countries. As Lord Goff put it in *Pinochet*, the doctrine of international immunities:

> can . . . be effective to preclude . . . process [in foreign countries] in respect of alleged crimes, including allegations which are misguided or even malicious—a matter which can be of great significance where, for example, a former head of State is concerned and political passion are aroused. Preservation of State immunity is therefore a matter of particular importance to powerful countries whose heads of State perform an executive role, and who may therefore be regarded as possible targets by governments of States which, for deeply felt political reasons, deplore their action while in office. (*R v Bow Street Stipendiary Magistrate and others, ex p Pinochet Ugarte*, House of Lords, Judgment of 24 March 1999 (1999) 2 All ER 97)

[5] The case is well known. It concerns a collision in the high seas, off the coast of Turkey, between the French mail steamer *Lotus* and the Turkish collier *Boz-Kourt*, which resulted in the sinking of the latter and the death of eight Turkish nationals. Turkey started criminal proceedings against, among others, Lieutenant Demons, a French national, who was the officer of the watch on the *Lotus*. After rejecting the objection raised by Lieutenant Demons that Turkey had no jurisdiction, the Criminal Court of Istanbul convicted him for involuntary manslaughter and sentenced him to 80 days' imprisonment and a fine. France's reaction of diplomatic protection led the case to come before the PCIJ, which had to decide whether the criminal proceedings against Lieutenant Demons had breached Art. 15 of the 1924 Convention on Lausanne on Conditions of Residence and Business and Jurisdiction. This provision required 'all questions of jurisdiction shall . . . be decided in accordance with the principles of international law'. France contended, inter alia, that the exercise of criminal jurisdiction by Turkey, which asserted its criminal jurisdiction on the basis of its national criminal code provision on the passive personality principle, was not in accordance with international law.

As is well known, the Court started from the assumption that '[r]estrictions upon the independence of states cannot be . . . presumed' and stated as follows:

Far from laying down a general prohibition to the effect that states may not extend the application of their laws and the jurisdiction of their courts to persons, property and acts outside their territory, it [international law] leaves them in this respect a wide measure of discretion which is only limited in certain cases by prohibitive rules; as regards other cases, every state remains free to adopt the principles which it regards as best and most suitable.[6]

This assertion was vigorously challenged by the dissenting judges. They opined that international law—far from being inspired by a laissez-faire approach—regulates directly the ambit of criminal jurisdiction of states and provides that it is mainly territorial. According to them, extraterritorial titles of jurisdiction could only be resorted to if this power was expressly provided for in an international rule, as was clearly the case for the active nationality principle.

Although the positivistic approach to international law, that inspired the majority in *Lotus*, seems to have been abandoned in contemporary legal thinking, the philosophical divide evinced in *Lotus* still persists in discussions concerning the ambit of states' jurisdiction. This divide is of course linked to one's own understanding of sovereignty and of the role and function of international law in a society whose primary subjects are sovereign states. A *factual* notion of sovereignty, according to which states are meta-legal entities whose formation is not regulated by international law, would lead one to believe that they were born free from obligations and rights, and that international law only intervenes to restrain their otherwise unfettered freedom. International law, however, would not attribute to them competences or powers (as Anzilotti put it, 'nothing is more repugnant [to states] than the notion that they exercise powers and authority granted to them by international law')[7] let alone in criminal matters. By contrast, those (like Kelsen) who propound a legal notion of sovereignty consider that international law regulates the formation of states, and that it confers upon them rights and obligations in relation to their territories only in accordance with the principle of sovereign equality. According to this view, criminal jurisdiction is principally territorial; only exceptionally, namely once a rule of international law so establishes, can states assert their criminal jurisdiction over facts committed outside their territories.

Clearly, following the majority view in *Lotus*, the exercise of extraterritorial jurisdiction over international crimes would always be possible unless one can point to the existence of a rule of international law prohibiting it. In *Lotus*, the judges did not provide a list of possible rules to that effect. They confined themselves to demonstrating that the exercise of criminal jurisdiction in the case at stake, reclassified by the Court as a form of territorial jurisdiction, was not forbidden by international law. In the end, therefore, the Court did not offer any clue at all as regards the possible impediments placed upon the exercise of extraterritorial

---

[6] Judgment, 7 September 1929, *The Case of the SS Lotus*, PCIJ, Series A, no. 10, 2ff at 19.
[7] 'Niente più ripugna [agli Stati] dell'idea di esercitare una potestà loro concessa dall'ordinamento internazionale', in D. Anzilotti, *Corso di diritto internazionale*, vol. I, 4th edn (Padua: Cedam, 1955), 53.

criminal jurisdiction. In addition, since it considered that after all the case con-cerned the exercise of *territorial* criminal jurisdiction, it could even have avoided the general statement concerning the restrictions to states' freedom that cannot be presumed. However, the fact remains that, from the point of view of the need to expand the jurisdictional reach of states for the repression of international crimes, the positivistic approach followed in *Lotus* would be the most suitable. According to this approach, there would exist a presumption in favour of the exercise of extra-territorial criminal jurisdiction, and it would be for the states challenging it to prove the existence of a specific prohibitive rule. This is perhaps rather paradoxical. The positivistic approach dominating the majority view in *Lotus* is indicative of a state-centric view of international law, which is at odds with the communitarian-ism that inspired the evolution of international criminal law.

The opposite (and I would say, more modern) approach, according to which criminal jurisdiction is principally territorial, obviously implies that in the matter of repression of international crimes one should point to a rule of international law allowing the exercise of extraterritorial jurisdiction. At the *treaty* law level, the task could be relatively easy since one can find rules allowing, if not obliging, the estab-lishment of extraterritorial jurisdiction on the basis of specific heads.[8] Nonetheless, a few problems still persist.

First, these treaties do not regulate the national criminal repression of all inter-national crimes: the list comprises genocide, grave breaches of the 1949 Geneva Conventions and Additional Protocol I, and torture, but leaves out crimes against humanity and those war crimes outside the grave breaches regime. For these crimes the question therefore remains of whether a rule of customary international law allows their extraterritorial domestic criminal repression. Secondly, the treaty regulation for the crimes mentioned above is not always crystal clear as regards the particular heads of extraterritorial jurisdiction, if any, which are allowed or imposed upon state parties.[9] Thirdly, since treaties can only derogate from rules of customary international law among state parties, the permissive or mandatory jurisdictional provisions can only be lawfully applied among contracting states: the exercise of extraterritorial jurisdiction over crimes committed by nationals of states not parties on the basis of such provisions would therefore violate customary international law vis-à-vis those states.

The *punctum pruriens* concerns, therefore, the content of customary international law on the matter. In this regard, it seems undisputed that customary international law allows extraterritorial criminal jurisdiction on the basis of the *active nationality* and the *protective* principles. In addition, elements of state practice clearly indicate

---

[8] See, eg, Art. 5 of the UN Convention Against Torture and Other Cruel, Inhuman or Degrading Treatment or Punishment.

[9] For genocide, Art. VI of the UN Convention against the Prevention and Repression of the Crime of Genocide imposes the exercise of criminal jurisdiction upon the territorial state. For grave breaches, again, the emphasis is on the duty to bring the alleged perpetrators before the courts of the state party to the Geneva Conventions and Additional Protocol I on whose territory they are found, but there is no express reference to the heads of criminal jurisdiction that the state must possess in this regard.

that the traditional opposition by common law countries to *passive personality*, at least as a basis to prosecute international crimes, has been overcome.[10] Things are more complex with respect to *universal jurisdiction*. Although there is a trend towards considering that universal jurisdiction is allowed for the prosecution of international crimes generally speaking, strong disagreement persists among states and legal experts as regards the need for a jurisdictional link to the forum state, in particular the presence of the suspect in the territory of the state.[11]

## 3. 'Pure' universal jurisdiction? A tentative solution in light of concern for respect of the principle of legality

The debate on whether the presence of the suspect in the territory of the state claiming jurisdiction is a necessary condition for universal jurisdiction is somewhat confused because the distinction between legislative and adjudicatory/enforcement jurisdiction is often not clearly maintained. As is well known, legislative jurisdiction indicates the authority of the state to determine the scope of application of its laws, in this case criminal legislation. Adjudicatory/enforcement jurisdiction refers to the ability of the state to apply its own laws to specific cases, through its courts and enforcement agencies. Clearly, legislative jurisdiction determines the scope of intervention of the judiciary and the enforcement agencies, since the latter cannot but intervene to apply and enforce a law that is applicable to a particular case. If adjudicatory/enforcement jurisdiction is by necessity territorial, in the sense that it can only be exercised within the territory of the state, legislative jurisdiction can extend to extraterritorial acts.

The issue with universal jurisdiction is whether the criminal legislation of a state can regulate acts committed abroad by foreigners against foreigners, when the suspect has never entered the territory of the state after the commission of the crime and there is no prospect that he will, at least not voluntary. This is what is called 'pure' or 'unconditional' universal jurisdiction. This broad form of (legislative) jurisdiction would imply a corresponding form of adjudicatory/ enforcement jurisdiction, in the sense that investigation and prosecution can be started without the presence of the accused in the territory of the state; in

---

[10] Some common law countries have clearly accepted the application of the passive personality principle (traditionally perceived by them as an exorbitant title of jurisdiction for the repression of ordinary offences) over war crimes, crimes against humanity, and genocide. See in this regard P. Gaeta, 'Il principio di nazionalità passiva nella repressione dei crimini internazionali da parte delle giurisdizioni interne', in G. Venturini and S. Bariatti (eds), *Diritti individuali e giustizia internazionale, Liber Fausto Pocar* (Milan: Giuffrè, 2009), 325.

[11] According to the 2010 UN Secretary-General's Report, 'The Scope and Application of the Principle of Universal Jurisdiction', as for the jurisdictional link, the uncertainty is greater since states adopt a variety of links for the assertion of universal jurisdiction and very few states, eg Spain, consider that 'unconditional' universal jurisdiction is allowed for the prosecution of international crimes. Disagreement also persists as regards the list of crimes: some states consider that universal jurisdiction is permitted under general international law over genocide, crimes against humanity, war crime, torture, and piracy, while other states deem that it is limited to piracy, genocide, and torture, or according to other states, to piracy only.

addition, the competent authorities could issue an arrest warrant and circulate it internationally (as was the case for Mr Yerodia, subject to an arrest warrant by Belgium) and they can issue a request for extradition if they know where the accused is located (as was the case with Pinochet, subject to an arrest warrant by Spain). If the domestic system allows it, a trial *in absentia* could be held and, in case of a conviction, an extradition for the enforcement of the sentence could be requested.

One of the major concerns with this very broad form of universal jurisdiction is respect for the principle of legality. True, one could contend that if the crimes with which the accused is charged were provided for in customary international law at the time of the commission of the offence this concern should not arise at all. However, respect for the principle of legality not only requires that the accused be aware that his act amounts to a criminal offence, but also that he knows the range of penalties attached to it, as provided by the maxim *nullum crimen, nulla poena sine lege*. The great disparity among states in sentencing policies and legislation could therefore impose in the state exercising pure universal jurisdiction a penalty which is excessive in comparison to the maximum penalty applicable in the territorial or the national state. For instance, for a war crime, the territorial state could provide for a penalty of, say, a maximum 20 years' imprisonment, while in the state exercising pure universal jurisdiction the same crime could receive the penalty of life imprisonment.

In order to bring the exercise of 'pure' universal jurisdiction into conformity with the principle of legality, one could envisage the obligation for the *forum* state to make the presence of the suspect in the territory of the state a requirement for the exercise of adjudicatory/enforcement jurisdiction. In other words, while the ambit of criminal law would extend to extraterritorial acts without a link with the forum state at the moment of their commission, this link would be required to trigger the adjudicatory/enforcement jurisdiction. The police and the prosecutor could therefore carry out investigations over the alleged commission of a crime abroad, if they wish, but criminal prosecution could be started only if the suspect enters the territory of the state after the alleged commission of the crime. His voluntary presence would imply that he subjects himself to the criminal jurisdiction of that state, knowing in advance that universal jurisdiction could be exercised in accordance with the criminal legislation of that state, which includes the range of penalties attached to the crime.

In this sense, the purpose of the presence requirement shall not be confused with the one traditionally assigned to it under the *forum deprehensionis* principle. In the latter case, the presence of the suspect in the territory of the state is a condition for determining the ambit of application of criminal law (and therefore of legislative jurisdiction), and as a consequence it amounts to a requirement for the act to be considered a crime under the legislation of the state. This means that, until the suspect is present in the territory, investigation (let alone prosecution) cannot be initiated because the criminal law of the forum state is not applicable at all. Interestingly, it is this form of *legislative universal jurisdiction* that is mandatory for contracting states under some treaties concerning international crimes, although they make it conditional to the decision not to extradite the alleged culprit found in the territory of the state.[12] From the point of view of respect for the principle of legality, this form of universal jurisdiction, that is termed 'conditional' or 'territorial' universal jurisdiction, would be even less problematical than in the scenario outlined above, since the criminal legislation of a state would regulate extraterritorial conduct only if the alleged wrongdoer has voluntary entered the territory of the state.

Theoretically, however, one could propound another solution to align universal jurisdiction (in its 'pure' and 'conditional' variant) with the principle of legality. The assumption is that, in the matter of repression of international crimes, the national criminal judge does not primarily act as an organ of his own state, but rather as an organ of the international community as a whole. In other words, in respect of conduct that is directly criminalized under customary international law, national criminal judges would realize a sort of *dédoublement fonctionnel*[13] to remedy the lack of a centralized and mandatory system of international criminal justice. When sitting in judgment over international crimes, they would simply apply and enforce international prohibitions directed at individuals, either when they are authorized by their national criminal system to apply directly customary international law in criminal matters, or when they need to have recourse to their own national criminal law implementing international criminal prohibitions. However, as is well known, the international rules on international crimes are far from being self-executing, in particular as regards an essential component of criminal rules: that of the penalty to be attached to the criminal behaviour. Each domestic system must therefore proceed, in this matter, to enact or to apply its own criminal legislation on penalties, with the ensuing inevitable disparity from state to state.

[12] A typical example is Art. 5(2) of the UN Convention Against Torture and Other Cruel, Inhuman and Degrading Treatment, which obliges a contracting state to establish its criminal jurisdiction 'in cases where the alleged offender is present in any territory under its jurisdiction and it does not extradite'. A similar provision is contained in almost all the treaties for the repression of so-called 'terrorist crimes' (an exception is the 1963 Tokyo Convention). On the face of it, these treaty provisions seem to provide that universal jurisdiction can be acquired only on condition that the alleged offender *is* in the territory of the state (provided that extradition is considered but not carried out), meaning that there is no possibility to launch a criminal investigation or to exercise any form of *adjudicatory jurisdiction* before he is found there. However, this would be an incorrect conclusion. The aim of these treaties is to create a jurisdictional web for the repression of given crimes, so that the alleged culprit cannot escape justice given that there will always be a state having criminal jurisdiction to prosecute. These treaties, therefore, do not preclude the possibility for contracting states to establish criminal jurisdiction acting on bases different from those imposed by the treaties themselves. The more is so if one considers that the relevant treaties also contain another provision which clarifies that any criminal jurisdiction exercised by contracting states in accordance with their internal law is not excluded (see, eg, Art. 5(3) of the UN Convention Against Torture). These provisions could therefore be interpreted as permitting unconditional universal jurisdiction, among contracting states, if this head of jurisdiction is provided for by national legislation.

[13] On Georges Scelle's theory of the *dédoublement fonctionnel*, see, among others, A. Cassese, 'Remarks on Scelle's Theory of "Role Splitting" (*dédoublement fonctionnel*) in International Law', 1 EJIL (1990) 210, and P.-M. Dupuy, 'Unity in the Application of International Law at the Global Level, and the Responsibility of Judges at the National Level: Reviewing Georges Scelle's "Role Splitting" Theory', in L. Boisson de Chazournes and M. Kohen (eds), *International Law and the Quest for Its Implementation: Liber Amicorum Vera Gowlland-Debbas* (The Hague: Martinus Nijhoff, 2010), 417.

It is therefore suggested that, when the domestic judge exercises universal criminal jurisdiction, he fills the lacunae of international criminal law on penalties by choosing the most favourable law among those applicable (namely the criminal legislation of the state of the *locus commissi delicti*, or that of the nationality of the accused, or its own laws). Admittedly, this would directly challenge the traditional wisdom according to which criminal judges cannot but apply the criminal legislation of their own countries. The incoherence of such a postulate with respect to the development of international criminal law, however, had already been demonstrated in the 1920s by Donnadieu de Vabres.[14] In addition, as forcefully demonstrated by one commentator,[15] there is no theoretical obstacle to the application, by the national judge, of a foreign criminal law, more so if it is the one *favor rei*.

The obligation for the state asserting and exercising 'pure' universal jurisdiction to have recourse, when necessary, to the most favourable applicable national criminal legislation would not only guarantee respect for the principle of legality, but would also constitute a tangible sign that the forum state is not driven by a sort of 'legal imperialism'—a concern expressed by some African states in some situations. Recourse to the criminal law of the territorial or national criminal legislation would also represent the logical consequence of the 'subsidiary' role of the principle of universal jurisdiction with respect to territoriality and active nationality, a subsidiary role advocated by many commentators and incorporated in some international treaties under the rule *aut dedere aut prosequi*. Finally, to allow national judges to apply foreign criminal legislation would not only avoid violations of the principle of legality, but would also help to create, in the field of criminal law, a true international community.[16]

## 4. In quest of a clarification

As stated above, exercise of universal jurisdiction, in particular in respect to former or sitting senior state officials, has raised concerns among some states, which fear

[14] R. Donnadieu de Vabres, 'Essai d'un système rationnel de distribution des compétence en droit pénal international', 19 Revue de droit international privé (1924) 48.

[15] T. Treves, *La giurisdizione nel diritto penale internazionale* (Padua: Cedam, 1973), 20–31.

[16] As Donnadieu de Vabres put it:

Si l'inculpé peut être jugé d'après des lois différentes, frappe de peines inégales suivant que les hasards de l'arrestation, les caprices de l'extradition l'auront amené à comparaître devant le juge territorial, le juge personnel ou le juge d'un Etat tiers, il n'existe pas de certitude dans la réglementation des rapports de droit pénal. La règle *Nulla poena sine lege*, sauvegarde essentielle de la justice et de la liberté individuelle, est violée dans son esprit, sinon dans sa lettre. Il est nécessaire, en droit pénal comme en droit civil, que la loi qui doit gouverner tel ou tel rapport soit déterminée suivant un principe de justice dans l'application soit constante, indépendante de la qualité du juge saisi. Le principe de Savigny, auquel MM. Lainé et Pillet ont donné un degré de précision supérieure, en admettant que la portée territoriale de chaque loi se détermine d'après sa 'nature', ou d'après son 'but social', était pressenti déjà, au XIV e siècle, par Bartole. Or Bartole ne prétendait pas en limiter l'application aux lois civiles : il l'étendait, certainement, aux lois criminelles. Et cette extension est nécessaire, si l'on veut réaliser, sur le terrain du droit pénal, la communauté internationale. ('Essai d'un système' cit, above n 14, at 53)

that it has been or will be used for political purposes. To smooth out these concerns, an important step has recently been taken at the level of the African Union and the European Union, which assigned to an Ad Hoc Experts group the task of preparing a report for fostering a better understanding of universal jurisdiction.[17] Other initiatives to clarify the scope of universal jurisdiction and the content of international immunities in cases of international crimes have been taken by the Institut de droit international, which in 2005 has adopted a resolution on this topic.[18]

Despite these recent developments, however, the issue has remained controversial. On several occasions the African Union members have asserted that there is the need 'for an international regulatory body with competence to review and/or handle complaints or appeals arising out of the abuse of the principle of universal jurisdiction by individual states.'[19] The UN General Assembly is currently dealing with the matter within its Sixth Committee, where representatives of some states have expressed strong concerns about the misuse of the principle of universal jurisdiction by certain national judicial bodies.[20] The General Assembly has therefore issued a resolution on the basis of the report of the Sixth Committee where it noted 'the views expressed by states that the legitimacy and credibility of the use of universal jurisdiction are best ensured by its responsible and judicious application consistent with international law.'[21] The General Assembly also decided to establish a working group of the Sixth Committee to undertake a thorough discussion of the scope and application of universal jurisdiction.[22]

It is to be hoped that the establishment of such a working group will constitute the first move by the General Assembly towards the process of codification and progressive development of the content of customary international law on the matter. The outcome of such a process could be either a draft convention to be submitted to states for ratification or, more plausibly, the adoption by the General Assembly of a declaration of principles, if possible by consensus. Time is indeed ripe for such a move, as a means to complement the establishment of international criminal courts and tribunals in the fight for accountability.

It is suggested, however, that any attempt to codify and progressively develop customary international law should take a comprehensive approach to domestic prosecution of international crimes, dealing with all titles of jurisdiction (not only with universal jurisdiction). It is only by taking this comprehensive approach that the question of universal jurisdiction can indeed be tackled in an appropriate and

---

[17] The Report was issued on 16 April 2009. For a comment on the Report and on the immediate cause that prompted the AU-EU to establish the ad hoc Expert Group, see J. Genuss, 'Fostering a Better Understanding of Universal Jurisdiction', 7 JICJ (2009) 945.

[18] Resolution on Universal Criminal Jurisdiction with regard to the crime of genocide, crimes against humanity and war crime, adopted at the Kraków Session of the Institute, available at: <http://www.idi-iil.org/idiE/resolutionsE/2005_kra_03_en.pdf >. For a comment see C. Kress, 'Universal Jurisdiction over International Crimes and the Institut de droit international', 4 JICJ (2006) 561.

[19] Decision on the Abuse of the Principle of Universal Jurisdiction, Doc. EX.CL/540(XVI), adopted by the Fourteenth Ordinary Session of the Assembly in Addis Ababa, Ethiopia, on 2 February 2010, point 6.

[20] See, eg, the statements by the representatives of Libyan Arab Jamahiriya and Rwanda at the 11th meeting of the UN Sixth Committee on 14 January 2001, A/C.6/65/SR.11.

[21] A/RES/65/33, 10 January 2011 (Preamble, fourth para.).     [22] Ibid, para. 2.

correct way, without losing sight of the whole picture. The draft codification convention, or the General Assembly resolution, should therefore clarify that—for the prosecution of international crimes—the territorial state is usually the *forum conveniens* state, but that this does not exclude the possibility to establish extraterritorial titles of jurisdiction, including universality. It should be clarified that the establishment of universal jurisdiction is possible, but that prosecution can be initiated only if the suspect enters the territory of the state. This would constitute an important guarantee for those who fear an abuse of universal jurisdiction. In addition, it must be recommended that—if a trial is commenced—the state exercising universality applies the criminal law of the territorial or national state if, as far as penalties are concerned, one of the two is more favourable to the accused. This would bring the exercise of universal jurisdiction into conformity with the principle of legality and would go some way towards challenging the suspicions of 'legal imperialism' levelled against it by some states. Universal jurisdiction could even been made subordinate to the offer to the territorial and national states to prosecute the case.

One could envisage the establishment of an institutional mechanism to monitor the correct application of the aforementioned rules and principles.[23] Admittedly, however, up to now domestic judicial authorities do not seem to have resorted to universal jurisdiction for any ulterior motive other than the prosecution of very serious international crimes. In addition, any international institutional mechanism would create a useless burden, which would discourage—instead of encouraging—domestic prosecution of international crimes; effective domestic prosecution of international crimes being a central component for the international community to become that which it ostensibly claims to be—a true community.

---

[23] See, eg, the proposals formulated by Kress, above n 18, at 584–5.

# 46

# Domestic Courts Should Embrace Sound Interpretative Strategies in the Development of Human Rights-Oriented International Law

*Massimo Iovane*

## SUMMARY

There are two significant trends in how domestic courts are applying international law: (i) they are exploiting all the creative potential of customary international law by pioneering the determination of new customary rules, or favouring the evolution of old ones. However, in so doing, they have often asserted the existence of international customs without sufficient reference to international precedents, or regarded international treaty rules as corresponding *ipso facto* to general international law; (ii) they constantly apply the interpretative methods of modern constitutionalism to solve the conflicts between international norms, or to propose an evolutive interpretation of customary and treaty norms on the protection of human rights. However, they tend to go too far, violating some well-established norms of customary international law and giving rise to a plethora of interpretations from state to state. The upshot of these trends is that recent national judicial practice marks a turning point in the formation of customary international law and general principles of law. Domestic courts have also developed a creative judge-made law. However, judges cannot use their freedom of interpretation in an arbitrary way. They would risk handing down illegitimate and ineffectual decisions. Moreover, judicial creativity may also run counter to the practice the executive organs of the various states adopt in their diplomatic intercourse. Too much discretionary power in the hands of the judiciary may, from the domestic point of view, also violate the democratic principle of the separation of powers. The only correction to these shortcomings is to adhere to strict methodological principles in setting out the grounds for any innovative decision. It is the fulfilment of these very conditions which characterizes courts as independent bodies in a rule-of-law-based legal system. Courts must respect precise formal constraints, such as the obligation not to exceed the limits of their competence and to give priority to norms of a higher rank.

According to legal hermeneutics formal criteria must be coupled with substantial control over the correspondence of the norms to the changing ethical convictions and expectations of the community, and the conformity of judge-made law with the existing legal system. The first type of control has been carried out especially by expanding on the content of general principles of law and *jus cogens*, whereas the second is expressed by the canons of balancing and proportionality.

## 1. Introduction: domestic courts and the systematic interpretation of international law in a human rights-oriented legal order

One of the main features of contemporary international law is the role played by domestic courts, leading to a broad-ranging doctrinal movement entirely devoted to analysing the causes and consequences of this widespread phenomenon over the last decades.[1] Broadly speaking, there appear to be two main reasons for the growing role of domestic courts in the interpretation and application of international law. In the first place, the escalating expansion of international law, now governing a much wider range of subjects than only a few decades ago. This has automatically resulted in the multiplication of cases where international treaties and customary rules are invoked before national courts and regularly applied by them. Secondly, and most importantly, increased reliance on international law by domestic courts is not due only to the quantitative increase in the number of claims brought before them. Rather, it is the content of contemporary international law which really makes a difference between the present and past roles of national judges. We are witnessing a crucial shift from classical international law, whose only purpose is the protection of a state's governmental power and the delimitation of this power vis-à-vis other states, towards the protection of human rights and fundamental liberties. Since rights and liberties concern individuals directly, they naturally turn to domestic courts as accessible fora for judicial protection of their rights under international law.

This 'humanization' of international law has profoundly influenced the general approach adopted by national judiciaries. In fact, courageous national courts have even dared to take a position on the eternal but theoretical question of the international personality of the individual, some asserting that international law

---

[1] See B. Conforti, *International Law and the Role of Domestic Legal Systems* (Dordrecht: Martinus Nijhoff, 1993); K. Knop, 'Here and There: International Law in Domestic Courts', 32 NYU J Int'l L & Pol (2000) 501ff; F. Francioni, 'International Law as a Common Language for National Courts', 36 Texas Int'l LJ (2001) 587ff; J. Charney, 'International Criminal Law and the Role of Domestic Courts', 95 AJIL (2001) 120ff; G. Betlem and A. Nollkaemper, 'Giving Effect to Public International Law and European Community Law before Domestic Courts: A Comparative Analysis of the Practice of Consistent Interpretation', 14 EJIL (2003) 569ff; W.W. Burke-White, 'International Legal Pluralism', 25 Mich JIL (2004) 965ff; S. Fatima, *Using International Law in Domestic Courts* (Oxford: Hart publ., 2005); Y. Shany, 'National Courts as International Actors: Jurisdictional Implications', 15 Federalismi. it (2009), available at <http://www.federalismi.it/>; E. Benvenisti and G. Downs, 'National Courts, Domestic Democracy, and the Evolution of International Law', 20 EJIL (2009) 59ff.

may create direct rights in favour of individuals,[2] and others that individuals must now be recognized as partial international subjects.[3] Clearly, such involvement of national judiciaries is not without implications for the certainty and uniformity of international law. As we shall see, there are two significant trends in how domestic courts are applying international law. In the first place, they are exploiting all the unifying and creative potential of customary international law by pioneering the determination of new customary rules, or favouring the evolution of old ones. However, in so doing, they have often affirmed the existence of international customs without sufficient reference to international precedents, or have declared international treaty rules as corresponding *ipso facto* to general international law. In the second place, they constantly apply the interpretative methods of modern constitutionalism to solve the conflicts between international norms, or to propose an evolutive interpretation of customary and treaty norms on the protection of human rights. In doing so, however, they tend to go too far, violating some well-established norms of customary international law and giving rise to a plethora of interpretations from state to state.

I shall examine these two trends in two dedicated sections, before turning to examine their main shortcomings, with some recommendations for future methodological improvement that may overcome the above-mentioned failings in an otherwise positive and innovative trend.

## 2. Domestic courts and the unifying potential and law-creating opportunities of customary international law

### (A) Challenging the traditional notion of customary law

Concerning customary law, post-Cold War judicial practice has slowly shifted its focus away from the jurisdictional immunity of foreign states that had largely characterized earlier case law. In the aftermath of the Second World War, domestic courts mostly had to deal with the perennial question of the *jure imperii* or *jure gestionis* nature of an activity performed by a foreign state or international organization. Moreover, to solve these questions, domestic courts chiefly relied on domestic legislation or their own precedents, cautiously adapting their previous findings to different claims.[4]

Diplomatic immunity was another topic typically addressed by domestic courts in this phase. However, the almost universal ratification of the 1963 Vienna Convention gave national judges common parameters to use when deciding

---

[2] See, eg, UK Court of Appeal, Civil Division, *Occidental Exploration and Production Co. v Ecuador* [2005] EWCA Civ 1116, at para. 19.

[3] German Federal High Court of Justice, 2 November 2006, *35 Citizens of the Former Federal Republic of Yugoslavia v Germany*, Appeal judgment, BGHZ 166, 384; III ZR 190/05; ILDC 887 (DE 2006), paras 7–8.

[4] On this practice see P.D. Trooboff, 'Foreign State Immunity: Emerging Consensus on Principles', 200 HR (1986-V) 235 at 266ff.

relevant questions in this field. The Convention's provisions were automatically considered to be equivalent to customary law without further examination. Moreover, domestic courts have often shown a tendency to extend the jurisdictional immunities of foreign organs without carefully considering the actual international practice.[5]

On the other hand, when required to reach a decision other than simply affirming or declining jurisdiction, domestic courts generally reacted by invoking a lack of uniform practice or sufficient consent by the states to establish the existence of customary norms.

Laying aside their traditional reticence, over the last decades domestic courts all over the world have undoubtedly been showing a greater inclination for research and the interpretation of international customary law. However, the notion of custom resulting from this practice largely departs from the traditional concept handed down by the general theory of law and endorsed by international law doctrine.

Before examining the relevant domestic case law, we should thus briefly recall that according to the notion developed by the general theory of law, custom is a spontaneous, informal, and unconscious source of law, which draws its effectiveness from the force of tradition.[6] Furthermore, it is commonly admitted that a customary norm must be based on widespread practice, consistently observed over a period of time by the members of a given community. Authoritative doctrine has long and rightly emphasized that the passing of time is important for the determination of customary norms especially in the field of private law, whereas this condition is not decisive in bringing about unwritten legal norms among entities exercising governmental powers such as states or state organs.[7] Nevertheless, the widespread occurrence and repetition of specific conduct remains a necessary condition for the establishment of a customary norm among the members of the international community, or in any other social environment. After all, regular repetition is crucial in deducing the element of *opinio juris ac necessitatis* attesting that the conduct in question is observed by the community *as a whole* out of a sense of legal obligation. Similarly, practice indicative of normative facts must necessarily consist of *concrete* acts by the members of the community in relation to a *specific* dispute or claim.[8] Concerning international law, weight has traditionally been given to official pronouncements of the executive, protests against an alleged violation of a customary rule, international judgments, or acquiescence. From this

---

[5] For recent examples of that tendency, see Bow Street Magistrates' Court, 14 January 2004, *Re Mugabe*, unreported decision ILDC 96 (UK 2004); Bow Street Magistrates' Court, 12 February 2004, *Re Mofaz*, unreported decision, ILDC 97 (UK 2004). The judicial practice referring to the 1961 Vienna Convention as automatically corresponding to customary law is so widespread that it would be superfluous to quote specific examples. Even in the field of the immunity of foreign states, some courts have referred to the as yet not in force 2004 UN Convention to infer customary international law. See, albeit unclearly, The Hague Court of Appeal, 27 July 2007, *X v Morocco*, Appeal judgment, 676984 CV EXPL 05-36544; ILDC 548 (NL 2007), paras 6.2.1–6.2.5.

[6] N. Bobbio, *La consuetudine come fatto normativo* (Padua: Cedern, 1942).

[7] N. Bobbio, 'Consuetudine (teoria generale)', in *Enciclopedia del Diritto IX* (Milan: Giuffré, 1961), 426, at 429.

[8] See the discussion on this point in M. Akehurst, 'Custom as a Source of International Law', 47 BYIL (1974–75) 197–275.

perspective, national decisions have long been considered pertinent practice only for inferring the actual content of customary rules on *jurisdictional immunity*.

On the other hand, the role of domestic judges in the determination of customary international law is normally described using a typically positivistic approach. Although a certain level of discretion is presumed whenever the existence and scope of unwritten norms are at stake, courts are expected to establish objectively both *diuturnitas* and *opinio juris* from a consistent set of precedents. In other words, they should behave as impartially and objectively as they do in the interpretation of written norms, thereby neutrally ascertaining and declaring the will of the state.

This conception of customary law perfectly fits the homogenous core of traditional international norms, which has remained unaltered for centuries. As recalled earlier, these norms only aim to protect every state's exclusive governmental power according to the spatial, functional, and personal criteria established by international law itself.

As already mentioned, the nature and intensity of contemporary international relations have dramatically changed with respect to this original pattern. So have those facts and methods which may reveal the existence of a normative practice. There are, however, some recurring and distinctive elements in the recent national courts' approaches which may help systematically to describe the overall approach by domestic courts.

First, the identification of customary rules is often accomplished by selecting convenient materials of an *abstract* kind, that is, those unconnected with previous official pronouncements over the existence of a disputed custom, and without the concrete observance by states of a pattern of behaviour in specific situations. Reference to diplomatic practice, which was once the main source of identification of customary law, is now scarcely to be found.

From the traditional point of view, these materials cannot in themselves establish customary law strictly understood as a normative *fact*, that is, as a source which draws its force from the tradition of a community and from a consistent series of *spontaneous actions* directly performed by the members of that community.

Indeed, new customary rules or the development of more traditional ones have often been affirmed or denied by simply quoting some materials which, far from consisting of spontaneous behaviour, are either mixed doctrinal and institutional products, such as the Draft Articles of the International Law Commission (ILC), or *written* and *formally adopted* sources, such as acts of international organizations, and multilateral treaties irrespectively of whether they have been ratified by the forum state, or whether they are currently in force.[9] Concerning treaty practice, it must also be stressed that domestic courts only refer to specific conventional norms in their abstractly formulated state, that is, irrespective of any concrete interpretation and application in state practice. From these sources, domestic courts try to mould a sort of international *opinio juris* which they treat as current customary

---

[9] Considering provisions in multilateral treaties as automatically expressing customary law is a tendency we have already stressed in relation to the interpretation of the Vienna Convention on Diplomatic Relations.

law. So it comes as no surprise that, particularly in the field of human rights, recent domestic decisions have affirmed the existence of certain specific international customs for the first time.[10]

Secondly, domestic courts have often sought confirmation of their conclusions about the existence and scope of customary law in earlier decisions by national and international courts on the same subject. In other words, they recognize the effectiveness of a given rule insofar as it is applied by other judges, and not in the repeated behaviour of a state.[11] In particular, reference to international case law by national judges has proved much more frequent and decisive in recent years, due to the growing establishment and activity of international tribunals. In accordance with the general content of domestic case law, this inter-judicial dialogue mostly occurs in relation to customary rules on the protection of human rights and the general interests of the international community as a whole.

## (B) The identification of customary rules on the prohibition of the use of force and on the protection of human rights

The method of blending institutional sources, abstract treaty provisions, and judicial precedents to infer the existence of customary norms covers a wide range of new topics in the field of human rights.

Interestingly, a series of recent decisions have ventured to affirm the customary nature of the prohibition of aggressive war, which is quite a surprising move [if we consider—given?] that resorting to armed force has long been considered, and still is, as a quintessentially non-justiciable subject.[12] The recent Iraqi scenario has offered the main opportunity for judicial pronouncements on this question. The Iraqi invasion of Kuwait was indeed regarded as a violation of customary law by the House of Lords in 2002 on the basis of 'a succession of resolutions passed by the UN Security Council under Chapter VII of the Charter of the United Nations'.[13] The House of Lords relied on the 1986 International Court of Justice (ICJ) decision in *Nicaragua v United States*[14] as judicial precedent to corroborate its conclusion on the unlawfulness of the Iraqi attack. In the well-known *Jones*

---

[10] See also Section 2(C) below. After all, the judicial origin of a normative practice is hardly new in the international legal order, where the development of customary law on the international responsibility of states and the treatment of aliens, began in judicial practice, ie decisions by international arbitral tribunals and claims commissions, expanding on general principles of civil law.

[11] See, eg, Supreme Court of India, 1 December 2000, *AP Pollution Control Board II v Prof. MV Nayudu (Retd) and Ors* [2000] Supp 5 SCR 249, at paras 8 ff (reference to the case law of the European Court of Justice, the European Court of Human Rights, the Inter-American Commission on Human Rights, the Philippine Supreme Court, the Constitutional Court of Colombia, and the Supreme Court of South Africa).

[12] See the case law mentioned in D. Amoroso, 'A Fresh Look at the Issue of Non-Justiciability of Defence and Foreign Affairs', 23 Leiden JIL (2010) 933 at 937.

[13] House of Lords, 16 May 2002, *Kuwait Airways Corp v Iraqi Airways Co. (Nos 4 and 5)*, Appeal judgment [2002] 2 AC 883; ILDC 243.

[14] ICJ, *Military and Paramilitary Activities in and against Nicaragua (Nicaragua v United States of America)*, Merits, Judgment of 27 June 1986, ICJ Reports 1986.

judgment of 29 March 2006,[15] the House of Lords recognized aggression as an internationally wrongful act and as an individual crime under customary international law, relying mainly on UN General Assembly resolutions and on the two draft Codes on crimes against the peace and security of mankind adopted by the ILC in 1954 and 1996.[16] The judgment of the Nuremberg Trial was also invoked to confirm the Lords' reasoning.

German courts have also recognized that the prohibition of the use of military force is part of customary international law, quoting the 1986 ICJ judgment on *Nicaragua* and the relevant provisions of the UN Charter.[17] Likewise on the recourse to armed force, it must also be noted that domestic courts autonomously proceeded to the qualification of an armed conflict as internal or international, either relying on the case law of international tribunals, notably the International Criminal Tribunal for the Former Yugoslavia (ICTY),[18] or directly interpreting the elements of the conflict in question.[19]

Turning specifically to the international protection of human rights, domestic courts have used the same type of precedents to affirm, sometimes for the first time, the customary law nature of norms such as those imposing the obligation of non-*refoulement* of asylum seekers,[20] the prohibition of racial discrimination,[21] and the recognition of fundamental guarantees to all victims of international

[15] *R v Jones and others* [2006] UKHL 16.

[16] Ibid, paras 12ff. In some sections of the judgment, the customary nature of the crime of aggression seems to be regarded as a corollary of the prohibition of aggressive war, the prohibition being recognized as a fundamental rule of general international law. For this aspect of the 2006 judgment connected with the unifying quality of general principles of law, see below.

[17] German Constitutional Court, *Parliamentary Group of the Party of Democratic Socialism in the German Federal Parliament v Federal Government*, Constitutional dispute between federal organs (*Organstreitverfahren*), BverfG, 2 BvE 6/99; ILDC 134 (DE 2001) paras 160 and 162; ibid, *Parliamentary Group of the PDS/Die Linke in the German Federal Parliament v Federal Government* (*The Tornado* case), dispute between supreme federal bodies (*Organstreitverfahren*), 2 BvE 2/07; ILDC 819 (DE 2007); Federal Administrative Court, *Attorney of the Federal Armed Forces v Anonymous (a Major of the Armed Forces)*, Final appeal, BVerwG 2 WD 12.04, 21 June 2005, para. 4.1.4.1.1. This court also clarified that the use of force not authorized by the Security Council or justified as an act of self-defence amounts to an act of aggression which violates an obligation of international *jus cogens* (paras 4.1.4.1.1 and 4.1.4.1.1b). However, in a more recent judgment, the German Constitutional Court, while confirming that the decision on war and peace is to be entrusted to the Federal Parliament, also affirmed that 'The notion of the "use of the armed forces" had to be defined in terms of constitutional law and did not depend directly on the international law qualification of the actual use to which the armed forces were put' (*Parliamentary Group of the Liberal Democratic Party in the German Federal Parliament v The Federal Government*, Final judgment, BVerfG, 2 BvE 1/03; ILDC 956 (DE 2008) para. 73Ia).

[18] German Federal Court of Justice, Third Criminal Law Senate, Revision judgment of 21 February 2001, *Sokolović* (*Complicity in Genocide* case), 3 StR 372/00; ILDC 564 (DE 2001).

[19] Bow Street Magistrates' Court, 13 November 2003, *Government of the Russian Federation v Akhmed Zakaev*, First instance, ILDC 259 (UK 2003); Dutch Council of State, Administrative Law Division, 20 July 2007, *A and ors v Minister of Immigration and Integration*, Administrative appeal, 200608939/1; LJN No BB0917; ILDC 910 (NL 2007).

[20] See House of Lords, 9 December 2004, *R (European Roma Rights Centre) v Immigration Officer at Prague Airport and another*, Appeal [2004] UKHL 55; ILDC 110 (UK 2004); High Court of the Special Administrative Region of Hong Kong, Court of First instance, 18 February 2008, *C and ors v Director of Immigration* [2008] 2 HKC 165; ILDC 1119 (HK 2008) paras 72–3.

[21] House of Lords, *European Roma Rights Centre*, n 20; United States Court of Appeals for the Ninth Circuit, 7 August 2006, *Sarei and ors v Rio Tinto and ors*, 456 F3d 1069; Turkish Cypriot com-

armed conflicts as prescribed by Article 75 of Additional Protocol I to the Geneva Conventions.[22]

## (C) New customary rules on international cooperation in judicial and cultural matters

Equally involved in the phenomenon under discussion is international cooperation in judicial and cultural cooperation. In this respect, I will mention two judgments from Italian case law.

In judgment no. 1072 of 17 January 2007,[23] the Court of Cassation did venture to affirm, albeit cautiously, the existence of a customary international law, valid both in time of peace and in time of armed conflict, roughly corresponding to the definition of terrorism set out by the Financing Convention.[24]

In the field of cultural relations, mention should be made of the decision of the Council of State of 23 June 2008. The highest administrative jurisdiction did not hesitate to determine the existence of a customary rule imposing the restitution of cultural artefacts removed from states which have been victims of military occupation and colonization. The obligation was inferred from diverse elements of international practice, as in the previous case, but this time the judges also tried a systematic interpretation of the customary rule in question. Indeed, they held that the obligation of restitution of art objects is a corollary of the interplay between the principle prohibiting the use of force and the principle of the self-determination of peoples.[25]

## (D) Excluding the existence of customary rules in some controversial topics

The method in question has been used not only to affirm new customary law, but also to exclude some controversial subjects from the current scope of customary law. In the field of disarmament, for instance, the 1996 ICJ Advisory Opinion on *Nuclear Weapons* was the only precedent quoted by a UK Court of Appeal in 2002 to reinforce its conclusion that the possession of nuclear weapons in pursuance of a policy of deterrence was not contrary to humanitarian principles of customary international law.[26] The same court considered the First Report of the ILC's

munity, Supreme Court, *National Unity Party v TRNC Assembly of the Republic*, 21 June 2006, No. 3, ILDC 499 (TCc 2006); High Court of Hong Kong, *C and ors v Director of Immigration*, n 20.

[22] Supreme Court of the United States, *Hamdan v Rumsfeld*, 548 US 557 at 632 (2006).

[23] *Corte di Cassazione (Sez. I penale)*, 11 October 2006, No. 1072, *Bouyahia Maher Ben Abdelaziz et al*, XVIII Italian YIL (2007) 325–7.

[24] Ibid, paras 2.1–4.1. On this judgment, see L. Aleni, 'Distinguishing Terrorism from Wars of National Liberation in the Light of International Law: A View from Italian Courts', 6 JICJ (2008) 525 ff.

[25] Council of State, 23 June 2008, No. 3154, *Associazione nazionale Italia Nostra Onlus v Ministero per i beni e le attività culturali et al*, XVIII Italian YIL (2008) 159ff.

[26] *Marchiori v Environment Agency and ors*, Appeal judgment [2002] EWCA Civ 03, ILDC 241 (UK 2002), 25 January 2002. See also Queen's Bench Division (Divisional Court), 2 October 2000,

Special Rapporteur on Diplomatic Protection and the ICJ's judgment on *Barcelona Traction* as conclusive evidence that the UK government was under no obligation to respond positively to the claimant's request for diplomatic assistance.[27]

Moreover, two important examples from German case law can be mentioned. In 2006, the Federal High Court of Justice ruled that customary international law does not confer a right to reparation on the victims of gross violations of human rights. This conclusion was entirely based on the lack of any reference to that right in the ILC Articles on the international responsibility of states and in the relevant international treaties.[28] On the other hand, the German Federal Constitutional Court relied on national and international judicial precedents in concluding that there was no customary obligation to refuse the extradition of a foreigner who had been lured out of his or her state of origin.[29]

Finally, when the Hague District Court had to prove that international customary law did not exclude universal jurisdiction in relation to Common Article 3 of the Geneva Conventions, it relied on the ICTY judgment in the *Tadić* case, and on the Institut de droit international's Kraków resolution on universal criminal jurisdiction.[30]

## 3. Recourse to the interpretative methods of modern constitutionalism to protect new interests and to solve normative conflicts in the field of human rights

### (A) Resort to the fundamental principles of international law as a specific source of general international law

Let us move now to the second element of the interpretative strategy of domestic courts. As I have already explained in the introduction, it involves resorting to the hermeneutical methods of modern constitutionalism to solve normative conflicts between international norms, and thus ensure the coherence of a legal order as a whole. Indeed, it is an approach which supreme and constitutional courts have introduced and constantly improve to expand on the norms and principles protecting fundamental values under democratic constitutions.

---

*Hutchinson v Newbury Magistrates' Court*, unreported, available at <http://www.tridentploughshares. org>; High Court of Justiciary of Scotland, *Re Nuclear Weapons* [2001] JC 143, HCJ.

[27] *R (On the application of Abbasi and Abbasi) v Secretary of State for Foreign and Commonwealth Affairs and Secretary of State for the Home Department* [2002] EWCA Civ 1598, Court of Appeal, 6 November 2002, para. 69. See also Queen's Bench Division, *R (Al Rawi and others) v Secretary of State for Foreign and Commonwealth Affairs* [2006] EWHC 972.

[28] Federal High Court of Justice, Third Senate for Civil Affairs, 2 November 2006, *35 citizens of the Former Federal Republic of Yugoslavia v Germany*, BGHZ 166, 384; III ZR 190/05; ILDC 887 (DE 2006), paras 9–13.

[29] *Yemeni citizens extradition* case, Individual constitutional complaint, BVerfG, 2 BvR 1506/03; ILDC 10 (DE 2003), 5 November 2003, paras 57–8.

[30] *Public Prosecutor v F*, First instance, Criminal procedure, LJN: BA9575, 09/750001–06; ILDC 797 (NL 2007), 25 June 2005, paras 15 and 18.

One can identify *three* well-known criteria belonging to the constitutional method of judicial interpretation that are increasingly being applied to create a uniform system of fundamental *international* values.

The first of these three criteria concerns the use of general principles of law to construct a framework of fundamental international values. Fundamental principles should not be confused with general principles as a form of *analogia juris*, which in international law chiefly consists in filling the lacunae in international law by resorting to common principles of domestic law.[31] Nor should they be automatically equated to the notion of international *jus cogens*, the effects of which impinge on the validity of international treaties and the consequences of an internationally wrongful act.[32] In liberal constitutions, whether written or unwritten, fundamental values are in fact expressed by a core of general principles of law, that is, provisions expressing essential concepts rich in meaning. The most common examples are respect for human dignity, equality, personal freedom, peace, or the right to a healthy environment. Unlike rules, general principles of law do not impose a specific course of conduct, but limit themselves to prescribing 'a direction that must be followed, a general trend that must be respected, and a value that must be taken into consideration'.[33] In fact, they perform an auxiliary and unifying function which enables constitutional and supreme courts to invoke fundamental principles of law whenever they need to adapt existing constitutional rules to the changing needs and convictions of society. Indeed, grounding a decision upon undisputed, albeit vaguely formulated principles makes it possible to preserve the coherence of the legal order, while suggesting an evolutive interpretation which might even border on the formulation of new rules.

International law is going through a similar process, as far as domestic courts are concerned. In some important decisions, national courts have indeed identified a number of general principles of law considered to be universally recognized as expressing the fundamental values of the international community. The international materials most frequently used by national judges to infer these fundamental principles of international law have been resolutions of international organizations, random provisions from treaties sometimes not even ratified by the *forum* state, and national and international decisions unconnected with the merits of the case in point. This is not exactly the kind of practice from which actual state behaviour can be discerned.

On the other hand, we are currently going through a period where fundamental values in national and international law are converging as they both concern topics such as human rights, peace, and the environment. This is part of the progressive internationalization of democratic life ongoing since the entry into force of the UN Charter. Consequently, general principles incorporating fundamental values are increasingly being identified by cross-referencing both international and domestic legal materials. In fact, international practice is often enmeshed in the

---

[31]  Indeed, this source has been invoked by domestic courts to establish general principles of international criminal law. See Court of Appeal, Criminal Division, 6 June 2003, *R v Safi and ors* [2003] EWCA Crim 1809; ILDC 253 (UK 2003).

[32]  See Section 3(B) below for the effects of *jus cogens* as they emerge from domestic case law.

[33]  F. Viola and G. Zaccaria, *Diritto e interpretazione* (Rome/Bari: Laterza, 1999), 385.

normative and judicial constitutional practice of states confirming the universality of the fundamental values in question.

From this heterogeneous material, domestic courts have particularly inferred the international principle of 'human dignity', sometimes also referred to as 'respect for elementary considerations of humanity', and the principle of 'sustainable development', more broadly referred to as the principle of 'the protection of the environment'.

There is a growing tendency across the domestic courts of several states to use these principles for innovative and uniform solutions under international law. Some national courts have indeed resorted to fundamental principles of international law to integrate the otherwise scanty customary regime of the prohibition of crimes against humanity as well as the protection of the environment, developing detailed provisions to the due-diligence-like structure of the relevant customary obligations on these topics. Moving from the general principles of human dignity and respect for elementary considerations of humanity, domestic courts have upheld, as part of international customary law, the right to compensation for the victims of gross violations of human rights,[34] the non-applicability of statutory limitation to war crimes and crimes against humanity,[35] the prohibition of arbitrary detention,[36] and the right to life, physical integrity, and human and dignified treatment.[37]

As mentioned above, fundamental principles are often identified by combining a blend of constitutional and international practice. This has proved particularly convenient for domestic courts which made use of the international principles of 'human dignity' and 'sustainable development' to justify the extensive interpretation of incompletely drafted constitutional and statutory provisions on the protection of human rights and the environment.[38]

## (B) Resort to the concept of normative hierarchy

Secondly, analogy with constitutional methods of interpretation has led a number of domestic courts to rely on the concept of hierarchy of different international norms in relation to the importance of legally protected values. In fact, recent

[34] Italian Court of Cassation, 29 May 2008, *Germany v Mantelli and ors*, Preliminary order on jurisdiction, No. 14201/2008; ILDC 1037 (IT 2008).
[35] Supreme Court of Argentina, 13 July 2007, *Mazzeo and ors*, M 2333 XLII; ILDC 1084 (AR 2007), para. 28.     [36] Court of Appeal, Civil Division, *Abbasi*, n 27, paras 59ff.
[37] South African Constitutional Court, 6 June 1995, *South Africa v Makwanyane and anor*, Case No CCT/3/94, ILDC 647 (ZA 1995), 1995 (3) SA 391 (CC), 1995 (6) BCLR 665 (CC), paras 33ff; ibid, 9 June 1995, *South Africa v Williams and ors*, CCT/20/94; ILDC 654 (ZA 1995), (1995) ZACC 6; Israeli Supreme Court sitting as a Court of Appeal, 12 April 2000, *Anonymous (Lebanese citizens) v Minister of Defence*, FCrA 7048/97; ILDC 12 (IL 2000), paras 19ff; German Federal Administrative Court, 28 February 2007, *Anonymous v Circuit of Saxon Switzerland*, Case No. 3 C 38/05; ILDC 951 (DE 2007), para. 36. The value of this judgment is, however, gravely diminished by the conclusion that the employment of forced labourers did not constitute per se a violation of the principles of humanity and the rule of law (paras 42–4).
[38] On this aspect, see the case law referred to in M. Iovane, 'La participation de la société civile à l'élaboration et à l'application du droit international de l'environnement', 112 RGDIP (2008) 465 at 494ff. See also E. Benvenisti, 'Reclaiming Democracy: The Strategic Uses of Foreign and International Law by National Courts', 102 AJIL (2008) 258ff.

judicial practice has made an important contribution to how the effects of peremptory norms of customary international law or *jus cogens* are assessed. In practice, domestic courts have not used the notion of *jus cogens* for either of the effects advocated by recent developments in the field of international law, namely the invalidation of treaties and the right of every state to adopt countermeasures for the violation of *erga omnes* obligations. However, domestic courts do use the greater importance of humanitarian values protected by a set of customary rules both to solve conflicts between conflicting customary rules and to establish the particular consequences of a regime of gross violations of human rights.[39] In other words, the effects of *jus cogens* have been decided on a case-by-case basis, using an interpretative method and not because they had been established by international law once and for all.

Concerning conflicts between international norms, a prominent example of this approach is the growing case law from lower and supreme courts affirming that the prohibition of gross violations of human rights, being a peremptory norm of customary international law, prevails over the norm regarding the immunity of foreign states from civil jurisdiction.[40] A similar reasoning has also been followed in some judgments concerning the immunity of foreign organs from criminal jurisdiction.[41]

---

[39] Some of these effects have already been pointed out by A. Cassese, *Diritto Internazionale* (Bologna: Il Mulino, 2006), 206ff.

[40] Italian Court of Cassation, *Ferrini v Germany*, Decision No. 5044/2004, Italian YIL; ibid, *Mantelli* case, n 34, in Italian YIL; ibid, *Milde* case, Decision No. 1072/2009, in Italian YIL. An interesting decision of a Belgian Court of Appeal affirmed that the provisions of the Vienna Convention on Diplomatic Immunity cannot be interpreted as preventing legal authorities in the host state from applying compulsory supervisory or protective measures for children in a situation of troubled upbringing, even if such children enjoy diplomatic immunity. Although the court later declared that it was applying the UN Convention on the Right of the Child as *lex posterior*, it was in reality resolving a conflict between conventional norms in the light of an international value (the protection of the child) possessing a higher rank: *Public Prosecutor v LC*, Appeal Judgment, *RW* (*Rechtskundig Weekblad*) 2002–03, no. 8, 301; ILDC 46 (BE 2002), 1 March 2002, para. 3.

[41] See, House of Lords, *R v Bartle and the Commissioner of Police for the Metropolis and Others, ex p Pinochet* (on appeal from a Divisional Court of the Queen's Bench Division); *R v Evans and Another and the Commissioner of Police for the Metropolis and Others, ex p Pinochet* (on appeal from a Divisional Court of the Queen's Bench Division) [1999] UKHL 17 at 199, per Lord Hope of Craighead:

> The principle of immunity *ratione materiae* protects all acts which the head of state has performed in the exercise of the functions of government.... There are only two exceptions to this approach which customary international law has recognised. The first relates to criminal acts which the head of state did under the colour of his authority as head of state but which were in reality for his own pleasure or benefit.... The second relates to acts the prohibition of which has acquired the status under international law of *jus cogens*.

See also *HSA et al v SA et al (Decision related to the indictment of defendant Ariel Sharon, Amos Yaron and others)*, Court of Cassation of Belgium, P.02.1139.F, 12 February 2003. According to the Court,

> il ressort de la combinaison des articles IV et VI de la Convention pour la prévention et la répression du crime de génocide que l'immunité de juridiction dont bénéficie un chef de gouvernement en exercice est exclue en cas de poursuite devant... les tribunaux compétents de l'Etat sur le territoire duquel l'acte a été commis ou devant la Cour criminelle internationale... (ibid at 7)

The judges also held that

The doctrine of act of state, which in some states prevents the courts from inquiring into the validity of public acts of a sovereign power performed within its own territory, has also been affected by international *jus cogens*. As the House of Lords put it in the *Kuwait Airlines* case, domestic courts must refuse to recognize acts of foreign states that violate customary norms of fundamental importance, such as the prohibition of the use of force.[42] Another English court also confirmed that gross violations of human rights will leave national judges free to express their view on a foreign state's clear breach of international law.[43] Turning to US case law, in 2006 the Court of Appeals for the 9th Circuit decided that systematic violations of the prohibition of racial discrimination constitute a violation of international *jus cogens* and could thus not be recognized as official sovereign acts for the purpose of the act of state doctrine.[44]

As regards the consequences on a domestic regime of gross violations of human rights, we may recall that the House of Lords affirmed the exclusion of evidence obtained by torture, having recognized that the prohibition of torture is included in international *jus cogens*.[45] Another typical effect of the notion of international *jus cogens* suggested by domestic courts concerns the refusal to extradite or deport persons at risk of being tortured in the receiving state, torture being considered in several judgments as contrary to the most fundamental principles of international justice. Extradition has been refused on these grounds despite the existence of an international convention on the judicial cooperation in force between the forum and the requesting state.[46] Following the same line of reasoning, the German Constitutional Court relied on the *jus cogens* character of the prohibition of genocide in applying the principle of universal jurisdiction to the prosecution of a Bosnian Serb in Germany.[47] Although not clearly set out, the *jus cogens* character of the prohibition of gross violations of human rights allowed the Supreme Court of Argentina to establish a harsher criminal regime for the perpetrators of such violations during the so-called 'Dirty War'.[48]

---

l'immunité attachée à la qualité officielle d'une personne n'entraîne pas son irresponsabilité pénale à l'égard des crimes de droit international énumérés par la loi du 16 juin 1993 relative à la répression des violations graves du droit humanitaire. (ibid at 8)

[42] House of Lords, *Kuwait Airways Corp*, n 13.

[43] Court of Appeal, Civil Division, *Abbasi*, n 27, para. 57.

[44] *Sarei v Rio Tinto*, n 21, at para. 17. The same principle has been recently confirmed, with regard to acts of torture, by the Federal Court of Australia, in *Habib v Commonwealth of Australia* [2010] FCAFC 12.

[45] *A (FC) and ors (FC) v Secretary of State for the Home Department, A and ors (FC) v Secretary of State for the Home Department (Joined Appeals)* [2005] UKHL 71.

[46] Bow Street Magistrates' Courts, *Zakaev* case, n 19. See also the cases recalled by Cassese, n 39, at 211ff.

[47] *Jorgić* case, German Higher Regional Court (*Oberlandesgericht*) of Düsseldorf, judgment of 26 September 1997, 2StE 8/96, unpublished, and German Federal High Court (*Bundesgerichtshof*), judgment of 30 April 1999, in 45 *Entscheidungen des Bundesgerichtshofes in Strafsachen*, 65–91.

[48] *Mazzeo and ors*, n 35, at paras 32ff.

## (C) Balancing and proportionality

We should finally recall that domestic courts have applied other hermeneutical devices typical of a constitutional approach, such as balancing or proportionality, to reconcile conflicts between divergent interests equally protected under international law, or to solve conflicts between international and domestic law. Clearly, these conceptual mechanisms are used by the courts in answer to the specific circumstances of each case. This highlights the creative role of the judiciary in reaching effective solutions for the differing international law issues they are called upon to address.

In relation to the first type of conflicting norms, balancing and proportionality were mentioned in the *Al Jedda* case, where the House of Lords stated in principle that the detainee's rights as protected under domestic and international law must not be restricted to any greater extent than strictly required by the state's imperative reasons of security.[49] This position has been more incisively applied by other courts in relation to UN Security Council sanctions against suspected terrorists. In these cases, some national judges did not hesitate totally or partially to quash executive orders implementing the relevant Security Council resolutions. Given that the orders did not provide any form of judicial review, they were considered as a violation of fundamental liberties protected by both constitutional and international law.[50]

The proportionality rule also played a major role in the recent case law of the Israeli Supreme Court on respect for human rights and humanitarian law by the Israeli Defence Force.[51] The recent US Supreme Court judgments in the so-called

---

[49]   *R (On the application of Al-Jedda) (FC) v Secretary of State for Defence*, Appeal judgment [2007] UKHL 58; [2008] 1 AC 332, 12 December 2007, House of Lords, Appellate Committee, paras 35–9. In a recent judgment by a Dutch District Court, the judges affirmed that the law implementing the Security Council resolution imposing sanctions on Iranian nationals was contrary to the internationally protected right of non-discrimination because it did not conform to the standard of objective and reasonable justification: *A and others v Netherlands (Ministry of Foreign Affairs and Ministry of Education, Culture, and Science)*, First instance judgment, LJN: BL1862/334949; ILDC 1463 (NL 2010), 3 February 2010, paras 4.6 and 4.10.

[50]   See the recent judgment by the UK Supreme Court, in which the Law Lords—confirming the High Court's approach in *Hay* [2009]—quashed in part the UK's *Al Qaida Order* because it removes the right of access to an effective remedy: *HM Treasury v Mohammed Jabar Ahmed and ors (FC)*; *HM Treasury v Mohammed al-Ghabra (FC)*; *R (On the application of Hani El Sayed Sabaei Youssef) v HM Treasury* [2010] UKSC 2, 27 January 2010, paras 81–2. In this regard, it is worth mentioning also the judgment rendered by the Canadian Federal Court in *Abousfian Abdelrazik v The Minister of Foreign Affairs and the Attorney General of Canada*, 4 June 2009, available at <http://decisions.fct-cf.gc.ca/en/dn/2009/01.html>. In that case the judge held that Canada had engaged in a conduct and specific acts that constituted a breach of Mr Abdelrazik's constitutional right to enter Canada, even though he was subject to an asset freeze and a travel ban under the relevant Security Council resolutions (ibid, paras 156 and 157).

[51]   See, among others, *Beit Sourik Village Council v Israel and the Commander of the Israeli Defence Force in the West Bank*, HCJ 2056/04; ILDC 16 (IL 2004); *Mara'abe and ors v Prime Minister of Israel*, HCJ 7957/04; ILDC 157 (IL 2005); *Public Committee against Torture in Israel and Palestinian Society for the Protection of Human Rights and the Environment v Israel and ors*, HCJ 769/02; ILDC 597 (IL 2006). Indeed, it can be said that the proportionality principle is quintessential to the Israeli case law (see A. Barak, *The Judge in a Democracy* (Princeton, NJ: Princeton University Press, 2008), 254ff).

*Guantanamo* cases may also be considered as an important example of the same tendency.[52]

Balancing and proportionality are also playing a significant role in the more traditional field of the jurisdictional immunity of states and international organizations. According to some Belgian decisions, the recognition of jurisdictional immunity of international organizations depends on whether the claimants are guaranteed 'reasonable alternative means' to protect their rights under the European Convention on Human Rights.[53] An English court also recognized immunity from execution of a central bank's funds in London, having ascertained that the claimant could enforce a judgment by the International Centre for Settlement of Investment Disputes (ICSID) elsewhere.[54] These judgments were delivered on the assumption that international law protects every individual's right to a fair trial.

In the same vein, the Brussels Labour Court of Appeal balanced diplomatic immunity and the right to a fair judgment, both protected by international law, in concluding that the initiation of proceedings by a summons was not a breach of the immunity, provided that the procedure was suspended for as long as the immunity was applicable in order to safeguard the efficient functioning of the diplomatic mission.[55]

Turning to a different topic, the German Constitutional Court invoked the principle of proportionality in deciding whether to extradite to India a foreigner who feared an excessively harsh punishment amounting to inhuman treatment.[56]

As for conflicts between international and domestic law, it is interesting how balancing and proportionality have been applied in some cases traditionally dismissed under the non-justiciability or political question doctrines by domestic courts. Such cases involve defence or foreign affairs decisions *by the executive of the forum state.* Instead of prejudicially refusing all judicial review over disputes relating to such matters, some national judges have justified their restraint by invoking the duty to respect the competences which every democratic constitution confers

---

[52] See, in particular, *Hamdan*, n 22, at 612. The same balancing approach has been followed by the House of Lords in some rulings concerning anti-terrorism measures. See, in particular, House of Lords, 16 December 2004, *A (FC) and others (FC) v Secretary of State for the Home Department* [2004] UKHL 56 (*Belmarsh* case); ibid, 31 October 2007, *Secretary of State for the Home Department v JJ and others (FC)* [2007] UKHL 45; ibid, 31 October 2007, *Secretary of State for the Home Department v MB (FC),* [2007] UKHL 46; ibid, 31 October 2007, *Secretary of State for the Home Department v E and another* [2007] UKHL 47 (*Control order* cases).

[53] Brussels Court of Appeals, 9th Chamber, 4 March 2003, *Lutchmaya v General Secretariat of the ACP Group,* Journal des Tribunaux 2003, 684; ILDC 1363 (BE 2003), paras 39 and 42; Brussels Labour Court of Appeals, 4th Chamber, *Siedler v Western European Union,* Journal des Tribunaux 2004, 617; ILDC 53 (BE 2003), para. 63; Court of First Instance, First Chamber, 1 December 2005, *SA Energies Nouvelles et Environnement v Agence Spatiale Européenne,* Journal des Tribunaux 2006, No. 6216, 171; ILDC 1229 (BE 2005), paras 12, 24, and 27.

[54] Queen's Bench Division, Commercial Division, 21 October 2005, *AIG Capital Partners Inc and CJSC Tema Real Estate Co. Ltd v Kazakhstan and ors,* Enforcement decision [2005] EWHC 2239; ILDC 94 (UK 2005).

[55] *BS and KG v AR and AR,* Appeal No. 42.534, ILDC 50 (BE 2002) (2003), *Tijdschrift Vreemdelingenrecht* 143, paras 76, 77, 78, and 80.

[56] *Extradition to India* case, n 29.

on the state's elected organs whenever decisions on matters of gravest public concern need to be taken. At the same time, they have also asserted their responsibility to ensure that all public power be lawfully conferred and exercised. Reference has expressly been made to the possible review of decisions by the executive affecting the human rights of specific individuals contrary to international law.[57]

I submit that judicial review of executive decisions under customary international law could reasonably develop along these tentatively balanced lines. In reality, the separation of powers is a key element of democratic regimes the advancement of which is advocated by international law itself. At the same time, the existence of some forms of checks and balances between the different powers, as well as between institutions and civil society, are also part of a rule-of-law-based system.

From this perspective, the legitimacy under customary international law of *general* decisions by the executive, such as launching an armed attack or the authorization to install a foreign military base, may preferably be challenged in the domestic legal order by Parliament or public opinion through the political measures of democratic control.[58] Indeed, such measures of control may include judicial intervention by the constitutional or the supreme court whenever those courts are formally entrusted with scrutiny of the executive's constitutional limits. Peace and the protection of human rights are in fact international law values incorporated in those very constitutions. Prominent examples of this situation come from the German Constitutional Court[59] and the Costa Rican Supreme Court.[60] Clearly, all these measures aim to prevent the governmental decision in question from being adopted, or else to obtain its withdrawal. In practice, domestic courts have mostly dismissed requests to determine the illegality of a declaration of war under customary international law, considering the decision to go to war to be a typical non-justiciable act.[61]

On the other hand, courts have cautiously found themselves examining international law in order to ascertain the possible consequences of the executive's external acts affecting individuals. One author has rightly pointed out that some courts have examined the legality of defence and foreign affairs decisions, such as the installation of a military base, establishing that the installation was not per se contrary to international norms on the prohibition of the use of force.[62] In two well-known cases, domestic courts did, however, implicitly rely on the illegality of an armed

---

[57] See, at this regard, the case law analysed by Amoroso, n 12, at 943ff.

[58] Confidence vote, parliamentary inquiry commissions, protests, etc.

[59] See the judgments of the German Constitutional Court quoted n 17.

[60] Two unreported judgments by the Costa Rican Supreme Court imposed on the government the withdrawal of their official endorsement of the imminent US/UK-led attack on Iraq. The military attack was, in fact, regarded by the Court as being contrary to the Costa Rican Constitution and Charter of the United Nations (Sala Constitucional de la Corte Suprema De Justicia), *Alvaro Cantero Valverde v La Ministra de la Presidencia de la Republica y el Ministro de Relaciones Exteriores y Culto*, Recurso de amparo, 2003; ibid, *Humberto Arce Salas, Kyra de la Rosa, Carlos Herrera Calvo, Peter Guevara Guth, Luis Guillermo Villanueva, Federico Malavasi y Carlos Salazar Ramirez v La Ministra de la Presidencia y El Ministro de Relaciones Exteriores*, recurso de amparo, 2003).

[61] In the *CND* case [2002] EWHC 2777, eg, the Queen's Bench Division of the High Court expressly ruled out the possibility of granting an advisory declaration on the unlawfulness of the impending decision to take military intervention against Iraq. For other cases, see n 11.

[62] Amoroso, n 12, at 945ff.

attack launched by their executive to draw such specific conclusions as the recognition of the right of conscientious objection,[63] and the proposition that aggression is in principle a crime disciplined by positive customary international law.[64]

## 4. Possible suggestions for the future

Stimulated by increasing claims by individuals seeking remedies against alleged violation of their rights, domestic courts have produced an imposing body of precedents, often richly structured through abundant reference to international practice. However, it is a phenomenon which has received contrasting appraisals by different scholars and has been assessed from different perspectives. Whereas some authors have hailed it as an advancement of the rule of law in international relations,[65] others fear that conflicting decisions on the same subject will strengthen fragmentation and ambiguity on the content of international law, undermining its efficiency and credibility.[66] Moreover, some scholars have privileged a more general and theoretical assessment of the practice, highlighting the position of domestic courts as a distinct collective power in the new globalized society, or as effective international actors alongside governments, international courts, and international institutions.[67]

While appreciating these theoretical suggestions, I would emphasize that recent national judicial practice marks a real turning point in the formation of unwritten international law, that is, of the only source of general international law.

As determined by the practice examined above, domestic case law is absorbing and overlapping with the two traditional sources of unwritten international law enumerated in Article 38(1)(c) of the ICJ Statute, that is, custom and general principles of law. Indeed, domestic courts have not limited themselves merely to applying existing customary law or general principles of law, but have mostly developed a creative judge-made law. In addition, this activism by domestic courts is matched by an analogous attitude on the part of international tribunals, both of which embody the present trend towards the judicialization of international law.

It is very likely that this rich interpretative practice by domestic courts will continue to spread in the near future, in spite of the many doctrinal hesitations still

---

[63] German Federal Administrative Court, *Attorney of the Federal Armed Forces v Anonymous*, n 17. [64] House of Lords, *Jones* case, n 15.

[65] Conforti, n 1; A. Nollkaemper, 'Internationally Wrongful Acts in Domestic Courts', 101 AJIL (2007) 760ff.

[66] See, among others, E.-U. Petersmann, 'Justice as Conflict Resolution: Proliferation, Fragmentation, and Decentralization of Dispute Settlement in International Trade', 27 U Penn J Int'l Econ L (2006) 273ff. As known, however, the issue of fragmentation has been mainly dealt with having regard to the proliferation of international tribunals (see, eg, P.S. Rao, 'Multiple International Judicial Forums: A Reflection of the Growing Strength of International Law or its Fragmentation?', 25 Mich JIL (2004) 929f. It has been authoritatively maintained that this anxiety is bereft of foundation (B. Conforti, 'Unité et fragmentation du droit international: "glissez, mortels, n'appuyez pas!"', 111 RGDIP (2007) 5ff.

[67] A.-M. Slaughter, 'A Global Community of Courts', 44 Harv Int'l LJ (2003) 191ff; Shany, n 1; Benvenisti and Downs, n 1.

favouring a diplomatic solution for individual claims under international law. As mentioned earlier, this attitude by domestic courts is matched by an analogous trend in international courts. Admittedly, this practice now raises the problems which have marked all manifestations of judge-made law and *Rechtsfortbildung* by the judiciary since the Middle Ages. Basically, it is a shared conviction that judges cannot use their freedom of interpretation to find innovative solutions in an arbitrary way. They would risk handing down an illegitimate and ineffectual decision with no impact on the case they have pronounced on, let alone on the evolution of the legal order as a whole. Moreover, this judicial creativity may also run counter to the practice which the executive organs of the various states observe in their diplomatic intercourse. Although this creativity is important for updating the content of fundamental liberties, too much discretionary power in the hands of the judiciary may, from the domestic point of view, also violate the democratic principle of the separation of powers.

As is also the case in relation to the interpretative practice of domestic norms protecting human rights, the only correction to these shortcomings is to adhere to strict methodological principles in setting out the grounds for any innovative decision. Indeed, it is the respect of these very conditions which characterizes courts as independent bodies exercising the judicial function in a rule-of-law-based legal system. Indeed, courts must respect precise formal constraints, such as the obligation not to exceed the limits of their competence and to give priority to norms of a higher rank. Besides these basic conditions, traditional theoretical methodology also mentions strict adherence to the criteria of reasonableness and consistency among the different arguments justifying the court's conclusions.

Modern hermeneutics has set out a series of specific criteria to be followed by the courts in the field of fundamental values, such as the protection of human rights and the environment, or the prohibition of crimes against humanity and the use of force. These norms constitute the thrust of contemporary international law, as they express the moral and political choices of the community as a whole.

As also happens under constitutional law, those norms need to be constantly integrated and updated, as well as harmonized with other conflicting values and general interests. For carrying out these inevitable interpretative activities, legal hermeneutics affirms that formal criteria must be coupled with substantial control over the correspondence of the norms in question to the changing ethical convictions and expectations of the community, and the conformity of judge-made law with the existing system of norms and principles.[68]

As we have seen, the first type of control has been carried out especially by expanding on the content of general principles of law and *jus cogens*, whereas the second is expressed by the canons of balancing and proportionality. Substantial controls are generally justified through abundant reference to precedents, scholarly opinions, and evidence from civil society organizations, as it normally happens in the common law tradition. Illustrations of both kinds of substantial controls are the English judgments on the use of force and aggression, the Italian Supreme Court's

---

[68] For further details on and references to these theories, see Iovane, n 38, at 495–8.

decisions on the relationship between sovereign immunity and gross violations of human rights, Belgian decisions on the relationship between the immunity of international organizations and the right of access to courts, and the Argentinean Supreme Court judgment on the crimes committed during the 'Dirty War'.

It is the reaction to the individual judgment which will decide whether all the formal and material criteria have been thoroughly respected and, consequently, whether the innovative solution proposed by a domestic jurisdiction has a chance of being successful. This reaction may come from a 'superior' or international judge, from the parties to the dispute, or from the international community as a whole. In reality, if the formal conditions on the competence and hierarchy of the sources are breached, the original decision is at risk of being quashed or revised by a higher court. Similarly, the lack of substantial controls over the existence and scope of a fundamental value will result in the decision or in an advisory opinion becoming a dead letter, that is, an isolated judicial act bearing no consequences on the development of international law. In some cases, an unreasonable decision which departs excessively from prior authorities may even give rise to an internationally wrongful act by the forum state. The Italian cases on the definition of terrorism or the obligation to return looted cultural heritage may have come too early, and were insufficiently justified on the basis of prior judicial practice. Consequently, it is very unlikely that they will be taken up by other courts deciding similar cases in the near future.

Conversely, the observance paid to a correct interpretative method will help the courageous attempts of domestic courts to produce long-standing effects. Within the context of a common law system grounded on the *stare decisis* principle, this means that an innovative decision on international law will become a precedent to be followed in future cases. In a civil law system, a well-balanced domestic decision advancing international law on controversial topics is more likely to be imitated to solve similar disputes by other courts in the same system. More importantly, an unchallenged and well-received domestic decision may be picked up by foreign and international courts thus becoming generally recognized case law, that is, a judicial authority upon which to ground future judicial solutions under general international law by domestic or international courts. As we have seen, this phenomenon is practically overshadowing the classical formation of general international law from the spontaneous practice of inter-state relations. Indeed, an innovative solution reached in the particular case may be spontaneously followed later by the international community as a whole, thus becoming a real customary rule.

# 47

# The Low Road: Promoting Civil Redress for International Wrongs

*Jaykumar A. Menon*

## SUMMARY

International law lacks muscle or, in other words, enforcement power; bones, that is, institutional infrastructure and capacity; and even heart, namely, the capacity to face up to some of the largest issues of our times. Civil litigation in domestic courts offers tremendous potential for redressing international wrongs, loosely defined to be of two types: (i) cross-border matters; these can be addressed either by applying rules of international law, or solely through domestic laws as applied across borders and (ii) acts that take place strictly domestically but that nonetheless violate international law, even if their physical aspects are limited to a small inquisition room. Redressing international wrongs through civil litigation has many advantages: (i) domestic courts have clear enforcement power; (ii) civil proceedings are of course initiated by the plaintiff—they are, in a sense, a form of 'bottom-up' activity in the legal world; (iii) domestic civil litigation has brought and will continue to raise issues that certain official hesitancies or deadlocks might otherwise quash; and (iv) while the handful of international courts and tribunals can hear only a limited number of cases per year, via the offices of domestic civil litigation international disputes can be adjudicated by literally thousands of domestic courts across the globe. Measures designed to improve upon the present conditions can be set out as follows: (a) existing educational efforts for current and future practising lawyers should be increased, and also broadened to include legislators and judges; (b) the collection of evidence in one country for use in litigation in another should be facilitated; (c) heads of jurisdiction should be broadened: for instance, often the jurisdictional peg is presence of the defendant's offices or person within the forum; property, however, can be an alternate base of jurisdiction; (d) statutes of limitation impose a major barrier to addressing undeniable injustices; to skirt around it one should resort to the standard doctrine of equitable tolling of the statute of limitations, which can be extended to encompass periods when the harm was undiscovered, or where the defendant was inequitably working to prevent discovery; and (e) civil litigation against corporations relating to their cross-border activity should be stepped up, although the exercise of restraint by plaintiffs and their lawyers, and decisions to sue only for bona fide grave injustices would be advisable.

# 1. Introduction[1]

If someone from a civilization more morally advanced than ours—whether from five hundred years hence, another world, or our imagination—were to behold our earth, what might they make of the current state of affairs? More likely than not, they might be most struck, and offended by, and pity us for, the depredation of the planet and its non-human beings, the billions of humans living without basic necessities in the face of others with plenty, the lack of political freedoms, the dearth of spiritual understanding. Of these problems, the first four are the province of international law which is, arguably, the conduit between our moral imagination, our better angels, and the use of power in our global society.

One could then ask: how adequate has the international law project been, as measured against the lofty but necessary[2] standard of solving these central problems? Or even more aggressively, from the perspective of an individual or entity suffering an injustice, what does all of this international law mean? The actions of the various international courts, the careful discussions of doctrine, the innumerable pages of books, journal articles, and commission findings. Precious little one could say, to be provocative, particularly from the standpoint of the average person who has suffered a wrong, as will be described below. Moreover, it will probably be decades, or centuries, or millennia, before we have a system of international law that can provide the concrete results that those who suffer injustice so desperately need.

In the meantime, what then? Despair? Or only slightly leavened despair, in which we take solace in enunciated but unheeded norms, and in glorious but gossamer hope spun by the legions of estimable scholars, activists, politicians, citizens, and civil servants who inexorably, yet terribly slowly, bring the world of international law, and the civilized conduct that it entails, into more concrete being?

# 2. The inadequacy of current international systems

The problem with international law is its ethereality. It lacks muscle—or in other words, enforcement power; bones, to wit, institutional infrastructure and

---

[1] The chapter title recalls the Scottish ballad 'Bonnie Banks O' Loch Lomond (You Take the High Road)':

Oh! ye'll take the high road and I'll take the low road,
And I'll be in Scotland afore ye.

[2] 'Reach what you cannot!', N. Kazantzakis, *Report to Greco* (New York: Simon & Schuster, 1965), 2.

capacity; and even heart—namely, the capacity to face up to some of the largest issues of our times.

First, the muscle. Enforceability is the Achilles heel of international law. One can enunciate norms. That of course is salutary. Then comes dialogue, discussion, castigation, occasional shame, periodic political mobilization. But what of the norms' direct enforcement? The rules of international law are disobeyed on a massive scale, as can be seen by the large-scale occurrences of torture, arbitrary detention, summary execution, violations of economic rights, and other violations that happen on a daily basis. Even the findings of international bodies—whether rulings of courts such as the International Court of Justice (ICJ), or conclusions of specific bodies such as UN human rights commissions—can be flouted. Even worse, they often lack even a theoretical possibility of being enforced.[3] This is not a scenario in which there are gaps in the enforcement of international law. Rather, it is its photographic negative: a world in which international law is only on occasion enforceable. And perhaps even more damningly, when international law is enforced it is often done so selectively, against the weaker actors, leaving the stronger players to act with impunity.

Secondly, there is a lack of bones, a dearth of institutional infrastructure and capacity. There are simply too few international bodies possessed of too little power to hear the vast number of legal plaints churned up by the world. For example, if a person suffered from a violation of their political rights in most countries on earth, or from a violation of their economic human rights in almost any country, to what international court, or to what doctrine of international law, could they turn and have a realistic chance of redress, or even of having their case heard at all?[4] The ICJ hears only cases between consenting states, international tribunals exist in only a handful of countries, and the International Criminal Court (ICC) has its jurisdictional limitations and acts only if the Prosecutor deems it necessary. While an empirical estimate would be difficult, although interesting, to create, one could hazard that less than 1 per cent of international wrongs are ever heard by or brought to the attention of any facet of the international adjudicatory system. For the other 99 per cent, the wronged have, from the existing system of international bodies and doctrines, only conceptual solace.

Thirdly, there is a lack of heart—namely, there is a failure to face up to some of the largest issues of our times. On a substantive level, an outside observer might

---

[3] Harold Koh points out that even domestic laws—eg the rules governing the parking of cars—often go unheeded and unenforced, 'How is International Human Rights Law Enforced?', 74 Indiana LJ (1993) 1397 at 1398–9. Thus, he argues, international and domestic law are of a piece, sharing similar difficulties with enforceability. The argument, however, is ultimately unpersuasive. In the parking violation situation there at least exists an entity charged with enforcing the law, with the legal authority to tangibly sanction or punish offenders, through fines, and the removal of drivers' licences. The entity may not always succeed, but at least it exists, and that with adequate staffing and the like it could achieve its goals. This is not the case with much of international law, where the enforcing entities often do not exist in the first place.

[4] Of course, the value of international law is not cabined to its worth in deciding cases in the courtroom. It is useful as a point of reference in negotiations and other venues. But, still, if international law is of little practical use for a person or entity who has suffered a wrong, and who seeks redress, or who even desires that the wrong not recur or continue, then that is a devastating shortcoming.

note that to date liability has not been imposed for some of the most colossal global wrongs. Whether it be slavery, the lack of basic necessities for billions of people as outlined so effectively by Thomas Pogge and others,[5] or the disproportionate historical emission of climate-altering gases, the failure to address these basic questions of justice, while at the same time honing in on wrongs committed by less powerful actors, serves to undercut the legitimacy of international law. The status quo is effectively impunity. Many of these wrongs are related to the North–South power dynamic that has dominated international relations over the past four or so centuries. And as the assent of the Great Powers is typically required to form a rule of international law, and as states are typically hesitant to constrain themselves, let alone impose upon themselves liability, there is a structural impediment within the current system of international law that systematically prevents it from addressing some of the largest injustices in the world. As a result, vast issues of global justice remain unredressed, with liability unimposed.

The prospects for addressing some of these core inadequacies of international law in the medium term (say, the next century) seem fairly bleak. Enforcement problems will persist. As for capacity, it will be a long time until we have a system of international courts and tribunals that can adjudicate even a fraction of the problems that arise. And the interests of some states will keep them from creating and deploying rules that assess liability over some of the central global wrongs.

There is, however, some hope, in those parts of the system that are more bottom up, that are relatively speaking more open source, and that leverage existing resources rather than requiring the creation of giant new systems. Hewing to the spirit of this volume, this chapter avowedly is not an exhaustive examination of a narrow slice of law, but rather aims, perhaps quixotically, to provoke, integrate, and make connections, perceive the larger scenario, and point to avenues of future change.

## 3. Transnational litigation: the potential and power of civil redress for international wrongs

Civil litigation in domestic courts offers tremendous potential for redressing international wrongs. International wrongs are loosely defined here to be of two kinds.

---

[5] See, eg, T. Pogge, *World Poverty and Human Rights: Cosmopolitan Responsibilities and Reforms*, 2nd edn (Cambridge: Polity Press, 2008), 2–3:

It is estimated that 830 million human beings are chronically undernourished, 1,100 million lack access to safe water, 2,600 million lack access to basic sanitation ... Each year some 18 million of [those below the World Bank's extreme poverty line] die prematurely from poverty-related causes. This is one-third of all human deaths—50,000 each day, including 29,000 children under age 5 ... The 2,533 million poor together accounted for only about 1.67 percent of all household consumption expenditure in 2004, while the 1,004 million people in the high income countries together accounted for 81%. Shifting 1/70 of the consumption expenditure from the latter group would provide the nearly $300 billion in annual additional consumption the former group needs to escape severe poverty.

First, there are border-crossing matters. These can be addressed either by applying rules of international law, or solely through domestic laws as applied across borders. Secondly, there are acts that take place strictly domestically but that nonetheless violate international law, even if their physical aspects are limited to a small inquisition room, or a square patch of grass.

Collectively, the addressing of these two types of international wrongs in domestic courts could be dubbed 'transnational litigation'.[6] The answer for how to address international problems through law lies, in part, in a shift in focus from 'international law' to 'transnational law', and an embrace of the activities of domestic courts as they grapple with international problems.[7]

Conceptually, transnational litigation, at its best, can be considered to play a role in creating a world where the rule of law, and the rights of people, traverse borders as easily as goods and capital. It can also be thought of as a baby step towards a global community that can support, temper, supplement, and countervail, a global market. Further, the resort to the judicial process is a time-honoured and justified technique for protecting the powerless when the political process has broken down

---

[6] A note on nomenclature: 'Transnational law' has been defined by Philip C. Jessup 'to include all law which regulates actions or events that transcend national frontiers. Both public and private international law are included, as are other rules which do not wholly fit into such standard categories', *Transnational Law* (New Haven, CT: Yale University Press, 1956), 2. 'Transnational legal process', as per Harold Koh, 'breaks down two traditional dichotomies that have historically dominated the study of international law: between domestic and international, public and private', 'Transnational Legal Process,' 75 Neb L Rev (1986) 181 at 183. It 'describes the theory and practice of how public and private actors—nation-states, international organizations, multinational enterprises, nongovernmental organizations, and private individuals—interact in a variety of public and private, domestic and international fora to make, interpret, enforce, and ultimately, internalize rules of transnational law', ibid at 183–4. Koh also speaks of 'transnational public law litigation' to refer to cases brought, eg, in the United States under the Alien Tort Statute and raising claims under international law. Ibid at 184. Here, I will use the term 'transnational litigation', as I am focusing on the litigation process, in a manner that includes both public and private law.

[7] There is also, although it is beyond the scope of what can be discussed in this chapter, the notion that much of domestic constitutional law is, in terms of the contents and substance of its rules, very similar to international law. Indeed, many portions of the domestic constitutional law of the various nations of the earth—at least that portion of constitutional law that relates to individual rights, as opposed to separation of powers, or federalism—can be thought of as a cognate to international law. To explain, many key rules of international law governing the relationship between the individual, state, and society have nearly identical counterparts in the domestic constitutional laws of many nations. Examples include certain rules governing freedom of association, proscriptions against summary execution, free exercise of religion, the requirements of a fair trial, and the like. The Universal Declaration of Human Rights itself was in part drafted by drawing from various domestic constitutional provisions. The provisions in the two bodies of law (domestic constitutional and international) are similar enough that acts that violate one will often violate the other. When that is the case, then there are, salutarily, two separate arguments to be made on behalf of the aggrieved— the international law argument and the domestic constitutional law argument. The former has more global resonance, and more 'grandeur'. The latter utilizes superior enforcement and case-processing capabilities. The point, then, of this little digression is that for those who are serious about making international law more real and enforceable, attention has to be paid to domestic constitutional law, as so many of the rules are so similar. If the goal is to create a fairer and more just society, and not to be overly concerned with form, then we should perhaps consider domestic constitutional law, where its rules are identical, as an integral part of international law, or at least, to borrow a phrase from the *Gita*, different paths to the same place.

or has been inadequate.[8] Civil redress for international wrongs is admittedly a vast area to traverse; given the space constraints the discussion here will be brief.[9]

## (A) The technical framework

To start, it is worth noting that obtaining civil redress for international wrongs is technically possible, and that the basic framework is already in place. Domestic courts can address international matters in two ways: (i) by applying domestic laws to matters of a cross-border character, using long-standing rules governing transnational litigation, or (ii) by directly applying rules of international law to a dispute.

With regard to the former, there are an array of well-established doctrines and procedures by which domestic courts can address cross-border wrongs via the application of domestic laws. These include the doctrine of transitory torts (where an action in tort can be brought, eg, in the jurisdiction where the defendant is domiciled, even if the injury took place elsewhere); cases related to cross-border business transactions, often pursuant to choice of law clauses; the entire field of conflicts of law; certain exceptions to the notion of sovereign immunity; treaties providing for the recognition and enforcement of foreign country judgments; traditional notions of jurisdiction, which allow for the assertion of jurisdiction by a domestic court over certain foreign defendants; and 'exorbitant jurisdiction', the exercise of which is valid under national law but would be considered overreaching under international law.[10]

Domestic courts can also directly deploy rules of international law to disputes. In the United States, this is permissible under the US Alien Tort Statute, which allows for suits for certain violations of international law such as torture, crimes

---

[8] Cf J.H. Ely, *Democracy and Distrust* (Cambridge, MA: Harvard University Press, 1980), 73–179, justifying judicial review, and the overturning of the legislative acts of a democratic government by unelected judges, on the basis that the legislative process can systematically fail to protect 'discrete and insular minorities', who lack adequate representation; see also *United States v Carolene Products*, 304 US 144, 152 N 4 p. 378: Article 73e (1938); R.M. Cover, 'The Origins of Judicial Activism in the Protection of Minorities', 91 Yale LJ (1982) 1287.

[9] While transnational litigation encompasses criminal cases in domestic courts concerning international matters, such as, eg, the criminal prosecution of Chile's former head of state Augusto Pinochet in Spain, in this chapter the focus will lie on transnational *civil* litigation. It should be noted, however, that many transnational civil suits under the US Alien Tort Statute, apply rules of international criminal law (concerning genocide, war crimes, and crimes against humanity) as their 'rules of decision'. As they are formally civil suits, they do not impose imprisonment as a sanction, they nonetheless explicitly deploy rules of criminal law.

[10] Exorbitant bases of jurisdiction have been commonly said to include France's Art. 14 jurisdiction, which provides French courts with jurisdiction in virtually all civil cases where the plaintiff is a French national, regardless of the domicile of the plaintiff or defendant, as well as the Swedish umbrella rule, where a defendant who leaves even minor personal property in Sweden forum is subject to full *in personam* jurisdiction (meaning that they can be sued for any amount, even in excess of the value of the property, and for matters unrelated to the property), to the same extent as if they lived in Sweden. It also includes the US 'tag jurisdiction', a symbolic relic of *capeas ad respondendum*, where the sheriff created jurisdiction by physically hailing the person into court. In 'tag jurisdiction' full *in personam* jurisdiction is created over the defendant simply by a process server touching (or nearly touching) a person with a summons and complaint while they are physically within the jurisdiction, even if they are merely flying over it in an aeroplane.

against humanity, and genocide, and which was originally used in the eighteenth century in cases involving privateers. However, it should be noted that the recognition and use of international law in US courts predates, and is independent of, the Alien Tort Statute's late twentieth-century renaissance.[11]

## (B) Key trends in transnational litigation

What we might call transnational litigation today has, certainly, been with us for millennia. The *lex mercatoria*, for example, governing commercial transactions between merchants throughout Europe, and applied in specialized local courts, began in medieval times. Even older is of course maritime law, a good portion of which governed conduct on the high seas, and was applied in domestic bodies. Older still is the heart of the matter, *jus gentium*, the law of nations, which was applied by Roman lawyers and magistrates in cases involving Roman citizens and foreigners.

In more recent times, there are a few trends of note. These will be outlined here briefly; their implications for the future will explored more fully below in Section 4.

As a root cause, cross-border interactions—be they flows of people, goods, services, or environmental phenomena—have increased. Further, international law has undeniably grown in prominence and impact, particularly after the Second World War, with the creation of the UN system, the Nuremburg Trials, the Universal Declaration of Human Rights, the Geneva Conventions, and numerous other international agreements. As a consequence, international law issues have further insinuated themselves into the legal sphere as a whole, including domestic litigation process and communities. International litigation sections of domestic bar associations, for example, are now commonplace.

With regard to evidence, we have seen an increasing array of devices for taking evidence from abroad, and incorporating cross-border facts into a case. Substantively, rules of customary international law have been imported into domestic cases, not only as a point of reference, but also as the 'rule of decision', or in other words, as the ultimate and formal standard against which conduct is measured.[12] In the United States, this practice became prominent in the modern era with the

---

[11]  See, eg, *Sosa v Alvarez-Machain*, 542 US 692, 730 (2004) ('For two centuries we have affirmed that the domestic law of the United States recognizes the law of nations'); *Banco Nacional de Cuba v Sabbatino*, 376 US 398, 423, 427 (1964) ('[I]t is, of course, true that United States courts apply international law as a part of our own in appropriate circumstances'); *The Paquete Habana*, 175 US at 700, 20 SCt 290 ('International law is part of our law, and must be ascertained and administered by the courts of justice of appropriate jurisdiction, as often as questions of right depending upon it are duly presented for their determination'). Also, treaties that are self-executing or that have been implemented by the appropriate domestic legislation provide causes of action that can be used in US courts, and customary international law is binding in certain circumstances. Moreover, for over two centuries US federal courts have followed the precept that any ambiguities in US statutes must be construed in a way that does not conflict with international law: *Murray v Schooner Charming Betsy*, 2 Cranch 64, 118 (1804).

[12]  Laws of foreign countries and international law have also been increasingly cited, although not as the rule of decision but rather as a point of reference or an aid in clarifying domestic law.

Alien Tort Statute case of *Filártiga v Peña-Irala*,[13] in which a Paraguayan national was allowed to sue his alleged torturer, a former Paraguayan official, in New York, for acts committed in Paraguay. In later years, other private actors such as corporations were also held to be subject to human rights suits via the Alien Tort Statute.[14] Further, on a more technical, but nonetheless very important level, there are a raft of key cases and doctrines concerning core procedural issues in transnational litigation, such as personal jurisdiction, choice of law, sovereign immunity, the act of state doctrine, and recognition of foreign judgments that must be considered whenever deciding or evaluating cases in the field.[15] And lastly, in terms of the sheer number of cases, transnational litigation, including both the more garden variety cross-border suits in tort and contract, and the domestic suits sounding in international law, seems to be greatly expanding.

## (C) Advantages

Given that it is possible to redress international wrongs through civil litigation in domestic courts, why might it be useful to do so? Below is a discussion of the avenue's advantages—enforceability, independent initiation, and capacity and scale. Each of these helps to surmount a core inadequacy of international law.

First, domestic courts have clear enforcement power, sufficient to satisfy even Austinians.[16] In civil litigation, domestic courts can issue injunctions, impose preliminary relief (ie, at an early stage, long before final judgment is issued), and impose monetary penalties, thus giving immediate and tangible effect to their judgments. Moreover, monetary awards go directly to the plaintiffs, and thus have a concrete compensatory effect. In these ways, civil litigation meets head-on one of the principal weaknesses of the international legal system—its limited capacity for enforcement.[17]

---

[13] 630 F2d 876 (2d Cir. 1980).

[14] While the law is a touch murky on this point, corporate liability for similar acts under more mundane principles of domestic tort law has never been in doubt.

[15] In the United States, these include *Asahi Metal Industry Co. v Superior Court*, 480 US 102 (1987) (personal jurisdiction, based on stream of commerce), *Burnham v Superior Court of California*, 495 US 604 (1990) (personal jurisdiction; 'tagging' a defendant transiently in the forum with service of process is sufficient to create personal jurisdiction), the Foreign Sovereign Immunities Act, 28 USC §§ 1330, 1332(a), 1391(f), and 1601–11; *Allstate Insurance Co. v Hague*, 449 US 302 (1981) (choice of law; US Constitution's due process and full faith and credit clauses require a minimum threshold of contacts in order for a state's law to be applied to a matter); *Banco National de Cuba v Sabbatino*, 376 US 398 (1964) (US courts are to abide by the act of state doctrine and respect certain acts of foreign states regarding their internal affairs); Uniform Foreign Money-Judgments Recognition Act, 13 ULA 39 (1986) (model legislation adopted in the majority of US states, requiring recognition of many foreign judgments).

[16] For them, law is simply the command of the sovereign, backed by the threat of sanction. See J. Austin, *The Province of Jurisprudence Determined* (1832) (W. Rumble ed., Cambridge: Cambridge University Press, 1995).

[17] In the economic realm, the presence of increased enforcement power can ripple throughout implicitly and explicitly negotiated social arrangements. In every business deal, eg, there is a tussle over how to allocate the economic surplus. There are a range of points where a deal could be struck that is beneficial to both sides, and in which economic value would be created. But typically the party with the most bargaining power can command most of the surplus, and push the price to a point

Secondly, civil proceedings are of course initiated by the plaintiff. They are, in a sense, a form of 'bottom-up' activity in the legal world. As such, they fit in with the larger trend in international law away from the centrality of the nation-state. In passing, it is interesting to note that this trend is arguably a return to an earlier state of international law, before the rise of the nation-state, when the gaze of international law rested more frequently upon private actors, such as sailors, merchants, and pirates.

Additionally, the plaintiff-initiated civil suit is one of the few institutional means in our society where would-be Davids can halt, confront, and exact redress from alleged Goliaths. The ability of, for example, Guantánamo detainee Shafiq Rasul to defeat US President George W. Bush in a case in the US Supreme Court,[18] or of a migrant worker to win an award from a huge corporation is, if one steps back from it, rather startling. These cases are rare, and even the victories can be Pyrrhic or insubstantial, but nonetheless, they serve to help to create certain open spaces for social movements, and to focus attention on injustices.

Further, because there is no ICC prosecutor or government official who must be persuaded to initiate a case, and who might be constrained by political concerns or a severe lack of institutional capacity, domestic civil litigation has brought and will continue to raise issues that certain official hesitancies or deadlocks might otherwise quash. The privately initiated suit thus has the potential to advance the development of international law further along certain key dimensions, many of them related to a key 'blind spot' that is inherent in the structure of international law, where the assent of the Great Powers is typically necessary to formulate a rule. It is only in civil litigation that the citizen has the power to force adjudication of international wrongs.

Fourthly, the issues of institutional capacity and reach in the international legal system are entirely transformed by considering domestic civil litigation. The handful of international courts and tribunals can hear only a limited number of cases per year, asserting jurisdiction over only a sliver of the planet, and fulfilling only a tiny fraction of the need. Via the offices of domestic civil litigation, however, international disputes can be adjudicated by literally thousands of domestic courts across the globe.

---

most favourable to it. The presence of increased enforcement power in the international realm would enhance the bargaining power of those whose rights were previously relatively unenforceable, and enable them to strike more favourable deals. It can also help to solve a market failure by providing a truly enforceable right to those affected by externalities, such as, eg, pollution produced by a private business deal in a context where regulation is lax. This can ultimately lead to a slew of practical effects: better resettlement policies for those being displaced by foreign-constructed dams; the use of safer equipment by those operating potentially explosive chemical factories or oil rigs; hesitance by a party to offer a bribe, especially if they may be subject to liability in their home country; or, conversely, more liability for those who chose not to make agreed upon payments to a foreign corporation. The dam, factory, and rig owners and deal strikers must now, due to the enforcement ability, realistically factor some of their externalities into the cost of doing business, and must deal with a more formidable counterparty in their negotiations.

[18] *Rasul v Bush*, 542 US 466 (2004).

# 4. Looking forward

For a system of international law to become far more enforceable, and to be able to redress a far greater percentage of wrongs than is currently the case, and to address some of its major blind spots, a few things must happen to bolster the existing transnational litigation system. These should take place in the sociological, procedural, and substantive realms. Given current trends, there is a fair degree of likelihood that they will actually transpire. And given that the basic framework for transnational litigation is already in place, both on a doctrinal (eg transitory torts) and institutional (eg the immense system of national courts) level, its potential for impact is large.

## (A) Sociological innovations

International law mavens and domestic civil litigators usually are communities apart. However, there is an increasing demand for knowledge of transnational litigation techniques, mirroring among other things the rise in cross-border activity in the global economy. Through continuing legal education, law school courses, conferences, and the like, alliances will form and knowledge can diffuse. Existing educational efforts for current and future practising lawyers should be increased, and also broadened to include legislators and judges. As a consequence, we will probably see a continued increase in the numbers of domestic civil suits pleading violations of international law causes of action, even more references to international law principles in domestic court decisions, and more cases filed where purely domestic laws are applied in innovative ways to address cross-border issues.

## (B) Procedural innovations

A series of what may be called procedural innovations would be of use. Through the continued adoption of more liberal discovery rules, such as a less frequent requirement of letters rogatory, the declining enactment and use of blocking statutes, and the more widespread acceptance of live video witness testimony, as well as purely technological devices such as the cheap and quick scanning and transmission of documents, the collection of evidence in one country for use in litigation in another may be facilitated. As a consequence, litigation in domestic courts over areas of transnational concern will be become easier and more common. These trends are in line with a general move away from legal formalism and toward more commonsense and pragmatic procedures, and also with the general increase in international commercial and non-commercial interaction. And even within current jurisdictional rules, as institutional defendants increase their global reach, and as individuals travel and live in a broader variety of places, they will also be subject to suit in a wider set of locales.

One specific area of opportunity lies in the field of attachment-based jurisdiction. In the human rights area, for example, it is often very difficult to find and assert jurisdiction over the alleged bad actor. Often the jurisdictional peg is presence of the defendant's offices or person within the forum. Property, however, can be an alternate base of jurisdiction. In *quasi in rem* suits in the United States, for example, a defendant's property within the forum can be attached and used as the basis for jurisdiction, even if the property has no connection to the suit, as long as the overall exercise of jurisdiction is deemed reasonable and meets due process standards. The fact that the court's award in a *quasi in rem* suit is capped by the value of the property helps to satisfy due process standards; other relevant factors include whether the plaintiff was resident within the forum. As more information surfaces about, for example, the bank accounts or homes of former dictators and torturers, then suits can be levied against that property for the violations committed by their owners. This technique, though intriguing, has been infrequently attempted thus far in human rights and other transnational litigation.

It would also be useful for adaptations to the domestic litigation model to be applied to the international arena. The hallmarks of the classic litigation model include strict rules concerning identifiable plaintiffs and identifiable defendants, causation, individualized justice, and statutes of limitation. For better or for worse, some of these constraints are relaxed in complex domestic litigation. This has occurred in areas such as mass torts and products liability, including the tobacco,[19] Agent Orange,[20] asbestos,[21] and DES pharmaceutical[22] cases. Largely due to national legislative inaction on these topics, courts have improvised solutions to fill the gap. This could be analogized to what is happening at the global level. There is inaction at the higher orders of affairs on certain key problems. In the absence of a global settlement, solution, or treaty (which can be thought of as global legislation), as a next-best alternative, litigation may have to be refashioned and step into the breach. There are a raft of innovative domestic litigation practices, such as multidistrict litigation, special masters, and market share liability, which allocates liability to a pool of defendants according to their share of the market for a defective product, that could be brought into the international arena. Could there not be, for example, a class action suit, utilizing a New York City-based or other law firm that specializes in plaintiff-side shareholder suits against large banks, that seized the overseas bank accounts of a dictator, and that ultimately deployed a special master to disburse the funds to those who had been victimized by that dictator,

---

[19] See Tobacco Master Settlement Agreement, available at <http://oag.ca.gov/tobacco/msa>, under which seven tobacco companies agreed to change their marketing practices, reveal previously secret documents, disband industry trade groups, and pay US states approximately $206 billion.

[20] For an overview of the Agent Orange Litigation on behalf of US military veterans see, eg, *In re Agent Orange Product Liability Litigation Multidistrict Litigation No. 381*, 818 F2d 145 (2d Cir. 1987); *In re Agent Orange Product Liability Litigation*, 597 FSupp 740 (EDNY 1984).

[21] See, eg, *Amchem Products, Inc. v Windsor*, 521 US 591, 599 (1997):

> In the face of legislative inaction, the federal courts—lacking authority to replace state tort systems with a national toxic tort compensation regime—endeavored to work with the procedural tools available to improve management of federal asbestos litigation. Eight federal judges, experienced in the superintendence of asbestos cases, urged the Judicial Panel on Multidistrict Litigation (MDL Panel), to consolidate in a single district all asbestos complaints then pending in federal courts.

[22] See, eg, *Martin v Abbott Laboratories*, 102 Wash2d 581, 606; 689 P2d 368, 383 (1984) (deploying 'market share liability' theory).

or at least returned the funds to the coffers of the successor government for distribution by that entity?

Another key procedural area is the simple but all-powerful statute of limitations. While statutes of limitation are helpful in that they provide peace of mind to defendants, they also impose a major barrier to addressing undeniable injustices. We will continue to see a bevy of attempts to skirt it. These include the standard doctrine of equitable tolling of the statute of limitations, which can extend the statute of limitations to encompass periods when the harm was undiscovered, or where the defendant was inequitably working to prevent discovery. Plaintiffs have also been resorting to national and state statutes such as California's business fraud statute[23] that do not impose a statute of limitations at all. Civil plaintiffs may also focus on causes of action for crimes against humanity and genocide, where a statute of limitations may not exist. Legislators should accommodate such efforts through focused acts such as those passed in California enabling certain slavery reparations suits,[24] or in California and Illinois forcing the disclosure of slavery data.[25] Through gambits such as the above, we may see procedural hurdles overcome, and the creation of rough answers for international problems that have to date defied solution.

## (C) Substantive innovations

The above sociological and procedural developments, coupled with civil plaintiff energy and judicial receptivity, may generate developments in a number of crucial substantive areas.

One such (cross-cutting) area is civil litigation against corporations relating to their cross-border activity. This is the inverse, if you will, of project finance and international trade. Cross-border suits relating to contractual matters are already commonplace. But we have seen several suits concerning environmental or human rights violations caused by extractive industries, particularly against oil and mining companies. In the United States, there have been suits which have proceeded far along to trial, and then settled. These include cases on behalf of relatives of executed environmental activist Ken Saro-Wiwa and others against Royal Dutch Shell

---

[23] California Business and Professions Code, § 17200.

[24] The California Second World War Slave Labor Victim Act, Cal. Code Civ. Proc. § 354.6, waived the statute of limitations for suits against private corporations that used slave labour during the Second World War. It was, however, struck down as unconstitutional, on that ground that it exceeded California's power to engage in foreign affairs: *Deutsch v Turner Corp.*, 324 F3d 692, 713–14 (9th Cir. 2003) ('the Constitution allocates the power over foreign affairs to the federal government exclusively, and the power to make and resolve war, including the authority to resolve war claims, is central to the foreign affairs power in the constitutional design'). However, not all legislation by US states related to wars is barred on foreign affairs grounds. See, eg, Holocaust Victim Insurance Relief Act, Cal. Ins. Code §§ 13800–7.

[25] The California Slavery Era Insurance Act requires insurance corporations licensed in California to disclose any slavery insurance policies issued by a predecessor firm: Cal. Ins. Code §§ 13810–13; Illinois Department of Insurance Slave Era Insurance Policies Registry, Public Act 093–0333, available at <http://www.insurance.illinois.gov/cb/cb0401_SlaveEraReport.htm>.

for its activities in Nigeria,[26] which settled in 2009 for $15.5 million,[27] and the case against Unocal for utilizing slave labour to build its pipelines in Burma, which settled in 2005.[28] Other cases of note include the suit against Texaco/Chevron for spilling oil into the Amazon region of Ecuador, initially filed in the United States, in which a court in Ecuador ultimately ordered Chevron to pay $8.6 billion in damages, and an equal amount in punitive damages.[29] Of course, there have also been suits against multinational companies in the countries where the damage occurred. In either case, whether the suits take place in the country of operations or the country of headquarters,[30] there are no inherent theoretical barriers to such suits,[31] and there is a great likelihood that they will increase in number, and be brought in a broader array of industries. Careful pleading, however, is required, as the procedural and substantive pitfalls are numerous. However, the exercise of restraint by plaintiffs and their lawyers, and decisions to sue only for bona fide grave injustices would be advisable.

We may also see suits that seek to impose liability or otherwise provide enforceable rulings in areas where the current international system cannot, or will not, tread. Domestic civil litigation may enable us to see the proverbial elephant in the room. This might happen in one of two ways. The first is through the creation or recognition of new types of rights and duties. This might happen through the rulings of the apex courts of various nations, providing enforceable rulings in emerging areas in advance of what the international system has been able to provide. In the famous *Oposa v Factoran* case in the Philippines,[32] which was a civil suit filed

---

[26]  *Wiwa v Royal Dutch Petroleum Co.*, 226 F3d 88 (2d Cir. 2000), *cert. denied* by *Royal Dutch Petroleum Co. v Wiwa*, 532 US 941 (2001).

[27]  See <http://wiwavshell.org/documents/Wiwa_v_Shell_Settlement_release.pdf>.

[28]  See <http://ccrjustice.org/newsroom/press-releases/historic-advance-universal-human-rights%3A-unocal-compensate-burmese-villagers>. Public relations fallout from the activist campaign concerning the environmental disaster from Shell's pipelines in Nigeria, and the associated Wiwa lawsuit, caused Shell to consider changing its very name, and to embark on a plan aggressively to court and fund NGOs to try to repair its image. See, eg, 'NGOs and BBC Targeted by Shell PR Machine in Wake of Saro-Wiwa Death', *The Guardian*, 9 November 2010, available at <http://www.guardian.co.uk/business/2010/nov/09/shell-pr-saro-wiwa-nigeria>.

[29]  *Maria Aguinda v Chevron*, 002–2003, Superior Court of Nueva Loja, Lago Agrio, Ecuador. See also *Jota v Texaco, Inc.*, 157 F3d 153 (2d Cir. 1998); 'Chevron's $17 Billion Ecuador Judgment May Be Unenforceable, Analysts Say', *Bloomberg News*, 15 February 2011.

[30]  For suits brought in the jurisdiction of the corporate headquarters, doctrines such as the US *forum non conveniens*, which allows a judge discretion to dismiss a suit despite the fact that jurisdiction exists, as long as there is an available alternate forum, do present a serious hurdle. It is not necessarily fatal, however. The doctrine in the United States is supposed to be exercised only in rare cases, with a presumption in favour of the forum selected by the plaintiff. Further, the presence of a US plaintiff, such as a person who has moved to the United States after the offence occurred, further tilts the analysis in favour of the selected forum. Additionally, if the forum state has an avowed policy interest in adjudicating issues under the law of nations, this can weigh in favour of the plaintiff's chosen forum. An example of this is the Alien Tort Statute, as supplemented by the Torture Victims Protection Act, which has been adjudged to reflect a US policy interest in favour of hearing cases concerning international human rights abuses, and has been factored into *forum non conveniens* rulings.

[31]  The status of corporate liability under the Alien Tort Statute is not wholly settled, but even if it were to be precluded, cross-border cases against corporations could still be brought under standard domestic tort and other law.

[32]  *Oposa v Factoran*, G.R. No. 101083 (30 July 1993).

by children concerning logging, the Supreme Court referred to 'inter-generational equity' as a key issue in protecting the environment.[33] This and other domestic court pronouncements may eventually inform or become recognized doctrines of international law, potentially even giving rise to the notion of 'crimes against future generations'. A second way is by addressing not so much emerging issues in international law, but rather areas that are quite clear but that the system has dared not, or chosen not, to address. For colossal issues such as slavery, climate change, or economic human rights, civil suits in domestic courts may be able to impose liability where international bodies, or even doctrines of international law, have not, due to resistance by nation-states.[34] But citizen litigation knows no such fetters. Addressing such large issues through a plaintiff-initiated litigation model can avert some of these political barriers. Admittedly, this smacks of Scylla and Charybdis—the freedom of the civil litigation approach brings with it the problem of piecemeal solutions, as well as an array of procedural hurdles, such as the statute of limitations, difficulties of causation and proof, and a lack of identifiable plaintiffs and defendants. These are not necessarily insurmountable, however.

With regard to slavery, the Holocaust Victim's Asset class action cases in the United States over the last decade for example, resulted in a $1.25 billion settlement, awarded to several classes of people.[35] These included those who had deposited assets with certain Swiss banks, where those assets were not returned; victims of Nazi persecution who had performed slave labour for companies which had deposited the revenues or proceeds of that labour into certain Swiss banks; and people who performed slave labour for Swiss entities. The cases have shown that large-scale civil redress for global historical wrongs such as slavery is indeed possible, and have inspired a new series of attempts to impose liability for slavery. The South African Apartheid Era litigation against German corporations that benefited from Apartheid is at the time of writing winding its way through US courts, having defeated motions to dismiss.[36] Cases against German corporations on behalf of the Herero people of Namibia, who at the end of the nineteenth century and the beginning of the twentieth had been placed in camps and then tortured, experimented upon, and placed into slave labour were, however, dismissed on a variety of grounds.[37] African American slavery reparations cases in the United States

---

[33] But see D. Gatmaytan, 'The Illusion of Intergenerational Equity: *Oposa v Factoran* as Pyrrhic Victory', 15 Georgetown Int'l Environmental L Rev (2003) 457 for a convincing discussion that the intergenerational standing language was not necessary for the resolution of the specific case and thus non-binding dicta. Even if so, the intergenerational equity point was nonetheless an innovative statement from a national supreme court that has resounded strongly in international law circles.

[34] Some of the resistance is legitimate. Nations may prefer to address such issues through international negotiations rather than through litigation. But sometimes the resistance is not legitimate. Powerful states may simply quash the issues, precluding any negotiated settlement, and leaving a glaring injustice substantially or even wholly unaddressed.

[35] *In re Holocaust Victim Assets Litigation*, 105 FSupp2d 139 (EDNY 2000).

[36] See *In re South African Apartheid Litigation*, 617 FSupp2d 228 (SDNY 2009).

[37] See *Hereros ex rel. Riruako v Deutsche Afrika-Linien Gmblt & Co.*, 232 Fed Appx 90, 2007 WL 1066949 (3d Cir. 2007); *The Hereros v Deutsche Afrika-Linien GMBLT & Co.*, 2006 WL 182078 (DNJ, January 24, 2006); *Herero People's Reparations Corp. v Deutsche Bank, AG*, 370 F3d 1192 (DC Cir. 2004).

have been brought for literally more than century to no avail, but there have been some developments in this area too. Cases have been filed against specific corporations that made use of African American slave labour.[38] This gambit provides an identifiable defendant and a relatively quantifiable measure of unjust enrichment. The cases have also benefited by being filed under state statues, such as the one in California, concerning fraudulent business conduct that do not have statutes of limitation. Further, with the use of corporate records, and advances in genealogical research, actual slaves and their descendants could be identified. Additionally, certain actions for the recovery of property are not subject to statutes of limitation in many common law jurisdictions. Also, as Professor Ogletree of Harvard points out, 'certainly, the slaves had a property interest in the money illegally obtained by their sale. A slavery reparations suit could demand the return of such funds.'[39] While many insist that the notion of reparations for African American slavery is simply too radical, an argument of unpaid labour is a conservative claim, consistent with the purest of free market societies. Nonetheless, large political hurdles, and perhaps more crucially, limits to the imagination, still remain. Large procedural hurdles persist as well. However, there is still a possibility that some of the actions could succeed, and impose liability that international bodies could not.

With regard to climate change, even though it is clear that the bulk of emissions over the last two centuries have come from the developed world, from a small minority of the world's population, and that the global North is disproportionately responsible for the gargantuan problem, assessing actual liability—meaning payment for damage done to date—through international negotiations and treaties has been difficult due to the clout of the large emitters. What is on the table is funding for green development and the like, falling far short of compensation for the damage done. While imposing liability for climate change through the civil litigation model is difficult due to a number of issues—such as a lack of identifiable offenders and victims, and a lack of previous knowledge about the existence and perniciousness of climate change—by borrowing from tobacco litigation and other domestic product liability suits, imposing liability may still be possible. Australian companies, for example, have been formally placed on notice by a non-government organization for their responsibility for climate change,[40] which going forwards may destroy the lack-of-scientific-knowledge defence, a variant of which was proffered to great effect for many years by the tobacco industry. A few US cases seeking liability for causing climate change, proceeding under the tort law doctrine of

---

[38] See *In re African-American Slave Descendants Litigation*, 471 F3d 754 (7th Cir. 2006).

[39] Charles Ogletree, 'Repairing the Past: New Efforts in the Reparations Debate in America', 38 Harv Civ Rts–Civ Lib L Rev (2003) 279 at 305.

[40] According to Climate Action Network Australia, on 30 July 2003, it notified the directors of selected Australian companies of the financial risks that climate change presents to their companies, and of their legal obligations to deal with those risks appropriately. See <http://www.climatelaw.org/media/2003Jul30/>.Twenty companies in New Zealand were also placed on notice. See 'Notice Served on Greenhouse Polluters', NZ Lawyer Online, 6 July 2007, available at <http://www.nzlawyermagazine.co.nz/Archives/Issue68/NewsandFeatures/News2/tabid/208/Default.aspx>.

public nuisance, are in their early stages.[41] And borrowing from US tobacco litigation, the idea of the US states as plaintiffs, seeking to recoup their tobacco-related health care costs from an identified set of defendants, could be analogized to a suit in which a developing country nation or nations are plaintiffs, seeking to recoup their climate-related adaptation costs.[42]

Certainly, if developing country sovereign nations were willing to be plaintiffs themselves, a number of issues currently blocked by Great Power reluctance and a lack of developing country could be addressed. For example, in the area of the developing country debt crisis, in which loans were provided by commercial banks to developing nation sovereign borrowers despite actual knowledge that proceeds were being stolen by the head of state—for example, Mobutu Sese Seko, who was widely known to be heading a 'kleptocracy', on the until now correct assumption that the nation itself would be bound to repay, we might see a civil suit against such banks in New York under garden variety tort and contract law on the grounds that they were complicit in a multibillion-dollar fraud. Ultimately, such suits, whether for climate change, debt, slavery, or other areas, offer the potential for radical breakthroughs. They may fail on procedural grounds, but not on whether the conduct was wrongful or not. As such, they will serve to keep such issues on the global agenda, and could be a bargaining chip in any overall settlement. But nevertheless, the possession of a potentially enforceable legal right by the wronged greatly increases their bargaining power, and even their ability to bring the offending party to the table.

## 5. Concluding remarks

There are, of course, limitations—domestic civil litigation is not a panacea. Domestic courts and legal processes have their own inadequacies, even for purely domestic matters. And in international matters, questions of evidence-gathering and of bias, become even more significant. And for cases taking place in countries with no strong tie to the matter, there are questions of overreaching, and even

---

[41] See, eg, *Connecticut v American Electric Power Co.*, 582 F3d 309 (2d Cir. 2009), *cert granted*, 131 SCt 813 (6 December 2010) (No. 10–174) (eight states, a city, and three land trusts separately sued the same six electric power corporations which owned and operated fossil-fuel-fired power plants in 20 states, seeking abatement of defendants' ongoing contributions to the public nuisance of global warming). But see *Native Village of Kivalina v Exxon Mobil Corp.*, 663 FSupp2d 863 (ND Cal. 2009) (denying claim of the governing body of Inupiat village of 400 people on Alaskan island against 24 power and utility companies for the costs necessary to relocate the residents away from the island, which allegedly is becoming uninhabitable due to climate change, on grounds that suit raised a political question). See also J. Hessler, 'A Temporary Solution to Climate Change: The Federal Common Law to the Rescue?', Note, 38 Hastings Const LQ (2011) 407.

[42] An alternative structure would have plaintiffs as domestic parties or domestic NGOs, provided they could prove standing. In either case, whether the plaintiffs were domestic parties or foreign states, the identification of defendants would still be a difficult issue. A possible answer would be for the suit to be against companies in a particularly greenhouse gas-intensive industry, comprising the bulk of emissions for a country, for emissions produced after the scientific knowledge of the harm was known, with liability apportioned according to their market share.

imperialism. Further, in civil cases there is of course no remedy of imprisonment. And lastly, litigiousness is not a boon.

But on the whole there is a powerful potential for international wrongs to be addressed not through constructing a separate and new system, but rather though the effective deployment of the intermeshed transnational web of domestic courts that is already in place. Indeed, to sum up, as the existing system of international bodies will be deficient in infrastructure and enforcement power for decades to centuries to come, and as states in power will usually not impede their own interests through the international legal system, the utilization of existing structures and mechanisms of domestic litigation by private plaintiffs becomes a very significant avenue for achieving global justice through law. To render a prediction, we may see massive activity in this area. It will be very interesting over the next decades to see how transnational litigation substantiates our ethereal system of international law.

# PART VI

# CONCLUSION

# 48

## Gathering Up the Main Threads

*Antonio Cassese*

This final chapter is not intended to summarize all the previous chapters. Each of them stands on its own, although all of them, or at least most of them, aim to suggest new avenues for change, in light of the present condition of the international society. This chapter will cast a net on the previous chapters, gather the main problems with which we have grappled in the book, and survey the solutions proposed from the discussion that has unfolded.

### 1.  Some general conclusions on the condition of world society

At least four conclusions can be drawn from the critical assessment of international institutions undertaken by the various contributors to this book.

### (A) States to continue playing a dominant role

In the next two or three decades, the basic architecture of world society is unlikely to change dramatically. As shown by Alvarez (Chapter 3) and Condorelli and Cassese (Chapter 2), states will continue to be the primary actors on the world scene. Their influence both within the world society and on the conditioning of intergovernmental organizations is not likely to dwindle. States still are, and will remain, the masters of the world society. The delegate of China, in his statement at the 2010 Kampala Review Conference of the International Criminal Court (ICC) Rome Statute, pithily restated this notion, when he said that 'countries are the basic and most important entities of international relationships and international activities; they shoulder the responsibility to continue social and economic development and satisfy people's needs.'[1] Although states no longer hold a 'decision monopoly' in international dealings,[2] they continue to run the show. They remain 'the makers of manners', to borrow a

---

[1] Statement of Chinese Delegation at the General Debate of the Review Conference of Rome Statute, available at <http://www.icc-cpi.int/iccdocs/asp_docs/RC2010/Statements/ICC-RC-gendeba-China-ENG.pdf>, at 4.

[2] This expression comes from the German original *Entscheidungsmonopol*, used by A. Bleckmann, *Grundgesetz und Völkerrecht* (Berlin: Duncker & Humblot, 1975), at 252, and refers to the monopoly of decisions on customary international law, held in Germany by the Constitutional Court.

well-known expression from Shakespeare.[3] This is also due to the fact that states do not exercise powers derived from the international legal order, contrary to what Hans Kelsen maintained.[4] As rightly pointed out by Dionisio Anzilotti back in 1928, states derive their authority from themselves.[5] This is made possible by their being both the founders of world society and the creators of the legal rules which govern it.

It is worth observing that some major powers are now increasingly taking conservative positions which give the impression that they would like a return of sorts to the Westphalian model, or at least to some of the main tenets of that system: insistence on the fundamental role of sovereignty, on states' right to non-interference, on maximum restraint on any collective enforcement of law. China and Russia, for instance, tend to adopt this position. A side effect of this neo-Westphalianism is that dictatorships such as those in Zimbabwe, North Korea, and Myanmar, are left substantially untouched by the world society and practically immune from any pressure exercised by it. The attitude shown in 2011 by the UN towards Syria is telling: faced with a state that blatantly massacred its own nationals over several months, the UN Security Council was only able on 3 August 2011 to issue a 'Presidential statement'[6] where among other things it stated that 'Those responsible for the violence *should* be held accountable' (emphasis added) and merely 'called upon' Syria 'to cooperate fully' with the High Commissioner for Human Rights, without even requiring Syria to allow a commission of investigation of the UN Human Rights Council to enter the country.[7] Here the return to

---

[3] Shakespeare, *Henry the Fifth* (Act V, Scene II): '...Dear/Kate, you and I cannot be confined within the weak/ list of a country's fashion: we are the makers of/manners, Kate; and the liberty that follows our/ places stops the mouth of all find-faults...'

[4] H. Kelsen, 'Les rapports de système entre le droit interne et le droit international public', 14 HR (1926-IV) 231 at 235–8, 241–8, 299–320.

[5]

> Le droit international est supérieur a l'État en ce sens qu'il constitue une limitation juridique de son pouvoir, mais non pas dans le sens que le pouvoir de l'État est une délégation du droit international; cette thèse non seulement n'est pas logiquement nécessaire: elle a contre elle-même l'expérience historique mais aussi—et principalement—la conviction des États, auxquels rien ne répugne davantage que l'idée d'exercer un pouvoir qui leur serait octroyé par l'ordre juridique international. (D. Anzilotti, *Cours de droit international*, I (G. Gidel trans., Paris: Sirey, 1929), at 51)

> See on this sentence by Anzilotti, L. Condorelli, 'Scholie sur l'idiome scellien des manuels francophones de droit international public', 1 EJIL (1990) at 232–4.

[6] S/PRST/2011/16/.

[7] On 29 April 2011 the Human Rights Council adopted Res. S-16/1 (passed with the contrary vote of nine states including China and Russia), whereby among other things the Council

> Request[ed] the Office of the United Nations High Commissioner for Human Rights to dispatch urgently a mission to the Syrian Arab Republic to investigate all alleged violations of international human rights law and to establish the facts and circumstances of such violations and of the crimes perpetrated, with a view to avoiding impunity and ensuring full accountability, and to provide a preliminary report and oral update on the situation of human rights in the Syrian Arab Republic to the Human Rights Council at its seventeenth session, and to submit a follow-up report to the Council at its eighteenth session, and also requests the High Commissioner to organize an interactive dialogue on the situation of human rights in the Syrian Arab Republic during the eighteenth session of the Council. (§ 7)

Westphalianism is striking: a country kills its own citizens in cold blood and the world society is merely able to issue exhortations (indeed, economic 'sanctions' against individuals,[8] or diplomatic 'sanctions'[9] taken by some Western countries plus the member states of the European Union were substantially inadequate or even toothless measures). Let me add that the position taken by the Security Council on that occasion substantially corresponds to China's general stand on the question of protection of civilians: on 7 July 2010 the Chinese delegate to the Security Council, addressing the issue of protection of civilians, stated that China intended to

> stress the responsibility of the states concerned and respect for their wishes. The responsibility of protecting civilians lies primarily with the national governments. While the international community can provide constructive help, it must do so in compliance with the provisions of the UN Charter, respect for sovereignty of the countries concerned and refrain from forcible intervention.[10]

With states the dominant actors on the international scene, non-state actors (intergovernmental organizations, non-governmental organizations (NGOs), multinational corporations, individuals, insurgents, and other violent groups holding some sort of control over human communities or even a territory) are not yet even playing second leads; they remain on the sidelines (see on this issue Bhuta, Chapter 6). They remain and are likely to remain secondary and partial international actors, and are still strongly conditioned by states' conduct. A telling example is that of the International Committee of the Red Cross (ICRC), an international subject that plays a crucial role in, among other things, monitoring states' behaviour or misbehaviour in international and internal armed conflict. The ICRC has to bow to state sovereignty in many respects, in particular by refraining from rendering its reports public on possible breaches of international humanitarian law by states. This is the price it has to pay for undertaking intrusive action in fields covered by states' sovereign prerogatives.

The initial and current relative marginality of non-state actors seems, however, destined to gradually diminish, on a par with the possible slow decline of state authority.

## (B) No hope for a reform of the United Nations

The second general conclusion of this book is that the present global organization, the United Nations, will not be reformed in the near future, whether in its

---

Call[ed] upon the Government of the Syrian Arab Republic to cooperate fully with and grant access to personnel from the mission dispatched by the Office of the High Commissioner. (§ 8)

[8] The United States and the European Union have imposed asset freezes and travel bans against various Syrian political and military and government officials.

[9] On 2 August 2011 Italy decided to recall the Italian Ambassador to Damascus in the face of the 'horrible repression of the civilian population' by the Syrian authorities. Italy also called upon other members of the European Union to follow suit. However, no other state heeded the Italian invitation.     [10] Reported in 10 Chinese JIL (2011) at 446–7.

structure or in its functioning. When discussing the UN Millennium Declaration during a speech he gave at the UN on 8 September 2000, the then President of the Czech Republic Václav Havel proposed a complete restructuring of the UN General Assembly, which, in his view, should be based on two pillars:

one constituted by an assembly of equal executive representatives of individual countries, resembling the present plenary, and the other consisting of a group elected directly by the globe's population, in which the number of delegates representing individual nations would, thus, roughly correspond to the size of the nations. These two bodies would create and guarantee global legislation.[11]

In his view, the Security Council should be answerable to these two assemblies. Its composition, however, would be different from the current one, and the veto power would be done away with altogether. Furthermore, the UN should have its own permanent military and police force.

I fear that the proposals sketched out by Havel, albeit not injudicious, will not materialize in the next decades, or even within this century. All the present relative merits and deficiencies of the UN are likely to remain for many years to come. Indeed, as rightly pointed out by Alston (Chapter 4), it will prove extremely difficult, if not impossible to reform the UN Charter through the amendment procedure envisaged in the Charter, save perhaps for the abolition of the Trusteeship Council, the fundamental revision of the Economic and Social Council (ECOSOC), and the upgrading of the Human Rights Council to the status of a principal organ of the UN. Similarly, provisions of the Charter are unlikely to be gradually modified by means of a customary process.

Nevertheless, some reforms which would not necessarily require amendments to the Charter could and should be introduced in order to streamline the organization. For instance, the UN bureaucracy, which at present is inflated, unwieldy, and slow, could be slimmed down. So, too, could the endless discussions in the various UN bodies and the production of useless documents that very few read, be reduced. The various 'minor institutional' adjustments proposed by Alston would indeed be beneficial. Moreover, it would be judicious to enhance the role of the heads of some independent organs, such as the Secretary-General and the High Commissioner for Human Rights, who should be chosen for their independence, gravitas, and moral authority. They could thus be impervious to the political pressure of states (in particular of the major powers) and wield greater moral leverage. Also, as suggested by Alston, greater use should be made of independent experts, and avenues of cooperation with civil society should be opened up.

## (C) World society is still governed by state interest

Thirdly, the international society is still grounded in the mere juxtaposition of its subjects—not in their solidarity, let alone their integration. Let us take up the metaphor conjured by Alf Ross in 1950 in his book *Constitution of the United*

---

[11] UN Doc. A/PV/8, at 1.

*Nations*.[12] World society, we could say, is like a densely forested area with many scattered wooden houses, an area prone to frequent fires. The inhabitants of the forest have been unable to undertake the most useful and logical step: setting up a fire brigade financed by the whole citizenry, equipped with all the necessary fire-extinguishing devices, and able to go wherever a fire breaks out without needing to obtain permission to enter every time a fire is raging on private property. Instead, owing to prevailing self-interests, to rifts and conflicting demands, the inhabitants have ultimately taken three steps only. First, they have decided that each of them will react to the fire in his own way and with his own equipment. The result of this is that the poor farmers easily succumb to fires, whereas those who have land, live-stock, sophisticated equipment, and financial means can easily put out the flames. The second step, taken after many fires have destroyed entire parts of the area, has been to set up a small body which in theory should represent all the inhabitants, but in practice is dominated by the few rich and powerful owners of land, who have a final say on most if not everything. This body can only decide whether a fire has broken out and, if the major members of the body are all amenable, authorize one or more inhabitants of the area to use their own extinguishers to go to the place where the blaze is raging. The third step consists of envisaging some palliatives: establishing communal institutions to help those most at the mercy of fires, to proclaim values with which all the inhabitants are expected to comply, or to morally exhort the collectivity to care about the common good. In this third scenario, however, the communal institutions are set up and dominated by a select number of members and therefore lack any autonomous power. They only wield moral authority and, subject to their financial constraints, act as charities intended to alleviate the plight of the needy.

Ross's metaphor reflects the reality of today's world. This world is radically dif-ferent from national societies where, as Herbert Spencer noted in 1874–96, social harmony is essentially based on division of labour and specialization of func-tions. Each individual devotes himself to a specific task and thereby automatically becomes linked to others by a solidarity bond.[13] As Émile Durkheim later added in 1893, societies based on the division of labour do not result

---

[12] A. Ross, *Constitution of the United Nations—Analysis of Structure and Function* (New York: Rinehart 1950), at 108–9, 137–9. See also A. Ross, *The United Nations—Peace and Progress* (Totowa, NJ: Bedminster Press, 1966), at 55–6.

[13] H. Spencer, *Principles of Sociology* (1874–96), 3 vols (New York: D. Appleton and Co., 1896; reprint, New Brunswick/London: Transactions Publishers, 2002), vol. 1, Part II, at 447–597. According to Spencer 'All kinds of creatures are alike in so far as each exhibits co-operation among its components for the benefit of the whole; and this trait, common to them, is a trait common also to societies' (ibid at 592). Spencer also insists on the notion that the division of labour is a phenomenon 'naturally arising in a society' (ibid, vol. 3, at 342, and see also 341; see, more generally, on 'speciali-zation of functions and division of labour', ibid at 340–61). Interestingly, Spencer contrasts societies with primitive hordes:

> At first there is no other life in the group than that seen in the lives of its members; and only as organization increases does the group as a whole come to have that joint life constituted by mutually-dependent actions. The members of a primitive horde, loosely aggregated, and without distinctions of power, cooperate for immediate furtherance of individual sustentation, and in a comparatively small degree for corporate sustentation. Even when,

in a myriad of juxtaposed atoms (*une poussière d'atomes juxtaposés*), among which only external and transitory contacts can be established; their members are instead united by bonds that go well beyond the brief moments in which they engage in exchanges between them. Each of the functions they discharge is always dependent on the others, and constitutes with them a solidarity system (*système solidaire*).

As Durkeim added: 'As the individual is not self-sufficient, he receives from society all that is necessary, since he works for society.'[14] This, according to Durkheim, is the process by which a society based on 'contractual solidarity' (*solidarité contractuelle*) is replaced by one based on 'organic solidarity' (*solidarité organique*).[15]

Durkheim and Spencer's paradigm is inapplicable at the international level. States tend to pursue national interests, and coalesce only where those interests converge. The spokesperson of the Chinese Foreign Ministry epitomized this tendency concisely when, on 13 July 2010, he stated that 'China's core interests refer to national sovereignty, security, territorial integrity and development interests'.[16] True, other states may take a different stand (eg recently the British Prime Minister underscored that his country, in addition to pursing national interests, also endeavoured to project onto the world community some national values such as liberty, security, and justice).[17] Nevertheless, *solidarity proper*, namely strongly shared concerns, moral bonds, feelings, sympathies, actions, resulting in collective action, still does not exist. The concept of 'common good' is not yet felt by the members of the international society. Only state interests and their occasional convergence regulate international relations.

Nevertheless, this has not excluded the gradual emergence, in recent times, of *community concerns*, namely the intent or will to pursue the implementation of universal values transcending the individual interests of each international actor. However, these values (peace, self-determination, human rights, the rule of law) essentially exist at the normative level, at the level of what *ought* to be done; they seldom actuate state undertakings.[18] One need only look at intergovernmental organizations

> the interests of all being simultaneously endangered, they simultaneously fight, they still fight separately—their actions are uncoordinated; and the only spoils of successful battle are such as can be individually appropriated. (ibid, vol.2, at 266)

[14] É. Durkheim, *De la division du travail social* ([1893] Paris: Presses universitaires de France, 1967), 8th edn, at 204.  [15] Ibid at 182ff.

[16] In 10 Chinese JIL (2011) at 433.

[17] On 12 November 2007 the British Prime Minister Gordon Brown stated:

> Of course the first duty of Government—our abiding obligation—is and will always be the safety of the British people, the protection of the British national interests...Yet the timeless values that underpin our policies at home—our belief in the liberty of all, in security and justice for all, in economic opportunity and environmental protection shared by all—are also ideals that I believe that it is in our national interest to promote abroad. (BYIL (2007) at 645; see also 646–7)

[18] In a way, the strong criticisms of the world society expressed in 1795 by I. Kant are to a large extent still valid today. Kant stated that

> We look with deep aversion upon the way primitive peoples are attached to their lawless liberty—a liberty which enables them to fight incessantly rather than subject themselves to the restraint of the law to be established by themselves; in short, to prefer wild freedom to a reasonable one. We look upon such an attitude as raw, uncivilized, and an animalic

such as the United Nations, the Council of Europe, the Organization of American States, the Arab League, and the meritorious UN special agencies, starting with the International Labour Organization (ILO) and finishing with the United Nations Educational, Scientific and Cultural Organization (UNESCO), which are the only institutions capable of addressing community concerns and realizing universal values but are ultimately bereft of any autonomous and independent authority distinct from that of the states backing them. It follows that any initiative they might launch aimed at addressing and redressing community concerns is ultimately amputated whenever it collides with the will of the important stakeholders. In the end, structural realities force these institutions to be more akin to the national bodies we call charities, that is, non-profit organizations intended to help those in need or distress, which do their utmost within the bounds of their normally modest financial resources.

In sum, everything indicates that Ferdinand Tönnies' classic distinction between 'society' (*Gesellschaft*) and 'community' (*Gemeinschaft*)[19] still holds true and can appropriately be applied to the aggregate of states and other international subjects. We can thus conclude that at the world level we are still faced with a *society* proper, where each member of the aggregate is more prone to pursuing its own interests than those of the whole group, and state relations are marked by reasoned calculation. It is an aggregate where, if one member does something for another, reciprocation is expected if not demanded, so that the entire life of the group is predicated on an exchange (*Tausch*) of self-serving performances rather than actions undertaken in the interest and on behalf of the aggregate.[20] In contrast, in a community proper, we are meant to find a homogeneity of view, common bonds, closeness and mutual aid, the coming together of like-minded subjects who share a common system of values. In a community 'each respected position can be regarded as a service to the community and each service to the community can be regarded as having its own dignity.'[21]

Thus, one is bound to acknowledge that, to date, the 'sociability' of states has not led them to create a community proper, the *societas generis humani* (society of mankind) dreamed by Grotius,[22] or what the Italian philosopher and politician

---

degradation of humanity (*viehische Abwürdigung der Menschheit*). Therefore, one should think, civilized peoples (each united in a state) would hasten to get away from such a depraved state as soon as possible. Instead, each state insists upon seeing the essence of its sovereignty (*Majestät*) (for popular sovereignty (*Majestät*) is a paradox) in this, that it is not subject to any external [legal] coercion (*keinem äusseren gesetzlichen Zwang unterworfen zu sein*). The lustre (*Glanz*) of its ruler consists in this, that many thousands are at his disposal to be sacrificed for a cause which is of no concern to them, while he himself is not exposed to any danger. (*Zum ewigen Frieden, Ein philosophischer Entwurf* (Königsberg: Friedrich Nicolovius, 1795), at 31; I have reproduced here the English translation of Carl J. Friedrich, in *The Philosophy of Kant, Kant's Moral and Political Writings* (C.J. Friedrich ed., New York: The Modern Library, Random House, 1977), at 442.

[19] F. Tönnies, *Gemeinschaft und Gesellschaft—Abhandlung des Communismus und des Socialismus als empirischer Culturformen* (Leipzig: Fues's Verlag, 1887), at 9–44 and 45–95.
[20] Ibid at 46–9.
[21] '*Jede Würde kann als Dienst [an der Gemeischaft] und jeder Dienst [an der Gemeischaft] kann als seine Würde betrachtet werden*', Tönnies, ibid at 21 (§ 8).
[22] See Grotius, *De Jure belli ac Pacis Libri Tres* (Paris: Apud Nicolaum Byon, 1625), at 439 (Liber II, Caput XX, Section XLIV), where Grotius confines himself to citing Cicero. More developments

Terenzio Mamiani, in Grotius' footsteps, termed 'the great universal city of humankind' (*la gran città universale del genere umano*).[23] We are equally far from Kant's dream of cosmopolitan law,[24] or from Giorgio La Pira's same dream. In 1947, this leading Italian jurist and politician, in his capacity as a member of the Italian Constituent Assembly, mentioned, after citing Francisco de Vitoria, the Latin tag *totus mundus est quasi unica res publica*, which he translated as follows: 'the whole world is coordinated as a single town' (*tutto il mondo è coordinato come un'unica città*).[25]

To return to the metaphor of fires and their extinguishment, no fire brigade has yet been established in the international society, lamentably, neither has any fire-extinguishing equipment, jointly owned by all community members, been made available.

## (D) Room for change and improvement

In spite of this dispiriting picture and the substantial fact that there is no chance in the next two or three decades to move away from the existing framework of world society, there is room both for enhancing some nascent 'communitarian' features of the international order and for legal change in many areas. This, however, will depend on the extent to which one can instil a strong sense of collective moral responsibility into policymakers and international subjects. As President Havel stated at the UN General Assembly:

Whenever I encounter any problem of today's civilization, I inevitably always arrive at one principal theme: that of human responsibility. This does not mean merely the responsibility of a human being towards his or her own life or survival; towards his or her family; towards his or her company or any other community. It also means responsibility before the infinite and before eternity—in a word, responsibility for the world. Indeed, it seems to

can be found in Grotius, *De Mari Libero* (Lugduni Batavorum: Ex officina Elzeviriana, 1633), in the Introduction (*Ad Principes Populosque Liberos Orbis Christianae,* no pagination, *passim*), and at pp 2 (Caput 1) and 74 (Caput XII).

[23] T. Mamiani, *D'un Nuovo Diritto Europeo* (Turin: Tipografia di Gerolamo Marzorati, 1860), at 10.

[24] Kant stated that 'the law of nations must be based upon a federalism of free states' (*Zum Ewigen Frieden, Ein philosophischer Entwurf* (Königsberg: Friedrich Nicolovius, 1795), at 30). In his view a pacific union (*foedus pacificum*, to be distinguished from a peace treaty (*pactum pacis*), which terminates a war whereas the pacific union ends all wars forever) would give birth to a 'free republic' of confederated peoples (*ein Staatenverein (Republik freier venbündeter Völker*, in I. Kant, 'Die Religion innerhalb der Grenzen der blossen Vernunft' (1793–94), 5th edn (K. Vorländer ed., Leipzig: Verlag von Felix Meiner, 1922), at 35 fn). In the world republic as envisaged by Kant states would no longer have a right to resort to war (*Zum Ewigen Frieden*, cit., at 37) although they would not subject themselves to public laws and to enforcement of such laws (ibid at 35). For Kant the fact that all peoples live on the earth and each people is obliged to live within certain borders results in the fact that evils and violence occurring in a part of our globe are felt in every other part of the globe (*Übel und Gewalttätigkeit an einem Orte unseres Globs an allen gefühlt wird*, in *Metaphysische Anfangsgründe des Rechtslehre* (1797), in Kant's *Gesammelte Schriften*, vol. VI (Berlin: Raimer Verlag, 1907), at 353).

On the development of Kant's ideas on cosmopolitan law, see the important considerations of G. Marini, 'Kant e il diritto cosmopolitico', 9 Iride (1996) 125–40.

[25] See Assemblea Costituente (Constituent Assembly), *Seduta pomeridiana dell'11 marzo 1947 (Afternoon sitting of 11 March 1947)*, at 1988.

me that the most important thing that we should seek to advance in the era of globalization is a sense of global responsibility.[26]

It would be sufficient for a group of major countries to take the lead and initiate the amelioration of the principal institutions in world society. The question, however, is whether the *political will* exists.

I believe that the suggestions made in this book are fairly realistic and constructive, particularly if compared with the utopian 2000 Millennium Declaration, a set of loose yet highly resounding proposals for the future, adopted by consensus by the member states of the UN, represented by their most senior organs.[27] The lack of any substantial implementation of the Millennium Declaration despite subsequent monitoring by the UN (through the 2010 Review Summit) and other international bodies (including the Organization for Economic Co-Operation and Development (OECD)) is a telling testament to the illusory nature of many goals it set forth.

## 2. What can be done to develop an international 'community' proper?

As stressed by Condorelli and Cassese (Chapter 2), although states continue to dominate the world order and steadfastly cling to the concept of self-interest, at least *two factors* militate in favour of limiting their overarching role and the gradual establishment of common values or common concerns. First, *human rights doctrines*, which are inherently universalistic and communitarian, are increasingly gaining a firm foothold in the world society. What is even more important, hand in hand with the increased rooting of the ideology of human rights, individuals have emerged as new actors in international society; they stake out demands and raise concerns that are at variance with those of states. They perforce bring about broad cracks in the architecture of world society and push for the establishment of a community where interests other than those of states are also protected.

The second factor testing the limits of a state-centric world society, is the increasing and dramatic impact of *globalization* both on inter-state relations and the intertwining of their domestic systems. The unimpeded movement all over the world of goods, services, technology, and information, means that no state can escape dramatic events which occur in other parts of the planet. One of the many consequences of globalization is that no individual state, not even the superpower, is able always to act unilaterally any longer. Globalization has therefore created an environment where a certain degree of reliance on other states is, in many instances, a given, and at the very least, some inter-state coordination is often undertaken prior to a policy's implementation.

---

[26] UN Doc. A/55/PV.8, at 2.

[27] It is, however, significant that no delegate of any major power took the floor in the General Assembly when the Declaration was being discussed. Their silence could perhaps be interpreted as a clear expression of scepticism.

Climate change is one illustration of a global problem which cannot be solved by the actions of one state alone. With its attendant consequences (rising sea levels, competition over water resources, mass migrations of peoples), climate change is bound to cause instability and affect most if not all states. It must, of necessity, be tackled not by single states but as a community problem. Other problems push in the same direction. For example, bloody and devastating civil wars in many states, particularly in African countries, result in the migration of thousands of civilians to wealthy countries, causing many socio-economic side effects, besides sometimes having repercussions on public order. These issues, again, cannot be settled by individual states, but must be grappled with collectively. In short, sovereign prerogatives of individual states are now eroded by these new extra-legal phenomena, which push for robust global or communitarian solutions.

I submit that, generally speaking, three main avenues should be taken to buttress the blossoming of 'communitarian' streaks in the world society.

First, an effort should be made to grant a more incisive role to intergovernmental organizations dealing with humanitarian matters (ILO, the UN Food and Agriculture Organization (FAO), the World Health Organization (WHO), UNESCO, the United Nations Industrial Development Organization (UNIDO); the United Nations Environment Programme (UNEP), UNICEF, the World Food Programme (WFP), the United Nations High Commissioner for Refugees (UNHCR), the the Office of the High Commissioner for Human Rights (OHCHR)) and which are the flag-bearers of 'communitarian concerns'. I will elaborate on this point at the end of this chapter.

Secondly, the core of fundamental values that must unite all states and are enshrined in norms of *jus cogens* should become a catalyst for a move towards a more just world order, as well as acting as the common denominator and a sort of glue for all members of the world society.

Thirdly, international civil society should develop a strong new ethos based on those fundamental values, and demand that states abide by them. Modern communication technology is likely to be of great assistance in this regard as a tool for mobilization. Since some of those values are still rudimentary in their formulation, international civil society's insistence that they be upheld and the gradual development of their tenets, might give a powerful push for compliance by states.

The birth in the world order of meta-individual concerns and universal values has been highlighted by some of the contributors to this book. Paulus (Chapter 8) has emphasized that 'community interests' (or, as I would term them, 'community concerns') have recently emerged, which share the following features: (i) they do not (only) affect individual interests or rights of certain states, but concern the community at large; (ii) they are of sufficient importance to avoid leaving their implementation to the usual interplay between states. Some, but not all of these 'community interests' also fulfil a third criterion: (iii) they give rights in certain matters to non-state actors which do not have the requisite international standing to seek enforcement themselves. 'Community interests' normally tend to implement universal values protected in international rules of *jus cogens*. In Paulus's view, there is no reason why 'community interests' should not be protected by the traditional means of reciprocity. He argues, however, that ultimately, international institutions are the ones which must address and bring to the fore collective concerns. This is the reason why, in his opinion, the need for the 'bilateralization' of community interests is the most important of all the insufficiently institutionalized areas of international law.

It has been advanced that the enhancement of some community features that can already be found in world society, even if chiefly at the normative level, cannot be achieved without also bolstering the significance and impact of universal values (peace, respect for human rights, self-determination of peoples, the rule of law) already enshrined as peremptory norms in the international legal order. In other words, the objective would be to attach to those norms the authority of constitutional principles operating at the supra-state level (see Peters, Chapter 10). However, as discussed below, in order to be minimally effective such a constitutionalization process cannot but go hand in hand with the strengthening of international institutions and their gradual detachment from state control.

In a similar vein, other contributors (Cassese, Chapter 11) have suggested the gradual formation of a world community predicated on human rights values, in spite of the different approaches to those same human rights.[28] To this end, a double-track approach should be taken, which deals both with the values at stake and with the means for translating them into living reality. As for values, emphasis must be laid on peremptory rules of international law (*jus cogens*) pertaining to human rights, which are at the summit of the international legal order and non-derogable. They could constitute a unifying set of fundamental standards embraced by all international subjects. Whatever the conflicts and divergences on other issues or on the daily international dealings of states *inter se*, these core values would remain a safe anchor for all international subjects, and a compendium of fundamentals with which all international subjects would identify. In sum, *jus cogens* could constitute the basic amalgam of international subjects until a fully fledged international community arrives at maturity.

However, some of the fundamental values enshrined in peremptory norms of international law are, to some extent, in a state of flux. For example, Yusuf (Chapter 30) pellucidly demonstrates the existence of what he terms 'socioeconomic' self-determination, which can become, and indeed is becoming, a principle enshrining the right of peoples freely to pursue their economic, social, and cultural development, and to participate, contribute to, and enjoy such development. In Yusuf's view two aspects of this new strand of self-determination are likely to assume growing legal importance in the twenty-first century: one based on the evolution of the principle of permanent sovereignty over natural resources, and the

---

[28]  Eg according to a Position Paper of China submitted at the 65th Session of the UN General Assembly,

> Governments of all countries of the world are duty-bound to promote and respect human rights…, taking into account their respective national conditions.…Due to different national conditions, countries have taken different approaches and adopted different models on human rights. It is undesirable to impose one uniform model in the promotion and protection of human rights. (Reported in 10 Chinese JIL (2011) at 440)

other related to the realization of the equal rights of peoples through the mitigation or elimination of the inequalities inherent in the international economic system. According to Yusuf, one can assume that, in the future, actions involving the exploitation of natural resources taken by non-representative or autocratic governments and manifestly contrary to the interests of the peoples concerned, could be open to challenge as violations of international law.

When handling fundamental principles, Zappalà (Chapter 9) warns that one should be careful, as they are not necessarily always reconcilable with each other. As had already been noted by Oscar Schachter in his groundbreaking work *International Law in Theory and Practice*,[29] these principles may, in certain instances, dictate conflicting lines of action when applied to realities on the ground. Nevertheless, Zappalà rightly concludes that, at present one can try, by dint of political savvy, to reconcile those principles both between themselves and with the traditional tenet of effectiveness. This would make it possible to deal with hitherto intractable problems such as the questions of Palestine and Western Sahara, and perhaps even the question of Kashmir and of the de facto government installed by Turkey in Northern Cyprus since 1974.

As for means for implementing these rules of *jus cogens*, three distinct avenues have been proposed (Cassese, Chapter 13). First, a robust system of inquiry should be developed which would be capable of verifying how and when violations occur. Secondly, authors of gross violations of those fundamental values should be held criminally responsible. Thirdly, international civil society should have an increased role in tenaciously and steadfastly pressuring all international subjects to abide by the law.

## 3. The need for legal change

The current legal regulation of international relations is highly deficient in many respects. First, the law governing resort to military violence and the use of force in armed conflicts has been deliberately left by states—the world's lawmakers— loose, opaque, and ambivalent, so as to give major powers a free hand in their actions. This is but one of several areas of international law which are still insufficiently or inadequately regulated. There is therefore a marked need for new and better legislation concerning all these fields.

---

[29] O. Schachter, *International Law in Theory and Practice* (Dordrecht/Boston/London: Martinus Nijhoff, 1991). According to the great international lawyer

> particular situations are covered by more than one principle. Principles can be said to intersect in those situations. They may point to different legal conclusions. Indeed, it has often been observed that principles like proverbs can be paired off into opposites. It is easy to find such opposites in international law: non-use of force versus self-defence, self-determination versus territorial integrity, freedom of the seas versus historic rights. (at 20)

Schachter goes on to note that 'Contradictory principles are not seen as defects in the law but as reflections of complex social realities' (ibid, at 21).

Secondly, in those areas of international law where legal standards are more mature and developed, monitoring and enforcement mechanisms capable of imposing compliance with the standards are meek, if they exist at all. Existing judicial and supervisory frameworks only apply to those states that have previously decided to accept them. If, instead, a state has decided to refuse or resist being overseen, no international body can impel it to live up to its international obligations. There is therefore a need to establish universal mechanisms capable of inducing abidance by international rules by all state and non-state actors.

Thirdly, for most international legal rules to become fully operational, it is imperative that they trickle down into domestic legal systems and be implemented by state authorities. It is lamentable, then, that so many states have structured their domestic legislative framework so as to filter international legal norms and apply them selectively, or even to find escape routes permitting them to eschew their application. There is therefore a strong need to make sure that all international legal imperatives promptly and effectively translate into standards of action by states, by obliging state authorities fully and faithfully to implement them domestically.

## 4. By what lawmaking tools should change be effected?

At present, if international subjects wish to change or supplement existing law, they dispose of the traditional lawmaking mechanisms: treaties, custom, and so-called soft law. The best instrument to produce legal change remains the treaty, on account of its indisputable advantages, namely that it creates written law with which contracting parties formally undertake to comply. Treaty-making is not always an easy exercise, however. On some matters, states prefer to remain free from any legal fetters, and in addition, treaties are of course only binding upon those states that ratify or adhere to them. Lastly, treaties are normally concluded between states, and thus all non-state actors remain in a legal limbo, in a vacuum of legal commitments.

Customary law, while marred by the disadvantage of not being written law, can prove more helpful in coping with the rapid pace of change in international relations. This is possible because it is now accepted that in many areas, particularly those touching upon human rights and humanitarian law, custom does not necessarily require a consolidated and consistent state practice, but can primarily result from *opinio juris*, whether it is laid down in UN General Assembly resolutions, statements or declarations of other intergovernmental organizations, or pronouncements of states. It is a trite observation that the merit of custom lies in its being general in scope and therefore capable of affecting the whole international society. Within this body of law, a privileged place belongs to that string of peremptory norms that are at the apex of the legal order and constrain states and other international subjects more incisively and penetratingly than other customary rules. Further development of *jus cogens* should be encouraged, so as to limit any conduct which could be in violation of international norms.

As for soft law, Viñuales (Chapter 27), Francioni (Chapter 34), and Ronzitti (Chapter 42) have considered it useful as a laboratory for the birth and testing of new standards that could then gradually evolve into hard law. In spite of the limitations inherent in this body of 'law', nascent standards initially deprived of legally binding force can prove helpful, for they offer guidelines to states and other international subjects and may subsequently ripen into legal rules proper.

One of the contributors to this book, Boyle (Chapter 14), has suggested that the Security Council should also exercise lawmaking functions, at least in some areas. Given the clashing interests and motivations of the five permanent members and the consequent need to reconcile such interests every time legislative action is to be taken by the body, it should not be excluded that such a normative function might perhaps be discharged in the interests of the world society at large and not of single members of the Council or of a segment of the world society. However, while in general we should be wary of entrusting an eminently political body with lawmaking functions, we could accept the exercise of such functions only on condition that the Security Council does not depart from strict compliance with peremptory norms. In this respect, it has been suggested by Fassbender (Chapter 5) that a set of practical realizations and initiatives by the Council could result in a sharp rise in the organ's effectiveness in enforcing universal values of international law.

The fact remains that the institutional mechanisms for producing legal change in the world society are slow and cumbersome. In particular, such mechanisms are unable to spawn rules that are immediately and undisputedly binding on all international subjects, thereby having a prompt and general impact on the whole society. States, in particular major powers, can always controvert or cast doubt about the existence of a fledgling customary rule and can thus easily avoid compliance. They can also call into question the emergence of a *jus cogens* norm, and in this case, it may prove difficult to persuade them of the existence of such a norm. Similarly, states can avoid multilateral treaties, or even ratify treaties and then fail to implement them within their domestic legal order (alas, a frequent occurrence in the world society).

In all these areas, a major 'substitutive' role can be played by international *courts*, as I will point out below. Also domestic courts, acting as guardians of international law, can contribute powerfully to the evolution and updating of traditional international law.

## 5. What areas are most in need of reform?

### (A) Resort to armed violence

The principal areas where there should be some progress concern armed violence: *jus ad bellum* (when to resort to armed force outside any authorization of the Security Council) and *jus in bello* (the regulation of violence in international and internal armed conflicts). These are the two areas most in want of legal regulation.

However, precisely because these are areas where states, and in particular major powers, are eager to retain as much latitude as possible, it is unlikely that any progress can be made.

With regard to resort to armed force, Sands (Chapter 28) suggests that one should focus on the 'operationalization' of the UN Charter rules, chiefly through domestic legal debate. In many countries, the interface between unlawful use of force and the crime of aggression has begun to generate increased debate. This growing sensitization to legal considerations by the public and political classes reflects the operationalization of Security Council resolutions in a domestic political context. In the same vein, Sands also points to international judicial consideration, given that the rules governing the use of force as well as the consequences of their violation have been the subject of recent judicial consideration before various international instances, chiefly the International Court of Justice (ICJ) but also an arbitral court established under the 1982 Law of the Sea Convention. A third way to operationalize the UN Charter rules would be through international legislative efforts, such as the definition of the crime of aggression agreed upon in 2010 by the Assembly of the States Parties to the Rome Statute. Legislative efforts are, of course, palliatives, because they are unlikely to lead to a revisitation or redefinition of the conditions under which a state can resort to force in self-defence. The 'legislation' passed at the Kampala Review Conference on the definition of aggression as an international crime can hardly be considered accurate and reflective of customary international law. In any event, it may not even enter into force until 2017. There is therefore little to expect regarding any lawmaking progress initiated by states. One can perhaps hold out greater hope that international courts may contribute to spelling out and circumscribing the requirements for self-defence.

Tams argues (Chapter 29) that there is no chance for a possible expansion of the right to resort to force in cases other than self-defence, even where the world society is faced with a human catastrophe, such as that of a state carrying out large-scale killings among its own population. In his view, there are a few options available. For one, the UN might internally be able to make more frequent and more effective use of its existing competences. Security Council practice, for example, may help to generate standards governing the auto-interpretation of equivocal terms of reference. Furthermore, a reinvigorated General Assembly might again assume a more active role in the field of peace and security. Outside the UN system, the most likely scenario is that the international society will continue to be recalcitrant in launching humanitarian interventions while at the same time tolerating breaches in exceptional circumstances. The only exception to this forecast is that one type of humanitarian intervention outside the UN system is likely to be accepted: *regional interventions* based on Article 4(h) of the African Union's Charter. Otherwise, we are here again faced with weak remedies. No major improvement on the existing condition is within view.

It appears that there might be more hope on the horizon when it comes to *jus in bello*. According to Melzer (Chapter 38), states and non-state actors should increasingly rely on the four general principles protecting civilians, which underlie the entire normative framework governing the use of force: necessity, proportionality, precaution, and humanity. In his view, whenever states resort to force, whether in self-defence against armed attacks, in the conduct of hostilities against belligerent adversaries, or in the exercise of their law-enforcement authority, it is always these four principles which circumscribe the permissible scope and intensity of their action. They could be regarded as a normative superstructure from which a unified legal regime governing the use of force can be extracted for all situations ranging from peacetime policing, to all-out international armed conflict. As for internal armed conflict, Sivakumaran (Chapter 40) argues that in order to ensure more extensive respect for civilians and for the human rights of all those involved in these conflicts, greater regard should be given to the ad hoc regulation of such conflicts through unilateral declarations, bilateral agreements, and the like, which—he opines—are more prevalent than may be thought. One way forward might reside in working out a new instrument designed to bind armed groups in all situations. The instrument would draw from international humanitarian law, international human rights law, and other relevant bodies of international law. Armed groups should be able to sign up to the instrument as signature coupled with participation in the lawmaking process may give them a greater sense of investment both in the process and in the norms that result from it. In Sivakumaran's opinion, this could potentially have a beneficial impact on compliance. The ICRC could prompt armed groups to declare that they will abide by this instrument and monitoring and enforcement of the instrument would take place through a number of mutually reinforcing and complementary means.

On a micro level, a related problem is the imposition of restraints on the use of weapons. Here, Ronzitti (Chapter 42) contends that improvements in international humanitarian law may not be the only way to achieve a satisfactory regime to regulate weapons. Arms control, non-proliferation, and disarmament instruments should be used to yield more potent results. The choice of instruments available is also important. As the indeterminacy and lacunae of customary international law make it ill-suited for disarmament, treaties are necessary for prohibiting the use of specific weapons. However, one should also rely on soft law for managing non-proliferation regimes and even arms control. As far as disarmament is concerned, in Ronzitti's view, treaties can set out the obligation of non-production and stockpiling, and soft law can help with monitoring, whenever treaty obligations on verification are difficult to negotiate. Moreover, soft law instruments may be transformed into hard law as soon as the political conditions render it feasible. In the framework of non-proliferation, Security Council resolutions are of paramount importance, although their impact is limited to states, since normally they do not apply to other international subjects. The overall prognosis is that there is little prospect for improvement in some areas. How many states are prepared and willing to ban lethal weapons, knowing that their use can make the difference in any armed conflict? This is indeed an area where there is the least hope of any major breakthrough.

If it proves impossible or extremely difficult to restrain the use of violence in armed conflicts, can one nevertheless hope that at a minimum, civilians may be compensated whenever they or their relatives are victims of unlawful use of violence? According to Pinzauti (Chapter 43) international rules are at present susceptible to an evolutive interpretation and may thus be construed in such a manner as to grant rights to individuals. As a consequence, victims would be entitled to compensation when they are the target of unlawful attacks. This is an area ripe for exploration, and which can generate interesting discussions and proposals, for example regarding: (i) the criteria and modalities by which individuals can claim compensation; (ii) domestic or international mechanisms to impel states to pay compensation; and (iii) if states fail to compensate, the enforcement of their obligation to pay, assuming such an obligation would have acquired the status of customary international law.

## (B) Other areas

Other areas of substantive international law where there is a great need for legal improvement include the development of poor countries, the environment, the regulation of international financial relations, terrorism, genetic manipulation, and the use of cyberspace.

In the chapter on the condition of development, Jouannet (Chapter 31) laments the disappointing application of legal norms stemming from major legal principles such as the right of peoples to self-determination, sovereignty over natural resources, and the right to nationalize against just compensation, which have helped to found and consolidate the sovereignty of newly independent states. Not only have these norms created a real dependence on aid from donor states and international organizations, but they also appear to have had virtually no impact on fostering the development of poor states. The same counterproductive effect has been felt from the application of double standards and the misapplication, whether deliberate or not, of policies on public support, cooperation, technology transfer, the principle of common but differentiated obligations, and the infamous Structural Adjustment Programmes (SAPs) run in authoritarian fashion under the leadership of large financial institutions. None of these legal and economic practices has proved to be adequate. International development law, as it has evolved in the post-Cold War era, no longer seems effective. In a way, Jouannet agrees in substance with the stern statement made in the UN General Assembly by the Governor-General of the Commonwealth of the Bahamas when discussing the 2000 Millennium Declaration.[30]

---

30

We are still for the most part trapped in a pernicious syndrome of the haves versus the have-nots, because those very factors which have contributed to improved standards for some have likewise contributed to the extreme impoverishment, dispossession and marginalization of millions of others around the world. Those same factors which have enhanced the existence of some have caused serious environmental degradation in the backyards of others and in some cases have actually threatened the peace and security of humanity to an unexpected degree, which is quite an ironic twist of fate when one considers the noble and lofty precepts which went into the establishment of the United Nations 55 years ago. (UN Doc. A/55/PV.8, at 8)

Jouannet argues that three options exist, in theory, to change the existing dire condition of development: (i) sticking to the neo-liberal pro-market paradigm—an economically efficient but socially unfair solution; (ii) jettisoning any model of development—a blind alley; and (iii) changing the rules of the global economic system, and creating a new and fair New International Economic Order (NIEO). This third option aims at changing the rules of the global economic system, recasting the Breton Woods financial institutions, changing the General Agreement on Tariffs and Trade (GATT) rules and revising the World Trade Organization (WTO) in a more equitable direction so that it finally refocuses relations between the various North(s) and South(s). This reform would not seek the mirage of equality between states, but to elevate the principle of fairness to the legal basis for all future discussions between the North and South, so as to change a profoundly unjust system. According to Jouannet, a new NIEO is the necessary condition for a sustainable human development that is effective.

As for international environmental law, Francioni (Chapter 34) rightly suggests that the original promise of the environmental movement be harnessed again, that is, the conceptualization and the legal treatment of the natural environment as a 'public good' to be administered in the interest of all and for the generations to come. He opines that two approaches are possible at the international level. The first would be consciously to shun the need for institutional reform as too costly and ineffective, and rely instead on market mechanisms of self-regulation and transnational private enforcement. The second approach would include carrying out a reform of the institutional system of environmental governance by creating effective multilateral institutions that can mirror what has been done in international economic law and human rights. The two approaches are not mutually exclusive, according to Francioni. They should be complementary because the first can hardly work without the second. Despite these general suggestions requiring decades if not longer to be brought into effect, the path suggested by Francioni seems to be the right one, and one would fervently hope that states and intergovernmental organizations will engage in that direction.

In the chapter on international financial relations, Howse (Chapter 33) advocates that issues arising from possible inconsistencies between measures taken in relation to International Monetary Fund (IMF) programmes on the one hand and WTO obligations on the other should be addressed through consultations and cooperation between the two bodies. In the field of trade restrictions for balance-of-payment purposes, Howse suggests that even though a developing country could address its balance of payments difficulties through exchange rate adjustments or tighter macroeconomic policies, it should not be expected to do so given the harm to development that may come from the resultant decline in needed imports. He argues that the concept of coherence reflected in the relevant WTO instruments and activities as concerns balance of payments and exchange matters is too narrowly focused on relations between the IMF and the WTO and does not include cooperation with those international institutions concerned with equity in development. In his view, the concept of coherence should be revised to reflect the relationship between equity and coherence as implied in the Millennium Declaration adopted in 2000 by the UN General Assembly (GA Res. 55/2) and related instruments. Here again, we have general guidelines for a possible amelioration of the existing condition: the question, however, arises of whether and when states and intergovernmental organizations are prepared to put into effect the suggested reform.

With regard to international investment law and arbitration, Reisman (Chapter 22) outlines five alternatives to respond to current stresses in the international investment infrastructure: (i) global integration (more and more direct foreign investment would be made worldwide, on the basis of economic rather than political considerations; in addition, there would be more decisions by international investment tribunals with respect to the quality of governance within states which hosted foreign investment); (ii) regional and sub-regional integration; (iii) recrudescence of protectionism and mercantilism; (iv) revival of the NIEO system; or (v) continuation of the present heterogeneous system. Reisman supports the first option as the most desirable, for its promise of enhanced production and the efficient use of the resources of our planet and the resulting interdependence which, one hopes, will act as a restraint on the use of violence.

As for the plague of terrorism, van Ginkel (Chapter 35) holds the view that the Security Council could decide on a definition of terrorism that would apply to all other resolutions in which the term is used, and would thus limit their scope; such definition could of course develop into customary international law over the years. Furthermore, in her view it should be possible to appeal the listing by the Council of an individual or an organization as 'terrorist' to an independent and impartial organ with the authority to order appropriate compensation, and in accordance with fair procedural principles. Van Ginkel also suggests three options for the possible establishment of an international tribunal for terrorism: (i) an ad hoc tribunal set up pursuant to a Security Council resolution; (ii) the broadening of the subject matter jurisdiction for the ICC; or (iii) the establishment of a special court for terrorism. In my opinion, while one can doubt whether the Security Council may be able to reach a generally accepted definition of terrorism—the more so because such a definition has already been set out by the Appeals Chamber of the Special Tribunal for Lebanon (STL) in its decision of 16 February 2011[31]—it is true that the listing procedure of terrorists or terrorist organizations needs judicial safeguards intended to protect the rights of the individuals or organizations involved. This is a measure that can easily be taken by the Council. As for the establishment of an international tribunal on terrorism, I submit that the best option would be to convert the STL into such a tribunal once it has discharged its functions, so as to maximize all the advantages of already having the necessary practical and logistical wherewithal available.

Genetic manipulation is a growing problem in the current world society. The rapid increase in scientific and technological advances in the areas of genetic

---

[31] Available at <http://www.stl-tsl.org/x/file/TheRegistry/Library/CaseFiles/chambers/20110216_STL-11-01_R176bis_F0010_AC_Interlocutory_Decision_Filed_EN.pdf>.

engineering or biotechnology, mainly applied to medicines and foodstuffs, poses considerable risks to biodiversity, human health, and the environment and has raised regulatory challenges under both regional and international law. The only hard law in this field is regional: the Council of Europe Convention on Human Rights and Biomedicine and all its additional protocols, and European Community Directive 98/44/EC of 6 July 1998 on the legal protection of bio-technological inventions. A string of UNESCO Declarations are not legally bind-ing and may thus be described as 'soft law'. According to El-Zein (Chapter 36), it would be problematic to draw up a single hard law instrument embracing all the questions that arise and linked to the extraordinary and rapid development of science and technology. However, the instruments of the Council of Europe and UNESCO reflect potential norms that could constitute 'building blocks' for the formation of customary international law. They could address the best balance between fast technology and secure law, ethical and legal norms, as well as norms in the trade field and in the field of medical or technological research. Again, these are general guidelines for the lawmakers, which are likely to be taken up only if the relevant states are amenable.

Finally, international regulation of the use of cyberspace constitutes an urgent matter, given the staggering advances of modern technology and the pressing need to protect the right to privacy and prevent crimes. According to Murray (Chapter 37) there are areas where international cooperation and perhaps even formalization of law through treaty obligations is likely to be successful. They include: (i) e-commerce where the UN Commission on International Trade Law (UNCITRAL) Model Law on Electronic Commerce has been extremely success-ful in bringing harmony and international recognition; (ii) intellectual property rights where a number of World Intellectual Property Organization (WIPO) treat-ies and others such as the recently finalized Anti-Counterfeiting Trade Agreement have been or are likely to be effective; and (iii) the field of criminal law. According to Murray the Council of Europe Convention on Cybercrime has been effective in providing cooperation on matters of illegal interception and computer-related fraud. However, in his view if lawyers want to create de facto control over content, this cannot occur through legal documents; it must be done through a web of terms and conditions of service and through Lessigian[32] code-based solutions. Content may be just beyond the direct control of the international legal community, as pre-dicted by the cyber-libertarians. Will states uphold these ideas and move forward towards a proper regulation of the matter?

---

[32] Namely based on Lawrence Lessig's books (*Code and Other Laws of Cyberspace*, New York: Basic Books 1999; and *The Future of Ideas: The Fate of the Commons in a Connected World*, New York: Vintage Books 2001).

## 6. How to ensure the trickle-down effect of international norms into domestic legal orders

State practice shows that the emergence of new or better international rules alone is insufficient to bring about any change. Some states evade international treaty obligations 'from the beginning', so to speak, by astutely using the mechanism of reservations and thereby either reducing the scope of their obligations or even stultifying these obligations. A case in point is the attitude taken by the Sultanate of Oman in 2006 when it made reservations to the 1979 Convention on the Elimination of all Forms of Discrimination Against Women,[33] an attitude similar to that taken by other states[34] which entered sweeping reservations based on a possible inconsistency of Convention provisions with shari'a law.

However, the more usual way of shirking international obligations is by acting at the domestic level. Indeed, in order to produce any legal effects international rules normally require implementation within the national legal order of contracting states. Many countries, however, are still reluctant to shape their legal system in such a manner as to render new legal imperatives (whether laid down in treaties or in customary rules) automatically enforceable domestically. They often 'filter' those international imperatives, or even refrain from implementing them within their domestic systems, or make their own legislation prevail over international rules. The United States is a case in point. Federal laws may supersede or repeal international treaties, and the value of customary international law is negligible. In *United States v Yunis* a Federal Court held that 'Our duty is to enforce the Constitution, laws and treaties of the United States, not conform the law of the land to norms of customary international law.'[35] Furthermore, as borne out by the authoritative *Restatement of the Law (Third)*, when the existence of a customary international rule is denied by the US executive, US courts defer to that policy stance in their own rulings. By extension, US courts attach special importance to the interpretation of a customary rule propounded by the executive branch,

---

[33] Oman entered a reservation to 'All provisions of the Convention not in accordance with the provisions of the Islamic sharia and legislation in force in the Sultanate of Oman.' It also made a reservation to Arts 9(2), 15(4), 16 (a), (c) and (f) and Art. 29(1). The United Kingdom rightly objected to such reservations in 2007, noting that

> a reservation should clearly define for the other States Parties to the Convention the extent to which the reserving State has accepted the obligations of the Convention. A reservation which consists of a general reference to a system of law without specifying its contents does not do so. (BYIL (2007) at 657)

The UK therefore objected to the general reservation reported above, as well as to other specific reservations, adding, however, that its objections 'shall not preclude the entry into force of the Convention' between Oman and the UK (ibid). As a result Oman is a party to the Convention even towards the UK but in practice may evade all the Convention provisions that it deems fit to disregard on the ground of the inconsistency that in its view may exist between those provisions and shari'a law.

[34] See the reservations entered by Brunei, Egypt, Mauritania, and Saudi Arabia.

[35] 924 F2d 1086, 1086ff (DC Cir. 1991); the sentence cited in the text is at 1091.

thereby renouncing any autonomous and final say in how to construe and apply international rules.[36]

The United Kingdom, like the United States, is loath quickly and automatically to apply binding international rules.[37] The same cautious attitude towards the implementation of international rules is taken by numerous other states, and as different from each other as Australia and South Africa. China's position is not dissimilar: international treaty rules are incorporated through an ad hoc procedure (whereas it would seem that customary rules are incorporated automatically); their rank is equal to that of ordinary Chinese laws, with the consequence that by passing new legislation the Chinese lawmakers can at any time repeal or modify rules of international origin.[38] Russia's situation is only seemingly different: despite the internationalist outlook of the 1993 Constitution,[39] in practice, given the authoritarian streaks of the current regime in Russia and the strong dependency of the

---

[36] See *Restatement of the Law Third—The Foreign Relations Law of the United States*, vol. 1 (St Paul, MN: American Law Institute Publishers, 1987), 59.

[37] The British stand in his respect was well set out in 1988 by Lord Templeman in the House of Lords' judgement in *Rayner v Department of Trade and Industry*:

> A treaty is a contract between the governments of two or more sovereign states. International law regulates the relations between sovereign states and determines the validity, the interpretation and the enforcement of treaties. A treaty to which Her Majesty's Government is a party does not alter the laws of the United Kingdom. A treaty may be incorporated into or alter the laws if the United Kingdom by means of legislation. Except to the extent that a treaty becomes incorporated into the laws of the United Kingdom by statute, the courts of the United Kingdom have no power to enforce treaty rights and obligations at the behest of a sovereign government or at the behest of a private individual. (3 All ER [1988] at 257; also in 81 ILR 670ff)

See also House of Lords, *Maclaine Watson v Department of Trade and Industry*, per Lord Oliver (3 All ER [1989] 523 at 544–5; also in 81 ILR at 701).

[38] See Wang Liyu, 'The Application of International Treaties and Agreements in the National Law of China', 93 Chinese YIL at 287–8; Wang Tieya, 'The Position of Treaties and Agreements in the Legal System of China', 94 Chinese YIL at 5–6. According to S. Guo, 'Implementation of Human Rights Treaties by Chinese Courts: Problems and Prospects', 10 Chinese JIL (2011) at 163,

> China's Constitution is silent on the general domestic status of treaties, making the status of treaties unclear in the Chinese legal system. Some scholars regard this silence as excluding treaties as part of Chinese law, while most Chinese international lawyers agree that the Constitution should expressly clarify the issue and its silence does not mean the rejection of direct effect of treaties in domestic law. Secondly, there are many specific laws and regulations concerning this issue in China, but they do not provide clear answers....Because of the silence of China's Constitution, scholars use different approaches to interpret such provisions. Some take the conflict between a treaty and domestic law as implying that the treaty has come into effect in the domestic legal system, while others think that the conflict is a precondition of the coming into effect of the treaty in domestic law. Some scholars have pointed out the difference between the application of treaties in Chinese courts and its effects in the Chinese legal system, arguing that the monist view on the relationship between treaties and domestic law cannot be inferred from provisions like Article 142 [of the General Principles of Civil Law].

[39] See, in particular, Art. 15(4) of the 1993 Constitution, which states:

> The generally recognized principles and norms of international law and the international treaties of the Russian Federation shall constitute part of the legal system. If an international treaty of the Russian Federation establishes other rules than those stipulated by the law, the rules of the international treaty shall apply.

judiciary on executive power, international law does not receive from the courts the consideration it should deserve.

In sum, major powers tend to take an extremely cautious attitude to international legal rules. If they ratify international treaties, it is not infrequent that they subsequently fail to implement them fully; or they even advance interpretations at variance with that upheld by international monitoring bodies and clearly dissonant with a plain reading of treaty rules. This has occurred in the case of the United States, which has espoused a highly questionable construction of the 1984 Convention on Torture before the UN Committee Against Torture (US delegates stated among other things that the Convention is not applicable in times of armed conflict).[40] Customary rules, by nature, are even easier than treaties for states to controvert. Worse, it is possible for states to deny they exist or to simply ignore them.

It would therefore seem crucial to suggest ways in which states should align their domestic systems with the legal standards of the world society, so as to ensure that those standards duly percolate through domestic law and are scrupulously observed. In Chapter 15, I have suggested four measures to achieve this, two of which would operate at the international level only. First, there should be an international judicial body endowed with compulsory jurisdiction over the national implementation of international treaties. This body should have a two-fold function. It should be charged with authoritatively establishing whether, in a specific instance, a state has breached an international rule which expressly or implicitly required amending national legislation, because it has failed to make the necessary legislative amendments that have led to the specific breach of the treaty. The judicial body should also be charged with finding whether states comply with international treaty provisions enjoining the parties to modify their legislation forthwith. In this case the judicial body would not need to wait for a specific breach of the treaty to occur, but would exercise its functions a short time after the treaty has entered into force. Plainly, this second function would be extremely relevant with regard to such treaties as the Rome Statute of the ICC, which automatically requires contracting parties to change their national legislation, something that not all the state parties to the Statute have done so far, without any international monitoring of such failure being carried out. The power to seize such a court should be granted not only to all parties to a multilateral treaty and any international body monitoring the implementation of the treaty, but also to any natural or legal person showing a direct legal interest in the implementation of the international rule. Secondly, an international monitoring body should be created in order to ascertain whether concerned states have followed up with the rulings of the court.

The remaining two mechanisms that I propose would function at the domestic level and would be more incisive. For one, every state should pass a constitutional

---

[40] See 'Report of the Committee Against Torture 2005–2006' (UN Doc. A/61/44), at 68–74. See also the comments by J.E. Alvarez, 'Torturing the Law', 37 Case Western Reserve JIL (2006) esp. 179–86.

provision stipulating that at any time a national piece of legislation is in conflict with an international treaty provision or a customary rule not contested by that state, such legislation is automatically repealed or, at a minimum, courts, administrative bodies and individuals are bound to disregard it (it can be noted that some European states such as Germany, Italy, Greece, the Netherlands, and Spain, already possess such constitutional or similar provisions). And, secondly, whenever there is a doubt or a dispute about whether national legislation conforms to international rules, national courts as well as natural and legal persons should be empowered to bring the case before an international court which has the jurisdiction to issue rulings on the matter with legally binding effect. Lamentably, the current condition of the world society renders the implementation of these suggested reforms very difficult. Based on the experience of some regional courts, I would submit that any progress in the not too distant future may only occur within regional groupings, not at the universal level.

The conundrum of how best to facilitate the observance of international norms at the domestic level cannot be resolved without also enhancing the role of national courts, which could be called upon to challenge national legislation or administrative acts inconsistent with international rules. According to Shany (Chapter 16), bolstering the role of domestic courts could dramatically increase the prospects of enforcing international obligations. In his view, the growing judicial treatment of international legal instruments by national courts may lead to increased international clarification of international legal standards. Furthermore, the democratic credentials of many domestic legal systems may confer upon their courts' decisions applying international law a greater degree of democratic legitimacy than that associated with the judgments of international courts. With a view to enhancing the role of domestic courts, Shany makes a few suggestions: (i) new and existing treaty regimes should prompt domestic courts to apply international law; (ii) states and international institutions should allocate more resources to develop the capacity of domestic courts to adjudicate cases involving international norms; (iii) a more rational set of principles governing the division of labour between domestic and international courts ought to be developed, especially in fields where international courts are inundated with cases; and (iv) new international standards should be developed that would try to regulate the application of international law in domestic courts.

## 7. Can one modernize international adjudicatory bodies?

At present, international courts are playing a momentous rule in expanding and clarifying the scope of international rules. In this respect the contribution of the ICJ and the (potential) role of the ICC, two permanent and potentially universal judicial institutions, must not be underestimated. Nevertheless, measures should be taken to transform the ICJ from a perfected arbitral court into a judicial court proper, settling disputes between states in the interests of peace and justice, on behalf not of two or more disputants, but of the whole international society. In this regard, Schabas (Chapter 20) de Hemptinne (Chapter 44), and I (Chapter 19) all propose various reforms to international adjudication. I have proposed a host of specific measures with regard to the ICJ, some of which could only be taken in the long term, whereas others can be put into effect in a relatively short time frame. Similarly, as suggested by Schabas some measures could significantly ameliorate the functioning and output of the ICC. In addition, as proposed by de Hemptinne, international criminal justice might be reorganized. On the one hand, a large number of international criminal cases should be decentralized on the basis of precise rules of jurisdictional allocation, that is, brought before local courts, or ad hoc internationalized tribunals, or possibly regional courts located as close as possible to the populations concerned. This process should go hand in hand with the establishment of truth and reconciliation commissions. On the other hand, a number of investigative and judicial activities of the ICC should be devolved, that is, conducted by the Court, not in The Hague, but in the countries concerned. In de Hemptinne's view, these two processes of *decentralization* and *devolution* should be implemented in parallel, on the basis of well-defined criteria.

Regional courts on human rights can also play an increasingly important role in disseminating respect for human rights and gradually expanding the scope of such rights to serve as a model to other courts in different regions of the world (see Evans, Chapter 21). I would add that a provision of the Protocol to the African Charter on Human and Peoples' Rights on the Establishment of an African Court on Human Rights and Peoples' Rights, of 9 June 1998 (which entered into force on 25 January 2004) is progressive enough to serve as a model for a gradual expansion of the jurisdiction of other human rights and international courts. Indeed, under Article 3(1) of the Protocol, the Court's jurisdiction extends not only to violations of human rights covered by the 1981 African Charter on Human and Peoples' Rights and its Protocol, but to any other human rights instrument ratified by the concerned African state or states.[41] This provision is of paramount importance. It signals that the African Court is vested with jurisdiction well beyond that founded on the 1981 African Charter. By that token, it furnishes significant judicial safeguards to other human rights treaties. The replication of this clause in other international instruments granting jurisdiction to international human rights courts would entail that any human rights treaty, whether or not it is endowed with its own oversight mechanism, could be further guaranteed by the human rights court. This targeted reform would lead the judicial enforcement of human rights treaties to make great strides.

Does the possible fragmentation of international law brought about by the existence of so many courts and tribunals impair the functioning of the law, given the likely divergences or even conflicts in interpretation? I do not think of this as a major problem, particularly if, in the field of inter-state dispute settlement, the ICJ

---

[41] 'The jurisdiction of the Court shall extend to all cases and disputes submitted to it concerning the interpretation and application of the Charter, this Protocol and any other relevant Human Rights instrument ratified by the States concerned.' This provision is restated in Rule 26(1)(a) of the Rules of the Court.

eventually comes to play the role of the highest international jurisdiction issuing well-argued decisions which can have precedential value for other courts. In order to ensure that interpretational discordances are harmonized, or at the very least reduced, Bennouna (Chapter 23) proposes an innovative solution, which would consist of the creation by the UN General Assembly of a new expert body, modelled on the International Law Commission, aimed at ensuring 'the progressive development of international law and its codification' (Art. 13, UN Charter). The task of this expert body would be to identify and analyse the potential divergences in the interpretation and application of general international law, as well as their consequences. It would submit its studies to the UN General Assembly, to international courts, as well as to the bodies entrusted with the codification of international law. Periodical studies, carried out by the expert body, would have the advantage of drawing the judges' attention to the issues relating to the diversified implementation of general international law by different international jurisdictions.

## 8. How can we bring about greater compliance with international imperatives through mechanisms other than international adjudication?

At present, the most suitable mechanisms for ensuring compliance with international rules are monitoring devices and fact-finding bodies.

As I have tried to argue in Chapter 24, monitoring differs from international adjudication and inquiry in a few crucial respects. First, the scrutiny (which is carried out through the examination of periodic reports, or on-site inspections, or contentious proceedings) is not triggered by a dispute between two or more parties, that is, as a result of a *private* action; it is instead inspired by a *collective* interest in supervising states' abidance by international standards. Secondly, it is not undertaken by an organ accepted ad hoc by, or set up ad hoc at the behest of, the states concerned; it is carried out by pre-existing international institutions. Thirdly, monitoring is not occasional, but permanent and automatic. It functions on a steady basis, that is, even before any violation occurs and regardless of whether or not a party complains about an alleged violation. Fourthly, the party or parties concerned are not free to give any follow-up to the result of supervision. Although often they are under no legal obligation to comply with the finding or assessment of the supervisory body, it is politically and morally difficult for them not to bow to that finding or assessment. In addition, in many instances, the international body is empowered to go so far as to scrutinize the state's implementation of corrective measures following the outcome of the monitoring exercise.

I have suggested that monitoring should be expanded and strengthened. It should be included in all multilateral treaties, and a committee of experts should be established within the UN entrusted with overseeing the implementation of multilateral treaties to be made in future. In addition, a follow-up to monitoring should be envisaged, to ensure that states take into account the reports of supervisory bodies. Monitoring should be strengthened in at least four areas: use of nuclear energy, human rights, environment, and armed conflicts. The chapters by Rockwood (Chapter 25), Clapham (Chapter 26), Viñuales (Chapter 27), and my own (Chapter 24) have dwelt on these specific areas.

The other mechanism for ensuring observance of international legal imperatives without coming up against strong resistance by states is fact-finding established not by states, along the lines of the traditional commissions of inquiry, but by international organizations, and not necessarily on the basis of the consent of the state or states concerned. Fact-finding mechanisms were born out of the attempt to perfect traditional commissions of inquiry, chiefly by disentangling such commissions from the will of the states concerned. In recent years the UN, through the Security Council, the Human Rights Council, or the Secretary-General, has launched various commissions composed of independent experts tasked with looking into specific matters or situations and reporting thereon. These commissions have many merits: (i) they are not dependent on the individual states involved in the matter at issue, but result from majority decisions of international bodies; (ii) they are made up of independent experts; (iii) they report to international organs, which may decide to take follow-up action; (iv) often, in addition to establishing facts, they also assess them in light of the relevant international standards, thereby determining whether the facts amount to violations of the those standards; and (v) they also often advise the 'parent body' on how to deal with the matter, that is, what possible steps should be taken in light of the commission's findings.

The benefits of institutional fact-finding subsist only if they are established by international organizations instead of states. I have identified, in addition, three initiatives in my chapter (Chapter 24), which can help international organizations to carve out for themselves a greater and more efficient role in their field of work. First, the UN Secretary-General should establish a roster of experts specializing in various fields and prepared to be called upon to undertake a mission. This would avoid the UN wasting any time in the selection and appointment of competent persons for a specific case. Secondly, a fund should be set up to finance fact-finding, so as to prevent states or organs from hampering or delaying missions on account of internal economic problems. Thirdly, regulations should be passed to outline the structure, powers, and functioning of fact-finding commissions, so that, once the need arises to investigate a situation, all the relevant rules are already in place. Commissions should be granted extensive powers and, in this respect, the Inquiry Commission on Darfur (established in 2004 by the UN Security Council) could be taken as a model. It was given three tasks: (i) to establish whether serious violations of human rights had been committed; (ii) to identify the perpetrators; and (iii) to propose accountability mechanisms. Its extensive powers allowed it to undertake an in-depth examination and also identify possible perpetrators and propose suitable means for achieving accountability. Thus the Commission, although charged with a highly sensitive mandate, was nevertheless in a position to examine the whole spectrum of problems and act as a pre-judicial body capable of clearing the ground for a court of law which would eventually be seized of the matter.

In sum, as noted in Chapter 24, both monitoring and institutional fact-finding are expressions of a new relationship that has developed in the world society between each individual state and society at large. States are no longer masters of the realm, but strongly dependent on multilateral relations and are subject to the pressure and weight of the collectivity. True, the world legal order does not yet have the various means that are available to central authorities in domestic legal systems. To induce compliance with international standards it therefore cannot resort to compulsory judicial determination, let alone collective enforcement. Monitoring and institutional fact-finding are thus the best way of bringing the weight of the community to bear on each member state, as well as other international legal subjects.

## 9.  Some tentative suggestions for action

Many measures have been propounded in this book with a view to ameliorating some prominent features of the current world society. Most of these measures hinge upon action to be taken by states or other international legal subjects such as intergovernmental organizations, or non-state entities such as insurgents or armed groups wielding authority and control over part of the territory and population of a sovereign state. The extent to which one can rely on these international actors to implement the initiatives set down in this book is, however, uncertain. States, particularly, are too much actuated by their own selfish concerns, by the necessity to safeguard military, economic, and commercial interests, by the urgency to heed national constituencies and their political and social desiderata.

In order to overcome the structural obstacles on the path to reforming the world order, headway needs to be made separately but simultaneously both at the level of international relations and at the domestic level.

Actions undertaken at the former level should try to enhance the non-political, professional dimension of many intergovernmental organizations so as to make them more efficient and responsive to common problems such as poverty, underdevelopment, climate change, and illiteracy. In addition, as suggested above, greater use of fact-finding bodies should be made in connection with the numerous situations where facts are contested by states or other international subjects. The powers of fact-finding bodies should also be expanded to allow them the flexibility to carry out their missions thoroughly and unimpeded. Furthermore, expansion of the hold of international law over non-state actors should be pursued so as to enhance the prescriptive range of international rules in a way that would no doubt be beneficial to a decrease in violence and to the smoother conduct of international dealings.

At the domestic level, national courts could contribute more to the regulation of international law and civil society should be encouraged to play a more incisive role.

Let me start with the international level.

## (A) Possible international remedial action

### (i) Detaching intergovernmental organizations from the sway of member states

It is common knowledge that intergovernmental organizations are substantially made up of two components: (i) a leadership that is normally chosen not only for its intellectual or professional quality, but also and primarily on political grounds or at least along lines where international political or ideological leanings carry great weight, and (ii) a bureaucracy consisting of staff members who are normally appointed on the basis of their professional qualities and their nationality so as to ensure 'an equitable national and geographical distribution'. The organizations' dependence on funding from member states, as well as the strong political element of the organizations' leadership inevitably spur these bodies to act as tools in the hands of the major contributing states, in essence, the major powers. Thus, often, the high professional quality of both the leadership and the staff panders to the international political game rather than the lofty ideals on which the organizations were created. If states are led gradually to grant more autonomy to international organizations, it might result in greater efficiency and, what is even more important, in those organizations working more proactively for the common good. In other words, they would better grapple with the major problems dogging the international society, thereby acting as 'instruments of communitarian concerns'. Although they would not be akin to national state agencies that work for the common good (since they would lack the necessary authority and autonomy), they would at least resemble national charities.

My proposal for increased autonomy and professionalism holds truest with regard to the intergovernmental organizations dealing with humanitarian matters and which—as I said earlier—are the flag-bearers of 'communitarian concerns' (ILO, FAO, UNESCO, UNIDO, UNEP, UNICEF, WFP, UNHCR, OHCHR). The organizations should be made more independent of the founding states and less dependent on states' financing (and conditioning). This can be achieved by allowing the organizations to raise funds from private bodies or individuals, provided close scrutiny of the spending of such funds is ensured by the organizations. Secondly, it would be crucial to enhance the professional and independent dimension of the organizations under discussion. In particular, the authority of the Secretary-General or the Director of the organization should be expanded and their appointment process reviewed. At present, these senior officials are often appointed not only on account of their professional experience but also, and chiefly, based on political considerations and, when one comes to political organizations, also because he or she is weak enough to yield to the pressure and demands of the major powers. In addition, the appointees normally seek a second or third mandate, a fact that impels them to be subservient to the major member states while in office. In my view, in order to enhance the professional quality of the organization's leadership, the head of the institution should be appointed only in light of his or her specific competence and experience, and should be allowed to fulfil only one mandate—possibly for longer than at present. To this end, it would not be necessary to amend the statute of the various organizations which allows a renewal of the mandate of the organization's head. A gentlemen's agreement could be made whereby the appointment shall not be renewed and the appointee shall not seek re-appointment.

In addition, the organizations under discussion should promote close dialogue with the civil society of member states, their constituency. It is a fact—a regrettable fact—that at present the contact point within the legal system of each member state of intergovernmental organizations is the member state's political leadership and its supporting bureaucracy. The messages, exhortations, condemnations, decisions, policy plans, and guidelines issued by an organization rarely trickle down to the citizenry, which as a rule remains incognizant and unaware of the action promoted at the international level. It is instead crucial for intergovernmental organizations to reach out to the whole population of each member state, its media, other news outlets, as well as non-governmental organizations. How many people know in Italy of the criticisms levelled against the Italian authorities by the Council of Europe Committee for the Prevention of Torture and Inhuman or Degrading Treatment,[42] or by the UN Human Rights Committee?[43] How many people in the United States are aware of the criticism levelled by the UN Committee Against Torture against the torture policy adopted in recent years by the US authorities?[44] How many Russian nationals are aware that the UN Human Rights Committee has been very critical of the Russian human rights record[45] and that the Council of Europe Committee Against Torture issued in 2007 a strong 'statement' on the conduct of Russian authorities in Chechnya?[46] By enhancing the impact of intergovernmental organizations on civil society, the former would gradually enhance their role as the main bearers of 'community concerns'. This trickling-down effect could be achieved by enjoining member states to disseminate in the media news about the action taken by intergovernmental organizations about each member state. If this proves to be complicated or hardly feasible, the organization press office could prepare short summaries of the highlights of the organization's action concerning each member state, and request the relevant governments to make public and disseminate such summaries.

### (ii) Encouraging recourse to independent investigatory bodies

A second area where changes in the international society would be welcome is that related to the ascertainment of truth with regard to controversial facts. It is a truism that states as well as other international subjects very frequently engage in heated disputes, which often occasion rifts about the existence, occurrence, or

---

[42] See the various reports of the Committee on Italy, the latest of which was issued in 2010 (CPT/INf/2010/14), available at <http://www.cpt.coe.int/documents/ita/2010-inf-14-eng.pdf>.

[43] See 'Report of the Human Rights Committee, 2005–2006', vol. 1, UN Doc. A/61-40, at 34–9, available at <http://daccess-dds-ny.un.org/doc/UNDOC/GEN/G06/449/87/PDF/G0644987.pdf?OpenElement>.

[44] See 'Report of the Committee Against Torture, 2005–2006', UN Doc. A/61-44, at 67–74.

[45] See 'Report of the Human Rights Committee 2009–2010', vol. 1, UN Doc. A/65/40, at 34–44.     [46] See CPT/Inf (2007) 17.

nature of factual circumstances. Controversies about facts (and often also about the relevant law) have increased at a staggering pace in recent decades, because international dealings have gathered pace under the push of globalization and the consequent interconnectedness of states and other international subjects. To date, the international society has been unable to cope with this new phenomenon, as states (and *a fortiori* other international subjects such as rebel movements) are reluctant to go before international courts. Consequently this role is eventually fulfilled at a *private* level, by authoritative NGOs, as Human Rights Watch and Amnesty International in the field of human rights. Furthermore, as noted above, the ICRC, an international body with enormous experience and competence in this area, has decided from the outset to bow to the typical requirements of the Westphalian structure. The ICRC keeps all its findings confidential by handing them over only to the state concerned, thereby depriving the international society of knowledge of what has actually occurred in some specific circumstances. True, in the last two decades the UN Secretary-General, the Security Council, or the Human Rights Council have instituted many commissions of inquiry that have proved helpful and significantly contributed to uncovering the truth. What is here proposed is a conspicuous multiplication of these fact-finding commissions or bodies. This, however, is not enough. To ensure uniformity, professionalism, and celerity, as suggested above, the competent UN bodies should adopt a general scheme for the establishment of such commissions, granting them ample powers of investigation, and setting up a roster of independent experts, from which the Secretary-General or the High Commissioner for Human Rights could draw at any time a new fact-finding mission as required and a panel also rapidly constituted.

### (iii) Bringing non-state actors under the sway of international law

At present most non-state actors are only tangentially restrained by international rules and, by the same token, derive little benefit from those rules. Individuals do have international obligations, chiefly those flowing from international criminal law (they are duty-bound not to engage in international crimes and, consequently, may be brought to trial if they breach those obligations). In addition, at least in one region of the world, Europe, they are entitled to bring cases before an international court with a view to protecting their own fundamental rights; at the universal level they can lodge complaints with the Human Rights Committee against states, provided such states have previously accepted to submit to the jurisdiction of that Committee. Otherwise the presence of individuals on the world scene is non-existent. Intergovernmental organizations, in addition to being submitted to the control of members states, as underlined above, are still not fully accountable for any action that conspicuously deviates from international rules. NGOs do not possess any legal entitlement to take part in international dealings, although most of them contribute in many ways to the action of states or intergovernmental organizations. As for multinational corporations, their activities are only restrained by 'guidelines' or 'codes of conduct', which normally are, however, non-binding. Such corporations thus have no obligations under international law and very few legal entitlements. The condition of rebels is not better. True, they may conclude international agreements, but otherwise they have few rights and obligations.

In addition, non-state actors are not subject to any international monitoring, let alone to international adjudication.

This state of affairs is plainly grounded in the notion proclaimed, or implicitly adhered to, by most states that they are the only crucial subjects of the international society, or at least the only subjects *pleno jure*, that is, enjoying full rights and obligations and entitled to have a say in world affairs. I would suggest that this condition is unfortunate and detrimental to international peaceful relations. Expanding the grip of international law to non-state actors would entail restraining violence by insurgents and other groups holding power within states, and limiting the negative impact of some activities of multinational corporations. Also, broadening the right of individuals to lodge complaints about their own rights with international bodies would result in limitation on states' misconduct towards their own citizens or any persons under their jurisdiction. Furthermore, making intergovernmental organizations internationally accountable for any misconduct, and also subjecting them to the jurisdiction of domestic courts whenever they seriously infringe upon rights of individuals, would contribute to enhancing the rule of law in international relations and significantly restraining possible abuses. In addition, awarding NGOs a stable legal foundation for their action and allowing at least some of them to participate in selected international action would mean taking advantage of the experience and competence of some important NGOs.

How to attain these goals? I have tried in Chapter 39 to suggest that granting rebels, subject to some strict conditions, the right to engage in armed activities without necessarily being considered as lawless bandits, but as lawful combatants, may induce rebels to comply with the rules of international humanitarian law. Sivakumaran in Chapter 40 sees merit in the need to develop an international agreement to which non-state belligerent actors can accede, and which codifies and progressively develops their human rights as well as their humanitarian law obligations.

Introducing by treaty restraints on intergovernmental organizations and also on certain activities of multinational corporations and making them accountable for possible abuses might prove feasible, at least in the long run. In particular, with regard to multinational corporations, I do not see why safeguards against possible abuses by such corporations should only be provided by states. Since they have now some legal entitlements (eg the right directly to vindicate their treaty-guaranteed investment protections), it would be only natural also to make them accountable, before international courts, for any abuse of their power or gross violation of human rights standards.

The possible expansion of human rights treaties setting up monitoring or adjudicatory mechanisms to which individuals may have access would no doubt make states accountable for any deviation from international rules protecting human rights.

As for NGOs, although Bhuta considers (Chapter 6) that granting them some participation in lawmaking functions is 'neither realistic nor self-evidently normatively desirable', the suggestion can be made that at least those which possess great experience and competence and are fully independent of states (eg Amnesty International and Human Rights Watch, to mention just two) should be empowered officially to carry out (i) fact-finding, as well as (ii) monitoring of state compliance with international obligations; they could also be requested (iii) formally to comment on draft treaties and propose texts or amendments to such treaties.

## (B) Possible domestic remedial measures

So far I have expounded the possible palliatives to which one can resort at the international level. I will now turn to the question of how national institutions might contribute to an amelioration of the present state of affairs.

Perhaps the best channels for change reside in two categories of bodies: domestic courts and international civil society. While at first glance they may appear to be disparate entities whose paths barely intersect, to my mind they are the best vehicles for change, and a closer look reveals that they have much more in common than meets the eye. We should perhaps pin our hopes for gradual change in the international society on these entities, which might be more inclined than states to reform and modernize international institutions. It is therefore worth briefly dwelling on them.

### (i) Enhancing the pivotal role of domestic courts as guardians of the international legal order

Domestic courts already fulfil, among other things, the important task of ensuring observance of international law. As rightly emphasized by Shany (Chapter 16), in spite of the many predictable hurdles, a myriad of advantages can come with the increased contribution of domestic courts. Such courts could dramatically raise the prospects of enforcing international obligations. As Shany states, 'since the enforcement facilities available at the domestic level are generally superior to the inadequate remedial and enforcement facilities existing at the international level, increasing the role of domestic courts in litigating international law cases is likely to lead to higher enforcement rates. This too has significant implications for the "bite" attendant to international obligations and for the international rule of law.' Shany has also emphasized the current growing role of the courts of the United States or the European countries as being instrumental in the more frequent application and implementation of international standards, particularly in the field of human rights: 'The recent experience of US courts dealing with a booming number of ATS [Alien Torts Statute] claims and the experience of European countries in receiving a growing number of requests to exercise universal jurisdiction illustrate the potential growth in the international law caseload, which changes in the laws governing the international law jurisdiction of domestic courts and in their actual practices may foster.' Menon also outlines the numerous ways national courts make it possible for individuals to receive compensation for international unlawful acts by states (see Chapter 47).

Of course one should not be oblivious to the many hurdles existing in the exercise of domestic jurisdiction. Some 'doctrines' stand out in this respect: that of state immunity from foreign jurisdiction (see thereon the chapter by Gaeta, Chapter 18); the doctrine of the act of state; the doctrine of political question; the doctrine of personal and diplomatic immunities of state agents; the practice, upheld in such states as the United States[47] and, until recently, France,[48] whereby in the event of doubts about the proper interpretation of international rules, domestic courts turn to the executive branch for the right construction of the rules at issue (a real abdication of the judicial role of courts); the doctrine whereby when state officials acting on behalf of an intergovernmental organizations breach international rules, responsibility for such breaches is borne by the organization and not by the state, with the consequence that, as normally intergovernmental organizations enjoy immunity from legal process, no one is ultimately held accountable.

Furthermore, the role of domestic courts in the application of international law is not entirely unproblematic. Often, it can be a cause for misgivings. As noted by Iovane (Chapter 46), domestic courts have often asserted the existence of international customs without sufficient reference to international precedents, or regarded international treaty rules as corresponding *ipso facto* to general international law. Moreover, they often apply the interpretative methods of modern constitutionalism to solve conflicts between international norms, or to propose an evolutive interpretation of customary and treaty norms on the protection of human rights. According to Iovane national courts frequently tend to go too far, violating well-established norms of customary international law and giving rise to a plethora of interpretations from state to state. Domestic courts have also developed a creative judge-made law. However, judges cannot use their freedom of interpretation in an arbitrary way. They would risk handing down illegitimate and ineffectual decisions. Furthermore, judicial creativity—as Iovane opines—may also run counter to the practice adopted by the executive organs of the various states in their diplomatic intercourse. Other problems have been highlighted by Shany (Chapter 16), who has identified a host of issues arising from the increasing application by domestic courts of international law.

In spite of all these difficulties, national courts may still help to fill an enormous gap by providing redress to individuals for wrongs caused by states. The chapter by Menon (Chapter 47) clearly illustrates this point and shows the many avenues open to individuals when they wish to receive judicial remedy for injuries caused by states.

---

[47] As pointed out, n 35, the US courts attach great importance to the views of the executive branch in interpreting customary international law. See *Restatement of Law Third*, §112, Comment c.

[48] Traditional French case law adhered to the notion that in matters of treaty interpretation it was for the Foreign Ministry to suggest to courts which interpretation was the appropriate one (see, eg, Court of Cassation, criminal section, *Glaeser* case, in Annuaire français de droit international (1977) at 969). The Court of Cassation, in its decision in *Banque Africaine de Développement v Bank of Credit and Commerce International and others* (19 December 1995), overturned this trend, holding that it was for the judge to construe treaty provisions relevant to the case at issue, without requesting the opinion of a non-judiciary institutions ('*sans qu'il soit nécessaire de solliciter l'avis d'une autorité non juridictionnelle*', in RGDIP (1996) at 652).

Let me add that it is a matter of relief to realize that, at present, national (but also international) courts are gaining momentum in their efforts to contribute to a better international law. National courts are gradually chipping away at traditional doctrines limiting the effectiveness and impact of such courts. Also international courts are more inclined than before to tone down or even set aside the authority of states in favour of the rights and concerns of individuals. A good illustration of this tendency are two recent cases brought before the European Court of Human Rights: *Al-Skeini and others v United Kingdom* and *Al-Jedda v United Kingdom* (judgments of 7 July 2011). There the Court, drastically departing from its previous case law which had culminated with *Banković and others v Belgium and others* (judgment of 12 December 2001), held that the human rights laid down in the European Convention on Human Rights must be observed by nationals of a contracting party (in this case, British nationals) even when they operate abroad, whether in Europe or elsewhere. Accountability for international breaches has thus been broadened, and the protection of individuals' rights enhanced.

As for national courts, they are challenging, more or less directly, more or less explicitly, the immunity of states from the jurisdiction of foreign courts: some of these courts are Italian,[49] some are British,[50] some Canadian,[51] as well

[49] See the various decisions of the Italian Court of Cassation. See, eg, *Ferrini v Germany*, 11 March 2003, no. 50 44, available at <http://www.haguejusticeportal.net/Docs/NLP/Italy/Ferrini_Cassazione_6-11-2003.pdf>; English translation at 128 ILR at 659ff (the Court held that while customary law prescribes immunity from jurisdiction of a foreign state for acts that embody its sovereign authority, such immunity must be lifted when such acts amount to international crimes; according to the Court violations of fundamental human rights encroach upon universal values protected by *jus cogens* norms, which lie at the top of the hierarchy of norms of the international legal order, and thus take precedence over conflicting law, including state immunity). On this case see C. Focarelli, 'Denying Foreign State Immunity for Commission of International Crimes: The *Ferrini* Decision', 54 ICLQ (2005) 951–68. Subsequently the Court issued a number of orders by which, besides ruling on the *Mantelli* case and the *Maietta* case (*Repubblica federale di Germania v Mantelli e altri*; *Daimler Chrysler v Mantelli e altri*; *Repubblica federale di Germania v Presidenza del Consiglio dei Ministri and Maietta*), order no. 14201 of 29 May 2008 (<http://www.cortedi-cassazione.it/Documenti/14201.pdf>), it pronounced on 11 other cases; there it held again that the relevant Italian judges enjoyed jurisdiction with regard to claims for financial compensation brought against Germany. The same Court of Cassation confirmed the *Ferrini* ruling in a judgment of 21 October 2008 (*Milde* (*Racciarini*) case, available at <http://www.icrc.org/ihl-nat.nsf/46707 c419d6bdfa24125673e00508145/938e2cb397e8da36c1257561003a1c4d/$FILE/Italy%20v.%20 Milde%202008.pdf>.

[50] See the judgment of the British High Court, *Mutua and others v Foreign and Commonwealth Office*, judgment of 21 July 2011. The claimants, Kenyan nationals, alleged torts by the British authorities governing Kenya in 1952 of trespass to the person, ie unlawful assault and battery (para. 113). The court held that the issue of whether the British government was liable, on the formulations of the claimants' case, was fit for trial. The court stressed that it was not deciding whether there *was* a system of torture of detainees in the camps in Kenya during the Emergency. The judge said: I merely decide that there is viable evidence of such a system which will have to be considered at trial' (para. 134).

[51] See the Superior Court of the District of Montreal, *Kazemi v Iran*, decision of 25 January 2011, at paras 211ff. Stephan Hashemi, the son of a Canadian photojournalist, Zahra Kazemi, who was allegedly tortured and killed in an Iranian prison in 2003, instituted civil proceedings before a Canadian court against the Islamic Republic of Iran, its Head of State, Chief Public Prosecutor, and Deputy Chief of Intelligence. He brought the action on behalf of his mother's estate and also

as French.[52] Other courts, in this case US courts, have dismissed the argument that senior state officials responsible for issuing policy guidelines are immune from civil jurisdiction when sued for torts in cases involving harsh conditions of detention, torture, and lack of legal remedies resulting from the implementation of those policies.[53] Although the importance of these cases is diminished by the fact that the plaintiffs had US nationality[54] (the US courts would not have taken the same stand were the plaintiffs foreigners), it seems remarkable

claimed for the emotional and psychological injuries he allegedly suffered in Canada as a result of his mother's detention and death and Iran's subsequent refusal to repatriate her body. The Court held, based on the wording of the State Immunity Act of Canada, the State of Iran, as well as its Head of State, the Ayatollah Ali Khamenei (provided that the latter acted in a public capacity) were immune from jurisdiction of any court in Canada (para. 98). However, according to the court that Canadian Statute 'expressly covers foreign states and heads of state and provides a general rule of immunity subject to specific exceptions, within which torts committed outside of Canada's territory do not feature' (paras 53 and 98). Hence the plaintiff could not sue a foreign country (Iran) for damage caused by Iranian agents in Iran to the victim, but only for the trauma caused in Canada (an 'attack on his physical integrity') by the torture and assassination of her mother (the victim) to her son (plaintiff Stephan Hashemi).

[52] The French Court of Cassation, *UTA* case, decision of 9 March 2011. The Court issued a very interesting ruling. In a case of terrorism against Libya it said that

les Etats étrangers et les organisations qui en constituent l'émanation ne bénéficient de l'immunité de juridiction, immunité relative et non absolue, qu'autant que l'acte qui donne lieu au litige ou qui leur est imputé à faute participe, par sa nature et sa finalité, à l'exercice de la souveraineté de ces Etats et n'est donc pas un acte de gestion; qu'en l'espèce, *il est reproché à la Jamahiriya non pas d'avoir commis les actes de terrorisme incriminés mais de ne les avoir ni réprimés ni désavoués, ou même de les avoir soutenus*; qu'ayant relevé que la responsabilité de cet attentat ne pouvait être imputée à cet Etat étranger et que seuls six de ses ressortissants d'un acte de terrorisme ne permet pas, à elle seule, d'écarter une prérogative de souveraineté avaient été pénalement condamnés, la cour d'appel a pu juger que la Jamahiriya pouvait opposer une immunité de juridiction dès lors que la nature criminelle.

The Court therefore rejected the appeal and upheld French jurisdiction over those terrorist acts. The Court added:

à supposer que l'interdiction des actes de terrorisme puisse être mise au rang de norme de *jus cogens* du droit international, laquelle prime les autres règles du droit international et peut constituer une restriction légitime à l'immunité de juridiction, une telle restriction serait en l'espèce disproportionnée au regard du but poursuivi dès lors que la mise en cause de l'Etat étranger n'est pas fondée sur la commission des actes de terrorisme mais sur sa responsabilité morale.

The Court therefore implicitly admitted that *jus cogens* norms may prevail over the customary rules on immunity of states from the jurisdiction of foreign courts.

[53] See US District Court for the Northern District of Illinois, *Ronald Vance and Nathan Ertel v Donald Rumsfeld*, 5 March 2010, available at <http://legaltimes.typepad.com/files/rumsfeld_suit. pdf>; US District Court, District of Columbia, *John Doe v Ronald Rumsfeld and others*, 2 August 2011, available at <http://legaltimes.typepad.com/files/rumsfeld_suit.pdf>.

[54] The US District Court, District of Columbia, in *John Doe v Ronald Rumsfeld and others* stated that 'The *Sanchez-Espinoza* court concluded that "the danger of foreign citizens" using the courts ... to obstruct the foreign policy of our government is sufficiently acute that we must leave to Congress the judgement whether a damage remedy should exist', 770 F2d at 209. In *Detainees Litigation*, the court likewise cautioned against allowing 'high-ranking military officials [to be] haled into our own courts to defend against our enemies' legal challenges ...', 479 F Supp 2d at 105 (at 18–19). The court then went on to note:

But Doe is a United States citizen and this case does not involve foreign citizen plaintiffs. The fear of allowing enemy aliens to engage domestic courts in continuing hostilities is not present here. Doe's American citizenship thus cuts strongly in favor of affording him

that the doctrine of civil liability of very high-ranking state officials for serious violations of human rights put into being while acting in their official capacity is taking a firm foothold in US courts. The principle is thus upheld that senior state officials do not enjoy any immunity when, in discharging their functions, they seriously breach fundamental human rights.

Other national courts have dismissed the theory that when the agents of a member state act on behalf of an international organization, it is the organization that is responsible for any breach of international law committed by those agents—the consequence of which is that the potential wrongdoers end up being sheltered from any judicial scrutiny. For instance, the Amsterdam Court of Appeals has affirmed the responsibility of the Netherlands for acting unlawfully in Srebrenica on 12 July 1995 when the Dutch battalion (*Dutchbat*) evicted Bosnian Muslims from their compound in Srebrenica, sending them off essentially to their deaths. It held that the *District Court of The Hague was wrong in rejecting* the claims of the two plaintiffs against the government of the Netherlands on the basis that the acts of *Dutchbat* could only be attributed to the UN. Reversing this ruling, the Court of Appeal held that the Dutch troops were under the effective control of the Dutch government, which therefore was liable.[55] A similar stance has been taken in other cases by the European Court of Human Rights.[56]

Other courts do not address state sovereignty, but the authority of the highest international political body, the UN Security Council. They challenge the power of the Council freely to decide, without any judicial safeguards, whether an individual or an organization is terrorist in nature and can accordingly be subjected to sanctions.[57] In other terms, these courts state that not even the Security Council can exercise its powers outside the ambit established by peremptory norms of international law, and its decisions can therefore be judicially scrutinized.

constitutional protections abroad and allowing judicial remedy for the constitutional violations he alleges. (at 19)

[55] Amsterdam Court of Appeal, judgment of 5 July 2011. English text in . . .

[56] See the two decisions of the European Court of Human Rights mentioned above in the text, as well as the judgment of the Amsterdam Court of Appeals in the *Srebrenica* case, n 55.

[57] See the various decisions of the European Court of Justice (*Yusuf and Al Barakaat v Council of the European Union and the Commission of the European Community*, T-306/01 Reports 2001, II-3533; *Kadi v Council of the European Union and the Commission of the European Community*, T-315/01, Reports 2005, II-3649, appealed and revised by the European Court of Justice, Reports 2008, I-6351). See also the decision of the Swiss Federal Tribunal in *Nada gegen Staatsekeretariat für Wirtschaft (SECO)*, Judgment of 14 November 2007, EuGRZ 2008, 66. See also the views of the UN Human Rights Committee in *Nabil Sayadi and Patricia Vinck v Belgium* (decision of 22 October 2008) at paras 10.1–10.13, and 11–13. See also the individual opinion (partly dissenting) of Sir Nigel Rodley and others (they among other things noted

the extravagant powers [that] the Security Council has arrogated to itself, including the obstacles it has created to the correction of error. It is more than a little disturbing that the executive branches of 15 Member States appear to claim a power, with none of the consultation or checks and balances that would be applicable at the national level, to simply discard centuries of States' constitutional traditions of providing bulwarks against exorbitant and oppressive executive action.

See also the remarks by Condorelli in Chapter 12 above.

Domestic courts have also been making a significant contribution in the field of international criminal law. The Statute of the ICC is rightly grounded in the notion of complementarity, according to which it falls to domestic jurisdictions to deal with international crimes, whereas the ICC can only step in when there is domestic inability or unwillingness to prosecute the crimes in question. This implies that it is primarily for national courts to enforce international rules prohibiting and criminalizing those gross violations of human rights which amount to core crimes. National courts, in addition to using traditional heads of jurisdiction such as territoriality, active or passive personality, or the protection of national interests, should increasingly resort to universal jurisdiction, although within the bounds suggested by Gaeta (Chapter 45). Belgian, Spanish, Dutch, and German courts have set a good example that other states could constructively emulate.

## (ii) Getting international civil society to play a more incisive role

International civil society, previously silent, has acquired great importance due to the spread of democratic principles, the role of media, and modern communication technology. It manifests itself chiefly through national and international public opinion as primarily articulated in media outlets, and organized groups such as NGOs and other non-profit organizations such as international charities.

The better-resourced NGOs fulfil many important functions. Very often, through inquiries or fact-finding, they substitute for states in establishing controversial facts, particularly if such facts relate to armed conflict. They propose legal instruments to international organizations, when states are loath to take such a step for fear of jeopardizing or meddling with interests of other states. They also assist individuals in seeking redress for wrongs before national or international courts. And frequently, they provide humanitarian assistance to the needy in lieu of, or together with, intergovernmental institutions or single states.

The other main set of actors in civil society, public opinion and media outlets, condition state authorities and can therefore have a considerable impact on the way the latter conduct their international dealings. As noted by Palma in his chapter (Chapter 7), national and international civil society can contribute powerfully to the observance of international guarantee procedures, to the identification of more advanced preventive, protective, and reparatory mechanisms, and to the definition of standards for the interpretation in practice of the human rights laid down in international treaties or customary international law. Authenticity, independence, and absence of profit interests can prove the right factors for prodding states more and more to heed universal values and sacrifice to some extent their self-interest. Public opinion, as sensitized by the media, NGOs, trade unions, political parties, and social movements, has become increasingly alert to global problems and community concerns. All these non-state entities can therefore exercise leverage over state authorities as well as on intergovernmental organizations. An illustration of the possible role of civil society is discussed by Sands (Chapter 28), when he emphasizes the impact public discussion regarding the resort to force has had in the United Kingdom, and suggests that public opinion should increasingly pressure states to place restraints on their use of military violence.

## 10.  Concluding remarks

It is apparent from the chapters in this book that the road to legal change is uphill and requires deployment of many efforts in order to ameliorate the present condition of world society. Clearly, there may be other options open to states and other international actors than those suggested here. The intent of this book, perhaps too ambitious, was to provide ideas and float proposals which could act as 'midwives' for social and legal change. Let us not forget the wise observations of George Scelle: 'Legal rules result from the blending of ethics and power' (*Les règles de droit viennent de la conjonction de l'éthique et du pouvoir*).[58] In this book, an effort has been made realistically to promote or enhance the 'ethical side' of the law. Whether or not one shares the suggestions set out here, one cannot deny that an effort must be made to set forth ideas conducive to a gradual amelioration of at least some features of world society. Admittedly, as rightly emphasized by Koskenniemi (Chapter 1), one should be careful not to project one's own ideologies and social bias into proposals for change. As he underlines, 'claims to humanity are always infected by the particularity of the speaker, the world of his or her experience, culture and profession, knowledge and ignorance.' Nevertheless, a critical attitude towards today's world is not only warranted, it is necessary. Similarly, proposals for change aimed at promoting universal values already consecrated at the international level seem justified, as long as they do not conceal specific interests—which is certainly not the case with the group of scholars whose chapters are assembled in this book. Ideas can play an important role, as affirmed by Victor Hugo in his celebrated phrase: 'one can resist an invasion of armies; one cannot resist the invasion of ideas' (*On résiste à l'invasion des armées; on ne résiste pas à l'invasion des idées*).[59]

We are comforted in our endeavours by the realization that a new wind of change is currently blowing in the world. As noted above, national and international courts are gradually gnawing at some of the previously unfettered prerogatives of states, with a view to upholding the new values rising in the world society, chiefly those relating to human rights. In sum, the world is rapidly moving and a new ethos is in the offing, if it is not already taking shape. It is an ethos more attuned to respect for human rights than to deference to state sovereignty. Our proposals for change could therefore find fertile ground; they can help new initiatives to ripen and new vistas to open up.

We have offered in this book a vast panoply of suggestions aimed at promoting reform and progress of the international society over the next two or three decades. These suggestions (some requiring much time and strong diplomatic and

---

[58] G. Scelle, *Manuel de droit international public* (Paris: Domat-Montchrestien, 1948), at 6.
[59] V. Hugo, *Histoire d'un crime—Déposition d'un témoin* ([1887] Paris: La Fabrique éditions, 2009), at 639. The book was written by V. Hugo in 1850–51, but published only in 1887.

political action, others susceptible of being realized in a short timespan) are hopefully less naïve or more realistic than those blithely set out in the 2000 Millennium Declaration adopted by so many heads of state and government gathered at the United Nations and barely implemented so far, in spite of the 2010 Review Summit and monitoring by the UN and other bodies. It is now for diplomats, politicians, national and international lawmakers, but also for NGOs and national and international public opinion to decide whether those suggestions are convincing and viable. It is for them to decide whether they are worth being implemented on the ground, or are nothing more than stillborn dreams.

# Index